A ... ed
... ls,
... el.

For more than 135 years our
guidebooks have unlocked the secrets
of destinations around the world,
sharing with travellers a wealth of
experience and a passion for travel.

**Rely on Thomas Cook as your
travelling companion on your next trip
and benefit from our unique heritage.**

Thomas Cook **rail** guides

EUROPE BY RAIL
THE DEFINITIVE GUIDE FOR INDEPENDENT TRAVELLERS

Edited by Nicky Gardner and Susanne Kries

Thomas
Cook

Your travelling companion since 1873

Published by Thomas Cook Publishing
A division of Thomas Cook
Tour Operations Limited
Company registration No. 3772199 England
The Thomas Cook Business Park
9 Coningsby Road
Peterborough PE3 8SB
United Kingdom

Telephone: +44 (0) 1733 416477
E-mail: books@thomascook.com
www.thomascookpublishing.com
Head of Travel Books: Lisa Bass
Production/DTP Editor: Steven Collins

Produced by hidden europe
Gardner u. Kries GbR
Geraer Str 14–c
D–12209 Berlin
Germany

E-mail: editors@europebyrail.eu
www.hiddeneurope.co.uk
Editors:
Nicky Gardner and Susanne Kries
Editorial assistants:
Paul Scraton and Greg Gardner

Book design and layout
by Gardner u. Kries GbR

Text: © 2012 Thomas Cook Publishing / hidden europe
Maps: © 2012 Thomas Cook Publishing / PC Graphics (UK) Limited

ISBN 978-1-84848-553-2

Cover design and cover layout: Thomas Cook Publishing
Front cover image: Cruising the Ligurian coast by train, a journey which forms part of
Route 33 in this book (photo © Siegfried Pascal / RailPictures.Net)

Printed and bound by Nutech Print Services, India

There is a website linked to this book at www.europebyrail.eu

ROUTES   49

Exploring France

Iberia: Spain and Portugal

The Alps: Austria and Switzerland

Italy

The Balkans and Adriatic

A WORD OF WELCOME

G reat festivals of culture and sport — and in the latter category there are few that rival the Olympics — have a wonderful capacity to focus the energy of railway companies. The first Japanese bullet train made its high-speed debut just in time for the Tokyo Olympics in 1964. Expo '92 in Seville was a powerful impetus for the development of Spain's rail network with the country's first new high-speed route, linking Madrid with Seville, opening on the eve of the Expo in April 1992. And Britain has demonstrated a rare capacity for enterprise and innovation in opening **High Speed 1**, linking London with the Channel Tunnel, well in advance of the 2012 London Olympics.

The sleek Eurostar trains that will bring athletes and spectators to London for the 2012 **Olympics and Paralympics** will of course not run back to France and Belgium empty. Thousands of Londoners might see an Olympic year as very good cause to forsake their capital and venture abroad. And why not by train?

A NEW AGE OF THE TRAIN

If the mid-19th century was the heyday of railway development, the early 21st century is a new golden age for **leisure travel** by train. Across much of Europe, the train is back in vogue. Rail travel is often modestly priced, generally very comfortable and appeals to the pieties of a new generation of travellers worried about environmental issues. It was surely not chance that the very first public Eurostar train to leave London's magnificently refurbished St Pancras International station in November 2007 was powered by two engines with the names *Tread Lightly* and *Voyage Vert*. The train comes with impeccable **green credentials**.

The audacity of 19th-century engineers ushered in the first era of rail travel. In 1841 **Thomas Cook** made his debut in the railway business, organising an excursion train to a temperance rally in the English Midlands. Within a few years, Thomas Cook had personally escorted several tours by train across the continent, taking his clients to Paris, the Rhineland and the Swiss Alps.

In 1873, Thomas Cook published his first rail timetable for **continental Europe**, promptly followed by his first two guidebooks — one devoted to Switzerland and the other to the Low Countries and the Rhine Valley. Both books were structured around descriptions of key routes, much like the present volume. The genius of the Victorian Age made the railway possible, but it took a man like Thomas Cook to bring travel to the millions. *Europe by Rail* reflects the authority and insight that Thomas Cook brought to his own explorations of Europe by train. When Thomas Cook escorted his first tours through continental Europe, train travel was slow and uncertain. Today, the railway has become the most consistently reliable means of transport across large parts of Europe.

Over the past few years, we have criss-crossed Europe by train, from fast journeys on **sleek expresses** (such as TGV and ICE services in France and

Germany respectively) to memorably slow meanderings on **remote branch lines**. We have written about slow trains through Bosnia, even slower trains through Bohemia and about the humdrum cream and red local trains that shuttle through our home city of Berlin. We have swapped stories with strangers on trains in Russia, we have been on trains marooned in deep midwinter snow in Scandinavia and we have slept soundly on trains that crept by dead of night around the back of silent factories in unnamed towns.

The train is fun — even when things do not always go utterly to plan. But planning is important on any journey and in this book we present 50 rail routes that between them cover the full gamut of European rail travel. There are routes where trains speed across great plains, routes where slow trains dawdle from one small town to another and there are routes where trains traverse harsh tundra and great mountain ranges. In addition to our **50 routes**, we offer **17 short side-tracks** — bite-size teasers that invite you to venture into lesser-known regions beyond our 50 routes.

Travel by train across Europe and you will inevitably be struck by the sheer variety of our continent. Our 50 routes reflect that mix. We include some high-speed hops, where you can cover a lot of ground fast. And wherever we can, we highlight slow trains that follow less-frequented rail routes. It is on such journeys that the **texture and detail of European life** is most easily appreciated, whether it be in the changing landscapes beyond the carriage window, the architecture of villages you pass through along the way or in the faces and the accents of folk with whom you find yourself sharing a railway carriage.

The opening of new rail routes has slashed journey times. Today's traveller can take a breakfast-time departure from London with Eurostar and by late afternoon be standing on the shores of the Mediterranean.

Traveller's choice: fast vs slow

The sleek silver trains on the new rail route that runs north-west from Frankfurt-am-Main slice determinedly through the wooded hills of the Taunus, defying the warp and weft of the landscape with moments of stroboscopic wonder, and depositing their distracted passengers in Cologne in little more than an hour. There are flashes of light between tunnels, angled glimpses of the sky and plenty of scope for headaches. It is a considerable technological feat, to be sure. But is being shot through the Taunus like a bullet actually better than sticking to the old rail route along the Rhine Valley to Cologne?

There the train follows the meandering course of the river, affording wonderful views of gabled villages, precipitous vineyards and romantic gorges presided over by formidable castles. True, the old valley route takes twice or thrice as long as the new fast line, but the experience is incomparably better. The slow rail journey along the Rhine features in **Route 18** in this book.

A judicious combination of daytime high-speed services and **overnight trains** allows longer journeys across the continent to be undertaken very comfortably by train. At their best, night trains are wonderful. Few are the experiences to compare with opening the blinds of the night sleeper in the morning to find a fragile blanket of morning mist over a foreign city. You can read more about night trains on p682.

The 18th-century English essayist **Samuel Johnson** claimed that "the grand object of travelling is to see the shores of the Mediterranean." And our cover image of an Italian train cruising along the coast of Liguria reinforces that distinctive perspective. But the imaginations of travellers today are less focused on a single region. The Med no longer commands attention to the exclusion of other parts of Europe. The routes in this book will take you far beyond the Arctic Circle and on mountain railways across the Pyrenees and the Alps. We shall lead you to **great cities** in eastern Europe and through Balkan byways to the shores of the Bosphorus. Some readers might try and undertake a dozen or more of these routes within a month. We would just sound a note of caution. That way madness lies. Better to focus a little, and take time to **stop off here and there** along the way.

Slow travel has come of age. You can read our *Manifesto for Slow Travel* (first published in 2009) at www.slowtraveleurope.eu. Savvy travellers nowadays realise that the journey is something to be savoured in its own right. Exploring Europe by rail is a great way to put slow-travel principles into practice. The pleasure of the journey need not be eclipsed by the anticipation of arrival. A lot has to do with choosing slower trains on at least some parts of your journey. For more on fast versus slow see the box on the opposite page.

Travel light if you possibly can. Heavy luggage and trains do not make good partners. Take this book along of course, and do not forget to take a train timetable. We noted above that Thomas Cook published the first European timetable way back in 1873. And the *Thomas Cook European Rail Timetable* (shown as 'ERT' in this book), a veritable masterpiece of compression, is still published monthly. An up-to-date copy of that timetable, and the *Thomas Cook Rail Map of Europe*, are natural companions to this volume. **Guidebook, map, timetable**: the three indispensable assets in the traveller's armamentarium have not changed since Thomas Cook first started encouraging folk to explore Europe by rail.

So are you game to join us on this journey? The best way to get started is to read 'How to use this book' (p14). You will find a useful map on p12 showing the routes (numbered 1 to 50) that form the core of this book. And you may like to know that we have a website to accompany this book at **www.europebyrail.eu**.

Enjoy the ride.

Nicky Gardner and Susanne Kries

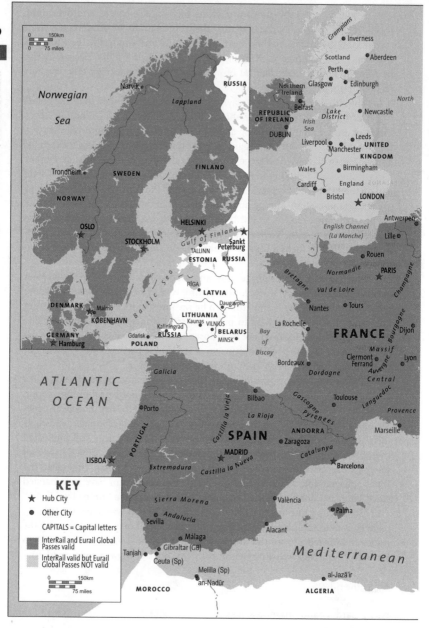

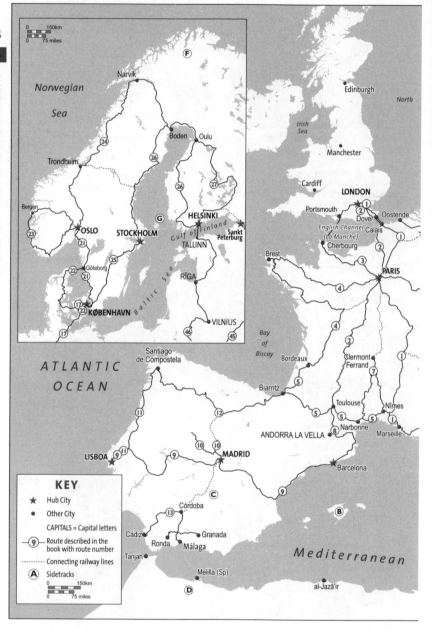

KEY

★ Hub City

● Other City

CAPITALS = Capital letters

⑨ Route described in the book with route number

········· Connecting railway lines

Ⓐ Sidetracks

0   150km

0   75 miles

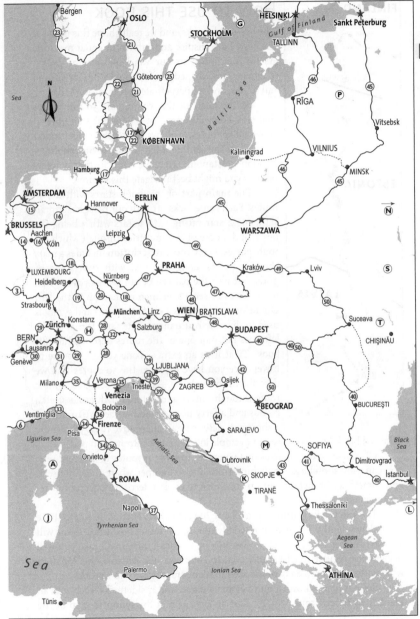

HOW TO USE THIS BOOK

The best guidebooks, and we really hope this is one of the best, both inspire and inform in equal measure. As we mentioned in our word of welcome on p7, Thomas Cook shaped his first books in 1873 around rail routes, and we perpetuate that tradition today.

At the heart of this volume are **50 rail routes** that criss-cross Europe. The general map on pp12–13 shows all 50 routes. It allows you to plot longer itineraries across the continent (eg. Lisbon to Stockholm or London to Istanbul). Here are a few further pointers on how you might best navigate this volume.

The **main part** of this book starts with the 50 routes. Each route kicks off with our personal appraisal using a **star rating** (1 to 3 stars with 3 being the best), and a note of the countries through which the route passes. Every **route description** includes a map, showing places along the way, with superimposed grids that give the pattern of rail services along that route. You can see a specimen route map to the left. On the opposite page is a key to the signs and symbols used in those 50 **route maps**. The sample map to the left does not plot one of the routes described in this book. Treat it as an extra — one you might like to travel once you have explored the 50 routes that we describe in this volume. As you can see, that sample route through Latvia and Estonia includes a stretch by bus and a ferry hop too. Sometimes we commend a short-cut, detour or an alternative route, shown by a dashed black line (you'll see an example in the map for **Route 1** on p51).

Of course no one dictates that you must follow our routes in their entirety. You can pick and choose, switching from one to another where they intersect, and sometimes branching out on your own to explore territory beyond our recommended routes.

The **sidetracks** features, 17 in all, might particularly encourage you to strike out independently. These are not strictly routes, but rather bold leaps. Some will lead to offshore islands (such as Sardinia or Corsica), others will take you well beyond the regular tourist trails, even to countries like Albania and Moldova which often get completely overlooked in many travel guides to Europe.

So 50 routes, all with a number and a name, and 17 sidetracks, each with an identifying letter (from A to T). Cast an eye again at the **synoptic map of the** routes (pp12–13) and you'll see that those letters appear on that map too, giving an indication of the area to which each sidetrack relates.

There are **26 major European cities** which deserve a more detailed look than we can comfortably accommodate within the route descriptions. We call these our **hub cities** and all 26 of them are shown with a distinctive star symbol in the maps of Europe on pp10–13. You will find the hub city descriptions arranged alphabetically on pp420–597 in this book (immediately after the 50 route descriptions).

If you want to get an overview of rail travel in Europe on a country-by-country basis, turn to our gazetteer on pp598–676. That **country gazetteer** also includes key facts on each country such as the currency and languages used, time zone, etc.

Routes (with sidetracks), hub city descriptions and the country gazetteer make up the three main elements of this volume. But there is much more besides. On pp16–32, preceeding our colour feature, we give a wealth of advice on **tickets**, **itinerary planning** and on links between the UK and continental Europe, concluding with thoughts on the revolution brought by **Eurostar**.

Tucked away towards the back of the book, after the country gazetteer, you'll find some real nuggets of information. Our **city links tables** show travel times between 37 principal places across Europe's rail network. And we also have a **rail pass directory**, sections on **night trains** and **cruise trains**, and an **A-Z of travel facts**.

Beyond the maps for each route, we also include 14 **regional maps** in the gazetteer that cover one or more countries. These maps are derived from the *Thomas Cook Rail Map of Europe*, which you might consider purchasing. Throughout the book we use **the abbreviation ERT** to refer to the *Thomas Cook European Rail Timetable* which makes a fine companion to this volume.

KEY TO ROUTE MAPS

GERMANY	country name
	international boundary
•WIEN	capital city
• Nauders	other city
✈	airport
	lake / sea

FEATURED ROUTES

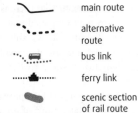

	main route
	alternative route
	bus link
	ferry link
	scenic section of rail route

ICONS USED IN THE BOOK

☎	telephone
⇌	rail station
🚌	bus
⛴	ferry service
✈	airport
ℹ	information
🛏	accommodation
✗	food and drink

PRICE GUIDE AND ACCOMMODATION COSTS

The question of how much money you need to explore Europe by train is a tough one. So much depends on length of journey, your expectations, the level of comfort to which you aspire or the degree of discomfort you are prepared to tolerate. **Train tickets** booked three months in advance might cost only a fraction of what you might pay if you buy tickets on the day of travel. We have made long journeys through Europe on just a pittance, taking advantage of special fare deals, opting for budget accommodation and surviving on a long litany of picnics. On other occasions, we have splashed out and enjoyed the comfort of crisp, clean sheets in air-conditioned sleeping cars and eaten in style in railway restaurant cars. We give more advice on train fares and ticketing matters in the tickets and rail passes sections of this book (pp21–27 and pp687–91 respectively).

Here the focus is on accommodation prices. **Hotel and hostel pricing policies** vary considerably across Europe. In many countries dynamic pricing is the norm, which means that there is virtually no set price, and the rates paid for the same room may vary wildly according to season, day of the week, or even the weather. Britain follows this approach, and it means that travellers may encounter extraordinarily good low-season deals, while prices rocket at times of peak demand. Visitors to the London Olympics might well have to pay top prices.

In many parts of Europe, the maximum price for which a room may be sold is clearly stipulated, and often subject to approval by the authorities. In some countries that may be the price that most travellers effectively pay. Elsewhere there is **regular discounting**, even to the extent that no one *ever* really pays the full list price. Negotiating your way through the tariff jungle is not easy. Where deep discounts on room rates are available, they may be reserved for clients who book weeks (or even months) in advance and prepay the full cost of their stay. A growing range of online booking engines may sometimes offer cheaper prices than you will be quoted by the hotel itself.

In the **table opposite**, we have assigned a classification to those European countries for which we provide accommodation options in our 50 routes and 26 hub city descriptions. No easy task, but it gives a rough-and-ready guide as to whether a country is cheap, mid-range or expensive when it comes to accommodation. And then in the listings we use **symbols** (€, €€, or €€€) to show what you might expect to pay for a room that is typical of the hotel or hostel in question.

Such a simple **classification** masks a wealth of difference. We have erred on the side of caution, and you may sometimes find a room costs rather less than we suggest. In major commercial centres (eg. Brussels, Hamburg or Zurich), top-end business hotels may discount so heavily on Friday, Saturday and Sunday nights that even travellers on only modest budgets can afford a weekend of rare luxury. And remember these are room prices, not the rate per person. Although hostels sell beds in dorms on a per-bed basis, in most European countries hotels sell, in the main, rooms for two people. Where single rooms exist, they will generally cost a lot more than half the rate for a twin or double. Solo travel can be an expensive business.

Hotel accommodation in cities often costs more than in more rural areas, though **Europe's blossoming hostel sector**, which offers discount accommodation in most cities, is less well represented in the rural regions of many countries. The new generation of independent hostels are not like the youth hostels of yesteryear. They attract clients of all ages and many offer private rooms. Capital cities are often more expensive than elsewhere in the country, but this rule is not infallible. Hotels in Rome can often be better value than those in Florence or Venice. Berlin is often significantly cheaper than Munich or Cologne.

Remember that these prices relate *only* to accommodation. Belarus and Russia are countries where rail travel is very cheap. Food, even in restaurants, can also be very affordable. But hotel prices are higher than you might expect. Folk flock to Andorra for cheap ciggies and alcohol, but that does not mean that hotels are any cheaper than in neighbouring Spain or France.

Table: Country classification and price bands per room

country group	price category	€	€€	€€€
low-price countries Bosnia and Herzegovina, Bulgaria, Kosovo, Macedonia, Romania, Serbia, Turkey, Ukraine		up to €30	€31–60	over €60
medium-price countries Belarus, Croatia, Czech Republic, Estonia, Greece, Hungary, Italy, Latvia, Lithuania, Poland, Portugal, Russia, Slovakia, Slovenia, Spain		up to €45	€46–90	over €90
high-price countries Austria, Belgium, Denmark, Finland, France, Germany, Liechtenstein, Luxembourg, Monaco, Netherlands, Norway, Sweden, Switzerland, United Kingdom		up to €60	€61–120	over €120

PLANNING YOUR ITINERARY

There is an untold pleasure in just breezing off without having given any real thought as to where you are bound. Some of the finest journeys are those which are least planned. Spontaneity brings its own rewards. But, as you'll quickly appreciate when you read our thoughts on train ticket deals (see p21), spontaneity is often a very expensive luxury. You can save a packet if you book at least some aspects of your journey in advance.

Even if money is no object, a modicum of **advance planning** still makes good sense. Missing the weekly train from Venice to Lviv may not trouble you at all. Venice is, after all, a splendid spot to hole up for a week if you have ample funds. But miss the only Saturday departure from a dreary small town in the Balkans, and finding that the next train out is not till Monday, may not be quite so much fun.

How much planning *you* need to do for *your* explorations of Europe by train has a lot to do with your **budget** and your **personal psyche**. Do you relish uncertainty? Will you be unduly troubled if you cannot easily find a place to stay overnight? Only you can answer such questions.

A key tool for planning your itinerary is the *Thomas Cook European Rail Timetable (ERT)*. A very useful website for **checking train times** across much of Europe is http://bahn.hafas.de (where you can use the pull-down menu to select English from the list of a dozen language options).

SOLO TRAVEL

The question of whether you travel alone is one that is ultimately a matter of personal choice. Solo travel can be immensely rewarding. The lone traveller is far more likely to strike up conversation with locals and fellow travellers. But an extended solo journey takes a certain grit and resilience, especially when all does not go quite as you might hope. There are times when being able to **share experiences** with a friend or partner can help make a journey take on new meaning. Bear in mind, too, that **accommodation costs** are heavily stacked against the single traveller.

BEWARE THE PACKED ITINERARY

By far the biggest mistake made by first timers embarking on a vacation exploring Europe by train is to bite off far more than is feasible. With so much on offer, it is all too tempting to say "Let's just throw in Florence. And Paris too."

Sketch out your **first tentative itinerary** and then halve the number of places you intend to visit. A two-night stop is hugely more rewarding than having just one night in a new city. Three nights is even better. If you opt for a fortnight of one-night stays, each morning setting off for a new city, Europe will collapse in a mishmash of blurred memories. Similarly, **long travel days** take their

SEVEN STEPS TO PERFECT PLANNING

Prepare a budget that includes estimates of accommodation, food and travel costs, including seat reservation fees and travel supplements for rail pass holders. Now add on a good allowance for incidentals. Entrance fees to galleries and museums and left-luggage charges may be hefty, not to mention coffees and cocktails.

Tune your expectations to match your budget. A gondola ride across the Grand Canal in Venice costs just a euro or two. But if you wish to be serenaded while drifting through Venice on your own private gondola, expect to pay upwards of €100. The grandest French clarets will not cost any less in a fine Bordeaux restaurant than at home. Even modest fare may test the depth of your wallet in some of Europe's more expensive countries such as Norway.

Review visa requirements earlier rather than later. If any country on your provisional itinerary might demand a visa, remember to make provision in your budget. For holders of EU passports, the sole journey in this book that requires visas to be procured prior to setting out is **Route 45**, where both the Republic of Belarus and the Russian Federation insist on a visa.

Consider money matters early. Do you have cash point (ATM) and credit cards to support your journey? Remember that even the most popular **credit cards** (VISA and Mastercard) may not be widely accepted in some European countries. Do you have a card that allows you to draw cash in local currency from your bank account? Know in advance what currencies you'll need at each stop on your itinerary. Give early thought as to where you'll pack cash to minimise the risk of loss or theft.

Think about luggage at the outset for how much you lug around will dramatically influence how manageable your itinerary is. A small amount of luggage, never more than you can comfortably carry without assistance, can be a wonderful asset. More just becomes a terrible burden. We know travellers who have survived long tours around Europe without a portable ice-bucket and a miner's lamp. But we judge a small torch, a corkscrew and appropriate plug adaptors to be essentials. There is no such thing as a universal packing list to suit all, but http://upl.codeq.info is a good start. And it's fun to play with.

Buy insurance early for, while it is a sound principle never to travel with something that you would be desperately sorry to lose, things do go astray. And medical cover is essential. If you are resident in any of the 31 European countries participating in the **EHIC scheme**, you should obtain a European Health Insurance Card before leaving home. The EHIC card is free. You should review whether it provides adequate cover, and you may consider top-up medical insurance.

Weather watching makes sense. Find out what sort of weather you can expect along the way. Bear in mind that an itinerary which includes both Arctic Norway and the Greek islands will traverse several climate zones. Check out the climate guides at www.weather2travel.com and explore the excellent graphics in the climate section of www.weatheronline.co.uk. And remember that places blessed with a wonderful climate may still turn out to have terrible weather on the week you visit.

toll as do several consecutive nights of overnight travel. There will be times when a ten-hour haul by day will allow you to cover a lot of ground. And it may be good fun, especially if you follow a route that takes in some great scenery. But if you have several such long days on the trot, the appeal of train travel will surely wane.

Careful planning can make a long travel day much more enjoyable. If you must make a ten-hour journey in a single day, then why not break it up into two legs of five hours each, and schedule a decent-length break at a midway point. A brisk walk or a relaxed lunch will leave you refreshed for the second stretch of the journey.

THE PLANE QUESTION

This book is all about exploring Europe by rail. But let's not be too purist about these things. If you do not mind flying, there are many itineraries where a **leg by plane** just makes good sense, whether at the start or end of your itinerary, or to shift quickly from one part of Europe to another in the middle of a long trip.

Before you start booking many sectors by plane, just consider what **alternatives** might be available. A long overnight journey by train may usefully bridge a gap. For example we've combined a week exploring the Alps with a subsequent week in Spain by using the excellent Elipsos hotel train between the two areas (www.elipsos.com). Similarly a long hop with a ferry might be a more relaxing way of crossing the Mediterranean, the North Sea or Black Sea than flying. We offer a few more thoughts on sea connections in **Sidetracks E** (p221).

But if you decide the plane really is the way to go, for one or more parts of your itinerary, then **research options carefully**. You can check out who flies where at www.whichbudget.com. Momondo is also good (www.momondo.eu). Other sites we have found useful for researching European flights and fares are www.alternativeairlines.eu, www.skyscanner.net and www.fly.com. Many of these sites allow you to specify your preferred currency for fare quotes.

URBAN OR RURAL?

What kind of Europe are you eager to discover? A Europe full of **cosmopolitan flair**, such as you might encounter in Paris, London and Rome, or a quieter, more rural Europe where the locals may even still have time for and interest in the visitors who come their way?

If you stick to the 26 hub cities in this book, you'll probably have a ball, but you'll see cities that are not always typical of the countries in which they are located. The wonderful thing about travelling by train is the European rail network can take you to backwaters frequented by few tourists. Make time for some of the **small towns** and **branch lines** that we mention in this book and you will be handsomely rewarded. And make time for slow trains that dawdle through the countryside, stopping off here and there along the way.

Getting the best deals on tickets

For almost any traveller exploring Europe by rail, **train tickets** will be one of the two principal categories of expenditure, the other of course being accommodation. How much you spend on tickets will be determined by your itinerary, whether you opt for second or first class and — in many countries — whether you can **book well in advance**. Across large parts of Europe, this last factor will dramatically influence how much you pay.

The rail fares jungle

Wouldn't it be a wonderful world if you could walk down to your local station in suburban London (or Oslo or Madrid) and buy a through train ticket to the other side of Europe? Sadly, Europe's railway administrations don't quite see it that way and travellers embarking on a complicated international itinerary must generally obtain a number of **separate tickets** to cover their entire journey.

Matters have improved over the last year or two, with tickets for many more routes now being available online. For those with the patience to check out a variety of different websites and agents, there are some fabulous deals there for the taking, especially for early bookers. In late 2011 we travelled from Alsace to southern Sweden and from Salzburg to London, in each case paying less than €50 per person for the journey. Those were exceptionally good offers and often one might have to pay very much more for the same trips. On p22, we list some of the principal websites and agencies that we have found useful in researching and buying rail tickets and passes for travel around Europe.

How far in advance can I book?

The key to **securing the best fares** is usually to book your tickets the moment they become available. One small caveat is that in a very few countries premium fares aimed at the business market may become available slightly prior to discounted tariffs. The forward-booking horizon for many rail networks across continental Europe is **three months** (give or take a few days).

But there are important exceptions to the general three-month rule. **Eurostar services** from London to Paris and Brussels are bookable four months in advance, while bookings for the seasonal Eurostar services from London direct to the French Alps (in winter) and to Avignon (in summer) may open as long as six months in advance. Most **European night trains** can be booked three months or even longer prior to travel. This applies in particular to many services that start or end in Germany (or cross Germany). But even here there are variations. Bookings for trains from Germany to Russia open only 60 days in advance. And that 60-day forward-booking horizon is the norm for all trains within Russia, Ukraine and Belarus. Finland is yet another exception with most tickets going on sale just 56 days in advance.

Whenever there are **major timetable changes**, generally on the second weekend in **December each year** across much of western and central Europe, ticket sales for the new timetable period will not open until the new schedules have been confirmed, and that may mean that, for a spell each autumn, the forward-booking horizon is shorter than normal.

BIG REWARDS FOR EARLY BOOKERS

Across much of continental Europe, though less so in eastern Europe and the Balkans than elsewhere, there has been a **revolution in rail tariffs** over the last

BOOKING TIPS

One thing that's clear from our review of rail tickets is that fares and ticketing are complicated matters, the high theology of which is understood by only a handful of people on the entire planet. The average travel agent will not be able to help you a lot, so if you need help, it is best to turn to specialists. A good source of online advice, geared mainly to the UK market, is Mark Smith, the much-quoted Man in Seat 61, whose website at www.seat61.com is a goldmine of good advice.

For booking journeys online, UK-based customers can turn to **Rail Europe UK** (www.raileurope.co.uk) — even if you are booking a journey that does not actually start or end in Britain. UK customers can call Rail Europe UK on ☎ 0844 848 4064. We have found Rail Europe UK to be very helpful. For non-UK customers (but still in Europe), www.tgv-europe.com is excellent. Both the Rail Europe UK and **TGV Europe** sites are particularly good for journeys that include a French train. For journeys that start, end in or cross Germany, **Deutsche Bahn** (DB) is a good bet. Many journeys can be booked at www.bahn.co.uk or www.bahn.de. For more complicated itineraries call the DB English-language call centre at ☎ +44 871 880 8066. Don't forget that the Eurostar UK website (www.eurostar.co.uk) will allow you to book more than merely tickets on Eurostar's direct services from London. Read more on p31.

We can recommend the following **UK-based agents** for their considerable expertise in European ticketing. They are also able to handle enquiries and bookings for clients based outside Britain: **Trainseurope** (www.trainseurope.co.uk, ☎ +44 871 700 7722), **Ffestiniog Travel** (www.festtravel.co.uk, ☎ +44 1766 772050), **European Rail** (www.europeanrail.co.uk, ☎ +44 20 7619 1083), **International Rail** (www.internationalrail.com, ☎ +44 871 231 0790) and **Rail Canterbury** (www.rail-canterbury.co.uk, ☎ +44 1227 450088). All these agents can advise on InterRail tickets (or book at www.interrailnet.com). Remember that these agents will often levy a booking fee and, for bookings made from outside the UK, may insist that tickets are sent by courier, which will incur additional charges.

In North America, **Rail Europe** (www.raileurope.com, ☎ +1 800 622 8600) will handle bookings for European rail travel, but often charges well over what you might pay for comparable journeys booked in Europe. The editors would appreciate feedback from readers on their experience in booking tickets with agents mentioned here. You can contact us at editors@europebyrail.eu.

few years, and particularly since 2005. Fares were traditionally based on the length of your proposed journey. While these kilometre-based tariffs still often apply to passengers who purchase their tickets on the day of travel, many countries now offer a vast range of cheaper options.

Let's take two routes of similar length. The regular **distance-based fares** from Paris to Leipzig or Amsterdam to Salzburg, both journeys of about 1,000 km, are similar — in each case about €160, the precise amount payable varying by the route you elect to follow. But canny travellers on a budget always book well ahead. Commit yourself in the few days after ticket sales open and you will almost certainly pay just €39 for either of our two sample journeys above. Even if you book just a week in advance, there is still a very good chance of bagging a good deal — no longer €39 but maybe €99.

Most rail operators in western Europe have fallen in love with **market pricing**, where the fare on offer is carefully tuned to reflect anticipated demand, and where the customer prepared to book well in advance and — most importantly — **commit to a particular itinerary** and specific trains can travel for a fraction of the regular fare. The best deals are always on off-peak services.

Of course, our Paris to Leipzig and Amsterdam to Salzburg examples both come from an area of Europe where rail tariffs are pricier than elsewhere across the continent. Move east a little and the same outlay of €160 will buy you a **fully flexible ticket** for a journey of over 2,000 km from Prague to Turkey. No need to book in advance and you can even stop off as often as you wish along the way within the one-month validity of your ticket.

Our general rule of thumb is that, in those areas where market pricing gives advantages to early bookers, you can normally expect to pay about one quarter of the regular fare if you book within a week or two of tickets being released for sale. The names given to these early deals vary confusingly by country and rail operator. But whether it be *prems* (on French TGV services), *smoove* (on Thalys trains), *minipris* (in Norway), *low-fixed* (in the Netherlands) or *Europa-Spezial* (on international journeys to or from Germany), the underlying message is that a very good deal is on offer.

OTHER DISCOUNTS

While every country offers **child discounts**, there are few across the board discounts for young people, students or seniors. Where such discounts do exist, they are usually calculated as a percentage reduction on the regular full fare, and are rarely as cheap as the bargain basement fares available to anyone who books well in advance. Eurostar is a happy exception and offers discounts to **young people** and **seniors** even on many discounted standard-class fares. And Hungary is a wonderful oddity and offers **free rail travel** (on all but a small number of express services) to all EU citizens aged 65 or older.

Many European rail operators offer reductions on their regular tariffs, and sometimes also on their discounted early-booking fares, to holders of selected **railcards**. Many such cards are marketed only within the countries where they are valid. Most of these railcards are valid for one year and can be purchased by anyone, so you do not need to be a local resident. Examples are the Swiss *Halbtax* card, the Czech *In-Karta*, the French *Carte Escapades*, the German *BahnCard* and the Dutch *Voordeelurenkaart*.

Many countries also have specific railcards aimed at the youth and senior-citizen markets. In France, for example, there is the *Carte 12-25* and *Carte Senior*. Other countries sell their **national railcards** to youths and seniors at a reduced price. The Austrian *Vorteilscard*, for example, normally costs about €100 for a year, but young travellers (under 26) and seniors get a discount of more than 70% on the regular card price. Many national railcards are affiliated to the **Railplus** scheme and thus give discounts on some international journeys too.

You have to be doing a lot of travelling over an extended period within a single country to make the purchase of such cards worthwhile. They are however an attractive option for residents or for those who frequently visit one particular country. For example, many British residents who are regular Channel-hoppers have realised that a French railcard can be a very sensible investment.

Second class or first class?

Most European local trains are one class only. Many regional trains and most express or long distance services offer **two classes of service**, often called second and first. The names vary. On Thalys trains for example, the two classes are called *Comfort 2* and *Comfort 1* respectively. In many countries, second class may be marketed as economy or standard. If you are buying tickets at a railway station, and you don't specify to the contrary, the booking clerk will generally assume that you wish to travel second class. Most booking websites also take second class as the default or norm.

A small number of trains offer three levels of services. On such trains, the middle of the three classes is usually roughly equivalent to first class, and the highest class is a premium product. AVE services in Spain operate on this model with the three classes called *turista*, *preferente* and *club*. Eurostar's services from London to Paris and Brussels have standard, standard premier and business premier. **Railjet** services operating on routes to and from Vienna have economy, first and premium classes.

Unless you really value creature comforts, the regular second- or standard-class carriages are more than adequate on most day trains (see box above right to find out more about what to expect in first class). The question of comfort levels on night trains is more complicated, and the simple distinction between first and second class no longer applies. See our feature on night trains (p682).

FIRST CLASS COMFORT

First class carriages may offer better legroom, extra space for luggage and a higher level of service. That may include snacks and drinks served at your seat (often at a price), complimentary newspapers, power sockets and free wi-fi access. Quite what you actually get for the extra outlay varies greatly by country and category of train. Generally if a train has air conditioning, then it is available in every carriage. But there is a dwindling minority of trains across Europe where only first-class carriages have air conditioning.

On a very small number of trains, passengers in first or premium classes may receive a **complimentary snack or meal**. Examples of where you can enjoy such perks include those TGV trains between France and Switzerland that offer the new *Lyriapremière* on-board service, all journeys on Thalys trains of over 45 minutes, and all Eurostar services (where passengers in both standard premier and business premier are offered complimentary snacks and drinks). In Spain, free meals are the norm on the principal express trains for holders of *preferente* and *club* tickets.

Whether you think it worth splashing out for first class is really a matter of personal choice. Bear in mind that first class affords much less opportunity for contact with locals.

The availability of first-class seating may be very limited on some routes. On certain long-distance daytime trains in central Europe and the Balkans, for example, just a small part of a single carriage is designated as first class — Munich to Zagreb and Belgrade to Budapest are examples.

The extra you pay for first class varies greatly. As a general rule, expect to pay about 50% more than for a second-class fare. In some countries you just pay a flat fare supplement on top of the regular price. Norway is an instance of this, where the upgrade to the higher class (called *NSB Komfort*) costs 80 NOK (€10), whatever the length of journey.

The question of class is more complex on **night trains**, where the basic distinction is between seats, couchettes and sleeping compartments. The highest sleeping compartment category will usually only be available to holders of first class tickets (plus the sleeper supplement). For more on night trains see p682.

FIRST CLASS BARGAINS

The real surprise for many travellers is that there are times when **first-class tickets may be cheaper than second-class**. Early bookers can sometimes take advantage of special offers, usually only available online, for heavily discounted first-class tickets. We have noted many instances of journeys in western Europe where the cheapest available ticket is in first class.

You are most likely to encounter this oddity some time after bookings first open, when budget-conscious travellers have already snapped up all the cheap second-class seats, but bookings in first class are still very light. This is most likely at weekends and during summer holidays — so when budget leisure travel is in high demand but there are fewer business travellers on the move.

RAIL PASSES OR REGULAR TICKETS

The question that many travellers ponder endlessly before, during and even after exploring Europe by rail is whether **investing in a rail pass** makes good financial sense.

Cast back a few years and an earlier generation of InterRail pass holders explored Europe's principal cities by day and slept by night on trains making long nocturnal hops across Europe. Others partied by night and slept on trains by day. Either way, the **InterRail pass** was a fine investment. Young backpackers with stamina could criss-cross Europe for a month and hardly pay a cent for accommodation.

Times have changed. Many European railway administrations have introduced **supplementary charges for pass holders** wishing to use even the most basic category of accommodation on overnight services. Some countries also levy a supplement for pass holders using premium daytime express trains. These supplements must usually be paid in local currency prior to boarding. In our view, the growing number of supplements gravely undermines the value of a pass, as the holder can no longer breeze through the station and avoid the queues at the ticket office. You can read more about supplements in the box (right).

A pass may make very good sense if you really intend to travel very intensively and cover long distances in those countries where rail tariffs are generally high. Bear in mind that Europe-wide passes (often referred to as **global passes**) are priced at a level that reflects the high prices of flexible walk-up tickets in countries such as Scandinavia, the Netherlands, France, Germany and Switzerland.

If your travel horizons lead you further east to areas where even flexible tickets are cheap, then a rail pass may be a poor investment. Even in Italy, they are not such a good deal — in part because the regular fares are very modestly priced, and also due to the hefty supplements demanded of pass holders using express services in Italy.

In those areas of Europe where market pricing offers potentially great deals for early bookers, travellers prepared to commit two or three months in advance will almost certainly pay less than pass holders. And yet every year, thousands of travellers do buy rail passes and never regret that decision.

The nub of the argument is that with a rail pass you purchase enormous flexibility. The **freedom to roam** at will does not come cheap, but can be incredibly liberating. Yet for those committed to keeping costs to a minimum, provided they are prepared to book well in advance and not change their itinerary, a rail pass may seem an expensive luxury.

Our comments on the relative merits of rail passes versus regular tickets relate mainly to global passes that cover a large part of Europe. If your geographical horizons are more limited, restricted to one country or even just one

SUPPLEMENTS FOR RAIL PASS HOLDERS

A rail pass does not necessarily entitle you to totally free travel. Many trains require that you pay a supplement. If you are keen to avoid **supplements**, always check at the ticket office before boarding. And be aware that on selected trains (eg. on TGV and Thalys services), there may be only a limited contingent of seats available for pass holders. Travellers who hop aboard without pre-checking availability, and without having paid for the necessary supplement, may be in for a big surprise as they are charged for the full fare for their journey.

Daytime travel supplements: Supplements, generally in the range of €4 to €10, sometimes more in first class, are payable on TGV services within France or between France and Switzerland, Germany or Italy; on Talgo services between France and Spain; on almost all express trains within Spain and Italy; and on the fastest premium services in the Czech Republic, Finland, Norway, Poland, Portugal and Sweden. In Italy, you may end up paying a €10 supplement for even a short hop. Romania and Greece both levy improbably high supplements on their fastest services. Pass holders may have to pay a €20 surcharge for a long journey across Romania. And a long journey on a premium Greek train may have you paying a €30 supplement.

The Thalys services linking Paris with Brussels, Amsterdam and Cologne carry hefty surcharges: €37 from Amsterdam to Paris and a pocket-draining €23 for the 30-minute run from Rotterdam to Antwerp. Eurostar simply won't accept rail passes, but does offer a **special pass holder fare** (see p31). Germany has in recent years become much more benign on the question of supplements. The only remaining daytime trains on which supplements are payable are half a dozen peak-time ICE trains branded as Sprinters and a handful of express trains to and from Paris.

Night train supplements: Most night trains require advance reservation and some sort of extra payment, even if you are willing to spend the entire night in a seat. Trade up to a **couchette** or **sleeping berth** and even pass holders will face a substantial supplement. Read more about night trains on p682.

part of a country, you may well find a more restricted pass that meets your needs perfectly. In the reference section at the end of this book (see p687) we give the low-down on the most commonly used rail passes. You'll find lots of nitty-gritty detail there.

At this stage, you may want to note just the bare facts. **InterRail** is designed for residents of Europe, while **Eurail** is designed for those who live outside Europe. The general **map of Europe** on pp10–11 in this book shows the extent of validity of the global InterRail and global Eurail passes. Check those maps and then refer to p687 to find out more about InterRail and p689 to find out more about Eurail.

There are some passes which are valid for a single country or just part of a country. You will find mention of these under the relevant country entry in the **gazetteer** section of this book (see pp598–676).

LINKS FROM BRITAIN

We include three routes that start in the UK. **Route 1** speeds to the continent using Eurostar, while **Routes 2** and **3** rely on ferry services to cross the Channel. Many will feel that Eurostar is the natural prelude to a journey around Europe by train (see our Eurostar feature on p30). But there are other options.

PLANES

The huge range of flights linking Britain with mainland Europe means that you can easily jet to the continent. Bear in mind that the bargain basement fares touted by some budget carriers might not be quite the great deals they first seem. Throw in taxes, booking charges and other extras, and that 'Fly to the Med for a Tenner' promotion may turn out not to be the perfect deal implied in the ad. To check out who flies where, turn to one of the specialist **aviation search** engines. We have found WhichBudget (www.whichbudget.com), Momondo (www.momondo.eu), and Alternative Airlines (www.alternativeairlines.eu) to be very reliable.

BUSES

Eurolines (www.eurolines.co.uk) operate direct services from London to Paris and Brussels, with their cheapest fares (£28 single or £39 return) undercutting Eurostar. There are also direct coaches, not always daily, from London to Amsterdam, Berlin, Budapest, Lyon, Munich and Vienna. Eurolines services from London either use P&O ferry services or the Eurotunnel shuttle for the hop over (or under) the English Channel. To learn more about long-distance coach travel on Eurolines' continent-wide network see www.eurolines.eu.

FERRIES

Britain has excellent passenger **ferry connections** with five countries in mainland Europe (Spain, France, Belgium, the Netherlands and Denmark). Travellers starting their journeys in northern England or Scotland may find the continental ferry links from Newcastle-upon-Tyne and Hull particularly useful. Sadly, Scotland lost its last direct ferry link with the continent in December 2010. The **table opposite** lists North Sea and eastern Channel routes. But if you are bound for north-west France or the Iberian peninsula, you should definitely consider the excellent network of routes operated by **Brittany Ferries** (www.brittanyferries.com). Key services useful for foot passengers wanting to connect to **Route 4** in France include Portsmouth to St-Malo and Plymouth to Roscoff. The Brittany Ferries services from Portsmouth and Plymouth to Santander in Spain, and a new Portsmouth to Bilbao route launched in 2011, all give the chance to bypass France to join **Route 12** in this book.

North Sea routes

From	To	Operator	ERT	Time
Newcastle	IJmuiden	DFDS	2255	14–15 hrs
DFDS Seaways operate connecting buses from Newcastle Central station to the ferry terminal at North Shields and from IJmuiden to Amsterdam Centraal (for **Route 15**)				
Hull	Europoort	P&O	2245	10–12 hrs
Connecting buses from Hull station to ferry terminal and from Europoort to Rotterdam Centraal station (for **Route 15**)				
Hull	Zeebrugge	P&O	2250	13–14 hrs
Connecting buses from Hull station to ferry terminal and from Zeebrugge to Bruges railway station (for **Route 14**)				
Harwich	Esbjerg	DFDS	2220	18–19 hrs
Short walk to boat from Harwich International station (ERT 15a and 200). Local bus from Esbjerg ferry terminal to train station (on a branch off **Route 21**) for direct train every 2 hrs to Copenhagen (ERT 705) for **Routes 17, 21, 22** and **25**				
Harwich	Hoek van Holland	Stena Line	2235	6–9 hrs
Short walk to boat from Harwich International station (ERT 15a and 200). Connects well with trains at Hoek van Holland (ERT 15a and 455) to join **Route 15** in Rotterdam				

Short sea and eastern Channel routes

From	To	Operator	ERT	Time
Dover	Calais	P&O	2110	75–90 mins
Foot passengers not conveyed on night services. Bus links to/from train stations at Dover and Calais. It is also possible to take a National Express Bus from London Victoria to the Dover ferry terminal (2 hrs 30 mins)				
Newhaven	Dieppe	LD Lines	2125	4 hrs
Alight at Newhaven Town station (NB. NOT the Harbour station) for the ferry terminal. Short walk from Dieppe port to train station for trains to Rouen and Paris (ERT 270a)				
Portsmouth	Le Havre	LD Lines	2165	3–8 hrs
Short taxi ride from Portsmouth & Southsea station (NB. NOT the Harbour station) to ferry terminal. Bus link to train station at Le Havre for direct trains to Paris (ERT 270)				
Portsmouth	Cherbourg	Brittany Ferries	2160	3–9 hrs
Alight at Portsmouth & Southsea station (NB. NOT the Harbour station) for a short taxi ride from there to ferry port. Bus link (Zéphir bus no. 8) to the train station at Cherbourg (for **Route 3**)				

THE EUROSTAR REVOLUTION

The 50 routes in this book focus firmly on the landscapes, cultures and sights of the countries through which they pass. And although we generally say little about the actual trains, we feel that Eurostar really deserves a mention in its own right. Many readers of this book will start or end their journeys in Britain; others will add on a short side trip to London as part of a longer tour of the European mainland. And the **Eurostar train service**, since it was launched in 1994, has subtly transformed Britain's relationship with its near neighbours on the continent. The move of Eurostar to its distinguished new London terminus in late 2007, happily coinciding with the opening of the new high-speed rail link from London to the Channel coast, reinforced the train's iconic status and its standing in the public imagination — on both sides of the Channel — as the most sensible way to travel between **London and the continent**. St Pancras was further enhanced by the reopening in 2011 by Marriott of the station hotel — now called the St Pancras Renaissance.

Eurostar's enviable success overturns the natural reticence that has often characterised England's relationship with its continental neighbours. French technological ingenuity was long directed to bridging the gap with its island neighbour. It was the Frenchman **Jean Blanchard** who in 1785 first crossed the Channel by balloon. Blanchard was alert to the symbolic importance of his pioneering journey. His balloon flight, just like the modern Eurostar trains, linked two nations that enjoy nothing more than spirited mutual ridicule. Shortly after Blanchard's flight, a French engineer proposed an undersea tunnel. Albert Mathieu-Favier's idea found no favour with the English who feared, perhaps not without good cause, that a tunnel might allow the French to invade England.

The following century and a half saw a good many precocious schemes to tunnel under the Channel, none of which succeeded in digging more than a short distance. The **engineering challenges** were immense, and the political hurdles even greater. British insularity resisted a fixed link. In 1928, one Scottish politician, giving evidence to a parliamentary committee in London, thought it no bad thing that the English Channel crossing by boat was "the worst sea journey in the world." The Earl of Crawford and Balcarres went on to hint that a tunnel would merely give succour to French proponents of nudity and German homosexuals eager to corrupt English morals.

TO FLANDERS AND BEYOND

Against such spirited opposition, is it not a matter of great wonder that some two dozen Eurostar trains now leave London every day bound for France and Belgium? It seems little short of a miracle that you can now scan the train departures board at **St Pancras** and, amid the lists of domestic departures to such prosaic spots as Luton and Leicester, continental destinations now feature.

Eurostar key facts

Route 1 of this book (see p50) kicks off by taking Eurostar from London St Pancras to Paris Nord. You can also use Eurostar as an alternative start to **Routes 2** and **3**, connecting with either of those routes in Paris.

Eurostar's second route from London is to **Brussels**, with many trains on that route stopping along the way at Calais-Fréthun (for a connection with **Route 2**) and Lille Europe. At Brussels you can connect onto **Route 14**. For just a small premium over the regular Eurostar fare to Brussels, you can extend your ticket's validity to cover any station in Belgium. You can then use your ticket, either on the day of arrival in Brussels or on the following day, for onward travel to any station in Belgium. So, whether your final destination be Bruges or Antwerp, a coastal resort or a village in the Ardennes, the onward rail journey on any Belgian Railways train is a good deal. The only restriction is that, on your onward journey beyond Brussels, you may not use Thalys or ICE services.

The **Lille Europe** stop made by some of the London to Brussels Eurostar services opens up a wealth of connection possibilities. Lille is a major hub on the French TGV network, and Eurostar passengers can change with ease onto direct trains to the south of France, Bordeaux and Alsace, so averting the need to change stations in Paris on itineraries from England to the French provinces. A number of Eurostar trains to and from London make additional stops at Ebbsfleet or Ashford International — very handy for travellers from Kent and East Sussex.

Eurostar offers a limited number of other direct trains from London to France, including winter services to the Isère Valley in the French Alps, a seasonal summer service to Avignon in the Rhône Valley, and an all-year direct train to Marne la Vallée-Chessy. The latter is particularly popular in the UK market for families visiting the **Disneyland resort**.

Book at www.eurostar.co.uk for one-way or return journeys starting in Britain. Fares to Paris and Brussels from London start at £39 one way and £69 return (there are small discounts for travellers aged 25 or less or 60 and over). You can also **book tickets** to any station in Belgium or the Netherlands, to many provincial cities across France and to Aachen and Cologne in Germany. At **www.eurostar.co.uk**, you can book tickets not just from London but also from over 300 other stations around Britain. Eurostar's French-language website at www.eurostar.fr offers much the same functionality but does not offer through fares to or from destinations in Britain beyond London. Tickets for most Eurostar services go on sale four months prior to travel, although for trains to the Alps, Marne-la-Vallée and Avignon tickets are often released very much earlier.

You can also purchase tickets for Eurostar services and onward connections from the various **agents and websites** mentioned on p22. It is worth checking around if you are travelling beyond a regular Eurostar destination. For example, for journeys from London to Germany, www.bahn.co.uk may offer more advantageous fares than those available on the Eurostar websites.

Eurail and InterRail passes are not valid for travel on Eurostar. Pass holders can however purchase a special ticket. It has the advantage of being flexible, but early bookers can secure regular tickets that undercut the pass holder fare.

Brussels rubs shoulders with Bedford. Choose the right time, and you might even see Avignon, Bourg-St-Maurice or Marne la Vallée-Chessy making a guest appearance amid the routine lists of trains bound for the English Midlands.

Eurostar re-engineers our travel horizons. It is possible to leave London in the afternoon and travel via Brussels to Cologne, arriving in the Rhineland city in good time to connect onto a **night train** to Warsaw, Minsk and Moscow. You'll be in Poland on the morning after departure from London. Or take Eurostar to Paris, arriving early evening in time to transfer onto comfortable night trains to Germany, Spain and Italy. Read more about night trains from Paris on p684. You can be in Venice, Madrid or Munich on the morning after you leave London.

The Eurostar journey itself is magic. To slide out of St Pancras early on a bright summer morning is a kaleidoscopic adventure. Watch for tantalising shadows at **Stratford** before a burst of sunshine as the train storms out of the London tunnels onto the Dagenham marshes. Speed past containers piled high on Thames-side industrial parks with glimpses of the slender bridge over the river at Dartford against a backdrop of blue sky. The route plunges under the Thames, out into a nowhere-world of north Kent industry and, just as disorientation threatens to set in, you are speeding over the **Medway Viaduct**. By the time you notice the first pang of morning hunger, the train has swept under the North Downs to emerge in a verdant vale of oast houses and picture-perfect villages. Then through the **Channel Tunnel**. In less than an hour from London, you are in France. On the right is the **forêt de Guînes**, a mere wisp of a wood where Jean Blanchard landed on his 1785 balloon flight from England to France. The entire Eurostar experience is pure cinema.

Whereas many of the slow train journeys described in this book breed a contemplativeness born of the immensity of landscape, Eurostar exhilarates by diminishing distance. Speed soaks up detail as poppies in the fields of Flanders become a red haze. It is quite simply a magnificent way to travel.

EXPLORING EUROPE

For many Londoners, the Eurostar fast rail service to the continent has been a journey of discovery, inviting them to rethink their relationship with their continental neighbours. London is now closer to Brussels than it is to Leeds or Manchester. And this book is full of such journeys of discovery with 50 carefully crafted routes that invite you to **rethink Europe**. Get a taste of what is to come with our sixteen page colour feature starting on the opposite page.

Note on colour feature
Every place included in our colour feature is on or close to one or more of the routes in this book. When a photo is credited to 'hidden europe', it comes from the collection of the editors of this book. All other images, each duly credited to the original photographer, were sourced through dreamstime.com.

Europe in colour:
journeys of discovery

BARCELONA

ABOVE: Most cities in Europe have fabulous markets for fresh produce. La Boqueria is in the heart of Barcelona (which is on **Routes 8** and **9**; photo © Tupungato). BELOW: The showpiece Finnish city of Tampere boasts a superb industrial heritage. It makes an excellent stopover when following **Route 26** (photo © hidden europe).

TAMPERE

COLOGNE

The Hohenzollern bridge is used by all trains crossing the Rhine to enter Cologne's main railway station from the east. The German city is on **Routes 16** and **18** (photo © Hiro1775).

VITEBSK

Enthusiasm for stern Soviet-style memorials has not waned in Belarus. Here, stone soldiers on Victory Square in Vitebsk, which is on **Route 45**, the longest of the 50 journeys described in this book (photo © hidden europe).

Trieste

Miramare Castle on the outskirts of Trieste, a city that features on **Routes 35** and **38** (photo © hidden europe).

La Mancha

Above: Red soils are one of the characteristics of Spain's La Mancha region. Explore tapas and more on **Routes 9, 10** and **13** and see also **Sidetracks C** (photo © hidden europe). Below: Gare do Oriente in Lisbon, Portugal, is on **Routes 9** and **11** (photo © Serban Enache).

Lisbon

Oslo

Above: Ice-cool design at Oslo's opera house, which opened in 2007. The Norwegian capital is on **Routes 21, 22** and **24** (photo © Masr). Below: Neoclassical lines and Habsburg style at the main station in Zagreb, a good place to break your journey when exploring **Routes 38** and **39** in this book (photo © Stelya).

Zagreb

ABOVE: Ride **Route 44** south from Mostar and you cannot miss the village of Počitelj with its distinctive mosque (photo ©Lianem). BELOW: Córdoba in southern Spain (**Route 13**) is most noted for its Moorish architecture, but the Puente Romano (Roman Bridge) is a reminder that long before Córdoba was a Muslim caliphate, the city was capital of the Roman province of Hispania Baetica (photo © Mauro Bighin).

CÓRDOBA

Dubrovnik

ABOVE: Dubrovnik, one-time capital of the Republic of Ragusa, is the most celebrated of Croatia's coastal towns. It is on **Routes 38** and **44** (photo © Jay Beiler). BELOW: Trakai is a Lithuanian landmark, easily visited as a day trip from Vilnius (which is on **Route 46** in this book; photo © Maruszkin).

Trakai

MOSTAR

ABOVE: Bridging the Neretva River in Mostar on **Route 44** (photo © Neyo).

EUROPE BY NIGHT

ABOVE: City Night Line, a subsidiary of the Deutsche Bahn, runs Europe's most extensive network of night trains (photo © hidden europe).

GENOA

BELOW: Style and tradition at the harbour in Genoa on **Route 33** (photo © hidden europe).

BUDAPEST

ST PETERSBURG

Above: Grand trains in grand stations are commonplace in central Europe. The *Tisza Express* (with through carriages to Russia) is preparing to depart from Budapest Keleti, an ornate station which you'll visit on **Routes 40, 42** and **48** (photo © Attila Vörös).

LEFT: Russian imitation of French style in the Grand Cascade at Peterhof. The palace complex features in our 'Best of St Petersburg' on p565. St Petersburg is on **Route 45** (photo © Javarman).

BRUSSELS

ABOVE: An exuberant city at the heart of Europe, Prague lies at the crossroads of **Routes 47** and **48** (photo © Steve Allen).

RIGHT: The Atomium in Brussels was designed by André Waterkeyn and constructed for the 1958 World Fair. Although very much a symbol of its time, it remains one of the main attractions in the Belgian capital. Brussels is on **Route 14** (photo © Quan Qi).

BORDEAUX

LEFT: Bordeaux lies at the centre of a region noted for its fine wines. This lively city on the Garonne River is on **Routes 4** and **5** in this book (photo © Vanessak).

BELOW: Featuring in this edition of *Europe by Rail* for the first time, the rail route from Lucerne to Interlaken is one of the finest in Switzerland. Here, the summit station at Brünig-Hasliberg, part of **Route 30** (photo © hidden europe).

SWITZERLAND

The ship-shaped Alcázar of Segovia, built on the site of a former Arab fortress, is one of the most distinctive palaces built after the Christian re-conquest of the Iberian peninsula. Segovia features on **Route 10** (photo © Dan Breckwoldt).

ISTANBUL

Istanbul may seem like the end of the line for travellers exploring Europe by train, but there are plenty of onward boat connections. The city is at the end of **Route 40** in this book (photo © Ahmet Ihsan Ariturk).

MENTON

LEFT: The most Italianate of the French Riviera towns, Menton is a wonderful place to spend a few days. The view here is looking east across the border to the coast of Liguria in Italy. Menton is on **Route 6** (photo © hidden europe).

BELOW: Although the German capital has smartened up in the 20 years since German unification, Berlin's edgy cultural scene is still a big draw. The city is on **Routes 16, 20, 45, 48** and **49** (photo © Mihaela Catalina Zaharescu).

BERLIN

HELSINKI

Eliel Saarinen's design (1914) for the main railway station in Helsinki. The city is on **Routes 26, 27** and **46** (photo © hidden europe).

SKOPJE

RIGHT: Certainly one of Europe's least-known capitals, Skopje is an excellent introduction to Macedonia and features on **Route 43** (photo © hidden europe).

LONDON

London's new gateway to the continent at St Pancras International opened in 2007. The station is a sensitive restoration of an 1868 design by William Barlow. **Route 1** in this book starts here (photo © Drew Macdonald).

SUCEAVA

Suceava on **Route 50** is the jumping-off point for visits to the local monasteries. This is the katholikon of Saint George at Voroneţ with its distinctive shade of blue in the building's exterior murals (photo © Radu Razvan Gheorghe).

ABOVE: Steam survives in western Poland (**Route 45**; photo © Remik44992). BELOW: The north Norwegian Lofoten island archipelago is easily visited in conjunction with **Route 24** (photo © hidden europe).

LOFOTEN

BELOW: The colourful Nyhavn waterfront in Copenhagen. The Danish capital is on **Routes 17, 21, 22** and **25** (photo © Christopher Grant).

COPENHAGEN

BIARRITZ

ABOVE: Stylish Biarritz in south-west France is a place to relax when exploring **Routes 5** and **12** (photo © Gregory Guivarch). BELOW: Steaming through the Harz Mountains in Germany. The Harz network of narrow-gauge lines can be visited as part of **Route 16** (photo © hidden europe).

HARZ

The Estonian capital of Tallinn is on **Route 46** (photo © Eerik Kaste).

TALLINN

Routes

Fifty key rail routes that together capture the very best that Europe has to offer. Our routes cover cities and landscapes from the Arctic to Andalucía, from the Baltic to the Bosphorus, from the Channel to the Carpathians. You can use our country index (p698) to check coverage on a country-by-country basis. Or refer to our place name index (p699–704) to identify principal towns.

Rail Route 1: From London to the Med

CITIES: ★★★ CULTURE: ★★ HISTORY: ★ SCENERY: ★★
COUNTRIES COVERED: ENGLAND, FRANCE

The Mediterranean has long held special appeal for northern Europeans. For the sun-starved English heading south, the natural route was always to cross the English Channel and travel south via **Paris** to the **Rhône Valley**. Forty years ago, travellers from London to Provence might have chosen to start their journey by climbing aboard one of the blue and gold Wagons-Lits sleeping cars that every evening left London Victoria station for Paris. The entire train was shipped on a ferry across the Channel. Eleven hours to Paris, changing stations there, and with time for a late breakfast at the stylish Le Train Bleu, a belle époque restaurant at the Gare de Lyon, before boarding a midday train that arrived in Marseille the same evening. That train journey, which in 1970 took 24 hours, can today be accomplished in just six or seven hours, using Eurostar from London via the Channel Tunnel and connecting at either Lille or Paris onto a French TGV service to the south. It is a superb way of reaching the south of France from London.

But might we suggest an alternative? **Eurostar** is definitely worth taking, for the run out of London is a dramatic piece of travel theatre. But having sped to Paris, why not dawdle through France? Instead of speeding south from Paris on a TGV, reaching Marseille in just three hours, why not take slower trains instead? Nowadays relegated to the status of a secondary route, the classic line **south from Paris** (via Sens and Dijon), which we describe in this chapter, is the Paris-Lyon-Méditerreanée (PLM), the company that introduced to the route such celebrated luxury trains as the *Côte d'Azur rapide* and *Le Train Bleu*.

As you move south, the scenery on this route becomes ever more compelling, and the journey culminates in a magnificent ride south along the Rhône Valley to the Mediterranean. If pressed to nominate our favourite spots for overnight stops on this route, we would opt for **Beaune** and **Avignon**. If you prefer to stop at places with more of a big-city feel, then **Dijon** and **Lyon** are your best bets.

LONDON — SEE P509

You will find a useful description of how Eurostar has transformed the journey from London to Paris on p30. The route from London speeds through the Garden of England to the **Channel Tunnel**. Your first glimpses of France are of **Flanders**, and the route then tracks south through Picardy to the French capital.

PARIS — SEE P538

The Eurostar service from London terminates at **Gare du Nord** in Paris. For the onward journey south from Paris, you need to change stations for the south-

Note

Hourly fast trains link Paris (Lyon) with Dijon (ERT 370), but the journey described in Route 1 relies on the slower TER services shown in ERT 371.

ROUTE DETAILS

London (St Pancras)–
Paris (Nord)

ERT 10

Type	Frequency	Typical journey time
Train	Every 1–2 hrs	2h15

Paris (Bercy)–Dijon

ERT 371

Type	Frequency	Typical journey time
Train	6 daily	3 hrs

Dijon–Beaune

ERT 377

Type	Frequency	Typical journey time
Train	Every hr	20 mins

Beaune–Lyon

ERT 377

Type	Frequency	Typical journey time
Train	Every 1–2 hrs	1h45

Lyon–Orange

ERT 351

Type	Frequency	Typical journey time
Train	Every 1–2 hrs	2h10

Orange–Avignon

ERT 351

Type	Frequency	Typical journey time
Train	Every 1–2 hrs	15 mins

Avignon–Marseille

ERT 351

Type	Frequency	Typical journey time
Train	Every hr	65 to 80 mins

KEY JOURNEYS

London–Lille

ERT 10

Type	Frequency	Typical journey time
Train	7–10 daily	1h30

Lille–Lyon

ERT 11

Type	Frequency	Typical journey time
Train	Every 2–3 hrs	3 hrs

Paris–Lyon

ERT 340

Type	Frequency	Typical journey time
Train	Every hr	2 hrs

Lyon–Marseille

ERT 350

Type	Frequency	Typical journey time
Train	Every 1–2 hrs	1h40

bound services that depart either from **Gare de Lyon** or from **Paris Bercy**. If you are keen to push on south at speed, make for the Gare de Lyon from where a TGV will whisk you non-stop to Dijon in just 100 minutes. But far better, if you can possibly afford the time, to take the TER train from Paris Bercy to Dijon — a three-hour journey that gets ever better with every mile that passes. Since December 2011, five trains per day on the classic Paris to Dijon route have been extended through to Lyon, a move by SNCF that surely pleased PLM purists.

The hop through Paris from Gare du Nord to Gare de Lyon or Bercy could not be easier. Look for RER Line D (shown in shamrock green on most Paris transport maps). Take any southbound train (bound for Melun or Malesherbes) and it is just two stops to Gare de Lyon. For Bercy, change at Gare de Lyon. It is then just one station on métro route 14 southbound (towards Olympiades) to Bercy.

If you shun the TGV and take the slower TER from **Paris Bercy to Dijon**, you will quickly discover why artists like Millet were so taken by the landscapes south-east of Paris. The train runs through the forests of **Fontainebleau** and between hills that become slowly more emphatic. Then the train cuts through a long tunnel and drops down steeply into the **Saône Valley** to reach Dijon.

DIJON

Dijon is an excellent introduction to **Bourgogne** (Burgundy), the region of France that is so intimately associated with the fine wines of the same name. The city's grandest building is the strikingly elegant **Palais des Ducs et des États de Bourgogne**, best viewed from the pl. de la Libération. The building reflects the great wealth of the Dukes of Burgundy and now serves as the town hall, also housing the **Musée des Beaux-Arts** (closed Tues, free entry). This is a superb collection of paintings, sculptures and tapestries. Don't miss the marvellously carved, gold-encrusted tombs in the **Salle des Gardes** (guardroom). Dijon's partly pedestrianised city centre is dotted with attractive squares and historic buildings. R. Verrerie has many half-timbered houses featuring ornate wood-carvings (some are now antique shops). Pl. de la Libération contains an elegant crescent of *hôtels particuliers* (17th-century mansions). There are more behind the palace, especially in r. des Forges, hub of the former jewellery and goldsmiths' quarter. The 13th-century Gothic **Église de Notre-Dame**, in r. de la Chouette, has a facade adorned with three tiers of arches. Look out for the lucky *chouette* (owl) on a corner buttress. Overhead, life-size figures on the 14th-century **Horloge de Jacquemart** (Jacquemart's clock) spring into action every quarter-hour. Beneath the **Cathédrale de St-Bénigne** is a fine Romanesque crypt.

ARRIVAL, INFORMATION, ACCOMMODATION

≋ Cour de la Gare, 5 mins west of the centre. The station is at the end of av. du Maréchal-Foch. 🚹 **Tourist offices**: 11 r. des Forges, ☎ 08 92 70 05 58 (premium rate), www.visitdijon.com, and at the train station. A suggested walking tour covering all the main sites is available. ◄ A cheap option, yet highly regarded, is the **Hôtel Victor Hugo**, 23 r. des Fleurs, ☎ 03 80 43 63 45 (www.hotelvictorhugo-dijon.com), €. Other reasonably-priced options include the charming **Hostellerie 'le Sauvage'**, 64 r. Monge, ☎ 03 80 41 31 21 (www.hotellesauvage.com), €€, a former staging inn, or **Le Jacquemart**, 32 r. Verrerie, ☎ 03 80 60 09 60 (www.hotel-lejacquemart.fr), €€. If you feel like sleeping in Napoleonic style go for the 4-star **Hostellerie du Chapeau Rouge**, 5 r. Michelet, ☎ 03 80 50 88 88 (www.chapeau-rouge.fr), €€€, built for the Emperor himself. **Hostel** (non HI): **Ethic étapes Dijon**, 1 blvd. Champollion, ☎ 03 80 72 95 20 (www.cri-dijon.com), is quite a way from the centre (🚌 3 will get you there) and has dorms from €18. **Campsite: Camping Municipal du Lac Kir**, 3 blvd. Chanoine Kir, ☎ 03 80 43 54 72 (www.camping-dijon.com), by a lake about 1 km from the centre (🚌 12 to CHS La Chartreuse; open April–October).

✗ There are lots of lively pizzerias and foreign restaurants, many with outside tables in summer, in the streets around pl. Émile Zola. Besides the fine wines of Burgundy, Dijon is famed for *moutarde* (mustard) and *crème de cassis* (used to make kir), *bœuf bourguignon* and *coq au vin* – the latter two dishes both worth trying here.

CONNECTIONS

Three trains a day run north to Nancy (taking 2 hrs 20 mins, ERT 379) to join **Route 3** (p66). En route you can change at Culmont for **Troyes** (1 hr 30 mins, ERT 380), an engaging market town in the heart of Aube-en-Champagne. Highlights include the cathedral and a wonderful modern art museum, but much of the pleasure is just strolling around and peeking into alleyways and courtyards. From Troyes you can continue north-west to return to Paris. In fact, for travellers wanting just a quick taste of provincial France, the triangular route Paris – Dijon – Troyes – Paris is a fine introduction, and one even more enhanced if while in Dijon you take time to ride south to Beaune and back.

WINE COUNTRY

The entire route south from Dijon to Avignon takes you through or close to some of France's most celebrated vineyards, producing wines that north of Lyon are generally classified as Burgundy and south of Lyon carrying a Rhône appellation. Tucked away within these general categories are some small properties that have world-class reputations. And nowhere is that more true than on the 20-minute train journey from Dijon to Beaune, which skirts the **Côte de Nuits**. The **vineyards** to the right of the train produce some of the most expensive wines in the world, among them the *grands crus* from Chambertin, Vosne-Romanée and Corton.

BEAUNE

Beaune is a charming old town of cobbled streets and fine mansions. The magnificent **Hôtel-Dieu**, r. de l'Hôtel-Dieu, with its flamboyant patterned roof of colourful geometric tiles, was originally built in the 15th century as a hospital for the sick and needy. Inside, don't miss the 15th-century *Polyptych of the Last Judgement*, showing sinners tumbling to an unpleasant fate. This building is the centre of the prestigious **Côte de Beaune** and **Côte de Nuits** wine trade; the tourist office lists local *caves* (wine cellars) that offer *dégustations* (tastings). The old ducal palace houses a museum dedicated to the subject: **Musée du Vin**, r. d'Enfer (closed Tues during Dec–Mar, €5).

ARRIVAL, INFORMATION, ACCOMMODATION

 Av. du 8 Septembre, east of town, just outside the old walls. **Tourist office**: Porte Marie de Bourgogne, 6 blvd. Perpreuil, ☎ 03 80 26 21 30 (www.beaune-burgundy.com). Located in a historic building, the **Hôtel de la Paix**, 45 r. du faubourg Madeleine, ☎ 03 80 24 78 08 (www.hotelpaix.com) is a 10-minute walk from the train station.

LYON

This big metropolis (population approx. 1.5 million) at the junction of the Saône and the Rhône has a lovely old centre, with a hive of charming streets and some truly amazing restaurants; it's rated as one of France's gastronomic high points, and as you might expect from a major university city, there's a lively buzz about the place.

The two rivers divide the city into three parts. On the west bank of the Saône is **Vieux Lyon**, the Renaissance quarter, while on the east bank of the Rhône is the modern business sector, with its high-rise offices and apartment blocks. In between the rivers lies the partly-pedestrianised city centre, dating largely from the 17th and 18th centuries. It runs from pl. Bellecour, where the tourist office stands, north to the old silk quarter of **La Croix-Rousse**.

Lyon is famous for its *traboules* — covered passageways between streets that once served as shortcuts for the silk traders and protected their precious cargoes from the weather. Most *traboules* are in **Vieux Lyon** and **La Croix-Rousse**. Lyon's best museums are the **Musée des Beaux Arts** on pl. des Terreaux (closed Tues) and the **Musée des Tissus et des Arts Décoratifs** (closed Mon), 34 r. de la Charité, recounting the history of the textile industry in Lyon. Old silk looms are still in use at **Maison des Canuts**, 10–12 r. d'Ivry (closed Mon & Sun). Just across Pont Galliéni over the Rhône from Perrache station is the poignant **Centre d'Histoire de la Résistance et de la Déportation**, 14 av. Berthelot (closed Mon & Tues).

Julius Caesar founded the Roman town of Lugdunum, on the hillside of Fourvière above Vieux Lyon. Take the funicular railway from near the cathedral up to the **Basilique Notre-Dame-de-Fourvière** for spectacular city views. Then walk down to the **Musée gallo-romain de Fourvière**, 17 r. Cléberg (closed Mon), which has mosaics, coins and jewels: the neighbouring **Théâtre Romain**, r. de l'Antiquaille, is the oldest Roman amphitheatre in France. Take the other funicular railway back down to the riverside.

ARRIVAL, INFORMATION, ACCOMMODATION

⇌ There are two main-line stations; many trains stop at both. **Lyon-Perrache**, pl. Carnot, is the more central (left-luggage facilities, 0615–2300, showers, money exchange offices, a restaurant and bar). For the tourist office, cross pl. Carnot, then follow r. Victor Hugo to pl. Bellecour (15 mins). **Lyon-Part-Dieu** (mainly TGVs) is on the east bank of the Rhône and serves the business district. It has similar facilities to Perrache. ✈ **Aéroport de Lyon-Saint Exupéry**: 32 km east of Lyon, ☎ 08 26 80 08 26 (www.lyon.aeroport.fr). The *RhôneExpress* (tram) runs every 15 mins until approx. 2400 between the airport and Part-Dieu rail station, taking 30 mins. ℹ **Tourist offices**: pl. Bellecour, ☎ 04 72 77 69 69 (www.lyon-france.com, métro: Bellecour). Additional branch in summer at av. Adolphe Max in Vieux Lyon.

Buses, funiculars, local trams and the **métro** are run by TCL (*Transports en Commun Lyonnais*). Get the map (*plan du réseau*) from the tourist office or any TCL branch; for information, ☎ 08 20 42 70 00 (http://tcl.canaltp.fr). The métro is modern, clean and safe. Four lines, A, B, C and D, criss-cross the city, operating 0500–2400. The two *funiculaires* (funicular trains) depart every 10 mins until 2200 (2400 for the Fourvière line) from Vieux Lyon métro station to either the hilltop Basilique or the Roman ruins. Buses generally run 0500–2100. Two tram lines, T1 and T2, both run through Perrache station, and T3 from Lyon-Part-Dieu (T1 links the two stations).

The weekly *Lyon Poche* lists the week's **events** (www.lyonpoche.com, French only). The best areas for **clubbing** are near the Hôtel de Ville and quai Pierre Scize. The 1,200-seat Lyon Opera House on pl. de la Comédie is a surprising mix of 18th- and 20th-century architecture. Lyon is the birthplace of Guignol, the original 'Punch and Judy'. Shows for kids and adults alike are on either at the Théâtre le Guignol de Lyon, 2 r. Louis Carrand in Vieux Lyon, ☎ 04 78 28 92 57, or in the open air in the Parc de la Tête d'Or.

🛏 There is a huge choice of **hotels** in every category and finding a room should not be difficult even at the height of summer. Try around the stations or in the Presqu'île quarter, north and south of the tourist office. **Hôtel Bayard**, 23 pl. Bellecour, ☎ 04 78 37 39 64 (www.hotelbayard.fr), €€, or the **Hôtel La Résidence**, 18 r. Victor Hugo, ☎ 04 78 42 63 28 (www.hotel-la-residence.com), €€, are good value. **Hostel** (HI): 41–45 montée du Chemin Neuf, ☎ 04 78 15 05 50 (www.fuaj.org/lyon), ideally located in the old quarter and with local character (métro: Saint Jean, then funicular or 🚌 28 from Part-Dieu rail station, 🚌 31 from Perrache to Vieux Lyon quarter, then the funicular to Les Minimes). **Campsite: Camping International de Lyon**, Porte de Lyon, 10 km north-west, ☎ 04 78 35 64 55 (www.camping-lyon.com), also has cabins and trailers to rent. Take the 🚌 89 from Gare de Vaise to Porte de Lyon.

✗ Lyon is renowned for its cuisine and boasts some of the best restaurants in France, serving fantastic food but often with prices to match. More traditional restaurants are known as *bouchons*, mainly found in **Presqu'île**, the area to the north of the tourist office, and **Vieux Lyon**, where simple, and often very good-value meals are served. Lyon has many specialities: *tablier de sapeur*, slices of tripe fried in breadcrumbs; *andouillette*, tripe sausages cooked in white or red wine; and *quenelles de brochet*, poached pike fish balls. Lyon has some wonderful street **markets**. There are food markets every day except Monday at **Les Halles** and **La Croix-Rousse**. On Sunday mornings don't miss the art and craft market, **Marché de la Création**, on the riverside by the cathedral in Vieux Lyon.

CONNECTIONS FROM LYON

Lyon is handily placed for heading east to explore the Alps by rail. For a superb route east into the Alps go via Culoz, Aix-les-Bains, Annecy and La-Roche-sur-Foron, where you can either continue to Geneva (p271) or take the narrow-gauge mountain railway from Chamonix-Mont Blanc to Martigny (ERT 572). There is also a much less interesting direct line from Lyon to Geneva (takes 2 hrs, ERT 346). **Culoz** is a gateway for the **Marais de Lavours**, a national park noted for its marshland habitats, while beyond the well-heeled lakeside spa of **Aix-les-Bains** (where excursion boats cross Lac du Bourget to the mystical monastery of L'Abbaye d'Hautecombe) is **Annecy**, an up-market, but still very beautiful, lakeside resort town in the heart of the Savoie Alps.

If you continue to Martigny, you switch to a metre-gauge line and climb into the mountains, with the option of a side trip on the **Tramway du Mont Blanc** (ERT 397) from St-Gervais-le-Fayet to (summer only) the Nid d'Aigle (2,386 m — and a 15-min stroll from the Bionnassay Glacier). Chamonix is placed beneath Mont Blanc, the highest peak in the Alps; the **Montenvers rack railway** (ERT 397) climbs 5 km to a height of 1,913 m, looking over the Mer de Glace, France's biggest glacier, which you can actually enter by way of a tunnel to visit the ice grotto. A great way of venturing into Italy is by travelling to Turin via Chambéry, Modane and through the 12.8 km **Fréjus tunnel** and past the Italian ski resort of Bardonecchia.

SOUTH FROM LYON

Lyon marks your first encounter with the **River Rhône**, and Route 1 beyond this point hugs the river for the journey south to Avignon. This is an oddly mixed landscape. Just south of Lyon huge oil refineries tower over historic villages. Nuclear power stations sit cheek by jowl with vineyards producing some of the Rhône's finest wines. The latter include the parched slopes of Côte Rôtie which you'll see high above the far bank of the river. A little further south the railway snakes between the tiered terraces of the Hermitage vineyards, the names of the principal growers highlighted in huge signs beside the tracks.

ORANGE

This northern gateway to Provence had a population of some 80,000 in Roman times and several sites from the period are still in existence. The **Arc de Triomphe** is the third largest Roman arch to have survived, and was originally in fact a gate to the ancient walled city. Dating from about 25 BC, it is a majestic three-arched structure lavishly decorated with reliefs depicting battles, naval and military trophies and prisoners, honouring the victories of Augustus and the setting up of *Arausio* (Orange) as a colony. Orange's most famous sight is its **Roman theatre**, dating from the 1st century AD and with the best preserved back wall in the Roman Empire, standing 37 m tall, a magnificent setting for the town's song and opera festival in summer. A museum (open daily) opposite the amphitheatre has some unique local Roman finds as well as some intriguingly incongruous scenes of British life painted by the Welsh artist Frank Brangwyn; some 800 of his paintings having been donated to the town. In the evening, walk around place Sylvain or place de la République for a drink or dinner.

ARRIVAL, INFORMATION, ACCOMMODATION

≋ Av. F. Mistral, 1.5 km east of the centre. ⊞ The main **tourist office** is across town, 5 cours Aristide Briand, ☎ 04 90 34 70 88 (www.otorange.fr). Another branch on pl. des Frères Mounet (open July–Aug only). ⊨ **Hôtel St Jean**, 1 cours Pourtoules, ☎ 04 90 51 15 16 (www.hotelsaint-jean.com), €€; the lobby is actually a cave. A good value option is the **Hôtel St Florent**, 4 r. du Mazeau, ☎ 04 90 34 18 53 (www.hotelsaintflorent.com), €.

AVIGNON

In 1305, troubles in Rome caused the Pope to move his power base to Avignon. Wealth flowed into the town — and remained after the papacy moved back to Rome 70 years later. The city walls, built to protect the papal assets, still surround the city and enclose just about everything worth seeing here. Jutting from the north-western section is **Pont St-Bénezet**, the unfinished bridge famed in song (*Sur le pont d'Avignon*), inevitably a tourist trap (€5.50 in high season), but now with a museum and a restored rampart walk leading up to the **Rocher des Doms** garden with its great views over both the bridge and the nearby town of Villeneuve-lès-Avignon. Take the steps from the gardens down to the Romanesque cathedral, **Notre-Dame-des-Doms**, dating from the 12th century and containing the tombs of Pope John XXII and Pope Benedict XII.

Adjacent is the most photographed sight in the city, the huge **Palais des Papes** (Papal Palace), boasting a 45-metre-long banqueting hall where cardinals would meet to elect a new Pope. In appearance it's more like a fortress than a palace and is still the most prominent landmark in the city. The Popes acquired the dignified **Petit Palais** in 1335, and a couple of centuries later it was adapted into a sumptuous residence for Cardinal Giulio della Rovere, the future Pope Julius II, who began the collection of Renaissance treasures that has now made the building into an art museum (€10.50 in high season).

Contemporary art is to be found at the **Collection Lambert** (5 r. Violette, closed Mon). In the middle of the Rhône lies **Île de la Barthelasse**, a favourite picnic island, with its own summer swimming pool. **Place de l'Horloge** is popular for its street entertainment and outdoor cafés.

LE FESTIVAL D'AVIGNON

For three weeks in July, Avignon hosts one of Europe's largest drama festivals (www.festival-avignon.com). Soak up the ambience and see theatrical events of all dimensions. Events are held outdoors or in venues ranging from the majestic Palais des Papes to quaint courtyards and barn-like warehouses.

ARRIVAL, INFORMATION, ACCOMMODATION

⇌ **Avignon-Centre,** just outside Porte de la République gateway in the city walls: head through this gateway and straight along cours J. Jaurès for the centre. Shuttle buses (ERT 351a) from this station link to Avignon-TGV station, 5 km to the south. **🖪 Tourist office:** 41 cours J. Jaurès, ☎ 04 32 74 32 74 (www.avignon-tourisme.com). Another branch at Pont St-Bénezet (Mar–Oct only). ⊨ During the drama festival in July (see box) everywhere gets completely booked up and you'd do better to stay at Tarascon or elsewhere, and travel in. At other times head into the Old Town, where you'll find a large number of reasonably priced pensions and hotels in the backstreets a few minutes away: try the **Innova,** 100 r. Joseph Vernet ☎ 04 90 82 54 10 (www.hotel-innova.fr), €. To step back to the future – just for a look as it's extremely expensive – visit **Cloître St Louis,** 20 r. du Portail Boquier, ☎ 04 90 27 55 55 (www.cloitre-saint-louis.com), €€€, a unique 4-star hotel. An oasis of calm just off Avignon's main street, it combines tradition and modernity; the old part is housed in original 16th-century cloisters and the new wing was designed by Jean Nouvel. **Hôtel Central,** 31 r. de la République, ☎ 04 90 86 07 81 (www.avignon-central-hotel.com), €€, has a lovely, Provence-style garden. **Hostels** (non-HI): **Auberge Bagatelle,** Île de la Barthelasse, ☎ 04 90 86 30 39 (www.campingbagatelle.com), 10-min walk from the centre; dorms from €15 and all-year 3-star camping facilities. The **Centre de Rencontres Internationales YMCA** is over the Rhône, in Villeneuve-lès-Avignon, 7 bis chemin de la Justice, ☎ 04 90 25 46 20 (www.ymca-avignon.com); 🚌 10 from the post office opposite Avignon-Centre station to Les Angles (stop: Monteau).

TO THE COAST

South from Avignon you are spoilt for choice with three routes south to Marseille. None wins any prizes for outstanding beauty, but whichever one you take, you will be struck by how the landscape opens out and becomes much more southern in demeanour. There are distant views of the arid **limestone peaks** of the Alpilles and on the route via **Arles** glimpses of flat delta landscapes that merge into the **Camargue.** Whichever route you opt for, our journey from London to the Mediterranean ends with an eyeful of the northern suburbs of Marseille — not always pretty but a reminder that the city of *pastis* and *bouillabaisse* is also a major industrial centre.

MARSEILLE — SEE P87

Rail Route 2: The Channel coast to the Midi

CITIES: ★★ CULTURE: ★★ HISTORY: ★★ SCENERY: ★
COUNTRIES COVERED: ENGLAND, FRANCE

Our route from **London** to south-west France is a classic journey in its own right. Of course you could get from London to Toulouse quicker — either by plane or by train, using Eurostar and with just one easy change of train in Lille. But our route here is more leisurely and takes in not just **Paris** but some of the finest cities in provincial France along the way. This route makes a bold transect across the middle of France, and you will surely notice the more southern flavours that become more evident as you approach **Toulouse**. Our favourite overnight stops on this route are at **Boulogne**, Paris and **Cahors**.

The journey starts at London's Victoria station, once dubbed 'The Gateway to the Continent'. If time is tight, you can always take Eurostar to Paris. You can then join this route in the French capital and follow it south-west across France to Toulouse. Or take Eurostar from London to Calais-Fréthun station from where a shuttle bus, run by Ligne BCD on behalf of the French railways, meets most trains to give a link with Calais town station where you can pick up this route.

But purists keen to follow the full route below should take the **Dover** to **Calais** ferry on the journey from London to Paris, although Newhaven to Dieppe is a credible alternative, and that too starts from London Victoria. Sadly, it is not possible to buy through rail-sea tickets from London to France anymore, so you will have to purchase one ticket for the train journey to the coast, another for the ferry and yet another for onward rail travel in France.

LONDON — SEE P509

TO THE KENT COAST

There is something rather special about starting a long journey on a humdrum commuter train, and you will surely have that feeling on the run down to Dover from Victoria. Leafy south London suburbs give way to unexciting industry along the Thames, surrendering eventually to gorgeous Kent countryside with views of Canterbury cathedral before the railway cuts through a range of chalk hills to Dover.

DOVER

Dover Priory railway station might seem like the most depressing place on earth, but don't underestimate the town itself which has a first-rate **local museum** (closed Sun off-season) and a very fine **castle** (closed Tues & Wed in winter). A visit to the castle, set in a commanding position overlooking the Straits of Dover,

Notes

A shuttle train connects main-line Les Aubrais–Orléans station to the town of Orléans. All trains from Limoges to Toulouse stop at Cahors.

ROUTE DETAILS

London–Dover ERT 100, 101

Type	Frequency	Typical journey time
Train	Every hr	1h09

Dover–Calais ERT 2110

Type	Frequency	Typical journey time
Boat	1–2 every hr	75–90 mins

Calais–Boulogne ERT 261

Type	Frequency	Typical journey time
Train	Every 1–2 hrs	35–40 mins

Boulogne–Amiens ERT 261

Type	Frequency	Typical journey time
Train	Every 2–3 hrs	1h30

Amiens–Paris (Nord) ERT 260

Type	Frequency	Typical journey time
Train	Every 1–2 hrs	1h15

Paris (Austerlitz)–Orléans (Les Aubrais) ERT 294

Type	Frequency	Typical journey time
Train	Every 1–2 hrs	1 hr

Orléans (Les Aubrais)–Limoges ERT 310

Type	Frequency	Typical journey time
Train	6–7 daily	2h20

Limoges–Toulouse ERT 310

Type	Frequency	Typical journey time
Train	7–8 daily	3h25

KEY JOURNEYS

London–Paris ERT 10

Type	Frequency	Typical journey time
Train	Every 1–2 hrs	2h15

Calais–Paris ERT 265

Type	Frequency	Typical journey time
Train	4–5 daily	2 hrs

Paris–Toulouse ERT 300, 310

Type	Frequency	Typical journey time
Train	5–6 daily	5h30

is a great prelude to crossing the Channel by ship. The castle is reached by bus 15 or 15A from the centre of town.

Not all **ferry** companies sailing from Dover to France accept foot passengers. Your best bet is **P&O** which conveys travellers without cars on daytime sailings only. Regular bus services connect Dover Priory train station and the ferry terminal (from about 0730 till early evening). A similar service in Calais, from mid-morning until early evening, links the P&O dock with Calais Ville station.

The 90-min crossing on the comfortable P&O ship is a highlight of this route. Remember to take time to stroll the decks, from where you'll have fine views of the **iconic white cliffs** that line the Kent coast at Dover. Arrival in Calais is a shade less romantic than in William Turner's famous picture of the steamer from England docking at Calais pier. A modern industrial port serves today's ships.

CALAIS

Ignore the English voices among the crowds, and there's a good French feel about the shops and restaurants along the main road from the port, especially on market day in pl. d'Armes (Wed/Sat) or blvd. Lafayette (Thur/Sat). Rodin's famous statue of the **Six Burghers of Calais** stands in front of the Flemish-style **Hôtel de Ville** (town hall), commemorating the English capture of the town in 1347. Opposite, in the Parc St-Pierre, is the **Musée de la Guerre**, devoted to a more recent conflict — World War II — and originally used as a bunker by German forces. The **Cité Internationale de la Dentelle et de la Mode**, located in a 19th-century lace factory at 135 Quai du Commerce, celebrates a local industry (closed Tues).

ARRIVAL, INFORMATION, ACCOMMODATION

≋ **Calais-Ville**, the main station, is almost opposite the Hôtel de Ville. The other station, **Calais-Fréthun**, is about 8 km south-west of Calais and is served by some Eurostar trains from London to Brussels. ⛴ **P&O** (Dover), ☎ 08 25 12 01 56 (☎ 08 71 664 2121 from UK, www.poferries.eu); 🚩 **Tourist office**: 12 blvd. Clemenceau; ☎ 03 21 96 62 40 (www.calais-cotedopale.com). ⊨ Plenty of hotels around r. Royale, such as the friendly, family-run **Hôtel du Beffroi**, 8 r. André Gerschell, ☎ 03 21 34 47 51, just off place d'Armes, €. Slightly more expensive, but equally well regarded is the **Hôtel Meurice**, 5 r. Edmond Roche, ☎ 03 21 34 57 03 (www.hotel-meurice.fr), €€. **Hostel** (HI): **Centre Européen de Séjour**, av. du Maréchal de Lattre de Tassigny, ☎ 03 21 34 70 20 (www.auberge-jeunesse-calais.com), 1 km from rail station.

BOULOGNE-SUR-MER

Boulogne-sur-Mer's **Basse Ville** (lower town) is unremarkable, though the port area is a constant hive of activity. One of the town's major attractions is **Nausicaá** (www.nausicaa.fr), an excellent (if expensive) aquarium on the seafront at blvd.

Sainte-Beuve. But by far the best thing in Boulogne is the **Ville Haute** (upper town), tantalisingly visible from the lower town within its well-preserved 13th-century ramparts. A walk around the **city walls** immediately transports you into medieval France, and provides fine views of the harbour. Besides the moated **château** (containing a history museum), the main sights are the 19th-century **Basilique Notre-Dame** with its landmark Italianate dome, and the ancient Hôtel de Ville on a charming cobbled square.

ARRIVAL, INFORMATION, ACCOMMODATION

≈ **Boulogne-Ville**, 1 km south of the centre; all buses stopping here go to the centre. **❏ Tourist office:** Parvis de Nausicaá, ☎ 03 21 10 88 10 (www.tourisme-boulognesurmer.com).

◄ Boulogne-sur-Mer has good-value hotels right in the heart of town. Try the reasonably priced, very central, 2-star **Hôtel de Londres**, 22 pl. de France, ☎ 03 21 31 35 63 (www.hotel-delondres.com), €€. For a great location close to the beach, try **Hôtel Alexandra**, 93 rue Adolphe Thiers, ☎ 03 21 30 52 22 (www.hotel-alexandra.fr), €–€€. **Hostel** (HI): The youth hostel is on pl. Rouget de Lisle, ☎ 03 21 99 15 30 (www.fuaj.org/Boulogne-sur-Mer), 100 m from the station.

AMIENS

Two world wars did great damage to what was a major industrial centre, sparing only the **Cathédrale Notre-Dame d'Amiens**, Europe's largest and arguably France's purest example of Gothic architecture. Sympathetically restored to their original character, the winding streets of the **St-Leu** district, straddling the Somme just north of the cathedral, date from medieval times. In summer, take a **boat trip** on the tiny canals criss-crossing the 'Hortillonnages' (market gardens), just beyond the cathedral. Jules Verne spent his last years in Amiens. You can visit his house (2 r. Charles-Dubois), and his grave in the Cimetière de la Madeleine (r. Saint-Maurice).

ARRIVAL, INFORMATION, ACCOMMODATION

≈ The main station, easily spotted near the austere post-war Tour Perret, lies about 500 m south-east of the cathedral. Turn right on blvd. d'Alsace-Lorraine and then second left on r. Gloriette. **❏ Tourist office:** 6 bis r. Dusevel, or 40 pl. Notre-Dame, ☎ 03 22 71 60 50 (www.amiens-tourisme.com). ◄ A basic but cosy option, close to the cathedral is the **Hôtel Victor Hugo**, 2 r. de l'oratoire, ☎ 03 22 91 57 91 (www.hotel-a-amiens.com), €, which is also 5 mins from the train station.

PARIS — SEE P538

You will arrive at Paris Nord. For the onward journey south, transfer to Austerlitz using métro route 5 (in the direction Place d'Italie). The run south from Paris is uninspiring, with the railway traversing open agricultural land until the forests that presage arrival in Orléans.

ORLÉANS

Orléans' older quarter, containing several Renaissance mansions, has been restored since World War II. Today Orléans makes much of its associations with **Jeanne d'Arc** (Joan of Arc, the Maid of Orléans), who saved the town from the English in 1429. Her statue takes pride of place in the spacious pl. du Martroi, and the nearby **Maison de Jeanne d'Arc**, pl. du Général de Gaulle, is a reconstruction of her lodgings with a museum recounting her life and the events of 1429. The annual **Fête de Jeanne d'Arc** (29 Apr to 8 May) features a living 'Jeanne' riding through the streets. The impressive **Cathédrale Sainte-Croix** (Holy Cross Cathedral) commemorates Jeanne in its 19th-century stained-glass windows. Guided tours of the roof include a panoramic city view.

ARRIVAL, INFORMATION, ACCOMMODATION

⇐ Gare d'Orléans, on the northern edge of the centre by pl. d'Arc **shopping complex**; r. de la République runs straight ahead to pl. du Martroi, in the heart of town. Gare d'Orléans is actually on a short spur, just off the main rail line, and through services stop only at nearby **Gare des Aubrais-Orléans** station. A train shuttle service (*navette*) linking the two stations connects with every through train; there is also a tram service. **🚌 Bus station** on r. M-Proust, **☎** 02 38 53 94 75, a block from Gare d'Orléans (connected by a covered passage). **🛈 Tourist office**: 2 pl. de l'Étape; **☎** 02 38 24 05 05 (www.tourisme-orleans.com).

‎   ➤ The streets around r. du Fg-Bannier and pl. Gambetta have some inexpensive hotels, such as the 2-star **Hôtel Le Saint-Aignan**, 3 pl. Gambetta, **☎** 02 38 53 15 35 (www.hotel-saintaignan.fr), €€. The central **Le Brin de Zinc**, 62 r. Saint Catherine, **☎** 02 38 53 38 77, €, has a restaurant. Close to the train station is the comfortable **Hôtel d'Arc**, 37 Ter r. de la République, **☎** 02 38 53 10 94 (www.hoteldarc.fr), €€.

LIMOGES

Capital of the Limousin region, Limoges is a large industrial city. Its delightful medieval centre is a web of dark, narrow streets filled with half-timbered houses, small boutiques, and antique and china shops. Surrounded by well-maintained botanic gardens — and overlooking the River Vienne — is the Gothic **Cathédrale de St-Étienne** (St Stephen's). The nearby Bishop's Palace contains some fine collections of porcelain and enamel (pl. de la Cathédrale; admission free), though it scarcely matches the magnificent array of porcelain and faïence on show at the **Musée Adrien-Dubouché**, pl. Winston Churchill, reopened in spring 2012 after renovation. Devotees of porcelain can take a tour of the **Bernardaud factory**, 1 km north of town (at 27 av. Albert Thomas, **☎** 05 55 10 55 91 (closed Sun; book ahead). Limoges was a centre of the Resistance during World War II. The **Musée de la Résistance et de la Déportation**, which relocated at the end of 2011 to r. Neuve Saint-Etienne, traces some of the Resistance operations.

ARRIVAL, INFORMATION, ACCOMMODATION

≈ **Gare des Bénédictins**, 500 m north-east of the Old Town (a wonderful example of art deco). ∎ **Tourist office**: 12 blvd. de Fleurus, ☎ 05 55 34 46 87 (www. limoges-tourisme.com). ⊨ Try **Familia**, 18 r. du Gén. Bessol, ☎ 05 55 77 51 40 (www. hotelfamilia.fr), €€. **Hôtel de la Paix**, 25 pl. Jourdan, ☎ 05 55 34 36 00 (www. hoteldelapaix87.fr), €–€€, is quiet and within walking distance of the station and town centre, and hosts a phonograph museum for the curious.

✘ Well-priced ethnic restaurants and student bars crowd the southern end of r. Charles Michels. Le Bistro d'Olivier at the **Halles Centrales** (covered market) does cheap, hearty lunches. Alternatively, stock up at the market, open daily until 1300.

CONNECTIONS FROM LIMOGES

Occasional trains run east to **Clermont-Ferrand** (ERT 326) to connect with **Route 7** (see p100).

CAHORS

An important Roman base on the tortuously winding River Lot, Cahors is famed for its red wine, which at its best rivals the vintages of Bordeaux. Its major monument, frequently depicted on wine labels, is the 14th-century **Pont Valentré**, a six-arched fortified bridge with three towers, west of the centre (reached via the r. du Président Wilson). Gallo-Roman remains dot the town, and medieval houses are grouped around the cathedral.

ARRIVAL, INFORMATION, ACCOMMODATION

≈ A 10-min walk west of the centre. ∎ **Tourist office**: pl. F-Mitterrand, ☎ 05 65 53 20 65 (www.tourisme-cahors.com). ⊨ For a special treat, the **Grand Hôtel Terminus** is a beautifully restored station hotel dating from the 1920s, 5 av. Charles de Freycinet, ☎ 05 65 53 32 00 (www.balandre.com), €€. The **Hôtel de la Paix**, 30 pl. St-Maurice, ☎ 05 65 35 03 40 (www.hoteldelapaixcahors.com), €, is located on a small square in the centre of town. Also recommended is the great value **Hôtel Jean XXII**, 2 r. Edmond Albe, ☎ 05 65 35 07 66 (www.hotel-jeanxxii.com), €. ✘ At night, head out to one of the cafés and restaurants on blvd. Léon Gambetta or r. Nationale.

CONNECTIONS FROM CAHORS

SNCF buses heading east from Cahors snake along one of the most beautifully sinuous sections of the Lot Valley to **Figeac**, a likeable old town that makes a pleasant base for a day or two. The bus passes through Conduché, from where it's a walk of just over 5 km past Cabrerets to **La Grotte du Pech-Merle**. This cave is one of Europe's great underground sights, not only for its stalactites and stalagmites, but also for its Stone

Age art. Also on the way are **Saint-Cirq-Lapopie** and **Cajarc**, quaint medieval villages well worth visiting.

On the rail line north from Figeac to Brive-la-Gaillarde, **Rocamadour** is the stunningly situated village (4 km from Rocamadour station) set on narrow ledges of a cliff face, where the famous Black Virgin has drawn pilgrims since the 12th century. The village actually looks more impressive from a distance. Wall-to-wall kitsch shops pander to the tourists and the devout who pack its main street for much of the year.

TOULOUSE

Now a lively university city and cultural centre, the capital of the Midi region is one of France's largest cities, not consistently attractive but with a wealth of medieval religious art. The pinky-red brick of many of the grandiose town houses has earned the city the epithet of the **Ville Rose**. The centre is walkable, but there is also a bus service, two short métro routes and a tram route, all run by **Tisséo**, ☎ 05 61 41 70 70 (www.tisseo.fr). Tickets cover all three modes, the best value being the *carnet* (pack) of ten, available from ticket booths or the main office; only single tickets are sold on board buses. Also consider the *Tribu* pass (for up to six people travelling together).

Many of the main attractions are in the **Old Town**, centred on **pl. du Capitole**, dominated by the 18th-century **Le Capitole** (town hall). The superb St-Sernin is the sole survivor of an 11th-century Benedictine monastery established to assist pilgrims en route to Santiago de Compostela (see p138). The **Musée des Augustins** showcases medieval sculptures rescued from long-gone city churches.

ARRIVAL, INFORMATION, ACCOMMODATION

≥ **Toulouse-Gare Matabiau**, north-east of the city; a 15- to 20-min walk from pl. du Capitole – or take the métro, stopping at **Marengo–SNCF**. 🚺 **Tourist office**: Donjon du Capitole, Square Charles de Gaulle, ☎ 05 61 11 02 22 (www.toulouse-tourisme.com).

🛏 If you fancy a splurge, check out the brand-new design hotel **Citiz**, 18 Allées Jean Jaurès, ☎ 05 61 11 18 18 (www.citizhotel.com), €€–€€€, right in the historic centre. Budget places can be found in the centre, around pl. Wilson (r. St-Antoine) and pl. du Capitole (r. du Taur and r. de Romiguières). There are cheap hotels around the station, but the area is best avoided. **Anatole France**, 46 pl. Anatole France, ☎ 05 61 23 19 96 (www.anatolefrancehotel.com), €, is centrally located. **Hostel**: La Petite Auberge de Compostelle, 17 r. d'Embarthe, ☎ 06 64 44 64 03 (www.gite-compostelle-toulouse.com), has dorm rooms with self-catering facilities right in the historic centre. ✗ Try **Casa Manolo**, 24 r. des Trois Piliers, open daily, a bodega with plenty of Spanish food, tapas and salads. In summer, treat yourself to a home-made ice cream from **Ô Sorbet D'Amour**, 28 r. Montardy.

CONNECTIONS FROM TOULOUSE

Continue south over the Pyrenees on **Route 8** (p104), or follow **Route 5** (p80) west to France's Atlantic coast or east towards Provence and the Riviera.

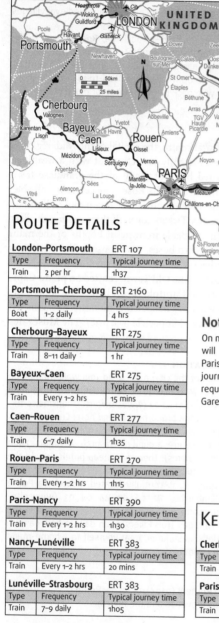

ROUTE DETAILS

London–Portsmouth   ERT 107

Type	Frequency	Typical journey time
Train	2 per hr	1h37

Portsmouth–Cherbourg   ERT 2160

Type	Frequency	Typical journey time
Boat	1–2 daily	4 hrs

Cherbourg–Bayeux   ERT 275

Type	Frequency	Typical journey time
Train	8–11 daily	1 hr

Bayeux–Caen   ERT 275

Type	Frequency	Typical journey time
Train	Every 1–2 hrs	15 mins

Caen–Rouen   ERT 277

Type	Frequency	Typical journey time
Train	6–7 daily	1h35

Rouen–Paris   ERT 270

Type	Frequency	Typical journey time
Train	Every 1–2 hrs	1h15

Paris–Nancy   ERT 390

Type	Frequency	Typical journey time
Train	Every 1–2 hrs	1h30

Nancy–Lunéville   ERT 383

Type	Frequency	Typical journey time
Train	Every 1–2 hrs	20 mins

Lunéville–Strasbourg   ERT 383

Type	Frequency	Typical journey time
Train	7–9 daily	1h05

Notes

On many journeys across France via Paris, it will be necessary to change stations in Paris. On Route 3, for example, through journeys from Cherbourg to Strasbourg require a change from Paris Lazare to the Gare de L'Est.

KEY JOURNEYS

Cherbourg–Paris   ERT 275

Type	Frequency	Typical journey time
Train	5–7 daily	3 hrs

Paris–Strasbourg   ERT 390

Type	Frequency	Typical journey time
Train	Every 1–2 hrs	2h20

Rail Route 3: Normandy to Alsace

CITIES: ★★★ CULTURE: ★★ HISTORY: ★★ SCENERY: ★
COUNTRIES COVERED: ENGLAND, FRANCE

Our route starts with a journey by train and ferry from **London** to **Normandy** as the prelude to a superb transect across France from the Cotentin peninsula to the **German border**. If we gave ratings for alcohol quality (as we do for scenery, see above) then this route would be the tops, with Calvados, Champagne and the wonderfully varied wines of Alsace all making star appearances along this route. It is a route that has a good dose of rural France, with some landmark cities along the way.

LONDON — SEE P509

It is a nice touch that a route that takes in some of the most fiercely contested battlefields of the 20th century starts with a war memorial at London's **Waterloo Station**, recalling the railway workers who died in World War I. The journey to Portsmouth is an easy 97-min run (ERT 107). The railway cuts through the North Downs at Guildford, which makes a good en-route stop. Beyond **Guildford**, the rail route affords great views of the wooded western Weald.

PORTSMOUTH

Portsmouth is still the premier naval city in Britain, and the landmark sight is the **Historic Dockyard**, which will appeal even to those with no interest in military matters. The wreck of the *Mary Rose*, a 16th-century warship recovered from the silts of Portsmouth Harbour, is the crowd-puller. A display hall for the *Mary Rose* is under construction and is due to open in mid-2012. If travelling directly on to **France**, alight at Portsmouth and Southsea station, for bus or taxi transfer to the Continental Ferry Port, which in April 2011 transformed into a smart new terminal. Brittany Ferries is the principal ferry operator on the route to Cherbourg, additional summer sailings are provided by Condor Ferries (ERT 2160). Daytime crossings take 4 hrs, nighttime ones up to 9 hrs.

CHERBOURG

Essentially a commercial and military port, Cherbourg played a key role in the **Battle of Normandy**. It was liberated by American troops three weeks after the landings on Utah Beach and used as a deep-water port. Hilltop **Fort du Roule**, overlooking the town and port, contains a museum commemorating the Allied liberation of Cherbourg and the Cotentin peninsula. A worthwhile recent attraction is the **Cité de la Mer**, housed in the former transatlantic ferry terminal, a grand art deco building. Its exhibits cover the theme of underwater exploration, and include Europe's largest aquarium plus a decommissioned nuclear submarine.

ARRIVAL, INFORMATION, ACCOMMODATION

≋ Pl. Jean Jaurès, at the south end of Bassin du Commerce (harbour). ⛴ The **Gare-Maritime** ferry port is north-east of the town centre; a shuttle bus runs between the two. There are cross-channel ferry services to the UK — Poole (ERT 2145), Portsmouth (ERT 2160) — and also to Rosslare in Ireland (ERT 2010). **🎦 Tourist office**: 2 quai Alexandre III (www.cherbourgtourisme.com), on the far side of Bassin du Commerce. Information also at Gare-Maritime on ferry arrivals and departures, ☎ 02 33 44 39 92.

🛏 The area north of the tourist office offers some cheap lodging options. Try the **Hôtel de la Renaissance**, 4 r. de l'Église, ☎ 02 33 43 23 90 (www.hotel-renaissance-cherbourg.com), €€, with views of the sea; or the **Hôtel Ambassadeur**, 22 quai de Caligny, ☎ 02 33 43 10 00 (www.ambassadeurhotel.com), €-€€, old-fashioned but comfortable, with views of the harbour. Just off the main square, the **Croix de Malte** is a modernised option, 5 r. des Halles, ☎ 02 33 43 19 16 (www.hotelcroixmalte.com), €€. **Hostel**: The official **youth hostel** (HI) is at 55 r. de l'Abbaye, ☎ 02 33 78 15 15 (www.fuaj.org), 3 km from the station by 🚌 3 or 5 to 'Chantier'. ✗ Lots of glass-fronted restaurants line the quayside road; there are cheaper options in the streets behind, where vestiges of the Old Town survive around pl. Centrale.

CONNECTIONS FROM CHERBOURG

A bus service (the bus station is opposite the rail station) heads down the Cotentin peninsula to the hilltop town of **Coutances**, via the villages of Martinvast and medieval Bricquebec, whose ancient fortress has a mighty keep housing a tiny museum.

BAYEUX

The first town liberated by the Allies after World War II, Bayeux escaped any damage to its fine medieval centre, dominated by the spires of the magnificent **Cathédrale Notre-Dame**. The world-famous **Bayeux tapestry** is a 70 m length of embroidered linen illustrating the Norman Conquest of England. It is thought to have been commissioned soon after the Battle of Hastings by the Bishop of Bayeux from an Anglo-Saxon workshop run by monks. The historical explanations, film shows and displays in the **Centre Guillaume-le-Conquérant**, where it is housed, rue Nesmond, interpret the scenes very thoroughly, but it is worth hiring a multilingual audio-guide as you walk round. The **Musée Mémorial de la Bataille de Normandie**, blvd. Fabian Ware, is one of the best museums in the area covering the Normandy campaign.

ARRIVAL, INFORMATION, ACCOMMODATION

≋ Pl. de la Gare, a 10- to 15-min walk south-east of the centre; upon exiting the station turn left on blvd. Sadi Carnot, bearing right until it becomes r. Larcher. Continue to r. St-Martin on the left: the tourist office is on the right. There are also buses into the centre from the bus station right by the train station. ⓘ **Tourist office**: Pont Saint-Jean, ☎ 02 31 51 28 28 (www.bessin-normandie.com). ⨝ The **Reine Mathilde** has simple rooms over a popular brasserie, 23 r. Larcher, ☎ 02 31 92 08 13 (www.hotel-reinemathilde.com), €€, while the **Hôtel d'Argouges**, 21 r. St-Patrice, ☎ 02 31 92 88 86 (www.hotel-dargouges.com), €€–€€€, is an upmarket option in an 18th-century building. The **youth hostel** (HI) is at 39 r. Général de Dais, ☎ 02 31 92 15 22, and doubles as a popular guesthouse.

CONNECTIONS FROM BAYEUX

Low tide at **Arromanches** (about 10 km from Bayeux, 🚍 75), reveals the remains of Mulberry Harbour – the artificial port and floating landing-stage for transporting troops and vehicles from the UK during D-Day operations. Visit the **Musée du Débarquement** for a comprehensive panorama of the events leading up to and during D-Day. A neat way of avoiding Paris is by changing at Caen for trains to Le Mans and Tours (ERT 271 and 275), both on **Route 4**.

ROUEN

Your first stop in Rouen should be the **Cathédrale Notre-Dame**, the subject of a series of Monet's paintings. An example of his work showing the west front can be seen at the attractively restored **Musée des Beaux Arts**, pl. Verdrel (closed Tues, free under 26s). A good-value joint ticket gives admission to two other Rouen museums. The old city centre, restored after war damage, has many colourful half-timbered buildings. At the end of the main street, r. du Gros Horloge, in pl. du Vieux Marché, a 20-m cross by the church marks the spot where Joan of Arc was burned at the stake in 1431. **La Tour Jeanne d'Arc**, r. du Donjon (closed Tues), is the only remaining tower of the castle where Joan of Arc was imprisoned just before her execution.

ARRIVAL, INFORMATION, ACCOMMODATION

⨝ R. Jeanne d'Arc, 1 km north of the centre. Either walk down into town (10–15 mins) or take the métro. The centre is pedestrianised, and all the main sights lie within walking distance of each other, so there's little point in buying a bus and métro day-pass. ⓘ **Tourist office**: 25 pl. de la Cathédrale, ☎ 02 32 08 32 40 (www.rouentourisme.com), right in front of the cathedral. ⨝ There are many affordable hotels in town, most in the north, but also in the Old City. Try **Hôtel le Cardinal**, 1 pl. de la Cathédrale, ☎ 02 35 70 24 42 (www.cardinal-hotel.fr), €–€€, or the **Hôtel des Carmes**, 33 pl. des Carmes, ☎ 02 35 71 92 31 (www.hoteldescarmes.com), €€. In a cobbled street, the **Hôtel de la Cathédrale** is a real charmer, 12 r. St Romain, ☎ 02 35 71 57 95 (www.hotel-de-la-cathedrale.fr), €€.

CONNECTIONS FROM ROUEN

Dieppe, reached in just over an hour from Rouen by train (ERT 270a) and with ferries to Newhaven in England, is an attractive coastal town. Its flint and sandstone **château**

is perched on the lofty white cliffs rising high above the shingle beach. The museum inside contains a fascinating collection of ivory artefacts carved by seafarers. The harbour is a lively area, lined with seafood restaurants. In the streets behind, a spectacular Saturday market (Pl. Nationale/Grande Rue/r. St Jacques) draws crowds from far and wide. **ℹ Tourist office**: 56 Quai Duquesne, ☎ 02 32 14 40 60 (www.-dieppetourisme.com). Accommodation includes **Au Grand Duquesne**, 15 pl. St Jacques, ☎ 02 32 14 61 10 (http://augrandduquesne.free.fr), €€, right by the market.

PARIS — SEE P538

MÉTRO CONNECTIONS

Trains from both Cherbourg and Rouen (and from the ports of Le Havre and Dieppe) arrive at **Paris St-Lazare** station, while trains for the Strasbourg direction leave from Paris-Est station. Allow 1 hr to cross Paris via the métro (lines 3 and 7, changing at Opéra) or use the RER line E from Haussmann St-Lazare to Magenta, close to **Paris-Est**.

NANCY

The historical capital of Lorraine is a stylish town, surprisingly little known for its architectural treasures. Its three main squares combine to create one of France's great masterpieces of town planning, commissioned by the Polish-born Duke of Lorraine, Stanislas Leszczynski, in the 18th century. Cream stone, ornate gateways and stately arches characterise the neoclassical **place Stanislas**, its entire south side taken up by the palatial Hôtel de Ville. Behind is the pl. d'Alliance, and to the north, through the Arc de Triomphe, the 15th-century pl. de la Carrière. In the early 1900s art nouveau made its mark on Nancy. Visit the **Musée de l'École de Nancy**, 36–38 r. du Sergent Blandan (closed Mon–Tues, 🚌 122 or 123 to Painlevé or Thermal) for fine examples of the style.

ARRIVAL, INFORMATION, ACCOMMODATION

🚊 Pl. Thiers, a 10-min walk from the town centre along r. Stanislas. **ℹ Tourist office**: pl. Stanislas, ☎ 03 83 35 22 41 (www.ot-nancy.fr). A couple of inclusive tourist passes give discounts on local museums and transport. Pick up a walking tour leaflet to see some of the best art nouveau buildings in town.

🛏 Housed in a beautifully restored building in the heart of the city, the **Hôtel des Prélats**, 56 pl. Monseigneur Ruch, ☎ 03 83 30 20 20 (www.hoteldesprelats.com), €€€, is well worth splashing out on. More affordable options include the **Hôtel de Guise**, 18 r. Guise, ☎ 03 83 32 24 68 (www.hoteldeguise.com), €€, or **Les Portes d'Or**, 21 r. Stanislas, ☎ 03 83 35 42 34 (www.hotel-lesportesdor.com), €€. **Hostel**: The 15th-century **Château de Rémicourt** (HI), 149 r. de Vandoeuvre, Villers-lès-Nancy, ☎ 03 83 27 73 67, is 4 km west of Nancy station (🚌 126/134/135 or tram line 1). Close by is **Camping Le Brabois**, av. Paul Muller, Villers-lès-Nancy, ☎ 03 83 27 18 28 (www.camping-brabois.com), open Apr–Oct; 🚌 122/125 from the station to Camping. ✗ Try pl. Stanislas and r. des Maréchaux for smart cafés and late-night bars.

LUNÉVILLE

Lunéville's chief glory is its massive 18th-century **château**, built by Duke Leopold of Lorraine in imitation of Versailles and graced with magnificent gardens, but its collections were destroyed by fire in 2003. However, some temporary exhibitions are held (free entry) and the tourist office is located within the château. The church of **St-Jacques**, pl. St-Rémy, has a unique baroque organ.

ARRIVAL, INFORMATION, ACCOMMODATION

≋ A 15-min walk from the centre. ⌕ **Tourist office**: Aile sud du Château, ☎ 03 83 74 06 55 (www.ot-lunevillois.com). ➼ **Hôtel du Commerce**, 93 r. d'Alsace, ☎ 03 83 73 04 17 (www.hotelducommerce-luneville.com), €, or **Hôtel Les Pages**, 5 quai des Petits Bosquets, ☎ 03 83 74 11 42 (www.hotel-les-pages.fr), €€, opposite the château.

STRASBOURG

The old capital of Alsace, once a mere fishing village, has grown into a most attractive city, successfully combining old with new. It's best known today as the seat of the European Parliament, housed in an imposing new building on the city outskirts. The prettiest bit of town is **Petite-France**, where 16th- and 17th-century houses crowd around narrow alleys and streams. The river is spanned by the picturesque **Ponts Couverts**, a trio of medieval covered bridges with square towers. The **Cathédrale Notre-Dame** is a Gothic triumph with a carved west front. Highlights include the 13th-century **Pilier des Anges** (Angels' Pillar) and the 19th-century **Horloge Astronomique** (astronomical clock), which strikes at 1230 each day. The tower, a 332-step climb, provides a marvellous city view.

ARRIVAL, INFORMATION, ACCOMMODATION

≋ Pl. de la Gare, 10-min walk to the centre. ⌕ **Tourist office**: 17 pl. de la Cathédrale, ☎ 03 88 52 28 28 (www.otstrasbourg.fr), with a branch at pl. de la Gare. The tourist offices sell a good value 3-day **Strasbourg Pass** (€13.40). ➼ Ideal for rail travellers, conveniently located close to the station, are the **Hôtel Monopole Métropole**, 16 r. Kuhn, ☎ 03 88 14 39 14 (www.bw-monopole.com), €€, and the **Mercure Strasbourg Gare Centrale**, 14–15 pl. de la Gare, ☎ 03 88 15 78 15 (www.mercure.com), €€–€€€. A good choice in the Old Town, nicely situated right beside the cathedral, is **Hôtel Patricia**, 1A r. du Puits, ☎ 03 88 32 14 60 (www.hotelpatricia.fr), €€. **Hostel:** The closer of the two official youth hostels (HI) is **René Cassin**, 9 r. de l'Auberge de Jeunesse, ☎ 03 88 30 26 46 (www.hihostels.com), 1 km from the station (🚌 2/15 to Auberge de Jeunesse). ✗ There are plenty of cafés and *winstubs* (traditional Alsatian restaurants) near the cathedral, on r. des Tonneliers and in the Petite-France quarter.

CONNECTIONS FROM STRASBOURG

Continue east over the border into Germany to Offenburg (ERT 912) on **Route 19** (p189). You can also continue south through Alsace to enter Switzerland at Basel (p261) on **Route 29** (ERT 385 and 390).

Rail Route 4: Western France

CITIES: ★★ CULTURE: ★★ HISTORY: ★ SCENERY: ★
COUNTRIES COVERED: FRANCE

The 19th-century English lawyer and explorer Charles Packe knew western France like the back of his hand, criss-crossing the region on journeys to and from his beloved Pyrenees. But he bemoaned how slow the trains were. Over 12 hours in 1862 by the fastest express from Paris to Bordeaux, and 20 hours with the slower trains. Today's traveller can speed from Paris to Bordeaux in little more than three hours. But Route 4 is for those less inclined to hurry. It takes in cathedrals and châteaux, long beaches and rocky coastlines. And along the way we explore some of Atlantic Europe's most historic regions: **Brittany** *(Bretagne)*, the Loire Valley and Aquitaine. Ideally this is a route to be spread over three or four days.

PARIS — SEE P538

The railway west from Paris to Chartres is one of the finest routes out of the French capital. It passes through Versailles and the Forest of Rambouillet and for the final run into Chartres follows the gentle valley of the River Eure.

CHARTRES

The city is famous for just one thing, the magnificent Gothic **Cathédrale Notre-Dame**, which replaced an earlier building destroyed by fire in 1194. It's known especially for the quality and brilliance of its 13th-century stained glass, dazzling even on the dullest of days, and the wealth of carved stone, notably around the west doorways. The rest of the town is a pleasant place with winding streets and a pleasant Old Town area by the **Eure**, with good views of the cathedral.

ARRIVAL, INFORMATION, ACCOMMODATION

⇌ Pl. Pierre Sémard. Follow the signs to the cathedral to reach the centre. 🚹 **Tourist office**: pl. de la Cathédrale, ☎ 02 37 18 26 26 (www.chartres-tourisme.com). 🛏 **Le Grand Monarque** is a safe and comfortable bet in a historic building with a bistro, 22

TO FRANCE BY FERRY

For travellers starting in Britain or Ireland who are prepared to sacrifice the first part of the route described here, there are excellent ferry connections across the western Channel direct to north-west France. Brittany Ferries sail Plymouth to Roscoff (ERT 2135) and Portsmouth to St-Malo (ERT 2180). They also have a summer Cork to Roscoff ferry (ERT 2015). Condor Ferries offer Weymouth to St-Malo and in summer also Poole to St-Malo (ERT 2100). Some of these Condor sailings are via the Channel Islands of Jersey and Guernsey.

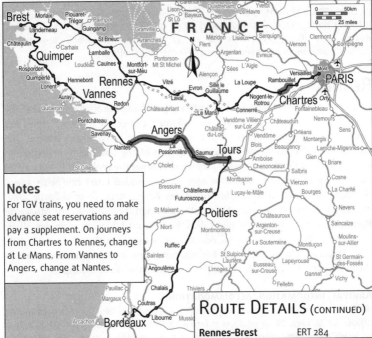

Notes

For TGV trains, you need to make advance seat reservations and pay a supplement. On journeys from Chartres to Rennes, change at Le Mans. From Vannes to Angers, change at Nantes.

KEY JOURNEYS

Paris (Montparnasse)–Bordeaux ERT 300

Type	Frequency	Typical journey time
Train	Every 1–2 hrs	3h15

Paris–Brest ERT 284

Type	Frequency	Typical journey time
Train	5–7 daily	4h40

ROUTE DETAILS

Paris (Montparnasse)–Chartres ERT 278

Type	Frequency	Typical journey time
Train	1–2 per hr	1h10

Chartres–Rennes ERT 278, 280

Type	Frequency	Typical journey time
Train	7 daily	2h40 to 3hrs

ROUTE DETAILS (CONTINUED)

Rennes–Brest ERT 284

Type	Frequency	Typical journey time
Train	10–12 daily	2h30

Brest–Quimper ERT 286

Type	Frequency	Typical journey time
Train	5–6 daily	1h10

Quimper–Vannes ERT 285

Type	Frequency	Typical journey time
Train	10–12 daily	1h15

Vannes–Angers ERT 280, 285, 289

Type	Frequency	Typical journey time
Train	5–6 daily	2h10 to 3 hrs

Angers–Tours ERT 289

Type	Frequency	Typical journey time
Train	7–8 daily	1 hr

Tours–Poitiers ERT 300

Type	Frequency	Typical journey time
Train	11–12 daily	1 hr

Poitiers–Bordeaux ERT 300

Type	Frequency	Typical journey time
Train	Every 1–2 hrs	1h45

pl. Épars, ☎ 02 39 80 15 15 (www.bw-grand-monarque.com), €€€. A cheaper option is **Logis L'Hotel**, 28 r. du Grand Faubourg, ☎ 02 37 18 52 77, €€, close to the cathedral. **Hostel** (non HI): 23 av. Neigre, ☎ 02 37 34 27 64 (www.auberge-jeunesse-chartres.com), 🚐 minibus service from near the tourist office.

RENNES

Brittany's commercial and administrative capital lacks the obvious appeal of the coast, but is worth at least a day trip. Following a huge fire in 1720, Rennes was largely rebuilt in stone, but some of its stripy half-timbered houses survive. The 17th-century **Parlement de Bretagne** was one of the few major structures to survive the first fire, but was less lucky when another fire broke out in 1994. After painstaking restoration, it is now open again (guided tours can be arranged through the tourist office). The **Musée des Beaux Arts**, 20 quai Émile Zola, houses a collection of French art from the 14th century onwards. The **Musée de Bretagne**, in a shiny new complex called the Champs Libres, 10 cours des Alliés, gives an excellent multimedia introduction to Brittany's history.

Route 4 continues west from Rennes, never quite touching the coast, to reach the naval port of Brest, from where it is a short hop south to Quimper.

ARRIVAL, INFORMATION, ACCOMMODATION

≋ Pl. de la Gare, a 15-min walk south-east of the centre or take the métro. 🚹 **Tourist office**: 11 r. St-Yves, ☎ 02 99 67 11 11 (www.tourisme-rennes.com).

🏠 The easiest place to find hotels is near the station, such as the **Hôtel de Nemours**, 5 r. de Nemours, ☎ 02 99 78 26 26 (www.hotelnemours.com), €€, or the **Hôtel Kyriad Rennes**, 6 pl. de la Gare, ☎ 02 99 30 25 80 (www.kyriad-rennes-centre.fr), €€. In the Old Town, check out the excellent **Hôtel des Lices**, 7 pl. des Lices, ☎ 02 99 79 14 81 (www.hotel-des-lices.com), €€. The **youth hostel** (HI), 10–12 Canal St-Martin, ☎ 02 99 33 22 33 (www.fuaj.org) is 2 km from the station (🚐 18 to Auberge de Jeunesse or, faster, the métro to pl. Sainte-Anne, then walk along r. de St-Malo). ✗ Pl. des Lices following through r. St-Michel right to r. St-Mélaine, and r. St-Georges and r. du Chapitre, are packed with a variety of multicultural restaurants.

QUIMPER

This is the most important town in south-western Finistère. The Gothic **Cathédrale St-Corentin** features a strangely off-centre nave. Close by are the **Musée Départemental Breton** (closed Mon) and the outstanding **Musée des Beaux-Arts** on 40 pl. Saint-Corentin (closed Tue except July–Aug), both of which capture the spirit of Brittany.

ARRIVAL, INFORMATION, ACCOMMODATION

≋ Av. de la Gare, east of town and a 15-min walk to the centre; turn right along av. de la Gare, cross the River Odet and turn left. 🚹 **Tourist office**: at pl. de la Résistance,

St-Malo and the North Coast

Regular buses link **Rennes** with many other Breton towns. The long-distance bus station is at blvd. Solférino (near the station). TGV and local trains run from Rennes to St-Malo (every 1–2 hrs, journey time 50–60 mins, ERT 281), most services stopping en route at Dol, where you can change for Dinan (ERT 282), a gorgeous fortified town with a 16th-century castle, a Romano-Gothic basilica and cobbled streets of timbered 15th-century houses.

The entire north coast of Brittany has fabulous scenery with rugged cliffs and unspoilt sandy beaches. Would only that the weather were just a little more clement! St-Malo is a good base for exploring the area. A highlight is the extraordinary island of Mont St-Michel with its fortress abbey. Bus connections from the train stations in Rennes and Dol are shown on ERT 269.

🖪 **Tourist office**: Esplanade St-Vincent, ☎ 08 25 13 52 00 (premium rate), www.saint-malo-tourisme.com. ⊨ A great little hotel is **La Rance**, 15 Quai Sébastopol, ☎ 02 99 81 78 63 (www.larancehotel.com), €€, close to the marina. The **Hôtel Quic en Groigne**, 8 r. d'Estrées, ☎ 02 99 20 22 20 (www.quic-en-groigne.com), €€, has small but pretty rooms within the Old Town walls. **Hostel**: Close to the beach and 1.5 km from the station, the **Centre Patrick Varangot** (HI), 37 av. du R P Umbricht, ☎ 02 99 40 29 80 (www.centrevarangot.com), has twin rooms as well as dorms.

☎ 02 98 53 04 05 (www.quimper-tourisme.com). ⊨ Sadly, Quimper is short on accommodation, and there's nothing cheap in the Old Town. Budget hotels by the station include **TGV**, 4 r. Concarneau, ☎ 02 98 90 54 00 (www.hoteltgv.com), €, **Le Derby**, 13 av. de la Gare, ☎ 02 98 52 06 91 (www.hotel-le-derby.fr), €, and **Le Pascal**, 19 av. de la Gare, ☎ 02 98 90 00 81, €€. **Youth hostel** (HI): 6 av. des Oiseaux, ☎ 02 98 64 97 97 (www.fuaj.org), 3 km from the station (🚌 1 to Chaptal); Apr–Sept.

Connections from Quimper

Douarnenez (40 mins north-west by CAT bus) is a working fishing port with lots of activity to watch on the harbour and quays. The major sight is **Le Port-Musée**, where you can explore a variety of vessels and watch demonstrations of skills such as boat-building and rope-making. At the tip of the peninsula (forming part of the **Parc Naturel Régional d'Armorique**), **Camaret** is a small resort and lobster fishing port; a jetty leads to a quaint 17th-century tower built by the military architect Vauban. Boat trips downriver from Quimper lead to the popular beach resort of Bénodet, from where other boats go to the **Îles de Glénan** (the path round the isle of St-Nicolas makes a pleasant walk) – or to **Concarneau**, a busy fishing port with a medieval *ville close* (walled island town).

Vannes

At the head of the island-strewn Golfe du Morbihan, Vannes makes a handy base for boat trips and for exploring southern Brittany. Its quaint walled town is a delight to explore. Near the **Cathédrale St-Pierre**, the ancient covered market of

La **Cohue** has been restored as an art and exhibition gallery. Behind the cathedral, you can walk along the foot of the old ramparts, past some well-preserved 19th-century washhouses.

ARRIVAL, INFORMATION, ACCOMMODATION
⇉ 2 km north-east of the centre: turn right onto av. Favrel et Lincy and left along av. Victor Hugo. Continue straight ahead for the old centre and the port. 🄱 **Tourist office**: Quai Tabarly, ☎ 08 25 13 56 10 (www.tourisme-vannes.com), near the port. ⋈ The town gets crowded in season, and hotels are often booked up. On the harbour front is **Le Marina**, 4 pl. Gambetta, ☎ 02 97 47 22 81 (www.hotellemarina.fr), €€.

ANGERS

This attractive wine-producing town is dominated by the massive striped walls of the 13th-century **Château d'Angers**, whose 17 towers now reach only half of their original height. The moat has been converted into formal gardens. Inside is a series of great 14th-century tapestries known as the *Tenture de l'Apocalypse* (the Apocalypse of St John). The nearby **Cathédrale St-Maurice** has a medieval facade and Gothic vaulting over an unusually wide nave, lit by stained glass. Across the river, the **Hôpital St-Jean** contains another spectacular tapestry, the 20th-century *Chant du Monde* (inspired by the Apocalypse) by Jean Lurçat. As well as wine, Angers produces the liqueur Cointreau (guided visits from the distillery museum on blvd. des Bretonnières, 🚌 7).

ARRIVAL, INFORMATION, ACCOMMODATION
⇉ About a 10-min walk south of the centre, or take 🚌 1. 🄱 **Tourist office**: 7–9 pl. Kennedy, ☎ 02 41 23 50 00 (www.angersloiretourisme.com). ⋈ The **Hôtel de l'Europe**, 3 Rue de Châteaugontier, ☎ 02 41 88 67 45 (www.hoteldeleurope-angers.com), €€, is reasonably priced and well located. For a treat, try the **Hôtel du Mail**, 8 r. des Ursules, ☎ 02 41 25 05 25 (www.hoteldumail.fr), €€–€€€.

CONNECTIONS FROM ANGERS
Infrequent trains run from Angers (taking 20–25 mins, ERT 289) to the town of **Saumur**, with its famous cavalry **riding school** (the Cadre Noir). The 14th-century château was originally a fortress for Louis I. It later became a country residence for the Dukes of Anjou, then a state prison, and now houses two museums. There are tours in English in summer. Vineyards surround the town, and mushrooms are grown in the caves that riddle the local hills, making good use of by-products from the riding school.

Most of the châteaux along the Loire Valley were originally medieval fortresses converted into luxurious country residences by 16th-century nobles. Some lie on bus routes or within range of railway stations (rail services may be erratic — the Saumur–Tours line provides the best access), but to visit others you really need a car — or if you're energetic, a bike, which you can take on most local trains to cover longer distances.

Boat trips from Vannes

Several companies offer boat tours and ferry services around the Morbihan coast and its many islands — you can reach the various departure points by bus. **Belle-Île** (reached from Quiberon, south of Carnac) is the largest of Brittany's offshore islands. It has a fine citadel, superb coastal scenery and beaches, good walking and picturesque villages. Within the Golfe du Morbihan is the **Île de Gavrinis**, which has an impressive decorated tomb beneath a grassy cairn. It can be reached by a boat (in season) from Larmor-Baden (south-west of Vannes).

Tours

The ancient university city of Tours is the largest city on the Loire, now restored to stately glory after damage during World War II. The classical architecture of pl. Jean Jaurès provides a focal point. The **Cathédrale St-Gatien**, in the style of Flamboyant Gothic, has some wonderful 13th-century stained glass, while the **Cloître de la Psalette**, to one side, has 13th- and 14th-century frescoes.

The 17th-century Archbishop's Palace contains the **Musée des Beaux-Arts**. In the evening, head for the heart of the Old Town, around the pl. Plumereau, which offers an excellent selection of inexpensive bars and restaurants, many occupying the carefully restored half-timbered houses that line this maze of mostly pedestrianised narrow streets.

Arrival, information, accommodation

≥ Pl. du Général Leclerc. Near the *Mairie* (town hall) in the city centre. **🚹 Tourist office**: 78–82 r. Bernard Palissy (opposite the train station), ☎ 02 47 70 37 37 (www.tours-tourisme.fr).

🛏 There are some cheap hotels around the station and the cathedral. The **Hôtel Ronsard**, 2 rue Pimbert, ☎ 02 47 05 25 36 (www.hotel-ronsard.com), €€, is a short walk from both, whilst the **Hôtel du Cygne**, 6 r. Cygne, ☎ 02 47 66 66 41 (www.hotel-cygne-tours.com), €–€€, is cheap and charming. The 2-star **Hôtel Mirabeau**, 89 bis blvd. Heurteloup, ☎ 02 47 05 24 60 (www.hotel-mirabeau.fr), €–€€, has a garden, perfect for alfresco breakfasts. The **youth hostel** (HI) is 2 km from the train station at 5 rue Bretonneau, ☎ 02 47 37 81 58 (www.fuaj.org); take 🚌 4 to Vieux Tours.

Futuroscope

Futuroscope could only ever have been created in France. This **theme park** with a twist, 9 km north of **Poitiers**, is dedicated to cinema, the moving image and multimedia. It offers more diversions than anyone could possibly do justice to in a single day. With a one-day ticket at €36 for adults (€17 from 1700), it's hardly cheap but memorably spectacular. See www.futuroscope.com which also has details of good-value short break options which include entrance to the park and overnight accommodation.

The TGV station for Futuroscope has direct trains to Paris and Lille. It takes about 1 hr 30 mins to reach the French capital.

POITIERS

For many visitors, Poitiers is simply the nearest place to **Futuroscope**, but the city has one of France's oldest universities and also lays claim to an impressive array of churches. Not for nothing is it known as the city of a hundred bell towers. The oldest, founded in 356, is the **Baptistère St-Jean**, place Ste-Croix. Nearby is the 12th- to 13th-century **Cathédrale St-Pierre**, r. de la Cathédrale, squat from outside, but inside, the nave soars to lovely 13th-century stained glass. Behind the cathedral is the **Église Ste-Radegonde**, r. Sainte-Croix, founded in the 6th century. It has fine Romanesque and Gothic additions and alterations. On summer evenings the facade of **Notre-Dame-la-Grande** is spotlit, recreating its colourful medieval appearance. Poitiers has a number of Renaissance and 18th-century buildings, as well as some high-tech modern civic architecture. One of Poitiers' best secular buildings is the 13th-century **Salle des Pas Perdus** inside the Palais de Justice.

ARRIVAL, INFORMATION, ACCOMMODATION

≠ Blvd. du Grand Cerf, about a 15-min walk from the centre; there is a pedestrian overpass shortcut. **i** **Tourist office**: 45 pl. Charles de Gaulle, ☎ 05 49 41 21 24 (www.ot-poitiers.fr). The free city map shows various self-guided walks. ⊨ Plenty of hotels both around Futuroscope and in the town, but not easy to find budget beds. Try the **Hôtel Central**, 35 pl. du Maréchal Leclerc, ☎ 05 49 01 79 79 (www. centralhotel86.com), €. **Youth hostel** (HI): 1 allée Roger Tagault, ☎ 05 49 30 09 70 (www.fuaj.org); 🚌 3 to Cap Sud. ✗ Restaurants on r. Carnot have regional specialities but tend to be expensive; the squares pl. du Maréchal Leclerc and pl. de Gaulle have a wider choice. The Poitiers region is noted for its goats' cheese.

CONNECTIONS FROM POITIERS

Poitiers has a train service to the historic port of **La Rochelle** (ERT 300), a popular sailing centre; it's elegant and striking, built in bright limestone, with gracious old squares, a fine town hall and arcaded Renaissance houses. Life focuses on the old harbour, which has some excellent fish restaurants. Two medieval towers preside over the harbour entrance, once linked by a protective chain. La Rochelle is a springboard for boat trips and island visits, notably to the **Île de Ré**, connected to the town by a 3 km toll bridge, offering beaches (some are naturist ones) and quiet picnic spots. It's reachable by bus, but best explored by bike.

BORDEAUX

Set on the **Garonne River** just before it joins the Dordogne and Gironde, Bordeaux is a busy, working city with an 18th-century core of monumental splendour surrounded by industrial gloom. A massive recent revitalisation programme has restored the handsome old centre and made it accessible to pedestrians.

Above all, the city is the commercial heart of one of the world's greatest wine-growing areas, surrounded by revered appellations such as **St-Emilion, Graves, Médoc** and **Sauternes**. The **Maison du Vin de Bordeaux**, opposite the main tourist office, arranges courses, tours and tastings, ☎ 05 56 00 22 85 (http://-ecole.vins-bordeaux.fr). Most of Bordeaux's main sights lie within easy walking distance, but a high-tech tram network is now in place.

Best of the city's historic buildings include the majestic neoclassical **Grand Théâtre**, on pl. de la Comédie, the **Musée National des Douanes**, housed in the 18th-century Customs House, and the elegant (private) **Hôtel de la Bourse**. Around the **Cathédrale St-André** are the superb 18th-century **Hôtel de Ville**, the **Musée des Beaux-Arts**, 20 cours d'Albret (nicely varied collection), which is currently undergoing extensive interior renovation and is due to open again in September 2012, and the **Musée des Arts Décoratifs**, 39 r. Bouffard (furniture, silver, pottery, etc.). Most of Bordeaux's museums are free of charge.

ARRIVAL, INFORMATION, ACCOMMODATION

⇒ **Gare St-Jean**, r. Charles Domercq. About 2 km south-east of the centre (tram line C runs from Quinconces to the station). ✈ **Bordeaux-Mérignac**, 12 km from the city, ☎05 56 34 50 50 (www.bordeaux.aeroport.fr). There are buses (Jet'Bus) every 45 mins to Gare St-Jean. ❿ **Tourist office**: 12 cours du XXX Juillet, ☎ 05 56 00 66 00 (www.bordeaux-tourisme.com), with an annexe at the station and one at the airport.

⊯ Many of the cheapest **hotels**, scattered around the grimy docks and the red-light district immediately around the railway station, can be a bit seedy. Nearer the centre, r. Huguerie is a good place to look for budget accommodation. Try the **Hôtel Touring**, 16 r. Huguerie, ☎ 05 56 81 56 73 (www.hoteltouring.fr), €€, or **Le Chantry**, 155 r. Georges Bonnac, ☎ 05 56 24 08 88 (www.chantry-bordeaux.com), €-€€, which has cheaper weekend rates.

✘ The quartier St-Pierre is a bustling district filled with small boutiques and cafés, and pl. du Parlement is a good place to look for restaurants. Look out for *guingettes* (waterfront seafood stalls) along the quai des Chartrons.

CONNECTIONS FROM BORDEAUX

Probably the main reason for coming to Bordeaux is to visit the great wineries spread out through the surrounding countryside. There are bus tours (ask at the tourist office), but also a local rail line to **Pointe-de-Grave** (ERT 307), with en-route halts at places with names that hint of great wines. **Margaux** and **Pauillac** are just two stations on that route. There are also train services to **La Rochelle** (taking 2 hrs 30 mins, ERT 292).

From Bordeaux you can follow **Route 5** through south-west France to the Midi and Provence. Or use Route 5 to connect onto **Routes 8** (at Toulouse) or **12** (at Biarritz) which both cross the border into Spain.

Rail Route 5:
From the Atlantic to the Mediterranean

CITIES: ★★ CULTURE: ★ HISTORY: ★ SCENERY: ★★
COUNTRIES COVERED: FRANCE

From Bordeaux our route runs south to chic Biarritz, before cutting south-east through to the Mediterranean. En route you skirt the northern foothills of the Pyrenees with the chance to pause at some of France's most appealing cities. There is **Lourdes**, with its bizarre yet moving non-stop pilgrimage scene, **Carcassonne** and its massive fortifications, and the lively university town of **Montpellier**. Nîmes and **Arles** are two of the great Roman sites of the Midi, and the finale, **Marseille**, is a big, bustling port, stronger in atmosphere than in sights. If you have time, stop off en route at **Tarascon** to admire the Château du Roi René, gloriously seated on the Rhône. You can lengthen and vary the journey by diverting onto **Route 7** (p100), heading up to Clermont-Ferrand before returning south through the Allier Gorge.

We think this route is at its best in spring or autumn, when on clear days you'll enjoy stunning views south to the Pyrenees. Summer heat in south-west France can be oppressive and skies are often less clear.

BORDEAUX — SEE P78

The two-hour train journey from Bordeaux to Biarritz that starts this route reveals a landscape not usually associated with France — a seemingly endless sandy pine forest.

BIARRITZ

The smart set have been coming to Biarritz since the splendid beaches and mild climate were 'discovered' in the mid-19th century by such visitors as Napoleon III and Queen Victoria. Although less grand now, it is still a fairly upmarket coastal resort with a string of good sandy beaches, great surfing and a casino.

ARRIVAL, INFORMATION, ACCOMMODATION

≋ **Gare de Biarritz-La Négresse**, 4 km from the centre, along a winding road: about a 40-min walk. Take 🚌 2 or 9 for a 20-min ride to the town hall. ✈ **Aéroport International de Biarritz-Anglet-Bayonne**, ☎ 05 59 43 83 83 (www.biarritz. aeroport.fr), 3 km from town; 🚌 6 from town centre (also links the airport to Bayonne). 🛈 **Tourist office**: 1 sq. d'Ixelles, ☎ 05 59 22 37 10 (www.biarritz.fr). Free maps and information on the Basque region. 🛏 **Hôtel Mirano**, 11 av. Pasteur, ☎ 05 59 23 11 63 (www.hotelmirano.fr), €€, is extremely well regarded. **Hostel** (HI): 8 r. Chiquito de Cambo, ☎ 05 59 41 76 00 (www.fuaj.org), 0.8 km from rail station, 🚌 2/9.

ROUTE DETAILS

Bordeaux–Biarritz   ERT 305

Type	Frequency	Typical journey time
Train	6–10 daily	2h10

Biarritz–Pau   ERT 325

Type	Frequency	Typical journey time
Train	6–8 daily	1h50 to 3 hrs

Pau–Lourdes   ERT 305, 325

Type	Frequency	Typical journey time
Train	Every 1–2 hrs	30 mins

Lourdes–Toulouse   ERT 325

Type	Frequency	Typical journey time
Train	8–9 daily	1h50

Toulouse–Carcassonne ERT 321

Type	Frequency	Typical journey time
Train	Every 1–2 hrs	1 hr

Carcassonne–Narbonne   ERT 321

Type	Frequency	Typical journey time
Train	Every 1–2 hrs	30 mins

Narbonne–Béziers   ERT 355

Type	Frequency	Typical journey time
Train	Every 1–2 hrs	15 mins

Béziers–Montpellier   ERT 355

Type	Frequency	Typical journey time
Train	Every 1–2 hrs	45 mins

Montpellier–Nîmes   ERT 355

Type	Frequency	Typical journey time
Train	Every 1–2 hrs	30 mins

Nîmes–Arles   ERT 355

Type	Frequency	Typical journey time
Train	7–8 daily	25 mins

Arles–Marseille   ERT 351, 355

Type	Frequency	Typical journey time
Train	Every 1–2 hrs	50 mins

Note

Most journeys from Biarritz to Pau require a simple change of train at Bayonne.

KEY JOURNEYS

Bordeaux–Lourdes   ERT 305

Type	Frequency	Typical journey time
Train	5–6 daily	2h40

Bordeaux–Marseille   ERT 320, 355

Type	Frequency	Typical journey time
Train	6 daily	5h45

Bordeaux–Toulouse   ERT 320

Type	Frequency	Typical journey time
Train	Every 1–2 hrs	2h10

Toulouse–Marseille   ERT 321, 355

Type	Frequency	Typical journey time
Train	7–8 daily	3h50

Toulouse–Nîmes   ERT 355

Type	Frequency	Typical journey time
Train	7–8 daily	2h45

PAU

This elegant and prosperous town is perched on a south-facing cliff above its river, enjoying panoramic views of the snow-capped **Pyrenees**. Pau has strong links with the British, who adored its favourable climate and flocked here in droves in the 19th century, bringing their much-loved pastimes (golf, rugby, steeplechasing and a casino) with them. Pau's attractions are easily walkable and a free map is available from the tourist office. Its **château** (reached via r. Henri IV from the pl. Royale, or by a free lift from pl. de la Monnaie) was the birthplace of the charismatic French monarch, Henri IV, and contains some of his personal possessions, as well as fine **Gobelin** tapestries and the **Musée Béarnais** (the provincial museum). Soak up more history at the **Musée Bernadotte** (closed Mon), 8 r. Tran, the birthplace of one of Napoleon's marshals, whose descendants are today's Swedish royal family.

ARRIVAL, INFORMATION, ACCOMMODATION

🚉 Av. Gaston Lacoste. On the southern edge of town. It's a tough 15-min uphill walk to the centre, but the funicular railway opposite the station will take you to pl. Royale for free. It operates every 3 mins, closed Sun mornings. 🚇 **Tourist office**: Hôtel de Ville, pl. Royale, ☎ 05 59 27 27 08 (www.pau-pyrenees.com).

📫 Try **Le Postillon**, 10 cours Camou, ☎ 05 59 72 83 00 (www.hotel-le-postillon.com), €€, or **Hôtel Central**, 15, r. Léon Daran, ☎ 05 59 27 72 75 (www.hotelcentralpau.com), €€; both are fine value.

LOURDES

The mountainous riverside setting of this famous pilgrimage centre is undeniably beautiful. Lourdes swarms with visitors (over six million a year), and every other building in town is a shop overflowing with kitsch **religious souvenirs**. For all that, a visit here is an unforgettable and sometimes moving experience even for the faithless. It all began in 1858, when the 14-year-old Bernadette Soubirous experienced visions of the Virgin Mary in a local grotto. A spring appeared, and word spread that its waters had miraculous curative powers. Today, water from the spring supplies local baths and drinking fountains. The 19 baths (rebuilt in 1955) are open to sick and healthy alike and hundreds of people plunge into them daily, many in search of cures for intractable ailments. Key locations associated with Bernadette can be visited in the town, including **Boly Mill**, where she was born, and the *cachot* (dungeon), where she lived during the time of the apparitions. Obtain a free map from the Forum information centre, **St Joseph's Gate**, off pl. Mgr Laurence. Bus excursions tour the surrounding area, including the **Parc National des Pyrénées**, which follows the Franco-Spanish border for 100 km; and the **Grottes de Bétharram**, vast underground caverns full of limestone formations.

ARRIVAL, INFORMATION, ACCOMMODATION

≋ Av. de la Gare. A 10-min walk north-east of the centre. 🚌 1 goes to the centre and the grotto. To reach the tourist office, turn right out of the station down av. de la Gare, and then left at the end along chaussée Maransin to pl. Peyramale. 🅱 **Tourist office**: pl. Peyramale, ☎ 05 62 42 77 40 (www.lourdes-infotourisme.com).

⊨ Paris aside, Lourdes has more hotels than anywhere else in France, including a huge number of budget and moderate establishments close to the station and around the castle. The tourist office has a list of all types of accommodation. Try **Hotel Antipodes Resort Saint Jean**, 1 av. du Paradis, ☎ 05 62 46 30 07, €–€€, or the **Hôtel Concorde**, 7 r. du Calvaire, ☎ 05 62 94 05 18 (www.concordelourdes.com), €€, for moderate lodging (both open mid-Apr till late Oct only). There are 13 **campsites**, including **Camping du Loup**, ☎ 05 62 94 23 60 (www.camping-du-loup-lourdes.com), open Apr to mid-Oct.

TOULOUSE — SEE P65

CARCASSONNE

From the 13th century, Carcassonne was the greatest stronghold of the Cathars, a Christian sect ruthlessly annihilated by crusaders sent out on the orders of Rome. The great **fortress** held out for only a month, but the structure survived for long afterwards, until being pillaged for building materials. Most of what you now see was restored in the 19th century by the architect Viollet-le-Duc. Today there are two distinct towns. On one side of the River Aude is the Ville Basse (Lower Town), which although modern and grid-like, dates from the 13th century. The more impressive **Cité** perches on a crag on the other bank of the river and is entered by two gates — Porte d'Aude and Porte Narbonnaise. If you are walking up from Ville Basse, look for the footpath beside St-Gimer, which leads to the 12th-century **Château Comtal** (Counts' Castle, guided tour only).

ARRIVAL, INFORMATION, ACCOMMODATION

≋ Behind Jardin André Chénier, in the Ville Basse, on the north bank of the Canal du Midi. It's a long walk to La Cité — about 30 mins and the last part uphill. 🚌 4 goes from the station to sq. Gambetta, then change and take 🚌 2 to just outside the walls of La Cité. ✈ 5 km from town (www.carcassonne.aeroport.fr); Agglo'bus 🚌 7 (3–8 services daily scheduled for each flight) to rail station and hotels. 🅱 **Tourist offices**: In the Ville Basse — 28 r. de Verdun, ☎ 04 68 10 24 30 (www.carcassonne-tourisme.com). In La Cité — Tour Narbonnaise, ☎ 04 68 10 24 36.

⊨ The most picturesque area to stay is in the Cité but hotels can be extremely expensive. A 10-minute walk from the medieval centre is the **Interhotel Les Oliviers**, 64 avenue du Général Leclerc, ☎ 04 68 26 45 69 (www.inter-hotel-carcassonne.fr), €€. **Hostel**: 10 km out of town, but well regarded by travellers is **Sidsmums Travellers Retreat**, 11 Chemin de la Croix d'Achille, Preixan, ☎ 04 68 26 94 49 (www.

sidsmums.com). **Camping**: **Camping de la Cité**, rte de St-Hilaire, ☎ 04 68 25 11 77 (www.campingcitecarcassonne.com), across the Aude, ask at the tourist office for bus routes (open mid-Mar to mid-Oct).

NARBONNE

A fine Midi town, lapped by vineyards and good beaches, Narbonne's most striking building is the magnificent Gothic **Cathédrale St-Juste-et-St-Pasteur**. It has some lovely stained glass and the views make it worth climbing the towers. Together with the adjacent **Palais des Archevêques** (Archbishops' Palace) this forms a remarkable group of civil, military and religious buildings. Flanked by medieval towers, the **Passage de l'Ancre** is a cobbled, L-shaped way between the cathedral and the old and new palaces; the new palace contains archaeological and art museums. Below ground is **L'Horreum**, 16 r. Rouget-de-Lisle, a well-preserved Roman granary.

ARRIVAL, INFORMATION, ACCOMMODATION

✈ A 10-min walk north-east of the centre: turn right along blvd. F Mistral to the river, and left along r. J Jaurès. 🛈 **Tourist office**: r. J. Jaurès, in a 16th-century mill, ☎ 04 68 65 15 60 (www.mairie-narbonne.fr), near the cathedral. Pick up a copy of the free *Escapades en Pays Narbonnais*.

🛏 Just a few minutes from the station is the charming **Hôtel Le Régent**, 13 r. Suffren, ☎ 04 68 32 02 41 (www.hotel-regent-narbonne.federal-hotel.com), with a terrace and a small garden, €–€€. Another good value option is **Hôtel de France**, 6 r. Rossini, ☎ 04 68 32 09 75 (www.hotelnarbonne.com), €–€€.

CONNECTIONS FROM NARBONNE

Trains to **Perpignan** take 50 minutes and run every 1–2 hrs (ERT 355); from there you can join **Route 8** (p104).

BÉZIERS

Vineyards spread from the outskirts of Béziers at the heart of the Languedoc wine country. Rising from the Pont-Vieux over the River Orb, the Old Town climbs to the 13th-century Gothic **Cathédrale de St-Nazaire**, which replaced an earlier cathedral burned down with 7,000 citizens locked inside during the Albigensian Crusade (1209). **Musée du Biterrois**, rampe du 96ème, has more cheerful exhibits on wine and local history.

ARRIVAL, INFORMATION, ACCOMMODATION

✈ For the centre of town, head straight up through the charming Plateau des Poètes. This is a lovely 19th-century park with statues and a dripping grotto topped by Atlas standing on two horses. When you reach the top, head along Allée Paul Ricquet, marked by an avenue of limes; the Old Town lies ahead and to the left. 🛈 **Tourist**

PONT DU GARD

The Pont du Gard is a spectacular Roman aqueduct 48 m above the Gard River (at a popular swimming spot), accessible by bus eight times a day from Nîmes. The site attracts two million visitors a year. Water was brought to the aqueduct from **Uzès**, a medieval village centred on a formidable castle, where today waxworks and holographic ghosts entertain visitors.

office: Palais des Congrès, 29 av. St-Saëns, ☎ 04 67 76 84 00 (www.beziers-mediterranee.com). Details of local wine festivals are available here. There's an additional branch at Place Lavabre, r. du 4 septembre, ☎ 04 67 36 06 27.

⤓ There are hotels near the station, but it's more fun to stay in the centre of town. Friendly and comfortable, **Hôtel des Poètes**, 80 Allées Paul Riquet, ☎ 04 67 76 38 66 (www.hoteldespoetes.net), €, is close to all the sights.

CONNECTIONS FROM BÉZIERS

West of town, the **Canal du Midi** leads from the Mediterranean to the Atlantic and there are day cruises through the locks and vineyards, while buses serve the long, sandy beaches not far from town.

MONTPELLIER

High-tech, young and trendy, Montpellier's main attraction is that it's simply fun to spend time in. As a university town, with 55,000 students to feed, Montpellier abounds with inexpensive eating places, bars and hotels. The **Vieille Ville** (Old Town) mixes cobbled streets with many 17th- and 18th-century mansions. To the west, the **Promenade de Peyrou** leads to an impressive clump of monumental sculptures, consisting of a triumphal arch, a hexagonal water tower and an equestrian statue of Louis XIV. Northwards lies the **Jardin des Plantes**, France's oldest botanic garden. For paintings, head to **Musée Fabre**, located in a town house (closed Mon).

ARRIVAL, INFORMATION, ACCOMMODATION

⇶ Gare St-Roch, a 5-min walk south-east of the tourist office (or take tram 1). 🛈 **Tourist office**: 30 allée J de Lattre de Tassigny, espl. Comédie, ☎ 04 67 60 60 60 (www.ot-montpellier.fr). ⤓ For a hotel in the historic centre, try **Hôtel du Palais**, 3 r. du Palais des Guilhem, ☎ 04 67 60 47 38 (www.hoteldupalais-montpellier.fr), €.

NÎMES

Nîmes boasts several superb Roman buildings. **Les Arènes**, ☎ 04 66 21 82 56, seating 23,000 in 34 elliptical tiers, is said to be the best preserved Roman amphitheatre in the world, and still stages concerts, theatrical events and bullfights (open daily). **Maison Carrée**, a well-preserved 1st-century temple, is now an exhibition centre (open daily). Next door is the futuristic **Carré d'Art**, a contemporary art gallery designed by Norman Foster (closed Mon). To the west, the 18th-century **Jardin de la Fontaine** (Garden of the Fountain), off av. J Jaurès, features a romantic Temple of Diana.

ARRIVAL, INFORMATION, ACCOMMODATION

⇒ Blvd. Talabot, a 10-min walk south-east of the centre: head down av. Feuchères to espl. C de Gaulle, then along blvd. Victor Hugo. 🚹 **Tourist office**: 6 r. Auguste, ☎ 04 66 58 38 00 (www.ot-nimes.fr). 🛏 A budget option is the **Hôtel Terminus Audrans**, 23 av. Feuchères, ☎ 04 66 29 20 14 (www.hotel-terminus-nimes.com), €–€€. Another good option is the more expensive **Hôtel Majestic**, 10 r. Pradier, ☎ 04 66 29 24 14 (www.hotel-majestic-nimes.com), €€–€€€. The popular **youth hostel** (HI), 257 Chemin de l'Auberge de Jeunesse, ☎ 04 66 68 03 20 (www.hinimes.com), is about 4 km from the station, 🚌 line i; 400-m uphill walk from bus stop to hostel.

ARLES

Ancient Rome meets Van Gogh and black bulls in Arles, the spiritual heart of Provence and a great place to relax and absorb history. Most major sights and museums are tucked into the sleepy Old Town and are easily accessible on foot. Arles is one of the best-preserved Roman towns in the world. **Les Arènes** is a mini Colosseum, less intact than the Roman amphitheatre at Nîmes but still used for bullfights. Summer theatrical productions are still staged at the **Théâtre Antique**. Elsewhere in town are the 4th-century **Thermes** (baths), r. du Grand Prieuré, of the otherwise vanished palace of Emperor Constantine and the seating and columns of the Théâtre Antique. Built next to a Roman racetrack, the modern **Musée de l'Arles et de la Provence antiques** has some superb Roman sarcophagi, mosaics and statuary (closed Tues). Art buffs should seek out the **Musée Réattu**, 10 r. du Grand Prieuré, which houses a collection of Picasso sketches (closed Mon), the **Espace Van Gogh**, an exhibition centre within the former hospital where the artist was treated after chopping off his ear, and **Alyscamps** (Elysian Fields), an ancient burial ground painted by Van Gogh and Gauguin. Unfortunately none of Van Gogh's works are still in the town, but the tourist office runs Van Gogh tours to some of the places that inspired his paintings. The **Église St-Trophime** has a west front regarded as one of the pinnacles of Provençal medieval stonework, depicting the damned descending naked into the flames of Hell while the Heaven-bound and robed saved people smirk self-righteously.

ARRIVAL, INFORMATION, ACCOMMODATION

⇒ Av. P Talabot. A few blocks north of Les Arènes: walk down av. P Talabot and along r. de la Cavalerie. 🚹 **Tourist office**: blvd. des Lices (🚌 4 from rail station), ☎ 04 90

VISITING THE CAMARGUE

Hourly buses run between Arles and **Saintes-Maries-de-la-Mer**, on the coast. This is the site of an annual Roma pilgrimage in late May and the main base for the Camargue. The **Camargue** is now a nature reserve, an area of marshland and rice fields where semi-wild white horses and black bulls roam free and lagoons are often pink with flamingos in summer. Horseback is the best way to get around; the **Saintes-Maries Tourist Office**, 5 av. Van Gogh, ☎ 04 90 97 82 55 (www. saintesmaries.com), can supply a list of some 30 farms with horses for hire. Cycling is a good alternative: bikes can be hired either from Saintes-Maries or from Arles (the tourist office, train station, or in Saintes-Maries at **Le Vélociste**, route d'Arles, pl. Mireille, ☎ 04 90 97 83 26).

18 41 20 (www.arlestourisme.com). Accommodation service. Differently themed walking tours and self-guided tours use symbols embedded in the pavement.

The *Petit Train d'Arles* (a road train) departs every day from Easter–Oct between 1000 and 1900 for a tour (with commentary) of the historic centre (about 40 mins), ☎ 04 93 41 31 09.

🛏 Close to Les Arènes is **l'Hôtel de l'Amphithéâtre**, 5 rue Diderot, ☎ 04 90 96 10 30 (www.hotelamphitheatre.fr), €€. Another good mid-range choice is the **Hôtel Gauguin**, 5 pl. Voltaire, ☎ 04 90 96 14 35, €€. The **youth hostel** (HI), open early Feb to mid-Dec, 20 av. Maréchal Foch, ☎ 04 90 96 18 25 (www.fuaj.org), is 1.8 km southeast of town, a 15-min walk from the town centre. **Camping**: **Camping-City**, 67 route de Crau, ☎ 04 90 93 08 86 (www.camping-city.com) is open Apr–Sept.

MARSEILLE

This earthy Mediterranean city is hectically vibrant, with a great music scene and superb fish-based cuisine. The busiest port in France, it's a melting pot of French and North African cultures. Marseille's grubby, rough-and-ready character appeals to some, while others will want to move on swiftly — though watch this space, because big regeneration schemes are changing the city, especially in the northern dock areas. There's a good métro and bus system and two new tram lines.

Full of small restaurants and street cafés, the **Vieux Port** (Old Port) is the hub of Marseille life and is guarded by the forts of St-Jean and St-Nicholas on either side of its entrance. From the **quai des Belges**, the main boulevard of **La Canebière** extends back into the city. Across the port from the steep narrow streets of Le Panier — the oldest part of Marseille — rises **Notre-Dame-de-la-Garde**, an impressive 19th-century basilica that is Marseille's most distinctive landmark (take 🚌 60 or the tourist train — it's a steep uphill climb otherwise). The golden Virgin atop the church watches over all sailors and travellers; the interior is full of paintings and mementos of the disasters the Virgin is supposed to have protected people from. In Dumas' novel of the same name the Count of Monte Cristo was imprisoned in **Château d'If** on one of the little **Îles de Frioul** just outside the harbour; it can be visited by boat on the Frioul-If-Express, ☎ 04 91 46 54 65 (www.frioul-if-express.com). Marseille also has some good beaches south of the Vieux Port.

The central (Vieux Port) area is walkable. Elsewhere, use the métro and buses, both run by **RTM** (*Régie des Transports de Marseille*). *Plan du Réseau* (from the tourist office and RTM kiosks) covers the routes: the map looks complicated but the system is easy to use. After 2100 the normal bus routes are replaced by a 10-route evening network called Fluobus, centred on Canebière (Bourse). Most of the city centre is safe but avoid wandering too far off the main streets at night particularly in the 6th *arrondissement* and around St-Charles.

ARRIVAL, INFORMATION, ACCOMMODATION

≋ **Gare St-Charles**, pl. Victor Hugo, is the main station, 20-min walk north-east of the **Vieux Port** (Old Port): head down the steps and straight along blvd. d'Athènes and blvd. Dugommier to La Canebière, then turn right; or take the métro, direction La Timone, station Vieux Port/Hôtel de Ville. Facilities include left luggage; open daily 0815–2100. ⛴ For information on ferries to Corsica, Sardinia and North Africa, contact **SNCM**, ☎ 3620 (+33 825 88 80 88 from abroad) (www.sncm.fr). The ferry terminal (Gare Maritime) is north of the Old Port; follow r. de la République.

→ **Marseille–Provence Aéroport**, ☎ 04 42 14 14 14 (www.mrsairport.com); at Marignane, 25 km north-west. Terminal 1 handles international flights. An airport bus runs between the airport and St-Charles railway station every 20 mins, taking 25 mins.

🚹 **Tourist office**: 4 La Canebière, ☎ 08 26 50 05 00 (www.marseille-tourisme.com). Various walking tours in English and other languages are available; check the tourist information website for the month's programme. ⛵ The tourist office has a free accommodation booking service. For cheap, functional and tranquil hotels, try around allées L Gambetta or south of the Vieux Port and Préfecture, but tread cautiously in the still rather dodgy streets south-west of the station (roughly the area bordered by blvd. d'Athènes, blvd. Charles Nédélec, cours Belsunce and La Canebière). Small, cosy and brand new, the **Pension Edelweiss**, 6 rue Lafayette,

---

MUSEUMS IN MARSEILLE

The streets of Le Panier lead up to the **Vieille Charité**, 2 r. de la Vieille Charité, an erstwhile workhouse now housing two museums covering African, Oceanian and American Indian art and Mediterranean archaeology (closed Mon). Also try **Musée Cantini**, 19 r. Grignan, ☎ 04 91 54 77 75 (métro: Estrangin Préfecture), which houses a considerable collection of modern art (closed Mon). For a more contemporary slant, visit **La Friche La Belle de Mai**, 41 r. Jobin, ☎ 04 95 04 95 04 (www.lafriche.org), a hip multidisciplinary arts centre in a converted tobacco factory in the north of the city.

AIX-EN-PROVENCE

Aix-en-Provence, the capital of Provence, and 30–40 mins from Marseille by train (ERT 362), is a charming university town. **Cours Mirabeau**, flanked by plane trees and dotted with ancient fountains, forms the southern boundary of **Vieil Aix**, whose markets are among the most colourful in Provence. To the south is the **Quartier Mazarin**, a grid of tranquil streets with elegant 17th-century houses. The **Cathédrale St-Sauveur** is an architectural mishmash, but has lovely Romanesque cloisters. Aix was the birthplace of Cézanne and inspired some of his work, although he despised the town, which ridiculed him and his art. Later it came to its senses and his studio, **Atelier Cézanne**, has been lovingly preserved (open daily). Using studs embedded in the pavement and a tourist guide, you can follow the main stages of Cézanne's life. Aix is also renowned for its **thermal springs**, e.g. 'Thermes Sextius', ☎ 04 42 23 81 82. The **station** is five minutes south of the centre: take av. Victor Hugo to La Rotonde; ❶ the **tourist office** is on the left, at 2 pl. du Général-de-Gaulle, ☎ 04 42 16 11 61 (www.aixenprovencetourism.com). ≋ The TGV station (with direct trains to Paris) is 9 km west of the town.

pen09 51 23 35 11 (www.pension-edelweiss.fr), €€, is a 2-min walk from the station. Nearer to the port, rooms tend to be pricier, though the **ETAP Vieux Port**, 46 r. Sainte, ☎ 08 92 68 05 82 (www.etaphotel.com), €–€€, is a good budget option a block from the harbour. **Hostels**: The **Vertigo Centre**, 42 rue des Petites Maries, ☎ 04 91 91 07 11 (www.hotelvertigo.fr) is one of Marseilles best-rated hostels and is a 3-min walk from the station. Another good option is the **Hello Marseille Hostel**, 12 rue de Breteuil, ☎ 09 54 80 75 05 (www.hellomarseille.com) in Vieux Port.

✗ The harbour and the streets leading from it are lined with North African and fish restaurants: **Cours Julien** is good for trendier, international fare, and more elegant restaurants are found along **corniche J F Kennedy**. Specialities include bouillabaisse; the authentic version of this fish stew contains *rascasse*, an ugly Mediterranean species, and is served with potatoes and croutons.

CONNECTIONS FROM MARSEILLE

Marseille is a major rail junction, from where some of the most scenic lines in France run. In addition to exploring **Route 6** (p90), east along the Riviera to Menton and the Italian border, you can take the slow route to Paris via the Allier Gorge.

Or make an excursion to Aix-en-Provence (see box). Beyond Aix, the line continues round the hills of the **Lubéron** (the subject of Peter Mayle's book *A Year in Provence*), and then through increasingly dramatic limestone scenery as you enter the foothills of the Alps.

Beyond **Gap**, you're really into the Alps proper; you can continue on to **Briançon** (ERT 362), a major centre for the mountains. Alternatively, stop at **Montdauphin-Guillestre** (between Gap and Briançon); from here there are connecting minibuses to the **Parc Régional de Queyras**, one of the most rural parts of the French Alps. Good bases are St-Véran (one of Europe's highest permanently inhabited villages) and Ceillac.

ROUTE DETAILS

Marseille–Cassis
ERT 360

Type	Frequency	Typical journey time
Train	Every 1–2 hrs	25 mins

Cassis–Toulon
ERT 360

Type	Frequency	Typical journey time
Train	Every 1–2 hrs	35 mins

Toulon–St-Raphaël
ERT 360

Type	Frequency	Typical journey time
Train	Every 1–2 hrs	1 hr

St-Raphaël–Cannes
ERT 361

Type	Frequency	Typical journey time
Train	Every 1–2 hrs	22–40 mins

Cannes–Nice
ERT 361

Type	Frequency	Typical journey time
Train	2 every hr	30–40 mins

Nice–Monaco (Monte Carlo)
ERT 361

Type	Frequency	Typical journey time
Train	2 every hr	24 mins

Monaco MC–Menton
ERT 361

Type	Frequency	Typical journey time
Train	1–2 every hr	12 mins

Menton–Ventimiglia
ERT 361

Type	Frequency	Typical journey time
Train	1–2 every hr	12 mins

KEY JOURNEYS

Marseille–Nice
ERT 360

Type	Frequency	Typical journey time
Train	Every 1–2 hrs	2h35

Nice–Ventimiglia
ERT 361

Type	Frequency	Typical journey time
Train	Every 1–2 hrs	50 mins

Ventimiglia–Milan
ERT 580

Type	Frequency	Typical journey time
Train	7 daily	4 hrs

Note

An interesting alternative ending to this route is marked as a dotted line on the map below. The timetable for trains from Nice via Breil-sur-Roya to Ventimiglia can be found in ERT 581. The route is served by about six trains a day. A change of train is always necessary at Breil-sur-Roya. Sospel, the last station prior to Breil on the route from Nice, makes an excellent en-route stop (ERT 581).

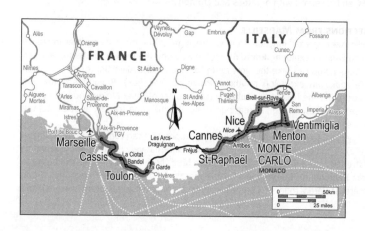

Rail Route 6:
Provence and the French Riviera

CITIES: ★ CULTURE: ★ HISTORY: ★ SCENERY: ★★★
COUNTRIES COVERED: FRANCE, MONACO, ITALY

The train journey east from **Marseille** to the Italian border and beyond is superb, a trip that rates alongside the Rhine Valley or some of the Swiss mountain routes as a true European classic. We have travelled this route a dozen times or more, and the most memorable journeys have all been at low sun angles. So this is an ideal journey for a summer morning before the crowds are up and about. The route has a grand, almost cinematic appeal when seen from the comfort of a TGV, but suddenly becomes more intimate when you experience it from one of the slower TER services that stop off at lesser stations along the way. Many trains on this route are double-deckers, so grab a place upstairs and on the seaward side (ie. on the right as you travel east from Marseille), sit back and enjoy the view.

This stretch of coast east of **Toulon** became the haunt of British aristocrats in the 19th century, heralding its new status as a sophisticated playground for the famous, beautiful or just plain rich. Grand hotels and casinos sprang up to cater for the incomers' tastes. Although parts of the **Côte d'Azur** have declined into untidy sprawls there's still an engaging mix of ostentatious villas, pretty waterside towns and fine beaches. **Cannes** and **Juan-les-Pins** are hot spots for nightlife, **Nice** is large, cosmopolitan and backpacker-friendly, whilst tiny, independent **Monaco** is super-compressed and super-rich. Behind the coast the land rises abruptly and you're into a different world with rugged mountains and ancient perched villages. Much of that mountainous hinterland is difficult to reach without a car.

MARSEILLE — SEE P87

The initial part out of this route is dismal, the views dominated by motorways and the low slung aluminium sheds that seem to have become the favoured architecture for the periphery of French cities. But suddenly the train emerges from a long tunnel near Cassis to give a tantalising glimpse of the Mediterranean — a hint of what is to come.

CASSIS

Centred around a pretty fishing harbour ringed with restaurants and an easy day trip from Marseille via bus or train, Cassis makes a handy base for seeing the spectacular *calanques*, rocky inlets that cut into the limestone cliffs. Coastal walks (including the long-distance path GR98 west to Cap Croisette) offer stunning views. The station is 4 km out of Cassis, and a bus (Mon–Fri only) meets most trains for the run into town. East of Cassis the railway skirts the vineyards of Bandol and passes the busy port of Toulon before cutting inland with superb views of the forested Massif des Maures to the east.

FRÉJUS AND ST-RAPHAËL

The ancient Roman port of **Fréjus** and the modern beach resort of **St-Raphaël** fuse to form one urban area, though each has its own identity, its own station and tourist office. St-Raphaël is the upmarket end and the main transport hub, with spacious beaches and a tiny Old Quarter. Fréjus-Plage is a strip of bars, restaurants and a giant marina lying between the sea and Fréjus town. The **Roman amphitheatre** (Arènes), r. Henri Vadon, is still used for bullfights and rock concerts. **Fréjus Cathedral**, pl. Formigé, was one of Provence's first Gothic churches, and has beautiful cloisters.

ARRIVAL, INFORMATION, ACCOMMODATION

🚄 **Gare de St-Raphaël** is central: for the sea, head down r. Jules Barbier to blvd. de la Libération. 🚌 **St-Raphaël bus station**: behind the rail station, av. Victor Hugo, ☎ 04 94 83 87 63. 🚹 **Tourist offices**: St-Raphaël, quai Albert 1er, ☎ 04 94 19 52 52 (www.saint-raphael.com); Fréjus, 249 r. J Jaurès, ☎ 04 94 51 83 83 (www.frejus.fr), dispenses a guide to the (widespread) Roman sites.

🛏 In Fréjus the **Atoll Hotel**, 923 Boulevard de la Mer, ☎ 04 94 51 53 77 (www. atollhotel.fr), €€, is good value. In St-Raphaël try **Hotel Le Thimothée**, 375 blvd. Christian Lafon, ☎ 04 94 40 49 49 (www.thimothee.com), €€. The **youth hostel** (HI) is in a large park 1.5 km from Fréjus at chemin du Counillier, ☎ 04 94 53 18 75 (www.fuaj.org), open Mar till mid-Nov. **Campsite: Parc Camping Agay Soleil**, 1152 blvd. de la Plage, Agay, ☎ 04 94 82 00 79, open Apr–Oct.

CONNECTIONS FROM ST-RAPHAËL

Hyères makes a pleasant excursion from St-Raphaël via Toulon; this charming old town, with a hilly medieval core set back from the sea, first attracted winter visitors in the late 19th century: Tolstoy, Queen Victoria and Robert Louis Stevenson enjoyed its mild climate.

HYÈRES

From Hyères you can catch a ferry to offshore islands – Île de Porquerolles (20 mins), Île de Port-Cros (1 hr) and Île du Levant (1 hr 30 mins) – which offer some of the most beautiful beaches in the Mediterranean. Take a bus from the town to the port at La Tour Fondue for the ferry to Île de Porquerolles (every 30 mins from 0900–1830 in summer, six a day off season), ☎ 04 94 58 21 81; Port d'Hyères for Port-Cros and Île du Levant, ☎ 04 94 57 44 07 (four ferries per day in summer, one per day off season). 🚹 Hyères **tourist office**: 3 av. Ambroise Thomas, ☎ 04 94 01 84 50 (www.hyeres-tourisme.com). Note that Île du Levant is a naturist island.

St-Tropez, a famously chic resort accessible by Suma bus (8–12 a day from St-Raphaël, ERT 358), can be tough to reach in hellish summer traffic (take the boat from St-Maxime instead) and it's grossly overpriced, but it does have a party atmosphere and a superb art gallery, the **Musée de l'Annonciade**, on the port (closed Tues).

CANNES

Cannes lives up to the Riviera's reputation as an overpriced, overcrowded fleshpot, but it's possible to enjoy it without spending a fortune. Looking good, spending money and sleeping little is the Cannes style, yet there's free fun to be had on the sandy beaches west of the port. Orientation is easy: the town stretches around the **Baie de Lérins**, the promenade is **La Croisette**. Everything is within walking distance and virtually all the cultural activities (including the film festival) centre on the hideous concrete **Palais des Festivals**. There are few specific sights, but try climbing r. St-Antoine to the hill of Le Suquet, the oldest quarter. The **Musée de la Castre**, housed in the citadel in the Old Town on the hill of Le Suquet, relates a history of Cannes (closed Mon off season).

ARRIVAL, INFORMATION, ACCOMMODATION

≥ 250 m from the sea and the Palais des Festivals: head straight (south) down r. des Serbes. **ℹ Tourist offices**: Palais des Festivals, 1 blvd. de la Croisette, ☎ 04 92 99 84 22 (www.cannes.travel). Also at the station (1 pl. de la Gare) and 1 av. P Sémard.

⤼ Some of the most exclusive hotels in the world overlook the Croisette. Try the streets leading from the station towards the seafront for more reasonably priced rooms: r. des Serbes, r. de la République or r. du Maréchal Joffre. Advance reservations recommended; during the festival rooms in Cannes are a highly prized commodity often booked from year to year. For celebrity spotting try the **Carlton InterContinental**, 58 La Croisette, ☎ 04 93 06 40 06 (www.ichotelsgroup.com), or the **Martinez**, 73 La Croisette, ☎ 04 92 98 73 00 (www.hotel-martinez.com), both €€€. If your budget won't stretch this far try the **Atlantis**, 4 r. du 24 Août, ☎ 04 93 39 18 72 (www.cannes-hotel-atlantis.com), €€, or the **Claremont Hotel**, 13 r. du 24 Août, ☎ 04 93 38 36 73 (www.claremontcannes.com), €€. **Hostel**: Check out the **Auberge le Chalit**, 27 av. Maréchal Gallieni, ☎ 04 93 99 22 11, a five-minute walk from the train station. **Camping**: **Parc Bellevue** (reached by train from Cannes, 67 av. M Chevalier, ☎ 04 93 47 28 97 (www.parcbellevue.fr); is convenient for the wide sandy beaches to the west of the town but not really for the centre (🚌 2), open Apr–Sept.

CONNECTIONS FROM CANNES

Off Cannes, the **Îles de Lérins** are an antidote to chic. **Île de St-Marguerite** is the larger of the two, and boasts the better beaches. At the north end, **Fort St-Marguerite** was commissioned by Richelieu and enlarged by Vauban in 1712. It is the legendary home of the mythical Man in the Iron Mask, made famous by the author Alexandre Dumas. There are daily ferry departures from the quai Laubeuf (close to rue du Port) operated by Trans Côte d'Azur (☎ 04 92 98 71 30), Planaria (☎ 04 92 98 71 38) and others.

ANTIBES

The biggest boats in the northern Med may moor here, but the likeable old town of Antibes is a pretty unpretentious place, with a relaxed atmosphere and a lively bar and restaurant scene. Take a walk along the port, and don't miss the **Musée Picasso**, looking over the sea from its home in the **Château Grimaldi**. Picasso worked here in 1946 and this excellent museum displays some of his most entertaining creations from that period (closed Mon).

ARRIVAL, INFORMATION

➤ For the centre, head down av. Robert Soleau to pl. de Gaulle. From here blvd. Albert 1er leads to the sea. **⊞ Tourist office**: 11 pl. du Gén-de-Gaulle, ☎ 04 97 23 11 11 (www.antibesjuanlespins.com). There is a branch at 55 blvd. Charles Guillaumont, ☎ 04 97 23 11 10. Free maps and accommodation information. Guided tours, ☎ 04 97 23 11 25 (90 mins, reservation only).

CONNECTIONS FROM ANTIBES

Juan-les-Pins, the playground of the coast, is where the Côte d'Azur's summer season was invented in 1921. It has sandy beaches (many are private, but there is still some public space), bars, discos and in July, the Riviera's most renowned jazz festival, Jazz à Juan. Just a 30-min walk or easy bus ride from Antibes — of which it is a suburb — it is a pleasant place to while away a few days.

NICE

Nice has been the undisputed queen of the Riviera ever since the 19th-century British elite began to grace the elegant seafront **Promenade des Anglais**. In those days Nice was Nizza and part of the Kingdom of Sardinia. The city was ceded to France in 1860. Hotels such as the **Negresco** capture the old Riviera style and are still as luxurious and imposing as ever, and not excessively expensive for a snack or a drink to sample how the other half lives. Standing apart from the belle époque hotels and villas, **Vieux Nice** (the Old Town) is the true heart of the city, and seems more Italian than French. It has wonderful outdoor markets, countless cafés and restaurants, and many of Nice's liveliest bars and discos.

Nice boasts some of the best museums in France. Most open 1000–1800, are closed on Tuesdays and are easily accessible by local bus. Best of the bunch is the **Musée Matisse**, 164 av. des Arènes de Cimiez (www.musee-matisse-nice.org), wonderfully set in a 17th-century villa amongst the Roman ruins of Cimiez. It houses Matisse's personal collection of paintings (🚌 15/17/20/22/25 from pl. Masséna). Next door **Musée et Site Archéologique de Nice Cimiez**, 160 av. des Arènes de Cimiez (www.musee-archeologique-nice.org), exhibits the copious finds dug up while excavating the Roman arenas in Cimiez (🚌 15/17/20/22/25 to Arènes). Matisse and fellow artist Raoul Dufy are buried in the nearby Couvent des Frères Mineurs. Also in Cimiez, the **Musée Marc Chagall**, av. du Dr Ménard, is a grace-

ART LINKS: THE MATISSE TRAIL

Bus 400 runs hourly from Nice to **St-Paul-de-Vence**, a picturesque village which houses one of the most interesting modern art museums in France, the **Fondation Maeght** (www.fondation-maeght.com), built by the Maeght family, friends of Matisse. The lovely garden is a sculpture park designed by Miró. **Vence**, 3 km further up the valley, is another delightful little town. Here Matisse was nursed by local nuns and repaid them by designing a simple yet breathtakingly beautiful chapel that he considered his masterpiece: **La Chapelle du Rosaire**, av. Henri Matisse (closed Fri & Sun, otherwise 1400–1730 and Tues & Thur also 1000–1130; ☎ 04 93 58 03 26). A mosaic by Chagall enlivens the Romanesque church.

ful temple to Chagall's genius — beautifully lit to display his huge biblical canvases (🚌 15/22; closed Tues, €7.50).

In the centre of town, the **Musée d'Art Moderne et d'Art Contemporain**, Promenade des Arts, is a white marble cliff rising above the street, and filled with striking pop art (🚌 3/4/6/7/9/10/16/17; closed Mon, free entrance). On summer nights, Nice parties till long after midnight, thanks to its many Irish-style pubs and live music venues, though younger visitors often gravitate to the beach.

ARRIVAL, INFORMATION, ACCOMMODATION

🚄 **Nice-Ville**, av. Thiers. Frequent services to all resorts along the Côte d'Azur. Left luggage and shower facilities. A 15-min walk to the town centre. ⛴ **SNCM**, quai du Commerce (on the east side of the port), ☎ 32 60 then say SNCM (premium rate). Regular crossings to Corsica (see p99). ✈ **Nice-Côte d'Azur**, 7 km west of the city, ☎ 08 20 42 33 33 (premium rate), www.nice.aeroport.fr. Airport buses (🚌 98) run along Promenade des Anglais to the Gare Routière (bus station) every 20 mins (0600–2350) and 🚌 99 to the Gare SNCF (rail station) every 30 mins (0750–2100); also 🚌 23 to the rail station every 20 mins (0600–2140). 🛈 **Tourist offices**: 5 Promenade des Anglais, ☎ 08 92 70 74 07 (premium rate), www.nicetourisme.com; also av. Thiers (at the rail station), and airport terminal 1. The Old Town quarter is manageable on foot, but to get between the various museums and sights requires transport. Bus services are good, most radiating from pl. Masséna. 🚌 Bus and Tram Information: Agence Masséna, 3 pl. Masséna, ☎ 08 10 06 10 06 (www.lignesdazur.com).

🛏 Try the highly rated **Villa Les Cygnes**, 6 av du Château de la Tour, ☎ 04 97 03 23 35 (www.villalescygnes.com), €€. Also popular, though more expensive, is **La Malmaison**, 48 blvd. Victor Hugo, ☎ 04 93 87 62 56 (www.lamalmaison.com), €€€, which is a short walk to both the beach and the Old Town. **Hostels**: There are a number of good hostel options in Nice, include the **Backpackers Hostel Chez Patrick**, 32 r. Pertinax, ☎ 04 93 80 30 72 (www.chezpatrick.com), 5 mins from the rail station. The **Villa Saint-Exupéry Gardens**, 22 av. Gravier, is some distance north of the centre but has excellent facilities (tram to Comte de Falicon, then they can pick you up if called in advance). Closer to the centre is the **Villa Saint-Exupéry Beach**, 6 rue Sacha-Guitry. The freephone (in France) number for both Villa Saint-Exupéry hostels is ☎ 08 00 30 74 09 (www.villahostels.com). The nearest **campsite** is **Camping Terry**,

INLAND BY TRAIN

Along the entire rail route that runs the length of the French Riviera there are just three opportunities for heading inland by train. And Nice is a good jumping off point for all three.

The old perfume town of **Grasse** is 1 hr 13 mins by direct train from Nice (ERT 361). Here you can visit perfume factories and see the villa of the painter Fragonard (www.fragonard.com; open daily), complete with cartoon frescoes and a collection of paintings, or shop and idle in the pl. aux Aires farmers' market and flower stalls.

For lovers of great scenery, there is a superb route through the hills to **Digne-les-Bains** (ERT 359). This narrow-gauge rail line is privately operated and holders of InterRail and Eurail passes cannot travel for free but receive a 50% discount on the regular fare. From Digne, you can travel south-west by fast bus to the TGV railway station at Aix-en-Provence, or take the local bus to Veynes (both bus routes are in ERT 359). From Veynes there are trains to Valence in the Rhône Valley (ERT 362).

Our third proposed inland digression is effectively an alternative ending to **Route 6**. Take the rail route that heads inland via **Sospel** to **Breil-sur-Roya** (ERT 581) from where trains run south through the precipitous Roya Gorge to reach the Ligurian coast and rejoin the main line at **Ventimiglia**. The small town of Sospel, beautifully located amid mountains in the Bévéra Valley, makes an excellent en-route stop. The route from Nice via Sospel and Breil to Ventimiglia, returning via the coast to Nice, makes an excellent one-day round trip.

768 route de Grenoble, St-Isidore, ☎ 04 93 08 11 58 (🚌 59 from Nice Gare Routière to La Manda).

✗ Something of a culinary paradise, Nice is influenced by its neighbour, Italy, and by the Mediterranean. Specialities are *pissaladière*, a Niçois onion tart garnished with anchovies and olives, *socca*, a traditional lunchtime snack of flat bread made from crushed chickpeas, and of course *salade niçoise*. Vieux Nice (the Old Town) is best for eating out — particularly the warren of streets running north from Cours Saleya and the cathedral. North of the Old Town, pl. Garibaldi boasts the best shellfish.

VILLEFRANCHE-SUR-MER

This incredibly steep little resort of precariously tall ochre houses has one of the deepest ports on the coast, so it's a major stop for cruise ships and also has the liveliest beach in the region. From Villefranche beach you can walk out onto St-Jean-Cap-Ferrat, a peninsula with gorgeous beaches plus some of the world's most expensive — and closely guarded — properties. The port is tranquil and lined with restaurants, many of them not excessively expensive. If you make it to **St-Jean-Cap-Ferrat**, don't miss the **Villa Ephrussi** (www.villa-ephrussi.com; open daily). Once owned by Béatrice de Rothschild, the house is a visual delight, and the exotica-filled gardens are stunning, with views down to Villefranche and Beaulieu.

🚈 Exit onto promenade des Marinières, turn right and follow signs to Vieille Ville (uphill). 🛈 **Tourist office**: Jardins François Binon, ☎ 04 93 01 73 68 (www.villefranche-sur-mer.com). 🛏 A pleasant budget hotel is the **Patricia**, 310 av. de l'Ange Gardien, ☎ 04 93 01 06 70 (http://hotel-patricia.riviera.fr), €–€€.

BEAULIEU-SUR-MER

'Beautiful place' (the name was bestowed by Napoleon) is a tranquil spot full of affluent retired people, and palms flourish profusely in its mild climate. Don't miss the **Villa Kérylos** (www.villa-kerylos.com; open daily) — built by two archaeologists at the turn of the 20th century, this is a faithful replication of a 5th-century BC Athenian home, complete with furnishings.

EZE

The perched village of Eze (as opposed to the sea-level Eze-sur-Mer) is a stiff climb from the station. It's inevitably a tourist trap, but you're rewarded by arguably the best views on the Riviera; cacti flourish in the botanic gardens.

MONACO (MONTE-CARLO)

Covering just a couple of square kilometres, this tiny principality has been a sovereign state ruled since 1297 by the Grimaldis, a family of Genoese descent. Later it grew rich on gambling and banking, and now high-rise buildings crowd round the harbour, some built on man-made platforms that extend into the sea. Whatever the geographical and aesthetic limitations of the place, its curiosity value is undeniable. Old Monaco is the extra-touristy part, with its narrow streets, the much-restored **Grimaldi Palace**, and the 19th-century **Cathédrale de Monaco**, containing the tombs of the royals, including Princess Grace. In av. St-Martin is the stimulating **Musée Océanographique**, in the basement of which is one of the world's great aquariums, developed by Jacques Cousteau (open daily). Monte-Carlo is the swanky part, with its palatial hotels, luxury shops and the unmissable, world-famous **Casino de Paris**, pl. du Casino, which is worth a look for the interior gilt alone. To the west, a pretty coastal path meanders into France from the modern marina district of Fontvieille to Cap d'Ail and, just beyond it, the lovely, unspoilt beach of **Plage Mala**.

🚈 Av. Prince Pierre: head straight down past pl. d'Armes to the port (with the palace off to the right), then turn left for the tourist office and casino (500 m); or take 🚌 4. 🛈 **Tourist office**: 2A blvd. des Moulins, Monte-Carlo. ☎ 92 16 61 16 (www.visitmonaco.com).

⋈ Budget accommodation is scarce — the youth hostel was demolished recently — but there are a few more moderate hotels within reach of the station. Otherwise, walk uphill from Monte-Carlo into the French settlement of Beausoleil, where there's a scattering of budget places. In Monte Carlo, a relatively reasonable option is the **Hôtel Alexandra**, 35 blvd. de la Princesse Charlotte, ☎ 04 93 50 63 13, €€–€€€. In Beausoleil, a good-value option is the **Azur**, 14 blvd. de la République, ☎ 04 93 78 01 25, €–€€, whilst a slightly more expensive option is the **Hôtel Villa Boeri**, 29 blvd. du Général Leclerc, ☎ 04 93 78 38 10 (www.hotelboeri.com), €€–€€€.

✗ Eating out in Monaco ranges from simple bistros and pizzerias to some of the most decadent restaurants in the world. Expect to pay big money in any of the restaurants around the casino. Sample typical snacks such as *socca* and *tourte* from a number of takeaway establishments, particularly around Place d'Armes.

CONNECTIONS FROM MONACO

La Turbie, just above Monaco, is accessible from Monaco by 🚌 114, or 🚌 116 from Gare Routière de Nice, (five–six times a day, but not Sat afternoon or Sun). The culminating point of the Roman road Via Aurelia, and marking the boundary between Italy and Gaul, La Turbie is renowned for the restored remnants of a huge statuesque tower of 6 BC known as the Trophée des Alpes (closed Sun).

MENTON

Looking into Italy, Menton is a retirement town of ample Italianate charm, endowed with long stony beaches and full of lemon, orange and olive trees. Wander around the hilly Old Town, constructed by the Grimaldis in the 15th century. The baroque **Église St-Michel** (St Michael's Church), built in 1640, is an attractive structure. In summer, the short curve of beach between the port and marina is lined with beach bars, some of them quite trendy.

ARRIVAL, INFORMATION, ACCOMMODATION

➹ Pl. de la Gare. West of the centre. For the sea (about 400 m), head down av. Edouard VII or r. Morgan. 🛈 **Tourist office**: inside Palais de l'Europe, 8 av. Boyer, ☎ 04 92 41 76 76 (www.tourisme-menton.fr). ⋈ Plenty of undistinguished 1- and 2-star places in the town centre. Rather better (and more expensive) is the 3-star **Hôtel Chambord**, 6 av. Boyer, ☎ 04 93 35 94 19 (www.hotel-chambord.com), €€€, with spacious rooms (closed last two weeks of Nov), or try the friendly **Hôtel Mediterranée**, 5 r. de la République, ☎ 04 92 41 81 81 (www.choicehotels.fr), €€. **Youth hostel** (HI): Plateau St-Michel, ☎ 04 93 35 93 14 (www.fuaj.org). **Camping St-Michel**, ☎ 04 93 35 81 23 (closed mid-Oct to mid-Feb) is 1.5 km from the station (take 🚌 6).

VENTIMIGLIA — SEE P286

CONNECTIONS FROM VENTIMIGLIA

At Ventimiglia you can join **Route 33** (p286).

If you are lucky enough to travel along Route 6 on a crisp clear winter day, you may get a glimpse of Corsica across the sea away to the south. The most likely vantage points are as the train runs east from Nice towards the Italian frontier. In our view this is the finest part of the Riviera coast, and it is made all the better when, against the backdrop of a crystal-blue sky, Corsica's **snowy mountains** rise up above the horizon. It is a little piece of magic that occurs all too rarely.

It is not for nothing that the Ancient Greeks called Corsica *Kalliste*, meaning 'the most beautiful'. And Corsica is easy to reach as a side trip from Route 6. The fastest **ferry crossings** are from Nice, some taking as little as four hours. Crossings from Toulon and Marseille take longer, but the latter is a good option if you are looking to make an overnight ferry journey. Outline schedules for all ferry routes to Corsica are in ERT 2565.

Prices on this large Mediterranean French island are higher than in mainland France, and rail passes aren't valid on trains. These might sound compelling reasons for giving Corsica a miss, but the island does have a largely **unspoilt coastline** and a wonderfully rugged and **mountainous interior**. For getting around, there is a limited narrow-gauge rail network (ERT 369), about 230 km of route operated by Chemin de Fer de la Corse (CFC), leading from the northern port of Bastia to Ajaccio on the west coast, and Calvi in the north-west. The stretch of line along the coast from **L'Île-Rousse** to **Calvi** runs through stunning scenery and gives access to old fishing villages such as Algajola. The island's deliciously antiquated cream-and-red railcars have recently been banished by modern rolling stock which has turned out to be less than perfectly efficient, so during 2011 buses were substituting for trains on some services.

Bus services are good and cover most corners of Corsica. The privately run website, www.corsicabus.org, has comprehensive public transport timetables for the entire island. Buses can be pricey. The two-hour journey from Calvi to Bastia costs €16 for example.

The best **beaches** are in the south-east, around Rondinara, Santa Giulia, Palombaggia and Pinarellu. **Bastia** has an interesting Old Port area and citadel, with fishing boats in the harbour and washing lines strung over dark, shuttered alleys. There's plenty of accommodation between the rail station and the port along av. du Maréchal Sébastiani. Inland and on the railway, **Corte** makes a good base for walking. Within the compact Old Town of **Ajaccio** is the birthplace museum of Napoléon Bonaparte, while the **Palais Fesch**, now sparkling after reopening in 2010, has the island's premier art collection. **Bonifacio** is a gorgeous place to arrive at by sea, as it clings close to a spur above the harbour. The maze of alleys contains lots of restaurants and hotels.

From Bonifacio you can continue by ferry to **Sardinia**, less than an hour away to the south (ERT 2565). Read our Sidetracks feature on p322 for more on Sardinia and onward links by ship to **Sicily**. If you return from Bonifacio to the north Corsica port of Bastia, you will find excellent shipping links to Italy, with services to Savona and **Genoa** (both on **Route 33**) and to Piombino and **Livorno** (both conveniently placed to join **Route 34**).

ROUTE DETAILS

Béziers–Millau   ERT 332

Type	Frequency	Typical journey time
Train	2–3 daily	1h55

Millau–Clermont-Ferrand   ERT 332

Type	Frequency	Typical journey time
Train	1 daily	5 hrs

Clermont-Ferrand–Nîmes   ERT 334

Type	Frequency	Typical journey time
Train	3 daily	6 hrs

KEY JOURNEYS

Béziers–Clermont-Ferrand   ERT 332

Type	Frequency	Typical journey time
Train	1 daily	7 hrs

Clermont-Ferrand–Paris (Lyon)   ERT 330

Type	Frequency	Typical journey time
Train	9 daily	3h30

Béziers–Nîmes   ERT 355

Type	Frequency	Typical journey time
Train	1–2 every hr	1h20 (via Sète)

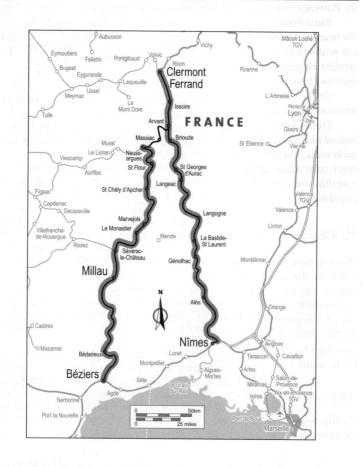

Rail Route 7: The heart of rural France

CITIES: ★ CULTURE: ★ HISTORY: ★ SCENERY: ★★★
COUNTRIES COVERED: FRANCE

This route is effectively an inverted V, with the apex and northernmost point at **Clermont-Ferrand**. The northbound leg from **Béziers** is often called the *ligne des Causses*, while the return journey south from Clermont back to **Nîmes** follows a route dubbed the *ligne des Cévennes*. Of course, it is not compulsory to follow Route 7 in its entirety, and from Clermont it is an easy journey north by direct train to Paris, whilst a quick hop south from Paris to Clermont allows you to continue south along either leg of Route 7. It is thus also replete with opportunities for travellers bound for the **Languedoc-Roussillon** region (via Béziers) or for **Provence** (via Nîmes and Marseille).

Rural France doesn't come any better than this, as the train slices through the heart of the **Massif Central**, the vast upland area of extinct volcanoes in central southern France. The one drawback is the infrequency of both rail and bus services, so you would really need several days to explore the area thoroughly but the views from the carriage window are definitely reason enough to make this trip.

On the northbound leg from Béziers towards Clermont-Ferrand you skirt the limestone heights of the Cévennes, a region of remote plateaux cut by huge gorges.

From Clermont, the route leads back south, through **Issoire** and **Brioude**, both of which have magnificent Romanesque churches. **Le Puy-en-Velay** is off the main route, but well worth a stopover. South of Langeac you travel through the spectacular **Allier Gorge** amid the wild, volcanic scenery of the Auvergne. It's not a wealthy area, and some of the medieval red-roofed villages look distinctly de-populated.

BÉZIERS — SEE P84

Winding north from Béziers, the railway skirts several great limestone areas. These are the barren *Causses* that give this route its name *ligne des Causses*. The railway cuts through the hills to reach the Tarn Valley. Just after the railway crosses the River Tarn (so now with the river on your right), you get a glimpse of one of Europe's landmark pieces of 21st-century architecture. The **Viaduc de Millau** (Millau Viaduct) opened in 2004 and cuts a slender arc across the sky, carrying a motorway across the entire Tarn Valley. Seen in the right light, it is as breathtaking as the finest Gothic cathedral.

MILLAU

Prettily situated at a confluence of valleys, this town is a good base for the Cévennes, one of the most ruggedly remote parts of the Massif Central uplands.

JUST WORTH NOTING

We would just add a cautionary note. These classic old-style rural railway routes suffered as French rail operator SNCF shifted its focus to high-speed routes in the 1980s and 1990s. Only now is the **railway infrastructure** on lines in Route 7 south of Clermont-Ferrand being brought up to modern standards. So trains are slow and, from time to time during 2012, the chances are that buses will replace trains for a spell to allow much-needed track renewal work to take place.

It is worth checking before travelling. Look in the latest edition of the *Thomas Cook European Rail Timetable* (ERT 332 and 334) for the current schedules or check on www.ter-sncf.com, where you'll find current timetables (*fiches horaires*) for all lines on Route 7 under the Auvergne region listings.

The historic centre is quietly attractive and almost traffic-free, with a spectacularly tall **belfry** (open mid-June to mid-Sept), the delightful arcaded **place Foch**, and a museum chronicling Millau's former glove industry (closed Sun and 1200–1400 off-season).

Within the Parc de la Victoire is the **Jardin des Causses**, with flora typical of the neighbouring limestone plateaux.

To the south-west of the city on the far bank of the Tarn is **La Graufesenque**, a 1st-century AD Gallo-Roman settlement with a kiln site where vast quantities of dark red pottery have been unearthed and are now on display in the museum (closed Mon, guided tours are available). The **Viaduc de Millau** can be visited by open-top bus. Details are available at the tourist office that also sells tickets for the bus tour.

Much of the area is hard to explore without your own transport, so best to hire a car for a day to visit stunning geological formations such as the impressive limestone gorges of the Tarn and the Jonte, the show cave of Aven Armand and the Chaos de Montpellier-le-Vieux.

If you want to avoid the crowds, get a good map and head for the windswept Causses that are such a feature of these Cévennes landscapes.

ARRIVAL, INFORMATION, ACCOMMODATION

≈ 10 mins from the centre: walk along av. A Merle and turn right at the T-junction.
☐ Tourist information: 1 pl. du Beffroi (by the big belfry), ☎ 05 65 60 02 42 (www.ot-millau.fr).

🛏 Hotels: nothing really in the historic core, but cheap and central is **Hôtel du Commerce**, 8 pl. du Mandourous, ☎ 05 65 60 00 56 (www.hotelmillau.com), €; or try the centrally located **Cévénol Hôtel**, 115 r. du Rajol, ☎ 05 65 60 74 44 (www.cevenol-hotel.fr), €€€, which also has a good pool. The **Hotel Ibis Millau**, r. du Sacré-Cœur, ☎ 05 65 59 29 09 (www.accorhotels.com), €€, is a reasonable mid-range option. **Hostel**: The hostel **Sud Aveyron Accueil** (HI), 26 r. Lucien Costes, ☎ 05 65 60 15 95 (www.fuaj.org) is 800 m from the railway station.

Through the hills

The railway does no more than flirt with the Tarn before cutting north through more limestone hills to reach the valley of the **River Lot** beyond. The landscape slowly takes on a darker demeanour as the white limestone gives way to ancient volcanic rocks. Almost any of the places along this route are good for a brief stop. **Marvejols** is an unassuming little spot with a lively Saturday market and medieval buildings. **St-Flour** has an extraordinary Upper Town perched on volcanic crags (a good 20-min walk up from the station, where most of the hotels cluster) with a cathedral built of lava rocks that resemble breeze blocks.

At **Neussargues-Moissac**, you can transfer onto a local train to **Aurillac** (50 mins, ERT 331), the principal town of the Cantal region, which has good onward rail connections to Toulouse (ERT 317), where you can join **Routes 2, 5** and **8**.

Clermont-Ferrand

Clermont, centre of the French rubber industry, and birthplace of Michelin tyres, is built of a dark volcanic stone, and is not exactly picturesque. But the centre has an absorbing maze of little lanes and alleys, dominated by the hilltop **Gothic cathedral**. The building to seek out is the 11th-century church of **Notre-Dame-du-Port**, place du Port, one of France's greatest examples of the local Romanesque style, displaying some wonderful stone carving inside and out.

Arrival, information, accommodation

⇒ The station is 1 km east of the old centre: turn left to square de la Jeune Résistance and take either av. de Grande Bretagne or av. Carnot. 🚹 **Tourist office:** pl. de la Victoire, ☎ 04 73 98 65 00 (www.clermont-fd.com). ⊨ Most hotels are uninspiring, but by the lively pl. Jaude is **Hôtel Foch**, 22 r. Maréchal Foch, ☎ 04 73 93 48 40 (www.hotel-foch-clermont.com), €€. A budget option close to the station is **Foyer Le Phare**, 7 av. de l'Union Soviétique, ☎ 04 73 92 46 40, €. **Hostel**: The **Auberge du Cheval Blanc Hostel** (HI), 55 av. de l'Union Soviétique, ☎ 04 73 92 26 39 (www.fuaj.org) is 100m from the train station.

Heading south

For the journey south back to **Nîmes** just sit back, relax and watch the Cévennes landscape slide by. The six-hour ride from Clermont-Ferrand to Nîmes is one of the very best in France. One of the thrice-daily services on this route continues through to Marseille. Highlights are the curved viaduct at Chamborigaud and the run down the Allier Gorge, where the train slows and you get glimpses of fierce chasms and chaotic rock-strewn slopes.

Nîmes — see p85

Notes

From Toulouse to Barcelona change trains at Narbonne. Collioure–Figueres: change trains at the border. Perpignan–Barcelona: journeys via the high-speed line (2 daily) currently require a change at Figueres Vilafant. Through services are expected to start in 2014.

ROUTE DETAILS

Toulouse–Foix   ERT 312

Type	Frequency	Typical journey time
Train	Every 1–2 hrs	1h10

Foix–L'Hospitalet   ERT 312

Type	Frequency	Typical journey time
Train	5–6 daily	1h20

L'Hospitalet–Latour de Carol   ERT 312

Type	Frequency	Typical journey time
Train	5–6 daily	30 mins

L'Hospitalet–Andorra la Vella   ERT 313

Type	Frequency	Typical journey time
Bus	2 daily	1h30 to 2h30

Latour de Carol–Villefranche   ERT 354

Type	Frequency	Typical journey time
Train	2–5 daily	3 hrs

Villefranche–Perpignan   ERT 354

Type	Frequency	Typical journey time
Train	6–8 daily	50 mins

Perpignan–Collioure   ERT 355

Type	Frequency	Typical journey time
Train	8–12 daily	25 mins

Collioure–Figueres   ERT 355, 657

Type	Frequency	Typical journey time
Train	4–5 daily	1h10 to 2h15

Figueres–Girona   ERT 657

Type	Frequency	Typical journey time
Train	Every 1–2 hrs	35 mins

Girona–Barcelona   ERT 657

Type	Frequency	Typical journey time
Train	Every 1–2 hrs	1h30

KEY JOURNEYS

Toulouse–Perpignan
(change at Narbonne)   ERT 321, 355

Type	Frequency	Typical journey time
Train	10–12 daily	2h30 to 3 hrs

Perpignan–Barcelona   ERT 13

Type	Frequency	Typical journey time
Train	3 daily	2h30 to 3 hrs

Toulouse–Latour de Carol   ERT 312

Type	Frequency	Typical journey time
Train	5–6 daily	3 hrs

Latour de Carol–Barcelona   ERT 656

Type	Frequency	Typical journey time
Train	4–5 daily	3h10

Rail Route 8: Across the Pyrenees

Cities: ★ Culture: ★★ History: ★ Scenery: ★★★
Countries covered: France, Spain

The **Pyrenees** mountain chain is one of the world's most emphatic national boundaries, a great wall of snow-capped peaks separating France from Spain. But the region is ill-served by railways. The magnificent outsize railway station at Canfranc, set amid dramatic mountains on the Spanish side of the border, is a reminder of a superb **cross-Pyrenean rail route** that closed in 1970 following an accident. Today the twice-daily slow train chugs up the valley from Zaragoza to Canfranc (ERT 654) but the onward journey through the Somport Tunnel into the Aspe Valley in France is by bus (ERT 324). If you don't mind that stretch on a bus, it is still a good route from Zaragoza to Gascony.

There remains just one international rail route that really tackles the mountains. This is the grandly named *transpyrénéen oriental* from **Toulouse** to **Barcelona**. There are no through trains, for the railway track gauge changes at the border, so passengers have to change from a French to a Spanish train at **Latour-de-Carol**. This is no great hardship for the station is in a wonderful mountain location at 1,230 m above sea level. This is a first-class journey, one that rates among Europe's most engaging rail trips, delightful at any time of year but at its best we think in spring or autumn when the mountain colours are unbeatable. The route we describe here starts at Toulouse and follows the Ariège Valley south via **Foix** to **Ax-les-Thermes** before climbing steeply up into the Pyrenees.

For travellers heading south from Paris, there is a very useful overnight train that leaves Paris Austerlitz each evening and reaches the Ariège Valley the following morning. It drops off at Foix, Ax, Andorre-L'Hospitalet and Latour-de-Carol.

Toulouse — see p65

The first part of the run south from Toulouse is unexceptional, but suddenly the railway cuts through a distinct ridge of hills called the Montagnes du Plantaurel to reach Foix.

Foix

This almost perfect-looking medieval town stands at the meeting of two rivers, with the three towers of its castle dominating the scene from a lofty crag. About 6 km north-west, take a boat trip (1 hr 30 mins) on the Labouiche, Europe's longest navigable underground river, and some 15 km south there are superb caves: admire 12,000-year-old cave paintings at the **Grotte de Niaux** (☎ 05 61 05 88 37, www.niaux.net; booking compulsory) and majestic stalactites and stalagmites in the **Grotte de Lombrives** (www.grotte-lombrives.fr).

🚄 10 mins north-east of town: follow the Ariège River and cross the bridge to the centre. 🅸 **Tourist office**: 29 r. Delcassé, ☎ 05 61 65 12 12, www.tourisme-foix-varilhes.fr. 🏨 The charming 2-star **Hôtel du Lac**, ☎ 05 61 65 17 17, Route nationale 20 (www.hoteldulac-foix.fr), €€, by the lakeside, can be reached by bus from the centre. Centrally located and overlooking the river is the **Hôtel Lons**, 6 pl. Georges Dutilh, ☎ 05 34 09 28 00, €, or try the popular bed and breakfast **Chapeliers Chambre d'Hôtes**, ☎ 05 34 09 05 48 (www.chapeliers.com), €–€€. **Camping** year round is at Camping du Lac. **Hostel** (non-HI): **Foyer Léo Lagrange**, 16 r. Noël Peyrevidal, ☎ 05 61 65 09 04 (www.leolagrange-foix.com), is conveniently situated in the town centre.

THROUGH THE MOUNTAINS

The hillsides tilt ever sharper as the railway climbs the **Ariège Valley**, especially south of Ax (where some southbound trains from Toulouse terminate). Tight curves and tunnels are the prelude to arrival at Andorre-L'Hospitalet, where you can alight for an infrequent bus connection to **Andorra** (ERT 313). The train continues south through the Puymorens Tunnel to reach Latour-de-Carol.

Here you face one of the most difficult decisions in this entire book. The main line south to Barcelona is very lovely, with mountain scenery giving way slowly to a more Mediterranean landscape. The direct trains from Latour-de-Carol take about 3 hrs to reach Barcelona's Sant Andreu Arenal station, from where it is but a short walk to Fabra i Puig métro station for route L1 (red route) to the city centre.

For those reluctant to forsake the hills quite so quickly, there is a fine alternative, and that is the route we follow in this description. From **Latour-de-Carol** the *Petit Train Jaune* (Little Yellow Train) runs east to Villefranche-de-Conflent (ERT 354). The 3-hr ride is sedate but spectacular. The **narrow-gauge route** skirts the Spanish exclave of Llívia, and serves several remote communities, among them Bolquère which at 1,593 metres has the highest SNCF railway station in France. During good weather in summer, you can ride the route in open-top carriages.

VILLEFRANCHE-DE-CONFLENT

On all journeys (in both directions) you need to change trains at Villefranche. This fortified village is a jumbled maze of narrow streets, well worth a wander if the next onward train is not for an hour or two. It is dominated by the enormous 17th-century **Fort Libéria**. Walk up to the UNESCO-listed fortification (open all year, admission charge) along the original soldiers' path (30 mins), coming back down via the more than 700 steps of the underground staircase that leads directly to Pont St-Pierre, the medieval village bridge.

Regular French local trains, now standard gauge, run east from Villefranche down the valley to Perpignan through rich agricultural country.

Perpignan

Unmistakably Catalan in character though unfortunately impossibly crowded in summer, Perpignan is the principal city of French Catalonia. Catalan is spoken hereabouts, and the *sardane*, Catalonia's national dance, is performed to music a couple of times a week in summer in the medieval pl. de la Loge, Perpignan's main square and still the hub of the city's life.

A 14th-century fortified gatehouse, **Le Castillet**, Place de Verdun, houses Casa Pairal (a museum of Catalan folk traditions; closed Tue), while the **Cathédrale St-Jean**, pl. Gambetta, is Gothically grand. The imposing Citadelle, to the south, guards the 13th-century **Palais des Rois de Majorque** (Palace of the Kings of Majorca).

ARRIVAL, INFORMATION, ACCOMMODATION

≋ Pl. Salvador Dali, 600 m from the centre: walk straight along av. Gén.-de-Gaulle to pl. Catalogne, and continue ahead to the centre; or take 🚍 1/20/21. 🚍 **Bus station:** av. du Gén. Leclerc, ☎ 04 68 35 29 02. There are regular services to the nearby beaches, especially in summer. 🚍 City bus 1 also goes to Canet beach.

🚹 **Tourist office**: pl. Armand Lanoux, at the Congress Centre (Palais des Congrès), ☎ 04 68 66 30 30 (www.perpignantourisme.com), a 30-min walk from the station.

🛏 There are lots of 1- and 2-star establishments along and off av. Gén.-de-Gaulle (leading from the station to the town centre). **Hôtel de la Loge**, 1 r. Fabriques d'en Nabot, ☎ 04 68 34 41 02 (www.hoteldelaloge.fr), €€, is centrally located. Or else, try **Hôtel Victoria**, 57 av. du Maréchal Joffre, ☎ 04 68 61 17 17 (www.hotel-victoria-perpignan.com), €€, or **Hôtel Aragon**, 17 av. Gilbert Brutus, ☎ 04 68 54 04 46 (www.aragon-hotel.com), €.

Hostel (HI): Parc de la Pépinière, av. de la Grande-Bretagne, ☎ 04 68 34 63 32 (www.fuaj.org), 600 m from the station (Mar to mid-Nov).

Collioure

Easily visited as a day trip from Perpignan, this is the most picturesque of the local ex-fishing villages, on a knob of land between two bays, and overlooked by a 13th-century château. Matisse, Braque, Dufy and Picasso all discovered Collioure, and artists still set up their easels here. The domed church steeple looks distinctly Arabic.

ARRIVAL, INFORMATION, ACCOMMODATION

≋ 400 m west of the centre, ☎ 04 68 82 05 89. 🚹 **Tourist office**: pl. du 18 Juin, ☎ 04 68 82 15 47 (www.collioure.com).

🛏 **Hôtel Madeloc**, r. Romain Rolland, ☎ 04 68 82 07 56 (www.madeloc.com), €€€, has a pool in a garden setting, but is pricey (as are other options). Open Apr–Oct. Better value, and right on the water, is the **Hôtel Boramar**, 19 r. Jean Bart, ☎ 04 68 82 07 06 (www.hotel-boramar.fr), €€.

FIGUERES (FIGUERAS)

The much-visited **Teatre-Museu Dalí** (www.salvador-dali.org, open daily except Mon during Oct to late May) is the only real attraction, honouring the town's most famous son. Whether you consider Dalí a genius or a madman (or both), the museum is likely to confirm your views of the Surrealist artist. Appropriately enough, it's a bizarre building, parts of which Dalí designed himself (including his own grave), a terracotta edifice sporting giant sculpted eggs.

ARRIVAL, INFORMATION, ACCOMMODATION

≥ Plaça de la Estació. Centrally located, with luggage lockers and a cash machine. A new railway station, called Figueres Vilafant, opened in early 2011. The new station serves as a temporary transit point for passengers arriving on French TGV trains and wanting to travel south to Barcelona and beyond. This station is less convenient for the city centre.

ℹ Tourist office: Pl. del Sol s/n, ☎ 972 50 31 55 (www.figueres.cat). There are also visitor information points beside the bus station across the plaza from the train station, and in Plaça Gala i Salvador Dalí, near the entrance to the Teatre-Museu Dalí. ⊨ Central, and close to the Dalí museum, is the **Hotel Plaza Inn**, C. Pujada del Castell 14, ☎ 972 51 45 40 (www.plazainn.es), €€.

GIRONA (GERONA)

The medieval Old Town stands on the east side of the River Onyar, connected by the Pont de Pedra to a prosperous new city in the west. From the bridge you can see the **Cases de l'Onyar** — a line of picturesque houses overhanging the river. In the heart of the labyrinthine Old Town is the superlative Gothic **cathedral**. Check out the **Banys Arabs** (Arab Baths), Romanesque with Moorish touches and dating from the 13th century. The **Museu d'Art**, housed in the splendid Renaissance Bishop's Palace, displays paintings and carvings from the Romanesque period to the 20th century. In the narrow streets of **El Call** (old Jewish quarter) is the **Bonastruc ca Porta Centre**, which contains a Museum of Jewish Culture.

ARRIVAL, INFORMATION, ACCOMMODATION

≥ In the new town; a 10-min walk from the river and Pont de Pedra. 🚌 **Bus station:** adjoins the railway station. **ℹ Tourist office**: C. Joan Maragall 2, ☎ 872 97 59 75 (www.girona.cat/turisme), centrally located close to the former Santa Caterina hospital. ⊨ Try around the cathedral, or head for Plaça de la Constitució. The **Equity Point Hostel**, Plaça Catalunya 23, ☎ 932 31 20 45 (www.equity-point.com) has dorms and family rooms.

BARCELONA — SEE P436

Reached by ferry from Barcelona or Valencia (both routes in ERT 2510), the perennially popular island of **Majorca** is the largest and most varied in the Balearic group. While Majorca (locally rendered as Mallorca) is massively touristy, it has some surprisingly beautiful scenery and unspoilt villages, particularly in the rugged northern mountains. The island capital, Palma, is at the hub of a gentle bay that has been densely developed, but the compact Old Town of Palma is a gem and includes a splendid Gothic cathedral, the Moorish palace and Arab baths. There's no shortage of excellent sandy **beaches** around Palma and the other resorts, though in summer many get impossibly crowded. The big resorts around Palma Bay are the best places for raucous **nightlife**, though Palma itself has much classier nightspots.

Narrow-gauge railway lines link Palma to Sa Pobla (57 mins), Manacor (66 mins) and Sóller (55 mins). Outline schedules for all these services are in ERT 674. Trains leave from the transport interchange on Plaça d'Espanya in Palma. Eurail and InterRail passes are not recognised on any of the island's railways. The train trip to the old fishing village of Port de Sóller is by far the most scenic of the three options. The **Ferrocarril de Sóller** (Sóller Railway) marked its centenary in 2011. The railway, funded through profits from the citrus trade, was built through difficult terrain and quite transformed access to remoter parts of Majorca. The one-way fare from Palma to Sóller is €10 and the return €17. Sóller station is improbably grand for somewhere in the outback, and the town itself a happy maze of little lanes where you can still just imagine what life on this beautiful island might have been like before it was engulfed by tourists. If you do head out by train to Sóller, it is worth taking the **local tram** that connects with the train and runs out to **Port de Sóller** with its jetties, beaches and laid-back cafés and bars. You have to pay extra for the tram: €2 one way or €4 return, but it is worth it.

Buses serve all the main towns and many villages across Majorca. Schedules are available from the Palma tourist information kiosk on Plaça d'Espanya. **Boat trips** offer one of the most pleasant ways of seeing Majorca. A popular cruise heads around the north-west coast from Port de Sóller to Sa Calobra. There's plenty of sightseeing elsewhere on the island, including some fine caves on the east coast. A must-see is the beautiful 14th-century **Monastery of Valldemossa** where Chopin and George Sand spent a winter.

🛏 The majority of accommodation is in the form of large hotels built for the package industry, although Palma does have a number of inexpensive *hostales*, a growing number of characterful converted properties (most of which are relatively expensive), and two youth hostels – near Palma and outside Alcudia. 🚹 The Palma **tourist offices** are at Parc de les Estacions building, Plaça d'Espanya, and Plaça de la Reina 2; ☎ 97 117 39 50 (www.illesbalears.es).

Ferries also serve the other Balearic islands. **Ibiza** is a brash nightlife haunt. **Menorca** is much more low-key, and popular with families and older tourists; seek out the island's intriguing Bronze Age sites. Tiny **Formentera** is comparatively undeveloped, with hostel accommodation in La Savina; Playa Illetas and Playa Levante are among the best beaches.

ROUTE DETAILS

Barcelona (Sants)–
Tarragona   ERT 652, 672

Type	Frequency	Typical journey time
Train	1–3 per hr	1h05

Tarragona–Valencia   ERT 672

Type	Frequency	Typical journey time
Train	12–14 daily	2h05

Valencia–Cuenca   ERT 669

Type	Frequency	Typical journey time
Train	4 daily	3h20

Cuenca–Aranjuez   ERT 669

Type	Frequency	Typical journey time
Train	3–5 daily	2 hrs

Aranjuez–
Madrid (Atocha)   ERT 661, 668a, 669

Type	Frequency	Typical journey time
Train	11–15 daily	35 mins

Madrid (Atocha)–
Cáceres   ERT 677

Type	Frequency	Typical journey time
Train	3–4 daily	3h55

Cáceres–Mérida   ERT 677

Type	Frequency	Typical journey time
Train	5–6 daily	1h10

Mérida–Badajoz   ERT 677, 678

Type	Frequency	Typical journey time
Train	6 daily	45 mins

Badajoz–Lisbon
(change at Entroncamento)   ERT 691, 690

Type	Frequency	Typical journey time
Train	1 daily	4h45

Notes

Most long-distance trains in Spain need advance reservations. Note that the only direct train from Madrid to Lisbon (and vice versa) is a night train. Daytime journeys between the two capital cities always require at least two changes of train. For travellers coming to Portugal from France, there is a very useful direct overnight train from Irún (on the French-Spanish border) to Lisbon. Connections at Irún to and from Paris by fast TGV are excellent, so making possible an easy overnight journey from Paris to Lisbon.

As you follow Route 9, remember that Spanish time is 1 hr ahead of Portuguese time. So put your watch back by 1 hr as you travel between Badajoz and Elvas.

KEY JOURNEYS

Barcelona–Madrid   ERT 650

Type	Frequency	Typical journey time
Train	1–2 per hr 1 daily	2h52 (day) 9 hrs (night)

Madrid–Lisbon   ERT 45

Type	Frequency	Typical journey time
Train	1 daily	10h15 (night)

Rail Route 9: Iberian cities

CITIES: ★★★ CULTURE: ★★ HISTORY: ★★ SCENERY: ★★
COUNTRIES COVERED: SPAIN, PORTUGAL

This journey across central Spain into Portugal links the three largest cities on the Iberian peninsula — **Barcelona** (p436), **Madrid** (p519), and **Lisbon** (p502). After hugging the coast from Barcelona to Valencia, the route cuts inland and then follows lesser rail routes west via Madrid to Portugal. Route 9 is a long journey, and you can speed things up a little by taking the new high-speed rail route from Valencia to Madrid (at the price of missing Cuenca). The whole journey requires a little planning, as daytime rail connections across the Portuguese border are not that great — although by night the *Lusitania* hotel train gives a very useful direct link from Madrid to Lisbon. Though if you stick to Route 9 as described here, you'll travel through parts of Spain less frequented by tourists. Our favourite part of this route is the section through the Extremadura, the name given to west central Spain. This is a deeply rural region of vast rolling sierras, forests and landscapes rich in wildlife; there are also some deeply atmospheric settlements largely untouched by the passage of time, notably **Cáceres**, **Trujillo** and **Mérida**.

Cuenca, Madrid and Mérida are obvious spots for overnight stops. The early part of Route 9 can also be used as a prelude to heading off south to Andalucía. You can read more on that in the **Sidetracks** section at the end of this route.

BARCELONA — SEE P436

TARRAGONA

The coast of Catalunya south-west of Barcelona is known as the Costa Daurada. It wins no prizes for beauty, yet tucked away in the ugly urban sprawl are some interesting spots. **Sitges** has quite a buzz as a hub of Catalonian counter-culture and as one of the most gay-friendly resorts in Europe. But the real star of this stretch of coast is Tarragona, where the ancient walled town (above the modern settlement) enjoys a glorious cliff-top position.

The city boasts a rich heritage of Roman sites — including the remains of temples, a substantial **amphitheatre** and the Roman **forum**, which now abuts modern housing. There is also a necropolis, where early Christians were buried, and a well-preserved aqueduct a couple of miles out of town. Along the foot of the 3rd-century BC Roman walls extends the **Passeig Arqueològic**, an archaeological walkway. Catalunya's foremost collection of Roman sculptures, temple friezes, bronzes and mosaics is housed in the **Museu Arqueològic**, Plaça del Rei 5 (closed Mon), while the neighbouring *Pretori*, a Roman palace, contains the **Museu de la Romanitat**, with historical displays ranging from Roman to medieval finds. **La Seu** (the cathedral), one of the finest churches in the region, exemplifies the transition from Romanesque to Gothic. To offset all that history, Tarragona has some great beaches.

ARRIVAL, INFORMATION, ACCOMMODATION

≋ Plaça de la Pedrera. Taxis and 🚌 2/24 take you into the Old Town. It's a 10-min walk uphill to the old centre: take C. de Orosio opposite, uphill; go right at the junction with C. d'Apodaca, and carry on up to the main street (Rambla Nova); the tourist office is left and immediately left again, while the Old Town lies ahead. **🖪 Tourist office**: (Regional) Carrer Fortuny 4, ☎ 977 23 34 15 (www.tarragonaturisme.cat). (Municipal) Carrer Major 39, ☎ 977 25 07 95 (near the cathedral), below the main town.

🛏 The best budget bets are in Pl. de la Font, a pleasant traffic-free square in the Old Town (also some good places to eat); here are two clean, adequate pensions – for sea views, try **Hostal Mediterrani**, C. de Orosio 11, ☎ 977 24 93 53, €–€€; right by the station, and **Hotel Noria**, Plaça del Font 53, ☎ 977 23 87 17, €€. The **youth hostel** (HI) is at C. Lluís Companys 5, ☎ 977 24 01 95 (www.reaj.com).

CONNECTIONS FROM TARRAGONA

Port Aventura is Spain's best adventure theme park (mid-Mar to early Jan). There are at least 12 trains a day from Tarragona, taking about 10 mins. For further details see www.portaventura.es. A more cultural diversion is to head to **Zaragoza** (ERT 650 for fast trains which require reservations, or ERT 652 for slow trains), where the key highlight is a spectacular Moorish palace known as the Aljafería, a reminder that the city was once the capital of an independent Muslim state known as the Taifa of Zaragoza.

VALENCIA

Continuing west from Tarragona, the rail route skirts mile after mile of golden beaches before crossing the watery flatlands that blend into the delta of the Ebro, which is Spain's largest river. Despite one or two remarkable sights, such as the fortified coastal city of Peñíscola, there is no particular reason to linger en route to Valencia.

Valencia is Spain's third city and the home of paella. It is a large and mostly faceless modern metropolis, but at its heart there's a bustling atmospheric Old Town with two medieval gateways (**Torres de Serranos** and **Torres de Quart**), pleasant squares, characterful run-down backstreets, crumbling baroque mansions and a handful of other historic landmarks. There's a sizeable student population and the nightlife is good.

Santiago Calatrava's stunning **City of Arts and Sciences** (www.cac.es), is the city's top attraction and a symbol of the 'new' Valencia. It's a gleaming, white, futuristic entertainment complex which encompasses an excellent hands-on science museum, a vast aquarium, an arts centre and a planetarium. The port and beach area were dramatically revamped for the 2007 America's Cup and Valencia is fast becoming one of the Med's most fashionable hot spots.

ZARAGOZA

The city boasts two cathedrals: La Seo is Romanesque and Gothic, and contains fine
Flemish tapestries and a Gothic reredos; more famous is the mosque-like 18th-
century **Basílica de Nuestra Señora del Pilar**, with its domes of coloured tiles, named
after the pillar bearing a tiny, much-venerated statue of the Virgin within the church
(where the Virgin Mary is said to have descended from heaven in a vision of St James
in AD 40). You get a good view from the tower (reached by lift, then stairs). The Plaza
del Pilar features an interesting water monument of South America: stand at the
closest point of the pool to the Basilica, crouch down, and you will see a clear outline
of the continent.

The **Museo Camón Aznar**, C. Espoz y Mina 23 (closed Mon), has a fine art
collection assembled by a devotee of Goya. Zaragoza's most impressive sight, the
Aljafería, is a stunning Moorish fortress-palace just outside the city centre; look out
for the ornate stucco oratory in the northern portico. Tours also take in the Gothic
quarters added by Ferdinand and Isabella. A modern attraction is the theme park
Parque Zaragoza (www.atraczara.com), 1 km north from the station on Duque de
Alba. Open Mar–Oct, there are ferris wheels, rollercoasters and houses of horror.

The Old Town, which contains the main sights, is easily covered on foot.
EMT buses operate throughout the city; most can be boarded in Plaça de l'Ajuntament (tickets from tobacconists and kiosks), a traffic-ridden triangle overlooked
by the copper-domed town hall. Two towers preside over the Plaça de la Reina:
the baroque spire of **Santa Catalina** and the **Miguelete**, which is the bell tower of
the cathedral; climb the spiral staircase to the top for a good view. Valencia's key
building is its **cathedral**, a mixture of styles ranging from Romanesque to baroque.
The city's finest building is the Gothic **Llotja de la Seda**, Plaça del Mercat (closed
Mon, free entry), a legacy of the heady days of the 15th-century silk trade, while
the nearby **Mercat Central** is a vast art nouveau market hall.

In summer, many cafés and bars in Valencia offer *orxata*, a sweet milky drink
made from *chufas*, or earth almonds, traditionally eaten with bread sticks (either
chewy, sweet *fartons*, or more brittle *rosquilletas*). The place to drink it is the
Horchatería Santa Catalina on Plaça Santa Catalina 6.

ARRIVAL, INFORMATION, ACCOMMODATION

≥ Valencia is famously complicated when it comes to train stations. Most trains from
Barcelona arrive at **Nord**, which has a magnificent art nouveau entrance hall. It is
centrally located (metro: Xàtiva; 🚌 5/8/10/11/14/19; lockers), 10 mins by rail from
Cabanyal station (🚌 81), which serves the ferries. Fast trains from Barcelona, as well
as the new fast AVE service from Madrid, serve **Joaquin Sorolla** (linked to Nord with a
free bus service). Trains to Cuenca and Aranjuez leave from **Sant Isidre** station.

🛈 **Tourist offices**: Regional: C. de la Pau 48, ☎ 96 398 64 22 (www.
comunitatvalenciana.com) and at Estació del Nord. Municipal: Pl. de la Reina 19, ☎ 96
315 39 31 and Plaça de l'Ajuntament 1, ☎ 96 352 49 08 (www.turisvalencia.com).

✉ Good budget areas are around Pl. de l'Ajuntament and Pl. del Mercat. The **Hostal Venecia**, C. en Llop 5, ☎ 96 352 42 67 (www.hotelvenecia.com), €€, is an excellent value 2-star hotel next to the town hall. The **Antigua Morellana**, C. En Bou 2, ☎ 96 391 57 73 (www.hostalam.com), €€, is friendly and well located. **Hostels**: Hôme have two funky, friendly hostels and a budget hotel (see www.likeathome.net for all three): the **Hôme Backpackers Hostal**, C. Vicente Iborra, ☎ 96 391 37 97, with dorm bunks from €12, the **Hôme Youth Hostel**, C. la Lonja 4, ☎ 96 391 62 29, and the **Hôme Deluxe Hilux** budget hotel, C. Cadirers, ☎ 96 391 46 91, €–€€.

HEADING INLAND

Devotees of scenic branch lines might consider a little diversion along the route that heads north from Valencia to Zaragoza via **Teruel**. Thrice-daily trains leave from Valencia Nord and dawdle over this rural route taking 4 hrs 30 mins for the full stretch to **Zaragoza** (ERT 670). Reserve seats in advance. Teruel, at about the midway point on the line, makes a marvellous stopover, with its intriguing mix of Muslim and Jewish history and the superb Mudéjar architecture that has earned Teruel a place on UNESCO's World Heritage List. The train schedules also allow Teruel to be visited easily as a day trip from Valencia.

Route 9 also turns inland at Valencia, departing from Sant Isidre station and following a minor rail route to Madrid, less dramatic than the route north to Teruel but still very pleasing. The only city of any size along the way is Cuenca.

CUENCA

For sheer physical drama, with its extraordinary position over two river gorges, Cuenca is a spectacular place to explore. Finely carved wooden balconies, armorial bearings, impressive doorways and breathtaking views are keynotes. Especially striking are the **Casas Colgadas**, the 13th-century tiered houses that hang over a chasm and form the city's emblem. Level ground is in pretty short supply, a notable exception being the arcaded **Plaza Mayor**, flanked by the **cathedral**, which dates from the 12th century and is more refined inside than its unfinished exterior suggests. It also houses an absorbing treasury with paintings by El Greco. The best museums are the **Diocesan Museum** and the **Museo de Arte Abstracto** (both closed Mon), the latter within one of the hanging houses and displaying Spanish abstract art. An iron footbridge in one of the gorges provides a much-photographed view of the hanging houses. Don't miss the very top of the town either: keep going right up, through an old gateway, for breathtaking views from the crags over the whole town.

ARRIVAL, INFORMATION, ACCOMMODATION

⇋ C. Mariano Catalina 10. It is a hard climb from the station to the Old Town and most prefer to take 🚌 1. The walk takes 20–25 mins: take the street diagonally left from the station, past a sign for Hostal Cortés in Ramón y Cajal. **⋈ Tourist office**: C. Alfonso VIII 2, ☎ 96 924 10 51 (www.cuenca.es).

⋈ Several cheap places are found between the station and the Old Town, including **Hotel Francabel**, Avenida de Castilla la Mancha 7, ☎ 96 922 62 22 (www. hotelfrancabel.es), €€. A few doors up is the comfortable **Hostal Cortés**, Ramón y Cajal 49, ☎ 96 922 04 00 (www.hostalcortes.com), €–€€. A nicely placed pension (with a lovely restaurant) below the Old Town is **Posada Tintes**, C. de los Tintes 7, ☎ 96 921 23 98, €. For a real splurge, try the **Parador de Cuenca**, Convento de San Pablo, Subida a San Pablo, ☎ 96 923 23 20 (www.parador.es), €€€, in a renovated convent and across a footbridge from the Old Town.

✗ Meaty variations occur on Cuenca's menus, most famously *morteruelo*, a spicy dish combining a multitude of meats, including game, chicken, pig's lard, cured ham and grated pig's liver. Something of an acquired taste, *zarajos* is roasted lamb's intestines, while *ajoarriero* is a more generally palatable dish of cod, eggs, parsley and potato; trout and crayfish are also on offer. *Resolí* is a liqueur made of orange peel, cinnamon and coffee.

ARANJUEZ

On the south bank of the Tagus, Aranjuez is famous for its spectacular **Royal Palace** and gardens (www.patrimonionacional.es, closed Mon, gardens open daily; free for EU passport holders on Wed), the inspiration for the world-famous *Concierto de Aranjuez*, or *Rodrigo's Guitar Concerto*. The structure dates from the 18th century and is a succession of opulently furnished rooms with marble mosaics, crystal chandeliers and ornate clocks. In the gardens are the **Casa del Labrador** (literally 'Farmer's Cottage', but more like the Petit Trianon at Versailles) and the **Casa de Marinos**, housing royal barges.

ARRIVAL, INFORMATION
≋ 1 km outside town and a 10-min walk from the palace. As you exit the station, take the road to the right and then turn left at the end. **⋈ Tourist office**: Plaza de San Antonio 9, ☎ 91 891 04 27 (www.aranjuez.es).

MADRID — SEE P519

From Madrid, Route 9 tracks west towards the sparsely populated **Extremadura** region, but it would be a pity to leave the Greater Madrid region without making a short detour to **Toledo**, just 30 mins by fast train (ERT 679) from the Spanish capital (see box on p117). Continuing west on the main route, most trains deviate from the main line to serve **Plasencia** of which there are superb views from the train. The journey from Plasencia south to Cáceres is utterly beautiful as the railway threads its way between huge reservoirs in the Parque Nacional de Monfragüe.

Cáceres

Not a lot of visitors make it out to this golden-stone World Heritage Site, though the storks do in incredible numbers — they have built nests on every conceivable perch. Its old centre has bags of charm, and is almost totally unspoilt. In medieval times Cáceres prospered as a free trade town, and was largely rebuilt in the 15th and 16th centuries; thereafter, it fell into decline and very little was added, hence the time-warp quality.

Ancient city walls surround a largely intact Old Town, with its Jewish quarter and numerous gargoyle-embellished palaces, displaying the heraldic shields of the status-conscious families who built them. The obvious starting point is the cobbled, partially arcaded Plaza Mayor, from which the gateway of 1726, known as the **Arco de la Estrella** (Arch of the Star), leads into the compact Old Town (easily explored on foot). You immediately reach the Plaza de Santa María, abutted by the **Concatedral de Santa María** (with an interesting cedarwood retable), the **Palacio Episcopal**, and the **Casa de los Golfines de Abajo** (one of the two mansions of the Golfine family). On the top of the town's hill, the **Church of San Mateo** has a fine array of nobles' tombs, while the nearby **Casa de las Cigüeñas** (House of Storks) was the only noble's house exempted from a royal decree and allowed to keep its fortifications.

Arrival, information, accommodation

⇝ At the far end of Avenida de Alemania. 🚌 **Bus Station**: C. de Túnez. The bus and train stations are not far from each other, about 3 km from the centre. 🚌 1 goes to Plaza Obispo Galarza, near the Plaza Mayor. From the station, cross the green footbridge over the road, then turn left 100 m for the bus stop (or walk up from here); a taxi to Plaza Mayor will cost about €5. Luggage lockers. 🛈 **Tourist office**: Plaza Mayor 3, ☎ 92 701 08 34 (www.turismoextremadura.com).

🛏 There's a good choice of hotels; the best area for both staying and eating cheaply is in the vicinity of Plaza Mayor. Try **Hostal Al-Qazeres**, Camino Llano 34, ☎ 92 722 70 00 (www.alqazeres.com), €–€€, the **Pensión Carretero**, Plaza Mayor 22, ☎ 92 724 74 82, €, or the **Hotel Castilla**, C. Ríos Verdes 3, ☎ 92 724 44 04 (www. hotelcastillacaceres), €€, central and reasonably quiet.

Connections from Cáceres: east to Trujillo

Don't miss **Trujillo** when visiting Cáceres (48 km to the east, reached by bus; journey 40 mins), a picture-perfect conquistador town overlooked by a 10th-century Moorish castle. From the bus station, a 10-min walk uphill leads to the **Plaza Mayor**, built on two different levels, connected by steps, and lined with magnificent palace-mansions, arcades and whitewashed houses. From Plaza Mayor, C. de Ballesteros leads up to the old walls, in which there is a gateway to the 13th-century Romanesque-Gothic church of **Santa María la Mayor**. A short distance away is the **Casa-Museo de Pizarro**, with a reconstruction of the 15th-century house of a *hidalgo* (nobleman) and an exhibition of the life of Pizarro. 🛈 **Tourist office:** Plaza Mayor (www.trujillo.es).

TOLEDO

A sense of history permeates every street of this famous UNESCO-listed walled city, perched on a hill and with the Río Tajo (River Tagus) forming a natural moat on three sides. Over the centuries Christian, Moorish and Jewish cultures have each left their mark on Toledo, which was a source of inspiration to El Greco, who lived and worked here for nearly 40 years.

The station boasts colourful tiles, chandeliers, stained glass, Moorish windows and art nouveau decoration, and is a sign of things to come. Cross the Tagus and you soon reach the **Alcázar** (old fortress), reopened in summer 2010 after years of renovation (closed Mon, free admission Sun). Another of the city's famous sights, the **Museo de Santa Cruz**, is located in the beautifully restored Renaissance hospice (C. Cervantes 3, ☎ 92 522 10 36, free, closed Sun afternoons). It has temporary art exhibits by local artists along with displays on fine arts (including El Greco's *Assumption of the Virgin*), archaeology and industrial arts.

Constructed over some 250 years, the heavily buttressed **cathedral** is one of the wonders of Spain for its stained glass, for the sculpture in the choir, for the tombs within its chapels, and for its works of art, notably the *Transparente* – an extravagant baroque creation of paintings and marble sculptures. In the Sacristy hang paintings by El Greco, Van Dyck, Goya and Caravaggio. In the old **Jewish quarter** to the south are the two spectacular surviving synagogues. **El Tránsito** is a 14th-century Mudéjar edifice with a ceiling of carved cedarwood, now home to the **Museo Sefardí**, a museum about Jewish culture (C. Samuel Leví, closed Mon, free entry Sun). The 12th-century synagogue of **Santa María la Blanca** is very different: its conversion into a Christian church did not affect the basic layout of the interior, with five aisles separated by horseshoe arches and supported by pillars with unusual capitals and stone carvings.

≋ Paseo de la Rosa, just north-east of the centre (🚌 5/61/62 to the Plaza de Zocodóver). It's more pleasant to take the 20-min walk in; cross the main road from the station, turn right and immediately fork left on a quiet road with no-entry road signs, then cross the 10th-century bridge known as the Puente de Alcántara, with the classic view of the town, and take the road rising opposite into town. 🚹 **Tourist office**: the main office is at Puerta de Bisagra, ☎ 92 522 08 43 (www.toledo-turismo.com).

🛏 It can be difficult to find somewhere to stay for summer weekends. The best cheap lodgings are in the Old Town, such as **Hotel Maravilla**, Pl. del Barrio Rey 9, ☎ 92 522 33 04 (www.hotelmaravilla.com), €€; **La Belviseña**, Cuesta del Can 7, ☎ 92 522 00 67, €; and **Hostal Descalzos**, C. de los Descalzos 30, ☎ 92 522 28 88 (www.hostaldescalzos.com), €€, a lovely inn with great views over the city from the patio jacuzzi. **Hostel**: The **Castillo de San Servando Hostel** (HI), Castillo San Servando, ☎ 92 522 45 54 (www.reaj.com), is on the outskirts of town in a medieval castle (near the station). **Campsite**: The **Circo Romano**, Avda. Carlos III 19, ☎ 92 522 04 42, is reasonably comfortable and only a 10-min walk from Puerta de Bisagra.

✗ The street Calle de Barrio Rey has a good range of inexpensive places to eat. Shops sell locally produced marzipan (*mazapán*).

MÉRIDA

Mérida has a remarkable collection of Roman ruins, a reminder that this remote city was one of the wealthiest and most important centres in Roman Spain. Head for the theatres, the **Casa del Mitreo** (Plaza de Toros) and the Roman bridge, and look in at the museum. It's worth getting the €9 ticket covering all the sites apart from the Roman Museum (buy at any site). Free attractions include the Roman bridge, the **Forum Portico** and the **Temple of Diana**. As you arrive by train from Cáceres, the appreciable remains of the Roman **aqueduct** are visible immediately on the left (north) side. Most points of interest lie to the south of the station, however. By the tourist office is the entrance to the 14,000-seater **Anfiteatro** (amphitheatre), and the acoustically perfect **Teatro** (theatre), still used for theatrical events, its magnificent colonnades rising two storeys and enclosing the back of the stage. The nearby **Museo Nacional de Arte Romano** (C. José Ramón Mélida; closed Mon & Sun afternoon) deserves a couple of hours. It includes some superb items such as a vast mosaic of a boar hunt and a statue of Chronos trapped by a snake. Beyond the **Alcazaba** — successively a Roman, Visigothic and Moorish fort — is the much-renewed **Roman bridge** (Puente Romano) over the Río Guadiana, 792 m long and with 60 arches.

ARRIVAL, INFORMATION, ACCOMMODATION

≋ In the centre of town. ❚ **Tourist office**: Paséo José Álvarez Sáenz de Buruaga, ☎ 92 433 07 22 (www.merida.es); map and free guide to the sights of Mérida.

┣ There's not a huge amount of budget accommodation in the town centre; good bets are **Hostal El Alfarero**, C. Sagasta 40, ☎ 92 430 31 83 (www. hostalalfarero.com), €€, and **Hostal Nueva España**, Avda. Extremadura 6, ☎ 92 431 33 56, €€ (between the station and Pza España).

OVER THE BORDER

From Mérida, the railway follows the Guadiana Valley west to **Badajoz** and the Portuguese border. There is a once-daily train across the border to Elvas in Portugal (ERT 691), operated by the Portuguese railways. An alternative is the regular local bus, where on most services you need to change buses at the border. If time is tight, you might consider a taxi for this short cross-border hop, but check prices carefully. It is a 15-min journey from Badajoz to Elvas. Remember that Portuguese time is one hour behind Spanish time.

Elvas has one of the most remarkable of all the Alentejo castles, and the cobbled streets of the town itself are an enticing introduction to Portugal. From Elvas it is an easy rail journey to Lisbon, changing en route at Entroncamento, where you can connect onto **Route 11** (see p124).

LISBON — SEE P502

Spain's high-speed rail network was inaugurated in 1992 with the opening of a fast link from Madrid to Seville. Since then, the network served by super-fast trains (known as **Alta Velocidad Española** or AVE services) has been progressively extended, with recent extensions to Málaga (2007), Barcelona (2008) and Valencia (2010). So with a little planning you can enjoy a Catalan breakfast in Barcelona, stop off for a leisurely lunch in Madrid and still be in Málaga in time for tapas.

Not everyone favours such speed. When the early Scottish traveller Henry David Inglis headed south from Madrid to Andalucía in 1830, he bemoaned the fact that the regular stage carriage took merely a week — too fast, he felt, to really do justice to the landscapes along the way. The old roads to **Andalucía** all converge on a single natural defile that strikes a huge gash through the mountains. The **Sierra Morena** may not tower to great heights, but the rugged demeanour of these mountains creates a formidable barrier to travellers bound for the south. God never intended anyone to reach the land of sherry, flamenco and Carmen without a struggle.

Despeñaperros is the name given to the great gorge that was, for travellers of yesteryear, the pre-eminent gateway to Andalucía. For men like Henry Inglis and other travellers to Andalucía in the first half of the nineteenth century, the seductive beauty of the gypsies of Andalucía was presaged in the cruel beauty of Despeñaperros. This was, and still is, a place with fierce relief, great black rocky walls and wild torrents — everything that was needed in fact to appeal to the Romantic imagination.

Take the modern high-speed line south to Andalucía, and it slices through the Sierra Morena like butter. You'll hardly notice the hills. But if you have a few hours to spare why not take the old rail route that runs through the gorge at Despeñaperros. This is truly one of Europe's finest rail routes, and is a creative way of linking **Barcelona** (on **Routes 8** and **9**) or **Madrid** (on **Routes 9** and **10**) with southern Spain (where you can join **Route 13** for a tour of Andalucía). Shun the fast line and instead ride through Despeñaperros, swapping the arid red plains of La Mancha for the fiery lushness of Andalucía.

Not many trains follow the **old Despeñaperros route**, but you can identify them from the timetable as services that stop at both Alcázar de San Juan and Linares-Baeza (ERT 661; half a dozen daily services in each direction). Pick of the bunch is the *García Lorca*, which we rate as Spain's most interesting train. The *García Lorca* leaves Barcelona just after eight every morning bound for Andalucía carrying through carriages for Málaga, Córdoba and Seville. The full run from Barcelona to Málaga takes over 12 hrs — a journey calculated to appeal to slow travellers.

Cast back to before the construction of the railway and Despeñaperros was the haunt of *banditti* who would waylay innocent travellers as they ventured south to Andalucía. It is a little tamer nowadays, but still the most exciting rail route south to Andalucía. South of Despeñaperros, you emerge into a land of dense olive groves and huge oleanders on the platforms of railway stations. Suddenly there are lush colours and Moorish architecture, and scenes outside the carriage window that seem taken directly from paintings by **Murillo** and **Velázquez**.

Rail Route 10: Historic Spain

CITIES: ★★★ CULTURE: ★★ HISTORY: ★★★ SCENERY: ★★
COUNTRIES COVERED: SPAIN

From **Madrid** an incongruously suburban-looking train climbs through the heart of the **Sierra de Guadarrama** to **Segovia**, one of the most exciting places in Spain. At Segovia station there is little hint of the nearby old city, but it soon comes into view after a short bus journey. From Segovia, retrace the route over the Sierra to the junction at Villalba de Guadarrama (or else take the direct bus from Segovia to Salamanca), and change trains, soon passing close to the vast complex of **El Escorial**, seen on the right-hand side of the train. Beyond the walled pilgrimage town of **Ávila** lies **Salamanca**, an elegant old university city built in a gorgeous yellow stone. Rail routes from there include west to Portugal and north to Zamora and Burgos. This route is a chance to see three of Spain's most historic cities. Throw in Toledo (just 30 mins by train from Madrid and described in **Route 9**) and you really will have seen the finest quartet of mid-sized cities that Spain has to offer. All four can be visited as day trips from Madrid.

MADRID — SEE P519

SEGOVIA

This romantic walled hilltop city has a tremendous setting, perched above the **Río Eresma** and looking out to the heights of the Sierra de Guadarrama. The **cathedral**, which towers majestically above the rest of the town, dates from the 16th century and was the last Gothic church to be built in Spain. One side chapel has great metal dragons supporting censers on each side of a ceramic altar. Segovia also has a fine clutch of smaller medieval churches, notably **San Esteban**, with its 12th-century tower; **La Trinidad**, an exceptional Romanesque church; **Vera Cruz** (closed Mon and lunchtime), a remarkably interesting church with a 12-sided nave and 15th-century murals (outside the city walls); and the **Monasterio de S. Antonio El Real**, noted for its 15th-century portal and painted wooden Calvary of the Flemish school.

Heading down towards the gorge that cuts around the town, you reach the **Alcázar** (castle), an amazing pile bristling with spiky towers. A massive fire in 1862 destroyed much of it, and most of what you see today is architectural bravado dating from the 1882 restoration. Fake it may be, but it does make an entertaining visit, with quaintly undersize suits of armour dotted around the rooms, and dizzying views from the tower. It's also worth following the riverside path from just below the Alcázar — a delightful semi-rural walk with views up to the Old Town.

Believed to have been built by Augustus, the **aqueduct** is one of Spain's most magnificent Roman monuments, with 166 arches spanning over 800 metres. It was

Route Details

Madrid (Chamartín)–Salamanca ERT 679

Type	Frequency	Typical journey time
Train	7–8 daily	2h40

Madrid (Chamartín)–Segovia ERT 679

Type	Frequency	Typical journey time
Train	5–7 daily	1h50

Segovia–Villalba ERT 679

Type	Frequency	Typical journey time
Train	5–7 daily	1 hr

Villalba–El Escorial ERT 679

Type	Frequency	Typical journey time
Train	1–2 per hr	11 mins

El Escorial–Ávila ERT 679

Type	Frequency	Typical journey time
Train	3 daily	1 hr

Ávila–Salamanca ERT 679

Type	Frequency	Typical journey time
Train	8–9 daily	1h10

Notes

It is also possible to travel from Madrid Chamartin to Segovia Guiomar station on a high-speed train, taking just 30 mins (ERT 663, 679). However, Guiomar station is located about 4 km from the centre of Segovia. The fast train route is much less scenic than the slow variant followed by Route 10.

constructed without mortar — and although partly repaired in the 15th century it is still intact.

ARRIVAL, INFORMATION, ACCOMMODATION

≋ The railway station is in the New Town; take 🚌 6 (it's much too far to walk) to the Old Town. 🚌 The **bus station** is a 15-min walk from the centre (also on 🚌 6). 🚪 **Tourist office**: Plaza del Azoguejo 1, ☎ 92 146 67 21 (www.turismodesegovia.com), by the aqueduct.

🛏 Stay in the Old Town. **Hostal El Hidalgo**, José Canalejas 3–5, ☎ 92 146 35 29 (www.el-hidalgo.com), €, has a pleasantly old-fashioned restaurant. Slightly cheaper are the **Pensión El Gato**, Plaza Salvador 10, ☎ 92 142 32 44, €, the **Hostal Juan Bravo**, C. Juan Bravo 12, ☎ 92 146 34 13, €–€€, and the **Hostal Taray**, Plaza San Facundo 1, ☎ 92 146 30 41 (www.hostaltaray.com), €. The youth hostel **Albergue Juvenil Emperador Teodosio** (HI), Paseo Conde de Sepúlveda 4, ☎ 92 144 11 11 (www.reaj.com), is open July to mid-Sept only. 🍴 Reasonable bars, cafés and restaurants in and around Plaza Mayor, the attractive central square of the Old Town.

El Escorial

Although it's some way from the station, you can easily see this vast grey palace, set beneath a hillside, from the railway. El Escorial is a magnificent 16th-century complex that includes a monastery, holding the tombs of the kings of Spain, and a library with nearly 3,000 5th–18th-century documents. Many notable works of art are on display in the complex, some forming an intrinsic part of the decor. The **palace** is of particular interest (closed Mon), read more about it on p525.

For something verging on the bizarre, **El Valle de los Caídos** (the Valley of the Fallen; regular buses from El Escorial) is a huge kitsch Fascist memorial to Civil War casualties. Built by Franco in the 1950s using political dissidents as slave labour, it is the largest cross in the world (150 m high), placed above a cave basilica holding the grave of Franco. A funicular gets you from the entrance of the basilica to the base of the cross.

Arrival, information, accommodation

⇶ About 2 km from town, uphill, so it's better to take a local shuttle bus to the centre.
🛈 **Tourist office**: C. Grimaldi 4, ☎ 91 890 53 13 (www.sanlorenzoturismo.org).
🛏 **Hostal El Retiro**, C. Aulencia 17, ☎ 91 890 09 46, €–€€, is central, a 15-min walk from the palace and monastery. A bit pricier is the **Hostal Cristina**, Calvario (nr Juan de Toledo), ☎ 91 890 19 61 (www.hostalcristina.es), €€, with a restaurant and garden.

Ávila

The highest city in Spain, Ávila is encircled by **medieval walls** in such a perfect state of preservation that the whole place looks like a cardboard model from a distance. Much of the walled town is surprisingly neglected and under-populated, though it's obviously the most atmospheric area to stay in. Throughout Spain and beyond, pilgrims are drawn to Ávila, indelibly associated with its native mystic and reformer **Santa Teresa de Jesús** (now the city's patron saint), canonised in 1622. Apart from the walls (part of which you can walk along the top of), Ávila's main attractions are the **cathedral**, the **Convento de Santa Teresa**, the **Basilica of San Vincente** and a number of other buildings associated with Santa Teresa. The cathedral and Basilica de San Vincente each deserve a visit, while **El Real Monasterio de Santo Tomás** on Plaza de Granada is a real time-warp of a monastery, which became the summer palace of Ferdinand and Isabella. There are three cloisters, in different styles, containing gardens graced with a romantic, overgrown air of repose.

Arrival, information, accommodation

⇶ In Avda. de José Antonio; there are luggage lockers. The bus and rail stations are 2 km out of town. 🚌 1/3/PV run from the railway station to the centre. 🛈 **Tourist office**: a visitor's reception centre (municipal) is on Avenida de Madrid 39, ☎ 92 022 59 69 (www.avilaturismo.com).

Cheap options within the old city walls include the **Hostal Don Diego**, C. Marqués de Canales y Chozas 5, ☎ 92 025 54 75, €, the **Hostal Cara Felipe**, Plaza del Mercado Chico 1, ☎ 92 021 39 24, €–€€, and the **Hotel Arco San Vicente**, C. López Núñez 6, ☎ 92 022 24 98 (www.arcosanvicente.com), €€. The youth hostel, **Albergue Juvenil de Profesor Arturo Duperier** (HI), Avda. de la Juventud, ☎ 92 022 17 16 (www.reaj.com), is open July to mid-Sept.

Salamanca

Salamanca is beautifully built in yellow stone and home to one of Spain's oldest universities. Virtually throughout the year there's a generous offering of concerts, exhibitions and other cultural events, many of them free.

Echoing to hundreds of footsteps, the **Plaza Mayor** is one of Spain's finest squares, a strikingly unified example of the baroque style. Walk south from here, past the **Casa de las Conchas** (House of Shells), a 15th-century mansion named after the carved shells embellishing its exterior, the motif of the Santiago pilgrimage.

Dating from 1243, the main part of the **university** (at the south end of Rúa Mayor) is the country's prime instance of the Plateresque style, seen on the ornamental facade, with its carvings of floral themes, royal heraldry, children, women and beasts. Inside you can look around the cloister, off which lie some of the oldest rooms, giving an idea of the university in medieval times, notably a dimly lit lecture hall austerely furnished with narrow, backless benches, and with a pulpit for the lecturer.

The two cathedrals stand side by side — the Romanesque **Catedral Vieja** (Old Cathedral), with wonderful frescos, cloisters and a 15th-century retable, and the **Catedral Nueva** (New Cathedral), displaying ornate relief carvings in the so-called Churrigueresque style. Nearby, the **Convento de San Esteban** is highly atmospheric. Just below the cathedrals, the **Casa Lis** (www.museocasalis.org) is a striking modernist edifice of glass and filigree ironwork, restored and now home to the city's collection of art nouveau, art deco and (for some reason) dolls. From here, you can walk down to the River Tormes and the **Puente Romano**, which is part of the Vía de la Plata.

ARRIVAL, INFORMATION, ACCOMMODATION

≥ Located centrally in Paseo de la Estación. There are luggage lockers plus a shopping and entertainment centre. 🚌 1/11. 🛈 **Tourist office** (provincial): Rúa Mayor, ☎ 92 326 85 71; (municipal): Plaza Mayor 32, ☎ 92 321 83 42 (www.salamanca.es).

Accommodation is plentiful; head for the Plaza Mayor, around which numerous pensions are signposted at the foot of staircases. A small and friendly choice is the **Microtel Placentinos**, C. de los Placentinos 9, ☎ 92 328 15 31 (www.microtelplacentinos.com), €€. The youth hostel **Albergue Juvenil** (HI) is at C. Escoto 13–15, ☎ 92 326 91 41 (www.reaj.com).

Rail Route 11: The Atlantic coast of Iberia

CITIES: ★★ CULTURE: ★★ HISTORY: ★★ SCENERY: ★★
COUNTRIES COVERED: PORTUGAL, SPAIN

Cast back to the mid-19th century and overland travel in Portugal was formidably difficult. The opening of the first railway in 1858 heralded a new era in Portuguese communication, giving inland communities access to the country's great ports at Porto (Oporto) and Lisbon.

Today, the railway is a fine way to take the pulse of Portugal and this route is designed to do just that. It starts in Lisbon and heads north, taking in the old university town of **Coimbra**, the port-producing city of **Porto** and the beautiful coastal resort of **Viana do Castelo**, lying close to sweeping golden beaches. From Porto it's worth spending a few days exploring the scenic and deeply rural Douro Valley. Then the route heads into Spain, traversing Galicia with its wild coast. The journey ends in the breathtaking Spanish pilgrimage city of **Santiago de Compostela**, where you can connect onto **Route 12**.

LISBON — SEE P502

TOMAR

Local trains, generally hourly, from Lisbon run directly to Tomar (journey time 2 hrs, ERT 699). These go via Entroncamento, itself halfway between Lisbon and Coimbra — so if you're heading north you can take the branch line to Tomar, then retrace to Entroncamento, where you change for Coimbra. Tomar is worth the detour.

THE KNIGHTS TEMPLAR

Begun as a military-religious order to guard pilgrim routes to the Holy Land in the 12th century, the Order of the Knights Templar had its own rules, its own confessors, and its own sizeable wealth. Known for their military skill more than their piety, the knights were especially successful in driving Moorish conquerors from Iberia.

King Philip IV of France, badly in need of some money, coveted the order's wealth and convinced the Pope that they were not only too worldly, but dangerous. The order was abolished in 1306 and Templar properties were distributed to the kings in whose countries they had holdings. But King Dinis remembered their bravery in ridding Portugal of the Moors and, with the Pope's approval, established a new Order of Christ. He invited all former Templars to join, in effect restoring to them all their properties in Portugal.

The Knights Templar built round churches in many parts of Europe, and these sites are linked to the legend of the Holy Grail — which might even have ended up in one of them.

ROUTE DETAILS

Lisbon (Sta Apolónia)–Coimbra (B)   ERT 690

Type	Frequency	Typical journey time
Train	16–19 daily	1h50 to 2h10

Coimbra (B)–Porto (Campanhã)   ERT 690

Type	Frequency	Typical journey time
Train	16–19 daily	1h05

Porto (Campanhã)–Viana do Castelo   ERT 696

Type	Frequency	Typical journey time
Train	4–6 daily	1h35

Viana do Castelo–Valença   ERT 696

Type	Frequency	Typical journey time
Train	4–6 daily	50 mins

Valença–Vigo   ERT 696

Type	Frequency	Typical journey time
Train	2 daily	55 mins

Vigo–Pontevedra   ERT 680

Type	Frequency	Typical journey time
Train	16–19 daily	30 mins

Pontevedra–Santiago de Compostela   ERT 680

Type	Frequency	Typical journey time
Train	16–19 daily	1 hr

KEY JOURNEY

Lisbon–Porto   ERT 690

Type	Frequency	Typical journey time
Train	Every 1–2 hrs	2h44

Notes

Lisbon to Santiago: change trains at Porto and Vigo. Fast trains call at Coimbra B station: a frequent rail shuttle connects Coimbra B with Coimbra station. Additional trains available Porto–Viana do Castelo by changing at Nine. Remember Portugal's time zone is 1 hr behind Spain's.

On a wooded hill above the Old Town of cobbled streets is the 12th-century castle and subsequent monastery of the Order of the Knights Templar (see p124), the **Convento de Cristo** (open daily). The structure was erected in 1160 for the master of the Knights Templar (responsible for keeping open pilgrim routes to the Holy Land during the Crusades), but from the 1320s became the seat of the Order of the Knights of Christ. Highlights include the Templars' Rotunda (the round chancel), modelled on the Holy Sepulchre in Jerusalem, and the magnificent Manueline-style window between the west end of the nave and Santa Barbara cloister. The window combines every maritime and nautical motif known to the Manueline style: ropes, shells, coral, fishing floats, seaweed, even an anchor chain. The Convento parking terrace overlooks **Nossa Senhora da Conceição**, perhaps Portugal's finest early-Renaissance church. While the outside is plain, the beautifully proportioned interior has finely carved Corinthian columns and faces with acanthus-leaf beards flanking the sanctuary arch. Other sights in the Old Town are the **Igreja de São João Baptista**, with two fine Manueline doorways and a richly carved altar covered in gold, and the 15th-century **Sinagoga**, housing the **Museu Luso-Hebraico**, a museum of Portuguese Judaism (open daily, admission free).

ARRIVAL, INFORMATION, ACCOMMODATION

≈ Located just south of the centre; hourly trains to Lisbon (ERT 699). 🚹 **Tourist office**: Av. Dr Candido Madureira, ☎ 249 322 427 (www.rtt.ipt.pt). ⍩ Your best bet for budget accommodation are Tomar's B&Bs, such as **Casa Das Flores**, R. Principal, ☎ 249 327 086 (www.casadasfloresportugal.com), €€, the **Casa Rosden**, Estr. Cochões, ☎ 249 382 730, €€, or the **Prado Sonolento**, En 238 No 4A, Portela de Nexebra, ☎ 249 362 493, €€.

COIMBRA

Coimbra was a centre of the Portuguese Renaissance and is the seat of one of the oldest universities in the world. Set on a hillside above the River Mondego, the town is packed with medieval character; in term time it has a lively, youthful air. Coimbra has its own version of the *fado*, a melancholy, monotonous and sentimental chant originally sung by sailors in the 18th century.

Although founded in 1290, the old university building is baroque, with a magnificent library resplendent in painted ceilings and gilded wood; you can also visit the grand **Graduates' Hall** and a small museum of sacred art. The 12th-century **Sé Velha** (cathedral) is a striking Romanesque building with a fine altarpiece and Gothic cloisters, while the **Monastery of Santa Cruz** contains a 16th-century Manueline cloister, an elaborately carved stone pulpit and the tombs of the first two kings of Portugal. Soak up the peaceful atmosphere of the **Jardim Botânico** (Botanic Gardens) south of the Old Town or take a boat trip from Parque Dr Manuel Braga (trips take 1 hr, not Mon & Jan) ☎ 239 433 770 (www.basofias.com).

≋ **Coimbra**, ☎ 808 208 208 (www.cp.pt), a 10-min walk from the centre or 🚌 4/29/ 103. **Coimbra B**, 3 km north-west of town, handles long-distance trains, including those from Lisbon; 🚌 5/29. Frequent trains between Coimbra and Coimbra B. For luggage lockers go to the Café Internacional. For the town centre, follow the road along by the river and fork left by the tourist office.

🛈 **Tourist office**: (regional) Largo da Portagem, ☎ 239 488 120, (municipal) Edifício da Biblioteca Geral da Universidade de Coimbra (University Library building), Praça da Porta Férrea, ☎ 239 834 158 (www.turismodecoimbra.pt).

🛏 The **Hotel Oslo**, Avda. Fernão de Magalhães 25, ☎ 239 829 071 (www.oslohotel-coimbra.com), €€, is good value and close to the station. The **youth hostel** (HI) is 3 km from the train station at Rua Doutor Henriques Seco 14, ☎ 239 822 955, (www.movijovem.pt), 🚌 6/7/29 from Largo da Portagem. **Campsite**: the municipal-run campsite offers excellent, modern facilities and is open 24 hours all year round. Rua da Escola – Alto Areeiro, St° António dos Olivais, ☎ 239 086 902 (www. arpurocampings.com), 🚌 38 from Largo da Portagem. ✗ Plenty of centrally placed cheap eateries, for example in the University Gardens and in Beco do Forno and Rua dos Gatos (alleyways between Largo da Portagem and Rua do Soto).

PORTO (OPORTO)

Portugal's seductive second city, spectacularly sited on the steep banks of the River Douro near its mouth, gives its name to the fortified wine the English-speaking world knows as port (fortuitously invented by two Englishmen who used brandy in an attempt to preserve Portuguese wine).

Get your bearings by climbing the **Torre dos Clérigos**, Porto's symbol, an 18th-century granite bell tower that gives a magnificent view. Below, the character-fully fading Old Town, with its pastel shades and changes in level, is strongly at-mospheric, notably in the **Ribeira** riverside area. The **Soares dos Reis Museum** (closed Mon), housed in the Carrancas Palace, is acclaimed for its collection of decorative arts, including Portuguese faience.

For an astonishing temple to money-making, take the guided tour of the centrally located **Palácio da Bolsa** (former Stock Exchange, now headquarters of the Chamber of Commerce, www.palaciodabolsa.pt), rather grey and boring-looking from outside but revealing a lavish interior which includes the Arabian Hall, a 19th-century gilded evocation of the Alhambra in Granada (see p145). The nearby **Church of Santa Clara** is a fine example of the Manueline style and has a dazzling baroque interior.

The vineyards themselves are a long way upriver in the magnificently scenic **Douro Valley**, but most of the port is aged in the numerous **port lodges** in the district of **Vila Nova de Gaia**, linked to the city centre by the double-decker coathanger-shaped Dom Luís I Bridge; walk over the top level for dizzying views. Many lodges offer **tours** with tastings and booking is not generally necessary.

Some are closed at weekends outside the main season. Some lodges levy a small charge, often as little as €3, but with the option to upgrade if you wish to taste more illustrious wines. Having visited many of the lodges, the three we especially recommend to get a sense of port and its history are those at Taylor's, Ramos Pinto (which has a wonderful small museum on wine) and Graham's, where the guides are especially good and show amazing prowess in many different languages. Moored on the river, small barrel-laden sailing craft (*barcos rabelos*), last used in 1967, serve as a reminder of how the young ports used to be brought downriver from the vineyards.

In 2005 Porto gained a new concert hall, the **Casa da Música**, a stunning design remarkable for its use of interior space. To the west of the town, amidst magnificent gardens, is the **Fundação de Serralves**, an art deco mansion with a fine collection of modern art (www.serralves.pt, closed Mon).

ARRIVAL, INFORMATION, ACCOMMODATION

≈ **Campanhã**, Rua da Estação, near the south-east edge of town, serves Lisbon trains (🚌 207 to centre); luggage lockers and cash machine. **São Bento**, near Praça da Liberdade, much more central (wonderful tiling makes it a sight in itself), handles local/regional services. Frequent connections between the stations, taking 10 mins. Leave **São Bento** station and turn right up Praça da Liberdade then go left to Avda. dos Aliados; tourist office is on your left, towards the top of this large square. ✈ **Francisco Sá Carneiro**, ☎ 229 432 400 (🚌 120/601/602 or Aero Bus from Avenida dos Aliados or take the metro); tourist office (www.ana.pt).

🛈 **Tourist offices**: (national) Praça Dom João I 43, ☎ 927 411 817; (municipal) Rua Clube dos Fenianos 25, ☎ 223 393 472, (Cathedral − Sé − Casa da Câmara) Terreiro da Sé, ☎ 223 325 174 (www.visitporto.travel). The free city map shows five **walking tours**: medieval, baroque, azulejos (tiles), neoclassical, and the garrett tour. 🚌 **Day passes** (€7) − cheaper than four separate fares − and **3-day passes** (€15) cover all transport and are sold at STCP kiosks. For information on public transport see www.stcp.pt. Diana run hop-on-hop-off **bus tours** (buy a ticket on board). The **Museu do Carro Eléctrico** is a vintage tram that tours the city from near the Church of São Francisco. ⛴ 50-min **boat trips** depart from Cais da Estiva (Ribeira) and near the Sandeman port lodge and tour the river.

🛏 For cheap lodgings, try the central area around Avda. dos Aliados. Avoid the dockside Ribeira. A friendly place with a variety of rooms from budget singles and quads to more comfortable doubles with private bathrooms is the **Pensão Residencial Duas Nações**, Praça G G Fernandes 59, ☎ 222 081 616 (www.duasnacoes.com), €–€€. Another good-value option is the **Albergaria Residência do Vice-Rei**, R. de Júlio Dinis 779, ☎ 226 095 371, €–€€. **Hostels:** There are a number of good hostels in Porto, most of which have private rooms as well as dorms. Some options include the **Oporto Poets Hostel**, Rua dos Caldeireiros 261, ☎ 223 324 209 (www.oportopoetshostel.com) and the **Porto Downtown Hostel**, Praça Guilherme Gomes Fernandes 66, ☎ 222 018 094 (www.portodowntownhostel.com). Newly renovated, the **Spot Hostel**, Rua Gonçalo Cristóvão 12, ☎ 224 085 205 (www.spothostel.pt) is a firm favourite on the

Braga

Braga, the nation's religious capital (**🅑 tourist office**: Avda. da Liberdade 1, ☎ 253 262 550, www.cm-braga.pt), has more than 300 churches as well as Portugal's oldest cathedral; it's the site of massive celebrations in Holy Week, and 5 km east is the pilgrimage site of **Bom Jesus do Monte**, with a 116-m climb up the monumental 'Staircase of the Five Senses' to its Chapel of Miracles and massive reliquary. Trains from Porto to Braga run approximately hourly (ERT 695); there are also direct trains and buses from Lisbon.

European hostelling circuit. **Campsites**: in Angeiras, around 20 km from Porto, is **Campsite Orbitur**, Rua de Angeiras, Lavra, ☎ 229 270 571 (www.orbitur.com); there are also two in Vila Nova de Gaia: **Camping de Salgueiros**, ☎ 227 810 500, and **Camping Marisol**, ☎ 227 135 942.

CONNECTIONS FROM PORTO

Allocate time to explore the mountain-backed **Douro Valley** east of Porto (ERT 694), with its many vineyards as well as some enchanting places accessible by train. **Amarante**, memorably placed by the River Tâmega, has photogenic houses with wooden balconies and iron grilles, and a monastic church with gilded baroque woodwork. **Vila Real**, placed on Corgo Gorge, has a host of 16th- to 18th-century patricians' houses. North-east of Porto, **Guimarães** (ERT 695a) was once the Portuguese capital and contains a rewarding medieval core within its industrial outskirts; **Paço dos Duques de Bragança** (still used as the president's residence) includes a town museum, and there's a fine wooden ceiling within the Banqueting Hall.

Viana do Castelo

This old fortress town is the Costa Verde's most pleasant resort, with the beach on one side of the River Lima and the charming little town — noted for its Renaissance and Manueline architecture, which appeared when trade began with the great Hanseatic cities of northern Europe — on the other. It's also a centre of Portuguese folklore and famous for its handicrafts.

With the exception of **Santa Luzia** on the top of the **Monte de Santa Luzia** (accessible by funicular from its beautifully restored station on Avda. 25 de Abril; excellent view), all interesting sights are walkable. The central square, **Praça da República**, has a 16th-century fountain that has been copied all over the region. Some choice examples of *azulejos* (tiles) can be seen in **Misericórdia Church** and the **Municipal Museum** (also showing glazed earthenware and furniture). Viana do Castelo's **Romaria** (in Aug) is the biggest festival in the country.

There are many unspoilt sandy beaches accessible by train on the line north to **Valença**. Our favourite is right by the railway line at Vila Praia de Âncora (alight at Âncora-Praia).

ARRIVAL, INFORMATION, ACCOMMODATION

≈ Avda. dos Combatentes near the town centre. **🛈 Tourist office**: Praça da Erva, ☎ 258 822 620 (www.cm-viana-castelo.pt). ⊨ Pensions are easy to find, but not that cheap; rooms in private houses are often a better bet. **Youth hostels** (HI): The modern **Viana do Castelo**, Rua de Limia, ☎ 258 800 260 (www.movijovem.pt) and **Gil Eannes Ship**, Doca Comercial, ☎ 258 821 582 (www.pousadasjuventude.pt), a former hospital ship for cod fishermen and a city landmark, now a floating hostel with 55 beds.

VALENÇA

Unsightly modern sprawl has marred the approaches to this ancient town by the Minho River, but it still has its fortress-within-a-fortress guarding the border with Spain. Much survives of the 17th–18th-century walls and there are narrow old streets of white houses. Good for a stopover for an hour or two. ≈ The station is on the east side of the New Town.

TUI

A bridge connects this tiered Spanish town to Portugal. Remember that clocks go forward by one hour as you cross from Portugal to Spain. Tui has grown around the lichen-encrusted **Cathedral of Santa Maria**. This impressive, austere Romanesque and Gothic building has a 13th-century cloister, carved choir stalls, an ornate 14th-century porch and fine Gothic sepulchres. Visit the churches of **San Bartolomé** and **San Telmo** if time permits.

ARRIVAL, INFORMATION, ACCOMMODATION

≈ Central. **🛈 Tourist office**: C. Colón, ☎ 98 660 17 89. ⊨ **San Telmo**, Avenida de la Concordia 84, ☎ 98 660 00 96, €.

VIGO

Spain's major fishing port lies on a beautiful sheltered bay. It's a clamorous, busy place built of grey granite, not immediately attractive except in the old, sloping quarter near the seafront. For a dose of art head to the centrally located **Marco – Museo de Arte Contemporánea de Vigo** on 54 Príncipe (www.marcovigo.com; closed Mon, free entry). **Castro Castle**, the ruined fort on a hill just above, provides a fine view. There are **beaches** and an **open-air pool** 2 km west at **Samil** that can be reached by 🚌 L10/C15A/C15B/C15C.

The wonderfully unspoilt **Islas Cíes** archipelago, reached by ferry from Vigo from mid-June to mid-Sept and during the Easter Week, is the main reason for stopping here. Designated a national park, the islands have white sands and rugged hilltops, with enough trails to provide a day's walking on the main two isles (which are joined together by a sandbank).

The third island is a bird sanctuary and is not open to visitors. Book ahead (☎ 98 643 83 58) to camp in summer. Ferries leave from Estación Marítima (☎ 98 622 52 72); visitors are limited to 2,000 per day, so go early in the day if you haven't reserved.

ARRIVAL, INFORMATION, ACCOMMODATION

⇌ Throughout 2012 and 2013 (and possibly even beyond), while a new city centre station is being constructed, trains to and from Vigo stop at Guixar, a very fine concrete and glass structure 1 km from the centre. Frequent buses into town. 🛈 **Tourist office**: C. Teófilo Llorente 5, ☎ 98 622 47 57 (www.turismodevigo.es); regional tourist office at C. Cánovas de Castillo 22, ☎ 98 643 05 77.

　　⊨ **Residencia Casais**, C. Lepanto 16, ☎ 88 611 29 56 (www.hostalcasaisvigo.com), €. **Hotel Atlántico Vigo**, Avenida García Barbón 35, ☎ 98 622 05 30 (www.hotelatlanticovigo.com), €€. **Youth hostel** (HI): **Residencia Juvenil Altamar**, C. Cesáreo González 4, ☎ 98 629 08 08 (www.xunta.es), 3 km from the rail station, dorm beds from €7.50; open July & Aug.

PONTEVEDRA

This typical old Galician town on the River Pontevedra began life as a port, but its importance dwindled as the old harbour silted up.

　　Although surrounded by a new city, the compact Old Town is pretty much intact, with parts of the original walls still visible around a maze of cobbled streets, arcaded squares with carved stone crosses and low houses with flower-filled balconies. **Iglesia de la Peregrina**, an unusual chapel in the shape of a scallop shell, is situated by the partly arcaded main square, Praza de la Ferrería, on the boundary between the Old and New Towns.

　　The Gothic facade of the **Convent of San Francisco** looks onto the Herrería. **Basílica de Santa María la Mayor** has an impressive Plateresque facade, which is floodlit at night. The 13th-century Gothic **Convent of Santo Domingo** by the **Jardines de Vincenti** is now in ruins but still evokes a certain splendour. It forms part of the **Provincial Museum**, other sections of which are at Praza de la Leña.

ARRIVAL, INFORMATION, ACCOMMODATION

⇌ Praza Calvo Sotelo, about 1 km from the centre; lockers. 🛈 **Tourist office**: C. General Gutiérrez Mellado 1B, ☎ 98 685 08 14 (www.visit-pontevedra.com).

　　⊨ Budget accommodation is limited; there are some *fondas* and *pensiones* near C. de la Peregrina and Praza de Galicia; try **Vedra Hotel**, Rua Profesor Filgueira Valverde 10, ☎ 98 686 95 50 (www.vedrahotel.es), €€, or the **Casa Maruja**, Avda. Santa Maria 12, ☎ 98 685 49 01, €.

SANTIAGO DE COMPOSTELA — SEE P138

Rail Route 12: The pilgrim route to Santiago

CITIES: ★★ CULTURE: ★★ HISTORY: ★★ SCENERY: ★★
COUNTRIES COVERED: FRANCE, SPAIN

If it were ever possible to make a pilgrimage by rail, this is it, for **Santiago de Compostela** (or just plain Santiago to most) has been the goal for millions of pilgrims over many centuries, walking the various routes from France and across northern Spain that have come to be collectively known as the **Camino de Santiago** or **The Route of St James**. Even for those of no or little faith, this transect across northern Spain is a very fine journey, much enlivened by some splendid scenery and some of Spain's most historic cities along the way.

The route starts in **Biarritz**, not because a luxurious seaside resort is a natural prelude to a pilgrimage, but more as a matter of convenience for users of this book. It provides a good link with **Route 5**, useful for travellers arriving from Paris via Bordeaux or coming from the Mediterranean coast of France.

San Sebastián stands on the coast beneath the green, rainy foothills of the Pyrenees in the **Basque** province, known to the assertively independent Basque people as Euskal Herria. Never conquered either by the Romans or the Moors, the Basques suffered appalling repression during the Franco period and their language was banned. This area has a reputation for the best cuisine in Spain.

Burgos and **León**, both with superlative cathedrals, lie in the great *meseta* (high plain) of Castilla y León (formerly known as Old Castile). To the north rise the **Picos de Europa**, not that well served by public transport, but offering some of the best mountain scenery in the country. By contrast, **Galicia**, comprising Spain's north-west corner, is lushly verdant and intricately hilly, with a complicated coastline buffeted by Atlantic gusts and characterised by fjord-like scenery.

BIARRITZ — SEE P80

The route south from Biarritz hugs the coast. The little town of **St-Jean-de-Luz**, halfway between Biarritz and the Spanish border, deserves a look. All trains stop at St-Jean. If you can avoid the high season crowds, this bustling fishing port is a fine place to linger. The train journey across the border to San Sebastián always requires a change of train en route. We suggest doing that at **Hendaye**. It was at this station that Hitler met Franco in October 1940. It is the only remarkable thing about an otherwise rather unlovely place. The onward journey to San Sebastián is with the frequent **EuskoTren** narrow-gauge railway (schedules at foot of ERT 689). EuskoTren does not accept rail passes, but the fare from Hendaye to San Sebastián is less than €2. An alternative is to choose one of the few French trains that continue from Hendaye over the bridge to Irún in Spain, where you can change onto a regular RENFE train to **San Sebastián** (less frequent than EuskoTren but rail passes are accepted).

Notes

Biarritz–San Sebastián: on main line trains change at Irún (southbound) or Hendaye (northbound). Additional journeys are available by local train, changing at Hendaye.

Reservations are needed on most express services in Spain.

Route Details

Biarritz–San Sebastián ERT 46

Type	Frequency	Typical journey time
Train	3–4 daily	1h20

San Sebastián–Vitoria ERT 689

Type	Frequency	Typical journey time
Train	7–8 daily	1h45

Vitoria–Burgos ERT 689

Type	Frequency	Typical journey time
Train	7–8 daily	1h20

Burgos–León ERT 681

Type	Frequency	Typical journey time
Train	2 daily	1h50

León–Astorga ERT 682

Type	Frequency	Typical journey time
Train	5–6 daily	30 mins

Astorga–Santiago de Compostela ERT 680, 682

Type	Frequency	Typical journey time
Train	1 daily	5h30

Santiago de Compostela–A Coruña ERT 680

Type	Frequency	Typical journey time
Train	16–20 daily	35 mins

Key Journeys

San Sebastián–Burgos ERT 689

Type	Frequency	Typical journey time
Train	4 daily	2h55

Burgos–Bilbao ERT 689

Type	Frequency	Typical journey time
Train	3–4 daily	3 hrs

SAN SEBASTIÁN (DONOSTIA)

Known as Donostia to the Basques, San Sebastián is an elegant resort, with tamarisks gracing the promenade that runs along a crescent-shaped bay. Formerly a whaling and deep-sea fishing port doubling as a stopover for pilgrims en route to Santiago de Compostela, San Sebastián really came into its own in the mid-19th century as a fashionable health resort.

Take time to wander the streets of the Old Town, or **parte vieja**, nestled at the foot of Monte Urgull. Although mainly rebuilt in the 19th century, it retains a characterful maze of small streets, tiny darkened shops and bars, arcaded plazas like the **Plaza de la Constitución**, which used to serve as a bullring, and churches such as the beautiful baroque **Basílica de Santa María del Coro**. Fishing is still much in evidence, with the daily catch on show on stalls in the fish market.

The **Museum of San Telmo**, which occupies a former Dominican monastery, opened its doors again to the public in April 2011 after years of renovation. The new pavilion blends neatly into the surrounding cityscape. At the far end of the quay you'll find the **Naval Museum** (closed Mon) and the renovated **Aquarium**. For superb views, climb **Monte Urgull** itself, topped by a much rebuilt fort (the **Castillo de la Mota**). Standing proudly near the top of the hill is the statue of the **Sagrado Corazón** (Sacred Heart), which watches over the city.

ARRIVAL, INFORMATION, ACCOMMODATION

≽ **RENFE: Estación del Norte**, Paseo de Francia. Cross the ornate María-Cristina Bridge, turn right, and it is a few mins' walk through the 19th-century area to the Old Town. **EuskoTren: Estación de Amara**, Plaza Easo. Beware of being hounded by unregistered hotel owners who group outside the station. Luggage lockers. **🛈 Tourist office**: C. Reina Regente 3, ☎ 94 348 11 66 (www.sansebastianturismo.com).

🛏 For budget accommodation head for the Old Town: hidden amongst the narrow streets are many *pensiones*. Try **Pensión Amaiur**, C. 31 de Agosto, ☎ 94 342 96 54 (www.pensionamaiur.com), €–€€, which offers spotless, comfortable rooms and a friendly welcome, or the newly refurbished **Adore Plaza**, Plaza de la Constitución 6, ☎ 94 342 22 70 (www.adoreplaza.com), €€. **Hostels**: In the Old Town, and within walking distance of the station is **Enjoy San Sebastian**, Treinta y Uno de Agosto 16, ☎ 069 990 14 51 (www.enjoyss.com).

✗ There are many superb backstreet tapas bars – monkfish kebabs, stuffed peppers and wild mushroom vol-au-vents may be on offer. There are two excellent markets: **La Bretxa**, on Alameda del Boulevard, and **San Martin**, near the cathedral on C. Loiola. For the best small **restaurants**, try the Old Town and the fishing harbour at the north end of Playa de la Concha.

HEADING SOUTH

Heading south from San Sebastián, our route cuts through the green hills of **Gipuzkoa**, a province where the Basque language and culture still thrive,

Spain's north coast by train

From Santander a quite remarkable rail route runs west along the north coast of Spain. The first stretch of the route, as far as Bilbao, is run by EuskoTren and services west of Bilbao are operated by FEVE. Rail passes are not recognised by either company. See ERT 686 for the frequent services from **San Sebastián to Bilbao** and ERT 687 for the very infrequent FEVE trains west of Bilbao. You may consider just making a day trip from San Sebastián to Bilbao, but if you have some days to spare, the north coast route **west from Bilbao**, while slow, is one of Europe's finest. It provides an alternative to Route 12 from San Sebastián to Galicia, skirting the coastlines of Cantabria and Asturias for much of the journey.

You might consider following Route 12 on the outward journey and then returning along the coast. Or vice versa. This **coastal journey** splits naturally into four stages, viz. San Sebastián − Bilbao − Santander − Oviedo − Ferrol. The one way fare for the entire run from San Sebastián to Ferrol is about €52. Our favourite stretch of this magnificent route is the section between Santander and Oviedo, where the railway cuts a narrow trail between the rugged Picos de Europa (to the south) and a dramatic coastline to the north. The small resort town of Llanes in the very middle of this stretch is an immensely tempting spot to alight and linger for a few days.

From Ferrol, there are five daily trains to A Coruña (see p140), whence there are frequent services to Santiago de Compostela (see p138). See ERT 682 for Ferrol to A Coruña and ERT 680 for A Coruña to Santiago.

Even if you are pressed for time, don't miss the excursion to Bilbao from San Sebastián. Bilbao's star attraction is the **Museo Guggenheim** art gallery, ☎ 94 435 90 00, www.guggenheim-bilbao.es (closed Mon, but open daily in July–Aug). Its titanium-clad geometric design is one of the most talked-about pieces of modern architecture. Bilbao's Old Town, on the right bank of the river and beneath the hillside, is pleasant for strolling around. **🅱 Tourist office**: Plaza Ensanche 11, ☎ 94 479 57 60 (www.bilbao.net/bilbaoturismo).

especially in remoter communities away from main roads. The next community of any size is the Basque capital: Vitoria-Gasteiz, though Basque speakers tend to refer to it simply as Gasteiz.

Vitoria-Gasteiz

Known for making playing cards and chocolate truffles, Vitoria-Gasteiz also has considerable charm if you ignore the ugly suburbs. The almost perfectly preserved centre of this medieval hill town has handsomely arcaded squares; at the centre of **Plaza de la Virgen Blanca**, a monument commemorates a nearby battle of 1813 in which Napoleon's army was defeated by the Duke of Wellington.

From here you can explore a tangled web of narrow streets, filled with inexpensive eateries as well as several fine churches and Renaissance palaces. Look out for the **Church of San Miguel**, beside the steps at the top of the large and open

Plaza de la Virgen Blanca, and the 16th-century **Palacio de Escoriaza-Esquível**, with its fine Plateresque-style patio. The **Catedral de Santa María** is currently closed for renovations until further notice (tours are available if you want to see how the restoration is progressing); its unfinished 20th-century replacement, the huge neo-Gothic **Cathedral of María Inmaculada** (open 1100–1400), stands amid parkland in the flat New Town.

From here you can stroll south to Paseo Fray Francisco 8, where a mansion houses the **Museo de Bellas Artes** (Museum of Fine Art; closed Mon, free entry).

ARRIVAL, INFORMATION, ACCOMMODATION

≈ Off C. Eduardo Dato, about four blocks from the cathedral and tourist office. 🛈 **Tourist office**: Plaza General Loma 1, ☎ 94 516 15 98 (www.vitoria-gasteiz.org/turismo). 🛏 Four star but reasonably priced: **Silken Hotel Ciudad de Vitoria**, Portal de Castilla 8, ☎ 94 514 11 00 (www.hotelciudaddevitoria.com), €€.

BURGOS

In medieval times Burgos grew rich on the wool trade, and in the 11th century the city became the capital of Christian Spain as well as the home of Rodrigo Díaz de Vivar, better known as **El Cid**, the romantic mercenary. During the Civil War in the 1930s, it again rose to fame as the Nationalist headquarters. It was here that Franco formed his Falangist government and (18 months later) declared a ceasefire that ended the war. Burgos has now grown into a large and busy modern city, but its heart is the atmospheric Old Town around the ruined castle (itself of little interest apart from the views from it).

The grand entrance to old Burgos is formed by the **Arco de Santa María**, a fortified 14th-century gateway, altered and decorated in 1536 to pacify Charles V, depicting his figure and those of the founder (Diego Porcelos) and El Cid (whose equestrian statue stands near the **Puente de San Pablo**). From here, it's a short walk to the bulk of the main attractions, eating places and hotels.

Foremost is the **cathedral**, consecrated in 1260 but not completed until the 18th century, making it the third largest cathedral in Spain (after Toledo and Seville), and also probably the richest. Amidst the splendour of the 19 chapels and 38 altars, positively dripping in gold leaf, is El Cid's unobtrusive tomb and a grotesquely real-looking crucifix, made in the 13th century with human hair, fingernails and a body of buffalo hide. Evening sees everyone promenade along the **Paseo del Espolón**, graced with fountains and statues and stretching along the river, with cafés and restaurants making the most of the atmosphere.

Two of Spain's most interesting monasteries are on the town's outskirts: the Cistercian convent of **Las Huelgas** (closed Mon), and the Carthusian monastery of **Santa María de Miraflores** (free, open daily), reached through a shady park, and full of art, including the carved tomb of Juan II and Isabel of Portugal and a lifelike wooden statue of St Bruno. Not all buildings are accessible to the public, but you can visit the monastery's 15th-century church.

ARRIVAL, INFORMATION, ACCOMMODATION

≈ About 1 km south-west of the cathedral on the far side of the Arlanzón River. 🚌 5/7/39. 🛈 **Tourist office**: Plaza Alonso Martínez 7, ☎ 94 720 31 25 (www.turismoburgos.org). ⊨ Close to the cathedral: **Hotel Norte y Londres**, Pl. de Alonso Martínez 10, ☎ 94 726 41 25 (www.hotelnorteylondres.com), €–€€.

CONNECTIONS FROM BURGOS

There are trains south-west to Salamanca (2 hrs 35 mins to 4 hrs, ERT 689) to join **Route 10** (p120). Some connections require a change of train at Palencia or Medina del Campo.

LEÓN

Nestling between the Bernesga and Torio rivers and surrounded by the rolling plains of the *meseta*, León was founded by the Romans, and over the years was ruled by Visigoths, Moors and Christians. In 1188, Alfonso IX summoned his first Cortes (parliament) here — one of the earliest democratic governments in Europe — but the court moved away permanently in the 13th century, and León became little more than a trading centre until 1978, when it was made the capital of the province of León. Today it's thriving once again. The major monuments are within easy walking distance of each other in the Old Town.

Of all the city's buildings, the most spectacular from the outside is the 16th-century, Plateresque-style **Monasterio de San Marcos** (now an upmarket parador, or state-run hotel, on Plaza de San Marcos), which was founded by Ferdinand and Isabella, the Catholic monarchs, as a pilgrim hostel and was later rebuilt as the headquarters for the Knights of Santiago. What is left of the old city is still bounded by fragments of the 14th-century city walls, which followed the line of the original Roman (and medieval) fortifications. Of the original 80 bastions 31 still stand. They are best seen around the cathedral and the **Royal Basilica of St Isidore**. Much influenced by the cathedrals of France, the **cathedral** has some of the finest medieval stained glass in Europe, even rivalling Chartres in brilliance.

ARRIVAL, INFORMATION, ACCOMMODATION

≈ **RENFE: El Norte**, C. de Astorga, on the west bank of the river. **FEVE**: Avda. del Padre Isla 48, near the Basilica de San Isidoro. Luggage lockers. 🛈 **Tourist office**: Palacio de los Guzmanes, C. Cid 1, ☎ 98 723 70 82 (www.leon.es).

⊨ The city has a wide range of hotels and guesthouses, ranging downwards from the ultra-luxurious **San Marcos** (see above), Plaza San Marcos 7, ☎ 98 723 73 00 (www.parador.es), €€€. Cheaper options include the **Hotel Quindós**, Gran Via San Marcos 38, ☎ 98 723 62 00 (www.hotelquindos.com), €€. **Hostels**: The **Miguel de**

Unamuno Hostel (HI), San Pelayo 15, ☎ 98 723 30 10 (www.residenciaunamuno.com) is right in the centre of town, not far from the cathedral.

CONNECTIONS FROM LEÓN

From León you can head north by bus (to **Posada de Valdeón** via **Riaño**) into the high mountains of the **Picos de Europa**, a stunning (often snow-capped) cave-riddled karst limestone wilderness that still shelters a few wolves and bears.

Said to have been the first sign of European land seen by sailors returning from the New World, the peaks rise almost vertically from the Bay of Biscay and offer magnificent views and walking, notably through gorges (such as the **Cares Gorge**). The scope for longer hut-to-hut walks is more limited, unless you're extremely fit and experienced in mountain walking; the area isn't huge (roughly 40 km across) but it's very easy to get lost in if you stray from the waymarked paths, and there are numerous sinkholes and other hazards. Unreliable weather is a further drawback: for much of the time the peaks are swathed in mist. Summer is obviously the time to go, though rooms get heavily booked up from late July to the end of August.

ASTORGA

Described by the Roman historian Pliny in the 1st century AD as a "magnificent city", this is now a small, gracefully decaying country town, capital of the bleak moorland region of La Maragatería. Sections of the 6 m Roman walls survive around the Old Town. Towering over it all, the 15th–17th-century **cathedral** displays an intriguing hotchpotch of late Gothic, Renaissance, baroque and Plateresque styles, with motley towers, one grey and the other pink. It's a frequent visit for pilgrims on their way to Santiago; next door, the flamboyant **Palacio Episcopal** (Episcopal Palace), designed by Gaudí in 1889, now houses the **Museo de los Caminos** (Museum of the Pilgrims' Way). Smaller buildings of interest centre on the **Plaza Mayor**.

ARRIVAL, INFORMATION, ACCOMMODATION

➣ Plaza de la Estación, about 1 km east of the town centre. Lockers. 🛈 **Tourist office**: Plaza de Eduardo Castro 5, ☎ 98 761 82 22 (www.ayuntamientodeastorga. com). From the station head straight on up Pedro de Castro, across to Enfermeras, then right through Plaza Obispo Alcolea and up Los Sitios. The tourist office is on your left near the Episcopal Palace.

🛏 Budget options include **Delfín**, Carretera Madrid-Coruña 417, ☎ 98 760 24 14, € (quite far from the centre); **Pensión Garcia**, Bajada del Postigo 3, ☎ 98 761 60 46, €; and **La Ruta Leonesa**, Carretera de León 82, ☎ 98 761 50 37, €.

SANTIAGO DE COMPOSTELA

A magnet for millions of **pilgrims** for the last thousand years, Santiago de Compostela hit the big time when the tomb of St James (*Sant' Iago*, Spain's patron saint) was discovered in 813, supposedly by a shepherd who was guided to the site by a star. Destroyed in 997 by the Moors, the town was rebuilt during the 11th century and began its golden age. In the 12th century, the Pope declared it a Holy City: for Catholics, only Jerusalem and Rome share this honour. The **Old Town** (contained within the medieval walls) is one of the most beautiful urban landscapes in Europe. It's not entirely given over to pilgrims, endowed as it is with a theatre, a concert hall and plenty of bars and clubs offering dancing and late-night drinking.

The Old Town contains a host of fine churches and monasteries as well as notable secular buildings tucked down the narrow side streets. The **cathedral** (started in 1075) is the obvious centre of attention. Its existing 18th-century baroque facade covers the original 12th-century facade, the *Pórtico de la Gloria* by Maestro Mateo, said to be the greatest single surviving work of Romanesque art in the world, with 200 exceptionally imaginative and detailed sculptures. To celebrate their arrival in the Holy City, pilgrims traditionally touch the base of the **Tree of Jesse** on the central column, accordingly known as the 'Pilgrim Pillar', and deeply worn down by millions of fingers over the centuries. On the other side of the pillar, facing the altar, is a figure of the sculptor Mateo, popularly known as the 'Saint of bumps on the head', as people knock heads with him in the belief that his talent is contagious. The interior is dominated by a silver Mexican altar and a dazzling 17th-century baroque altarpiece.

Four plazas surround the cathedral, each architectural gems in themselves. On the largest, the pigeon-populated Praza do Obradoiro, stand the impressive **Hostal de los Reyes Católicos** (the former hospital for pilgrims, now a *parador*) and the classical **Pazo de Raxoi** of 1772 (now the town hall).

Along one side of Praza da Quintana is the austere facade of the **Mosteiro de San Paio de Antealtares**. Entrance to the church and the monastery's **Museum of Sacred Art** (closed Sun) are via the steps at one end of the square. Another landmark is the 16th-century **Monastery of San Martiño Pinario** (whose monks used to give new clothes to pilgrims who looked worse for wear after their journey), though the interior is no longer open to the public.

The Old City is tiny and everything of interest is easily accessible on foot. A tourist train tours the sights of interest, leaving Praza do Obradoiro every 20 mins (July and Aug only; less frequent during the rest of the year).

ARRIVAL, INFORMATION, ACCOMMODATION

≋ Rúa do Hórreo, 1 km south of the Old Town. 🚌 6 goes into the centre, but it's quicker to walk. Luggage lockers, accommodation service and cash machine. ✈ 10 km from the centre, ☎ 98 154 75 00; bus takes 25 mins. 🚌 Bus station: **Estación Central de Autobuses**, Praza Camilo Díaz Baliño, 🚌 5 runs every 16 mins from Praza de Galicia. There is a good local bus system and route plans are posted at most stops. **Taxis**: There are taxi ranks at the bus and train stations; ☎ 98 158 24 50 or 98 159 84

A Coruña

Frequent rail services link Santiago with the large maritime city of A Coruña (taking about 1 hr 5 mins) whose Old Town is on an isthmus between the beach and the harbour. The town's main attractions (after its beaches) are the **Castelo de San Antón**, which now houses an Archaeology Museum (closed Mon), and the **Torre de Hércules**, a 2nd-century UNESCO-listed Roman lighthouse, restored in the 18th century and still in use today, standing at the extreme north of the isthmus. Contemporary attractions include the **Domus**, or Museum of Mankind, designed by Arata Isozaki, with lots of touchy-feely exhibits, and, just around the headland, the **Aquarium**, with a huge subterranean tank and outdoor seal pool.

≷ **San Cristobal** railway station is about a 30-min walk from the centre (or take 🚌 5); 🄱 **Tourist office**: Praza de María Pita 6, ☎ 98 192 30 93 (www.turismocoruna.com). ⊨ Budget accommodation includes **Hostal Mara**, Rúa Galera 49, ☎ 98 122 18 01 (www.hostalmara.com), doubles from €38; **Carbonara**, Rúa Nueva 16, ☎ 98 122 52 51 (www.hostalcarbonara.com), doubles €36; and **Roma**, Rúa Nueva 3, ☎ 98 122 80 75 (www.pensionroma.com), doubles from €42; July to Sept only.

88. 🄱 **Tourist office**: Rúa do Vilar 63, ☎ 98 155 51 29 (www.santiagoturismo.com). From the station turn left up Rúa do Hórreo, to Praza de Galicia.

⊨ During the three weeks leading up to the feast of St James on 25 July, the town is absolutely packed and you should book well in advance. Accommodation ranges from the 5-star **Hostal de los Reyes Católicos**, Praza do Obradoiro 1, ☎ 98 158 22 00 (www.parador.es), €€€, a magnificent 16th-century pilgrim hostel built by Ferdinand and Isabella, to an array of small, relatively inexpensive guesthouses in both the old and new parts of the city. For budget accommodation in the Old Town, try around Rúa do Vilar and Rúa Raiña. **Hospedaje Ramos**, Rúa Raiña 18, 2nd floor, ☎ 98 158 18 59, €, is very central, with small, basic rooms. Other good-value places are **Hospedaje Sofia**, Rúa del Cardenal Payá 16, ☎ 98 158 51 50, €; **Hostal Pazo de Agra**, Rúa da Caldeirería 37, ☎ 98 158 35 17 (www.hostalpazodeagra.com), €; **Hospedaje San Jaime**, Rúa do Vilar 12, 2nd floor, ☎ 98 158 31 34, €; **Pensión Badalada**, located close to the cathedral, Rúa Xelmírez 30, ☎ 98 157 26 18 (www.badalada.com), €; **Hostal Fornos**, Rúa Hórreo 7, ☎ 98 158 51 30 (www.fornossantiago.com), €.

Hostels: The **Meiga Backpackers**, Rúa dos Basquiños 67, ☎ 98 157 08 46 (www.meiga-backpackers.es) is ideally located in the heart of the city. The **youth hostel** (HI), ☎ 98 155 89 42, is out towards the airport. **Campsites**: **Cancelas**, Rúa do 25 de Xullo 35, ☎ 98 158 02 66 (www.campingascancelas.com), is the best option, being only 2 km from the centre (🚌 6 from Praza de Galicia).

✗ There are plenty of budget restaurants around the Old Town, especially on the streets leading south from the cathedral. Slightly further out of town, the Praza Roxa area, near the university, is very cheap.

CONNECTIONS FROM SANTIAGO

Pay a visit to **A Coruña** or carry on to Lisbon by taking **Route 11** in reverse (p124).

Rail Route 13: Exploring Andalucía

CITIES: ★★★ CULTURE: ★★★ HISTORY: ★★ SCENERY: ★★
COUNTRIES COVERED: SPAIN

Andalucía (often styled Andalusia in English) conjures up classic images of Spain — beaches and olives groves, rugged sierras, flamenco music, lively fiestas, hilltop castles and beautiful towns full of picture-perfect white houses. The Moors left evidence of their occupation in the form of spectacular monuments such as the Alhambra in **Granada** and the Mezquita in **Córdoba**, and there's also a very rich Catholic heritage.

Sit on the left-hand side of the train as you leave the port of **Málaga**, for the views soon become stupendous as you snake along the Garganta del Chorro, a huge chasm 180 m deep, only visible from the train. Note that the fast AVE trains that speed north from Málaga do not run through the El Chorro gorge.

The scenery is less special after the little rail junction of Bobadilla, but westwards lies **Ronda**, one of the most spectacular of the aptly named *Pueblos Blancos* ('white towns') of Andalucía, perched improbably on a precipice. There's more of the same at **Arcos de la Frontera**, reachable by bus from Ronda and Cádiz. **Antequera** merits a stop for its remarkable prehistoric dolmens, but top of most travellers' must-see lists is **Granada**. From there, you could take a bus up to **Capileira**, the highest village in the Sierra Nevada range, and look down on Granada. **Cádiz** is an atmospheric old port, but much of the rest of the coast, at least along the built-up Costa del Sol, is a mess.

A visit to the region can tie in with a boat trip to Morocco (see the Sidetrack on p153).

MÁLAGA

The sixth largest city in Spain and a busy working port, Málaga is also the communications centre for the holiday coasts on either side. At first sight it isn't pretty, with high-rise modern apartment blocks built up close together within close range of a dismal-looking canalised river. But the centre is a hundred times more cheerful and resolutely Spanish in character, with a tree-lined main boulevard, dark back alleys, an atmospheric covered market and traditional shops and bars where Spanish (not holidaymakers' English!) is very much the first language. Restaurants are relatively inexpensive and lively, and the city has a real sense of place far removed from the tourist excesses of much of the rest of the Costa del Sol.

Málaga's past is most evident in the area near the port. The long, shady walks of Paseo del Parque are overlooked by the **Alcazaba** (🚌 35 from Paseo del Parque), a fort built by the Moors on Roman foundations; it has the character of the Alhambra in Granada, albeit on a smaller scale, and the views extend over the city to the coast. Its neighbour, the **Gibralfaro** castle (separate entrance), is of Phoenician origin, reconstructed later by the Moors, and offers even better views. At Paseo del Parque there is an open-air theatre, which sometimes stages free productions in summer (ask at the tourist office for details).

Just off the Paseo is the **Cathedral**, set in a secluded square and built between the 16th and 18th centuries. Close by, in Calle San Agustín, is the city's star attraction, the **Museo Picasso** (www.museopicassomalaga.org), where you can admire over 150 of the master's works in a 16th-century palace (closed Mon). Picasso was born in Málaga in 1881 and you can visit his birthplace, now the **Museo Casa Natal**, on the Plaza de la Merced (http://fundacionpicasso.malaga.eu) with works of art and personal effects. **Plaza de la Merced** is the city's liveliest and most attractive square with several good bars and restaurants. Fans of contemporary art might also like to visit the **Centro de Arte Contemporáneo** on Calle Alemania (http://cacmalaga.org). It has a small permanent collection of art and is highly regarded for the quality of its temporary exhibitions. Málaga buzzes after dark, with most action around the Plaza de la Merced and Plaza Uncibay.

ARRIVAL, INFORMATION, ACCOMMODATION

⇄ Explanada de la Estación (luggage lockers and accommodation services; for currency exchange go to the nearby bus station), a 20- to 30-min walk from the centre of town. 🚌 3 goes to Alameda Principal and Paseo del Parque near the centre. Local trains for the coastal resorts leave from here as well (at a different level). Note this coastal rail route is also served by another more centrally located station, **Centro Alameda**. ✈ 8 km from the city, ☎ 91 321 10 00. There is a **tourist office** in the main hall. Trains to Málaga run every 30 mins, taking about 10 mins. **i** **Tourist offices**: (municipal) Casa del Jardinero-Park, Avda. Cervantes 1, ☎ 95 213 47 30, (www.malagaturismo.com); (regional) Pasaje de Chinitas 4, ☎ 95 221 34 45.

🛏 There is a good choice of hotels, including a small *parador* set in the gardens of the Gibralfaro castle (🚌 35 from Paseo del Parque) above the town. Budget accommodation is functional, but lacking in any obvious regional charm. Good areas for cheap lodgings are around the Plaza de la Constitución (north-west of the cathedral) and immediately off either side of the Alameda Principal (although the south side is less salubrious). In high season, central Málaga is lively at night (all night); the only solution is to ask for a room away from the street, or buy earplugs. **Hostal Domus**, C. Juan Valera 20, ☎ 95 229 71 64 (www.hostaldomus.com), €–€€, is friendly and central. **Pensión Juanita**, C. Alarcón Luján 8, ☎ 95 221 35 86 (www.pensionjuanita.es), €. **Hostels**: There are a number of good options in Malaga, including **Picasso's Corner**, C. San Juan de Letrán 9, ☎ 95 221 22 87 (www.picassoscorner.hostel.com), which has double rooms as well as dorms, the **Melting Pot Hostel**, Avenida Pintor Joaquín Sorolla 30, ☎ 95 260 05 71 (www.meltingpothostels.com) and the official youth hostel, **Albergue Juvenil de Málaga** (HI), Plaza Pío XII 6, ☎ 95 230 81 70 (www.reaj.com).

Campsite: the nearest is 12 km away in **Torremolinos**, Carretera Cádiz-Barcelona Km 228, ☎ 95 238 26 02, reached by 🚌 Málaga–Benalmádena or train.

Notes

AVE high–speed trains run Madrid–Córdoba–Sevilla and Madrid to Málaga on dedicated high-speed lines. Special fares apply and reservations are compulsory.

For journeys from Málaga to Ronda, Algeciras and Granada, a change of train is almost always necessary at Bobadilla. If you are travelling on from south-west Andalucía to Morocco, we recommend you use the ferry from Tarifa rather than Algeciras. Boats from Algeciras now serve Tangier Med Port (a new port approx. 45 km east of Tangier). There is a (free) bus connection from Tangier Med to Tangier. But Tarifa is the better choice of departure port from Spain as the FRS shipping services from Tarifa run to the city of Tangier itself. FRS provide a free bus from Algeciras to Tangier.

KEY JOURNEYS

Málaga–Madrid ERT 660

Type	Frequency	Typical journey time
Train	10–12 daily	2h35

Málaga–Granada ERT 673

Type	Frequency	Typical journey time
Train	1 daily	2h50

Málaga–Córdoba ERT 660

Type	Frequency	Typical journey time
Train	13–17 daily	1h05

Málaga–Seville ERT 660

Type	Frequency	Typical journey time
Train	4–6 daily	1h55

Málaga–Algeciras ERT 673

Type	Frequency	Typical journey time
Train	2 daily	4h10

ROUTE DETAILS

Málaga–Ronda ERT 673

Type	Frequency	Typical journey time
Train	2–3 daily	1h55

Ronda–Granada ERT 673

Type	Frequency	Typical journey time
Train	3 daily	2h35

Granada–Córdoba ERT 660

Type	Frequency	Typical journey time
Train	2 daily	2h20

Córdoba–Seville ERT 660

Type	Frequency	Typical journey time
AVE	20–29 daily	45 mins

Seville–Cádiz ERT 671

Type	Frequency	Typical journey time
Train	10–14 daily	1h55

✖ There are several good **restaurants** around the cathedral, especially along C. Cañón. Seafood and *gazpacho* are good bets. **Paseo Marítimo** and the seafront in Pedregalejo are the best areas for seafood restaurants. Málaga gives its name to an inexpensive sweet fortified red wine. Convent *dulces* are cakes made by nuns throughout Andalucía: in the morning nuns of **Santa Clara** at C. Cister 11 (just east of the cathedral) sell these.

CONNECTIONS FROM MÁLAGA

For a trip to the Costa del Sol see the box below. Another popular excursion is by boat (75 mins) to **Benalmádena Costa** (alternatively you could catch the C1 train to Benalmádena). This smart marina resort has bars, restaurants and family attractions. Benalmádena 'Pueblo', the original village 5 km inland, is a charming if somewhat stage-managed traditional whitewashed village.

Málaga is also at the centre of a bus network reaching out to many smaller resorts. Eastwards, it is possible to reach **Nerja** and other assorted seaside towns all the way to Almería. Nerja is a relatively peaceful resort, built around an Old Town that still feels distinctly Spanish, about 50 km from Málaga. Buses run approximately every hour, the journey taking 1 hr 30 mins. It is noted for its panoramic views of the coast, especially from the promenade known as the **Balcón de Europa**.

Just east of the town is the **Cuevas de Nerja**, a series of large caverns full of breathtaking rock formations (**🅱 tourist office**: C. Carmen 1, ☎ 95 252 15 31; www. nerja.org).

RONDA

Ronda is a small town in the rugged Serranía de Ronda, split in two by a dizzying gorge, with white houses clinging to the rim, and spanned in quite spectacular fashion by an 18th-century bridge known as the **Puente Nuevo**. The view from the bridge is hair-raising, even more so when you learn that it was from here in 1936, during the Civil War, that 512 prisoners of the Republicans were hurled to

THE COSTA DEL SOL

A frequent train service runs west from Málaga (Centro–Alameda and RENFE stations) along the **Costa del Sol**, connecting it to the airport and the busy resorts of Torremolinos, Benalmádena and Fuengirola. **Torremolinos** is a tacky, exuberant, concrete high-rise resort, with a plethora of discos, fish and chip shops and bars, much of it run by a huge expat population. The western part of the resort is more attractive, frequented by Spanish holidaymakers. There are abundant beach facilities along the expansive stretch of grey sands.

Further west, **Fuengirola** is another sun and sand haunt, slightly calmer than Torremolinos, but equally ugly. **Marbella**, with its many beaches, charming Old Town and glitzy Puerto Banús marina, is further but a more attractive option in every way. You can go by train from Málaga airport to Fuengirola, then take a bus to Marbella.

their deaths, an incident adapted by Ernest Hemingway in *For Whom the Bell Tolls*. It was in Ronda that Pedro Romero invented the modern style of bullfighting — on foot rather than from horseback — and his father is said to have invented the red rag that provokes the bull! Near the bullring is the **Alameda**, a public garden beside the gorge, enjoying breathtaking views of the surrounding area, with olive groves stretching into the hilly distance.

On the other side of the bridge is the old Moorish quarter, with the attractive **Casa del Rey Moro** (House of the Moorish King), an early 18th-century mansion. You can visit the gardens, designed in 1912, and the mines, which provided Ronda with water as early as the 14th century.

ARRIVAL, INFORMATION, ACCOMMODATION

≋ A 10- to 15-min walk to the centre. Luggage lockers and accommodation service.
🛈 Tourist office: (municipal) Plaza de Blas Infante, ☎ 95 218 71 19 (www.turismoderonda.es); (regional) Plaza de España 1, ☎ 95 287 12 72.

🛏 You'll pass plenty of inexpensive places as you walk in from the station. Options include **Hotel IGH San Francisco**, C. María Cabrera 18–20, ☎ 95 287 32 99 (www.ighsanfrancisco.com), €€; **Hostal Virgen del Rocio**, C. Nueva 18, ☎ 95 287 74 25 (www.hostalvirgendelrocio.com), €; and the **Hotel Ronda**, Calle Ruedo de Doña Elvira 12, ☎ 95 287 22 32, €€.

GRANADA

Founded, according to legend, by a daughter of either Noah or Hercules, what is not in doubt is that in 1492 Granada was the last of the great Moorish cities to succumb to Ferdinand and Isabella's ferocious Christian Reconquest. The main reason for visiting is to see its fabulous fortress-palace, the **Alhambra**, resplendent on its lush hilltop. If you don't fancy the pleasant but often hot walk uphill from town catch a bus from Plaza Nueva (every 12 mins).

Most of the exterior of the Alhambra dates from rebuilding in the 13th–14th centuries and is reasonably simple, giving no hint of the decoration inside. There are three principal sets of buildings: the **Alcazaba** (Fortress), the **Alcázar** (Palace), and the **Generalife** (Summer Palace and Gardens), with a combined entrance fee (www.alhambradegranada.org).

The number of visitors to some areas of the Alhambra is now being limited to 8,000 per day with timed tickets, so it is advisable to arrive in the morning (or reserve your tickets in advance at any branch of La Caixa bank, through any of their yellow Servicaixa machines, or through www.alhambra-tickets.es) if you don't want to face a very long wait to get in. The Generalife shelters a stunning garden with patios and running water; the Moors used their irrigational expertise to divert the River Darro to supply the pools and fountains.

The main Christian edifice in the complex is the 16th-century **Palace of Charles V**, which houses the **Museum of Fine Arts** and the **National Museum**

of Hispano-Islamic Art. Saturday evenings see a parade of newly-married couples being photographed beside the ramparts.

In the city below the Alhambra, the **Capilla Real** (Royal Chapel) deserves a visit for the tombs of the Catholic monarchs, Ferdinand and Isabella, and their daughter and her husband; displayed in the Sacristy are some notable paintings from the private collection of Queen Isabella. Next door, the Cathedral was completed in the early 18th century, and boasts a gloomily impressive classical grandeur. The **Albaicín** quarter, on the hill opposite the Alhambra, out from the hectic whirl of the city centre, retains some Moorish atmosphere and is a rewarding and tranquil place for a stroll in its maze of stepped alleys.

If you're willing to splash out for the experience, **Al Andalus Baths**, C. Santa Ana 16, ☎ 95 822 99 78 (www.hammamspain.com), provide the chance to bathe in therapeutic waters for 2 hrs in Alhambra-like surroundings; massages are on offer for a very reasonable price.

ARRIVAL, INFORMATION, ACCOMMODATION

⇌ Avda. de los Andaluces. Lockers. 🚌 30 takes you from the Plaza Nueva to the Alhambra. From the station it's a 20-min walk to the centre or take 🚌 4/6/11. The **tourist office** is by the cathedral. 🚌 3/4/6/9 go to the Gran Vía and the centre from the main road up the hill from the station; they run every 20 mins. ✈ 17 km from Granada on Ctra. de Málaga, ☎ 95 824 52 00. Only nine buses a day to the airport (bus info at ☎ 95 849 01 64).

🖪 **Tourist offices**: (municipal) C. Virgen Blanca 9, ☎ 90 240 50 45 (www.granadatur.com); (regional) Plaza Mariana Pineda 10, ☎ 95 824 71 28 (www.turismodegranada.org). The 3-day **Bono Turístico Granada Card** costs €25.00, including numerous sights (among them the Alhambra) and five bus rides.

🛏 Budget accommodation is plentiful, especially off Plaza Nueva, Plaza de la Trinidad, Gran Vía de Colón and on the streets north of Plaza Mariana Pineda. Cuesta de Gomérez leads directly up to the Alhambra and is lined with *hostals*. The **Britz**, Cuesta de Gomérez 1, ☎ 95 822 36 52, €–€€, has several rooms overlooking the Plaza Nueva. Next to the Cathedral and the Capilla Real is the **Hotel Carlos V**, Plaza de los Campos 4, ☎ 95 822 15 87 (www.hotelcarlosvgranada.com), €€. At the top end of the scale, the *parador* is located in the former convent **Parador de San Francisco**, Real de la Alhambra, ☎ 95 822 14 40 (www.parador.es), €€€, in the Alhambra complex.

Hostels: Popular backpacker hostels include **Oasis**, Placeta Correo Viejo 3, ☎ 95 821 58 48 (www.hostelsoasis.com), the **Funky Backpackers Hostel**, Calle del Conde de las Infantas 15–17, ☎ 95 880 00 58 (www.funkybackpackers.hostel.com), and the **Makuto Guesthouse**, Calle Tiña 18, ☎ 95 880 58 76 (www.makutoguesthouse.com). **Campsite: Sierra Nevada**, Avda. de Madrid 107, ☎ 95 815 00 62 (www.campingsierranevada.com), is very central and not too far from the bus station. They also have a two-star motel with doubles from €59.50; 🚌 3 from Acera de Darro.

✗ Plaza Nueva and the streets around it are where the locals eat: not always cheap, but fair value. A glass of Arabian tea in one of the *teterías* (tea shops) on Calderería Nueva will invoke the Moorish spirit.

GUADIX

Guadix (east of Granada) is an old walled town with a sandstone cathedral, and remarkable for its cave district, the **Barrio Santiago**. Around 10,000 cave dwellings, most with mod cons, have been cut into the pyramids of red rock. Some inhabitants will show you their homes, often for an exorbitant fee; you can find some deserted caves, and there's a museum near San Miguel Church. Frequent buses run from Granada to the town centre and there's a less frequent train service (the station is some way out). The journey by train takes about 1 hr (ERT 673), while the bus takes a little longer.

CONNECTIONS FROM GRANADA

The rail connections from Granada to Córdoba are not that good (though there is a direct bus taking 4 hrs, three services a day) and you could instead opt to take the train to **Linares-Baeza**, for the connecting bus to **Baeza** (ERT 661), which has a sleepy charm in its Renaissance squares and palaces; from there you can take a bus on to **Úbeda**, a stunning Renaissance town, linked by bus to Córdoba and Seville. You can also head on by train from Linares-Baeza through spectacular desert to **Almería**, a landscape that's been used as a location for 'Spaghetti Westerns'.

Buses from Granada zigzag up onto the **Sierra Nevada**, the great mountain mass that looms over the city. A good place to stay here is **Capileira**, the highest village in the range. There are several places to stay among its whitewashed houses, and it boasts spectacular views.

CÓRDOBA

The main attraction of this former capital of the Moorish caliphate is undoubtedly the **Mezquita**, the grandest and most beautiful mosque ever built in Spain. Córdoba has a really strong atmosphere of the past, with one of the largest medieval townscapes in Europe, and certainly the biggest in Spain, offering a harmonious blend of Christian, Jewish and Moorish architecture. There's a distinctly Moorish character, with a labyrinth of whitewashed alleys and gorgeous patios, as well as a fascinating Jewish quarter.

The huge Mezquita (it's free to attend Mass in the cathedral section of the building) was founded in the 8th century by Caliph Abd al Rahman I and was enlarged over the next 200 years. At the foot of the bell tower, the delicately carved **Puerta del Perdón** leads through the massive outer walls to the **Patio de los Naranjos** (Courtyard of the Orange Trees), a courtyard with fountains for ritual cleansing. Inside the mosque, the fantastic forest of 850 pillars, joined by two-tiered Moorish arches in stripes of red brick and white stone, extends over a vast area. The pillars are not identical: materials include alabaster, marble, jasper, onyx, granite and wood; some are smooth, others have ribs or spirals; most are Roman in origin and were shipped in from places as far apart as France and North Africa, then cut to size. The capitals are equally varied. After the Moors departed, the

Christians added the cathedral within the complex, incongruous but stunning, and blocking out the light that was an integral part of the design. The Third Mihrab once housed the original copy of the Koran. Unlike the other two, it survived Christian vandalism and its walls are covered in mosaics of varied colours and friezes of texts from the Koran. Its unusual off-centre position in the *qibla* (the south-facing holy wall) is the result of the final enlargement of the mosque in the 10th century, which, because of the proximity of the river in the south and the palace in the west, had to be made on the east side.

The **Puente Romano** is a bridge of mainly Moorish construction, but the arches have Roman foundations. Downstream are the remains of an Arab waterwheel, which originally transported water to the grounds of the Alcázar. The **Torre de la Calahorra** (on the other side of the river) is a high-tech museum with a model of the Mezquita as it was before the Christians got to work on it.

The **Alcázar de los Reyes Católicos**, on the north bank, retains the original Moorish terraced gardens and pools. In August, these stay open until midnight, perfect for an evening stroll. Less gloriously, this was the headquarters of the Spanish Inquisition for over three centuries.

The **Judería** is the old Jewish quarter, a maze of lanes surrounding a tiny synagogue in C. Judíos. Open doorways provide tantalising glimpses of chequered courtyards filled with flowers; to get a better look visit the town in May, when the **Festival de los Patios** (a 'best-kept patio' competition) takes place.

ARRIVAL, INFORMATION, ACCOMMODATION

⇶ Glorieta de las Tres Culturas. Tourist office and taxis at the station. 1 km north of the main area of interest; 20–30 mins on foot, or take 🚌 3 (every 15 mins). Luggage lockers and cash machine. 🔢 **Tourist offices**: (provincial) C. Torrijos 10 (Palacio de Congresos y Exposiciones), ☎ 95 735 51 79 (www.andalucia.org); (municipal) C. Rey

WALKING TOUR OF CÓRDOBA

This walk encompasses the main attractions of Córdoba in a couple of hours. Begin at the Plaza del Potro, see the fountain, the **Museo de Bellas Artes** and the inn, **La Posada del Potro**, where Cervantes is thought to have stayed. Walk down Paseo de la Ribera, along the banks of the Río Guadalquivir. Turn right down Cano Quebrado to take in Córdoba's most famous sight, the **Mezquita**. Carry on along to the riverside Ronda de Isasa; on reaching an Arab waterwheel on your left, with the **Alcázar** off to your right, go down Santa Teresa de Jornet. Go back onto Ronda de Isasa/ Avenida del Alcázar and continue alongside the river. Turn left onto Puente San Rafael, cross the bridge, and turn left to head back in the direction you just came, but on the opposite side of the river. Call at the **Museo Torre de la Calahorra** and afterwards cross Puente Romano and continue straight ahead into the little shops and inexpensive cafés of the **Judería**.

Heredia 22, ☎ 90 220 17 74 (www.turismodecordoba.org). There are three further information points: opposite the Alcázar, in the train station, and at Plaza de las Tendillas. The provincial information office is right next to the Mezquita.

🛏 Cheap places are near the station, in and around the Judería (Jewish Quarter) and off Plaza de las Tendillas. Plaza de la Corredera, although cheap, is a less savoury area. Calle Rey Heredia has lots of cheap accommodation (the street changes name five times), including the **Hostal Triunfo**, C. Corregidor Luis de la Cerda 79, ☎ 95 749 84 84 (www.hostaltriunfo.com), €€, which is a clean and light 2-star *hostal* near the Mezquita. **Hostal Luis de Góngora**, C. Horno de la Trinidad 7, ☎ 95 729 53 99, €€, is lacking in traditional charm, but is clean, quiet and comfortable. Other budget options include: **Pensión Los Arcos**, C. Romero Barros 14, ☎ 95 748 56 43 (www.pensionlosarcos.com), €€; **Hostal Lineros 38**, C. Lineros 38, ☎ 95 748 25 17 (www.hostallineros38.com), €€. **Hostels**: A well-regarded backpacker hostel is **The Terrace,** Calle Lucano 12, ☎ 95 749 29 66. The youth hostel is the **Albergue de Córdoba** (HI), Pl. de Judá Leví, ☎ 95 735 50 40 (www.reaj.com), located in the Jewish Quarter, near the Mezquita. ✖ There are a number of restaurants around the Judería. Budget eateries can be found along C. Doctor Fleming or in the Judería.

SEVILLE (SEVILLA)

Of all the Andalucian cities, Seville has the most to see. The capital of Andalucía, it's a romantic, theatrical place, with a captivating park, a gigantic cathedral and two very important fiestas, the **April Feria** and the processions of **Holy Week**. Columbus sailed from Seville to discover the New World, and *Don Giovanni, Carmen, The Barber of Seville* and *The Marriage of Figaro* were all set here. The downside is the high level of petty crime: be on the alert for bag-snatchers and pickpockets.

The prime sights are in a very small area, but the secondary ones are quite widespread. All but the keenest walkers will probably want to hop on a bus or two along the way. Most places of interest are in the Barrio de Santa Cruz. A pleasant place for a stroll, it lives up to the idealised image of Spain; white and yellow houses with flower-bedecked balconies and romantic patios. The focal point is the **Giralda**, a minaret that has towered over the Old City since the 12th century and which now serves as belfry to the cathedral. Built by the Almohad rulers 50 years before Ferdinand and Isabella's Christian Reconquest, it consists of a series of gentle ramps designed for horsemen to ride up; it's in excellent condition and worth climbing for the views.

The **cathedral** is the largest Gothic structure in the world, simply groaning with gold leaf. The **Capilla Mayor** has a vast gilded retable, which took 82 years to complete. The **Sacristía Mayor** houses the treasury and **Sacristía de los Cálices** contains Murillos and a Goya. A huge memorial honours Christopher Columbus (who may or may not be buried here!) while outside is the pretty **Patio de los Naranjos** (orange-tree courtyard).

The **Alcázar** (www.patronato-alcazarsevilla.es) was inspired by the Alhambra of Granada (see p145), but has been marred by later additions. Within is the **Salón de Embajadores**, where Columbus was received by Ferdinand and Isabella on his return from the Americas, and there are also shady, interconnected gardens separated by arched Moorish walls. The neighbouring **Casa Lonja** contains a collection of documents relating to the discovery of the Americas.

There's more 16th-century history captured in the relatively unvisited but very atmospheric **Casa de Pilatos** on Pl. di Pilatos (a 5- to 10-minute walk from the cathedral). It is a wonderful confection of Mudéjar, Gothic and Plateresque styles and takes its name from the unlikely story that it is a replica of Pontius Pilate's house in Jerusalem. There are gorgeous courtyards and rooms, plus fine paintings by Spanish masters including Goya.

The **Hospital de la Caridad**, C. Temprado, was commissioned by a reformed rake, reputed to have been the real-life inspiration for Don Juan. The church contains several works by Valdés Leal, depicting death in ghoulishly disturbing ways; there are also paintings by Murillo.

Nowadays, the 18th-century **Fábrica de Tabacos** (on C. de San Fernando south of the Alcázar) houses parts of the university, but it was once a tobacco factory, employing over 10,000 women (supposedly including Bizet's gypsy beauty, Carmen). South-east of the factory is **María Luisa Park**, a delightful mixture of wilderness areas and formal gardens laid out for a trade fair in 1929 and shaded by trees from Latin America. It contains the **Plaza de España**, which was the central pavilion (now municipal offices, but on an incredible scale and with some eye-catching ceramics), and Plaza de América, a peaceful place that is home to the **Archaeological Museum**, containing a famously rich Roman section (closed Mon, free for EU citizens). The Latin American countries that exhibited at the fair each built a pavilion in their own national style, most of which survive.

The **Museo de Bellas Artes** (closed Mon, free for EU nationals), Pl. del Museo (between Santa Cruz and Cartuja), has a collection of 13th–20th-century Spanish paintings, second only to that in the Prado in Madrid. The decorative **Maestranza** (bullring), near the river, dates from the 18th century. To find out when fights are held call ☎ 95 421 03 15, but there's also a worthwhile museum here so you can get a peek of the structure inside.

ARRIVAL, INFORMATION, ACCOMMODATION

🚄 **Estación Santa Justa**, Avda. Kansas City; 15-min walk from the centre. 🚌 27 goes from the station to Plaza de la Encarnación; 🚌 70 goes to Plaza de España. Tourist office and taxis. Luggage lockers; the locker area is open 0600–2400. Currency exchange, cash machines and tourist information booth. 🚌 There are two bus stations: **Prado de San Sebastián**, Plaza Prado de San Sebastián, ☎ 95 441 71 11, is mainly for buses to Andalucía; **Plaza de Armas**, Avda. Cristo de la Expiración, ☎ 95 490 80 40, is for buses elsewhere. **City buses**: 🚌 C1 and C2 are circular routes around the

Seville's Nightlife

Seville is the home of flamenco and it's easy to find, but you should be selective because it is often staged specially for tourists. If you ask around, you should be able to find more genuine (and cheaper) performances. There are various clubs with flamenco evenings, but they can be quite expensive, especially during festival time in the spring. An excellent one to try is **El Gallo** in Barrio de Santa Cruz.

Seville is packed with lively bars, clubs and discos, notably in the **Los Remedios** district in the south of the city and on C. Betis next to the river, but little seems to happen until close to midnight. If you're looking for activity and atmosphere a little earlier in the evening, try the other side of the river, where there is a range of tapas bars, some of which have live music.

town. Many buses pass through Plaza de la Encarnación, Plaza Nueva and Avda. de la Constitución. If you're making more than four trips, buy a **Tarjeta Turística** day-ticket for €5. **Taxis**: There's a rank on Plaza Nueva. To order a taxi, ☎ 66 384 22 59 or 95 458 00 00. ✈ **San Pablo Airport**, 12 km east of town, ☎ 95 444 90 00; tourist information desk, ☎ 95 478 20 35. Trains to Seville take 15 mins; taxis cost about €18. Express buses take 30 mins to the centre. 🚉 **Tourist offices**: (regional) Avda. de la Constitución 21B, ☎ 95 478 75 78 (www.andalucia.org); (municipal): Plaza de San Francisco 19, Edificio Laredo, ☎ 95 459 29 15 (www.turismosevilla.org or www.visitasevilla.es). **Centro de Información de Sevilla**, Plaza del Triunfo 1, ☎ 95 421 00 05. There are also tourist information booths in strategic locations, including the station.

🛏 During Holy Week and the April Fair accommodation is very difficult to obtain, and must be prebooked. On the whole, staying in Seville tends to be expensive. For the least pricey lodgings, try the Barrio de Santa Cruz: C. Archeros, the streets around Plaza Nueva (C. Marqués de Paradas or C. Gravina), or down towards the river. Also in Santa Cruz is **Hostal Sierpes**, C. Corral del Rey 22, ☎ 95 422 49 48 (www.hsierpes.com), €€. **La Casa de la Luna**, C. Mariana Pineda 9, ☎ 95 421 83 89 (www.lacasadelaluna.es), €, is small and plain but located right next to the Alcázar. **Hostal Aguilas**, C. Aguilas 15, ☎ 95 421 31 77, €, has clean rooms. **Pensión Alcázar**, C. Dean Miranda 12, ☎ 95 422 84 57 (www.pensionalcazar.com), €€, all rooms en suite, is right next to the Alcázar wall. **Hotel Simón**, García de Vinuesa 19, ☎ 95 422 66 60 (www.hotelsimonsevilla.com), €€, is in a former 18th-century mansion. **Hostels:** Try first to get a bed at **Oasis Backpackers**, Plaza Encarnación 29 1–2, ☎ 95 429 37 77 (www.hostelsoasis.com). Other good options include the **Samay Sevilla**, Avda. Mendez Pelayo 13, ☎ 95 510 01 60 (www.samayhostels.com) and the **Albergue Juvenil de Sevilla** (HI), C. Isaac Peral 2, ☎ 95 505 65 00 (www.reaj.com), located 2 km from the station.

✗ Seville is probably the best place to sample such typical Andalucían dishes as *gazpacho* (chilled tomato and pepper soup) and *pescaíto frito* (deep-fried fish). Eating out can be expensive, but there are a few places with excellent menus for reasonable prices. The liveliest bars and restaurants, frequented by students, are in Barrio de Santa Cruz. Perennially popular is the Plaza Alfalfa, with a wide choice of bustling bars and nightspots. For a meal with a view, try restaurants on the other side of the river

JEREZ DE LA FRONTERA

Just before you reach Cádiz on the train from Seville you pass through the station for Jerez. This town has given its name to sherry and the bodegas are the town's main attraction; it's also home to Spanish brandy. Here you will find such familiar names as Harvey, González Byass and Domecq. Most bodegas offer tours (varying prices, reservations necessary for some; many close in Aug) that finish with a tasting. Sherry also appears in the local cuisine; try kidneys in sherry sauce.

by the Puente de San Telmo. Or buy your own food at the **Mercado del Arenal**, C. Arenal and C. Pastor, the town's largest market.

CONNECTIONS FROM SEVILLE

Itálica (closed Mon, free to EU nationals) is a substantial excavated Roman town at **Santiponce**, about 9 km from Seville, with remains of streets, baths and mosaics. The 25,000-seater amphitheatre is particularly interesting. Itálica was first founded by Publius Cornelius Scipio, and it was thought to be the home of Trajan and Hadrian in the 2nd century AD. Buses leave Pl. de Armas every 30 mins and cost €1.

CÁDIZ

Like Venice, that other once-great naval city, Cádiz is approached by a causeway and all but surrounded by water. Its tight grid of streets, squares and crumbly ochre buildings exudes an atmosphere of gentle decay, but it's all the better for that, and really comes into its own during the huge **carnival** in February (one of the best in Spain) and in the evening, when the promenaders come out and the bars open. Colourful tiling is a feature of the pavements, parks and even the **Catedral Nueva** (New Cathedral), which was rebuilt, like much of the rest, in the city's 18th-century heyday. However its origins go back to 1100 BC when it was founded by the Phoenicians; the port was of vital importance at the time of the conquest of the Americas (which was why Sir Francis Drake attacked it). You can get a panoramic view of it all from **Torre Tavira**, both from the top of the tower and in the camera obscura below, via a mirror and lens on the roof.

ARRIVAL, INFORMATION, ACCOMMODATION

➤ The **main station** is at Plaza de Sevilla. 🚩 **Tourist office:** (municipal) Paseo de Canalejas, ☎ 95 624 10 01 (www.sevilla.org); (regional) Avenida Ramón de Carranza, ☎ 95 620 31 91 (www.andalucia.org). ⊨ **España**, Marqués de Cádiz 9, ☎ 95 628 55 00 (open Mar–Oct), €–€€; **Hostal Canalejas**, C. Cristóbal Colón 5, ☎ 95 626 41 13 (www.hostalcanalejas.com), €€, is very central; or **Hostal San Francisco**, C. San Francisco 12, ☎ 95 622 18 42 (www.amaparhostales.com), €€, which is a step away from all the main sights. A friendly hostel is the **Cadiz Inn Backpackers**, Calle Botica 2, ☎ 95 626 23 09 (www.hotelincadiz.com).

Route 13 explores a part of Europe that has been deeply influenced by settlers from North Africa. In its heyday (in the 8th and 9th centuries AD), the network of Muslim caliphates and emirates collectively known as **al-Andalus** covered a much larger area than modern Andalucía, extending beyond the Iberian peninsula and the Pyrenees to **Septimania**, the region of south-west France around Narbonne. This veil of Moorish settlement gave Arab mariners control of much of the western Mediterranean and the **Strait of Gibraltar**.

Historically the links between Andalucía and North Africa have been forged by seafarers, but that may change in the years ahead as Morocco and Spain debate the possibility of a rail tunnel linking Europe to Africa. Don't hold your breath. If it ever comes to pass, the first trains from **Madrid to Marrakech** won't be running before 2030. So meanwhile it's the boat, and you are spoilt for choice. From Málaga (on Route 13), there are excellent links to Melilla (ERT 2595), one of two autonomous Spanish cities on the coast of North Africa which, along with some other tiny fragments of Spanish territory on the Moroccan coast and some inshore islands, are all that is left of **África Española**.

Melilla wins no prizes for beauty, but it is a curious political oddity (as indeed is Gibraltar on the European side of the water). From Melilla you can walk across the Moroccan border to the railway station at **Beni Nzar**. You'll find train times at the website of Moroccan rail operator ONCF. Just go to www.oncf.ma (English-language interface available).

More common jumping-off points for Africa, each with shorter crossings than from Málaga, are **Algeciras** and **Tarifa**. If you are bound for **Tangier**, Tarifa is the best bet, for services from there go to Tangier city rather than the out-of-town port. See the note on p143. From Algeciras, there are frequent crossings (1 hr) to **Ceuta** (the second Spanish city in North Africa). As in Melilla, you can walk into Morocco, along the way seeing the fierce fences that surround this little outpost of Europe in Africa to deter migrants who judge that Ceuta or Melilla might be an easy route into the European Union.

Of course there is one port on Route 13 that, in terms of its historic status as a great mercantile centre, quite eclipses anywhere we have yet mentioned in this Sidetracks feature. And that is **Cádiz**. During more than 500 years under Moorish rule, Cádiz was very bound into Mediterranean and North African trade, but since the Spanish settlement of the Americas, Cádiz has set its sights on the Atlantic. That is reflected in modern shipping schedules, for Cádiz has no scheduled service to the African mainland. But Cádiz has something special for those with a dose of sea fever. It has **ferry links to the Canary Islands**. Modern cruise ferries take 30 hrs to Lanzarote, 38 hrs to Las Palmas de Gran Canaria, 49 hrs to Santa Cruz de Tenerife, and 63 hours to Santa Cruz de La Palma (ERT 2512). If all those hours afloat have not quashed your appetite for ocean waves, connect at Las Palmas de Gran Canaria to the weekly ferry to **El-Aaiún**, principal city of the contested desert territory of **Western Sahara**. It is a place so far from Europe and any rail routes that any further description lies beyond the province of this book.

Rail Route 14: Belgium and Luxembourg

CITIES: ★★★ CULTURE: ★★ HISTORY: ★★ SCENERY: ★
COUNTRIES COVERED: BELGIUM, NETHERLANDS, LUXEMBOURG

For an earlier generation of British rail travellers, **Ostend** was often their first glimpse of the continent, arriving by boat from Kent and immediately joining trains at Ostend that carried through carriages to cities like Moscow or Milan and popular holiday destinations such as the Austrian Tyrol and the Adriatic coast of what was then Yugoslavia. Belgium was somewhere that these colourful trains of yesteryear trundled through en route to more exotic destinations.

But take another look at Belgium, and its tiny neighbour Luxembourg. For years, we ignored them and yet latterly they have asserted themselves as worthwhile destinations in their own right. This route is a tremendous introduction to two countries that we now judge to be among the most interesting in Europe. So give Belgium a chance, and you'll really find that the country offers its own surreal exotica. Don't so much as even think of just dashing through.

Not a mountain in sight for the first half of Route 14, but the hilly Ardennes that straddle the Belgium-Luxembourg border make up for that. There are fine townscapes aplenty though, notably the handsome cities of **Bruges**, **Ghent** and **Antwerp**, each boasting impressive legacies of medieval prosperity, and each deserving at least a day or two. Luxembourg itself arguably has the most striking natural setting of any European capital. And, along the way on this route, we make a little foray over the Dutch border to visit cosmopolitan **Maastricht**, the arty capital of the province of Limburg. If time is tight there are regular fast trains from Ostend, Bruges and Ghent to both Brussels and Liège (all in ERT 400) allowing you to make quick progress to the latter part of **Route 14**.

Ostend (Oostende)

The only regular cross-Channel ferry service to Ostend nowadays is from Ramsgate and quite bizarrely refuses to carry travellers without cars, so foot passengers and cyclists are barred from this service. Even if Ostend is not the

Arriving in Belgium

It is worth bearing in mind that travellers arriving in Belgium on Eurostar (from the UK or France) or on Thalys trains (from France, the Netherlands and Germany) can use certain tickets for onward travel to any station in Belgium (using regular Belgian domestic rail services). On **Eurostar and Thalys** you can book tickets either just to Brussels or to Brussels ABS/TGB (any Belgian station/toutes gares Belges). The latter option comes with just a modest supplement over the regular Brussels fare and, if your onward journey extends for any distance at all, can be an extremely good deal. On Thalys trains this option is also valid via Liège and Antwerp, provided of course that you select the destination Liege ABS/TGB or Antwerp ABS/TGB.

ROUTE DETAILS

Ostend–Bruges	ERT 400, 410	
Type	Frequency	Typical journey time
Train	2 per hr	15 mins

Bruges–Ghent	ERT 400, 410	
Type	Frequency	Typical journey time
Train	3 per hr	25 mins

Ghent–Antwerp	ERT 410	
Type	Frequency	Typical journey time
Train	2 per hr	50 mins

Antwerp–Brussels	ERT 420, 421	
Type	Frequency	Typical journey time
Train	5 per hr	50 mins

Brussels–Liège	ERT 400, 430	
Type	Frequency	Typical journey time
Train	2–3 per hr	1h05

Liège–Maastricht	ERT 436	
Type	Frequency	Typical journey time
Train	Every hr	30 mins

Liège–Luxembourg	ERT 444	
Type	Frequency	Typical journey time
Train	Every 2 hrs	2h30

Note

To travel directly from Ostend to Luxembourg, just one change of train is necessary. That can be at either Brussels Midi or at Liège.

KEY JOURNEYS

Ostend–Brussels	ERT 400	
Type	Frequency	Typical journey time
Train	Every hr	1h15

Brussels–Paris	ERT 18	
Type	Frequency	Typical journey time
Train	1–2 per hr	1h22

Brussels–Amsterdam	ERT 18	
Type	Frequency	Typical journey time
Train	1–2 per hr	fast train 1h53 slow train 2h45

Brussels–Cologne	ERT 20	
Type	Frequency	Typical journey time
Train	Every 2 hrs	1h50

transport hub it once was for ferry and rail travellers, yet it remains our favourite spot on the coast of Belgium, a place to linger at the fish market on Visserskaai, enjoy first-rate seafood and catch the flavour of seaside Belgium. Stroll the Albert I Promenade down past the casino to the covered arcades that lead to the Thermae Palace hotel and you'll realise that this town is a gem.

The **Noordzeeaquarium** (on the front) displays the flora and fauna of the North Sea. The studio where the Expressionist painter James Ensor worked has become a museum devoted to him (**James Ensorhuis**, Vlaanderenstraat 27, closed Tues), and many of his possessions are among the exhibits in **Museum voor Schone Kunsten** (Fine Arts Museum), Leopold de Waelplaats (closed Mon). **Museum voor Moderne Kunst aan zee Oostende** (Modern Art Museum by the Sea Ostend), Romestraat 11, contains modern paintings and sculptures (closed Mon).

ARRIVAL, INFORMATION, ACCOMMODATION

≥ Adjacent to the port, a 20-min walk from the tourist office (or 🚌 5). Note: there are currently no foot passenger ferry services to Ostend. 🛈 **Tourist office**: Monacoplein 2, ☎ 059 70 11 99 (www.visitoostende.be). Sells the A–Z brochure and town map. 🛏 The **Hotel Serge**, Brusselstraat 15, ☎ 059 80 34 34, is good value and central. The youth hostel **De Ploate** (HI), Langestraat 82, ☎ 059 80 52 97 (www.vjh.be), is 1 km from train and bus stations.

FLANDERS LANDSCAPES

Heading inland from Ostend towards Bruges and beyond you will cross the Flanders landscapes that have so powerfully influenced artists over the centuries. On a dull day the region might seem dismal in the extreme, but with a little sunshine it comes alive to reveal a delicate mix of willow-lined canals, water meadows, brick barns and windmills. Throw in a few storm clouds on the horizon and Flanders becomes beguilingly beautiful.

BRUGES (BRUGGE)

A powerful trading city 500 years ago, Bruges became an economic backwater and the industrial age largely passed it by. Located in the heart of Flanders, Bruges is one of northern Europe's most impressive surviving medieval cities. A boat trip on the extensive and pretty canal system is a good introduction to the town, with frequent departures from quays along **Dijver**, which, along with **Groene Rei** and **Rozenhoedkaai**, provide some of the vintage views of Bruges.

Markt, Bruges' large, lively and impressive main square, is surrounded by guild buildings, many of which have been converted into restaurants and bars. The **Burg**, the other main square, features the **Heilige Bloed Basiliek** (Basilica of the Holy Blood), with an early 12th-century stone chapel below a 16th-century chapel (closed Mon afternoons, Oct–Mar). Dijver is the central canal; Dijverstraat

THE LONGEST TRAMLINE IN THE WORLD

Ostend lies at the midway point of the coastal tram that runs the length of the Belgian coast from **Knokke-Heist** (on the Dutch border) to **De Panne** (on the French border). This entire 70-km sweep of coast is an essay in surrealism from René Magritte's magnificent murals in the casino at Knokke to the gnomes at **Plopsaland** (near De Panne). In between these two end points there are giant bananas dangling from flagpoles, piers that lead nowhere, and sedate belle époque hotels where the sea view has been blocked by monstrous apartment blocks. The coastal tram is the longest tram route in the world. The entire run takes 2 hrs 30 mins with 70 stops along the way. The quaintest spot on the route is **De Haan**, just 20 mins up the coast from **Ostend**. Trams run at least every 20 mins in each direction (ERT 406). A one-way ticket along the entire route is €3, and a day pass for unlimited travel costs €6.

(scene of a weekend antiques and flea market) is home to several museums. **Groeningemuseum** (closed Mon) houses a fine collection of Flemish art from the 15th century to date. **Bruggemuseum-Gruuthuse** (closed Mon), on the same side of the street, was a 16th-century palace. A visit to Bruges would not be complete without a walk around the walled religious village of the **Begijnhof**. The houses where Beguine nuns lived, as well as other single women or widows who opted for living within the community, are neatly arranged near the **Minnewater**, a tranquil, swan-populated lake.

ARRIVAL, INFORMATION, ACCOMMODATION

≼ A 20-min walk south-west of the centre; buses stop in front (tickets and a free route map from the De Lijn kiosk). To the right as you leave the station is a branch of the tourist office. **🛈 Tourist office**: (municipal): Concertgebouw (Concert Hall), 't Zand 34, and at the railway station, ☎ 050 44 46 46 (www.brugge.be). (Provincial): Koning Albert I-Laan 120, Sint-Michiels, ☎ 050 30 55 00 (www.westtoer.be).

🛏 Two reasonably-priced B&Bs are **iRoom**, Verversdijk 1, ☎ 050 33 73 53 (www.iroom.be), €€, and **Charming Brugge**, Komvest 13, ☎ 050 20 16 02 (www.charmingbrugge.be), €€. **Hostels**: Some good options for dorm rooms are the **Bauhaus-St Christopher's**, Langestraat 133–137, ☎ 050 34 10 93 (www.bauhaus.be), **Snuffel Backpacker Hostel**, Ezelstraat 47–49, ☎ 050 33 31 33 (www.snuffel.be) and the **Lybeer Traveller's Hostel**, Korte Vuldersstr. 31, ☎ 050 33 43 55 (www.hostellybeer.com), a renovated Catholic rectory in Bruges' medieval city centre.

GHENT (GENT)

Ghent is a pleasant Flemish university city, rich in culture and very lively during term time. The 12th–17th-century **guildhouses** along the **Graslei quay** and the old houses by the **Kraanlei quay** provide two of the city's classic views. There are summer boat trips on the river. **Sint-Baafskathedraal** (St Bavo's Cathedral), resplendent with marble statuary and a baroque organ and pulpit, contains Van

Eyck's multi-panelled masterpiece *The Adoration of the Mystic Lamb*, painted in 1432 and considered to be the most important work of church art in Belgium (entry fee). **Gravensteen**, Sint-Veerleplein, the 12th-century 'Castle of the Counts', has a museum that displays a selection of gruesome instruments of torture, with illustrations of how they were used. Allow plenty of time for the fascinating **Het Huis van Alijn** (Alijn House), Kraanlei 65 (closed Mon), which spreads through three converted almshouses.

ARRIVAL, INFORMATION, ACCOMMODATION

⇌ Gent-St-Pieters: south of the centre (tram 1/10/11/12: Korenmarkt). De Lijn bus/tram information to the left as you exit. 🛈 **Tourist office**: Botermarkt 17A (in the crypt of the Belfry), ☎ 09 266 56 60 (www.visitgent.be).

🛏 **Bed In Gent**, Lucas Munichstraat 18, ☎ 09 224 35 79 (www.bedingent.be), €€, is a good value B&B close to the station. The official youth hostel (HI) is **De Draecke**, Sint-Widostraat 11, ☎ 09 233 70 50 (www.vjh.be). Another option is the environmentally-friendly **Ecohostel Andromeda**, Bargiekaai 35, ☎ 0486 67 80 33 (www.ecohostel.be), which is on a boat, a 10-min walk from the centre of town.

ANTWERP (ANTWERPEN/ANVERS)

Belgium's second city, Antwerp has an extensive old Flemish quarter, a rich Jewish heritage and is at the cutting edge of diamonds and fashion. Nowhere else in Belgium is so thoroughly dedicated to being cool. If that isn't enough, the famously tolerant city on the **River Schelde** has Belgium's best club scene. Antwerp hit the headlines in 2011 with the opening in May of the **Museum aan de Stroom**, Hanzestedenplaats 1 (www.mas.be; closed Mon) in the Eilandje district of the city's old port. It is dedicated to the city's connections with the world. Just hop on 🚊 17 at the central station and alight at Van Schoonbekeplein.

The **Diamantmuseum**, Koningin Astridplein 19–23 (walkable from Centraal station), covers all aspects of the diamond trade, one of the cornerstones of Antwerp's appreciable fortunes (closed Wed). Perhaps Antwerp's most astonishing survival is the unique **Plantin-Moretus Museum/Stedelijk Prentenkabinet**, Vrijdagmarkt 22–23 (closed Mon), a perfectly preserved 16th–18th-century printer's works and home built by the famous printer Plantin; don't spend too long on the first few rooms — the most interesting parts come later on.

The **cathedral** is Belgium's largest (free multilingual tours; entrance on Handschoenmarkt), built 1352–1521. Grote Markt is home to the 19th-century **Brabo Fountain** (which depicts the legend of the city's founding), elaborately gabled guildhouses and the Renaissance **Stadhuis** (Town Hall).

ARRIVAL, INFORMATION, ACCOMMODATION

⇌ **Antwerpen-Centraal**, 2 km east of the centre, linked by metro-tram to the centre. The station is an extraordinarily eclectic but striking piece of architecture. 🛈 **Tourist**

office: Grote Markt 13–15, ☎ 03 232 01 03 (www.antwerpen.be). From Centraal, take metro 2/15 to Groenplaats (direction: Linkeroever), near the cathedral.

◄ Some cheap places near Centraal (beware that some rent by the hour). **Mabuhay**, Draakstr. 32, ☎ 03 290 88 15 (www.mabuhay.be), €, is an Asian-style gay-friendly Bed & Breakfast hotel in the hip Zurenborg area. **Number 20**, St Thomasstraat 20, ☎ 04 974 36 319 (www.bedandbreakfast-antwerpen.be), €€, is a small, stylish B&B in the centre.

Hostels: Abhostel, Kattenberg 110, ☎ 04 735 70 166 (www.abhostel.com), is a super-friendly hostel run by a passionate backpacker. **Youth hostel** (HI): **Op Sinjoorke**, Eric Sasselaan 2, ☎ 03 238 02 73 (www.vjh.be).

BRUSSELS— SEE P459

LIÈGE (LUIK/LÜTTICH)

Change at Liège Guillemins for the detour to **Maastricht**. Liège is an industrial city that sprawls along the west bank of the River Meuse. Guillemins railway station, 2 km from the city centre, is a stunning piece of architecture. Designed by Santiago Calatrava, the building is best appreciated from the road outside rather than from the platforms. Route 14 makes a detour to Maastricht in the Netherlands and returns to Liège.

MAASTRICHT

Tucked into the southern, mildly hilly corner of the Netherlands, the provincial capital of Limburg and busy university town has a captivating atmosphere with its lively squares, distinctive stone houses and arty boutiques. You can get a great view from the tower of **Sint Janskerk**, next to huge **Sint Servaasbasiliek** (see the 11th- and 12th-century crypts).

The most atmospheric church is the elaborately decorated Romanesque **Onze-Lieve-Vrouwe Basiliek**. At **Museumkelder Derlon**, there are *in situ* remnants of Roman Maastricht, while centuries-old **fortifications** abound in and around the city, notably at **Fort Sint Pieter**. **St Pietersberg Caves** are the result of centuries of excavation of marl stone, which have left a labyrinth of more than 20,000 passages; you can visit two sections (daily guided tours in English in July and August; for details call ☎ 043 325 21 21).

ARRIVAL, INFORMATION, ACCOMMODATION

⇾ A 10-min walk east of the centre. **🛈 Tourist office: VVVTourist Office**, Kleine Staat 1, ☎ 043 325 21 21 (www.vvvmaastricht.nl). ◄ Cheap options around the station and in the Markt area. **Youth hostel** (HI): **Stayokay Maastricht**, Maasboulevard 101, ☎ 043 750 17 90 (www.stayokay.com). **Campsite: Camping Dousberg**, Dousbergweg 102, ☎ 043 43 21 71 (www.dedousberg.nl).

Through the Ardennes

The journey to Luxembourg from Liège takes a very rural branch line via Gouvy and Clervaux (ERT 444). We rate this route that runs south through the increasingly rugged Ardennes region from Liège into Luxembourg as the finest 2-hr train journey in the Benelux region. Not a stretch on which to fall asleep!

Luxembourg (City)

One of Europe's smallest capitals, Luxembourg is a pleasant place to pass a day or two. The city was founded in Roman times and is dramatically sited on a gorge cut by the rivers **Alzette** and **Pétrusse**. It falls naturally into three sections: the **old centre** (north of the Pétrusse Valley and home to most of the sights), the **modern city** and **station** (south of the gorge), and **Grund** (the valley settlement), reachable by deep escalators or lift from the central part of town. Descending to Grund ('the ground') is like entering a different, darker city, and it is this area that houses most of Luxembourg's racier nightlife.

The **Cathédrale Notre-Dame**, a 17th-century Jesuit church, contains the simple stone crypt that is the tomb of Duke John the Blind (King of Bohemia and Count of Luxembourg), backed by statues of mourners. Bronze lions flank a gate through which can be seen the burial chapel of the Grand-Ducal family. From pl. de la Constitution there is access to the **Pétrusse casemates**: the underground passages that formed part of the city's original defences (open Easter, Whitsun and school holidays). Tours take 45 mins and you need to be reasonably fit. If you're in doubt, opt for the similar casemates at **Rocher du Bock** (open Mar–Oct), which are easier. The entrance is on r. Sigefroi, the site where Count Siegfried built the **original fortress**, later expanded, especially by the French in the 17th century.

Arrival, information, accommodation

≋ **Gare Centrale**, a 15-min walk south of the centre. 🚺 **Tourist office**: 30, pl. Guillaume II, ☎ 22 28 09 (www.lcto.lu) in the Old Town. ⊨ Most of the cheaper hotels are near the station. A good moderately priced option is the **Bristol**, 11 r. de Strasbourg, ☎ 48 58 29 (www.hotel-bristol.lu), €–€€. Not cheap, but located right on Place d'Armes in the old centre is the 3-star **Hotel Français**, 14 pl. d'Armes, ☎ 47 45 34 (www.hotelfrancais.lu), €€–€€€. Another central option is the **Hotel Piemont**, 56 Route d'Esch, ☎ 25 42 01 (www.hotelpiemont.com), €€. **Hostels:** The **Luxembourg City Hostel** (HI), 2 rue du Fort Olisy, ☎ 22 68 89-20 (www.youthhostels.lu) is 3 km from the station. A low-cost shuttle bus service is offered from both the train station and the airport, or take 🚌 9 to Vallée d'Alzette and then walk 150 m down the hill.

Camping Kockelscheuer, Route de Bettembourg 22, Kockelscheuer, ☎ 47 18 15 (www.camp-kockelscheuer.lu), is south of the centre, 4 km from Gare Centrale and 200 m from the 🚌 18 stop; open Mar–Oct. ✗ Good mid-range options are in the old centre. Pl. d'Armes is full of cafés, with open-air entertainment on most summer evenings. There's a regular food market in pl. Guillaume II (Wed and Sat 0800–1200).

Rail Route 15: Dutch circle

CITIES: ★★ CULTURE: ★ HISTORY: ★★ SCENERY: ★
COUNTRIES COVERED: NETHERLANDS

Contrary to popular belief, the Netherlands and Holland are not synonymous. Holland is that part of the country which borders the North Sea between Amsterdam and Rotterdam and extending east thereof. And Route 15 is in effect a grand tour of Holland, the region of the country so full of dykes, canals, gabled houses, glasshouses and windmills that it lives up to every Dutch stereotype. Holland is beautiful, but very densely populated.

Our circular tour takes in the best of Holland and makes a short foray east to include the historic city of **Utrecht** and the sandy heathlands of **Veluwe** where the occasional ripple in the landscape shows that the Netherlands are not all pancake-flat. We think the real highlights of this tour are canal-laced towns like **Delft** and **Gouda** (famous for porcelain and cheese respectively), **Haarlem** (definitely worth a stop for the Frans Hals Museum) and the laid-back university town of **Leiden**.

An early start allows you to follow the entire length of Route 15 in a long day, securing along the way a wonderful medley of Dutch impressions. If you decide to do that, buy the **Dagkaart** (Day Card) that affords unlimited rail travel in the Netherlands for a day for €47. Better, though, to allot two or three days to this route, stopping off along the way. The key to really enjoying this route is to eat copious quantities of **Hollandse appeltaart** — in our view no other apple pie reaches quite the same pinnacle of perfection as that found in small towns in Holland.

AMSTERDAM — SEE P421

HAARLEM

The late Gothic **St Bavo/Grote-Kerk** (1370–1520), with its soaring 80-m wooden lantern tower, contains a notable 16th-century screen and the famous Christian Müller baroque pipe organ (1738), on which both Handel and Mozart played; it's still used for regular concerts. The Antwerp-born painter Frans Hals is buried here. He spent most of his life in Haarlem, and much of his work is in the **Frans Hals Museum**, Groot Heiligland 62 (www.franshalsmuseum.nl, closed Mon). The Netherlands' oldest public museum, which first went on view in 1784, is the **Teylers Museum**, Spaarne 16, an entertaining miscellany of old scientific instruments, fossils, gemstones, coins and above all a fine display of drawings (by Raphael, Michelangelo, Rembrandt and others).

ARRIVAL, INFORMATION, ACCOMMODATION

≋ A 10-min walk north of the centre. 🚻 **Tourist office**: Verwulft 11, ☎ 0900 616 1600 (premium rate), www.vvvzk.nl. ⋈ The **Stayokay Youth hostel** (HI), Jan Gijzenpad 3,

☎ 023 537 3793 (www.stayokay.com/haarlem) has both dorms and private rooms. Otherwise accommodation generally is limited; there's a better choice in Zandvoort.

CONNECTIONS FROM HAARLEM

Zandvoort (11 mins by train) is a busy beach resort (casino; sandy beaches near the station) and has plenty of cheap pensions. 🚻 **Tourist office**: Bakkerstraat 2B, ☎ 023 571 7947 (www.vvvzk.nl).

LEIDEN

Birthplace of Rembrandt, this delightful old university town has a medieval quarter, centred on the vast Pieterskerk, plenty of studenty haunts and some excellent museums, covering archaeology (**Rijksmuseum van Oudheden**, Rapenburg 28), local history and art (**De Lakenhal**, Oude Singel 28–32), changing exhibitions from around the world (**Voor Volkenkunde**, Steenstr. 1) and milling (within a windmill; **Molenmuseum de Valk**, 2e Binnenvestgracht 1). In the **Boerhaave**, Lange St Agnietenstr. 10, is an anatomical theatre, complete with skeletons and displays of early medical paraphernalia. The university, founded in 1575, includes the world's oldest botanic gardens (**Hortus Botanicus**).

ARRIVAL, INFORMATION, ACCOMMODATION

➹ A 10-min walk north-west of the centre. 🚻 **Tourist office**: Stationsweg 41, ☎ 071 516 6000 (http://portal.leiden.nl). ⊨ **Nieuw Minerva**, Boommarkt 23, ☎ 071 512 6358 (www.nieuwminerva.nl), €€, is a stylish 3-star canalside hotel in the centre.

CONNECTIONS FROM LEIDEN

Keukenhof Gardens (near Lisse; 🚌 54 in season from Leiden): the showcase of the Dutch bulb industry (late Mar–late May; best in April), noted for tulips, narcissi and hyacinths; take a picnic because the cafés are invariably overcrowded (www.keukenhof.nl).

THE HAGUE (DEN HAAG, 'S-GRAVENHAGE)

The administrative capital of the Netherlands is a pleasant town, spread over a wide area of parks and canals and centred around **Binnenhof**, the home of the **Dutch parliament** (guided tours; tram 1/2/3/6/8/9/10/16/17, 🚌 4/22). The 13th-century **Ridderzaal** (Knights' Hall) hosts official ceremonies. Installed in a rotunda, the remarkable **Panorama Mesdag**, Zeestr. 65 (tram 10 — peak hours only — or 🚌 22/24; closed Mar), consists of a realistic circular view of the North Sea resort of **Scheveningen** (itself a district of The Hague) painted by Hendrik Mesdag, his wife and some friends in 1881.

Most of the city's palaces can be viewed only from the outside. An exception is the huge **Vredespaleis** (Peace Palace), Carnegieplein 2 (tram 1, 🚌 24), which

Notes

For train journeys from Arnhem to Apeldoorn, change at Zutphen.
Travelling from Apeldoorn to Amsterdam, it is necessary to change trains
at Amersfoort on some connections.

Route Details

Amsterdam–Haarlem   ERT 450, 496

Type	Frequency	Typical journey time
Train	6 per hr	16 mins

Haarlem–Leiden   ERT 450

Type	Frequency	Typical journey time
Train	4–6 per hr	19 mins

Leiden–The Hague   ERT 450

Type	Frequency	Typical journey time
Train	4–6 per hr	12 mins

The Hague–Delft   ERT 450, 471

Type	Frequency	Typical journey time
Train	4 per hr	12 mins

Delft–Rotterdam   ERT 450, 471

Type	Frequency	Typical journey time
Train	6 per hr	12 mins

Route Details (continued)

Rotterdam–Gouda   ERT 465, 481

Type	Frequency	Typical journey time
Train	4–6 per hr	18 mins

Gouda–Utrecht   ERT 481

Type	Frequency	Typical journey time
Train	4–8 per hr	19 mins

Utrecht–Arnhem   ERT 468

Type	Frequency	Typical journey time
Train	2–4 per hr	37 mins

Arnhem–Apeldoorn   ERT 475, 498

Type	Frequency	Typical journey time
Train	2 per hr	46 mins

Apeldoorn–Amsterdam   ERT 480

Type	Frequency	Typical journey time
Train	2 per hr	1h05

houses the International Court of Justice and the Permanent Court of Arbitration; it is a strange architectural mishmash, with a display of items donated by world leaders. There are normally tours Mon–Fri 1000–1500 (up to 1600 during summer; advance booking only, ☎ 070 302 4137).

ARRIVAL, INFORMATION, ACCOMMODATION

🚆 **Centraal (CS)** is a 5-min walk from the centre and serves most Dutch cities. Fast services for Amsterdam and Rotterdam use **HS** (Hollandse Spoor) station (1 km south). Centraal and HS are linked by frequent trains and by tram 10/17. ⓘ **Tourist office**: Koningin Julianaplein 30, ☎ 070 363 5676 (www.denhaag.com). Buy a proper street map, as the free small ones are deceptive in scale. 🚌 There is an excellent bus and tram network. 🛏 A B&B close to the beach in the Scheveningen district is the **Villa Suisse**, Haarlemsestraat 10, 070 356 1567 (www.villasuisse.nl), €€. Another good bet is the **Stayokay Youth Hostel** (HI), Scheepmakersstraat 27, ☎ 070 315 7888 (www.stayokay.com), a 5-min walk north-east of HS station.

DELFT

Long famed for Delftware porcelain and birthplace of the artist Vermeer, Delft is an elegant town with old merchants' houses lining the canal. It has a number of porcelain factories where you can watch production; the oldest is **De Koninklijke Porceleyne Fles** (Rotterdamseweg 196; closed Sun, Nov–late Mar), but more central is **Aardewerk-atelier de Candelaer** (Kerkstr. 14).

Stedelijk Museum Het Prinsenhof (the Prince's Court), St Agathaplein 1, includes silverware, tapestries, paintings and Delftware. Across the road is **Nusantara Museum**, with a collection of art from the former Dutch East Indies.

Nieuwe Kerk (New Church) houses the huge black-and-white marble mausoleum of Prince William, and its 109-m spire provides great views. A nice way to see Delft is by horse-drawn tram from Markt, or by canal cruise.

ARRIVAL, INFORMATION

🚆 A 5-min walk south of the centre. ⓘ **Tourism Information Point**, Hippolytusbuurt 4, ☎ 015 215 4051 (www.delft.com).

A HAGUE DUO

The Hague has a remarkable pair of galleries, either of which would alone justify a journey to the Dutch city. The **Royal Picture Gallery** (Mauritshuis), Korte Vijverberg 8 (tram/bus: to Binnenhof; closed Mon), is a Renaissance mansion on the famous Hofvijver (Courtpond) which has a superb collection of paintings by Flemish masters, including Rembrandt and Vermeer. A few steps from the Mauritshuis is the **Escher in het Paleis** museum, Lange Voorhout 74, showcasing the work of Dutch graphic artist M C Escher. It includes a mind-bending multimedia exhibit which takes you inside some of Escher's more impossible creations.

Rotterdam

The city was virtually flattened in World War II, but much of its modern architecture is strikingly innovative (**Lijnbaan** was the European pioneer of shopping precincts, for example). Situated at the delta of the rivers **Rhine**, **Maas** and **Waal**, **Europoort** is the world's largest container port; **harbour tours** operated by **Spido**, Willemsplein 85, ☎ 010 275 9988 (www.spido.nl), metro: Leuvehaven, tram 7 from central station (stop: Willemsplein).

The **Museum Boijmans Van Beuningen**, Museumpark 18/20, ☎ 010 441 9400 (metro: Eendrachtsplein, tram 7; closed Mon), is massive and high quality, with applied and fine art (including clocks, lace and paintings by Dalí, Magritte, Rembrandt, Van Gogh and Bosch). **Maritiem Museum Rotterdam**, Leuvehaven 1, ☎ 010 413 2680 (metro: Beurs, tram 8/23/25, 🚌 32/49; closed Mon exc. July–Aug & school holidays), is the country's oldest and biggest maritime museum.

The 185-m **Euromast**, Parkhaven 20 (metro: Dijkzigt, tram 7/20), towers over the trees in **Central Park** (www.euromast.nl). It is the highest structure in the Netherlands. Even from the first platform you have panoramic views of the waterfront, but go right to the top on the **Space Adventure**, a simulated rocket flight. After blast-off you go into 'orbit' and have breathtaking views as the capsule ascends and revolves slowly to the top. **Abseiling** is possible May–Sept and there are even two pricey suites if you fancy sleeping overnight at the top of the tower.

ARRIVAL, INFORMATION, ACCOMMODATION

≋ **Centraal**, on the northern edge of the centre (blue metro line). 🚹 **Tourist office**: Coolsingel 195–197 (5-min walk from Centraal; follow the signs), ☎ 0900 403 4065 (premium rate), www.rotterdam.info. *R'uit* is a free monthly listing. VVV sells advantageous combination tickets (travel and attractions and reduction in restaurants). 🚌 **RET**: Coolsingel 141, ☎ 0900 92 92 (www.ret.nl).

The Rotterdam metro has fully embraced the new *OV-Chipkaart* electronic ticketing system and *strippenkaarten* are no longer valid. Metro stations are indicated by a large yellow M. Only two lines matter for the centre: blue (north–south) and red (east–west), intersecting at Beurs. Trams fill the gaps in the metro; summer-service tourist tram no. 10 visits all the main places of interest. Buses are more useful away from the centre.

🛏 Plenty of middle-range options, including **H2otel**, Wijnhaven 20a, ☎ 010 444 5690 (www.h2otel.nl), €€, the quirkily-named **Cherrycake & Chocolate**, Maaskade 88b, ☎ 0621 8374 20 (www.cherrycake.nl), €€, and **Het Hemelrijck**, 1e Pijnackerstraat 99c, ☎ 0641 3274 18 (www.hemelrijck.com), €€. **Hostels**: Well-regarded is the **Hostel Room Rotterdam**, Van Vollenhovenstraat 62, ☎ 010 282 7277 (www.roomrotterdam.nl), or else try **Stayokay Rotterdam** (HI), Overblaak 85–87, ☎ 010 436 5763 (www.stayokay.com/rotterdam), now spectacularly located inside the city's famous cube houses, created by Dutch architect Piet Blom in 1984. **Campsite**: **Stadscamping Rotterdam**, Kanaalweg 84, ☎ 010 415 3440 (www.stadscamping-rotterdam.nl), west of Centraal (🚌 33), is open all year.

Head south to Antwerp (ERT 420) to join **Route 14** (p154).

GOUDA

This quaint place exemplifies small-town Holland, with a ring of quiet canals around ancient buildings. The 15th-century **Stadhuis** (Town Hall) is the oldest Gothic municipal building in Holland, while **Sint Janskerk** (the Netherlands' longest church) is famed throughout the country for its 64 superb 16th-century stained-glass windows. The old **Waag** (weigh-house) in Marktplein (the market square) opens for trading on Thursday morning, 1000 until around 1230 (mid-June to early Sept). Gouda cheese comes in several grades (the extra-mature is hard and deliciously strong), while syrup waffles (or *goudse*) are another speciality.

ARRIVAL, INFORMATION

⇶ A 10-min walk north of the centre. **🛈 Tourist office**: Markt 27, ☎ 0900 468 3288 (www.vvvgouda.nl).

UTRECHT

Tree-lined canals encircle the Old Town at the heart of this historic city, not a major tourist destination but worth a brief visit. **Domtoren**, the 112-m cathedral tower (🚌 2/22, but the 10-min walk from railway station takes less time), is the tallest in the Netherlands, and gives a marvellous view — if you can face 465 steps. Utrecht is the headquarters of Dutch Railways (NS), and home to the **Nederlands Spoorwegmuseum** (Railway Museum), Maliebaanstation 16 (closed Mon, 🚌 3). The highly entertaining **Nationaal Museum van Speelklok tot Pierement**, Steenweg 6 (10-min walk from Utrecht Centraal), covers mechanical musical instruments from music boxes to barrel organs, with demonstrations given (closed Mon). To the east of the centre, the **Rietveld Schröderhuis**, Prins Hendriklaan 50 (closed Mon), dates from 1924 and represents one of the most radical architectural designs of its day, with an open plan divided by internal sliding doors, and ingenious use of light and space.

ARRIVAL, INFORMATION, ACCOMMODATION

⇶ **Centraal**: west of the centre, separated from the old quarter by the Hoog Catharijne indoor shopping centre. There are several outlying stations; don't get off until you reach Centraal. **🛈 Tourist office**: Domplein 9 (in the city centre), ☎ 0900 12 8732 (premium rate), www.utrechtyourway.nl.

⊨ The **Hostel B&B**, Lucas Bolwerk 4, ☎ 06 5043 4884 (www.hostelutrecht.nl), part of a non-profit budget accommodation organisation; free internet access, TV in all rooms, 15 mins from rail station.

ART AND NATURE

De Hoge Veluwe National Park to the north-west of Arnhem encompasses dunes, fens, heath, forest and added attractions. The visitors' centre in the park houses **Museonder**, an underground museum devoted to every form of subterranean life; 🚌 108 (from Ede, Wageningen and Apeldoorn or 🚌 105 from Arnhem, then change onto the 🚌 108 in Otterlo). Entrances: Otterlo (🚌 105 from Arnhem), Hoenderloo (🚌 108 from Apeldoorn, Ede and Wageningen) and Schaarsbergen (🚌 105 from Arnhem). Once at a gate, buy a map and borrow a white bicycle (free) as there's a lot of ground to cover. The **Kröller-Müller Museum**, Houtkampweg 6 (www.kmm.nl, closed Mon; a good 35-min walk from the Otterlo entrance, but 🚌 106 stops there on its way between Otterlo and Hoenderloo), has one of Europe's best modern art collections, notably 278 paintings by Van Gogh (including *The Potato Eaters* and *Café Terrace at Night*), although only 50 or so are on show at any one time. The adjacent **Sculpture Garden** and **Sculpture Forest** contain works by Rodin, Epstein and Moore, plus Dubuffet's extraordinary *Jardin d'Émail*.

ARNHEM

Attractions are scattered, but an excellent bus network makes reaching them easy. Attractions include **Burgers' Zoo**, Antoon van Hooffplein 1 (🚌 3, plus 🚌 13 in summer), a zoo with safari park, pride of place going to a giant greenhouse, and **Nederlands Openluchtmuseum**, Schelmseweg 89 (🚌 3, plus 🚌 13 in summer), an extensive and delightful open-air museum.

At **Oosterbeek**, the **Airborne Museum**, Hartenstein, Utrechtseweg 232 (8 km west of the centre, 🚌 1), is devoted to Operation Market Garden, the Allied debacle of Sept 1944 that was immortalised in the film *A Bridge Too Far*. You can find photographs, film footage, and weapons and equipment from both sides.

ARRIVAL, INFORMATION, ACCOMMODATION

⇌ On the north-western edge of town. 🛈 **Tourist office**: Stationsplein 13, ☎ 0900 190 4022 (premium rate), www.vvvarnhemnijmegen.nl.

🛏 The **Hotel-Pension Parkzicht**, Apeldoornsestr. 16, ☎ 026 442 0698, €€, is walkable from the station. Centrally located and a good budget place is the **Rembrandt**, Patersstr. 1–3, ☎ 026 442 0153, (www.hotelrembrandtarnhem.nl), €. **Youth hostel** (HI): Diepenbrocklaan 27, ☎ 026 442 0114 (www.stayokay.com/arnhem), 4 km north of the station (🚌 3 towards Alteveer: Ziekenhuis Rijnstate). You'll see a sign with the HI logo; 30 m further on steps climb a forested hill to the hostel. Two **campsites**: **Camping Warnsborn**, Bakenbergseweg 257, ☎ 026 442 3469 (www.campingwarnsborn.nl), Apr–Oct (north-west of the centre, 🚌 2), and **De Hooge Veluwe**, Koningsweg 14, ☎ 026 443 2272 (www.droomparkhoogeveluwe.nl), Apr–Oct, by the Hoenderloo entrance to the park (🚌 2 towards Schaarsbergen).

AMSTERDAM — SEE P421

Rail Route 16: Across northern Germany

CITIES: ★★★ CULTURE: ★ HISTORY: ★★★ SCENERY: ★ (GENERALLY — BUT ★★★ FOR THE HARZ MOUNTAIN SECTION)
COUNTRIES COVERED: GERMANY

"A very agreeable place for visitors," wrote Thomas Cook of Aachen in the 1874 edition of his handbook for travellers to the Rhineland. And that's still true today, making the town a fine introduction to Germany. Aachen, the gateway to Route 16, boasts a very proud past. And Berlin, endpoint of this long route from west to east, is also a crucible of European history. The main rail route linking Aachen with Berlin — let's not beat about the bush — will hardly inspire you with fine scenery. Six hours on Germany's sleek silver ICE trains is all it takes. There's a delicate beauty here and there, particularly around the **Weser Hills** and in the watery flatlands of **western Brandenburg**. But ultimately this is a journey where few will be spellbound by the scenery beyond the carriage window.

But if you cut off the main line to the south and meander through the Harz Mountains as we suggest, you will find some of Germany's most delectable hill country with picture-perfect villages. The **Harz Mountains** lie astride the former border that until 1990 separated the two German States, and tucked away in the pretty valleys of the Harz are some of Germany's best preserved small towns. We include two of them in this tour, **Goslar** and **Quedlinburg**. Both feature on UN-ESCO's List of World Heritage Sites. The narrow-gauge rail network of the eastern part of the Harz Mountains (see box on p173), operated in the main by steam trains, is a superb way of exploring the region. Slow travel at its best.

You can forsake Route 16 at **Hannover** to follow **Route 17** to Hamburg and Copenhagen. Or follow this route right through to Berlin from where you can pick up more of our recommended itineraries: **Route 45** via Warsaw to Russia, **Route 49** via Kraków to Ukraine, and **Route 48** south via Prague to Budapest.

AACHEN

A frontier town close to where the borders of Belgium, the Netherlands and Germany converge, Aachen (formerly known as Aix-la-Chapelle) was already a great city 1,000 years ago when Emperor Charlemagne the Great enjoyed the thermal springs and made it the capital of his empire. The new **Route Charlemagne** links the main historic sights of Aachen, all easily covered on foot. Download an excellent brochure at www.route-charlemagne.eu.

The Aachener Dom is the oldest cathedral in northern Europe and inspiring more for its historical associations than for any great beauty. You can see **Charlemagne's gilded tomb** and the imperial throne. After years of renovation, the **Internationales Zeitungsmuseum** (International Newspaper Museum), Pontstr. 13, opened its doors again in July 2011 (www.izm.de; closed Mon). The museum has

Notes

Journeys from Wernigerode to Quedlinburg require a change of train in Halberstadt.

Choose your Berlin alighting point carefully. Many trains arriving in the German capital from the west stop more than once in Berlin. Halts may include Spandau (in the western suburbs), Berlin Hauptbahnhof and Berlin Ostbahnhof. Some trains may serve Berlin Südkreuz instead of Ostbahnhof. Services from Magdeburg always stop at Potsdam, Berlin Wannsee, Berlin Zoo, Hauptbahnhof and Ostbahnhof.

The **Harz narrow-gauge rail network** (HSB) is not shown on the map above, but you can connect onto it at Wernigerode and Quedlinburg. And, if you have an appetite for slow travel, you can ride between the two using HSB trains that loop south through the mountains. Read more in the box on p173. Typical travel times are:

Wernigerode to Nordhausen: 2h45
Wernigerode to Brocken: 1h40 to 2 hrs
Wernigerode to Quedlinburg: 4h30 to 6 hrs
Quedlinburg to Brocken: 5h40 to 6h30
Quedlinburg to Nordhausen: 3h05 to 3h40

The times of most HSB trains are shown in ERT 867. Services run daily throughout the year, but are significantly less frequent in winter than during the summer months.

ROUTE DETAILS

Aachen–Cologne ERT 802, 807, 910

Type	Frequency	Typical journey time
Train	2–3 per hr	53 mins

Cologne–Düsseldorf ERT 800, 802

Type	Frequency	Typical journey time
Train	4 per hr	30 mins

Düsseldorf–Hannover ERT 800, 810

Type	Frequency	Typical journey time
Train	Every hr	2h35

Hannover–Goslar ERT 860

Type	Frequency	Typical journey time
Train	Every hr	1 hr

Goslar–Wernigerode ERT 860

Type	Frequency	Typical journey time
Train	Every 2 hrs	43 mins

Wernigerode–Quedlinburg ERT 860, 862

Type	Frequency	Typical journey time
Train	Every hr	40 mins

Quedlinburg–Magdeburg ERT 862

Type	Frequency	Typical journey time
Train	Every hr	1h09

Magdeburg–Berlin ERT 839

Type	Frequency	Typical journey time
Train	Every hr	1h40

KEY JOURNEYS

Cologne–Berlin ERT 800, 810

Type	Frequency	Typical journey time
Train	Every hr	4h20

a collection of over 200,000 newspapers. Nowadays, in a post-Schengen Europe largely free of border controls, Aachen thrives as the main city in the three-country Euregio district. The quirky **Dreiländerpunkt** (three-country point) on the edge of town is worth a visit in fine weather. Take bus 25 or 33 to Vaals Grenze from where it is a 10-minute uphill walk.

ARRIVAL, INFORMATION, ACCOMMODATION

➤ **Aachen Hbf**, Bahnhofplatz 2A, about 1 km from the city centre. 🚶 **Tourist office**: in the centre at Elisenbrunnen, Friedrich-Wilhelm-Pl., ☎ 0241 180 2960 (www.aachen.de). Hotel booking service, ☎ 0241 180 2950. Daily guided tours start here.

🛏 Medium-priced hotels include the two adjacent sister hotels **Am Bahnhof**, Bahnhofplatz 8, ☎ 0241 354 49 (www.hotel-ambahnhof.de), €–€€, and the pricier **Hotel Stadtnah**, Leydelstr. 2, ☎ 0241 474 580 (www.hotelstadtnah.de), €€. Another good option is the **Art Hotel Aachen**, Adenauerallee 209, ☎ 0241 608 360 (www.art-hotel-aachen.de), €€, just south of the centre. The HI youth hostel **Euregionales Jugendgästehaus** is out of town at Maria-Theresia-Allee 260, ☎ 0241 711 010 (www.aachen.jugendherberge.de), 🚋 2 from Aachen Central station, direction Preuswald, stop Rhonheide. The nearest **campsite** is **Camping Hoeve de Gastmolen**, 7 km west of the centre at Vaals in the Netherlands, ☎ 43 306 5755 (www.gastmolen.nl); open mid-Mar to late Oct.

COLOGNE — SEE P178

DÜSSELDORF

Too often derided as being too commercial and industrial, Düsseldorf has moved markedly upmarket, its transition exemplified by the Königsallee (generally termed the 'Kö'), one of the most elegant shopping streets in Germany. The city has a substantial Japanese population, who appear to have learnt the art of drinking beer in the same quantities as German natives — especially the local 'Alt'. Most of the areas of interest are along the Rhine, itself spanned by the graceful **Rheinkniebrücke** (bridge) with the **Rhine Tower** prominent on the skyline. Marked by the **Schlossturm**, all that remains of the original 14th-century castle, the **Altstadt** (Old Town), is small and walkable. Within it is **Flingerstr.**, a quaint pedestrianised shopping precinct, somewhat more affordable than Königsallee. One of the most attractive corners is the **Marktplatz** (Market Square), brimming over with outdoor cafés and restaurants.

Düsseldorf boasts a world-class collection of modern art, split between three venues: The **K20** at Grabbepl. 5, the **K21** at Ständehausstr. 1 and the **Schmela Haus** at Mutter-Ey-Str. 3 (see www.kunstsammlung.de; closed Mon). The city is also the unlikely birthplace of **German punk**. Along with Hamburg and Berlin, Düsseldorf nurtured the nascent punk culture, most notably at the Ratinger Hof, which is still an important music venue in the city's Altstadt.

➤ **Düsseldorf Hbf**, about 2 km from the east bank of the Rhine, is near most places of interest. ✈ 7 km from city; S-Bahn line 11 runs every 20–30 mins. ☒ **Tourist office**: Marktplatz 6, ☎ 0211 1720 2844 (www.duesseldorf-tourismus.de). There is another office at the main railway station. Both offer a room booking service.

🛏 Close to the station, the **Max Hotel Garni**, Adersstrasse 65, ☎ 0211 386 800 (www.max-hotelgarni.de), €€, is very well regarded. **Hostel**: The independent **Backpackers Düsseldorf** is at Fürstenwall 180, ☎ 0211 302 0848 (www.backpackers-duesseldorf.de), take 🚌 725 from the train station to Corneliusstrasse.

HEADING EAST

The main rail routes north-east from Düsseldorf skirt once heavily industrialised valleys (the Ruhr, Wupper and Emscher). Much of this area has been creatively rescued from its industrial past with impressive new green landscapes. The route then opens out onto the **Westphalian plain**. You can detour via the old cities of **Münster** and **Osnabrück**, both with a rich religious history, Münster Protestant and Osnabrück Catholic. They are on the route shown on the map on p169, but the fastest ICE trains speed east on a more southerly route through Bielefeld.

HANNOVER

The city is gritty and industrial, but with some fine historical buildings and some world-class landscape gardens. A great route for first-time visitors is **Der Rote Faden** (the Red Thread), a red line painted on the pavement that tracks a 4.2 km (2 hr) path through the city centre and can be easily followed on foot; pick up a free map and explanatory leaflet from the tourist office. From the station, Bahnhofstr. leads to the **Kröpcke piazza**, in the heart of the largely reconstructed **Altstadt**; the Kröpcke clock is the most prominent rendezvous in town. The high-gabled, carefully restored **Altes Rathaus** is a splendid edifice with elaborate brickwork. Alongside is the **Marktkirche**, with 14th- to 15th-century stained glass and a bulky tower that is the city's emblem.

Across town, over the Friedrichswall, is the high-domed **Neues Rathaus** located in a pleasant garden and reflected in a small lake. An absolute must-see is the **Royal Herrenhäuser Gardens**, 10 mins from Kröpcke (U-Bahn: Herrenhäuser Gärten) — four once-royal gardens, two of which are the English-style landscaped Georgengarten and the formal Grosser Garten with spectacular fountain displays in summer.

Hannover's reputation as a business centre may deter younger travellers, but the city boasts a lively youth culture. For nightlife check out the **Kulturzentrum Faust** (www.faustev.de), a former factory building by the River Leine (U-Bahn: Glocksee). Cheap eats (daytime only) are available at the **Markthalle** on Karmarschstrasse (ethnic cuisine and the omnipresent wurst and pizza).

Arrival, information, accommodation

➽ **Hannover Hbf**, central location about 600m north-east of the Altstadt. A major hub, where the main east–west (Berlin to Cologne) and north–south (Hamburg to Munich) routes cross. 🅑 **Tourist office**: Ernst-August-Pl. 8 (next to Hbf), ☎ 0511 1234 5111 (www.hannover-tourism.de).

🏨 Many conventions take place here, so cheap accommodation can be hard to find, although prices drop further away from the centre. A reasonably-priced option in the centre is the **Intercityhotel Hannover**, Rosenstrasse 1, ☎ 0511 169 921–300 (www.intercityhotel.de), €€. The HI **youth hostel** is at Ferdinand-Wilhelm-Fricke-Weg 1, ☎ 0511 131 7674 (www.jugendherberge.de), U-bahn 3/7 to Fischerhof. The independent **Hostel Hannover**, Lenaustrasse 12a, ☎ 0511 131 9919 (www.hostelhannover.de), is three stops from the rail station on tram 10/17 (stop: Goetheplatz).

Connections from Hannover

You can join **Route 17** (p174) here. Hourly trains (ERT 900, 1 per hr) from Hannover to Würzburg give a useful link onto **Route 18** (p178) to Linz in Austria. At Würzburg you can also join Route 18 northbound to follow the Main and then the Rhine valleys via Mainz and Koblenz back to Cologne. Route 16 now heads south-east into the **Harz Mountains**, the finest stretch of the entire journey, but if time is tight you can skip the hills and head directly east via Helmstedt (the former crossing point into East Germany on the transit rail route to West Berlin) to Magdeburg (ERT 866, hourly, takes 80 mins).

Goslar

Goslar has a well-preserved medieval centre full of half-timbered houses. It owed its prosperity to silver and lead mining in the Middle Ages. At its heart is the **Marktplatz**, presided over by the Rathaus and Marktkirche. It is all very fine, but in our view a shade too touristy. Quedlinburg (further east on Route 16) offers the same architectural feast but without the crowds. But Goslar is a good jumping-off point for hikes into the hills to the south.

Arrival, information, accommodation

➽ Centrally located on the edge of the Old Town. 🅑 **Tourist office**: Markt 7, ☎ 05321 780 60 (www.goslar.de). 🏨 5 mins from the centre is **Gästehaus Möller**, Schieferweg 6, ☎ 05321 230 98, €. The HI **Goslar Hostel**, Rammelsberger Str. 25, ☎ 05321 222 40 (www.jugendherberge.de) is 4 km from the rail station, on the foothill of the Rammelsberg.

Wernigerode and Quedlinburg

Wernigerode is yet another historic half-timbered town, notable for what might well be the finest **town hall** (Rathaus) in all Germany. That, and the extravagant castle, justify a stop. The town is also the start of the journey by steam train (ERT

THE HARZ MOUNTAIN RAILWAYS

Wernigerode and Quedlinburg, both on Route 16, offer a connection to Europe's most extensive narrow-gauge steam railway network, the **Harzer Schmalspurbahnen** (HSB): 161 km of deliciously scenic lines winding through the picturesque Harz Mountains. We spent three days with gorgeous early autumn weather exploring HSB routes in 2011 and were taken aback by the sheer beauty of the region. The big draw is of course the 34-km run from **Wernigerode** to the summit of the **Brocken**, but we found the less celebrated lines even more beautiful – and with trains that were happily empty.

The main axis of the HSB network is the **Harzquerbahn**, running south from Wernigerode to Nordhausen, where you can connect onto regular regional trains from Halle to Kassel (ERT 865). The Harzquerbahn also links at Eisfelder Talmühle with the narrow-gauge **Selketalbahn**, which runs through the scenic Selke Valley to Alexisbad before crossing the hills to Quedlinburg. A branch line, the **Brockenbahn**, reopened in 1992 for the first time since World War II, connects with the Harzquerbahn at Drei-Annen-Hohne, from which it ascends 19 km to the exposed summit of the Brocken. Dress warmly! For **timetables and fares**, see the HSB website (www.hsb-wr.de; see also ERT 867). Rail passes are not accepted on these lines, although HSB has its own passes which are good value if you are lingering in the area: 3 days unlimited travel on the entire HSB network is €44, 5 days is €49. A 3-day pass on the Selketalbahn is €17. Travel times are slow: see the note on p169.

867) to the top of the **Brocken**, at 1,141 m the highest summit hereabouts (see box above). Further east is the most engaging small town in the region. **Quedlinburg**, with its remarkable ensemble of **medieval buildings**, knocks spots off the Bavarian competition, and still seems undiscovered by non-Germans despite its UNESCO World Heritage status. From Quedlinburg, trains run hourly to Magdeburg (ERT 862), where you can rejoin a main line east towards Berlin.

ARRIVAL, INFORMATION, ACCOMMODATION

≈ A 15-min walk north of the city centre. 🛈 **Tourist office**: In Wernigerode: Marktpl. 10, ☎ 03943 553 7835 (www.wernigerode-tourismus.de). In Quedlinburg: Marktpl. 2, ☎ 03946 905 624 (www.quedlinburg.de).

🛏 Pensions are the best bet for reasonably priced accommodation in Wernigerode, including **Pension Kristall**, Karl-Marx-Str. 12, Elbingerode, ☎ 03945 441 235 (www.pensionkristall.de), €. A good-value and central option in Quedlinburg is the **Pension Nikolai**, Pölkenstrasse 22, ☎ 03946 528 093 (www.pension-nikolai.de), €. **Hostels**: In Wernigerode, the eco-friendly **Harz Hostel**, Schmatzfelder Str. 50-52, ☎ 03943 501 826 (www.harz-hostel.de) is 500 m from the main train station. For dorm beds in Quedlinburg, try the **youth hostel** (HI), Neuendorf 28, ☎ 03946 811 703 (www.jugendherberge.de).

BERLIN – SEE P450

Rail Route 17: To the Baltic

CITIES: ★★ CULTURE: ★ HISTORY: ★★ SCENERY: ★
COUNTRIES COVERED: GERMANY, DENMARK

Hannover is easily accessible from Amsterdam (ERT 22), Cologne (ERT 810) and Frankfurt (ERT 900) and also features on **Route 16** in this book. And here it is the starting point for a tour of three great cities that were members of the 13th- to 16th-century trading association known as the Hanseatic League — **Bremen, Hamburg** and **Lübeck**. Beyond Lübeck you can continue by a train that is loaded onto a ferry to cross to Denmark — in our opinion one of the best ways to travel to Copenhagen from western Europe.

HANNOVER — SEE P171

ROUTES NORTH

Our main route tracks north-west from Hannover (ERT 813) and follows the Weser Valley to Bremen. If Bremen does not appeal as a first stop, there is an alternative and shorter route from Hannover to Hamburg via **Celle** (ERT 900, 903). Overlooked by a magnificent 16th-century castle, Celle is among the best-preserved medieval towns in northern Germany. It also boasts one of the few synagogues in Germany to have been spared destruction by the Nazis. ✉ **Youth hostel** (HI), Weghausstr. 2, ☎ 05141 532 08 (www.jugendherberge.de/jh/celle). ❏ **Tourist office:** Markt 14–16, ☎ 05141 1212 (booking reservation service).

BREMEN

Bremen is one of Germany's foremost maritime cities. It boasts rich Hanseatic connections and traded on its links with the Americas. Bremen's wealth was based on trade in coffee and cotton and many of its 15th- and 16th-century buildings survive. Together with **Bremerhaven**, its outer harbour downstream towards the mouth of the Weser River, Bremen is one of the Länder (states) that make up Germany, continuing a proud tradition of self-government that dates back to the Middle Ages. The **Altstadt**, on the north-east bank of the river, is the main area of historical interest. The wide Marktplatz is dominated by the **Rathaus**, a 15th-century structure overlaid with a Renaissance facade. It's worth joining a tour to see the splendid interior. Don't miss the quirky statue of the **Four Musicians of Bremen** on Marktplatz, which recalls a Grimm Brothers' tale.

The 11th-century twin-spired **St Petri Dom**, Sandstr. 10–12, is sombrely beautiful. In the **Bleikeller** (basement, open Easter–Oct) are some ghoulish corpses, believed to be of men who fell from the roof during construction, and preserved from decay by the lack of air. To the south side of Marktpl. is **Böttcherstrasse** with

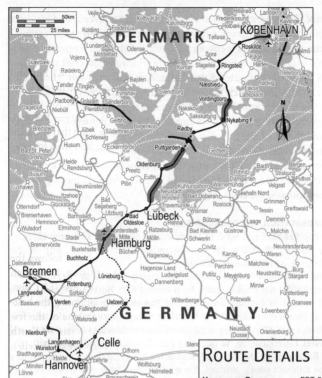

ROUTE DETAILS

Hannover–Bremen   ERT 813

Type	Frequency	Typical journey time
Train	2 per hr	59 mins

Bremen–Hamburg   ERT 800, 801

Type	Frequency	Typical journey time
Train	2 per hr	55 mins

Hamburg–Lübeck   ERT 825

Type	Frequency	Typical journey time
Train	1–2 per hr	41 mins

Lübeck–Copenhagen   ERT 50

Type	Frequency	Typical journey time
Train	4–6 daily	4h05

Hannover–Celle   ERT 900, 903

Type	Frequency	Typical journey time
Train	1–2 per hour	25 mins

Celle–Hamburg   ERT 900, 903

Type	Frequency	Typical journey time
Train	Every hour	1h09

KEY JOURNEYS

Hannover–Hamburg   ERT 900

Type	Frequency	Typical journey time
Train	2–3 per hr	1h14

Hamburg–Berlin   ERT 840

Type	Frequency	Typical journey time
Train	1–2 per hr	1h40

Hamburg–Copenhagen   ERT 50

Type	Frequency	Typical journey time
Train	4–6 daily	4h43

its eclectic mix of Jugendstil (Germany's version of art nouveau) and art deco. Today it houses cafés and artisans' workshops as well as Bremen's main casino.

The **Schnoorviertel** area (between the Dom and the river) consists of well-preserved 16th- to 18th-century buildings, many of which are now **craft shops**. Just to the east is the newly renovated **Kunsthalle**, Am Wall 207 (www.kunsthalle-bremen.de; closed Mon), which houses an impressive art collection including works of the Old Masters and French and German Impressionists.

Among other highlights are **Beck's Brewery** (English-language tours at 1400, Thur–Sat) and the fascinating excursion into the realms of science at the **Universum Science Center**, Wiener Str. 2 (www.universum-bremen.de). The **ErlebnisCARD Bremen**, available for 1 or 2 days (€8.90/10.90 one adult and two children, or €17.50/22.00 for up to five people), provides free bus travel as well as significant discounts on the city's attractions.

ARRIVAL, INFORMATION, ACCOMMODATION

⇶ **Bremen Hauptbahnhof**, just north of the main area of interest. 🛈 **Tourist office:** in main railway station, ☎ 01805 101 030 (www.bremen-tourism.de). Also at the junction of Obernstr. and Liebfrauenkirchhof.

🛏 **Hotel Gästehaus Walter**, Buntentorsteinweg 86–88, ☎ 0421 525 950 (www.hotel-walter.de) has double rooms from around €60. **Hostels**: There are quite a few hostel options in Bremen, including the **Townside Hostel**, Am Dobben 62, ☎ 0421 780 15 (www.townside.de), the **GastHaus Bremer Backpacker Hostel**, Emil-Waldmann-Strasse 5–6, ☎ 0421 223 8057 (www.bremer-backpacker-hostel.de), and the **Grand Hostel**, Feuerkuhle 30, ☎ 0421 643 7209 (www.thegrandhostel.com).

✗ The **Ratskeller** (in the Rathaus) has been a bar since the early 15th century and offers 600 different wines, although it is quite pricey. Cheap eating places can be found on and around Ostertorsteinweg.

CONNECTIONS FROM BREMEN

Germany's answer to Glastonbury, the huge **Hurricane festival**, takes place at Scheessel, just east of Bremen (direct train) in late June each year. Located 110 km north of Bremen, uninspiring **Cuxhaven** is the jumping off point for the journey to the extraordinary island of Helgoland. Trains from Bremen take 1 hr 30 mins (every hour, ERT 815). En route you pass through **Bremerhaven**, and it is worth stopping here for the fine **Deutsches Schiffahrtsmuseum** (German Ship Museum; www.dsm.museum; closed Mon in winter), where exhibits include square-riggers and a U-boat. From Cuxhaven, ferries sail to the remote island of **Helgoland**, with pleasant walks above its red craggy cliffs. Once a British possession, it was swapped for Zanzibar in 1890, and was nearly bombed to bits by RAF target practice in the immediate post-war years; it was reconstructed in 1952 and is now a busy little holiday resort. Bracing sea air and great views. **Youth hostel**: **Haus der Jugend Helgoland**, Postfach 580, 27487 Helgoland, ☎ 04725 341 (www.jugendherberge.de/jh/helgoland); Apr–Oct.

HAMBURG — SEE P485

LÜBECK

If you only have time to visit one of the old **Hanseatic towns**, make it Lübeck, a city that has cut a dash in commerce, trade and the arts for seven centuries. The 12th-century **Altstadt** (Old Town), on a moated island in a river, has been beautifully restored. Between this and the main station is Lübeck's emblem, the twin-towered **Holstentor**, a 15th-century structure and now museum, that was one of the four city gates. Get your bearings by taking the lift up the 50-m spire of the Gothic **Petrikirche** (itself now an art gallery). Nearby, **Theater Figuren Museum**, Kolk 14, is devoted to theatrical puppets, while behind the handsome facades of Grosse Petersgrube is the **Music Academy**. Both places give regular public performances. The Marktplatz is dominated by the striking L-shaped medieval **Rathaus**, typical of Lübeck's architectural style of alternating red unglazed and black glazed bricks, a trick later copied by the Dutch. Opposite the east wing is **Niederegger Haus**, Breitestr., renowned for displays of **marzipan** (the town's speciality and produced since the Middle Ages). Opposite the north wing is the brick-built 13th-century **Marienkirche** that was the model for many in the area. **Buddenbrookhaus**, the inspiration for Thomas Mann's Lübeck-based saga of the same name, is a museum at Mengstr. 4. For a different perspective on Lübeck, consider a boat trip to nearby Travemünde.

ARRIVAL, INFORMATION, ACCOMMODATION

⇝ **Lübeck Hbf**, a 10-min walk west of the Old Town. ➔ **Flughafen-Lübeck**: ☎ 0451 583 010 (www.flughafen-luebeck.de), new train station at airport or local bus every 20 mins to Lübeck. 🛈 **Tourist office**: Holstentorpl. 1, ☎ 0451 889 9700 (www.luebeck-tourismus.de). ⊨ There are several reasonably priced hotels around the station (Hbf). If you want to stay in the Altstadt, try the **Hotel zur alten Stadtmauer**, An der Mauer 57, ☎ 0451 737 02 (www.hotelstadtmauer.de), €€, or the **Hotel an der Marienkirche**, Schüsselbuden 4, ☎ 0451 799 410 (www.hotel-an-der-marienkirche.de), €€.

Hostels: The **Vor dem Burgtor Hostel** (HI), Am Gertrudenkirchhof 4, ☎ 0451 334 33 (www.jugendherberge.de) is on the edge of the Altstadt. Also well-located is the **Rucksack Hotel Lübeck**, Kanal Strasse 70, ☎ 0451 706 892 (www.rucksackhotel-luebeck.de).

ONWARD TO DENMARK

From Lübeck it is a shade over 4 hrs to **Copenhagen** (ERT 825, 720) on either the German ICE or Danish EC train. The entire train is shipped on a ferry for the 45-min sea crossing to Denmark. On peak travel days this is one route where trains can be very full, so it is worth reserving a seat. The trip from Lübeck to Denmark is through flat country with lovely water meadows and occasional glimpses of Baltic inlets, really one of our favourite rail routes in Europe.

COPENHAGEN — SEE P472

Rail Route 18:
From the Rhine to the Danube

CITIES: ★★ CULTURE: ★ HISTORY: ★★ SCENERY: ★★★
COUNTRIES COVERED: GERMANY

If pressed to nominate one route in this book as our favourite, this one would be a strong candidate. We'd say ideally take a week for this journey, if possible using mainly local trains (*Regionalzüge* in German), and stopping off here and there along the way. But many travellers are pressed for time, and even if you have only a day or two exploring Route 18, you will still find your time well spent.

The route starts with one of Europe's classic rail journeys, as the route south from **Cologne** hugs the River Rhine and then, once past **Koblenz**, follows the dramatic **Rhine Gorge**. Our route then runs up the Main Valley before cutting through forested Bavarian hill country to reach the Danube. There are **vineyards** aplenty along the way and plenty of picturesque old towns too. There are many opportunities for digressions along rural branch lines that parallel the main route.

The starting point of this route is Cologne, less than 2 hours by fast train from Brussels (ERT 20), and about 3 hours from both Paris (ERT 20) or Amsterdam (ERT 28). Cologne also features on **Route 16** in this book. Travellers from Britain can leave London on a morning departure on Eurostar and with just one change of train in Brussels be in Cologne to start Route 18 by early afternoon.

COLOGNE (KÖLN)

During World War II, nine-tenths of what was Germany's largest **Altstadt** (Old Town) was flattened by bombing, and the quality of reconstruction has been patchy. But there's much to enjoy, in the cathedral, churches and museums, and Kölners themselves have an irresistible verve, exemplified in the city's pre-Lent **carnival**, reaching its peak on Shrove Tuesday. The twin spires of the **Dom** (cathedral), one of the world's greatest Gothic buildings, soar over the Rhineland capital, and greet the visitor arriving at Cologne's main station. Climb the tower for a splendid view of the city, the River Rhine and a largely industrial hinterland. Lively Cologne has a large Turkish minority. The city boasts excellent beer (look for the local *Kölsch*).

The city's Roman traces include remnants of the original 5th-century city wall. The excellent **Römisch-Germanisches Museum**, Roncallipl. 4, holds many of the finds of the ancient town, including an arched fortress gate and the famous Dionysus Mosaic. By the 13th century, Cologne was a thriving metropolis of 40,000 people, protected by Europe's longest city walls — a 6-km rampart pierced by 12 massive gates. Within the original city wall stand a dozen Romanesque churches, Germany's finest such architectural concentration. The most striking are **Gross St Martin**, overlooking the Rhine in the Altstadt, and **St Aposteln**. From 321 until

KEY JOURNEYS

Cologne–Frankfurt — ERT 910, 911

Type	Frequency	Typical journey time
Train	2–3 per hr	1h04 (high-speed line) 2h20 (Rhine Valley route)

Frankfurt–Munich — ERT 920

Type	Frequency	Typical journey time
Train	Every hr	3h11

Notes

Travelling south from Cologne along the Rhine Valley, choose your train carefully. Most ICEs heading out of Cologne towards Frankfurt-am-Main take a new fast route to the east of the Rhine Valley. Ignore services that don't stop at Koblenz, as the finest of the classic Rhine Gorge scenery lies immediately south of Koblenz, upstream towards Mainz.

ROUTE DETAILS

Cologne–Bonn — ERT 800, 802

Type	Frequency	Typical journey time
Train	4 per hr	19 mins

Bonn–Koblenz — ERT 800, 802

Type	Frequency	Typical journey time
Train	3 per hr	32 mins

Koblenz–Frankfurt — ERT 911, 914

Type	Frequency	Typical journey time
Train	1–2 per hr	1h25

Frankfurt–Würzburg — ERT 920, 921

Type	Frequency	Typical journey time
Train	1–2 per hr	1h10

Würzburg–Nuremberg — ERT 900, 920, 921

Type	Frequency	Typical journey time
Train	2 per hr	54 mins

Nuremberg–Regensburg — ERT 920, 921

Type	Frequency	Typical journey time
Train	Every hr	51 mins

Regensburg–Passau — ERT 920, 921

Type	Frequency	Typical journey time
Train	Every hr	1h03

Passau–Linz — ERT 962

Type	Frequency	Typical journey time
Train	Every 1–2 hrs	1h10

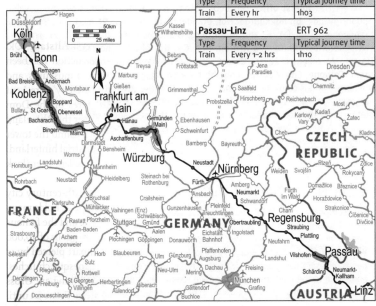

1424, the city was home to one of the most important Jewish communities in Germany. The remains of a *mikvah* (a Jewish ritual bath) dating from 1170 are preserved under a glass pyramid in the middle of the square of the City Hall. Nearby, in Bischofsgartenstr., is a modern complex incorporating the **Philharmonie**, the **Agfa-Foto-Historama**, covering all things photographic, and the **Museum Ludwig** (closed Mon), which houses 20th-century works including those of Kirchner, Beckmann and Dix and an excellent collection of pop art (Warhol, Lichtenstein and more). The outstanding **Wallraf-Richartz-Museum**, with superb 14th- to 16th-century paintings by the Cologne school and an excellent café, is at Martinstr. 39, about a 10-min walk from the **Dom**. For information about all these museums, and more, check out www.museenkoeln.de. The **Kwartier Lateng**, Barbarossa Pl. (U-Bahn lines 12/15/16/18), and the **Südstadt** are good places to chill out. The Altstadt has several good music venues. There are two good monthly listings mags: *Live!* (free) and *Kölner Illustrierte* (€1).

ARRIVAL, INFORMATION, ACCOMMODATION

≈ **Köln Hbf**, centrally placed, right by the cathedral with a huge shopping centre, left luggage, information desk, currency exchange and service point; station closes 0100–0400. ➔ **Flughafen Köln–Bonn**, south-east of the city. Information ☎ 02203 404 001 (www.koeln-bonn-airport.de). S-Bahn trains take 15 mins and run every 20 mins, direct to Köln Hbf (see ERT 802). **ℹ Tourist office**: Kardinal-Höffner Pl. 1, ☎ 0221 221 304 00 (www.koelntourismus.de) by the Dom. Also at Köln–Bonn airport.

🛏 The **Tourist office** can book hotels (www.koelntourismus.de). Good value options include: **Brandenburger Hof**, Brandenburger Str. 2–4, ☎ 0221 122 889 (www.brandenburgerhof.de), €, and **Hotel Berg**, Brandenburger Str. 6, ☎ 0221 912 9162 (www.hotel-berg.com), 100 m from Hbf, €€. **Hostels:** Try the **Station Backpackers Hostel**, Marzellenstr. 44–56, ☎ 0221 912 5301 (www.hostel-cologne.de), the **Meininger Cologne City Centre**, Engelbertstrasse 33–35, ☎ 0221 924 090 (www.meininger-hotels.com) or the more central of the two HI hostels, **Köln-Deutz**, Siegesstr. 5A, ☎ 0221 814 711 (www.jugendherberge.de), a 15-min walk from the station, over the Hohenzollernbrücke, a couple of blocks south of Deutz station.

✗ A typical Cologne dish is *Sauerbraten*, a 'sour roast', with beef soaked in vinegar and stewed, served with *Kartoffelklösse* (potato dumplings) and apple sauce. *Blootwoosch* (black pudding) makes a snack served with mustard on a bread roll,

GETTING AROUND COLOGNE

The comprehensive public transport system includes U-Bahn (underground), S-Bahn (surface suburban trains), trams and buses. **Day Tickets** valid for up to five people are still great value for two people travelling together. The 24-hr **Köln Welcome Card** (available from tourist offices and hotels) exists in three different bands, offering free public transport within Cologne and the region, up to 50% off admission to the city's museums and attractions, and further reductions. The card is available for a single person (€9/13/24) or a group of up to five people (€19/29/49).

known as 'Cologne caviar'. A dish that sounds like half a chicken (*Halve Huhn*) is actually just a cheese roll. Many local beer-pubs (*Brauhäuser*) offer good-value food.

BONN

With its small-town atmosphere, it is hard to believe that Bonn was still a capital city just 22 years ago. Packed with students and top-notch cultural attractions, Bonn is a lively stopover for a day or two. All the central areas are very walkable, and the pubs near the river do a roaring trade at night. Deprived of its capital city status, Bonn now makes the most of its musical connections, of which Beethoven is the biggest. The **Beethoven-Haus-Museum**, where the composer spent the first 22 years of his life, is at Bonngasse 20 and contains his instruments and a rather sad collection of ear trumpets testifying to his irreversible decline into total deafness.

Just west of the rail station, the **Rheinisches Landesmuseum**, Colmantstr. 14–16 (www.rlmb.lvr.de), has everything from old skulls to Celtic gold. The **Museumsmeile** (Museum Mile) is a complex south-east of the main station, easily reached by U-Bahn lines 16/63/66/67/68 (stop: Heussallee/Museumsmeile) or 🚌 610/611 (stop: Bundeskanzlerpl.). It includes (all closed Mon) **Museum Alexander Koenig** (Natural History Museum; www.zfmk.de), the **Kunst- und Ausstellungshalle** (for art exhibitions; www.kah-bonn.de), the **Kunstmuseum Bonn** (City Art Gallery; www.kunstmuseum-bonn.de), the **Haus der Geschichte**, Willy-Brandt-Allee 14 (www.hdg.de), with excellent and very self-critical displays on German history (free entry) and the **Deutsches Museum Bonn** (for German technology; www.deutsches-museum.de/bonn). To recover from museum-fatigue, head for the Altstadt or Südstadt for beer aplenty. **Brauhaus Bönnsch** (at Sterntorbrücke 4) is an excellent pub that brews a local beer called Bönnsch, with local food specialities to match.

ARRIVAL, INFORMATION, ACCOMMODATION

🚆 **Bonn Hbf**, beside the bus terminal and right in the centre, near the pedestrian precinct. 🄸 **Tourist office**: Windeckstr.1/am Münsterpl., ☎ 0228 775 000 (www.bonn.de). There is a hotel booking service: ☎ 0228 910 4170 (www.bonn-region.de). 🛏 **Hotel Aigner**, Dorotheenstr. 12, ☎ 0228 604 060 (www.hotel-aigner.de), €; **Bergmann**, Kasernenstr. 13, ☎ 0228 633 891 (www.hotel-bergmann-bonn.de), €. **Hostels**: There are a couple of options, for example **Bonn Hostel** (HI): Haager Weg 42, ☎ 0228 289 970 (www.bonn.jugendherberge.de) or **Max Hostel**, Maxstrasse 7, ☎ 0228 8234 5780 (www.max-hostel.de).

KOBLENZ

Koblenz is a name intimately associated with travel: it was here that Karl Baedeker started publishing his famous guidebooks to Europe in 1823. The

Moselle and Rhine rivers meet here at the **Deutsches Eck** (the German Corner), marked by a massive, heavy-handed monument to Kaiser Wilhelm I. The pleasant gardens that line the banks of both rivers combine to provide an attractive 8-km stroll. **Ehrenbreitstein** (across the Rhine, ferries in summer) is dominated by an enormous **fortress**, begun in the 12th century, but grown to its present size during the 16th century. The **Sesselbahn** (cable car) operates Easter–end Oct. As well as providing a fantastic view, the fortress contains two regional museums and a youth hostel. A big firework display (**Rhein in Flammen**) is staged here on the second Saturday in August.

ARRIVAL, INFORMATION, ACCOMMODATION

⇌ **Koblenz Hbf**, Bahnhofpl. 2, south-west of the centre, a 25-min walk downhill (or 🚌 1) to the riverside area from which cruises (*Rheinfähre*) depart. 🄱 **Tourist office**: Bahnhofspl. 17 (opposite rail station), ☎ 0261 313 04 (www.touristik-koblenz.de). It provides boat schedules and a city map that includes listings. There is another tourist office in the historic Rathaus (town hall), Jesuitenpl. 2.

🛏 The **Hotel Jan van Werth**, v.-Werth-Str. 9, ☎ 0261 365 00 (www.hoteljanvanwerth.de), € and **Hotel Grebel**, Planstr. 7–9, in the Güls district, ☎ 0261 425 30 (www.hotel-grebel.de), €, are reasonable. A chain hotel, but close to the station and good value, is the **Ibis Koblenz**, Rizzastrasse 42, ☎ 0261 302 40 (www.accorhotels.com), €€. **Hostels**: The HI **youth hostel** is housed in the Festung, ☎ 0261 972 870 (www.jugendherberge.de), and is popular, so book well ahead. The downside is that the ferry and chairlift both stop very early so, after taking a bus (🚌 7/8/9/10) to Charlottenstr., you end the day with a long uphill climb. **Campingplatz Rhein-Mosel**, Schartwiesenweg 6, ☎ 0261 827 19 (www.camping-rhein-mosel.de) is at Lutzel, across the Mosel. There's a ferry across during the day.

🗶 Some food bargains are found by indulging in the *Stehcafés* (standing cafés) and beer gardens on the banks of the Rhine, just by the **Deutsches Eck**.

SOUTH FROM KOBLENZ

From Koblenz to **Frankfurt-am-Main**, express trains all keep to the west bank of the Rhine (ERT 912). Devotees of slow travel can choose between local trains on either bank of the Rhine (both ERT 914 where the upper table shows east bank trains) or even travel upsteam by boat (ERT 914a). Any of the **riverside villages** along this stretch of the Rhine are marvellous spots to linger. Our favourites are **St Goar** on the west bank opposite the famous **Lorelei rock**, and **Lorch** on the east side of the river. Ferries cross the river at almost every village, allowing travellers to mix and match the two routes.

FRANKFURT-AM-MAIN

After the rural demeanour of the Rhine Gorge, Frankfurt with its brash Manhattan-style skyline comes as a shock. The city that is home to the European

Rhine versus Moselle

Travellers at Koblenz face big decisions. Most continue up the Rhine and indeed that is just what Route 18 does. But you can also forsake the Rhine in favour of the Moselle, following the lesser river upstream towards **Trier** and Luxembourg. Ideally do both, by making a side trip some way along the Moselle Valley, then return to Koblenz before continuing south through the Rhine Gorge. The Moselle Valley is softer, gentler and prettier than the rugged Rhine and we think it would be a big mistake to skip the Moselle. It takes less than 2 hours to reach either Trier or **Traben-Trarbach** from Koblenz. The latter involves an easy change of train at Bullay (ERT 915). Opt for Traben-Trarbach if you want to catch the flavour of a classic Moselle wine town. Traben-Trarbach nestles on the bank of the sinuous Moselle surrounded by vineyards.

Trier is less of a wine town, less evidently connected to the Moselle than Traben-Trarbach, but offers a big dose of history and culture. The highlight in Trier is the **Porta Nigra** (Black Gate), one of the most impressive Roman structures north of the Alps. You can also see Emperor Constantine's throne room and part of a Roman street in the huge **Konstantin-Basilika**, Konstantinpl., part of the Imperial Palace, and the largest surviving single-hall structure of the ancient world. Backing onto it is the picture-perfect pink, white and gold rococo **Kurfürstliches Palais** in gardens with fountains (and a café). This area leads directly to the **Rheinisches Landesmuseum**, Weimarer Allee 1 (www.landesmuseum-trier.de).

Close by are the **Kaiserthermen**, a huge complex of well-preserved imperial baths, and the **Amphitheatre** (c. AD 100), where crowds of up to 20,000 watched gladiatorial combat. Sedate Trier was the birthplace of Karl Marx, and the house where he was born at Brückenstr. 10 has a superb exhibition on his life and work (closed Monday mornings Nov–Mar). ⬛ **Tourist office**: Porta Nigra, ☎ 0651 978 080 (www.trier.de). ◄ **Hilles Hostel**, Gartenfeld Strasse 7, ☎ 0651 710 2785 (www.hilles-hostel-trier.de) has private doubles and singles, as well as dorm rooms, and is close to the main station.

From Trier, it is less than an hour by train to Luxembourg City (ERT 915), where you can join **Route 14**, speed west to Paris by fast TGV service (ERT 390) or head south through Alsace to Strasbourg and Switzerland (ERT 385).

Central Bank and Germany's largest stock exchange doesn't rely on tourism, but the traffic-free boulevards with shops, parks and the leafy banks of the River Main, which flows through the centre, make Frankfurt very pleasant to stroll around. Römerberg, a square of half-timbered and steeply gabled buildings, is at the heart of the **Altstadt** (Old Town). Along one side is the **Römer**, the medieval town hall, which has been meticulously restored.

A short walk to the east leads to **Kaiserdom**, Domstr., the red-sandstone Gothic cathedral with its dome and lantern tower, where emperors were crowned (www.dom-frankfurt.de). Frankfurt was the birthplace of Germany's most famous writer, Goethe. The **Goethe Haus**, Grosser Hirschgraben 23, is a careful post-war reconstruction of the house where he was born in 1749 (www.goethehaus-frankfurt.de). The old **Sachsenhausen** district, reached by crossing the Alte Brücke (Old Bridge), has a village-like feel with its cobbled alleys of half-timbered houses. To the north (U-Bahn 6/7 to Westend) are the botanic gardens, **Palmengarten**, Zeppelinallee, with lily ponds and conservatories of orchids and cacti. Twelve of the city's 40 museums are gathered on the south bank of the river along Schaumainkai, known as **Museumsufer** (Museum Bank).

ARRIVAL, INFORMATION, ACCOMMODATION

⇌ Hauptbahnhof (Hbf), almost a city unto itself, bustles day and night and has good cafés and shops. The city centre is a 15-min walk straight ahead along Kaiserstr. **✈ Flughafen Frankfurt-Main** (9 km south-west of the city) is Germany's busiest airport. ☎ 069 6900 (www.frankfurt-airport.de). S-Bahn line 8 to Frankfurt Hbf leaves the airport every 15 mins; the journey takes 12 mins (ERT 917a). Long-distance trains leave from Frankfurt Flughafen Fernbahnhof. Direct services are available to Cologne, Dortmund, Hamburg, Nuremberg, Stuttgart, Munich, Freiburg and Basel. Note that Ryanair flies to the misleadingly named **Frankfurt Hahn** airport (www.flyhahn.com); buses connect with flights (journey 2 hrs, €12; to Cologne, 2 hr 15 mins, €15; and Heidelberg, 2 hr 20 mins, €20). **🛈 Tourist office**: at Hauptbahnhof (Hbf) and also at Römerberg 27, ☎ 069 2123 8800 (www.frankfurt-tourismus.de). Hotel booking service: ☎ 069 2123 0808.

✉ The **Hotel Cult**, Offenbacherlandstr. 56, ☎ 069 9624 460 (www.hotelcult.de), €–€€, is stylish and reasonably priced. Close to the train station is the highly recommended **Five Elements Hostel**, Moselstrasse 40, ☎ 069 2400 5885 (www.5elementshostel.de). A little further out is the **Haus der Jugend Hostel** (HI), Deutschherrnufer 12, ☎ 069 610 0150 (www.jugendherberge-frankfurt.de). **Campsite: City Camp Frankfurt**, An der Sandelmühle 35, in Heddernheim, ☎ 069 570 332 (www.city-camp-frankfurt.de).

✗ A range of cuisines are represented, and there's a plentiful choice of *Lokale* (taverns) serving local and regional treats like *Eisbein* (stewed pork knuckle), *Handkäse mit Musik* (sour cheese garnished with onions and caraway seeds) and

GETTING AROUND FRANKFURT

Travel within Frankfurt is easy, with an efficient combination of S-Bahn (overground) and U-Bahn (underground) trains, trams and buses all run by **RMV**, the regional transport authority. Directions to the system, in six languages, including English, are on the blue automatic ticket machines at all bus stops, tram stops and stations. **Transport information:** ☎ 01805 768 46 36. Buy **tickets** (valid for all RMV transportation) at newspaper booths and blue machines. If you are making more than two trips a day, it's worth buying a day pass. The **Frankfurt Card**, available from tourist offices for 24 hours (€8.90) or 48 hours (€12.90), gives unlimited travel on all public transport, including local and S-Bahn trains to the airport, as well as half-price admission to 20 museums, 20% discount on river cruises, plus other benefits. To book a taxi, ☎ 230 001, 250 001, 230 033 or 545 011. The shortest taxi rides cost about six times as much as a single RMV ticket. Bikes can be hired at the rail station.

Sauerkraut. Above all, of course, there's the original *Frankfurter* – long, thin and tastiest eaten at a *Schnell Imbiss* (street stall) in a fresh roll. You'll find a good selection of restaurants along Fressgasse and the narrow streets running north. For the more informal *Lokale*, head south of the river to the **Sachsenhausen** district around Schweizerstr., or the cobbled Grosse Rittergasse and Kleine Rittergasse. Try the heady *Äppelwoi* cider and enjoy the local *Hochheimer* wine.

HIGHLIGHTS AND EVENTS

For hints on happenings and clubs, look to the following listings magazines: *Prinz* (www.prinz.de), *Kultur News, Frizz* or *Strandgut* (www.strandgut.de). Kleine Bockenheimer Str. has a good jazz scene. Try the **Jazzkeller** (www.jazzkeller.com; from 2100, closed Mon). An evening 'must' is to wander over the Main bridges to **Sachsenhausen** to the many pubs where the local tipple, called *Äppelwoi*, is consumed in truly impressive quantities. There's an alternative scene in the city's Bockenheim district, where, particularly in Leipziger Str., you'll find a good choice of cheap cafés. Each year in mid-October, the city hosts the world's largest book fair.

CONNECTIONS FROM FRANKFURT

Frankfurt is a major international rail junction and has services to **Amsterdam** (ERT 28), **Vienna** (ERT 28), **Paris** (ERT 30), **Berlin** (ERT 902) and **Switzerland** (ERT 73).

INTO BAVARIA

Frankfurt is just a stone's throw from the Bavarian border. Our route heads up the Main Valley and **Aschaffenburg**, the first stop for many fast trains, already oozes Bavarian atmosphere. From Aschaffenburg, there is an especially beautiful alternative route to Würzburg (ERT 926 to Lauda, then ERT 922 to Würzburg).

WÜRZBURG – SEE P204

NUREMBERG (NÜRNBERG)

The poet Longfellow had mixed feelings about Nuremberg, calling it "a quaint old town of toil and traffic." Nowadays the city of *Lebkuchen* (a speciality Advent gingerbread) and *Bratwurst* is trying to cast off its associations with Nazi rallies and war trials. Heading north from the station, you immediately enter the Old Town with its impressive **Stadtbefestigung** (city wall). Beyond the **Schöner Brunnen** (Beautiful Fountain), the spacious **Hauptmarkt** (market square) makes a perfect setting for one of Germany's liveliest Christmas markets. For a good view of the whole city, seek out the terraces of the **Kaiserburg** fortifications above the north-west corner of the Old Town. Below it nestles Nuremberg's prettiest corner, including the gabled **Albrecht Dürerhaus**. The artist Dürer lived here from 1509 until his death in 1528. It is furnished in period style and contains several of his woodcuts (closed Mon). The **Germanisches Nationalmuseum**, Kartäusergasse 1 (www.gnm.de), founded in 1852, houses the country's largest collection of German art and culture (closed Mon, free entry Wed 1800–2100). Hitler's mass rallies were held in the vast **Reichsparteitagsgelände** (in the Luitpoldhain, in the south-eastern suburbs), a huge area with a parade ground, stadium and the shell of a massive congress hall that was never completed. One of the remaining parts, the Zeppelin grandstand (S-Bahn line 2 to Frankenstadion) hosts an exhibition called *Faszination und Gewalt* (Fascination and Violence).

After World War II, the surviving Nazi leaders were put on trial in the city's court, Fürtherstr. 110, on the western outskirts (U-Bahn line 1 to Bärenschanze). The tourist office has a brochure on Nazi Nuremberg.

ARRIVAL, INFORMATION, ACCOMMODATION

≋ **Nürnberg Hbf**, on the southern edge of the Old Town, a 5-min walk to Hauptmarkt via the underpass. **❶ Tourist office**: Konigstr. 93 (opposite the railway station), ☎ 0911 233 60 (www.tourismus.nuernberg.de) and at Hauptmarkt 18. Hotel booking service. ◢ Clean, comfortable and close to the station, the Nuremberg city branch of **Motel One**, Bahnhofstrasse 18, ☎ 0911 2743 170 (www.motel-one.com), €–€€€, is a good option for those travelling on a budget. If you are looking for a **hostel** try either the **Lette'm Sleep**, Frauentormauer 42, ☎ 0911 9928 128 (www.backpackers.de) or the **Nuremberg Youth Hostel** (HI), Burg 2, ☎ 0911 2309 360 (www.jugendherberge.de), which is housed in the 500-year-old former imperial stables.

✗ The Tiergartenpl. is a good place to go in the evenings, with music, nightlife and drinking. Don't forget to taste some *Lebkuchen* (spiced gingerbread), a local speciality that, though widely exported, still tastes best here.

ONWARD FROM NUREMBERG

Our route now leaves the Main Valley and cuts through low hills to the Danube Valley. Alternatively, an exceptionally beautiful rural route leads through the hills of Franconia and Saxony direct to **Dresden** (ERT 880). You can also head east on **Route 47** to Prague and the Tatra Mountains. There are twice daily direct trains to Prague (ERT 885) as well as an express bus run by Deutsche Bahn. Nuremberg also has hourly fast trains to **Berlin** via **Leipzig** (ERT 851). Just 45 mins north of Nuremberg on the Berlin route is Bamberg, arguably the most beautiful small town in Bavaria. It makes an easy day trip from Nuremberg. The most striking areas of Bamberg are just a 15-min walk from the station.

REGENSBURG

Sitting at the confluence of the Regen and the Danube, Regensburg has leapt to prominence since its Old Town (Altstadt) was awarded UNESCO World

Heritage status in 2006. With the knobbly twin towers of the grey stone **cathedral** dominant on the skyline, and a cheerful huddle of stone houses and red roofs, Regensburg boasts 1,300 listed buildings of historical importance. It has preserved its medieval character particularly well. Pretty pastel plasterwork, in pinks, yellows and greens, and decorative towers on many of the former patrician houses in the narrow streets lend it a southern feel. The town had strong trading links with Venice in the 13th century, when its merchants grew rich from the selling of silk, spices and slaves. They competed to have the biggest house (often incorporating its own chapel) in the style of an Italian fortified palace with the highest tower on top — these were never defensive, just status symbols. The most striking of the 20 surviving towers is the **Baumburger Turm**, Watmarkt, though the highest is the nine-storey **Goldener Turm**, Wahlenstr. Some of the chapels have been turned into restaurants but the tiny **Maria-Läng Kapelle**, Pfarrgasse, is still in use.

Domstadt, the church area, centres on **Dom St Peter**, the magnificent Gothic cathedral. Started in the 13th century, its 105-m spires were completed six centuries later. It has fine stained glass, medieval and modern, and its own interior well. The exterior of **Alte Kapelle**, Alte Kornmarkt, belies the wealth of rococo decorations within, including a marble altar and superb frescoes. The **Porta Praetoria** archway, Unter den Schwibbögen, is part of 2nd-century Roman defences. The south-western part of town was formerly the monastic quarter and many of the old buildings survive. At the far end, the former Benedictine monastery of **St Emmeram** was once a great centre of learning. The 12th-century 14-arch **Steinerne Brücke** over the Danube gives the best view of the medieval spires, towers and battlements along the waterfront. **Schloss Thurn und Taxis**, Emmeramspl., consists of Benedictine buildings that were turned into luxurious residences in Napoleonic times. Hourly cruises around the city are available from Easter to the end of October with Regensburger Personenschifffahrt Klinger (www.schifffahrtklinger.de; €7.50 or €4.80 with student card).

ARRIVAL, INFORMATION, ACCOMMODATION

≋ **Regensburg Hbf**, a 10-min walk from the historic centre, or take the *Altstadtbus*. 🛈 **Tourist office**: Altes Rathaus, Rathausplatz 4, ☎ 0941 507 4410 (www.regensburg.de). Accommodation booking service.

🛏 Two options on the same street are the **Hotel Zum Fröhlichen Türken**, Fröhliche-Türken-Str. 11, ☎ 0941 53651 (www.hotel-zum-froehlichen-tuerken.de), €, and **Am Peterstor**, Fröhliche-Türken-Str. 12, ☎ 0941 54545 (www.hotel-am-peterstor.de), €–€€. **Hostels**: The **Brook Lane Hostel**, Obere Bachgasse 21, ☎ 0941 690 0966 (www.hostel-regensburg.de) is centrally located and also has double rooms. The **Youth hostel** (HI) is at Wöhrdstr. 60, ☎ 0941 57402 (www.jugendherberge.de), on an island in the Danube, a 5-min walk from the centre.

✗ Regensburg hosts two annual beer festivals, one in May (Maidult) and one in late August (Herbstdult). With a high student population, there's a good choice of eateries in the city centre. The 850-year-old **Historische Wurstküche**, Weisse Lamm Gasse 3, by the Danube, is Germany's oldest sausage house and sells nothing else; note the flood marks on the walls. **Alte Linde Biergarten**, Müllerstr. 1, on an island, is a lovely beer garden overlooking the Old Town.

PASSAU

The captivating cathedral city of Passau is a watery place, with the flood-prone city sitting at the confluence of the Danube, Inn and the Ilz rivers. With the exception of the **Veste Oberhaus**, a castle high on a hill across the Danube, everything of interest is within close range. The oldest part lies between the Danube and Inn; most of it postdates a major 17th-century fire and is an enjoyable jumble of colour-washed stone walls, assorted towers, and baroque, rococo and neoclassical styles. Like Regensburg, it is quite Italian in feel.

Check out **Stephansdom** (St Stephen's Cathedral) which has one of the world's largest church organs with over 17,000 pipes. Veste Oberhaus, the former palace of the bishops, is on a peninsula between the Danube and the Ilz. It's a steep walk, but regular bus services run from the rail station and Rathauspl. The stronghold, which offers a view over the confluence of the rivers, is now a museum documenting the history of Passau and its surroundings (closed in winter).

Another, more accessible viewpoint is the **Fünfersteg** footbridge, looking over the Inn towards the **Innstadt** on the opposite bank. River ferries leave from the quayside, along Fritz-Schäffer-Promenade, in front of the Rathaus, and offer day and longer trips up and down the Danube.

ARRIVAL, INFORMATION, ACCOMMODATION

⇌ **Passau Hbf**, west of the centre, a 10-min walk to the right along Bahnhofstr. **ⓘ Tourist offices**: Main office: Rathauspl. 3, ☎ 0851 955 980 (www.passau.de). Also a branch at Bahnhofstr. 28, opposite the rail station. Room reservation service.

🛏 The **Hendl House Hotel** is located in the Old Town at Grosse Klingergasse 17, ☎ 0851 33069 (www.hendlhousehotel.com), €–€€. **Youth hostel** (HI): **Veste Oberhaus**, Oberhaus 125, ☎ 0851 493 780 (www.jugendherberge.de) is in the castle across the Danube. Cross the bridge by the docks and be prepared for a steep climb, or take 🚋 1/2/3/4 to the door.

✗ Reasonably-priced restaurants spill out onto the promenades beside the Danube in summer, particularly around Rathauspl.

ONWARD TO AUSTRIA

Our route crosses the Austrian border and cuts through rolling hills to regain the Danube Valley at Linz. For more on Linz see p284. At Linz you can continue east on **Route 32** to Vienna and Slovakia, or follow Route 32 westbound to Salzburg, the Austrian Tyrol and Switzerland.

Rail Route 19: Bavaria and the Black Forest

CITIES: ★★ CULTURE: ★ HISTORY: ★★ SCENERY: ★★★
COUNTRIES COVERED: GERMANY

This tour takes in some of southern Germany's most spectacular rail routes. It is a tour for all seasons, and, if you like snowy landscapes, Route 19 would be as good in winter as in mid-summer. The high point is the stretch of railway that cuts through the **Schwarzwald** (Black Forest) leaving the Rhine Valley at Offenburg and running, via a tortuous series of hairpins and tunnels, over the hills to the **Bodensee** (Lake Constance) at Germany's border with Austria and Switzerland.

The prelude is no less distinguished, heading out from Munich to the beautifully sited old university town of **Heidelberg** via **Augsburg** (a starting point for visiting the amazing **Ludwig II castles** near Füssen) and **Ulm** — with its stupendously tall cathedral spire. **Stuttgart** has one of the world's greatest modern buildings in the Neue Staatsgalerie. You can shorten the route by going directly from Stuttgart to Konstanz, taking in the improbably perfect-looking hill town of **Rottweil**. And we throw in another alternative, the beautiful Danube Valley railway south-west from Ulm, that can be used to make this route into a circular tour.

MUNICH — SEE P526

AUGSBURG

Just a stone's throw from Munich, Augsburg nowadays is overshadowed by its larger Bavarian neighbour. But there was a time when Augsburg was respected as one of the largest and most influential centres in all Europe. Be it as a hub for finance and trade, in its social programmes to alleviate poverty or as a centre of Jewish life and culture, Augsburg towered above its rivals. The key to this was two families, the Welsers and the Fuggers who, in the early 16th century, dominated Augsburg life. The main sights are within walking distance of the central pedestrianised Rathausplatz, with its distinctive onion-domed **Rathaus** (painstakingly rebuilt after World War II). There's a great view from the adjoining **Perlachturm** (70 m, open May–Oct). A short stroll east down narrow alleys leads to the **Fuggerei**, a pioneering 'village' that the Fugger brothers built in 1516 as accommodation for the poor, who were requested to pray for the Fuggers in lieu of paying rent. Augsburg's merchants lived in style in the stately mansions that still set the tone of Maximilianstr., where the **Schaezler Palace**, an 18th-century rococo edifice with a sumptuous banquet hall, now houses the state art gallery. There is a predictably imposing cathedral on the hilly north side of the city centre, and, just a stone's throw from the Hauptbahnhof (on Halderstr. 8), one of Germany's most remarkable synagogues.

⇗ **Augsburg Hbf**, a wonderful building just a 10-min walk west of the city centre.
🚉 **Tourist office**: Rathausplatz 1, ☎ 0821 502 070 (www.augsburg-tourismus.de).
Reservations for accommodation.

🛏 An inexpensive option is **Pension Märkl**, Schillstr. 20, ☎ 0821 791 499 (www.
pension-maerkl.de), €; a bit pricier is **Pension Herrenhäuser**, Georgenstr 6,
☎ 0821 346 3173 (www.pensionherrenhaeuser.online.de), €. **Hostels**: Just south of
the cathedral is the **Übernacht Hostel**, Karlstrasse 4, ☎ 0821 4554 2828 (www.
uebernacht-hostel.de). Also within walking distance of the Old Town is the **Jugendherberge Augsburg** (HI), Unterer Graben 6, ☎ 0821 780 8890 (www.djh.de).
✗ There's no shortage of places to eat in the Old Town, mostly offering hearty local
Swabian or Bavarian dishes. Plenty of jolly beer cellars too.

CONNECTIONS FROM AUGSBURG

Among Bavaria's star attractions are the Royal Castles (see box below), built at
preposterous expense by King Ludwig II in the 19th century. The easiest way of getting
to **Neuschwanstein** and **Hohenschwangau** is to take the train to **Füssen**, an attractive
old town beneath the mountains, served by trains from Augsburg (2 hrs, ERT 935).
🛏 There's an HI youth hostel in Mariahilferstr. 5, ☎ 08362 7754 (www.
jugendherberge.de/jh/fuessen). From Füssen, numerous buses make the short
journey to the castles.

For **Linderhof**, there are regular buses from **Oberammergau** (reached from
Munich via Murnau, 2 hrs, ERT 895 then 897), a touristy but attractive small Alpine
town celebrated for its Passion Play, performed only every ten years (the next one is
in 2020). In the meantime you can visit the theatre and see the props and costumes.

KING LUDWIG'S CASTLES

Just over the road from Schwangau (and 4 km from Füssen), Hohenschwangau and
Neuschwanstein are within walking distance of each other (involving a modest
climb). Tudor-style **Hohenschwangau** (www.hohenschwangau.de), built in the early
19th century by Maximilian II, was an attempt to recreate the romantic past and was
adorned with Wagnerian references by his son, King Ludwig II. Ludwig surpassed his
father by building the fairy-tale neo-Gothic **Neuschwanstein** on a rocky outcrop high
above (www.neuschwanstein.de). It is best seen from the dizzying heights of the
Marienbrücke, a bridge spanning a huge gorge. This most famous of his castles was
never finished – hence the Throne Room without a throne, and doorways leading to
suicidal drops. The third castle, **Linderhof**, 20 km east, is a small French-style
château, modelled on the Petit Trianon at Versailles near Paris. The outstanding
oddity is the king's dining table, engineered to be lowered to the kitchens and then
raised again for him to dine entirely alone.

A fourth castle is **Herrenchiemsee** on a wooded island on the Chiemsee south-
east of Munich. Built in the style of Versailles, this building has a hall of mirrors but
remains unfinished (train from Munich to Prien am Chiemsee; ERT 890, hourly, 1 hr,
then ferry). He lived here for only a week, before mysteriously drowning.

Notes

Route 19 includes two alternatives, both via pretty routes, that can be used to abbreviate the journey. Both are shown as dotted lines on the map above. Ulm to Immendingen takes 2h09 and trains run every 2 hrs (ERT 938). Hourly trains from Stuttgart to Singen take 1h54 to 2h20 (ERT 940). If you wish to travel directly from Konstanz to Heidelberg, change at Karlsruhe.

KEY JOURNEYS

Konstanz–Heidelberg   ERT 912, 913, 916

Type	Frequency	Typical journey time
Train	Every hr	4h03

Heidelberg–Munich   ERT 912, 930

Type	Frequency	Typical journey time
Train	Every hr	3h03

Stuttgart–Munich   ERT 930

Type	Frequency	Typical journey time
Train	1–2 per hr	2h21

ROUTE DETAILS

Munich–Augsburg   ERT 905, 930

Type	Frequency	Typical journey time
Train	3–4 per hr	38 mins

Augsburg–Ulm   ERT 930

Type	Frequency	Typical journey time
Train	2–3 per hr	46 mins

Ulm–Stuttgart   ERT 930

Type	Frequency	Typical journey time
Train	3–4 per hr	56 mins

Stuttgart–Heidelberg   ERT 912, 924

Type	Frequency	Typical journey time
Train	Every hr	1h56 (via Heilbronn)
Train	1–2 per hr	39 mins (direct)

Heidelberg–Karlsruhe   ERT 912, 913

Type	Frequency	Typical journey time
Train	1–2 per hr	36 mins

Karlsruhe–Baden Baden   ERT 912, 916

Type	Frequency	Typical journey time
Train	1–2 per hr	19 mins

Baden Baden–Triberg   ERT 916

Type	Frequency	Typical journey time
Train	Every hr	1h08

Triberg–Konstanz   ERT 916

Type	Frequency	Typical journey time
Train	Every hr	1h32

Alternatively you can go by **Europabus** (🚌 190), which follows the celebrated Romantic Road from Frankfurt to Füssen via Würzburg, Rothenburg, Dinkelsbühl, Nördlingen, Augsburg and several other historic towns (20% discount for holders of Eurail and German Rail passes; reservation strongly recommended, ☎ 0171 653 2340, www.romanticroadcoach.de; one bus daily, May–Oct; ERT 927).

ULM

This instantly appealing old town on the Danube has a quaint quarter known as **Fischer- und Gerberviertel**, the old fishing and tanning district, with half-timbered houses and bars and cafés beside the Blau, a rushing tributary. Most places of interest are on the north bank of the Danube and the main attractions are easily walkable. You can hardly fail to notice the soaring spire of the **Münster** (cathedral), all 161 m of it. Dominating a huge traffic-free square, the cathedral represents Gothic architecture at its mightiest. Climb the tower on a clear day to survey the terrain from the Black Forest to the Alps.

Many buildings that were hit in a bombing raid of 1944 have been carefully restored, including the 14th-century **Rathaus** (town hall) on the market square, with its intricate astronomical clock. One especially fine Renaissance building houses the **Ulmer Museum**, Marktpl. 9 (www.museum.ulm.de), notable for its early Ulm paintings and an outstanding 20th-century collection. Towards the Danube, the **Metzgerturm** (Butchers' Tower), formerly a prison, is known as the leaning tower of Ulm (36 m high) as it is about 2 m off the vertical. From there, follow a path to a pleasant riverside walk dotted with sculptures and another up onto a stretch of the old city walls. Ulm was the birthplace of Einstein, marked by a memorial opposite the rail station.

ARRIVAL, INFORMATION, ACCOMMODATION

🚆 **Ulm Hbf**, a 5-min walk to the centre through the pedestrian zone. **🚹 Tourist office**: Stadthaus, Münsterpl. 50, ☎ 0731 161 2830 (www.tourismus.ulm.de). Free hotel booking service. 🛏 There are several reasonably priced central hotels, including **Gästehaus Heigeleshof**, Heigeleshof 3, ☎ 0731 602 6468 (www.statt-hotel.de) and **Pension Jäger**, Söflinger Str. 210, ☎ 0731 389 643, €. **Youth hostel** (HI): Grimmelfingerweg 45, ☎ 0731 384 455 (www.djh.de); 🚌 4 to Schulzentrum. Internet access: **Albert's Café**, Kornhauspl. 5, or free at the public library, next to the Rathaus.

✖ The old fishermen's quarter near the Danube has a selection of restaurants in picturesque spots. The wood-panelled **Allgäuer Hof**, Fischergasse 12, ☎ 0731 674 08 (www.erstes-ulmer-pfannkuchenhaus.de), features traditional pancakes on large platters, with a choice of over 40 toppings.

ONWARD FROM ULM

From Ulm, there is an especially beautiful rail route to the south-west that follows the **Danube Valley** upstream to Donaueschingen (ERT 938). The small

StuttCard and VVS 3-Tage ticket

The StuttCard (valid 3 days; €9.70) allows free or reduced admission to nearly all state museums, reductions at other attractions including the zoo, planetarium, mineral baths, theatres and nightclubs, plus savings on city tours.

The **VVS 3-Tage Ticket** allows three consecutive days' travel on Stuttgart's public transport system (rapid-transit railway, city trains and buses). For the inner zone (€10.30) or entire Stuttgart region (€13.90). Available on proof of hotel reservation only. Best value is the combined **StuttCard Plus** card (€18/22).

riverside towns of **Munderkingen** and **Beuron**, the latter with its striking Benedictine abbey, both make pleasant spots to pause on this rural journey.

Our main route cuts through the Swabian hills north-west of Ulm to reach the Neckar Valley and the Swabian city of Stuttgart.

Stuttgart

Surrounded by green hills, the capital of Baden-Württemberg is best known as the home of the Daimler-Benz and Porsche motor factories. The traffic-free centre, radiating from the huge **Schlossplatz**, with its pavement cafés, buskers, fountains and gardens, is an inviting place to stroll. Along one side is the **Neues Schloss**, the former palace of the Württemberg kings, now offices. The **Württembergisches Landesmuseum**, Schillerplatz, occupies the Altes Schloss opposite, an imposing Renaissance palace (www.landesmuseum-stuttgart.de, closed Mon). Its exhibits range from 19th-century crown jewels and Swabian sculptures to an intact Celtic grave and Renaissance clocks. Round the corner, the **Market Hall** groans with delicacies (closed Sun).

A **flea market** is held on Karlspl. on Saturdays. The **Schlossgarten** park stretches all along the city centre as far as the River Neckar and then joins the Rosensteinpark, with the **Natural History Museum** (closed Mon) and the **Wilhelma**, a large zoological/botanic garden with about 9,000 animals, buildings in Moorish style and a large lily pond.

The British architect James Stirling has firmly put the city on the map with his **Neue Staatsgalerie**, the postmodern wing of the **Staatsgalerie**, Konrad-Adenauer-Str. 30–32 (www.staatsgalerie.de, closed Mon), with its audacious use of materials. It's the setting for one of the world's largest Picasso collections. Motor enthusiasts can head for the **Mercedes-Benz Museum**, Mercedesstr. 100, Bad Cannstatt (S1 to Neckerpark), where one hundred historic models are on show (closed Mon).

Racing cars make up the bulk of the exhibits in the smaller **Porsche Museum**, Porscheplatz 1 (S6 to Neuwirtshaus), in the northern suburb of Zuffenhausen (closed Mon).

≋ **Stuttgart Hbf**, 5-min walk from the centre, along Schlosspl. 🖪 **Tourist office**: directly on coming out from the rail station underpass, at Königstr. 1a, ☎ 0711 22280 (www.stuttgart-tourist.de). Free accommodation booking service.

🛏 The small **City Hotel**, Uhlandstrasse 18, ☎ 0711 210 810 (www.cityhotel-stuttgart.de), €€, is in a great location for a reasonable price. Clean, cheap and close to the Hauptbahnhof is the **Hotel Pflieger**, Kriegerstrasse 9, ☎ 0711 221 878 (www.hotel-pflieger.de), €-€€.

Hostels: Alex 30 Hostel, Alexanderstrasse 30, ☎ 0711 838 8950 (www.alex30-hostel.de), from Hbf, U-Bahn 5/6/7/8/15 or S-Bahn 15 to Olgaeck. **Jugend-gästehaus Stuttgart**, Richard Wagner Str. 2, ☎ 0711 241 132 (www.backpacker-hostel.net), take tram 15 to Bubenbad. **Youth hostel** (HI): Haussmannstr. 27, ☎ 0711 6647 470 (www.djh.de), a 15-min uphill walk from the rail station (🚌 42 or tram 15 to Eugensplatz).

CONNECTIONS FROM STUTTGART

From Stuttgart you can head south to Singen (2 hrs, ERT 940) and change trains there to Konstanz (ERT 916). This is a very pretty line through the **Neckar Valley**. On the way, **Rottweil** warrants a stop. It's a delightful little market town, squeezed on a spur of the Neckar River with tremendous views.

Punctuated by the medieval Schwarzes Tor (Black Gate), the pedestrianised Hauptstrasse has a striking array of colourful Renaissance and baroque houses displaying a wealth of carvings and murals, and projecting oriel windows. The town is also the provenance of the ferocious Rottweiler dog, descended from Roman guard-dog stock and formerly used by local butchers to pull carts. 🖪 **Tourist office**: Hauptstr. 21-23, ☎ 0741 494 280 (www.rottweil.de).

HEIDELBERG

Heidelberg's romantic setting, beneath wooded hills along the banks of the River Neckar and overlooked by castle ruins, makes it a magnet for tourists and movie-makers. Expect packed streets in the summer high season. The town has a long history and is home to Germany's oldest university, founded in 1386, but there's little that's ancient in the centre, as most of it was rebuilt in the 18th century following wholesale destruction by Louis XIV's troops in 1693.

The city's most famous sight is the part-ruined pink sandstone **castle**, high above the town. From its terraces, you get a beautiful view over the red rooftops and the gently flowing river.

Many fine old mansions are scattered around the **Altstadt** (Old Town). The buildings around Marktpl. include the Renaissance **Haus zum Ritter** and the 14th-century **Heiliggeistkirche** (Church of the Holy Spirit). Universitätspl., which has the **Löwenbrunnen** (Lion Fountain) in the centre, is the location of both the 'old' and 'new' universities. Until 1914, students whose high spirits had got out of hand were confined to the special students' prison round the corner in

DAY TRIPS FROM HEIDELBERG

Summer cruises on the River Neckar depart from the quay by the Stadthalle (town hall). Along the banks, half-timbered villages nestle in woods below old castles on rocky crags. Within a few minutes you reach **Neckargemünd** and then **Neckarsteinach**, which boasts four ruined castles.

    Schwetzingen (frequent train service, change at Mannheim) is renowned for the 18th-century **palace**. The building itself is not vastly interesting, but its extensive gardens (at their colourful best in May) are an amazing rococo wonderland of statues, follies, mock ruins, tricks of perspective and fountains.

Augustinerstr. 2. Incarceration was regarded as an honour and self-portraits are common in the graffiti on the walls.

    Across the river, over the Alte Brücke, the steep **Schlangenweg steps** zigzag up through orchards to the **Philosophenweg** (Philosophers' Path). This is a scenic lane traipsing across the hillside, so-called because the views allegedly inspired philosophical reflection.

ARRIVAL, INFORMATION, ACCOMMODATION

≈ **Heidelberg Hbf**, 10-min walk to the edge of the pedestrian district; or 25 mins to the heart of the Old Town (or 🚌 33). 🅱 **Tourist office**: Willi-Brandt-Pl. 1, directly in front of the rail station, ☎ 06221 19433 (www.heidelberg-marketing.de). Accommodation booking service. The **HeidelbergBeWelcome Card** is valid for city travel, castle admission and various discounts (for 1, 2 or 4 days, €11/13/16, including funicular ride to the Schloss). Guided walking tours of the Altstadt (Old Town) in English (Fri & Sat at 1030, Apr–Oct) from Marktplatz. There are also themed guided tours, such as 'Heidelberg in the Time of Romanticism', or 'Student Life in Heidelberg': check with the tourist office for details. 🚌 A network of buses and trams serve the pedestrianised Altstadt, where a funicular ride saves the 300-step climb up to the Schloss. It's also possible to tour by bike; rentals available from **Eldorado**, Neckarstaden 52, ☎ 06221 654 4460 (www.eldorado-hd.de), particularly pleasant for exploring the banks of the Neckar.

    🛏 Heidelberg is a prime tourist destination, so the later you book during the summer, the further from the centre you will find yourself. The **Goldener Hirsch**, Kleingemunder Str. 27, ☎ 06221 800 211, €, is away from the Altstadt, with simple rooms. **Pension Jeske** is located in the Old Town, Mittelbadgasse 2, ☎ 06221 23733 (www.pension-jeske-heidelberg.de), €. **Hostel: Lotte – The Backpackers**, Burgweg 3, ☎ 06221 735 0 725 (www.lotte-heidelberg.de), is a cosy new hostel/guesthouse that opened in July 2011. A popular place for backpackers is **Steffi's Hostel** located at Alte Eppelheimer Str. 50, ☎ 06221 778 2772 (www.hostelheidelberg.de).

    ✗ The **Altstadt** is very touristy and its restaurants lively with a student atmosphere. Many spill out onto the traffic-free streets. This is also the **nightlife** hub. You are spoilt for choice along Heiliggeiststr. and Untere Str. *Kneipen* (pubs) are an important part of Heidelberg life and in term time they fill up with students. For details of what's on, have a look at the listings magazine *Heidelberg aktuell* (www.heidelberg-aktuell.de).

HIGHLIGHTS AND EVENTS
Highlight of the summer is the castle festival, when opera, theatre and dance performances are staged outdoors in the cobbled courtyard; Romberg's romantic operetta *The Student Prince* is the permanent fixture. For tickets, ☎ 06221 582 0000 (www.theaterheidelberg.de). Grand fireworks displays are held on the first Saturday in June, July and Sept.

CONNECTIONS FROM HEIDELBERG
Heidelberg is served by trains to **Frankfurt** (55 mins, ERT 911), where you can join **Route 18** (p178).

KARLSRUHE

A major university city, Karlsruhe's most interesting sight is the huge **Schloss**, home of the Margraves and Grand Dukes of Baden until 1918. Built in 1715 by Margrave Karl Wilhelm, it's an enormous neoclassical pile with extensive formal gardens. From the tower, you see clearly how he designed the entire city to radiate out from it like a fan. Karlsruhe's grace derives from that ambitious urban plan.

Inside the Schloss, the wonderfully eclectic **Badisches Landesmuseum** (www.landesmuseum.de, closed Mon; free entry Fri 1400–1800) covers prehistory to the present day. The Orangerie merits a look for its 19th- and 20th-century European art. You'll need more time for the **Kunsthalle**, Hans-Thoma-Str. 2–6 (www.kunsthalle-karlsruhe.de, closed Mon), a wide-ranging collection from the 15th to 19th centuries and notable above all for its German primitives, among them Grünewald's astonishingly powerful *Crucifixion*; later German works include a fine set of paintings by the Black Forest artist Hans Thoma.

Marktplatz, the enormous central square near the Schloss, is dominated by a pyramid of red sandstone, under which Karl Wilhelm is buried. The **ZKM** (Centre for Art and Media Technology), Lorenzstr. 19 (www.zkm.de), is an experience-oriented media museum and interactive art gallery (tram line 2 or 🚌 55 from the station). There's enough for a full day's visit (closed Mon–Tues).

Directly across from the rail station and right next to the tourist office is the **Stadtpark-Tiergarten**. The park is a very pleasant way to cross town (particularly handy for getting to the Schloss). There is a boating lake and, in season, outdoor cafés and a blaze of flowers. For something less sedate, head for the pubs and clubs around Kaiserstr. For nightlife pointers try www.karlsruhe.eins.de.

ARRIVAL, INFORMATION, ACCOMMODATION
🚆 **Karlsruhe Hbf**, a 25-min walk south of the centre (tram 3/4/5/6 from Marktpl.).
✈ **Karlsruhe Baden Airport** ☎ 07229 662 000 (www.badenairpark.de), served by

Ryanair flights from London, Porto and Rome, is actually nearer to Baden-Baden; regular buses to Karlsruhe and Baden-Baden.

🛈 Tourist office: Bahnhofpl. 6, ☎ 0721 3720 5383 (www.karlsruhe-tourism.de), opposite the rail station. Also at Weinbrennerhaus am Marktplatz. Free room-booking service. There are good bus and tram services. Rhine cruises operate Easter–Nov from the western edge of town. **⊨ Pension Stadtmitte**, Zähringer Str. 72, ☎ 0721 389 637 (www.pensionstadtmitte.de), €, and **Pension am Zoo**, Ettlinger Str. 33, ☎ 0721 336 78 (www.pension-am-zoo.de), €. **Youth hostel** (HI): Moltkestr. 24, ☎ 0721 282 48 (www.jugendherberge-karlsruhe.de), west of Schlossgarten (tram 2 or 4 to Europaplatz).

BADEN-BADEN

The city is the European spa town par excellence. Ever sniffy about modernity, the locals kept the railway at a distance and the station is inconveniently distant from the town. Almost oppressively elegant and full of visitors dripping with money, Baden-Baden is a throwback to an earlier age.

But it has a compelling appeal, and nowhere else in Germany offers the same opportunities for people-watching (or even snaring a rich, aged spouse). The city has snob-appeal and everything is overdone, but it's all the more fabulous for that. You half expect to bump into the Russian tsar or a Hungarian countess as you stroll into the Casino.

A long boulevard of plane trees and manicured parkland known as the **Lichtentaler Allee** is the resort's principal promenade. At the renovated art nouveau **Trinkhalle** (Pump Room), Kaiserallee 3 (www.in-der-trinkhalle.de), romantic murals depict the town's history as a spa; here you will find the tourist office and a bistro. There is a small well inside where you can try the saline waters.

Indulging in a spa treatment is a memorable experience that won't break the bank; at the historic **Friedrichsbad** (www.roemisch-irisches-bad.de) you get a three-hour session (whirlpools, saunas, steam rooms and hot and cold baths), massages extra. It has a marvellous Roman-Irish bath, which combines bathing in thermal spring water with exposing the body to warm dry air (nudity mandatory). Underneath the building you can see traces of the original Roman baths. The **Caracalla-Therme**, Römerpl. 1 (www.caracalla.de), is a complex with currents, whirlpools and hot and cold grottos; upstairs (nudity mandatory) has saunas, steam rooms and suntan areas. Inside, the huge pool is under a Roman-style dome and outside, both hot and cold pools are embellished by fountains. Take your own towel.

The casino in the neoclassical **Kurhaus**, Kaiserallee 1, is Germany's oldest and biggest. Redecorated in French style in 1853, it claims to be the world's most beautiful casino. Marlene Dietrich is said to have promoted it thus. There are daily tours 0930–1200 (from 1000 Oct–Mar). Gambling starts at 1400, strict dress code (jackets and ties available for hire); admission is €5. Definitely worth a look. Over 21s only.

ARRIVAL, INFORMATION, ACCOMMODATION

≋ Baden-Baden station is at **Oos**, 8 km north-west of town; 🚌 201 runs every 10 mins 0500–2000, then every 20 mins until 2300. 🚹 **Tourist office**: Trinkhalle (Pump Room), Kaiserallee 3 (city centre); ☎ 07221 275 200 (www.baden-baden.de).

🛏 As the baths and casino attract many wealthy visitors, most hotels are glossy and expensive. A popular mid-range choice is the **Hotel am Markt**, Marktplatz 18, ☎ 07221 2704-0 (www.hotel-am-markt.de), €€. More options include the **Hotel Deutscher Kaiser**, Merkurstrasse 9, ☎ 07221 270-0 (www.deutscher-kaiser-baden-baden.de), €€, and the **Hotel Haus Reichert**, Sophienstrasse 12, ☎ 07221 908-0 (www.hausreichert.de), €€.

To get a taste of the luxury that made Baden-Baden famous, the elegant and over 165-year-old **Brenner's Park-Hotel & Spa**, Schillerstrasse 4-6, ☎ 07221 900-0 (www.brenners.com), €€€+, is a journey back in time. The rooms will be beyond the budget of most, but nevertheless it is well worth a look. The youth hostel **Werner-Dietz-JH**, Hardbergstrasse 34, ☎ 07221 522 23 (www.djh.de) is to the west of the city; take 🚌 201/205 or 216 to Grosse Dollenstrasse and then a seven-minute walk.

CONNECTIONS FROM BADEN-BADEN

It is easy to head south to **Switzerland**, with about a dozen direct trains to Basel each day (ERT 912). **Freiburg im Breisgau** (see box opposite) makes an excellent en-route stop. Baden-Baden is also a jumping off point for France, using local trains via Offenburg to Strasbourg (ERT 916 to Offenburg, then ERT 912 for the short hop over the Rhine to France). In Strasbourg, you can pick up fast trains to Paris (ERT 390) and follow **Route 3** in this book across France to Normandy (p66). Route 19 now leaves the Rhine Valley and cuts south-east into the hills, along the way taking in some spectacular scenery. This is a fine section for window-gazing.

TRIBERG

Cuckoo-clock shops have arrived here with a vengeance, and there is a fabulous array of south German kitsch in Triberg. At the heart of the **Schwarzwald** (Black Forest) and known for the purity of its air, the touristy spa town has been a centre for cuckoo-clock making since 1824, when Josef Weisser started his business in the **Haus der 1000 Uhren** (House of a Thousand Clocks). The **Schwarzwald-museum** (www.schwarzwaldmuseum.de) is full of woodcarvings, some splendid local costumes and inevitably clocks.

Apart from timepieces, **Triberg** is an appealing centre for walking; one walk is to the highest waterfall in Germany, which cascades down 163 m in seven stages and is floodlit at night.

ARRIVAL, INFORMATION, ACCOMMODATION

≋ 1.5 km north-east of the town. 🚹 **Tourist office**: at the Schwarzwaldmuseum, Wallfahrtstr. 4, ☎ 07722 866 490 (www.triberg.de). Accommodation reservation service. 🛏 The **Hotel Central**, Hauptstr. 64, ☎ 07722 4360 (www.hotel-central-

FREIBURG IM BREISGAU

Freiburg lies off our main route, but the city is too good to be excluded on that count. It is certainly worth a detour. Nestling at the western edge of the Black Forest, Freiburg spreads around its Gothic cathedral. With most sights in the **Altstadt** (Old Town), it's very walkable so long as you don't fall into the numerous *Bächle* (gulleys) that run along the streets. This old drainage system was used as a fire precaution and for watering livestock and even now, particularly after a storm, the old gulleys still fill with water. Freiburg's famously easy-going atmosphere is immediately apparent; the university is very much the life and soul of the city. The university quarter, west of the Münsterplatz, is the area to head for to find student cafés and lively bars.

Topped by a 116-m spire, the red sandstone **Münster** (cathedral) has a Romanesque-Gothic interior illuminated by 13th- to 16th-century stained glass — many sections depicting the guilds who paid for them. From the tower you get a vertigo-inducing panorama.

On Münsterpl., the **Historisches Kaufhaus**, an arcaded merchants' hall, is flanked by two handsome baroque palaces, **Erzbischöfliches Palais** and **Wentzinger-haus**. The latter was the house of the 18th-century artist Christian Wentzinger and is now a museum on the town's history. A short stroll away, Rathauspl. is notable for the **Neues Rathaus**. A bridge links **Altes** and **Neues Rathaus** (old and new town hall). The nearby red and gold **Haus zum Walfisch** (Franziskanerstr.) is a recreation of the elegant house (bombed in World War II) where Erasmus lived for two years. The **Augustiner**, Augustinerpl. 1–3, the town's best museum, contains religious and folk art from the Upper Rhine area.

≼ **Freiburg Hbf**, a good 10-min walk west of the centre. ☒ **Tourist office**: Rathausplatz 2–4, ☎ 0761 388 1880 (www.freiburg.de). Free accommodation booking service ☎ 0761 8858 1145. ⍾ There are plenty of cheaper places (€–€€) to stay (and restaurants too) around the **Altstadt**, such as **Hotel Schemmer**, Eschholzstr. 63, ☎ 0761 207 490 (www.hotel-schemmer.de), €. Hostel accommodation is available at **Black Forest Hostel**, Kartäuserstr. 33, ☎ 0761 881 7870 (www.blackforest-hostel.de); take tram 1 to Oberlinden. **Youth hostel** (HI): Kartäuserstr. 151, ☎ 0761 676 56 (www.djh.de), at the extreme east of town (tram 1 to Römerhof). **Campsite: Hirzberg**, Kartäuserstr. 99, ☎ 0761 350 54 (www.freiburg-camping.de), near the youth hostel.

triberg.eu), €, has a location that lives up to its name. **Youth hostel** (HI): Rohr-bacherstr. 35, ☎ 07722 4110 (www.djh.de).

KONSTANZ

The Swiss border cuts through the southern part of this town on the **Bodensee** (Lake Constance). Leafy gardens extend along the water's edge and there's a pleasant Old Quarter, **Niederburg**, where alleys wind between half-timbered buildings with decorated facades. The harbour is the departure point for lake cruises and ferries. At the mouth of the marina is the 9-m-high **Imperia**, a controversial statue depicting a courtesan holding the king in one hand (representing the State) and in the other the Pope (representing the Church), thus questioning who has the real power. In the Marktstätte (Market Place), elaborate frescoes on the Renaissance **Rathaus** depict the town's history, and children clamber on the bronze beasts of a decidedly jolly 19th-century fountain. Jan Hus was martyred here in 1415; the **Hus Museum**, Hussenstr. 64 (free, closed Mon) contains an exhibition about the life of this influential Czech reformer.

ARRIVAL, INFORMATION, ACCOMMODATION

≈ Between Bahnhofpl., the eastern boundary of Altstadt, and the **Bodensee** (Lake Constance). 🚹 **Tourist office**: Bahnhofpl. 43, ☎ 07531 133 030 (www.konstanz-tourismus.de); includes accommodation service. Bicycles can be hired from **Kultur-Rädle Radverleih** which has its office at the station, ☎ 07531 273 10 (www.kultur-raedle.de) or **Pro Velo**, Konzilstr. 3, ☎ 07531 293 29. 🛏 The centre of town is more expensive than the outlying villages, although there are some clean and affordable options, one being **Hotel Sonnenhof**, Otto-Raggenbass Str. 3, ☎ 07531 222 57 (www.hotel-sonnenhof-konstanz.de), €. A cheaper alternative, situated close to Hbf, is **Pension Graf**, Bodanstrasse 3, ☎ 07531 128 6890 (www.hotel-pension-graf.de). Right by the train station is the upmarket **Hotel Halm**, Bahnhofplatz 6, ☎ 07531 121 803 (www.hotel-halm-konstanz.de), €€–€€€.

Hostels: The youth hostel is called **Otto-Moericke-Turm** (HI), Zur Allmannshöhe 16, ☎ 07531 32260 (www.jugendherberge-konstanz.de), 🚌 4 to Allmannsdorf-Jugendherberge. **Campsite**: **Campingplatz Klausenhorn**, Hornwiesenstr. 40–42, Dingelsdorf, ☎ 07533 6372 (www.camping-klausenhorn.de), open Apr–early Oct or **Campingplatz Litzelstetten-Mainau**, Grossherzog-Friedrich-Str. 43, ☎ 07531 943 030, which is near the shore opposite Mainau island, open Easter–Sept.

LAKE CONSTANCE

The quay on the Bodensee (Lake Constance), behind the rail station, offers a wide choice of boat trips and cruises on the lake and the Rhine (into which it flows nearby). Most services are seasonal. The main operator is **Bodensee-Schiffs-betriebe**, Hafenstr. 6; ☎ 07531 364 0389 (www.bsb-online.com). **Lindau** (3 hrs 30 mins by ferry) has rail services to Ulm and Augsburg (ERT 935). Other ferry destinations include **Meersburg**, an atmospheric hillside town with a picturesque **Markt** and an old inhabited castle; **Unteruhldingen**, which has an open-air museum (with recreations of neolithic dwellings) and a basilica that's fully worth the 20-min uphill walk; **Überlingen**, a strikingly attractive town with a Gothic **Münster** and a fine moat walk; and the island of **Reichenau**, which has three 9th-century monasteries, each surrounded by a village. Linked by a footbridge to the mainland, and reached by boat services from Konstanz, **Mainau** is a delightful 45-hectare island, where a lush and colourful garden surrounds an inhabited baroque palace that was used by the Teutonic Knights for more than five centuries.

Rail Route 20: From Bavaria to Prussia

CITIES: ★★ CULTURE: ★ HISTORY: ★★ SCENERY: ★★
COUNTRIES COVERED: GERMANY

This route does more than just link two important German cities: **Munich** and **Berlin**. It explores Germany's cultural heartland, taking in superb towns in northern Bavaria, and historic cities in eastern Germany like **Weimar** and **Leipzig**. If you are pushed for time, just choose one Bavarian stopover then head straight for eastern Germany. Cutting the corner from **Würzburg** on the direct route to **Erfurt** (ERT 870) is one option. It won't save you a lot of time, but will give you a glimpse of the beautiful hill country of southern **Thuringia**, plus many wonderful half-timbered buildings along the way.

Forget any preconceptions you may have about the former German Democratic Republic. It isn't all run-down industry. Eastern Germany boasts some of Europe's most memorable cities.

MUNICH — SEE P526

EICHSTÄTT

For a great view of the town, make the steep but pretty 15-min climb from the station up a wooded hillside to the **Willibaldsburg**, a splendid white palace built between the 14th and 18th centuries. A recent addition to this is the **Hortus Eystettensis**, a garden based on the plants documented in the definitive 16th-century illustrated horticultural work. The Burg also houses the **Jura-Museum** of natural history, with a notable collection of fossils from the Altmühl Valley.

The bustling market square consists of pretty gabled buildings, shops and pavement cafés, while nearby the **Residenzplatz** is a serene complex of pale green and white 18th-century mansions in a semicircle around the imposing **Residenz**, the former bishops' residence, which is now used by the town council as offices and reception rooms. The adjoining light and airy Gothic **Dom** (cathedral) is notable for its stained-glass windows by Hans Holbein and intricately carved 500-year-old Pappenheim altar.

ARRIVAL, INFORMATION, ACCOMMODATION

⇌ **Eichstätt Stadt** is served by a shuttle train from **Eichstätt Bahnhof** on the main line, a 9-min journey. The tourist office is a 3-min walk over the bridge from Eichstädt Stadt station. 🚩 **Tourist office**: Dompl. 8, ☎ 08421 600 1400 (www.eichstaett.info). Information on the **Naturpark Altmühltal**, the surrounding area, is at: Notre Dame 1, ☎ 08421 987 60 (www.naturpark-altmuehltal.de).

🛏 Spaces in guesthouses are easy to find. **Gasthof Goldener Adler**, Westenstr. 76, ☎ 08421 4488, €; **Gasthof Ratskeller**, Kardinal-Preysing Pl. 8, ☎ 08421 901 258 (www.ratskeller-eichstaett.de), €, is slightly more expensive. **Private rooms** are also

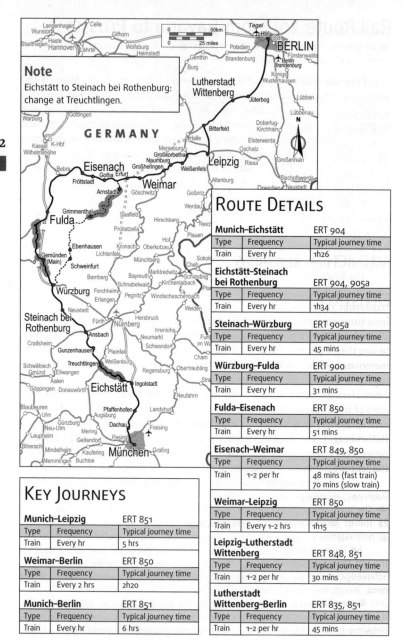

Note

Eichstätt to Steinach bei Rothenburg: change at Treuchtlingen.

ROUTE DETAILS

Munich–Eichstätt — ERT 904

Type	Frequency	Typical journey time
Train	Every hr	1h26

Eichstätt–Steinach bei Rothenburg — ERT 904, 905a

Type	Frequency	Typical journey time
Train	Every hr	1h34

Steinach–Würzburg — ERT 905a

Type	Frequency	Typical journey time
Train	Every hr	45 mins

Würzburg–Fulda — ERT 900

Type	Frequency	Typical journey time
Train	Every hr	31 mins

Fulda–Eisenach — ERT 850

Type	Frequency	Typical journey time
Train	Every hr	51 mins

Eisenach–Weimar — ERT 849, 850

Type	Frequency	Typical journey time
Train	1–2 per hr	48 mins (fast train) 70 mins (slow train)

Weimar–Leipzig — ERT 850

Type	Frequency	Typical journey time
Train	Every 1–2 hrs	1h15

Leipzig–Lutherstadt Wittenberg — ERT 848, 851

Type	Frequency	Typical journey time
Train	1–2 per hr	30 mins

Lutherstadt Wittenberg–Berlin — ERT 835, 851

Type	Frequency	Typical journey time
Train	1–2 per hr	45 mins

KEY JOURNEYS

Munich–Leipzig — ERT 851

Type	Frequency	Typical journey time
Train	Every hr	5 hrs

Weimar–Berlin — ERT 850

Type	Frequency	Typical journey time
Train	Every 2 hrs	2h20

Munich–Berlin — ERT 851

Type	Frequency	Typical journey time
Train	Every hr	6 hrs

available (brochure at the tourist office). **Youth hostel** (HI): Reichenaustr. 15, ☎ 08421 980 410 (www.djh.de), 10 mins from the rail station (closed Dec–Jan).

ROTHENBURG OB DER TAUBER

Change trains at **Steinach bei Rothenburg** for the 14-min journey to Rothenburg ob der Tauber. This little town may deserve the title 'Jewel of the Romantic Road' (see box p204) but Rothenburg's fêted status among overseas visitors to Germany comes at a price. It can be impossibly packed in high season. The town is situated on a rocky outcrop surrounded by **medieval walls**, its pastel-coloured steep-gabled houses — some half-timbered — are the stuff of picture books, especially in summer, when window boxes trail with flowers.

As early as 1902, the local council, showing commendable foresight, imposed a preservation order, so physically not much has changed since the 15th century — if you ignore all the tourist shops, galleries, restaurants and crowds, which can dilute the atmosphere. One of the best walks is around the intact (and roofed) town walls, which are long enough for you to lose most of the hordes of visitors.

On **Marktplatz**, there is usually some entertainment, whether a musical concert or a theatrical performance. The glockenspiel on the 15th-century **Ratstrinkstube** (City Councillors' Tavern), now the tourist office, re-enacts on the hour (1100–1500 and 2000–2200) the historic scene in 1631, during the Thirty Years War, when Mayor Nusch rose to the challenge of knocking back a gallon of wine to save the town from destruction. The **Meistertrunk** festivities at Whitsun commemorate his feat. Climb the more than 200 steps (very steep and narrow at the top) onto the **Rathaus tower's** roof for a dizzying view (Apr–Oct). Then walk down Herrngasse to the **Burggarten**; graced by a remarkable 15th-century backdrop of the town, these shaded gardens were the site of a castle destroyed in an earthquake in 1356. Well might you question why there is so much hype over Rothenburg. It's lovely, but no more so than dozens of other Bavarian communities: Feuchtwangen, Ansbach, Dinkelsbühl and Eichstätt are examples. For Rothenburg nightlife try the area around Ansbacher- and Adam-Hörberstrasse.

ARRIVAL, INFORMATION, ACCOMMODATION

≋ The town centre is a 10-min walk straight ahead, then follow 'Stadtmitte' signs.
🏢 **Tourist office**: Marktpl. 2, ☎ 09861 404 800 (www.rothenburg.de), includes accommodation service. Guided tours in English at 1400 from Marktpl., Apr–Oct.

🛏 There is plenty of choice, including private houses, both inside and outside the Old Town walls. Good-value hotel options include the **Hotel Roter Hahn**, Obere Schmiedgasse 21, ☎ 09861 974-0 (www.roterhahn.com), €€, and the **Altes Brauhaus**, Wenggasse 24, ☎ 09861 978-0 (www.altesbrauhaus.com), €€. **Youth hostel** (HI): **Rossmühle und Spitalhof**, Mühlacker 1, ☎ 09861 94160 (www.djh.de), located in a former horse mill in the Old Town. **Campsite: Tauber-Romantik Stadtteil Detwang**, Detwang 39, ☎ 09861 6191 (www.camping-tauberromantik.de), open Easter–Oct.

GERMANY'S ROMANTIC ROAD

The Romantic Road (Romantische Strasse) is the best known of Germany's themed tourist routes. It is a marketing ploy devised in 1950, and has been a huge hit with American and Japanese visitors. The route runs from **Würzburg** to **Füssen**, taking in along the way such notable tourist towns at Rothenburg and Dinkelsbühl. The southern end of the route at Füssen is on the edge of the Alps and a magnet for castle lovers, as mad **King Ludwig's famous follies** are nearby (see also p190). From early May until late October, Deutsche Touring (Europabus) run a daily luxury coach the full length of the Romantic Road (see ERT 927). It is a pricey excursion. Würzburg to Füssen is €80. You can also use this bus for intermediate hops (eg. Rothenburg to Munich is €36). 10% discount for students, under 21s and over 60s. Eurail pass holders receive a 20% discount on the regular fares.

WÜRZBURG

Würzburg is a university town where in autumn the *Winzerfest*, a traditional annual harvest festival, celebrates the (justly famous) Franconian wines. The rebuilt domes, spires and red roofs are seen at their best from the terrace battlements of **Festung Marienberg**, an impressive white fortress on a wooded hill above the River Main. Converted to baroque style in the 17th century, little remains inside, though the **Mainfränkisches Museum** (www.mainfraenkisches-museum.de, closed Mon) displays a large collection of works by Franconian artists, including superb 16th-century woodcarvings by one of the city's most famous sons, Tilman Riemenschneider. The Festung is best reached by 🚌 9 (Apr–Oct), a 10-min ride; otherwise it's a 40-min walk.

The marketplace is notable for the **Marienkapelle**, a 14th-century church with more Riemenschneider carvings, and the richly decorated 18th-century **Haus zum Falken**, which houses the tourist office. The town's main sight is the massive sandstone **Residenz** on the eastern edge of town. Built as the new palace of the prince-bishops in the 18th century by Balthasar Neumann, it has been given World Heritage Site status. Statues line the roof facade, symbolising the Church's wealth and power. The rooms are sumptuously decorated with frescos and sculptures by leading artists of their day, including the Venetian master Tiepolo (guided tours in English, daily at 1100 and 1500). Evening bevvies aplenty in and around Sander-str., popular with students, and for clubs move on to the old harbour area.

ARRIVAL, INFORMATION, ACCOMMODATION

🚊 **Würzburg Hbf**, at the foot of vineyards on the northern edge of the town centre, a 15-min walk. 🛈 **Tourist offices**: Am Congress Centrum, ☎ 0931 372 335 (www.wuerzburg.de) and in the **Falkenhaus**, Markt, ☎ 0931 372 398 (ticket booking service). For internet cafés try **Café Franz**, Franz-Ludwig-Str. 6.

🏨 There is no shortage of hotels in all categories. Moderately priced is **Pension Siegel**, Reisgrubengasse 7, ☎ 0931 52941 (www.pension-siegel.com), €. If you are looking to splurge, try the **Schlosshotel Steinburg**, Auf dem Steinberg, ☎ 0931 97020 (www.steinburg.com), €€€. **Hostels**: Close to the train station is the **Babelfish Hostel**, Haugerring 2, ☎ 0931 304 0430 (www.babelfish-hostel.de), €. The official **youth hostel** (HI) is at Fred-Joseph-Platz 2, ☎ 0931 42590 (www.djh.de), on the bank of the Main, below Festung; tram to Löwenbrücke then 500-m walk. **Campsite: Kanu-Club**, Mergenheimer Str. 13b, ☎ 0931 72536 (www.kc-wuerzburg.de), tram 3/5 to Juden-bühlweg.

CONNECTIONS FROM WÜRZBURG

Würzburg is on **Route 18** (p178). At Würzburg you can also cut north-east using a direct *Regionalbahn* (regional train) to rejoin Route 20 at Erfurt (ERT 870). The scenery along this short cut is initially unexceptional with the railway broadly following the Main Valley, but north of Schweinfurt (where the train reverses), the landscape becomes progressively hillier. The 1-hr section north of Mellrichstadt is the finest stretch as the railway cuts through the wooded hills of Thuringia — part of what was until 1990 still East Germany.

FULDA

This city in the Rhön area comes with a baroque theme, although the town goes back over 1,250 years. A modern fountain plays in the rose garden outside the twin-towered Italianate 18th-century **Dom** (cathedral), where pilgrims come to see the revered tomb of St Boniface within the crypt; the dagger that killed him and the codex with which he tried to shield himself are exhibited in the crypt museum. It's worth taking a peek at the adjacent **Michaelskirche**, one of the oldest churches in Germany. In the **Stadtschloss** (City Palace), the private apartments of the prince-abbots who once lived there are open to visitors and an impressive array of Fulda porcelain is on show.

Fulda is full of history but the modern town has a lively pulse too. Head for cosy pubs in the Old Town or enjoy the city's nightlife on weekends in the Fun-park, Keltenstr. 20 (www.funpark-deutschland.de). Foodies should try the local Rhön region speciality, *Zwibbelploatz*, a tasty sort of onion pizza served with potato soup. It's the Fulda dish of choice on Fridays, when Catholic tradition prescribed a meat-free meal.

ARRIVAL, INFORMATION, ACCOMMODATION

≋ A 7-min walk north-east from the centre. **❸ Tourist office**: Bonifatiuspl. 1, ☎ 0661 102 1814 (www.tourismus-fulda.de), arranges guided tours lasting 1 hour, at 1130 and 1500, or tours lasting 2 hours, Fri/Sat/Sun at 1400 (Apr–Oct), starting at the tourist office.

⊨ Cheaper guesthouses near the station include **Pension Wenzel**, Heinrichstr. 38–40, ☎ 0661 753 35 (www.hotel-pension-wenzel.de), €, and **Pension Hodes**, Peterstor 14, ☎ 0661 72862 (www.pension-hodes-fulda.de), €. More luxurious, ex-pensive, but wonderfully located is the **Maritim Hotel am Schlossgarten**,

Pauluspromenade 2, ☎ 0661 2820 (www.maritim.de), €€€. **Youth hostel** (HI): Schirrmannstr. 31, ☎ 0661 733 89 (www.djh.de).

EISENACH

For a first taste of eastern Germany, Eisenach is a tad dour, but things are on the up with some of the city centre's fine old buildings now having a facelift. The real reason to visit is the splendid **Wartburg**, a medieval castle on a hill on its southwest edge (12 mins by 🚌 10 from the rail station, and then 227 steps), the seat of the Landgraves of Thuringia (www.wartburg-eisenach.de). It dates from 1067 with many later additions, making it an attractive complex where half-timbered buildings surround two courtyards. **Wagner** stayed there and used it as the setting for his opera *Tannhäuser*, and **Martin Luther** translated the New Testament into German there — in just 10 weeks — while being held in secret for his own protection in 1521–22 after being excommunicated.

The 15th-century **Lutherhaus**, Lutherpl. 8, is where Martin Luther lodged as a boy; the present half-timbered structure encloses the original house. **Bachhaus**, Frauenplan 21, the former Bach family home is furnished in period style with documents and old musical instruments. A large statue of Bach stands just inside the big triple-galleried **St Georgenkirche**, Markt, where he was christened.

Eisenach was where East Germany's second most famous car (after the robust Trabant), the Wartburg, was manufactured until 1991. The **Automobile Welt Eisenach** (the Museum of Car Production), Friedrich-Naumann-str 10, ☎ 03691 772 12 (closed Mon) deserves a look.

ARRIVAL, INFORMATION, ACCOMMODATION

🚆 Turn right outside for the town centre, a 5-min walk. **🅕 Tourist office**: Markt 24 (in the Stadtschloss), ☎ 03691 792 30 (www.eisenach-tourist.de). 🛏 There is a reasonable selection of both *Pensionen* and *Gasthöfe* starting from about €25, such as **Gasthof am 'Storchenturm'**, Georgenstr. 43a, ☎ 03691 733 236 (www.gasthof-am-storchenturm.de), €, or **Pension St Peter**, Am Petersberg 7, ☎ 03691 872 830 (www.stpeter-eisenach.de), €. Good mid-range options are the **Hotel Haus Hainstein**, Am Hainstein 16, ☎ 03691 2420 (www.haushainstein.de), €€, and the **Hotel Villa Anna**, Fritz-Koch-Strasse 12, ☎ 03691 23950 (www.hotel-villa-anna.de), €€. **Youth hostel** (HI): **Artur Becker**, Mariental 24, ☎ 03691 743 259 (www.djh.de; 🚌 3/10 to Liliengrund, 100 m), about 1 km from the city centre.

GOTHA

This attractive little town, gateway to the **Thüringer Wald** (Thuringian Forest), was the home of the Saxe-Coburg-Gotha dynasty, ancestors of the English royal family. It's also known as the 'Residence City' — a label dating from the mid-17th century, when Duke Ernst I chose the Duchy of Gotha as his residence.

The main **market square** is surrounded by immaculately restored and colourful Renaissance and half-timbered buildings, among them the 16th-century terracotta **Rathaus**.

The plain white exterior of **Schloss Friedenstein**, on a hill overlooking the town centre, gives no hint of the ornate decor inside. Built by Duke Ernst I in 1634, after the Thirty Years War, it now houses the municipal museum. The **Ekhof-Theater** is Germany's oldest baroque theatre in its original state, and aptly hosts an annual summer baroque music festival.

ARRIVAL, INFORMATION, ACCOMMODATION

≋ At the southern end of town (tram 1/2/4 to the centre; alight at Huttenstr., then walk up Erfurterstr.). 🚩 **Tourist office**: Hauptmarkt 33, ☎ 03621 5078 5712 (www.gotha.de); accommodation booking service. ⋈ There are a good number of pensions and private rooms at inexpensive to reasonable prices as, for example, the centrally located **Pension Regina**, Schwabhäuser Str. 4, ☎ 03621 408 020 (www.pension-regina.de), or the smaller **Pension am Schloss**, Bergallee 3a, ☎ 03621 853 206 (www.pas-gotha.de).

CONNECTIONS FROM GOTHA

Tram 4 (the Thüringerwaldbahn) from the rail station goes to Tabarz in the Thüringer Wald, a 1-hr ride past **Marienglashöhle**, which has lovely crystalline caves.

ERFURT

Sited on the River Gera, the Thuringian capital has shot to prominence as a tourist attraction, with its substantial variety of attractive old buildings from mills to monasteries, much spruced up since German unification. A flight of 70 steps leads up to **Dom St Marien**, the hilltop Gothic cathedral beside the Domplatz, a large market place and useful tram stop.

An array of decorative buildings surround **Fischmarkt**. Markstr. leads off it to **Krämerbrücke**, a 14th-century river bridge lined with old houses and shops, best seen from the river itself. In the 15th century, Erfurt was noted for its altarpieces and a superb example can be seen in **Reglerkirche**, Bahnhofstr. To find out more on local traditions, visit the **Museum für Thüringer Volkskunde**, Juri-Gagarin-Ring 140a (closed Mon). For evenings, check out the **Studentenclub Engelsburg**, Allerheiligenstr. 20/21 (www.eburg.de) or the Museumskeller, Juri-Gagarin-Ring 140a (www.museumskeller.de).

ARRIVAL, INFORMATION, ACCOMMODATION

≋ **Erfurt Hbf**, a 10-min walk along Bahnhofstr., or tram 3/4/6, to the centre. ✈ **Flughafen Erfurt**, ☎ 0361 656 2200 (www.flughafen-erfurt-weimar.de), city rail line 4 departs every 10 mins from Hbf, taking 20 mins. 🚩 **Tourist office**: Benediktspl. 1, ☎ 0361 664 00 (www.erfurt-tourismus.de), accommodation booking service,

☎ 0361 664 0110. **ErfurtCard** (valid 2 days €12.90) provides free transport, a complimentary city tour and entry to city museums.

⇥ A pleasant small pension is the **Pension Reuss**, Spittelgartenstr. 15, ☎ 0361 731 0344 (www.pension-reuss.de), €. A nice hotel in a good location is the **Hotel Lindenhof,** Lindenstrasse 7, ☎ 03677 680088 (www.hotel-lindenhof.de), €€.

Hostels: There are a couple of good independent hostels in Erfurt, as the **Opera Hostel**, Walkmühlstr. 13, ☎ 0361 6013 1360 (www.opera-hostel.com), and the **Re4Hostel**, Puschkinstr. 21, ☎ 0361 6000 110 (www.re4hostel.com). **Youth hostel** (HI): Klingenstr. 4, ☎ 0361 562 6705 (www.djh.de), tram 6 to Steigerstr.

WEIMAR

Smart shops, pavement cafés and a lively **Onion Fair**, which takes over the town for the second weekend in October, are outward signs of Weimar's vitality. But, famously, Weimar is steeped in German culture, having been the home of two of the country's greatest writers, Goethe and Schiller, as well as the composers Bach, Liszt and Richard Strauss, the painter Lucas Cranach and the philosopher Nietzsche. It was also where the ill-fated pre-Nazi Weimar Republic was founded. A replica 1925 bus, the **Belvedere Express** (www.belvedere-express.de), takes in the main sights (there are three stops).

The entire town centre, with its wide tree-lined avenues, elegant squares and fine buildings, is designated a historic monument. After decades of neglect, extensive renovation for its role as European City of Culture in 1999 — coinciding with the 250th anniversary of the birth of Goethe — has revived its gracious character. Architecture fans should not miss Weimar's **Bauhaus** connections. Look out for the **Haus am Horn** (Am Horn 61), a modernist prototype of Bauhaus demeanour that relieves the tedium of Weimar's baroque mansions.

The baroque mansion where Goethe lived, **Goethehaus**, Frauenplan 1 (closed Mon), displays furniture, personal belongings and a library of 5,400 books. A stroll across the little River Ilm in the peaceful **Park an der Ilm** leads to the simple **Gartenhaus**, his first home in town and later his retreat. Goethe himself became a tourist attraction: people travelled from afar to glimpse the great man.

In the **Marktplatz** a plaque marks the house in the south corner where Bach lived when he was leader of the court orchestra. The **Liszthaus** (closed Mon and Nov–Mar), on the town side of the park at Marienstr. 17, is the beautifully maintained residence of the Austro-Hungarian composer Franz Liszt. The 200th anniversary of his birth was celebrated in 2011. He moved to Weimar in 1848 to direct the local orchestra and spent the last 17 summers of his life here. His piano and numerous manuscripts are on display.

Schiller stayed in Weimar for the last three years of his life at **Schillerhaus**, Schillerstr. 12, and his rooms are much as they were then (museum is closed Mon). Statues of Schiller and Goethe stand in the nearby Theaterpl. outside the imposing **Deutsches Nationaltheater**, where many of their plays were first performed.

Ten kilometres north of Weimar is the memorial museum and site of **Buchenwald concentration camp**, a grim reminder of the horrors of the Nazi regime during World War II (closed Mon).

ARRIVAL, INFORMATION, ACCOMMODATION

⇶ A 20-min walk north of the centre (🚌 6/7). 🄸 **Tourist office**: Markt 10, ☎ 03643 7450 (www.weimar.de). Also in the Welcome-Center at Friedensstr. 1. They can arrange hotel and private accommodation. City tours 1000 and 1400 (Mar–Oct). The **Weimar Card** gives three days' worth of free public transport and free or reduced admission to museums, exhibitions and performances at the German National Theatre and city guided tours all for €10.

🛏 A good choice in the centre of town is the **Hotel Kaiserin Augusta,** Carl-August-Allee 17, ☎ 03643 2340 (www.hotel-kaiserin-augusta.de), €€. **Hostels**: There are plenty of hostels in town, including the student-run **Hababusch Hostel** in the Old Town, Geleitstr. 4, ☎ 03643 850 737 (www.hababusch.de) and the **Labyrinth Hostel**, Goetheplatz 6, ☎ 03643 811 822 (www.weimar-hostel.com).

Weimar also has four (HI) **youth hostels** (www.djh-thueringen.de), including **Germania**, Carl-August-Allee 13, ☎ 03643 850 490, just 2 mins away from the station, and **Am Poseckschen Garten**, Humboldtstr. 17, ☎ 03643 850 792, in the centre of town.

LEIPZIG

Leipzig has been a cultural centre for many centuries, famous particularly for its music: numerous great 19th-century works were premiered at the **Gewandhaus**, Augustuspl. 8, beside the broad ring road encircling the **Innenstadt** (city centre). It makes a good starting point for a stroll around the pedestrianised centre, whose streets of long-neglected buildings and arcades are fast acquiring rows of smart shops, restaurants and offices. Yet Leipzig retains some of the grace of an old European city.

In 1989, the mass demonstrations and candlelit vigils in **Nikolaikirche**, Nikolaikirchhof 3, were the focus for the city's peaceful revolt against the East German state authorities. The **Stasi 'Power and Banality' Museum**, Dittrichring 24, in the former Ministry of State Security, reviews the apparatus of State surveillance and control.

Marktplatz is the centre for many of Leipzig's outdoor activities, including free concerts and impromptu beer fests. The fine Renaissance **Altes Rathaus** has survived and now houses the **Stadtgeschichtliches Museum**, covering the city's history. From Leipzig a trip can be made to **Colditz**, an attractive little town dominated by its castle (**youth hostel** (HI): Schlossgasse 1, ☎ 034381 450 10) — made notorious as a prisoner-of-war camp in World War II.

Leipzig is second only to Vienna for its musical tradition, being the home of Bach, Mendelssohn and Schumann. The **Gewandhaus Orchestra, Opera House** and **Thomanerchor** (St Thomas's Church Choir), which was conducted by Bach for 27 years, have a world-class reputation.

ARRIVAL, INFORMATION, ACCOMMODATION

⇒ On the edge of the Innenstadt (city centre), a 10-min walk to the middle. Known as the **Hauptbahnhof Promenaden Leipzig** and built in 1915, the station is an attraction in its own right, and is one of Europe's biggest and most impressive, recently refurbished and attired with a glossy shopping mall. Also part of the facelift is the magnificent *Deutsche Bahn* waiting room, complete with bar, stained-glass overhead ceiling and rich wooden interior. ➤ **Leipzig-Halle Airport**, ☎ 0341 224 1155 (www.leipzig-halle-airport.de): trains every 30 mins (takes 14 mins to main station, ERT 866). **ℹ Tourist office**: Katharinenstr. 8, ☎ 0341 710 4260 (www.ltm-leipzig.de), north of Marktplatz. Online accommodation booking service (zimmer@ltm-leipzig.de), or phone ☎ 0341 710 4255.

There is a good tram network from the rail station, but most things of interest are within the pedestrianised city centre. The **Leipzig Card**, including travel and museum discounts, is available for one or three days (€8.90/18.50).

▦ The tourist office can provide a list of pensions, including the **Herberge Zur Alten Bäckerei**, Zur Alten Bäckerei 12, ☎ 0341 415 300 (www.herberge-zur-alten-baeckerei.de), €. The **Motel One**, Nikolaistrasse 11, ☎ 0341 3374 370 (www.motel-one.com), €–€€, is central and stylish. **Hostels**: The **Central Globetrotter Hostel**, Kurt-Schumacher-Str. 41, ☎ 0341 149 8960 (www.globetrotter-leipzig.de), is close to the station. Another good option is the **Hostel Sleepy Lion**, Käthe-Kollwitz-Str. 3, ☎ 0341 993 9480 (www.hostel-leipzig.de), which is clean, friendly, central, open 24 hrs and highly recommended; singles, doubles and dorms; bike hire. New in 2011, the **Hostel Unschlagbar**, Karl-Liebknecht-Straße 1a, ☎ 0341 256 680 70 (www.unschlagbar-leipzig.de),is located in Leipzig-Süd, the popular student and nightlife district a short walk south of the city centre. **Youth hostel** (HI): Volksgartenstr 24, ☎ 0341 245 700 (www.djh.de), tram 1 towards Schönefeld, alight Löbauerstrasse, then a 300-m walk.

✗ Restaurants crowd the pavements around Kleine Fleischergasse, such as **Zills Tunnel**, Barfussgässchen 9, ☎ 0341 960 2078 (www.zillstunnel.de), a typical Saxon beerhouse serving traditional dishes. Famed because Goethe featured it in Faust, having dined there as a student, is the 16th-century wood-panelled **Auerbachs Keller** restaurant in the exclusive Mädler shopping arcade off Grimmaische Str. 2–4, ☎ 0341 216 100 (www.auerbachs-keller-leipzig.de). Lots of cafés crowd around the Marktpl., with music spouting out of most of them. **Spizz**, Markt 9 (www.spizz.org), does jazz nights, as well as an excellent breakfast.

LUTHERSTADT WITTENBERG

The country between Leipzig and Berlin is largely uninspiring, but dotted away here and there are a few interesting towns. Pick of the bunch is Lutherstadt Wittenberg, served by many of the fast trains en route from Leipzig to the German capital. Wittenberg is intimately associated with the Protestant reformer **Martin Luther**. The town is worth a visit not merely on account of its Luther

Bauhaus architecture

Lutherstadt Wittenberg is a good jumping off point to visit Dessau, the UNESCO World Heritage city that is so popular with fans of 20th-century architecture, but curiously unknown among a wider public. Dessau is the Bauhaus town par excellence. If you took a peek at the Haus am Horn in **Weimar** (see p208) and liked it, then it is really worth making time for Dessau where the Bauhaus legacy is very much richer than in Weimar. Trains from both stations at Wittenberg run at least hourly to **Dessau**, about 40 mins distant (ERT 848). The main Bauhaus building is just a 4-min walk from the back entrance of Dessau Hauptbahnhof. Catch it on a good day, and the glass curtain facade looks superb against a blue sky.

Other Bauhaus highlights include the **Meisterhäuser** (Masters' Houses), a 20-min walk from the station. These classic Bauhaus buildings were once the homes of the architects, artists and designers who brought such revolutionary impetus to the Bauhaus movement. The roll call of illustrious residents includes **Paul Klee**, **Wassily Kandinsky** and **Walter Gropius**. And don't miss the **Kornhaus Restaurant**, a classic piece of Bauhaus style, on the bank of the Elbe. Take 🚋 11 from Hauptbahnhof directly to Kornhaus, or for journeys that do not run via Kornhaus alight at Elballee, from where it is a 10-min walk.

There is no need to return to Lutherstadt Wittenberg to continue your journey, for Dessau is served by direct local trains to Leipzig (ERT 848) and Berlin (ERT 847).

connections and the inevitable memorials to the reforming pastor, but also as a chance to see a former East German town that is a little off the beaten track. The **Haus der Geschichte** (House of History) at Schlossstr. 6 gives rich insights into everyday life in the German Democratic Republic from 1949 to 1989.

Nearby is the **Schlosskirche**, the church to whose door Martin Luther famously pinned his theses denouncing the abuses of power within the hierarchy of the Catholic Church. No surprise therefore that Wittenberg has iconic status in the Protestant world as the community that challenged the hegemony of Rome. Yet that has not attracted the crowds.

ARRIVAL, INFORMATION, ACCOMMODATION

≋ The main station is a 15-min walk east of the centre. Frequent buses, or hop on any Dessau-bound train for the 2-min ride to the more centrally located station called **Lutherstadt Wittenberg Altstadt**. 🚺 **Tourist office**: Schlosspl. 2, ☎ 03491 498 610 (www.wittenberg.de). ⊨ Central and good value is the **Hotel Goldener Adler**, Markt 7, ☎ 03491 404 137 (www.wittenberghotel.de), €–€€. For more luxury, try the **Hotel Alte Canzley**, Schloßplatz 3, ☎ 03491 429 190 (www.alte-canzley.com), €€–€€€. The **youth hostel** (HI), Schloßstr. 14/15, ☎ 03491 403 255 (www.djh.de) is also well located in the heart of the Old Town.

BERLIN — SEE P450

Rail Route 21: Two Scandinavian capitals and Sweden's west coast

CITIES: ★★ CULTURE: ★ HISTORY: ★★ SCENERY: ★
COUNTRIES COVERED: DENMARK, SWEDEN, NORWAY

It is an easy journey from **Copenhagen** to Oslo. DFDS offers an overnight sailing between the two capitals (ERT 2360). But it is also a fine train trip, one that takes in lakes, forests and some very appealing coastal scenery. The rail journey kicks off by crossing the **Øresundsbroen**, the spectacular international bridge that connects Danish and Swedish territory. With stops in **Malmö** and **Gothenburg** (Göteborg), the route takes in two very different Swedish cities. Much of the route between those two towns hugs Sweden's western seaboard, then north of Gothenburg the railway turns inland for the 4-hr journey north to **Oslo**. The entire route is 703 km long. Gothenburg makes an ideal stopover at the midpoint in the journey.

COPENHAGEN — SEE P472

Route 21 shares a common start with **Route 25**, and the two routes run in parallel as far as Lund (see p236/238 for descriptions of Malmö and Lund). Beyond Lund, the two routes diverge, Route 25 heading north-east towards Stockholm and our train running north-west through rolling agricultural land towards Gothenburg.

HELSINGBORG

Don't be put off by the subterranean train station. Helsingborg is well worth a stop. During much of the Middle Ages, Helsingborg was Danish and functioned as an important garrison town; the massive fortified keep, the **Kärnan**, still dominates the place.

The bustling port is a pleasant enough base, with an Old Quarter to explore. But you should also pay a visit to the rewarding 15th-century **Church of St Maria** and the entertainingly eclectic **Stadsmuseet** (Town Museum). On the east side of town **Fredriksdal**, Gisela Trapps väg 1, is an open-air museum of reconstructed buildings.

ARRIVAL, INFORMATION, ACCOMMODATION

≋ Next to the ferry terminal. **🚻 Tourist office**: Dunkers kulturhus, Kungsgatan 11, ☎ 042 10 43 50 (www.helsingborg.se).

🛏 Cheap, and close to the train station and the ferry terminals, is the **Stadsmotellet**, Hantverkaregatan 11, ☎ 042 127 955 (www.stadsmotellet.se), €€. **Hostel**: The youth hostel **KFUM Nyckelbo** (HI), Scoutstigen 4, ☎ 042 920 05 (www.nyckelbo.se), is a 10-min bus ride from the centre of town.

ROUTE DETAILS

Copenhagen–Malmö   ERT 703

Type	Frequency	Typical journey time
Train	Every 20 mins	35 mins

Malmö–Helsingborg   ERT 737

Type	Frequency	Typical journey time
Train	Every 30 mins	42–54 mins

Helsingborg–Varberg   ERT 735

Type	Frequency	Typical journey time
Train	1–2 per hr	1h40

Varberg–Gothenburg   ERT 735

Type	Frequency	Typical journey time
Train	1–2 per hr	43 mins

Gothenburg–Halden   ERT 770

Type	Frequency	Typical journey time
Train	2–3 daily	2h06

Halden–Fredrikstad   ERT 770

Type	Frequency	Typical journey time
Train	Every 1–2 hrs	35 mins

Fredrikstad–Oslo   ERT 770

Type	Frequency	Typical journey time
Train	Every 1–2 hrs	1h08

KEY JOURNEYS

Copenhagen–Gothenburg   ERT 735

Type	Frequency	Typical journey time
Train	13–18 daily	3h10 to 3h45

Copenhagen–Oslo   ERT 735, 770

Type	Frequency	Typical journey time
Train	1–2 daily	8h12

Gothenburg–Oslo   ERT 770

Type	Frequency	Typical journey time
Train	2–3 daily	4 hrs

Notes

A change of train is always necessary at Gothenburg on journeys from Copenhagen to Oslo. All long-distance trains in Sweden and Norway tend to be reservation-only. Supplements apply on the high-speed X2000 trains in Sweden. There is also a daily overnight ship from Copenhagen to Oslo (ERT 2360).

You can take the ferry across to **Helsingør** in Denmark (itself served by frequent trains to Copenhagen, taking 47 mins; ERT 703), best known for **Kronberg Slot**, the Elsinore of Shakespeare's *Hamlet*.

VARBERG

Varberg made its mark in the late 19th century as a **bathing station**, and has some appealing period survivals, notably the **wooden pavilion** (Societetshuset) in the **park**, and the rectangular bathing section of 1903, with changing rooms and sunloungers ranged around a tamed expanse of sea water. The dominant feature of this spa-like port is the moated 13th-century **castle**, which doubles as a youth hostel (**Fästningens Vandrarhem** non-HI, ☎ 0340 868 28, www.fastningensvandrarhem.se) with plenty of idyllic beaches (including nudist ones) within close range. Within walking distance south of the town is **Apelviken Bay**, popular with surfers.

GOTHENBURG (GÖTEBORG)

The huge cranes and shipyards that greet visitors arriving at Scandinavia's biggest port mask the fact that this is one of Sweden's most attractive old cities, one that grew rapidly when Dutch merchants settled here in the early 17th century. Boat tours take in the best of the waterside views from the old canals, while elsewhere there are atmospheric squares and numerous leafy parks that have earned Gothenburg the nickname 'Garden City'. To get your bearings, go up **Skanskaskrapan** (Skanska Skyscraper), a striking red and white skyscraper, 86 m high, which has a lookout (**Göteborgsutkiken**; opening hours vary) with a small café (June–Aug only) near the top, giving superb harbour views. It's situated in **Lilla Bommen**, itself a charming area, with shops and craft workshops. Dominating the whole scene here, however, is the spectacular modern waterside **Göteborgs Operan** (Gothenburg Opera House) with performances of opera, ballet and concerts; guided tours ☎ 031 10 80 00 (www.opera.se).

Kungsportsavenyn, usually known simply as 'Avenyn' (The Avenue), is the hub of the city, a 50-m-wide boulevard lined with lime trees, shops and eateries, further enlivened by buskers and ad hoc street stalls. It leads up to **Götaplatsen**, the city's cultural centre, fronted by Carl Milles' fountain of **Poseidon**. Just off Avenyn is **Trädgårdsföreningen**, Nya Allén, a fragrant park full of flora and birdsong, speckled with works of art and other attractions.

The city's oldest secular building (1643) is **Kronhuset** (Crown Arsenal; closed Sun), Postgatan 6–8. Around it is **Kronhusbodarna**, a courtyard bounded by handicraft boutiques in 18th-century artisans' dwellings. Other good places for browsing are the **Antikhallarna** antique market in Västra Hamngatan, and **Haga**

GOTHENBURG DIVERSIONS

The popular **Liseberg Amusement Park**, Örgrytevägen 5 (www.liseberg.se; tram 4/5/6/8/13), Scandinavia's largest amusement park, is dominated by the 150-m-high **Spaceport**, which offers panoramic views. Among the 30 or so gut-wrenching rides is one of Europe's longest roller coasters. You'll find a wide selection of lively bars and clubs centred around Avenyn where things get going around midnight, and places stay packed until 0500. At the **Göteborgskalaset** (Gothenburg Festival) in early Aug the town cuts loose and there's all-night partying in the streets.

Nygata, a renovated historic area of cobbled streets, lined with craft, second-hand, antique and design shops, as well as cafés and restaurants. Opposite, the **Feskekörka** resembles a 19th-century church, but is actually a thriving fish market, open Tues–Sat, also Mon in summer, and has a good seafood restaurant.

Some city museums close on Mondays but open daily in summer. Don't miss the **Göteborgs Maritima Upplevelsecentrum** (Gothenburg Maritime Centre), Packhuskajen (open Mar–Nov), the **Konstmuseet** (Art Museum; closed Mon), Götaplatsen, and the **Universeum** (the National Science Discovery Centre; open daily), Södra vägen 50.

ARRIVAL, INFORMATION, ACCOMMODATION

⇌ **Göteborg Centralstation**, a short walk north-east of the centre, has a bureau de change (open daily), magazine outlets, lockers, showers and reasonably priced eateries. Most buses stop at Nils Ericsonsplatsen, next to the station. **Nordstan** is a huge shopping mall opposite the station, to which it is linked by a pedestrian tunnel.
✈ **Landvetter Airport** (20 km south-east of Gothenburg), ☎ 031 94 10 00 (www.landvetter.com); buses every 20 mins Mon–Fri and every 20–30 mins Sat & Sun to Centralstation. ⛴ **Stena Line**, ☎ 031 704 00 00 (www.stenaline.se), to/from Germany (**Kiel**), sail from Majnabbehamnen, 15 mins west of town; Stena ships to/from Denmark (**Frederikshavn**) sail from Masthuggskajen, at the west end of the centre.
🛈 **Tourist offices**: Kungsportsplatsen 2, ☎ 031 368 42 00 (www.goteborg.com) and a branch at Nordstadstorget, in Nordstan. Pick up the free *Göteborg Guide* which contains listings and tips and has a good town map. The centre's attractions are quite close together. The excellent **tram** network helps if you don't feel like walking.
🛏 You can book private rooms as well as hotels through the tourist office (for a small fee). Mid-range options include the **Nice B&B**, Utlandagatan 18, ☎ 031 20 21 50 (www.hotelnice.se), €€, the central **Palace Hotel**, Södra Hamngatan 2, ☎ 031 80 25 21 (www.palace.se), €€, and the **Kville Hotel**, Kvilletorget 24, ☎ 031 744 14 40 (www.kvillehotel.se), €€. **Hostels**: There are three reliable HI youth hostels; **Torrekulla Turiststation**, in Kållered, ☎ 031 795 14 95; **Slottsskogens Vandrarhem**, Vegagatan 21, ☎ 031 42 65 20 (www.slottsskogenvh.se); and **Stigbergsliden**, Stigbergsliden 10, ☎ 031 24 16 20 (www.hostel-gothenburg.com).
✗ The **seafood** is excellent, most restaurants clustering along the waterfront. For other types of cuisine, try around Avenyn or in Linnéstaden. The **Nordstan** complex offers a lot of eateries, including fast-food outlets and a good supermarket, Hemköp,

which has a deli section in the basement of the big store known as **Åhléns City**. Try the indoor **Stora Saluhallen market**, Kungstorget, for a tempting range of goodies.

CONNECTIONS FROM GOTHENBURG

Services run north-east to Stockholm; for a longer route to the Swedish capital via the southern shore of Lake Vänern use the **Herrljunga–Hallsberg** service via **Mariestad** (ERT 736).

HALDEN

Halden is an old border post on the attractive **Iddefjord**, overlooked by the star-shaped **Fredriksten Fort**, a huge 17th-century castle east of the town. Other highlights include the **Fredrikshalds Theater**, with its fully restored baroque stage, and **Rød Herregård**, a furnished 18th-century manor house with an enviable collection of art.

ARRIVAL, INFORMATION, ACCOMMODATION

≋ On the south bank of the river. 🚹 **Tourist office**: Torget 2, ☎ 69 19 09 80 (www.visithalden.com). ⊨ **Grand Hotell**, Jernbanetorget 1, ☎ 69 18 72 00 (www.grandhotell.net), €€–€€€. **Youth hostel** (HI): **Halden Vandrehjem**, Flintveien, ☎ 69 21 69 68, 2 km from the station, open late June–early Aug.

FREDRIKSTAD

With three sides of its edges still protected with fortified walls, Fredrikstad guarded the southern approaches to Oslo and has survived as one of the best-preserved fortress towns in Scandinavia. It's conducive to wandering, particularly around the walls and along the cobbled alleys of **Gamlebyen** (the Old Town) over on the east bank. **Fort Kongsten** is a pleasant 15- to 20-min stroll.

ARRIVAL, INFORMATION, ACCOMMODATION

≋ A 5-min walk south-east of the centre. 🚹 **Tourist office**: Tøyhusgaten 41, ☎ 69 30 46 00 (www.opplevfredrikstad.com). ⊨ Try the **Victoria Hotel**, Turngaten 3, ☎ 69 38 58 00 (www.hotelvictoria.no), €€, or **Hotell Fontenen**, Nygaardsgaten 9–11, ☎ 69 30 05 00 (www.hotelfontenen.no), €€; both central.

OSLO — SEE P532

CONNECTIONS FROM OSLO

You may wish to return to Copenhagen by ship (ERT 2360) and there is also a useful daily ship to Kiel in northern Germany (ERT 2372). Or continue on by train through Norway following **Route 23** west to Bergen (p224) or **Route 24** north to Trondheim (p228). There are twice-daily direct trains to Stockholm (ERT 750, 6 hrs).

Rail Route 22: Circling the Kattegat

CITIES: ★★ CULTURE: ★ HISTORY: ★★ SCENERY: ★
COUNTRIES COVERED: DENMARK, SWEDEN

The **Kattegat** is the body of water that lies east of the Danish province of Jutland and essentially separates Denmark from Sweden. In quiet weather the shores of this sea are mellow. There are royal castles and lovely sandy beaches backed by ribbons of forest. But watch a storm roll in, and the Kattegat coast becomes memorably dramatic. Route 22 heads west from Copenhagen to explore Denmark's two largest islands: **Sjælland** (Zealand) and **Fyn** (Funen). On Zealand we stop at **Roskilde**, the former capital of Denmark, and a place really to feel the pulse of Danish history. Then we continue west, stopping at **Odense**, to reach Jutland. The northern part of **Jutland**, especially once you get beyond **Aalborg**, is one of the remotest corners of Denmark — a windblown region that is an antidote to the big city buzz of chic Copenhagen. There are sand dunes and salt marshes, towns that once lived from herring and now rely mainly on tourists. Last stop in Denmark on Route 22 is **Frederikshavn**, a busy commercial port, from where you take a ship over the Kattegat to **Gothenburg**, Sweden's foremost maritime city. If you want to get a taste for one of the islands in the Kattegat, the obvious choice is **Læsø**, easily reached with a 90-min ferry crossing from Frederikshavn. At Gothenburg, you can connect onto **Route 21**.

COPENHAGEN — SEE P472

ROSKILDE

Roskilde was Denmark's first capital, and it is rich in history, with a magnificent brick cathedral that is the traditional burial place of Danish royalty. The impressive **Viking Ship Museum**, 1 km north of the centre on the shore of **Roskilde Fjord**, exhibits the intact remains of five original ships and shows a film about their excavation in the 1960s. Just next door is the museum harbour where, in the summer months, visitors are allowed in to the workshops to try their hand at maritime crafts and even venture out onto the fjord in a reconstructed Viking longship. The famous open-air **Roskilde music festival** is held in June/July (www.roskilde-festival.dk) and features some of the biggest international rock groups as well as lesser-known Scandinavian bands.

ARRIVAL, INFORMATION, ACCOMMODATION

≥ At the southern edge of the central area. 🚊 **Tourist office**: Stændertorvet 1, ☎ 46 31 65 65 (www.visitroskilde.com). ⛴ A reasonably priced B&B not far from the train station is the **Soviro**, Skovbovængets Allé 17, ☎ 46 32 05 45 (www.soviro.dk), €–€€. **Youth hostel** (HI): Vineboder 7, ☎ 46 35 21 84 (www.rova.dk), just west of the Viking Ship Museum by the sea.

ODENSE

Odense, a busy manufacturing city, is the largest settlement on the island of **Fyn** and the third largest city in the country. Throughout Denmark it's known as the birthplace of Hans Christian Andersen, who turned to writing fairy tales after failing in his ambitions to be an actor and novelist. Andersen's childhood home, **Barndomshjem**, Munkemøllestræde 3–5, has a couple of period-era rooms crammed with his belongings, but there's far more material in the extensive **H C Andersen Hus**, Bangs Boder 29, the site where he was born in 1805, including manuscripts, paper cuttings and his celebrated top hat (both closed Mon except end of June to end of Aug). Two excellent art museums are **Fyns Kunstmuseum** (Funen Art Museum; closed Mon), Jernbanegade 13, a superb collection of Danish art, and **Kunsthallen Brandts**, Brandts Torv 1 (closed Mon), a large, open gallery space comprising photography, printing and fine-arts museums with both permanent and temporary exhibits. Carl Nielsen, Denmark's greatest composer, was born near Odense in 1865, and is commemorated by the **Carl Nielsen Museet** at Claus Bergs Gade 11 (by the concert hall; opening times vary).

ARRIVAL, INFORMATION, ACCOMMODATION

⇄ The railway forms the northern boundary of the city centre. 🖪 **Tourist office**: Rådhuset, Vestergade 2, ☎ 63 75 75 20 (www.visitodense.com). 🖼 For cheaper private rooms, check out the B&B options in Odense, such as **Allehus**, Tietgens Allé 3, ☎ 22 83 18 92 (www.bbengvej9.dk), €–€€. The **Cab Inn Odense**, Østre Stationsvej 7, ☎ 63 14 57 00 (www.cabinn.com), €€, is a budget hotel right next to the train station. On the same street is the **Danhostel Odense City Hostel** (HI), Østre Stationsvej 31, ☎ 63 11 04 25 (www.cityhostel.dk); closed mid-Dec to early Jan.

ÅRHUS

Denmark's second largest city is an active port and commercial and cultural centre, but even so most sights are within easy walking distance. Old Århus holds the monopoly on nightspots as well as a few museums, including the **Kvindemuseet** (Women's Museum, closed Mon Sept–June), Domkirkepladsen 5, examining the role of women through history, the **Besættelsesmuseet** (open

TO DENMARK'S NORTH SEA COAST

From Odense there are hourly direct trains to **Esbjerg** (1 hr 20 mins, ERT 705) on the west coast of Jutland. The fishing port may not be a prime destination in its own right, but it is the jumping-off point for excursions to the North Frisian Islands and for exploring Denmark's eerily beautiful west coast. Just south of Esbjerg is our favourite town in Denmark, the little city of **Ribe**, with its lofty cathedral, picture-perfect lanes and timber-framed houses. Frequent trains take just 37 mins from Esbjerg to Ribe (ERT 709). Esbjerg also has a direct ferry link with England (ERT 2220).

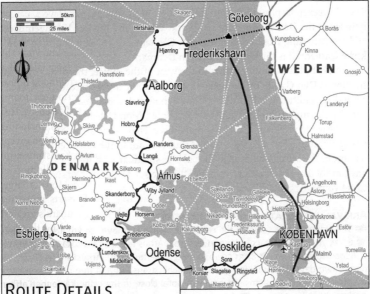

ROUTE DETAILS

Copenhagen–Roskilde	ERT 700, 704, 720	
Type	Frequency	Typical journey time
Train	4–5 per hr	20 mins

Roskilde–Odense	ERT 700	
Type	Frequency	Typical journey time
Train	Every 30 mins	1h10

Odense–Århus	ERT 700	
Type	Frequency	Typical journey time
Train	2 per hr	1h35

Odense–Esbjerg	ERT 705	
Type	Frequency	Typical journey time
Train	Every 1–2 hrs	1h20

Århus–Aalborg	ERT 701	
Type	Frequency	Typical journey time
Train	1–2 per hr	1h35

Aalborg–Frederikshavn	ERT 701	
Type	Frequency	Typical journey time
Train	Every hr	1h10

Frederikshavn–Gothenburg	ERT 2320	
Type	Frequency	Typical journey time
Ferry	4–6 daily	3h15

Notes

There are also up to three HSS Fast Ferry services daily in summer between Frederikshavn and Gothenburg, taking 2 hrs. The port of Hirtshals (shown on the map above) is a one-hour journey from Aalborg, with an easy change of train at Hjørring. At Hirtshals, there are connections with the Smyril Line shipping services to the Faroe Islands and Iceland (ERT 2285). Read more in the Sidetracks on p221. Hirtshals also has useful direct shipping links to Norway (ERT 2350, 2366).

KEY JOURNEYS

Copenhagen–Gothenburg	ERT 735	
Type	Frequency	Typical journey time
Train	8–18 daily	3h45

Copenhagen–Esbjerg	ERT 705	
Type	Frequency	Typical journey time
Train	Every 1–2 hrs	2h55

Tues & weekends, plus Tues–Sun June–Aug), Mathilde Fibigers Have 2, paying homage to the Danish Resistance in World War II, and the free **Vikingemuseet** (Viking Museum; closed Sat–Sun), Skt. Clemens Torv 6. The imposing **Domkirke** (cathedral) is the longest church in Denmark.

Next to the botanic gardens to the west of the centre, the city's major attraction is **Den Gamle By**, an open-air ethnographic museum featuring close to a hundred traditional half-timbered Danish homes. Located about 10 km south of the city the superb **Moesgård Museum** (closed Mon Oct–Mar) is home to the 2,000-year-old preserved Grauballe man, discovered in a nearby peat bog in 1952 (www.moesmus.dk); take 🚌 6 from Århus station. In the town centre, you can use any of the 250 city bikes at 30 special bike stands around town, free of charge, any time of day (insert DKr.20 coin into the bike's slot). Return to a stand after use to get your DKr.20 back.

ARRIVAL, INFORMATION, ACCCOMMODATION

🚆 The station is just south of the centre. ✈ **Århus Lufthavn**, 40 km away in Kolind, ☎ 87 75 70 00 (www.aar.dk); airport bus from Århus takes 45 mins. **🛈 Tourist office**: Banegårdspladsen 20, ☎ 87 31 50 10 (www.visitaarhus.com). **ÅrhusCard**, available for one or two days (DKr.119/149), gives free public transport and free or reduced entry to attractions and museums. 🛏 A budget hotel close to the cathedral is the **Cab Inn Aarhus**, Kannikegade 14, ☎ 86 75 75 00 (www.cabinn.com), €€. **Hostels**: Youth Hostel **Danhostel Århus Vandrerhjem** (HI), Marienlundsvej 10, Risskov, ☎ 86 21 21 20 (www.aarhus-danhostel.dk); closed late Dec to mid-Jan. An independent hostel option is the **City Sleep-In**, Havnegade 20, ☎ 86 19 20 55 (www.citysleep-in.dk).

AALBORG

Herring brought prosperity to this north Jutland town in the 17th century, and the legacy of that boom is the handsome Old Quarter with finely preserved merchants' houses, such as the spectacularly ornate **Jens Bangs Stenhus**. **Kunsten** (Museum of Modern Art, closed Mon) is home to one of the nation's foremost collections of 20th-century art — and has a sculpture garden too. The museum is located at Kong Christians Allé 50 (take 🚌 15). After the sun goes down, **Jomfru Ane Gade** is the street to hit for restaurants, music and bars (be sure to sample the local spirit, Akvavit). The **Aalborg Carnival** takes place in late May every year and throughout the summer open-air rock concerts are held in Mølle Park and in Skovdalen.

ARRIVAL, INFORMATION, ACCOMMODATION

🚆 A short walk south down Boulevarden from the town centre. **🛈 Tourist office**: Østerågade 8, ☎ 99 31 75 00 (www.visitaalborg.com). 🛏 There are some reasonable budget hotel options in Aalborg, including the central **Cab Inn Aalborg**, Fjordgade, ☎ 35 36 11 11 (www.cabinn.com), €€, and the **Zleep Hotel**, Hadsundvej 182, ☎ 70 23

56 35 (www.zleephotels.com), €€. **Hostel**: The youth hostel (HI): **Aalborg Vandrer-hjem**, Skydebanevej 50, ☎ 98 11 60 44, (www.danhostelaalborg.dk), is 3 km from Aalborg centre, close to the marina. Accommodation in four-bed rooms or in one of 30 cabins on an island sleeping five to seven.

Frederikshavn

Really just a place to change from train to boat. ⚓ Sailings to **Gothenburg** depart from the international ferry terminal 400 metres south of the train station. But there are some alternatives. To really feel the wind in your hair, head for the pretty Danish island of **Læsø**. The ferry leaves from a pier 200 metres from the station. Expect rustic delights, and houses thatched with seaweed. If you want to head straight to Oslo (to connect with **Routes 23** and **24**), Stena Line have a useful overnight ferry to the Norwegian capital (ERT 2368).

Gothenburg — see p214

SIDETRACKS E: SHIPPING LINKS

The little branch railway that runs down to the port of Hirtshals at the north tip of the Jutland peninsula looks inconspicuous on the map at the start of Route 22 (see p219). Yet that short train ride is the prelude to one of Europe's most extraordinary journeys by ship.

For travellers less inclined to fly, the dense web of **ferry services** in European waters is an invaluable complement to the rail network. Sometimes an overnight or longer stretch on a ferry can be marvellously recuperative. Did you know, for example, that three **Spanish ports** (Barcelona, Alicante and Almería) all have regular shipping links with Italy? Book a decent cabin, climb aboard and enjoy a relaxing mini-cruise across the Mediterranean. See ERT 2518 for services from Almería and Alicante (Alacant) to Italy, ERT 2520, 2537 and 2580 for ships from **Barcelona** directly to Italy, and ERT 2675 for ships from Barcelona to Italy that stop off in Sardinia en route.

Other long-distance ferry routes that we've used to good effect on our travels are those linking **England** with both **Denmark** (ERT 2220) and **Spain** (ERT 2140 and 2175). These services allow a long hop from Britain to parts of the continent that might not easily be reached by train within a day.

Yet the star of the show, when it comes to a long ferry route through open sea, is the shipping service that starts at the unassuming little port of **Hirtshals** in Denmark. Since October 2010, Hirtshals has been the mainland port-of-call for the Smyril Line link to the **Faroe Islands** and Iceland (ERT 2285). Every week the Smyril ship *Norröna* casts off from Hirtshals for its long journey to some of Europe's remotest island outposts. The ship serves Tórshavn in the Faroes and Seyðisfjörður in eastern **Iceland** (www.smyrilline.fo). In winter, go prepared for a wild crossing. But it beats the plane any day. See our gazetteer listings for the Faroe Islands (p618) and Iceland (p631).

Rail Route 23:
Norwegian fjords and mountains

CITIES: ★★ CULTURE: ★ HISTORY: ★ SCENERY: ★★★
COUNTRIES COVERED: NORWAY

This circular route takes in some of Norway's best mountain and coastal landscapes. The trip incorporates two lines, connected by a catamaran voyage between Bergen and Stavanger. From Oslo the route steadily climbs, past the year-round resorts of **Gol** and **Geilo**, and up to the holiday centre of Ustaoset (990 m), followed by a bleak but magnificent mountainscape of icy lakes and rocky, snow-capped ridges. Shortly after leaving Finse, the train enters a 10-km tunnel to emerge near Hallingskeid. The next stop is **Myrdal**, where you can divert to the hugely popular loop, via train, boat and bus, to the north via **Flåm** dubbed *Norway in a Nutshell* that offers superb fjord views and the chance of meeting a troll or two. The main line then descends to the lakeside town of **Voss**. Thereafter, the scenery is a little less wild, although still impressive.

After you've had a look around the quaint harbour city of Bergen, the catamaran to Stavanger is fast and enjoyable. Even the last leg back to Oslo runs through consistently pleasant countryside, with lots of lakes and forest, along the way serving the cities of **Kristiansand** and **Kongsberg** — both well worth a visit.

If the Oslo–Bergen train is fully booked, or cheap fares are all sold, make Bergen–Oslo reservations and do the circuit in reverse, which has the advantage of saving the really dramatic scenery for the final part of the journey.

OSLO — SEE P532

VOSS

Mountains rise straight out of the lakeside resort, itself just 56 m above sea level. Sights are pretty much limited to the 13th-century baroque-embellished **church**, as most of the town is modern and geared towards winter sports; its après-ski atmosphere is distinctly lively. A cable car, **Hangursbanen**, runs up to 600 m, covering a height difference of about 570 m in 4 mins. For water sports, contact the Voss Rafting Senter, ☎ 56 51 05 25 (www.vossrafting.no, open all year, for rafting May–Oct).

ARRIVAL, INFORMATION, ACCOMMODATION

➽ 5-min walk from town centre. **🛈 Tourist office**: Uttrågata 9, ☎ 56 52 08 00 (www.visitvoss.no), a 3-min walk from the railway station, has plenty on hiking.

🛏 **Youth hostel** (HI): Evangerveien 68, ☎ 56 51 20 17 (www.vosshostel.com), closed mid-Dec till mid-Jan, call ahead in autumn. Located by the lake, 1 km from the town centre.

KEY JOURNEYS

Oslo–Bergen   ERT 780

Type	Frequency	Typical journey time
Train	3–5 daily	6h40

Oslo–Stavanger   ERT 775

Type	Frequency	Typical journey time
Train	2–4 daily	8 hrs

Note

Seat reservation is compulsory on most Norwegian long–distance trains.

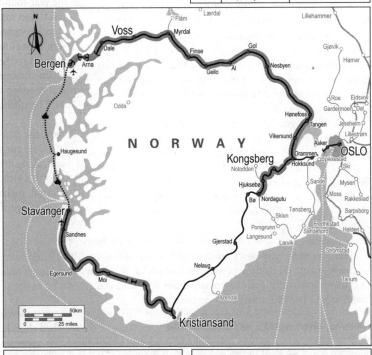

ROUTE DETAILS

Oslo–Voss   ERT 780

Type	Frequency	Typical journey time
Train	3–5 daily	5h30

Voss–Bergen   ERT 781

Type	Frequency	Typical journey time
Train	9–14 daily	1h15

Bergen–Stavanger   ERT 2240

Type	Frequency	Typical journey time
Ship	1–2 daily	4h30

ROUTE DETAILS (CONTINUED)

Stavanger–Kristiansand ERT 775

Type	Frequency	Typical journey time
Train	3–7 daily	3 hrs

Kristiansand–Kongsberg ERT 775

Type	Frequency	Typical journey time
Train	3–5 daily	3h30

Kongsberg–Oslo   ERT 775

Type	Frequency	Typical journey time
Train	1–2 per hr	1h25

BERGEN

An old Hanseatic port, Norway's extremely appealing second city is the gateway to some of the country's most magnificent fjords. Placed on a peninsula and surrounded by mountains, Bergen has meandering cobbled streets lined with gabled weatherboard houses and dignified old warehouses.

The city centres on the waterfront **Fisketorget**, a working fish (and various other things) market open Mon–Sun 0700–1900 June–Aug and Mon–Sat 0700–1600 Sept–May. At the centre of the Old Quarter, **Bryggen** contains a fine row of medieval houses designated a UNESCO World Heritage Site.

Tiny **Theta Museum**, Enhjørningsgården Bryggen, was the clandestine one-room centre for Resistance operations in World War II, until it was discovered by the Nazis in 1942. When the **Bryggens Museum** was being constructed, the remains of the original city of 1050–1500 were found and incorporated. Other museums in town are the art museums and those housed in the university, which also runs the botanic garden.

Gamle Bergen (Old Bergen), at **Sandviken**, is an open-air museum of some three dozen 18th- and 19th-century wooden houses and shops, many furnished in period style, located on cobbled paths and streets. You can wander round for nothing, but have to join a tour if you want to see the interiors. Yellow buses, 🚌 20/23/24, take 10 mins from the tourist office. You can get almost everywhere on foot in Bergen, but take the **Fløibanen** (funicular) from the centre up Mt Fløyen (320 m), for a panoramic view. At the top there's scope for pleasant picnics and walks in the woods.

Classical music lovers may like to visit **Troldhaugen**, home of Edvard Grieg, Norway's greatest composer. Crammed with memorabilia, it is little altered since his death in 1907. Open daily in summer, and weekdays all year except Easter and Dec; there's a museum and concert hall. Buses from the main bus station to Hops-broen, from where it's a walk of 15–20 mins.

ARRIVAL, INFORMATION, ACCOMMODATION

🚆 **Strømgaten**, a 10-min walk east of the centre; walk straight ahead down Marken and keep going. ⛴ Most **ferries** and local boats leave from Strandkaiterminalen and Skoltegrunnskaien. Hurtigruten leaves from Nøstet. Flaggruten catamarans to Stavanger leave from Strandkaien, on the east side. Their office is in Strandkai-terminalen, ☎ 55 23 87 00 (www.tide.no). Pick up a boarding pass 30 mins before departure.

🛈 **Tourist office**: (the best outside Oslo) Vågsalmenningen 1, ☎ 55 55 20 00 (www.visitbergen.com). The **Bergen Card** (valid 24/48 hrs for kr.200/260, from tourist offices, station, hotels and campsites) offers free local transport, free or discounted admission to most of the attractions, and 'a surprise on the menu' at selected restaurants. If you want to wander further afield on foot, or even on skis, **Bergen Turlag** (Bergen Touring Association), in DNT office, Tverrgt 4–6, ☎ 55 33 58 10 (www. bergen-turlag.no) can provide walking maps for the surrounding mountains. Bergen

Norway in a Nutshell

Let's face it. This little circuit is pure tourism, and one of those little adventures that have nothing to do with the real Norway. But it's fun and along the way you'll have a myriad of chances to take pics that will surely impress the folks back home.

The journey leaves the Oslo to Bergen route at **Myrdal** where you board a local train for a breathtaking journey to Flåm, taking about an hour (ERT 781). Rail passes are not valid on this short stretch of railway down to Flåm, but rail-pass holders do receive a 30% discount on the regular fare.

The descent offers superb views of towering cliffs, chasms and cascades. There are 16 tunnels on the route, including one where the line makes a 360° turn completely within the mountain. Most trains stop briefly at the spectacular **Kjosfossen waterfall**. From Flåm, take a ferry for the 2-hr journey along the Aurlandsfjord and **Nærøyfjord** (ERT 781a). After you disembark at **Gudvangen** (accommodation available), the bus back to Voss (also shown in ERT 781a) follows an incredibly steep and breathtakingly dramatic road out of the valley. From 1 May to 30 Sept there are also direct boats from Flåm to Bergen (5 hrs 10 mins, ERT 782).

has plenty of **nightlife**. **Ole Bulls Plass**, south-east of the quay, is good for bars, as is the area behind Torget. There are more student-frequented bars and cafés up towards the university. Look out for events at the **Kulturehuset**, on an old wharf to the south.

🚢 Advance booking recommended – Bergen is often chock-full of tourists and conference-goers. The **Marken Gjestehus**, Kong Oscarsgt 45, ☎ 55 31 44 04 (www.marken-gjestehus.com), has singles, doubles and dorm rooms and is a 2-min walk from the centre of town and the station. Also well-located, in sight of the tourist office, is the **YMCA**, Nedre Korskirkealmenningen 4, ☎ 55 60 60 55 (www.bergenhostel.com).

✖ There's a supermarket next to the YMCA on Nedre Korskirkealmenningen. Buy fruit and delicious smoked salmon or prawn sandwiches from the **fish market**. The large red-and-white building on Zachariasbryggen contains several mid-market restaurants.

By boat from Bergen

The regular catamaran service from Bergen to Stavanger, upon which Route 23 relies for the journey south from Bergen, is called the Flaggruten (ERT 2240, www.flaggruten.no). It is less a coastal voyage than an island cruise, with the vessel picking a route through inshore waterways amid a maze of islands, stopping off here and there at small ports along the way. It is, quite simply, superb. If you are travelling at a busy time, reserve a seat in advance.

Connections from Bergen

From Bergen there are regular day trips by boat to nearby fjords. The most popular give you a chance to explore **Hardangerfjord** (south of Bergen), **Nordfjord** (north of

Bergen), which twists over 100 km to the foot of the **Briksdal Glacier**, and the **Sognefjord** (north of Bergen) which is the longest (205 km) and deepest (1,300 m) in Norway. Bergen also has thrice-weekly sailings to Hirsthals in Denmark (20 hrs, ERT 2237).

And for truly dedicated mariners with a week to spare, Bergen is the jumping-off point for the Hurtigruten service to all points north (ERT 2240). A ship leaves Bergen every evening for the 6-day voyage to Kirkenes, in the Barents Sea near Norway's short frontier with Russia.

STAVANGER

The centre is small and easily walkable, with an excellent pedestrianised cobbled shopping area, and there's a good bus network to reach outlying attractions. **Gamle Stavanger** (the Old Town) is the area on the west side of the harbour. It's lovely for a stroll, with cobbled walkways and rows of early 18th-century wooden houses at crazy angles. The impressive stone **Domkirke** (St Svithun's) was established in 1125 and is the only church in Norway to have kept its original medieval atmosphere. You can also peek inside **Ledål**, a mansion of 1800 still used by the royal family when visiting the town, and **Breidablikk**, an 1880s ship-owner's house. **Valbergtårnet**, a 19th-century watchtower perched on top of a hill in the centre, provides an excellent view of the harbour.

Stavanger is well-placed for day trips to the **Ryfylke fjords**: head for Pulpit Rock (Preikestolen), which has a sheer drop of 600 m (ferry to Tau, then bus to the base of the rock; or via sightseeing boats into the steep-walled Lysefjord). Some 5 km west of town, at Ullandhaug, the **Jernadergarden** is an Iron Age farm (350–550 AD), excavated and reconstructed: 🚌 6/7/x60 from the Sparkassen, opposite the cathedral.

ARRIVAL, INFORMATION, ACCOMMODATION

⇄ Jernbanevej, 10 mins from the harbour and tourist office; round the left side of the lake and straight on. ⛴ **Flaggruten,** ☎ 55 23 87 00 (www.flaggruten.no), catamarans for Bergen leave from Hurtigbåtterminalen. **Fjord Line,** ☎ 51 46 40 99 (fjordline.com) sail for Hirtshals (Denmark). **i Tourist office**: Domkirkeplassen 3; ☎ 51 85 92 00 (www.regionstavanger.com). Exchange, cash machine next door.

🛏 Essential to reserve in advance – Stavanger is often booked out for conferences and is short on cheap hotels. Try the **Stavanger Lille Hotel**, Madlaveien 7, ☎ 51 53 43 27 (www.slh.no), €€, or **Tone's Bed and Breakfast**, Peder Claussøns gt 22, ☎ 51 52 42 07 (www.tones-bb.net), €–€€.

KRISTIANSAND

Regular ferries from Hirtshals in Denmark (ERT 2350) serve this bustling port and resort at the southern tip of Norway. In summer, the town's pleasant beaches are busy. Much of the town was laid out in the 17th century by Christian IV, after whom it is named. His plan included the **Christiansholm Festning**, Strand-promenaden, built to guard the eastern approach to the harbour; the circular fortress is now the major sight (open mid-May to mid-Sept) with views to match. Forming the north-eastern part of the Old Quarter, **Posebyen** has many carefully preserved little wooden houses, while the neo-Gothic **Domkirke** (cathedral), Kirkegt, of 1885 asserts a massive presence. The **fish market** on the quay is a good place to pick up some smoked salmon or prawns for a picnic lunch.

Dyreparken (20 mins from the centre of Kristiansand by 🚌 O1/M1) is a vir-tually cageless zoo and Norway's most visited attraction. There is also an amuse-ment park with a special children's area (Cardamom Town).

Arrival, information, accommodation

🚆 On the west side of the centre, a few blocks from the tourist office, along Vestre Strandgate. 🅱 **Tourist office**: Rådhusgt 6, ☎ 38 12 13 14 (www.visitkrs.no). Also information kiosk at Torvet (Lower Market Square) mid-June to early Aug. ⊨ Just 150 m from the train station is the **Centrum Budget Hotel**, Vestre Strandgate 49, ☎ 38 70 15 65 (www.budgethotel.no), €€.

Kongsberg

Silver put the town on the map following the discovery of silver deposits of unique purity in the early 17th century in the nearby mountains. Kongsberg also established Norway's **National Mint**. Mining remained the town's raison d'être for three centuries: most of the mines (*sølvgruvene*) closed early in the 19th century, but the last one survived up to 1957.

Just out of town are the disused **silver mines** at **Saggrenda** (8 km west, 🚌 410); tours (daily mid-May–Aug; Sat, Sun in Sept; Sun in Oct) take you by train into the mountain to 560 m below sea level. In the town centre a striking legacy of the silver-boom heyday is the **Kongsbergkirke**, a sumptuous triumph of baroque church architecture on the grand scale. Close to Nybrufoss waterfall is the **Norsk Bergverksmuseum** (Norwegian Mining Museum), housed in an old smelting works. **Den Kongelige Mynts Museum** (Mint Museum) is an offshoot of the industry: coin production moved to Kongsberg in 1686 (the National Mint is still here).

The 32 buildings that form the **Lågdalsmuseet** (folk museum, 10-min walk south of the centre) date mainly from the 18th and 19th centuries and include Nor-way's only remaining turret-barn.

Arrival, information, accommodation

🚆 On the west side of the river, next to the tourist office. 🅱 **Tourist office**: Schwabes-gate 2, ☎ 32 29 90 50 (www.visitkongsberg.no). ⊨ The **Kongsberg Bergmannen Hostel** (HI), Vinjesgate 1, ☎ 32 73 20 24 (www.hihostels.no/kongsberg), is just south-west of the town centre.

Rail Route 24:
Arctic adventure: north to Lapland

CITIES: ★ CULTURE: ★★ HISTORY: ★ SCENERY: ★★★
COUNTRIES COVERED: NORWAY, SWEDEN

The real appeal of this popular route into the **Arctic Circle** is undoubtedly the scenery and the real sense of remoteness that you encounter along the way. Townies may get jittery with such vast expanses of wilderness and begin to yearn for concrete (which is there aplenty in some of the townships of northern Norway). In summer you will experience perpetual daylight, but this is a journey for winter too, when the subdued, sometimes even ethereal, character of very short days bring a special quality to the landscape.

The scene outside the carriage window evolves from gentle and bucolic near **Oslo** to breathtakingly dramatic in the northernmost reaches, which are inhabited by reindeer and by the **Sámi** (the more common term Lapp is considered a tad derogatory) — the Nordic region's original, traditional inhabitants. Distances here are serious: Norway is an extremely long country — 1,752 km from tip to tip — and sections of the route take as long as 10 hours. In particular, the recommended side trip from **Dombås** to **Åndalsnes** is an epic one, plunging through tunnels, across bridges, past cascading waterfalls and the highest vertical canyon in Europe.

There is a short stretch of this route, between Fauske and Narvik, that relies on a bus link. There is also the possibility of taking a ship from Bodø to the Lofoten Islands and then continuing by bus to Narvik. From **Narvik**, Route 24 continues over the scenic Ofoten line through awesomely remote terrain over to **Boden** in Sweden.

OSLO — SEE P532

HAMAR

This tiny town, set on Lake Mjøsa, is worth a stop for the **Hedmarksmuseet** (www.hedmarksmuseet.no), a regional open-air museum, a 2-km walk north of the centre, with some 65 historic buildings and the ruins of a medieval cathedral, which had been under cover for a decade to protect it from pollution. On the same site is a herb garden emulating a medieval monastery garden and an art centre where you can observe traditional artisanry.

ARRIVAL, INFORMATION, ACCOMMODATION

⇌ On the southern edge of the centre. 🛈 **Tourist office**: Vikingskipet, Åkersvikveien 1, ☎ 62 51 75 03 (www.hamarregionen.no). In the Vikingskipet (Viking Ship) of the Hamar Olympiske Anlegg (Hamar Olympic Arena). ⊨ 2 km from the centre is the **Hamar Vikingskipet Hostel** (HI), Åkersvikveien 24, ☎ 62 52 60 60.

Notes

If you wish to follow the suggested detour to Åndalsnes, shown as a dotted line on the map to the left, note that the branch-line journey takes about 1h20 (one way). See ERT 785. The direct route between Oslo and Boden includes a change of train in Stockholm. Travellers from Trondheim to Narvik not wanting to visit Bodø can connect onto the Bodø to Narvik bus at Fauske (55 km east of Bodø).

ROUTE DETAILS

Oslo–Hamar — ERT 783, 785

Type	Frequency	Typical journey time
Train	Every 1–2 hrs	1h23

Hamar–Lillehammer — ERT 783, 785

Type	Frequency	Typical journey time
Train	Every 1–2 hrs	50 mins

Lillehammer–Dombås — ERT 785

Type	Frequency	Typical journey time
Train	2–5 daily	1h50

Dombås–Trondheim — ERT 785

Type	Frequency	Typical journey time
Train	2–3 daily	2h35

Trondheim–Bodø — ERT 787

Type	Frequency	Typical journey time
Train	2 daily	9h55

Bodø–Narvik — ERT 787

Type	Frequency	Typical journey time
Bus	2 daily	6h30

Narvik–Gällivare — ERT 761

Type	Frequency	Typical journey time
Train	2 daily	4 hrs

Gällivare–Boden — ERT 761

Type	Frequency	Typical journey time
Train	3 daily	2 hrs

KEY JOURNEYS

Oslo–Trondheim — ERT 785

Type	Frequency	Typical journey time
Train	4 Mon–Fri & Sun; 2 Sat	6h40

Oslo–Boden (via Stockholm) — ERT 750, 760, 761

Type	Frequency	Typical journey time
Train	1 daily	20–23 hrs

Boden–Stockholm — ERT 760, 761

Type	Frequency	Typical journey time
Train	2 daily	13 hrs

Stockholm–Narvik — ERT 760, 761

Type	Frequency	Typical journey time
Train	1 daily	18h30

LILLEHAMMER

Lillehammer is both a major **skiing** centre and an appealing lakeside town, typified by winsome wooden houses that cling to the hillside. It hosted the 1994 Winter Olympics and many of the facilities can now be visited — and in some cases used. In winter, the downhill and cross-country ski trails and skating rinks are some of the best maintained in the country. Many are open during the summer too — including chairlifts, summer ski-jumping and an Alpine bobsled track, and the surrounding area is laced with paths ideal for hiking.

ARRIVAL, INFORMATION, ACCOMMODATION

≋ West of the centre. **🛈 Tourist offices**: Jernbanetorget 2, ☎ 61 28 98 00 (www.lillehammer.com). ⊨ For rail travellers, the **Lillehammer Vandrerhjem Stasjonen** (HI), Jernbanetorget 2, ☎ 61 26 00 24 (www.stasjonen.no) is perfectly located next to the station. A little out from the centre is the **Ersgaard Gjestehuset**, Nordsetervegen 201, ☎ 61 25 06 84, €€.

DOMBÅS

The branch line to **Åndalsnes** (ERT 785) diverges at this popular centre for winter sports. The journey out to Åndalsnes is reason enough for a visit, but it also gets you to **Geirangerfjord**, arguably the most stunning of all the Norwegian fjords. The green-blue water wends its way for 16 km between cliffs (of up to 1,500 m) and past tumbling waterfalls. Get a bus from Åndalsnes to **Hellesylt** or **Geiranger** (at opposite ends of the fjord) and take the ferry between them (70 mins), then bus back to Åndalsnes — or on towards **Ålesund**, which is architecturally quite a surprise, for the town boasts some first-class art nouveau buildings.

ARRIVAL, INFORMATION, ACCOMMODATION

≋ Station: a few mins walk from the centre. **🛈 Tourist office**: Frichgården, ☎ 61 24 14 44 (www.rondane-dovrefjell.no). ⊨ **Youth hostel** (HI): Trolltun Gjestegård, ☎ 61 24 09 60 (www.trolltun.no), 2 km from rail station.

TRONDHEIM

Norway's first capital was founded in 997 by the Viking king **Olav Tryggvason** whose statue adorns a column in the market square. Trondheim still has strong royal connections. Monarchs are crowned in the cathedral and the city has been the seat of the monarchy since the 12th century. Trondheim is Norway's third city and a major **university town**, with more than 20,000 students giving it some of the best nightlife in Norway. The narrow streets of the compact centre make a pleasant strolling ground, but after dark, prepare to find out how Norwegians party.

At Hunderfossen, 15 km to the north (10 mins by train), you can try out the 1994 Olympic luge and bobsleigh tracks (up to 60 mph; on wheels in summer), or 'play, learn and experience' at the **Hunderfossen Family Park** (open summer; www. hunderfossen.no). Worth it if only to get a photo next to the 12-metre-high trolls. We exaggerate not! Several operators run rafting and canoeing trips in the **Gudbrandsdal Valley**, ranging from a half-day taster to an epic two-day voyage down the Sjoa River. Ask for details at tourist offices in Lillehammer or Dombås.

Sjusjøen, reached by regular buses from Lillehammer, is a lakeside sports town set high up on a plateau where the snow stays till late in the year. A couple of ski rental shops can kit you out for cross-country skiing and sell you a map of the vast network of groomed tracks (*løype*). In summer, it's a good place for water sports. ⊨ The youth hostel (HI): **Fjellheimen**, Sjusjøen, ☎ 62 34 76 80 (www.sjusjoen-fjellheimen.no), is a large complex by a lake, perfect for nature exploration.

The **Nidaros Domkirke** (cathedral), Bispegata, is cavernously Gothic in design, and well worth seeing for its decorative stonework and elegant stained-glass windows. Northwards from the cathedral lies **Torvet** (main square), while further on at the water's edge is **Ravnkloa**, home to a fish market. From here, hourly boats run, usually mid-May to mid-Sept, to the island of **Munkholmen**, a monastery-cum-fortress-cum-prison; it's now a popular place for swimming.

Trondhjems Kunstforening (Trondheim Art Gallery, www.tkf.no; closed Mon), Bispegata 9a, exhibits some of Norway's greatest art, including a few works by Munch, while the **Nordenfjeldske Kunstindustrimuseum** (National Museum of Decorative Art), Munkegata 5, has a collection of contemporary arts and crafts (closed Mon, late Aug–late May). Other sights include the **Gamle Bybro** (Old Town Bridge), with views of the wharf and its 18th-century warehouse buildings.

ARRIVAL, INFORMATION, ACCOMMODATION

⇟ North of the centre; also the bus station, a 15-min walk to the tourist office (cross the bridge, after three blocks turn right on to Olav Tryggvasonsgata and left up Munkegata). 🛈 **Tourist office:** Munkegata 19, ☎ 73 80 76 60 (www.trondheim.com); entrance from Torvet (market square). ⊨ The **Trondheim InterRail Centre**, Elgesetergate 1, ☎ 73 89 95 38 (www.tirc.no), is an excellent option in the summer months, although it is only open from mid-June to mid-August. During the rest of the year, try **Pensjonat Jarlen**, Kongensgt. 40, ☎ 73 51 32 18 (www.jarlen.no) or the **Trondheim Vandrerhjem Hostel** (HI), Weidemannsvei 41, ☎ 73 87 44 50 (www.trondheim-vandrerhjem.no), 2 km east (🚌 63 Singsaker; infrequent Sat–Sun).

AROUND TRONDHEIM

Don't miss **Ringve Museum**, Lade Allé 60, 3 km east of town: 🚌 3/4: Fagerheim (from Munkegata towards Lade). This national music museum holds an astounding collection of antique musical instruments (open daily mid-June to mid-Sept, otherwise only Sun; free admission Nov–Mar). The assortment of buildings at **Trøndelag Folkemuseum**, Sverresborg, includes turf huts and a small stave church from 1170; buses from Dronningensgate (D1): 🚌 8 towards Stavset; 10 mins.

CONNECTIONS FROM TRONDHEIM

If the lure of the North means less to you, there is a useful rail route to Sweden from Trondheim operated by Veolia (rail passes accepted). Twice-daily trains run via **Storlien** to Östersund C (4 hrs, ERT 760), from where there are direct trains to Stockholm and an overnight train to Gothenburg. At **Östersund C** (overnight stay required) you can also connect onto the summer-season Inlandsbanan train south to Mora and north to Gällivare (ERT 753).

NORTHWARD BOUND

One of the most remarkable rail trips we have made in Europe was a June overnight journey from Trondheim to Bodø. Yes, the sun did set, but only just, and the 'simmer dim' had a peculiar quality all of its own. Since then, we have made this same journey by day in deep mid-winter and it was every bit as engaging as on the first occasion. This line is called **Nordlandsbanen** and is the only rail route that crosses the **Arctic Circle** on Norwegian territory (ERT 787).

Here is an instance where the journey is the thing. There is no particular reason to break the 10-hr journey to Bodø. The towns along the way are unprepossessing and it comes as a surprise that they are quite industrial. Mosjøen has an aluminium smelter while a little farther north Mo-i-Rana (usually dubbed Mo for short) has a steel works. End of the line is **Bodø**. If you are not stopping off, but heading on north at once, then transfer from train to bus at Fauske, reached about 40 mins before Bodø. Bus times on to Narvik are in ERT 787.

BODØ

Bodø is a busy little port and departure point for ferries to the Lofoten Islands. The **Domkirke** (cathedral) is notable for its unusual detached spire, while the **Norsk Luftfartsmuseum** (Norwegian Aviation Museum), Olav V gata, has a good collection of airliners from various eras.

WITNESSING THE NORTHERN LIGHTS

The Aurora Borealis, or Northern Lights, is a stunning natural spectacle of glowing light in the sky, an atmospheric phenomenon caused by collisions between air molecules and charged particles from the sun that explode upon entering the earth's atmosphere. It occurs sporadically in winter throughout northern Scandinavia, and your best chance of catching this spectacular natural aurora is during crisp, clear conditions with ideally no moon.

THE LOFOTEN ISLANDS

Bodø is the best place to catch a ferry to the spectacular Lofoten Islands, a chain of improbably jagged glacially-sculpted mountains that shelter **fishing villages**, farms, sheep and thousands of birds (including puffins). This is the Norwegian scenery at its best — mild climate, comparatively uncrowded and the sense that you are with nature at its purest. It is excellent terrain for walking, horseriding and cycling (it is possible to hire bicycles), and there are some great boat trips — including to the beautiful cliffside bird colonies of **Værøy** and to **Trollfjord**. Røst and Værøy support colonies of puffins; both have accommodation.

The islands' main town is Svolvær (pop. 4,500), on Austvågøy. 🚩 **Tourist office**: Svolvær Torg, ☎ 76 06 98 07 (www.lofoten.info). Don't miss the picturesque fishing village with the modest name of **Å**, 5 km south of Moskenes, with cottages, an **HI hostel** (Å Vandrerhjem, ☎ 76 09 11 21, www.lofoten-rorbu.com) and a campsite. Fishing, caving and hiking trips can all be arranged here.

The northbound **Hurtigruten ship** leaves Bodø at mid-afternoon daily for the Lofoten ports of **Stamsund** and **Svolvær**. A later boat is faster and serves Svolvær only, but is much less comfortable (see ERT 2240). Other ferries from Bodø serve Moskenes, Røst and Værøy. From Svolvær, there are direct buses to Narvik via the new Lofast Highway (see footnote ERT 787) that uses a series of bridges and undersea tunnels to link the principal islands of the Lofoten chain to the mainland.

ARRIVAL, INFORMATION, ACCOMMODATION

🚆 300 m east of the tourist office. 🚩 **Tourist office**: Sjøgata 3, ☎ 75 54 80 00 (www.visitbodo.com). ⛴ Hurtigruten cruises and ferries to the islands leave from quays on the road near the station. 🚌 Long-distance bus station is 300 m from the tourist office further along Sjøgata.

📨 For central budget accommodation, try **Opsahl Gjestegaard**, Prinsens gate 131, ☎ 75 52 07 04 (www.opsahlgjestegaard.no), €€.

NARVIK

This small modern port wins no prizes for its architecture, though the setting is magnificent. Narvik was invaded in 1940 by the Germans in a bid to control shipments of iron ore; within days the British destroyed the German fleet and the Allies recaptured the town. The first section of the **Nordland Røde Kors Krigsminnemuseum** (Red Cross War Museum) commemorates the town's important role in World War II as well as the work of the Resistance. Narvik's prosperity owes virtually everything to the Ofoten railway line, which transports iron ore from Sweden, then ships it out to sea from town; the **Ofoten Museum** provides a thorough overview of the industry and its history.

For panoramic views towards the Lofoten Islands, take the *Fjellheisen* (cable car) up **Fagernesfjellet**, at the top of which is a restaurant, lookout station and a host of walking trails; allow 2 hrs to hike up without the lift.

⇶ A 10- to 12-min walk south-west into the city centre. ➿ Bus station is in the city centre. **🛈 Tourist office**: Stasjonsveien 1 (at the railway station), ☎ 46 92 24 66 (www.destinationnarvik.com).

⇥ Norumgården, Framnesveien 127, ☎ 76 94 48 57 (www.norumgaarden. narviknett.no), €€, a B&B in a 1920s villa. **Breidablikk Gjestehus**, Tore Hundsgate 41, ☎ 76 94 14 18 (www.breidablikk.no), €, is a moderately priced pension up the hill from the main road. **Spor 1 Gjestegård**, Brugata 2a, ☎ 76 94 60 20 (www.spor1.no), €, is just as cheap and has very friendly owners.

GÄLLIVARE

Iron and copper ore mining dominates the scene in this Swedish town, and tours (contact the tourist office for details) enter the open-cast copper mine and the underground iron mine. In Malmberget (the site of the mines north of town) are the museum village, **Kåkstan**, and the **Mining Museum**.

Gällivare is also a good place to immerse yourself in the Sámi (Lapp) culture, whose heritage is reflected in the (current) name of its mid-18th-century church, **Lappkyrkan**. About 2 km from the centre of town, up the road to Dundret, **Vägvisaren** is a small family business specialising in adventures based on Sámi culture. The top of Dundret, the 820 m hill that looms to the south of the town, is a **nature reserve** with panoramic views. It's 7 km to the top and you should allow at least 3 hrs to come down (it can take twice that), but you can get great views from 4 km. When the **Midnight Sun** is visible there are bus tours to the top.

ARRIVAL, INFORMATION, ACCOMMODATION

⇶ On the western edge of town. **🛈 Tourist office**: Storgatan 16, ☎ 0970 166 60 (www.gellivare.se). **⇥ Hotell Dundret**, Tingshusgatan 3, ☎ 0970 550 40 (www. hotelldundret.se), €. The **Vandrarhemmet Rallarrosen STF** (HI) youth hostel, Barnhemsvägen 2A, ☎ 0970 143 80 (www.stfturist.se) is a short walk from the train station.

CONNECTIONS FROM GÄLLIVARE

Gällivare is the northern end of the superbly scenic Inlandsbanan, which runs 1,067 km through central Sweden from Mora (summer-only service, overnight stop required at Östersund; ERT 753).

For a 100-km sample, ride from Gällivare to **Jokkmokk** (2 hrs). There's only one train a day in each direction, giving you rather longer than you might need there; alternatively, daily buses from Gällivare allow you a 5-hr stay. Jokkmokk grew from a Sámi mission into a sizeable town and its prime role today is to keep the Sámi culture alive. **🛈 Tourist office:** Stortorget 4, ☎ 0971 222 50.

BODEN — SEE P243

Whether you approach Narvik on a direct overnight train from Stockholm or on the bus that runs up the Norwegian coast from Bodø and Fauske, you are sure to have that distinct feeling of having reached somewhere very far from civilisation. **Narvik** is the end of the line, and the spectacular **Ofoten railway** that runs over the mountains from Sweden (part of Route 24) is the northernmost rail journey included among the 50 routes in this book. It is not, as it happens, the northernmost passenger railway in Europe by any means. That prize goes to a route that runs west towards the Norwegian border from the Russian Arctic port of **Murmansk** (Мурманск).

End of the line does not mean end of the road, and true adverturers can continue beyond Narvik to explore Norway's two northernmost *fylker* (or counties): **Troms** (or Romsa in the Sámi language) and **Finnmark** (Finnmárku in Sámi). If you are tempted to head north from Narvik, don't underestimate the formidable distances involved.

Four times each week, there is a bus connection from Narvik to **Kirkenes**, the last community of any size in Norway before the border with Russia. The journey takes 28 to 31 hrs, depending on the day of the week. That long haul includes an 8-hr overnight stop in **Alta**, a superbly located but utterly dreary town on Altafjord. An alternative route north is by the regular coastal shipping service called **Hurtigruten**. Ships operate daily in each direction, but do not serve Narvik. You can board the Hurtigruten boats in Bodø, whence it is 67 hrs around the northern Norwegian coast to the Barents Sea port of Kirkenes. If you are in Narvik, your best bet is to take the direct bus to **Tromsø** (4 hrs) and join the Hurtigruten boat there. Tromsø to Kirkenes by ship takes 40 hrs. Hurtigruten schedules are shown in ERT 2240.

Travel right to the furthest reaches of eastern Finnmark and you'll realise that remoteness is utterly relative. Experience those long bus and boat journeys to Kirkenes, and now Narvik will retrospectively glow in your memory as a bustling hub of northern life. Kirkenes is further east than Istanbul, while **Vardø**, the administrative capital of Finnmark, is further east than Cairo. Like Kirkenes, Vardø is on the Hurtigruten. The town, located on a small offshore island linked by undersea tunnel to the mainland, cut a dash in 17th-century Europe by burning lots of witches. More than a hundred in all, which encourages one to speculate quite what so many witches were doing on a rather inhospitable island in the **Barents Sea**. Nowadays there's witchcraft of another kind in the array of electronic gadgetry that sits atop a hill on the mainland. Officials say the radar facility is there to keep an inventory of satellites in the heavens above. Locals say the dishes point only at Russia.

For Russia really is just over the horizon. Kirkenes is the best jumping-off point for journeys into Russia. A 15-min drive from Kirkenes harbour and you can be eye-to-eye with a **Russian border** guard across a wire-mesh fence. If you have a Russian visa, you can cross the frontier at **Boris Gleb** (Борисоглебскй). Direct buses run daily from Kirkenes to Murmansk in Russia (5 hrs, ERT 789) where you can hop on a train for the 27-hr journey to St Petersburg and join **Route 45**, following it in reverse direction back to Germany.

Rail Route 25: Historic Swedish cities

CITIES: ★★ CULTURE: ★ HISTORY: ★★ SCENERY: ★
COUNTRIES COVERED: DENMARK, SWEDEN

This is not a long route, and slick Swedish X2000 trains speed from **Copenhagen** to **Stockholm** every two hours, taking just 5 hrs for the 644 km journey. Even at such speed the forest and lake landscapes of southern Sweden are sheer delight. If speed is not your style, semi-fast services traverse the same route too, usually involving a change of train in **Malmö**, and taking up to 7 hrs for the journey between the two capitals. Real slow-travel enthusiasts can follow the entire route on local trains, which actually connect very well. But with four changes and a journey time of 12 hrs, this option is really only for those keen to savour every passing tree.

COPENHAGEN — SEE P472

MALMÖ

Sweden's fast-growing third city (pop. 260,000) is a lively place, with plenty of good bars, clubs and coffee houses, and an excellent festival in August. Capital of the Skåne province, Malmö was part of Denmark for much of the Middle Ages and came under Swedish sovereignty in 1658: even today the Skåne accent has something of a Danish tinge. Most recently, many young Danes have moved here to avoid strict Danish marriage laws.

Enclosed by a canal that loops round through a park and doubles as the castle moat, the city's well-groomed historic centre dates back to Danish times and features a pair of fine cobbled squares. Leaving the station southwards along Hamngatan, you soon reach the large central square, **Stortorget**, presided over by the statue of Carl Gustav, who won Skåne back from Denmark. The square is flanked on the east by the 1546 **Rådhuset** (town hall), itself on the line of Södergatan, the main pedestrianised street. Just behind stands **St Petri Kyrka** (St Peter's Church) — Sweden's second-largest church — its whitewashed Gothic interior complementing its baroque altar and medieval frescos. Off Stortorget's south-western corner lies **Lilla Torg**, a smaller and slightly more charming square with medieval brick and timber facades, outdoor cafés and restaurants; live music sparks up the atmosphere on summer evenings.

From here walk a few minutes west to the formidable 15th-century fortress, **Malmöhus Slott**, open daily 1200–1600, whose circular towers and assorted buildings hold a set of captivating museums covering a range of themes — including city history, military exhibits, art and natural history.

If the weather permits, kick back in one of the three **great parks**, Kungsparken, Slottsparken and Pildammsparken; or head down to the 3-km long

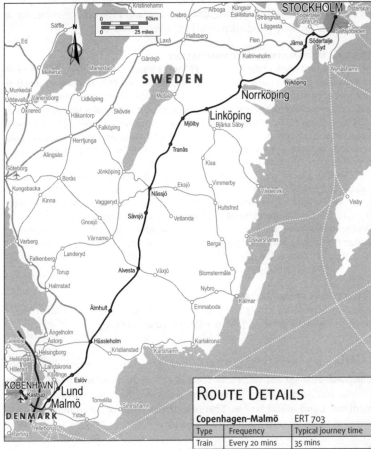

ROUTE DETAILS

Copenhagen–Malmö — ERT 703

Type	Frequency	Typical journey time
Train	Every 20 mins	35 mins

Malmö–Lund — ERT 730, 735, 737, 745

Type	Frequency	Typical journey time
Train	6 per hr	12 mins

Lund–Linköping — ERT 730

Type	Frequency	Typical journey time
Train	Every 1–2 hrs	2h30

Linköping–Norrköping — ERT 730

Type	Frequency	Typical journey time
Train	Up to 3 per hr	25 mins

Norrköping–Stockholm — ERT 730

Type	Frequency	Typical journey time
Train	1–2 per hr	1h15

KEY JOURNEYS

Copenhagen–Stockholm — ERT 730

Type	Frequency	Typical journey time
Train	5–6 daily	5h02

Stockholm–Oslo — ERT 750

Type	Frequency	Typical journey time
Train	2 daily	6h05

Stockholm–Helsinki — ERT 2465

Type	Frequency	Typical journey time
Ferry	2 daily	17 hrs

Ribersborg beach, within walking distance. You can pick up provisions for a picnic at the excellent Saluhallen covered market in Lilla Torg.

ARRIVAL, INFORMATION, ACCOMMODATION

≋ **Malmö C**, just north of the Old Town. 🄸 **Tourist office**: Centralstation, ☎ 040 34 12 00 (www.malmotown.com). Get the useful free *Malmö This Month* two-monthly guide for events and listings. For information on the Malmö Festival in August see the website (www.malmofestivalen.se). Consider getting the **Malmökortet** (Malmö Card), valid for 1/2 days (SEK170/200) for one adult and two children (under 16) for free local buses, free admission to the castle, all of Malmö's museums and a bus tour, plus savings on sightseeing trips, shopping, entertainment and eating out. The Malmö Card is available from the tourist office and Forex offices.

⊨ The tourist office can make free hotel bookings. The **Formule 1 Hotel**, Lundavägen 28, ☎ 040 93 05 80 (www.hotelformule1.se), €, is a no-frills budget option to the east of the city centre. More expensive, but right next to the train station, is the **Comfort Hotel**, Carlsgatan 10c, ☎ 040 33 04 40 (www.choicehotels.se/comfort), €€. **Hostels**: The **STF Malmö City Hostel** (HI), Rönngatan 1, ☎ 040 611 62 20 (www.stfturist.se/malmocity), is modern and central. Another option for a bed in a dorm, is the private **Rut & Ragnars Hostel**, Spånehusvägen 77, ☎ 040 611 60 60 (www.rutochragnars.se).

CONNECTIONS FROM MALMÖ

Malmö to Gothenburg X2000 trains take 2 hrs 45 mins (supplement payable). There are also slower trains, taking 3 hrs 10 mins. See **Route 21** (p212).

LUND

The handsome ancient university town is one of the most rewarding spots to visit in southern Sweden. A religious centre in the 12th century, much of **medieval Lund** is still visible. There's a decent range of accommodation and plenty of studenty eating and drinking haunts.

ARRIVAL, INFORMATION, ACCOMMODATION

≋ A 5-min walk west of the centre. 🄸 **Tourist office**: Kyrkogatan 11, ☎ 046 35 50 40 (www.lund.se). ⊨ **Youth hostel** (HI): **Vandrarhem 'Tåget' Lund**, Vävaregatan 22, ☎ 046 14 28 20 (www.stfturist.se), 300 m from the station — known as 'The Train', it's possibly the only hostel in the world made up of railway carriages.

LINKÖPING

The town's prime attraction is **Gamla Linköping** (www.linkoping.se), Malmslättsvägen, an ambitious living museum that seeks to recreate 19th-century Linköping, much of which was painstakingly relocated piece by piece and rebuilt here. It includes a small chocolate factory, as well as working craft shops, houses, street lamps and old signs. Try to visit when the buildings are open; otherwise you may have to content yourself with viewing them from the outside. Linköping's **Domkyrka** is one of Sweden's oldest cathedrals, with a 107-m green spire visible from far outside the town, and containing fine stone carvings along the south doorway. The north doorway is a survival of the original Romanesque building that was later substantially extended (particularly in the 19th century). There is a very striking bronze baptismal font, a lovely 14th-century crucifix and some stunning modern art. The latter include the *Afzelius tapestries* (1938) and the *Tree of Life* (1997).

Flygvapenmuseum (Airforce Museum), next to Malmen military airfield, 6 km west of Linköping (🚌 13 from Resecentrum, the central train/bus station, www.sfhm.se), is an assemblage of some 60 military aircraft dating from 1912 — several of the cockpits are open to sit in and try your hands at the controls (www.flygvapenmuseum.se).

ARRIVAL, INFORMATION, ACCOMMODATION

⇶ A 5-min walk east of the centre. 🖪 **Tourist office**: Storgatan 15, ☎ 013 190 00 70 (www.visitlinkoping.se). ⊨ **Hostel**: The youth hostel **Linköpings Vandrarhem & Hotell** (HI), Klostergatan 52A, ☎ 013 35 90 00 (www.lvh.se), also offers private rooms and apartments, and is central.

NORRKÖPING

Norrköping is a prosperous textile centre, with a museum celebrating the town's industrial legacy. For most visitors, however, the main reason for a stop is **Kolmårdens Djur och Naturpark** (Kolmården Zoo and Safari Park; www.kolmarden.com), open early May–early Oct. The zoo is the largest in Europe and consists of two separate sections: the main zoo (with a dolphin show) and the safari park. The cable car is great for views of the landscape. It's 30 km north-east of town, 🚌 432 (roughly hourly) takes about 50 mins. 🚌 481 runs 10 km to **Löfstad Slott** (Löfstad Castle), a lavish 17th-/18th-century mansion on vast manicured grounds that has remained unchanged since the last owner died some 60 years ago (www.lofstad.nu). Rock carvings depicting wild beasts, human figures and sailing ships — and dating from 1500 to 500 BC — can be seen at **Himmelstalund**, 2 km west of the centre of Norrköping.

ARRIVAL, INFORMATION, ACCOMMODATION

⇶ Norrköping C, a 5-min walk north of the centre. 🖪 **Tourist office**: Dalsgatan 9, ☎ 011 15 50 00 (www.upplev.norrkoping.se). ⊨ **Youth hostel** (HI): **Turistgården**, Ingelstagatan 31, ☎ 011 10 11 60 (www.turistgarden.se).

STOCKHOLM — SEE P568

Rail Route 26: Around the Gulf of Bothnia

CITIES: ★ CULTURE: ★ HISTORY: ★★ SCENERY: ★★
COUNTRIES COVERED: SWEDEN, FINLAND

Route 26 is more than merely a quick hop between Stockholm and Helsinki. Indeed, if time is tight there are comfortable overnight ships that link the two capitals (ERT 2465). Route 26 makes a great loop around the **Gulf of Bothnia**, the northernmost extension of the Baltic. The Gulf waters are shallow, brackish in the south and almost salt-free at the northern end. The journey turns out to be more challenging than you might think, for the rail network along **Sweden's east coast** is patchy (but rapidly improving, with a new rail link from Sundsvall to Umeå due to open in August 2012) and there is no passenger service across the border from Sweden to Finland. But, if you do not mind a bus or two, this is a fine trip, with several interesting cities and some blissful scenery along the way.

Devotees of oddball diversions may like to visit the world's northernmost IKEA or head off north from the main route to cross the Arctic Circle.

STOCKHOLM —SEE P568

UPPSALA

Our view is that if there is one city in Sweden that absolutely should not be missed, it is Uppsala, home of the country's oldest university as well as its foremost ecclesiastical centre. The 16th-century **Uppsala Slott** (Red Castle), overlooking the town, was built by King Gustav Vasa, who broke ties with the Vatican and pointed his cannons directly at the archbishop's palace. Beneath the castle is what's left of the Old City. Ingmar Bergman's film *Fanny and Alexander* was filmed here (Bergman himself was also born in Uppsala). The central sights are easily walkable.

Dominating the skyline are the twin towers of Scandinavia's largest church, the French-Gothic **Domkyrka**. Completed in 1435, it took 175 years to build and was heavily restored in the 18th and 19th centuries. Virtually every inch of the church's side chapels is covered with tapestries or wall and ceiling paintings; the most impressive chapels are those of St Erik, Gustav Vasa and the botanist Linnaeus (see p242). Founded in 1477, the **old university building (Gustavianum)** features an anatomical chamber where the public dissection of executed convicts was a 17th-century tourist attraction. It is open to visitors (closed Mon). Books, manuscripts and maps are on display in **Carolina Rediviva Universitets-biblioteket** (library), Dag Hammarskjölds väg 1. Most notable here is part of the 6th-century *Codex Argenteus* (Silver Bible) — a rare example of the extinct Gothic language, penned on purple vellum parchment — and the original manuscript of Mozart's *Die Zauberflöte* (*The Magic Flute*).

Notes

On the journey from Luleå to Kemi, change buses at Haparanda. Advance your watch by one hour as the bus crosses the border bridge between Haparanda (Sweden) and Tornio (Finland).

Sundsvall to Umeå: trains are expected to start using the new Bothnia railway line (Botniabanan) from late summer or autumn 2012. In anticipation of the opening of this new rail route, the map below already shows this leg as a train journey. Prior to the opening of the new route, the stretch from Sundsvall to Umeå is by bus as shown in the route details to the right.

ROUTE DETAILS

Stockholm–Uppsala	ERT 758, 760, 765	
Type	Frequency	Typical journey time
Train	1–2 per hr	40 mins

Uppsala–Sundsvall	ERT 760	
Type	Frequency	Typical journey time
Train	5–6 daily	2h45

Sundsvall–Umeå	ERT 768	
Type	Frequency	Typical journey time
Bus	7 daily	4h05

Umeå–Luleå	ERT 761, 768	
Type	Frequency	Typical journey time
Bus	7–10 daily	4h10
Train	4 daily	3h30 to 4h40

Luleå–Kemi	ERT 769	
Type	Frequency	Typical journey time
Bus	4–6 daily	3h10 to 4h30

Kemi–Oulu	ERT 794	
Type	Frequency	Typical journey time
Train	6 daily	1 hr

Oulu–Tampere	ERT 794	
Type	Frequency	Typical journey time
Train	9–10 daily	5h20

Tampere–Turku	ERT 795	
Type	Frequency	Typical journey time
Train	7–9 daily	1h44

Turku–Helsinki	ERT 791	
Type	Frequency	Typical journey time
Train	Every 1–2 hrs	2 hrs

KEY JOURNEYS

Stockholm–Luleå	ERT 760, 761	
Type	Frequency	Typical journey time
Train	2 daily	12h45

Stockholm–Turku	ERT 2480	
Type	Frequency	Typical journey time
Ship	4 daily	11 hrs

The great 18th-century professor of botany, Linnaeus (Carl von Linné), developed the definitive system of plant and animal classification. His former residence is now a museum, **Linnémuseet**, in the small **Linnéträdgården** (Linnaeus' Garden), Svartbäcksg. 27. Also worth a visit is the larger **Botaniska Trädgården** (Botanic Garden), Villavägen 8.

Gamla Uppsala (Old Uppsala), 5 km north, was the cradle of Swedish civilisation and thought to be the centre of a pre-Christian pagan cult. Hundreds of tombs are dominated by huge grassy mounds, resting places of three 6th-century kings. Alongside them are the **Uppsala Kyrka** (church) and a small museum village.

ARRIVAL, INFORMATION, ACCOMMODATION

⇶ Uppsala C. East of the centre, a 5-min stroll to the tourist office: walk straight up Bangårdsgatan to the river, turn right and cross the second bridge – the **⊞ tourist office** is halfway along the block on Fyristorg 8, ☎ 018 727 48 00 (www.uppsala.to).

⊨ **Uppsala Room Agency**, ☎ 018 10 95 33 (Mon–Fri 0900–1700), can book private rooms. **Samariterhemmets Gästhem**, Samaritergränd 2, ☎ 018 56 40 00 (www.samariterhemmet.se), €€, run by the Church of Sweden, is probably the cheapest hotel. **Hotel Uppsala**, Kungsg. 27, ☎ 018 480 50 00 (www.profilhotels.se), €€, is a comfortable business hotel. **Grand Hotell Hörnan**, Bangårdsg. 1, ☎ 018 13 93 80 (www.grandhotellhornan.se), €€€, is old-style classy and more expensive. **Youth hostel** (HI): **Sunnersta Manor**, Sunnerstavägen 24, ☎ 018 32 42 20 (www.sunnerstaherrgard.se), 5 km to the south (🚌 20 to Herrgårdsvägen). (Non-HI): **Uppsala City Hostel**, St Persgatan 16, ☎ 018 10 00 08 (www.uppsalacityhostel.se), right in the city centre.

SUNDSVALL

Spread over the mainland and onto the island of Alnö, the town is primarily a timber port, though it does maintain a charming centre dominated by grand, late 19th-century limestone and brick structures built after a disastrous fire in 1888 that destroyed most of Sundsvall's wooden buildings. The **Kulturmagasinet** is an interesting complex of restored warehouse buildings, now housing a small local museum, a gallery, a café and a library. For a look at a unique modern church interior, have a peek inside the red-brick **Gustav Adolfs Kyrka**. Otherwise, head out of the centre to the medieval **Alnö gamla kyrka** (🚌 1 to Alnö), a church with several well-preserved 16th-century frescos; or to **Norra Bergets Hantverks- och Friluftsmuseum**, an open-air museum with an eclectic mix of panoramic views.

ARRIVAL, INFORMATION, ACCOMMODATION

⇶ A 10-min walk from the main square. **⊞ Tourist office:** Stora Torget, ☎ 060 658 58 00 (www.visitsundsvall.se). ⊨ **Lilla Hotellet**, Rådhusgatan 15, ☎ 060 61 35 87 (www.lilla-hotellet.se), €€, an old sweet factory, and now a lovely, homely and inexpensive hotel in the centre. The **Sundsvall City Hostel**, Sjögatan 11, ☎ 060 12 60 90 (www.sundsvallcityhostel.se), located in the centre, has dorms and private rooms.

UMEÅ

Umeå is a rapidly growing university town with a youthful population and is northern Sweden's largest town. A popular activity is shooting the nearby rapids in rubber rafts (mid-May to mid-Sept). One place really worth lingering is **Gammlia**, a complex of seven museums, including a ski museum and an excellent open-air museum with buildings from all over the region; most sections open only in summer.

ARRIVAL, INFORMATION, ACCOMMODATION
≉ A 5-min walk north of the centre. Luggage lockers. **🚹 Tourist office:** Renmarkstorget 15, ☎ 090 16 16 16 (www.visitumea.se). Free hotel reservation service. ⋈ Inexpensive options are **Tegs Hotell**, Verkstadsgatan 5, ☎ 090 12 27 00 (www.tegshotell.se), €, or **Pensionat Pendlaren**, Pendelgatan 5, ☎ 090 12 98 55 (www.pendlaren.com), €. **Youth hostel** (HI): Västra Esplanaden 10, ☎ 090 77 16 50 (www.umeavandrarhem.se).

BODEN

Primarily a rail junction and once Sweden's largest garrison town, Boden is a pleasant enough place to wait between trains. Fearing attack by Russia after the 1809 invasion of Finland, the Swedes erected a mighty complex of fortresses. The **Rödbergsfortet** was built a little later, in the early 20th century, but is nonetheless impressive.

ARRIVAL, INFORMATION, ACCOMMODATION
≉ **Boden C**. A 20-min walk north-east of the centre. **🚹 Tourist office:** Kungsgatan 40, ☎ 0921 624 10 (www.upplevboden.nu). Pick up a copy of the mostly Swedish-language *Bodenturist*.
⋈ The **Hotell Niva**, Kungsgatan 4, ☎ 0921 558 60 (www.hotellniva.se), €€, is close to the station, as is the **youth hostel** (HI): **Bodens Vandrarhem**, Fabriksgatan 6, ☎ 0921 133 35 (www.bodensvandrarhem.com).

CONNECTIONS FROM BODEN
For those with a real taste for epic journeys, carry on far into Lapland and the Arctic Circle by taking **Route 24** in reverse (p228), or by returning to Stockholm via Gällivare and taking the **Inlandsbanan** (p234; ERT table 753). Between Boden and Kemi are Haparanda and Tornio — effectively one town but in two time zones, linked by bridges. **Haparanda** has latterly become a popular spot for Russians (mainly from Murmansk Oblast) to come shopping. It is IKEA that pulls the cross-border crowds.

ROVANIEMI

If you feel the need to dance on the Arctic Circle, Kemi is the jumping-off point for the short train journey to Rovaniemi (1 hr 20 mins, ERT 794), the capital of the Finnish province of **Lapland**. Thoroughly destroyed in 1944 and subsequently redesigned and rebuilt by Alvar Aalto, it feels quite distant from its Sámi roots, but it has the impressive **Arktikum** (Science Centre and Museum of the Arctic Regions) at Pohjoisranta 4 (www.arktikum.fi). You can take a 10-min bus ride north to the Arctic Circle.

🛈 **Tourist office:** Lordi's Square, Maakuntakatu 29–31, ☎ 016 346 270 (www.visitrovaniemi.fi). 🛏 The **Guesthouse Borealis**, Asemieskatu 1, ☎ 016 3420 130 (www.guesthouseborealis.com), €, is a favourite with young travellers or try the **youth hostel** (HI): **Hostel Rudolf**, Koskikatu 41–43, ☎ 016 321 321 (www.rudolf.fi); check in/out at **Clarion Hotel Santa Claus**, Korkalonkatu 29.

KEMI

This tiny, laid-back town has a few draws: the **Jalokivigalleria** (Gemstone Gallery), at the end of Kauppakatu (open summer 0900–1700, rest of the year Mon–Fri 1000–1600; also home to the tourist office) has excellent gemstone displays. Kemi is also the spot where, after a stretch by bus, Route 26 takes to the rails again.

ARRIVAL, INFORMATION, ACCOMMODATION

🚆 A 5-min walk east of the centre: straight along Kauppakatu. 🛈 **Tourist office**: Kemin Kaupungin Matkailutoimisto, Kauppakatu 29, ☎ 040 568 2069 (www.kemi.fi/matkailu), in the Gemstone Gallery.

🛏 **Hotelli Merihovi**, Keskuspuistokatu 6–8, ☎ 016 4580 100 (www.merihovi.fi) is smart and comfortable, while **Hotelli Palomestari**, Valtakatu 12, ☎ 016 257 117 (www.hotellipalomestari.com), €€, has a more chain-like feel but is similar in price.

OULU

The mostly modern town (pop. 140,000) of **Oulu** is one of Finland's high-tech industry hubs. A few of the centre's older buildings such as the city hall recall the 19th-century tar boom — in which Oulu was also a world leader — and a short walk away is the **Science Centre Tietomaa**, Nahkatehtaankatu 6 (www.tietomaa.fi), an interactive science and technology museum that's entertaining even for non-kids.

There's an assemblage of Sámi artefacts and other local miscellanea at the nearby **Pohjois–Pohjanmaan Museo** (Northern Ostrobothnia Museum), Ainola Park (closed Mon, free Fri). The town's harbour-side market square looks out to a number of wooded islands, linked to the town by bridge.

≋ Rautatienkatu, east of the centre. From Kemi there are about six–eight trains daily, taking around 1 hr 5 mins. **❿ Tourist office**: Oulun Kaupungin Matkailuneuvonta, Torikatu 10, ☎ 044 703 1330 (www.oulutourism.fi). Walk six blocks along Asemakatu, then left on Torikatu. Get *Oulu This Week* and *Look at Oulu* (plus free map). ➤ **Best Western Hotel Apollo**, Asemakatu 31–33, ☎ 08 5221 (www.hotelapollo.fi) close to the railway station, free wi-fi. **Nallikari Camping**, Leiritie 10, ☎ 044 7031 353 (www.nallikari.fi), has holiday cottages and camping cabins as well as tent pitches, and is open year-round.

CONNECTIONS FROM OULU

An alternative, but longer, way to Helsinki is by taking **Route 27** (p248) in reverse.

TAMPERE (TAMMERFORS)

Finland's second city was once the nation's industrial fulcrum, but the atmospheric red-brick factory buildings and warehouses have since been converted into museums, galleries and shopping centres, and **Tampere** today stands as a surprisingly attractive place, flanked by lakes and graced with abundant green spaces. Exit the station and head a few streets to the right to reach the granite **Tuomiokirkko** (cathedral), Tuomiokirkkonkatu, built in 1907 with resplendent frescos and stained glass. From the station, Hämeenkatu leads across the **Tammerkoski**, a series of rapids that connect the city's two largest lakes and provide it with hydroelectric energy.

To the north you'll see the former **Finlayson factory**, now a centre for crafts and artisan works. More on the life of the factory's workers can be found at **Amurin työläismuseokortteli** (Amuri Museum of Workers' Housing; open mid-May to mid-Sept; closed Mon), Satakunnankatu 49, where 32 houses and shops from the workers' district are preserved with a genuinely lived-in feeling. Close by, the **city library** in Hämeenpuisto, is a curvaceous masterpiece of modernism by Reima and Raili Pietilä, built in 1986. There's also a **Lenin Museum** in Hämeenpuisto, near the end of Hämeenkatu. This marks the spot where Lenin met Stalin in the early 1900s — Lenin lived in Tampere after the 1905 revolution.

Two of Tampere's galleries give an excellent survey of Finnish art: the **Hiekka Art Museum**, Pirkankatu 6 (closed Mon, Fri & Sat), contains earlier works amassed by goldsmith Kustaa Hiekka, including some of his jewellery, while the lakeside **Sara Hildén Art Museum** (20-min walk or 🚌 16 north-west of the centre; closed Mon Sept–May) displays some of the nation's finest modern art through changing exhibitions.

ARRIVAL, INFORMATION, ACCOMMODATION

≋ A 5-min walk east of the centre; left-luggage office. **❿ Tourist office**: Rautatienkatu 25A, at the train station, ☎ 03 5656 6800 (www.visittampere.fi). Walk up Hämeenkatu and turn left just before the bridge: it's on the riverside. *Tampere* is a free comprehensive listing that includes a map; there's also a self-guided walking tour. ⊨ An affordable option is **Omenahotelli Tampere**, Hämeenkatu 28, ☎ 0600 18018 (premium rate) (www.omenahotels.com), €€, comfortable and right in the centre of the city, or try **Hotel Cumulus**, Koskikatu 5, ☎ 03 242 4111 (www.cumulus.fi), centrally located and on the river. **Hostels**: Opened in 2010, the **Tampere Dream Hostel**, Åkerlundinkatu 2a, ☎ 045 2360 517 (www.dreamhostel.fi), is quickly becoming a backpacker favourite. An alternative is the **Hostel Sofia**, Tuomiokirkonkatu 12a, ☎ 03 254 4020 (www.hostelsofia.fi).

TURKU (ÅBO)

Finland's oldest city and its capital until 1812, Turku is home to the country's oldest university and is a vibrant commercial and cultural centre, with a pulsating nightlife. Turku's cathedral is the seat of the Lutheran Archbishop of Finland and very much the centre of Protestant life in Finland.

Turku's much-rebuilt but nonetheless impressive **Tuomiokirkko** (cathedral) is easily spotted by the tower's distinctive face, the result of several fires over the centuries; look out for some intriguing tombs, including that of **Karín Månsdotter**, a local flower girl who became Queen of Sweden in 1568. The **Sibelius Museo** (Sibelius Museum), Piispankatu 17, displays over 350 musical instruments, as well as memorabilia of the great composer revered throughout Finland (although he had no connection with Turku itself); concerts are sometimes given here (closed Mon).

South of the cathedral, **Luostarinmäki**, near Vartiovuori Hill, is an 18th-century area of town that has been turned into an open-air museum, busy with artisans' workshops.

ARRIVAL, INFORMATION, ACCOMMODATION

⇌ **Turku** is north-west of the centre, a 15-min walk from the tourist office. One or two trains continue to **Satama** (Hamnen; the harbour). **Kupittaa** is also fairly central, but not as well equipped as Turku. ⚓ At the south-west end of town. 🚎 1 (to the main square) is more frequent than the trains, and also goes to the airport. 🅸 **Tourist office**: Aurakatu 4, ☎ 02 262 7444 (www.turkutouring.fi).

⊨ **Hotelli Artukaisten Paviljonki**, Messukentänkatu 11, ☎ 02 284 4000 (www.artukaistenpaviljonki.fi), €€, is good value. Bed and breakfast: **Hotel Harriet**, Käsityöläiskatu 11, ☎ 040 910 3333 (www.hotelharriet.fi), €€. **Youth hostel** (HI): **Hostel Turku** near the Radisson at Linnankatu 39, ☎ 02 262 7680 (www.turku.fi/hostelturku). **Linnasmäki**, Lustokatu 7, ☎ 02 412 3500 (www.linnasmaki.fi). open mid-May to mid-Sept (4 km from centre).

HELSINKI — SEE P491

Route 26 from Stockholm to Helsinki relies on trains and buses to make a great loop north around the Gulf of Bothnia. But there is an alternative route from **Stockholm to Finland**, and that is by boat. Several shipping services link the two countries, but one we particularly recommend is shown as a dotted line in the Route 26 map on p241. Its appeal is that it takes in the **Åland Islands**, a complex archipelago of more than five thousand islands, rocky islets and skerries that lie halfway between Sweden and Finland.

The Ålands really are a place apart, politically linked to Finland but with a large measure of independence, and Swedish speaking. They have many of the trappings of statehood, with their own flag, postage stamps and vehicle licence plates. Although part of the European Union, this scatter of islands lies outside the EU's fiscal regime — a little accounting curiosity that means that Swedes head to the Ålands for great duty-free deals. They stock up on cigarettes, aquavit and snuff — yes, snuff, for the Swedes have an appetite for ground tobacco unmatched by any other nation in Europe.

The **ships** that set sail for Åland and Finland from Swedish ports are the epitome of Scandinavian comfort and style. Expect a dozen variations on the pickled herring theme and the smörgåsbord. This is a far cry from the open rowing boats that used to leave the Swedish coast carrying over to Åland the mail that was eventually bound for Russia. From 1638, this was part of the postal route from Stockholm to the Swedish city of Åbo (now Turku in south-west Finland). After Sweden ceded both Finland and Åland to Russia in 1809, the **Åland mail route** became one of the main arteries for conveying post to St Petersburg — the safe passage of the mail was entrusted to Åland's farmers and fishermen.

Over in the Åland Islands there are everywhere reminders of the old postal route. On two of the smaller islands in the archipelago, **Vårdö** and **Kumlinge**, there are old wooden signposts which are denominated in Russian *versta* (верста), a unit of distance measurement that was used in tsarist times. One *versta* was slightly more than one kilometre.

Most ferries from Stockholm to the Finnish mainland ports of **Turku** (ERT 2480) and **Helsinki** (ERT 2465) stop off in the Ålands by dead of night. And they stop for one reason only. That brief Åland port of call allows the on-board shops to offer **tax-free goods**. Those bound for the Åland Islands who prefer not to arrive in the middle of the night have several options, with sailings at sensible times from coastal ports north of Stockholm over to Åland.

Pick of the bunch is the Viking Line service (ERT 2470), which starts with a short bus journey from Stockholm's city bus terminal (near the main railway station) to **Kapellskär**, where you switch onto a ferry for the crossing to Mariehamn, the capital of the Åland Islands. **Mariehamn** is the *least* interesting spot in the islands, but if you can take time to venture out and explore the more easterly islands in the archipelago, you will be in for a real treat. **Ålandstrafiken** (www.alandstrafiken.ax), have an excellent network of ferries and buses that you can use to plot a course east to mainland Finland.

Rail Route 27: Karelian lakes and forests

CITIES: ★ CULTURE: ★★ HISTORY: ★ SCENERY: ★★
COUNTRIES COVERED: FINLAND

If countries have a soul, then Finland's is tucked away somewhere in the forests of Karelia. Route 27 is a remarkable journey through rural Finland that has as its highlight a chance to visit the country's eastern borderlands with Russia. Karelia is just one part of a route that also takes in the **Finnish Lakeland** before heading north through the Kainuu region to **Oulu** on the **Gulf of Bothnia**, from where you can join **Route 26** which provides an alternative way back to Helsinki. Or, if you prefer, you can follow Route 26 in the reverse direction across the border into neighbouring Sweden.

Route 27 is not one to rush. Take three or four days over it if you can. Linger at quiet country stations, watch the forests slide by the window of the slow train, and sense something of the landscapes immortalised in the music of Sibelius and in the Finnish national epic, the *Kalevala*.

HELSINKI — SEE P491

PARIKKALA

This small town right on the border with Russia is first and foremost a place to change trains. It is the start of the branch line to **Retretti** and **Savonlinna**. But this pleasant community on the shore of **Lake Simpele** is worth a wander. One day Parikkala hopes to attract cross-border visitors from Russia, but until the border crossing opens to the public, the town remains a sleepy Karelian backwater. Only trucks working the lucrative cross-border timber trade are authorised to use the Parikkala border crossing to and from Russia.

RETRETTI

There are two very good reasons for breaking your journey at Retretti. The first is that Retretti is home to a bold cultural initiative of a kind that could only ever have been devised in Finland.

Here, in the middle of the wilderness, is a remarkable **arts centre**. Retretti plays on the word 'retreat' and this place really is a retreat from civilisation, but one graced by fine art. Rotating **exhibitions** are displayed in subterranean galleries (www.retretti.fi; usually open early June to late Aug). At €16 (€10 for students), admission is pricey but worth every cent.

The other reason to stop at Retretti is that it is a great spot to explore the bizarre landscape left by melting **glaciers** at the end of the last Ice Age. Just follow the trail along the ridge towards Punkaharju.

ROUTE DETAILS

Helsinki–Parikkala   ERT 797

Type	Frequency	Typical journey time
Train	4–6 daily	3h20

Parikkala–Retretti   ERT 797

Type	Frequency	Typical journey time
Train	5–6 daily	28 mins

Retretti–Savonlinna   ERT 797

Type	Frequency	Typical journey time
Train	5–6 daily	26 mins

Parikkala–Joensuu   ERT 797

Type	Frequency	Typical journey time
Train	4–6 daily	1h10

Joensuu–Kuopio   ERT 798, 799

Type	Frequency	Typical journey time
Train	2–3 daily	3h15

Kuopio–Oulu   ERT 798

Type	Frequency	Typical journey time
Train	3–4 daily	4 hrs

KEY JOURNEY

Helsinki–Oulu   ERT 794

Type	Frequency	Typical journey time
Train	7–8 daily 2–3 overnight	6–7 hrs (day) 9h15 (night)

Notes

When travelling by train from Joensuu to Kuopio, change trains at Pieksämäki. The following journeys can also be made by bus: Parikkala to Retretti & Savonlinna; Savonlinna to Pieksämäki; Joensuu to Kuopio.

ARRIVAL, INFORMATION

⇄ Just 300 metres from the centre. ⛴ During high summer there is a boat from Retretti/Punkaharju to Savonlinna at 1540. The service is operated by the *SS Heinävesi*, a ship that is now over 100 years old. The journey takes 2 hrs 15 mins (€25). Alternatively, just return to Retretti station and take the train west to Savonlinna.

SAVONLINNA

Sited among several lake islands linked by walking bridges, this small town was hugely fashionable with the Russian aristocracy (including the tsars) in the mid-19th century. The must-see is **Olavinlinna**, the best-preserved medieval castle in the Nordic countries, built originally in 1475, still largely intact and full of character. The courtyard is the venue for the town's other major draw, the annual international **Opera Festival** (July: tickets go on sale the previous Nov, ☎ 0600 10 800, www.operafestival.fi); the tourist office may have last-minute tickets.

ARRIVAL, INFORMATION, ACCOMMODATION

⇄ **Savonlinna–Kauppatori** station is the first stop and more central than the main station. 🛈 **Tourist office**: Puistokatu 1, ☎ 0600 300 07 (www.savonlinna.travel). ⊨ A small, poetic B&B a few kilometres from the centre is the **Ilola**, Ilokallionkatu 13, ☎ 050 3090 501 (www.madeinlove.fi), €€. **Youth hostels** (HI): Most central is **Vuorilinna**, Kylpylaitoksentie, ☎ 015 739 5 430 (www.hihostels.com), June–Aug only. The *SS Heinävesi* (mentioned above under Retretti) moored in the harbour has a number of cabins available.

CONNECTIONS

Savonlinna is the end of the railway line. For onward travel by train you need to return to Parikkala to continue north to **Joensuu**. If you don't mind two hours on a bus, there is a useful bus link twice or thrice daily to the major railway junction at **Pieksämäki** (times in footnote to ERT 799), from where you continue north by train to Kuopio.

JOENSUU

Worthy of a few hours' stop, Joensuu is the capital of Finnish Karelia (the eastern part of Karelia, east of the border, now known as the Republic of Karelia, is part of the Russian Federation). Joensuu has plenty of 19th-century wooden buildings, the excellent **North Karelian Museum**, an art nouveau **town hall**, Lutheran and Orthodox **churches** and the university's **botanic gardens** west of the centre, with an engaging butterfly and insect collection.

ARRIVAL, INFORMATION, ACCOMMODATION

⇄ 600 m east of the city centre; cross the Pielisjoki River and walk along Siltakatu. 🛈 **Tourist information**: **Karelia Experts**, Koskikatu 5, ☎ 0400 239 549 (www.jns.fi). ⊨ The **Hotel Karelia**, Kauppakatu 25, ☎ 013 252 6200 (www.hotellikarelia.fi), €€, is

Orthodoxy in Finland

The Orthodox Church of Finland is a reminder that the country still has a touch of the East. The Church enjoys an equal status to the much larger Lutheran community. You'll find Orthodox churches across Finland, but the spiritual heartland for Orthodox Finns is the deeply rural region east of Kuopio towards the Russian border. **New Valamo Monastery,** ☎ 017 570 111 (www.valamo.fi) in Heinävesi is much cherished by all Finns, Orthodox or not. Monks migrated here during World War II from the 800-year-old monastery of the same name just over the border in Russian Karelia. You can stay at the monastery's hotel or guesthouse. The **Orthodox Lintulan Luostari** (Lintula Convent), ☎ 017 563 106, 20 km away in Palokki (open daily 0900–1800 June–Aug, and on request in May and Sept), offers more modest accommodation. A full-day guided tour from Kuopio is the easiest way to visit both.

centrally located, or else try **Sokos Hotel Kimmel**, Itäranta 1, ☎ 020 1234 663 (www.sokoshotels.fi), €€. There are three HI **hostels**: the nearest to the station, and the only one open all year, is **Finnhostel Joensuu** in the Eastern Finland Sport Institute, Kalevankatu 8, ☎ 013 267 5076 (www.islo.fi). Slightly cheaper and 1 km north of the centre is **Partiotalo**, Vanamokatu 25, ☎ 013 123 381 (www.youthhostel-joensuu.net), June–Aug only.

Kuopio

The town, an important ecclesiastical centre and the headquaters of the Orthodox Church of Finland, has a splendid lakeshore location. The main reason to stop here is the outstanding **Suomen Ortodoksinen Kirkkomuseo** (www.ortodoksinenkirkkomuseo.fi, the Finnish Orthodox Church Museum) at Karjalankatu 1, about 1 km north-west of the centre. But it is closed for a major refurbishment throughout 2012 and won't reopen until at least July 2013.

But Kuopio still warrants a stop with a brace of quaint cathedrals (one Lutheran, one Orthodox) and the **Old Kuopio Museum** (an open-air ethnographic museum; closed Mon). In June (14–20 in 2012), the **Kuopio Dance Festival** (www.kuopiodancefestival.fi) fills the town with dozens of lively performances. There are lake cruises aplenty in summer, even including a boat service that makes the 10-hr journey to Savonlinna.

Arrival, information, accommodation

≋ About 500 m north of the city centre. ⓘ **Tourist office:** Haapaniemenkatu 17 (by the market square), ☎ 017 182 584 (www.kuopioinfo.fi). ⊨ The **Hostelli Hermanni**, Hermanninaukio 3E, ☎ 040 910 9083 (www.hostellihermanni.fi), €, is a 10-min walk south of the centre and has both cheap rooms and dorm beds. **Youth hostel** (HI): **Puijon Maja**, Puijontornintie, ☎ 017 255 5250 (www.puijo.com), 2 km from the centre.

Oulu — see p244

Rail Route 28:
Across the Alps: Bavaria to northern Italy

CITIES: ★ CULTURE: ★ HISTORY: ★ SCENERY: ★★
COUNTRIES COVERED: GERMANY, AUSTRIA, ITALY

This route is a very useful fast hop south over the **Alps** from southern Germany to Italian sunshine. But it is also worth doing in its own right for, within a journey of just 434 km, Route 28 packs in an astonishing variety of scenery. **Munich** and **Verona** could hardly be more different. Each city deserves a few days of exploration. Along this route, the Alps change in character almost from one valley to the next. **Innsbruck** makes a marvellous overnight stop along the way (where there is a connection with **Route 32**).

MUNICH — SEE P526

GARMISCH-PARTENKIRCHEN

Once two quiet Bavarian villages at the foot of the 2,962-m **Zugspitze**, Germany's highest mountain, **Garmisch** and **Partenkirchen** were officially united to host the 1936 Winter Olympics. Though now separated only by the railway line, they retain individual personalities. **Partenkirchen** is more modern and upmarket while **Garmisch** has much more of a traditional Bavarian character — the most appealingly rustic part is around Frühlingstr.

Garmisch is Germany's most popular ski resort, with downhill and cross-country skiing on offer. Having hosted the FIS Alpine World Ski Championships in February 2011, the place is also great for mountain walking, climbing and biking during the summer months. The **Olympic Ice Stadium**, Olympiastr., built in 1936, stays open virtually year-round.

The **Zugspitzbahn** cog railway leaves from Olympiastr. 27, not far from the railway station, to a point near the summit of the Zugspitze. It's a 75-min journey. On the way, it stops at **Eibsee**, an idyllic mountain lake, where you can transfer to the **Eibseebahn** cable car (often crowded) to reach the summit (10 mins); alternatively, take the easy 7-km path round the lake itself. Meanwhile, the train continues up through a winding 4.5-km tunnel to the **Zugspitzplatt** and the Sonn-Alpin Restaurant (2,600 m), from where the **Gletscherbahn** cable car goes the final stage to the summit (2,962 m). The views are impressively far-ranging in decent weather.

Several other summits around are accessible by chairlifts or cable cars from the town, giving plenty of scope for walks. These include **Eckbauer** (1,238 m), from where you can follow a path down through the woods to the entrance of the **Partnachklamm**, one of the most dramatic of all Alpine gorges, and descend to the ski stadium.

Notes

The Munich to Innsbruck stretch described in Route 28 is that via Garmisch-Partenkirchen. It is exceptionally beautiful. But if you are in a rush the Munich to Innsbruck trains via Kufstein are faster.

ROUTE DETAILS

Munich–Garmisch Partenkirchen — ERT 895

Type	Frequency	Typical journey time
Train	Every hr	1h25

Garmisch Partenkirchen– Mittenwald — ERT 895

Type	Frequency	Typical journey time
Train	Every hr	22 mins

Mittenwald–Innsbruck — ERT 895

Type	Frequency	Typical journey time
Train	Every 2 hrs	57 mins

Innsbruck–Bolzano — ERT 595

Type	Frequency	Typical journey time
Train	Every 2 hrs	2h05

Bolzano–Verona — ERT 595

Type	Frequency	Typical journey time
Train	1–2 per hr	1h30

Innsbruck–Lienz — ERT 596

Type	Frequency	Typical journey time
Train	2–3 per day	3h30 via San Candido

Bolzano–Merano — ERT 597

Type	Frequency	Typical journey time
Train	Every hr	40 mins

Merano–Malles — ERT 598

Type	Frequency	Typical journey time
Train	1–2 per hr	1h10

KEY JOURNEYS

Munich–Innsbruck — ERT 895, 951

Type	Frequency	Typical journey time
Train	7 daily 8 daily	2h51 via Garmisch 1h52 via Kufstein

Innsbruck–Verona — ERT 595

Type	Frequency	Typical journey time
Train	4 daily	3h40

Munich–Verona — ERT 70

Type	Frequency	Typical journey time
Train	4 daily	5h35

Munich–Salzburg — ERT 890

Type	Frequency	Typical journey time
Train	1–2 per hr	1h42

≋ Centrally located between Garmisch and Partenkirchen. **🛈 Tourist office:** Richard-Strauss Pl. 2, ☎ 08821 180 700 (www.gapa.de). ⋈ This is a popular ski resort, with plenty of rooms. Least expensive options are private rooms, such as **Huber Hildegard**, Schwalbenstr. 4, ☎ 08821 3443, €. A mid-range option is the **Gasthof Fraundorfer**, Ludwigstrasse 24, ☎ 08821 927-0 (www.gasthof-fraundorfer.de), €€. **Hostels**: the **Hostel 2962**, Partnachauenstr. 3, ☎ 08821 9575-0 (www.hostel2962-garmisch.com), has both dorms and private rooms, or else try the **Garmisch-Partenkirchen Hostel** (HI), Jochstr. 10, ☎ 08821 967 050 (www.djh.de), which is 4 km from town in Burgrain (🚌 3/4/5).

254 MITTENWALD

Close to the Austrian border, **Mittenwald** is perhaps the most attractive town in the German Alps, with an abundance of character in its gabled, whitewashed houses, hung with green shutters and sporting creaky wooden balconies. Elaborate outside murals are another striking feature, but the town's main claim to fame is in its violins. Matthias Klotz (1653–1743), a pupil of the great Amati, began Mittenwald's tradition of high-quality violin making that continues to this day.

ARRIVAL, INFORMATION, ACCOMMODATION

≋ 5 mins east of the town centre. **🛈 Tourist office:** Dammkarstr. 3, ☎ 08823 339 81 (www.mittenwald.de). ⋈ **Youth hostel** (HI): Buckelwiesen 7, ☎ 08823 1701 (www.djh.de).

INNSBRUCK

The 800-year-old Tyrolean capital on the River Inn is a bustling, amiable Austrian city overlooked by the **Karwendel Mountains** to the north and the Patscherkofel Mountains to the south — making it an excellent base for walks and other activities in the Alps (guided hikes start daily June–Oct, leaving 0900 from the Congress Hall; free with Club Innsbruck Card, which you get when you stay overnight anywhere in Innsbruck — not to be confused with the Innsbruck Card).

The **Hungerburgbahn** cog railway, which ascends from the **Alpenzoo** on the edge of the city on to the Hungerburg plateau — a superb place for walks and views — opened in 2007, following the earlier rebuild of the Nordkettenbahn, which takes visitors from the Congress Centre up onto the Hafelekar.

The **Altstadt** is dotted with 15th- and 16th-century buildings, many with elaborate stucco decorations and traditional convex windows to catch extra light on the narrow streets. Its most famous sight is the 15th-century **Goldenes Dachl**, Herzog-Friedrich-Str. 15 (www.goldenes-dachl.at), a roof of 2,657 gilded copper tiles covering a balcony, which Emperor Maximilian I (the subject of an exhibition inside) added in 1500 to the **Neuhof**, the residence of the Tyrolean princes. The **Stadtturm** (City Tower) opposite the balcony offers views across the rooftops to the mountains. Nearby is the **Dom zu St Jakob**, a striking baroque cathedral.

The **Hofburg** (Imperial Palace), Rennweg (www.hofburg-innsbruck.at) has a sumptuous ballroom lined with portraits of Empress Maria Theresa's family, who also feature in 28 larger-than-life bronze statues on Emperor Maximilian's grand tomb in the 16th-century **Hofkirche**, the Court Church. Near the **Hofgarten** (Court Gardens), the revamped **Tiroler Volkskunst Museum** (www.tiroler-landesmuseum.at) concentrates on Tyrolean culture, displaying traditional costumes and wood-panelled rooms. The **Tiroler Ferdinandeum**, Museumstr. 15 (closed Mon), is more diverse, with beautiful stained glass, medieval altars and works by Cranach and Rembrandt.

ARRIVAL, INFORMATION, ACCOMMODATION

≈ **Innsbruck Hauptbahnhof (Hbf)** is centrally located; left luggage, showers, tourist information. Walk down Salurner Str. and then right at the 1765 triumphal arch into Maria-Theresien-Str. ↗ **Innsbruck Airport**, ☎ 0512 225 250 (www.innsbruck-airport.com), 4 km west of the city centre (🚌 F from the station). 🛈 **Tourist office:** Burggraben 3, ☎ 0512 59 850, edge of the Altstadt (www.innsbruck.info); branch at the station. Accommodation booking service; money exchange, concert tickets, ski/cable-car passes and Innsbruck Cards. 24 hr ticket for use on trams and buses (www.ivb.at). Bikes can be hired from Inntour, Leopoldstrasse 4, ☎ 0512 5817 4217 (www.inntour.at). All-inclusive **Innsbruck Card**, covering local transport (including one ascending and one descending journey on lifts, funiculars and cable cars), the *Sightseer* tourist bus and entrance to all museums and other attractions; valid 24, 48 or 72 hours (€29/34/39); from tourist offices, cable cars and museums. Children (age 6–15) pay half-price.

🛏 The family-run 4-star **Hotel Sailer**, Adamgasse 6–8, ☎ 0512 5363 (www.sailer-innsbruck.at), €€, notable for its Tyrolean restaurant and decor, is handy for the station. **Hostels**: Extremely popular with backpackers is **Nepomuk's B&B Backpackers Hostel**, Kiebachgasse 16, ☎ 0512 584 118 (www.nepomuks.at). Another good option is the **Fritz Prior Schwedenhaus Hostel** (HI), Rennweg 17b, ☎ 0512 585 814 (www.hostel-innsbruck.com). **Campsite**: **Camping Innsbruck Kranebitten**, Kranebitter Allee 214, ☎ 0512 284 180 (www.campinginnsbruck.com), west of town (🚌 O).

✕ The Altstadt area is generally expensive. **Café-Konditorei Munding**, Kiebachgasse 16 (www.munding.at), is the oldest Tyrolean café and pastry-shop, and serves fabulous cakes. Try the studenty music bar **Zappa**, Rechengasse 5.

OVER THE BRENNER PASS

Our journey crosses **Route 32** in Innsbruck, which you can follow east through Salzburg and Vienna to Slovakia, or west through the Austrian Tyrol to Liechtenstein and Switzerland. If you decide to stick with Route 28, then you will

BORDER HOPPING THROUGH THE ALPS

Bolzano is a good starting point for some very rural cross-border adventures. The first leg is by train to **Merano** (ERT 597), a lovely little German-speaking spa town well worth a brief stop. Then take the **Vinschgaubahn** (ERT 598), a local railway which happily reopened in 2005, to Malles, from where there are onward bus connections to Nauders and Landeck (ERT 954), where you can join **Route 32**. From Nauders, there are also regular buses to Scuol Tarasp in the remote Lower Engadine area of eastern Switzerland (also shown in ERT 954). From Scuol Tarasp, there are direct trains (ERT 546) to **Pontresina** at the northern end of the Bernina Pass (on **Route 29**). Another bus route into Switzerland is direct from Malles to Zernez (times in the footnote to ERT 546), a route that runs along the **Müstair Valley** and traverses Switzerland's only national park. From **Zernez**, take the train back to Pontresina. Bus and rail services on the interconnecting routes mentioned in this box are all generally hourly. Sample overall travel times: Bolzano to Landeck 4 hrs 30 mins, Bolzano to Pontresina via either Val Müstair or Scuol Tarasp 5 hrs.

head south over the Brenner Pass into Italy. By Alpine standards, the Brenner is a very modest affair. No great tunnels as on the Simplon and Gotthard routes and no great heights as on the Bernina. The Brenner route tops out at just 1,370 metres, but what it lacks in height is made up for by the beauty of the landscape.

If you have the time, take slow trains south from Innsbruck, changing at Brennero and usually Bolzano too to reach Verona. Once over the top, you can cut off to the east at Fortezza to follow a beautiful branch line back over the border at San Candido to reach the Austrian town of Lienz (ERT 596).

BOLZANO (BOZEN)

Although in Italy and with street names in Italian, **Bolzano** looks decidedly Austrian, with its pastel-coloured baroque arcades and Austrian menu items; for centuries Bolzano was part of the South Tyrol region of Austria. Set beneath Alpine slopes in a deep valley, it's handy for exploring the **Dolomites**. Piazza Walther is the focus of the town's outdoor life.

ARRIVAL, INFORMATION, ACCOMMODATION

⇒ A 5-min walk south-east from the town centre. Buses stop at an area by a small park, reached by crossing the main road outside the station and turning left.

🚺 **Tourist office:** (municipal) Piazza Walther 8, ☎ 0471 307 000 (www.bolzano-bozen.it). ⊨ The **Hotel Regina**, via Renon 1, ☎ 0471 972 195 (www.hotelreginabz.it), €€, is next to the train station.

VERONA — SEE P299

Rail Route 29:
From the Jura via the Engadine to Milan

CITIES: ★★ CULTURE: ★ HISTORY: ★ SCENERY: ★★★
COUNTRIES COVERED: SWITZERLAND, ITALY

This route includes as its climax the **Bernina railway**, in our view far and away the finest of the three north-south rail routes that link Switzerland with Italy. Just for the record the other two are the Gotthard (described in **Route 31**) and the Simplon (highlighted as an attractive option running south from **Route 30** at Spiez via Brig; see p269). While the Gotthard and Simplon routes tunnel through the mountains, the narrow-gauge Bernina railway (since 2008 included on UNESCO's World Heritage List) climbs high over a mountain pass, at Ospizio Bernina reaching an elevation of 2,253 metres. If you are bound for **Milan** or elsewhere in northern Italy, the Bernina route is quite a detour, but it is extra time well spent. Route 29 is great at any time of year, but the Bernina stretch is really at its very best in deep mid-winter.

The route starts in **Lausanne** (also on **Route 30**) then heads north-east through the vineyards clinging to the hilly shores of Lac de Neuchâtel, where **Yverdon** and **Neuchâtel** are pleasantly set lakeside towns, and lake views are a feature from the right (south) side of the train as far as **Biel**. Beyond the watch- and clockmaking town of Delémont, the scenery is less remarkable between the cities of **Basel** and **Zurich**. Thereafter, things step up a couple of gears as the hills close in. Near **Sargans** you pass within a stone's throw of the tiny Principality of Liechtenstein (more on which in **Route 32**). **Chur** lies at the foot of an astonishing climb high up into the **Alps**, using the little red trains of the Rhätische Bahn. The chic resort of St Moritz is at the heart of the **Engadine**, the huge straight valley of the Inn that cuts across the Grisons (Grischun or Graubünden), Switzerland's Romansch-speaking canton. From there it is up and over the Bernina route to **Poschiavo** and on to **Tirano** in Italy where there are direct trains to Milan that, along the way, skirt the shores of Lake Como.

LAUSANNE

A city of two moods, half Alpine and half Riviera, Lausanne is perched on the hills above Lake Geneva. Some of the best views of this university city are from the cathedral high above the Old Town. The steepness of the place is part of its appeal, and if you don't fancy the trudge up from the lakeshore suburb of **Ouchy**, with its grand hotels and large park, up to the Old Town, there's a useful metro (actually a funicular) linking all three in a few minutes. The partly pedestrianised Old Town is small enough to be explored on foot.

The upper metro terminal (Flon) is located just south of the main area of interest and dominated by the 15th-century steeple of the 13th–14th-century **Église**

St-François (St Francis' Church). The **Cathédrale de Notre-Dame**, a 10-min walk up into the town, was consecrated in 1275. Italian, Flemish and French craftsmen all had a hand in its construction, and it is accepted as a perfect example of Gothic architecture. The night watch is still called from the steeple every hour from 2200 to 0200.

The **Musée historique de Lausanne**, Pl. de la Cathédrale 4 (closed Mon except in July and Aug), in **l'Ancien-Evêché** (the bishop's palace until the early 15th century), exhibits a large-scale model of 17th-century Lausanne. Also by the cathedral is another fortified bishops' residence, the **Château St-Marie**, now the seat of the cantonal government (partly open to the public). **Escaliers du marché**, a wooden-roofed medieval staircase, links the cathedral square to **Pl. de la Palud**, an ancient square surrounded by old houses.

West of the cathedral, the Florentine-style **Palais de Rumine**, Pl. de la Riponne, was built by a Russian family at the turn of the last century. It now houses a number of museums, including the cantonal museum of fine art. Take a 10-min walk north-west (or 🚌 2) to the **Collection de l'Art Brut**, av. des Bergières 11 (www.artbrut.ch), housed in the **Château de Beaulieu** (closed Mon except July–Aug). This compelling post-war gallery was founded by a local collector, who sought the works of anyone who was not a trained or formal painter, from amateur dabblers to the criminally insane.

North of the centre is the **Fondation de l'Hermitage**, Route du Signal 2 (www.fondation-hermitage.ch), an early 19th-century villa full of period fixtures and fittings, which hosts top-quality touring exhibitions of contemporary art (closed Mon). The view from the villa gardens, over the city and the lake to the Alps, is magnificent. For more lake views, take 🚌 16 to the **Forêt de Sauvabelin**, 150 m above the city centre. This 140-acre beech forest offers a choice of walking paths, a viewing tower and a deer reserve around a small lake.

The **quai de Belgique** is a shady, flower-lined, waterside promenade, looking towards the Savoy Alps. The 13th-century keep of **Château d'Ouchy** is now a hotel. Baron Pierre de Coubertin, founder of the modern Olympics in 1915, chose Lausanne as the headquarters of the International Olympic Committee. The unique **Musée Olympique**, quai d'Ouchy 1, is a large modern complex, cleverly designed to retain the natural beauty of its surrounding park. Boats can be hired near the 'cruise' pier.

ARRIVAL, INFORMATION, ACCOMMODATION

🚆 Between the centre and Ouchy, connected by metro. Left luggage facilities and bike rental. **ℹ Tourist office:** av. de Rhodanie 2, ☎ 021 613 73 73 (www.lausanne-tourisme.ch) and at the rail station. A walking tour (not always in English) of the Old Town leaves from the Town Hall at 1000 and 1500, Mon–Sat (May–Sept).

🛏 There's plenty of budget accommodation. The **Pension Ada-Logements**, av. de Tivoli 60, ☎ 021 625 71 34 (www.kobo.ch/ada-logements), €, is centrally located

ROUTE DETAILS

Lausanne–Neuchâtel — ERT 505

Type	Frequency	Typical journey time
Train	Every hr	41 mins

Neuchâtel–Biel — ERT 505

Type	Frequency	Typical journey time
Train	2 per hr	16 mins

Biel–Basel — ERT 505

Type	Frequency	Typical journey time
Train	Every hr	1h04

Basel–Zurich — ERT 510

Type	Frequency	Typical journey time
Train	3–4 per hr	1h05

Zurich–Chur — ERT 520

Type	Frequency	Typical journey time
Train	2 per hr	1h15

Chur–St Moritz — ERT 540

Type	Frequency	Typical journey time
Train	Every hr	2 hrs

St Moritz–Poschiavo — ERT 547

Type	Frequency	Typical journey time
Train	Every hr	1h45

Poschiavo–Tirano — ERT 547

Type	Frequency	Typical journey time
Train	Every hr	43 mins

Tirano–Milan — ERT 593

Type	Frequency	Typical journey time
Train	Every 2 hrs	2h30

Tirano–Lugano — ERT 543

Type	Frequency	Typical journey time
Bus	1 daily	3 hrs (summer only)

KEY JOURNEYS

Geneva–Zurich — ERT 500, 505

Type	Frequency	Typical journey time
Train	1–2 per hr	2h43

Zurich–Milan — ERT 550

Type	Frequency	Typical journey time
Train	7 daily	3h41

and not far from the station. **Hostels: Lausanne GuestHouse & Backpacker,** Épinettes 4, ☎ 021 601 80 00 (www.lausanne-guesthouse.ch), €, has twins and dorms, all facing the lake, or try the **youth hostel** (HI), Chemin du Bois-de-Vaux 36, ☎ 021 626 02 22 (www.youthhostel.ch/lausanne), on the lakeside west of Ouchy (🚌 2 from Ouchy metro station to Bois-de-Vaux then a 5-min walk). **Campsite: Camping de Vidy,** Chemin du Camping 3, ☎ 021 622 50 00 (www.campinglausannevidy.ch).

CONNECTIONS FROM LAUSANNE

Frequent **SBB** trains link the waterfront towns. **Compagnie Générale de Navigation sur le lac Léman (CGN),** av. de Rhodanie 17, ☎ 0848 811 848 (www.cgn.ch), operate ferries from Ouchy (and paddle steamers in summer) to **Geneva** (western end of the lake), **Évian** (in France, southern shore), and **Montreux.**

NEUCHÂTEL

Set steeply beside the 38-km-long lake of the same name, **Neuchâtel** slopes down from the castle to its Old Town. At the heart of the Old Town, itself characterised by Renaissance fountains and defensive towers, is **Place Pury**; markets are held in the adjacent **Place des Halles**. It's well worth the walk up to the top of town, past the **Tour des Prisons** (Prison Tower), used as a dungeon until 1848, for the views from the town's monumental set pieces. The imposing **château**, built from the 12th to 16th centuries, now functions as the cantonal office; free guided tours take you within, though there's not much of historical interest inside nowadays. A walkway leads from there to the **Église Collégiale** (Collegiate Church), featuring a splendid 14th-century monument to the Counts of Neuchâtel (www.collegiale.ch). Museums include the **Musée d'art et d'histoire** (www.mahn.ch), boasting three 18th-century automata — a draughtsman, writer and musician — the latter representing a female harpsichordist (closed Mon, free on Wed).

ARRIVAL, INFORMATION, ACCOMMODATION

🚆 1 km north of the centre. 🛈 **Tourist office**: Hôtel des Postes, ☎ 032 889 68 90 (www.neuchateltourisme.ch). 🏨 The **Hôtel des Arts**, rue J.L. Pourtalès 3, ☎ 032 727 61 61 (www.hotel-des-arts.ch), €€, is a short walk south of the station.

CONNECTIONS FROM NEUCHÂTEL

Twice-hourly trains, taking 40 mins (ERT 511), link Neuchâtel with Berne, where you can join **Route 31** (p273).

BIEL (BIENNE)

Beside **Lake Biel**, the busy clock-making town (home to Omega watches since 1879) is unique in Switzerland in that French and German share equal billing — you will even hear one person talking in French and the other answering in

LAKE BIEL AND ST PETERSINSEL

Lake Biel (Bielersee or lac de Bienne) has a nearby beach, but its main attraction is St Petersinsel (St Peter's Island), a nature reserve reached by a 50-min boat trip from Schifflände, 800 m west of Biel station. A monastery on the island has been converted into the **St Petersinsel Restaurant & Klosterhotel,** ☎ 032 338 11 14 (www.st-petersinsel.ch), where in 1765 the Swiss-born French philosopher Jean-Jacques Rousseau spent a blissful time, which he recorded in his *Confessions* and in the *Reveries of a Solitary Walker*.

German. French speakers know the town as Bienne. Biel's **Old Town** has a wealth of medieval architecture, with turrets and arcades characteristic of the Bernese style, and prettily painted wrought-iron signs. Some of the best of it is along Burggasse and the Ring, a fine old square with a 16th-century fountain in the middle.

ARRIVAL, INFORMATION
≈ Hauptbahnhof, town centre. The Old Town is a 10-min walk via Bahnhofstr. and Nidaugasse, while the lake is 5 mins away, behind the station via Badhausstrasse. 🚩 **Tourist office:** Bahnhofpl. 12, ☎ 032 329 84 84 (www.biel-seeland.ch).

BASEL (BÂLE)

Wedged into the corners of Switzerland, France and Germany, this big, working city (the second largest in the country after Zurich) has long been a crossroads for European culture.

If you are making day trips to Basel it's worth considering the **Basel Card**, which gives free admission to museums, the zoo, sightseeing tours and ferries, plus discounts at shops, theatres, concerts, clubs, boat trips and taxis (S Fr.20 for 24 hrs, S Fr.27 for 48 hrs and S Fr.35 for 72 hrs). Visitors staying in a hotel or youth hostel receive a mobility ticket, which gives free bus and tram travel during your stay.

Of the six bridges across the River Rhine, **Mittlere Brücke** offers the best views. The medieval centre is on the south bank, in Grossbasel. Kleinbasel is the small modern area on the north bank. Admission to museums generally costs around S Fr.7.

Just south of the Rhine, Münsterpl. is dominated by the 12th-century red sandstone **Münster** (cathedral), which has decorative twin towers, a Romanesque portal surrounded by elegant carvings, and a rose window featuring the wheel of fortune. Housed within a Gothic church on Barfüsserplatz, the **Historisches Museum** has 13th- to 17th-century artefacts, including Luther's chalice; the 18th- to 19th-century sections of the collection are in the **Haus zum Kirschgarten**, Elisabethenstr. 27/29, about 300 m north of the SBB station (both closed Mon).

The one sight not to miss is the world-class **Kunstmuseum** (Fine Arts Museum; closed Mon; tram 2 from the SBB rail station), St Alban-Graben 16 (www.kunstmuseumbasel.ch), in a building constructed in 1932–36 to house the art treasures the town had been accumulating since the 17th century, including important works by the 15th-century Basel master Konrad Witz, the world's largest collection of works by the Holbein family, and modern contributors such as Van Gogh, Picasso, Braque and Dalí.

The permanent collection of the **Museum für Gegenwartskunst** (Museum of Contemporary Art), St Alban-Rheinweg 60, includes pieces by Stella, Warhol and Beuys (closed Mon). The 16th-century **Rathaus** (Town Hall) has an ornate and very picturesque red facade that includes an enormous clock. It towers over Marktplatz, the long-standing heart of Basel.

Of the three main surviving medieval city gates, **St Alban-Tor**, St-Alban-Graben, takes second place to the splendid 14th-century **Spalentor**, Spalengraben. Near here, in Spalenvorstadt, is the pick of the town's older fountains, the **Holbein-Brunnen**, based partly on a Holbein drawing and a Dürer engraving. The **Zoologischer Garten**, Binningerstr. 40 (www.zoobasel.ch), west of the SBB station, has gained a reputation for breeding armoured rhinos, but is also known for its collections of pygmy hippos, gorillas and penguins.

ARRIVAL, INFORMATION, ACCOMMODATION

≽ Basel is a frontier town for both France and Germany. The main station, **Bahnhof SBB**, is a 10-min walk south of the city centre (5 mins by tram from the front of the station), and handles Swiss and main-line German services, with a useful hourly direct train north to Karlsruhe (1 hr 48 mins, ERT 912) to join **Route 19**. Facilities include left luggage, bike rental, showers, a post office and a supermarket. A separate adjacent station, **Bâle SNCF**, hosts all French services and boasts a large, suspended and animated Tinguely sculpture.

Both stations evoke the heady old days of train travel. For a spell there were even direct overnight trains from here to London (shipped on a ferry across the Channel). No longer, but it is an easy run north to **Strasbourg** (1 hr 20 mins, ERT 385) to connect with **Route 3**.

✈ In France, 9 km way to the north-west; 20 mins by 🚌 50 (frequent services) to rail station (www.euroairport.com). 🚍 **Tourist office:** Stadtcasino, Barfüsserpl., ☎ 061 268 68 68 (www.basel.com) and at the SBB rail station.

TINGUELY IN BASEL

Tinguely is the Fribourg-born sculptor whose works typically resemble parodies of machines, manically juddering into action, seemingly against the odds. His Fasnachts-Brunnen/Tinguely-Brunnen, Theaterpl., is an extraordinary fountain (1977) that looks like a watery scrapyard. The **Museum Tinguely**, Paul Sacher-Anlage 2 (www.tinguely.ch), celebrates his life and work (closed Mon).

DAVOS

From Chur, hourly narrow-gauge trains (1 hr 35 mins, ERT 545) take you to Davos (two stations: Davos Dorf and Davos Platz, the latter being the more central). Change trains at Landquart. Information on the ski resort is available from the tourist office, Talstrasse 41, ☎ 081 415 21 21 (www.davos.ch). Davos is the highest town in Europe (1,560 m).

Although rather dominated by modern concrete and glass and lacking in genuine Alpine atmosphere, Davos is an excellent centre for walking: a favourite easy excursion is to take the funicular up to the Alpine Garden at Schatzalp, where 800 plant species flourish. **Schatzalp** has a summer toboggan run and toboggans are for hire. Alternatively, take the cable car to Jakobshorn for superb views from waymarked paths that lead to the top. ⊨ **Youth Palace Davos** (HI), Horlaubenstrasse 27, ☎ 081 410 19 20 (www.youthhostel.ch/davos) is open all year.

⊨ Moderate hotels in the Old Town include the **Rochat**, Petersgraben 23, ☎ 061 261 81 40 (www.hotelrochat.ch), €€€. The **Haus zur Sonnenwende**, St Jakobs-Str. 351, ☎ 061 271 16 89 (www.haus-zur-sonnenwende.ch), €€, and **Casa La Luz**, Kembserweg 8, ☎ 061 321 38 00 (www.bed-andbreakfast.ch), €€, are central and easy on the wallet.

Hostels: Two options within walking distance of the station are **BaselBackPack**, Dornacherstr. 192, ☎ 061 333 00 37 (www.baselbackpack.com) and the **YMCA Hostel**, Gempenstr. 64, ☎ 061 361 73 09 (www.ymcahostelbasel.ch).

ZURICH — SEE P593

CHUR

A cathedral city as well as capital of the canton of Grisons (population 33,000), **Chur** (pronounced 'Koohr') has an appealing Old Town. Green and red footprints mark recommended walking tours of Chur (details from tourist office). With a fair range of places to eat and stay, it makes a feasible stopover. Its Romanesque-Gothic cathedral, built 1150–1272, has a dark, impressive interior with an exceptional Gothic triptych of carved and gilded wood made by Jakob Russ between 1486–92. The **Bündner Kunstmuseum** (Museum of Fine Arts) on Postpl. has works by artists associated with Grisons (www.buendner-kunstmuseum.ch; closed Mon).

ARRIVAL, INFORMATION, ACCOMMODATION

≋ North-west of the town centre; cycle hire and left-luggage facility. **🛈 Tourist office:** Bahnhofplatz 3, ☎ 081 252 18 18 (www.churtourismus.ch). ⊨ The **Hotel Franziskaner**, Kupfergasse 18, ☎ 081 252 12 61 (www.hotelfranziskaner.ch), €€, is central.

St Moritz

Even in the face of opposition from the likes of Zermatt and Davos, **St Moritz** still pretty much leads the way as a Swiss sports resort, with a breathtaking location and a sunshine record (322 sunny days a year) unrivalled by anywhere else in the country.

St Moritz divides into **Dorf** (village) on the hill, and **Bad** (spa) 2 km downhill around the lake. You find the main hotels, shops and museums in St Moritz Dorf (including the **Engadine Museum**, offering an absorbing look at the furniture and house interiors of the Engadine). The centre for downhill skiing is **Corviglia** (2,486 m), but even if you're not skiing it's worth the 2-km funicular trip for the views and a glimpse of the 'beautiful people' at play. From there, take the cable car up to **Piz Nair** (3,057 m) for a panorama of the Upper Engadine.

ARRIVAL, INFORMATION, ACCOMMODATION

≋ Near the centre of town. 🛈 **Tourist office:** Via Maistra 12, ☎ 081 837 33 33 (www. stmoritz.ch). ⋈ Accommodation and food are generally less expensive in St Moritz Bad than in St Moritz Dorf. **Youth hostel** (HI): Via Surpunt 60, St Moritz Bad, ☎ 081 833 39 69 (www.youthhostel.ch/st.moritz); postbus to Hotel Sonne then 5-min walk.

CONNECTIONS FROM ST MORITZ

Take the *Glacier Express* (see p269), one of the great scenic rail journeys of the Alps from St Moritz to Zermatt via Andermatt and Brig (ERT 575).

Over the Bernina Pass

Now for the highlight of Route 29, the Bernina rail route to **Tirano** in Italy. Our experience is that the old carriages on the regular local trains are much more fun than the slick observation cars on the trains shown in the schedules as *Bernina Express*. And no supplement is payable to ride the slow train routinely used to travel between remote communities along the route. So opt for the slow train (2 hrs 27 mins to Tirano), throw open the window, take a deep breath of mountain air and enjoy the ride. It is pure magic. After ice fields and fierce mountain peaks over the Bernina Pass, the line loops down steeply to **Poschiavo**, a lovely town of southern demeanour with a central piazza surrounded by dignified Italianate houses.

The Swiss Bernina trains terminate at Tirano. Change there to regular Italian train services onward to Milan (ERT 593). If your appetite for good scenery has not been entirely satiated by the Bernina route, then pause at **Colico**, at the north-east end of **Lago di Como** and continue by boat to Como (ERT 599).

Milan — SEE P296

Rail Route 30: Swiss lakes and mountains

CITIES: ★★ CULTURE: ★ HISTORY: ★ SCENERY: ★★★
COUNTRIES COVERED: SWITZERLAND

This is a **new route** introduced in *Europe by Rail* for 2012. In our opinion, it is the best one-day train journey in Switzerland, even having the edge over the much vaunted *Glacier Express* from Zermatt to St Moritz. And the latter won't give you a free ride with a Eurail or Interrail pass, whereas rail pass holders can travel Route 30 without having to pay supplements. But do just note that the suggested side trip from Interlaken up to the top of the Jungfraujoch, Europe's highest railway station, is run by a private operator that will still levy a charge to holders of rail passes.

When **Thomas Cook** escorted his first tours to Switzerland, his itineraries focused on the territory traversed by Route 30. To English travellers in the Victorian period, Switzerland meant the Alps. This understanding of Switzerland was not peculiar to the English. The Alps are still as essential an element as ever of the Swiss psyche, even if more Swiss citizens now live in Zurich apartment blocks than on farms in remote Alpine valleys. The myth of the Dörfli under the shadow of an alp is a very powerful image, and many Swiss folk who live in cities still claim that their hearts lie in a small village in the hills.

This route nicely explores the **Switzerland of the imagination** — a place full of Alpine pastures. With some of Europe's most efficient rail services penetrating even into **remote Alpine valleys**, there is plenty of scope for really getting off the beaten track on this route.

We start in **Zurich**, heading south for a brief but tantalising encounter with Lake Lucerne, before striking south-west into one of the most serenely beautiful parts of the Alps. You'll see a lot of the **Bernese Oberland** on this route. Our favourite section is the steep drop down to Montreux on the shores of **Lake Geneva**. West from **Montreux** we cruise through the Lavaux Vineyards to reach Lausanne, before the final leg along the lakeshore to Geneva.

There is an oddity about this journey which may appeal to rail buffs but may be judged a modest inconvenience by others. You will have to change trains along the way. There are two **narrow-gauge sections** of line: the 74-km Zentralbahn from Lucerne to Interlaken Ost and the 62-km Montreux-Berner Oberland-Bahn leg from Zweisimmen via Gstaad to Montreux.

The various operators that ply different sections of Route 30 are cooperating to develop new rolling stock with wheels that slip ingeniously from standard-gauge to narrow-gauge track and back again — a piece of engineering magic which will allow through trains from about 2016.

Journeys on the Lucerne to Interlaken and Montreux axis, the central portion of Route 30, are now being marketed under the banal name **Golden Pass** (with a slick nine-language website at www.goldenpass.ch).

ZURICH – SEE P593

The first part of the run out of Zurich speeds under the balconies of multicoloured apartment blocks, before plunging into a long tunnel. There are stops in lakeside **Thalwil** and affluent **Zug** before, less than an hour after leaving Zurich, the train arrives at Lucerne for the first of several changes of train along the route. At **Lucerne** you can connect conveniently onto **Route 31**.

LUCERNE – SEE P274

Beyond Lucerne, the hills slowly close in. After skirting the **Sarnersee**, the railway climbs steeply to **Brünig Pass**, where the summit station is called Brünig-Hasliberg. This is an extraordinary spot, not so much for the scenery as for the huge **bric-a-brac shop** now housed in the station buildings. Austrian cook Joseph Hechenberger has run the place for twenty years, and when we stopped off at Brünig in April 2011, Hechenberger's stock included a ship's bell, an artificial leg, a life-size model of Jesus Christ with a penguin, and a fabulous collection of books ranging from Karl May to Karl Marx (and a very handsome edition of *Sexual Splendours of the Erotic East*). This delicious emporium is open every day of the year.

From Brünig, it's downhill all the way to **Meiringen**, a town that claims to be the birthplace of meringue (the confection rather than the Caribbean musical genre). From Meiringen, opt for a seat on the left for lovely lake views on the run west, skirting the north shore of the Brienzersee, to Interlaken.

INTERLAKEN

This lively resort, strategically placed between two lakes, boomed in the 19th century when it became popular with British visitors as a base for exploring the mountains, and fanciful hotels sprang up along the Höheweg, the town's principal avenue (which links the two stations). It's still virtually unrivalled in the country as a centre for **scenic excursions**. You don't need transport for getting around town, but hiring a bike to explore the adjacent lakeshores can be fun. Horse-drawn carriages (at a price) are available for hire outside both stations. From the **Höheweg** a wonderful, uninterrupted view extends across the undeveloped meadow where the original 12th-century monastic site of the town once stood, to **Jungfrau** (4,158 m) and other peaks looming beyond — especially magnificent in the later afternoon Alpenglow.

One of the period pieces in town is the distinctive 19th-century **Kursaal** (Casino), which in addition to gambling (high rollers should note that the ceiling for bets is only S Fr.5) stages concerts and folklore evenings (www.casino-kursaal.ch). Across the River Aare is the old part of town known as **Unterseen**,

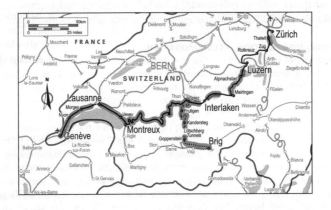

Key Journey

Zurich–Geneva	ERT 500, 505	
Type	Frequency	Typical journey time
Train	2 per hr	2h42

Notes

Follow Route 30 in its entirety from Zurich to Geneva and it'll take the best part of a day. But, as you'll see from the key journey cited above, main-line trains from Geneva back to Zurich are very much faster. There are two fast options from Geneva to Zurich. Although neither has the adventurous appeal of Route 30 through the mountains, both are very fine journeys. One train each hour on the Geneva to Zurich axis runs via Berne (see p273), the other hourly train runs via Neuchâtel and Biel with a beautiful sweep along the north shore of Lake Neuchâtel (following part of Route 29).

On Route 30 there are two stretches of metre-gauge railway, one between Lucerne and Interlaken and the other between Zweisimmen and Montreux, both requiring changes of train at the start and end of each section. Zweisimmen is not shown on the map above. It lies west of Spiez.

Route Details

Zurich–Lucerne	ERT 555	
Type	Frequency	Typical journey time
Train	2 per hr	45 mins

Lucerne–Meiringen	ERT 561	
Type	Frequency	Typical journey time
Train	Every hr	1h17

Meiringen–Interlaken (Ost)	ERT 561	
Type	Frequency	Typical journey time
Train	2 per hr	40 mins

Interlaken (Ost)–Spiez	ERT 560	
Type	Frequency	Typical journey time
Train	3 per hr	21 mins

Spiez–Zweisimmen	ERT 563	
Type	Frequency	Typical journey time
Train	1–2 per hr	44 mins

Zweisimmen–Montreux	ERT 566	
Type	Frequency	Typical journey time
Train	Every hr	2h05

Montreux–Lausanne	ERT 570	
Type	Frequency	Typical journey time
Train	4 per hr	20 mins

Lausanne–Geneva	ERT 570	
Type	Frequency	Typical journey time
Train	5 per hr	40 mins

with the oldest buildings in the region. Cross the bridge and walk along the river to **Marktplatz**, with its 17th-century town hall and palace, 14th-century church and the **Touristik Museum** (charting the rise of Interlaken's tourist industry).

ARRIVAL, INFORMATION, ACCOMMODATION

⇌ **Ostbahnhof** is on Lake Brienz, a 10-min walk from the centre. **Westbahnhof**, by Lake Thun, is central. The two stations are 15 mins apart on foot, 4 mins by rail. It is the Ostbahnhof that connects with the railway to Jungfraujoch. From Berne, Westbahnhof is the first stop and the journey, by hourly trains, averages 50 mins. 🔢 **Tourist office:** Höheweg 37, ☎ 033 826 53 00 (www.interlaken.ch). ⊨ There's no shortage of hotels, many catering largely for tour operators, but private rooms can be better value. A reasonably priced hotel is **Arnold's Bed & Breakfast**, Parkstr. 3, ☎ 033 823 64 21 (www.arnolds.ch), €€. **Hostels:** An excellent choice is **Backpackers Villa Sonnenhof**, Alpenstr. 16, ☎ 033 826 71 71 (www.villa.ch), with twins, triples, quads and dorms. The **Balmer's Herberge**, Hauptstr. 23, ☎ 033 822 19 61 (www.balmers.com), is a 15-min walk from both stations, in the suburb of Matten (🚌 5/15). The official **youth hostel** (HI): Aareweg 21, am See, ☎ 033 822 43 53 (www.youthhostel.ch/boenigen), is a 20-min walk east from Ostbahnhof, in the village of Bönigen on Lake Brienz (🚌 1). Seven **campsites** are within easy walking distance, so ask the tourist office for details.

TO SPIEZ AND BEYOND

Route 30 runs west from Interlaken to Spiez with fine views over the Thunersee en route (sit on the right). Crossing the main Brig to Berne railway at Spiez (see box opposite), Route 30 climbs the Simmern Valley. Hills roll into more hills and

TO EUROPE'S HIGHEST STATION

A popular excursion from Interlaken is the 2 hr 20 min journey to **Jungfraujoch**, the highest railway station in Europe at 3,454 m. Services (ERT 564) leave from Interlaken Ost at least hourly, and two changes of train are usually necessary: firstly in either **Lauterbrunnen** or **Grindelwald** and then always in **Kleine Scheidegg**. The earlier you start, the better, to increase the chance of clear views. Dedicate a whole day to the trip, if the weather warrants it, as stops can be made en route.

This trip is undeniably breathtaking, but also very expensive (S Fr.186.20 return, passes not valid), although you can save around 25% by splashing out on a 'Good Morning Ticket' (valid only on the first train of the day and from May to October you must start your descent from the Jungfraujoch by 1200). On a good day, you'll see the best of Switzerland on this route. The little rack-and-pinion railway then goes into the face of the Eiger, emerging from the long tunnel at the 3,454 m summit. If you are put off by the high fares, consider at least travelling as far as **Kleine Scheidegg**, much more modestly priced at S Fr.74.20 return, but no discounts for early risers. This little community, dominated by the **North Face of the Eiger**, is a great place for mountain walks (including many easy strolls amid dramatic scenery).

South from Spiez: towards the Simplon

Spiez has a lovely setting and is a major rail hub. If you are not spellbound by Route 30 (and the best is yet to come), there are frequent northbound trains from Spiez to Berne (see p273). It is a 30-min journey (ERT 560). ⊨ If you are tempted to stay in Spiez, the **Hotel Restaurant Seegarten Marina** has an unbeatable location on the lake at Schlachenstr. 3, ☎ 33 655 67 67 (www.seegarten-marina.ch), €€.

South from Spiez the main line towards Italy plunges through the long **Lötschberg Base Tunnel** (opened in 2007). It is boring. But happily the old Lötschberg mountain route south via Kandersteg to Brig survives and it is superb. Hourly BLS trains serve the route (ERT 562). Kandersteg makes a good midway stop on the run to Brig. This one-time village turned into mountain resort is perfectly sited for exploring the **Bernese Oberland**. Everything's geared to outdoor activities, with year-round walking trails and winter sports. Pick of the walks is up to the Oeschinensee, a stupendously sited mountain lake (walk up or take the chairlift), or take the Sunnbüel cable car and walk up to the Gemmi Pass.

Leaving Kandersteg, the BLS train dives into the old Lötschberg Tunnel, which transformed travel through this region when it was opened in 1913. It is a fraction of the length of its 2007 counterpart. Emerging from the tunnel, there are fine views south into the Rhône Valley. The first place of any size is **Brig**, a mainly German-speaking town and a major transport hub for the entire Valais region. Brig once made its living as gateway to the **Simplon Pass** route to Italy and nowadays it boasts fine rail links in all directions. The vast Italianate palace of **Stockalper Castle** is the largest private building ever erected in Switzerland. The castle was constructed in 1658–1668 by Kaspar Stockalper, a merchant who made a fortune controlling the flow of goods between France, Lombardy and Switzerland. ⇥ Just north of the town centre. 🛈 **Tourist office**: Bahnhofplatz 3, ☎ 027 921 60 30 (www.brig-belalp.ch).

From Brig you can continue south through the **Simplon Tunnel** into Italy, proceeding along the shores of Lake Maggiore (p278) to Milan (p296) (a 1 hr 50 mins to 2 hr 15 mins trip — see ERT 590).

One of the great scenic Alpine routes is east from Brig over a network of **narrow-gauge lines** to St Moritz, where you can connect with **Route 29** over the Bernina Pass into Italy. This route east from Brig is used by the *Glacier Express*, a premium service aimed fair-and-square at the tourist market. The *Glacier Express* runs Zermatt – Brig – Andermatt – Disentis – Chur – St Moritz (ERT 575). The scenery is superb, but our feeling is that you're better off to use the local trains that follow the same route (shown in ERT 576 for Zermatt – Brig – Chur and ERT 540 for Chur – St Moritz). Reservations are compulsory on the *Glacier Express*, and there is a hefty supplementary charge. With the local trains, you can hop on and off at will. Seats cannot be reserved on those local services. Whether on the *Glacier Express* or the regular trains, just note that holders of **Eurail and InterRail pass** holders cannot travel for free on that section of the mountain narrow-gauge network operated by the **Matterhorn-Gotthard Bahn** (MGB). This is the rail route from Zermatt, a car-free resort town in the shadow of the Matterhorn, via Brig and Andermatt to Disentis.

An excursion from Montreux

Easily reached by train, by boat or a pleasant walk of 3 km south along the lakeshore from Montreux, **Château de Chillon** (www.chillon.ch) is an impressive and well-preserved medieval castle. Famously, the Reformationist Bonivard was chained to a pillar in the dungeon here for four years, an event immortalised in verse by **Byron** in *The Prisoner of Chillon*; the poem itself brought the castle to public notice, and it's become the most visited attraction in Switzerland.

the train traverses several ridges, passing the resort town of Gstaad, before a spectacular descent down to Montreux on the shores of Lake Geneva. Stylish Gstaad is a pleasant spot to pause for a couple of hours. ⇥ For an overnight stay in Gstaad the Hotel Restaurant Alphorn, Gsteigstrasse, ☎ 33 748 45 45 (www.gstaad-alphorn.ch), €€, is a good small and family-owned option.

Montreux

The best-preserved of the **Lake Geneva** resorts, Montreux is blessed with a mild climate, with palm trees, magnolias and cypresses along its long waterfront promenade — a lovely place for strolling. Smart hotels make the most of the views, while the rest of the town rises in tiers up the hillside. The effect is slightly spoiled by a garish casino.

Arrival, information, accommodation

⇶ In the centre of town. 🄱 **Tourist office:** r. du Théâtre 5, ☎ 0848 86 84 84 (www.montreux-vevey.com). ⇥ The **Hotel Bon Port**, Rue du Théâtre 4, ☎ 021 962 80 70 (www.montreux.ch/bon-port), €€, is reasonably priced and close to the water. **Youth hostel** (HI): Passage de l'Auberge 8, ☎ 021 963 49 34 (www.youthhostel.ch/montreux). Just 150 m from Territet rail station (2 km from Montreux station); 🚌 1 from Montreux's main station. Closed mid-Nov–mid-Feb.

Lac Léman (Lake Geneva)

Our route west from Montreux skirts Switzerland's largest lake for much of the 85 km journey to Geneva. Best of the scenery is between Vevey and Lausanne where the railway skirts the **Lavaux Vineyard Terraces**, affording good views of a cultural landscape that dates back to medieval times and is deservedly included on UNESCO's World Heritage List. There are some lovely set-piece villages which are delightful places to stop. Our favourite is Saint-Saphorin, the first stop west of Vevey. It is served by hourly local trains on the S1 lakeshore route.

Lausanne — see P257

Geneva (Genève, Genf)

Geneva is a cosmopolitan, comfortably prosperous city, with promenades and parks beautifying the shores of **Lac Léman** (**Lake Geneva**). The River Rhône splits the city into two distinct sections, with the international area on the Rive Droite (right bank, to the north) and the compact Old Town on the Rive Gauche (left bank, to the south).

On Rive Droite (🚌 5/8/14/F/Z) is Pl. des Nations, near which most of the international organisations are grouped. The **Musée International de la Croix-Rouge**, av. de la Paix 17 (www.micr.org), is a stern building with high-tech exhibits tracing the history of the Red Cross and its Islamic offshoot, the Red Crescent. Profoundly moving, it covers natural disasters and man's inhumanity to man. Close by, the **Palais des Nations**, av. de la Paix 14, is home to the European headquarters of the United Nations, which replaced the League of Nations in 1945; there are guided tours. Between here and the lake is the lovely **Jardin Botanique**, a perfect place for a quiet stroll (once you're away from the main road) and featuring a rock garden, a deer and llama park and an aviary.

On Rive Gauche, south of the centre, the **Jardin Anglais**, on the waterfront, is famous for its **Horloge Fleurie** (floral clock), while the city's trademark, the 140 m high fountain (**Jet d'Eau**), spouts from a nearby pier.

At the heart of the Old Town is the lively Place du Bourg-de-Four, Geneva's oldest square. Take rue de l'Hôtel de Ville to the 16th-century Hôtel de Ville (town hall), where the first Geneva Convention was signed in 1864. Adjacent is the former arsenal and the 12th-century **Maison Tavel**, Geneva's oldest house and now an evocative museum, with several period rooms and exhibits covering the 14th–19th centuries.

The original medieval Gothic facade of the **Cathédrale de St-Pierre** has incongruous 18th-century additions. Most interior decorations were stripped out in the Reformation, but there are some frescos in the neo-Gothic Chapelle des Maccabées. Calvin preached here and his chair has been saved for posterity. The north tower, reached by a 157-step spiral staircase, offers a great view of the Old Town. Beneath the cathedral is the **Site Archéologique**, where catwalks allow you to see the result of extensive excavations, including a 4th-century baptistery and a 5th-century mosaic floor. Two blocks south, the vast marble **Musée d'Art et d'Histoire**, r. Charles-Galland 2 (www.ville-ge.ch/mah), has several rooms in period style, Hodler landscapes and the famous painting *The Fishing Miracle*, by Witz, which portrays Christ walking on the water — of Lake Geneva.

The 19th-century **Petit Palais**, Terrasse St-Victor 2, has an impressive array of modern art and includes works by Cézanne, Renoir and the Surrealists. Nearby, the **Collections Baur**, r. Munier-Romilly 8 (www.collections-baur.ch), contains some lovely Japanese and Chinese objets d'art, ranging from samurai swords to jade and delicate porcelain.

≋ **Gare de Cornavin** is the main station, a 10-min walk north of the centre (🚌 5/8/9). **Gare Genève Eaux-Vives**, south-east of the lake, is the terminal for SNCF trains from Annecy and St Gervais (30-min walk from Cornavin station or tram 16). **Metro Shopping**, a large complex that includes the 'Alimentation Automatique', is open Sun. The Aperto supermarket is open 0600–2200 every day.

✈ The airport has its own station (Genève Aéroport), with frequent trains into central Geneva taking 6 mins; services continue to all major cities in Switzerland. 🛈 **Tourist office**: r. du Mont-Blanc 18 (in main post office), ☎ 022 909 70 00 (www.geneve-tourisme.ch). Travellers' Information Office also at Gare de Cornavin, ☎ 022 732 00 90. *Genève Guide Pratique* and *Info-Jeunes* are free guides definitely worth picking up. *Genève Agenda* is the free weekly city entertainment guide.

There are numerous internet cafés, one in the main station, with prices typically around S Fr.5/hr. At **Laundrenet**, r. de la Servette 83, ☎ 022 734 83 83 (www.laundrenet.com), you can do your washing while you surf.

🛏 Most **hotels** are expensive, but there are plenty of hostels and private rooms. From 15 June to 15 Sept, the CAR (Centre d'Accueil et de Renseignements), located in a trailer in the pedestrian area opposite the station, offers accommodation booking and other advice to young people. There are a handful of hotels listed that are within walking distance of the centre, offering a room with shower from around S Fr.70, including **De la Cloche**, r. de la Cloche 6, ☎ 022 732 94 81 (www.geneva-hotel.ch/cloche), €. Other options include the **Hôtel du Lac**, r. des Eaux Vives 15, ☎ 022 735 45 80, €€, the **Hôtel St-Gervais**, r. des Corps-Saints 20, ☎ 022 732 45 72 (www.stgervais-geneva.ch), €€, and the **Hôtel Hermitage**, r. de la Tour-Maîtresse 8, ☎ 022 310 30 24 (www.hotelhermitage.ch). **Hostels**: The **City Hostel Geneva**, r. Ferrier 2, ☎ 022 901 15 00 (www.cityhostel.ch) is close to the train station. In the same neighbourhood is the **Auberge de Jeunesse Genève** (HI), r. Rothschild 30, ☎ 022 732 62 60 (www.genevahostel.ch). **Campsites: Camping Pointe-à-la-Bise**, Chemin de la Bise, Collonge-Bellerive, ☎ 022 752 12 96, open Apr–Oct, 7 km north-east, close to Lac Léman (🚌 E); **Camping d'Hermance**, r. du Nord 44, Hermance, ☎ 022 751 14 83, open Apr–Sept, 14 km north-east (🚌 E).

✗ Capitalising on the proximity to France, Geneva claims to be the culinary centre of Switzerland. The majority of places, however, cater for the international business market. Good places to look for reasonably priced restaurants are on the r. de Lausanne (turn left out of Gare de Cornavin) and around place du Cirque (blvd Georges-Favon). Otherwise, try **Café du Centre**, place du Molard 5 (in the Old Town) or **Aux Halles en l'Ile**, place de l'Ile 1, where you can listen to jazz. **Parc des Bastions** is also great for picnics.

CONNECTIONS FROM GENEVA

Frequent trains cross the border to France including TGV services to **Paris** and **Mâcon** (ERT 341), **Lyon** (ERT 346) and **Marseille**, **Nice** and **Montpellier** (ERT 350, 355, 360). Geneva to Paris takes 3 hrs 10 mins. There is a particularly beautiful local rail route along the French (ie. south) side of the lake to Évian-les-Bains, departing from Eaux-Vives station in Geneva (ERT 363).

Rail Route 31:
The Gotthard route to Ticino and beyond

CITIES: ★ CULTURE: ★★ HISTORY: ★ SCENERY: ★★★
COUNTRIES COVERED: SWITZERLAND, ITALY

The Gotthard route over the Alps is an absolute classic, but one that is set to change forever with the opening of the new Gotthard Base Tunnel in about 2017. No longer will great express trains need to manage the steep grades and tight curves of the traditional Gotthard route. True, the Gotthard does not match up to the majesty of the Bernina route from Switzerland to Italy (covered in **Route 29**) but the latter is slow. The Gotthard route will speed you across the Alps in comfort, with some great mountain scenery along the way.

The opening part of Route 31 skirts **Lake Lucerne**, an irregularly shaped body of water surrounded by flattish land around the dignified old resort of Lucerne itself. Then there is the long slow climb up to the tunnel. Beyond the **Gotthard Tunnel**, the landscape changes abruptly, as you enter the canton of **Ticino**, to an emerald-green valley dotted with rustic granite houses and tall campaniles as you head towards the Italian border. **Lugano** has the atmosphere of a smart Italian provincial town, and makes a good base for excursions.

BERNE (BERN)

One of Europe's more relaxed capitals, Berne is rightly fêted as a wonderfully appealing city. Its handsome Old Town, tucked into a big meander of the River Aare, features on the **UNESCO World Heritage List**. Berne was made for walking, so do just that, taking time to admire the medieval houses of yellow sandstone, the choppy roofscape, the handsome arcaded streets that make up Europe's largest covered shopping promenade, and the city's numerous fountains. The Alps are often visible in the distance, though the immediate rural hinterland of the city is unremarkable. From the main station, the first of 11 monumental fountains is the **Pfeiferbrunnen**, on Spitalgasse, a flamboyant 16th-century creation with technicolour carvings and flowers around the base. Münsterpl. is home of the Gothic **Münster** (Cathedral), which has a magnificent depiction of the Last Judgement above the main entrance and superb 15th-century stained glass. The 100-m steeple (Switzerland's highest) provides a good view if you feel like climbing its 344 steps (www.bernermuenster.ch).

Back on the main street (by now Gerechtigkeitsgasse), you pass Gerechtigkeitsbrunnen, where the blindfolded Goddess of Justice stands over the severed heads of historical figures. Cross the river by the 15th-century **Nydeggbrücke** and climb the hill facing you to look back on the picture-postcard view of the city. The **Kunstmuseum**, Hodlerstrasse 12 (www.kunstmuseumbern.ch; closed Mon), has a fine display of works by the Swiss artists Ferdinand Hodler and Paul Klee (of whom this is the world's largest collection). You'll find work by, among others, Fra Angelico, Matisse, Kandinsky, Cézanne and Picasso.

The other major museums are around Helvetiapl., south of the River Aare, across the Kirchenfeldbrücke (tram 3/5). **Kunsthalle**, Helvetiapl. 1, hosts temporary exhibitions of contemporary art (www.kunsthalle-bern.ch). Close by, the **Naturhistorisches Museum**, Bernastr. 15 (www.nmbe.ch) features Barry, the St Bernard dog who rescued over 40 people, as well as African animals and the inevitable bears. The apartment and workplace of **Albert Einstein**, a one-time resident of Berne, is at Kramgasse 49.

ARRIVAL, INFORMATION, ACCOMMODATION

≥ **Hauptbahnhof** (Hbf) is at the western end of the old centre. **🚻 Tourist office:** Hauptbahnhof, ☎ 031 328 12 12 (www.berninfo.com). Its bilingual brochure *Bern Guide* contains plenty of useful information. ⊨ Cheap accommodation is not plentiful but at least most of it is quite central. In the thick of things is **Hotel Glocke Backpackers Bern**, Rathausgasse 75, ☎ 031 311 37 71 (www.bernbackpackers.ch), €. The 2-star **Arabelle**, Mittelstr. 6, ☎ 031 301 03 05 (www.arabelle.ch), €€, is also well located. **Youth hostel** (HI): Weihergasse 4, ☎ 031 326 11 11 (www.youthhostel.ch/berne), a 10-min walk from the rail station, just below Bundeshaus.

✗ The area around Spitalgasse and Zeughausgasse is good for menu browsing. The best-value lunch is at the pleasant **EPA** department store at Marktgasse 24. On Gerechtigkeitsgasse, at No. 62, is the **Klötzlikeller**, Berne's oldest wine cellar (dating from 1635), serving meals (www.kloetzlikeller.ch). For a picnic with a view, cross the Nydeggbrücke to the lovely **Rose Garden**.

LUCERNE (LUZERN)

This resort straddles the River Reuss, itself crossed by quaintly roofed medieval footbridges, at the end of Lake Lucerne. Old-fashioned hotels attest to the town's long standing as a holiday place. There's a major music festival mid-Aug to Sept.

Old Lucerne is characterised by its many elaborately painted houses, its cobbled squares, its fountains, its Renaissance town hall by the Kornmarkt, and the two bridges over the Reuss. As you cross the 14th-century **Kapellbrücke**, a wooden-roofed footbridge that straggles crookedly over the river, you pass under a succession of 111 triangular-shaped paintings depicting local and national history. Halfway across, the bridge goes through a sturdy 13th-century octagonal **Water Tower**, which has undergone several changes of function over the centuries, including use as a prison. A little further down the river is the other medieval roofed bridge, the **Spreuerbrücke**, also lined with 17th-century paintings, in this case depicting the macabre Dance of Death.

Near the south end of Kapellbrücke, the **Jesuit Church** is plain from the outside, but has a gorgeous pink-and-white baroque interior dating from 1677. **Nölliturm**, near the north end of Spreuerbrücke, is a fortified gate at one end of a

Notes

Note the alternative renderings of place names, both used with equal currency in this part of Switzerland where locals shift easily from one language to another. So Bern or Berne and Luzern or Lucerne. Brunnen to Lugano requires a change at Bellinzona. Lucerne to Brunnen: a change may be required at Arth–Goldau.

Route Details

Berne–Lucerne		ERT 565
Type	Frequency	Typical journey time
Train	Every hr	1 hr

Lucerne–Brunnen		ERT 550
Type	Frequency	Typical journey time
Train	Every hr	45 mins

Brunnen–Lugano		ERT 550
Type	Frequency	Typical journey time
Train	Every hr	2h23

Lugano–Milan		ERT 550
Type	Frequency	Typical journey time
Train	8 daily	1h02

Key Journey

Berne–Milan		ERT 560
Type	Frequency	Typical journey time
Train	3 daily	3 hrs

well-preserved stretch of **Musegg Wall**, the old fortifications. You can follow this all the way (and climb three of its nine surviving towers) as it curves east to end just off Löwenpl.

The graceful twin-spired **Hofkirche** (Cathedral), off Schweizerhofquai, has an organ with 4,950 pipes and a 10-ton bell. The city's mascot, the **Löwendenkmal** (Lion Memorial), Löwenstr., is a massive but movingly portrayed dying lion carved in the cliff-side, commemorating the Swiss Guards massacred at the Tuileries in Paris during the French Revolution. Nearby is the **Gletschergarten** (Glacier Garden), Denkmalstr. 4, a bed of smooth rocks pitted with holes, created by glacial erosion. There's an ingenious mirror-maze here too.

Anyone with an interest in transport in all its guises and vintages should make for the **Verkehrshaus** (Swiss Transport Museum), Lidostr. 5 (www.verkehrshaus.ch), 2 km east of town (near the campsite), reached by a pleasant lakeside walk (or 🚌 6/8); it's one of Europe's leading museums on the theme, with exhibits covering locos, vintage cycles, space rockets and more, plus an IMAX movie theatre, a 360-degree cinema with a huge, almost vertigo-inducing screen.

Other Lucerne highlights are the **Picasso Museum**, Am Rhyn-Haus, Furrengasse 21, just off the old Kornmarkt square, with a small collection of his later paintings and photographs of the artist. The **Richard Wagner Museum**, Wagnerweg 27 (www.richard-wagner-museum.ch), by the lake, 1.5 km south-east of the centre (🚌 6/7/8 or walk east along the lake from the station), occupies the house where the German composer lived during the time he wrote the scores for *Siegfried* and *Die Meistersinger von Nürnberg*.

ARRIVAL, INFORMATION, ACCOMMODATION

🚆 On the south bank of the River Reuss, where it meets Lake Lucerne, a few minutes walk over the bridge to the Old Town. In the basement is a '24-hr shopping' automat, for emergency rations. 🛈 **Tourist office:** Zentralstr. 5 (in station), ☎ 041 227 17 17 (www.luzern.com). Pick up a copy of the *Luzern City Guide*, which is free and full of useful information. Ask about the **LucerneCard**.

🛏 Lucerne is a popular tourist destination, so advance booking is advisable for its limited range of cheap options, especially in summer; some of the 19th-century hotels surrounding the Old Town can be noisy. Try the **Tourist Hotel,** St Karliquai 12, ☎ 041 410 24 74 (www.touristhotel.ch), €€, or the **Pickwick**, Rathausquai 6, ☎ 041 410 59 27 (www.hotelpickwick.ch), €€. **Hostels: Backpackers Lucerne**, Alpenquai 42, ☎ 041 360 04 20 (www.backpackerslucerne.ch), offers student-style accommodation by the south shore of the lake (12-min walk from station) and is highly recommended. Another option is the **Lion Lodge**, Zürichstr. 57, ☎ 041 410 0144 (www.lionlodge.ch).

Youth hostel (HI): Am Rotsee, Sedelstr. 12, ☎ 041 420 88 00 (www.youthhostel.ch/luzern), is situated by the lake north-west of town (🚌 18 to Jugendherberge or 🚌 19 to Gopplismoosweg). **Campsite: Camping International Lido**, Lidostr. 19; ☎ 041 370 21 46 (www.camping-international.ch) (🚌 6/8/24 to Verkehrshaus), on the north shore of the lake.

DAY TRIPS FROM LUCERNE

You can get to most of the settlements around Lake Lucerne, which covers 114 square km, by regular local boat services, as well as excursion cruises in summer; contact **Schifffahrtgesellschaft Vierwaldstättersee**, Werftestr. 5, ☎ 041 367 67 67 (www.lakelucerne.ch), or book through the tourist office. These boats combine nicely with walks as well as rack-railway and cable-car trips. From **Alpnachstad** (reached by steamer), south of Lucerne, take the world's steepest rack railway (climbing a 48% gradient) up **Mt Pilatus** (2,132 m). Supposedly haunted by the spirit of Pontius Pilate, the summit is also accessible by cable car from **Kriens** (🚌 1) on the southern outskirts of Lucerne – giving scope for a circular tour of the mountain. From Vitznau, on the eastern shore, Europe's oldest rack railway ascends **Mt Rigi** (1,800 m), where the summit view from **Rigi-Kulm** at sunrise (including the Jungfrau and Titlis) has attracted generations of tourists, including Victor Hugo. There's also a cable car from the sunny waterside resort of **Weggis**; if you prefer to walk, there's a 4-hr route from Weggis, or you can take the cable car up from **Küssnacht** to within a 2-hr hike of the summit.

✗ There are reasonably priced restaurants and cafés all round Lucerne's many squares and waterside promenades. The town's speciality is *Kügelipasteti*, a large meat and mushroom vol-au-vent covered in rich sauce.

BRUNNEN

Brunnen has a wonderful location at the meeting of lakes **Uri** and **Lucerne**. The bustling resort is well set up for most watersports, as well as walking on Lake Uri's shores. Brunnen can claim to be the cradle of the nation's history. Here the states of Unterwalden, Uri and Schwyz were sworn together as the Confederation in a declaration on 1 Aug 1291 in **Rütli Meadow** by the lake, an event immortalised in the legend of William Tell as told by Schiller in 1804. 1 Aug is Swiss National Day, celebrated nationwide with bonfires lit on high spots and the Rütli Meadow floodlit. The **Swiss Way** is a 35-km walkers' route round the lake, divided into 26 sections; each section represents a canton or half-canton, with the length of each determined by the proportionate populations of each canton.

ARRIVAL, INFORMATION, ACCOMMODATION
≋ Close to the town centre. 🛈 **Tourist office:** Bahnhofstr. 15, ☎ 041 825 00 40 (www.brunnentourismus.ch). 🛏 A mid-range hotel with a great view is **Hotel Bellevue Brunnen**, Axenstr. 2, ☎ 041 820 13 18 (www.bellevue-brunnen.ch), €€.

LUGANO

Lugano, the largest town in the Italian-speaking canton of Ticino, is a handsome and sophisticated lakeside resort. The lakeside promenade is a popular place to

THE ITALIAN LAKES

Locarno on Lake Maggiore is 1 hr 10 mins by train from Lugano (change at Bellinzona; ERT 550). ⊨ **Youth hostel** (HI): via Varenna 18, ☎ 091 756 15 00 (www.youthhostel.ch/locarno). From the town, the scenic **Centovalli** (Hundred Valleys) route runs to Domodossola in Italy (ERT 528). The 53-km line clings to dramatic hillsides, soars across dozens of steep valleys (hence its name), over spectacular bridges and viaducts to **Santa Maria Maggiore**. Afterwards, continue exploring Switzerland via the major rail junction at **Brig**, 42 km north of **Domodossola** through the **Simplon Tunnel**. North-east of Lugano, just beyond Gandria, is the Mediterranean-flavoured Menaggio. In Italy, this Lake Como town provides lovely views over the water. To get to the other bank, there are frequent trains from Lugano to Como (about 35 mins). Continuing on the Italian side, the train skirts the shore, providing views of Italian villages on both sides of the lake.

stroll or rollerblade in July and August, when vehicles are banned from it. At its eastern end is the **Parco Civico** (Municipal Park), the pleasant setting for summer concerts and graced with fountains, statues and trees. Swimmers can head for the lido (to the east of the river), with its pool and sandy beaches. Funiculars climb the two mountains guarding the bay: up **Monte Brè** (930 m) from **Cassarate** and up **San Salvatore** (912 m) from **Paradiso**, both 20-min walks from the centre (or take 🚌 1).

The arcaded Via Nassa is the main pedestrianised shopping street, where you can take your pick of such Swiss specialities as expensive wristwatches or chocolate in all its national varieties. There's more worthwhile art in **Thyssen-Bornemisza**, a collection of 19th- and 20th-century paintings and watercolours housed in the **Villa Favorita**, Riviera 14 (Fri–Sun, Easter–Oct), while the **Cantonal Art Museum**, Via Canova 10 (www.museo-cantonale-arte.ch), also has many 20th-century works.

ARRIVAL, INFORMATION, ACCOMMODATION

🚋 At the top of the town. From it a funicular descends to the centre (otherwise a 6-min walk), halfway down to the lake. 🚹 **Tourist office:** Palazzo Civico, Riva Albertolli, ☎ 091 913 32 32 (www.lugano-tourism.ch); on the lakeside opposite the central landing stage. Accommodation booking service.

⊨ Try the **Rosa**, v. Landriani 2–4, ☎ 091 922 92 86 (www.albergorosa.ch), €€. **Youth hostel** (HI): **Lugano-Savosa**, v. Cantonale 13, Savosa, ☎ 091 966 27 28 (www.dieoase.ch); take 🚌 5 from station to Crocifisso then a 3-min walk. Generally, Paradiso (the southern part of Lugano) is slightly better value.

✗ There are several restaurants along the lakeside, as well as around the main square, the Piazza Riforma.

MILAN — SEE P296

Rail Route 32: Tyrolean transect

CITIES: ★★ CULTURE: ★★ HISTORY: ★ SCENERY: ★★★
COUNTRIES COVERED: SWITZERLAND, LIECHTENSTEIN, AUSTRIA, SLOVAKIA

Route 32 is a tremendous west to east transect that nicely combines reasonable speed with superb scenery. The full route is over 900 km long and could at a pinch be covered in a day, particularly as the new Austrian Railways RailJet trains now speed from **Zurich** to Vienna in just 8 hrs. But Route 32 is too good to be rushed and we suggest you take your time and stop off here and there along the way. The route takes you from the middle of **Switzerland** to the banks of the **Danube** in Slovakia, passing through four major Austrian cities: **Innsbruck**, **Salzburg**, **Linz** and **Vienna**.

Our favourite section of scenery on this mountainous route is the 2-hr stretch east from Feldkirch to Innsbruck, where the railway follows the Arlberg route through the heart of the Austrian Tyrol. And for devotees of microstates, Route 32 has something special. It is the sole route in this book to traverse Liechtenstein territory (see the Sidetracks at the end of this route).

ZURICH — SEE P593

Our route leaves Zurich heading south-east, initially following the same railway line as **Route 29**, skirting the Walensee before turning north at Sargans to briefly hug the Rhine Valley. Until **Buchs**, the railway stays in Swiss territory, with Liechtenstein on the far bank of the Rhine. At Buchs the train reverses and then crosses the River Rhine into **Liechtenstein**, where it traverses the full length of the principality's sole rail route in just 9 mins.

FELDKIRCH

There are two very good reasons for pausing at Feldkirch. First, it happens to be a very pleasant small town. For first-time visitors to Austria, it is a great introduction to the country. Second, Feldkirch is by far the best jumping-off point to **explore Liechtenstein** by bus. Although there are bus connections into the principality from Sargans and Buchs, we think the approach from Feldkirch is just very much prettier. For more on day trips and longer excursions into Liechtenstein see p285.

Nestling in against the hills, Feldkirch is a place to linger, enjoy coffee and cake and wander though the nicely arcaded main streets. It is worth climbing up to the **Schattenburg**, not so much for the contents of the museum now housed in the old fortress, but more just for the view. Don't miss **St Nikolaus Cathedral**, locally referred to as the Domkirche, with its odd double nave and flamboyant 1960s stained-glass windows.

ROUTE DETAILS

Zurich–Feldkirch — ERT 951

Type	Frequency	Typical journey time
Train	6 daily	1h30

Landeck–Malles — ERT 954

Type	Frequency	Typical journey time
Bus	Every 1–2 hrs	1h53 (via Nauders)

Feldkirch–Landeck — ERT 951

Type	Frequency	Typical journey time
Train	13 daily	1h10

Landeck–Innsbruck — ERT 951

Type	Frequency	Typical journey time
Train	Every 1–2 hrs	48 mins

Innsbruck–Kitzbühel — ERT 960

Type	Frequency	Typical journey time
Train	Every 1–2 hrs	1h20

Kitzbühel–Salzburg — ERT 960

Type	Frequency	Typical journey time
Train	Every 1–2 hrs	2h31

Salzburg–Linz — ERT 950

Type	Frequency	Typical journey time
Train	2 per hr	1h08

Linz–Vienna — ERT 950

Type	Frequency	Typical journey time
Train	2–3 per hr	1h34

Vienna–Bratislava — ERT 996

Type	Frequency	Typical journey time
Train	Every 1–2 hrs	1h10 (via Marchegg)

KEY JOURNEYS

Zurich–Innsbruck — ERT 86

Type	Frequency	Typical journey time
Train	4 daily	3h26

Innsbruck–Salzburg — ERT 951

Type	Frequency	Typical journey time
Train	Every 1–2 hrs	1h50

Salzburg–Vienna — ERT 950

Type	Frequency	Typical journey time
Train	2 per hr	2h45

Notes

Innsbruck to Kitzbühel: a change of trains at Wörgl is necessary on certain journeys. Additional connections are available between Zurich and Feldkirch, but these require two changes of train (at Sargans and Buchs). The fast trains shown in the key journeys table above from Innsbruck to Salzburg do not follow the line of Route 32, but take a shorter route that traverses German territory.

➤ The railway station is 700 m north-east of the town centre. It is an easy walk, following Wichnergasse beside the railway line. **🛈 Tourist information** (here called the Fremdensverkehrsamt), Schmiedgasse 1–3, ☎ 05522 734 67–3212, is tucked away in a little courtyard between Raiffeisenplatz and Schlossergasse.

🛏 The **Hotel Bären**, Bahnhofstr. 1, ☎ 05522 355 00 (www.hotel-baeren.at), €€, is close to the station. Another mid-range option is the **Central Löwen Hotel**, Schloß-garten 13, ☎ 05522 720 700 (www.central-hotel-loewen.at), €€. The **youth hostel** (HI) is at Reichsstr. 111, ☎ 05522 731 81 (www.hostelfeldkirch.com).

ST ANTON AND LANDECK

St Anton and Landeck are the principal stopping points for express trains following the beautiful **Arlberg rail route** from Feldkirch to Innsbruck. St Anton is an upmarket winter-sports resort (very pricey in season). Landeck is unremarkable, and would hardly warrant a stop, were it not for its key position in the Tyrolean transport network. From here you can catch a bus south, following the **Inn Valley** to Nauders (ERT 954), from where there are onward bus connections to the **Engadine** area of eastern Switzerland and to **Malles** in Italy (all in ERT 954). Read more on p256.

INNSBRUCK — SEE P254

Fast trains between Innsbruck and Salzburg deviate from the route described here and travel without stopping for about an hour across German territory. This applies to services shown in ERT 951. The slower trains between Innsbruck and Salzburg shown in ERT 960 follow Route 32, and stay within **Austria**. If you can afford the time we recommend you take that slower route. At Innsbruck you can connect onto **Route 28**, heading north to Munich or south to Verona.

KITZBÜHEL

With its mountain backdrop, this pleasant old town, with tree-lined streets of steeply gabled pastel-coloured buildings, is one of Austria's prettiest and largest ski resorts (though the snow's not that reliable; main season Christmas–Easter). The **Museum Kitzbühel**, Hinterstadt 32 (www.museum-kitzbuehel.at), occupies the town's oldest house and displays paintings by Alfons Walde (a contemporary of Klimt). Don't miss the **Kitzbüheler Hornbahn** cable car to the summit of the Horn; near the top, some 120 species of flowers bloom from May to October in an **Alpine Flower Garden**, 1,880 m high (free guided tours 1100 and 1330, July and Aug). The ski elite arrive in January for the **Hahnenkamm Ski Competition**, a World Cup leg, down one of the world's trickiest ski runs. At the top of the

Hahnenkammlift, the **Bergbahn Museum** reveals the history of skiing in Kitzbühel since 1893 (free entry).

The tourist office organises free guided hiking and bike trips (register one day before). A 2.5 km walk leads to the **Schwarzsee**, a good bathing lake. In summer, hikers can buy lift passes valid for 3 days in a week or 6 in a ten-day period.

ARRIVAL, INFORMATION, ACCOMMODATION

⇥ Kitzbühel Hbf, Bahnhofpl. 2. A 10-min walk to the town centre; go straight across the River Ache, left along Achenpromenade, then follow signs right for the centre. Bike hire at the station: rates for 1, 3 or 7 days (reduction with a rail ticket).

🚩 Tourist office: Hinterstadt 18, ☎ 05356 666 60 (www.kitzbuehel.com), next to the Rathaus (town hall). Free accommodation service, free street and hiking maps. **⇥** Try the **Pension Hörl**, Josef-Pirchl-Str. 60, ☎ 05356 63 144, €. The **Jugendhotel Noichl**, Wieseneggweg 3, ☎ 0664 783 0457 (www.noichl.com), has dorm accommodation.

SALZBURG

Wonderfully sited between the Alps and the lakes of the Salzkammergut, Salzburg is renowned as Mozart's birthplace and is where *The Sound of Music* was filmed in 1964. Much of the city's appearance dates from the 17th century, when many of the old buildings were pulled down and others given a baroque makeover to create Italian-style squares with spectacular fountains. Salzburg's entire **Old City** (Altstadt) is designated a UNESCO World Heritage Site and much of it is sweetly beautiful, although some find it cloying, and the crowds can be oppressive. The compact centre is largely pedestrianised; the main shopping street is narrow Getreidegasse, bordered by elegant old houses, decorative wrought-iron signs and medieval arcades, which now house jewellery shops or boutiques. **Mozarts Geburtshaus**, No. 9, where the composer was born in 1756 and spent most of his first 17 years, is now a museum. In nearby Residenzpl. is the **Residenz** (hourly tours), the former Prince-Archbishop's palace, built after the need for fortification had passed. Mozart conducted in its grand rooms. Opposite stands the Neue Residenz, home to the **Salzburg Museum** (www.salzburgmuseum.at). The **cathedral**, in adjacent Dompl., is considered the finest early baroque church north of the Alps.

On **Mönchsberg** (Monk's Mountain), high above the Altstadt, looms the formidable **Festung Hohensalzburg**, Mönchsberg 34 (www.hohensalzburg.com; entry fee), once the stronghold of the Archbishops of Salzburg. Built over six centuries, it's almost perfectly preserved, with medieval torture chambers, early Gothic state rooms, and a 200-pipe barrel organ that booms out once the 7th-century 35-bell carillon of the **Glockenspiel**, Mozartpl., has pealed (at 0700, 1100 and 1800). The castle can be reached on foot from Festungsgasse behind the cathedral, or by the **Festungsbahn**, Austria's oldest cable railway dating from 1892. Alternatively, the **Mönchsbergaufzug** (Mönchsberg Lift) operates from Gstättengasse 13 (by Museumpl.) and takes you to the uncompromisingly minimalist contemporary art museum, the **Museum der Moderne**, from whose café terrace there are breathtaking views over the city. Across the river is **Schloss Mirabell**, Mirabellpl., built in the 17th century for Prince-Archbishop Wolf Dietrich's mistress, Salome Alt, who bore him 15 or 16 children. It houses the **Marble Hall**, a magnificent venue for chamber music concerts. The garden is a tranquil oasis, one of the most instantly recognisable locations from *The Sound of Music*. Nearby is the Mozart-Wohnhaus, Makartpl. 8, where the Mozart family lived from 1773 to 1787.

ARRIVAL, INFORMATION, ACCOMMODATION

⇌ **Salzburg Hbf**, Südtiroler Pl. 1, 20-min walk from the old centre (🚋 1/2/5/6/51 to Staatsbrücke, the main bridge). The station is being entirely rebuilt, so expect some chaos throughout 2012. Tourist information, accommodation service, left luggage, money exchange, shops. ✈ **Salzburg Airport**, 4 km west of the city; ☎ 0662 8580 (www.salzburg-airport.com), 🚋 2/8 every 15 mins connects station with airport; journey time about 25 mins. Taxis to the city centre: ☎ 0662 8111.

🛈 **Tourist offices**: Auerspergstr. 6, ☎ 0662 889 870 (www.salzburg.info); accommodation service (fee). Branches at the station and Mozartplatz 5. The **Salzburg Card** provides admission to most of Salzburg's attractions, free public transport and other discounts; valid 24, 36 or 72 hrs (peak season €25/34/40; off-peak €22/30/35). **SalzburgerLand Card**: Free access to over 180 attractions in the region for six or 12 days (€46/55; www.salzburgerlandcard.com). Bus and trolley tickets: from vending machines or tobacconists; more expensive from driver (punch ticket on boarding). Day passes also available. ⤳ During festivals, it pays to book early as accommodation often gets very scarce. Centrally located are **Junger Fuchs**, Linzergasse 54, ☎ 0662 875 496 (www.pensionjungerfuchs.com), €, and **Schwarzes Rössl**, Priesterhausgasse 6, ☎ 0662 874 4260 (www.academiahotels.at), €€; July–Sept only. **Hostels:** The **Yo-Ho**, Paracelsusstr. 9, ☎ 0662 879 649 (www.yoho.at) is a non-HI hostel a few minutes' walk from the station and is extremely popular.

✗ **Café Tomaselli**, Alter Markt 9, is elegantly authentic. Also try the **Augustiner-Bräu beer garden**, Augustinerg. 4, where beer is brewed by the monastery.

CULTURE AND EVENTS

The big event is the Salzburg Festival, mid-July to late Aug. For major performances, tickets must be booked months ahead from **Kartenbüro der Salzburger Festspiele**, Herbert-von-Karajan-Pl. 11, Postfach 140, 5010 Salzburg, ☎ 0662 8045 500 (www. salzburgfestival.at). Last-minute standing tickets sometimes available in the **Kleine Festspielhaus**. Events linked to the festival include an opening Fackeltanz (torch-dance) in the Residenzpl. (free) and performances of *Jedermann* ('Everyman'); standing tickets only sold at the Dompl. door 1 hr before start. Other events include Mozart Week in late Jan, a Nov Jazz Festival and an Easter Music Festival. In addition, there's always a concert on somewhere in the city. The **Salzburger Marionetten-theater**, Schwarzstr. 24, ☎ 0662 872 406, (www.marionetten.at), presents operas 'performed' convincingly by puppets that 'sing' to recordings.

LINZ

Austria's industrial third city is gradually reinventing itself with ultra-modern museums and events, such as the annual classical *son et lumière* **Klangwolken**. **Ars Electronica Center**, Hauptstr 2 (www.aec.at; Tue, Wed, Fri 0900–1700, Thur 0900–2100, Sat & Sun 1000–1800), is Europe's only museum dedicated to virtual reality. Facing it across the river, the sleek **Lentos Kunstmuseum**, Ernst-Koref-Promenade 1, glows with changing colour after dark. **Hauptplatz** blends colourful baroque and rococo facades around the baroque marble **Trinity column**.

In 1938, Hitler — who grew up here — stood on the balcony of Hauptplatz 1 (now the tourist office) to inform the Austrians that the Nazis had annexed their country. The 17th-century **Alter Dom**, Domgasse, one of the city's two cathedrals, is simple outside, restrained baroque within. The other, the huge neo-Gothic **Neuer Dom**, Herrenstr., can hold 20,000 people. **Landhaus**, Promenade 24, is where the astronomer Johann Kepler developed the third law of planetary motion. Across the river, the **Pöstlingbergbahn**, the world's steepest rack railway, chugs from tram 3 terminus at Landgutstr. 19 to a fortress and pilgrimage church (every 30 mins, Mon–Sat 0600–2200, Sun 0730–2200).

ARRIVAL, INFORMATION, ACCOMMODATION

⇶ Electronic information service, left-luggage lockers (24 hrs), shops. For the centre, take tram 3 to Hauptpl. (10 mins). **🔋 Tourist office**: Hauptpl. 1, ☎ 0732 7070 2009 (www.linz.at/tourismus). **Linz Card** (1 day €15, 3 days €25) gives unlimited travel within the city, free admission to all museums and various other discounts. The **Linz Museum Card** (€12) qualifies you to one visit to each of Linz's 12 museums. Steamboat trips and cruises (Apr–Oct) are operated from the quay by **Donauschiffahrt Wurm & Köck**, Untere Donaulände 1, ☎ 0732 783 607 (www.donauschiffahrt.de).

🛏 **Goldenes Dachl**, Hafnerstr. 27, ☎ 0732 775 897, €, is central and affordable; **Wilder Mann**, Goethestrasse 14, ☎ 0732 656 078, €–€€, is reasonable and close to the station. The **youth hostel** (HI) is at Stanglhofweg 3, ☎ 0732 664 434 (www.jugendherbergsverband.at); 🚎 17/19/45 (to Goethekreuzung, then 7-min walk). ✗ The pedestrian zone around **Hofgasse** is busy at night and has plenty of reasonable eateries. **Klosterhof**, Landstr. 30 (www.klosterhof-linz.at), boasts Austria's biggest beer garden. Sample Linzer Torte (almond cake topped with redcurrant jam).

CONNECTIONS FROM LINZ

Join **Route 18** (p178) by taking the train over the German border to Passau (ERT 950; 1 hr 15 mins).

VIENNA — SEE P581

From Vienna there are two rail routes east to Bratislava. We strongly recommend that you use the more northerly of the two, shown in ERT 996. This route is more rural and just east of Marchegg affords good views of the water meadows that surround the Danube. The **Marchegg** route is also hugely more convenient for arrival in Bratislava, as it drops you at the main city centre station (called Hlavná). The alternative route from Vienna to Bratislava (ERT 997) deposits you at **Petržalka** station, a rather dismal lump of concrete in a soulless Bratislava suburb that decorates the only fragment of Slovakian territory on the south bank of the Danube.

BRATISLAVA — SEE P398

SIDETRACKS H: EXPLORING LIECHTENSTEIN

"There's really not a lot there," replied the barman in Feldkirch when we said we were walking to Liechtenstein. And that's the common view of Liechtenstein. Undeterred we walked through Austrian drizzle to the village of **Fresch** and followed a tiny lane that led up the hill to the principality. No formalities at the border. In fact, no humans at the border. This is the back road into Liechtenstein, the route followed by 400 Russian soldiers who in early May 1945 sought refuge in neutral Liechtenstein. Quite how 400 Russian soldiers came to be wandering around western Austria in the dog days of the Second World War is itself an intriguing tale, but not one for here.

The first building in Liechtenstein is a pub, just as it was in 1945 when **General Boris Smyslovsky** and his ragtag force arrived (accompanied by a Polish ballerina, a Swiss journalist and a lost Englishman). The feat of the innkeepers in rustling up tea and sandwiches for 400 guests who arrived unexpectedly at three in the morning defies belief. We had less luck. Closed Wednesdays and Thursdays said the sign on the door, which seemed a tad harsh, given our efforts to re-enact the Russian invasion of Liechtenstein.

That was the only disappointing moment we have ever experienced in Liechtenstein. The **Alpine principality** is more than just cowbells and questionable bank accounts. The word on Liechtenstein, rehearsed in so many guidebooks, is that the only reason to go to Liechtenstein is to tick it off on the list of countries you have visited. This is nonsense and a myth perpetuated by those who have spent just an hour or two in the capital Vaduz. Liechtenstein deserves much, much more. True, **Vaduz** is an odd place, verging on the sterile. But no country should be judged on its capital alone, and certainly not Liechtenstein.

Of course, it is not compulsory to walk from **Feldkirch**. Occasional local trains from Feldkirch to Buchs (Switzerland) stop en route at one or more of the four railway stations of the principality. Or better still, catch the lemon Liechtenstein bus that leaves every 30 mins from the station forecourt at Feldkirch and spend the day roaming Liechtenstein by bus. A one-day bus pass for all zones costs €12 (schedules at www.lba.li). Our favourite route is 🚌 21 that climbs high into the hills above Vaduz. Alight at Steg and listen to the cowbells. And on the way back down visit the museum in **Triesenberg**.

Rail Route 33: Liguria and Tuscany

CITIES: ★★ CULTURE: ★★ HISTORY: ★ SCENERY: ★★
COUNTRIES COVERED: ITALY

Starting just on the Italian side of the frontier with France, and so a natural follow-on from **Route 6** (p90), Route 33 follows the full length of the **Italian Riviera**, along the way affording a wonderful sequence of seaside panoramas.

Behind the coast, the hills generally rise steeply into wild country, but the coastal littoral itself is seductively mellow. Vineyards, olive groves and palms flourish in the mild climes that attracted English visitors to **Liguria** in the 19th century. **Genoa** is gritty but engrossing, and **Pisa** is a fine introduction to **Tuscany**.

VENTIMIGLIA

Ventimiglia is a scruffy frontier town that the French invade on Friday mornings for the famous market. There is a crumbling steep Old Town, a thriving cut-flower and olive-oil industry, but little to detain visitors beyond the superb market, the place to stock up on bags, clothes, Parmesan cheese, oil and picnic lunches.

ARRIVAL, INFORMATION, ACCOMMODATION

≈ In the town. **B** **Tourist office:** Via Cavour 61, ☎ 0184 351 183 (www.turismoinliguria.it). ☒ The B&B **Casa Lorenzina**, Corso Toscanini 30, ☎ 347 161 1045 (www.casalorenzina.it), €€, is friendly and welcoming.

SANREMO

The prime resort of the western Riviera is located in the long gentle arc of a bay. It has a pleasant Old Town, with its narrow streets, steep steps and arches. The **Nobel Villa**, C. Cavalotti 112, was the house of the Swedish inventor Alfred Nobel, who established the international prizes named after him; it is open to the public. In early March each year the town is filled with singers and musicians for Italy's massively popular annual musical event: the Festival di Sanremo. East from Sanremo the railway skirts the coast (as shown on our front cover).

ARRIVAL, INFORMATION, ACCOMMODATION

≈ In the town. **B** **Tourist office:** Largo Nuvoloni 1, ☎ 0184 590 59 (www.visitrivieradeifiori.it). Internet Point Sanremo, Pza C. Colombo 42.

☒ Modest rooms can be found at **hotels** like the **Villa Maria**, Corso Nuvoloni 30, ☎ 0184 531 422 (www.villamariahotel.it), and the central **Alexander**, Corso Garibaldi 123, ☎ 0184 504 591 (www.hotelalexandersanremo.com), which is an art nouveau affair in gardens. **Campsite: Villaggio dei Fiori**, Via Tiro a Volo 3, ☎ 0184 660 635 (www.villaggiodeifiori.it), offers tent space as well as bungalow accommodation (open all year).

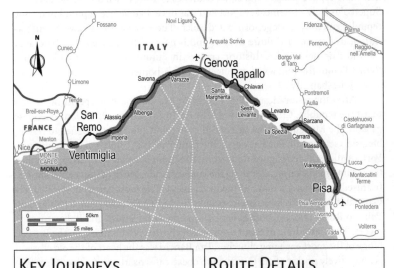

KEY JOURNEYS

Nice–Genoa	ERT 361, 580	
Type	Frequency	Typical journey time
Train	6–7 daily	3h15

Nice–Pisa	ERT 361, 580, 610	
Type	Frequency	Typical journey time
Train	5 daily	7h15

ROUTE DETAILS

Ventimiglia–Sanremo	ERT 580, 581	
Type	Frequency	Typical journey time
Train	1–2 per hr	15 mins

Sanremo–Genoa	ERT 580	
Type	Frequency	Typical journey time
Train	1–2 per hr	1h50 to 3 hrs

Genoa–Rapallo	ERT 610	
Type	Frequency	Typical journey time
Train	Up to 2 per hr	30 mins

Rapallo–Pisa	ERT 610	
Type	Frequency	Typical journey time
Train	Every 1–2 hrs	1h45

Notes

For the key journeys from Nice to Genoa and Pisa, as indeed for all journeys from the French Riviera to anywhere in Italy beyond Ventimiglia, you will need to change trains at Ventimiglia. That one still normally needs to change trains thus seems quite out of kilter with the modern affection for open borders and seamless cross-border rail services. The only passenger train that travels along the Ligurian coast and continues into France is the weekly Moscow to Nice service inaugurated in autumn 2010. Sadly, this deliciously exotic train is not available for local journeys along the coast.

Genoa (Genova)

Sandwiched between the mountains and the sea, **Genoa** is a concertina of a city, with slate-topped palaces and squat churches bearing down on the old port. 'La Superba' is Italy's foremost seaport and was once, like Venice, a proud maritime republic ruled by a Doge, or elected ruler. The city gained a huge facelift as European Capital of Culture in 2004 and is now gritty but gorgeous. As one of the most densely packed historic centres in Europe, Genoa is unfathomable. Renzo Piano, the renowned architect, sees his hometown as a 'secret, inward-looking Kasbah city'.

After the restoration of the waterfront, Genoa now has a port worthy of a maritime republic. Clustered around the **Porto Antico** are a traditional Genoese galleon, the **Museum of the Sea** and the superb **Aquarium**, designed to resemble a ship setting sail. Further west is the **Lanterna** (1544), Italy's oldest lighthouse. Porto Antico, the redesigned waterfront, functions as a new city piazza, with bars tucked into medieval arcades along the landward side. Much of the centre is pedestrianised, set among a maze of medieval alleys. The most patrician street is **Via Garibaldi**, lined with Renaissance palaces, including **Palazzo Bianco** (No. 11) and **Palazzo Rosso** (No. 18), both galleries bursting with Flemish and Italian masterpieces. The **Cattedrale di San Lorenzo**, which survived bombing by the British, is one of the most engaging churches. **Pza Banchi** was the heart of the old city and is now a lively pocket of old Genoa, with cheap cafés nearby and places to try typical pasta and pesto dishes. The **Palazzo Ducale**, on Pza Matteotti, was once the seat of the Doge, but now houses chic cafés and an exhibition centre. A funicular from Pza del Portello whisks you to **Sant'Anna**, high on the hill. If you fancy a swim, there are a few *bagni*, private beaches with facilities such as showers, on Corso Italia (Albaro area), like Bagni Lido at No. 13.

Nervi, a few stops along the line from Brignole station, is a delightful escape, with its dramatic coastline, beautiful promenade, and several revamped art museums.

ARRIVAL, INFORMATION, ACCOMMODATION

🚉 There are two main stations. **Principe** (take 🚌 41 to get to the city centre) and **Stazione Brignole** further east (🚌 40 to the centre). Trains to the north use both stations; use 🚌 37 to transfer between them. ✈ **Cristoforo Colombo Airport** (7 km to the west), 12–14 buses daily to the two main rail stations and Piazza de Ferrari.

🅱 **Tourist office**: Genova Turismo, Stazione Porta Principe, ☎ 010 246 2633 (www.turismoinliguria.it). Internet: *1pc4you*, Pza Durazzo 12/N (near Stazione Principe).

🛏 Cheap accommodation is easy to find, but can be tacky. Try the outskirts of the Old Town, near Brignole. Convenient for the station is **Essiale B&B**, Via Gropallo 14/2, ☎ 335 56 86 326 (www.essiale.com), €€. **Youth hostel** (HI): **Ostello di Genova**, Via Costanzi 120n, ☎ 010 242 2457 (www.ostellogenova.it), 🚌 35/40 from Piazza Principe.

A MONASTIC DIVERSION

Pavia, north of Genoa on the line to Milan, is reached by train in about 1 hr 15 mins (hourly; ERT 610; ⇄ a 10-min walk from the centre, or take 🚌 3/6). It's a quietly attractive old town, known for its medieval towers, churches and peaceful squares. The highlight of the area and one of the great buildings of Italy is the **Certosa di Pavia**, a Carthusian monastery, 8 km to the north. It has an incredible facade of Carrara marble. Cistercian monks now live there and maintain a vow of silence. The monastery can only be seen by joining a guided tour.

Buses from Pavia are frequent (from Pza Piave), then there's a 1.5-km walk to the entrance. 🅘 **Tourist office:** IAT Pavia, Piazza Petrarca 4, ☎ 0382 597 001 (www.pavese.pv.it). 🛏 Try the **Hotel Aurora**, Via Vittorio Emanuele II 25, ☎ 0382 236 64 (www.hotel-aurora.eu), €€.

✖ The cheapest places for lunch are in the dock area, but most close in the evening. For Saturday night fever, head for the student-filled Via di San Bernardo and Stradina Sant'Agostino, or stroll down pedestrianised Via di San Lorenzo.

RAPALLO

Icing-coloured belle époque hotels overlook the palm-shaded promenade that defines Rapallo's long seafront. Anchoring the far end of this classic Riviera scene is a picture-perfect stone **castle** almost surrounded by water. Admire the view from the cafés that overlook the beach below. The only must-see is **Museo del Merletto** (Tues–Sat), whose examples of handmade lace includes high-fashion clothing, set among the rare plants and trees of **Parco Casale**. Footpaths and a **funicular** (from Pzle Solari) climb to the **Santuario Basilica di Montallegro**, a shrine with expansive views over the Gulf of Paradise.

ARRIVAL, INFORMATION, ACCOMMODATION

⇄ Near the promenade. 🅘 **Tourist office:** Lungomare V. Veneto 7, ☎ 0185 230 346. 🛏 The **Albergo Mignon Posta**, V. Boccoleri 12/1, ☎ 0185 230 230 (www.hotelmignonposta.it), €€, is central.

PISA — SEE P290

CONNECTIONS FROM PISA

Either venture into **Tuscany** on **Route 34** or carry on along the coast to Rome (ERT 610). On the way to Rome you can visit the island of **Elba**; change at Campiglia for Piombino, then take the 1-hr ferry crossing to Elba (ERT 2699). Elba has clear waters, fine beaches and a ragged coastline of capes and bays, though in summer it gets very tourist-ridden; there are attractive villages to explore, plus Napoleon's villa and a cable car up to a 1,019-m summit. Buses serve the island's villages and resorts. Accommodation is plentiful (incl. campsites), but it gets heavily booked in July & Aug. 🅘 **Tourist office**: Calata Italia 26, Portoferraio, ☎ 0565 914 671 (www.aptelba.it).

Rail Route 34: The heart of Tuscany

CITIES: ★★★ CULTURE: ★★ HISTORY: ★★ SCENERY: ★★
COUNTRIES COVERED: ITALY

This trip winds through the heart of **Tuscany**, culturally one of richest and least spoilt parts of Italy, with its green hills striped with olive groves and vineyards, as well as historic towns and cities overflowing with Renaissance art and architecture. It takes in premier-league tourist destinations like **Pisa**, **Florence** and **Siena**, but also makes space for cities that are a little off the beaten track, such as Lucca and Orvieto.

The entire route can be undertaken using local trains, for which no advance booking is necessary and where no supplements are payable by holders of rail passes. Route 34 starts in Pisa, where there is a connection with **Route 33**. And from the end point of Route 34 in Orvieto, it is but a short hop south to Rome where you can join **Routes 36** or **37**.

PISA

The **Leaning Tower of Pisa** rates among the world's most familiar landmarks, part of a magnificent triumvirate of buildings around the **Campo dei Miracoli** (Field of Miracles), by the Cathedral and Baptistry. Some of Italy's finest medieval sculptures are here, many by Nicola and Giovanni Pisano (father and son) and other Pisanos (unrelated). The unusual architecture, characterised by distinctive stripes of marble and by blind arcades, is thought to emanate from the Pisans' contact with the Muslims of North Africa and Spain.

The 11th-century, four-tiered **Duomo**, one of Italy's finest cathedrals, was the first Tuscan building to use marble in horizontal stripes, a design device popularised by the Moors.

The original bronze entrance, **Portale di San Ranieri**, was cast around 1180 and is by Bonanno, one of the designers of the Leaning Tower itself. A fire destroyed much of the interior in the 16th century, but some of Cosmati's lovely floor survived, as did the 14th-century mosaic of *Christ Pantocrator* by Cimabue, in the apse, and a magnificent sculpted pulpit by Giovanni Pisano (1300).

Construction of the circular **Baptistry** stopped when money ran out. The three lower storeys consist of Romanesque arcades. The top half, in Gothic style, with pinnacles and a dome, was added later (again by the prolific Pisanos, in the 1260s). It has a pulpit superbly carved by Nicola Pisano, whose design produced a whole series of similar pulpits during this period.

The **Leaning Tower** (Torre Pendente) began life in 1173, as a campanile for the Duomo. When it was 10 m high it began to tilt and the architect fled. Construction continued, however, with successive architects trying unsuccessfully to restore the balance.

Note

On journeys from Siena to Orvieto a change of train at Chiusi is necessary.

KEY JOURNEYS

Pisa–Florence
(via Empoli)   ERT 613

Type	Frequency	Typical journey time
Train	1–2 per hr	1h05

Pisa–Florence
(via Lucca; change at Lucca) ERT 614

Type	Frequency	Typical journey time
Train	13–15 daily	2h10

Florence–Rome
(by Alta Velocità)   ERT 600

Type	Frequency	Typical journey time
Train	1–2 per hr	1h30

ROUTE DETAILS

Pisa–Lucca   ERT 614

Type	Frequency	Typical journey time
Train	13–15 daily	25 mins

Lucca–Florence   ERT 614

Type	Frequency	Typical journey time
Train	Every hr	1h20

Florence–Siena   ERT 613

Type	Frequency	Typical journey time
Train	9–14 daily	1h30

Siena–Orvieto   ERT 611, 620

Type	Frequency	Typical journey time
Train	7 daily	2 hrs

≋ **Centrale**, south of the River Arno and a 20-min walk from the Leaning Tower, or CPT 🚌 1/3. ➜ Pisa's **Galileo Galilei Airport** is the main regional hub for international flights, ☎ 050 849 111 (www.pisa-airport.com), served by buses and trains from the city centre. Details of the train service are shown at the foot of ERT 613.

🅱 **Tourist offices**: Piazza Vittorio Emanuele II 16, ☎ 050 422 91 (www.pisaunicaterra.it); Piazza Arcivescovado 8, and at the airport, ☎ 050 502 518. A special one-week ticket covers entry to the major museums and monuments in Pisa. **Internet**: Koinè, Via dei Mille 3/5.

🛏 Budget hotels: try **Pensione Rinascente,** Via del Castelletto 28, ☎ 050 580 460 (www.rinascentehotel.com), €, near Borgo Stretto, or **Hotel Roseto**, Via Pietro Mascagni 24, ☎ 050 42596 (www.hotelroseto.it), €€, just a few steps from the station. **Hostel** (non HI): **Centro Turistico Madonna dell'Acqua**, Via Pietrasantina 15, ☎ 050 890 622, 🚌 3. **Campsite: Campeggio Torre Pendente**, Viale Cascine 86, ☎ 050 561 704 (www.campingtorrependente.it), 1 km west of the Leaning Tower, signposted from Pza Manin (open summer only).

LUCCA

Despite its considerable beauty, **Lucca** never feels overrun, and has a leisurely, provincial feel. Bicycles are much used by the locals. The city comes alive in summer, when major rock concerts take place in key squares. Outside summer, Lucca is tranquil, with streets that are dotted with palaces, towers and handsome early churches, most of them dating from the city's heyday (11th–14th centuries). Start with a stroll around part of the 4 km of the 16th–17th-century walls — the most complete in Italy — that enclose the Old City and are themselves encircled by a green belt, a buffer between the medieval and modern towns. Some bastions have been restored and you can get a good idea of the town's original layout. The **Pza Anfiteatro** is an oval of medieval tenements clustered around the site of a **Roman amphitheatre**. Parts of the original arches and columns are visible in the buildings themselves, and the shape of the oval is effectively a fossilisation of the theatre.

The Romanesque **Duomo di San Martino**, in the south of the centre, has individually designed columns and loggias: look out for an exquisite early 15th-century **Tomb of Ilaria del Carretto** (by Jacopo della Quercia) and Tintoretto's *Last Supper*. Further north-west, **Casa Puccini** was the boyhood home of the opera composer Puccini, and is open to the public. The central **Church of San Michele in Foro**, on the site of the ancient Roman forum, has a dazzling Pisan Romanesque facade, studded with mosaics, and surmounted by a huge bronze of Archangel Michael. Near the western city wall is the **Pinacoteca Nazionale**, housed in **Palazzo Mansi**, Via Galli Tassi 43. The 17th-century palace is of rather more interest than the pictures it displays, and the overdecorated interior includes a particularly spectacular gilded bridal suite.

Further east from Palazzo Mansi is **Palazzo Guinigi**, Via Guinigi, a rambling complex of interconnected medieval buildings. A climb of 230 steps leads up a turreted tower with an oak sprouting from the top, giving a fascinating view over the city's rooftops. The main museum, **Museo Nazionale Guinigi**, east of the centre on Via della Quarquonia, contains a huge and varied collection of local Romanesque and Renaissance art.

ARRIVAL, INFORMATION, ACCOMMODATION

➤ Just outside the city walls, an easy walk to the centre. There are frequent trains from **Pisa** (20 mins), **Viareggio** (20 mins) and **Florence** (1 hr 20 mins). **🚺 Tourist office**: Piazza S. Maria 35, ☎ 0583 919 91 (www.luccatourist.it). It also has an internet point.
🛏 Finding space is often a problem, so book ahead. The local tourist office (APT) can help you find last-minute accommodation. **Hotels: Hotel Moderno**, Via Vincenzo Civitali 38, ☎ 0583 55840 (www.albergomoderno.com),€; and **Hotel Diana**, Vicolo della Dogana 18/20, ☎ 0583 492 202 (www.albergodiana.com), €. **Youth hostel** (HI): **San Frediano**, Via della Cavallerizza 12, ☎ 0583 469 957 (www.ostellolucca.it). **B&B Ai Cipressi**, Via di Tiglio 126, ☎ 0583 496 571 (www.aicipressi.it). There are several B&Bs so check the Lucca tourist office website.

FLORENCE — SEE P479

FLORENCE — SEE P479

SIENA

Spread over low hills and filled with robust terracotta-coloured buildings, **Siena** has changed little since medieval times. Indeed, this most beautiful of Tuscan cities has contracted inside its walls in places — look out from just behind the **Campo**, the main square, and there's a vista down a green, rural valley, as pretty as a wine label. The city was Florence's tireless enemy for much of the Middle Ages, competing with it for supremacy politically, economically and artistically. Now it's a delightful place to visit, for its artistic treasures as well as just for the pleasures of discovering its myriad sloping alleys. The fan-shaped Campo dates from 1347 and is regarded as the focus of the city's life. The arcaded and turreted **Palazzo Pubblico**, on the south side, still performs its traditional role as the town hall, and its bell tower, the 102-m **Torre del Mangia**, soars above the town, with dizzying views. Part of the Palazzo Pubblico houses the **Museo Civico**, whose Sala della Pace and Sala del Mappamondo contain treasures of Lorenzetti and Martini among others. To the west stands the **Duomo**, the cathedral, with its striped marble facade studded with Renaissance sculpture. Inside, the floor comprises 56 separate sections, on which over 40 artists worked for nearly two centuries; other highlights are the elaborate pulpit by Nicola Pisano and a Donatello bronze. The **Museo dell'Opera del Duomo** contains masterpieces of painting and sculpture.

SAN GIMIGNANO

San Gimignano, located 32 km to the north-west, with half-hourly buses from **Siena** via Poggibonsi, is a perfect medieval hill town, although overrun with tourists. As a medieval Manhattan in miniature, it originally sported 70 towers. The towers, of which 14 survive, were partly defensive and partly status symbols.

Pza del Duomo has some of the finest medieval buildings, while the **frescos** by Gozzoli in the Church of Sant'Agostino and the four fresco cycles in the Collegiata (cathedral) also stand out. 🚹 The **tourist office** is on the main square while an internet café (Internet Train) is on Pza delle Erbe.

Terzo di Città (south-west of the Campo) has some of the city's finest private palaces, such as the **Palazzo Chigi-Saracini**, Via di Città 89. In the past, the city was divided into 60 *contrade* (wards named after animals), of which 17 remain, each with its own church, museum and central square with a fountain featuring the relevant animal.

Rivalry between wards is strong, reaching a head in the famous twice-yearly **Palio**, a no-holds-barred horse race around the Campo (which is regarded as neutral territory) on 2 July and 16 Aug. Only ten horses can participate, so lots are drawn to decide which wards will be represented; the whole event is regarded as a matter of honour by the locals, with rehearsals for days beforehand and excitement mounting to fever pitch. Races last only 90 seconds or so, but are preceded by a two-hour procession and a lifetime of passion. Get there early if you want to watch — standing in the centre is free, if crowded.

ARRIVAL, INFORMATION, ACCOMMODATION

🚆 2 km north-east (in a valley below the town). It is a tedious 45-min walk uphill to the centre, but there are regular shuttle buses (tickets from the machine by the entrance). 🚌 Long-distance buses (covering all Tuscany), run by Sena, Lazzi and Train, leave from **Pza Gramsci bus station**. 🚹 **Tourist office**: Pza del Campo 56, ☎ 0577 280 551 (www.terresiena.it). There are also booths in the train and bus stations. **Internet**: there are various points in Via di Pantaneto, like Net Runner, ☎ 0577 449 46.

🛏 Private rooms are best value, but you often have to stay at least a week and they can be full of students in term time. **Hotels**: budget hotels are often full. For the Palio (early July and mid-Aug), either book well ahead or stay up all night (many do). At other times, if the tourist office can't help, try the **Cooperativa Siena Hotels** promotion booth Piazza Madre Teresa di Calcutta 5, ☎ 0577 288 084 (www. hotelsiena.com). One of the cheapest hotels is **Tre Donzelle**, Via delle Donzelle 5, ☎ 0577 280 358 (www.tredonzelle.com), €. **Youth hostel** (HI): **Ostello Guidoriccio**, Via Fiorentina 89, ☎ 0577 522 12 (www.ostellosiena.com), 2 km north-west of the centre (🚌 7/10/15). **Campsite**: **Campeggio Colleverde**, Strada di Scacciapensieri 47, ☎ 0577 332 545 (www.sienacamping.com), 2 km north (🚌 3/8, both from Piazzade/ Sale). For rural accommodation in the superb surrounds of Siena check out www.agriturismo.it.

ORVIETO

Orvieto, like Lucca, is less beset by the tourist hordes. Set in a valley of vineyards, this striking cliffside town is perched above a raised tufa-stone plateau. Dominating the town is the vividly striped **Duomo**, Pza Duomo, built in honour of a 13th-century miracle. With its triple-gabled exterior of gilded mosaics, bronze doors and bas-reliefs by Lorenzo Maitani, as well as its outstanding interior frescos by Luca Signorelli depicting the *Last Judgement* (in the **Cappella di San Brizio** in the right transept), it is one of the great churches of Umbria. Several grand buildings near the Duomo now contain museums.

The **Pozzo di San Patrizio**, Viale San Gallo, near the funicular terminal, is an astonishing cylindrical well with a diameter of 13 m and a depth of 62 m. A double-helix mule ramp runs around the interior. The well was completed in 1537 to provide an emergency water supply for the city.

ARRIVAL, INFORMATION, ACCOMMODATION

≋ By the bus station and connected by funicular 'Bracci' to Pza Cahen in the Old Town (takes 2 mins; every 10 mins weekdays 0720–2030, Sun and public holidays 0800–2030), from where you can walk or take any of the frequent buses (🚌 Line A or B) to the centre. 🛈 **Tourist office:** Pza Duomo 20, ☎ 0763 341 772 (www. orvietoonline.com). Local bus tickets and the combined travel and sightseeing ticket, **Carta Orvieto Unica**, can be purchased here (see further down). Pick up the current version of *Welcome to Orvieto* for useful listings. **Internet:** Caffè Montanucci in Corso Cavour 21, near the Cathedral. The **Carta Orvieto Unica** (www.cartaunica.it), allows access to nine major sites in the town, including the Cathedral, the Pozzo di San Patrizio and the Cappella di San Brizio. The card also allows free use of the local electric minibus service (🚌 Lines A and B).

🛏 If you want to experience the atmosphere of Orvieto at night, the best-located central hotels (both inexpensive) are **Virgilio**, Piazza del Duomo 6, ☎ 0763 394 937 (www.orvietohotelvirgilio.com), €€, or **Duomo**, Via Maurizio 7, ☎ 0763 341 887 (www.orvietohotelduomo.com), €€. The **Maitani**, Via Maitani 5, ☎ 0763 342 011 (www.hotelmaitani.com), €€€, is worth splashing out on.

✗ Orvieto is famous for its **wines**. Best known are the crisp fruity whites made from Trebbiano grapes. *Orvieto Classico* wines are fermented and stored in the underground passages and caves that honeycomb the soft local tufa, and are often sold under the Cardeto label (the largest Umbrian wine cooperative). Taste before you buy in local bars and *enoteche* (wine bars) such as the atmospheric **La Bottega del Buon Vino**, Via della Cava 24–26, which is also a restaurant. Orvieto is full of good places to eat, though prices are high. There are picnic facilities in the **Parco delle Grotte** near the Pza Duomo. The public gardens of the **Rocca**, near the funicular terminal, can be enjoyed free, and have fine views over the **Paglia Valley.**

CONNECTIONS FROM ORVIETO

Carry on to Rome (p555); this route goes via **Orte**, where you can change for trains to **Spoleto** (see ERT 615 and 625).

Rail Route 35:
From Lombardy to Friulia and Istria

CITIES: ★★★ CULTURE: ★★★ HISTORY: ★★★ SCENERY: ★
COUNTRIES COVERED: ITALY, SLOVENIA

This route takes in six glorious north Italian cities from **Milan** in the west to Trieste in the east — a veritable feast of art and architecture. The scenery along much of the route is unspectacular, but it picks up on the run into Trieste where the railway skirts the northern edge of the Adriatic. With such illustrious cities as **Verona**, **Vicenza**, **Padua** and **Venice** along the way, this route is, at one level, quintessential Italy.

But at its eastern extremity Route 35 packs a few surprises for **Trieste** is in many respects the most un-Italian of cities. In Trieste there are hints of the **Habsburg world**, and then we hop over the border into Slovenia, where in Piran Italianate flair rubs shoulders with the Slavic world. If you really are a city lover, then Route 35 is for you.

MILAN

Italy's second largest city is the country's economic powerhouse as well as its commercial, banking, fashion and design centre. Milan is less aesthetically appealing than Florence or Rome. But Italy's most cosmopolitan city boasts Romanesque churches, grand galleries, a superb museum of Northern Italian art (the Brera) and one of the boldest cathedrals in Christendom.

Milan's signature building is the **Duomo**, on Pza Duomo. This extravagant Gothic cathedral, overflowing with belfries, statues and pinnacles, has stairs leading to rooftop views. Leading off the square is the **Galleria Vittorio Emanuele II**, an iconic 19th-century iron and glass shopping arcade lined with chic cafés and boutiques. Beyond lies **Pza Scala**, home of La Scala, the world's most celebrated opera house (www.teatroallascala.org).

The **Pinacoteca di Brera**, Via Brera 28 (metro: Lanza), is Milan's finest art gallery, featuring Italian artists of the 14th–19th centuries, including masterpieces by Mantegna, Raphael and Caravaggio. In addition, the **Pinacoteca Ambrosiana**, Pza Pio XI 2 (metro: Duomo or Cordusio), presents works by Caravaggio, Raphael and Leonardo da Vinci.

Milan's most celebrated work of art is Leonardo's *Last Supper* (1495–1497), occupying a wall of a Dominican monastery refectory next to **Santa Maria Delle Grazie**. The 'Da Vinci Code' phenomenon ensures that the crowds continue to flock here, trying to unravel the 'mystery' through Leonardo links. Tickets must be booked ahead: ☎ 02 9280 0360 (www.cenacolovinciano.net).

Before leaving Milan, escape the urban chaos by visiting two peaceful spots. Milan's most beloved church is not the Cathedral but the largely Romanesque

Notes

Several additional bus connections are available from Trieste to Piran (except on Sundays) with an easy change of bus at Koper. In the summer months (usually from late June to mid-September), Trieste Lines (www.triestelines.it) offer the chance of travelling by sea from Trieste to Piran and back. The journey time is just 30 mins, but do note that services are limited and may not run at all on Mondays and Tuesdays. Schedules for 2012 were not yet available as this book went to press. In 2011 the fare from Trieste to Piran was €7.05 single.

KEY JOURNEYS

Milan–Venice · ERT 605

Type	Frequency	Typical journey time
Train	1–2 per hr	2h35

Venice–Zagreb · ERT 89

Type	Frequency	Typical journey time
Train	1 night train	7 hrs

ROUTE DETAILS

Milano (Centrale)–Verona · ERT 605

Type	Frequency	Typical journey time
Train	1–2 per hr	1h22

Verona–Vicenza · ERT 605

Type	Frequency	Typical journey time
Train	1–2 per hr	25 mins

Vicenza–Padua · ERT 605

Type	Frequency	Typical journey time
Train	1–2 per hr	16 mins

Padua–Venice (Sta Lucia) · ERT 605

Type	Frequency	Typical journey time
Train	1–2 per hr	30 mins

Venice (Sta Lucia)–Trieste · ERT 601

Type	Frequency	Typical journey time
Train	Every hr	2h05

Trieste–Piran

Type	Frequency	Typical journey time
Bus	1 daily (not Sun)	1h30

TRIP TO TURIN (TORINO)

West of Milan (ERT 585) lies one of Italy's most elegant — and overlooked — cities, the capital of the Dukes of Savoy, who made it a showplace of broad avenues, baroque architecture and spacious squares. Always a well-kept and prosperous city, Turin has been undergoing a renaissance since its successful makeover for the 2006 Olympic Winter Games. The celebrations of the 150th anniversary of the **Unity of Italy** took place in the city in 2011 (Turin was the first capital city before Rome).

Turin is far more patrician than Milan, but its arcaded streets invite strolling, while its belle époque cafés invite lingering, ideally over a hot chocolate or a Martini, two drinks the city has perfected. As for sights, the city itself is the main attraction, with its elegant arcades, grand squares and cosy cafés.

The **Sacra Sindone**, the Holy Shroud (www.sindone.org) is displayed only rarely (check the website) in the cathedral. The most memorable sights are the magnificently revamped **Egyptian Museum**, second only to the one in Cairo, and the **Cinema Museum**, one of Italy's most enthralling experiences. The latter is set in the **Mole Antonelliana**, the symbol of the city, and Turin's most bizarre building, which started out as a synagogue, before becoming the cinema museum and acquiring a surreal glass elevator, which speeds visitors to the top for views stretching towards the Alps.

🛏 **Casa della Mobilità Giovanile**, Corso Venezia 11, ☎ 011 250 535 (www.openzero11.it), and **Ostello Torino**, Via Alby 1, ☎ 011 660 2939 (www.ostellotorino.it). Budget Hotel: **Albergo Alba**, Via Maria Vittoria 34, ☎ 011 812 0208 (www.albergoalba.it).

Sant'Ambrogio, a basilica begun in the late 4th century by St Ambrose, Milan's patron saint and former bishop. So smooth in speech was St Ambrose that honey liqueur was named after him.

The other urban retreat is the castle and grounds of **Castello Sforzesco**, on Pza Castello, a fortress housing eclectic galleries and museums, displaying everything from arms and musical instruments to Egyptian art and works by Michelangelo. (Note that museums — including the Brera — are closed on Mon.)

ARRIVAL, INFORMATION, ACCOMMODATION

🚄 Most long-distance trains arrive at **Stazione Centrale**, Piazza Duca d'Aosta, although a limited number of services use **Porta Garibaldi**. Both stations are north of the city centre. ✈ There are three airports (www.sea-aeroportimilano.it) serving Milan: **Malpensa**, about 50 km north-west, **Linate**, 7 km from the city, and **Bergamo** (www.orioaeroporto.it), 45 km north-east. Intercontinental flights land at Malpensa; the other airports share international, charter and domestic air travel. Fast trains link Malpensa Terminal 1 with both Stazione Nord (Cadorna) and Milano Centrale (both services run every 30 mins, taking 40 to 45 mins, ERT 583). Travellers flying Alitalia travel free. Malpensa Shuttle, ☎ 0331 258 411 (www.malpensashuttle.it) operates a service to Malpensa airport from Stazione Centrale. Buses leave for Malpensa every 20 mins. The shuttle also runs between Malpensa and Linate every 30 mins. Starfly,

☎ 02 5858 7237 (www.starfly.net), at Linate airport, operate a service to and from Stazione Centrale every 30 mins. Regular shuttle buses connect Bergamo airport with both **Bergamo** (journey time 15 mins) and **Milan** (journey time 1 hr) **central railway stations**. 🛈 Main **IAT Milano Tourist Office:** Pza Duomo 19/A, ☎ 02 7740 4343 (www. ciaomilano.it). Branch: Stazione Centrale. **Internet access:** Some *Mondadori* book-shops have internet points; there is one in Piazza del Duomo (open daily).

🛏 Lodging in Milan is expensive, but there are places to stay around Stazione Centrale, even if the area is rather seedy, despite the revamped station itself. **Hotel Virgilio**, Via P L da Palestrina 30, ☎ 02 669 1337 (www.virgiliohotel.it), €€, and **Hotel Rallye**, Via Benedetto Marcello 59, ☎ 02 2940 4568 (www.hotelrallye.net), €€, are both family-run hotels near Centrale. To splash out, choose the lovely inn known as the **Antica Locanda Solferino,** Via Castelfidardo 2, ☎ 02 657 0129 (www. anticalocandasolferino.it), €€€. **Hostel:** Brand new and run by experienced travellers, the **Ostello Bello**, Via Medici 4, ☎ 02 3658 2720 (www. ostellobello.com), has dorms and private rooms a short walk from the Duomo.

VERONA

Placed on an S-bend of the **River Adige** and best explored on foot, this beautiful city of pastel-pink marble thrives on the story of *Romeo and Juliet* (see below), but the real attractions are its elegant medieval squares, fine Gothic churches and massive Roman amphitheatre, the **Arena**, which comes alive during the annual opera festival in July and August (ticket office ☎ 045 800 5151, www.arena.it; the cheapest seats are unreserved, so arrive early). Dominating the large Pza Bra, it has 44 pink marble tiers that can accommodate 20,000 people — incredibly, the singers and orchestra are perfectly audible. By day, explore the Arena to savour the feeling the gladiators must have had while waiting for combat.

Via Mazzini, which leads off Pza Bra, is one of Italy's smartest shopping streets. This leads to Pza delle Erbe, which is surrounded by faded Renaissance palaces. Originally the Roman forum, the square is now a daily market. An arch-way leads to a serener square, Pza dei Signori, the centre of medieval civic life, and framed by the 15th-century **Loggia del Consiglio** and the crenellated **Palazzo del Capitano**.

Via Cappello was the supposed home of Juliet Capulet (of *Romeo and Juliet* fame), though the famous balcony immortalised in the play was only added in 1935. Her statue, an even more modern addition, stands in the courtyard near the balcony. Although now a romantic shrine, this spot owes less to history than to legend (and Verona's astute sense of marketing). The **Castelvecchio Museum** be-side the river deserves a look for its weapons and jewellery. Beyond it, **San Zeno Maggiore**, the most elaborate Romanesque church in northern Italy, boasts a Madonna altarpiece by Mantegna and magnificent 11th to 12th-century bronze doors. On **Piazza Duomo**, Verona's striped red and white marble Cathedral blends Romanesque and Gothic, forming a lovely backdrop to Titian's *Assumption*.

Apart from the amphitheatre, the city has numerous other Roman remains, including **Porta Leona** and the carved **Porta Borsari**, each a short walk from **Piazza delle Erbe**. Go across the river, over the partly Roman **Ponte Pietra**, Verona's best-known bridge.

On the opposite bank are the remains of the **Roman theatre** (where plays were performed, as opposed to the amphitheatre, which held coarser public entertainments); although smaller than the amphitheatre, there's rather more to see, as entrance includes admission to the **Archaeological Museum**, housed in an old convent with great views of the city

ARRIVAL, INFORMATION, ACCOMMODATION

🚄 **Stazione Porta Nuova**, a 15- to 20-min walk south of the centre (🚌 11/12/13/14 from stop A). Bike hire available. ✈ There are two airports: the main one is **Valerio Catullo**, www.aeroportoverona.it (buses every 20 mins); Ryanair flights go to the more remote **Brescia** airport (buses connect with flights). 🄳 **Tourist offices:** Via Degli Alpini 9; ☎ 045 806 8680 (www.tourism.verona.it). Also at the station. The **Verona Card** (€15/20) is a 2- or 5-day combined sightseeing/travel card valid for public transport and entry to the major sights. **Internet:** *Veron@Web*, Via Roma 17.

🛏 One of the central, best-value budget options is **Locanda Catullo**, Via Valerio Catullo 1, ☎ 045 800 2786, €–€€, graciously old-fashioned but friendly. Also central is the 2-star **Sanmicheli**, Via Valverde 2, ☎ 045 800 3749 (www.sanmicheli.com), €€, close to the station or try the **La Tana B&B**, Vicolo Volto Cittadella 8, ☎ 045 894 0016 (www.latana.info), €€. **Hostel**: **Villa Francescatti** (HI), Salita Fontana del Ferro 15, ☎ 045 590 360 (www.ostelloverona.it), 3 km from the station, take 🚌 73 (🚌 90 on Sun) to Pza Isolo. ✗ For reasonably priced restaurants, look along Corso Porta Borsari, in the streets around Pza delle Erbe or the Veronetta district on the east bank of the Adige. The Pza delle Erbe's **food market** is also useful.

CONNECTIONS FROM VERONA

Venture north into the Dolomites from Bolzano, or head via Innsbruck to Munich (**Route 28**, p252). Services (1 hr 45 mins, ERT 595) to Bologna link with **Route 36** (p304) via Florence, where you can join **Route 34** (p290).

VICENZA

This prosperous city was largely rebuilt in the 16th century to designs by Andrea di Pietro della Gondola, better known as Palladio, who moved here from Padua at the age of 16 to become an apprentice stonemason. He gave his name to the Palladian style of architecture, which applied elegant Romanesque concepts to classical forms. His first public commission was the imposing **Basilica**, on Pza dei Signori, hub of the city. This medieval palace was in danger of collapsing until he shored it up brilliantly with Ionic and Doric columns.

Corso Palladio, the long, straight, main street, is lined with palaces. The **Teatro Olimpico** at the eastern end was Palladio's last work. Based on the design of ancient Roman theatres and opened in 1585, it is the oldest indoor theatre in Europe and still in use from May to early July, and from Sept to early Oct. The acoustics are superb.

Palladio's most famous villa, **La Rotonda,** is on a hillside about 1.5 km southeast of the centre (🚌 8/13). It has a round interior under a dome set in a cube of classical porticoes, a design often copied. Nearby is the **Villa Valmarana**, an 18th-century country house notable for its Tiepolo frescos and dwarfs on the garden wall.

ARRIVAL, INFORMATION, ACCOMMODATION

⇝ A 10-min walk south of the centre (🚌 1/7). **🅑 Tourist office:** Pza Matteotti 12, ☎ 0444 320 854 (www.vicenzae.org); branch at Pza dei Signori 8.

🛏 The cheapest **hotels** are away from the centre or in noisy locations, so it's worth considering 2-star places like **Hotel Vicenza**, Strada dei Nodari 5–7, ☎ 0444 321 512. Book ahead for summer and autumn. **Youth hostel** (HI): Via Giuriolo 9, ☎ 0444 540 222 (www.ostellovicenza.com), 🚌 1/2/4/5/7 (stop nearby).

Campsite: **Campeggio Vicenza**, Strada Pelosa 241, ☎ 0444 582 311 (20 mins by 🚌 1 to Torri di Quartesolo from the station). ✗ For eating out, look around Pza dei Signori.

PADUA (PADOVA)

The dignified Old Town has attractive arcaded streets and traffic-free squares. **Prato della Valle**, Italy's largest square, hosts a Saturday market. In the **University**, founded in 1222, you can see the wooden desk used by Galileo, who taught physics there, and visit the old anatomical theatre. Giotto's glorious depiction of the lives of Mary and Jesus in the **Cappella degli Scrovegni** (Scrovegni Chapel) in Corso Garibaldi alone justifies a visit to Padua (booking via www.cappelladegliscrovegni.it).

ARRIVAL, INFORMATION, ACCOMMODATION

⇝ At the northern edge of town, a 15-min walk to the centre or 🚌 3/12/18. **🅑 Tourist office:** IAT point: Stazione Ferroviaria (in the station), ☎ 049 875 2077 (www.turismopadova.it). Branches in Galleria Pedrocchi and Piazza del Santo. **Padova Card**, valid 48/72 hrs for €16/€21, allows admission to 12 city sites and free local transport (www.padovacard.it).

🛏 There is a wide choice of places to stay (try around Pza del Santo), though booking is advisable. A good option in the Old Town is the **Hotel Donatello**, Via del Santo, ☎ 049 875 0634 (www.hoteldonatello.net), €€. **Youth hostel: Città di Padova**, Via A. Aleardi 30, ☎ 049 875 2219 (www.ostellopadova.it); 🚌 3/8/12/18.

VENICE — SEE P575

TRIESTE

Arriving by train in Trieste from Venice is something special. Sit on the right and you'll see Miramare Castle (more on which below). Italy's atmospheric easternmost city looks more Austrian than Italian, a reminder of its former role as the entrepôt of the Austro-Hungarian Empire (up to 1918). Rebuilt in the 19th century in a grand gridiron plan, it relishes its role as a crossroads between east and west. Trieste is stately rather than intimate, with six-storey palazzi and art nouveau and classical facades. It's set on a beautifully curving bay, with the rugged limestone heights of the arid Carso an impressive backdrop to the city.

Trieste is a major coffee port, and café life is part of its lifeblood. Perhaps the most evocative place is **Caffè San Marco**, Via Cesare Battisti 18, with its high-ceilinged art nouveau interior. One of Trieste's oldest cafés, the **Caffè degli Specchi** (1839), occupies the majestic central square, Pza dell'Unita d'Italia, presided over by the vast Palazzo del Comune del Governo, aglow with its mosaic ornamentation. City sights include more than a dozen museums, including the **Museo di Storia ed Arte** (with a wide range of art and archaeology relating to Trieste), and the **Civico Museo Sartorio**, an opulent former family residence filled with objets d'art. A pleasant area for strolling is the **Capitoline Hill**, the heart of Roman and medieval Trieste. On top, beside the remains of the Roman forum, stands the 11th-century **Cathedral of San Giusto**, founded in the 5th century on the site of a Roman temple and containing early medieval mosaics and frescos.

Narrow alleys drop down to V. Teatro Romano, named after the restored ruins of a **Roman theatre**. One of the best aspects of Trieste is its scope for **excursions**. Cycling around town is feasible (bicycle hire at the station and on the quay at Stazione Maritima). For a taster of the Carso, take the wonderfully old-fashioned **Villa Opicina tram** from Pza Oberdan (ultra cheap; tickets sold at the booth). For a walk with intermittent views of the city far below, get off at the tall obelisk at the top, and walk along the track by the map board.

ARRIVAL, INFORMATION, ACCOMMODATION

⚞ **Stazione Centrale**, Pza della Libertà 8. Adjacent to the bus station. ➤ **Trieste Airport** (www.aeroporto.fvg.it), 33 km west, 30 mins by air bus (pay on board) or

MIRAMARE CASTLE

A short bus ride west from Trieste (🚌 36 towards Grignano) leads to Castle Miramare, a white marble pile in a stunning coastal location. Built 1856–60 for Maximilian of Habsburg as a love nest for him and Charlotte of Belgium, it reveals astonishingly ornate marquetry interiors.

There's free entry to the surrounding park, which slopes down from the main road (get off the bus after going through two tunnels; retrace through one tunnel to reach the park gates). It is laced with trails and has many rare Mediterranean broadleaf trees, as well as a pond and a grotto.

AQUILEIA

A recommended side trip from Trieste is westwards to Aquileia (train to Cervignano, then change for a bus, direction Grado; also direct buses, direction Grado, from Trieste Airport/Ronchi dei Legionari). Sited on a fertile wine-growing coastal plain, Aquileia has striking remains of a **Roman town**, notably in the form of a huge mosaic floor in the basilica (the largest early Christian monument in western Europe, surpassing anything even in Rome), a burial ground, remains of a port and houses, and a very extensive museum of finds that include some remarkably life-like sculpted heads. 🛏 The friendly HI **youth hostel** is in the centre of town at Via Roma 25, ☎ 0431 91024 (www.ostelloaquileia.it); it may be closed Nov–Mar, so check beforehand; internet, bike hire.

cheaper 🚍 51 (buy a ticket in the bar upstairs in the airport) to Trieste bus station. Also buses to Monfalcone rail station for trains to Venice. 🅱 **Tourist office:** Pza Unità d'Italia 4b, ☎ 040 347 8312 (www.turismofvg.it). **Internet**: Bar Unità, near Piazza dell'Unità d'Italia.

🛏 A quiet, comfortable mid-priced **hotel** in a side street near the station is **Hotel Italia**, Via della Geppa 15, ☎ 040 369 900 (www.hotel-italia.it); €€. There are cheaper 1-star options such as the **Nuovo Albergo Centro**, Via Roma 13, ☎ 040 347 8790 (www.hotelcentrotrieste.it), €, a centrally located family-run ex-pension. There are also **B&Bs** (full list from the tourist office) from around €30, such as **B&B Aachen**, Via Cesare Battisti 24, ☎ 0338 228 7085. The HI **youth hostel** is 5 km out of town on the coast near Miramare Castle and has dorms only; **Tergeste**, Viale Miramare 331, ☎ 040 224 102 (www.aighostels.com), 🚍 36 (from the rail station, turn left, cross the road, then left again 50 m to the bus stop).

CONNECTIONS FROM TRIESTE
For a short local excursion take the regular ferry over to Muggia (30 mins), a fine little port on the Slovene border. Or head into Slovenia following **Route 38** (p323) to Ljubljana and on to the beautiful Dalmatian coastal cities of Split and Dubrovnik.

PIRAN

Route 35 ends with a short hop over the border by local bus to Piran in Slovenia, a slip of a place that we rate as one of the loveliest communities around the Adriatic. The marvellously well-preserved old port once belonged to **Venice**. It's a huddle of tiny lanes and stepped alleys full of washing lines and prowling cats.

ARRIVAL, INFORMATION, ACCOMMODATION
⛴ Piran reached by ferry from Trieste in summer, also served by 🚍 from Trieste, roughly every 2 hrs (Monday-Saturday only), plus buses every 20 mins if you change in Koper. 🅱 **Tourist office:** Tartinijev trg 2, ☎ 05 673 4440 (www.portoroz.si).

🛏 The centrally located HI **youth hostel** makes a great place to stay: **Hostel Val & Garni Hotel**, 38 Gregorčičeva Ulica, ☎ 05 673 2555 (www.hostel-val.com).

Rail Route 36: South to Umbria and Lazio

CITIES: ★★★ CULTURE: ★★★ HISTORY: ★★ SCENERY: ★★
COUNTRIES COVERED: ITALY

From the graceful old university city of **Bologna**, Route 36 ventures south through **Tuscany** into verdant **Umbria**, with its mystical atmosphere and medieval hilltop towns. It was the landscape of northern Umbria that Dante evoked in his accounts of the Garden of Eden. Art and history gently intermingle in the great pilgrimage city of **Assisi**, the Umbrian capital of **Perugia**, and in **Spoleto**, which we value as the most instantly appealing city on this route, a place where one might easily linger for a few days of rest. This is not a route to be rushed. **Florence** and **Rome** both demand several days each. Although fast train options are the best bet on the northern part of the route from Bologna to Florence, thereafter you can complete the entire route on local or regional services that need no advance booking and carry no supplements for rail pass holders.

BOLOGNA

Bologna is the capital of **Emilia-Romagna**. The city's long-standing role as a major transport hub has been enhanced by Italy's new Alta Velocità spinal rail route that links the cities of the north with Rome and Naples. The Milan to Bologna section opened in December 2008 and the section south from Bologna to Florence opened one year later. Schedules for these high-speed services are in ERT 600.

The city mastered the art of living in medieval times, when a pink-bricked settlement clustered around **Europe's oldest university**, founded in 1088. In terms of tourism, the only reason that Bologna has languished is because Florence is a looming presence over the hills. The streetscape has real dignity in its arcades, red- and ochre-coloured buildings, stucco facades, greatly varied porticos, church spires, palaces and medieval towers, the latter built as status symbols by the city's wealthy nobles. The university's first permanent home is today in **Palazzo Poggi**, Via Zamboni.

The two adjoining 13th-century squares, Pza Maggiore and Pza Nettuno, make the obvious central starting point. Around them lie the **Palazzo Comunale** (the town hall, which now houses Bologna's modern art collection), the 15th-century **Palazzo del Podestà**, the **Palazzo dei Banchi** and the **Basilica di San Petronio**. The Fountain of Neptune (1567) spouts in the north-west corner. The Pza Santo Stefano, also known as the Piazza delle Sette Chiese, is a complex of many churches, complete with cloisters and courtyards, that has retained its ancient atmosphere.

The two most distinctive towers still standing are the 98-m **Asinelli** (with a dizzying panorama from the top) and its tilting partner, the **Garisenda**, by Pza di

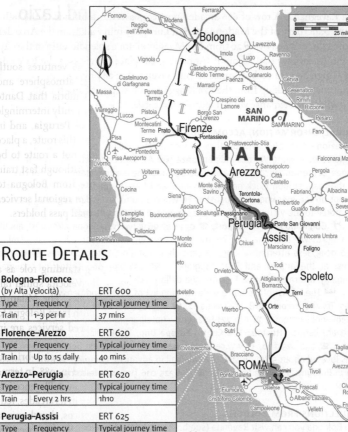

Route Details

Bologna–Florence

(by Alta Velocità)		ERT 600
Type	Frequency	Typical journey time
Train	1–3 per hr	37 mins

Florence–Arezzo

		ERT 620
Type	Frequency	Typical journey time
Train	Up to 15 daily	40 mins

Arezzo–Perugia

		ERT 620
Type	Frequency	Typical journey time
Train	Every 2 hrs	1h10

Perugia–Assisi

		ERT 625
Type	Frequency	Typical journey time
Train	8 daily	20 mins

Assisi–Spoleto

		ERT 625
Type	Frequency	Typical journey time
Train	8 daily	45 mins

Spoleto–Rome

		ERT 625
Type	Frequency	Typical journey time
Train	13 daily	1h45

Key Journey

Florence–Rome

(by Alta Velocità)		ERT 600
Type	Frequency	Typical journey time
Train	1–3 per hr	1h35

Notes

In the route details (left) we show the fast trains that use the new line from Bologna to Florence. Purists who really want to stick to Route 36 should take the IC service which follows the old line via Prato. Departures are every 2 hrs and the journey takes 1 hr from Bologna Centrale to Firenze Rifredi. You can also travel by local trains from Bologna to Florence, again following the old route via Prato. If you use local trains, you'll need to change at Prato. Allow 2 hrs for the entire journey. The local trains from Prato will bring you into Florence SMN station, which is better placed for the city centre.

Porta Ravegnana. A row of 666 arcaded porticoes ascends a hillside to the 18th-century **Sanctuary of the Madonna di San Luca**, a 35-min walk from the **Arco del Meloncello** (reached by 🚌 20 from Pza Maggiore), for a splendid vista of the city and the Apennines that adjoin it. Another great place for views is the **Parco di Villa Ghigi**, an area of Apennine foothills given to the city by a former rector of the university. Walk up from the Pza Maggiore and step out from the city centre into a wild, open expanse with vineyards and cattle.

ARRIVAL, INFORMATION, ACCOMMODATION

🚆 **Stazione Centrale,** a distinctive neo-classical building, is 1 km north of Pza Maggiore; walk along Via dell'Indipendenza (🚌 A). Expect a festival of construction as a new subterranean station is constructed under the existing station. It's not chance that the main station clock no longer works and forever reads 10.25. That was the moment on the morning of 2 August 1980 when a bomb exploded killing 85 people. A memorial to the victims stands by the renovated station entrance.

➔ **Gugliemo Marconi Airport,** ☎ 051 647 9615 (www.bologna-airport.it), about 8 km north-west of the city centre. Aerobus (www.atc.bo.it) every 12–15 mins (0600–0015; less often after 2115) to Centrale rail station, taking 20 mins. 🛈 **Tourist offices:** at the airport and Pza Maggiore 1, ☎ 051 239 660 (http://iat.comune.bologna.it). **Internet:** Everest Telecom, Via della Zecca 3.

📨 The tourist office has a wide-ranging list of hotels and *pensioni* in all categories. Try the **Accorsi B&B**, Via Licinia 12, ☎ 845 454 40, €, or the **Hotel Panorama**, Via Giovanni Livraghi 1, ☎ 051 221 802 (www.hotelpanoramabologna.it), €€, both of which are central. **Hostels:** The **Centro Europa Uno**, Via Emilia 297, San Lazzaro di Savena, ☎ 050 625 7007 (www.centroeuropauno.it), is your best bet for a dorm bed, and is located about 5 km outside the city (call in advance). **Camping: Centro Turistico Città di Bologna**, Via Romita 12/4°a, ☎ 051 325 016 (www.hotelcamping.com), open all year.

CONNECTIONS FROM BOLOGNA

From Bologna you can visit Ravenna (see box) or take the line along the Adriatic coast to **Ancona** (ERT 630) and **Brindisi** (ERT 631), though this trip isn't Italy at its best. On the way you could pause at **Rimini**, a somewhat charmless resort but with an excellent beach, fine Roman bridge and lively nightlife; it's a 40-min bus trip (ERT 630) from Rimini to the tiny independent republic of **San Marino**, memorably perched on the slopes of **Monte Titano**. Other worthwhile detours include **Peschici**, east of **San Severo** on the **Gargano massif** (a rugged limestone coast), and the area around **Monopoli** (notable for its *trulli* – curious drystone, white-domed structures of feudal origins). **Brindisi**, the port near the 'heel' of Italy, has a useful ferry to **Pátra** (Πάτρα) in Greece (ERT 2775).

The old **Bologna** to **Milan** rail route (ERT 615; 2 hrs 20 mins), rather sidelined by the fast route opened in 2008, runs via **Modena**, a quietly attractive old town with a Romanesque cathedral and with a fine collection of art and illuminated manuscripts within the Palazzo dei Musei. Just another half hour beyond Modena is **Parma**, a household name for its ham and cheese, and worth a stop for the frescoed Baptistry,

RAVENNA

Ravenna (1 hr 20 mins; ERT 621) was the centre of Byzantine rule in Italy during the 6th and 7th centuries AD. The most impressive reminders of these periods are Ravenna's famed **mosaics** (the major sights cluster in the north-west corner of the Old Town). The 6th-century octagonal **Basilica of San Vitale** features depictions of the Byzantine Emperor Justinian and Empress Theodora. In the grounds are the **Mausoleum of Galla Placidia**, decorated with richly coloured mosaics, and the **National Museum**. The **Basilica of Sant'Apollinare Nuovo** dates from the same period; its walls are lined with green and gold mosaics showing processions of saints and virgins. ⇌ The station is about 500 m east of town. 🚻 **Tourist office**: Via Salara 8, ☎ 0544 357 55 (www.turismo.ravenna.it). ⇥ **Youth hostel** (HI): **Dante**, Via Nicolodi 12, ☎ 0544 421 164 (www.hostelravenna.com), 🚌 1/11/70 or 10-min walk south-east from the rail station.

the sensuous Correggio frescos in **Camera di San Paolo** and the art in the **Galleria Nazionale** in the **Palazzo della Pilotta**. The Alta Velocità high-speed train service (ERT 600) will speed you from Bologna to Milan in little over an hour, but you'll sadly not see a lot along the way.

FLORENCE — SEE P479

AREZZO

Arezzo was a major settlement in Etruscan, Roman and medieval times. Always a wealthy city, today its economy rests on jewellers, goldsmiths and antiques. Much of the centre is modern, but there are still attractive winding streets in the hilltop Old Town, with its Renaissance houses and the handsome Pza Grande.

One of the masterpieces of Italian Renaissance painting and the city's major attraction is Piero della Francesca's brilliant fresco cycle of the *Legend of the True Cross* (1452–66), on display in the 14th-century **Church of San Francesco**, Pza San Francesco, ☎ 0575 352 727, in the centre of the Old Town (reservation required).

The spacious **cathedral**, begun in 1278 and lit by 16th-century stained glass, is adorned by Piero della Francesca's fresco of Mary Magdalene, near the organ. The **Museo Statale d'Arte Medievale e Moderna**, Via San Lorentino 8, contains an exceptional collection of majolica as well as sculptures dating from the 10th to 17th centuries (closed Mon). **Santa Maria delle Grazie**, Via Santa Maria delle Grazie 1, is a particularly fine 15th-century church that contains a high altar by Andrea della Robbia.

There's less to detain you in the lower town, though you may like to pause at the **Museo Archeologico**, Via Margaritone 10, in an old monastery not far to the east of the station; it has a collection of Roman Aretine ware (50 BC to AD 60–70 terracotta with a shiny red glaze and adorned with bas-relief), Etruscan bronzes and 1st-century BC vases. Nearby is a ruined Roman amphitheatre, the **Anfiteatro Romano**.

ARRIVAL, INFORMATION, ACCOMMODATION

⇌ In the modern sector, south-west of the centre: walk up the hill to the Old Town. 🖪 **Tourist office**: Piazza della Repubblica 28 (by the station), ☎ 0575 377 678 (www. apt.arezzo.it). Information Centre at Via Ricasoli. **Internet**: **Informagiovani**, Pza G. Monaco 2 (Mon–Sat). ⌖ Rooms are difficult to find over the first weekend of every month, but otherwise generally fine. There are several budget options in the centre, including the **Hotel Cecco**, Corso Italia 215, ☎ 0575 209 86 (www.hotelcecco.com), €, the **B&B Antiche Mura**, Piaggia di Murello 35, ☎ 0575 204 10 (www.antichemura.info), €€, or the **B&B I Due Gigli**, Via Cavour 170, ☎ 338 866 19 34 (www.iduegigli.it), €, in the heart of town. The **Foresteria Arezzo I Pratacci**, Via Edison 25, Zona Pratacci (2 km from city centre), ☎ 0575 383 338 (www.foresteriaarezzo.com), offers budget accommodation and use of the kitchen.

PERUGIA

Warlike and belligerent, the splendid capital of **Umbria** was smitten by strife almost until the 19th century and has a host of monuments of very martial demeanour.

Ignore the unattractive modern suburbs and head straight for the almost intact medieval centre, by bus or escalator. From **Pza Italia** the pedestrianised Corso Vannucci, lined with fortified palaces, cafés and shops — the centre of activities for a cosmopolitan crowd almost around the clock — runs north to the city's heart in **Pza IV Novembre**, where the **Duomo** (cathedral) is located. All the other major sights are within easy walking distance of here.

The **Duomo** is a large, plain, medieval building, supposedly home to the Virgin Mary's wedding ring. In the centre of the square is the 13th-century Fontana Maggiore, a fountain sculpted by Nicola and Giovanni Pisano. Facing the fountain, the somewhat forbidding **Palazzo dei Priori**, Perugia's civic headquarters since 1297, has a great Gothic portal and long rows of windows. Fan-like steps lead up to the Sala dei Notari, covered with an entertaining array of frescos.

The **Galleria Nazionale dell'Umbria**, on the fourth floor, contains works notably by Pinturicchio and Perugino, and is Italy's most important repository of Umbrian art (closed Mon); it also has a few Tuscan masterpieces, including Piero della Francesca's *Madonna and Saints with Child* and a triptych by Fra Angelico. See also the **Collegio della Mercanzia**, with its magnificent 15th-century carvings, while the restored frescos of the **Collegio del Cambio** (the Bankers' Guild) are considered to be Perugino's finest works.

San Domenico, Pza G Bruno, is an enormous church with several outstanding works of art. Authorship of the 14th-century **Tomb of Pope Benedict XI** is unknown, but it's clearly the work of a master sculptor. Here, too, is a

St Francis and the Basilica di San Francesco

San Francesco (St Francis) expressed the wish to be buried simply, but the news of his death (in 1226) brought a flood of donations from all over Europe and construction of the Basilica di San Francesco, at the western end of the Old Town, began in 1228. It has a choice collection of masterpieces, making it something of an art gallery in itself; several great artists were employed, inspiring each other into innovative forms of painting that departed from the rigid Byzantine conventions. The basilica consists of two churches: the lower church, designed for peaceful meditation by the saint's tomb, and the soaring upper church, intended to mollify the faction who wanted a glorious monument. The upper church suffered severe damage during the 1997 earthquake, but has been completely restored.

magnificent 15th-century, stained-glass window. The **Museo Archeologico Nazionale dell'Umbria**, in the monastery alongside San Domenico, includes Etruscan and Roman artefacts. And don't miss the 10th-century **Basilica of San Pietro**, south-east of the centre (Borgo XX Giugno).

Arrival, information, accommodation

➤ **FS** (State Railway), 4 km south-west of the centre (an uphill walk) or 15 mins by bus (🚌 G/R/TD/TS/Z4) to Pza Italia. Tickets from a forecourt booth or machine by the entrance. The private **FCU** (Ferrovia Centrale Umbria) railway terminal is **Stazione Sant'Anna**, from which you can get a *scala mobile* (escalator) to Pza Italia. 🛈 **Tourist office**: Pza Matteotti 18, ☎ 075 573 6458 (www.regioneumbria.eu). **Internet**: at **Perugia Web**, Via Ulisse Rocchi 30, near the cathedral.

🛏 There is plenty of cheap, central accommodation, but book ahead if you're coming during the Umbria International Jazz Festival (ten days every July: www.umbriajazz.com). A couple of central options: **Alla Residenza Domus Minervae**, Via Pompeo Pellini 19, ☎ 075 573 2238, €–€€, and the **B&B Le Naiadi**, Via Luigi Bonazzi 17, ☎ 075 573 3497 (www.beblenaiadi.com), €€. **Hostels**: 5km from the train station, but extremely well regarded, is the **Perugia Farmhouse Hostel**, Strado Torre Poggio 4, ☎ 0339 562 0005 (www.perugia-farmhouse.it). Other options closer to the centre are the **Ponte Felcino Hostel** (HI), Via Maniconi 97, ☎ 075 591 3991 (www.ostellopontefelcino.com; take 🚌 8 from Perugia station), and the **Ostello di Perugia**, Via Bontempi 13, ☎ 075 572 2880 (www.ostello.perugia.it).

Assisi

One name is irrevocably linked with **Assisi** — St Francis. Born here in 1182, he practised what he preached: poverty, chastity and obedience, leading to a love of God and an appreciation of all living things. He founded the Franciscan Order, and his home town became (and remains) a major pilgrimage centre, concentrated around the **Basilica di San Francesco**, erected in his memory and adorned with some of the most magnificent frescos in Italy (see box above).

St Francis' life initiated a wealth of art and architecture in Assisi. Still largely medieval, and clinging to a side of **Monte Subasio** high above the green Umbrian countryside, the town is instantly familiar from the landscapes in the frescos of the Umbrian painters.

The Pza del Comune, in the centre of the Old Town, is dominated by the 1st century AD **Tempio di Minerva** — a Roman temple partly incorporated into what is now the Church of Santa Maria. To the east of the centre, below the cathedral, is the **Basilica di Santa Chiara**. Santa Chiara (St Clare) was an early friend of St Francis and, with his guidance, established the Order of the Poor Clares, the female equivalent of the Franciscans. The old fortress, known as **Rocca Maggiore**, towers dramatically above the northern edge of the city, providing panoramic views of the town and surrounding countryside.

The **Basilica di Santa Maria degli Angeli**, near the station, surrounds a chapel used by St Francis and the spot where he died. Much more evocative, if you fancy a 4 km forest walk to the north-east, is **Eremo delle Carceri**, on the slopes of Monte Subasio. It was here, in caves, that the original Franciscans lived. See the cell used by St Francis and the altar from where he addressed the birds.

ARRIVAL, INFORMATION, ACCOMMODATION

⇶ This is not in Assisi proper, but in Santa Maria degli Angeli, about 5 km south-west and uphill all the way. Buses run to the centre every 35 mins. 🄸 **Tourist office:** Pza del Comune, ☎ 075 813 8680 (www.regioneumbria.eu). It provides a map in English and has information about accommodation, including pilgrim hostels.

◄ There is plenty of accommodation of every grade, but booking is advisable — essential for Easter, the Feast of St Francis (3–4 Oct) and Calendimaggio (a medieval celebration of spring held in early May). Central options include the **San Rufino**, Via Porta Pertici 7, ☎ 075 812 803 (www.hotelsanrufino.it), €, the **Hotel Pallotta**, Via San Rufino 6, ☎ 075 812 307 (www.pallottaassisi.it), €–€€, and the **Hotel La Fortezza**, Vicolo della Fortezza 19, ☎ 075 812 418 (www.lafortezzahotel.com), €–€€. The **youth hostel**, **Ostello della Pace** (HI), Via di Valecchie 177, ☎ 075 816 767 (www.assisihostel.com) is a 10-min walk from the centre of town.

CONNECTIONS FROM ASSISI

Spello (10 mins by train, ERT 625) is the epitome of an Umbrian hill town, with tiers of pink houses, cobbled alleys, churches and Roman gateways. The 13th-century church of **Santa Maria Maggiore** contains a chapel full of brilliantly restored frescos by Pinturicchio and a 15th-century ceramic floor. Spello is generally much quieter than Assisi. From the station it's a short walk up to the Old Town.

SPOLETO

Founded by Umbrians in the 6th century BC, **Spoleto** has an interesting mix of Roman and medieval sights, the most spectacular being the cathedral, adorned on its entrance facade with eight rose windows of differing sizes. Its campanile, propped up by a flying buttress, was constructed from various bits of Roman masonry and other un-medieval elements — and yet still manages to present itself as a perfect blend of Romanesque and Renaissance styles. Within, a baroque makeover rather ruined the effect, though Fra Filippo Lippi's magnificent frescos depicting the life of the Virgin are timeless.

Also of interest is **Cappella Eroli**, with a *Madonna and Child* by Pinturicchio, and the Cosmati marble floor. After several centuries of power the town fell into obscurity until being chosen (in 1958) to host Italy's leading performing arts festival in June/July, the **Spoleto Festival** (www.festivaldispoleto.com), which transforms the tranquil town into an unrecognisably invigorated place; prices, inevitably, soar.

Part of the small **Teatro Romano**, Pza della Libertà, at the southern end of the old centre, has been carefully restored and is now used for festival performances. Another section is occupied by the **Convent of Sant'Agata**, which houses a small collection of Roman artefacts. A walk through the **Arco di Druso** (AD 23), 100 m north, leads to Pza del Mercato, which was the Roman forum and is still a marketplace and the hub of Spoleto's social life.

Nearby, the small **Pinacoteca Comunale** is housed in the **Palazzo Rosari Spada** on Corso Mazzini, a visit to which requires a guide (closed Tues). The decor is magnificent and some of the paintings are outstanding, especially in the Umbrian section. The **Rocca**, a huge 14th-century castle to the south-east of town, guards one of the finest engineering achievements of medieval times, the **Ponte delle Torri**: a 240-m long bridge, supported by ten arches 80 m high. From it there are magnificent views of the gorge below and there's a pleasant 2-km walk (turn right) leading to **San Pietro**, with a facade adorned by some of the region's finest Romanesque sculpture.

ARRIVAL, INFORMATION, ACCOMMODATION

≋ In the Lower Town, with a long uphill walk south to the medieval town (or 🚌 D to Pza della Libertà — tickets from the station bar). Free city map from the station newsstand. 🄸 **Tourist office**: Pza della Libertà 7, ☎ 0743 238 911 (www.regioneumbria.eu). **Internet**: **Spider Service**, Via Porta Fuga 11.

🛏 Book well ahead during the summer arts festival. At other times it should be possible to find a bed in the centre of town without too much problem. Try the **Athena Hotel**, Via Giuseppe Valadier 3, ☎ 0743 225 218, €, the **Aurora Hotel**, Via dell' Apollinare 3, ☎ 0743 220 315 (www.hotelauroraspoleto.it), €–€€, or the centrally located **B&B Casa degli artisti**, Piazza Sansi 5, ☎ 0743 221 694 (www.bblacasadegliartisti.it), €€. If Spoleto is full, try Foligno, 26 km north-east and linked by trains that run until late; it has a **youth hostel** (HI): **Ostello Palazzo Pierantoni**, Via Pierantoni 23, ☎ 0742 342 566 (www.ostellofoligno.it).

ROME — SEE P555

Rail Route 37: Bound for Sicily

CITIES: ★★ CULTURE: ★★ HISTORY: ★★ SCENERY: ★★
COUNTRIES COVERED: ITALY

This is a route full of the flavours of the Italian south. When the English poet Shelley arrived in Naples, he remarked that it seemed to be a city of almost Sicilian demeanour. But it is a long haul, about six hours on the fastest trains, from Naples to Messina, the first port of call in Sicily. On this route, we make tracks south from **Rome**, explore **Naples** and its hinterland and then continue south to Sicily, skirting the coastline of the **Tyrrhenian Sea** along the way. Towards the 'toe' of mainland Italy, the train is shunted onto a ferry from Villa San Giovanni to **Messina** on the island of Sicily. This is the last remaining place in southern Europe where passenger trains take to ships in this manner. The only other place where you will encounter this is on two Baltic crossings.

Successive invasions of Romans, Arabs, Normans, French and Spanish have shaped the Sicilian character; the land is a strange mixture of fertile plains, volcanic lava fields and virtual desert, while **Mount Etna**, the great volcano, is omnipresent, smoking in the background.

ROME — SEE P555

The easy route south from Rome is to hop on the premium Alta Velocità (AV) train that will dash the more than 200 km to Naples in just 70 mins (ERT 600). It is far better, if you can afford the time, to take the slower coastal route (ERT 640). The finest scenery is around **Formia**. Our favourite spot along this coast is Minturno, where the train station is called Minturno-Scauri. Not shown in ERT 640, it is one stop south of Formia, and served only by local trains (including the stopping services from Rome to Naples which run every 2 hrs). **Minturno** is a little gem with some striking Roman remains, including a fabulous aqueduct, and a very atmospheric Old Town, full of tiny alleys.

NAPLES (NAPOLI)

There's nowhere quite like **Naples** — the city is a glorious assault on your senses. It may have a notorious reputation as a city of crime, but its ebullience, history, cuisine and range of treasures make it a compelling stop on a southern Italian journey. The old central axis, known as **Spaccanapoli**, is a superb immersion into the Neapolitan maelstrom, so break yourself in with a pizza and a peaceful gallery visit first. Then venture out and explore dark, crumbling, medieval alleys, with washing lines strung above and cooking smells everywhere. Watch housewives haul up bucketfuls of shopping by ropes linked to high tenement windows. Out on the streets, you can wander for hours in the city's various

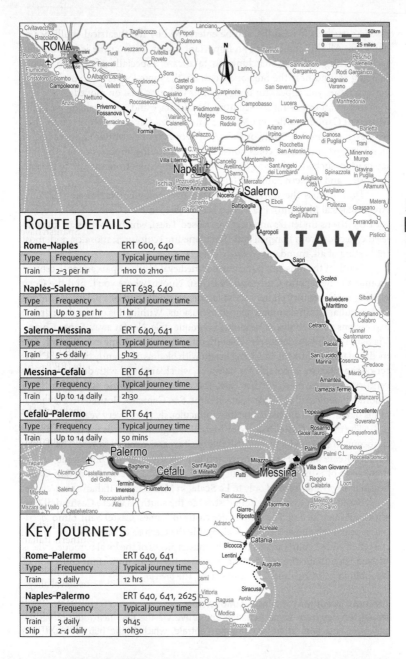

ROUTE DETAILS

Rome–Naples — ERT 600, 640

Type	Frequency	Typical journey time
Train	2–3 per hr	1h10 to 2h10

Naples–Salerno — ERT 638, 640

Type	Frequency	Typical journey time
Train	Up to 3 per hr	1 hr

Salerno–Messina — ERT 640, 641

Type	Frequency	Typical journey time
Train	5–6 daily	5h25

Messina–Cefalù — ERT 641

Type	Frequency	Typical journey time
Train	Up to 14 daily	2h30

Cefalù–Palermo — ERT 641

Type	Frequency	Typical journey time
Train	Up to 14 daily	50 mins

KEY JOURNEYS

Rome–Palermo — ERT 640, 641

Type	Frequency	Typical journey time
Train	3 daily	12 hrs

Naples–Palermo — ERT 640, 641, 2625

Type	Frequency	Typical journey time
Train	3 daily	9h45
Ship	2–4 daily	10h30

districts, such as the **Sanità**, and be entertained by the theatrical ebullience of daily life. All this comes with an important caveat. Petty crime is rife, notably pickpocketing and bag-snatching, so take care, especially after dark. Avoid hanging around near the Stazione Centrale: the more lost-tourist you look, the easier a target you appear for dodgy youths whizzing past on mopeds.

Set in an imposing 18th-century Royal Palace and a huge shady park, the **Museo di Capodimonte**, Via Miano 2 (metro: Pza Cavour or Montesanto, then 🚌 C63/R4 from Pza Dante or 🚌 178/M2/201 from Pza Museo) houses one of Italy's largest and richest collections of art — including important works by Italian masters such as Titian and Botticelli, art from Naples from the 13th to the 19th centuries, and modern paintings (closed Wed).

Do not miss the world-class **Museo Archeologico Nazionale** (National Archaeological Museum), Pza Museo Nazionale 19 (metro: Cavour or Museo; free for EU citizens under 18s and over 65s; closed Tues), which contains an unparalleled collection from Pompeii and Herculaneum: sculptures, mosaics, and, most interesting of all, mundane everyday objects.

South of the museum is the heart of medieval Naples, **Spaccanapoli**, centred around Via Benedetto Croce and Pza Gesù Nuovo, where you'll find the **Gesù Nuovo**, a 16th-century church whose facade, originally part of a palace, is studded with peculiar basalt diamond-shaped extrusions. Within, it is one of the extreme expressions of the ebullient Neapolitan baroque style. Not far away, **Santa Chiara**, Via Santa Chiara 49, dates from the 14th century. In it are some exceptionally fine medieval tombs. Attached to it and bright with blooms, the gently decaying **Cloister of the Clarisse** is notable for its walks, which are lined with decorative 18th-century majolica tiles. Further east, the cavernous **Duomo** (Cathedral), Via Duomo, is dedicated to Naples' patron saint, San Gennaro. Housed here is a phial of his blood, which allegedly liquefies miraculously twice every year.

The massive **Castel Nuovo** (or Maschio Angioino) guards the port. The castle, begun in 1279, is chiefly recognisable for its massive round towers. The nearby **Palazzo Reale** was the seat of the Neapolitan royalty. Vast and handsome, within it are acres of 18th- and 19th-century rooms. The adjacent **Teatro di San Carlo**, begun in 1737, ranks second only to **La Scala**, in Milan, in the Italian opera league.

Santa Lucia, the waterfront district to the south, is where **Castel dell'Ovo** sticks out into the bay. The third major castle in Naples, **Castel Sant'Elmo**, occupies a peak high above the city — alongside the **Certosa di San Martino**. Inside the latter, whose courtyard is one of the masterpieces of the local baroque style, is **Museo Nazionale di San Martino**, which contains an important collection of Neapolitan paintings and Christmas cribs, the *presepi*.

ARRIVAL, INFORMATION, ACCOMMODATION

🚄 All services from Rome (whether you arrive via the new fast route or via the slower coastal line) arrive at **Stazione Centrale**, which is the hub for most long

DAY TRIPS FROM NAPLES

Naples is somewhat upstaged by its surroundings, notably the Neapolitan Riviera — including the beautiful but often crowded resorts of Sorrento, Positano and Amalfi, and the island of Capri, just a short boat ride away — as well as the astonishing **Roman remains** of **Herculaneum** and **Pompeii**. And above the ensemble towers mighty Vesuvius, the volcano that has so powerfully shaped the history of this region. All the spots we mention here can be reached in day trips from Naples.

Exploring the area is easily done by train, bus and ferry. The **Circumvesuviana** (www.vesuviana.it) is a private venture operating a network of half a dozen rail lines (half-hourly service on most routes, ERT 623) linking Naples, Sorrento, Pompeii and Ercolano (for Herculaneum). There are also regular trains and buses to Salerno (see p317), from where there is a ferry to Amalfi.

The **Sorrento Peninsula** is unbeatable if you like beaches, ancient sites, boat trips and stunning coastal scenery. Not many European cities the size of Naples have all these right on the doorstep. The best approach is by ferry — from Salerno to Amalfi, or from Naples to Sorrento and on to Capri. Here you will see villages and towns perched beneath towering limestone cliffs that will have you wondering how anyone ever managed to build on them. The settlements are linked by a network of tiny stepped paths, making it outstanding terrain for walking. Scenically, **Amalfi** has the edge over **Sorrento**. There are some great walks in and around Amalfi. Take the frequent bus from Amalfi up to **Ravello** and return by one of several very attractive paths. This delicious hilltop village has stupendous views. Lying just off the Sorrento Peninsula, the island of **Capri** is renowned for its wonderful setting, with bougainvillea, cacti and jasmine growing everywhere around the Greek-looking dome-roofed white houses.

Also on the Circumvesuviana railway and a short ride from Naples, **Pompeii** (station: Pompei, adjacent to the site) is very touristy, but nonetheless mesmeric and eerie. This substantial Roman town, excavated from the volcanic ash that buried it, gives a real feel for life at the time. You can see original graffiti on the walls and chariot ruts in the road, wander into houses and courtyards, identify shop counters and even lose the crowds in some of the more remote areas. Indeed the scale of the place is almost daunting. Highlights include the **Forum**, the **Forum Baths**, the **Villa of the Mysteries**, the outdoor and indoor theatres, the **House of Loreius Tiburtius** and the **House of the Vettii** (both with marvellous wall paintings), and the **Lupanar**, the restored main brothel, complete with erotic frescos. On arrival at the site you can join guided tours, which can be worthwhile as features are not well signed once you are within the site. Many of the best sculptures, mosaics and paintings have ended up in the National Archaeological Museum in Naples.

Herculaneum (station: Ercolano; 10-min walk downhill to the site) was a wealthy Roman suburb, buried in AD 79 by the eruption of **Mount Vesuvius**. It was engulfed by mud rather than ash. Excavations have revealed an astonishing time capsule, with many house facades virtually intact. Unlike Pompeii, some upper storeys are in evidence. You can see half-timbered buildings and even balconies, and some remarkable bathhouses, still roofed and with benches in position.

distance trains. Most Circumvesuviana services, including those to Pompeii and Sorrento, start at **Napoli Porta Nolana** station (often locally referred to as Circumvesuviana) and then stop 2 mins later at Piazza Garibaldi, which is very close to the main-line station at Centrale. The two stations are linked by a moving walkway.

✈ **Capodichino** (www.portal.gesac.it) is 7 km north of the centre. There are taxis and a bus service to the city centre (Pza Garibaldi), approximately every 20–30 mins. For airport information, ☎ 081 789 6111.

🛈 **Tourist office**: Pick up a town map at the city tourist office and a copy of the monthly listing *Qui Napoli*. **Ente Provinciale per il Turismo** (EPT) provides information about hotels; its main office is at Pza dei Martiri 58, ☎ 081 410 7211 (www. eptnapoli.info), and it maintains a spartan but helpful office in the Stazione Centrale. See also www.inaples.it for useful tourist information.

The city centre is best explored by foot, but if you tire there is an excellent metro network. Three **funicular** railways (Funicolare di Montesanto, Centrale and Chiaia) link the Old City with the cooler Vómero Hill – take the funicular from Montesanto metro station to admire the views. Buy train **tickets** at kiosks and validate them in the machines near each platform. Buy bus tickets from news kiosks, tobacconists and bars. Day passes (€3.60) and cheaper weekend passes are available. A local transit ticket is valid for 60 mins (€1.20).

🛏 The tourist office can help with accommodation but confirm prices with the hotel before committing yourself. **La Concordia**, Piazzetta Concordia 5, ☎ 081 412 349 (www.laconcordia.it), €€, is a friendly, good-value B&B. Cheap hotels cluster in and around the noisy, un-salubrious Pza Garibaldi. **Hotel San Pietro**, Via San Pietro ad Aram 18, ☎ 081 286 040 (www.sanpietrohotel.com), €€, is a large block just west of Pza Garibaldi (with the station behind you, take Corso Umberto leading diagonally left; the hotel is signed off to the right). Good value, with a big street market close by (so can be noisy). Also west of Pza Garibaldi is **Pensione Mancini**, Via Pasquale Stanislao Mancini 33, ☎ 081 553 6731 (www.hostelpensionemancini.com), €, a fair budget option which also has dorm facilities. For other **B&Bs**, see www.bed-breakfast-napoli.com, a comprehensive website featuring several B&Bs in both Naples and surrounding areas.

The HI **youth hostel**, **Ostello Mergellina**, 23 Salita della Grotta, ☎ 081 761 2346 (www.ostellonapoli.com), is behind the Stazione Mergellina. **Non-HI**: **Fabric**, Via Bellucci Sessa 22, Portici, ☎ 081 776 5874 (www.fabrichostel.com), is a sought-after hostel set in a former fabric factory; it has a bar, restaurant, internet and regular events. Equally popular is the central and friendly **6 Small Rooms**, Via Diodato Lioy 18, ☎ 081 790 1378 (www.6smallrooms.com). **Hostel of the Sun**, Via Melisurgo 15, ☎ 081 420 6393 (www.hostelnapoli.com), is central and clean, a 20-min walk or 🚌 2 from the main station; get off at Via Depretis near **Hotel Mercure**. **Campsites** are mainly in Pozzuoli (on the metro), west of Naples. **Camping Internazionale Vulcano Solfatara**, Via Solfatara 161, ☎ 081 526 2341 (www.solfatara.it), is the nearest.

CONNECTIONS FROM NAPLES

There is a particularly attractive rail route that cuts east from Naples through the heart of rural **Basilicata** to **Taranto** and the east coast. Trains are not frequent (see ERT 638), but we rate the 4 hr journey from Naples to Taranto as one of the finest in southern

Italy. From Taranto there are frequent local train services to Brindisi and Bari, each of which offer good onward connections by ship across the Adriatic. From Bari there are regular ferries to Dubrovnik in Croatia (ERT 2795), which is on **Route 38**, Bar in Montenegro (ERT 2738) and Durrës in Albania (ERT 2880). Both Bari and Brindisi have frequent ships to Corfu, Igoumenítsa (Ηγουμενίτσα) and Pátra (Πάτρα) in Greece (ERT 2755, 2765, 2770, 2775).

There are direct ships from Naples to Palermo (8–10 hrs, ERT 2625) as well as a number of other services to Sicily. The summer season hydrofoil to **Trapani** on the north-west corner of Sicily makes an en route stop at the remote island of Ustica, well worthy of a stop if you want to escape from modernity for a day or two. And for something really special, we recommend the twice-weekly sailings from Naples to Milazzo operated by Siremar (16–22 hrs, ERT 2570).

These sailings stop at various islands in the Aeolian archipelago, a great arc of volcanoes off the north coast of Sicily. Thought by the ancients to be the home of Aeolus, the God of the Winds, the **Aeolian Islands** have wonderful scenery and rich marine life including turtles, hammer fish and flying fish. Lipari, the main island, has an old walled town, while the isles of Vulcano and Stromboli are classic conical volcanos. These are Sicily's loveliest islands. The Siremar schedule often includes an utterly memorable night-time stop at **Stromboli**.

SALERNO

Spread around a crescent bay, Salerno is recommended as a stop for visiting **Paestum** or **Amalfi**. The city goes back a long way. It belonged to Greece in ancient times, and was then a Roman settlement. In medieval times it was celebrated for its **School of Medicine** — the *Code of Health*, written here in verse in the 12th century, was for some time held to be the definitive pronouncement on the subject. World War II devastation, left Salerno a shadow of its former self, the best of what remains being the atmospherically dilapidated centre around **Via dei Mercanti**, spanned by an 8th-century arch, and the cathedral — with its superb mosaic-covered 12th-century pulpit and the Salerno ivories (depicting Bible scenes) from the same period in the Cathedral Museum.

≈ South of the old centre (turn right out of the station); a 10-min walk. **ⓘ Tourist office**: Pza V. Veneto 1 (near the station), ☎ 089 231 432 (www.turismoinsalerno.it).

✉ There are a number of inexpensive **B&Bs** in the old part of town, including **Cometa**, Via Mario Avallone 34, ☎ 089 337 527 (www.bbcometa.com), €, and the **Salerno Centro**, Piazza Portanova 10, ☎ 089 296 1315 (www.salernocentro.it), €€. **Youth hostel** (HI): **Ostello di Salerno**, Ave Gratia Plena, Via Canali, ☎ 089 234 776 (www.ostellodisalerno.it); 500 m from the rail station.

MESSINA

Messina, Sicily's nearest port to the mainland, was the victim of an earthquake in 1908 that shook for two months and claimed 84,000 lives, and of a massive attack by US bombers in 1943. But even those events can't take away its glorious setting beneath the mountains. Much has been rebuilt in a stable, squat style. The well-constructed **cathedral**, Pza del Duomo, has an ornate Gothic central entrance portal and mosaics in the three apses.

Try to catch the moving figurines on the clock tower as it chimes at midday, and climb the tower for the view.

ARRIVAL, INFORMATION, ACCOMMODATION

≈ Trains from the mainland arrive on FS ferries at **Stazione Marittima**, and continue to **Stazione Centrale** – departure point for city and long-distance buses. **ⓘ Tourist office:** Via Calabria 301, ☎ 090 674 236 (near the station) and Pza Cairoli 45, ☎ 090 293 5292 (www.messina-sicilia.it).

✉ There's limited budget accommodation. Try **B&B Don Gaspano**, Via Antonino Torre 27, ☎ 090 933 534 (www.dongaspano.com), €–€€, or, slightly more upmarket, the **Villa Morgana**, Via Consolare Pompea, ☎ 090 325 575 (www.villamorgana.it), €€. **Camping**: The nearest campsite is **Nuovo Camping dello Stretto**, Via Circuito, Torre Faro, ☎ 090 322 3051 (www.campingdellostretto.it), open June–Sept. Also, **Camping Il Peloritano**, ☎ 090 348 496 (www.peloritanocamping.it), in Rodia, is about 20 km from Messina but reachable by bus, open Mar–Oct.

CEFALÙ

Crammed between a rocky promontory and the sea, this idyllic fishing port and beach resort is a great place to rest, with plenty of restaurants, walks and views, and charming corners, particularly on Corso Ruggero. The Arab-Norman **cathedral**, a twin-towered, fortified medieval structure, dominates the town from its position just beneath the **Rocca**, the rock that protects it. It contains some of Sicily's best-preserved — and earliest (1148) — mosaics. Dating from the time of the Norman kings, these are the work of Byzantine craftsmen. See the *Christ Pantocrator* in the main apse: it is one of the great works of medieval Sicilian art.

SICILY'S EAST COAST

From Messina, there is a good train service south along the east coast of Sicily to **Siracusa** (3 hrs, ERT 641), along the way serving Taormina and Catania and skirting the lower slopes of Mount Etna. Real devotees of volcanic scenery can take a local private railway called the Circumetnea which runs for 111 km around the base of the mountain. No Sunday services. See ERT 644 and www.circumetnea.it.

The **Museo Mandralisca**, Via Mandralisca 13, contains, along with a variety of artefacts including some Greek ceramics, an important painting by Antonello da Messina, *Portrait of an Unknown Man* (1460). Above the town, on the Rocca — ascend from Pza Garibaldi — a ruined **medieval fortification** provides magnificent views out over Cefalù and the coast. The attractive beach offers shallow bathing.

ARRIVAL, INFORMATION, ACCOMMODATION

≽ Via A. Moro, a 10-min walk from Corso Ruggero. **𝐢 Tourist office:** Corso Ruggero 77, ☎ 0921 421 050 (www.cefalu.it). **Internet**: Kefaonline, Pza S. Francesco 1.

➡ A wide range of accommodation, though in August things get heavily booked. A budget option is **Locanda Cangelosi**, Via Umberto I 26, ☎ 0921 421 591 (www.locandacangelosi.it), €, near Piazza Garibaldi. The **B&Bs Casa al Duomo**, Via Lo Duca 27, ☎ 368 78 68 771, €–€€, centrally located, and **Ale Robi Cefalu'**, Via Porpora 17, ☎ 0921 422 780 (www.alerobi.it), €, are other options. **Campsites: Costa Ponente Internazionale**, ☎ 0921 420 085 (Apr–Oct) and, beside it, **Sanfilippo**, ☎ 0921 420 184 (www.campingsanfilippo.com) — both 3 km west of town at Contrada Ogliastrillo (heading for La Spisa).

PALERMO

Framed by an arc of mountains behind the city overlooking the sea, Palermo is a melting pot of styles, cultures and civilisations. The city, and western Sicily in general, is steeped in Arab-Norman architectural values rather than Greek or Roman styles.

Parts of Palermo are dilapidated, the legacy of wartime bombing and criminal neglect, but a renaissance has been ever more evident over the last decade — albeit a Sicilian renaissance, so one with as many false starts as bold leaps. Palermo has a seductive atmosphere, with its ancient labyrinth of alleys, ornate churches and souk-like markets. More North African than Italian, the **Vucciria** in the side streets south-east of Pza San Domenico, or the vibrant **Ballarò** in Pza Ballarò (near the station), signal Palermo's status as a meeting place of two continents.

Palermo's unmissable sights include the **Palazzo Reale o dei Normanni** with its lavishly ornamental mosaics by Arab and Byzantine craftsmen (1150). Its ceiling is the finest surviving example of Fatimid architecture anywhere. The Palazzo

Excursion from Palermo

Some 10 km from Palermo, and a shortish ride on 🚌 389 from Pza Indipendenza, **Monreale** is a hill town perched on a hill south-west of the city. The **cathedral,** austere outside, reveals nothing of its glories — but inside it's absolutely covered with Byzantine mosaics executed during Norman times in the 12th century and of the highest standard of craftsmanship. If you see no other church in Sicily, see this one. The cloister has some quirky carved capitals, and the climb to the tower takes in some hair-raising rooftop views.

is also home to **Cappella Palatina**, created in 1132, an east-meets-west chapel of Moorish splendour, with its coffered ceilings equalled by shimmering Byzantine mosaics. Nearby, on Via dei Benedettini, is **San Giovanni degli Eremiti**, a Benedictine abbey, which incorporates a Byzantine basilica, a mosque, Norman cloisters and an Arab 'garden of delights'. The **Duomo**, on Corso V Emanuele, is yet another hybrid, part-Christian, part-Moorish.

The rich legacy of the ancient Greeks can be studied in one of southern Italy's best museums, the **Museo Archeologico Regionale**, at Pza Olivella 24; highlights include the panels of relief sculpture from temples at **Selinunte**. Other mosaics in the city can be seen in the **Martorana** in Pza Bellini (12th century).

The other great milestone of Sicilian style is the baroque: the local Palermitan baroque is ornate and ebullient. In Palermo, the richest examples of it can be seen in the interiors of the little oratories of **Rosario di San Domenico** at Via dei Bambinai, and of **Santa Zita**, behind the **Church of Santa Zita** at Via Valverde 3. In both, the stucco artist Giacomo Serpotta (1656–1732) unleashed the full throttle of his exuberance. His remarkably realistic stucco figures run riot around the walls.

One intriguing area stretches north from the main rail station to the **Teatro Massimo**, the huge opera house on Piazza Verdi (see www.teatromassimo.it for details). It is well worth taking the guided tour (Tues–Sun except during rehearsals). During the opera season, if you can avoid a peak day, get a dirt-cheap ticket to a production. If the building looks familiar it's because it featured in the film *The Godfather III.*

For a peaceful oasis from the city's din, head to the **Orto Botanico** (Via Lincoln 2b, entrance fee), a luscious botanic garden full of exotic species such as the *Ficus magnolioides* with its bizarre aerial roots (more on www.ortobotanico.unipa.it). Another peaceful spot is **Piazza Marina**, just off the waterfront. Lined with restored palaces and restaurants, and overlooking tranquil gardens, this is the loveliest square in Palermo's historic centre. The neighbouring waterside is being restored but even the picturesquely decaying port has huge charm.

City buses run on a 2 hr time limit no matter how often you transfer (buy tickets from booths near bus stops, and stamp your ticket as soon as you board), making it cheap to get to outlying places. On the west side of town the **Convento dei Cappuccini** (Pza Cappuccini) is a 1-km walk from Pza Indipendenza: the Capuchin friars here have created extraordinary catacombs, with embalmed corpses dressed up and displayed according to their station (soldier, monk, lawyer, etc) — definitely a sight for the strong of stomach.

ARRIVAL, INFORMATION, ACCOMMODATION

≋ **Stazione Centrale**, in Pza Giulio Cesare, is at the southern end of the city. Located in the same square, and in the streets around it, are some of the termini of local, provincial and long-distance bus services. **Stazione Marittima**, Via Francesco Crispi, in the east, by the port, is the focus for most ferry services. 🚻 **Tourist office:** Pza Castelnuovo 34, ☎ 091 605 8351 (www.palermotourism.com). Another tourist information point is at ✈ Falcone e Borsellino Airport (www.gesap.it), reached by rail link from Stazione Centrale (ERT 5). Walking is the best way of getting around.

    🛏 Cheap accommodation is easy to find, though much of it is tacky. **Hotel Verdi**, Via Maqueda 417, ☎ 091 584 928 (www.albergoverdi.it), €€, is on an atmospheric, if busy, street in the city centre. The mid-range is well catered for. **Hotel Regina**, Cso Vittorio Emanuele 316, ☎ 091 611 4216 (www.hotelreginapalermo.it), €€. **Youth hostel** (HI): **Baia del Corallo**, Via Plauto 27, ☎ 091 679 7807 (www.ostellopalermo.it); 1 km from station.

    Away from the city, at Sferracavallo (connected by 🚌 101) near the sea, are two **campsites**: **Camping Trinacria**, Via Barcarello 25, ☎ 091 530 590 (www.campingtrinacria.it), and **Camping degli Ulivi**, Via Pegaso 25, ☎ 091 533 021 (www.campingdegliulivi.com).

CONNECTIONS FROM PALERMO

Palermo is not quite the end of the line. If you are tempted to explore Sicily by train a little more, Palermo is a good jumping-off point. There are local trains to **Trapani** and **Marsala** (both ERT 646). And there is a network of lines that plunge through the hills of central Sicily. The direct train (not Sat and Sun) from Palermo to Catania takes this route, and with a little creativity you can devise itineraries from Palermo to **Siracusa** that take in parts of Sicily's south coast (see ERT 645, 647, 648). **Ragusa** makes a great place for an overnight stop on the south coast. The tumbled streetscape of the lower town looks like something out of a film set.

    Palermo has a rich range of shipping links that include services to offshore Ustica and summer hydrofoil services along the coast to **Cefalù** and **Milazzo** (all in ERT 2570). Those local links apart, there is a weekly overnight ship to **Sardinia** (14 hrs, ERT 2675) and almost daily ferries to **Naples** (8–11 hrs, ERT 2625). Grandi Navi Veloci have a daily ship to **Genoa** (20 hrs, ERT 2547). This latter service uses very comfortable cruise ferries and is a relaxing way of returning north after the long rail journey south to Sicily.

    If the train appeals more, there are daily direct overnight trains with sleeping cars and couchettes from Palermo to Rome, Milan, Turin, Florence and Venice (all ERT 640). Palermo also has direct shipping links with Tunisia, and since 2010 much enhanced shipping connections with Malta.

When Sicilian winter weather became too overbearing for the English writer DH Lawrence and his wife Freda, the couple took a break in Sardinia (Sardegna), taking care to make bacon sandwiches and prepare a thermos of tea before setting out from their home in Taormina in the east of Sicily. First they took the train to Messina ("dreary, dreary hole" wrote Lawrence), and then journeyed by train along the north coast, following — although they did not know it — Route 37 in this book. DH Lawrence wrote a wonderful account of the couple's journey by train through Sicily, the crossing by ship from **Palermo** to Cagliari and their nine days exploring Sardinia, much of the latter by train. *Sea and Sardinia* was published in 1921 and remains a classic piece of travel writing. It is witty, insightful and tells us as much about Lawrence as it does about Sardinia. Definitely a volume to pack if you are bound for Palermo and think you might be tempted to board the ferry for Sardinia.

In Lawrence's day, the boat ran just fortnightly. Nowadays there is a service from Palermo leaving on Saturdays, and a second **weekly boat** on Sunday nights from Trapani. Both routes are operated by Tirrenia (see ERT 2675). The Sicilian port of Trapani is 2 hrs 30 mins by direct train from Palermo (ERT 646). Both ferry routes take you to **Cagliari**, by far the largest and most modern-looking city on the island. Cagliari was much rebuilt following wartime bomb damage, but there's a compact Old Town inside the imposing 13th-century walls, with a warren of brick-paved lanes and two Pisan towers, **Nuraghic artefacts** in the National Archaeology Museum (closed Mon) and a **Roman amphitheatre**. As the capital of Sardinia, Cagliari offers the greatest opportunity to sample the fine cuisine and wines that are so characteristic of the island.

From Cagliari, one rail route heads west and another heads north. The latter is much the finer of the two options. DH Lawrence perfectly caught the flavour of rail travel in Sardinia when he wrote: "It is a queer railway. I would like to know who made it. It pelts up hill and down dale and round sudden bends in the most unconcerned fashion." The **rail network** is more limited today than it was when Lawrence visited, but it's still fun. Outline schedules are shown in ERT 629. Sardinia's second city, Sassari, is an obvious place to head for. It is a busy commercial, administrative and university town. You can experience real Sardinian life here in the knot of medieval streets before taking the train on to either **Porto Torres** or **Olbia**, both of which offer a wealth of onward shipping connections.

You might, by way of example, consider taking the regular ferry from Porto Torres to **Barcelona**, a longish route across the Mediterranean that thrives because of the long-standing cultural and trade links between **Catalunya** and north-west Sardinia. At Barcelona you can connect onto **Routes 8** and **9**. Another very useful link from Porto Torres is to **Marseille** (for **Routes 1, 5** and **6**). Both Porto Torres and Olbia have ferries to **Genoa** (for **Route 33**). Details of all ferry routes mentioned above are in ERT 2675. If travelling through Sicily and Sardinia has not exhausted your appetite for islands, then Corsica beckons. The French island is less than an hour from Sardinia by boat (ERT 2565). Read more about **Corsica** in another Sidetracks feature on p99.

SIDETRACKS J: BY SEA TO SARDINIA

Rail Route 38:
From Slovenia south to the Dalmatian coast

Cities: ★★ Culture: ★★ History: ★★ Scenery: ★★
Countries covered: Italy, Slovenia, Croatia

This route starts with a half-hour bus journey then cleverly combines trains and ferries to take in the finest stretch of the Dalmatian coast of Croatia. The journey includes the Slovenian capital **Ljubljana**, then follows a scenic rail route down the Sava Valley towards the Croatian capital, **Zagreb**. The journey from Zagreb south to the country's second city, Split, takes in some wild limestone *karst* terrain and skirts the border with Bosnia and Herzegovina to the east. Split itself is a relaxed city with a Roman palace, and is a good base for ferry excursions to the **islands**. From here take the ferry to the wonderfully preserved town of **Dubrovnik**, one of the jewels of the Adriatic.

Trieste — see p302

Sadly there are no cross-border train services into Slovenia from Trieste Centrale. But buses for Sežana depart about eight times every weekday from the nearby bus station (actually more frequently than the timetables at www.autostazionetrieste.it imply). But note that Sunday services are sparse. There are also twice-daily direct buses from Trieste to Ljubljana (once only on Sundays).

Sežana

The new bus station is just a three-min walk from the train station. A short walk around Sežana is a nice reminder that on that short bus journey up from Trieste, you have crossed one of Europe's great cultural frontiers and are now definitely in the Slavic world. *Burek* replaces pizza as a favoured snack, and there are memorials to the Yugoslav Partisans (who liberated Sežana). The **botanical park** at the top end of town is a nice spot to while away an hour while waiting for the onward train. Sežana lies at the southern end of a remarkable rural rail route to Bled and Jesenice (ERT 1302), described in **Route 39** (see p333).

If you wish to stop en route from Sežana to Ljubljana, the obvious choice is Postojna, famous for its remarkable cave complex. **Postojna** is also a place to connect onto **Route 39** southbound to the port city of Rijeka. You will find a further note about Postojna on p332 (see the section about connections from Rijeka).

Ljubljana

The capital of Slovenia is a lively university town dominated by a hilltop fortress. The **River Ljubljanica** divides the city into two parts, joined in the city centre by

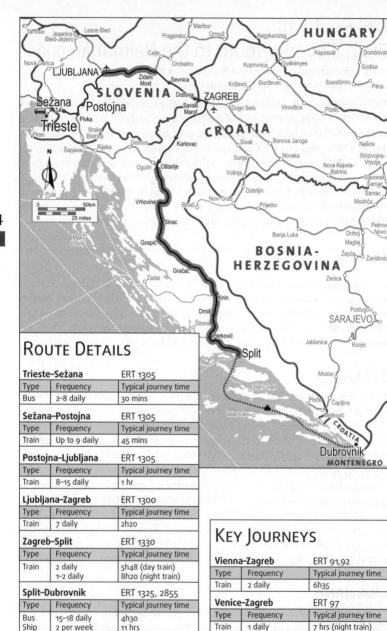

ROUTE DETAILS

Trieste–Sežana
ERT 1305

Type	Frequency	Typical journey time
Bus	2–8 daily	30 mins

Sežana–Postojna
ERT 1305

Type	Frequency	Typical journey time
Train	Up to 9 daily	45 mins

Postojna–Ljubljana
ERT 1305

Type	Frequency	Typical journey time
Train	8–15 daily	1 hr

Ljubljana–Zagreb
ERT 1300

Type	Frequency	Typical journey time
Train	7 daily	2h20

Zagreb–Split
ERT 1330

Type	Frequency	Typical journey time
Train	2 daily	5h48 (day train)
	1–2 daily	8h20 (night train)

Split–Dubrovnik
ERT 1325, 2855

Type	Frequency	Typical journey time
Bus	15–18 daily	4h30
Ship	2 per week	11 hrs

KEY JOURNEYS

Vienna–Zagreb
ERT 91,92

Type	Frequency	Typical journey time
Train	2 daily	6h35

Venice–Zagreb
ERT 97

Type	Frequency	Typical journey time
Train	1 daily	7 hrs (night train)

an attractive and unique triple bridge, the **Tromostovje**. This links the city's old heart, **Stari Trg**, on the right bank, built below the hilltop castle, to **Novi Trg** on the left bank. The Old Town, on the **right bank**, is an inviting maze of cobbled streets with historic buildings. Recent years have witnessed a renaissance with the opening of numerous shops, restaurants and bars, many with river views and generally reasonably priced. It is a gentle stroll up to the **castle**, which gives a good view of the city below. Baroque **St Nikolas's Cathedral**, Ćiril-Metodov Trg, abuts the Bishop's Palace. Beyond, on Vodnikov Trg, lies the **central food market** (Mon–Sat 0600–1800), good for picnic shopping.

On the river's **left bank**, the 17th-century Franciscan **church** dominates **Prešernov Trg**. Within, the high altar is the work of Italian architect and sculptor Francesco Robba. The left bank of the city serves a generous portion of museums, including the **National Museum** and the **Museum of Modern Art**. If suffering from an overdose of Middle European culture, chill out on the green expanse of **Tivoli Park** (good for picnics).

ARRIVAL, INFORMATION, ACCOMMODATION

≽ Trg Osvobodline Fronte 6 (Trg OF), a 15-min walk from the main street, Slovenska Cesta. ✈ **Ljubljana Brnik Airport** (served by easyJet), 26 km, 45 mins by bus (hourly Mon–Fri 0500–2000; every 2 hrs Sat & Sun 1000–2000; www.lju-airport.si). 🛈 **Tourist offices:** Adamič-Lundrovo nabrežja 2, ☎ 01 306 1215 (www.visitljubljana.si); branch in the station, ☎ 01 433 9475. Guided tours of the city meet in front of the Town Hall daily at 1000 from Apr–Oct and usually 1 hr later during the winter months.

⇥ A good-value choice in the centre of town is the **Bed & Breakfast Petra Varl**, Vodnikov trg 5a, ☎ 01 430 3788 (www.petravarl.com), €€. The **Hostel Celica**, Zavod Šouhostel Metelkova 8, ☎ 01 230 9700 (www.hostelcelica.com), is housed in a former prison, and is an excellent choice located in the heart of the popular artist-run Melalkova quarter. ✗ The riverside zone between Stari Trg and Novi Trg is the centre for friendly bars and reasonably priced eating places.

ZAGREB

Zagreb has a distinctly Austro-Hungarian flavour, both in architecture and, on first impression, the restrained manners of its citizens. Its oldest and most beautiful quarter is **Gornji grad** (Upper Town), with the cathedral-dominated Kaptol area. To reach it, begin from Trg Bana Jelačića, the main square, and follow Ilica, to reach Tomićeva, where you can take the funicular up to Strossmayer promenade for one of the best views over the city. A cannon is fired daily at 1200 from Lotrščak Tower.

Next take Ćirilometodska to **St Mark's Church**, noted for its extraordinary 'coat of arms' red, white and blue tiled roof, and follow Kamenita to pass through an archway, housing a shrine complete with altar, flowers and flickering candles. Turn left up Radićeva, and take one of the series of steep wooden stairways to your right, which link the upper town to Kaptol. In the cathedral look for the inscription of the Ten Commandments on the northern wall, written in 12th-century Glagolitic characters unique to the old Slavic language. Zagreb's fine art collection is in the **Mimara Museum**, Rooseveltov Trg 4 (closed Mon).

Despite its straight-laced image, Zagreb is culturally progressive. The early summer street festival *Cest is D'Best* is great, free and literally everywhere. The cult alternative venue **Mochvara** (www.mochvara.hr) on the banks of the Sava River is unlike any other, and for a distinctly urban local experience of cheap drinks and good music, find your way to **Krivi put** (The Wrong Way), at the bottom of Runjaninova (next to the Botanic Gardens).

ARRIVAL, INFORMATION, ACCOMMODATION

≋ In the centre of town. Left luggage and exchange offices. Bar and newspaper kiosks. ✈ **Zagreb Airport** (served by EasyJet and Germanwings) (www.zagreb-airport.hr) is 15 km south of Zagreb, in Pleso. A scheduled bus runs 0700–2000 from the main bus station, journey time 25 mins. Outside these hours buses run to connect with flights. ⓘ **Tourist offices:** Trg Bana Jelačića 11, ☎ 0800 53 53 (www.zagreb-touristinfo.hr), in the main town square. Other branches at the railway station and the airport. Pick up a copy of *Zagreb Info A–Z, Zagreb in Your Pocket* and *Events and Performances*, all free and published in English. **Internet access:** Preradovićeva 25, Teslina 12, Trg Petra Preradovića 5 and Masarykova 26 (courtyard entrance).

⊨ **Hotels** can be quite expensive. Check with the tourist office for private rooms, or try the **Camera Felice**, Trg Vladka Mačeka 2, ☎ 01 377 8301 (www.camera-felice.com), €€, close to the station, or the **Jägerhorn**, Ilica 14, ☎ 01 483 3877 (www.jaegerhorn.hr), €€–€€€, Zagreb's oldest hotel, in the heart of the Old Town. **Hostels**: A small but wonderfully central private youth hostel, **Fulir Hostel**, Radićeva 3, ☎ 01 483 0882, is just off the main square (www.fulir-hostel.com). Other good options are the **Hobo Bear Hostel**, Andrije Medulićeva 4, ☎ 01 484 6636 (www.hobobearhostel.com), and the **Funk Hostel and Bar**, Poljička 13, ☎ 01 631 4530 (www.funkhostel.hr).

✗ The central and certainly most obvious destination for coffee by day and beer by night is popular Tkalča (i.e. Tkalčićeva street), leading from Trg Bana Jelačića up to Gornji grad. The farmers' market at **Dolac**, overlooking Trg Bana Jelačića, is the best and most colourful place to shop for mostly organic veggies, as well as souvenirs.

For an evening of food and drink in a typical central European beer hall, visit **Pivnica Medvedgrad**, Božidara Adžije 16. Try *rezano*, a half-dark and half-light beer on tap.

SPLIT

Split's old core is built around the remains of **Diocletian's Palace**, constructed 2,000 years ago for the Roman emperor's retirement. The waterfront **Riva** buzzes all day with a string of pavement cafés. The traffic-free Old Town consists of narrow paved alleys, opening out onto ancient piazzas. From here the tourist

TROGIR

The UNESCO World Heritage-listed city of Trogir lies a short bus ride west from Split. Wander around the narrow cobbled streets, stopping off at the cathedral and the Kamerlengo Fortress. The waterfront fills at night with pavement cafés and seafood restaurants in summer and there are regular boat excursions to the nearby islands.
🅸 **Tourist office**: Trg Ivana Pavla II 1, ☎ 021 881 412 (www.trogir.org).

office's self-guided walk leads through town; a series of information boards highlight Split's Roman roots, the **Cathedral of St Duje**, and the various buildings dating back to periods of Venetian and Austro-Hungarian domination. Climb the cathedral bell tower for fine views.

Continue through the area of **Varoš**, where steep winding steps take you to the wooded Marjan peninsula. Split's best museums are the **Museum of Croatian Archaeological Monuments** and the **Meštrović Gallery**, both in Šetalište Ivana Meštrovića. Ivan Meštrović was a Split-born sculptor whose work can be seen all over the country and overseas, with one of the most striking examples the hulking statue of Grgur of Nin on the northern edge of Diocletian's Palace.

ARRIVAL, INFORMATION, ACCOMMODATION

🛳 The train station, bus station and ferry port are all next to each other, overlooking Gradska Luka, the town harbour. Left luggage; supermarket. The historic centre is just 100 m away. ✈ **Split Airport**, ☎ 021 203 5555 (www.split-airport.hr), 25 km from Split, 6 km from Trogir. Buses to and from Split every 20 mins. 🅸 **Tourist office**: Peristil 1, ☎ 021 345 606 (www.visitsplit.com), situated close to the seafront (or Riva).

🛏 Well-located and at a reasonable price, **Vila Gold**, Matosiceva 19, ☎ 021 345 286 (www.split-vila-gold.hr), offers rooms (€€) and apartments (€€€). Right in the centre of the Old Town, **Al's Place**, Kruziceva 10, ☎ 098 918 2923 (www.hostelsplit.com), is a friendly backpackers hostel, just 10 mins from the train station. The **Tschaikovsky Hostel**, Ulica Petra Iliča Čajkovskog 4, ☎ 99 195 0444 (www.tchaikovskyhostel.com), opened in 2011 and is a 20-min walk from the train station and ferry port.

🍴 Simple eating places offer a fixed menu at budget prices. For typical Dalmatian food join the locals at **Kod Jose**, Sredmanuska 4, behind the market, or **Kod Fife**, Trumbićeva obala 11. For a cheap stand-up lunch with locals try *ribice*, tiny fishes deep fried and served with a glass of red wine, in a canteen-style establishment opposite the fish market (**Ribarnica**), Kraj Sv. Marije 8. Get ultra-fresh fruit and veg and local smoked cheeses at **Stari Pazar**, the colourful open-air green market held just outside the main walls, Mon–Sat 0800–1400, Sun 0800–1100.

THE ISLANDS OF CROATIA

The onward journey from Split to Dubrovnik is a stunning journey on a ship that weaves it way between some of Croatia's most beautiful islands. In summer, frequent services allow easy island hopping. The **Jadrolinija** (www.jadrolinija.hr) fast service from Split to Dubrovnik (ERT 2855) takes 8 to 10 hrs, always stopping en route at Korčula and usually also at either Stari Grad (on the island of Hvar) or at Sobra (on the island of Mljet). The direct bus from Split to Dubrovnik (ERT 1325) is faster than the ship but no cheaper. We strongly recommend the sea route. If you do take the bus, though, note that the road route traverses a little finger of Bosnian territory at Neum.

If you want to break your journey between Split and Dubrovnik, **Hvar** is the obvious choice. This island is awash with lavender, other wild herbs and flowers, with the highlight the impressive Venetian settlement of **Hvar Town**. The waterfront buzzes all summer long with holidaying Italians, outdoor concerts and clubs. A few ferries from Split service the waterfront in Hvar Town directly, but most of the larger Jadrolinija boats call at **Stari Grad**, where buses transfer passengers over to Hvar Town. ☑ **Tourist office**: Arsenal, Trg Sveti Stjepana, ☎ 021 741 059.

Dubrovnik

Dubrovnik is one of the most impressive medieval fortified cities on the Mediterranean. The best way to get a feel of the place is to walk the full 2 km circuit of the walls (open summer 0900–1930, winter 1000–1500), but do avoid the hottest hours, especially if you've sampled Dubrovnik's atmosphere to the full the night before. For centuries Dubrovnik was a refined and prosperous trading port, which managed to keep its independence by paying off various would-be conquerors. Buildings such as the **Rector's Palace**, the **Sponza Palace** and **Jesuit Church** still bear witness to this glorious past. There's a major festival, mid-July to mid-Aug, with outdoor theatre, jazz and classical music.

ARRIVAL, INFORMATION, ACCOMMODATION

🚌 Put Republike 19, 24 hr left luggage. ✈ **Dubrovnik Airport** is 20 km south of Dubrovnik and 5 km from Cavtat, 30 mins by bus. ⛴ **Gruž Port**, Gruška obala, the Jadrolinija coastal service ☎ 020 418 000, runs Split–Dubrovnik, twice per week, journey time 7–10 hrs depending on stops, Kn115. ☑ **Tourist office**: Brsalje 5, ☎ 020 312 011 (www.tzdubrovnik.hr). **Internet** access is available at Black Jack in Stari Grad and Dubrovnik internet centre, Pile (next to the tourist office).

🛏 A lovely spot in Lapad, with great views from the terrace, is the **Begovic Boarding House**, Primorska 17, ☎ 020 435 191 (www.begovic-boarding-house.com), €–€€, which offers dorms, doubles and apartments. Free pickup from the ferry terminal and the bus station.

✗ Try along Prijeko, parallel to the central street, Placa, the main area for eating out within the city walls. **Lokanda Peskarija**, Na Ponti (next to town harbour fish market) offers simple but finger-licking seafood fare at surprisingly moderate prices. For the cheapest beer in summer months contact the friendly lads with a fridge under Porporela lighthouse, on Old Town pier.

Comb the various online travel forums that focus on Adriatic travel and there is one question that recurs with unfailing regularity: "How do I get from Dubrovnik to Greece without going through Albania?" And of course the travel pundits who haunt those virtual communities give all the right advice. There are direct boats from Dubrovnik to Bari (ERT 2795), from where there is an onward ship to Greece (ERT 2755) serving Kérkira (Corfu), Igoumenitsa (in the Thesprotia area of north-west Greece) and Pátra (in the northern Peloponnese, about 200 km west of Athens). But few on those online forums query why one would ever want to avoid Albania. True, a couple of days making an Adriatic dog-leg to reach Greece by ship from Dubrovnik would surely be very relaxing. But to skip Albania (and for that matter Montenegro too) is to miss two of Europe's most intriguing countries.

There are 5 to 8 buses daily (according to season) from Dubrovnik to Montenegro, all serving **Herceg Novi**, and some continuing beyond. Montenegro certainly deserves a few days. Highlights include the lovely **Bay of Kotor**, a great fjord surrounded by high mountains, and the mountain town of **Cetinje** (Цетињ), which flourished in the late 19th century as the capital and principal centre of Montenegrin culture. It is not for nothing that many Montenegrins still refer to Cetinje as the honorary capital of their country, which naturally irks folk in **Podgorica** (Подгорица), the rather drab valley town that now officially serves as capital city. Bus services around Montenegro are extremely reliable, and you can check schedules for principal routes at www.autobusni-kolodvor.com. Although Montenegro has no direct rail links along the coast with either Croatia or Albania, there is a good train service from Bar on the coast via Podgorica to Belgrade (ERT 1370). This is an exceptionally beautiful route that skirts wild canyons and boasts, in the truss bridge over the Mala Rijeka, the highest **railway viaduct** in Europe.

Ulcinj (Улцињ), the southernmost coastal town in Montenegro (reached by one daily direct bus from Dubrovnik, leaving the Croatian city at 1030 each morning) is the best jumping-off point for Albania. There is a morning bus at 0600 from Ulcinj across the border to **Shkodër**, from where regular minibuses (locally called a *furgon*) run to the capital **Tirana**. The *furgon* is the mainstay of inter-urban transport in Albania, but you should not miss the chance to sample Albanian trains. Don't expect great comfort, but you'll be in for a memorable treat (schedules in ERT 1390).

Albania's famously antiquated trains are a great way of getting around the country, but they are of no help in crossing the borders. Not a single train service links Albania with its neighbours. From Tirana there are direct buses to Athens and Skopje, giving connections onto **Routes 41** and **43** respectively. If the thought of a long international bus journey does not appeal try the ferry from **Saranda** to **Corfu** (schedules at www.ionian-cruises.gr; click on 'lines'). In 2011, this service ran May to Oct every afternoon except Mon, with a pricey one-way fare of €19 for the 75-min crossing. There are also ferries from **Durrës** to Bari in Italy. One creative option is to take a train from Tirana to **Pogradec** (at 7 hrs 30 mins, with a change of train in Durrës), from where it is just 1 hr by minibus to Ohrid (Охрид) in Macedonia.

Rail Route 39: Through Habsburg Europe

CITIES: ★★ CULTURE: ★★ HISTORY: ★★★ SCENERY: ★★
COUNTRIES COVERED: AUSTRIA, SLOVENIA, CROATIA

Salzburg and **Osijek**, the two end points of this route might seem at first sight to have little in common, yet both were once cities that marked the extremities of the Austro-Hungarian Empire, presided over by Habsburg monarchs. Osijek's Hapsburg pedigree dates back to the late 17th century, while Salzburg, having enjoyed spells of independence and suffered annexation by the neighbouring Kingdom of Bavaria, only became definitely part of Austria-Hungary in 1866.

History does not always make a sound basis for exploring the contemporary world, but Route 39 is an exception. On the face of it, our journey takes in places that are extraordinarily varied, but there is a Habsburg theme to our meandering through Austro-Hungarian crown lands and territories, including Carinthia, Carniola and Slavonia.

Along the way there are two capital cities, Ljubljana and Zagreb, and some remarkable scenery. The **Julian Alps** of northern Slovenia are the high point and we include an optional alternative along the remote branch line that takes in the best of Slovenia's mountain landscapes. And the great thing about this route is that, if you tire of Habsburg history, there are rich opportunities for diving off and connecting onto other routes. There are connections with **Route 38** at both **Ljubljana** and **Zagreb**. From **Rijeka**, there are excellent boat connections, in particular the Jadrolinija service (ERT 2855) which hops south along the Croatian coast to Split and Dubrovnik, with occasional services then continuing across the Adriatic to Bari in Italy (ERT 2795).

SALZBURG — SEE P282

The rail route south follows the Salzach Valley before cutting through the **Tauern Tunnel** to reach Austria's southernmost province of Kärnten (Carinthia), a part of the country that has a Slovene-speaking minority. After **Villach**, the railway tunnels under the Karawanken Alps to reach **Jesenice**, the first stop in Slovenia. Don't be put off by the monstrously ugly railway station and the pollution of the nearby metal smelters. Slovenia gets better! At Jesenice, you can connect onto the branch railway to Sežana (ERT 1302).

BLED

Though popular with visitors, **Lake Bled** in the Julian Alps and on the edge of the Triglav National Park is one of the most stunning stretches of water in Europe. Take lakeside walks, laze on the beaches or hire a rowing boat. In winter you can skate on the lake and there's plenty of skiing in the surrounding hills.

Notes

If you can possibly spare the time, we strongly recommend the alternative route (shown as a dotted line on the map below) from Bled to Pivka via Nova Gorica and Sežana, even if it means doubling back to take in Ljubljana. On some journeys from Bled Jezero to Sežana, a change of train is necessary at Nova Gorica. From Nova Gorica you can, if you wish, easily cross the border into Italy. The town effectively spans the frontier and it is 3 km from Nova Gorica to Gorizia Centrale station, for direct trains to both Trieste and Venice (ERT 601).

ROUTE DETAILS

Salzburg–Lesce Bled	ERT 1300	
Type	Frequency	Typical journey time
Train	3 daily	3h40

Lesce Bled–Ljubljana	ERT 1300	
Type	Frequency	Typical journey time
Train	12–17 daily	45 mins to 1 hr

Ljubljana–Rijeka	ERT 1305	
Type	Frequency	Typical journey time
Train	2 daily	2h45

Rijeka–Zagreb	ERT 1310	
Type	Frequency	Typical journey time
Train	3 daily	4 hrs

Zagreb–Osijek	ERT 1340	
Type	Frequency	Typical journey time
Train	4 daily	4h30

Bled Jezero–Sežana	ERT 1302	
Type	Frequency	Typical journey time
Train	Up to 4 daily	3h45

Sežana–Ljubljana	ERT 1305	
Type	Frequency	Typical journey time
Train	Up to 9 daily	1h50

KEY JOURNEYS

Salzburg–Ljubljana	ERT 1300	
Type	Frequency	Typical journey time
Train	3 daily	4h20

Ljubljana–Zagreb	ERT 1300	
Type	Frequency	Typical journey time
Train	7 daily	2h20

≈ Main station **Lesce-Bled**, 4 km east of the town of Bled. Frequent buses. **❸ Tourist office**: Cesta Svobode 15, ☎ 04 574 1122 (www.bled.si). ⋈ There are plenty of options in town, including **Penzion Mayer**, Želeška Cesta 7, ☎ 04 576 5740 (www.mayer-sp.si), €€, and the good value **Garni Penzion Berc,** Želeška Cesta 15, ☎ 04 574 1838 (www.berc-sp.si), €. There is an excellent **Youth Hostel** (HI), Grajska Cesta 17, ☎ 04 574 5250 (www.youth-hostel.si), just a five-minute walk from the lake, or try the **Traveller's Haven Hostel**, Riklijeva Cesta 1, ☎ 04 139 6545 (www.travellers-haven.si).

✗ There are a variety of restaurants in Bled centre, including a number of cheap and cheerful pizza places. Food is also available in summer on the outdoor terraces of local pubs.

LJUBLJANA — SEE P323

RIJEKA

This major ferry port is something of an industrial eyesore, but it does have an impressive Austro-Hungarian-era core, complete with grand 19th-century architecture and pavement cafés. **Trsat Castle** offers sweeping views of the city and the Adriatic stretching out below. The heart of the city is along the Korzo, with its shops, restaurants and cafés. Down by the waterfront a sprinkling of bars buzz on late into the night. Rijeka trades on its ambiguously international past. Within the last 100 years it has been part of Austria-Hungary, Italy, Yugoslavia and now Croatia. From 1920 to 1924 it enjoyed a spell of independence as the major city of the Free State of Fiume.

ARRIVAL, INFORMATION, ACCOMMODATION

≈ The main railway station is west of the centre. ➔ **Rijeka Airport** (served by easyJet) is 30 mins by city bus every two and a half hours before flight departure. **❸ Tourist office**: Korzo 33, ☎ 051 335 882 (www.tz-rijeka.hr).

⋈ Budget options are limited; ask at the tourist office about **private rooms.** The **Hotel Continental**, Šetalište Andrije Kačića Miošića 1, ☎ 051 372 009 (www.jadran-hoteli.hr), €€–€€€, is well-located but pricey. The **Hostel Rijeka** (HI), is on Šetalište XIII. divizije 23, ☎ 051 406 420 (www.hfhs.hr). ✗ The cafés on the Korzo serve snacks and salads, while there are pizzerias and fast-food outlets along its length.

CONNECTIONS FROM RIJEKA

Visit **Postojna** (1 hr 30 mins, ERT 1305, on the line between Rijeka and Ljubljana) to see the spectacular **Postojna Cave**, one of the largest cave systems in the world, with 23 km of underground passages adorned with stalactites and stalagmites. It's a 2-km walk from Postojna station. A **miniature railway** guides visitors through the chambers, where temperatures average 8°C the year through (woollen cloaks are available for hire at the entrance). Don't miss the 'human fish', a family of eyeless and colourless amphibians unique to the caves. Tours leave half-hourly in summer, hourly the rest of

INTO THE MOUNTAINS

From Bled, Route 39 follows the Sava Valley downstream to Ljubjlana. But there is an intriguing alternative. You can travel south-west through the mountains and rejoin Route 39 at **Rijeka**. The stretch from **Bled Jezero** to **Nova Gorica** (1 hr 40 mins, ERT 1302) is Slovenia's most scenic mountain rail route. The line leaves the main line at Jesenice and serves Bled Jezero, Bled's second railway station, which is a grand Swiss-Alpine-hut-style structure reached by footpath from the north-west of the lake. The railway runs via **Most na Soči** on its way to the modern city of Nova Gorica. The best of the scenery is the hour either side of Most na Soći. With half a dozen trains in each direction Mon–Fri (fewer at weekends), day trips are possible on this dramatic route past the craggy peaks, lakes and gorges of the Julian Alps. You can continue on through Nova Gorica (a town straddling the Italian border) to Sežana (also ERT 1302), from where you can travel east to Ljubljana (ERT 1305) or, if you are prepared to skip the Slovenian capital, to Rijeka to rejoin Route 39 there. The latter requires a further change of train at Pivka (also in ERT 1305).

the year. The **Postojna Blues Festival** takes place at the entrance during spring months. 🛈 **Tourist information**: Postojnska Jama Turizem, Janska Cesta 30, ☎ 05 700 0100 (www.postojnska-jama.si).

KARLOVAC

Trains run frequently through Karlovac and yet few travellers get out here. This often-overlooked city is tucked in the dividing line between the mountains to the south and the **Zagreb plains** to the north and has good road and rail connections to the capital. Karlovac, the town on four rivers, was a pivotal stronghold for the Austro-Hungarians in their battles with the **Ottoman Empire** and the sturdy fortress that makes up the Old Town is a legacy of those days. In the 1990s the hastily assembled Croatian forces managed to halt heavily armed Serb forces from advancing on to Zagreb, but war damage at the heart of Karlovac has now largely been repaired.

ARRIVAL, INFORMATION, ACCOMMODATION

🚆 Vilima Reinera 3, a 15-min walk from the city centre. 🛈 **Tourist office**: Petra Zrinskog 3, ☎ 047 600 606 (www.karlovac-touristinfo.hr). **Internet access:** VIP centre shop, Gundulićeva 8, and Knjižnica za mlade (Youth library), Banjačićeva 8. 🛏 **Private rooms** (*sobe*) are available through the tourist office, or try the **Hotel Carlstadt**, Vraniczanyeva 1, ☎ 047 611 111 (www.carlstadt.hr), €€. 🍴 There are several good riverside eateries, especially on Camp Korana.

CONNECTIONS FROM KARLOVAC

Turanj (15-min bus ride south) is a small town that was the scene of the dramatic resistance of Croatian defence forces during the Homeland War in the 1990s. Today an open-air war museum dedicated to the events of 1991–95 is sited there. On show is a motley collection of military hardware including a poignant bullet-riddled old tractor that was converted into an armoured vehicle in those desperate days. Across the road from the museum a simple marble memorial remembers the dead.

ZAGREB — SEE P325

OSIJEK

Until the 1990s the largest city in the region of Slavonia, Osijek was a thriving, cosmopolitan hub, but by 1991 it was a city under siege, holding out against the Yugoslav Army and Serbian volunteers. Today, peace has returned and Osijek is recovering some of its lustre with cafés and bars along the Drava River buzzing again and many of the damaged buildings repaired. Osijek's centre is dominated by the river, the voluminous spires of the **Church of St Peter and St Paul** and the ornate fin de siècle buildings that line the grand **Europska Avenija**. Continue along this thoroughfare to **Tvrđa**, an 18th-century fortress built by the Austro-Hungarians to keep out the Ottoman threat.

ARRIVAL, INFORMATION, ACCOMMODATION

⇆ Bartul Kašića. ✈ **Osijek Airport** is 20 km from central Osijek. The airport bus operated by Taxi Cammeo leaves from Trg Lavoslava Ružičke (outside the railway station). For times check www.osijek-airport.hr or ☎ 031 205 205. 🅸 **Tourist office**: Turistička Zajednica, Županijska 2, ☎ 031 203 755 (www.tzosijek.hr). **Internet**: VIP internet café, L. Jeagera 24, ☎ 031 212 313.

🛏 Very limited budget options; best bet are **private rooms** (*sobe*), booked through the tourist office. Mid-range hotel **Central**, Trg Ante Starčevića 6, ☎ 031 281 399 (www.hotel-central-os.hr), €€, while not quite lush, is very central indeed. The **Tufna Hostel**, Franje Kuhaca 10, ☎ 031 215 020 (www.tufna.hr), has good-value dorm beds, as well as an in-house bar and club. ✕ Down by the Drava River is the pinnacle of summer action with a floating pizzeria and a string of bars. For a traditional fill don't miss local speciality *fiš paprikas* (a spicy fish stew), or a *meze* of smoked meats that includes the renowned Slavonian spicy smoked salami, *kulen*.

CONNECTIONS FROM OSIJEK

In 1991 **Vukovar** (40 mins by bus from Osijek or direct daily train from Zagreb, ERT 1320) was a charming baroque town with a mixed Serb and Croat population. Then came the most brutal siege of the war when the Yugoslav Army and Serb militia subjected Vukovar to months of shelling and infantry attacks that cost the life of up to 2,000 citizens and defending forces, with around the same number of people still listed as 'missing'. Today the town, its **war cemetery** and the **massacre site** on Vukovar's outskirts provide a painfully vivid picture of what happened, and are essential stops for anyone with an interest in the most savage conflict in Europe since World War II. For tourist information ask at the Hotel Dunav on the waterfront.

Rail Route 40: The slow route to Istanbul

CITIES: ★★ CULTURE: ★★ HISTORY: ★★ SCENERY: ★★
COUNTRIES COVERED: HUNGARY, ROMANIA, BULGARIA, TURKEY

Mention a train journey through the **Balkans** to **Istanbul** and people's thoughts will immediately turn to the *Orient Express*, the uncrowned Queen of European trains which, even in its heyday, was nowhere near as smart as film-makers might have you believe. Not since 1962 has the *Orient Express* run through from Budapest to Istanbul and, even when it did still connect the two cities, it took a rather different route from that we describe here. So forget any idea of dowager duchesses dining in mahogany-panelled restaurant cars decorated with lace curtains and crystal chandeliers. Route 40 is for travellers with no pretensions to grandeur and who don't mind enduring a little grit and grime along the way. True, it helps to have a spark of romantic adventure in your soul as we travel through **Transylvania**, cross the **Danube** and eventually ride through **Thrace** on our way to the shores of the Bosphorus.

At over 1,700 km, this is the second longest route in this book. Only **Route 45** is longer. If you are prepared to travel virtually non-stop, you can complete the entire journey in just 36 hrs, using the *Ister* overnight train from **Budapest** to **Bucharest**, and changing there onto the *Bosphor* to Istanbul. Two consecutive nights on trains may not be the best way to see the Balkans. And go prepared, for although there is a restaurant car on the *Ister*, south of Bucharest you'll need to have your own provisions. An alternative one-change connection is available from Budapest to Istanbul, travelling via **Belgrade** and **Sofia** rather than Romania, which clips a little off the journey time (see key journey details on p336).

Our view is that you could easily spin Route 40 out to a week, stopping off in Transylvania and then visiting Bucharest before heading south and making overnight stops here and there in Bulgaria.

BUDAPEST — SEE P465

The journey across Hungary crosses the **Alföld**, which means simply plain. It is a word that accurately describes this two-dimensional landscape. The first hints of serious relief are not till after the Romanian border. The first town in Romania will be either **Arad** or Oradea. The routing of trains from Hungary to Romania varies, and our map for Route 40 shows the route via **Oradea**. That via Arad is slightly further south. At either Arad or Oradea, you can connect on **Route 50**, which meanders north-east through the hill country of northern Romania and enters Ukraine.

The first two recommended stops on this route are both in Transylvania, a region of **Romania** that was irrevocably defined in the European and American psyche by Bram Stoker with his 1897 novel *Dracula* and the subsequent efforts of

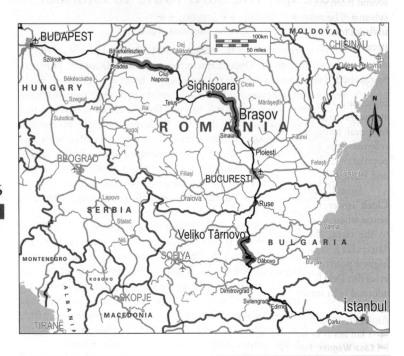

KEY JOURNEYS

Budapest–Bucharest   ERT 1280

Type	Frequency	Typical journey time
Train	2–3 daily	14–16 hrs

Budapest–Istanbul   ERT 61

Type	Frequency	Typical journey time
Train	1 daily	36 hrs (via Bucharest)
Train	1 daily	32 hrs (via Sofia)

Notes

Some direct trains from Budapest to central Romania cross the Hungarian-Romanian border further south and travel via Arad. Journey times are similar via both routes.

ROUTE DETAILS

Budapest–Sighişoara   ERT 1600

Type	Frequency	Typical journey time
Train	3 daily	11 hrs

Sighişoara–Braşov   ERT 1600

Type	Frequency	Typical journey time
Train	9–11 daily	2h15

Braşov–Bucharest   ERT 1600

Type	Frequency	Typical journey time
Train	11–13 daily	3 hrs

Bucharest–Veliko Târnovo   ERT 61, 1525

Type	Frequency	Typical journey time
Train	1 daily	5h50

Veliko Târnovo–Istanbul   ERT 1525, 1550

Type	Frequency	Typical journey time
Train	1 daily	13h45

several Hollywood directors. Just remember that Stoker never once visited Transylvania. The only vampires likely to attack you nowadays are entrepreneurs keen to fleece tourists by invoking many spurious and a few credible Dracula connections.

SIGHIŞOARA

Sighişoara is a wonderful Transylvanian town with winding streets, covered stairways and breathtaking architecture against a backdrop of spectacular medieval fortifications. It was settled by ethnic Germans, hereabouts often referred to as Saxons, from the 12th century. There is a tiny residual German population today, much outnumbered by other ethnic minorities such as Roma and Hungarians. The latter call their hometown **Segesvár**.

From the commercial centre, you enter the Old Town by the 14th-century **Clock Tower**, now a history museum (closed Mon). Beyond this is an ancient house where Vlad the Impaler (aka Dracula) was reputedly born about 1431, and to the right, the 15th-century church of the **Dominican Monastery**, Piața Muzeului 8, famous for its bronze baptismal fonts dating back to 1440. At the highest point of the citadel and reached by a roofed wooden stairway is the **Biserica din Deal** (Church on the Hill), Str. Scolii 7, built in Gothic style 1345–1525 and adorned with some remarkable frescos.

ARRIVAL, INFORMATION, ACCOMMODATION

≋ 1 km north of the centre. 🚺 **Tourist office**: Octavian Goga 8, ☎ 0265 770 415. ⊨ **Casa Wagner**, Piața Cetății 7, ☎ 0265 506 014 (www.casa-wagner.com), €€, up in the medieval city, is the most popular place in town: reserve well in advance. A cheaper pension, **Casa Saseasca**, Piața Cetății 12, ☎ 0265 772 400 (www.casasaseasca.com), €–€€, on the other side of the square, is just as good. Cheaper still are pensions in the lower town: the **Hera**, Str. Eminescu 62, ☎ 0265 778 850 (www.pensiunea-hera.ro), €, has both 2- and 1-star rooms. **Hostels: Nathan's Villa Hostel**, Str. Libertatii 8, ☎ 0265 772 546 (www.nathansvilla.com), is 250 m west of the station and slightly better than the **Burg Hostel** (HI), Strada Bastionului 4–6, ☎ 0265 778 489 (www.burghostel.ro), in the medieval city.

BRAŞOV

Baroque buildings dominate much of the beautiful centre of Braşov, another very fine Transylvanian city, while imposing gates guard the road into the Schei quarter to the south-west, where once the local Romanian population lived. Until the late 17th century, they were barred from living within the city proper, which was the preserve of the ethnic German population. In central Piața Sfatului (Council Square) stands the old **Town Hall**, now the local **History Museum** (closed Mon); from its tower trumpeters sounded the warning of

AROUND BRAŞOV

It is an easy 40-min bus ride from Braşov to **Bran Castle**, south-west of the city. The castle was built by German settlers, but comes in handy for the local tourism authorities as a key prop in the Dracula story, although the building's link with Vlad the Impaler is tenuous. But Bran is nonetheless worth a visit, for the wild setting makes this the prototypical Transylvanian castle.

Immediately south from Braşov, Route 40 cuts through the hills and the railway gives easy access to ski resorts. All trains stop at **Predeal** and Sinaia, respectively 30 and 60 mins south from Braşov. Predeal is all very low key and hardly worth the stop. But **Sinaia** is something special, a gracious old-style mountain resort, set in a gorgeous location on the eastern flank of the Bucegi Mountains. It makes a very good rural stopover for a day or two. ⇝ It's a stiff climb up the steps from the station into town. ⊨ The **Cerbul**, B-dul Carol I 19, ☎ 0244 310 290 (www.cerbul.ro), €, and the **Intim**, Str. Furnica 1, ☎ 0244 315 555, €, are both acceptable, if rather plain, hotels. Don't miss Sinaia's two set-piece attractions, **Peleş Castle** (closed Mon) and **Pelişor Palace** (closed Mon and Tues).

impending attack, by Tatars or Turks, for many centuries. Nearby, the **Biserica Neagra** (Black Church, closed Sun) overshadows the same square with its Gothic pinnacles. Dating from the 14th century, this is one of the greatest monuments of Transylvania's Saxon (German) community, and displays historic prints and fine carpets brought by merchants from Turkey. You can get great views of the city and surrounding mountains from the summit of **Mt Tâmpa**, reached by a cable car or by footpaths; the base of the hill is fortified with a wall and bastions.

ARRIVAL, INFORMATION, ACCOMMODATION

⇝ Blvd Gării 5, about 2 km north-east of the Old Town. 🚋 4 runs from the station to Piaţa Livada Poştei on the edge of the Old Town. **Wasteels**, at the station, ☎ 0268 424 313, sell rail tickets for even the most complicated itineraries (Mon–Fri 0800–1900, Sat 0800–1400). 🛈 **Tourist information**: Centrul de Informare Turistica Brasov, Piaţa Sfatului 30 (inside History Museum), ☎ 0268 419 078 (www.brasovtourism.com).

⊨ The cheapest sleep in central Braşov is the 1-star **Aro Sport**, Str. Muresenilor 12, ☎ 0268 477 664, €, while the **Postavarul**, Republicii 62, ☎ 0268 477 448, €, is better located but a little more expensive; enter through the grander Coroana (www.aro-palace.ro for both hotels). The best hostel is the **Kismet Dao**, which moved in early 2011 to its new location in Braşov's historic centre, Str. Neagoe Basarab 8, ☎ 0268 514 296 (www.kismetdao.com). **Hostel Mara** (HI), Piaţa Sfatului 11, ☎ 0746 968 216 (www.hostelbrasov.ro), is right on the central square.

BUCHAREST (BUCUREŞTI)

Bucharest was once known as 'The Paris of Eastern Europe', for its decadent lifestyle and for the elegant mansions lining its 19th-century **boulevards**.

However, the city has been vandalised over the years by successive generations of planners. Perversely for many people, the city's main sight is the so-called **People's Palace**, now officially known as the Palace of Parliament, a huge edifice whose construction required the demolition of a quarter of the city's historic centre. B-dul Unirii, lined with fountains and trees, leads from Piaţa Unirii (hub of the metro system), which offers the major vista of the Palace. Tours of the interior start from the south door (daily 1000–1600); these pass through a succession of grandiose public halls with chandeliers, marble and mirrors. The construction costs almost bankrupted the country. One wing contains Bucharest's newest museum, the **National Museum of Contemporary Art**, or MNAC, displaying works by Romania's contemporary artists (closed Mon & Tues). Most other sights are along Calea Victoriei, the historic north-south axis, which is also lined by smart shops. Near its mid-point is Piaţa Revoluţiei, scene of the most dramatic events of Ceauçescu's overthrow during Christmas 1989; here the **Atheneum** concert hall faces the former Royal Palace, now the **National Art Museum** (closed Mon & Tues). To the south along Calea Victoriei is the **National History Museum** (closed Mon & Tues), which houses Romania's finest archaeological collection and National Treasury. To the north of Piaţa Revoluţiei are the **Peasant Museum** (closed Mon) which has the city's best souvenir shop, the **Art Collection Museum** (closed Mon & Tues) and the **George Enescu Museum** (closed Mon).

The **Bucharest History and Art Museum** (closed Mon), housed in the 19th-century Sutu Palace on Piaţa Universitatii, forges some links with the legend of Dracula, in fact the local prince **Vlad Tepeş** (Vlad the Impaler). Angry protests in June 1990 against the hijacking of the 1989 revolution by the functionaries of the communist regime were centred on Piaţa Universitatii. You can still see political graffiti here, as well as memorials to those killed in both the revolution and the aftermath. To the west of the city in a pleasant leafy suburb is **Cotroceni Palace**, home of the president of Romania. There is a medieval art collection here (closed Mon). Bucharest has a large number of pleasant parks: to the north in the largest, Herăstrău Park, is the open-air **Village Museum**, Sos. Kiseleff 28–30, open daily. This fascinating collection of re-erected buildings brought from all over the country includes churches, houses, watermills and windmills. Elsewhere, the quintes-sential Bucharest experience is to walk through the **Lipscani** district north of Piaţa Unirii, visiting the tiny 15th- and 16th-century Romanian Orthodox churches.

ARRIVAL, INFORMATION, ACCOMMODATION
≋ Virtually all trains use the **Gară de Nord**, 2 km north-west of the city centre on Calea Griviţei. This is chaotic, crowded and a place to keep a careful eye on your luggage and your pockets. It is served by the metro (*metrou*), although you'll have to change trains to reach the city centre. Other stations are mostly for local or seasonal trains. **Tickets** can also be purchased up to 24 hrs in advance at **Agenţia de Voiaj**

SNCFR, Str. Ion Brezoianu, ☎ 021 313 2644 (closed Sun). ✈ **Henri Coanda Airport**, ☎ 021 204 1000, 19 km north of the centre, handles almost all international flights. 🚌 783 takes you to the city centre (Piața Unirii) every 15 mins (30 mins at weekends), costing about €1 and taking 45 mins. ✈ **Baneasa Airport**, 6 km north of the centre, handles Bucharest's budget airline traffic. 🚌 131 runs every 10 mins to Piața Romana. A standard Bucharest transport ticket is all you need.

ℹ There is a **tourist information office** at the Gară de Nord, but it offers little beyond very simple maps and promotional flyers. Free wi-fi is available in and around Piața Universității as well as in most cafés, bars and restaurants. The **metro** (0500–2330) is efficient and fast, linking central Bucharest to the **Gară de Nord** and the suburbs. There are three main lines and most city maps carry a metro plan. **Magnetic tickets** (for a minimum of two trips) must be bought as you enter a station and passed through a turnstile; there are also better-value 10-trip and day tickets.

Buses, trams and **trolleybuses** run throughout the city, although it can be hard to work out their routes, as maps are rare. They are run-down and crowded, but very cheap. Buy any number of tickets before boarding from the grey aluminium kiosks by most stops. Express buses, including those to the airports, require special magnetic tickets. **Taxis** are plentiful and inexpensive. Just make sure you get in one displaying its tariffs on the driver's door and always make sure the meter is running. There is no central reservation agency so try to book accommodation before you arrive in Bucharest. You may be offered space in a hostel and a free lift by a tout at the Gară de Nord: always ignore them. No hostels send personnel to the station.

🛏 Budget hotel options in Bucharest have all but disappeared and are now limited to the excellent, cheap 2-star **Hello Hotel**, Calea Grivitei 143, ☎ 037 2121 800 (www.hellohotels.ro), €, next to the slightly more expensive **Ibis**, €€, across the road from the station. Also close to the station is **Coco's**, Str. Dinicu Golescu 29, ☎ 021 311 0535, €. **Hostels** are a growing business in Bucharest. Some worth checking out are: **Butterfly Villa Hostel**, Str. Dumitru Zosima 82, ☎ 0747 032 644 (www.villabutterfly.com), the **East Hostel**, Sfintii Voievozi 1, ☎ 0721 099 328, and the **Midland Youth Hostel**, B-dul Regina Elisabeta 30, ☎ 021 317 0362 (www.themidlandhostel.com). ✗ Eating well is not expensive in Bucharest, or you can opt for pizzas/hamburgers, or patisseries/cafés. **Panipat** is a chain of good if pricey takeaway bun shops (pizzas and pastries). The area around **Piața Universității** has several cafés frequented by students and young people.

CONNECTIONS FROM BUCHAREST

Bucharest is a major rail hub for the eastern Balkan region. There are direct trains to the Black Sea coast cities of **Constanța** (4 hrs) and **Mangalia** (6 hrs; both in ERT 1680), daily overnight services to **Chișinau**, capital of Moldova (ERT 1670), **Kiev** and **Moscow** (both in ERT 98) and also direct daytime and overnight trains to **Sofia** (ERT 61).

ACROSS THE DANUBE

It is a curiosity of Route 40 that you hardly see the Danube. Bridging the Danube between Romania and Bulgaria was quite a challenge for early **railway engineers**, and for many years rail travellers bound for Turkey from central Europe would travel by train to Constanţa, on the Black Sea coast of Romania, east of Bucharest, and then transfer to a ship for the final part of the journey. Today, trains rumble across the 2.8 km long **Danube Bridge** from Giurgiu in Romania to Ruse in Bulgaria. Route 40 then cuts a 380-km line across Bulgaria to the Turkish border at Svilengrad.

VELIKO TÂRNOVO (ВЕЛИКО ТЪРНОВО)

If you stop at just one place in Bulgaria en route to Istanbul, make it Veliko Târnovo, from 1185 to 1396 the seat of the Bulgarian Emperors, whose sway over the region was abruptly terminated by Ottoman invasion. No other community in Bulgaria so nicely captures the vicissitudes of Bulgarian history.

The town perches on hills about the tight and intricate meanders of the River Yantra. **Tsarevets Hill** (sometimes floodlit at night) has the restored ruins of the medieval citadel. Nearby are Byzantine churches and the **Samovodska Charshiya** (Bazaar), a photogenic area of restored workshops interspersed with modern jewellers, souvenir shops and cafés.

ARRIVAL, INFORMATION, ACCOMMODATION

≋ Neither the bus nor the rail station is central. 🚌 5/13 run from the train station to the centre. Trolleybuses 1/2 and 🚌 12 go from the bus terminal to the centre. Trains from Sofia to Varna stop at **Gorna Oryahovitsa** just 7 km north of Veliko Târnovo (eight local trains per day connect to the town), or take the shuttle bus to Gorna Oryahovitsa bus station from which 🚌 10 goes into town every 20 mins. 🚪 **Tourist office**: Hristo Botev str. 5, ☎ 062 622 148 (www.velikoturnovo.info), next to the Hotel Etar.

🛏 Often booked up, as the town is popular with Bulgarians. Possibilities include **Hotel Etar**, ul. Ivailo 2, ☎ 062 621 838 (www.hoteletar.com), €, or **Hotel Lucky**, ul. Nikola Pikolo 3, ☎ 062 651 224 (www.hotel-lucky.com), €. **Hostels**: There are also quite a few hostels in town. Two to try first are the **Nomad's Hostel**, ul. Gurko 27, ☎ 062 603 092 (www.nomadshostel.com) and the **Hostel Mostel**, ul. Iordan Indjeto 10, ☎ 0897 859 359 (www.hostelmostel.com).

DIMITROVGRAD (ДИМИТРОВГРАД)

This railway junction in south-east Bulgaria is an extraordinary place. It is a new town created in the 1950s as a showpiece socialist city. Since Bulgarian independence, it has fallen on hard times with high unemployment and a declining population. But the main public buildings from the 1950s are classics of their kind. Not worth the stop, you might think, but if you alight here to connect to **Route 41** (to Greece), do take an hour or two to look around.

ISTANBUL — SEE P496

For many travellers using this book, Istanbul will be the end of the line. It is one of those places where the map ends and there seems to be little choice but to turn back and retrace your steps towards home. But pause and think! Asia beckons. The railway tunnel under the Bosphorus will not be open for a few years yet, but why not take the ferry over to Asia? Head for the train station at **Haydarpaşa** (called **Haydarpaşa Garı** in Turkish) to get a whole new perspective on rail travel.

The station is one of the most magnificent buildings in the Greater Istanbul area. It deftly combines solid German architecture with Turkish interior design. Look for the beautiful gently voluted ceilings in some of the interior halls. And gaze at the departure boards listing such exotic trains as the *Eastern Express* to Kars or the *Van Gölü Express* to Tatvan. Both **Kars** and **Tatvan** are in the far east of Turkey. The journey to Kars, just under 2,000 km, takes 36 hours (ERT 1575).

Wednesday evening is the best time of the week to visit Haydarpaşa Garı, for it is then that Tahran is listed on the departure board. Tahran is the Turkish rendering of the Iranian capital **Tehran**, and at just a shade before midnight every Wednesday the *Transasya Express* leaves Haydarpaşa for Tehran (ERT 1575).

If ever you are tempted to hop aboard, make sure you have an Iranian visa, and pack a good book or two, for you'll not be in Tehran until late Saturday. Vita Sackville-West's *Passenger to Teheran* springs to mind as recommended reading, though Sackville-West's legendary journey to Persia was not on the train from Turkey. The one-way first-class fare from Haydarpaşa to Tehran is a snip at just €39.40. Not bad for a 66-hour journey. In addition, you'll need to pay a further €9.90 for a couchette.

For a spell in 2010, there was a direct rail link **between Turkey and Iraq**. True, you couldn't travel all the way from the Bosphorus to Baghdad. The train service was a once-weekly overnight train linking Gaziantep in south-east Anatolia (Turkey) with Mosul in northern Iraq. En route, the train crossed the Al-Qamishli district of north-east Syria. Sadly, it was withdrawn after just a few weeks with the train's promoters remarking that there just did not seem to be a lot of demand for rail travel to Iraq these days. *Quelle surprise!* But this route is one to watch for the future. With the continuing improvement of the security situation in Iraq, the **Gaziantep** to **Mosul** train would be a candidate for reinstatement. Until the invasion and occupation of Iraq in 2003, train connections between Turkey and Iraq were excellent, with regular services from Gaziantep to **Baghdad** and sometimes even through carriages from Haydarpaşa to Iraq.

Apart from the trains to Iraq which cut through Syria en route, Turkey still has other regular connections with Syria. The weekly direct service from **Haydarpaşa to Aleppo** has run intermittently and, although it was on hold in 2010 and 2011, it may (or indeed may not) resume in 2012.

Meanwhile, local trains connect Gaziantep with Aleppo in five hours, and a weekly overnight train provides a direct link from Mersin and Adana to Aleppo. In Aleppo there are good onward connections to **Damascus**. You will find schedules for journeys in this Sidetracks at www.seat61.com/Turkey2.htm or www.tcdd.gov.tr.

SIDETRACKS L: ONWARD TO ASIA

Rail Route 41: Northbound from Greece

CITIES: ★★ CULTURE: ★★ HISTORY: ★★★ SCENERY: ★★
COUNTRIES COVERED: GREECE, BULGARIA

Greek trains have improved enormously in recent years. That's the good news. Less welcome is **Greece's current isolation** from the rest of Europe's rail network. Unless the cross-border rail link from Thessaloniki north into Bulgaria is restored for 2012, you'll need to take a bus for that leg of the journey. Look for updates on www.europebyrail.eu. That little inconvenience apart, Route 41 is a lovely journey. You may wish to detour on the journey north through Greece to take in some of the country's landmark sites: **Delphi, Mt Olympus** and the monasteries at **Metéora**. There is some great scenery as you head north through Greece. Our favourite part is the stretch just north of Amfiklia (170 km from Athens), where the railway picks a route through the eastern foothills of Mt Gióni and Mt Iti and crosses the spectacular Gorgopotamos viaduct.

Beyond Greece's second city, Thessaloniki, the route enters **Bulgaria**. The Struma Valley, just north of the Greek border, followed by the bus route (and, if they resume in 2012, the trains too) is strikingly beautiful with fine views of the **Pirin and Rila Mountains**. Next stop is **Sofia**, capital of Bulgaria, before moving east to **Plovdiv**, Bulgaria's second city, and a place that many travellers find more appealing than Sofia. Route 41 then continues further east through the **Plain of Thrace**, but with the **Rhodopes Hills** defining the southern horizon, to provide a connection to **Route 40** (south to Istanbul and north to Budapest).

This 1,100 km long route is well worth following in its own right, but it is also a useful first leg for travellers returning from Greece to northern and western Europe by rail. Long gone are the days when you could board a train in Athens that would take you directly to Venice, Cologne or Moscow. But Route 41 connects at Thessaloniki with **Route 43** to Belgrade, whence an onward ribbon of routes described in this book will conduct you further north.

ATHENS — SEE P430

LIVADEIÁ (Λιβαδειά)

Overlooked by a **sandstone castle** tower, Livadeiá (Levadiá in ERT) is a common stopover for travellers bound for Delphi, 56 km to the west. In ancient times those heading to the Oracle at Delphi could stop at Levadia's Oracle of Zeus Trofonios on **Profitis Ilias**, one of the two hills overlooking the town.

ARRIVAL, INFORMATION, ACCOMMODATION

≥ 3 km from the centre, but taxis are available. ⊞ **Tourist office**: Diikitirio, ☎ 226 108 6336 (www.livadia.gr). ⋈ Accommodation is scarce. Two options are **Hotel Livadia**,

Note

Rail services across the Greek-Bulgarian border were suspended in 2011 and may not be restored for 2012. So a bus is recommended for the stretch from Thessaloniki to Sofia.

ROUTE DETAILS

Athens–Levadia   ERT 1400

Type	Frequency	Typical journey time
Train	10 daily	1h25

Levadia–Larissa   ERT 1400

Type	Frequency	Typical journey time
Train	8 daily	2h40

Larissa–Thessaloniki   ERT 1400

Type	Frequency	Typical journey time
Train	20 daily	1h20 to 1h35

Thessaloniki–Sofia

Type	Frequency	Typical journey time
Bus	2–4 daily	5–8 hrs

Sofia–Plovdiv   ERT 1500

Type	Frequency	Typical journey time
Train	11 daily	2h20

Plovdiv–Dimitrovgrad   ERT 1550

Type	Frequency	Typical journey time
Train	6 daily	1h50

KEY JOURNEYS

Athens–Thessaloniki   ERT 1400

Type	Frequency	Typical journey time
Train	7 daily	5h20

Sofia–Bucharest   ERT 61

Type	Frequency	Typical journey time
Train	2 daily	9h35

Delphi

Delphi (buses from Livadeiá and Athens) is synonymous with its Oracle, the greatest spiritual power in ancient Greece, said to be situated over the centre of the world (amusingly also referred to as the 'belly button of the world'). This belief was strengthened by leaking volcanic gases, which induced lightheadedness and trance-like stupors. People came from far and wide to seek wisdom; prophecies were given so ambiguously that they could never be proved wrong. The most dramatic aspect of the **Temple of Apollo** (the Oracle), however, is its location, perched on the slopes of **Mt Parnassus** and reached by the paved, zigzagging **Sacred Way**. Delphi is one of the largest remaining ancient sites in Greece, with a host of other ruins, notably a **Stadium** and an **Amphitheatre**.

Thousands of visitors make for Delphi, so come early (or out of season). **🛈 Tourist office**: Municipality of Delphi, ☎ 226 508 2900. ➽ Accommodation is a problem: in high season hotels and pensions are often full, while many of them are closed off season. The **Sibylla Hotel**, 9 Pavlou & Friderikis Str, ☎ 226 508 2335 (www.sibylla-hotel.gr), €€, is a friendly, low-cost, family-run hotel, just up from the tourist office, and has great views. Another good option on the same street is the **Hotel Fedriades**, 46 Pavlou & Friderikis Str, ☎ 226 508 2370 (www.fedriades.com), €€. Alternatively, stay in the pretty village of Arahova (11 km east of Delphi), which is a popular winter-ski resort where prices actually drop during summer.

4 Papaspyrou Ave, ☎ 226 102 3611, €€, or the **Hotel Erato**, 3rd km Avenue, ☎ 226 102 0351 (www.hotelerato.com), €€.

Lárisa (Λάρισα)

Lárisa is the starting point for some outstanding day trips.

Arrival, information, accommodation

➽ 1 km from the centre. **🛈 Tourist office**: GNTO, 18 Koumoundourou str, ☎ 241 250 919 (www.visitgreece.gr). ➽ **Hotel Dionissos**, 24 L. Katsoni, ☎ 241 023 0101 (www. dionissoshotel.gr), €€. If you fancy splashing out, the **Larissa Imperial**, 182 Farsalon str, ☎ 241 068 7600 (www.larissaimperial.com), €€€, offers five-star luxury.

Connections from Lárisa

Nine trains run daily from Lárisa to **Vólos** on a branch line, taking 50 mins (ERT 1425). Apart from the waterfront **Archaeological Museum** there's little of note in the ugly industrial port of Vólos, where Jason set sail in the *Argo* in search of the Golden Fleece. But the town is the main base from which to explore the lush forests and charming old villages of the mountainous **Pilion peninsula** to the east (best done by car, or take either of two bus routes from Volos); or you can take a ferry to the **Sporades Islands** (of which **Skiathos** is the most beautiful and most touristy).

The major tourist attraction in central Greece, the hilltop monasteries of the **Metéora**, are reached on foot from **Kalambáka**, to which there are two direct **trains** a day from Lárisa; additional journeys are possible by changing at **Paleofársalos**

(ERT 1408). The journey takes about 1 hr 20 mins to 2 hrs. Paleofársalos is on the main rail route between **Athens** and **Thessaloniki**, if you want to visit Metéora without going to Lárisa.

Litóhoro (Λιτόχωρο)

Litohoro is the access point for **Mt Olympus** (2,917 m), home of the ancient gods: it actually has nine peaks. You don't need special equipment (other than suitable footwear) for the full ascent, but it does demand real fitness and takes two days — treat it with respect, as more people die here than on any other Greek mountain. Book a bunk in one of the mountain refuge dormitories (hot meals available) through the EOS office. Getting to the top involves taking a taxi or hitching a lift to the car park 6 km from Litóhoro, at the 1,000 m level, then hiking through ravines to the refuge at around 2,000 m. It is best to spend the night here before making the demanding trek to the summits. The final stretch to **Mitikas**, the highest peak, requires strong nerves.

Arrival, information, accommodation

⇴ Near the coast, 5 km east of town. Buses link the station with the town. **🚻 Tourist office**: Odos Ag. Nicolaou 15, ☎ 235 235 0103 (www.dion-olympos.gr), mid-May–end Aug. Out of season, visitors can try the Town Hall next door at Odos Ag. Nicolaou 17, ☎ 235 235 0100. ⊨ **Papanikolau Pension**, Nikolau Episkopou Kitrous 1, ☎ 235 208 1236, €€, has cosy furnished studios for 2–3 people. **Hostel**: A beachside hostel that is popular with both backpackers and hikers is **Summit Zero**, Gritsa, port of Litohoro, ☎ 235 206 1406 (www.summitzero.gr).

Thessaloniki (Θεσσαλονίκη)

The second largest city in Greece was founded in 315 BC. Many of the interesting sights are within a 10- to 15-min walk of the **Plateia Aristotelous**, an elegant pedestrian-only square giving onto the sea and rimmed by popular open-air cafés. The Old Town was destroyed by fire in 1917 and suffered a severe earthquake in 1978.

Thessaloniki today is a modern, busy city, laid out along a crescent bay — yet it's a worthwhile place to stop over, with some elegant corners and a lively night scene (thanks primarily to the large number of young people who study here). A good area to eat and go out at night is **Ladadika**, a short taxi ride west of the centre, where former warehouses have been refurbished to house countless bars, tavernas and small clubs. Alternatively, try the bustling tavernas that line the narrow alleys of **Athinos**, just off Plateia Aristotelous in the centre.

Thessaloniki (Saloníki) became strategically vital to the Romans, straddling the **Via Egnatia**, their highway between Constantinople and the Adriatic, and later to the Byzantines and their Turkish conquerors. It was one of the greatest cities of the Ottoman Empire, rejoining Greece only in 1913. On the seafront promenade, the **White Tower**, the most prominent surviving bastion of the Byzantine-Turkish city walls, stages an exhibition tracing the city's history.

A five-min walk north-east from here, the vast **Archaeological Museum** (www.amth.gr) houses finds from different parts of Macedonia. Next door, the highly regarded **Museum of Byzantine Culture** (www.mbp.gr) displays religious icons of sultry-eyed saints. The city's Roman heritage includes remains of the **Forum**, Odos Filipou, the **Palace of Galerius**, Plateia Navarinou, the **Baths**, the 4th-century **Rotonda**, and the **Arch of Galerius**, beside Odos Egnatia, near Plateia Sintrivaniou. The city also has a fine collection of Byzantine churches (giving Thessaloniki status as a UNESCO World Heritage Site), the most notable of which are the restored 4th-century **Agios Dimitrios**, and the 8th-century **Agia Sofia**, decorated with stunning golden mosaics. Those who enjoy food shopping should also check out the colourful **Modhiano covered market**.

ARRIVAL, INFORMATION, ACCOMMODATION

✈ 1 km west of the centre. 🚌 3 from the station to the centre, via Plateia Aristotelous. 🛈 **Tourist office**: Tsimiski 138, ☎ 231 254 834. Information desk at the station. **Tourist police**: Odos Dodekanissou, near Plateia Dimokratias, ☎ 231 055 4871. ⇥ The cheaper hotels mostly cluster along Egnatia, the continuation of Monastiriou, east of the station. Some good, moderate options include the **Hotel Emporikon**, Sygrou 14, ☎ 231 051 6666 (www.hotelemporikon.gr), €€, and the **Hotel Atlantis**, Egnatia 14, ☎ 231 054 0131 (www.atlantis-hotel-thessaloniki.com), €€. **Hostel** accommodation is available at the **Thessaloniki Youth Hostel**, 44 Al. Svolou, ☎ 210 225 946, or the **Backpacker's Refuge**, Botsari, ☎ 698 343 3591 (www.backpackers-refuge.biz.ly).

THE STRUMA VALLEY

Route 41 crosses into Bulgaria, where the first settlement is **Kulata**. The small communities on the Bulgarian side of the frontier made a good living through not-always-legal cross-border trading, which has waned since Bulgaria joined the EU in 2007. Look out for particularly fine scenery for the two hours north of Kulata as the bus and train follow the Struma Valley upstream towards Sofia. The landscape is very mixed with lush vineyards ceding to rock-strewn terrain, and the vegetation changing from Mediterranean to more continental species. The railway came late to this region and the train stations are often inconveniently distant from the communities they allegedly serve.

SOFIA (СОФИЯ)

When Bulgaria was liberated from Ottoman rule in 1878, Sofia became its capital, and imposing public buildings, squares and parks were created. Though Sofia is one of the oldest cities in Europe, it is still one of its least-known capitals. Traces of Thracians, Romans, Byzantines, Slavs and Ottoman Turks can all be seen here. The city takes its name from the restored 6th-century **Basilica of St Sofia**, which stands in a central square. The main sights are easily covered on foot. Sofia nowadays is a lively, changing city with many new cafés, bars, restaurants and small family-run hotels. Its excellent museums, art galleries and concerts and **Mt Vitosha** (about 30 mins from the centre by public transport), all deserve a visit.

The **Alexander Nevski Memorial Church**, with its neo-Byzantine golden domes dominating the skyline, is the most photographed image of Sofia. Don't miss the superb collection of Bulgarian icons in its crypt. Nearby, the tiny **Russian Church** is an exuberant, vividly decorated gem, its gold domes contrasting with its emerald-green spires. If you only have time for one museum, visit the **National History Museum** (*marshrutka* 21 from the National Palace of Culture), which has the fabulous Thracian gold treasures. In the foothills of Mount Vitosha, **Boyana Church**, with its sophisticated 13th-century frescos, is also on UNESCO's World Heritage List.

ARRIVAL, INFORMATION, ACCOMMODATION

≼ **Central Station**, Bul. Mariya Luiza, 1.5 km north of the centre. Buses, taxis, tourist information, currency exchange. Be extra cautious here, as petty crime is common. ✈ **Sofia Airport**, 11 km east from the centre; ☎ 02 937 2211–3.

🛈 **National Tourist Information Centre**, Pl. Sveta Nedelya 1, ☎ 02 933 5811 (www.bulgariatravel.org). **Alma Tour**, ul. Serdika 12, ☎ 02 805 6800 (www.almatour.net), offers all kinds of tourist services. For information on hiking and a variety of alternative holidays, try **Zig Zag Holidays**, Bul. Aleksandar Stamboliyski 20V, ☎ 02 980 5102 (www.zigzagbg.com). Train and bus **tickets** are sold by the **Transport Service Centre**, underneath the National Palace of Culture, Pl. Bulgariya, ☎ 02 932 4280.

🚌 **Central Bus Station**, Bul. Mariya Luiza 100, 200 m east of the central railway station. Significantly cleaner, 24 hr left-luggage, ATMs, cafés and fast-food outlets. Central Sofia is compact with a good network of **trams, trolleybuses** and **buses**; buy tickets (single trip) from drivers, kiosks or street vendors. A one-day pass is good value if you're planning more than three rides, but single tickets are extremely cheap. Trams 1/7 run from the station along Bul. Mariya Luiza and Bul. Vitosha through the town centre. Buses cover the city comprehensively.

🛏 There are a wide range of accommodation options in the city, and the tourist office can help with bookings. Extremely well-regarded, and at a decent price, is **Scotty's Boutique Hotel**, Ekzarh Yosif str 11, ☎ 02 983 6777 (www.scottyshotel.eu). Also worth checking in the **Red House B&B**, ul. Ljuben Karavelov 15, ☎ 02 988 8188 (www.redbandb.com), €–€€. There are numerous **hostels** in Sofia, but standards vary. Three of the best places in town are the **Hostel Mostel**, Makedonia Blvd. 2a, ☎ 0889 22 32 96 (www.hostelmostel.com), the **Art Hostel**, ul. Angel Kanchev 21/a, ☎ 02 987 0545 (www.art-hostel.com), and the **Be My Guest Hostel**, 13 Ivan Vazov Str., ☎ 02 980 2142 (www.bemyguesthostel.com). ✗ Sofia's restaurants have increased in number and quality, but prices (for foreign visitors) remain low. Side streets off Bul. Vitosha, particularly to the east, have a mixture of western fast-food outlets and international cuisine. In the foothills of **Mount Vitosha**, several traditional taverns serve **local specialities**.

PLOVDIV (ПЛОВДИВ)

Plovdiv was described by the Greek writer Lucian in the 2nd century AD as "the largest and most beautiful of all cities in Thrace." When Bulgaria was unified in 1885, Sofia became the country's capital and Plovdiv's influence dwindled. As the second city, Plovdiv has uninspiring suburbs of industrial buildings and tower blocks, but the characterful **Old Town** is a different world, with coarsely cobbled streets and a charm that Sofia lacks.

    Buses and **trolleybuses** run throughout Plovdiv, but much of the hilly Old Town is only accessible on foot. It's a 10- to 15-min walk north-east along tree-lined Ivan Vazov, diagonally across from the station, to the central square. Archaeological finds date Plovdiv to around 4000 BC, and the city was occupied by Thracians and Philip II of Macedon before the Romans took over in 72 BC. Remains include the partially restored 2nd-century marble **Roman Theatre**, one of Bulgaria's best archaeological sites, recently accommodating various festivals, concerts and other cultural events. The remains of the **Roman Forum**, including marble floors, can be seen in the central square near Hotel Trimontium. The city's most important contribution to recent Bulgarian culture are the National Revival period houses, scattered around the Old Town. Don't miss the **Ethnographic Museum**, Arghir Kuyumdzhiouglu House, with its wonderful wooden ceilings and interior; it also has many exhibits of traditional craftwork.

ARRIVAL, INFORMATION, ACCOMMODATION

≽ 1 km south-west of the centre on Bul. Hristo Botev. **🛈 Plovdiv Tourist Information Centre**, Pl. Tsentralen 1, ☎ 032 620 229 (www.plovdiv-tour.info), offers maps, booklets, and arranges accommodation.

    🛏 Plovdiv has a few modern hotels and numerous guesthouses to choose from at very affordable prices, such as the **Alliance Hotel**, Vasil Aprilov boulv. 7, ☎ 032 646 333. For **hostel** accommodation, try the **Hiker's Hostel**, ul. Saborna 53, ☎ 0989 9898 266 (www.hikers-hostel.org), or the **Hostel Plovdiv Guesthouse**, ul. Saborna 20, ☎ 0932 622 432 (www.plovdivguest.com).

EAST TO DIMITROVGRAD

From Plovdiv, you can continue across the Plain of Thrace to Dimitrovgrad (see p341) to connect with **Route 40** to Istanbul. If you want to head north into Romania on Route 40, you can also connect at Dimitrovgrad, but there is also a useful direct train from Plovdiv to Veliko Târnovo (5 hrs, ERT 1525), which is also on Route 40.

Rail Route 42:
Two Danube capitals and the Vojvodina

CITIES: ★★ CULTURE: ★★★ HISTORY: ★★ SCENERY: ★
COUNTRIES COVERED: HUNGARY, SERBIA

This is one of the shortest routes in this book, but it is nonetheless a key link in Europe's rail network. For travellers **bound for the Balkans**, the 350 km hop from the Hungarian capital to Belgrade is often a standard leg in their itinerary.

Leon Trotsky travelled on this line in 1912, when he was heading south to report on the Balkan Wars. He nicely captured the essence of the journey with the observation in his diary that "although the railway line from Budapest to Belgrade proceeds mainly in a southerly direction, from the cultural standpoint one moves eastward." Trotsky went on to remark on the multilingual and motley kaleidoscope of cultures that he saw as his train paused at wayside stations along the route.

This is not a route that wins any prizes for dramatic scenery. It traverses landscapes that are often pancake flat. The **Pannonian Plain** is the dried-up bed of a vast inland sea that once lay between the Carpathian Mountains and the uplands of southern Serbia. Despite the unremarkable scenery, this route is very interesting, mainly on account of the changing cultural landscapes. Our favourite section is without doubt the two-hour stretch from the Serbian border south to **Novi Sad** through the Autonomous Province of **Vojvodina**. Although the route has Danubian landscapes aplenty, you will not see a lot of the river itself, but there is a dramatic crossing of the **Danube** at Novi Sad.

With a choice of one night- and two daytime direct trains on the route, we would strongly suggest making the journey by day, ideally using the trains which in each direction leave at about 10 in the morning. These are train numbers 343 (southbound) and 342 (northbound), both named after Ivo Andrić, the Nobel Prize-winning author whose prose so vividly captured life and culture in **Yugoslavia**. These trains are not great international expresses, but they are full of local character. Both services are usually composed of just three Hungarian carriages that crawl rather than dash between the two capitals with two dozen stops along the way. Subotica is the obvious place to break your journey.

BUDAPEST — SEE P465

Heading south from Budapest, you might well wonder why Hungarians refer to this great plain as *puszta,* a term that has only derisory connotations. This is no arid wasteland at all, but a varied landscape with areas of productive farmland, prairie-like grasslands, forests and great saline depressions, often filled with brackish waters. There is something of the **Hungarian soul** in these sweeping landscapes. They have inspired Csontváry's art and Sándor Petőfi's poetry.

ROUTE DETAILS

Budapest–Kiskőrös — ERT 1295

Type	Frequency	Typical journey time
Train	Every 2 hrs	2 hrs

Kiskőrös–Subotica — ERT 1295

Type	Frequency	Typical journey time
Train	3 daily	1h50

Subotica–Novi Sad — ERT 1360

Type	Frequency	Typical journey time
Train	Up to 12 daily	2 hrs to 2h30

Novi Sad–Belgrade — ERT 1360

Type	Frequency	Typical journey time
Train	Up to 13 daily	1h30

Budapest–Szeged — ERT 1290

Type	Frequency	Typical journey time
Train	Every hr	2h25

Szeged–Subotica — ERT 1377

Type	Frequency	Typical journey time
Train	Up to 3 daily	1h50

Budapest–Pécs — ERT 1200

Type	Frequency	Typical journey time
Train	Every 2 hrs	2h50

KEY JOURNEY

Budapest–Belgrade — ERT 61, 1360

Type	Frequency	Typical journey time
Train	3 daily	7h40

KISKŐRÖS

If Shakespeare is the literary figure who captures all of England, then **Sándor Petőfi** does the same for Hungary. The poet and revolutionary was born in Kiskőrös, and there is hardly a Hungarian alive who has not made a pilgrimage to Petőfi's birthplace. Unless you are a real Petőfi fan, we would say it is hardly worth the stop, but you'll get serious kudos from Hungarian fellow passengers if you can recite a line or two of Petőfi's *Nemzeti dal*, which holds revered status as Hungary's national poem. An hour or two south of Kiskőrös, the train approaches the border with Serbia. **Kelebia** is the last stop in Hungary, and the train waits here for 30 minutes. Kelebia is a curious small town that is split in two by the international border. This is one of those old-style frontiers where passports really are properly checked.

SUBOTICA (СУБОТИЦА)

Subotica is a strange introduction to Serbia, but it is a very fine place to start exploring the **Vojvodina**, that region of northern Serbia which celebrates its peculiarly multicultural character. This is a town full of surprises, and top of the list is the extraordinary **mix of languages** you will hear in the streets, typical of

DIVERSIONS: PÉCS AND SZEGED

There is a useful alternative route from Budapest to Subotica that takes in the Hungarian city of Szeged en route. There are regular direct trains from Budapest to Szeged (ERT 1290). From Szeged there is a thrice-daily connection to Subotica, taking 2 hrs for the 43-km journey, with a change of train along the way (ERT 1377). Szeged is one of a pair of university cities in southern Hungary that deserve to be far better known. The other is Pécs, which is less easily accommodated on journeys from Budapest to Serbia, but makes a fine stopover for travellers heading from Budapest to Bosnia. Budapest to Pécs is just three hours by train (ERT 1200). From Pécs, there is a daily direct train, the Drava, to Sarajevo via Osijek (ERT 1345 and 1350), thus providing useful connections with **Route 39** (in Osijek) and **Route 44** (in Sarajevo).

Pécs is in an enviable location at the foot of the Mecsek Hills. The city deftly blends Habsburg with Ottoman style. Many of the principal buildings have served more than one empire, a trend exemplified in the former **Gazi Kasim Pasha Mosque** which is now a Catholic church. Other highlights include a striking synagogue and a gallery devoted to the painting of **Kosztka Csontváry** (closed Mon). That gallery alone justifies the journey to Pécs. It contains vast canvases with a mystical quality that, once seen, will remain with you forever.

Szeged on the Tisza River cannot quite rival Pécs for location, but it has the same distinctive buzz that comes from having a high student population. It beats Pécs when it comes to **nightlife**. Szeged offers a good dose of Jewish heritage and a very fine central area. Like Pécs, more than enough to justify a one-night stopover on routes south from Budapest.

Serbia's semi-detached northern province which has several official languages (see box on next page). The town has a **Habsburg** feel to it, more central European than Balkan in character. Indeed, enjoying coffee and cake in the many outdoor cafés you might easily imagine you were in a provincial city in Austria.

Subotica offers an extraordinary feast of **art nouveau** architecture, among them the overly fussy **town hall** and the more restrained **synagogue**. Near the railway station is another striking art nouveau building, the **Raichle Palace**, which houses a gallery of modern art (closed Sat afternoon and Sun).

ARRIVAL, INFORMATION, ACCOMMODATION

⇖ On the eastern fringe of the town centre. **⚑ Tourist office**: Trg slobode 1, ☎ 024 670 350 (www.visitsubotica.rs). The town centre is compact with all the principal sights on the west side of the railway line and within easy walking distance of the station. ⊨ **Hotel Gloria**, Dimitrija Tucovića 2, ☎ 024 672 010 (www.hotelgloriasubotica.com), €€, near the Franciscan Church is pure luxury. The family-run **PBG Hotel**, Harambašićeva 19–21, ☎ 024 556 542 (www.pbghotel.co.rs), offers double rooms from €30, whilst the four-star **Vila Royal Crown**, Somborski put br. 75, ☎ 024 533 666 (www.vilaroyal.rs), €€€, is a five-minute taxi ride from the centre.

SOUTH THROUGH THE VOJVODINA

The train journey south from Subotica traverses pretty Vojvodina agricultural landscapes with villages clustered around monumental churches. There are Slovaks, Croats, Rusyns and many other ethnic groups. The first station stop south of Subotica is named **Bačka Topola** (Бачка Топола) on Serbian maps, but the Hungarians who form the majority of the population in the town call it Topolya. Next stop is **Vrbas** (Врбас), a town full of Rusyns, Montenegrins and Serbs. This is one of Europe's most strikingly multi-ethnic areas.

NOVI SAD (НОВИ САД)

The Vojvodina capital is a bustling city, though it takes a vivid imagination to understand why the locals call it the Serbian Athens. The city has a central European feel and its population reflects the complex ethnic mix of the Vojvodina region. The city suffered terribly in the NATO bombing of Yugoslavia in 1999, rather surprisingly in view of the fact that the authorities in Novi Sad and much of the local population had little time for the Milošević government in Belgrade. The city is striking for its eclectic collections of churches, the most impressive of which is the **Orthodox Cathedral**. Don't miss the **Bishop's Palace** just by the cathedral.

Mention Novi Sad to young people across Europe and you'll quickly discover that the Danube city is intimately associated with one annual event: the **State of Exit** music festival that is staged every July in the **Petrovaradin Fortress**, located

LANGUAGES OF VOJVODINA

When the English lexicographer Samuel Johnson observed that language is the dress of thought, it is possible that he hadn't reckoned with the Vojvodina region of northern Serbia. For this area traversed by Route 42 has a prolific variety of languages spoken within a relatively compact area. If Dr Johnson is to be believed, then this must be one of the most thoughtful parts of Europe.

The **cultural mosaic** of Vojvodina is sometimes difficult for outsiders to fathom. Six official languages with daily or weekly newspapers in all of them, and a long tradition of multilingual education suggest that Vojvodina is something quite extraordinary. Beyond the **six official languages** (Serbian, Hungarian, Rusyn, Slovak, Romanian and Croatian) a handful of other tongues crop up in isolated villages. But multicultural Vojvodina is not always a place full of happy interactions between its constituent communities. If you take time to explore the region, you'll discover that specific villages are often home to just one language group — many of whose members might well be hard pushed to have any sensible conversation with speakers of another language living in the next village down the road.

on the east bank of the Danube opposite Novi Sad. With its origins in the anti-Milošević protests of Novi Sad students, the festival has matured over the last ten years to become one of Europe's most dynamic music events.

Music apart, Petrovaradin Fortress definitely deserves a visit. It is a pleasant walk across the new **Varadinski most** (Varadin Bridge) to reach the fortress, where you can wander amid turreted bastions, and even explore some of the underground passageways. It is all very atmospheric. The **Novi Sad Museum** (closed Mon), well worth a visit, is housed in an erstwhile barracks within the fortress. Even if you do not get over to Petrovaradin, you'll get a glimpse of the fortress as you leave Novi Sad on the Belgrade-bound train as it crosses the **Drumsko-železnički most**, an improvised structure that carries rail and road traffic over the Danube. It is a temporary solution to replace bridges destroyed by NATO bombing in 1999. To the right of the train, as it rumbles over the blue girder bridge, you'll see Petrovaradin Fortress in the distance.

ARRIVAL, INFORMATION, ACCOMMODATION

⇛ The railway station is north-west of the city centre, and the main sights are a 15-min walk from the station, or take 🚌 4 from the station to the centre. 🛈 **Tourist office**: Ul. Modene 1, ☎ 021 661 7343 (www.turizamns.rs). 🛏 The cosy **Hostel Sova**, Ilije Ognjanovića 26, ☎ 021 661 5230 (www.hostelsova.com) is highly recommended by backpackers and independent travellers, and offers dorm beds for €12 and doubles from €36. Located in the heart of Novi Sad is the **TAL Centar**, Zmaj Jovina 23, ☎ 021 661 3813 (www.talcentar.rs), €€. The **Boutique Hotel Arta**, Heroja Pinkija 12, ☎ 021 6804 500 (www.boutiquehotelarta.rs), €€€, is a stylish, but more expensive option.

BELGRADE — SEE P444

Rail Route 43:
Through the heart of the Balkans

CITIES: ★ CULTURE: ★★ HISTORY: ★ SCENERY: ★★★
COUNTRIES COVERED: SERBIA, MACEDONIA, GREECE

Thriller writers who set their novels on slow trains wandering through ill-defined Balkan territories probably had routes like this one in mind as they plotted out their stories. This is a fine run south through former Yugoslavia to Greece. In 2011, the financially-beleaguered Greek government severed all rail connections with the rest of Europe. Unless cross-border trains are restored in 2012 (check for updates on www.europebyrail.eu), you'll need to take a bus for the final stretch of Route 43 from Skopje to Thessaloniki.

Oddly, the two direct daily trains from Belgrade to Skopje retain names that might suggest they are still destined for Greece: the *Hellas Express* and the *Olympus*. The latter is the better choice, for the journey from Belgrade to Skopje, capital of Macedonia, is worth doing by day. There is some great scenery. The route affords a **wonderful transect** through the hill country of southern Serbia, skirting (but not crossing) Kosovo's eastern border, before slipping over the frontier into **Macedonia**. Skopje deserves an overnight stop.

The journey south from Skopje (whether by bus or, if the rail link is revived, by train) meanders through lush Macedonian valleys before entering Greece for the final hour of the journey to **Thessaloniki**.

BELGRADE — SEE P444

Within twenty minutes of leaving Belgrade on the southbound train, you are passing **Rakovica** (Раковица), famous for the Orthodox monastery and infamous for its abandoned factories. Skirting low wooded hills, the rail route drops down into the **Morava Valley** which it then follows upstream for some hours almost to the Macedonian border. The river has from time to time inflicted terrible flooding on communities along the valley. These are unremarkable places, yet this meandering valley is seen by many Serbs as constituting the historic heartland of Serbian life and culture. Parts of central Kosovo are accorded similar iconic status.

Niš (Ниш)

There is no special reason to break your journey until Niš, a major regional centre and the largest city in southern Serbia. At first sight this gritty industrial centre may not seem to have much to offer, but a high student population makes for a relaxed atmosphere and lively nightlife. Niš has a couple of very unusual sights. Devotees of dark tourism should not miss the **Skull Tower** (Ćele Kula), a grisly

Note

Rail services across all Greek borders were the victim of Greece's economic woes in 2011. They were suspended and may not be restored for 2012. So a bus is recommended for the leg from Skopje to Thessaloniki.

ROUTE DETAILS

Belgrade–Niš — ERT 1380

Type	Frequency	Typical journey time
Train	Up to 7 daily	4h10

Niš–Skopje — ERT 1380

Type	Frequency	Typical journey time
Train	2–3 daily	4h45

Skopje–Thessaloniki

Type	Frequency	Typical journey time
Bus	1 daily	3h30

memorial on the edge of town erected by Ottoman forces who suppressed a Serbian uprising here in 1809. The skulls of dead Serbian forces were mounted on a tower as a cautionary reminder of the folly of contesting Ottoman supremacy in the region. A chapel protects the remains of the tower. 🚌 1 from the city centre gets you to the Skull Tower.

Only slightly less dark than the Skull Tower is the Nazi **concentration camp**, located north of town on Bulevar 12 Februar in the Crveni Krst (Red Cross) district of Niš, which offers frightening insights into the horrors of war. Between 1941 and 1944, many Roma, Jews and Yugoslav communists were interned and murdered here. The site now hosts a museum (closed Mon).

Arrival, information, accommodation
🚃 The railway station is 2 km out of town, but frequent bus services (🚌 1/5/6/10) will get you into town. 🄸 **Tourist office**: Voždova 7, ☎ 018 523 118 (www. nistourism.org.rs), centrally located and another branch is at Istanbul Gate, at the entrance to the fortress at Tvrdjava, ☎ 018 250 222. 🛏 An extremely well-regarded choice is the **Hotel Panorama Lux**, 51 Svetolika Rankovića Str, ☎ 018 561 214 (www. panoramalux.co.rs), €€. **Hostel**: A popular choice for backpackers is the **Downtown Hostel**, Kej Kola Srpskih Sestara, ☎ 018 526 756.

Southern Serbia
Continuing up the **Morava Valley**, the rail route passes through a region that was once renowned across Europe for its textiles. Watermills powered a vibrant lace and woollen industry, but today most of the mills have closed, leaving a scene of economic desolation. Travelling south towards the Macedonian frontier, the last stations in Serbia — Vranje (Врање) and Preševo (Прешево) — are inconveniently distant from the communities they affect to serve. It is no surprise, therefore, that most locals use buses rather than trains for travel between towns in this region. Border formalities take place at **Preševo** (Serbia) and **Tabanovce** (Macedonia). At the latter, the locomotive is usually changed, and a little railway ritual of yesteryear is played out as men in overalls walk the length of the train carefully tapping each wheel — presumably to check it is still intact. Wheel tapping seems in general to be a profession in decline but it is alive and well at some frontier crossings in the Balkans.

Through Macedonia
It takes less than four hours to cross **Macedonia** by train. It is just 250 km from the border with Serbia at Tabanovce (Табановце) to the Greek frontier at **Gevgelija** (Гевгелија). Of course Macedonia deserves more than merely four hours as it affords many insights into one of Europe's least-known countries. Macedonia is smaller than Belgium, and yet encompasses a considerable variety

of landscapes and peoples — it is not for nothing that chefs across Europe take the very name Macedonia as a byword for variety, viz. *macédoine de légumes* in France or *macedonia de frutas* in Spain.

Virtually the entire run south from Tabanovce through Macedonia follows the valley of the **River Vardar** and its tributaries. The Vardar defines Macedonia and it is pre-eminently a Macedonian river. It rises in the hills east of the border with Albania, and then makes a great loop across northern Macedonia, passing through the capital **Skopje** before turning south towards Greece. At that border, the name of the river changes to Axios. The journey through Macedonia, whether by train or by bus, affords glimpses of distant mountains and close-up views of seductively beautiful vineyards as well as fields of sunflowers, tobacco and grain crops. Highlight of the run, a little over an hour south from Skopje, is the remarkable **gorge** through which the Vardar cuts near **Demir Kapija** (Демир Капија) — the name is derived from Turkish and means 'iron gate', a hint at the former importance of the great limestone bluffs on either side of the river in securing the defence of the settlements to the north.

SKOPJE (СКОПЈЕ)

There are two sides to the Macedonian capital. The hub of business life lies south of the Vardar River in a part of the city which is modern, chaotic and generally Christian. Walk over the **old stone bridge**, itself the most well-known Macedonian landmark, to the north bank of the Vardar and you'll discover quite another Skopje, a city that is ancient, in the main Muslim and even more chaotic than the south bank. For all the bustle, Skopje is a great place just to wander. North-bank highlights are the **Kale Fortress** and the **Mustafa Pasha Mosque**, opposite the main entrance to the fortress, which has an especially lovely rose garden. From the mosque there are good views over the **Old Bazaar**. Dive into this area to discover back lanes, several very fine mosques, old Ottoman inns (often with wonderfully secluded courtyards overlooked by wooden balconies) and a covered market. Don't miss the **National Gallery** housed in an old Turkish bath (Daut Pasha Amam) just north of the stone bridge — worth a visit as much for the remarkable building as for the art it houses (closed Mon).

On the south bank, the not-to-be-missed sight is the **Museum of Skopje** on Mito Hadzivasilev Jasmin at the south end of Macedonia Street. It is in the city's former main railway station, a building that was much more elegant that the disastrous modern structure that replaced it.

ARRIVAL, INFORMATION, ACCOMMODATION

≽ The new train station looks anything but new and is on the south side of the Vardar River in a run-down part of town, close to the bus station (15-min walk south-east of the stone bridge). Frequent buses into the centre, invariably overcrowded.

➔ **Alexander the Great Airport**, 20 km east of Skopje, flight information: ☎ 02 314 83

33 (www.airports.com.mk). **?** **Tourist office**: in the Old Bazaar, ☎ 02 311 68 54 (www. exploringmacedonia.com). Where English fails, try German. Skopje has a large number of foreigners working in international organisations. ✉ Good value and in the centre of town is the **Hotel Vila Silia**, Vostanicka 30, ☎ 02 273 55 62 (www.hotelvilasilia. com.mk), €€ or the slightly more expensive boutique **Hotel Victoria**, Str Slave Delovski 18, ☎ 02 310 76 00 (www.hotelvictoria.com.mk), €€. **Hostels**: There are some good options in Skopje, including the **Art Hostel**, Tome Arsovski 14, ☎ 02 322 37 89 (www.art-hostel.com.mk). Newly opened and close to the bus and train stations, try the **Shanti Hostel**, Rade Jovcevski Korcagin 11, ☎ 70 620 320.

THESSALONIKI — SEE P346

SIDETRACKS M: KOSOVO

Skopje is the jumping-off point for visiting Kosovo by train (ERT 1375). There is an afternoon direct train from Skopje to the Kosovan capital **Priština**. A morning service from Skopje across the border into Kosovo is shown in some schedules but at the time of writing (autumn 2011) is suspended. These trains are operated by the **Kosovan Railways**, Hekurudhat e Kosovës (HK), which now run services previously managed by United Nations Interim Administration Mission in Kosovo (UNMIK). The rolling stock used by HK is a curious mix donated by various European countries. On one journey we rode in Swedish carriages hauled by a Norwegian locomotive. Italian soldiers patrolled the train to maintain order — not that they were needed, and nowadays HK services operate without military escorts.

As Europe's newest country, albeit one not universally recognised by the international community, Kosovo deserves a visit. Priština is a capital city in the making, a messy place with an eclectic jumble of architecture. But the town has a buzz about it and is surprisingly cosmopolitan, helped in this respect by the sizeable contingent of international agencies and the growing number of embassies that jostle for space. ✉ For accommodation in Pristina, check out the newly-renovated **Hotel Begolli**, Maliq Pashë Gjinolli str. 8, ☎ 038 244 277 (www.hotelbegolli.com), €–€€.

For a first time visit to Kosovo, we recommend **Peć** (Pejë in Albanian) over Priština. It is served by twice-daily direct trains from the capital (ERT 1375). Peć is in a superb location surrounded by hills, has much old Ottoman architecture and is an ecclesiastical centre for Orthodox Serbs. You can visit the **Peć Orthodox Patriarchate**, a UNESCO World Heritage Site, which is 2 km west of town. This is the mother church of the entire Serbian Patriarchate, as important to many Serbs as Rome is to Catholics. Beyond the convent and church lies the beautiful Rugova Valley. A day or two in Peć will surely set you thinking about the issues of religion, nationhood and identity that lie at the very heart of the Kosovo conundrum.

The rail journey from Skopje north into Kosovo is generally safe nowadays, and both Peć and Priština are very much open to visitors. We would just caution about travelling into northern Kosovo. Return south to Skopje to continue your journey. And take some satisfaction from having visited one of the most out-of-the-way corners of the Balkan region.

Rail Route 44: A Bosnian journey

CITIES: ★★ CULTURE: ★★ HISTORY: ★★ SCENERY: ★★★
COUNTRIES COVERED: SERBIA, CROATIA, BOSNIA AND HERZEGOVINA

Route 44 is a heartfelt tribute to a changing **Balkan region**. A quarter century ago, this entire route lay within the territory of Yugoslavia, the federal state that, after the split between Tito and Stalin in 1948, developed its own very distinctive brand of socialism. With the disintegration of Yugoslavia, triggered by the secession of Croatia and Slovenia in June 1991, the region experienced a very dark decade of civil strife. But from the embers of chaos have emerged a number of separate nation states that have generally learnt to mutually respect each other and often work very positively together. And there is no better symbol of this new order than the new train service that since December 2009 has linked **Belgrade** with **Sarajevo**. From the capital of Serbia to the capital of Bosnia and Herzegovina, along the way traversing Croatian territory. It is this new train service that makes this route now very easy to follow. Our preferred en route stops, definitely each worth a day or two, are Sarajevo and **Mostar**.

The scenery along the first part of Route 44 through Serbia and Croatia is unexceptional, but once over the **River Sava** the railway follows the Bosna Valley upstream through increasingly hilly country all the way to Sarajevo. Beyond Sarajevo you are in for a treat. Just sit back and watch the landscape unfold, revealing a beautiful mix of lakes, gorges and mountains. Rail travel in Europe does not get any better than this.

BELGRADE — SEE P444

Breakfast time at **Belgrade station** is one of the few moments of the day when this transport hub really comes to life. Of course there are commuters arriving — though nowhere near as many as decant from the coaches and minibuses in the adjacent bus station. There are also passengers awaiting the departure of the morning trains to Hungary and Montenegro. And then there are those intent on trying a flagship new train service for the Balkans. The once-daily train to Sarajevo departs a little after 0800 (check ERT 92 for current timings).

This is no grand express. Indeed the train hardly looks big enough to carry such a hefty burden of meaning and expectation. On the one occasion that we used this train, it had just three carriages: one Serbian and one from each of the Bosnian entities that co-exist so uneasily that each has its own railway administration. Coffee, drinks and snacks were served in the Serbian carriage, sandwiched between the two Bosnian cars.

The journey out from Belgrade to the Croatian border is through undemanding country. This is the southern part of the **Vojvodina**, the autonomous region of Serbia which is covered more thoroughly in **Route 42**. The little ripple of

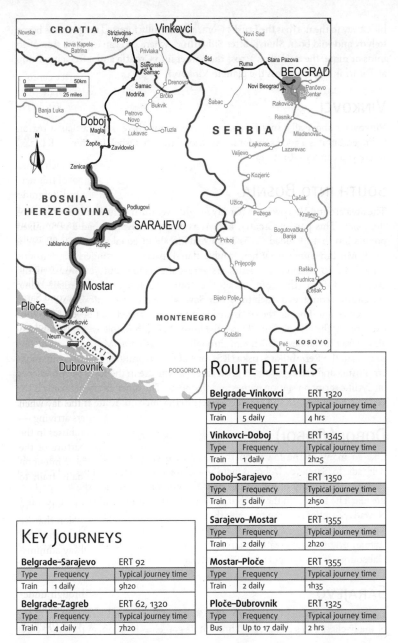

ROUTE DETAILS

Belgrade–Vinkovci — ERT 1320

Type	Frequency	Typical journey time
Train	5 daily	4 hrs

Vinkovci–Doboj — ERT 1345

Type	Frequency	Typical journey time
Train	1 daily	2h25

Doboj–Sarajevo — ERT 1350

Type	Frequency	Typical journey time
Train	5 daily	2h50

Sarajevo–Mostar — ERT 1355

Type	Frequency	Typical journey time
Train	2 daily	2h20

Mostar–Ploče — ERT 1355

Type	Frequency	Typical journey time
Train	2 daily	1h35

Ploče–Dubrovnik — ERT 1325

Type	Frequency	Typical journey time
Bus	Up to 17 daily	2 hrs

KEY JOURNEYS

Belgrade–Sarajevo — ERT 92

Type	Frequency	Typical journey time
Train	1 daily	9h20

Belgrade–Zagreb — ERT 62, 1320

Type	Frequency	Typical journey time
Train	4 daily	7h20

hills away to the north is the Fruška Gora, a beautifully forested range that is home to lynx and wild boar. Shortly after **Šid** (Шид), where you can expect a stop of 20 mins or more, the train slips across the border into **Croatia** and, after a brief stop at Tovarnik, speeds across the plain to Vinkovci.

VINKOVCI

Vinkovci is above all a spot for changing trains, and there is no particular reason to linger. But it is a good spot for taking a local train to **Osijek** (44 mins, ERT 1345) where you can join **Route 39**.

SOUTH INTO BOSNIA

The area around Vincovci was fiercely fought over during the terrible conflicts of the 1990s. This part of Croatia, known as **eastern Slavonia**, had a very mixed population that included Serbs and Croats in about equal measure and even a small Muslim minority. When trouble flared in late 1991, underlying tensions exploded into violence that left scars across the region. But you would hardly credit that from the comfort of the train which trundles through tame agricultural country to reach the **River Sava** where it crosses into Bosnia.

Once into Bosnia, the landscape is at first unchanged, but beyond Modriča (Модрича) the hills close in. This is the Bosna Valley, now followed by the railway all the way to Sarajevo. Upstream through Doboj as far as Maglaj (Маглај), the route is in the **Republika Srpska (RS)**, one of the two entities that make up modern Bosnia and Herzegovina. A good clue that you are in the RS is the prevalence of Cyrillic script on station names and signposts. The other entity in Bosnia is the **Federation of Bosnia and Herzegovina (FBH)**, which our route enters at Maglaj.

DOBOJ (Добој)

Like so many of the towns on the more than eight hour train journey from Belgrade to Sarajevo, Doboj is hardly a place you'd want to linger. The town captures the futility of war. It lies near the boundary between the two parts of Bosnia. The town is in the **RS**, but some of the surrounding hills are in the FBH. Nowadays Doboj is home to many thousands of Serbs displaced from the FBH. The town is dominated by a great **fortress**, visible from the train. This citadel has Roman origins, was greatly enlarged under Ottoman rule and later served the Habsburgs. It is a symbol of shifting patterns of civil power in this region.

SARAJEVO

Put succinctly, Sarajevo is superb. The capital of Bosnia and Herzegovina is one of the liveliest cities in Europe. Throw in its gorgeous location, at the junction of two rivers (the Bosna and the Miljacka) and surrounded by hills, and you have a place that deserves to be much better known. Sarajevo was brought to breaking point from 1992 to 1995, when it endured the longest siege in modern European history. From that low point, it has bounced back to become a Balkan star.

The city is safe, compact and easy to explore on foot. And it is a place where you can just linger, taking advantage of the city's fine café culture. Our favourite part of the city is **Baščaršija**, just east of the centre, which was for four centuries the hub of Ottoman life in the city. Today it is an evocative mix of markets and mosques. Far and away the nicest street is **Farhadija** which runs west from the middle of Baščaršija. Farhadija is busy at any time of day, but is at its best early evening when many local families come here to stroll and meet friends.

ARRIVAL, INFORMATION, ACCOMMODATION

➤ The railway station is a feast of glass and concrete west of the centre next to the bus station. Tram no. 1 departs every few minutes from outside the station, making a circuit of the entire central area as far east as Baščaršija, running counter-clockwise before returning past the **Jewish Museum** and **Roman Catholic cathedral** to the station. Even if you are only changing trains, it is well worth making this loop on the tram. 🚉 **Tourist office**: near the New Serbian Orthodox church on Zelenih beretki (down the alleyway by the Central Café), ☎ 033 22 07 24 (www.sarajevo-tourism.com).

➤ For cheaper private rooms, try guesthouses and pensions such as the **Guesthouse Halvat**, Kasima Efendije Dobrače do 5, ☎ 033 23 77 14 (www.halvat.com.ba), €€, or the **Kandilj Pension**, Bistrik 12a, ☎ 033 57 25 10, €€. **Hostels**: For dorm beds, try one of Sarajevo's hostels such as the **Hostel City Center**, Saliha Hadzihuseinovica Muvekita 2/3, ☎ 033 20 32 13 (www.hcc.ba). A new hostel that has been getting great reviews is the **New Age Hostel**, Muse Cazima Catica 18, ☎ 033 44 61 00 (www.hostelnewage.ba), just north of the Old Town.

SOUTH TO HERZEGOVINA

If you stop overnight in Sarajevo, the chances are you'll be at Sarajevo station early next morning for the onward journey south. There are just two trains a day on the route from Sarajevo to Mostar and the coast (ERT 1355). The journey to Mostar is fabulous and we can think of no finer way to experience a summer morning in the Balkans. The train climbs direct from Sarajevo, cutting through the **Bjelašnica Mountains**, where the 1984 Winter Olympics were held, before dropping down steeply to the **Neretva Valley** which the railway line follows for the entire route to the coast. Just after Konjic, the railway skirts beautiful **Lake Jablaničko** before cutting through wild canyons to reach Mostar.

MOSTAR

When the **Stari most** (old bridge) at Mostar finally succumbed to the attacks and collapsed into the Neretva Gorge in November 1993, it wasn't just bricks and mortar that tumbled into the abyss. With the bridge went the last vestige of hope for many of Mostar's inhabitants. The old structure was one of the most striking pieces of Islamic architecture in all Europe. For observers in western Europe, who had tired of media pictures of mass graves and long lines of displaced refugees, the painful gap where once had stood the bridge at Mostar became the symbol of a country that was being rent asunder.

Mostar today is a very different place from the dark days of the 1990s. The sullen roar of war has been replaced by peace, and Mostar's old bridge has been re-built. The bridge and the **cafés** that cluster in a jumble on the banks of the Neretva are now happy spots to linger. Enjoy a Turkish coffee and ponder the common misfortunes of the communities that make up modern Bosnia and Herzegovina. Mostar is back in business and desperately needs visitors. Make it a priority to spend at least a night here. The main sights are conveniently clustered in the **Stari Grad** (Old Town) around the landmark bridge.

ARRIVAL, INFORMATION, ACCOMMODATION

≽ The railway station is in the Pasjak area on the east bank of the river well north of the Old Town. There is a regular bus into town. 🛈 **Tourist office**: close to the old bridge on the west side of the river at Rade Bitange 5, ☎ 036 58 02 75 (www.bhtourism.ba/eng/mostar.wbsp). ⊨ A cosy pension, just a short walk from the Old Town is the **Villa Sara**, Sasarogina br. 4, ☎ 036 55 59 40 (www.villasara-mostar.com). There are plenty of small and comfortable **hostels** in Mostar, including the **Hostel Majdas**, 39 Franje Milicevica, ☎ 061 38 29 40 (www.hostelmajdas.com) and the **Hostel Magdalena**, Trk Ivana Krndelja br. 16, ☎ 061 60 99 11.

TO THE COAST

It is just an hour or two from Mostar down to the coast. Along the way you'll see the small walled village of **Počitelj**, which is remarkably unchanged from Otto-man days. The train crosses into Croatia at Metković, from where most services run non-stop to the Adriatic port of Ploče, along the last part of the route with fine views over the marshy wetlands of the Neretva delta.

After such a superb journey, **Ploče** is a dismal anti-climax. Fortunately there are hourly buses south to **Dubrovnik**, which is also on **Route 38**. Note that the evening train from Mostar misses the last bus to Dubrovnik. Buses leave from out-side the train station, taking between 2 hrs and 2hrs and 20 mins, depending on the bus operator (see ERT 1325). Sit on the right side of the bus for great views of the coast on the 110 km journey. Curiously, the coastal highway (called the **Magistrala**) crosses briefly back into Bosnia and Herzegovina around **Neum**, where a thin sliver of Bosnian territory reaches the Adriatic.

DUBROVNIK — SEE P328

Rail Route 45: Eastbound to Russia

CITIES: ★★★ CULTURE: ★★ HISTORY: ★★★ SCENERY: ★
COUNTRIES COVERED: GERMANY, POLAND, BELARUS, RUSSIA

Route 45 is the longest journey described in this book, a little under 2,000 km in all, starting in **Berlin** and ending in Russia's magnificent second city and erstwhile capital, **St Petersburg**. Lenin's wife Nadya Krupskaya, who accompanied the Bolshevik leader on his historic journey from Switzerland to Russia in the spring of 1917, remarked on how Lenin was lost in thought for most of the long trip from Berlin to St Petersburg. Lenin, it must be said, did not follow Route 45 but took a circuitous itinerary via Sweden and Finland. Such were the difficulties of travel in a Europe rent asunder by the First World War. Today you can hop onto a train in Berlin and arrive in St Petersburg about 36 hrs later — not a single change of train and air-conditioned comfort the whole way. A different world from 1917, when Lenin, Nadya and their comrades even ended up **travelling by sledge** for part of their journey.

Route 45 hardly crests any great hills for the entire route, but don't imagine that it is pancake flat. Gently undulating fits the bill. Sit back, relax and discover **the pacific beauty of birch forests**. And the journey, topped and tailed by two great European cities (Berlin and St Petersburg) is punctuated by several superb way stations. Warsaw deserves a couple of days and we highly recommend both **Toruń** (Poland) and **Vitebsk** (Belarus). Neither city is much visited by foreigners, yet both deserve a place in the premier league of European tourism. And each is intimately associated with one person: Toruń with the early 16th-century astronomer **Nicolaus Copernicus** and Vitebsk with the 20th-century painter **Marc Chagall**. So a Christian scientist and a Jewish artist, and that very nicely distils the essence of Route 45. The cities on this route are places that spawned new ways of looking at the sky and the stars, novel approaches to art and, in the case of St Petersburg, a whole new take on politics. The city was the cradle of the 1917 revolutions that deposed the Russian monarchy and brought the Bolsheviks to power. Route 45 is above all a journey for travellers sensitive to the **intellectual history** of Europe.

Take along a **Russian dictionary** and **phrase book**, and if you master the transliteration of the **Cyrillic alphabet**, you'll find your experience of that part of the route after you cross the River Bug into Belarus immensely more enriching. Be aware that you may encounter very few English speakers in Belarus and rural Russia. So have a few key phrases in Russian ever ready on the tip of your tongue. And don't forget to get any necessary visas (see the box on the next page).

BERLIN — SEE P450

Direct trains to St Petersburg all leave from the Hauptbahnhof in Berlin, and may be used *only* by travellers bound for Brest and beyond. **Brest** is the first railway station in Belarus, just over the border from Poland. If you plan to stop off in Poland, and we strongly suggest you do, then take one of the five daily express services that leave Berlin for **Poznań** and **Warsaw** (you can choose between the four times daily Berlin-Warsaw Express or, for early risers only, the pre-dawn *Jan Kiepura*).

Most trains stop at Frankfurt (Oder), before crossing a high bridge over the River Oder to reach Polish territory. From there it is a pleasant run through sparsely populated forests to Poznań.

POZNAŃ

The capital of **Wielkopolska** is one of Poland's most engaging and oldest cities. It was the seat of Poland's first bishop in the 10th century. A long-held status as a great mercantile centre (it's still an important centre for trade fairs) has contributed to the architectural heritage of its Old Town.

The city's focal point is **Stary Rynek**, a spacious square with gabled burghers' houses and a spectacular multicoloured 16th-century Renaissance **Town Hall**, where at midday two mechanical goats emerge from above the clock to lock horns. Inside is the **Chamber of the Renaissance** with its beautifully painted, coffered ceiling (1555) and the **Poznań Historical Museum** (free Sat). In the partly reconstructed **Royal Castle** on Przemysław Hill is the **Museum of Applied Arts**, with a wide-ranging collection through the ages, and a cellar full of poster art.

Several churches form an outer ring around the market square. Of those, the baroque **Poznań Parish Church** (Kolegiata Poznańska) at the southern end is dedicated to St Mary Magdalene. The **Jesuit College** next door, once Napoleon's residence, now hosts Chopin concerts. A short walk north-east of the centre is **Ostrów Tumski**, the oldest part of the city on an island in the River Warta; here stands the cathedral, fronted by a huge but gentle statue of Pope John Paul II.

BEFORE SETTING OFF

Most travellers will need to do some pre-planning before embarking on Route 45. Both **Russia and Belarus demand visas of most visitors** and these must be secured in advance. The visa requirement for Russia is waived only for holders of passports from selected Latin American nations, some western Balkan countries and some (not all) members of the Commonwealth of Independent States. For Belarus, the visa regime is even tighter than for Russia and some travellers who might not need a visa for Russia do require one for Belarus. Note that holders of EU passports, as well as visitors from North America, anywhere in Africa or Australasia and from India, China and Japan *all* require a visa for *both* countries. Visa regimes can change from year to year, so do check the current situation carefully before leaving home. The **consular sections** of the embassies of the **Republic of Belarus** and the **Russian Federation** in your home country will be able to advise.

Route Details

Berlin–Poznań — ERT 1001

Type	Frequency	Typical journey time
Train	5 daily	2h40

Poznań–Toruń — ERT 1020

Type	Frequency	Typical journey time
Train	4–5 daily	2h15

Toruń–Warsaw — ERT 1020

Type	Frequency	Typical journey time
Train	7–8 daily	2h55

Warsaw–Brest — ERT 1050

Type	Frequency	Typical journey time
Train	4 daily	4–5 hrs

Brest-Minsk — ERT 1950

Type	Frequency	Typical journey time
Train	5–6 daily	4h25

Minsk-Vitebsk — ERT 1920

Type	Frequency	Typical journey time
Train	8 daily	4h20 to 6 hrs

Vitebsk-St Petersburg — ERT 1920

Type	Frequency	Typical journey time
Train	3–4 daily	9–11 hrs

Notes

Remember that you will need advance reservations to board any train bound for Belarus or Russia in Germany or Poland. As you cross the border from Poland to Belarus, advance your watch by one hour in summer, two hours in winter. And clocks go forward a further hour on entering Russia.

Key Journeys

Berlin–Warsaw — ERT 56

Type	Frequency	Typical journey time
Train	4 daily	5h25

Warsaw–St Petersburg — ERT 94

Type	Frequency	Typical journey time
Train	2–5 weekly	31–32 hrs

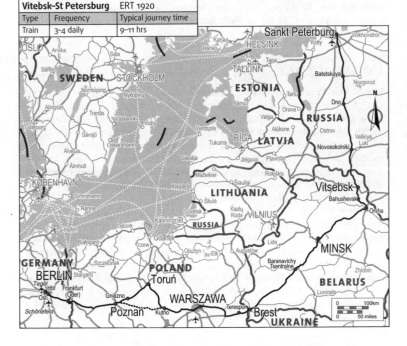

Poznań has two zoos and a vast palm house (in the botanic garden). Fifteen km south of the city is the 75-sq-km **Wielkopolski Park Narodowy** (a national park), easily accessible by train. Almost all museums in Poland are closed Mon.

Arrival, information, accommodation

≽ **Poznań Główny**, 24-hr rail information office, tourist information, cash machines, currency exchange, left luggage and shops; a 10-min walk to the centre or take trams 5/8. Buy tickets from one of the kiosks at the western exit. All international and domestic trains call here. **🚹 Tourist offices**: Stary Rynek 59/60, ☎ 61 852 6156, and the city information centre in the Arkadia shopping centre, ul. Ratajczaka 44, ☎ 61 851 9645 (www.poznan.pl). Get the map of Poznań, plus the *Welcome to Poznań & Wielkopolska* monthly magazine (with information in English). The PPWK-published map of Poznań is useful for travel outside the centre (shows bus routes).

🛏 If you can possibly splash out to stay at the **Brovaria**, Stary Rynek 73, ☎ 61 858 6868 (www.brovaria.pl), €€, and can secure one of the few rooms that overlook the Stary Rynek, then it is worth every złoty. There are a number of budget hotels on the edge of the city which offer cheap accommodation, such as **Gold**, ul. Bukowska 127A, ☎ 61 842 0774 (www.goldhotel.pl), €, or **Strzeszynek** at ul. Koszalińska 15, ☎ 61 848 3129, €. **Hostels**: The central **Fusion Hostel**, ul. Św. Marcin 66/72, ☎ 61 852 1230 (www.fusionhostel.pl), is fashionably designed, but caters to small budgets, offering rooms and dorms. New in 2011, **La Gitarra Hostel**, Aleje Karola Marcinkowskiego 20a, ☎ 61 852 2074 (www.lagitarra.com), is a promising addition to Poznan's hostel scene. Or try the **Frolic Goats Hostel**, ul. Wrocławska 16/6, ☎ 61 852 4411 (www.frolicgoatshostel.com).

Polish steam

Poznań Główny is one of the last remaining main-line stations in Europe where you can still see steam locomotives regularly hauling scheduled standard-gauge passenger trains. Two local trains daily from **Poznań** to **Wolsztyn** (ERT 1099) are usually **steam hauled**, though not in July or August or at other times when the risk of lineside fires is unduly high. The two departures from Poznań most consistently rostered for steam have been those around 0900 and 1700, though times for 2012 may vary. These services usually leave from Platform 4A, tucked away at the west end of the station. Other steam-hauled services (including occasional freight trains) may be seen in the Wolsztyn area.

That **Wolsztyn** has survived as an outpost of standard-gauge steam trains, long after they disappeared elsewhere in Europe, is the result of a remarkable cooperation between the Polish railway authorities and British train enthusiasts (www.thewolsztynexperience.org). The latter have provided financial support to ensure that the **locomotive depot** at Wolsztyn is kept operational. Local Polish staff retain the necessary skills to keep old locomotives in good order. The **steam trains** seen around Wolsztyn are immensely evocative of a bygone age of European rail travel. The area is often blanketed in winter by deep snow and in such conditions the engines are seen at their best.

Connections from Poznań

From Poznań, there are hourly trains south to **Wrocław** (2 hrs 35 mins to 3 hrs, ERT 1070) where you can connect onto **Route 49**. Route 45 leaves the eastbound main line towards Warsaw, deviating off to the north to take in Toruń. If you want to skip Toruń and head directly to Warsaw, there are plenty of direct trains from Poznań Główny to the Polish capital (2 hrs 40 mins, ERT 1005).

Toruń

This UNESCO World Heritage City on the **River Wisła** (Vistula) is second only to Kraków in terms of Poland's architectural heritage. Toruń has two distinct claims to fame: one is its gingerbread (which comes in dozens of varieties), the other great astronomer Nicolaus Copernicus (1473–1543), who broke new ground in arguing that the Sun, and not the Earth, is the centre of the solar system. The obvious starting point is the **Rynek Staromiejski** (Market Square). Its main building, the 14th-century **Ratusz** (Town Hall), houses the **Muzeum Okręgowe** (District Museum) and has panoramic views. Copernicus' house and alleged birthplace at ul. Kopernika 15–17 is now the **Nicolaus Copernicus Museum**, its interior recreated as it was in his day.

Toruń hosts many annual international festivals, including the **Probaltica** (music festival) and the **Kontakt** theatre festival in early May, the **Gingerbread Festival** in June, the **Artus** outdoors Jazz Festival in July and the **International Puppet Theatre Festival** in October.

Arrival, information, accommodation

≥ **Toruń Główny**, left luggage (main hall, window 7), restaurant; take 🚌 22/27 to the Old Town. **Toruń Miasto**, on a branch line, is more convenient for the city centre. 🚩 **Tourist office**: Rynek Staromiejski 25, ☎ 56 621 0931 (www.it.torun.pl).

🏨 Mid-range hotels in Torun include the **Petite Fleur**, Piekary 25, ☎ 56 621 5100 (www.petitefleur.pl), €€, and the **Hotel Polonia**, Plac Teatralny 5, ☎ 56 622 3028 (www.polonia.torun.pl); both centrally located. **Hostel**: The inexpensive **Orange Hostel** is centrally located in the Old Town, Prosta 19, ☎ 56 652 0033 (www.hostelorange.pl; free internet access and use of kitchen). **Campsite**: Tramp, ul. Kujawska 14, near the train station, ☎ 56 654 7187, open May to mid-Sept, huts and small hotel open year round, mini-golf.

Connections from Toruń

Toruń Główny is a good jumping-off point for journeys north to Poland's **Baltic coast**, where the star attraction is undoubtedly **Gdańsk** (4 hrs 30 mins, ERT 1020), the beautiful former Hanseatic port city that nurtured the early growth of the Solidarity social movement in the 1980s. It was in the Lenin shipyards in Gdańsk that **Lech Wałęsa** sowed the seeds of political change that bore fruit across central and eastern Europe in 1989. There are also good rail links from Toruń to Olsztyn (ERT 1020) and the **Mazurian Lake District**, a seductively beautiful area of Poland replete with opportunities for hiking and water sports. A daily train from Toruń to Suwałki (7 hrs 40 mins, ERT 1020 and 1045) meanders through rural Mazuria and provides a useful link onto **Route 46** north through the Baltic States to Finland.

WARSAW — SEE P587

There is not a lot to detain you on the run east from Warsaw to the border with Belarus. If you pause at any of the small communities beyond Łuków, you will surely be struck by how eastern they feel. **Biała Podlaska** is the most interesting of these small towns, a place on the main railway line from Paris to Moscow that has been trampled over by too many invading armies. Unsung, even unlovely you may say, and yet somehow immensely interesting. The town is surrounded by crumbling agricultural estates, but the real highlight is the decaying **castle**, once the home of the Radziwiłł family, in the heart of Biała Podlaska.

You will hear **Belarusian voices** too, a reminder that in this part of Europe political boundaries, often imposed from outside, do not always coincide with linguistic and cultural frontiers. What you will no longer hear in these small towns of eastern Poland are **Yiddish voices**. Prior to the Second World War, Jews numbered more than 50% of the population of this part of the country.

Last stop in Poland is **Terespol**. The very size of the station building, a dated piece of 1960s modernism that still bustles with peak-capped officials and sniffer dogs, is a reminder that this is one of Europe's great remaining borders. The very existence of the military border zone that extends along the valley of the **River Bug** has provided a measure of protection for the delicate environment of the area. So the 20-minute journey from Terespol to Brest, when the train rumbles slowly over girder bridges spanning the river and adjacent reed beds and wetlands, affords superb views of a **watery wilderness** below. Once over on the east bank of the river, there is (on the right-hand side) a magnificent view of the **striking red fortress** that dominates the city of Brest.

In Brest, trains arriving from Poland are shunted into a shed, jacked up, and the wheel bogies swapped for the wider gauge versions necessary on the broader railway tracks that are the norm throughout the former Soviet Union.

BREST (БРЕСТ)

Look out of the carriage window and you know at once that you have entered another world. Suddenly Cyrillic script has eclipsed the Latin alphabet used in western and central Europe. Brest is the main western **gateway to Belarus**, and the city's 19th-century fortress underlines Brest's role as the guardian of a main east-west trade route. Venture out from the railway for your first real glimpse of Belarus and you'll almost certainly be struck by the youthful energy and gentle dynamism of Brest. The star-shaped **fortress**, once dominated by four great gateways (of which just two remain), with a citadel in the centre, is the principal sight and a place to lose yourself for hours. It is open daily until nightfall, and is at its best in the quiet of a June evening when low sun angles emphasise the red hues of the stonework. The city centre has excellent shopping and at its southern fringe blends into a **riverside park** with some lovely willows and ducks aplenty.

ARRIVAL, INFORMATION, ACCOMMODATION
≋ **Brest Tsentralny** railway station is at the north end of the city centre. ❽ Quite unusually for Belarus, you'll find a **tourist information office**, ☎ 162 01 071 tucked away on the first floor of the **Hotel Intourist** at Masherov Prospekt 15, ☎ 162 202 083, €€, an unattractive ex-Soviet pile on Masherova Prospekt, but a safe place to stop overnight. ⊨ Another obvious choice is the **Hotel Bug**, 2 Lenina Str, ☎ 162 236 170, €, right opposite the train station on the corner of Lenina. Sadly, the interior doesn't match up to the rather inviting exterior but it is extraordinarily good value. An alternative is the **Hotel Belarus**, Bulvar Shevchenko, ☎ 162 221 648, €€.

CONNECTIONS FROM BREST
There are one or two daily direct overnight trains to **Vitebsk** (14–17 hrs), later on Route 45, if you don't mind sleeping through most of Belarus and missing the capital Minsk.

MINSK (MIHCK)
The capital of Belarus has that same unhurried feel that you encountered in Brest. It is, for many visitors, one of the most appealing aspects of Belarus. Minsk has the predictable array of monuments and museums that come with a country very determined to assert its own distinctive identity and its separateness from its dominant eastern neighbour, Russia. Highlights include the **Belarusian State Museum of the Great Patriotic War** on Nezavisimosti 25a (closed Mon) and the **Museum of the History and Culture of Belarus** on Karla Marksa 12 (closed Wed). Don't expect sparkling displays or any glitz. Both museums rely on old-style curatorial techniques. Minsk is a great place just to wander, and you'll find splendid Stalinist architectural ensembles around **Independence Square** and along the main thoroughfares that run north-east from Independence Square towards **Victory Square**, on the far side of the River Svislach.

ARRIVAL, INFORMATION, ACCOMMODATION
≋ The main station on Pryvokzalnaya Square is right in the heart of the city, a stone's throw south from Independence Square. The city is very walkable, but do take a ride on the impressively efficient **metro**. A token for a one-way journey, purchased at the ticket window on entering any station, costs 950 Belarusian rubles (less than €0.20). ❽ **Tourist office**: Prospekt Pobediteley 19, ☎ 17 226 9900.
⊨ The **Hotel Express**, 4 Pryvokzalnaya, ☎ 225 64 63, €, right by the main station, is strictly for the really desperate. That it is cheap is the best that can be said of it. The **Hotel Belarus**, 15 Storozhevskaya, ☎ 209 76 93 (www.en.hotel-

belarus.com), €€, is a good mid-range choice but be aware that prices vary considerably with many grades of room. The hotel is in a great location in parkland just north of the city centre. The **Hotel Orbita**, on Pushkin St, ☎ 252 39 33 (www. orbita-hotel.com/eng), €€, is another safe choice, with some cheap basic rooms and then the whole range up to luxury suites. It is also possible to rent private apartments, which can work out cheaper than hotels. Other mid-range hotels include **Hotel Sputnik**, 2 Brilevskaya, ☎ 220 36 19 (http://en.sputnik-hotel.com), €€, and **Hotel Yubileynaya**, 19 Pobediteley, ☎ 226 90 24, €€. Minsk also has some luxury five-star hotels, priced like their counterparts elsewhere in the world, which require a serious splurge: **Hotel Minsk**, 11 Nezavisimosti, ☎ 209 90 78 (www.hotelminsk.by) and the **Hotel Victoria**, 59 Pobediteley, ☎ 204 88 44 (www.hotel-victoria.by), both €€€, are two such options.

Connections from Minsk

Minsk is one of eastern Europe's principal transport hubs. Take your pick of direct trains to Venice or Paris, Sofia or Siberia. Users of this book might find the direct trains to Lithuania and Ukraine most useful, providing a link at Vilnius onto **Route 46** and at Lviv onto **Routes 49** and **50**.

Vitebsk (Витебск)

The last major city in Belarus before the Russian border is Vitebsk. Put at its simplest, Vitebsk is superb. The birthplace of **Marc Chagall** was an important centre of Jewish life in the 19th century, a place that was still just within the permitted area of Jewish settlement (called the Pale), yet within striking distance of both Moscow and St Petersburg. Most of the main sights are on the east bank of the Western Dvina. The conspicuous exception is the old Jewish quarter which is on the west bank just 8 mins walk north-east of the railway station. The house on **Pokrovskaya** where Chagall lived as a child is nowadays a museum devoted to his work (closed Mon).

Across the river, on the east side of Kirova Bridge, there is a quartet of first-rate churches of which two of the most impressive are the newly renovated Orthodox **Market Church** (sometimes called the Resurrection Church) and the homely little wooden church on the river bank devoted to Alexander Nevsky. The latter looks as though it has been there for centuries, but actually was only built in 1993. The other two are the **Annunciation Church**, right beside and dwarfing the wooden church, and the **Church of the Dormition of Mary** which stands boldly on a bluff overlooking the river. It is worth walking up for the fine view, even though the interior is currently closed for renovation. Strike north from this last church past the old governor's palace to the **Marc Chagall Art Centre** on ul. Putna (closed Mon), which has a decent collection of memorabilia connected to Chagall, including some etchings and lithographs. Sadly, none of Chagall's more famous paintings are on display in his home city.

⇌ The railway station building is one of the last gasps of Stalinist design, and most travellers nowadays walk round it rather than through it. The station is 1 km west of the centre on the west bank of the Western Dvina River. Just walk up ul. Kirova towards Kirova Bridge. 🅱 The **tourist office** is in the Hotel Vetrazh on Chernyakovsky Prospekt 25/1, ☎ 212 21 72 04. 🍴 The **Hotel Eridan**, 21/17 Sovetskaya str, ☎ 212 36 24 56 (www.eridan-vitebsk.com), €€, is in a prime spot by the Marc Chagall Art Centre while the **Luchesa**, Stroiteley Avenue, ☎ 212 29 85 00 (www.luchesa.by), €€, 2 km south of the centre, pitches more to the business market but is still good value. Otherwise, try the **Hotel Vetrazh**, Chernyakovsky Prospekt 25/1 , ☎ 212 27 22 75, €€.

NORTH TO RUSSIA

Travelling north from Vitebsk through gently undulating country and **endless forests**, you cross the border into Russia. You may not get quite the same reception in St Petersburg as the rapturous welcome that awaited Lenin and his wife Nadya in 1917. But, whether this be your first visit to Russia or you are an old hand at Russian travel, you'll surely have that distinctive feeling of now being in a Europe very different from the one you left behind in Berlin.

ST PETERSBURG — SEE P562

SIDETRACKS N: SIBERIA BECKONS

Travelling widens your horizons, so they say. And as you travel east across Europe, you inevitably become much more aware of the vast areas that lie beyond the regions with which you profess some familiarity. In Cologne, you might glimpse a train bound for Vienna or perhaps you'll see the smart blue and red carriages of the train bound for Moscow. But the real **widening of horizons** comes in Berlin, when suddenly you realise that you could catch a direct train from the German capital to dozens of destinations across Russia. Europe's most outlandish train leaves Berlin every Saturday afternoon bound for **Saratov** and beyond (ERT 1980). During the summer months, it has through carriages to Sochi and Adler on Russia's Black Sea coast. The Russian Riviera still pulls the summer crowds and will no doubt establish its credentials as a winter resort too when Sochi hosts the Winter Olympics in 2014.

But whatever the time of year, that Saturday train from Berlin always has through carriages to Siberia. Yes, you really can travel by direct train from Berlin to **Novosibirsk**, a four-day journey that will take you beyond the Ural Mountains into Asia from whence you could travel on directly to China, Mongolia or North Korea. Such journeys are the marathons of rail travel, strictly for addicts and not to be attempted before you've tackled some of the longer routes in this book and know that you have an appetite for endless days on trains. As you travel Route 45, look at other trains along the way. You may see the direct train from Poland to **Kazakhstan**, and once in Belarus, the chances are you'll see carriages bound for the **Russian Arctic**.

Rail Route 46: Exploring the Baltic States

CITIES: ★★ CULTURE: ★★ HISTORY: ★★ SCENERY: ★
COUNTRIES COVERED: POLAND, LITHUANIA, LATVIA, ESTONIA, FINLAND

For many travellers from western Europe, the three Baltic States are a first encounter with post-Soviet space. Estonia, Latvia and Lithuania are all now members of both the European Union and the Schengen area, but they only seceded from the Soviet Union well after the fall of the Berlin Wall. Their status as autonomous independent republics secured widespread international recognition after the August 1991 coup attempt in Moscow.

So Route 46 is an adventurous journey through **recent European history**, one that along the way links five capital cities (including those of the three Baltic States) and takes in some serenely beautiful landscapes. It is a journey that will test the patience of rail travellers (see box on p377), and there are some legs where buses are just far more practical than rail services. And for the final leg of Route 46, from **Tallinn** to **Helsinki**, you have to take one of the frequent boat services across the **Gulf of Finland**. So this really is a multi-modal journey involving trains, buses and ships.

Route 46 can also be used as an alternative to **Route 45** from Warsaw to St Petersburg, one that does not cut through Belarus and so avoids the need to secure a Belarusian visa (but does not of course obviate the need for a Russian visa to visit St Petersburg). From both **Riga** and **Vilnius** there are direct overnight trains to St Petersburg (ERT 1820). The direct rail service from Tallinn to St Petersburg has not run since 2008, but frequent buses link the two cities in about 7 hrs (ERT 1870). From Helsinki, the Allegro train service launched in December 2010 will speed you to St Petersburg in just 3 hrs 36 mins (ERT 1910).

WARSAW — P587

The sole remaining train from Warsaw to Lithunia is the *Hańcza*, taking its name from Poland's deepest lake which is in the beautiful region of forest and lakes through which the train passes shortly before crossing the border into Lithuania. While the first part of the journey, running north-east from Warsaw, is humdrum, the scenery really picks up beyond Białystok.

NORTH-EAST POLAND

If you have time to explore the remote areas of north-east Poland through which the train passes en route to the Lithuanian border, three places served by the *Hańcza* all warrant a visit and serve as good bases for exploring the surrounding countryside. They are Białystok, Augustów and Suwałki, and all have plenty of direct trains from Warsaw apart from the *Hańcza*.

Route Details

Warsaw–Białystok ERT 1040

Type	Frequency	Typical journey time
Train	10–12 daily	2h30

Białystok–Kaunus ERT 1040

Type	Frequency	Typical journey time
Train	1 daily	5h30

Kaunus–Vilnius ERT 1811

Type	Frequency	Typical journey time
Train	10–12 daily	1 hr

Vilnius–Riga ERT 1800

Type	Frequency	Typical journey time
Bus	8 daily	4h30

Riga–Tartu ERT 1800 or 1880

Type	Frequency	Typical journey time
Bus	3 daily	4 hrs
Train	1 daily	5 hrs (change Valga)

Tartu–Tallinn ERT 1880

Type	Frequency	Typical journey time
Train	3–4 daily	3 hrs

Tallinn–Helsinki ERT 2410

Type	Frequency	Typical journey time
Ship	Up to 10 daily	2–3 hrs

Key Journeys

Warsaw–Vilnius ERT 1040

Type	Frequency	Typical journey time
Train	1 daily	9h30

Riga–Tallinn ERT 1800

Type	Frequency	Typical journey time
Bus	7 daily	4h25 to 5 hrs

Notes

On journeys from Białystok to Kaunus, and from Warsaw to Vilnius, it is necessary to change trains at Šeštokai. Put your watch forward by one hour as you cross from Poland into Lithuania. For the final leg from Tallinn to Helsinki there are also high-speed craft connecting the cities up to 7 times daily taking 1h30.

Białystok is a major provincial centre and railway junction, a one-time Jewish *shtetl* that has become a place of pilgrimage for Esperanto speakers. Dr L L Zamenhof, inventor of the artificial language, hailed from the town. Out of town, near the border with Belarus, there are a number of Tatar villages. Three hundred years or more after their ancestors arrived, these people nowadays think of themselves as being totally Polish, but curiously the villages still have mosques.

Augustów is well placed for exploring the unspoilt forests east of the town. This area, known as the *puszcza*, is wonderful country for walking and cycling. The dense network of waterways also makes canoeing a good option. Suwałki, even closer to the Lithuanian border, also has good access to the surrounding lakes and forests. A striking feature of this region of Poland is how historically it was such a melting pot of peoples and cultures. Tucked away in the forests around Suwałki, you will still find Old Believer villages, peopled by conservative Orthodox Christians who fled from Russia to escape the Nikonian reforms of the 17th century. From Suwałki, it is an hour on the *Hańcza* to Šeštokai in Lithuania. As the railway tracks in Lithuania are built to the Russian gauge, a little wider than in Poland, this is the end of the line for the *Hańcza*, and you need to change trains.

KAUNAS

Kaunas was the capital of independent Lithuania from 1920 to 1940, and retains an air of elegance as Lithuania's second city. Laisvės, the city's pride and joy, is a pedestrianised, tree-lined boulevard, bordered with shops and cafés that reflect increasing prosperity. Near the Vytautas the Great War Museum at Donelaičio 64, the MK Ciurlionis National Art Museum (www.ciurlionis.lt) on Putvinskio houses a vast collection of modern Lithuanian and folk art. The nearby Devils Museum is a collection of over 2,000 depictions of devils from all over the world, generally attesting to the Lithuanian sense of humour, but with an edgy admixture of more political fodder, such as the demons Hitler and Stalin dancing over Lithuania (all three museums closed Mon). A walk eastwards, along Putvinskio, leads to the funicular, which ascends the 'green hill' for a fine view over the city; you can pay using a trolleybus ticket. Perkūnas House on Aleksoto g. 6 is the finest example of late Gothic architecture in the town, and houses handicraft displays at weekends.

ARRIVAL, INFORMATION, ACCOMMODATION

➤ Kaunas' railway station, rather grander than any of the trains that serve it, is south-east of the city centre — immediately opposite the terminal for long-distance coaches. Frequent trolleybuses into town. **🅱 Tourist office**: Laisvės alėja 36, ☎ 37 32 34 36 (http://visit.kaunas.lt).

🛏 Budget hotels in good locations include the **Apple Economy Hotel**, M. Valančiaus 19, ☎ 37 32 14 04 (www.applehotel.lt), €, which is close to the castle, and the **Metropolis**, Daukanto 21, ☎ 37 20 59 92 (www.metropolishotel.lt), €. Two slightly

Baltic trains

As you travel through Lithuania, Latvia and Estonia you will frequently hear locals explaining away their sometimes abysmal rail services, with particularly poor cross-border links, as a consequence of the three countries having until 21 years ago been part of the **Soviet Union**. 'All lines led to Moscow, and only to Moscow', is a common refrain. But the truth is otherwise.

Cast back to 1989, and the *Chaika Express* day train ran from Tallinn via Riga to Vilnius. From Vilnius there were also direct trains to Warsaw and Berlin. In the new post-independence piety of the 1990s, when car ownership in the Baltic States rocketed, the region's railways were left to rot. Many routes closed, and elsewhere the lack of investment in infrastructure meant that line speeds were so reduced that buses easily outpaced trains — so giving weight to the view that trains were an unfortunate relic of the Soviet period.

Nowadays, there is only one train a day from **Poland** to **Lithuania**, and that requires a change of trains just north of the Polish border at Šeštokai for onward travel to the main Lithuanian cities of Kaunas and Vilnius. Don't be misled by the direct overnight train from Warsaw to Vilnius shown in some timetables. Since 2005, this 'train' is actually a bus and surely not a comfortable way of getting a good night's sleep.

Just one train a day runs from **Lithuania** north into **Latvia**, and frankly we would not recommend it if your destination is Riga. From Vilnius to Riga takes 15 hrs (ERT 1820 and 1850) including an enforced overnight stop at Daugavpils, Latvia's dreary second city which really does not have a lot going for it. So, unless you are a real diehard for rail travel, better to take the express bus which takes just 4 hrs 30 mins (ERT 1800) from Vilnius to Riga.

The situation on the **Latvian-Estonian border** is pretty dismal too. The cross-border rail link, closed after independence, has been revived, and three trains daily now run from Riga to Valga in Estonia. But there, only one of the three connects with an onward Estonian train to Tartu and Tallinn. The same applies in the reverse direction. The journey from Tallinn to Riga or vice versa is just over 8 hrs (see ERT 1880 for timings). Yet it is a journey worth making, one which is therapeutic in its relaxed pace, affording along the way a close engagement with passing forests and remote villages. If you are in a rush, take the bus (4 hrs 25 mins to 5 hrs ERT 1800).

Yet all is not doom and gloom in Baltic rail travel. A **new rail link** connecting Vilnius city centre with the airport opened in 2008 (ERT 1812). A couple of minor branch lines in Lithuania have recently reopened. A partnership programme with Finnish Railways led to the renewal of outdated infrastructure from **Tartu** (Estonia) to the Latvian border and the route was reopened in 2010.

And planners are now sketching out ideas to transform rail travel in the Baltic States. The **Rail Baltica project** would see a new axis linking Warsaw with Tallinn. If ever it comes to pass, express trains might one day speed from Warsaw to Tallinn in just ten hours, and then we shall all look back and fondly remember the good old days when Route 46 required grit and determination. But there is yet time. Even if Rail Baltica goes ahead, the first trains will not run before 2020.

more expensive options, are the **Centre Hotel Nuova**, Savanoriu 66/31, ☎ 37 24 40 07 (www.centrehotel.lt), €€, and the tongue-twisting **Kunigaikščių Menė**, M. Dauksos 28, ☎ 37 32 08 88 (www.hotelmene.lt). **Hostel**: **City Hostel**, Kęstučio 91, opened in 2011 in the Old Town and has dorms and a double room, ☎ 60 76 85 85 (www.city-hostel.lt).

VILNIUS

With its cobbled winding streets, the heart of the Lithuanian capital is instantly appealing. This is the least visited of the three Baltic capitals and Vilnius' appeal lies partly in its comparative obscurity. The main street that bisects the town, **Gedimino**, could be a useful place to start and return to as it connects the old and new parts of Vilnius.

Cathedral Square, the focal point of the city, witnessed mass anti-Soviet demonstrations in the run-up to independence in 1991. **Sts Stanislav and Vladislav Cathedral** was built on an ancient site dedicated to the god of thunder. Rebuilt eleven times, it received its classical facade in 1783–1801. Within its St Casimir's Chapel are the splendid tombs of the members of the Polish-Lithuanian royal dynasty. Sts Johns' Church, the university church, has the striking **belfry**, which is among the highest buildings of the Old Town. The Gediminas Tower in Arsenalo st. 5 is all that remains of the royal castle and now contains the **Gediminas Castle Tower Museum**. Take the funicular from the bottom of Gediminas Hill up to the tower. From the tower's observation platform you get wonderful views of the Old Town. Adjacent to the Sts Stanislav and Vladislav Cathedral is **Kalnų Park**, a shady streamside sanctuary. T Kosciuškos leads eastwards from the north side of the park to **Sts Peter and Paul's Church**, the finest baroque church interior in Vilnius, with over 2,000 stucco figures.

From Cathedral Square, Gedimino leads westwards into modern Vilnius, terminating at the Parliament building. Adjacent to the **Lithuanian Music and Theatre Academy** are the old KGB headquarters, now home to the **Museum of Genocide Victims**, Gedimino 40 (entrance from Aukų 2A; conducted tours of the cells, sometimes by former inmates, Wed–Sun). **Vilnius Picture Gallery** can be found at Didžioji 4, where tickets for all the branch galleries can be purchased (student and other concessions available).

Note that museums and galleries are usually closed on Mon. Avoid the districts of Užupis and Kalvarijų late at night.

ARRIVAL, INFORMATION, ACCOMMODATION

🚆 The railway station is at Geležinkelio 16 (24 hr currency exchange close by). Luggage lockers are available at the station, but given the complexity of coins needed to operate them, it is easiest to use the proper baggage store at the 🚌 bus station over the road. Vilnius is less good for international bus connections (particularly to Poland) than Kaunas. From both the bus and railway station it is a 10-min walk into the city centre, or take trolleybus 1/2/5/7.

TRIPS FROM VILNIUS

Trakai, the old medieval capital (**⚑ tourist office**: Vytauto 69, ☎ 5 285 1934), has an impressive (restored) castle, dating from the 14th century, on a picturesque lake. The castle is open daily (frequent buses and trains; just under 1 hr).

Don't miss **Grutas Park**, the sculpture graveyard for the Lenins, Stalins and their local acolytes who used to dominate every town and village square in Lithuania. Also a large museum dedicated to the Soviet period. Take any bus bound for Druskininkai and say 'Grutas' to the driver so that he puts you off at the right stop, about 90 mins after leaving Vilnius.

⚑ **Tourist office**: Vilniaus 22, ☎ 5 262 96 60 (www.vilnius-tourism.lt). The staff will book accommodation and arrange guides. Other branches are at the railway station and at Cathedral Square (summer only). Buy *Vilnius in Your Pocket,* a guide to the city's sights, hotels, restaurants and bars (also online at www.inyourpocket.com). The most attractive part of the city, the Old Town, is best explored on foot. Public transport runs 0500–2300. Buy tickets at kiosks (cheaper) or from the driver.

🚅 Mid-range hotels worth checking out include the **Ecotel Vilnius**, Slucko 8, ☎ 5 210 27 00 (www.ecotel.lt), €€, and the **Ambassador**, Gedimino 12, ☎ 5 261 54 50 (www.ambassador.lt), €€. **Hostels**: Possibly the best-located of the hostels is the **Hostelgate**, Šv. Mikalojaus 3/1, ☎ 638 328 18 (www.hostelgate.lt). New for 2011, **Jimmy Jumps House/Hostel**, Savičiaus gatvė 12–1, ☎ 607 88 435 (www. jimmyjumpshouse.com), is within walking distance of the train station. Another hostel worth trying is the **Hostel Filaretai**, Filaretu 17, ☎ 5 215 46 27 (www.filaretaihostel.lt). ✗ The cheapest food is from supermarkets or the colourful food market at Hales Turgaviete on the corner of Pylimo and Bazilijonu.

RIGA (RĪGA)

Of the Baltic Republics, Latvia has the strongest remaining links with Russia, and roughly 30% of its inhabitants are Russian speakers. You'll hear Russian all the time on the streets of Riga. Nevertheless, the country and its capital have asserted their independence from Russia, and Riga has witnessed a growth in tourism. Riga has four elements — a 17th-century **Hanseatic town** preserved as the historic core, a large monumentally Parisian-style quarter of boulevards, parks and **art nouveau** architecture and the odd Stalinist building beyond the fortifications, a Soviet industrial and urban wasteland and finally a new financial centre of glass skyscrapers. There is no need to stray from the northern shore unless you want to cross the bridge to look at the Old Town's church spires from a distance. You can walk the Old Town but you might need public transport for the Parisian-feeling area.

Riga's **Old Town** is a mass of winding streets, attractive old buildings and a great number of worthwhile churches. Don't miss the **cathedral** and the other large churches of the Old Town, the **Central Market** or **Riga Castle**. Adjacent to the rail and bus stations is the eye-opening Central Market on Nēģu iela. Housed in five huge former Zeppelin hangars, it's a mixture of meat, varieties of bread, dairy products, vegetables and anything else edible. The approaches often consist of lines of women selling things like outdated lingerie to make a bit of money.

Cross the road by the tunnel and proceed up Aspazijas bulv. On the right is the beautifully restored **National Opera**, and the old moat, set in a linear park on the site of the old fortifications. The wide expanse of **Brīvības bulv.** on the right, leads to the **Freedom Monument**. A guard is mounted (and changed) every hour by the new Latvian Army. Turn left down Torņa iela. The **Pulvertonis** (Gunpowder Tower) on the left now houses the **Latvian War Museum** (closed Mon & Tues). The road continues past the surviving (but much restored) section of the Old Town wall, dating from the 13th century. It ends with the picturesque Swedish Gate, built in 1698, ironically just 12 years before Riga fell to Peter the Great.

Riga Castle dates from 1330 and contains the official residence of the President of Latvia and museums of Latvian history, foreign art and Latvian culture. On the cobbled cathedral square, the cathedral is the largest place of worship in the Baltics, and is renowned for its organ. In Mazā Pils iela, **The Three Brothers** are the most famous of Riga's old houses, dating from the 15th century. For an excellent view of the city, ascend the tower of **St Peter's Church** on Skārņu iela. **Town Hall Square** still hosts a large monument to the Latvian Red Riflemen who were Lenin's bodyguard and fought with the Bolsheviks, but its highlight is the restored **House of the Blackheads**, a lay order of bachelor merchants. It was blown up by the Soviets in 1948 to clear the square of any German links but was rebuilt in the 1990s. The **Occupation Museum** (free) at Strēlnieku laukums 1 displays the sufferings of the Latvian people under the Nazi and Soviet regimes.

ARRIVAL, INFORMATION, ACCOMMODATION

⇌ On the south-eastern edge of the city centre. International trains are booked at windows 1–6, immediate departure tickets for local services from windows 7–12. Bear in mind that the station is now Riga's largest shopping centre, in which trains are largely an irrelevance. Most people come here to buy designer clothes, try exotic foods or to arrange mortgages. Banks here are open seven days a week. Avoid exchange bureaux (Valūtas maiņa), which often give terrible rates.

🚌 Bus station: Near the rail station, adjacent to the Central Market, ☎ 9000 0009 (www.autoosta.lv). There is a tourist office, left luggage and a day hotel with a waiting room and shower facilities. 🛈 **Tourist office**: Rātslaukums 6, ☎ 6703 7900 (www.liveriga.com). On sale here (and in some hotels) is the **Riga Card**, which offers free admission to major sights and unlimited city transport journeys (24 hrs for 12Ls, 48 hrs for 14Ls, 72 hrs for 18Ls). You can buy a 0.70Ls ticket from the driver of **trams, trolleybuses** and **buses**, or purchase cheaper electronic e-talons tickets for a specific number of rides or a time period ranging from one to five days at newsstands around Riga. Large pieces of luggage cost an extra 0.80Ls. If you must take a cab, call **Lady Taxi**, ☎ 2780 0900, a reliable service that only employs women drivers.

📧 For an excellent budget hotel beyond the Central Market, try **Dodo Hotel**, Jersikas iela 1, ☎ 6724 0220 (www.dodohotel.lv), €–€€. **Jakob Lenz Guesthouse**, Lenču iela 2, ☎ 6733 3343 (www.guesthouselenz.lv), €€, is a good central option. **Hostels**: There are quite a few good hostels in Riga, including **Friendly Fun Franks Hostel**, 11 Novembra Krastmala, ☎ 2599 0612 (www.franks.lv) and the **Argonaut Hostel**, Kaleju iela 50, ☎ 614 7214 (www.argonauthostel.com). Newly-opened, the **Cinnamon Sally Backpackers**, Merkela 1, ☎ 2204 2280 (www.cinnamonsally.com), has quickly established itself as one of the leading hostels in the city.

✗ The streets of the Old Town have seen a rapid increase in the number and variety of bars and restaurants. There are eating places to suit all pockets from Russian fast-food joints (serving *pelmeni*, a Russian-style ravioli) to local specialities and branches of familiar Western chains. The LIDO chain of Latvian self-service buffets offers hearty local fare for very reasonable prices. The national drink is **Riga Black Balsam**, a potent herbal liquor with a bitter taste, which is often drunk with coffee or blackcurrant juice. It can be bought at any bar or supermarket. Don't forget to try the local rye and sourdough breads known as *rupjmaize* and *saldskābmaize*.

TARTU

Tartu is Estonia's foremost university town, built into a wooded hill, with picturesque views. Avoid it on Mondays and Tuesdays when most museums are closed. The concrete river bridge replaces the original stone bridge of 1784, which symbolised Tartu and which was bombed by the Russians in 1944. It is hoped that the original may be rebuilt in due course. The **Tartu Citizens' Museum**, Jaani 16, is an 1830s town house. **St John's Church** at Jaani 5 has been totally restored, including its terracotta statues. The university was founded by King Gustav Adolphus of Sweden in 1632 (whose statue is behind it) but the classical university building dates from 1809.

The **Town Hall Square** is probably the most photographed spot in Tartu. At one end is the bridge and at the other the fine neoclassical Town Hall, built in 1778–84. Notice the leaning house (No. 18) — one wall is built on the foundation of the town wall, the other isn't. Take time out to explore **Toomemägi**, the hill behind the Town Hall. You can cross the 'sighing bridge' to ascend 'kissing hill'. There's a sacrificial stone upon which Tartu students burn their notes at the end of final exams. The excellent **Estonian National Museum**, Kuperjanovi 9, covers everything a museum should, but look out for the collections of gloves and beer tankards. It has also opened the grounds of Raadi Manor house, to the east of Tartu, to the general public.

ARRIVAL, INFORMATION, ACCOMMODATION

🚆 Tartu's station building has been under redevelopment for some years. The station is 1.5 km south-west of the city centre. The platform is accessible from the south end and tickets are bought on the train. The simplest way into the town centre is right along Vaksali, and then left along Riia, or by local bus. 🚌 Bus station: Soola 2, junction of Riia and Turu, the Town Hall Square is only a 10-min walk. 🛈 **Tourist office:** Raekoja plats 9, ☎ 372 740 0782 (www.visittartu.com). 🛏 The **Hotell Tartu**, Soola 3, by the bus station ☎ 372 731 4300 (www.tartuhotell.ee), €€, has a number of dorm rooms as well as private ones, but the communal areas are certainly those of a hotel and not a hostel. **Vaksali 4**, Vaksali 4, ☎ 372 510 4698 (www.hostel4.ee), is beside the old railway station so a short bus ride into town or a 20-min walk. The official **youth hostel** (HI), is the **Hiie Hostel**, Hiie 10, ☎ 742 1236 (www.bed.ee), a 15-minute walk from Tartu town hall.

TALLINN

Over the past few years, Tallinn has become something of a tourist mecca both for Finns on booze cruises and western Europeans exploring further afield. Said by some to be the Prague of the Baltic States, the old parts of the town are compact, manageable and a delight to explore on foot both during the day and at night. **Nightlife** in Tallinn goes on into the small hours particularly on the long summer nights (the summer season is very short so the locals and visitors need to take advantage of it while it is there). **Live music** is common and there is a vibrant atmosphere on the streets.

The increase in tourist traffic has led to a sharp rise in the number of shops with top-quality local goods (linen, leather, suede and woollen products) and a wide variety of craft stalls and stores selling local specialities. The old part of Tallinn is thick with attractive **cobbled streets**, picturesque painted houses, medieval churches and fortifications. Against a stretch of the medieval wall surrounding the **Old Town**, which can be entered through a number of gates, there is a craft market, specialising in traditionally patterned fishermen's knitwear and multi-bobbled hats. Katariina käik is a medieval alley tenanted by craftswomen and is lined with ancient gravestones. **Tallinn City Museum**, Vene 17, has a section on modern history, with videos bringing to life the drama of 1989–1991 (closed Tues). From here it's a short walk through the **Vana Turg** (Old Market) into the Raekoja plats (Town Hall Square), with its outdoor cafés on the cobbles, and watched over by the Gothic town hall of 1404 (sporting Vana Toomas, or Old Thomas, the city guardian, on its tower — which can be climbed).

St Nicholas Church at Niguliste 3 houses medieval art, including a striking 15th-century *Dance of Death*, while the **Orthodox Cathedral of Alexander Nevsky** of 1900 is worth a look if you've never seen the interior of a Russian church. No hint of Estonia here. Across Lossi plats is **Toompea Castle**, the seat of government: walk around its 18th-century facade (hiding the medieval structure) and see **Tall Hermann**, the tower from which the Estonian flag, banned in the Soviet era, now proudly flies. From here Toomkooli leads to the cathedral (called the Toomkirik), Tallinn's oldest church, founded by the Danes and much rebuilt. It contains fine gravestones and crests of Swedish and German noblemen, plus a memorial to one of many Scottish Jacobite naval officers who left Britain and joined the Russian service (closed Mon). Nearby **Toompea Hill** has two good viewpoints, one over the Old Town and the other looking towards the harbour.

Returning to the **Orthodox Cathedral**, Pikk Jalg (long leg) drops between the walls of Toompea and Tallinn proper (the two communities didn't get on). The charming gate leads to Pikk. On the corner is the Church of the Holy Ghost, with a memorial to British sailors who helped in the fight for Estonian independence in 1918–20. The **Estonian History Museum** is on Pirita tee 56 in Maajamäe Palace (closed Mon & Tues).

ARRIVAL, INFORMATION, ACCOMMODATION

≋ Near Tallinn's Old Town and harbour at Toompuiestee 37. It has been recently renovated, inside it has an upmarket restaurant and day spa. A 10-min walk to the Old Town or take tram 1 or 2. 🚌 Bus station: Lastekodu 46, ☎ 125 50, some distance from the centre (take tram 2/4 or 🚌 17/17a). To be sure of a seat, buy tickets before travel. Some bus journeys can now be booked online (www.bussireisid.ee).

🛈 Tourist office: Niguliste 2/Kullassepa 4, ☎ 645 77 77 (www.tourism.tallinn.ee), good for timetables for buses, trains and ferries to Finland, and for current information on museum opening hours and concerts. Poor for guidebooks and cards, which are best bought over the road at Raamatukoi bookshop. The tourist office sells the **Tallinn Card**: includes admission to major sights, unlimited city transport journeys, a boat trip in Pirita Harbour, a city tour and discounts in some restaurants. Good value for longer stays (available for 1/2/3 days for €24/32/40). **Trams** connect harbour, rail and bus stations with Viru väljak (Viru Square); there are also buses and trolleybuses. Tickets can be bought from the driver but are half the price if bought in booklets of ten from kiosks; 24 and 48 hour tickets offer further savings.

🚢 The **Hotel Economy**, Kopli 2c, ☎ 667 83 00 (www.economyhotel.ee), €–€€, is close to the train station. Other budget hotel options include the **Braavo**, Aia 20, ☎ 699 97 77 (www.braavo.ee), €€, and the **Bed & Breakfast Rex**, Tartu mnt. 62, ☎ 50 78 650, €. **Hostel** options are many and varied. Some of the best-regarded hostels in town include the **Oldhouse Hostel**, Uus 22–1, ☎ 6411 464 (www.oldhouse.ee), the **Alur Hostel**, Lai 20, ☎ 6466 210 (www.alur.ee), and the **Flying Kiwi Backpackers**, Nunne 1, ☎ 5821 3292 (www.flyingkiwitallinn.com).

ONWARD BY SHIP

The final leg of Route 46 is the voyage from Tallinn to Helsinki. There are four different operators with a range of **hydrofoil** and fast **ferry services**. This competition is sustained by the huge number of Finns who see a shopping expedition to Tallinn as the ideal day out from Helsinki. Crossing time is 90 mins by hydrofoil and 2–3 hrs by ship (ERT 2410).

HELSINKI — SEE P491

As you travel the length of Route 46 through the Baltic States, you are forever in the shadow of Russia, the great territory away to the east, but not so far away as to be out of sight and out of mind. As we designed Route 46, we wanted to link places that have had, over the last two centuries and more, a tempestuous relationship with their eastern neighbour. During the heyday of railway construction in the 1850s, the entire stretch you follow in Route 46 was part of the **Russian Empire**. Warsaw was in *Tsarstvo Polskoye*, the Polish Tsardom, that had been created at the Congress of Vienna in 1815, when Poland was effectively partitioned (yet again) with chunks given to Prussia, Russia and Austria-Hungary. The Polish Tsardom was no more than a province of Russia, and any pretence at autonomy was a fiction.

Further north, the regions of the three **Baltic States** through which Route 46 passes were variously parts of the Baltic governorates of the Russian Empire, respectively known as **Curonia, Livonia** and **Estonia**. And Helsinki, where Route 46 ends, was the blossoming capital of the **Grand Duchy of Finland**, which was another territory in the Russian Empire. The capital had been moved to Helsinki in 1827 to boost Russian control over the allegedly autonomous principality. The Russian tsar was keen, too, to quash Swedish influence in Finland, and the previous capital Turku (on Route 26 in this book) was judged to be too close to Sweden (culturally, politically and linguistically) for comfort. Thus power shifted from Turku to Helsinki, and a new capital was created in the image of St Petersburg, oozing the same neoclassical style that makes the Russian city so appealing.

During the **Cold War** years, when Europe was divided, it would have been difficult for western visitors for follow Route 46 at all. There was little western tourism in the three Soviet Republics that sung their way to independence in 1990 and 1991. For many years in the post-war period there was not even a ferry link across the Gulf of Finland from Tallinn to Helsinki. Poland was of course very considerably overshadowed by the Soviet Union, and even neutral Finland had a web of links, based mainly on trade and commerce, with its giant neighbour to the east. The **Finno-Soviet Friendship Pact**, concluded in 1948, mediated Finland's relationship with the Soviet Union, and indeed the wider world, for over four decades.

So, as you climb aboard the once-daily train from Poland to Lithuania at the start of Route 46, it is worth savouring the moment. You are embarking on a journey that 30 years ago would have been next to impossible. But Russia's influence has not disappeared entirely from the regions through which you'll pass. All three Baltic States have sizeable **Russian minorities**, not always, it has to be said, accorded the rights that the EU would insist are given to other minorities. Russians are now often second-class citizens in places where once they ruled the roost. And curiously, Finland and Russia are nowadays closer than they ever were. Since December 2010, it has been possible to board one of the new fast **Allegro trains** in Helsinki and be in St Petersburg 3 hrs 36 mins later (ERT 1910). Day trips between Helsinki and Russia are now commonplace. Railways often cement international relations far better than kings or politicians ever could.

Rail Route 47:
From Bavaria to the Tatra Mountains

CITIES: ★★ CULTURE: ★★ HISTORY: ★★ SCENERY: ★★★
COUNTRIES COVERED: GERMANY, CZECH REPUBLIC, SLOVAKIA, POLAND

There have always been historic links between **Franconia** and the city of **Kraków** in southern Poland. Indeed, pop into the lovely Marian Basilica (*Bazylika Mariacka*) in Kraków's main square and much is made of the fact that the striking carved wooden altarpiece in the church was created in the 15th century by a master craftsman from the Franconian capital of Nuremberg. Veit Stoss (Wit Stwosz), who carved that celebrated altarpiece, probably took many weeks for the journey when he set out from **Nuremberg** for Kraków in 1477. Nowadays, you could follow Route 47 between the two cities in just a couple of days.

Our route has as its highlight one of central Europe's least-known mountain ranges, namely the **Tatras** that straddle the border between Slovakia and Poland. And that's not all, for along virtually the entire length of this 1,150 km route, the scenery is never dull. Route 47 gives a credible alternative to **Routes 45** and **49** for travellers heading east from Germany towards Russia and Ukraine, and along the way it takes in some very fine cities, notably **Prague** and Kraków. The opportunities for branching out from Route 47 are legion. While travelling through **Bohemia**, it would be a pity to miss the **spa towns** of the northern Czech Republic, and we especially recommend the hill country of north-east **Slovakia** with its distinctive wooden churches. This latter area is easily reached by venturing east from the Tatra Mountains.

NUREMBERG — SEE P185

The train journey through the hills east from Nuremberg **into the Czech Republic** is superb. The twice daily direct trains from Nuremberg to Prague follow this route, and additional connections are available if you are happy to make one easy change of train at Schwandorf (ERT 885 and 886). Sadly, too many travellers miss this cross-border rail route because the German and Czech Railways operate a non-stop bus service from Nuremberg to Prague. Taking only 3 hrs 40 mins to speed along the boring motorway between the two cities, and crossing into the Czech Republic at Waidhaus, the bus undercuts the travel time by train by more than an hour. Take the bus if time is all that matters. But if you have the slightest interest in landscape and culture, then the train is the way to go.

The train follows the **Pegnitz Valley** east from Nuremberg before cutting through the Bayerischer Wald (Bavarian Forest) to reach the Czech border at Furth im Wald. From there the train descends steeply towards Domažlice, the first stop in the Czech Republic. This is **Chod country**. The Chods were an early version of

ROUTE DETAILS

Nuremberg–Domažlice   ERT 885, 886

Type	Frequency	Typical journey time
Train	2 daily	2h10

Domažlice–Prague   ERT 885

Type	Frequency	Typical journey time
Train	4 daily	2h45

Prague–Žilina   ERT 1160

Type	Frequency	Typical journey time
Train	11 daily	5h15 to 6 hrs

Žilina–Poprad Tatry   ERT 1180

Type	Frequency	Typical journey time
Train	Every 1–2 hrs	1h55

Poprad Tatry–Zakopane   ERT 1183

Type	Frequency	Typical journey time
Bus	2–4 daily	2 hrs

Zakopane–Kraków   ERT 1066

Type	Frequency	Typical journey time
Train	5–8 daily	3 hrs to 3h30

KEY JOURNEYS

Nuremberg–Prague   ERT 76

Type	Frequency	Typical journey time
Train	2 daily	5hrs
Bus	5–6 daily	3h40

Prague–Poprad Tatry   ERT 1180

Type	Frequency	Typical journey time
Train	3 daily	7 hrs

Notes

The only advantage of the bus on the Nuremberg (Nürnberg) to Prague (Praha) stretch is speed. The rail journey wins hands down when it comes to scenery. InterRail and Eurail passes are valid on the bus service. The bus has a small lower deck section reserved for first class passengers. The second class area on the upper deck is very much nicer and allows better views.

border guards. They made a decent living by keeping an eye on the borderlands where Bohemia runs up against Bavaria. Imagine a militia armed with bagpipes which kept Bavarian aspiration in check and so secured the independence of Domažlice.

DOMAŽLICE

The small towns of south-west Bohemia, many of them just a stone's throw from the border with Bavaria, are a part of Europe that remains well off most tourist trails. Domažlice, a one-time stronghold of Hussite reformers, is well worth visiting in its own right, but is also an excellent base for exploring this area. The town's nicely **elongated main square**, lined by arcades, is a place to linger and watch life go by. The **town's museum**, located in the renovated castle, tells the story of the region, explaining the history of the local Chod minority, and making much of a fine collection of **bagpipes** that ranges from the Magyar *duda* to the Swedish *säckpipa*.

ARRIVAL, INFORMATION, ACCOMMODATION

≋ Domažlice has two railway stations. The direct trains from Munich, Nuremberg and Prague all stop only at the main station, simply called Domažlice, 1 km east of the centre. Many local trains, including those from Furth im Wald, also serve Domažlice mesto, a small halt located 500 metres south of the main square. **🖪** The very helpful **tourist office** is next to the town hall in the main square (www.domazlice.info). ⊨ **Penzion Konšelský šenk,** at Vodní 33, ☎ 379 720 200 (www.konselskysenk.cz), €, just south of the square, is great value and has a very good restaurant. Otherwise try the **Penzion Family**, Školni 107, ☎ 379 725 962, €€.

CONNECTIONS FROM DOMAŽLICE

For devotees of slow trains, and we mean very slow trains, this region is well served by a dense network of **rural railway lines**. Many of these routes are operated by antiquated red railbuses that trundle through the forests stopping off here and there at tiny wayside halts. You can take small branch lines north, staying on the Czech side of the border with Germany, to reach **Mariánské Lázně** (more famously known in film and literature by its erstwhile German name of Marienbad) and the other spa towns of northern Bohemia (see Sidetracks on p393). Our favourite small town in the region is **Horšovský Týn**, easily reached by train from Domažlice (see box p388).

PRAGUE – SEE P548

East from Prague, Route 47 parallels **Route 48** for a spell, both journeys following the Labe (Elbe) Valley upstream through eastern Bohemia. At Česká Třebová, Route 48 cuts south through the hills towards Bratislava and Budapest, while our journey continues east through **northern Moravia** into Slovakia.

This leg from Prague to Žilina is one of the longest stretches between cities in this book, generally 5 to 6 hours by rail depending on which train you choose. Sometimes there are times when it is good to just sit back and enjoy the journey. This is one such moment. **North Moravia** has a reputation for grime and industry, not entirely deservedly. The valley floors do indeed have their share of industrial settlement, but all around there is delectable hill country. The region has a very strong sense of regional identity, to the extent that many inhabitants firmly describe themselves as Moravian rather than Czech.

If you are tempted to make a break on this long stretch, opt for **Olomouc**, a lively university city at about the midway point between Prague and Žilina. Quite how Olomouc has been so overlooked by the Czech tourism industry is a mystery, for the Moravian city has all the charm of Prague but without the crowds and high prices that characterise the Czech capital.

East of Olomouc, there are two rail routes **east to Žilina**, a more northern option via the industrial city of **Ostrava** and a southern route that crosses the border into Slovakia at **Horní Lideč**. It is this southerly route that is shown on our route map (p386). It is the faster and prettier of the two options.

ŽILINA

The first place of any size in Slovakia is Žilina, a city that has something of the Slovak soul, for the town is intimately associated with the development of Slovak national consciousness in the late 19th century. A pilgrimage here is mandatory for every Slovak schoolchild. **Budatín Château** (incorporating the regional museum) is almost on the doorstep; **Orava Castle**, situated on a high rock above the Orava River, is further afield. The onward train journey to both **Banská Štiavnica** and Kremnica, former mining towns with exquisite architecture, is spectacular.

Žilina is an ideal base for exploring the Malá Fatra mountain ranges and the **Kysuce Nature Reserve**. As a well-known Slovak holiday area, the region is criss-crossed with well-marked paths of varying lengths and difficulty. The **Vrátna Valley** is one of the most renowned beauty spots — take the chairlift to Snilovské

EXCURSION FROM DOMAŽLICE

Horšovský Týn is just a dozen kilometres north of Domažlice, but the magnificently circuitous train journey between the two towns takes 90 mins. Horšovský Týn is dominated by a great castle, a one-time palace for the local bishop. Unlike Domažlice, which welcomed the Hussites, the episcopal town of Horšovský Týn made a fierce stand against the reformers. Topography has always been the town's greatest ally, making it easy to defend, and its steep slopes nowadays contribute to the appeal of the place. Even the main square is on a slope.

Excursion to Trenčín

Just an hour south of Žilina on the non-stop fast trains (ERT 1180) Trenčín is a charming old town on the river Váh, totally dominated by the great **castle** on a crag overlooking the town. The massive reconstructed castle is open daily for guided tours. The views are spectacular. Down in Trenčín itself, Mierové námestie (the main square) is lined with trees and pastel-coloured houses and includes several cafés, pubs and a pizzeria. Trenčín also makes a good base for hiking in the **Považský Inovec woods**. There is a sparsely-served branch line from Trenčianska Teplá (8 km from Trenčín) to **Trenčianske Teplice spa** (with pseudo-Turkish baths) on the narrow-gauge railway. Try the Hammam baths (men only) and the **Zelena žaba** spring-water baths, the marked walks up to Čvrigorec and, if you're in town in the summer, the international art, film and music festivals. ⇌ Trenčín station is a 15-min walk east through the park to the centre. 🚪 **Tourist office**: Mierové nám. 2, ☎ 032 16 186 (www.visittrencin.sk). 🛏 The best source of accommodation is via the helpful tourist office – booking ahead is strongly recommended.

Sedlo for stunning views. Stop-offs on the way to Poprad-Tatry include **Liptovský Mikuláš**, for its beautiful lake. Part of the Slovak karst system, **Demänovská dolina** boasts some astonishing underground stalactite and stalagmite caves (hourly bus from Liptovský Mikuláš).

Arrival, information, accommodation

⇌ North-east of the centre, on Národná ulica. 🚪 **Tourist office**: Republiky 1, ☎ 041 723 3186 (www.tikzilina.sk). 🛏 You can stay cheaply at **Penzión Majovey**, Jána Milca 3, ☎ 041 562 4152 (www.slovanet/majovey), €€, or the **Hotel Slovakia**, Nám. Ľudovíta Štúra 2, ☎ 041 562 3265 (www.hotelslovakiazilina.com), €€.

Connections from Žilina

Five trains per day make the short run through from Žilina to **Martin**, taking 30 mins (ERT 1185). Plenty more journeys are possible by changing at Vrútky. Martin is an outstanding base for walking or skiing in the Malá and Velká Fatra mountains, and for visiting the open-air **Slovak Village Museum** (at Jahodnícke háje; closed Mon except July–Aug), 3 km away.

Poprad-Tatry

Poprad, sandwiched between the High and Low Tatra Mountains, is un-distinguished, though the main railway station is a faded but still very good example of the distinctive bold style of architecture known as Slovak East Modernism. In Czechoslovakia, Slovak architects always had the edge over their Czech counterparts.

Poprad is first and foremost a place to change trains, it being the natural gateway to the magnificent Tatra Mountains. On the edge of Poprad, the little village of **Spišská Sobota** (3 km east of the station and easily reached by local bus) is a very fine example of a settlement created by craftsmen from Saxony who arrived here in the 14th century. The pristine little square and church with its intricate altar carvings are superb.

ARRIVAL, INFORMATION, ACCOMMODATION

⇒ 800 m north of the town centre. **⛊ Tourist office**: Štefániková 99/72, ☎ 052 772 1700 (www.poprad.sk). ⛵ For rooms in both Poprad and the wider Tatra region **Tatranská informačná kancelária**, ☎ 052 442 3440, can arrange accommodation, and the Popradská informačná agentúra, has information about chalets, pensions and hotel accommodation. The High Tatras are very busy in the summer and ski seasons, so book ahead. If you want to stay in the Poprad area before heading for the hills, then make for the Spišská Sobota district. **Penzión Sabato**, at Sobotské námestie 1730, ☎ 052 776 9580 (www.sabato.sk), €€, in Spišská Sobota is first class. Close to the train station, is the **Penzión Aqualand**, Štefánikova 893, ☎ 052 776 3049 (www. aqualand.sk), €€.

EXPLORING THE TATRAS

The arrival of the railways from Prague, Bohumín and Košice in the last two decades of the 19th century suddenly opened up the Tatra Mountains for popular travel. To cope with the crowds, **narrow-gauge railways** were built into the hills and these routes are still the mainstay of local transport serving the Slovakian side of the mountain range. Today, these lines seem more tram-like, but they operate under the banner *Tatranská elektrická železnica* (Tatra electric railway), and are often branded as TEŽ. You can connect onto the TEŽ network at Poprad and also at **Štrba**, a little place on the main line west of Poprad served by all but the fastest trains on the Žilina to Poprad route.

From Poprad and Štrba, TEŽ services (ERT 1182) climb into the stunning alpine **High Tatra Mountains**, stopping at Starý Smokovec, Štrbské Pleso and Tatranská Lomnica for spas, hiking and skiing. Although the main Tatra range is only 40 km long, paths of varying difficulty, generally very well waymarked, provide a wealth of choice for walkers and skiers. But take care in winter, for severe weather can sweep in very quickly, confounding even the most mountain-savvy walker. Access to certain high areas, including **Gerlachovský štít** (at 2,654 metres the highest peak in the Tatras and in the entire Carpathian mountain chain) is generally restricted to those accompanied by registered mountain guides. An exception is made for members of a national Alpine club affiliated to *Union Internationale des Associations d'Alpinisme (UIAA)*.

The main Tatra communities served by TEŽ services are places wholly dedicated to mountain tourism. It is worth doing the whole TEŽ circuit, taking in **Štrbské Pleso, Starý Smokovec** and **Tatranská Lomnica**. Starý Smokovec is the grandest of the three, with many over-the-top timbered Alpine villas and some extravagant late 19th-century hotel architecture. Sadly, you will also find some modern concrete monstrosities. If your aim is to head high without effort, then make for Tatranská Lomnica, from where a cable car will whizz you to the top of Lomnický štít, 2,634 metres and the second highest Tatra summit.

The hill country of north-east Slovakia

The Tatra Mountains are hard to leave, but if you have a day or two free, head yet further east for a glimpse of a real outpost of Europe. A network of small railway lines (not all shown in the *Thomas Cook European Rail Timetable*) penetrate the deep valleys of **Carpatho-Ruthenia**, home to one of Europe's hidden minorities, the **Rusyns** or Ruthenians.

Travelling east from the Tatras, before you reach the Rusyn settlements, do pause at **Bardejov** (ERT 1196). It is a pristine medieval town that looks as though it was built last week. It is a fine example of a township founded by migrants from Germany who settled through this mountainous region in the 13th century.

Heading further east, you'll start running across the wooden churches and folk architecture of the Rusyns, particularly around **Humenné** (ERT 1194). The town itself isn't remarkable, but there is an excellent outdoor museum (ask for the Skanzen, open daily May–Oct) with fine examples of Rusyn-style cottages and a Greek-Catholic church, an unusual variant of Christianity common in Rusyn areas, and also found in other places along the fracture line between Roman Catholicism and Orthodoxy (for example in eastern Poland and western Ukraine). The Greek Catholics, often called Uniates, use the Byzantine Rite but recognise the Pope.

From Humenné, you can head north (still ERT 1194) to Medzilaborce, a place in the very back of beyond that has a memorably bizarre museum devoted to the life and work of **Andy Warhol**, ul. Andyho Warhola 749/26 (closed Mon).

Into Poland

There are some tantalising gaps in Europe's rail network that we have run across in this book. Remember the paucity of rail links over the border from Italy into Slovenia in **Routes 35** and **38**. And the complete lack of any railway to Dubrovnik, which meant resorting to a boat in Route 38 and a bus in **Route 44**. And there is no railway line that conveniently links the Slovakian and Polish side of the Tatra Mountains. Yes, you could make a very circuitous journey, with half a dozen changes of train and in 20 hrs reach **Zakopane** from Tatranská Lomnica.

Better, we think, to take the **bus** which takes just 70 mins (ERT 1183). Services start in Poprad and serve Starý Smokovec and Tatranská Lomnica before heading over the hills into Poland. The border crossing is at Łysa Polana, an eerie spot deep in the **Białka Valley** that in winter seems to survive for months without any direct sunlight. Note that this cross-border bus service may be suspended during winter snowstorms.

Zakopane

Every Pole knows Zakopane, a resort town in the **Tatra Mountains**, three hours south of Kraków by train. It's the place to which the Kraków intelligentsia came (and still come) to rest and play.

With beautiful late 19th-century villas, wooden churches, leafy avenues and easy access to Poland's highest mountains, Zakopane is a year-round resort: excellent **winter sports**, **rock climbing** and **summer hiking**.

For information on access to wilderness areas, ask at the PTTK office (ul. Krupówki 12, ☎ 18 201 24 29), the tourist information or the less central Tatra National Park Information Centre (ul. Chałubińskiego 44). If you're hiking into the mountains, book mountain huts well ahead (or risk ending up sleeping outside), and take your own food.

The high season, when the **trails and huts** are very busy, runs from late June to late August. May, early June and September usually offer good hiking conditions without the crowds, but be aware that winter snow may linger well into spring at higher elevations, especially on north-facing slopes.

As for day hikes from Zakopane, one of the best is to the summit of **Giewont** (a 7-hr round walk); there's also a cable car up to **Kasprowy Wierch** (1,985 m) from Kuznice, from where there's a ridge path that hugs the Slovakian border. Keep an eye open for approaching bad weather, and don't venture out into the High Tatras without a good map and equipment. The less energetic may like to take the modern funicular railway from the centre of town to Gubałówka (1,120 m) for excellent views south to the main Tatra range; there are cafés at the top.

From Zakopane you can also venture to the **Pieniński National Park**, with its time-warp villages and castles. A great favourite is to go rafting in the Dunajec River Gorge (Apr–Oct).

The office at ul. Jagiellónska 107b, ☎ 18 262 556 01 in Krościenko n/Dunajcem (www.pieninypn.pl) organises rafting trips and excursions by bus to places of interest such as the spa town of **Szczawnica**, which makes a good base and has accommodation.

ARRIVAL, INFORMATION, ACCOMMODATION

≋ Left luggage, currency exchange. It's a 15-min walk south-west to the town centre.
🚌 Buses from Kraków arrive very close by.

🚹 **Tourist office**: ul. Kościuszki 17, ☎ 18 201 2211 (www.promocja.zakopane.pl); arranges accommodation and has useful maps. 🛏 Book ahead, especially during the peak winter season. Mid-range hotels include the **Hotel Daglezja**, ul. Pilsundskiego 14, ☎ 18 201 4041 (www.daglezja.com.pl), €€, the **Helios Hotel**, ul. Sloneczna 2a, ☎ 18 201 3808 (www.hotel-helios.pl), €€, and the **Orbis Giewont**, ul. Kościuszki 1, ☎ 18 201 2011 (www.accorhotels.com), €€–€€€.

Budget travellers should check out the **hostels** in Zakopane, including the **Goodbye Lenin Hostel**, Chłabówka 44, ☎ 18 200 1330 (http://zakopane.goodbyelenin.pl), free wi-fi, and the **Flamingo Hostel**, Krupówki Str 24, ☎ 18 200 0222 (http://zakopane.flamingo-hostel.com).

KRAKÓW — SEE P406

In the north-west corner of the Czech Republic, close to the German border, are three towns that are truly outstanding examples of European spa culture. All have their origins in the **Austro-Hungarian spa tradition**, and all were once favoured holiday destinations for Europe's royalty. These are not places for Bohemian excess. On the contrary, perfect order reigns supreme. But fear not! Colonic irrigation is not mandatory, and these three towns are just wonderful places to hole up and relax for a day or two.

The three are, from the smallest to the largest, and with their old German-language names in brackets: Františkovy Lázně (Franzensbad), Mariánské Lázně (Marienbad) and Karlovy Vary (Karlsbad). Each has its own charm. **Františkovy Lázně** is a tiny picture-perfect community with the air of an outdoor sanatorium and a nice line in erotic sculptures. Fertility treatments are one of the town's specialisations and this gives Františkovy Lázně a more youthful air than the other spa towns mentioned here.

Mariánské Lázně is three times as big and has a feast of belle époque decadence, a lovely Russian Orthodox church and is surrounded by some beautiful parks and woodland. In **Karlovy Vary**, very much larger than the other two, the real world intrudes on the pursuit of health and recuperation, and there's a bustle about the town, especially during the annual film festival which takes place in July each year. ⊨ The **Hotel Embassy**, Nová Louka 21, ☎ 353 221 161 (www.embassy.cz), €€, is extremely friendly and located right in the heart of the spa zone. The excursion up the funicular railway (called the 'Diana') to the viewing tower is a must in Karlovy Vary.

All three spa towns offer good-value hotels, often more geared to long-stay clients nursing their ailments than passing trade, but if space is available casual guests are accepted. Plan for leisurely days taking the waters, going for healthy walks, and enjoy afternoon tea and waltzes aplenty! If you really want to catch the spa atmosphere, head for one of the two smaller towns mentioned here. If you're uncertain whether you can cope with such unalloyed commitment to healthy living, Karlovy Vary makes for a good compromise. At least there you can sup on something stronger than the spa waters. Try the **Jan Becher Museum** on T G Masaryka 57, which provides an interesting history of the locally produced Becherovka spirit, as well as ample opportunity to sample the product itself.

For direct trains from Prague to Mariánské Lázně (3 hrs 15 mins) see ERT 1120. From Mariánské Lázně, a very beautiful minor railway runs through the **Bohemian hills** to Karlovy Vary, taking around 80 mins for the journey (see ERT 1123). There are also direct trains from Prague to Karlovy Vary (3 hrs 20 mins, see ERT 1110). Františkovy Lázně is just a short hop by train from both Mariánské Lázně and Karlovy Vary, in each case usually requiring a change of train at Cheb. Similarly, the 4 hr journey from Prague to Františkovy Lázně also requires a change of train in Cheb. To escape from this trio of spa towns, Františkovy Lázně also has a useful direct train north into Germany every two hours, over yet another exceptionally scenic route (ERT 1122). It runs to **Zwickau**, from where there are good onward connections to Dresden (on **Route 48**) and Berlin (on **Routes 16, 20, 45** and **49**).

Rail Route 48: Four capitals in a day

CITIES: ★★★ CULTURE: ★★ HISTORY: ★★ SCENERY: ★★
COUNTRIES COVERED: GERMANY, CZECH REPUBLIC, SLOVAKIA, HUNGARY

The 1,000-km rail journey from **Berlin** to **Budapest** can easily be undertaken within a single day, ideally using the *Hungaria*, a train which oozes history. Cast back to the Cold War days, and the *Hungaria* carried East German families off for summer holidays in Hungary — where Lake Balaton was the favourite destination. It was also the train that transported government officials and party stalwarts carrying fraternal greetings between the Warsaw Pact capitals. The *Hungaria* was much favoured by spies too. In the 1980s, it still carried through carriages from Sweden to Yugoslavia, both non-aligned countries, and the train was a good spot for discreet exchanges of intelligences as it trundled through the countryside.

In 1981, the *Hungaria* left Berlin just before 7 in the morning, and so it does today. But the Europe traversed by that train has been utterly transformed over the last 30 years. The **Iron Curtain** has gone and borders have melted. Nowadays you can travel from Berlin to Budapest without once being asked to show your passport — such are the freedoms secured through the Schengen treaties. And the train that once served three capitals (Berlin, **Prague** and Budapest) now stops at four. The velvet divorce that divided Czechoslovakia gave **Bratislava** capital city status on 1 January 1993.

The route is dominated by great river valleys, with the blue and white carriages of the *Hungaria* following the **Elbe Valley** (Labe in Czech) on its route south to Prague. The latter part of the journey plays cat and mouse with the **Danube**, never actually crossing the river, but on several occasions running close by the river banks. Indeed at one point, just north of Bratislava, you can look across the river to Austria in the distance.

The entire route is well served by high-quality train services, generally running at 2 hr intervals. There are two other trains that follow Route 48. The *Jan Jesenius* is the second day train, not quite as characterful as the *Hungaria*, and there is also the *Metropol* night train for those who prefer to sleep their way across central Europe.

BERLIN — SEE P450

DRESDEN

The capital of Saxony for four centuries, Dresden will long be remembered as one of the great tragedies of World War II. In February 1945, the city was carpet-bombed by the Allies, and some 35,000 people died. But despite the devastation, the city has risen from the ashes, and is once again a major cultural destination

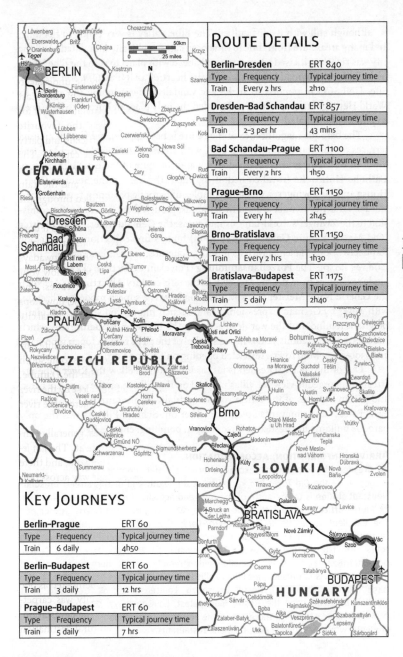

ROUTE DETAILS

Berlin–Dresden — ERT 840

Type	Frequency	Typical journey time
Train	Every 2 hrs	2h10

Dresden–Bad Schandau — ERT 857

Type	Frequency	Typical journey time
Train	2–3 per hr	43 mins

Bad Schandau–Prague — ERT 1100

Type	Frequency	Typical journey time
Train	Every 2 hrs	1h50

Prague–Brno — ERT 1150

Type	Frequency	Typical journey time
Train	Every hr	2h45

Brno–Bratislava — ERT 1150

Type	Frequency	Typical journey time
Train	Every 2 hrs	1h30

Bratislava–Budapest — ERT 1175

Type	Frequency	Typical journey time
Train	5 daily	2h40

KEY JOURNEYS

Berlin–Prague — ERT 60

Type	Frequency	Typical journey time
Train	6 daily	4h50

Berlin–Budapest — ERT 60

Type	Frequency	Typical journey time
Train	3 daily	12 hrs

Prague–Budapest — ERT 60

Type	Frequency	Typical journey time
Train	5 daily	7 hrs

— although still with its difficulties. The **Elbe Valley** is very prone to flooding, and many areas have from time to time been catastrophically inundated. And the city was rightly criticised when it pressed ahead with plans to ruin the Elbe Valley by building a new road bridge through the heart of a UNESCO World Heritage Site. UNESCO responded to such civic vandalism by stripping the city of its World Heritage status — making Dresden the only place in Europe to have been so publicly humiliated.

The baroque magnificence of the centre is best appreciated from the raised terraces on the south bank of the Elbe, with views of the **Residenzschloss** (the tower of which gives another good view), and the spire of the early 18th-century Catholic **Hofkirche** (royal cathedral).By the cathedral are the **Semper Opera House** and the **Zwinger**, a gracious complex of baroque pavilions, fountains and statuary. It is free to walk around the grounds, though there is a charge for admission to the Zwinger's world-famous museums: the **Gemäldegalerie Alte Meister** (Old Master Picture Gallery; closed Mon) houses fine collections that include Raphael's *Sistine Madonna* with its immortal cherubs, and Dürer's *Portrait of Bernhard von Reesen*. The **Porzellansammlung** (Porcelain Collection; closed Mon) includes examples from nearby Meissen. In the 16th-century **Albertinum** (Arsenal), the **Galerie Neue Meister** (New Masters Gallery) is a superb modern collection, with works by German Expressionists and French Impressionists. A particularly poignant reminder of the war destruction is the Lutheran **Frauenkirche**, which has been entirely rebuilt, and is now a symbol of the city's rebirth (open 1000–1200 and 1300–1800 Mon to Fri, restricted opening on Sat and Sun).

Out of the centre, Dresden is just as interesting. Follow the **River Elbe** upstream for gorgeous views of villas perched on the hillside on the opposite bank, and within minutes of the centre you are virtually into countryside as you head east. Forests and vineyards aplenty. Further on, **Schloss Pillnitz** was the only baroque building in Dresden to have escaped bombing; entry is free.

Arrival, information, accommodation

⇌ **Dresden Hbf**, left luggage, exchange facilities, hotel information. Follow signs for Prager Str. — the Old Town is 1 km away at the south end of this street. **Dresden-Neustadt station** is to the north of the river and actually closer to the Elbe than Hbf. ⓘ **Tourist office**: Kulturpalast, Schlossstrasse, ☎ 0351 5016 0160 (www.dresden.de). The excellent value 48 hr **Dresden-City-Card**, €24, allows free public transport, reduced or free admission to main museums plus reductions on city bus and walking tours. ⊨ The **Hofgarten 1824**, Theresienstr. 5, ☎ 0351 250 2828 (www.hofgarten1824.de), €–€€, is good value and extremely central. There are a number of excellent **hostels** in Dresden, including **Lollis Homestay**, Görlitzer Str. 34, ☎ 0351 810 8458 (www.lollishome.de), **Hostel Louise 20**, Louisenstr. 20, ☎ 0351 889 4894 (www.louise20.de), and the **Hostel Mondpalast**, Louisenstr. 77, ☎ 0351 563 4050 (www.mondpalast.de). All three are in the Neustadt, a neighbourhood popular with students, which has many cafés, bars and restaurants.

Trains to **Prague** take 2 hrs 15 mins for the 191-km journey; there are six services a day (ERT 60 and 1100). There are also good eastbound trains to Poland, with thrice-daily fast services to **Wrocław** (3 hrs 35 mins, ERT 1085), where you can join **Route 49**. These trains stop at **Görlitz** just before crossing the River Neisse into Poland. For more on Görlitz and the Neisse Valley see p404. Just 40 mins east of Dresden, on that same route to Poland, is **Bautzen**. It is a town that just deserves to be better known. Bautzen has a super Altstadt and a quirky cathedral. One end of the building is used by the town's Protestant community and the other end by Catholics. Bautzen is also a major centre of **Upper Sorbian culture** and language. Street signs are all bilingual.

Dresden has excellent **night-train services**, with direct trains to Amsterdam, Budapest, Cologne, Vienna and Zurich.

THE ELBE GORGE

The stretch of the Elbe Valley upstream from Dresden has the finest scenery on Route 48. Heading south, sit on the left side of the train. You may wish to consider taking slow trains for the cross-border leg from Dresden to **Děčín**. While the fast services take just 45 mins, the slow trains take twice the time and usually require an en-route change of train at **Bad Schandau**, a small town in southern Saxony that has become a mecca for hikers wanting to explore the sandstone hills that tower over the Elbe Valley. A ferry across the river links the station with the town centre. The train slips across the border into the Czech Republic at **Schöna**. The landscape south towards Prague becomes slowly more industrial, but still full of interest. These landcapes of northern **Bohemia** inspired Smetana's music *Má vlast* (which means 'My Country').

PRAGUE — SEE P548

PRAGUE — SEE P548

From the Czech capital, the train heads past Kolín (for a connection for Kutná Hora, with its medieval Old Town huddled around a superb Gothic church), through the Bohemian-Moravian uplands to **Brno** in South **Moravia**. This is a land of rolling hills, dotted with elegant châteaux and medieval castles where many Czech and foreign films are set, peaceful nature reserves and areas with karst limestone scenery and underground caves. It's also the main Czech wine-growing region (with attractively painted wine cellars dotting the hills).

BRNO

High-rise blocks and an unmistakably industrial look might tempt you to skip Brno, which expanded in the 19th century as a textile-making centre. But the town does have a scattering of good sights (most are closed Mon, and are either cheap or free) within 1 km of the station in the largely traffic-free centre. The neo-

Gothic **Katedrála sv. Petra a Pavla** (Cathedral of Sts Peter and Paul) crowns Petrov Hill, while the 13th-century **Špilberk Castle** was the most notorious prison in the Austro-Hungarian Empire — you can visit the horrifying prison cells (closed Mon). A little way south-west is the **Augustinian Monastery**, where in 1865 the monk Mendel studied genetics, breeding pea plants in the garden. Garden and plants remain, and there's also a small museum, the **Mendelianum**, Mendlovo náměstí 1 (closed Sat and Sun; take tram 1 from the station).

The **Old Town Hall**, Radnická 8, is a combination of Gothic, Renaissance and baroque style and displays a 'dragon', a stuffed crocodile from 1608. Brno's most bizarre sight is the crypt of the **Kapucínský klášter** (Capuchin Monastery) close to the station, containing 150 mummified bodies, air-dried since 1650 (closed entirely 15 Dec to 15 Feb, otherwise open daily except off-season Mondays).

ARRIVAL, INFORMATION, ACCOMMODATION

➤ South of the city centre; exchange facilities, left luggage. For the town centre, head across the road in front of the station and up Masarykova street. 🛈 **Tourist office**: Old Town Hall, Radnická 8, ☎ 542 211 090 (www.ticbrno.cz), and at the rail station.

🛏 Reserve well in advance as Brno is a trade fair city and its hundreds of hotels and pensions tend to book up months ahead. **Penzion na Starém Brně**, Mendlovo nám. 1a, ☎ 543 247 872 (www.penzion-brno.com), €€; **Pension Venia**, Riegrova 27, ☎ 549 240 915 (www.klecka-ag.cz), €€. The **Travellers' Hostel**, Jánská 22, ☎ 545 212 263 (www.travellers.cz), is centrally located but only open July&Aug; free internet access. The helpful staff at the tourist office can provide you with comprehensive accommodation info, and are happy to arrange this for you.

BRATISLAVA

Overshadowed by Prague, it has sometimes been hard for the Slovak capital to make its mark. But the city is superbly placed midway between Prague and Budapest, and is less than an hour by train east of Vienna. Bratislava fans always argue that the city has all the merits of Prague without the crowds. There will not be a lot to detain you in the dreary suburbs, but the **Old Town (Staré Mesto)** is a gem. The main sights cluster within the old city walls on the east side of **Staromestská**. West of that is a prominent hill topped by the rather austere castle (Bratislavský hrad). The Danube riverfront is dominated by the modernist New Bridge (Nový most) that leads over to the huge **Petržalka** estate.

The Old Town is full of atmospheric lanes. In and around Ventúrska, Michalská and Panská you'll find excellent baroque palaces. Look out for the **Mozartov dom** (which has only the most tenuous of links with the composer), the rococo **Mirbach Palace** and the **Pálffyho Palace** that houses part of the Bratislava City Gallery (closed Mon). Noteworthy Gothic structures include the Franciscan church and the striking tower of **St Klara's Convent** (today not a convent at all but a library). Climb St Michael's Tower at Michalská 22 (closed Mon) for a great

EXCURSIONS FROM BRATISLAVA

There are two mid-sized Slovakian towns that make easy day trips from the capital. Trnava is just 30 mins from Bratislava, and Piešťany is another 30 mins beyond Trnava. The two can easily be combined into a great day trip, stopping off first at Trnava before continuing to Piešťany.

Trnava is somewhat ludicrously dubbed the 'Slovak Rome', though the link is hard to identify. It is a picturesque walled university town boasting 12 churches and a maze of unspoilt, cobbled lanes. While you're there don't miss **Trojičné námestie**, with its fine houses and public buildings and plague column. The huge rococo **Univerzitný kostol**, on Invalidská, is one of Trnava's most interesting and elegant churches, but it's just as rewarding to wander the town's leafy alleyways and squares. ⇌ The centre is a 10-min walk up Hospodárska, then right down Bernolákova Divadelná. **🛈 Tourist office**: Trojičné námestie 1, ☎ 033 323 6440 (www.trnava.sk). ⇥ Cheap accommodation is thin on the ground: if you are travelling in a group, try **Hotel Inka**, ul. Vladimíra Clementisa, ☎ 0805 590 5111 (www.hotelinka.sk), €€–€€€, or **Hotel Nukleon**, J. Bottu 2, ☎ 033 55 21 0956 (www.hotelnukleon.sk), €€.

Piešťany could not be more different from Trnava. It offers cures, elegant cafés and peaceful, riverside parks. Recently renovated, its smartest spa hotels (€€€) are now largely populated with holidaying well-heeled Russians. Take a leisurely swim in the **Eva** pool, sample the granny-filled cafés on Winterova and explore the tranquil parks on **Kúpeľný island**, so relaxing it's almost comatose. ⇌ A 15-min walk north-west of the centre (signposted). **🛈 Tourist office**: Tourist Information Centre, Pribinova 2, ☎ 033 771 9621 (www.pic.piestany.sk). ⇥ South of the centre and on the lake is the reasonably-priced **Rybarsky Dvor**, Bratislavska 151, ☎ 0918 664 991 (www.rybarskydvor.sk), €€. A cheaper option, 3 km from the centre, is the **Pension Tematin**, Krizna 350, ☎ 033 797 0479 (www.tematin.sk), €–€€.

panoramic view. At the west side of the Old Town stands the Gothic **St Martin's Cathedral**, nowadays rather hemmed in by **Staromestská**. Immediately on the west side of Staromestská, under the shadow of the castle, is Bratislava's old Jewish Quarter. The castle itself houses extensive museums (all closed Mon).

Bratislava's Old Town is full of bars, cafés and restaurants that spill out onto the streets on sunny evenings, with the highest concentration on **Ventúrska**. If you're determined to stay out until the wee hours it pays to wander to the outskirts of the Old Town where there are some options. **Nu Spirit Bar** (Medená 6; www.nuspirit.sk) has live jazz, as well as soulful house and funk DJs. **Radosť** (Obchodná 48; www.mojaradost.sk) is an underground chill-out bar and club, with DJs playing electro and house. The non-smoking dance club **Remix** is located centrally at Ventúrska 16 (open from 2100, www.remixbar.sk).

ARRIVAL, INFORMATION, ACCOMMODATION

⇌ Bratislava has two main train stations. The chief one, **Hlavná stanica**, is served by virtually all services to other Slovak destinations. It is 1.5 km north of the Old Town and trams 2/3/8/13 provide reliable links. The station has exchange facilities, cafés and left luggage. A second station at **Petržalka** (3 km south of the city centre on the south side of the Danube) has fewer facilities, but it is the terminus for fast trains to and from Vienna via Kittsee. An alternative link with Vienna (via Marchegg) is slightly slower but uses the much more convenient Hlavná stanica. ✈ Bratislava Airport, with its new terminal building opened in June 2010, is about 9 km from the city centre. 🚌 61 connects the airport with the main railway station (every 15-20 mins, taking 25 mins).

ℹ Tourist office: BKIS, Klobučnícka 2, ☎ 02 5443 3715 (www.visit.bratislava.sk) and also at Terminal B of the airport. 🛏 Budget accommodation is hard to find in Bratislava. Book early for the **Gremium Pension**, Gorkého 11, ☎ 02 2070 4874 (www.penziongremium.sk), €€. More upmarket is the **Hotel Spirit**, Vancurova 1, ☎ 02 5477 7561 (www.hotelspirit.sk), €€€, which is very near the rail station. Cheaper beds are available in Bratislava's hostels. The **Hostel Blues**, Špitálska 2, ☎ 905 20 40 20 (www.hostelblues.sk), is centrally located, and also has double rooms, €–€€. Other hostels worth checking out include the **Hostel Possonium**, Sancova 20, ☎ 02 2072 0007 (www.possonium.sk) and the **Downtown Backpackers** (HI), Panenska 31, ☎ 02 5464 1191 (ww.backpackers.sk).

✗ Head for the old heart of town to find decent places to eat – **Michalská** and **Hlavné námestie** are lined with lively cafés, pubs and bars serving snacks, wine, coffee and sticky cakes. Panská and the charming streets and squares close by boast some good restaurants, pizzerias and gallery cafés. Check out the latest eateries in *The Slovak Spectator* (www.spectator.sk), the weekly English-language newspaper.

Connections from Bratislava

It's just over 1 hr to Vienna (ERT 996 and 997), and just over 2 hrs 30 mins to Budapest (ERT 1175).

Towards Hungary

The scenery through the Danube Lowlands east from Bratislava is largely unexceptional, so what follows comes as a surprise. Shortly after leaving the last station in Slovakia at **Štúrovo**, there is a magnificent view south across the Danube to Esztergom in Hungary. The vista is dominated by **Esztergom Basilica**, the tallest building in Hungary and an impressive symbol of ecclesiastical power in the Danube town that for 250 years served as capital of Hungary. Seen in the right light, we would really rate that view of Esztergom from Slovakia as one of the finest anywhere on Europe's rail network.

Within a few minutes, the train crosses into Hungary (but still does not cross the Danube) and there is suddenly a superb stretch with the train running through small **Hungarian villages** surrounded by vineyards. Not many long train journeys across Europe have quite such a rousing finale.

BUDAPEST – SEE P465

Rail Route 49: Through Silesia to Galicia

CITIES: ★★ CULTURE: ★★ HISTORY: ★★★ SCENERY: ★
COUNTRIES COVERED: GERMANY, POLAND, UKRAINE

Route 49 is a journey through European history, one that starts in **Prussia** and traverses **Silesia** to reach the former Austro-Hungarian eastern province of **Galicia** (not to be confused with the region in north-west Spain still known today as Galicia). Along the way, our route takes in two particularly fine Polish cities, beautiful **Wrocław** and busy **Kraków**. The end point is **Lviv**, a Ukrainian city which has a superb Old Town centre — a place that is rather akin to Kraków, but without the crowds.

Like every route in this book, this journey is not just about getting from A to B. There is a daily direct train from **Berlin** to Kraków that precisely follows the first half of this route (but see box p403). That train is called the *Wawel*, thus picking up the name of the hill in Kraków that is so intimately associated with Polish royalty and nationhood.

The *Wawel* arrives in Kraków early evening, where it is an easy change onto the onward overnight train (running alternate nights only) that will have you in **Lviv** by early the next morning. Do it that way and you'll speed from Berlin to Lviv in less than 20 hrs. Better, though, to linger and take a few days along the way. Kraków deserves at least a couple of days. Other obvious choices for stopovers are Wrocław and **Przemyśl**. If you want to make an interesting rural diversion, it is an easy journey south from Kraków to visit the **Tatra Mountains**. Another option, much earlier in the route, is to follow the German-Polish border up the Neisse Valley to **Görlitz** and **Zittau**. Route 49 links with **Route 47** (in Kraków) and **Route 50** (in Lviv).

BERLIN — SEE P450

The journey out of Berlin on the sole daily direct train to Silesia is through an apocalyptic landscape of neglected railway sidings and abandoned factories, but the route quickly gains open country and within an hour you are skirting the watery **Spreewald**. This area of eastern Germany is called the **Lausitz** (Lusatia in English) and is home to a very distinctive linguistic and cultural minority called the **Sorbs**. They speak a Slavonic language closely related to Czech, and you will see Sorbian place names alongside the more familiar German renderings at stations along the route.

This area of eastern Brandenburg has suffered much rural depopulation since German unification in 1990, with the disappearance of traditional industries like textile production, glass making, and opencast mining for low-grade lignite fuel. The train pauses to change locomotives at **Cottbus** (Chóśebuz in Sorbian), a place that styles itself as being the safest place on earth. 'No earthquakes, no

Notes

The hourly slow trains from Berlin to the Polish border at Forst always require a change of train at Cottbus. Station names in parts of eastern Germany are also rendered in the local Sorbian language. So Chóśebuz for Cottbus and Baršć for Forst. Remember to advance your watch by one hour as you cross from Poland into Ukraine.

ROUTE DETAILS

Berlin–Forst
ERT 838, 854, 1086

Type	Frequency	Typical journey time
Train	1 daily	2h02 (direct)
	Every hr	2h23 (via Cottbus)

Forst–Wrocław
ERT 1086

Type	Frequency	Typical journey time
Train	1 daily	3h40

Wrocław–Kraków
ERT 1075

Type	Frequency	Typical journey time
Train	12–14 daily	4h40

Kraków–Rzeszów
ERT 1075

Type	Frequency	Typical journey time
Train	12–14 daily	2h30

Rzeszów–Przemyśl
ERT 1075

Type	Frequency	Typical journey time
Train	14–16 daily	1h40

Przemyśl–Lviv
ERT 1056

Type	Frequency	Typical journey time
Train	2 daily	2h20 to 3h45

KEY JOURNEYS

Berlin–Kraków
ERT 58

Type	Frequency	Typical journey time
Train	1 daily	10 hrs

Warsaw–Kraków
ERT 1065

Type	Frequency	Typical journey time
Train	Every 1–2 hrs	2h40

Kraków–Lviv
ERT 1056

Type	Frequency	Typical journey time
Train	2 daily	6–10 hrs

Dresden–Wrocław
ERT 1085

Type	Frequency	Typical journey time
Train	3 daily	3h30

hurricanes, no avalanches, no dangerous animals', runs the blurb. It often elicits the knowing rejoinder 'No jobs either'.

Forst (Baršć in Sorbian)

Forst lies on the west bank of the **River Neisse**, which since 1945 has marked the border between Germany and Poland. It was once Germany's equivalent of Manchester, the epicentre of the great **textile industry** that was so important to much of Lusatia and Silesia. Today it is awesome in its desolation.

Yet there is a quiet beauty in the rows of abandoned mills, the architecture of many of which is redolent of mill towns in north-west England. The town has a very good little museum detailing the history of the textile industry in Forst (on Sorauer Str. 37, east of the station, closed Mon in winter).

Arrival, information, accommodation

⇝ About 800 m south-west of the city centre. 🄱 **Tourist office**: Cottbuser Str. 10, ☎ 03562 669 066 (www.forst-information.de). ⊨ There are some reasonably priced pensions in Forst, including the **Hotel Pension Haufe**, Cottbuser Strasse 123, ☎ 03562 28 44 (www.hotel-haufe.com), €–€€, **Pension Am Kegeldamm**, Kegeldamm 13, ☎ 03562 69 12 45 (www.cafe-am-kegeldamm.de), €, and the **Pension Am Bahnhof**, Bahnhofstrasse 5, ☎ 03562 79 49, €.

Connections from Forst

A private rail operator, **ODEG** (www.odeg.info), operates an hourly rail service from Forst to Zittau, sometimes requiring a change of train in Cottbus. Rail passes are accepted. Sleek modern railcars with big windows glide up the rural Neisse Valley to **Görlitz** (1 hr 40 mins) and **Zittau** (2 hrs 25 mins). Times are shown in part in ERT 854. Görlitz, right on the Polish border, has one of the finest city centres in central Europe with a dazzling array of Renaissance, Gothic and baroque architecture.

The best of the show is on and around the **Untermarkt** where you'll find courtyards with an almost Mediterranean demeanour. Trams 2 or 3 run direct from the station to the centre of Görlitz. The Hotel Börse on the Untermarkt is a real touch of luxury (€€–€€€), but also offers simpler rooms in an annexe around one of the nearby courtyards (€–€€). Details on www.boerse-goerlitz.de.

The best of the **Neisse Valley** scenery is south of Görlitz along the final part of the route to Zittau. En route the railway criss-crosses the **German-Polish border**. Zittau is another little-visited gem of a town and the jumping-off point for the **narrow gauge railway** (ERT 853) into the mountains immediately south of Zittau. This service still has steam trains running day-in day-out all year round. For more extended explorations of the Görlitz-Zittau region the **Euro-Neisse ticket** allows unlimited travel for a day in south-east Saxony and well over the borders into the Czech Republic and Poland: €11.50 for 1 person, €23 for 2 to 5 people (details on www.zvon.de).

If you do head up the Neisse Valley to Görlitz and beyond, there is no need to retrace your steps to Forst to continue east into Poland. There are thrice-daily direct train services from Görlitz to Wrocław (2 hrs 17 mins, ERT 1085), again using very attractive state-of-the-art railcars. At Wrocław you can rejoin Route 49.

THROUGH LOWER SILESIA

East of Forst, the route to Wrocław traverses a forest wilderness that holds little promise for agriculture. Small Polish towns like Żary seem like the end of the world, but every community has a tale to tell. The baroque composer Telemann lived in Żary for a while, while the astronomer Johannes Kepler resided in nearby Żagań. The latter town was immortalised in the film *The Great Escape*, which told the tale of how 80 British airmen escaped from the Stalag Luft III camp in Żagań. Today a museum in Żagań (closed Mon) commemorates this episode.

WROCŁAW

Poland's fourth largest city is the capital of **Lower Silesia** and is culturally one of the most interesting oddballs in this part of Europe. Prior to World War II, it was a predominantly German city, then known as Breslau, which was ceded under the 1945 Potsdam Treaty to Poland.

The Germans left, quickly to be replaced by thousands of Polish migrants from the **Lwów** region. Today Lwów is the Ukrainian city of Lviv, the end point of Route 49. So east from Wrocław this route follows (in reverse) the route of one of the great forced migrations of post-war Europe.

With the city's airport latterly much favoured by budget carriers, Wrocław is no longer so off the beaten track as it was just five years ago. We rate it as being almost as good as Kraków, but happily without Kraków's high prices. The **central area** is compact and easily covered on foot. The city is defined by its river, the Odra, which skirts the northern edge of the city centre. Apart from the stunning main square dominated by the magnificent **town hall**, our favourite part of Wrocław is the ecclesiastical and university district north-east of the centre. Head over Piaskowy bridge onto Wyspa Piasek and then right over the colourful **Tumski bridge** to reach the **cathedral**. Back on the south side of the river, you can easily spend many happy hours exploring the various streets around the central Rynek (main square).

One highlight not to be missed is the **Racławice Panorama** in a striking modern building in Słowackiego Park about 1 km east of the Rynek (closed Mon in winter). The Panorama was produced for an exhibition in Lwów in 1893 and thus predates the heyday of cinema.

Its portrayal of one of the rare glorious moments in Polish military history, the Battle of Racławice where Polish peasants armed with scythes and pitchforks outwitted better-equipped Russian forces, evokes a great sense of reality that must have been truly dramatic when first viewed by late 19th-century Poles who had no experience of media we now take for granted. It still stirs the hearts of all with a drop of Polish blood in their veins. The Panorama accompanied the post-war mass movement of Polish exiles from Lwów to Wrocław, and is the most tangible expression of the historic connections between the two cities.

ARRIVAL, INFORMATION, ACCOMMODATION

≋ Wrocław's main station is a Disneyesque confection about 1 km south of the heart of the Old City. 🄸 The main **tourist office** is on the central square in the Old Town at ul. Rynek 14, ☎ 71 344 31 11 (www.wroclaw.pl).

⊨ Close to the market, the **Cilantro B&B**, ul. Pomorska 32/26-29, ☎ 71 793 86 82, €–€€, is a good budget option, or else try the three-star **Hotel Duet**, ul. Sw Mikolaja 47–48, ☎ 71 785 51 00 (www.hotelduet.pl), €€. There are a number of decent **hostels** in town, such as the **Babel Hostel**, Kollataja 16/3, ☎ 71 344 12 06 (www.babelhostel.pl), **Nathan's Villa Hostel**, ul. Swidnicka 13, ☎ 71 344 10 95 (www.nathansvilla.com), and the **Cinnamon Hostel**, Str. Kazimierza Wielkiego 67, ☎ 71 344 58 58 (www.cinnamonhostel.com).

CONNECTIONS FROM WROCŁAW

As a major rail hub, Wrocław has excellent onward connections. There are thrice-daily direct services to **Dresden** (3 hrs 25 mins, ERT 1085) to connect with **Route 48** and frequent trains to **Poznań** (2 hrs 30 mins, ERT 1070) to join **Route 45** to Russia.

If you are in a rush to reach the end of Route 49, there is on alternate nights a direct sleeper train from Wrocław to Lviv in Ukraine. Wrocław is also the gateway to the **Karkonosze Mountains** that straddle the Polish-Czech border. For access to the hills, take the train to Szklarska Poręba Górna (4 hrs 42 mins, ERT 1084). In late 2010 this route was extended over the border to Harrachov in the Czech Republic (ERT 1141).

Kraków

Kraków is by far the most popular tourist destination in Poland, and justifiably so. The city's main square rivals St Mark's in Venice as one of the finest piazzas in Europe. Kraków was once Poland's capital, and, though it lost that status in 1596, so much of Polish history has been forged in Kraków. After Poland was partitioned, Kraków was briefly an independent city-state, and then became part of the Austro-Hungarian province of **Galicia**. During the 20th century, Kraków was Poland's pre-eminent **city of ideas**. Be it in the arts, politics, commerce or in church affairs, Kraków has always punched above its weight.

But Kraków is also an important centre of industry. It is home to the huge steelworks at **Nowa Huta**, just north-east of the city. As a tourist attraction, Nowa Huta district provides a completely different experience from its romantic counterpart, but this fascinating, carefully designed socialist suburb is more than concrete blocks and just a tram-ride away from the beaten path.

The city's main sights are concentrated on the north bank of the **River Wisła** (Vistula). Focal points are the Old Town Square, Wawel Hill with the castle and cathedral, and the old Jewish quarter, Kazimierz. All are within walking distance of each other.

The **Old Town Square** (Rynek Główny) is a gem, but to experience it at its best you will have to see it at dead of night or at dawn on a sunny spring morning. No other space in Poland is so utterly dedicated to tourists, and the impact of the square's magnificent architecture is often lessened by the sheer number of visitors. The centrepiece is the **medieval cloth hall** (Sukiennice), a fine covered market in 16th-century Renaissance style. The distinctive colonnades were added much later. Nowadays the Sukiennice houses stalls that trade in jewellery, amber and pricey souvenirs, while on the upper floor there is a gallery of 19th-century Polish art (www.muzeum.krakow.pl; closed Mon).

All that remains of the Gothic town hall is the **Ratusz** (City Hall Tower), Rynek Główny 1, which has a fine view from the top and houses one of the stages of the Ludowy Theatre. In the opposite corner of the square, **St Adalbert's**, built in Romanesque style but since partially redecorated in baroque fashion, is the oldest and smallest church in Kraków. Within the vaults is an exhibit dedicated to the history of the Old Town Square.

Further north, **Bazylika Mariacka** (St Mary's Basilica) has a wooden Gothic altar, 13 m high and adorned by 200 figures, created by Wit Stwosz, the 15th-century master carver of Nuremberg. Legend has it that a watchman was shot down from the church tower by Tartar invaders. The *hejnał*, the melody he trumpeted to sound the alarm, is repeated hourly. For military architecture explore the **Floriańska Gate** and **barbican**.

Central Europe's second oldest **university** was founded in 1364. Distinguished students include the Polish astronomer Nicolaus Copernicus and Pope

John Paul II. **Collegium Maius**, ul. Jagiellońska 15, is the oldest college, a magnificent example of Gothic architecture in which 35 globes are on display, one dating from 1510 and featuring the earliest illustration of America, marked 'a newly discovered land'. Tours (1000–1420 Mon–Fri, 1000–1440 Sat, till 1800 Apr–Oct on Tues & Thur; closed Sun) take in the alchemy rooms (supposedly Dr Faustus's laboratory), lecture rooms, the assembly hall and professors' apartments.

Kraków's most important sites are the dramatic **cathedral** and fortified **Royal Castle** (both built by King Casimir the Great), high on **Wawel Hill** and bordered by the Wisła River. The Gothic cathedral of 1320–64 replaced an 11th-century church whose relics are displayed in the castle's west wing. The most striking of the 19 side chapels is the gold-tiled, domed Renaissance **Zygmuntowska** (Sigismund's Chapel), built 1519–31. Climb the tower for a great view plus the 2.5 m diameter **Zygmunt Bell**, rung on church or national holidays. The Royal Castle, chiefly a Renaissance structure of 1502–36, has a superb courtyard with three-storey arcades. Displayed in the **Royal Chambers** you can see 142 exquisite Arras tapestries, commissioned in the mid-16th century.

An easy 20-min walk due south from the Old Town Square will bring you to **Kazimierz**, once a separate community outside the walls of Kraków, and later the city's Jewish quarter. Steven Spielberg's film *Schindler's List* captured something of Jewish life in Kraków, while recent years have seen a bit of a Jewish revival in Kazimierz. There are several synagogues and a number of restaurants that proclaim their Jewish credentials (some not as kosher as they may seem). Check out the **Synagoga Stara** (Old Synagogue) at ul. Szeroka 24 (closed Mon afternoon), the Jewish centres at ul. Skawińska 2, ul. Miodowa 24, ul. Meiselsa 17 and ul. Szeroka 2 (exhibition, bookshop, a restaurant with Jewish food and music; organises guides to Auschwitz). Kazimierz is also home to one of the world's greatest and most important **Jewish Culture** festivals, held in the summer.

ARRIVAL, INFORMATION, ACCOMMODATION

≥ **Kraków Główny** (main station) is a short walk north-east of the centre. Currency exchange, accommodation information, left luggage (0500–2300), luggage lockers (24 hrs), showers, restaurant. Head left from the station, turn right down Basztowa, enter the large underpass and head for the *Planty/Basztowa* exit to the right. **Główny** has services to **Oświęcim** (for the Auschwitz museum), **Zakopane** and **Wieliczka**, as well as long-distance trains.

▐ Tourist office: main offices: ul. Szpitalna 25, ☎ 12 432 01 10, in the town hall, ☎ 12 433 73 10 and on ul. św. Jana 2, ☎ 12 421 77 87 (www.krakow.pl/en). Full information, tickets and a monthly listings magazine (English supplement) can be obtained from the tourist information office at ul. św Jana 2.

◄ If you've travelled around Poland and become used to good-value accommodation, prepare for a shock if you arrive in Kraków in high season. Market rules apply, and prices rocket. See www.hotelsinpoland.com for bargains and www.jordan.pl for specific details of accommodation and tourist offices in the city. It's common to be

Excursions from Kraków

The foothills of the Polish Tatra Mountains fringe the southern outskirts of Kraków. It is a pleasant train journey to Zakopane (3 hrs, ERT 1066), though buses are much faster. Read more about the Tatra Mountains in **Route 47** (p390). For a shorter venture into the hills, take the local train to **Kalwaria Zebrzydowska** (45–65 mins), where the **UNESCO listed Mannerist style park** is a superb 17th-century celebration of Christ's life and passion.

It is a major pilgrimage venue for Polish Catholics and in the run-up to Easter hosts some sparking ecclesiastical theatre, culminating in Good Friday processions. From Kalwaria a local railway and frequent buses connect to **Wadowice**, less than half an hour away and birthplace of the late Pope John Paul II, whose status as local hero is unchallenged in these parts.

Auschwitz (now **Oświęcim**), synonymous with the atrocities of the Holocaust, was the largest Nazi concentration camp. Between 1.5 and 2 million, mainly Jewish, men, women and children were transported here in cattle trucks from across Europe to meet brutality and death. Piles of glasses frames, shoe-polish tins, baby clothes and monogrammed suitcases confiscated from the victims are on display. Screenings of liberators' films are regularly shown in several languages.

Nearby **Birkenau** (free bus from the main museum) was an even more 'efficient' Nazi death factory. **National Museum of Auschwitz–Birkenau**, ul. Więniów Oświęcimia 20, ☎ 33 844 81 00; free admission). Access to Auschwitz I site for individuals may be restricted at times, so join a guided tour. Frequent buses from PKS bus station (around 20 daily, take 1 hr 40 mins; much easier than going by train). Tours are organised by tourist information centres and many hotels. Accommodation: International Youth Meeting House and Education Centre, ul. Legionów 11, Oświęcim, ☎ 33 843 21 07 (www.mdsm.pl).

The Royal Wieliczka Salt Mine, Daniłowicza 10, ☎ 12 278 73 02 (www.kopalnia.pl). Mined for over 700 years, it has 560 km of tunnelling. It's a dazzling spectacle, with 40 chapels carved entirely from salt, larger-than-life salt statues and an underground lake. Guided tours in English; allow at least 2 hrs. Entry is pricey. To get there from Kraków, hop on 🚌 304, departing from ul. Kurniki opposite Galeria Krakowska.

approached by individuals at the station — check location and price; pay only when you've seen the place. A centrally located option is the **Hotel Saski,** ul. Sławkowska 3, ☎ 12 421 42 22 (www.hotelsaski.com.pl), €€ (note the antique lift); **Ascot Hotel**, ul. Radziwiłłowska 3, ☎ 12 384 06 06, €€, a mid-range hotel with free web access just outside the Old Town walls. Bargains at pricier hotels can often be netted via the web or tourist offices in the city.

There are also some comfortable and reasonably priced **apartments**: **Redbrick**, ul. Kurniki 3, ☎ 12 628 66 00 (www.redbrick.pl), is minutes away from Kraków Główny station and the Old Town, and has fully-equipped apartments for up to six people and a reception ready to assist guests 24 hrs.

Independent **hostels** include **Nathan's Villa**, ul. Św. Agnieszki 1, ☎ 12 422 35 45 (www.nathansvilla.com; free internet), just 2 mins from the Castle, and **Deco Hostel**, equally central at ul. Mazowiecka 3A, ☎ 12 631 07 45 (www.hosteldeco.pl; free internet, breakfast included). Proximity to the rail station is handy but sometimes noisy, the **Hotel Alexander II**, Ul. Zamenhofa 14, ☎ 12 351 50 50, (www. alexhotel.pl), €–€€, was newly refurbished in 2011. **Youth hostels** (HI): ul. Grochowa 21, ☎ 12 653 24 32; **Hostel Atlantis**, ul. Dietla 58, ☎ 12 421 08 61 (www.atlantishostel.pl), one of the top hostels in town. There are also plenty of student rooms available during the summer. Try **Bydgoska**, ul. Bydgoska 19, ☎ 12 636 80 00 (www.bydgoska.bratniak. krakow.pl), or **Żaczek**, al. 3 Maja 5 (www.zaczek.bratniak.krakow.pl).

✗ Rynek Główny and the surrounding streets are packed with restaurants. For premium locations on the Old Town Square, expect to pay premium prices. Make for the small streets around the university to find the best deals. Excellent Polish-Mediterranean cuisine at the **Farina**, ul. św. Marka 16, ☎ 12 422 16 80 (www.farina. com.pl) close to the Old Town Square.

Przemyśl

If you stop at just one place between Kraków and Lviv, make it Przemyśl, a small town on the River San just short of the Ukrainian border. Frontier-hopping shoppers have boosted the economy of this **border town** that has a delightful town centre just a 5-min walk south-west of the railway station. The main square (Rynek) doesn't match up to those in Wrocław and Kraków, but the real draw in Przemyśl are the **churches**, where you will find western-style Roman Catholicism merging gently into Eastern Orthodoxy. The Uniate or **Greek Catholic Church** bridges the divide and commands a great following in this area of eastern Poland.

Przemyśl is a chance to experience another side of Poland before taking a deep breath and leaping over the border into the territory of the former Soviet Union. Make sure that you have your passport to hand and check that the visa requirements have not changed. In late 2011 no visas were required of tourists holding passports from EU countries, Switzerland, Canada, the US or the Commonwealth of Independent States.

Arrival, information, accommodation
≽ About 400 m east of the city centre. 🅱 **Tourist office**: ul. Grodzka 1 (close to the main square), ☎ 16 675 26 63 (www.przemysl.pl).

🛏 Try the **Hotel Gromada**, ul. Wyb. Marsz. J. Pilsundskiego 4, ☎ 16 676 11 11 (www.gromada.pl), €€. Other mid-range options include the **Hotel Marko**, ul. Lwowska 40, ☎ 16 678 92 72 (www.hotelmarko.pl), €–€€, and the **Hotel Albatros**, ul. Ofiar Katynia 26, ☎ 16 678 08 70 (www.albatros.przemysl.pl), €€.

Lviv (Львів)

If Lviv were just 100 km further west, it would be in the premier league of European tourist destinations. The problem is while Poland is hip, a country that oozes youthful chic from every cobblestone, Ukraine is much less so, and Lviv's attempts to style itself as 'the new Kraków' have yet to really bear fruit. While Kraków pulls the crowds, Lviv slumbers.

The two cities share a common history, both having been part of the Austro-Hungarian province of Galicia. And both have that same **Italianate flair** in their central square and some of the surrounding courtyards. The centre of Kraków was the very first place in Poland to be inscribed on the UNESCO List of World Heritage Sites. That was back in 1978. Lviv had to wait another 20 years to receive the same accolade.

Lviv boasts a galaxy of **fine churches** and civic buildings. 'Must sees' include the **Armenian Cathedral** and the over-the-top baroque **St George's Cathedral**. The latter has served as the mother-church of the Ukrainian Greek Catholic Church which dominates religious affairs in western Ukraine. Its followers, often called Uniates, use Orthodox liturgies but are in union with Rome. It's a detail that underlines the west European orientation of this part of Ukraine.

Above all, Lviv is a fine place just to wander. The **Italian Yard** is a spot to linger over coffee. Or watch the sunset from **Vysoky Zamok** (Castle Hill) when the view of the city takes on a dreamy quality. For a more macabre take on life (or death), don't miss Lychakivsky Cemetery, a magnificent wooded parkland east of the city full of crumbling memorials to poets, philosophers and soldiers.

ARRIVAL, INFORMATION, ACCOMMODATION

≋ West of the city centre. Trams 1 and 9 get you to the town centre at Rynok Square.

🛈 **Tourist office**: On the main square at Rynok 1, opposite the Neptune Fountain, ☎ 32 254 60 79 (www.lviv.travel, www.lwiw.info).

🛏 Lviv is happily very cheap. Get a place in a 6-bed dorm at the **Central Square Hostel**, 5 Rynok Square, ☎ 32 254 61 69 (www.cshostel.com), in a plum spot on the main square, for just 120 UAH (about €12), much less off-season. Or trade up to the **George Hotel**, Mickiewich sqr 1, ☎ 32 232 62 36 (www.georgehotel.ukrbiz.net), where the cheapest rooms are just €35 including breakfast. Pick of the hotels is definitely the **Zamok Lewa** (Lion's Castle), Glinka str. 7, ☎ 32 297 15 63 (www.lioncastlehotel.com), in a leafy compound a 20-min walk south of the centre, which has doubles for €70 (including breakfast). Other budget options include the **Old Ukrainian Home**, Lepkoho 12, ☎ 32 272 76 11 (www.homehostels.org), and the **Retro Hostel Shevchenko**, Shevchenka prosp. 16, ☎ 32 240 37 61.

CONNECTIONS FROM LVIV

The city is blessed with a great hinterland that is well worth exploring. Lviv Ecotour (www.lvivecotour.com) organises day-trips and longer tours for English speaking visitors. Apart from nearby spots like the handsome town of **Zhovkva** (Жовква), the Carpathian wilderness beckons.

If Lviv feeds your appetite for exploring Ukraine, read our Sidetracks feature opposite. Alternatively, you can now follow **Route 50** (p412) in reverse south towards the border with Romania and beyond.

Routes 49 and 50 give a taste of Ukraine. Both feature in this book for the first time. Ukraine of course deserves more. If you enjoyed Lviv, you may be tempted to head east. Long train journeys are a quintessential part of the Ukraine experience. This country is vast, twice the size of Poland and almost five times larger than England.

The daily train from **Lviv** to **Simferopol** (Сімферополь), 1,500 km away in the Crimea (but still part of Ukraine), takes 24 hrs. Handier options from Lviv are Kiev (Київ; 9 hrs, ERT 1750) and the Black Sea port of **Odessa** (Одеса; 12 hrs, ERT 1750). Remember that all long-distance journeys in Ukraine must be pre-booked

The *Thomas Cook European Rail Timetable* includes limited schedules for Ukraine. For fuller information on rail travel in the country, check out www.poezda.net, which summarises all main line and long-distance train services in the territories of the former Soviet Union. If you have ever dreamt of travelling from Sochi to Samarkand or from Vorkuta to Vladivostok, then poezda.net was made for you. *Poezda* is simply the Russian word for 'train'.

After Lviv, **Kiev** is the obvious next step. The Ukrainian capital is set on wooded hills around the River Dniepr and has an altogether grander and more eastern demeanour than Lviv. It boasts impressive squares, graceful boulevards and magnificent churches and museums. Star of the show is the **Kyievo-Pechers'ka lavra**, in English dubbed the Monastery of the Caves, one of highest-ranking ecclesiastical foundations in the Orthodox world. It includes a number of churches, a newly rebuilt cathedral, a curious tiered bell tower, and a vast complex of underground corridors that travel writers of yesteryear often suggested led to Moscow. Be not fooled. If you are bound for Moscow, it's better to take the train.

Spend any time in Kiev and you'll appreciate how much Ukraine is split. You'll realise in retrospect that Lviv was very western in orientation. Kiev is different. There's a more palpable eastern influence and more Russian spoken. Move further east and the Russian thread becomes yet more dominant. In the Crimean port city of **Sevastopol** (Севастополь), for example, ethnic Russians outnumber Ukrainians by three to one.

With Lviv and Kiev under your belt, it now makes sense to head to the Crimea. From Kiev it is 15 hrs to Simferopol (ERT 1770) and 2 hrs longer to Sevastopol. **Simferopol** is the better choice for a first-time visit to the region. It has a first-class transport curiosity in **trolleybus number 52** that leaves from the station forecourt. It looks just like any other trolleybus. But this is the longest trolleybus route in the world. It is a formidable run, with the old trolleybus rattling along country roads, high over **Angarskyi Pass** in the hills south of Simferopol before descending steeply to the coast at Alushta, from where it hugs the beach to the coastal resort of **Yalta**.

Much earlier in this book, way back in **Route 14**, we extolled the merits of the **coastal tram route in Belgium** (see p157), which happens to be the longest tram route in the world. The trolleybus to Yalta seems to us to be the perfect complement to that Belgian tram. And the ideal way to conclude one of the last Sidetracks in this book. Travellers who have ridden both are surely a rare breed.

Rail Route 50: Exploring the Carpathians

CITIES: ★★ CULTURE: ★★ HISTORY: ★★ SCENERY: ★★
COUNTRIES COVERED: SERBIA, ROMANIA, UKRAINE

Route 50 is for pros. If you are one of those folk who habitually start reading a book from the back rather than the front, might we offer a word of advice? If you have never set foot on a train in Europe before, Route 50 would not be a good first excursion. At 1,173 km, Route 50 is not particularly long. Route 1 from London to Marseille is actually longer. It is merely that Route 50 really takes you off the beaten track. It is a chance to see regions of Europe less frequented by tourists.

En route from **Belgrade** to Lviv, our journey crosses areas whose very names evoke a sense of history: **Banat**, **Transylvania** and **Bukovina**. Along the way we traverse the **Carpathian Mountains** and the final section of the route, in southwest **Ukraine**, is through hilly country, culminating in the beautiful city of **Lviv** — a place so brimming with elegance and style that you would hardly credit that it was until 1991 within the Soviet Union.

Do just check before setting out that Ukrainian **visa rules** are unchanged. In autumn 2011, no visas were required of tourists holding passports from all EU countries, Switzerland, Canada, the US or the Commonwealth of Independent States.

Take along both Romanian and Ukrainian (or Russian) **phrasebooks**. You will be travelling through areas where you cannot rely on always finding English speakers (though you can get a long way with French in Romania). And once in Ukraine, it really is a huge asset if you can at least transliterate Cyrillic signs — if only to up the chances of not boarding the wrong train. And don't even think of embarking on Route 50 without a supply of toilet paper tucked away in your luggage.

This is a route that deserves time. Yes, you could do the journey in three days with an overnight stop in **Timişoara** (Romania) and then two overnight train journeys, but Route 50 deserves more. Take a week and give Route 50 its due. You will discover that it is arguably the finest route in this book.

BELGRADE — SEE P444

The only direct train from the Serbian capital to Romania leaves Belgrade mid-afternoon bound for Bucharest. This train will take you direct to Timişoara (ERT 1365). But you can be a little more creative by leaving Belgrade earlier in the day, and taking a bus from Belgrade to **Vršac**. The route is operated by Stup Vršac and buses run at least hourly.

The journey to Vršac, whether by bus or by train, cuts across the sandy heathland and forest area known as Deliblatska Peščara. It gives a hint of the delicate beauty that was once much more widespread across this region.

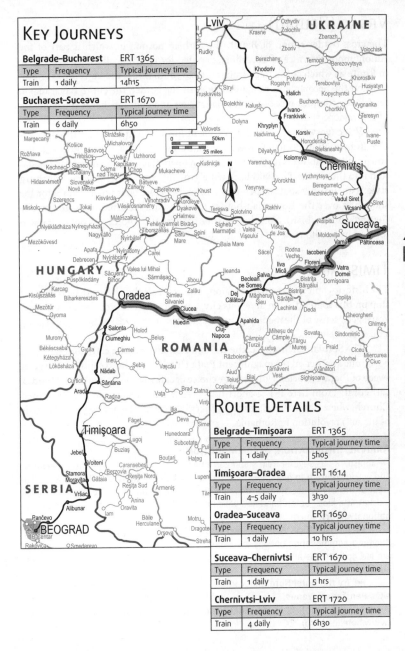

Key Journeys

Belgrade–Bucharest   ERT 1365

Type	Frequency	Typical journey time
Train	1 daily	14h15

Bucharest–Suceava   ERT 1670

Type	Frequency	Typical journey time
Train	6 daily	6h50

Route Details

Belgrade–Timişoara   ERT 1365

Type	Frequency	Typical journey time
Train	1 daily	5h05

Timişoara–Oradea   ERT 1614

Type	Frequency	Typical journey time
Train	4–5 daily	3h30

Oradea–Suceava   ERT 1650

Type	Frequency	Typical journey time
Train	1 daily	10 hrs

Suceava–Chernivtsi   ERT 1670

Type	Frequency	Typical journey time
Train	1 daily	5 hrs

Chernivtsi–Lviv   ERT 1720

Type	Frequency	Typical journey time
Train	4 daily	6h30

Vršac (Вршац)

The cross-border region of **Banat**, the Serbian portion of which is part of the Autonomous Province of Vojvodina, is noted for its ethnic diversity (read more in **Route 42** which cuts a track from north to south across the Vojvodina region). Both on the Serbian and Romanian sides of the border, the entire Banat region reveals the complex mix of peoples, languages and cultures that is the hallmark of this region.

Vršac (www.vrsac.com) is an excellent introduction to Banat. It has a sizeable Romanian minority. Throw in a smattering of Hungarians and Roma and you'll realise that this is no ordinary Serbian town. It is a 20-min hike from the station into the centre. This laid-back **wine growing** town with its faded **Habsburg style** is an amiable spot to spend an afternoon before boarding the train for the short hop over the Romanian border to Timişoara (referred to as Temišvar / Темишвар in Serbian). Note that the time changes at the border — put your watch forward by one hour.

Timişoara

The historic capital of the Banat region, Timişoara, is the obvious first overnight stop on this route. It is a marvellous city, a perfect place to stop for a day or two. You'll get a sense of the medley of cultures that have shaped Timişoara by visiting a quartet of churches.

The **Serbian Orthodox cathedral** and **Roman Catholic cathedral** stand opposite one another on the magnificent **Piaţa Unirii**. Then head south via the great sweep of **Piaţa Victoriei**, with its huge choice of cafés, to the **Romanian Orthodox cathedral**. From here it is a short hop over the Bega Canal to the **Reformed Church**, where Calvinist pastor Lászlo Tökes is credited with having sown the seeds of the 1989 revolution in Romania.

ARRIVAL, INFORMATION, ACCOMMODATION

≋ Timişoara has several train stations. The one at which you'll arrive from Belgrade, and will leave from to head north to Arad and beyond, is **Timişoara Nord**, about 1 km west of the city centre. Regular trolleybuses link the station with the city centre (buy a ticket at a kiosk beforehand and validate it on the trolleybus). ✈ **Traian Vua International Airport**, 10 km out of town, 🚌 26 to city centre (www.aerotim.ro).

🛈 **Tourist office**: Alba Iulia str. 2, ☎ 0256 43 79 73 (www.timisoara-info.ro). Budget accommodation options are limited and, as the train from Serbia only arrives around 9pm, this is an instance where we definitely recommend booking a room in advance.

🛏 Try the **Hotel Nord**, Bulevardul General Ion Dragalina 47, ☎ 0256 49 75 04, €€, **Pensiunea Venus**, Str. Liviu Rebreanu 59, ☎ 0256 27 50 90 (www.venus.pensiune.info), €, or the **Hotel Tresor**, Str. Radu Tudoran 18, ☎ 0256 22 87 54 (www.hoteltresor.ro), €€.

Timişoara has excellent connections east to Bucharest (8 to 9 hrs, ERT 1620), where you can join **Route 40** to Istanbul. There are also direct trains, both by day and overnight, to **Suceava** (13 to 15 hrs, ERT 1650) where you can pick up the final leg of this route north into Ukraine.

Through the Romanian Banat

North from Timişoara, our route skirts the Hungarian frontier, a reminder that Magyar influences are a powerful force in Banat, both historically and today. **Arad** and **Oradea** are the two cities of note in these flatlands. Both warrant a stop.

Arad

Arriving from Timişoara, most trains stop at Aradu Nou — not the place to alight as the station is inconveniently distant from the centre of Arad. Stay on the train for the extra 9 mins it takes to reach the main station (take 🚎 1/2/3 to the city centre). Arad has a feast of Habsburg style and is dominated by a vast **citadel**, built to remind Ottoman forces that this was Habsburg territory.

Oradea

Two hours further north Arad's big sister, Oradea, is full of Hungarian flavours. It is a city of evocatively fading baroque and secessionist buildings. A trio of **synagogues** attest to the city's Jewish connections, but the real star is the enormous **Roman Catholic cathedral** just 5 mins walk from the train station. As with Arad, Oradea is a great place to while away a few hours between trains.

Connections from Arad and Oradea

The links of these two Banat cities to Hungary are reflected in the rail schedules. From Arad there are fast trains every 2 hrs to **Budapest** (4 hrs, ERT 1280). Oradea has four fast trains daily to the Hungarian capital (also 4 hrs, ERT 1275). Oradea also has a useful late-afternoon slow train to **Debrecen** in Hungary (3 hrs, ERT 1277) where there is a very good connection on to the late-evening *Tisza Express* to **Lviv** (to join **Route 49**), **Kiev** and **Moscow** (timings for all three in ERT 97). Note that berths on the *Tisza* must be reserved in advance.

Oradea is on **Route 40** from Budapest to Istanbul. Some direct trains from **Budapest** to Transylvania are routed via Oradea, while others travel via Arad.

Cluj-Napoca (Cluj)

East from Oradea, you quickly have a sense of heading into the hills, although the main range of the **Eastern Carpathians** is not till well beyond Cluj-Napoca. The railway from Oradea to Cluj skirts the northern edge of the Apuseni Mountains, an area of dramatic wild country. The finest part of the route is the 68 km stretch between Aleşd and Huedin.

Cluj-Napoca is the unofficial capital of **Transylvania**. Less hyped than the famous trio of southern Transylvanian cities (Sibiu, Sighişoara and Braşov), and with less evidence of Saxon settlement than those more southern cities, Cluj-Napoca has the scent of Hungary in every alley and every square. In the late 19th century, Cluj oozed belle époque style and there is still more than a hint of that in the town today. The key sights are all on the south side of the river in the Old Town.

ARRIVAL, INFORMATION, ACCOMMODATION

➴ The main station is a 20-min walk north of the Old Town (walk down south along Strada Horea). 🚹 **Tourist office**: Blvd. Eroilor 6–8, ☎ 0264 45 22 44 (www.romaniatourism.com/cluj.html).

🛏 The **Pension Déjà vu**, Str. Ion Ghica 2, ☎ 0264 35 49 39 (www.deja-vu.ro), €€, is a 5-minute walk from the Old Town. There are a couple of **hostels** in Cluj-Napoca; the **Transylvania Hostel**, Str. Iuliu Maniu 26, ☎ 0264 44 32 66 (www.hotelcluj.com), and the **Retro Hostel** (HI), Str. Potaissa 13, ☎ 0264 45 04 52 (www.retro.ro).

EAST TO BUKOVINA

The journey east from Cluj-Napoca to Suceava crosses the main range of the Carpathians and takes a little planning. It is definitely a route for daylight hours, for the scenery is superb. On most days, there is really only one option with a departure from Cluj just after midday.

The best of the landscape is the hour immediately beyond **Lunca Ilvei**, where all trains stop before tackling the steep mountain route ahead. Many authorities suggest that it was in these hills that Bram Stoker placed **Count Dracula's** fictional castle.

Once over the mountains, the railway descends into the Romanian region known as **Moldavia** — not to be confused with the Republic of Moldova, an independent country that lies further east beyond the River Prut. This area of northern Moldavia is often called **Bukovina**, recalling the former Habsburg territory which included part of south-west Ukraine and the northernmost part of present-day Moldavia. Suceava is the principal town of the Romanian Bukovina.

SUCEAVA

There is only one real reason to visit industrial Suceava. It is the jumping-off point for tours of the UNESCO-listed **painted monasteries** of southern Bukovina. Suceava itself is a shade run-down, but of note are the **Monastery of St John** (south-east of the city centre), the **Armenian church** (in the centre) and the **Armenian monastery** at Zamca (north-west of the centre). Suceava comes to life every Thursday morning when it hosts a market that attracts many traders from Ukraine and Moldova.

ARRIVAL, INFORMATION, ACCOMMODATION

≉ The old main station, locally referred to as Iţcani, is a crumbling Habsburg pile well out of the centre. It is shown as **Suceava Nord** in timetables. **Suceava station**, locally called Burdujeni, is north-east of town, and is much more convenient for the centre. Its distinctive red building is one of the most handsome in town. There is a regular *marshrutka* (minibuses, often called maxi-taxis in Romania) link to the centre.

🛈 **Tourist office**: Str. Ştefan cel Mare 23, ☎ 0230 55 12 41. ✉ Monica Zavoianu runs a good, centrally located **hostel, High Class** (HI), Str. Mihai Eminescu 19, ☎ 0723 78 23 28 (mobile) (www.classhotel.ro) that caters to the needs of travellers keen to see the painted monasteries. She organises excellent one-day tours. Other options to try are **Irene's Hostel**, Str. Armeneasca 4, ☎ 0744 292 588 (mobile), www.ireneshostel.ro, and the **Pensiunea Leaganul Bucovinei**, Blvd. Sofia Vicoveanca Nr. 18, ☎ 0740 828 888 (www.leaganulbucovinei.com).

INTO UKRAINE

From Suceava, you can join the once-daily train to **Chernivtsi** in Ukraine (ERT 1670). On certain days, this train carries through sleeping cars to Lviv (ERT 98). The journey from Suceava to Chernivtsi takes 5 hrs for just 90 km, so making this one of Europe's slowest trains. The tardiness is because the carriages are adapted to run on the wider Ukrainian-gauge tracks at the border. If you cannot bear the slow speed, there are regular *marshrutkas* to Chernivtsi, generally taking 3 to 4 hrs for the journey, which includes time for border formalities. A daily bus leaves Suceava for Chernivtsi around 1 pm.

CHERNIVTSI (ЧЕРНІВЦІ)

Chernivtsi's distinctive green-domed railway station gives a hint of the city, which is one of the most attractive in Ukraine. Take some time to explore this remarkable place before joining the train to **Lviv**. The gracious style of Chernivtsi reflects its former status as cosmopolitan capital of the Bukovina region. This is a city that has, over the last hundred years, been variously part of **Austria-Hungary** (until 1918), the **Kingdom of Romania** (from 1918 until 1940) and the **Soviet Union** (from 1944 to 1991). Since 1991 it has been part of an independent Ukraine.

As the crucible of so much European history, Chernivtsi distils the complex mix of cultures that we have experienced while travelling the 50 routes in this book. And it is appropriate that Chernivtsi be the last city described in the routes section of this volume. For the city that claims to be the very heart of Europe is close to the **geographical centre** of the continent.

Chernivtsi has many pastel-coloured buildings that still have heaps of belle époque charm. Don't miss the green **opera house** and blue **town hall**. Among the many other remarkable buildings in Chernivtsi are the old **Armenian cathedral** (now a concert hall), the **Orthodox cathedral** with its curiously twisted towers and the **University**, a huge red-brick affair with Moorish elements that seems like something out of a fairy tale. There are guided tours every afternoon of the principal halls and galleries inside the building. The university gives the city much of its buzz, but there is another vital ingredient to the Chernivtsi mix. Some 5 km north-west of town is **Kalynivsky market**, a huge open-air bazaar that every day attracts thousands of visitors. *Marshrutkas* run out to the market every few minutes from the city centre. Even if you profess to have no interest in shopping, go out to Kalynivsky. It is pure theatre, even if sometimes a trifle muddy.

For a glimpse of rural Bukovina life, take trolleybus 4 out to the **Folk Architecture Museum** (closed Mon).

ARRIVAL, INFORMATION, ACCOMMODATION

≈ 1.5 km north of the city centre on vul. Gagarina; trolleybus 3 runs between the railway station and the bus station south of the city centre. ☐ There is a **tourist information office** in the Hotel Bukovina (see below), ☎ 0372 58 56 26. ⊨ If you want to stay overnight, the **Hotel Bukovina** in the heart of the city on Holovna 141, ☎ 0372 58 56 25 (www.hotel.cv.ua), €€, is a safe bet. Otherwise try the **Hotel Magnat**, L. Tolstoy 16a, ☎ 0372 52 64 20. **Hostel** accommodation is available at **TIU Chernivtsi Backpackers**, Sheptytskogo 2 Apt. 3, ☎ 0508 85 70 49 (www.hihostels.com.ua).

BEYOND CHERNIVTSI

Chernivtsi may be the last place described in our routes, but it is not the end of the line. From Chernivtsi there are direct trains to **Lviv** (ERT 1720) where you can join **Route 49**. En route to Lviv you may decide to stop off for a night or two in Ivano-Frankivsk (Івано-Франківськ), a good base for heading south into the Ukrainian part of the Carpathian wilderness and a town well worth exploring in its own right.

But if you have followed Route 50 all the way from Belgrade to Chernivtsi, then you are clearly an independent spirit and no longer need our guiding hand. Cast an eye over the departure boards at Chernivtsi station and take your pick. Lviv is the tame option. You might opt instead for **Moscow** or track east towards **Odessa** on the Black Sea coast of Ukraine. Or take the daily train to the Crimea. Or even **Moldova** (see next page). The next 50 routes are yours to decide and plan alone, for now the world is your oyster.

LVIV — SEE P409

The most interesting train of the day from **Chernivtsi** is the morning train to Moldova. Devotees of the absurd will love this train, and it really deserves to be much better known. It is one of just a handful of trains in the *Thomas Cook European Rail Timetable* that are shown as conveying fourth-class carriages.

When was the last time you travelled fourth class? For us the very thought evokes images of migrant workers travelling in open wagons through Manchuria a hundred years ago.

Austere Prussia certainly had fourth-class carriages for the workers, but they were scrapped in 1928. Travel writers of yesteryear took care to ensure that they enjoyed the bourgeois comforts of second class while travelling on routes through Prussia, but often commented on the merriment of life in the densely populated fourth-class part of the train. Wordsmiths have always been quick to add a little colour and romance to peasant and proletarian affairs.

The train to Moldova does not have the elaborate social structure of Prussian trains, where each had his or her place according to his rank in society. It is pure and simple fourth class, just as the illustrious Mr Cook advises in his timetable. On Russian trains we have run across fourth class where it is called *obshchi* — the very name suggests a mobile version of the muddy peasant villages of pre-Revolutionary Russia which were called *obshchina*.

You may find a few folk with mud on their boots on Train 610 at 8.45 am from Chernivtsi to **Moldova**, but they will not be peasants. The chances are that they are traders returning from a few days of good business at the huge market on the edge of Chernivtsi. The 173 km run from Chernivtsi to **Ocniţa** takes over five hours, along the way thrice crossing the border between Ukraine and Moldova, giving scope for some fine bureaucratic theatre as passport checkers and customs men go about their business on the train. Along the way there are some fine views across the Prut Valley to Romania on the opposite bank.

And fourth class or *obshchi*? It is absolutely fine. True, there is no samovar at the end of the carriage and no-one to turn down the bed. Hard seats, dirty windows and a lot of diesel fumes. But it is cheap and no-one complains.

If you just want a quick taste of Moldova, you should alight at **Lipcani**, a rather ramshackle border town. A new bridge over the road was opened in early 2010, so you can use that to cross into Romania for a bus to Suceava.

Alternatively, you can have about four hours in Lipcani before returning on the late afternoon train back to Chernivtsi in Ukraine.

If you are intent on exploring Moldova stay on the train to **Ocniţa** for a connection to the capital **Chişinău**. Don't expect luxury. Moldova is Europe's poorest country, and its railway infrastructure is pitifully backward. Indeed, it has no regular electric passenger trains at all — a status it shares with Kosovo, Albania, Iceland and Wales. Now there's a thought to ponder.

Hub Cities

the places hard to miss...

Our 26 hub cities are places through which you are likely to pass more than once if you regularly explore Europe by train. Many of these cities feature in several of our 50 routes. Our hub city descriptions are designed to help those who opt for a longer stay, but they also contain the essential facts for travellers who are merely passing through or stopping off for a few hours.

For a summary of rail connections between our hub cities (and selected other major points on Europe's rail network) see our city links tables on pp678–681.

Amsterdam

Amsterdam has always been a city that has attracted outsiders, whether tourists, philosophers, immigrants or hippies. Romantic and laid-back, what makes Amsterdam so special is its combination of a beautiful setting with a vibrant and youthful street life that reflects Dutch society's culture of tolerance. Yes, the red-light district and the 'coffee shops' will not be to everyone's taste, but thankfully Amsterdam is much more than just sex and smoking, and if you give yourself the time to explore you will discover a city that is home to marvellously varied **museums and galleries**, as well as leafy parks and a network of canals lined with elegant gabled brick houses that rivals Venice in its beauty.

The city centre is wonderful for walking, and the Amsterdam Tourist Board has a series of signposted walking routes to help you find your way. It is useful to grab one of their maps from the tourist office, however, as Amsterdam's layout can be confusing; bear in mind that *gracht* means 'canal' and that the centre follows the horseshoe shape dictated by the ring canals. That entire **central area** of the city was inscribed on the UNESCO World Heritage List in 2010.

The **Singel canal** confines the old centre, with the red-light district around the handsome Oude Kerk (Old Church), and the Royal Palace at the Dam. Seek out the Keizersgracht, the Herengracht and the houseboats along the Prinsengracht, and explore the **Jordaan**, an enticing area of shops, bars and restaurants that lies to the west of the ring canals. At night Amsterdam can be magical (get hold of entertainment listings, as there's lots going on). The canals seem to come alive, with the largest lit by twinkling lights and the glow from windows.

Above and beyond its attractions, though, Amsterdam is about its atmosphere, its bars and cafés, its cheap and cheerful Indonesian restaurants, the street markets and quirky shops, and its friendly locals. Amsterdam's **Centraal Station** is well-connected with the rest of Europe, with direct links to Brussels, Paris and Cologne. Amsterdam is the start and end point for **Route 15** (p161) in this book.

TRAVEL BASICS

⇌ **Centraal** (www.ns.nl) is the terminal for most trains and a 5-min walk north of Dam (the central area); beware of opportunistic thieves that hang around there. There's a manned left-luggage facility, as well as lockers, but the baggage area is closed 0100–0500. ✈ **Amsterdam Airport Schiphol** ☎ 020 794 0800 (www.schiphol.com) is about 14 km south-west of town. Transfers by train to/from Centraal are the cheapest: every 10 mins 0600–2400 (hourly 2400–0600); journey time 15 mins.

For getting around the city, you can cross Amsterdam's central canal hub on foot in about an hour and walking is a pleasant way of getting around. In terms of regular public transport, the tram is the easiest and the most popular option. The tram network (www.gvb.nl) covers the city centre, with 15 lines running regularly until 0030. When travelling on trams you must buy an OV *chipkaart*, which you can purchase on board the tram.

There's a **metro** within the city centre, designed mainly to access the suburbs. Three lines (51, 53 and 54) travel between Centraal Station, **Nieuwmarkt** and **Waterlooplein**, the city centre stops most likely to interest visitors. In general, it is a good idea to pick up a free English-language *Tourist Guide to Public Transport* from any tourist office when you first arrive. It explains everything you need to know.

Otherwise just do as the locals do and get on your bike, although be warned; Amsterdam is full of expert bikers and it is not an experience for the faint-hearted. A way of breaking into Amsterdam cycling gently is to join a group such as Mike's Bike Tours, Kerkstraat 134, ☎ 020 622 7970 (www.mikesbiketoursamsterdam.com). MacBike (five locations, including Centraal Station), ☎ 020 620 0985 (www.macbike.nl), is open daily and prices for **bike rental** start at €9,50 per day, although the longer period you book, the cheaper the daily rate becomes.

INFORMATION

🅱 The **main tourist office** is run by the Amsterdam Tourism & Convention Board and can be found in a wooden building opposite Centraal at Stationsplein 10, ☎ 020 201 8800 (www.iamsterdam.com). There is also a booth in Centraal (in the international area, platform 2B), and branches at Leidseplein (corner of Leidsestraat), and Amsterdam Airport Schiphol (Arrivals Hall 2).

Amsterdam is something of a cyberpunk mecca and is chock full of **internet cafés** with impressive hacker-sounding names such as The Mad Processor (www.madprocessor.nl). Typical costs for internet access are €1–2 per hour, though some charge more for non-members. Underworld, Voetboogstraat 7 (www.underworld-amsterdam.page.tl), runs a more grown-up operation than most; find them close to the big shopping street Kalverstraat.

ACCOMMODATION

Amsterdam is a small, old city but a popular one and there isn't really enough accommodation to deal with the huge numbers of visitors flocking into Amsterdam on peak days. Book well ahead, especially at weekends and in summer, and don't expect to find anything really cheap.

🛏 With each room decorated by a different artist, the **Winston,** Warmoesstraat 129 (Central Amsterdam), ☎ 020 623 1380 (www.winston.nl), €–€€, is a stylish and at times provocative place to stay. Other reasonably-priced options include the **Museumzicht,** Jan Luykenstraat 22 ll, ☎ 020 671 2954 (closed Jan–Feb), €, and the floating hotel **Amstel Botel,** NDSM Shipyard, Pier 3, ☎ 020 626 4247 (www.amstelbotel.nl), €€. A converted 1672 canal house is home to the **Keizershof**, Keizersgracht 618,☎ 020 622 2855 (www.hotelkeizershof.nl), €€. Other mid-range options in the centre of the city include the **Agora**, Singel 462, ☎ 020 627 2200 (www.hotelagora.nl), €€, the **Seven Bridges,** Reguliersgracht 31, ☎ 020 623 1329 (www.sevenbridgeshotel.nl), €€, and the **Singel Hotel,** Singel 13–17, ☎ 020 626 3108 (www.singelhotel.nl), €€. At the higher end, celebrity hang-out **The Dylan**, Keizersgracht 384, ☎ 020 530 2010 (www.dylanamsterdam.com), €€€, is based around a 17th-century former theatre, whilst those willing to splurge will love the old

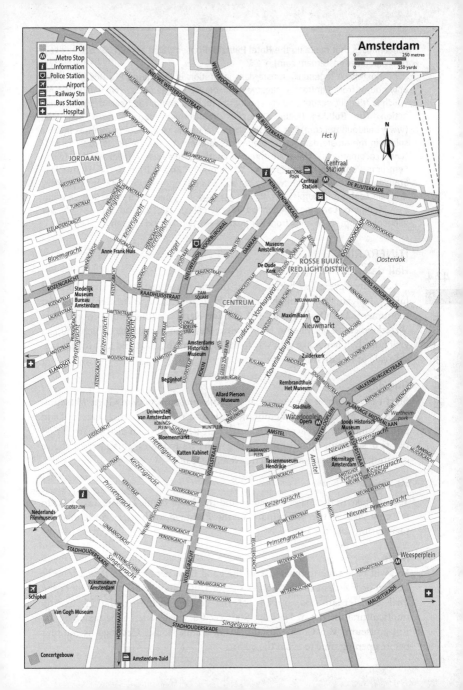

canal houses that make up the **Hotel Pulitzer**, Prinsengracht 315–331, ☎ 020 523 5235 (www.pulitzeramsterdam.com), €€€.

Hostels: A legendary Amsterdam institution is the **Flying Pig Hostel**, located only 500 m from Centraal at Nieuwendijk 100, ☎ 020 420 6822 (www.flyingpig.nl), which is friendly, secure and cheap. Stylish, modern and in the heart of the nightlife action, **The Bulldog Hotel**, Oudezijds Voorburgwal 220, ☎ 020 620 3822 (www.bulldoghotel.com) has beds from €27. A trendy new addition that has made a splash in the Amsterdam hostel scene is **Cocomama**, Westeinde 18, ☎ 020 627 2454 (www.cocomama.nl). There are three **HI youth hostels** (www.stayokay.com), two in Centrum: **Vondelpark**, Zandpad 5, ☎ 020 589 8996; tram 1/2/5: Leidseplein; **Stadsdoelen**, Kloveniersburgwal 97, ☎ 020 624 6832; tram 4/9/16/24/25: Muntplein, €, while **Zeeburg**, Timorplein 21, ☎ 020 551 3190, is 15 mins by tram east of Centrum.

Camping: **Camping Vliegenbos**, Meeuwenlaan 138, ☎ 020 636 8855 (www.vliegenbos.com) is 10 mins from Centraal on 🚌 32 or 33 and is open Apr–Sept.

ITINERARIES

Half day

If you only have a few hours, forget the big museums; you'll never do them justice. Instead, walk through the red-light district and visit Amsterdam's oldest monument, the **Oude Kerk**, and **Zuider Kerk**, a 17th-century church near Waterlooplein. Continue on to **Museum Het Rembrandthuis**, which you can visit quickly. Then make your way to the **Herengracht** canal and look for a canal-side café or restaurant.

One day

Start early and beat the crowds at the **Rijksmuseum** or **Van Gogh Museum**. Then visit **Museum Het Rembrandthuis** and red-light district, take in **Dam Square** and head west across four canals to reach the **Jordaan** district. You'll find plenty of shopping opportunities, along with bars and cafés, plus a terrific choice of eating places for an atmospheric evening meal.

Two days

You can take in the major museums and the **Anne Frank House**. Take time to relax by visiting the **Vondelpark** or the **Plantage**, with more museums, the planetarium and the zoo.

More

You will have time to make use of the good train network and take a train to **Leiden** or **Haarlem** to see another side of Dutch life. You can see more of the 'real' Amsterdam too, outside of the centre, including the fascinating multicultural district of **De Pijp**. Start each day with one of the major sights: Rijksmuseum, Van Gogh Museum, Anne Frank House. Get there 15 minutes before opening time to avoid the queues.

The best of Amsterdam

Amsterdams Historisch Museum (Historical Museum)
Lively exploration of the fascinating history of this unique city located at Kalverstraat 92 (www.ahm.nl).

Van Gogh Museum
People travel from around the world to see this, the finest collection of Van Gogh's work all housed in one place and much else besides. Located on Museumplein (www.vangoghmuseum.nl) close to Rijksmuseum.

Anne Frank Huis (Anne Frank House)
This museum and house is an essential (and moving) stop for a first-time visitor to the city, situated in the centre at Prinsengracht 263–267 (www.annefrank.org).

Rijksmuseum
The grandest of Amsterdam's two most popular art museums, with an unrivalled collection that includes portraits by Dutch masters Rembrandt and Vermeer.

Dam Square
This huge square at the hub of city life is not especially picturesque, but its historical interest cannot be questioned.

Jordaan district
Once an overcrowded working-class slum, this is now one of the prettiest quarters of the city, relaxing but fun and great for photography.

Begijnhof
An amazing historical old square — home to the city's oldest house — that survives in the heart of Amsterdam.

Museum Amstelkring (Ons' Lieve Heer op Solder)
A fascinating historical museum in the heart of the red-light district, just 5 mins walk from Dam Square, with a once secret Catholic church at the top (www.opsolder.nl).

Museum Het Rembrandthuis (The Rembrandt House Museum)
The home and studio of the city's artistic genius on Jodenbreestraat 4, 5 mins walk from Amsterdam Centraal Station. Both ordinary and extraordinary at the same time (www.rembrandthuis.nl).

De Oude Kerk (The Old Church)
The oldest building in Amsterdam, with stained-glass windows from the 1550s, and the finest of the city's several old churches (www.oudekerk.nl). Located on Oudekerksplein in Amsterdam's red-light district south of Amsterdam Centraal.

Exploring Amsterdam

The canals are an integral part of Amsterdam and provide an excellent way to appreciate the city: **boat trips** can be very cheap and have multilingual commentaries. Most people embark at Centraal, but you can board at any stop; there are quays in each area of interest — get tickets at any quay where Rondvaart/Rederij boats are moored.

Amsterdammers are exceedingly fond of the **Vondelpark** and make full use of its 45 hectares (111 acres) all year round and especially in summer. Millions of people visit the park every year, which has been providing green relief to the city dwellers ever since it opened in 1865. The park is the biggest in the city and is filled with trees, pathways, ponds and lakes teeming with wildlife, children's playgrounds, a bandstand, a rose garden and the **Nederlands Filmmuseum** ☎ 020 589 1400 (www.filmmuseum.nl). There are regular concerts in the bandstand in summer and activities for children on Wednesday afternoons.

The **red-light district** is usually the one area of a city most visitors avoid. In Amsterdam it's the opposite; the place is filled not only with prostitutes and live sex shows but with tourists who come simply to stand and stare. The girls sit openly in the windows of little apartments, dressed or, more accurately, undressed, in a range of outrageous and skimpy outfits. It is not a place to go if you are easily shocked. The area itself is quite a picturesque part of Amsterdam, with its narrow canal-side streets, but it is not a good idea to get your camera out. The girls, and their minders in the streets around, don't take kindly to having their picture taken. The city has recently embarked on a clean-up of the area, closing some of the windows and renting out various buildings to upmarket shops and boutiques. The police keep the district fairly safe, but do watch out for pickpockets.

South-east of Dam lies the heart of the erstwhile Jewish quarter which flourished for more than 300 years and formed 10% of the population until being almost annihilated by the Nazis. The **Joods Historich Museum** (Jewish Historical Museum), Nieuwe Amstelstraat 1 (www.jhm.nl), celebrates this community, and its collection of art, documents and antiques has been greatly expanded by the gift of two important private family collections.

THE FRINGE

Amsterdam is renowned for its libertarian views on, among other things, marijuana and homosexuality, and there is a nationwide gay and lesbian organisation (☎ 020 623 6565; 1200–1800 Mon–Fri, 1600-1800 weekends; www.switchboard.nl, Dutch only) that gives information about gay venues nationwide.

The city has many 'smoking' **coffee shops** (often with such words as 'free', 'happy', 'high' or 'space' in their name) where hash and pot can be purchased and smoked (usually to the accompaniment of ear-shattering music). But this apparently wayward aspect of Dutch life is changing. New legislation (piloted in Maastricht in autumn 2011 and due to be implemented nationwide in 2012) will bar non-residents from the coffee shops. Since the general smoking ban came into force, even in the coffee shops you will be required to smoke in specially designated areas.

The red-light district, in and around Oude Zijdsachterburgwal, is always an eye-opener in the evening, with prostitutes posing in windows; **the Erotic Museum** makes the experience that much more memorable if you don't mind the sleazy exterior (well, you probably wouldn't be here if you did!).

The **Nederlands Scheepvaartmuseum**, Kattenburgerplein 1 (www.scheep-vaartmuseum.nl) is an exceptionally rich maritime museum with particular emphasis on the adventures of the VOC — the buccaneering Dutch East India Company, the world's most powerful trading organisation during the 17th and 18th centuries. The museum is housed in a 17th-century arsenal, and features complete vessels, the most spectacular of which is a convincing 18th-century East Indiaman replica, *The Amsterdam*. Normally you can watch costumed personnel performing shipboard work, though occasionally it sails away to duties elsewhere.

AMSTERDAM ON A BUDGET

If you're looking to enjoy Amsterdam without spending too much money, you'll find plenty to do. Some of the top sights in the city are free, such as the **Begijnhof**, the **Bloemenmarkt** (Flower Market) and the hidden treat, the **Hollandsche Manege**, or Dutch Riding School, Vondelstraat 140, ☎ 020 618 0942 (www.dehollandschemanege.nl).

If you love music, culture and partying, the best way to enjoy the city cheaply is to visit during one of its many festivals. Try the **Amsterdam Roots Festival** on the third Sunday in June, or check out free open-air theatre in the **Vondelpark** from June to August. The **Uitmarkt** is a season of culture with music and theatre performances taking place all over town. Be prepared for large crowds.

If you're a bargain-hunting museum lover, you should come during the second weekend in April for National Museum Weekend. Entry to the city's museums over the weekend is free, although you'll have to struggle through the crowds. At other times it's a good idea to buy the **I amsterdam Card** (www.iamsterdam.com) from a tourist office, which combines a public transport ticket with discounted entry to many museums and other attractions (prices and validity: €39 for 24 hrs, €49 for 48 hrs, €59 for 72 hrs).

The **canal-side paths** make for beautiful strolls and there is always a cheap and cheerful café or bar in which to take a break. **Street markets** are an endless source of free fun and good photographs. Put together a picnic at the food markets and take it to one of the city's many parks to stroll, relax and eat. Head to a street stall for some cheap, filling snacks, including the Dutch favourite: herring.

FOOD

Amsterdam is buzzing with great places to eat, with everything from cheap cafés to the finest gourmet cuisine. Much on offer is international — there are excellent Italian, Japanese, Chinese, Indian, African, American and Caribbean restaurants — but traditional cuisine from the Netherlands and other countries close by, such as Belgium, Scandinavia and Germany, is also popular.

One international speciality you shouldn't miss is **Indonesian food**. There is a large Indonesian population in Amsterdam thanks to the close trading ties between the Netherlands and the East Indies, and there are countless restaurants serving this tasty and spicy cooking. Try the *rijsttafel* (rice table), a selection of twelve or more beef, seafood and vegetable dishes served with rice. It can be extremely filling, so save it for when you're really hungry. It is worth noting that many restaurants start to wind down by 2200, when last orders are taken. If you like to eat late, your choice will be somewhat limited and you should first check out opening hours.

If you want to buy your own groceries there's a good Albert Heijn supermarket on the corner of Singel and Koningsplein (nicely situated for picnics next to the floating flower market). For a sit-down meal at a reasonable price, try one of the many traditional '**brown cafés**'. Around Spui it's mega touristy; there are better places in backstreets and along the quieter canals, while the areas near Nieuwmarkt, Dam and De Pijp (especially along Albert Cuypstr.) are the best for Far Eastern cuisine.

CULTURE AND NIGHTLIFE

You'll find it hard not to have fun in Amsterdam. Whatever you want to do, you can usually do it — and that includes a few things you can't do in too many other cities. Amsterdam is beautiful by day but comes into its own after dark. The infamous red-light district near Centraal Station might not be everyone's idea of a fun time, but it undeniably has its own kind of neon attraction and you shouldn't miss it.

The **Leidseplein** near the Jordaan district is the place where teenagers hang out in bars and cafés and is a lively place to go for fast food. A trendier area is Spuikwartier, around Spuistraat, packed with bars, clubs, restaurants and some of Amsterdam's best brown cafés.

For music, dance and drama performances of all sorts, Amsterdam can't be beaten. Weekly listings can be found in *Time Out* and on the excellent English language website (www.underwateramsterdam.com). Make sure you look for flyers in bars and music shops advertising local clubs and special gigs.

Some recommended venues in the city include **Paradiso**, Weteringschans 6–8, ☎ 020 626 4521 (www.paradiso.nl), for rock, jazz and dance music, depending on the evening. **De Melkweg** (The Milky Way), Lijnbaansgracht 234a, ☎ 020 531 8181 (www.melkweg.nl) is particularly good for jazz and attracts some seriously stylish dudes — but you won't be turned away if your threads are a little more worn. **Studio 80**, Rembrandtplein 17, (www.studio-80.nl), is conveniently located in the heart of the nightlife district, and has a reputation as the city's most cutting-edge and underground techno club.

Major venues for classical music and opera are the **Muziektheater**, ☎ 020 625 5455 (www.hetmuziektheater.nl) at Waterlooplein and the **Concertgebouw** on Museumplein (which has free lunchtime concerts on Wednesday). If you want to catch a **movie**, foreign films are invariably subtitled, so there's a good choice of showings in English. There is a concentration of cinemas around the Leidseplein. Two spectacular art deco picture palaces are **Tuschinski** near the Rembrandtplein (screen 1 is the most impressive) and **The Movies** on the Haarlemmerstraat near the Jordaan.

EVENTS

If Amsterdam is a party town any night of the year, it's double the fun when there's a festival going on. One of the biggest and best parties is the Queen's Day on 30 April and the city's streets are heaving around that time. Throughout the year, particularly in summer, there are many music, theatre and film festivals. Here are just a few of the best:

Carnival takes place every February in the Brabant region, roughly two hours from Amsterdam. The weather doesn't quite rival Rio's, but there is a buzz about the place and a lot of action on the streets. **Koninginnedag** (Queen's Day) — the biggest and best celebration in Amsterdam, is held on 30 April. Book accommodation far in advance. **Amsterdam Gay Pride** celebrations commence at the start of August and include a unique Gay Pride Boat Parade on the canals. The streets are packed and you should expect to see some extravagant outfits and outrageous behaviour. (www.amsterdamgaypride.nl).

The **Grachtenfestival** (Canal Festival) is a classical music festival that sees internationally renowned musicians performing along canals and the river. It's usually held over the last two weeks of August. A spectacularly inventive multimedia festival held within an industrial backdrop, **Robodock** brings together international designers, architects, theatrical performers, musicians and robots. Usually held mid-September, Robodock returns in 2012 after a year off in 2011 (www.robodock.org). One of Europe's biggest **New Year** celebrations is in the Dutch capital. Beware the local custom of throwing fireworks.

OUT OF TOWN

Amsterdamse Bos, Amstelveenseweg 264 (www.amsterdamsebos.nl), on the southern fringe of the city, is an 80-hectare park, pleasant for swimming, rowing, canoeing, cycling and walking (200 km of tracks). **Enkhuizen** (www.enkhuizen.nl) is 1 hour by train from Amsterdam (ERT 459), and was cut off from the sea when the Zuider Zee was dammed to create Lake Ijsselmeer. The boat for the **Zuiderzee Museum** leaves from behind the station, and the ticket includes both the boat and museum.

The indoor section, **Binnenmuseum**, contains traditional costumes and fishing craft, while the open-air section, **Buitenmuseum**, consists of whole streets rescued from fishing villages. You can enter any house with an open door and ask questions if you find someone at home.

Athens (Αθήνα)

Modern Athens is a noisy, bustling, exhilarating but exhausting city of over 4 million people. Revamped for the 2004 **Olympic Games**, it is now less polluted and more pedestrian friendly, and with its countless trendy bars and restaurants (notably in the areas of Psyrri and Gazi) offers one of the best nightlife scenes in Europe.

Yet many Athenians live a laid-back, village-style life amid the concrete apartment blocks, and hardly a corner is without a tiny café or taverna. Street-crime rates are remarkably low and it's a conspicuously friendly place. Its enduring appeal lies in the great sights of the ancient city where the seeds of Western democracy, philosophy, medicine and art were planted.

You can visit most of the sights on foot as the city is quite compact and best seen early in the morning to avoid the worst of the heat and crowds. Athens is on **Route 41** (p343) of this book.

TRAVEL BASICS

All trains now use **Lárisa Station** (Stathmós Larísis), Theodorou Diligiani, ☎ 210 529 7777. It is about 2 km north-west of Syntagma (metro: Stathmós Larísis). You can buy international rail tickets at the train station. The port at **Piraeus** serves the Greek islands. Visit www.greekferries.gr for routes and ferry times or book at one of the many agencies in Piraeus. The port is 8 km south-west of Athens and is served by the metro (green line). If you are island hopping, Thomas Cook's guidebook *Greek Island Hopping* combines a guide to every Greek island with ferry timetable information.

The new **Eleftherios Venizelos Airport** is 27 km north-east of the city centre and served by both Olympic Airways and international airlines (www.aia.gr). For international flight information, ☎ 210 353 0000. There are connections to Lárisa Station by both metro and suburban rail, although depending on the time you arrive, a change of trains may be necessary. Central Athens has become increasingly walkable thanks to the 'Archaeological Promenade', a 4 km long pedestrian-only way, which leads from the Acropoli metro station, skirts around the foot of the Acropolis, past the Ancient Agora, then continues from Thissio metro station, east along Adrianou to Monastiraki metro station, and west along Ermou to Kerameikos metro station.

Metro tickets (covering 1 zone, 2 zones or all lines, valid 90 mins) are available from station kiosks or self-service machines; validate them in the machines at station entrances. Buy tickets for **trolleybuses** and **buses** from blue booths near bus stops or from kiosks throughout Athens. Validate tickets on board. The 24 hr ticket is valid for the metro, trolleybuses and buses; validate ticket once only, on the first use.

INFORMATION

The office of the **Greek National Tourism Organisation** (GNTO) is at Tsoha 7, ☎ 210 870 7000 (www.gnto.gr); sightseeing information leaflets, fact sheets, local and regional transport schedules and up-to-date opening times of sights. There are also GNTO offices in the city centre at Amalias 26 (near Syntagma Square) and at Eleftherios

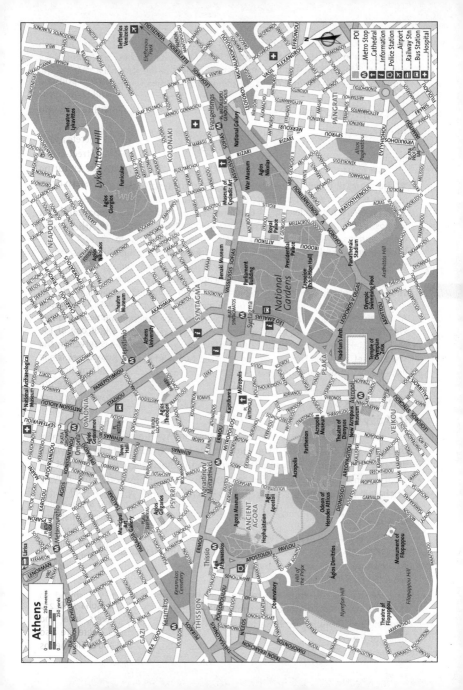

Venizelos Airport. **Internet cafés** are less plentiful than in most other European capitals. The most reliable are Café4U at Ippokratous 44 in Exarcheia (open 24 hrs non-stop), Museum Internet Café at Patission 46 next to the National Archaeological Museum, and Plaka Internet World at Pandrosou 29 in Plaka.

ACCOMMODATION

The Hellenic Chamber of Hotels provides a booking service for Athens hotels. They can be contacted before arrival at Stadiou 24, 10564 Athens, ☎ 213 216 9900 (www.grhotels.gr).

⊨ **Hotels**: Much beloved of budget travellers, the **Acropolis House**, Kodrou 6, ☎ 210 322 2344 (www.acropolishouse.gr), €€, is in a quiet Plaka street, with plenty of other options around if they happen to be full. The **Adonis Hotel**, Kodrou 3, ☎ 210 324 9737 (www.hotel-adonis.gr), €€, is modern, small and friendly, whilst the **Athens Studios**, Veikou 3a, ☎ 210 923 5811 (www.athensstudios.gr) offer a range of great value options, from self-catering studios and apartments to dorm beds for backpackers. **Hostels**: Hostels cluster in the Plaka area, noisy but ideally located for the main sights, or between Victoria and the stations (where the tackiest accommodation is found). Some of the cheapest 'hostel' accommodation near the station is extremely overcrowded in high season with tight-budget travellers.

However, except in the height of summer, you should have plenty of options. Among the best budget choices in the Plaka area are the **Student and Travellers Inn**, Kidathineon 16, ☎ 210 324 4808 (www.studenttravellersinn.com), and **Athens Backpackers**, Makri 12, ☎ 210 922 4044 (www.backpackers.gr). Alternatively, try **Athenstyle Hostel**, 10 Agias Theklas, ☎ 210 322 5010 (www.athenstyle.com), in the lively nightlife district of Psyrri.

ITINERARIES
Half day

You can't see it all so don't even try: focus on the **Acropolis**. Approach it from the south side, and go early if you can. The site and museum will take you at least an hour. Turn right when you exit, down into the **Plaka** district, where there are plenty of places to have a coffee or glass of wine and buy souvenirs. A little further on is **Monastiraki Square** for a touch of authentic Athenian street life.

One day

If you have a full day, consider your afternoon options after the half-day suggested above. In winter and on holidays, the **National Archaeological Museum** closes at 1500, not giving time to squeeze this in. In summer it stays open later, so head there.

Most other museums and archaeological sites close at 1500 all year round, so if there is one you want to see, go straight there after the Acropolis and save your strolling and shopping for the afternoon. With only time for one evening meal, head for **Psyrri**.

THE BEST OF ATHENS

The Acropolis
One of the world's greatest ancient sites, and the starting point of any traveller's tour of the city. And all the better since the sparkling new Acropolis Museum opened in 2009 (www.theacropolismuseum.gr; closed Mon). Metro: Acropoli.

National Archaeological Museum
The greatest collection of Greek antiquities anywhere and one of the finest museums in the world. Metro: Victoria.

The Plaka
This district below the Acropolis is unashamedly touristy, but still attractive and Athenian too.

Psyrri
Visitors go to the Plaka, but Athenians flock to the Psyrri district, right next door, for an evening out.

Syntagma Square
The heart of modern Athens, in front of the Parliament buildings and the National Gardens.

Museum of Cycladic Art
A specialist collection of beautiful objects, beautifully displayed. The museum is close to Syntagma Square and the Parliament. Closed Tues.

Monastiraki Flea Market
See it on Sunday morning if you can, though there's always something happening here. Located in the Old Town, Monastiraki metro station is closest.

The Olympic Stadiums
The stadium for the 1896 Olympics is right in the city centre, and a visit to the 2004 stadium shows you how times have changed.

Two days

If you have a few days, save the National Archaeological Museum for the second morning after trying out our one-day programme above. After a few hours here you may have museum fatigue, but outdoor sites such as the **Roman Agora** or **Kerameikos Cemetery** can still be enjoyed. Visit **Lykavittos Hill**, too, for good views over the Acropolis. You could also dine here in the evening, and enjoy the night-time city scene.

More

If you have more than two days, make use of the extra time by exploring further afield. Take the metro to the bustling port area at **Piraeus** and have a seafood lunch, or catch a bus out to **Akrotirio Sounio** (Cape Sounion) for the sunset. A trip to Delphi or Nafplion will take a full day, as will a visit to the nearest Greek islands.

ATHENS ON A BUDGET

Athens is one of Europe's cheapest capital cities, and while you could spend a lot of money by booking the best accommodation and restaurants, most of the attractions and general prices are still inexpensive for visitors. And if you do want to see Athens on a budget, it's quite easy with a little thought and planning.

Syntagma Square is at the very centre of Athens, and here each day you can enjoy the almost hypnotic **Changing of the Guard** ceremony in front of the Parliament building at the top of the square. The guards in their traditional costumes are very photogenic, and the ceremony takes place hourly at about 20 minutes before the hour. The Sunday morning changing is the main ceremonial one of the week, with full orchestral accompaniment, and though this is often said to be at 1100, it usually begins at 1040, like all the others, so don't be late. From Syntagma it's a short walk through the **Kolonaki district** (expensive, but window shopping costs nothing!) to the foot of **Lykavittos Hill**. Walk to the top, up the winding paths for the best free view in the city: the Parthenon sitting on top of the Acropolis. Day or night, it's magic.

FOOD

Some of the best Greek food is the *meze*, the Greek equivalent of Spanish tapas. It includes typical starter dishes such as *taramasalata*, *tzatziki* (a yoghurt, cucumber and garlic dip) and aubergine salad. These dishes come on small plates and you can make an entire meal from them if you order several. Ask the waiter for a selection of *meze* for one or two people, or more, but make sure you're hungry, as the Greeks have big appetites!

There are countless inexpensive tavernas in Athens where you can get good Greek staples such as moussaka, stuffed peppers, stuffed aubergines, lamb and beef stews, grilled chicken and pork. These days Greek food is often sophisticated as well as hearty. Be adventurous. Head for the Psyrri and Gazi districts.

CULTURE AND NIGHTLIFE

Going out is central to Greek and therefore Athenian culture. There are big noisy bars and small intimate ones — and clubs that play music running the gamut from top 40 hits to soft jazz, from hard rock to Greek popular music. In the summer, some clubs close down and revellers head out to the open-air venues in the city's beach-resort suburbs. All those places serve alcohol but beware: as Greece has not adopted a standard measuring system, you often get treble the quantity of measures back home. And the friendlier the bartender the more alcohol will end up in your bloodstream.

Although every type of **music** is catered for it's advisable to check the local listings magazines. Some clubs are devoted to one kind of music; others have different styles on different nights. There are fewer choices available in summer,

VISITING THE ISLANDS

If you have more than a couple of days in Athens, you might want to fit in a visit to some of the nearby Greek islands. It's a refreshing break from the city, which is why many Athenians take advantage of the opportunity. On summer weekends the islands and the boats can be very busy indeed, so travel during the week if you can and book your ferry ticket in advance.

There are five islands within easy reach of the port of Piraeus, although not many visitors bother with the island of Salamis (or Salamina), as it is so close to the mainland and the industry around Piraeus that it doesn't give the true Greek island experience. For that you have to go a little further, into the four **Argo-Saronic islands** that are the main attractions for Athens: Aegina, Poros, Hydra (or Idra) and Spetses (or Spetsai).

With fast hydrofoils, these islands are very easy to reach. Aegina takes just 40 minutes, making it the most popular, while the furthest, Spetses, is about 2 hours away. It makes it quite feasible to go and have lunch on Aegina, visit Spetses for the day, stay there overnight and come back the next day.

partly due to lack of air conditioning and partly to musicians working the much busier tourist resorts on the Greek islands.

While Athens has a lively theatre scene and a **National Theatre** company (www.n-t.gr), most performances are in Greek. You might get to see a visiting theatre group. So check the listings while you're there. There is also a **Greek National Opera** company (www.nationalopera.gr), and several halls putting on classical concerts. Dance is popular too, from contemporary work via classical ballet to Greek traditional dance, notably at the **Dora Stratou Theatre** (www.grdance.org) at the foot of Filopappou Hill.

EVENTS

Carnival (February/March) is not as big in Greece as it is in, say, Venice or the Caribbean, but they do still celebrate. You'll find music in the streets of Athens, especially around the Plaka district, with children in costumes and people hitting each other over the head with plastic hammers.

The biggest religious celebration in Greece is **Easter**, and a time when it's a joy to be there, religious or not. There are processions through the streets, shown live on TV. Greek Easter usually falls in April, though not always, and the ecclesiastical calendar of the **Greek Orthodox Church** is different from that espoused by western Christianity.

Beginning in late May and running through till early October, the **Athens Festival** is the big annual arts festival. As well as the best in Greek classical dance and theatre, recent visitors have included the Bolshoi Ballet, the English National Ballet, the Berlin Symphony Orchestra and the Musiciens du Louvre. Many events take place in the ancient Odeon (Theatre) of Herodes Atticus.

Barcelona

This may be 'officially' Spain's second city after Madrid, but Barcelona is the capital of **Catalunya**, and its real sense of regional pride, energy and style make it a capital city to rival any in Europe. Over the past two decades it has become one of Europe's most visited destinations, and every year millions of travellers and tourists descend on Barcelona to marvel at the **modernist** architecture of **Antoni Gaudí**, explore the museums and galleries devoted to the likes of Picasso and Miró, promenade along the wide boulevards of the Eixample, or get lost in the narrow streets and alleyways of the old **Gothic Quarter** (Barri Gòtic).

Beyond the art and the architecture, Barcelona has plenty more to divert you. There are few better places in Europe to eat out, whether you find your dinner in tiny backstreet *tapas* bars and the food stalls of the **Boqueria market**, or restaurants helmed by award-winning chefs. Football fans should most certainly make a pilgrimage to the **Camp Nou**, home of local heroes FC Barcelona. Tickets for the games may be hard to come by, but the museum at the stadium is an attraction in its own right.

As with any city as popular as Barcelona, things are not entirely rosy. The summer months can be oppressively crowded, especially around famous landmarks such as Gaudí's **Sagrada Família**, and those crowds are a tempting target for the city's pickpockets and bag-snatchers, which have given Barcelona a sadly justified reputation for petty crime. None of this should put you off, however, as Barcelona would be a highlight on any tour, and a perfectly wonderful destination in its own right. Cosmopolitan, prosperous and confident, Barcelona has been forward-looking ever since it hosted the Olympic Games back in 1992 and is firmly established as one of Europe's truly great cities. Barcelona is well connected by train to the rest of Spain, and also to Paris, Zurich, Montpellier, Geneva and Milan. You will find Barcelona on **Routes 8** (p104) and **9** (p110) of this book.

TRAVEL BASICS

≋ There are two main stations: the central **Estació de França**, Avda Marquès de l'Argentera (metro: Barceloneta), for most regional trains and certain long-distance national and international services; and **Estació de Sants**, Plaça dels Països Catalans, ☎ 90 224 02 02, about 3.5 km from the Old Town (metro: Sants-Estació), for suburban, regional and international trains as well as those to the airport. ▭ **Estació de Autobuses Barcelona Nord**, Carrer d'Alí Bei 80, ☎ 90 226 06 06 (www.barcelonanord.com; metro: Arc de Triomf) and **Estació de Sants**, Plaça dels Països Catalans, ☎ 93 490 40 00 (www.eurolines.es; metro: Estació de Sants).

⛴ From **the port**, ferries leave for the Balearics, Tangier in Morocco and the Italian ports of Civitavecchia and Livorno. For details, contact Trasmediterránea, ☎ 90 245 46 45 (www.trasmediterranea.com). ✈ **Aeroport del Prat** is 12 km south-west of the city, ☎ 90 240 47 04 (www.aena.es). RENFE trains run every 30 mins, between about 0600 and 2330, to and from Estació de Sants (journey time: 19 mins) and Estació

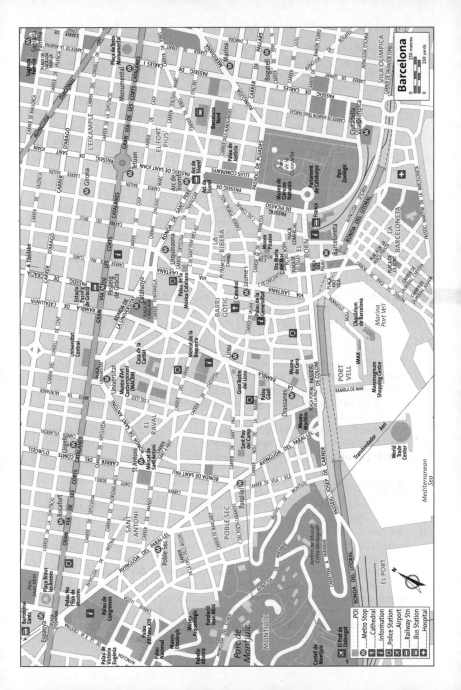

Passeig de Gracia (26 mins). The Aerobús bus service runs every 6–15 minutes (0530–0015 from Plaça Catalunya; 0600–0100 from airport). For information: ☎ 93 415 60 20. You can find an official city map online at www.bcn.cat/guia.

Once in town, the **metro** service, ☎ 93 318 70 74 (www.tmb.cat), will get you around quickly and easily. It has seven colour-coded lines, and trains are designated by the name of the last stop. There is a flat rate for all journeys, regardless of distance or location, as long as you stay within the city limits. You have to pay again if you transfer between two lines. The metro runs Mon–Thur, Sun & holidays 0500–2400, Fri 0500–0200, Sat 24 hrs. The metro also runs non-stop overnight between 31 Dec/1 Jan, 23/24 June, 14/15 Aug and 23/24 Sept.

The **Bus Turístic** (tourist bus) runs every day 0900–2000 Apr–Oct (approx every 6–10 mins) and until 1900 Nov–Mar (approx every 30 mins). Pick up a map and guide from the tourist office, which outlines the monuments and sights, and buy a ticket on-board. The routes start from Plaça de Catalunya, though to avoid the queues you might do better to walk on to the next stop and then start from there. You can hop on and off as many times as you please.

INFORMATION

🄸 There are **tourist Information** centres throughout the city, including at Plaça de Catalunya 17 (underground, opposite the El Corte Inglés department store); City Hall, C. Ciutat 2; Estació de Sants. During the summer months there are also street information services; look out for staff in red and white uniforms with the standard 'i' on their sleeves. You can also get city information by phone ☎ 93 285 38 34 or online at www.barcelonaturisme.com. If you are in town for a few days, you might consider getting the **Barcelona Card**, which gives free public transport travel and discounted or free admission to certain attractions (2–5 days, €27.50–€45).

It has never been easier to **get online in Barcelona** since wi-fi access is available in over 500 municipal buildings, such as libraries, cultural centres, the airport and museums. Plenty of bars and cafés offer wi-fi access to their customers as well. If you don't have a laptop with you, there are internet cafés dotted around the city. Try **Abre Barcelona**, Aribau 308, ☎ 93 202 02 74 (www.abrebarcelona.com).

ACCOMMODATION

Barcelona has as wide a range of hotels as any major European city, but be aware that prices are fairly high compared to the rest of Spain. In the summer it is definitely worth reserving in advance, or at the very least, arriving early in the day. There are many reasonably priced *pensiones*, particularly in the areas just off La Rambla in the Raval neighbourhood.

🛏 **Guesthouses**: For style on a budget, try the **Sol y K Guesthouse**, C. Cervantes 2 2–1, ☎ 93 318 81 48 (www.solyk.com), €, in the Gothic Quarter or the **Gat Raval**, C. Joaquín Costa 44, 1º, ☎ 93 481 66 70 (www.gatrooms.es), €–€€, in the Raval. For those seeking home comforts, the **Sagrada Família**, C. Napolis 266, ☎ 651 89 14 13 (www.sagradafamilia-bedandbreakfast.com), €, is a cheap and cosy option. **Hotels**: Chic and surprisingly affordable, the **Banys Orientals**, C. Argenteria 37 (www.

THE BEST OF BARCELONA

La Sagrada Família
This eccentric church is an architectural marvel, the foremost symbol of the city and Gaudí's most celebrated creation.

Museu Picasso
A comprehensive collection of early artworks by Pablo Picasso, from childhood sketches to Cubism, housed in five medieval palaces. Located at Montcada 15–23, metro L1 (Arc de Triomf) or L3 (Liceu) (www.museupicasso.bcn.cat), closed Mon.

Parc Güell
Antoni Gaudí's flamboyant hilltop park is an extraordinary piece of landscape design, great for family picnics and far-reaching views.

La Rambla
The most famous boulevard in Spain and the hub of city life for locals and visitors.

Museu Nacional d'Art de Catalunya (MNAC)
One thousand years of Catalan art under one roof situated at the Parc de Montjuïc — don't miss the decorative arts and photography displays. Take metro L1 or L3 (Pl. Espanya) or at the MNAC stop of the Bus Turístic (www.mnac.cat), closed Mon.

Manzana de la Discordia
Three *modernista* masterpieces in one city block in the Eixample: Gaudí's *Casa Batlló*, Puig i Cadafalch's *Casa Amatller* and Domènech i Montaner's *Casa Lleó Morera*.

Fundació Joan Miró
A dazzling gallery devoted to one of Barcelona's finest artists up on Montjuïc hill (www.fundaciomiro-bcn.org), closed Mon.

hotelbanysorientals.com), €€, can be found in the heart of trendy El Born. Other mid-range options include: **El Jardi**, Pl. Sant Josep Oriol 1, ☎ 93 301 59 00 (www.hoteljardi-barcelona.com), €€, and the **Market Hotel**, Passatge Sant Antoni Abad 10, ☎ 93 325 12 05 (www.markethotel.com.es), €€. Boutique-style at boutique prices, the **Casa Camper**, C. Elisabets 11, ☎ 93 342 26 80 (www.casacamper.com), €€€, is worth treating yourself to, as is the intimate boutique hotel **Neri**, C. Sant Sever 5, ☎ 93 304 06 55 (www.hotelneri.com), €€€.

    Hostels: The funky **Equity Point chain** (www.equity-point.com) is a boon for backpackers, with three excellent locations: Centric Point (Passeig de Gràcia 33, ☎ 93 215 65 38), Gothic Point (C. Vigatans 5, ☎ 93 268 78 08) and Sea Point (Plaça del Mar 1–4, ☎ 93 224 70 75), all with doubles and dorms, mostly en suite. If you don't mind a party atmosphere, the **Kabul Hostel** at Plaça Reial 17, ☎ 93 318 51 90 (www.kabul.es), is legendary on the backpacker scene for those who like to make friends and don't mind too much how little they sleep. The **Sant Jordi** (www.santjordihostels.com) chain of hostels have won awards, with the **Hostel Sant Jordi Alberg**, Roger de Lluria 40, ☎ 93 342 41 61, being especially recommended. Another good option in the same chain is the **Mambo Tango**, Poeta Cabanyes 23, ☎ 93 442 51 64 (www.hostelmambotango.com). There are 12 **camping sites** within easy reach of Barcelona.

BARCELONA'S BEACHES

Barcelona's beaches offer bathers and sun-worshippers some of the cleanest city sea-bathing in the Mediterranean, with nearly 5 km of broad, sandy beaches stretching from Barceloneta northwards. Facilities include lifeguards, public toilets and showers (some accessible for people with disabilities), beach bars, shops and restaurants. On Platja de la Barceloneta there is a new beach centre and small library (with some publications in English) that lends out magazines and newspapers along with beach toys in the summer months. The most central beaches are fringed by the Passeig Marítim — the palm-lined boardwalk linking La Barceloneta to La Vila Olímpica, the 'twin towers' of the Arts hotel and the Mapfre building, signposted by Frank Gehry's glittering copper *Fish* sculpture — the city's maritime symbol.

Camping Tres Estrellas, Carretera de Castelldefels C-31, km 186,2, ☎ 93 633 06 37 (www.camping3estrellas.com). Can be reached by the 🚌 94/95 from Plaça d'Espanya or Plaça de Catalunya. **La Ballena Alegre**, Autovía de Castelldefels, ☎ 90 251 05 20 (www.ballena-alegre.es) has bungalows as well as tent pitches.

ITINERARIES

Half day

If you have only a few hours, start your visit promenading along the city's most famous boulevard, **La Rambla**. Then explore the dark atmospheric streets and enchanting squares of the **Barri Gòtic**. Art lovers should also visit the remarkable collections of **Museu Picasso** in the neighbouring La Ribera district.

One day

Having completed the half-day itinerary, you are now at the heart of the fashionable **La Ribera district** with its myriad hip fashion boutiques, galleries and design shops, so add some shopping to your day. Alternatively, visit the beautiful church of **Santa Maria del Mar** or take in a museum. The **Museu d'Història de Catalunya** is especially interesting. For dinner, head back to the trendy bars and bistros of La Ribera or enjoy more traditional dishes and some of the city's finest seafood in the **Barceloneta** district.

Two days

The extra day provides plenty of time to explore the city's **museums** and spectacular *modernista* **architecture**. The Eixample district contains many of the most famous buildings. Shopaholics will also enjoy Passeig de Gràcia — the Champs-Élysées of Barcelona — for its exclusive shops and designer boutiques. There are also some excellent tapas bars here for a light lunch, before heading off to admire Gaudí's most celebrated sights — **La Sagrada Família** and **Parc Güell**. Or visit **Montjuïc** hill and spend the day marvelling at such major museums as the **Museu Nacional d'Art de Catalunya** (MNAC) and the **Fundació Joan Miró**.

Return to the Old Town for dinner in the Barri Gòtic. You may also have time to explore the rejuvenated waterfront, including **Port Vell** with its impressive Maremàgnum shopping complex.

More

A longer stay enables you to soak up the café culture of the Old Town, venture out to the football stadium (the Camp Nou), top up your tan on the beaches and visit some of the outlying districts of town, including **Pedralbes** with its monastery and museums, and **Mont Tibidabo** in the Collserola hills.

EXPLORING BARCELONA

Just off La Rambla, the **Barri Gòtic** (Gothic Quarter) is Barcelona's oldest district, brimming with atmospheric streets, alleyways and hidden squares, and flanked by countless buildings of historical interest. The Barri Gòtic is something of a misnomer as the district combines its splendid Gothic architecture with Roman, Romanesque and Renaissance elements, making it a fascinating area to explore.

Barcelona's main covered market, the **Mercat de la Boqueria**, is a veritable showcase for Catalan gastronomy, from fruit, herbs and vegetables to meat, fish and crustaceans. The cavernous market hall is best entered through an impressive wrought-iron gateway off La Rambla. Inside it's a riot of noise and activity, as market sellers, local shoppers, restaurateurs and tourists all jostle for the best buys of the day. It is an excellent place to stock up for a picnic or simply to soak up the flavours, colours and fragrances.

The quaint old district of **Barceloneta** was traditionally the home of seamen and port workers, and the clock tower on the Moll de la Barceloneta was once a lighthouse. Although the area has been greatly gentrified in recent years, the criss-cross grid of ancient narrow streets still holds children playing football while locals sit and chat, their washing fluttering overhead on the balconies. The heart of the district is the Plaça de la Barceloneta, with the beautiful baroque church of Sant Miquel del Port, and the enormous adjacent square of Plaça de la Font with the newly rebuilt municipal market.

South of the city, the vast hill of **Montjuïc** is named 'Mountain of the Jews' after an early Jewish necropolis here. In 1929 it was the venue for the International Expo, and in 1992 it was the main site of the Barcelona Olympics. Today, with its top-notch sports facilities, together with some of the city's finest museums and galleries, it is a popular place for both locals and visitors at weekends.

BARCELONA ON A BUDGET

Some museums offer free entry at certain times: the **Museu Picasso** is free every Sunday from 15.00 (and all day on the first Sunday of the month); **Museu**

Frederic Marès offers free admission from 15.00 every Wednesday and Sunday; and the **Museu d'Història de Catalunya** is free on the first Sunday of the month.

In many ways, the entire city resembles a giant outdoor gallery, with over 400 open-air monuments and sculptures to enjoy. Shopping fanatics on a budget can enjoy some of the world's finest window-shopping, especially on **Passeig de Gràcia**, the Diagonal and in La Ribera and El Born. There are also several worthwhile **markets** to browse, including an antiques market in Plaça del Pi on Thursdays; the weekend art market in Plaça Sant Josep Oriol; the Sunday coin and stamp market in Plaça Reial; the huge flea market of Els Encants at Sant Antoni; and the sensational food market of La Boqueria from Monday to Saturday.

The city squares are also great places to sit and watch the world go by: feed the pigeons in Plaça de Catalunya; listen to the buskers in Plaça Sant Josep Oriol; and watch the *sardana* dancers perform in Plaça de la Seu on Saturday at 1800 or in Plaça Sant Jaume I on Sunday evenings. It's also fun to people-watch on La Rambla, and enjoy the lively street entertainment every few paces.

FOOD

Catalan cooking derives from peasant fare, with grilled meats and casseroles alongside Spanish staples such as *paella*, *serrano* ham, salt cod and dozens of *tapas* dishes. *Crema Catalana* is a delicious local dessert, like egg custard with caramelised sugar on top. Catalunya is also famous for its champagne-style sparkling wine, cava — the speciality of establishments known as *Xampanyeries*.

In general, modern, upmarket and avant-garde establishments are to be found in the **Eixample**, while the Raval specialises in economic Asian restaurants and curry houses. The **Gothic Quarter** has food of all stripes, from dark old *tascas* to funky fusion start-up restaurants run on a shoestring. Local wines are widely on offer everywhere at a very reasonable price.

For a taste of the sea, try **Barceloneta**, the old fishermen's neighbourhood and still home to restaurants serving some of the best seafood anywhere in Europe. Away from the Old Town, the Olympic Village is packed with modern bars and restaurants. The *Guía del Ocio* (published weekly) and *Time Out Barcelona* have good coverage of restaurants and are available from most newsstands.

CULTURE AND NIGHTLIFE

Barcelona is a city of night owls, and the vibrant club scene is among the best in Europe. There is plenty to choose from every night, and weekends here start on Thursday. A typical evening begins around 2030 with *tapas* and aperitifs in a local bar, followed by a leisurely dinner around 2230. The usual starting time for opera, ballet and concerts is around 2100, or 2200 for theatre. After midnight, music bars become crowded. Around 0300 the clubs and discos fill up and the famous Barcelonan night movement sweeps across the city until dawn. For those who just

ANTONI GAUDÍ

For many people, Gaudí alone is sufficient reason to visit Barcelona. He designed many of its most characteristic buildings; throughout the city, mansions, parks, schools, gateways, lamp posts and sculptures provide a constant reminder of his genius. Particularly striking are Casa Milà, with its extraordinary rippling facade devoid of straight lines and right-angled corners, and Casa Batlló, an imaginative example of the fusion of architecture with the decorative arts of the *époque*.

Gaudí's most emblematic structure is the still unfinished Temple Expiatori de la Sagrada Família, the city's iconic church that he spent over 40 years creating, personally going out into the street to raise funds among the passers-by to facilitate its construction.

don't want to stop, there are 'afters' bars that take the party all the way to lunchtime the next day.

The **main nightlife areas** are El Born and La Ribera, with their many small bars, and the chic nightspots of L'Eixample. However, the Barri Gòtic and El Raval are also lively and some of the more exclusive bars and clubs are further afield — on Montjuïc hill and the lower slopes of Tibidabo. To find out what's on, the *Guía del Ocio* (www.guiadelociobcn.es) has comprehensive listings.

One of the world's most extraordinary concert halls, the tiled **Palau de la Música Catalana**, C. Sant Pere Més Alt, ☎ 90 244 28 82 (www.palaumusica.org) is an astonishing modernist building with a huge stained-glass dome, designed by Montaner and finished in 1908; tours are available, or attend a concert. Several **cinemas** show screenings in the original version with subtitles, including the Boliche, Casablanca-Gràcia, Verdi and the Yelmo Icària Cineplex. Look for VO (*versió original*) in the listings.

EVENTS

Throughout the year religious processions, festivals and traditions turn the city of Barcelona into an open-air theatre. The **Festival de Santa Eulàlia** is celebrated on 12 February with a week of traditional parades, *gegants* (giant figures), concerts, *sardanes* (Catalan folk dances) and *castellers* (human castles). Many events are focused on children.

The **Primavera Sound** is a five-day music festival at the end of May filling the vast Parc del Fòrum with enormous crowds and big names from all music genres (www.primaverasound.com). The **Sant Joan** celebrations on the evening of 23 June offer solstice bonfires, the *Nit del Foc* (night of fire) in Barceloneta and all-night beach parties.

La Mercè, the city's main week-long fiesta, takes place around the 24 September. Events include free concerts, fireworks, an air show, traditional parades and *sardanes* all finished off with the wildest *correfoc* (fire run) of the year.

Belgrade (Београд)

Wandering around Belgrade's relaxed **Old Town**, with its chic restaurants, galleries and boutiques, it's almost impossible to imagine that just over a decade ago the city was suffering a NATO bombardment. Today the Serbian capital is generally a serene metropolis, particularly as two of its main districts are pedestrianised — the Roman-era streets around **Knez Mihailova**, home to many of the city's best shops, eateries and museums, and the bohemian restaurant district **Skadarlija**. Despite — or perhaps because of — what they have endured over the years, Belgrade's citizens now seem focused on life's simple pleasures, socialising at the many tiny bars and clubs dotted around, shopping or just sitting and watching the world go by in a café or in **Trg Republike**.

Visit this city and you'll be seeing it on the cusp of its transformation into a bustling centre of tourism and commerce. As a destination, Belgrade ticks all the boxes. It's positively brimming with culture — not only is the city a living historical site in itself, but it boasts **museums** on everything from African art and the football club **Red Star Belgrade** to the weird and wonderful gifts given to President Tito during his decades in power. There are plenty of pleasant outside spaces for strollers to enjoy, from the car-free centre to various city parks and gardens, topped off by the showpiece **Kalemegdan Fortress** and its park, a large green area popular with families, couples and walkers. And, after the sightseeing, there's a wealth of cafés, restaurants and bars in which to unwind or party until sunrise.

Belgrade is well placed for journeys encompassing the Balkans, the Adriatic, eastern and central Europe. You will find Belgrade on **Routes 42** (p350), **43** (p355), **44** (p360) and **50** (p412) of this book.

TRAVEL BASICS

≋ Most main-line trains, including all international services, serve **Beograd** station (often called Beograd Glavna) in the heart of the city at Savski trg 2. It has left-luggage facilities, a currency exchange, and a tourist information centre. Many local trains serve **Beograd Centar**, a bit more than 1 km south of Beograd station. ✈ Belgrade's **Nikola Tesla Airport** is 18 km west of the city centre; flight information, ☎ 011 209 4444 (www.beg.aero). The national carrier JAT Airways runs a shuttle bus (Line A1) from the airport to Trg Slavija, with stops in Novi Beograd and the main train station. 🚌 72 also runs to the airport from Zeleni venac market.

The city has an integrated and comprehensive public transport system of **buses**, **trolleybuses** (except in Novi Beograd) and **trams**. Tickets cost around 40 or 60 dinars, depending on where you're going, if you pay on board, and about two-thirds that if you buy them in advance from a kiosk. Fares are slightly higher if you're travelling between 0000 and 0400. Make sure you punch your ticket once on board or it won't be valid. There is also a limited **metro** service. Things can get pretty packed during rush hour. Major transport hubs are at Trg Republike and Trg Slavija. The transport system has a useful website with more information (www.gsp.rs).

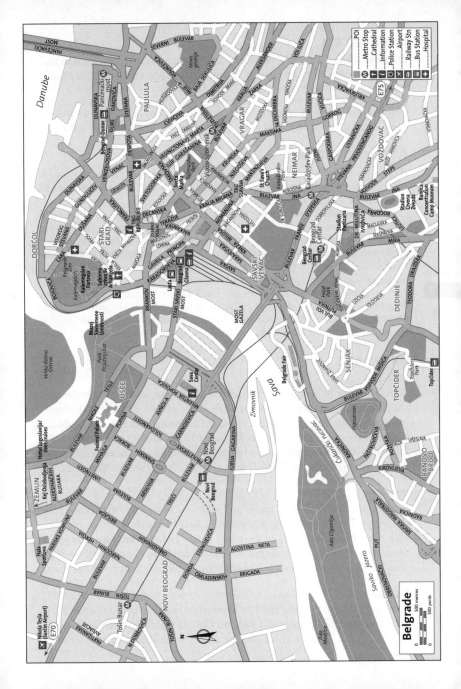

Information

ℹ Tourist offices are at the main railway station, ☎ 011 361 2732, on Knez Mihailova 6, ☎ 011 328 1859 (www.tob.co.rs), at Terazije — a pedestrian subway by the Albanija Tower — and also at the airport. The Tourist Organisation of Belgrade also posts a comprehensive list of monthly events and other useful information about the city on their website. **Internet access** is available at the many internet cafés common in the city, and an increasing number of bars, cafés and hotels are offering wi-fi access.

Accommodation

There is a concentration of cheap places around the train station, although the area is not the best. If you are finding it difficult to find a room, the Tourist Organisation of Belgrade (see above) can help.

✉ **Hotels**: Beer lovers will enjoy **Kasina**, Terazije 25, ☎ 011 813 5441, €€, a hotel that has its very own brewery. One of the city's most famous landmarks, the **Moskva**, Terazije 20, ☎ 011 268 6255 (www.hotelmoskva.rs), €€€, is more expensive, but the art nouveau building offers rooms of character and class. **Hostels**: Many of the newer hostels offer private rooms as well as the traditional dorms. Try: **Madness Hostel**, Brace Jugovica 7 (www.bgmadness.com), the **Spirit Hostel**, Brace Baruh 20b, ☎ 011 29 200 55 (www.spirithostel.com) and the small but extremely welcoming **Hostel Belgrade**, Kralja Milana 17, ☎ 011 63 7238 130 (www.hostelbelgrade.com). New on the Belgrade hostel scene, having opened in the summer of 2011, is the **Good Morning Hostel**, Takovska 36-38, ☎ 011 329 5031 (www.goodmorninghostels.com).

Itineraries

Half day

Start with a walk along **Knez Mihailova**. Unless the weather is terrible you should stroll around **Kalemegdan** and take some panoramic shots of the town. It's a short walk from here to the Orthodox Cathedral and **Princess Ljubica's Konak**. If it really is too cold or wet for the park (provided it's not Monday), the **Ethnographic Museum** on Studentski trg and the **Military Museum** are nearby and do-able in less than an hour. If you're having dinner, head to **Skadarlija**.

One day

In a day you can do all of the above, and have time to see something outside the Old Town. That could be the impressive **St Sava's Church** or, if you prefer to pack more in, you could go to the much nearer **Federal Parliament** building, which is opposite St Mark's Church and **Tašmajdan Park**. If you have the energy, round the day off with a visit to one of the basement bars in the centre of town.

Two days

Your next priority should be the **Tito Memorial Complex**. It's quite a trek but it takes you near the Red Star and Partizan football stadiums, where you may be able to catch a game or check out the Red Star museum, and the street of

THE BEST OF BELGRADE

Kalemegdan
Combining history, green space and a laid-back vibe, Kalemegdan Park and Fortress encapsulate three of the best things about modern Belgrade.

Princess Ljubica's Konak
Built by Prince Obrenović for his wife Ljubica, this is a superb example of 19th-century Serbian architecture, just to the south of the Kalemegdan.

Skadarlija
The bohemian style of Skadarlija's early Roma settlers is clear in the city's cobbled restaurant district.

Federal Parliament building
Both a stunning structure and the symbolic place where Milošević was forced out of Serbian politics. Overlooking the Pioneer Park.

A Red Star Belgrade match
With 50,000 Serbs passionately cheering on their team, watching a match at the so-called Serbian 'Marakana' stadium is a great experience.

Floating nightclubs
Belgrade's chic set get dressed up and hit the riverboat clubs, ready for a night of catchy Serbian turbo-folk.

Tito Memorial Complex
The fascinating collection of diplomatic gifts that Tito amassed during his time as Yugoslav leader shows why a statesman never has to worry about home decor.

St Sava's Church
Well over 100 years from conception, it's still not finished, but the church is imposing from afar and magnificent close up. Close to Slavija Square.

embassies. You can also head over the river to take in Novi Beograd's **Museum of Contemporary Art**, restaurants and nightlife and enjoy a concert or show.

More

Now you can factor in the markets, parks and smaller museums that give a more authentic taste of Belgrade, and relax a while at Kalemegdan or Ada Ciganlija. You can also see something else of Serbia: its second city **Novi Sad** can be visited on a day trip, or you could overnight there and explore more of the area, including the beautiful monasteries of **Fruška Gora National Park**.

BELGRADE ON A BUDGET

Belgrade is a city that's **perfect to walk around**, and it's quite possible to have a fulfilling day or two without spending very much at all. Many of the city's main attractions are outside and, provided the weather is fine, you can easily take in the atmosphere by strolling around pedestrianised streets such as Knez

Mihailova and Skadarska, and doing a spot of window shopping or people-watching. There are also several **parks and public spaces** where you can spend a pleasant few hours. Kalemegdan costs nothing unless you want to go up its clock tower, and Ada Ciganlija island, Tašmajdan Park and Hajd Park — further south on the way to the Tito Memorial Complex and the football stadiums — will also leave the wallet untroubled. A wander along the **riverside** is another enticing option on a sunny day.

Many of the **museums**, such as the Fresco Gallery on Cara Uroša 20 (closed Mon) and the Tito Memorial Complex, have free entrance. Several of the paying attractions also offer free days and weekends, but there seems to be no hard-and-fast rule about when these are. Some of the most important sites in the capital are its **religious buildings**, St Sava's and the Cathedral among them, for which there is no entrance fee. The ornate Cathedral is fascinating, while the monumental St Sava's is also surrounded by charming gardens, from which there are superb views.

Food

In Serbia, as in much of the Balkans and eastern Europe, meat is king. Since it is considered a luxury, many people cannot understand why anyone would willingly forgo it. That said, Belgrade is becoming increasingly international, and caters to a wide range of foreign palates, with Italian food particularly prevalent. A few vegetarian options appear on most menus.

If you really want to experience true Serbian cuisine, **hearty meat** is the way to go: lamb, veal, beef and pork are popular choices. A typical starter consists of smoked meats, often with a spicy dip. For the main course, the methods of cooking meat are multifarious: it can come roasted, grilled, in a stew, kebab, patty, or as a sausage. Belgrade's history has left its mark on the city's cuisine, which borrows heavily from **Turkish cookery**.

Vegetables feature in salads or combined with meat, such as peppers, courgettes or cabbage leaves stuffed with meat and rice. Other commonly used vegetables include aubergine and tomato as well as onion (sometimes raw) and garlic. **Fish** also features, particularly in the riverside restaurants of Novi Beograd, although the distance from the city to the sea pushes the price up somewhat.

Culture and nightlife

Belgraders have a big appetite for fun, which is manifested in their city's nightlife. In the 1990s, after the fall of communism, techno music caught on in a big way, as did **turbo-folk** (see box opposite), an all too-catchy combination of traditional Serbian song, electronic beats and Oriental influences.

Today there is a raft of good **dance clubs**, and raft is perhaps an appropriate term: many of the city's nightspots are housed in boats floating on the river — called *splavovi* — which bang out their rhythms into the early hours. These venues

TURBO-FOLK

Turbo-folk is something of a contradiction in terms: a blend of turbo – or high-energy, modern dance beats – and old-fashioned Serbian folk music. Although the name has been about since the late 1980s, it was in 1993 that it resurfaced with a vengeance. Against the backdrop of the Balkan Wars and their resulting hardships, Serbs were looking for both **national reaffirmation** and **escapism** from their country's plight – and they found them in music. The BBC summed it up, reporting that "in 1990s Serbia, there were two things on the radio: one of them was war and the other was turbo-folk."

With Middle Eastern, Roma, Turkish and Greek influences plus dashes of rock&roll, dance, soul, house and garage, the music was raunchy and provocative. Massive in Serbia, the music quickly spread around the rest of the **Balkans**. It was soon attracting criticism from various quarters, derided by many as lowbrow, tacky, pornographised and glorifying violence and crime. Singer-songwriter Rambo Amadeus, who first coined the term, joked, "I feel guilty for turbo-folk in much the way Albert Einstein felt guilt over Hiroshima and Nagasaki." But the phenomenon has defied its detractors, retaining its popularity long after the end of the hostilities that spawned it. Tens of thousands of fans attend the concerts, and CDs and DVDs of the music are among the country's bestsellers. Turbo-folk can also be heard – usually rather loudly – in the floating clubs, or *splavovi*, of Novi Beograd.

are frequented by Belgrade's new money, out to parade its wealth. The calibre of the clientele is not always of the highest — don't be alarmed if you are frisked for guns at some of the establishments. That said, they are still worth a visit to see the flashier side of Belgrade's post-communist culture. Other clubs are housed in small basement settings, and these tend to be less pretentious.

But not all nightlife is of the frenetic kind. **Cafés and bars** often keep late hours and it's not unusual to see people strolling around Knez Mihailova or sitting with a coffee and a cake well after midnight. There is often **entertainment in public spaces**, with concerts frequently staged in Trg Republike.

EVENTS

Belgrade goes movie mad in late winter/early spring with its **International Film Festival (FEST)**, which often features the big Oscar contenders, starting at the end of February. Both celebrating the city and reflecting on its chequered history, the **Belgrade Days** festivities in April include parades, theatre, a museum night, an ancient-crafts fair plus concerts, sporting events and exhibitions.

The annual **Belgrade Summer Festival (BELEF)** encompasses a wide array of art performances and activities held across the city in July and Aug, including dance, drama, music and the visual arts. In September it is time for the **Belgrade International Theatre Festival**. One of the top European theatre festivals, past participants include such luminaries as Ingmar Bergman and Steven Berkoff.

Berlin

Rich history, fabulous art, alternative culture — all in the broadest sense — combine to make the city of Berlin a destination that is a little out of the ordinary. The city's turbulent past and cosmopolitan citizens are its main draw; at every corner a piece of modern history plays out in front of you — whether it's the intrigue of the **Cold War** or the violent trauma of **Nazism**, it's all represented here.

But Berlin is more than just wars and destruction. Reunification in 1990 brought new hope to the German metropolis, and civic construction continues to boom. Visit this city once and you'll see some incredible views; return a few months later and the skyline will have changed considerably. Berlin is a city that is always evolving, never stagnant, and this is nowhere more apparent than the thriving **cultural scene**, which combines world-class orchestras and theatre companies, some of Europe's best electronic music, a café culture that can rival any in Europe, and an eclectic art scene that has drawn artists from around the world to the city to create and showcase their work.

Rail travellers will most likely enter the city through the Hauptbahnhof, a stunning glass and steel construction that opened for the World Cup in 2006 and is worth visiting in its own right. Indeed, it can be said that Berlin as a city only truly came of age in the era of the railways, and its rich history in this regard is reflected in some wonderful **railway architecture**, including the Hamburger Bahnhof, now converted into a museum of modern art, the red-brick Oberbaumbrücke lifting the elevated U-Bahn tracks across the **River Spree**, and the ruined facade of the Anhalter Bahnhof that stands as a reminder of the city's sometimes destructive history.

Also worth searching out is the small memorial by the Friedrichstrasse station. It shows the two sides of the railway's role during the Nazi era in Germany, from the evacuation of 10,000 Jewish children to England in 1938 on the one side, to the many others who were deported by train to the concentration and extermination camps of the Third Reich on the other. Berlin is featured on **Routes 16** (p168), **20** (p201), **45** (p365), **48** (p394) and **49** (p401) of this book.

TRAVEL BASICS

≷ Berlin's impressive new **Hauptbahnhof** (Hbf) is the city's main railway hub. It offers a good range of passenger facilities, with shops and cafés that, unusually for Germany, are open seven days a week. There is a left-luggage office, a bank and a Deutsche Bahn travel centre where multilingual staff can assist with timetable queries and seat reservations. Note that the railway platforms are not all on the same level, so changing trains, particularly if you are unfamiliar with the station, might take a while. Avoid tight connections. The Hauptbahnhof is served by long-distance services, by regional trains and by S-Bahn services. Every long-distance train that serves the Hauptbahnhof also stops at one of the city's other main stations, but quite which one will depend on the

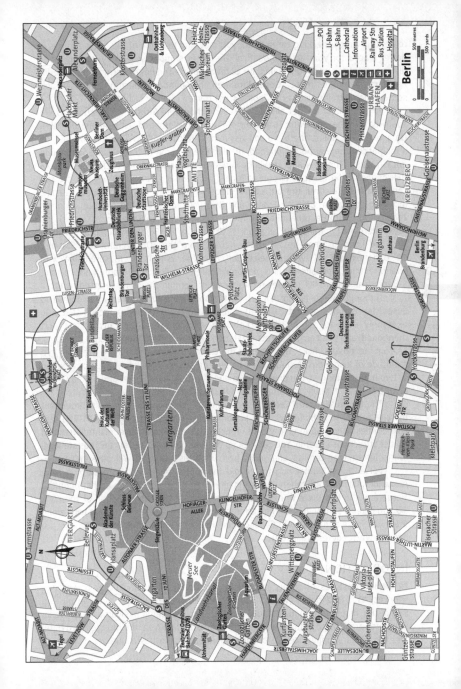

route. It is worth checking carefully for you may find that one of the other stations is better placed for your accommodation. The other stations served by various long-distance services and night trains are **Ostbahnhof** (Ost), **Südkreuz** (marked as Berlin Papestrasse on older maps), **Gesundbrunnen** and **Spandau**. Selected night trains and some regional trains also serve Zoologischer Garten (Zoo) or Lichtenberg.

✈ The major budget airlines all serve **Schönefeld Airport** (SXF), about 20 km south-east of the city centre (trains 0430–2300 to Zoo, Hbf and Ost stations; ERT 847). On 3 June 2012, unless there are any last-minute hitches, SXF will morph into BER, as a magnificent new airport is opened, making use of some of the existing Schönefeld infrastructure. The new airport will be called **Berlin Brandenburg** (BER for short). As BER opens, Berlin's second airport at **Tegel** (TXL), about 12 km north-west of the city centre, will close. Until the big switch, Tegel is home to many traditional airlines, including Lufthansa, BMI, Air France and British Airways. 🚌 The TXL bus connects Tegel Airport with Hauptbahnhof (20 mins), S-Bahn Brandenburger Tor (28 mins) and Alexanderplatz (35 mins). For all airports, ☎ 0180 500 0186; www.berlin-airport.de.

🚌 Long-distance buses: These depart from the ZOB (Central Bus Station), ☎ 030 301 0380 (www.zob-reisebuero.de). The ZOB is at Masurenallee 4–6, Charlottenburg, opposite the International Conference Centre (U-Bahn: Kaiserdamm; S-Bahn: Messe Nord/ICC). Buses run to all major German cities and selected resorts.

Although Berlin is big, the efficient **public transport system** that combines buses, trams, underground (U-Bahn) and surface trains (S-Bahn) means that it is extremely easy to get around. Tickets are valid on all the means of transport mentioned, and you can get tickets on station platforms, from machines on the trams, or from bus drivers. Ticket machines in the U- and S-Bahn stations are available in a multitude of languages. A single allows travel on buses, trains and trams for a period of two hours as long as you only travel in one direction. A day ticket and a 7-day ticket is for travel on all public transport during that period.

The **Berlin Welcome Card** allows unlimited use of public transport throughout the city and its suburbs for 48 or 72 hrs or 5 days (€16.90/€22.90/€29.90). The card also entitles you to up to 50 per cent reduction on city tours, museums, theatres and tourist attractions in Berlin. You can pick up the welcome card at train and bus stations, tourist information centres, and online from www.visitberlin.de/welcomecard.

For a cheap sightseeing trip, avoid the tourist buses and take 🚌 100 from Alexanderplatz to Zoo Station. Travelling along the Unter den Linden and through the Tiergarten, the bus takes in most of Berlin's central sights at a fraction of the cost. 🚌 200 takes a similar, but slightly different route. For daily (Mar–Oct) **boat trips** along the River Spree and Landwehr Canal contact Reederei Bruno Winkler 349, ☎ 030 349 9595 (www.reedereiwinkler.de).

INFORMATION

ℹ **Berlin infostores** offer city information, accommodation and ticket reservation services, ☎ 030 250 025 (www.visitberlin.de). From these offices you can pick up Berlin city maps, information about events, and the Berlin Welcome Card. Berlin infostores are located at the Hauptbahnhof, Kurfürstendamm 22, the Brandenburg Gate, and the Alexa shopping centre at Alexanderplatz. Berlin has a number of **internet**

THE BEST OF BERLIN

Brandenburger Tor (Brandenburg Gate)
Once a symbol of power, now one of freedom and reunification.

Museumsinsel (Island of Museums)
Explore the past at the Pergamon Museum, Alte Nationalgalerie, Altes Museum and the stunningly restored Neues Museum.

Reichstag (Parliament Buildings)
The German capital has been the epicentre of national events ever since the day it was built.

Hackescher Markt (Hackescher Market)
Berlin's hottest complex of boutiques, galleries, bars and cafés. Go for the day or spend the entire weekend.

Filmmuseum Berlin
You'll become a fan of German cinema after a visit to this amazing museum at Potsdamer Platz chronicling the history of the industry from *Metropolis* to *The Lives of Others*.

Tiergarten
Located west of the Brandenburg Gate, this is one of the finest urban parks in Europe.

Jüdisches Museum (Jewish Museum)
Daniel Liebskind's museum dedicated to the history of German-Jewish culture is a masterpiece. If you have time to visit just one museum, then choose this one. Located at Lindenstrasse 9–14, U-Bahn: Hallesches Tor.

Topographie des Terrors (Topography of Terror)
The 'final solution' plan to destroy Europe's Jews was drawn up on this site. The original buildings have been replaced by a stunning new museum; the horror, however, remains. Located at Niederkirchnerstrasse 8, U-Bahn: Potsdamer Platz, S-Bahn: Anhalter Bahnhof.

cafés scattered across the city centre, and an increasing number of bars, cafés and public spaces offer free wi-fi, including the Sony Center at Potsdamer Platz.

ACCOMMODATION

⨝ Berlin has some wonderful **hotels** and, although prices are creeping up, the German capital remains surprisingly reasonable. Hotels in Mitte are best placed for the majority of Berlin's sights, and some recommended options in the neighbourhood include the small, family-run **Hotel Honigmond**, Borsigstrasse 28, ☎ 030 284 4550 (www.honigmond-berlin.com), €€, and the stylish and friendly **Circus Hotel**, Rosenthaler Strasse 1, ☎ 030 2000 3939 (www.circus-berlin.de), €€. For a decidedly no-frills but functional and cheap alternative, the new **EasyHotel**, Rosenthaler Strasse 69, ☎ 030 400 065 511 (www.easyhotel-berlin.com), €, is in an excellent location, whilst throughout the city branches of **Motel One** offer decent rooms at reasonable prices. The best located is at Dircksenstrasse 36, ☎ 030 2005 4080 (www.motel-one.com), €€, close to Alexanderplatz. If you are in the mood to treat yourself, the **Casa Camper**, Weinmeisterstrasse 1, ☎ 030 2000 3410 (www.casacamper.com), €€€, has brought their extremely popular boutique hotel concept to Berlin from Barcelona, whilst the **Hotel Adlon Kempinski**, Unter den Linden 77, ☎ 030 226 10 (www.hotel-adlon.com), €€€€, remains the ritziest location in town, directly on Unter den Linden by the Brandenburg Gate. Located in an old factory, the hip **Michelberger Hotel**, Warschauer Strasse 39, ☎ 030 2977 8590 (www.michelbergerhotel.com), €€, in Friedrichshain offers extremely good-value private rooms in a funky setting.

Berlin's **hostels** deservedly have the reputation of being some of the best in Europe, and are also an excellent option for those looking for private rooms as well as the more traditional dorm bed. There are a huge number of hostels to choose from, and the choice might simply come down to where you wish to be based. Some of the best include the **East Seven Hostel**, Schwedter Strasse 7, ☎ 030 9362 2240 (www.eastseven.de) and the **Pfefferbett**, Schönhauser Allee 176, ☎ 030 9393 5858 (www.pfefferbett.de), in Prenzlauer Berg. Full marks also to **The Circus Hostel**, Weinbergsweg 1a, ☎ 030 2000 3939 (www.circus-berlin.de) and **Wombats**, Alte Schönhauser Strasse 2, ☎ 030 8471 0820 (www.wombats-hostels.com), both in Mitte. If you are interested in checking out the punky, alternative scene of Kreuzberg, the following two hostels are worth a look: **The Grand Hostel**, Tempelhofer Ufer 14, ☎ 030 2009 5450 (www.grandhostel-berlin.de) and the **Jetpak Alternative**, Görltitzer Str. 38, ☎ 030 6290 8641 (www.jetpak.de).

ITINERARIES

Half day

Stuck for time? Worry not. It's easy to see the bulk of Berlin's biggest sites in just a few hours. Start your day at the **Reichstag** and climb Sir Norman Foster's dome. From there, head to the **Brandenburg Gate** to see the symbol of reunification featured in so many news reports during the destruction of the Berlin Wall. Follow the **Unter den Linden** past Friedrichstrasse, stopping in any of the museums along the way, such as the **Deutsches Historisches Museum**. End up at the **Berliner Dom** to savour the architectural splendour.

BREWER'S BERLIN TOURS

A great way to get a handle on Berlin's main points of interest is to take a walking tour, which will provide you with an excellent overview of the city and a checklist of places to return to for the rest of your time in Berlin. There are many different walking tour companies available, but one of the most highly-regarded are Brewer's Berlin Tours who run many different tours in the city, from the 3-4 hour 'free tour' (tips for the guide are appreciated), to the marathon all-day tour that lasts 7-8 hours in the company of their excellent guides (€15; €12 for students). They also offer themed tours, such as a Third Reich Tour, and trips to Potsdam. Find more information on their website: www.brewersberlintours.de.

One day

Begin your day at **Potsdamer Platz** to see how Berlin has grown over the past couple of decades. Step inside the **Filmmuseum** for a look at the masterpieces of German cinema, then follow Ebertstrasse up to the **Brandenberg Gate** and the **Reichstag**. Follow the Unter den Linden to the **Museumsinsel** for explorations of the four museums that call the island home, then hop along Bodestrasse towards **Hackescher Markt** for a relaxing coffee (or something a little stronger).

Two days

With two days you can get a much better impression of what the city has to offer. To get a good overview of the main sights, use the first day for a **walking tour**. On day two, explore **Charlottenburg** — including shopping along Kurfürstendamm, plus trips to the museums and the sights surrounding Schloss Charlottenburg. If you have time, choose a walk around the trendy neighbourhood of **Prenzlauer Berg** for a sense of 'real' Berlin. Alternatively, head down to **Kreuzberg** and visit the stunning Jüdisches Museum and soak up the atmosphere of one of Berlin's most eclectic districts.

More

Get more out of Berlin by getting out of town. A visit to **Potsdam** (see p458) will expose you to Prussian splendour, while **Sachsenhausen** provides grim reminders of the nation's Nazi past (also p458). If the weather is fine, head to one of the lakes that are still within Berlin's city limits, such as the **Wannsee** in the south-west, or **Müggelsee** in the south-east.

EXPLORING BERLIN

During the summer Berliners like nothing better than spending a lazy evening cuddled up on long benches in one of the city's leafy **beer gardens**. The oldest, and still one of the best, is the **Prater Garten**, which can be found at the north end of Kastanienallee in Prenzlauer Berg. Another great option is the **Café am Neuen See**, which sits by a small lake at the heart of Berlin's Tiergarten. The open-air **East Side Gallery** is one of the few remaining stretches of the original Berlin Wall. The artworks, which are dedicated to the promotion of peace, were restored in 2009 to celebrate 20 years since the fall of the Berlin Wall (www.eastsidegallery.com).

The **stadium** of the 1936 **Olympics** was made famous by two things: the triumphs of sprinter Jesse Owens, who won four gold medals, and *Olympia*, a documentary of the Games made by Leni Riefenstahl, infamous for her compelling record of a rally at Nuremberg, *Triumph des Willens* (*Triumph of the Will*). Built in the epic style loved by all Nazis, the stadium was restored in time to host matches for the 2006 World Cup (www.olympiastadion-berlin.de). Guided tour €10.

No longer a working synagogue, the **Neue Synagoge** remains a symbol for the shattered history of Berlin's once-thriving Jewish community. It was built between 1857 and 1866, and was inaugurated in the presence of Bismarck. The beginning of the end arrived when the building was targeted by Nazis on Kristallnacht in 1938. An exhibition discussing Jewish life and the remains of the structure remind today's travellers of yesterday's tragedies.

BERLIN ON A BUDGET

Consider yourself prudent with the euros? Then you're in luck. Many of Berlin's most inspiring sights are absolutely free (or close to it). On warm days, one of the best Berlin experiences is a day in **Tiergarten**. Sunbathe on the grassy lawns, or take a stroll along the paths. You might even spot a deer during your walk. For inspiring views, head over to the **Siegessäule** (victory column). Fans of director Wim Wenders' film *Wings of Desire* will immediately recognise the column from which viewpoint the angels used to watch over the citizens of Berlin.

Continue east to enter the **Reichstag** — the German parliament buildings. When the Nazis took control of Germany in 1933 they burnt down the building. Russian graffiti and bullet holes can still be seen in the walls, left by the conquering military forces. It's free to enter and climb up into Sir Norman Foster's stunning glass dome, though you may have to queue. From the Reichstag it's just a few steps south to see the **Brandenburg Gate** made famous as the backdrop to the reunification celebrations in 1989 when the Wall was dismantled.

Finally, one of the best things to do is simply to wander through Berlin's various neighbourhoods, each with its own distinctive flavour. **Prenzlauer Berg** is trendy and popular with the Berlin creative set, and features some great small galleries and craft shops, as well as chic second-hand stores and a wealth of fine cafés. Elsewhere, **Charlottenburg** is regal in tone, whilst for a multicultural experience, head over to **Kreuzberg**, home to ageing punks and many of Berlin's Turkish community.

FOOD

Berlin has come a long way from the days when a *bratwurst* and a pretzel were considered haute cuisine. Waves of Asian and Middle Eastern immigration and a long period of occupation by Western forces helped to change all that. Chefs are abandoning the standard pork-leg-and-two-veg dishes of yesteryear in favour of delicately spiced fusions. Many of Berlin's most acclaimed restaurants serve international cuisine and are located in the wealthier neighbourhoods of Charlottenburg and Mitte. Establishments in and around Friedrichstrasse are particularly chic and popular. Prenzlauer Berg and Friedrichshain also offer great culinary possibilities. That said, eateries will be more basic in look and feel. Luckily, the prices will reflect this lack of investment in swish interiors. It's curious to note that the humble doner kebab was created not in Turkey but in the Turkish neighbourhood of Kreuzberg, where they are especially tasty.

CULTURE AND NIGHTLIFE

Berlin has long enjoyed a reputation for being a bit lively of an evening (think Cabaret and the Kit Kat Klub), and, over the past decade, the city has established itself as Europe's most happening capital. The **electronic music** scene is especially prominent; hundreds of venues play host to world-class DJs, and bands from around the world take to one of the city's many stages night after night. At the same time Berlin hosts some **world-famous orchestras** and **opera companies** and, if you speak some German, the Berlin theatre scene is as varied as it is (at times) provocative. As ever with Berlin, it is the contrasts that make this city fascinating.

Whilst in town, pick up a copy of *Tipp* or *Zitty* magazines, which provide comprehensive listings of what is on around town. They are only in German, but it is easy to work out what is going on where. As with so much else in the city, the style of nightlife depends greatly upon which district you are in. The bars around the Savignyplatz in **Charlottenburg** for example offer high-end cocktails with prices to match, whilst the cafés and late-night watering holes of the Simon-Dach-Strasse in **Friedrichshain** are a lot more laid back and less hard on your budget.

Other neighbourhoods worth exploring in the evening are **Kreuzberg**, which still retains something of its 1980s punk roots (especially along the Oranienstrasse) and **Prenzlauer Berg** where the leafy streets of old workers' houses are filled with cosy bars and cafés (try Kastanienallee or the streets around the Kollwitzplatz). **Schöneberg** is the centre of Berlin's gay and lesbian scene, and the bars and cafés around Nollendorf Platz are worth exploring. Please note that Berlin's clubs tend to start late and finish as the sun is cracking the flags. So don't arrive early, and take your time in one of the city's many lovely cafés or bars, or you might find yourself the only one on the dance floor.

For top-class classical music, or to catch a film in English, head to Potsdamer Platz. Just down the street is the Philharmonie, the home of the world-renowned **Berliner Philharmoniker** orchestra, whilst beneath the canopy of the Sony Center you will find the **Cinestar Original**, a multiplex that shows only original versions of films.

EVENTS

The tourist offices in Berlin can provide a full list of all the events in the city and surrounding areas. There's a comprehensive calendar at www.berlin.de, but here are some of the highlights.

Now over 60 years old, the **Berlinale**, Berlin's international film festival is one of the world's most important film events (February, www.berlinale.de).

A TRIP TO POTSDAM

Potsdam has an eye-opening array of landscaped gardens and palaces, 30 km south-west of Berlin (Regional Express [RE], 24 mins from Hbf, also serves Ost-bahnhof, Friedrichstr. and Zoo, every 30 mins, ERT 839). The seat of the Hohenzollern kings in the late 17th century and now a UNESCO World Heritage Site, it is best known for the compact rococo Sanssouci Palace (1745–47) set in the huge **Park Sanssouci**. Arrive early to ensure a place on the guided tours.

A leisurely walk through the park reveals the breathtaking Chinese Tea House (1754–57), the pagoda-like Drachenhaus, Schloss Charlottenhof and the so-called *Römische Bäder* (Roman Baths). And don't miss the centre of Potsdam with its lovely Dutch Quarter.

Brightening up a weekend each May, the multicultural **Karneval der Kulturen** is inspired by the Caribbean colour of the Notting Hill Carnival in London (www.karneval-berlin.de).

The annual gay and lesbian pride parade is now one of Berlin's most flam-boyant street parties. Gay and straight people take part in the **Christopher Street Day Parade**, usually held on the Saturday closest to 22 June (www.csd-berlin.de). At the **Fête de la Musique** on 21 June you'll hear music of all genres spilling out of every bar, café and music venue (www.lafetedelamusique.de). Don't bother try-ing to have an early night — join in!

Traditional **Christmas markets** spring up all over the city from the end of November up until 26 December (www.weihnachtsmarkt-deutschland.de). Thou-sands take part in the celebrations of **Berlin's New Year's Eve** at the Branden-burger Tor. Expect a night of live music, DJs, food, drink and street partying galore (www.silvester-berlin.de).

OUT OF TOWN — SACHSENHAUSEN

Sachsenhausen is a district of Oranienburg, a town just north of Berlin, that contains a former **concentration camp** with the same name. The camp was reopened one last time on 23 April 1961 as a national memorial, with a museum and memorial hall/cinema chronicling its devastating past. They can be found at either end of the parade ground, where prisoners were forced to watch executions on the gallows. Next to the cinema is a prison and the bleak remains of the Station Z extermination block. A map allows visitors to trace the path of new arrivals. Hire an English audio guide, as all the labels are in German only.

Oranienburg is located at the end of the S1 S-Bahn line. From Mitte, the journey takes approximately 40 minutes. Follow the signs to **Gedenkstätte Sachsenhausen**, ☎ 03301 200 200 (www.gedenkstaette-sachsenhausen.de) after leaving the station. The walk should take about 20 minutes. The Gedenkstätte is closed on Mondays.

Brussels (Bruxelles, Brussel)

As the hub of the European Union and NATO, and with residents who can trace their origins around the world, Brussels is an exceptionally cosmopolitan city. It may not be regarded as the most glamorous or romantic of Europe's capitals — after all, its two most famous monuments are a statue of a urinating boy and an outsized 1950s atomic model — but take some time to explore and you will find some great art galleries, abundant greenery, a majestic central square, and many excellent restaurants. There is also a wealth of art nouveau architecture, and it is well worth seeking out the squares **Ambiorix** and **Marie-Louise**, both just north of Schuman station, as well as the **Avenue Louise**, which houses several buildings by the great Victor Horta.

Brussels is well placed for journeys by rail into the Netherlands, Germany and France, and with its **Eurostar terminal** has a direct link to the United Kingdom. The old joke goes that the rest of Belgium is basically the suburbs of Brussels, and the country's size means it is perfectly possible to use Brussels as a base to explore the rest by day trip. Brussels is featured on **Route 14** (p154) of this book.

The city is officially bilingual and so street names appear in two versions (e.g. French *Rue Neuve* is Dutch *Nieuwstraat*); this chapter uses the French ones.

TRAVEL BASICS

≽ Virtually all long-distance trains stop at both **Midi** and **Nord** (change at Rogier from metro line 2 or at De Brouckère from line 1), but many omit **Centrale** (metro line 1: Centrale; 5-min walk from Grand Place). The facilities at all three include baggage lockers, eating places and newsagents that sell international papers. Midi/Zuid (metro line 2) is the terminal for **Eurostar** services from London (fastest journey: 1hr 51 mins) and the Thalys train from Paris (1 hr 25 mins); train information office ☎ 07 079 79 70 (daily 0600–2200; www.b-rail.be).

✈ **Brussels International Airport**, ☎ 02 753 77 53 (www.brusselsairport.be), at Zaventem is 14 km north-east of the centre; an express rail link operates from soon after 0500 until around 2330 (four times an hour to all three main stations; journey time 20 mins).

The **city centre** is compact and walking is the best way to get around. The **metro, tram and bus network** is efficient. Individual tickets (€1.80, €2 if bought on board) can be purchased from bus drivers or in metro stations, and multi-ride tickets from tourist offices, metro stations and some newsagents; 5-trip tickets are sold (€7.30) and 10-trip tickets (€12.50). The 1-day travelcard (€4.50) gives unlimited travel on all city transport (covering two people at weekends). Stamp your ticket in the machine by the metro entrance or on board buses before travelling.

INFORMATION

🛈 Brussels Tourist Information Office, Tourism & Congress (BI-TC), can be found at the Hôtel de Ville, Grand Place, ☎ 02 513 89 40 (www.brusselsinternational.be). There are

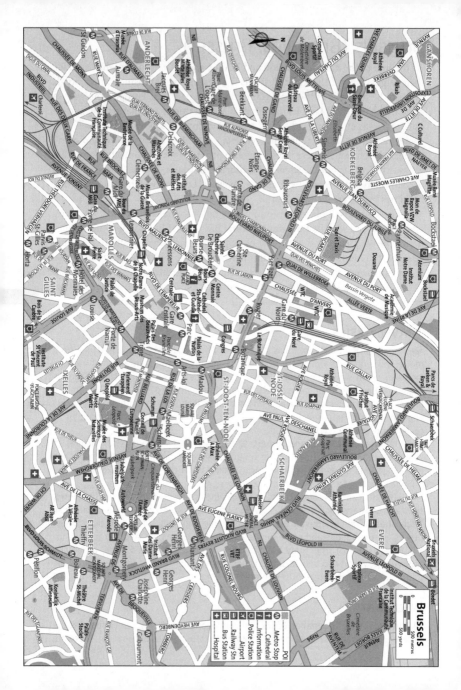

also branches at Midi Station and the airport. The **Brussels Card** covers public transport and admission to 30 museums for €24 (24 hours), €34 (48 hours) and €40 (72 hours). The *Brussels Guide & Map* is the most comprehensive tourist booklet available from the tourist office and bookshops. The English-language weekly *The Bulletin* has a useful 'What's On' supplement (www.bulletin.be). Brussels being the international place that it is, you're never far from an **internet café** or wi-fi point. Internet cafés offer excellent value for money too, at only €1–2 per hour.

Accommodation

There is a fair choice of accommodation in Brussels to suit every budget, although during the week the more upmarket hotels are priced very much for business travellers on expense accounts. If you are struggling, the **Brussels Tourist Information Office** can help you find a room.

📧 **Hotels**: A good budget option is **La Vieille Lanterne**, Rue des Grands Carmes 29, ☎ 02 512 74 94 (www.lavieillelanterne.be), €€, overlooking the Mannekin Pis, or for a quirky and eccentric choice, try **Les Bluets**, Rue Berckmans 124, ☎ 02 534 39 83, €. Both comfortable and stylish, **Noga**, Rue du Béguinage 38, ☎ 02 218 67 63 (www. nogahotel.com), €€, is well located, whilst for those looking to splash out, **Stanhope**, Rue du Commerce 9, ☎ 02 506 91 11 (www.stanhope.be), €€€, is located in three classic town houses with individually designed rooms. Another central and good value option is **Floris Arlequin Grand'Place**, Rue de la Fourche 17–19, ☎ 02 514 16 15 (www.florishotels.com), €€. Brand new and incredibly stylish, the **Pantone Hotel**, 1 Place Lox, ☎ 02 541 48 98 (www.pantonehotel.com), €€–€€€, is two metro stops from the main station. **Hostels**: The independent **Sleep Well** hostel, Rue du Damier 23, ☎ 02 218 50 50 (www.sleepwell.be) is bright and friendly, whilst another option for finding a dorm bed for the night is the **Centre Vincent Van Gogh**, Rue Traversière 8, ☎ 02 217 01 58, which is clean and simple, but can feel a little institutional. HI Hostels in the city include the **Auberge de Jeunesse Jacques Brel**, Rue de la Sablonnière 30, ☎ 02 218 01 87 (www.laj.be). You need to take metro line 2 to Madou, so it is a little way from the centre of the city.

Itineraries

Half day

Head straight for the **Grand Place** and explore the guild houses that line this lovely square. From here, join a tour of the historic **Hôtel de Ville** and then grab some *frites* from one of the nearby vendors.

One day

Begin your visit by taking in the beauty of the Grand Place. Head south out of the square to visit the **Manneken Pis** — you'll know you're there when you spot the crowds. Have lunch in a local café and then head over to **Lower Town** to enjoy the shopping opportunities; making sure you don't miss **Les Galeries Saint Hubert** arcade with its mix of luxury boutiques, antique bookshops and cafés.

THE BEST OF BRUSSELS

Grand Place
Brussels' main square, described by Victor Hugo as the most beautiful square in Europe. Stunning, definitely a place to linger for an hour or two.

Manneken Pis
He may just be a boy having a wee, but to many he's the symbol of a nation. Located at the junction of Rue de l'Étuve and Rue du Chêne not far from the Grand Place.

Musée Horta
A graceful example of the contribution to art nouveau made by Belgium's favourite architect at 25, rue Américaine, tram 81/91/92/97 (place Janson) or 🚌 54, open 1400–1730 (www.hortamuseum.be). Admission €7, closed Mon.

Atomium
This enormous model of an atom remains a popular tourist destination. The views from the top are superb. Take metro line 6 to Heysel (www.atomium.be).

Parc du Cinquantenaire
The city's favourite green space built by Léopold II.

Musée Magritte
More than 200 works by René Magritte are packed into this stylish new museum on Place Royale (www.musee-magritte-museum.be). Admission €8, closed Mon.

Chocolate
Sweet, sinful and oh so delicious. The museum dedicated to its development is worth sinking your teeth into (www.mucc.be). Close to the Grand Place.

Centre Belge de la Bande Dessinée (Belgian Comic Strip Centre)
In the land of Tintin and Hergé, don't miss this excellent collection of contemporary comic strips, 10 mins north-east of the Grand Place on rue des Sables (closed Mon).

Toone
Much-loved puppet theatre with outlandishly satirical shows performed by highly detailed marionettes.

Two days
Two days is the average length of a stay in Brussels. Pack your first day with the suggestions above and then head straight to **Upper Town** on the morning of your second day. Here is where you will find the best art galleries and museums in the city. Then head out to Heysel and ponder whether you can make sense of the Atomium.

More
To experience all that Brussels has to offer, you need to leave the Petit Ring. Spend a day in **Ixelles** for colourful African culture and unique boutiques. Visit the **EU Quarter** to understand the inner workings of the European democracy and bureaucracy, and feast on fine art at the new **Magritte Museum**.

Brussels on a budget

You don't need to break the bank to have a good time in Brussels, most of the city's finest sights are absolutely free. **Grand Place** is the heart of the city and a stop to admire the architecture won't cost you a cent. The guild houses that circle the square showcase the Golden Age of the city when merchants ruled the nation. **Manneken Pis**, the symbol of the city, is also free of charge and just a few steps south of the square on Rue de l'Étuve.

Brussels has plenty of **glorious parks** in which to enjoy a day strolling through the shaded lawns. The most interesting is the Parc du Cinquantenaire. King Léopold II had the park built in order to commemorate the 50th anniversary of the founding of the Belgian nation. These days it is surrounded by a number of cultural institutions allowing visitors to combine a walk in the woods with a bit of inspiring art and architecture.

Food

Belgians have long had a reputation for being hard-working, yet keen to celebrate when the occasion arises. The best reward for them after a long day at the office is a well-prepared meal — and they will work long and hard to ensure that only the best is dished up. The cuisine of Brussels is heavily influenced by the flavours of Belgium's regions. **Fresh seafood** from the coast, **game** from the Ardennes, **rich sauces** from Wallonia and, of course, **beer**. What really differentiates the cooking of Brussels from that of Belgium's other regions is its variety. Nowhere else has such a large ethnic community offering the flavours of the Congo, East Asia, India and more.

The classic Belgian dish is **moules et frites**, which is typically a bowl of steamed mussels in either a clear, herbed broth or tomato-based sauce served up with crisp fries (or 'chips' by any other name) and a dollop of mayonnaise. You can find this dish at almost every café and restaurant in the city — and each will keep their sauce ingredients a closely guarded secret. Other seafood varieties to look out for include oysters, small, sweet-tasting shrimp from the North Sea and eels from the rural canals that dot the countryside.

Culture and nightlife

Brussels may be a hard-working town but it likes to play hard too. Locals think nothing of spending an evening **sipping local brews** in a bar, especially when they have such a variety of beers to choose from. City bars don't have an official closing time and many stay open until the wee hours of the morning.

Brussels also has a thriving **live music scene**, and as the home of the saxophone, Belgium is well known for its **jazz** venues. The octogenerian Toot Thielemans and the late great Django Reinhardt both cut their teeth in the clubs of Brussels. **World music** is another speciality of the city. A night in this happening

KNOW YOUR BEER

There is a brew to suit every occasion, taste and meal. While there are few breweries in Brussels, the city is the best place to plan a beer-tasting tour as the bars offer the widest selection of bottles from the most breweries. The beer museum on Grand Place, the **Musée des Brasseurs Belges**, is a good place to go for a brief overview of the industry, with a day trip to Leuven an absolute must if you want to challenge your taste buds further. When embarking on a tasting session at a Belgian bar, you'll find that a typical establishment will usually have on tap a draught lager such as Stella Artois or Maes and a wheat beer such as Hoegaarden. Wheat beer is generally considered to be more of a summer drink and is usually served in large tankards. The Holy Grail of beers are the Trappist varieties produced by Trappist monks in the towns of Chimay, Westmalle, Orval, Rochefort and Westvleteren. These beers are for the pros and pack a killer alcoholic kick. A standard variety will be dark brown and creamy.

community will expose you to African, Asian and South American sounds with a strong focus on the music of Belgium's former colony, the Congo. The biggest festival of world sounds is the **Couleur Café** festival in June.

Find out what's happening from *The Bulletin Unlimited*, a weekly English-language paper, or have a look at the free *Brussels Your Guide to the Night* published by the tourist office or the free list of musical performances that includes clubs and discos, jazz, opera, films, etc.

Clustered around **Fernand Cocq** and the lower end of **ch. d'Ixelles** are lots of bars with music, many staying open until the early hours. The area around Grand Place is also lively at night.

EVENTS

The tourist offices for Brussels and the surrounding region can provide a full list of events. The **Brussels International Festival of Fantastic Film** (www.festivalfantastique.org) is a two-week film festival dedicated to horror and sci-fi held in April. Prepare yourself for the gore! Three days of **non-stop jazz** in May take over almost all the bars, clubs and stages in the city. Shuttle buses run between the major venues. Each year more than 250,000 people come to listen to the music performed by both amateurs and professionals (www.brusselsjazzmarathon.be). Belgium's split personality is reflected in a duo of festivals, the **Festival of Flanders** and the **Festival of Wallonia**. Both festivals take place in June and are above all one big celebration of culture.

Classical music is the core focus of both festivals with concerts planned throughout the country across the summer months (www.festivaldewallonie.be & www.festival.be). Every 21 July, Belgians recognise their **National Day**, the celebrations featuring pageantry, military displays and royal family sightings.

Budapest

Budapest is a grand city, and was always the most westernised of the Warsaw Pact capitals. In the two decades since the **fall of the Iron Curtain** it has demolished many of its communist monuments, while moving others, such as the Liberation Monument, to be reassembled in a statue park. Within a medley of Habsburg and Ottoman influences, Budapest is now a city to indulge yourself, in **spas**, Hungarian cuisine, and the city's thriving cultural scene.

The grey-green **Danube** splits the city into Buda, on the west bank, and Pest on the east. Buda is the photogenic, hilly Old Town, with its pastel-coloured baroque residences, gas-lit cobblestone streets and hilltop palace, while Pest is the thriving, mostly 19th-century commercial centre, with the imposing riverside State Parliament building, its wide boulevards and **Vörösmarty tér**, the busy main square. Between Buda and Pest, Margaret Bridge gives access to **Margaret Island** (Margit-sziget), a green oasis and venue for alfresco opera and drama in summer.

Budapest has excellent rail connections to the rest of central Europe, the Balkans and destinations further east, and if your enthusiasm for railways moves beyond the train as a means of transport, don't miss the **Railway History Park**. Budapest is on **Routes** 40 (p335), 42 (p350) and 48 (p394) of this book.

TRAVEL BASICS

✈ There are three major stations: **Nyugati pályaudvar** (Western Station), designed in 1877 by the Eiffel firm from Paris (tourist office; accommodation; exchange; left luggage); **Keleti pályaudvar** (Eastern Station; accommodation; exchange; K&H Bank Mon–Sat; left luggage 24 hrs); and **Déli pályaudvar** (Southern Station; post office; accommodation; exchange; left luggage). All three are fairly central, close to hotels and on the metro: Keleti and Déli on line 2, Nyugati on line 3. Railway customer service: ☎ 1 444 4499. ➔ **Ferihegy Airport** ☎ 1 296 7000 (www.bud.hu), 16 km east from the centre, has two terminals. There's a rail service 2–3 times an hour from the airport station, near Terminal 1, to Budapest Nyugati station, taking 25 mins, with shuttle buses to Terminal 2.

The **metro** is fast and inexpensive and runs 0430–2330. All three lines intersect at Deák Ferenc tér: M1 (yellow), M2 (red) and M3 (blue). M4 (green) will open in late 2011. Metro tickets are available from kiosks or machines inside stations. All **tickets** must be stamped in the machines at the station entrance. A single is 320Ft; the ticket (*vonaljegy*) is valid for all kinds of public transport. Transfer ticket for two rides (*átszállójegy*) 490Ft: validate on both metro trains. One-day and seven-day travel passes (1,550Ft, 4,600Ft), valid for all kinds of public transport, are available. You can also save a small amount by buying tickets in blocks of 10 or 20. For areas not on the metro, the **bus, trolleybus and tram system** is very useful as it covers the city extensively. A similar method for ticket stamping exists, with machines on board. From Apr to Oct, boat services operate from the southern end to the northern end of Budapest, from Boráros tér to Pünkösdfürdö, daily 0900–1715. **The Funicular** (Siklö) from the Buda side of the Chain Bridge to Buda Castle runs daily 0730–2200.

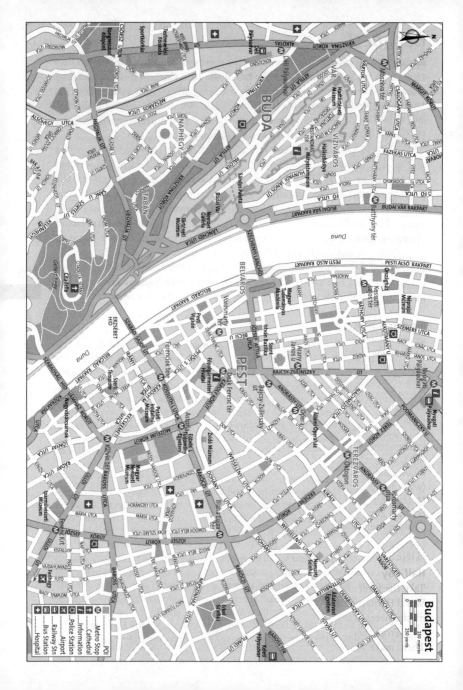

INFORMATION

🛈 Budapest tourist office (local representation of the national tourist information Tourinform): branches at Ferihegy Airport Terminals 1 and 2 and in the city at Süto utca 2 (Deák Ferenc tér), open 0800–2000, ☎ 1 438 8080, and Liszt Ferenc tér 11, open 1200–2000, ☎ 1 322 4098 (www.budapestinfo.hu). **The Budapest Card**, available at hotels, tourist offices, travel agencies, the airport and main underground stations, allows free travel by public transport, ample discounts in restaurants, and reductions on more than 60 sights throughout Budapest (valid for 24/48/72 hours, costing 5,500Ft/6,900Ft/8,300Ft for one adult accompanied by a child up to 14).

For the fastest public **internet access** in Budapest, the central Private Link Hungary, József körút 52, ☎ 1 334 2057, offers discounts for IYH members and students (24 hrs). One of the few actual internet cafés is Kávészünet, Garibaldi utca 5, with good music, cakes and sandwiches.

ACCOMMODATION

Budapest has a wide range of hostels and hotels in all categories, as well as pensions and private rooms. The latter can be cheaper than hotels, although they are usually way out from the centre of town. You can book private rooms through the tourist offices.

🛏 **Hotels**: **Hotel Benczúr**, Benczúr utca 35, ☎ 1 479 5650 (www. hotelbenczur.hu), €€, lies parallel to the elegant Andrássy út, offering a central location. **Hotel Carlton** is ideally located below Castle Hill, Apor Péter utca 3, ☎ 1 224 0999 (www.carltonhotel.hu), €€€. **City Hotel Pilvax**, Pilvax köz 1–3, ☎ 1 266 7660 (www.taverna.hu), €€, is very centrally located by the river. Basic and well located near the Opera by Andrássy út is **Medosz Hotel**, Jókai tér 9, ☎ 1 374 3000 (www.medoszhotel.hu), €€. For no-frills but a great location, the **easyHotel Budapest Oktagon**, VI. Eötvös utca 25/a (online booking only at www.easyhotel.com) offers great value for money.

Budapest has a choice of **hostels** to rival any city in Europe. Some of the best independent hostels include the **Art Guest House**, V. Podmaniczky utca 19 (doorbell ART), ☎ 1 302 3739, the **Citadella Hotel and Hostel**, XI. Citadella sétány, ☎ 1 466 5794 (www.citadella.hu), and the **Hostel Marco Polo**, VII. Nyár utca 6 ☎ 1 413 2555 (www.marcopolohostel.com). You could also try the top rated **Lavender Circus Hostel**, Muzeum Krt. 37, ☎ 70 618 4536 (www.lavendercircus.com), the **Carpe Noctem Vitae**, Erzsébet körút 50, ☎ 20 365 8749 (www.carpenoctemhostel.com) and the Hoscar-award winning **Budapest Bubble**, Bródy Sándor u. 2, ☎ 70 397 7974.

ITINERARIES
Half day

Take the funicular up to the carefree and car-free **Castle district**, a UNESCO World Heritage Site. If it's raining, take an hour to check out the world-renowned masterpieces at the **Hungarian National Gallery**.

From there, it's on to Buda Castle and the neo-Gothic **Matthias Church**. Then, make your way to the sun-bleached **Halászbástya** (Fishermen's Bastion), and climb the turrets, which afford possibly the finest views of Pest from across the Danube.

One day

If you have a full day, walk along the embankment, admiring the boat traffic along the Danube as you cross **Margit híd** (Margaret Bridge). Pick up tram 2 at Jászai Mari tér, which will take you on a riverside circuit, passing some of the most important buildings of the town. You'll take in the **Országház** (Houses of Parliament), grand hotels such as Gresham Palace and, finally, the **Corvinus University of Budapest**. From there, you get a beautiful view of Gellért Hill across the Danube. Cross the **Szabadság híd** (Liberty Bridge) and end your day by visiting the Danubius Hotel Gellért, which has one of the most luxurious **thermal baths** in Budapest.

Two days

To get a closer look at Budapest, you can see all the above sights, plus take in some other areas of interest. If the weather's nice, or you have children, go to the **Városliget** (City Park), which has some grandiose spaces to explore, including

THE BEST OF BUDAPEST

Országház (Houses of Parliament)
Laid prominently along the east bank of the Danube, the city's political powerhouse seems to possess a spire for every day of the year.

Houses of Worship
Szent István Bazilika (St Stephen's Basilica), Mátyás Templom (Matthias Church) and Nagy Zsinagóga (Great Synagogue) — lavishly decorative houses of God reflecting the diverse paths of religion in Budapest.

Budavári Sikló (Buda Castle Funicular)
Lends new meaning to the phrase 'hanging out'.

Halászbástya (Fishermen's Bastion)
The bird's-eye view over Pest from Castle Hill is stunning, and so is the neo-Romanesque structure that you mount to enjoy it.

Váci utca
The buzzing heart of Budapest positively throbs with atmospheric pubs, charismatic bars and beautiful boutiques; every visitor should get with the Váci vibe at some point in their trip.

Gellért Fürdő (Gellért Baths)
Relaxing muscles that you didn't even know were tense while soaking up the decadent ambience of this art nouveau baths and spa complex is the best way to purge yourself of that last scintilla of stress. Located in the Danubius Hotel Gellért on Kelenhegyi út 2–4 (www.gellertbath.com).

The spas of Budapest

Budapest boasts ten spas, offering mixed and segregated bathing, endless treatments and often stunning architecture at affordable prices. Széchényi fürdő (Széchényi Baths) is one of the most famous baths. Located in the City Park, its neo-baroque building houses several indoor and outdoor pools. Just south of Buda Palace, the art nouveau Gellért has a much-photographed 'champagne' bath and nearby the Rudas fürdő (Rudas Baths) (Döbrentei tér) are an amazing time warp (men only). Further north the Király fürdő (Király Baths) (Fő utca 84) were built in the 16th century — their green cupolas are a reminder of the Turkish occupation. For further details ask at the tourist office.

the **Museum of Fine Arts** and **Hősök tere** (Heroes' Square), or to **Margaret Island**, a tranquil oasis in the middle of the Danube.

More

With three or more days, you can see all the above sights, as well as climb **Gellért Hill**, stop off at the **Sziklatemplom** (Cave Church) and go on to the Citadel. With a bit more time, you'll be able to catch an opera performance in the evening or take a day trip to Hungary's favourite little town, **Szentendre** (see p471).

Budapest on a budget

Budapest is brimming with museums, with admission for adults ranging from only 800–1,200 Ft and some even offering free admission to permanent exhibitions. The most impressive include the **Magyar Nemzeti Múzeum** (Hungarian National Museum, VIII. Múzeum körút 14–16, ☎ 1 338 2122), the **Hungarian National Gallery** and the **Museum of Fine Arts**. Budapest's most beautiful **churches** are free to visit, including Szent István Bazilika (St Stephen's Basilica), and you can even get a close look at the macabre sight of St Stephen's shrivelled-up forearm, displayed in a small glass cabinet.

For a unique insight into Hungarian history, visit **Kerepesi Cemetery** (VIII Kerepesi temető), close to Keleti train station. This is the final resting place of the famous and the revered; the cemetery is filled with elaborate statues, striking frescos and massive mausoleums. It's a sober opportunity for historical, artistic and personal reflection. **Margaret Island** is Budapest's playground, smack in the middle of the Danube. This 2.5 km of gentle parks and leafy picnic spots is part of the green belt of Budapest. Here you can wander the tree-lined paths, passing thermal spas, landmark monuments and ancient ruins.

Food

Rich, spicy and meat- or fish-based, Hungarian cuisine is delicious. Cold fruit soups make wonderful starters, followed by game, goose, pike, perch, pork, goulash soup or paprika chicken, washed down with sour cherry juice, *pálinka* spirit or *Tokaji aszú* wine.

Budapest's elegant coffee houses offer irresistible cakes, pastries and marzipans. You can be sure of finding a lively café, bar or restaurant on or near Liszt Ferenc tér and Ráday utca, all of which compare very favourably with Western prices. There are plenty of eateries in the Castle district too, although this can get a bit more pricey. Finally, ask your hotel or hostel staff for their recommendations — after all, the locals know best!

CULTURE AND NIGHTLIFE

Budapest is open non-stop for a good time and offers **something for everyone**, from calm cafés to brash and bawdy transvestite shows. Most of the action happens in Pest: Liszt Ferenc tér and Ráday utca brim with fashionable venues and restaurants. Be prepared to walk between venues, where you'll find jazz, blues, rock, disco, gypsy, Balkan and Hungarian folk music, all elbowing for your attention at the smoky, raucous clubs and bars. Most **bars** are open until 0200; **clubs** continue until 0400, though some stay open until dawn.

Budapest has a great club scene, featuring everything from hip hop to salsa grooves, and the cover charges are very reasonable. One of the most unique venues can be found at the **Király fürdő** (King's Baths). On regularly scheduled evenings, they turn into a steamy, trip-hop splash pad, with light reflecting off the steam as you groove in the water.

The *borozó* (wine cellar) is a Budapest institution. These smoky cavernous rooms are usually filled with older men drinking cheap, but decent, wine and arguing over politics. Women, especially single women, will not feel welcome. The *söröző* (beer house) is more of a social place, where you can find good, affordable food and a more mixed group of locals, expats and foreign travellers.

To find out exactly what is going on, check **monthly listings guides** and English-language newspapers such as *Time Out Budapest, Budapest Funzine* (www.funzine.hu) or *Where Budapest*, a free monthly information guide that is available in most hotels and hostels.

EVENTS

The tourist season in Budapest kicks off with the month-long **Spring Festival**, featuring world-class performers of classical music, opera, literature and theatre in a variety of glittery Budapest venues. There's also a series of open-air events, including parades and markets (wwww.festivalcity.hu).

The Worldwide Music Day (closest weekend to Midsummer Day, 21 June) is big throughout Hungary — every town features some kind of concert. Budapest opens its doors (and ears) to jazz, folk and rock musicians in the Városliget, Népliget and Klauzál parks. Every weekend in early summer (late June–mid-Aug),

Vasúttörténeti Park

Remember the hours you spent playing with a train set as a child? Those were the days, and the Vasúttörténeti Park (Railway History Park) is the place to pursue your childhood fantasy, and try your hand at being a conductor. There's plenty to gawk at: more than 100 old locomotives, including 50 vintage engines. Using a simulator modelled on the most powerful electric engine in Hungary, you can travel at 140 km per hour. Once you've practised, you'll have the chance to drive a real steam engine on a track 800 m long. If you get hungry with all the excitement, the Nostalgia Café serves light refreshments. From April to October, a vintage diesel shuttle train runs between Nyugati and the park. **Railway History Park**, XIV. Tatai út 95 ☎ 1 450 1497, closed Mon and Dec–Mar.

the arts take over the **Lánchíd (Chain Bridge)**, which connects Buda and Pest, with a lively promenade of painters, musicians, dancers and musical groups (www.festivalcity.hu).

From noon on 24 December until the evening of 26 December, the whole city shuts down to celebrate Christmas (**Karácsony**). Even if you're not into carp, the traditional Christmas meal eaten on Christmas Eve, try it just this once. Presents are exchanged on Christmas Eve, after dinner. Fireworks blast all over town on **Szilveszterest** (New Year's Eve), and public transport runs all night to take you to the pre-, post- and post-post-midnight parties. The next day is an opportunity for re-affirming healthy resolutions.

Out of town — Szentendre

Szentendre, a mere 20 km north of the hustle and bustle of Budapest, is a perfect day trip for those interested in escaping the heat of the capital and dipping their toes into Hungarian culture. In a town with a population of 20,000, it's rare to see ancient churches, historical and contemporary museums, small galleries, chic cafés, affordable restaurants and hotels, and tacky souvenir shops all comfortably sharing the same space. Grand **baroque houses** teeter on haphazardly built streets; unexpected alleyways lead just as often to a grandmother's kitchen as to an Orthodox church; and artists strive to capture the mottled hues of yesteryear.

A suburban train known as the HÉV will take you from Batthyány tér to **Szentendre** in just 45 minutes. Trains marked 'Szentendre' run every 20 minutes throughout the day, until 2300. Buy your tickets at the station. You can also get to Szentendre by boat. This is the most recommended and romantic route, which follows the gently curving **Danube** from Budapest to Szentendre in a little over 90 mins. The boat leaves the Mahart quay at Vigadó tér each day at 1030 and 1430. A return boat leaves the quay at Szentendre at 1700 and 1900. Buy your tickets at the quayside.

Copenhagen (København)

Copenhagen is a refined and vibrant city of gorgeous Renaissance architecture, cobbled pedestrian walks and meandering **canals and lakes**, with a distinct, easy-going and friendly atmosphere that is a joy to take in, especially in the summertime. Cruise boats tour the canals that thread through a historic core revealing an appealing diversity of open spaces, spires, towers and statuary. **Cycling** is encouraged here, and the outdoor, almost Mediterranean, feel is compounded by an effervescent street life and excellent nightspots. For an evening of mindless pleasure, do not miss the **Tivoli Gardens** and its stomach-churning rides, giant puppets, kitsch merry-go-rounds and all the fun you would expect of the fair in what is one of Europe's oldest, and best-loved amusement parks.

Copenhagen is also the rail link between **Scandinavia** and the rest of Europe. A **train ferry** — a wonderful experience in itself — links Hamburg to Copenhagen via Rødby and Puttgarten (ERT 50 and 720) whilst trains to Malmö and beyond in Sweden cross on the Øresund Fixed Link (ERT 703, 730, 735 and 737). Copenhagen is on **Routes 17** (p174), **21** (p212), **22** (p217) and **25** (p236) of this book.

TRAVEL BASICS

➔ The main rail station is **København Hovedbanegård** (København H) (www.dsb.dk), with an S-train (local train) station of the same name. There are dozens of shops and cafés in the large, bright concourse, including a supermarket, an internet café, a post office, a bureau de change and a newsagent stocking international newspapers. There is a left-luggage office (*bagagebokse*) and toilets and showers. Buses to districts in and around Copenhagen stop right outside and the city centre is a 5-min walk away.

⛴ Take the train to **Helsingør** and catch the 20-min Scandlines ferry, ☎ 33 15 15 15; www.scandlines.com (leaves every 20 mins; less often during the night) to Helsingborg on the Swedish side. There are also direct trains every 20 mins to Malmö (much quicker than the ferry and a spectacular run over the bridge).

✈ **Copenhagen Airport Kastrup**, ☎ 32 31 32 31 (www.cph.dk), is 8 km southeast of town. There is a tourist information desk, car hire desk, train ticket office, bank and hotel reservations desk in the arrival hall. Trains to København H every 10 mins (☎ 04 45 01 45) taking 12 mins, and the metro every 4–6 mins (0500–2400 daily; every 15 mins, but every 20 mins at night), taking 15 mins to Nørreport; you must buy your ticket before boarding the train.

Buses, trains and the driverless **metro** (0500–0030 and night buses) all form part of an integrated system in the Copenhagen area and tickets are valid on all. Night bus fares are double. Most attractions are central, so for a single journey you will probably only need the cheapest ticket, Dkr.24, which covers travel in two zones for 1 hr. Alternatively, buy a 24-hr transport pass (for two zones Dkr.70, all zones Dkr.120), or a *klippekort* ten-ride ticket (Dkr.140). These tickets must be validated in the machines on board buses and on S-train platforms. Bus tickets can be purchased on board, but train tickets must be purchased at one of the automated machines at the station.

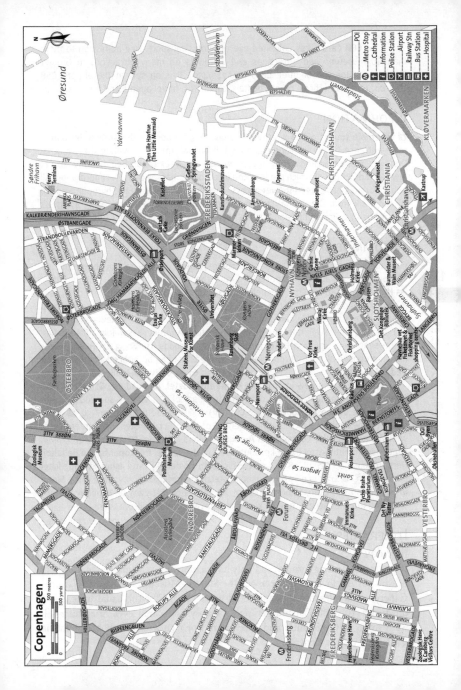

The **CPH Card** gives unlimited use of public transport, free admission to more than 60 museums and attractions and discounts on many attractions in Greater Copenhagen for one or three days (DKr.229/459). It is on sale at the airport, DSB stations, HT ticket offices, hotels, hostels, campsites, travel agents and tourist offices.

INFORMATION

ℹ The **main tourist office** is on Vesterbrogade 4A, opposite the station, by Tivoli's main entrance (www.visitcopenhagen.dk). It has information covering the whole of Denmark. Get a map and a copy of *Copenhagen this week* (published monthly; also at www.ctw.dk), both of which are free and incorporate masses of useful information. All public libraries have **free internet access**. The most central is by the harbour, a 10- to 15-min walk from the central station at Søren Kirkegaards Plads 1, ☎ 33 47 47 47 (www.kb.dk). Some hotels and hostels have free wi-fi, as do many cafés.

ACCOMMODATION

Copenhagen has a wide range of accommodation options, although turning up without a reservation – especially during the summer months – can be risky. **⊨ Hotels: The Cab Inn City**, Mitchellsgade 14, ☎ 33 46 16 16 (www.cabinn.com), €€, is central and clean although the rooms are small. Newly opened in 2011, the **Wake Up Copenhagen**, Carsten Niebuhrs Gade 11, ☎ 44 80 00 00 (www.wakeupcopenhagen. dk), €€, is a short walk from the main train station. Another reasonably priced option is the simple yet spotless **Hotel Jørgensen**, Rømersgade 11, ☎ 33 13 81 86 (www. hoteljoergensen.dk), €€. A room in a bed & breakfast can be booked through **Dansk Bed & Breakfast**, Sankt Peders Stræde 41, ☎ 39 61 04 05 (www.bbdk.dk).

Hostels: Brand new in 2011, the **Generator Hostel**, Adelgade 7, ☎ 78 77 54 00 (www.generatorhostels,com) is right in the heart of the city. A gorgeous 'design hostel' is the **Danhostel Copenhagen City** (HI), H C Andersens Boulevard 50, ☎ 33 11 85 85 (www.danhostel.dk), the most central of the official hostels. The others, less-well situated, are the **Copenhagen Amager**, Vejlandsallé 200, ☎ 32 52 29 08 (www. copenhagenyouthhostel.dk), 4 km south-east of the centre, the **Copenhagen Bellahøj**, Herbergvejen 8, ☎ 38 28 97 15 (www.youth-hostel.dk), and **Ishøj Strand**, Ishøj Strandvej 13, ☎ 43 53 50 15 (www.ishojhostel.dk). A backpacker favourite is the **Sleep in Heaven** in Nørrebro, Struensegade 7, ☎ 35 35 46 48 (www.sleepinheaven.com) with free internet access, free lockers and showers, and a chill-out room.

ITINERARIES
Half day

If you're just passing through and only have a morning or an afternoon — where do you go? Art lovers must seek out the **Statens Museum for Kunst** (National Gallery) while pleasure seekers should head straight for the **canal tour** — sit down and cruise the Copenhagen sights, if only from canal level. Anarchists will want to go to **Christiania** and beer lovers won't go wrong with a visit to the **Carlsberg Visitor Centre**.

The best of Copenhagen

Tivoli Gardens
An evening of pure fun and pleasure, ending on Wednesdays and Saturdays with a firework display. The main entrance is close to Copenhagen's main railway station on Vesterbrogade 3 (see box on p476).

Ny Carlsberg Glyptotek (Carlsberg Sculpture Centre)
Enjoy a coffee in the winter gardens surrounded by stunning sculptures. The museum is located in the centre on Dantes Plads 7 (www.glyptoteket.dk), closed Mon, free Sun.

Christiania
Have a stroll through this unique social experiment and enjoy a picnic on the lakeside, sip on a beer with the curious array of locals and visitors, or just browse through the market stalls.

Assistens Kirkegård (Assistens Cemetery)
The most beautiful garden in Copenhagen situated in Nørrebro. Visit Hans Christian Andersen and other famous folk in their place of rest (www.assistens.dk; Danish only).

Canal boat cruise
Take a waterborne tour around the city with DFDS Canal Tours (www.canaltours.dk; leaving from Nyhavn or Gammel Strand) or the cheaper Netto-Bådene (www.havnerundfart.dk, leaving from Holmens Kirke or Nyhavn).

Smørrebrød
Danish speciality, best enjoyed in a traditional city centre café.

One day
Start your day with a **Danish breakfast** — Danish pastries, croissants, black bread and mild Danish cheese and fresh fruit. Fill your morning with one of the half day suggestions, and maybe your afternoon with one of the others. Alternatively, stroll over to **Strøget**, shop your way down to Kongens Nytorv and lunch at Nyhavn, where you can choose one of the Nyhavnside cafés.

In the afternoon head down Gothersgade towards **Nørreport**, where you can while away the time in Kongens Have, the Botanic Gardens or Rosenberg Slot, admiring the crown jewels and wondering why anyone would want cutlery made of glass. Grab a bite to eat, and then after dinner, head over to **Tivoli** for a ride or just wander about catching the performances and the sound-and-light show.

Two days
With a couple of days, **Slotsholmen** could take up a morning, doing the tour of the royal residence, admiring the Black Diamond and perhaps picnicking in the Royal Library Gardens. The afternoon might be dedicated to some serious culture, perhaps the **Statens Museum for Kunst**, or the **Nationalmuseet**

(National Museum). Dinner followed by a performance at the **Opera House**, arriving by water taxi, would round off the highbrow evening or you could go on to one of the city's **clubs** which are just getting started around 0100.

Save your serious shopping for your second or third morning, checking out some of the trendier shops in Nørrebro and Frederiksberg, but spend the afternoon in **Christiania**, a place like nowhere else. If you like it stay for the evening — there's usually music of some kind going on, or just hang out in a bar. Or else one of the **canalside restaurants** would make a pleasant evening, followed by a stroll back to the city centre and a late-night bar somewhere behind Illum department store.

More

On a longer stay you ought to visit some of the **smaller art collections**, spend an afternoon strolling along the harbour to **Amalienborg** to see the Queen's winter residence, then on to the Gefion Fountain, the English Church and the Little Mermaid. A week would allow a day trip to **Roskilde** to visit the Viking Ship Museum and one to **Helsingør** to see the castle Hamlet never lived in. You could easily while away half a day viewing art and lunching at Louisiana — art in a garden.

COPENHAGEN ON A BUDGET

There are lots of things you can do in Copenhagen which are completely free. Most of Copenhagen's museums have **free entrance on Wednesdays**. All of the churches are free and there are plenty of architectural and design wonders to be seen among them. Be sure to visit **Vor Frelsers Kirke** in Christianshavn with its beautiful golden spiral steeple, which offers great views over the city. The magnificent **Grundtvigs Kirke** (at På Bjerget 14B) just outside the Nørrebro

TIVOLI

One of the oldest amusement parks in Europe, Tivoli is also one of Copenhagen's top tourist attractions. Although the park opens at 1100, it is at its best in the evening. As darkness falls and the fairy lights hover over your head, the bandstands fill with music and the rides start to whirl. You will feel like you are ten years old again, if only for a while. Save Tivoli for a warm night and enjoy a meal that will coincide with the nightly performances — programmes are posted up outside. Don't miss the sound-and-light show, on 30 mins before the gardens close. Every Friday evening during the summer season a free concert, Friday Rock, is put on for visitors at 2200 (entrance fee to Tivoli still applies). On special occasions, such as Tivoli's official birthday on 15 August, there are firework displays. Tivoli is open 33 weeks each year: in spring and summer, during a ten-day spell in late October plus the last six weeks of the year (www.tivoli.dk).

district in Nordvest was designed by the influential lighting and furniture designer Kaare Jensen-Klint, and his father.

Visit the **National Library** to see late 20th-century cutting-edge design in the form of the Black Diamond and to view the 17th-century architecture of the original library building next door. All of the **parks** have a unique layout and offer something special. A less likely place to relax, but one that is well used by joggers, sunbathers and picnickers is the beautiful Assistens Kirkegård, which is in fact a cemetery. As well as some of Denmark's most famous deceased, it contains a wonderful assortment of trees from all around the globe.

There are pleasant walks to be had **along the harbour** to Kastellet and **Den Lille Havfrue** (the Little Mermaid), and around **Christiania**, where you will come across some of the craziest-shaped houses you could ever imagine. Another popular spot to relax is around the **Three Lakes**. If you want to soak up the atmosphere of **Nyhavn**, with its expensive canal-side cafés, grab a beer from the supermarket and sit by the canal. If you are lucky you will find some of the **city's free bicycles** and you can cycle around the city for nothing but a Dkr.20 returnable deposit.

FOOD

Copenhagen This Week (online at www.ctw.dk) and *Playtime* have many listings for restaurants and cafés; the latter is full of tips for eating on a budget. Brunch is a popular weekend ritual, and you can get a large brunch platter at many places from DKr.50–100. Nyhavn with its outdoor tables is pretty at night, but expensive. Traditional Danish fare is not cheap, but it's worth visiting one of the cellar restaurants (off Strøget) to sample the mainly Danish specialities.

There are many good cafés and takeaways in the smaller streets around Vor Frue Kirke including Turkish, Greek and Italian restaurants offering good-value buffet menus. **Vesterbro** and **Nørrebro** (Skt Hans Torv and Blågårdsgade) are good areas for lively, cheapish eateries and bars buzzing with students and young professionals. The best foodies' shopping street, Vaernedamsvej, has all manner of exotic groceries, delis, bakers and cheesemongers. There are also plenty of Netto and Fakta discount supermarkets dotted around the city.

CULTURE AND NIGHTLIFE

With a young, fun-loving population and a constant flow of visitors, the city's nightlife scene leaves nothing to be desired. Like its range of restaurants, Copenhagen's **club scene** has grown to match its increasing wealth and its ethnic and libertarian influences. Most musical tastes are catered to and clubs and discos exist to suit every lifestyle, wallet and age group. Clubs get going quite late, especially at weekends when they are empty until well past 0100. This may be because drinking all night and into the early hours would be prohibitively

COPENHAGEN JAZZ FESTIVAL

Copenhagen's most celebrated music event is the annual Jazz Festival, a local institution since 1978. It takes place over ten days in July, starting on the first Friday. Whether you're a serious jazz enthusiast, or merely like the casual vibes of good jazz, don't miss this event. During the festival, every possible space in the city becomes a venue. The big names play at the **Opera House**, the **Gamle Scene**, the **Playhouse** and **Koncerthuset**, but cafés, parks, public squares, churches, and even museums are a stage for the hundreds of performers who flock here. You will hear all kinds of jazz, from traditional to experimental. The big concerts can be expensive, but they're worth it. Cafés and clubs only charge a small entrance fee, and open-air events are free. Some of the best small performances are those by Denmark's home-grown jazz musicians.

Copenhagen is a wonderful place to be in summer anyway. But the Jazz Festival takes life out onto the streets, and a sunny, laughing, relaxed chaos hits the city. The music and atmosphere have become so popular that the city now holds another festival, Autumn Jazz, in early November. The city's accommodation gets packed during the festivals, so make sure you book early. **Copenhagen Jazz Festival**, Sankt Peder Stræde 28C, ☎ 33 93 20 13 (www.jazz.dk).

expensive. Many clubs have a lower age limit of 21. If you prefer violins and flutes to ear-splitting hip hop and house, you'll be pleased to know that Copenhagen offers many opportunities to enjoy classical concerts. It's easy to find out what's on in Copenhagen during your stay, and to buy tickets for forthcoming performances. The English language weekly newspaper *Copenhagen Post* has information about events in the city. Find free copies in cafés and shops or check www.cphpost.dk.

EVENTS

There are plenty of events taking place in Copenhagen throughout the year, and what follows is just a selection. You can find out more online at: www.visitcopenhagen.dk. The **Dyrehavsbakken (Bakken Amusement Park)** officially opens for the season on the last Thursday in March. Hundreds of motorcyclists congregate in Nørrebro and head out to Bakken in convoy. The **May Day Parade** to Fælledparken by trade unionists and workers involves speeches, music events, food stalls and lots of ale.

The **Copenhagen Marathon**, an athletic mainstay in the Copenhagen calendar since 1980, circles the city on a Sunday in mid-May. The **Whitsun Carnival** Parade from Strøget to Fælledparken means three days of Latin American fun and world music. **Copenhagen Pride Week** takes place in mid-Aug. From mid-Nov to Christmas, the **Tivoli Christmas Market** provides an opportunity for Christmas shopping, ice skating, good eating and a glass of *gløgg* (mulled wine).

Florence (Firenze)

One of the greatest of Italy's old city-states, Florence has one of the richest legacies of art and architecture in Europe. It is so popular that, from Easter till autumn, its narrow streets are tightly crammed and major sights get extremely crowded during this period. Be prepared to wait in line to enter the **Galleria Uffizi** — Italy's premier art gallery — or to see **Michelangelo's David** in the Galleria dell'Accademia. Nevertheless, few would omit Florence from a tour of Tuscany, and it's really rewarding providing you don't overdo the sightseeing, remember to take an afternoon siesta, and keep an eye on your valuables.

There are plenty of other galleries of world status if you don't feel able to cope with the Uffizi crowds. Try the **Museo dell'Opera del Duomo**, the **Palazzo Pitti** museums or the **Bargello**. Enjoy the city by walking around: take in the **Ponte Vecchio**, the **Duomo**, the banks of the Arno or the huge Piazza Santo Spirito. For shots of the city worthy of the many postcard sellers around town, head up to the Piazzale Michelangelo for great views over the rooftops. Florence has train connections to both the north and the south of Italy, and connections to Milan link the city by train to the rest of Europe. Florence is on **Routes 34** and **36** of this book.

TRAVEL BASICS

⇶ **Santa Maria Novella** (SMN) is Florence's main rail hub. It is a short walk from the city centre; facilities include left luggage, currency exchange and an accommodation service. The Milan/Florence/Rome high-speed trains call at Santa Maria Novella. ✈ **Amerigo Vespucci Airport**, 7 km north-west of the city, ☎ 055 306 1300 (www. aeroporto.firenze.it) handles mainly domestic and some European services. **Pisa's Galileo Galilei Airport** (84 km) is the main regional hub for international flights (www.pisa-airport.com). There are 5–8 trains daily between the airport and Florence's Santa Maria Novella rail station (1 hr, ERT 613).

Most sights are in the compact central zone and the best way to see them all is on foot. You can cover much of the city in two days. You can also rent **bicycles** from the municipal rental location at Pza della Stazione, next to the SMN station, and at several other outlets around the city. Florence's **buses**, Azienda Trasporti Autolinee Fiorentine (ATAF), run from 0515–0100. There is an ATAF information office opposite the main entrance of the SMN rail station, ☎ 800 424 500. Buy **tickets** for one, two or four trips from the ATAF office at the station, from ticket machines at the main stops, or from newsstands, tobacconists, or bars displaying the ATAF logo. Validate them in the machine immediately upon boarding. Bus tickets last for one hour from the time the machine stamps them (change of bus on same ticket permitted). A 24-hr pass is less than five single tickets, while multi-day passes are worthwhile if you take more than three trips a day. A single ticket is €1.20, a day pass €5, and a three-day pass €12.

INFORMATION

🛈 **Tourist offices:** The **Agenzia per il turismo di Firenze** (APT) has its head office at Via Manzoni 16, 50121 Firenze, ☎ 055 23 320 (www.firenzeturismo.it). There are also

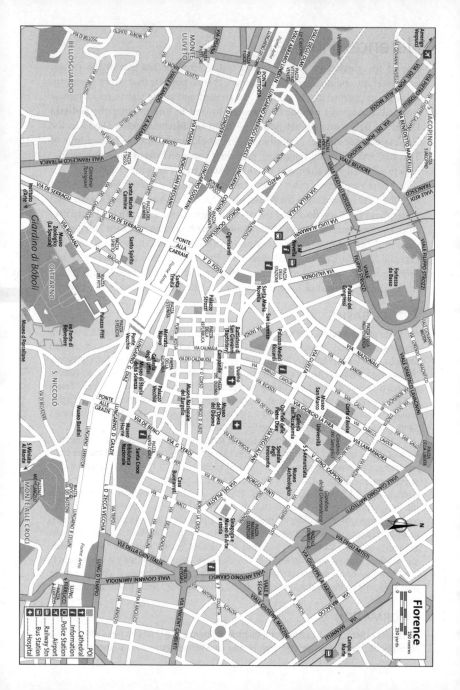

tourist information offices at Borgo Santa Croce 29r, ☎ 055 234 0444, at Pza Stazione 4, just across the street from the train station, at the airport and a combined City and Province of Florence office at Via Cavour 1r, ☎ 055 290 833.

You pay an entrance fee for every building you visit in Florence – even some of the churches have instituted small admission fees for tourist visits. Combined entrance tickets are available for some museums, and queues can be avoided at the state museums by reserving visiting times in advance through Firenze Musei, (www.firenzemusei.it).

Internet cafés are plentiful and mostly offer student discounts. Internet Train, a chain of internet points, sells credit on magnetic cards that can be used at outlets throughout Italy (www.internettrain.it). There are branches at Via Guelfa 54/56; Via dell'Oriuolo 40r (near the cathedral); Borgo San Jacopo 30r (near Ponte Vecchio); Via Porta Rossa 38 (near Mercato del Porcellino); and Via de'benci 36r (near Santa Croce church).

ACCOMMODATION

Florence is one of Europe's most popular tourist destinations, and although this means that there is plenty of accommodation on offer, things can get pretty full during the summer months. ⌅ Near the station is the family-run **Hotel Nuova Italia**, Via Faenza 26, ☎ 055 287 508 (www.hotel-nuovaitalia.com), €. **Hotel Abatjour**, Viale Cadorna 12, ☎ 055 485 688 (www.abatjour-florence.it), €, is a central bed and breakfast in an art nouveau building while **Hotel Bretagna**, Lungarno Corsini 6, ☎ 055 289 618 (www.hotelbretagna.net), €–€€, is an ex-pension near the Ponte Vecchio. The **Casci**, Via Cavour 13, ☎ 055 211 686 (www.hotelcasci.com), €€, is a small, friendly hotel in a 15th-century *palazzo*. More upmarket, the **Gallery Hotel Art**, Vicolo dell'Oro 5, ☎ 055 272 63 (www.lungarnohotels.com), €€€, is a boutique design hotel just off the north end of the Ponte Vecchio.

Hostels: The **Gallo d'Oro**, Via Cavour 104, ☎ 055 552 2964 (www.ostellogallodoro.com) is a central, efficient, friendly and highly popular hostel with library, wi-fi, bar and restaurant, so book in good time. Other good options within walking distance of the train station are the **Leonardo House**, Via del Trebbio 4, ☎ 055 285 477 (www.leonardohouse.it) , and the **Archi Rossi Hostel**, Via Faenza 94, ☎ 055 290 804 (www.hostelarchirossi.com). **Youth hostels**: **Ostello di Firenze** (HI), Viale A Righi 2/4, ☎ 055 601 451 (www.ostellofirenze.it) and **Ostello Santa Monaca** (non HI), Via Santa Monaca 6, ☎ 055 268 338 (www.ostello.it). **Campsites** are at **Camping Michelangelo**, Viale Michelangelo 80, ☎ 055 681 1977 (open all year), and **Camping Villa Camerata**, in the grounds of the Ostello di Firenze (see above, open year round).

ITINERARIES
Half day

Book in advance to get priority entrance to the **Uffizi**. You haven't got time to dally, so head straight for the *Primavera* and the *Birth of Venus*, probably the best of Botticelli's many works, then have a look at Titian's *Urbino Venus*. Head out to **Mercato Nuovo**, rub the snout of the bronze boar in the Il Porcellino fountain in order to return to the city, then pick up some gifts for those at home. Swing south from there to **Ponte Vecchio**, where you can admire or even buy some of the jewellery. Get a taxi up to **Piazzale Michelangelo** and take your camera.

One day

Spend longer in the Uffizi and really appreciate the great art it contains. Pre-book the **Accademia** and go and marvel at *David* before taking in Michelangelo's other works. Lunch in one of the cafés in **Piazza della Repubblica** — the people-watching is great fun. In the afternoon check out the market and **Ponte Vecchio** and head on to **Palazzo Pitti** to wonder at the brash Medici riches. As dusk approaches, enjoy the cool of the evening with a walk across Ponte alle Grazie and join the crowds taking photos of Ponte Vecchio with the setting sun behind it. Walk quickly up to **Piazzale Michelangelo** to take in the gorgeous nightscapes.

Two days

With a couple of days there is time to relax and enjoy much more of the sights listed earlier. Still get to the museums early though, in order to avoid the long queues. Add the **Bargello** to your list of museums and check out **Museo San Marco**, **San Lorenzo** and **Santa Croce**. The **Museo Leonardo da Vinci** makes a pleasant change from all the art and you can explore some of the small streets around Santa Croce and the Mercato Centrale, checking out the leather workshops and restaurants. The streets between the **Duomo**, the river and the railway station are filled with gorgeous little shops so you can spend at least an early evening shopping.

More

With longer in the city, you can put away the map and begin to look like a local. There is time to get out for a proper exploration of **Oltrarno**, the **Boboli Gardens**, the weird and wonderful wax museum **La Specola** and to enjoy dinner in one of the squares on the south side of the river. Consider a day trip to **Siena** for its medieval feel and quieter atmosphere. Visit **Pisa** and pose for a classic photo pretending to hold up the tower.

FLORENCE ON A BUDGET

Life can be expensive in Florence. Most museums have an entrance charge and some charge an additional fee to jump the queue. Even churches may charge quite high prices to pay for upkeep. But Florence does offer a fair range of activities at no cost whatsoever. For those with strong willpower, **window-shopping** is an inexpensive way to spend an afternoon.

The views from **Piazzale Michelangelo** are completely free, as is the walk through pleasant parkland up to it. Visit **Parco delle Cascine** to check out the

The best of Florence

The Uffizi
Home to some of the most moving and beautiful works of art in the world (on Piazzale degli Uffizi, a 10-min walk from Santa Maria Novella station; closed Mon).

The Duomo
This Florentine icon dominates the city.

Santa Maria Novella
One of the finest Italian Rationalist buildings, this railway station is a place to linger.

Museo San Marco
Where Savonarola lived and where Fra Angelico's beautiful paintings still retain their original simplicity and intensity (Piazza San Marco 3).

Ponte Vecchio
The bridge spanning the River Arno where all that glitters probably is gold.

Michelangelo's David
An inspiring, passionate creature carved from a vast piece of marble, housed in the Galleria dell'Accademia (Via Ricasoli 58–60, closed Mon).

Piazzale Michelangelo
Get out of town, enjoy the fresh air and admire the views of the whole city.

football matches and enjoy a bit of people-watching. Take a stroll along the river. The city's markets are a worthwhile experience and touching the snout of the bronze boar in **Mercato Nuovo** costs nothing but will, they say, one day bring you back to the city. Many important artworks are in the city streets and can be viewed at no expense. Look up at street corners to see frescos installed by the city's ancient guilds, or wander thorough **Piazza della Signoria** to see an amazing collection of statues.

Food

Thanks to its large student population, Florence has a fair range of reasonably priced eating places, found down small alleys, or close to the station, including in Via Spada, south-east of Pza Santa Maria Novella. Even better is just across the river, where the Santo Spirito district is vibrant, bohemian and student-orientated, while the adjoining San Frediano district is where (hungry!) Florentine craftsmen are based. Although you can opt for fixed-price (*prezzo fisso*) meals, you will do better in price, atmosphere and quality in a small trattoria.

An even cheaper option is the *tavola calda*, an uninspired but acceptable buffet-style self-service restaurant where you can choose a single dish or a full meal. These are found all over town, and service charges are included in the price displayed for each dish.

VIEWS OF FLORENCE

Despite the crowds, the view of the old city straddling the banks of the Arno from the Ponte Vecchio is still much as the Florentines' ancestors knew it, while from the top of the cathedral dome there's a magnificent view across the city's rooftops. A wider view of the city can be had from San Miniato al Monte, an art-filled church overlooking the city from behind the Boboli Gardens. A stirring walk up from the river, Piazzale Michelangelo gives spectacular views over Florence and the surrounding area. Aim to reach the summit as dusk falls to see an amazing sunset, or even better, get up early and watch the sun rise over the city.

As in other Italian towns, drinks taken standing or sitting at the bar are a great deal cheaper than those consumed at a table, and restaurants outside the main sightseeing semi-circle are usually cheaper than those close to the main sights.

CULTURE AND NIGHTLIFE

Florence offers plenty to do and see, especially on the street. On summer evenings, street performers take over the Pza della Signoria, the Pza del Duomo and the Via Calzaiuoli. Opera is also popular, though it is an expensive way to spend an evening. The English-language listings guide *Florence: Concierge Information* can be picked up at upmarket hotel desks. *Firenze Spettacolo* (www.firenzespettacolo.it), the monthly listings guide available at newspaper stands and bookshops, has a section in English.

A lively youth culture boosted by a floating summer population ensures that there are plenty of clubs and discos. Admission prices are high, however, and drinks are expensive. The scene changes in the summer when many locales move outdoors to the city squares, which become venues for music, dance and cinema. Admission is free, though consumption of at least one drink is expected.

EVENTS

Whatever time of year you visit Florence, you are sure to come across one of the city's many excellent festivals and special events. The **Carnevale Fiorentino** (Florentine Carnival) offers colourful processions and confetti throwing in the ten days before Lent. In May, the city invites you to join the popular **Fabbrica Europa** festival of music and dance (www.ffeac.org). For luck in love, buy a cricket and release it from its tiny cage on the first Sunday after Ascension at the **Festa del Grillo** (Festival of the Cricket).

In November, Florence's international film and documentary festival, the **Festival dei Popoli** (People's Film Festival), welcomes guests at various locations around the city (www.festivaldeipopoli.org). Pick up local crafts or enjoy the entertainment at the **Mercato di Natale** (Christmas Market; www.florencenoel.it).

Hamburg

Hamburg's long maritime history and its status as Germany's media capital means that it has grown to become one of the country's richest, most cosmopolitan and sophisticated cities. It has everything you would expect of a port city — with a multicultural population, red-light district centred on the infamous **Reeperbahn**, and a waterfront of hulking warehouses and storerooms — but the city is much more than that. For a start, Hamburg is surprisingly green, with leafy streets and pleasant parks, and its location on the water provides plenty of opportunities to take boat trips on the **Alster Lakes** or around the **harbour**. As Germany's second largest city after Berlin, Hamburg also offers up a wealth of cultural attractions, including a vibrant and hedonistic nightlife, a fine collection of museums, and plenty of events and festivals taking place throughout the year.

Hamburg is also home to a fascinating combination of **historic and modern architecture**, including many of those warehouses now renovated to house some of the city's top cultural and tourist attractions. Take some time and you will also discover Germany's finest culinary scene, which happily has something to offer all budgets. For rail travellers Hamburg is the perfect link between the rest of Germany and **Scandinavia**, and the main railway station has connections to all over Europe. Hamburg is on **Route 17** (p174) of this book.

TRAVEL BASICS

⇌ The **Hauptbahnhof** (Hbf) handles most long-distance trains. It's huge, central and on the U-Bahn and S-Bahn. It houses the main tourist office and a wonderfully cosmopolitan selection of eateries. The station's main exit is on Kirchenallee. **Altona**, in the west of the city, is the terminal for most trains serving Schleswig-Holstein.

✈ **Hamburg International Airport**, ☎ 040 507 50 (www.ham.airport.de), is 8 km from the town centre. Rapid-transit S-Bahn line S1 runs every 10 mins for most of the day and takes 25 mins to and from Hamburg Hbf. The Airport Express bus to the Hauptbahnhof takes 25 mins and runs every 20 mins. Ryanair use ✈ **Lübeck airport** (bus connects with flights; 75 mins to Hamburg). Lübeck airport now has its own railway station. Central Hamburg is small enough to be walkable. 🚌 HVV (Hamburg Transit Authority) run efficient **buses**, **U-Bahn** (underground) and **S-Bahn**, as well as a night bus service to most city districts. Enquiries: ☎ 040 194 49 (www.hvv.de). The price of single tickets depends on your destination, but if you think you will be making good use of the HVV network, the day tickets starting from €6.80 are decent value.

INFORMATION

🛈 The **main tourist office** can be found at the back of Hauptbahnhof, ☎ 040 3005 1300 (www.hamburg-tourism.de). Make sure to pick up the free *Map of Hamburg — Tips and Sights at a Glance*, also *St Pauli Tips from A-Z*, plus *Top Info* magazine, which includes a map of the city rail system, full details of Hamburg travel cards and an

outline guide to the city's attractions. Other tourist offices are at the port, between piers 4 and 5 on the St. Pauli Landungsbrücken, and at the airport (Airport Plaza, between terminals 1 and 2). The **Hamburg Card** can be bought from tourist offices and includes free travel on public transport, free or reduced admission to museums and sights, and reductions of up to 25% on sightseeing, lake and harbour tours. A one-day card (€8.90) and a three-day card (€20.50) are available, as well as a five-day card for €35.90. An increasing number of cafés and bars are offering wi-fi access for those travelling with a laptop.

ACCOMMODATION

Budget **hotel** options include the **Rock'n'Roll Hotel Kogge**, Bernhard-Nocht-Strasse 59, ☎ 040 312 872 (www.kogge-hamburg.de), €, and the extremely popular **Hotel Schanzenstern**, Bartelsstrasse 12, ☎ 040 439 8441 (www.schanzenstern.de), €. Hamburg has a wealth of mid-range options, including the stylish **25 Hours Hotel**, Paul-Dessau-Strasse 2, ☎ 040 855 070 (www.25hours-hotel.com), €€. Others worth considering include the **Hotel Boston**, Missundestrasse 2, ☎ 040 589 666 700 (www.boston-hamburg.de), €€, **Fritzhotel**, Schanzenstrasse 101–103, ☎ 040 8222 2830 (www.fritzhotel.com), €€, **Hotel Hafen Hamburg**, Seewartenstrasse 9, ☎ 040 311 130 (www.hotel-hamburg.de), €€, and the **Junges Hotel**, Kurt-Schumacher-Allee 14, ☎ 040 419 230 (www.junges-hotel.de), €€.

At the higher end, Hamburg has the usual range of 4- and 5-star international hotels, but for a bit of luxury combined with some individuality, take a look at **East**, Simon-von-Utrecht-Strasse 31, ☎ 040 309 930 (www.east-hamburg.de), €€€, or the **Hotel Side**, Drehbahn 49, ☎ 040 309 990 (www.side-hamburg.de), €€€.

For those looking for a dorm bed and some **hostel** atmosphere, check out the **Superbude**, Spaldingstrasse 152, ☎ 040 380 8780 (www.superbude.de), dorms from €16, doubles from €59. Other options include the **Meininger Hostel**, Goetheallee 3–11, ☎ 040 3802 3089 (www.meininger-hotels.com), dorms from €12, whilst the **Kiezbude Hostel**, Lincolnstr.2, ☎ 040 7421 4269 (www.kiezbude.com) is located in the St Pauli district, close to the nightlife. New for 2012 is the **Generator Hostel**, Steintorplatz 3, ☎ 020 7388 7666 (www.generatorhostels.com) which is located in the heart of St Georg and a short walk from the main station. Rooms in private homes can be booked through **Privatzimmervermittlung 'Bed & Breakfast'**, Markusstr. 9, ☎ 040 491 5666 (www.bed-and-breakfast.de).

ITINERARIES
Half day

Go to the lakeside at **Jungfernstieg** and take a one-hour tour of the picturesque Alster Lakes. The views back to the city centre are excellent and you will get a commentary, not only about the Alster and its grand houses, but about the city, too. Back on shore, take the U-Bahn U3 (or S-Bahn S1/S3) from Jungfernstieg station to **Landungsbrücken** to enjoy a panoramic view of the docks. Take a walk along the front on the floating landing stages, grabbing a fish sandwich en route.

One day

If you would rather see big ships than big houses, take a harbour tour instead of the lake tour, then drive around the **Alster** on a one-hour bus tour. Both depart from the Landungsbrücken, so you can step from one straight to the other. While you are at the docks, however, you may wish to make the short detour (10-min walk) to **Deichstrasse** to see Hamburg's oldest surviving buildings, where you can also get lunch, then cross the river to the **Speicherstadt** warehouse complex, where the Spice Museum is recommended.

Two days

With more time in hand you can start to get under the skin of this fascinating city. It's a good idea to begin with a bus tour that will orientate you and introduce sights you may like to return to. Take both the lake and harbour boat trips, and visit Deichstrasse and Speicherstadt. Fit the **History Museum** in as soon as possible to give you background information and take a bird's-eye view from one of the church towers. Ride the Maritime Circle Line to the **BallinStadt Museum** complex. If it is the weekend, you *must* visit **St Pauli** by night (although bars are lively throughout the week). Art lovers should beat a path to the **Kunsthalle**.

More

Once you've done everything recommended above, it's time to broaden your horizons. **Hagenbeck's Zoo** isn't just for kids. See where the wealthy Hamburgers live by taking the 36 bus along the Elbchaussee to **Blankenese**. Visit **Lübeck** (on **Route 17**, p177). If you're here in summer and the weather is good, do as the Hamburgers do, hire a bike at the Hauptbahnhof and visit the Altes Land countryside on the south side of the Elbe downstream from the city.

HAMBURG ON A BUDGET

Hamburg is one of the wealthiest cities in Europe but you don't have to spend a fortune to enjoy it. Some university-owned museums, including the **Zoology Museum**, Martin-Luther-King Platz 3, ☎ 040 428 383 880, have no admission fee; whilst when the weather is good you can walk in the city parks, along the Elbe, and in the summer even relax on the beach, all for nothing. The largest and most accessible of Hamburg's parks is just north of the centre, the **Planten un Blomen**, which has beautiful botanic gardens, among other attractions.

You should also explore Hamburg's fascinating mix of architectural styles and its most eye-catching buildings. It is free to visit the city's most famous church, the **Michaeliskirche**, although there is a small charge to climb the tower. A contrast comes from the acclaimed post-modern steel-and-glass warehouse style offices of one of Germany's largest publishers, the **Grüner + Jahr Pressehaus**. You can't miss it, and you wouldn't want to.

THE BEST OF HAMBURG

Spend a night in St Pauli
It's tacky, fun for many and offensive to some. You haven't seen Hamburg until you've 'walked along the Reeperbahn'.

Harbour Tour
Hamburg owes its prosperity to its maritime trade, making a trip around the harbour essential. The scale alone is impressive. Boats leave from St Pauli Landungsbrücken.

Cruise on the Alster Lakes
Take an Alster-Kreuz-Fahrt on a sunny day. Hop off to visit fashionable lakeside cafés or to picnic in the Alsterpark. Boats leave from Jungfernstieg pier (see www.alstertouristik.de).

Museum für Hamburgische Geschichte (Hamburg History Museum)
A good option for a rainy day, the museum is very informative and all exhibits have English captions. Located at Holstenwall 24 (U-Bahn: St Pauli), closed Mon.

Fischmarkt (Sunday Fish Market)
Even non-German speakers will smile at the banter at this lively Sunday morning event. Live music, souvenirs and great food bargains.

Take in a concert or a jazz session
Hamburg has world-class ballet and opera companies, as well as some wonderful little jazz bars that belong to a scene for which Hamburg is justifiably famous.

Food

Hamburg rightly claims to be the gastronomic capital of Germany. It's not surprising that a place that's been the country's gateway to the world for centuries should offer a vast range of national cuisines, or that its media capital should boast some superb restaurants.

Prices tend to reflect the areas in which they are located, but the places around the Rathausmarkt are not exorbitant and it's a good place to watch the world go by. Kirchenallee, Altona, Univiertel and Schanzenviertel are popular with students, and therefore great spots to find some cheap eats.

Some local specialities include the *Hamburger Pannfisch mit Bratkartoffeln* (German fish & chips), *Hamburger Aalsuppe* (Eel soup) and *Labskaus*, a kind of seaman's hash involving corned beef and herring with mashed potato and beetroot, often topped with a fried egg.

Culture and nightlife

Hamburg comes alive at night, and at the last count the city could offer bars, clubs and discos galore, not to mention cinemas, theatres and the hundreds of restaurants, local pubs and cafés. A lively English-language theatre scene is

TRIPS BY BOAT AND TRAM

In a city dominated by water, a boat trip is an essential part of the Hamburg experience. English-language harbour tours (lasting an hour depart daily at noon from March to November from Landungsbrücken, pier 1; ☎ 040 3178 2231. The Alster, divided into the Binnen- (inner) and Aussen- (outer) Alster is a 455 hectare stretch of water that contributes to the city's relaxed ambience. The shortest Alster cruise takes about an hour, looping through the inner and outer lakes, but there are longer voyages such as the 3-hour trip (late Apr–late Sept) to Bergedorf. These tours also depart from the ⛴ Landungsbrücken, piers 1–9.

The Hummelbahn Tram is a 1920s-style tram with multilingual guides that covers the major sights in 90 mins (daily, Apr–Sept); ☎ 040 792 8979. There are a number of walking tours in summer (ask at the tourist office for details). These feature the warehouse district, the St Pauli district and a tour of the city highlights.

centred around the long-established **English Theatre**, Lerchenfeld 14, ☎ 040 4199 5739. Visitors who prefer to go to an opera or watch a ballet are catered for at the **Hamburg State Opera** and **Hamburg Ballet**, Grosse Theaterstrasse 25, box office ☎ 040 356 868, both of international class and housed in a common venue.

In the **St Pauli** quarter, north of the Elbe riverfront, raunchy sex-show clubs tout their delights next to casinos, discos, tattoo parlours and some of Hamburg's best restaurants.

The **Reeperbahn**, St Pauli's main drag, has been going strong for generations, though there is now an element of gentrification, with a growing number of bars popular with the bohemian and media set.

Locals also gravitate towards the bars and cafés of the **Schanzenviertel**, which is strategically located between St Pauli and the university district. To find out what's going on in the city, pick up a free copy of *Hamburg: Pur* from the tourist office. It is in German, but nevertheless it is easy to work out what's happening where.

EVENTS

This is just a small selection of many of the events and festivals that take place in Hamburg throughout the year (visit www.hamburg-tourism.de for a more detailed look at what's going on). Heiligengeistfeld, St Pauli, is home to a month-long funfair thrice annually (23 Mar–22 Apr, 20 July–19 Aug and in November 2012; www.hamburger-dom.de).

Enjoy three days of rock, pop and indie played open air in late September on the Spielbudenplatz as well as in a plethora of clubs on and around the Reeperbahn at the **Reeperbahn Festival** (www.reeperbahnfestival.com.). Tickets (available online) start at €29.50 for a one-day pass.

Helsinki (Helsingfors)

Built on a series of peninsulas Helsinki is first and foremost a **city of the sea**. It has a gritty, north-meets-east flavour, but in recent years this modern city has become one of the most culturally pulsating capitals in Europe. It became a capital in 1812 while the Grand Duchy of Finland was part of the Russian Empire. Helsinki was rebuilt in a grand grid in the 19th century.

With its public buildings standing proud upon great granite steps, the architecture has a distinctively **Russian air** — the city itself was originally modelled on St Petersburg. The wide boulevards are lined with cobbles and tramlines and exude a unique sense of space, while visible from many streets is the onion dome of the **Eastern Orthodox cathedral**.

Those interested in railway architecture should certainly not miss Saarinen's **Helsinki Railway Station**, a theatrical design dominated by the granite giants that flank the main entrance. The station has direct trains to Russia (ERT 1910). The Finnish capital is on **Routes 26** (p240), **27** (p248) and **46** (p374).

TRAVEL BASICS

⇞ **Helsinki Central Railway Station** is central. International newspapers are available at R-kioski, the VR (Finnish Railways; ☎ 0600 41902 premium rate line; www.vr.fi) information office is open 0630–2100 daily, and there are several eateries and food kiosks. ⟶ **Helsinki-Vantaa Airport**, ☎ 0200 14636 (premium rate) (www.helsinki-vantaa.fi), 20 km north, has an exchange bureau. Finnair buses, Elielinaukio (www.finavia.fi), depart from the railway station (platform 30). The journey takes about 30 mins and costs €6.20.

⛴ There are many **cruises**, both within Scandinavia and to Tallinn (Estonia) and Germany. The big companies are: **Silja Line**, ☎ 0600 15700 (www.tallinksilja.fi) and **Viking Line**, ☎ 0600 41577 (www.vikingline.fi), both of which run several trips daily to Stockholm. **Tallink** (part of the same company as Silja Line), ☎ 0600 15700 (www.tallinksilja.fi), has the cheapest ferries and catamarans to Tallinn. Buses to the city centre go from the ferry terminal.

🚌 Many of the sights are in the area between the station and Kauppatori, and trams are a quick way of reaching most of the others. Tourist tickets (from the tourist office, HKL offices and vending machines) give unlimited city travel on **buses, trams, metro** and **local trains** for one day, three or five days. Single tickets for city centre travel are sold on the tram or bus but are cheaper if bought from HKL offices and R-kiosks, where you can also purchase ten-trip tickets. Tickets are valid for one hour.

INFORMATION

🚩 The main **tourist office** is at Pohjoisesplanadi 19, ☎ 09 3101 3300, (www.visithelsinki.fi); five blocks from the station, south on Keskuskatu, left on Pohjoisesplanadi. Most leaflets are free and include a street map. Get the free booklet *Helsinki – Visitors Guide*. **'Helsinki Helps'** (students wearing green and carrying green bags with an 'i') wander around the centre 0900–2000 (June–Aug), to provide general guidance in perfect English. They know more about goings-on for younger travellers than the tourist offices. **The Helsinki Card** is available from the tourist office, the airport, passenger ferry terminals, the main rail station and hotels. It provides free public transport (including some ferry trips), a city sightseeing tour, free admission to more than 60 museums and sights and many other discounts (including restaurants, concerts and car rental): 24/48/72 hrs (€35/45/55).

ACCOMMODATION

Helsinki Expert Hotel Booking Centre, ☎ 09 2288 1400 (www.helsinkiexpert.fi), is at the railway station (central hall) and books hotels, youth hostels and apartments (closed Sun except during summer months). ⊨ For **hotels**, try the **Hotel Anna**, Annankatu 1, ☎ 09 616 621 (www.hotelanna.com), €€, and **Omenahotelli Helsinki Eerikinkatu**, Eerikinkatu 24, ☎ 0600 180 18 (www.omenahotels.com), €€, near the Kamppi shopping centre. More upmarket is the sleekly-designed boutique hotel **Glo**, Kluuvikatu 4, ☎ 09 5840 9540 (www.palacekamp.fi), €€€.

HI **hostels** are **Eurohostel**, Linnankatu 9, ☎ 09 622 0470 (www.eurohostel.fi), 2 km east of the station. At the Olympic stadium you will find the **Stadion Hostel**, Pohjoinen Stadiontie 4, ☎ 09 477 8480 (www.stadionhostel.fi). Independent hostels (non-HI) are **Hostel Erottajanpuisto**, Uudenmaankatu 9, ☎ 09 642 169 (www. erottajanpuisto.com), in the centre of town, and **Hostel Suomenlinna**, Suomenlinna, ☎ 09 684 7471 (www.leirikoulut.com) on a pristine, peaceful island only a 15-min ferry ride from the centre of town.

Rastila Camping, Karavaanikatu 4, ☎ 09 3107 8517 (www.hel.fi/rastila), is open all year and also has cottages for two to six people. It's 14 km east of town.

ITINERARIES
Half day

Begin at the **market**, right on the harbour, for a preview of what you'll see on tonight's menu and to mix with the hearty, good-humoured Finns. Make a detour east to see the interior of **Uspenski Cathedral** before heading uphill from the market to **Senaatintori** (Senate Square).

Head west on Aleksanterinkatu, past the smart shops, entering no. 44, the Pohjola Insurance Building, for a dose of **Finnish art nouveau**. Don't miss the big square bordered by the National Theatre, the Ateneum (National Gallery) and the landmark **railway station**.

One day

If you have completed the morning's whistle-stop tour and have acquired a feel for the architecture, design and lively buzz of the city, use the afternoon to take a boat to the fortress island of **Suomenlinna**. The 15-min trip gives good city views. Once you're on the island you can explore the fortress buildings, watch the excellent film, visit the museums and craft studios, and walk the island paths for views of the city, surrounding islands, and the ships in the Gulf of Finland.

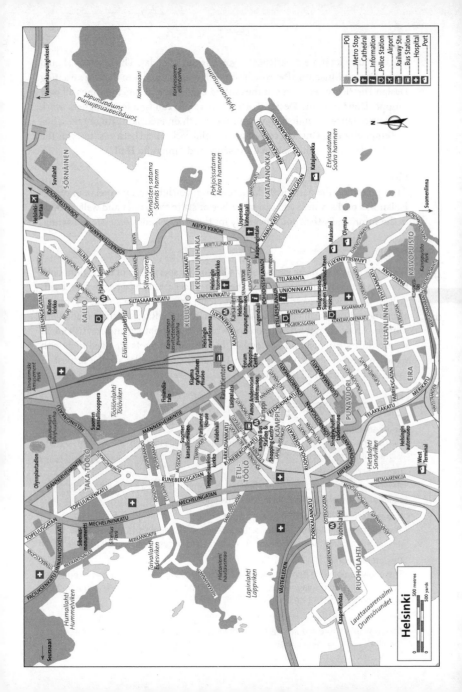

Two days

You can add a lot more experiences if you have another day. The first stop should be the **Design Museum** after which you will want to wander in the city's exciting Design District to see what's at the cutting edge before it hits the shops all over Europe. Don't miss the **Design Forum**, where you can find top designers' work in all price ranges. Window-shop your way north on Fredrikinkatu or take a bus to **Temppeliaukio Church**, carved out of solid rock. Head back east towards the unmissable tower of the **National Museum** and **Finlandia Hall**.

More

After pounding the pavements for a few days, you'll be ready to relax in one of **Helsinki's parks**, where you can snowshoe or ski in the winter and walk or cycle in the summer. By then you'll be ready for the other Finnish obsession, a **sauna**.

FOOD

Whilst in Helsinki, make sure you try some of the specialities of the region, both from the water and the land. Baltic **herring**, *silakka*, is the favourite fish, fried, grilled, baked with layers of potato and cream or pickled as a snack. Herring is also smoked or marinated in a way similar to gravadlax, which is made with salmon. Arctic char, trout, salmon and whitefish are popular, and crayfish are in season during August and September. In autumn, markets are piled high with woodland mushrooms (mostly) from **Lapland**. Chanterelles are the tastiest of these, but you'll see all sorts, in meat dishes or served on their own. Sausages

THE BEST OF HELSINKI

Suomenlinna Fortress
One of the world's largest sea fortresses, and a World Heritage Site to boot, on an island out in the harbour.

Uspenski Cathedral
One of Europe's largest Orthodox churches is dramatic and inspiring and a good place to learn a little about the Finnish Orthodox Church.

Kauppatori (Market Square) and Harbour
The real heart of Helsinki, where locals, visitors, craftspeople and traders meet. Take a boat trip around the harbour and enjoy some tasty fresh fish cooked to order.

Design Museum
The evolution of style periods expressed in numerous materials and objects. Brilliant design, brilliantly displayed (www.designmuseum.fi). Located at Korkeavuorenkatu 23, closed Mon except during the summer months.

Art nouveau buildings
Take a walking tour around Helsinki's fabulous art nouveau architecture, starting at the city's central railway station.

ART NOUVEAU

At the turn of the 20th century, a unique combination of events, ideas and talents propelled Finland and its capital city into the spotlight of European design. Finland's rising intellectual and artistic community, already seeking its own national identity, was further inspired by the Arts and Crafts Movement popular in Europe at the time. Today, the results of that golden age of Finnish art make Helsinki a living museum of art nouveau. Helsinki was experiencing a rapid growth spurt, so housing and public buildings were in great demand — and so were these brilliant young architects to design them. Dozens of their landmark buildings cluster in easy-to-visit neighbourhoods. One of Europe's signature buildings in this style is Saarinen's Helsinki Railway Station, whose dramatic straight lines are accented by monumental sculptures. The interior is a triumph of art nouveau, combining elegantly simple structure with flowing lines of natural ornamental designs.

(*makkara*) are the snack food of choice, and you'll find them sizzling on grills in markets and street stalls. *Mustamakkara* is a black sausage from Tampere, and is usually served with sweet-tart lingonberry jam.

CULTURE AND NIGHTLIFE

With almost 10% of its population being university students, Helsinki is among Europe's hippest cities, with non-stop nightlife that's all the better for being largely undiscovered by foreigners.

Don't worry about feeling left out though, since almost everyone under 40 speaks excellent English. Variety is the name of Helsinki's game, with everything from clubs run by film directors to jazz clubs, gay clubs, raucous pubs and heavy-metal **karaoke** bars. Clubs are not the only place where young Finns spend a night out. Live performances are everywhere: arena rock shows, experimental metal, pop and a summer packed with festivals. Helsinki is also home to top-class venues for **opera, ballet** and **classical music**. When you arrive in Helsinki, pick up a copy of the twice-monthly *City Lehti* for listings of current happenings — it's free at most shops and hotels.

EVENTS

There are events taking place all year round in Helsinki. The **April Jazz/Big Band Jazz Festival** takes place at concert halls, restaurants and other relaxed (and even ad hoc) venues (www.apriljazz.fi).

On 12 June, Helsinki marks the day of its foundation with free concerts at Kaivopuisto Park. In late Aug to early Sept, the **Helsinki Festival** features prominent international artists in various venues and a festival tent. The **Flow Festival** combines music from all over the world, from jazz to rock and electronica on a long weekend in August (www.flowfestival.com).

Istanbul

Europe's largest city, Istanbul, is a bustling metropolis of over 12 million people. The city always has one eye on Asia, just on the other side of the **Bosphorus**. To the ancient Greeks, the city was Byzantium. The Emperor Constantine christened it Constantinople, relocating his capital here from Rome in 330 AD. In 1453 it fell to the Ottoman Sultan Mehmet II, and became the glittering, cosmopolitan capital of an even greater empire stretching from the Danube to the Red Sea — the city was as much Greek, Armenian and Balkan as Turkish. The city was renamed by **Kemal Atatürk**, father of modern Turkey, in 1923. The Asian side is usually called Anadolu Yakası. The European side is itself split by the **Golden Horn** (Haliç), an inlet off the Bosphorus. Most of the historic tourist sights are in Sultanahmet, south of the Golden Horn.

For rail travellers following **Route 40** (p335) in this book and approaching through the Balkan region, Istanbul presents a wonderful end-of-the-line kind of sensation. This is one of Europe's nerve ends. Your train trundles through the city's western suburbs, which seem to go on for ever. Then the railway pierces the wall of the Old Town. It slides past mosques and hammams, and you might glimpse little courtyards where women sit in the shade. The train makes a great loop around the **Topkapı Palace**, once the political hub of the whole **Ottoman world**, and then comes sedately to a halt in Sirkeci station, the station immortalised in prose and in the film *Murder on the Orient Express*. And there really is a touch of the Orient about Istanbul. Dedicated explorers can cross the Bosphorus by ferry to Haydarpaşa and continue east by train to Anatolia and the Levant. The romance of the ferry will be eclipsed by a new undersea rail tunnel, known as the Marmaray, expected to open by 2013.

TRAVEL BASICS

≈ There are two rail terminals. **Sirkeci Station**, ☎ 0212 520 6575, near the waterfront at Eminönü (express tram or 10-min walk beside tram line to Sultanahmet) serves trains to Europe via Greece or Bulgaria. The bureau de change in the station will exchange only cash (not traveller's cheques), but there are others immediately outside and automatic cash dispensers in the forecourt. For rail services to Asian Turkey and beyond use **Haydarpaşa Station**, ☎ 0216 336 4470, across the Bosphorus (by ferry). Note that in Greek rail timetables, Istanbul is still referred to (in Greek script) as Constantinopolis.

✈ **Atatürk Airport**, ☎ 0212 465 3000, is in Yeşilköy, 25 km west of Istanbul. The Havaş bus service, ☎ 0212 444 0487, to the airport departs from Taksim, in front of the THY Sales Office (Cumhuriyet Avenue 14), every half hour from 0400–0100. Havaş buses to Taksim depart from the airport every half hour from 0400–2100, and every 10 minutes from 2100–0100. ✈ **Sabiha Gökçen Airport**, ☎ 0216 585 5000, is in Pendik/Kurtköy, on the Anatolian side of Istanbul, 40 km to Kadıköy and 50 km to Taksim. There is one express tram line, running from Kabataş (one connection of the

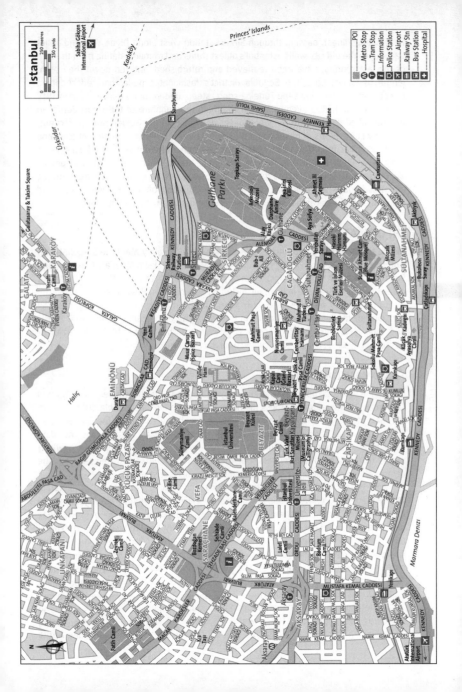

ferry/seabus lines), passing through Sirkeci station west along Divan Yolu and Millet Cad, out to the old city walls. Istanbul's oldest trams and tramline, dating from the turn of the last century, have been reprieved and refurbished, and run down the 1.2 km length of İstiklâl Cad., the Beyoğlu district's fashionable pedestrianised shopping street. They connect with the Tünel, a short, steep, underground railway built in 1875 to connect the hilltop avenue – then the main thoroughfare of the smart European quarter called Pera – with the warehouses and docks of the Golden Horn waterfront.

🚌 Large fleets of **buses** cover most of Istanbul, but routes can be confusing and there is no bus map. The yellow **taxis** offer a simpler alternative to the buses. Fares are not expensive, but ensure that the driver starts the meter when you get in. 🚢 **Ferries** run regularly across the Bosphorus, between Karaköy on the European side and Haydarpaşa and Kadıköy; and between Eminönü on the European side and Üsküdar. Schedules can be confusing, so ask for details at the tourist office.

INFORMATION

🛈 The **tourist office** has branches at Atatürk Airport; Karaköy Maritime Station; Hilton Hotel, Cumhuriyet Cad., Harbiye; Sultanahmet Meydani; Taksim Meydani Maksem; and Sirkeci Station, ☎ 0212 518 8754. Tourist police, ☎ 0212 527 4503. There are **internet cafés** nearly everywhere in Istanbul, including Sultanahmet, Beyoğlu and Kadıköy. The local municipality provides free wi-fi access in the main avenue in Beyoğlu, İstiklâl Cad. One of the best internet cafés in Beyoğlu, where you can also find good music and food is **Omayra Café**, near the Galatasaray High School, İstiklâl Cad. Aznavur Pasajı, Kat:3, ☎ 0212 244 3002 (www.omayracafe.com).

ACCOMMODATION

Most of Istanbul's top-range hotels congregate north of the Golden Horn around Taksim and Harbiye, areas of less historical interest and a considerable distance from the main sights. Yet there are plenty of hotels and hostels south of the Golden Horn, with a particular concentration of hotels of all categories in Sultanahmet, including good three-star hotels to youth hostels. You might encounter some folk hawking rooms to arriving rail passengers, but these establishments are often far from the centre. A safer bet is to get some information at the tourist office.

🛏 **Hotels**: In Sultanahmet, try the **Peninsula**, Akbıyık Caddesi, Adliye Sokak 6, ☎ 0212 458 6850 (www.hotelpeninsula.com), €–€€, with friendly management and a roof terrace, or the **Şebnem**, Akbıyık Caddesi, Adliye Sokak 1, ☎ 0212 517 6623 (www.sebnemhotel.net), €–€€, a family-run, friendly guesthouse with small but tasteful rooms and superb sea views from the rooftop. Another option is **Hotel Antique**, Küçük Ayasofya Cad., Oğul Sok 17, ☎ 0212 516 4936 (www.hotelantique.com), €€. Agatha Christie stayed in **Pera Palas**, Meşrutiyet, Caddesi 52, ☎ 0212 222 8090 (www.perapalas.com), €€€, where it is believed she wrote *Murder on the Orient Express* in room 411.

There are plenty of **hostel** options in Sultanahmet, of varying quality, but standards are improving. Those worth checking out include the **Cheers Hostel**, Zeynepsultan Cami Sokak 21, ☎ 0212 526 0200 (www.cheershostel.com), the **Agora**

THE BEST OF ISTANBUL

Mosques
Not all of them, but the Blue Mosque and Süleymaniye Camii are two of the most impressive and beautiful.

Topkapı Palace & Harem
Principal residence and pleasure palace of the Ottoman sultans.

Ayasofya
Former church, former mosque, a massive dome and monumentally fascinating.

Pummelling pleasures at a hammam
Tension and fatigue scrubbed and massaged away in an ancient steam bath.

Cruising the Bosphorus
Straddle Europe and Asia with a trip up the Bosphorus. The principal terminus is Eminönü, but boats also leave from the opposite side at Karaköy.

Buzzing bazaars
The hyperreal Spice Bazaar and, if you want a bazaar experience on a mega scale, the Grand Bazaar as well.

Afternoon tea at Pera Palas Hotel
Time travel to the 1890s and get your antioxidants in style. You will find the hotel, built by the Wagons-Lits company for Orient Express passengers, at Meşrutiyet Caddesi 52, in the city's Beyoğlu district.

Hostel and Guesthouse, Akbiyik Cad. Amiral Tafdil sk. No. 6, ☎ 0212 458 5540 (www. agoraguesthouse.com), and the **Metropolis Hostel**, Akbiyik Caddesi, Terbiyik Sokak 24, ☎ 0212 518 1822 (www.metropolishostel.com). In Galata, try the brand new **Bada Bing Hostel**, Kemeralti Caddesi, ☎ 0212 249 4111 (www.badabinghostel.com). Another hostel in Kadıköy, on the other side of the Bosphorus, and near lively nightspots, is only a short walk from the Harem Bus terminal and the Haydarpaşa Railway Station: **Hush Hostel**, Caferağa Mah. Miralay Nazım Sok. No. 20, ☎ 0216 330 9188 (www. hushhostelistanbul.com).

ITINERARIES

Half day

It would be a mad rush to see both sides of the **Golden Horn**; by staying in **Sultanahmet** you can explore this historic site and enjoy a walk beginning at the **Blue Mosque**. Even a quick visit inside will reveal its splendour and the same could be done for nearby **Ayasofya**, best reached by walking through **Arasta Bazaar** for some shopping on the hoof. From here it is five minutes to a tram stop on **Divan Yolu Caddesi** — cafés, restaurants and bars here offer refreshment — buy a ticket at the booth and hop on a tram for a short ride to Eminönü. Here you will see the Golden Horn and sense the majesty of the city and, if there is still time, pop into the nearby **Spice Bazaar** for some oriental razzmatazz.

One day

The half-day itinerary above could easily stretch into a day's activity just by slowing down the pace. The extra time would also allow for a **Turkish bath** at Çemberlitaş before boarding a tram to Eminönü. Alternatively, instead of a hammam, take your lunch at one of the many restaurants underneath the Galata Bridge while gazing at the busy sea traffic. There might still be time to take in the **Istanbul Modern** (a giant Modern Art museum), five minutes by taxi from the northern side of Galata Bridge.

Two days

Visit the **Topkapı Palace** and its harem and enjoy some leisurely shopping in the byways off **İstiklâl Caddesi**. Take in some after-dark entertainment by way of a rooftop restaurant overlooking the Bosphorus, a bar or club to unwind in or, in summer, a taxi out to Ortaköy for one of the chic, waterside restaurants.

More

Once you have enjoyed all of the above, you will have time to take a **boat trip up the Bosphorus**, or another day trip out of the city. After all that, you will really appreciate that **Turkish bath**.

ISTANBUL ON A BUDGET

Sultanahmet's cityscape at night is there for the taking and the lit-up exteriors of the Blue Mosque and Ayasofya are an experience in themselves. Even a very small donation will cover a visit to the **Blue Mosque**. No one minds if you wander into the period-piece **Pera Palas Hotel**, pretending you have just stepped off the Orient Express, or, with the famous train in mind, visit the free **Orient Express Museum** at the railway station. Every Thursday, entrance to the **Istanbul Modern** is free. Enjoy an evening taking one of the regular boats from Eminönü to Kadıköy for the small price of a ticket on the **ferry** (2TL each way). Along the way you will experience the splendour of the Bosphorus and the city at night. Disembarking at Kadıköy you **set foot in Asia** and the atmosphere can be soaked up on a short walk before catching a boat back.

FOOD

Istanbul's eating options are as varied and colourful as the city itself. During daytime, you can head for the **Grand Bazaar**, where there are lots of indoor and outdoor cafés, or İstiklâl Caddesi and the streets off it. Located near two seas, Istanbul is naturally a great place for seafood, though it is relatively expensive. It's also good for vegetarians, with plenty of meat-free dishes and wonderful fresh fruit. The best place to eat is in **Çiçek Pasajı** (Flower Passage), off pedestrianised İstiklâl Caddesi, where a covered arcade and the alleys around it

DAY TRIPS TO PRINCES' ISLANDS

Nine islands in the Sea of Marmara make up the Princes' Islands. There are no cars — only horse-drawn carriages — so the islands make a peaceful break from the city traffic. **Heybeliada** is perhaps the prettiest island, while **Büyükada** is the largest and most cosmopolitan with plenty of hotels, restaurants, cafés and a nice sandy beach, Eskibağ at Haliki bay. Small boats will transport you from the pier to the beach for free. The **St George Monastery**, or Aya Yorgi Monastırı, dating back to Byzantine times, is situated at Yücetepe, which is the highest point on Büyükada. Ferries depart from the docks at Kabataş or Kadıköy and stop at the four largest islands: Kınalıada, Burgazada, Heybeliada and Büyükada.

are packed with restaurant tables. The cheapest places are in the lane behind the arcade, called **Nevizade**. Some small restaurants off the streets above İstiklâl Caddesi, like Kallavi Street, offer delicious home food at reasonable prices.

If you like street food, you can try the new and more hygienic street-carts offering various cheap eats. Try *simit*, a roll with a hole; fish sandwiches at the Eminönü and Kadıköy waterfronts; *nohutlu pilav*, rice with chickpeas; *kokoreç*, skewers of grilled lamb tripe; the familiar döner kebab, a roll of lamb on a vertical skewer, and *gözleme*, Turkish crêpe.

CULTURE AND NIGHTLIFE

Istanbul's thriving nightlife is to be found on the north side of the Golden Horn in the side streets off İstiklâl, in the **Beyoğlu** area, and in **Ortaköy**, which has a huge number of bars and restaurants, with the benefit of a Bosphorus view. If you prefer to have a leisurely stroll, try a Bosphorus walk along from Bebek to Rumeli Hisari or the ancient city walls. On the other side of the Bosphorus, in Kadıköy, you can visit **Kadife Sokak**, also known as Barlar Sokağı, for good music and live performances. This is a smaller and calmer area compared to Beyoğlu, but quite cosmopolitan and frequented by young people. Many bars in this street hold art performances.

EVENTS

The website of the Istanbul Foundation for Culture and Arts, www.iksv.org, is a good source of information for the cultural events listed here and more. The **International Istanbul Film Festival** kicks off in early April in a number of venues, mainly in Beyoğlu (www.iksv.org). The start of July sees the launch of the two week **International Istanbul Jazz Festival**, which reverberates through many a club across the city. Despite the corporate sounding name, **Rock n' Coke** is Turkey's largest open-air music festival, bringing together international and Turkish acts to an airfield close to Istanbul (www.rockncoke.com; in July).

Lisbon (Lisboa)

The Portuguese capital is a city on a human scale, and its immediately likeable atmosphere is the gateway to a rich cultural background. History and politics are inscribed on its soul and written into its unique geography. Get up high on the Elevador de Santa Justa and look out over the cobbled, hilly streets and hotchpotch of roofs and alleyways that cover Lisbon's seven hills. At one end of the city you'll see the **Castelo de São Jorge**, towering over an area that forms a powerful historical and architectural reminder of the city's reclamation from the Moors. At the other end of Lisbon, the 1960s Padrão dos Descobrimentos is a monument to its maritime glories.

Located at the mouth of the **Rio Tejo** (River Tagus), the city has a rich gastronomy influenced both by the sea and by its imperial history. In the streets you'll smell roasting chestnuts and freshly baked custard tarts, and in the restaurants they'll serve up salted cod or fresh sardines washed down with young *vinho verde* wine and fiery after-dinner *ginginha*. Fado music and other sounds fill the air in the historic **Bairro Alto**. However you like to spend your days and evenings, immerse yourself in Lisbon's unique, enticing atmosphere and you're sure to find something to entertain you. Lisbon has direct overnight trains to Madrid, to the Basque region of northern Spain and to Hendaye in France (for onward connections to Paris). Lisbon also has direct trains to destinations throughout Portugal. You will find Lisbon on **Route 9** (p110) and **Route 11** (p124) of this book.

Travel basics

⇌ **Santa Apolónia Station**, on the banks of the Tagus near Alfama, is the main station, handling all international trains and those to east and north Portugal; accommodation desk, luggage lockers. All trains to and from Santa Apolónia also call at the **Gare Intermodal do Oriente**, where there is an interchange with the metro system. From Oriente take the metro (changing at Alameda) to Rossio or Baixa-Chiado, the main areas for accommodation.

Cais do Sodré station doubles as the quay for the Tagus ferries and as the station handling the local coastal services. For general rail enquiries, ☎ 80 820 82 08 (www.cp.pt). 🚌 **Express bus services** to the Algarve and Porto are run by Renex, ☎ 21 895 68 36 (www.renex.pt) departing from Arco do Cego and Oriente. Terminal Rodoviario do Arco do Cego, Av. Duque De Avila 12. ✈ **Lisbon Portela Airport**, ☎ 21 895 68 36 (www.ana.pt) is 7 km north of the city, with no train link; take the Aerobus (every 20 mins; daily 0745–2015; buy tickets from the driver; tickets valid for any bus, tram or funicular that day), which stops at various points in the city, including Cais do Sodré station and Restauradores.

Public transport in Lisbon is cheap, efficient and varied, consisting of buses, trams, the metro and funiculars (*elevadores*) between different levels of the city. Make a point of getting a walking map of the labyrinthine Alfama district. The metro is fast, frequent... and cool! Trams are still an integral part of the city and easy to use. Tickets for single trips on buses and trams operated by Carris cost €1.45 on board.

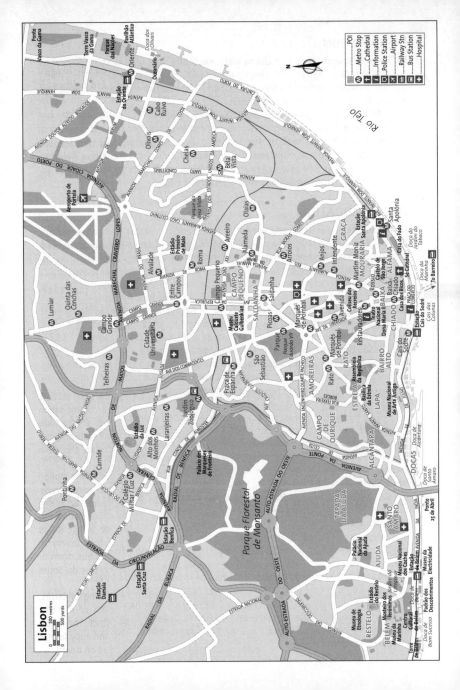

INFORMATION

ℹ The main **tourist office** is in **Lisboa Welcome Center**, at Rua do Arsenal 15, next to the city hall, ☎ 21 031 27 00 (www.visitlisboa.com); as well as an exhibition gallery, the new Welcome Center also has workstations with **internet** access. Most hotels and hostels also have internet and computers.

For intensive sightseeing, the **Lisboacard** (valid for 1/2/3 days for €17.50/ €29.50/€36) gives unrestricted metro access and free travel on most buses, trams, funiculars and lifts, as well as free entry to 25 museums and monuments and discounts of up to 50% at other places of interest. Available from the Lisboa Welcome Center (see above), and also at Turismo de Lisboa booths at Lisbon Airport (arrivals hall), and at the Santa Apolónia railway station.

ACCOMMODATION

Accommodation is scarcest and priciest at Easter and in summer; out of season you may be able to find a room for around €30–35, but around €40–50 at busier times. The website www.insidelisbon.com has a good selection of cheaper pensions.

🛏 **Hotels**: The vast majority of cheap places are in the centre of town, on and around Avda Liberdade or the Baixa. In the latter, head for the three squares Praça da Figueira, Praça dos Restauradores and Praça Dom Pedro IV. Reasonable no-frills places are **Pensão Ibérica**, Praça da Figueira 10, ☎ 21 886 57 81, €€; **Pensão Residencial Praça da Figueira**, Travessa Nova de São Domingos 9, ☎ 21 342 43 23 (www. pensaopracadafigueira.com), €€, with internet and laundry, plus a range of rooms; and **Pensão Beira Minho**, Praça da Figueira 6, ☎ 21 346 18 46, €€.

The perenially popular **Duas Naçoes Residence**, Rua da Vitória 41, ☎ 21 346 07 10 (www.duasnacoes.com), €€, is very good value, with breakfast and TV; one month advance booking is generally recommended but you might try your luck and just turn up.

Over the past couple of years Lisbon has developed a reputation as being home to some of the best independent **hostels** in the world. Mostly small and owner-operated, the following hostels all offer dorm beds in extremely pleasant surroundings, and are a great place to meet fellow travellers. Check out: **Lisbon Lounge Hostel**, Rua São Nicolau 41, ☎ 21 346 20 61 (www.lisbonloungehostel.com), **Oasis Backpackers Hostel**, Rua de Santa Catarina 24, ☎ 21 347 80 44 (www. oasislisboa.com), **Travellers House Hostel**, Rua Augusta 89, ☎ 21 011 59 22 (www. travellershouse.com), **Living Lounge Hostel**, Rua de São Nicolau 41, ☎ 21 346 10 78 (www.lisbonloungehostel.com), the **Rossio Hostel**, Calçada do Carmo 6, ☎ 21 342 60 04 (www.rossiohostel.com), and the **Lisbon Poets Hostel**, Rua Nova da Trindade 2, ☎ 21 346 10 58 (www.lisbonpoetshostel.com). The official **youth hostel** (HI) is at Rua Andrade Corvo 46, ☎ 21 353 26 96 (www.movijovem.pt).

Campsites: **Parque da Câmara Municipal de Monsanto Lisboa Camping**, Estrada da Circunvalação (on the road to Benfica), ☎ 21 762 82 00 (www.lisboacamping.com), is very pleasant and 4-star amenities include a pool (🚌 from Rossio to Parque Monsanto Florestal); **Clube de Campismo de Lisboa**, Costa da Caparica, ☎ 21 290 01 00 (www.clubecampismolisboa.pt) is 5 km out of town, with a beach (🚌 from Praça de Espanha metro station).

THE BEST OF LISBON

Castelo de São Jorge (Castle of St George)
See the castle's dry moat, towers, lookouts and squares for an idea of the city's history. The castle is located in Alfama, the oldest neighbourhood of Lisbon, and can be reached by the historic tram 28 (see below) followed by a short walk.

Tram no. 28 ride
A quick and easy way to see the Bairro Alto, Baixa and Alfama without a tour guide. You can start from Basilica da Estrela and ride all the way to Graça (approx 45 mins) but take your time and jump on and off along the way.

Alfama district
A tangle of narrow streets; take in the cathedral, castle, Jewish quarter, museums and great city views.

Torre de Belém (Belém Tower) and Mosteiro dos Jerónimos
The Torre de Belém is a superb example of Manueline architecture; look out for the stone ropes, heraldic motifs and carved rhinoceros. The Mosteiro dos Jerónimos (Hieronymites Monastery) is an architectural masterpiece in the heart of the historic Belém neighbourhood. The district of Belém is to the west of the centre and best reached by tram 15.

Fundação Calouste Gulbenkian (Calouste Gulbenkian Foundation)
Modern art, lush gardens and musical history in the making. North of the centre, the foundation hosts both a museum and the centre of Modern Art (both closed Mon). The closest metro stations are São Sebastião and Praça de Espanha.

Elevador de Santa Justa
Ride the funicular for great views over the city. The funicular links the Bairro Alto with Baixa, and has a viewing tower at the top. You will find it at the junction of Rua do Ouro and Rua da Santa Justa, and the closest metro station is Baixa-Chiado.

ITINERARIES
Half day
Jump on the vintage **tram no. 28**, which clatters along the narrow streets through several key districts. There are *paragens* (stops) along the route in Campo Ourique, Estrela, Bairro Alto, Baixa, Alfama and Martim Moniz. Hop off at Alfama and visit **Castelo de São Jorge** to take in its spectacular city views. If you have time, stop for a coffee in the Largo das Portas do Sol before heading back.

One day
Take tram 28 up to the Alfama and visit the Castelo de São Jorge, stopping for lunch in or around the castle. Wind your way back downhill past the Jewish quarter and the **Casa dos Bicos** (Rua dos Bacalhoeiros), then head for the **Baixa** for some shopping. If your feet are tired from Lisbon's hills, take the **Elevador de Glória** from Praça dos Restauradores up to the Bairro Alto and walk to the Solar do Vinho do Porto, sink into an armchair and enjoy a well-earned glass of port.

Two days

A little bit of extra time means that you can really explore the one-day options suggested above, and maybe linger in particular districts. Spend some time soaking up the atmosphere of the **Bairro Alto** and **Chiado**, visiting the Convento do Carmo and Museu do Chiado and making time for its cafés and for a very Portuguese evening of **fado**, before heading off to a club in the renovated Docas. A whole day is needed to take in the sights of **Belém**. The Mosteiro dos Jerónimos and Torre de Belém should be at the very top of your list, but make sure you don't miss the Centro Cultural de Belém, and the Padrão dos Descobrimentos (Discoveries Monument).

More

Visit the **Fundação Calouste Gulbenkian**, find a retreat in one of the **city parks**, such as the lush Jardim Botânico and Parque Eduardo VII, or take a boat trip on the River Tagus. Make time for a trip to **Sintra** to see the Castelo dos Mouros and the Palácio da Pena, or head to **Cascais** and **Estoril** for beaches, watersports, golf, a young crowd and plenty of vibrant nightlife.

LISBON ON A BUDGET

Exploring Lisbon on foot is a tiring but worthwhile experience. As it is built on seven hills — Castelo, Estrela, Graça, Monte, Penha de França, Santa Catarina and São Pedro de Alcântara — it gives you a vista of the city at no cost. At various points around the city, *miradouros* (belvederes or viewing points) have been built to enhance the view and let you relax as you take in the sights. After climbing the steep Alfama streets to the **Castelo de São Jorge**, you'll be rewarded with fabulous views from the first castle square across the Baixa and Chiado. Look out for the ruins of the Convento do Carmo, the domes of Igreja de Santa Engrácia and **Basílica de Estrela** as well as the Parque Eduardo VII and the River Tagus. Just a walk downhill from the castle, you'll find two adjacent viewing points, Portas da Sol and Santa Luzia, from where you can peer over the rooftops of the Alfama to the river. At Santa Luzia, look for the old *azulejos* tiles to see an image of Lisbon prior to the 1755 earthquake.

On the other side of the hill, on **Largo da Graça**, is another viewing point with similar views to the castle. It's much more romantic here and you can look up towards the castle, relax in the shade of the pine trees and gaze over the rooftops of the Mouraria quarter. Walk to the top of the slanting Parque Eduardo VII to get a great view of the park's formal gardens and straight down the Avenida da Liberdade.

From the *miradouro* at **São Pedro de Alcântara** in the Bairro Alto, there's a panoramic view of the castle, Baixa and Avenida da Liberdade. For a view in the opposite direction, head to **Santa Catarina** at the other end of the Bairro Alto,

Fado

Fado remains at the forefront of Lisbon's musical identity. Whether you love or hate the melancholic sounds of fado music, it attracts thousands of tourists and locals to the restaurants and bars of the Bairro Alto and Alfama every year.

There are two forms of fado: one form developed among the privileged students of the University of Coimbra, while the other arose among the working classes in Lisbon and was sung by social outcasts. It was often called *fado do marinhero* (sailors' song), referring to the seafarers during the Golden Age of Discovery who yearned for their homeland. Fado is sung by a solo vocalist and usually accompanied by a *viola* (Spanish guitar) and a *guitarra* (pear-shaped, 12-string Portuguese guitar). Lisbon's most famous *fadista* is Amália Rodrigues, who rose to fame in the 1950s and 1960s, but others have followed in her wake.

from where you can see the Basilica da Estrela, the districts of Lapa and Madragoa, and over the roofs to the port.

Food

Eating in Lisbon is a real pleasure, as the Portuguese love their food, menus are full of variety and portions are generous. Traditional Portuguese restaurants compete with a large number of international eateries. Try one of the Brazilian restaurants, which often have buffet menus that include cold meats and fish, as well as hot meat from the spit. There are plenty of pizzerias, steakhouses, Chinese and even a few Indian restaurants.

Vegetarians sometimes find it easier to eat in the international restaurants, as the local diet doesn't regularly include options for non-meat eaters; a smattering of vegetarian restaurants does exist though. Lisbon's proximity to the sea means that fish and seafood feature high on the menu, but there are plenty of meat dishes as well.

Soup is the mainstay of the Portuguese diet and you'll find it on many menus as a starter, particularly *caldo verde* (a delicious cabbage soup made from chicken stock and a slice of the spicy *chouriço* sausage) and *sopa de legumes* (vegetable soup). *Bacalhau* (salt cod) is a common local speciality and you'll often see it hanging up in the shops. The most popular recipe is *bacalhau com natas*, salt codfish with cream and potatoes. Cafés are your best option for less formal dining; try one of the *cervejarias* (café/bar) for snacks such as *tosta mixta* (toasted cheese and ham sandwiches) or steak with crab claws (they'll give you a hammer to crack them).

Culture and nightlife

There's no shortage of entertainment in Lisbon, but don't expect the Portuguese to be falling out of the pubs. They know how to have fun, but generally stay well

SINTRA

Sintra is great to see if you have more than a couple of days in the Lisbon area. Surrounded by the green and rocky hills of the Serra da Sintra, its palaces, castle, houses and museums are among the country's top attractions. A UNESCO Heritage Site since 1995, the Romans, Moors and Portuguese royal family all adored it here, and with the advent of the Lisbon–Sintra railway in the 19th century it became a summer resort for the middle classes. You can easily walk around the **Vila Velha** (historic centre), dominated by the Palácio Nacional, but it is easier to take a bus or car to see the **Palácio da Pena** and some of the other attractions.

Getting around Sintra is easy – bus 434 runs every 20 mins from the train station to the **historic centre** and the Palácio Nacional, the Castelo dos Mouros, Palácio da Pena and back to the station. Rossio Station in Lisbon is the most central station for reaching Sintra; trains run every 10 mins and the journey only takes 40 minutes.

in control. Part of the reason is that they eat well and drink slowly. Dinner can be taken around 2000 or 2100 and accompanied by music in a **fado** bar, or you can enjoy a drink before heading out to a club. **Clubs** don't generally get going until midnight. You can wine, dine and dance all over the city but the labyrinthine streets of Bairro Alto, such as Rua Diário de Noticias and the adjacent alleys, are traditionally the most popular place to go out drinking and clubbing.

Lisbon offers a good choice of **live music**, including fado clubs where you can eat and drink, jazz clubs, as well as larger venues, such as the Coliseu dos Recreios and Pavilhão Atlântico, where international artists play, be it classical, pop, rock or opera.

There are also **open-air events** throughout the year. The tourist office publishes *Follow Me Lisboa*, a monthly magazine in English that highlights forthcoming live events and festivals.

EVENTS

Every February, the **Carnival** brings colourful festivities to the streets of the city, with carnival floats, fancy dress and dancing. In May and June the **Festas de Lisboa** and the **Festas dos Santos Populares** are popular saints' days which fill the areas of Bairro Alto, Chiado, Baixa and Alfama with parades, music and dance.

Music is the order of the day during the summer months, with the world-renowned **Estoril Jazz Festival** and the **Super Bock Super Rock** bringing the sound of live music to the city, whilst the **Cascais Summer Festival** is a celebration of the warmer months, lighting up the neighbourhood with fireworks and nightly entertainment. In November, the **Arte Lisboa** contemporary art fair sees artists and galleries from around the world descending on the exhibition centre in the Parque das Nações.

London

London is one of the world's great cities. Spreading along the banks of the **River Thames**, it has been a capital city (variously of England and the UK as a whole) since Roman times. London may be the showcase for British history and culture, but it is also a city of great diversity, with a dynamic mix of residents and visitors from around the globe. Ethnic minorities make up around a third of the population, and more than 270 nationalities call London home.

They have given the capital its vibrant blend of customs and cuisines. Back in the 18th century, Dr Samuel Johnson famously wrote that "in London there is all that life can afford." That still holds true today. You can shop for designer clothes and luxury goods in smart **West End** stores, or hunt for bargains in the many markets around the capital. You can eat in curry houses, noodle bars and trendy cafés, or dine on elegant French, Asian or modern British cuisine. London has **palaces**, monuments and some of the world's finest museums containing a wealth of art and artefacts. London is also a magnet for the **performing arts**. Theatre, opera, classical music and dance in the city are world class. After dark, you can dance till dawn in the city's famous nightclubs, and hear live music every night of the week. Balancing the urban landscape is a **paradise of parks**, squares and gardens that adds up to the largest amount of green space of any city in Europe. There's something for everybody to love in London, a city that never fails to impress. In 2012 all eyes will be on London as the city hosts the Summer Olympics (see box on p511).

The Eurostar services to continental Europe leave from the refurbished **St Pancras International Station**, which was originally built in 1868. The first train to Paris rolled out from St Pancras in 2007. The combination of renovated historic architecture — including the glorious Barlow train shed — and the new developments make the station a destination in its own right and well worth visiting. London is on **Routes 1** (p50), **2** (p59) and **3** (p66) of this book.

TRAVEL BASICS

≋ There are 16 main-line rail stations (all linked by underground trains) in central London. The most important are **Victoria** (trains to Gatwick and the south coast); **Waterloo** (south-west, including Portsmouth for ferries to France and Spain; London Visitor Centre Tourist Office); **Liverpool Street** (eastern England, including services to Harwich for ferries to the Netherlands and Denmark); **King's Cross** (north-east and Scotland); **Euston** (West Midlands, north-west and Scotland); **Paddington** (west and Wales); and **St Pancras International Station** (Eurostar services to the continent, plus Sheffield and East Midlands). For information about trains to continental Europe, consult the *Thomas Cook European Rail Timetable* or contact **Rail Europe**, ☎ 0844 848 4064 (www.raileurope.co.uk). 🚌 **Victoria Coach Station**, 164 Buckingham Palace Rd, is the main London terminal for long-distance buses; the main operator is National Express, ☎ 0871 781 8181 (or book online at www.nationalexpress.com).

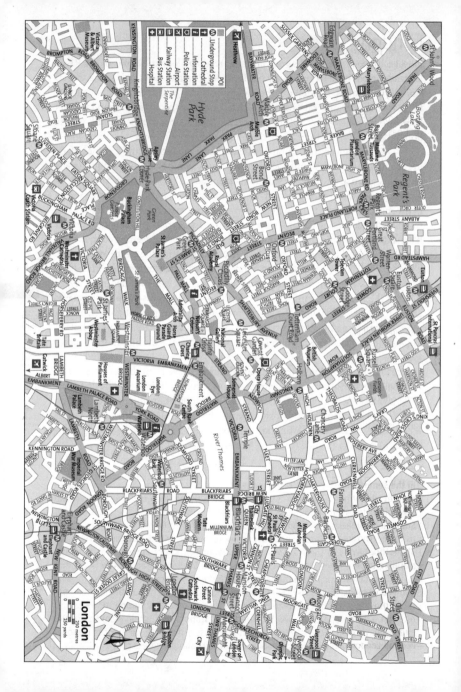

✈ **Heathrow Airport**, ☎ 0844 335 1801, is 24 km west of Central London. The Piccadilly line underground (journey time 1 hr) serves all five terminals. The Heathrow Express is more expensive, but takes just 15–20 mins to reach Paddington and runs every 15 mins. Heathrow Connect, also to Paddington, is cheaper but slower, taking 25 mins. A taxi to the centre costs about £50–70. ✈ **Gatwick Airport**, ☎ 0844 335 1802, is 45 km south of London. Gatwick Express trains run non-stop up to every 15 mins (rail passes not valid), from London Victoria, taking 30 mins; other trains (not called Gatwick Express) are slower but cheaper. National Express buses run up to every 30 mins from Victoria Coach Station taking 1 hr 25 mins. Taxis cost £90–100 to Central London. Other international airports are: ✈ **Stansted** (trains to London Liverpool Street station take 45 mins), ✈ **City** (Docklands Light Railway to Bank, takes 22 mins) and ✈ **Luton** (shuttle bus to Luton Airport Parkway rail station for services to London St Pancras or King's Cross Thameslink).

The **London Underground** ('the Tube') is extensive, efficient and often quickest way to get around, but can be impossibly crowded during rush hours. Most lines operate Mon–Sat 0500–0030, Sun 0730–2330. Each line is colour-coded and named. Indicators on the platforms and on the front of the trains show the destination. Keep your ticket handy: there are occasional inspections and they are inserted into the turnstiles at the beginning and end of your journey.

London's bright **red double-decker buses** have become a tourist attraction in their own right, and heritage Routemaster buses still run on parts of routes 9 and 15 (linking Trafalgar Square with Kensington and Tower Hill respectively). The roads are often congested and travel can be slow, but some routes (e.g. 🚌 9/11/12/15/88) are excellent for sightseeing and the view from the top deck is always great. Most services run 0500–0030, with many routes now operating 24 hr services. Keep your ticket until you reach your destination as there are random checks. Buses sometimes cover only part of the route, so check the final destination display on the front or back.

The famous **'black cabs'** may be painted in other colours, but their shape remains distinctive. Fares are metered and not cheap; there are extra (metered)

2012 OLYMPIC GAMES

In the summer of 2012 the Olympics come to London, and even if you do not have a ticket, the atmosphere in the city should be something to behold. The Olympics take place from 27 July until 12 August, and are followed from 29 August to 9 September by the Paralympics. Tickets may be like gold dust, but certain events such as the cycling road race (Men – 28 July, Women – 29 July) can be watched for free. The official website (www.london2012.com) has **good information** for anyone planning to be in the city during the two events.

Of course, during this period **accommodation** in the city will be at a premium, and you would be well advised to book long in advance. One neat new service that might provide a solution is www.campinmygarden.com, a website where members offer up a pitch for your tent in their own garden at very reasonable prices. They already have dedicated pages for the different Olympic venues, including those beyond London.

charges for baggage, for more than one passenger, and for travelling in the evening (after 2000) or at weekends; drivers expect a tip of 10% of the fare (but you don't need to tip minicabs that you order by phone). There are taxi ranks at key positions, but you can also hail them in the street. When a taxi is available, the roof-light at the front is illuminated.

INFORMATION

ℹ The **main tourist office** is the **Britain and London Visitor Centre**, 1 Lower Regent St, near Piccadilly Circus (underground: Piccadilly Circus; www.visitbritain.com). It provides comprehensive multilingual information, has a hotel booking service for the whole of the UK, can book guided tours, shows and events and sells transport passes. The **King's Cross St Pancras Travel Information Centre** can help with travel information, tickets, and tours from London.

ACCOMMODATION

London has an enormous range of accommodation, from world-renowned hotels with sky-high prices to bed and breakfast establishments and backpacker hostels. As London is such a large city, we have focused our hotel listings on places reasonably close to St Pancras International Station. The hostels are more spread out, but have been chosen as some of the better places in London to find a dorm bed for the night. Although much has been done to make the neighbourhood around St Pancras/King's Cross safer, it is always worth being cautious, especially at night.

⊨ Hotels: The Midland Grand Hotel opened in 1873 to welcome rail travellers to and from St Pancras. In 2011 it was fully refurbished and re-opened as the magnificent **St Pancras Renaissance**, Euston Road, ☎ 0800 221222 (www.stpancrasrenaissance. com), €€€+. Perfectly positioned for a quick getaway on Eurostar, it is a chance to experience the grandeur of the golden age of rail travel. Some good bed and breakfast options include the pleasant and clean **Jesmond Dene Hotel**, 27–29 Argyle Street, ☎ 020 7837 4654 (www.jesmonddenehotel.co.uk), €€, and the good value **Celtic Hotel**, 61–63 Guildford St, ☎ 020 7837 6737 (www.celtichotel.com), €€, which is located close to the British Museum on Russell Square. If you are looking to treat yourself, two well-located design hotels that are worth checking out are **Number 16**, 16 Sumner Place, ☎ 020 7589 5232 (www.firmdale.com), €€€, and **The Rockwell Hotel**, 181 Cromwell Road, ☎ 020 7244 2000 (www.therockwell.com), €€€. Another decent choice close to St Pancras/King's Cross is the **MacDonald Hotel**, 45–46 Argyle Square, ☎ 020 7837 3552 (www.macdonaldhotel.com), €–€€.

Hostels: Some places that are well-regarded by backpackers and other independent travellers include the **St Christopher's Camden**, 48–50 Camden High Street, ☎ 020 7407 1856 (www.st-christophers.co.uk), **Palmer's Lodge**, 40 College Crescent, ☎ 020 7483 8470 (www.palmerslodge.co.uk), the **Astor Hyde Park**, 191 Queensgate Mews, ☎ 020 7584 3019 (www.astorhostels.co.uk), and the **Piccadilly Backpackers**, 12 Sherwood Street, ☎ 020 7434 9009 (www.piccadillyhotel.net). Among the best value for cheap accommodation are the seven **Hostelling International** youth hostels in London (www.yha.org.uk).

THE BEST OF LONDON

Tower of London
Centuries of history and the Crown Jewels lie within the massive walls of this London landmark. The Yeoman Warders, or 'Beefeaters' relay much of the information in entertaining tours. Take the underground to Tower Hill.

London Eye
Relax and be thrilled as the glass pod carries you to the top for stunning panoramas of the city on the largest observation wheel in the world, close to the Westminster Bridge (underground: Waterloo, Westminster).

Covent Garden
The old covered market is now one of the liveliest spots for shopping and dining, and close to much of the city's entertainment (underground: Covent Garden).

British Museum
Not far from Oxford Street, the British Museum offers up remarkable treasures from ancient times and from around the world (underground: Holborn).

St Paul's Cathedral
A London landmark, the dome of St Paul's is the second-largest in the world. There is also much to admire in the splendid baroque interior, from the frescos on the dome to the ironwork screens and carved choir stalls (underground: St Paul's).

Tate Modern
London's impressive modern art gallery is set in the former Bankside power station on the banks of the Thames, close to London Bridge.

Boat cruise on the Thames
Discover London's landmarks on an entertaining riverboat cruise. Catch a boat from a number of piers along the river — Westminster Pier is a good starting point.

Westminster Abbey
The crowning place of monarchs through the ages, it has some of London's finest medieval architecture. Also nearby are the Houses of Parliament and St James's Park. The closest underground stations are Westminster or St James's Park.

National Gallery
On the north side of Trafalgar Square, the gallery houses a superb collection of art that spans eight centuries (underground: Charing Cross, Leicester Square).

ITINERARIES

Half day
Stick to the central area to see several highlights in a short time. Begin at **Covent Garden**, with its lively scene around the historic covered market. Then stroll through the charming backstreets to **Trafalgar Square**, just a few minutes away. Spend an hour or so seeing the highlights in the **National Gallery**. You could also pop in to the **National Portrait Gallery**. Then wander down to the Victoria Embankment for some fine riverside views, and carry on to **Westminster** for a

close-up look at Big Ben, the Houses of Parliament and Westminster Abbey. Return to Covent Garden or Soho for a wider choice of cafés and restaurants.

One day

With the other half of the day to spare, walk across Westminster Bridge to the **London Eye** for the most fantastic views over the city. If you've booked a time slot in advance, you won't have to waste time queuing. From here it's about a half-hour walk along the river promenade to the **Tate Modern**. Have a snack at the gallery's café and take in some of the collection. Then walk across the Millennium Bridge to **St Paul's Cathedral**. Take the tube to Holborn and stroll through the streets of Covent Garden back to the piazza.

Two days

With a couple of days you can get a much broader impression of the city. Both the **Tower of London** and the **British Museum** are highlights, but will require at least two hours (or more) each to do them justice. A boat cruise on the **River Thames** is fun and can get you to or from the Tower. A stroll in **Hyde Park** makes a refreshing change from urban sightseeing. A great idea would be to head for the east of London which, with exciting areas such as **Brick Lane** and **Spitalfields**, is almost a mini-city in itself.

More

At least a week is needed to get **beyond the surface** attractions and begin to get a feel for the real London. Once you've hit the main sights, fan out to some of the areas around the city centre, where you'll discover the breadth and depth of London's architecture, history and multicultural lifestyle. Spend some time exploring the streets of Southwark, Chelsea or Hampstead, enjoying their markets, pubs and cafés.

Exploring London

One thing that sets London apart from other cities is the healthy amount of green space in the city centre. The largest is **Hyde Park**, which, together with the adjoining **Kensington Gardens**, stretches 2.5 km east to west. It's criss-crossed by paths for walking, running and biking, and you can hire boats for paddling about on the Serpentine, the central artificial lake. Take in the free art exhibitions at the little Serpentine Gallery on the west side. At the north-east corner is the famous Speakers' Corner, where earnest eccentrics voice their views and battle the hecklers every Sunday morning.

The **Borough Market**, set under Victorian railway arches, is the most atmospheric and arguably the best food market in London. During the week and early morning hours it operates as a wholesale produce market, as it has done since

BRICK LANE AND SPITALFIELDS

Brick Lane is synonymous with a market, curry houses and a best-selling novel, and now this narrow East End street is officially trendy. For the past 40 years or so Brick Lane has been the centre of the local Bengali community, who are slowly being phased out by the young blood settling in the area. The hippest part is further north around the **Old Truman Brewery**, which has been redeveloped as a music, art and design centre with trendy cafés, bars, markets, fashion and vintage shops nearby. (underground: Liverpool Street, Aldgate East).

One of the city's most fascinating areas, Spitalfields was the heart of the old **East End**. The focal point of the area is the covered **Old Spitalfields Market**, one of London's leading fashion stops, where a multimillion-pound regeneration has seen polished restaurants, shops, boutiques and galleries added to this thriving consumer hub. (underground: Liverpool Street).

the mid-18th century. But Thursday to Saturday it opens its doors to thousands of food lovers, who come for the sprawling array of restaurants and stalls selling organic meats and veg, poultry, game, cheeses, seafood, coffee, tea, sweets and foodstuffs from Spain, Italy and beyond (8 Southwark Street, ☎ 020 7407 1002, www.boroughmarket.org.uk; open Thur 1100–1700, Fri 1200–1800, Sat 0900–1600; underground: London Bridge).

If you've got some time to kill at King's Cross station, it's worth taking a short stroll to see the **British Library**, Britain's largest 20th-century public building, which opened in 1998. A handsome forecourt fronts the library, which is graced by a giant glass column filled with antique books, changing exhibitions and massive storerooms holding every tome published in the UK since 1911 (96 Euston Road, ☎ 020 7412 7000, www.bl.uk; underground: King's Cross).

LONDON ON A BUDGET

London may be an expensive city, but there are plenty of ways to enjoy yourself while spending very little, or, in many cases, nothing at all. Britain's capital has some of the **finest museums in the world**, and they're **free**. You can ogle antiquities in the British Museum, drool over the decorative arts at the V&A, and admire the great masters at the National Gallery and National Portrait Gallery. Other top freebies include the main collections of Tate Britain and the Tate Modern, the Natural History Museum, the Science Museum, the Imperial War Museum, the National Maritime Museum and the Museum of London.

There are many **great churches** that cost nothing to admire, and many have free lunchtime concerts throughout the year. St Martin-in-the-Fields (Trafalgar Square), St Bride's (Fleet Street) and St Mary-le-Bow (Cheapside) are especially noteworthy. The Royal Academy of Music (Marylebone) and the Royal College of Music (South Kensington) offer free lunchtime concerts during term time.

Browsing in London's **street markets** costs nothing, and it's a great way to pick up the flavour of the city. The capital's **wonderful green spaces** — Hyde Park, St James's Park, Regent's Park and Hampstead Heath, to name a few — are also part of the London experience and can be freely enjoyed by all. While children under 11 can ride London's buses and the tube for free, the only free transport for adults is on foot. But you'll see more that way and keep fit, too.

Food

London is a superb hunting ground for food, with restaurants of every conceivable type, from traditional British to those of countries few could pinpoint on a map. The cost is equally varied: from fast-food chains, where you can get something filling for about £4, to places that will easily set you back £100 for a couple of courses plus drinks. The **Covent Garden** and **Soho** districts (there's an endless choice of Chinese places in the Gerrard St/Wardour St area of Soho) offer the best array of **West End** restaurants. The Queensway, Victoria, Leicester Sq., Panton St and Earls Court areas are very lively, especially in the evenings, with innumerable cheap eateries of all types, including some of the eat-your-fill variety. Italian, Chinese, Indian, Greek and Turkish restaurants are common and many are excellent, with a wide range of cheap dishes on offer. Many do takeaways and there are still plenty of fish and chip shops.

Food in pubs and **wine bars** is usually good value though pubs in the centre are often unpleasantly crowded. For upmarket food shopping, visit Fortnum & Mason, Piccadilly, and the Food Hall in Harrods, Knightsbridge. Alternatively visit Borough Market on the South Bank for more down-to-earth prices but equally tasty fare. There are **pubs** on virtually every street, including historic inns reputed to have been frequented by everyone from Ben Jonson to Charles Dickens.

Culture and nightlife

There are several publications listing London's entertainments, of which the best are the weekly magazine *Time Out*, the daily *Evening Standard* and the free *TNT Magazine* (help yourself from special stands in central areas).

Almost everything is on offer in terms of **nightlife**, including casinos, jazz clubs, discos, straight and gay clubs and pub entertainment. Most clubs offer one-night membership at the door and often have a dress code, which might be a jacket and tie or could just depend on whether you look trendy enough. Jeans and trainers are usually out. The larger rock venues (such as the London Apollo in Hammersmith and the O2 Arena) are all a little way from the centre, as are many of the pubs with live entertainment.

London is one of the world's greatest centres of **theatre and music**. In addition to the **National Theatre** and the **Barbican**, the London home of the Royal

Shakespeare Company, there are about 50 theatres in central London. West End theatre tickets are expensive, but there is a half-price ticket booth, Leicester Sq. (the south side), for same-day performances. To book ahead, go to the theatre itself — most agents charge a hefty fee. Seats for big musicals are hard to come by, but it's worth queuing for returns.

There's a wide range of **classical music**, from free lunchtime performances in churches to major symphonies in famous venues. The Proms are a huge summer-long festival of concerts held at the Royal Albert Hall, with the cheapest tickets sold on the day to 'Promenaders' who stand at floor level; the flag-waving 'Last Night' is massively popular.

Other major classical music venues are the Barbican Hall and the **Royal Festival Hall**. The latter, part of the South Bank Centre (underground: Embankment, then walk over Hungerford Bridge) is a stylish 1950s hall where there's lots going on in the daytime in the way of free foyer concerts, jazz and exhibitions, and there's an inexpensive self-service restaurant downstairs. The cheapest tickets for concerts are in the 'choir' behind the orchestra, where the sound is a bit distorted but you are really close to the musicians.

Also on the South Bank are the National Theatre, BFI (British Film Institute) (where you can get temporary membership if you just want to see one film) and the BFI London IMAX Cinema, boasting a gigantic screen (Britain's largest). For mainstream **cinema**, the Odeon Leicester Square is the venue for recent releases, British and world premieres.

It's also well worth catching a play at Shakespeare's **Globe Theatre** on the south bank of the Thames in Southwark's Bankside, where it's very cheap to get a ticket for standing space (or 'groundling').

EVENTS

As you might expect, London has its fair share of wonderful events which are worth seeking out if you are in town at the right time. In February, the **Chinese New Year** brings colourful dancing dragons, fireworks and celebrations to the neighbourhood around Gerrard Street, whilst **St Patrick's Day** (17 March) offers a taste of Ireland to the centre of the city. Of course, London is famous for allowing visitors a glimpse of good old British pageantry, such as **Trooping the Colour** (second Sat June), the **State Opening of Parliament** and the **Lord Mayor's Show** (second Sat Nov).

Other free spectacles include: the **Flora London Marathon** (Apr: the world's largest, truly international); the **University Boat Race** (Sat near Easter: a traditional contest between Oxford and Cambridge universities); and the **Notting Hill Carnival** (which takes over a wide area for three days over the summer bank holiday weekend in late Aug — the largest of its type in Europe, noisy and fun, but don't take any valuables).

Out of town

As you would expect for a capital city, London has excellent transport connections to the rest of the country, and there are many interesting places within a couple of hours which make them good for a day trip or an overnight stay. **Stratford-upon-Avon** (2 hrs 20 mins from Marylebone station; ERT 128) is famous as the home of William Shakespeare.

The main places connected with the Bard are his birthplace (within a small timber-framed house), Anne Hathaway's Cottage (the thatched cottage of his wife, located 1.7 km from the centre of town), Mary Arden's House (his mother's childhood home) and the Royal Shakespeare Theatre (productions by the Royal Shakespeare Company).

The university cities of Oxford and Cambridge are also within easy travelling distance of London. The colleges of **Cambridge** (70 mins; quickest service from King's Cross; ERT 196/197) offer architecturally-rich variations scattered around the city and combine a cloistered tranquillity with some lovely walks along the river (popular for punting — an ancient boating tradition). In many ways **Oxford** (1 hr from Paddington; ERT 132) is similar to Cambridge, with a river to explore and many ancient colleges with pretty gardens. Seek out the free Ashmolean Museum, with a superb collection of art and artefacts.

On the south coast, **Brighton** (55 mins from Victoria; ERT 103) has developed quite a reputation in recent years for its cool living and nightlife and is a particular magnet for the gay and lesbian community as well as one of the best places to go to experience the traditional English seaside resort. The maze-like old fishing quarter, now full of eateries, boutiques and antique shops, is known as the Lanes — not to be confused with the North Laine, a line of pedestrianised shopping streets at the heart of trendy, alternative Brighton.

Two cities that are well worth a visit, and could be used as alternative starting points to London for routes in this book are Canterbury and Portsmouth. Seat of the head of the Church of England, **Canterbury** (on **Route 2**, see p59) has some gems, notably the cathedral and its precincts, which miraculously escaped wartime bombing that obliterated part of the centre (unimaginatively rebuilt) but left some old streets intact. Poor Priests' Hospital now houses a good museum covering the city's heritage. (Canterbury is 1 hr 25 mins from Victoria; ERT 100/101).

Portsmouth (**Route 3**, see p66) is the hub of Britain's navy, but for visitors, the bulk of interest is in the Historic Dockyard (www.historicdockyard.co.uk), where three historic craft are on show: HMS *Victory*, the flagship of Nelson, HMS *Warrior*, launched in 1860 and at the time the most powerful naval ship in the world, and the *Mary Rose*, for which a new exhibition hall is being built (opening in 2012). Portsmouth is 1 hr 35 mins from Waterloo (ERT 107). For public transport in Britain, browse www.traveline.info or ☎ 0871 200 2233; for train times and journey planning see www.nationalrail.co.uk ☎ 0845 748 4950.

Madrid

Madrid occupies a location at the very centre of Spain, and deliberately so. In 1561 Philip II chose Madrid as his capital to avoid inflaming regional jealousies. Beyond the medieval Old Quarter, the majority of Madrid was built from the 19th century on, and much of the city is given over to relentless, drab high-rise buildings. But the charm of Madrid is not necessarily its architecture. What Madrid is good at is its street- and nightlife, with the smart, fun-loving Madrileños taking their evening *paseo* along **Calle del Carmen** and **Calle de Preciados**; thereafter the city keeps going late into the night.

The other main attraction of the city is the fine collection of museums. The **Prado** is one of the world's great art galleries, and you could spend days exploring the collection in order to feel like you have done it justice. Elsewhere, the **Centro de Arte Reina Sofía** houses a superb collection of modern art, including a masterpiece of anti-war painting; Picasso's *Guernica*. The Royal Palace and its gardens are worth exploring, as is the lovely green space of the **Retiro**. More than anything though Madrid is a place where you can simply enjoy the atmosphere — on the city streets, in its many squares, or at the counter of a tapas bar.

All distances in Spain are measured from Puerta del Sol, and if all roads lead to Madrid, then a quick look at a map gives you the feeling that this applies to the railways too. As well as the routes covered in this book to Barcelona and Lisbon (**Route 9**, p110) and Segovia and Salamanca (**Route 10**, p120), Madrid also has connections to Valencia (ERT 668), Granada (ERT 661), Córdoba and Sevilla (ERT 660) and other destinations throughout Spain and Portugal.

TRAVEL BASICS

≥ **Puerta de Atocha Station**, Glorieta del Emperador Carlos V (metro: Atocha Renfe), just south of the city centre, is Madrid's most prestigious station and the terminal for high-speed trains to the south (Córdoba, Málaga, Seville and Valencia) and north-east (Zaragoza and Barcelona). The magnificent original 19th-century building now shelters tropical gardens. The main **RENFE office** is at C. Alcalá 44. For general RENFE information: ☎ 90 224 02 02 (www.renfe.es). However, most trains to the north-west and north of Spain and those to France via Irún/Hendaye and the overnight train to Lisbon, start and finish their journeys at Madrid's other main station, **Chamartín**, Calle Agustín de Foxá (metro: Chamartín), in the suburbs, 8 km north of the centre.

✈ **Madrid Barajas Airport**, ☎ 90 240 47 04 (www.aena.es), 12 km north-east of town, is served by suburban trains (Cercanías line C1), running every 30 mins (0559 to 2228) from terminal T4 to Chamartín (12 minutes), Atocha Cercanías (26 minutes) and Príncipe Pío (38 minutes), serving all stations en route.

Public transport: With services every 5 mins (0600–0130) and colour-coded lines marked according to the destination, the **metro** is easy to use. Free maps are available from ticket offices, tourist offices and many hotels. Single tickets cost €1 (pay on entry; valid until you leave the system) (www.metromadrid.es).

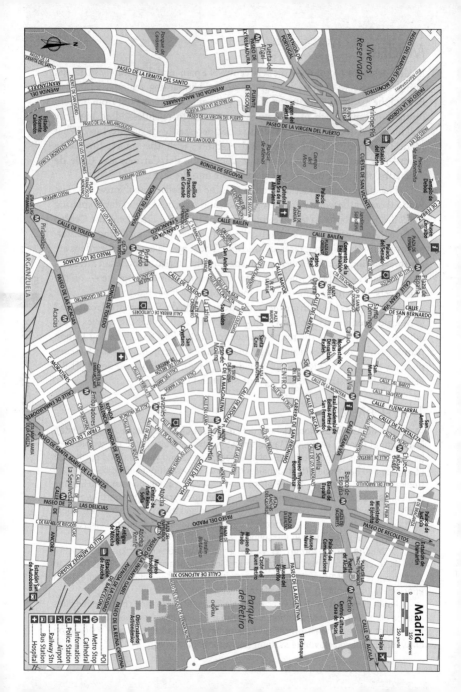

The EMT **city bus** system is comprehensive, efficient and the same price as the metro, but not as easy to master. Single-ride tickets cost €1 (pay on boarding). You can get a map of the whole system (*Plano de los Transportes*) from tourist offices, bookshops and the EMT booths on Plaza de la Cibeles or Plaza del Callao. There are also route plans on the bus stops (*paradas*).

The regular city buses mostly operate 0600–2400 (there are a few night services from Puerta del Sol and Plaza de Cibeles, with stops marked 'N', which run every 30 mins to 0200 and then every hour until 0600, but late at night it's safer to use taxis).

INFORMATION

ℹ The **main tourist office** is at C. del Duque de Medinaceli 2, ☎ 91 429 49 51. There are also branches at Plaza Mayor, Atocha station and the airport. In summer, there are temporary tourist stands around the city. General tourist information is available at ☎ 90 210 00 07 (or online at www.turismomadrid.es). Another useful site is www.esmadrid.com.

The **Madrid Card** includes free entry into more than 50 museums, as well as other discounts and priority access at certain attractions allowing you to jump the queues. It is available for 1/2/3/5 days and costs €32/€42/€52/€85.

ACCOMMODATION

If you don't mind sharing a bathroom, you can get a big choice of accommodation offering doubles for under €50. Your best bet may be to take the metro to Sol and then head south-east towards the Plaza de Santa Ana, where there are a number of pleasant streets that are close to the action but less seedy and noisy than the other large accommodation area just north of Sol.

✉ **Hotels**: On the Plaza Santa Ana is the mildly eccentric **Hostal Delvi**, Plaza Santa Ana 15, 3rd floor, ☎ 91 522 59 98 (www.hostaldelvi.com), €–€€. Close by is the bright and colourful **Hostal Alaska**, C. Espoz y Mina 7, 4th floor, ☎ 91 521 18 45 (www.hostalalaska.com), €, the **Hostal Cervelo**, C. Atocha 43, ☎ 91 429 95 94 (www.hostalcervelo.com), €, and the small, family-run **Hostal Armesto**, C. San Agustín 6, 1st floor, ☎ 91 429 90 31 (www.hostalarmesto.com), €€.

For those looking to splurge, the **Room Mate Mario**, Camponares 4, ☎ 91 548 85 48 (www.room-matehoteles.com), €€€, is an intimate, design-conscious choice. If money is no object, it would be hard to find a more spectacular place to rest your head than the **Palacio San Martín**, Plaza de San Martín 5, ☎ 91 701 50 00 (www.intur.com), €€€, a 19th-century palace converted into a luxurious hotel with stunning views from the rooftop restaurant.

With so many reasonable options in the city, it might be tempting to ignore Madrid's **hostels**, but these are often the best places to meet like-minded travellers, and so are particularly good for those travelling alone. Some of the best independent hostels in the city include the **Hostal Metropol**, C. Montera 47, 1st floor, ☎ 93 231 20 45 (www.equity-point.com), the award-winning **Cat's Hostel**, C. Cañizares 6, ☎ 91 369 28 07 (www.catshostel.com) and the **Way Hostel**, C. Relatores 17, ☎ 91 420 05 83 (www.wayhostel.com). Newly opened in autumn 2011 is **The Living Roof Hostel**, C. Costanilla de San Vicente 4, ☎ 91 523 05 79 (www.thelivingroofhostel.com).

ITINERARIES

Half day

If you feel like walking you can see the best of the **Old Town** in two or three hours, including some window-shopping and a coffee break. If it's winter or wet, you'll probably be better off going directly to the Prado, the Thyssen-Bornemisza or the Centro de Arte Reina Sofía.

One day

A whole day in Madrid will give you a chance to relax over a leisurely lunch to break up the sightseeing. Half the day can be spent exploring the streets of the Old Town as outlined above and the other half in **El Prado**, the city's main art gallery. Take in a flamenco show in the evening.

Two days

You'll be able to fit in El Prado and either the **Reina Sofía** or the **Thyssen-Bornemisza** galleries along with a visit to the **Palacio Real**. Allow some time for wandering around the Old Town, visiting the **Retiro** park and shopping in the Salamanca quarter.

More

As well as the three main art galleries and the Palacio Real, you'll have time to see lesser-known gems, such as the **Monasterio de las Descalzas Reales** or the **Las Ventas bullring**. Away from the Old Town, a stroll up the Paseo del Prado and the Castellana could easily fill a whole afternoon. Day trips might include **El Escorial** and at least one of the nearby monumental cities — **Segovia** and **Toledo** are closest.

MADRID ON A BUDGET

Prices in Madrid for everything from a t-shirt to a taxi have soared in recent years but it takes only a little knowledge and imagination to see how you can happily spend time in the city without needing wads of cash.

To begin with, there are **atmospheric boulevards and squares** to wander around, where the charm is in the buildings, monuments, statues and street life rather than in attractions you have to pay to get into. The best place to stroll is the **Old Town** and in particular, if you don't want to be tempted by shops, **La Latina quarter**, south-west of the Plaza Mayor towards the Plaza de la Paja and Plaza de San Andrés.

On Sunday mornings, the streets of La Latina are occupied by the **Rastro street market**, which is almost more enjoyable to explore if you can't afford to buy

THE BEST OF MADRID

Medieval Madrid
There's a maze of quaint old streets to explore heading south and west from the city's principal square of the Puerta del Sol. Particularly picturesque is the Plaza de la Villa halfway down the Calle Mayor.

Plaza Mayor
This arcaded rectangle is at the heart of the Old Town, a place to stroll around or have a coffee in the sunshine. The Plaza Mayor is close to the Puerta del Sol, and therefore is not only in the heart of the city, but a few steps away from Point Zero, from where all distances in Spain are measured.

Palacio Real
The extravagantly ornate 18th-century royal palace of Spain is to the west of the medieval heart of the city, set alongside the graceful gardens of the Campo del Moro.

Museo del Prado
Spain's internationally famous collection of great art, with particular emphasis on Goya and Velázquez (see box on p524).

Museo Thyssen-Bornemisza
This outstanding gallery not far from the Prado offers a condensed tour through the history of Western art (www.museothyssen.org); closed Mon.

Centro de Arte Reina Sofía
A superb collection of modern Spanish art, pride of place being reserved for Picasso's anti-war masterpiece *Guernica*. Don't miss the room devoted to the bizarre and often provocative work of Salvador Dalí (metro: Atocha); closed Tues.

Parque del Retiro
The former grounds of a palace, Madrid's biggest park is a place to amble down tree-shaded avenues or go boating. The Retiro is a short walk from Madrid's art museums and has its own metro stop.

El Escorial
The most popular day out from Madrid is to King Felipe II's massive palace-cum-monastery crammed with art (see box on p525).

anything. The busy **Gran Vía** is another interesting street to promenade along, mainly to look at its monumental buildings and shop windows.

When you get tired of streets, there are gardens. The **Retiro** is the largest and most obvious but there are plenty more, some little frequented. Closest to the city centre are the **Jardines de Sabatini** (off the Plaza de Oriente), a raised terrace garden handy for a picnic.

Food

Madrid offers a full range of regional dishes from all over Spain; for local fare look for **Castilian-style** roasts and stews, tripe in spicy sauce (*callos a la* *madrileña*) and *cocido* (often served on Tues) — a satisfying concoction — part soup, part meat and veg, cooked in a broth, and often served as two or three separate courses. Restaurants don't really get going until well after 2200, late even by Spanish standards. The **Old Town**, south-west of Plaza Mayor, is full of 'typical' Spanish bars and restaurants built in cellars and stone-walled caves, where *Madrileños* tend to head towards after the evening *paseo* (stroll). However, as with the tapas bars surrounding Plaza Mayor, some of these tend to be touristy and overpriced.

A better area is around **Plaza de Santa Ana**: Calles Echegaray, Ventura de la Vega and Manuel Fernández González all host a number of quality budget restaurants, and Plaza de Santa Ana itself is great for tapas. Pork lovers can't leave Madrid without visiting the **Museo del Jamón**. A restaurant, not a museum, its walls are covered in huge slabs of meat, and diners can feast on Iberian ham in any conceivable shape or form. There are several branches throughout the city, including Gran Vía 72 and Calle Atocha 54.

CULTURE AND NIGHTLIFE

Madrid has a pulsating nightlife, centred on its numerous restaurants, bars and dance venues. Live music can easily be found. At weekends, many bars stay open until 0300 and some close much later than that. Discos tend to have a cover charge, but bars with dance floors don't.

The **Malasaña** area (metro: Bilbao/Tribunal) is good for music and bars, and is mainly popular with a younger crowd. It centres on Plaza Dos de Mayo, Calle de Velarde and Calle de Ruíz.

Although **flamenco guitar playing**, dancing and singing belong to Andalucía, Madrid is said to have the best performers around, though some of it is aimed at tourists, with prices to match. Huertas (metro: Antón Martín) is the area around Plaza de Santa Ana and has a huge variety of bars that stay open pretty

SPANISH ART AT THE PRADO

One of the world's greatest art collections, the Museo del Prado, got even more impressive following the unveiling of its new extension in 2010. Designed by Rafael Moneo, the extension has increased the site by a whopping 50 per cent and allowed an overhaul of some of the more cramped galleries, including the museum's biggest crowd-puller, the Velázquez rooms.

The collection is still mostly housed in the neoclassical **Palacio de Villanueva**, built in 1785 on the orders of Carlos III, and is particularly strong on Spanish art. If you haven't got time to explore it all, head for the sections on the country's two most famous artists, Velázquez and Goya. **Information**: Paseo del Prado, ☎ 91 330 28 00 (www.museodelprado.es), open 0900–2000 Tues–Sun (metro: Atocha or Banco de España). Admission charge (free every day after 1800).

EL ESCORIAL

Everybody's number one day trip from Madrid has to be to this massive palace-cum-monastery. King Felipe II had it built by architect Juan de Herrera when the Spanish empire was at the height of its power and wealth. In size and scope, it is truly daunting, although the austere and sober outside is at odds with the fineries within. You could do El Escorial in a morning or afternoon but if you have the time, give yourself the best part of a day to enjoy it. El Escorial is on **Route 10** (p122).

There are four parts to the palace complex (closed Mon): the **monastery**, the **church**, the **library** with its magnificently decorated vaulted ceiling (whose holdings are said to rival those of the Vatican), and the **Friars' Garden** – a good place to stroll when you need to get your breath back. To see everything you can either join a guided tour (which takes about 45 minutes) or follow the signs around yourself, in which case you'll need up to two hours. **Getting there**: 🚌 664/661 (Autocares Herranz) from Moncloa metro station (about 1 hr). Or take the train (line C-8) from Atocha or Chamartín stations (50 mins plus a 2 km walk).

much through the night. Paseo del Prado (metro: Atocha/Banco de España) is rather more upmarket, with smart and expensive café-bars. Chueca has a lively gay scene, particularly along Calle de Pelayo.

The *Guía del Ocio* (www.guiadelocio.com) is a weekly Spanish-language publication with listings of what's on in Madrid; it is sold at newsstands. Useful free handouts from tourist offices and hotels include the English-language *In Madrid* (www.in-madrid.com) and *Madrid Connect* (www.madridconnect.com).

EVENTS

As the capital of Spain and a cultural centre, Madrid has a wide range of events taking place throughout the year. Visit the website www.turismomadrid.es for a full calendar of events.

Some of the highlights include the **Carnaval**, which takes place in the run-up to Lent with fancy-dress parties, parades and a comic conclusion with the *Entierro de la Sardina* (Burial of the Sardine) — a parade which takes place on Shrove Tuesday. During Easter Week (**Semana Santa**), processions of spookily hooded penitents bearing images of Christ and the Virgin wander through the city. The best place to see the floats is La Latina quarter on Maundy Thursday and Good Friday.

In August and September, the **Verbenas de San Cayetano, San Lorenzo** and **La Paloma** take place, with street parties organised in the neighbourhoods of Lavapies, Rastro and La Latina. Expect traditional dress, dancing and sangria-sodden barbecues. On **Noche Vieja** (31 December) the Puerta del Sol is packed with revellers celebrating the coming of the New Year. The tradition is to eat twelve grapes — one for each chime at midnight — and then wash it all down with *cava*, the Spanish equivalent of champagne. Don't forget your lucky red underwear!

Munich (München)

The less you know about Munich, the easier it is to define. Right — it's the **Oktoberfest** city, full of ruddy-cheeked people in lederhosen singing '*ein prosit, ein prosit*' with foaming steins raised. But after a few trips — or even a few days — you'll soon discover that Munich is **more than just beer**. Munich is affluent and stylish, with a world-class cultural scene, **superb museums**, and some of Germany's best restaurants. It is also laid-back in a way other German cities are not, and boasts a vibrant counter-culture that comes as a welcome respite from Bavarian formality. Munich's location is also a huge asset, with easy access to **lakes and mountains**, and superb transport connections to Italy, Switzerland, Austria and destinations further south as well as the rest of Germany.

You will find Munich on **Routes 19** (p189), **20** (p201) and **28** (p252) of this book. Beyond these, Munich also has direct rail links with Paris (ERT 32), Berlin (ERT 851), Budapest (ERT 65), Belgrade via Ljubljana and Zagreb (ERT 62), Salzburg (ERT 890), Verona (ERT 70) and Zurich (ERT 75).

TRAVEL BASICS

⇌ **München Hauptbahnhof** (Hbf), Bahnhofpl. (about 1 km due west of Marienplatz in the city centre), is Munich's main railway station, and southern Germany's most important rail hub, with excellent day and night train connections via Austria into Italy, Slovenia, Croatia and Hungary. Travel enquiries: ☎ 0180 599 6633 (www.bahn.de).

✈ **Franz Josef Strauss Airport**, 30 km north-east of Munich city centre, is a major intercontinental hub with two terminals served by over 60 airlines. Flight information: ☎ 089 9752 1313 (www.munich-airport.de). S-Bahn lines S1 and S8 run every 10 mins from the rail station via the Ostbahnhof and city centre to the airport (see ERT 892). If you're starting a rail trip from here, note that up to five people can travel anywhere in Bavaria in a day for the price of one ticket, €29 from ticket machines or purchased online, otherwise €31, including the airport S-Bahn station. For the city centre, get off at Marienpl. It takes 48 mins by S1 or 38 mins by S8 to get to the airport.

The city centre, pedestrianised apart from trams and cycles, is easy to explore on foot, being only a 20-min walk across. For trips further afield, use the excellent **public transport system** of buses, trams and trains: S-Bahn (overground) and U-Bahn (underground). All transport runs 0430–0200. City transport **tickets** can be used on trains, buses or trams; they must be validated in the blue box the first time you board, or you are liable to be fined on the spot. Buy them at stations, newsagents, hotel desks and campsites (single and strip tickets can also be bought on board buses and trams). The price of a single ticket depends on the number of zones you'll be travelling.

INFORMATION

🛈 The **main tourist office** is at Bahnhofplatz 2, outside the main railway station. There are also branches in the city centre in the town hall on Marienplatz and at the airport. For information call ☎ 089 2339 6500 (www.muenchen-tourist.de). The main tourist office offers an accommodation service, hotel listing, city map and theatre bookings.

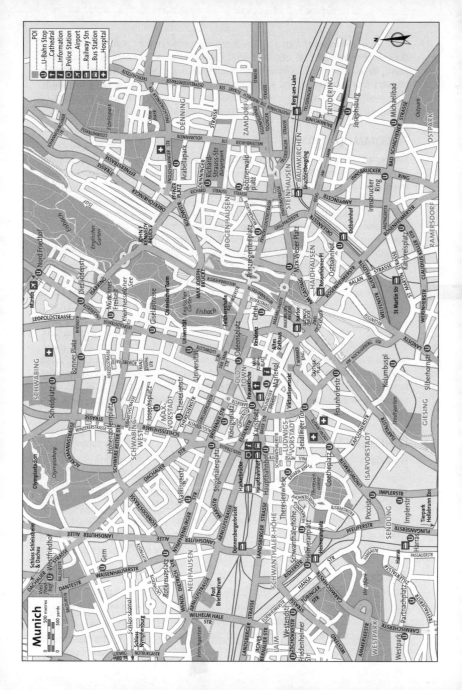

For a **walking tour** with a knowledgeable English-speaking guide, try one of *The Original Munich Walks*, ☎ 089 5502 9374 (www.munichwalks.com), or *Munich Walk Tours*, ☎ 089 2423 1767 (www.munichwalktours.de), which also covers Dachau, a brewery tour, a cycle tour and a Third Reich Tour. You can **get online** easily in Munich, with most hostels offering internet access or wi-fi, and there are internet cafés throughout the city, especially in the neighbourhood around the main train station.

ACCOMMODATION

Finding accommodation is rarely a problem except during the city's biggest tourist attractions, the annual Oktoberfest beer festival (mid-Sept–early Oct) and Fasching, the Bacchanalian carnival that precedes Ash Wednesday.

🛏 The biggest choice of **hotels** is around the rail station in streets like Schillerstr. and Senefelderstr.; it's a rather drab area but handy for the centre. Mid-range ones include **Hotelissimo Haberstock**, Schillerstr. 4, ☎ 089 557 855 (www.hotelissimo.com), €€, and **Leonardo Hotel München City Center**, Senefelderstr. 4, ☎ 089 551 540 (www.leonardo-hotels.com), €€. Other moderately priced hotels include the **Hotel Andi München City Center**, Landwehrstr. 33, ☎ 089 552 5560, €€; and **Hotel Herzog**, Häberlstr. 9, ☎ 089 5999 3901 (www.hotel-herzog.de), €€. A charming, family-operated hotel, if a little more expensive, is the **Hotel Pension Mona Lisa**, Robert-Koch-Str 4, ☎ 089 2102 8380 (www.hotelmonalisa.de), €€, which is just off the Maximilianstrasse, and close to the Englischer Garten.

You'll find plenty of budget accommodation with several independent **hostels**, most of which are close to the main train station. Try the **Euro Youth Hotel**, Senefelderstr. 5, ☎ 089 5990 8811 (www.euro-youth-hotel.de), or the **Easy Palace City Hostel**, Mozartstrasse 4, ☎ 089 558 7970 (www.easypalace.de). Two other hostels worth a look are The **Wombats City Hostel**, Senefelderstraße 1 ☎ 089 5998 9180 (www.wombats-hostels.com), and the **4 You München**, Hirtenstraße 18, ☎ 089 5521 660 (www.the4you.de).

ITINERARIES
Half day

Begin or end at **Marienplatz**, to see the Glockenspiel perform. Look inside Peterskirche and, if it's a clear day, get a good view from its tower (or from that of the Rathaus). Enjoy a stroll through the **Viktualienmarkt**. North of the Rathaus, a street leads to Odeonsplatz, on the way passing the enormous royal Residenz. Just beyond it is the Hofgarten. Leave time to visit a **beer hall**, perhaps the Hofbräuhaus or the Augustinerkeller, closer to Marienplatz.

One day

After wandering around the **Old Town**, allowing time for a look at the rococo Asamkirche, and a stroll down Sendlinger Strasse, choose one of the royal palaces to tour. The **Residenz** is so big that you will need to decide which half to see — morning and afternoon tours are different. On a nice day, opt for

THE BEST OF MUNICH

Glockenspiel
The giant animated clock in the tower of the Neues Rathaus performs two or three times daily. Located in Marienplatz in the very heart of the city, this is also a good place to start your explorations of the city.

Schwabing
Join students, artists, musicians and Munich's young crowd on the city's left bank. Schwabing is north of the centre, and a good way to get there is to take the U-Bahn to Münchner Freiheit.

Beer garden or beer hall
Enjoy a drink with the locals. The Hofbräuhaus and the Augustiner beer halls in the centre of the city are the most famous, but try the Augustiner hall at the brewery itself (Landsbergerstrasse 19, S-Bahn: Hackerbrücke) which is much less touristy.

Haus der Kunst and Lenbachhaus
Munich houses a treasury of 20th-century art, including works of the Blue Riders. The Haus der Kunst is close to U-Bahn station Lehel at the southern end of the Englischer Garten, whilst the Lenbachhaus is by Königsplatz.

Deutsches Museum
One of the world's best science and technology museums, with lots of hands-on fun as you poke at the exhibits and play with the toys. On Museums' Island, close to S-Bahn station Isartor.

Viktualienmarkt
Try Bavarian specialities or pick up the makings of a picnic from around the world at one of Europe's finest produce markets, right in the heart of the city. Exit Marienplatz to the east and then walk around the corner... you can't miss it!

Nymphenburg, where you get the bonus of the gardens and the pretty little Amalienburg. Head for **Schwabing** in the evening for dinner and the nightlife.

Two days
With a bit more time, you might want to see whichever royal palace you didn't opt for the first day, and indulge in some of the **fine art museums** in Munich. Take a walk in Schwabing to see the art nouveau houses. Spend an evening sampling the nightlife of Munich's arty gay/lesbian neighbourhood around **Gärtnerplatz** or take in a concert or opera performance.

More
Push the buttons and ring all the bells at the **Deutsches Museum**, stroll in the **Englischer Garten** at least as far as the Chinese Tower — resting over a beer and maybe lunch in their beer garden. Make a pilgrimage to **Dachau**, but don't limit it to the concentration camp. See the pretty town and its hilltop castle, and if art

is your thing, don't miss the civic art museum. With even more time, you can head out of the city and take a trip to see some of Bavaria's stunningly beautiful countryside, and perhaps the kitsch charm of **King Ludwig's castles**.

MUNICH ON A BUDGET

Schwabing, the area of Munich where artists and the intelligentsia lived at the turn of the 20th century, was filled with everything new and exciting in those heady years before World War I. Along with the new wave of Expressionist painting which threw out all the old rules came a new wave of architecture and decoration. Known elsewhere as art nouveau, in Germany it was called **Jugendstil** — young style. The houses that line the streets on either side of **Leopoldstrasse** create a free art gallery, with building after building designed by some of the movement's foremost names. Another way to enjoy Munich without spending (much) money is to head to the green spaces of the **Englischer Garten**. Go first to the **Viktualienmarkt** to stock up on supplies for a picnic, and then explore the park itself, especially the **Chinese Tower** which stands proudly at the heart of the park, towering over an enormous beer garden. Grab a beer and unpack your supplies — in Munich's beer gardens you are allowed to bring your own food.

FOOD

Good eating areas include Schwabing, Gärtnerpl. and, across the River Isar, Haidhausen. An entertaining place for cheap snacks is the open-air **Viktualienmarkt**, a food market where a score of traditional taverns dispense beer, schnapps, sausage and soup — look out particularly for the tasty *Schwarzwaldschinken* (Black Forest smoked ham), black on the outside and red inside. The city's favourite titbit, particularly popular for mid-morning second breakfast washed down with beer, is *Weisswurst*, a boiled white sausage flavoured with herbs and spices. Munich is famous for its bread, but even more for its **beers**. The main varieties are *Helles* (normal), *Dunkles* (dark) and the cloudy orange-coloured *Weissbier* made from wheat instead of hops. There are beer halls

DACHAU

The significance of the name will never fade. Dachau has a very attractive old centre, but visitors come to this town north-west of Munich for something else: Dachau was the Nazis' first concentration camp. The camp itself is now a memorial, known as the KZ Gedenkstätte (www.kz-gedenkstaette-dachau.de; closed Mon; free entry). It commemorates the 35,000 inmates, mostly Jews and political prisoners, who died there between 1933 and 1945. The museum has an excellent audiovisual presentation, in English at 1130, 1400 and 1530 (S-Bahn 2 from the rail station to Dachau; then 🚌 726 to the Memorial).

Escaping the city: Munich excursions

There is some particularly fine countryside immediately south-west of Munich, easily accessible by S-Bahn from the city centre. The **Fünf-Seen-Land** (Five Lakes Area) is a firm favourite with locals wanting to escape the city. Two of the lakes, **Ammersee** and **Starnberger See**, are sufficiently close to town that you can easily make a summer evening excursion out to the lake shore. Starnberg (on route S6, 31 mins from the underground platforms at Munich Hauptbahnhof) makes a good first trip, with fine lake-shore promenades, evening boat trips and, if the weather is on your side, superb views south towards the Bavarian Alps. If Starnberg appealed, try **Herrsching** next (48 mins on S8 from Hbf). Much the same appealing mix, slightly less posh and more scope for swimming.

and gardens all over the city; the touristy **Hofbräuhaus**, am Platzl 9, is the most famous. **Augustiner Gaststätten**, Neuhauserstr. 27 (www.augustiner-restaurant.com), is the home of Munich's oldest brewery.

Culture and nightlife

Munich, for all its Bavarian conservatism, rocks after dark, with more than enough noisy beer halls, cool bars and hot sounds. Most of Munich's entertainment venues are on the southern and western sides of the city. For the young and the restless, especially of university age, **Schwabing** is the place to be. And for alternative lifestyles, the place to be is in the **Glockenbachviertel**, around Gärtnerplatz. The exact antithesis of the traditional beer hall scene, which hasn't changed much in the last century, Munich's relatively new and thriving gay and lesbian life centres here. Its lively scene is generally an open one, so gay or straight, you're welcome. This, and the artists and musicians who call this neighbourhood home, make the Glockenbachviertel a centre for nightlife and entertainment.

Events

The one event that towers over all others when it comes to perceptions of Munich is of course the **Oktoberfest**, which actually begins in September. A celebration of beer and communal drinking, there is much going on around the beer tents with fairground rides and costume parades. Another event that takes place throughout the year and that is well worth seeking out is **Fasching**, Munich's carnival, which is celebrated with parties and events throughout the city in the last three days before Shrove Tuesday. In late April the Oktoberfest grounds at the Theresienwiese become the location for the **Spring Festival**, with lots of music and beer. In late June the film world comes to town for the **Munich Film Festival**. The summer months are filled with cultural events throughout the city — check with the tourist office for more information or visit www.muenchen.de.

OSLO

Hemmed in by water, forests and rolling hillsides, this **former Viking capital** is now a pleasant and laid-back modern-looking city. It is not a big place — nor is it as architecturally captivating as the other Scandinavian capitals — but it is definitely worth a stop before venturing out to experience Norway's great outdoors. The city has a number of outstanding art museums — with attractions such as Edvard Munch's *The Scream* — as well as great harbour views from the **Akershus fortress** and a lively nightlife in the central districts of **Grünerløkka** and **Grønland**.

Oslo is connected by ferry to Germany and Denmark, and you can catch trains via Sweden to Denmark and on to the rest of Europe. Oslo is also the starting point for some spectacular train journeys to the Norwegian fjords, mountains and on to the Arctic which are covered in the routes section of this book. You will find Oslo on **Routes 21** (p212), **23** (p222) and **24** (p228).

TRAVEL BASICS

≋ The main rail station is the very central **Oslo Sentralstasjon** (known as Oslo S). All long-distance trains stop here, as well as some local services. This modern construction feels more like an airport than a train station, and it is crammed with facilities of every kind. The NSB (Norwegian State Railways; ☎ 81 50 08 88; www.nsb.no) ticket office opens daily 0700–2300. The **T-bane** (metro) is to the right as you leave the station.

⛴ There are usually **daily sailings** to Germany (Kiel) by **Color Line**, ☎ 81 00 08 11 (www.colorline.no) and to two Danish ports. **DFDS Seaways** sail daily to Copenhagen, ☎ 21 62 13 40 (www.dfdsseaways.no) and **Stena Line** sail to Frederikshavn, ☎ 23 17 91 00 (www.stenaline.no). 🚌 Long-distance buses: these use **Bussterminalen**, Schweigaardsgate 10, ☎ 23 00 24 00, which is easily reached from Oslo S by an enclosed walkway. Information about *Nor-way bussekspress* is given on www.nor-way.no, ☎ 81 54 44 44, or www.lavprisekspressen.no; for general information and bookings, ☎ 67 98 04 80.

✈ **Gardermoen** (50 km north; www.osl.no). This is a stunning example of sleek Scandinavian modern architecture. Airport express trains take 20 mins to Oslo, ☎ 81 50 07 77 (www.flytoget.no); buses take 45 mins but are cheaper. You can also travel north from here direct to Lillehammer and Trondheim (ERT 783 and 785). Ryanair flights go to **Oslo Torp**, which has bus connections with Ryanair flights (booking not necessary); buses leave Oslo's main bus terminal around 3 hrs before flight departure, ☎ 67 98 04 80 (www.torpekspressen.no).

Oslo's centre is relatively small and outlying attractions are easily reachable on the excellent **public transport** system. Get the (free) public transport map, *Sporveiskart Oslo*, from the station or tourist office. Single tickets are valid for 1 hr. Multi-ride tickets include day cards (*dagskort*) and 7-day cards (*ukekort*). Oslo's metro lines converge at Stortinget and Jernbanetorget (T-bane: Oslo S). Most trams converge at Oslo S and most city buses around the corner on Schweigaardsgate (on Vaterland, by Oslo S). Most westbound buses and trams (including those to Bygdøy

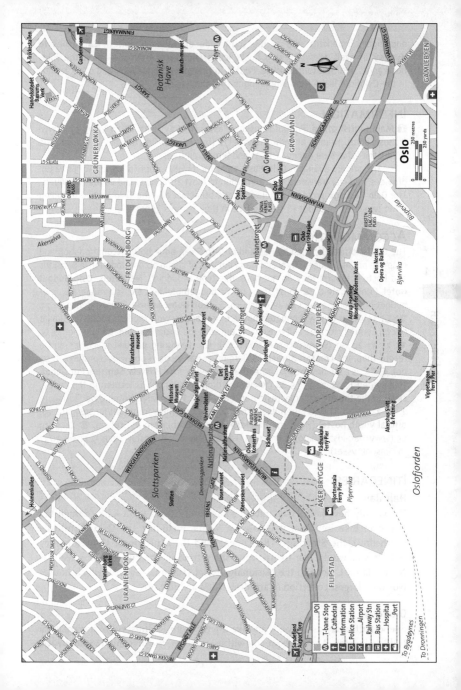

and Vigelandsparken) stop at the south side of Nationaltheatret. ⛴ **Ferries to Bygdøy** as well as sightseeing boats leave (Apr–Sept) from pier 3 on the Rådhusbrygge, near the tourist office. Ferries to Hovedøya, Langøyene and other islands in the Oslofjord leave from Vippetangen (🚌 92/93/94).

INFORMATION

🚹 **Main tourist office**: Fridtjof Nansens Plass 5 (by City Hall), ☎ 81 53 05 55 (www.visitoslo.com). Branch at Jernbanetorget 1 (by Oslo S). Get the latest official *Oslo Guide*, the *What's on* events listings and a map, all free.

The widely available **Oslo Pass**, valid for 24/48/72 hrs (price kr.230/340/430), provides free city transport, free admission to most attractions and various discounts. The **Oslo Package** provides hotel room and breakfast and the Oslo Pass — including up to two children under 16 staying free in their parents' room.

.ACCOMMODATION

The tourist offices by the City Hall and at Oslo S can book hotel accommodation and rooms in private houses. They also hand out lists of cheap accommodation in pensions and hostels, though they do not book this type of lodging. 🏨 **Hotels**: **Oslo Budget Hotel**, Prinsengate 6, ☎ 21 01 40 55 (www.budgethotel.no), €€, is a moderate, low-budget hotel only 200 m away from Oslo S. **Thon Hotel Astoria**, Dronningensgate 21, ☎ 24 14 55 50 (www.thonhotels.no), €€, is classier, with modern rooms at similar prices. Centrally located and reasonably priced is the **Cochs Pensjonat**, Parkveien 25 N, ☎ 23 33 24 00 (www.cochspensjonat.no), €€. Featuring pin-ball machines and a record shop, the **Comfort Xpress**, Møllergata 26, ☎ 22 03 11 00 (www.comfortxpress.no), €–€€, is a hip new budget hotel that opened in 2011. **Hostels**: **Sentrum Pensjonat**, Tollbugaten 8, ☎ 22 33 55 80 (www.sentrumpensjonat.no), is located in the centre, close to the theatre, cinema, restaurants and bars. **Perminalen Hotel**, Øvre Slottsgate 2, ☎ 23 09 30 81 (www.perminalen.no), is only two mins from Karl Johans gate. An official **youth hostel** (HI) is the **Haraldsheim**, Haraldsheimvn 4, Grefsen, ☎ 22 22 29 65 (www.haraldsheim.no), 4 km from Oslo S (T-bane 4/6 'Sinsen', tram 17 or 🚌 31/32 to 'Sinsenkrysset').

ITINERARIES

Half day

If you only have half a day, put on some comfy shoes for a walk through the centre to take in some of Oslo's top sights, including the **Oslo Domkirke** (Cathedral), the **Stortinget** (Parliament) and the **Museum of Contemporary Art**. If you would like to use your short time in the city to get a feel for Norwegian art, head to the **Nasjonalgalleriet** (National Gallery) which houses Norway's largest collection of art, design and architecture.

One day

Spend half a day as above, then take a ferry from Rådhusbrygge (by the City Hall) to Bygdøy. As you alight you will see the *Gjøa*, the first ship to traverse the

THE BEST OF OSLO

Norsk Folkemuseum (Norwegian Folk Museum)
Over 150 buildings make up Europe's largest open-air museum. You will find the museum on the Bygdøy peninsula; take the ferry from pier 3 on Rådhusbrygge, close to the tourist office.

Akershus Castle
This centuries-old fortress is still used for state occasions and contains the Resistance Museum, which gives a startlingly forthright account of the German occupation of Norway.

Kon-Tiki Museum
Thor Heyerdahl mesmerised the world with his balsa-log raft voyages across the Pacific Ocean in 1947. On permanent display are the raft itself, artefacts from that voyage and the papyrus boat, the *Ra II*. The museum is also on the Bygdøy peninsula.

Vikingskipshuset (Viking Ship Museum)
The Viking ships on display — the *Gokstad, Tune* and *Oseberg*, all dating from 800–900 — are the best-preserved in any museum. The Viking Ship Museum is on the Bygdøy peninsula, close to the Folk Museum.

Munch-museet (Munch Museum)
Edvard Munch's body of work is well represented here, along with the works of many other Norwegian artists (T-bane: Tøyen).

Vigeland Park
Located in Frogner Park, this is one of Oslo's most remarkable attractions. The 212 dramatic bronze, granite and iron sculptures of Gustav Vigeland depict his vision of humanity in all its forms. To get there, catch the metro line to Majorstuen, just north of the city centre.

Nasjonalmuseet (National Museum of Art, Architecture and Design)
Only a short walk from Karl Johans gate is one of Norway's largest collections of important pieces of art, design and architecture spread over several places. Be sure to take a stop at the National Gallery, on Universitetsgata 13, in the Edvard Munch Hall to see the world famous *Skrik* (*The Scream*). Closed Mon, free entrance.

North-West Passage in 1903-1906. Just past the *Gjøa* is a large plaza, onto which three major maritime museums face: the **Fram Museum**, the **Kon-Tiki Museum**, and the **Norwegian Maritime Museum**. After exploring at least one of these museums, it is worth the extra 1 km walk to perhaps the best of them all: the **Viking Ship Museum**. If you still have time, you can continue north to the **Norwegian Folk Museum**.

Two days
Take more time over the museums listed above, and then head out to explore the other sights that Oslo has to offer. Definitely worth checking out are the **Munch Museum**, the **Holmenkollen Ski Jump**, **Vigeland Park** and **Gamlebyen**. Oslo

also has many smaller museums dedicated to just about anything you can imagine. Spend at least one evening wining and dining with the locals in **Grünerløkka**.

More

If you have lots of time, you can easily spend several more days taking in what Oslo has to offer. If you feel a need to **get away from the city**, however, you can discover Norway outside Oslo. A great way to get away from it all is the **coastal cruise north** from Bergen. You can go as far north as time and funds allow.

OSLO ON A BUDGET

Although Oslo isn't considered the most expensive city in the world, the cost of living here is definitely on the high side — luckily, there are a whole host of possibilities on offer depending on the weather, ranging from museums to parks to winter sports.

In summer, you can't go wrong with a trip to the park. **Vigeland Park** is one of Norway's most visited attractions, and is filled with more than 200 sculptures by noted artist Gustav Vigeland. The same artist also designed the clever layout of the park: set off exploring the paths and admiring the sculptures, and you'll be entertained for a couple of hours or more.

When snow is lying on the ground, take the bus out to **Akebakken** to watch — or join in with — the thrill-seekers sledding down from Grefsenkollen. Alternatively, it's **free to skate** on one of the many outdoor ice rinks which appear around Oslo during the winter months; the only small cost involved is for skate rental. Most rinks are open every day from December to March.

For those who love cultural attractions the **Astrup Fearnley Museum of Modern Art** is home to an extensive collection of post-war art from Norwegian and international artists. For an historical overview of the city, you can't go wrong with a visit to the **Oslo City Museum**, which is set in the distinguished Frogner Manor. Here, the house and grounds alone would make the trip worthwhile; entry to the museum, which sets out Oslo's history using models, photographs, objects and paintings, is free. Entrance to the exhibitions of the National Museum is also free.

FOOD

Traditional Norwegian food comes mostly from the sea. *Laks* (salmon), whether grilled, smoked or marinated, is very popular, as is *reker* (boiled shrimp), *sild* (herring), and *torsk* (cod). Boiled potatoes and other vegetables are normally served alongside meat or fish.

You can expect to see pickled herring and *brunost* (a sweet brown goat's cheese) on breakfast buffets along with breads and cereals. A favourite Norwegian dessert is *moltebær syltetøy* (cloudberry jam), served warm with ice cream. *Eplekake* (apple cake) with fresh cream is also popular.

Oslo does have its share of excellent restaurants, but they can be pricey. For something a little different, you can try a **reindeer, moose** or **whale steak**. Vegetarians and vegans, admittedly, will find the city a challenge, as most menus are based on fish and meat. At the bottom of the food chain are food wagons and street kiosks, where you can get hot dogs, hamburgers and soft drinks. Next up are the *konditoris*, or bakeries, which sell coffee, fresh pastries and sandwiches. Most have a few tables where you can sit and enjoy your food as you watch the street scene. For more substantial meals, try the *kafeterias*, which serve traditional, simple meals at reasonable prices.

CULTURE AND NIGHTLIFE

Oslo has a well-developed café culture, but also has a number of newer student-style bars and clubs. Many cafés can be found along the stretch between the station and the palace and in the capital's trendy area of **Grünerløkka** to the north-east; hip, atmospheric, lively and doing its best to avoid gentrification. **Grønland** is a grungy area east of the train station with the cheapest beer in town. The **Aker Brygge**, by the harbour, has waterfront bars, but is a bit more touristy and expensive.

Drinking anywhere in Oslo is expensive; alcohol is cheaper from supermarkets, but they can't sell it after 2000 (Sat 1800). Wine and spirits are only sold at special Vinmonopolet shops, e.g. at Oslo S, Jernbanetorget 1. Well-known **operas** are performed at the new opera house, Den Norske Opera & Ballett, Kirsten Flagstads pl 1, while the **Oslo Konserthus**, Munkedamsvn 14, stages folklore events in midsummer. **Movies** are usually shown in their original language.

EVENTS

Some of the highlights of Oslo's annual events calendar include the **World Cup Biathlon** (March), when some of the best athletes in the world gather for this combined skiing and shooting event. 17 May is **Constitution Day**, when the country celebrates with parades and other festivities, whilst mid-June sees bands from Norway and around the world take to the stage at the **Norwegian Wood Rock Festival**.

During the last week of June it is **Oslo Gay and Lesbian Pride Week**, with concerts, exhibitions, and parties taking place all across the city, whilst **midsummer night** on 21 June is the occasion for bonfires and celebrations throughout the country. In November stars gather for the **Oslo International Film Festival**, whilst in December all eyes are on the city for the announcement of the **Nobel Peace Prize Award**. To check out the latest listings, pick a free copy of *Natt & Dag* or *What's on*, both available at tourist offices.

Paris

Paris has always held great allure — it's been a byword for style, glamour and romance since railway tourism began and the British started to go there for weekends in the 19th century. Everyone is familiar with the city through films, photographs and paintings. Café accordion songs celebrate everything from its bridges to its womenfolk. In the 19th century Baron Haussmann transformed the city for Napoleon III, sweeping away many of its crowded slum *quartiers* and replacing them with tree-lined **boulevards** too wide to barricade. Today, these stately avenues of elegantly matching, shuttered buildings and imposing monuments form the framework of much of modern Paris. The city is divided into 20 numbered *arrondissements*, or districts, which spiral from the centre in a clockwise pattern as far as the orbital ring road (Boulevard Périphérique). The **Louvre** area is referred to as the first (1er), the Opera district is the second (2e), and so on. The geometrical layout and long vistas make it fairly easy to get your bearings on the western side of the city. If you stand amid the nonstop whirl of traffic at the **Arc de Triomphe**, you can look right along the ruler-straight Grand Axe, or main axis. To the west looms the huge archway heralding the modern business sector of **La Défense**. In the other direction you look past the obelisk in the Place de la Concorde through the **Jardin des Tuileries**, where old ladies toss crumbs to plump pigeons, to the glass pyramid at the entrance of the Louvre, one of the world's biggest and best art museums.

Paris is now very much a city for young people. Students traditionally hang out in the **Latin Quarter** on the **Left Bank**, so-called because studies at the Sorbonne were originally in Latin. The once seedy area around Bastille has shaken off its revolutionary past to become one of the city's trendiest nightspots with a multitude of bars and restaurants. Older quarters such as **Le Marais** and **Montmartre** remain warrens of picturesque old streets. Parisian night views (from a riverboat, the top of the **Eiffel Tower** or the steps in front of **Sacré-Cœur**) are part of the experience too. In the peak holiday month of August, Parisians desert their city en masse, leaving it strangely quiet.

Paris has multiple rail connections to destinations throughout Europe, and has a number of different train stations to serve them. Check the information below and consult the *European Rail Timetable* to make sure you go to the right one. Rail history buffs might be interested in the fact that the home of one of Paris's most famous museums — **Musée d'Orsay** — is a grand structure that was built as a train station for the World Fair in 1900. You will find Paris on **Routes 1** (p50), **2** (p59), **3** (p66) and **4** (p72) of this book.

TRAVEL BASICS

⇌ There are **seven main rail stations** in Paris, all with tourist information and some with left luggage. Each has its own métro stop; all except Montparnasse and Gare de

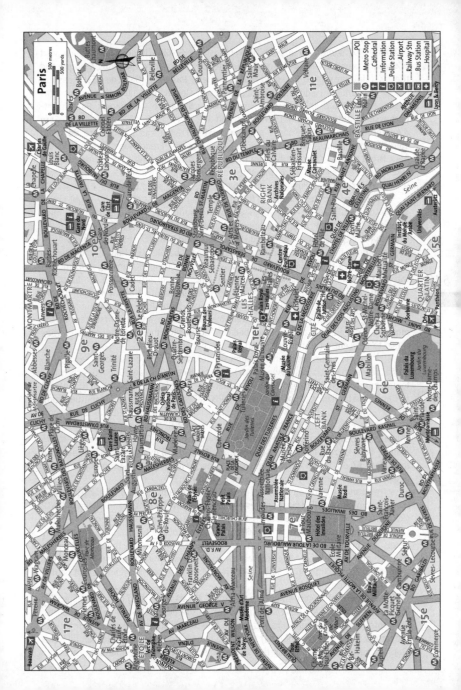

l'Est are also served by express RER trains. For SNCF schedule information visit www.sncf.com. **Paris-Nord** (Gare du Nord): for Belgium, the Netherlands, Cologne and the UK (via Eurostar or Boulogne/Calais ferries). **Paris-Est** (Gare de l'Est): eastern France, Luxembourg and Germany. **Paris-Bercy**: slower regional trains to Dijon (as described in Route 1), Lyon and Nevers. **Gare St-Lazare**: Normandy. **Gare Montparnasse**: Brittany, Versailles, Chartres and TGV services to the south-west. **Gare d'Austerlitz**: Loire Valley, south and south-west France and Spain. **Gare de Lyon**: south-eastern France, the Jura, Auvergne, Provence, the French Alps, Switzerland and Italy. **Night trains** to the south leave from Gare d'Austerlitz and to Italy from Gare de Lyon. Travellers by TGV trains through France may not need to pass through Paris; there's a bypass line calling at Roissy-Charles-de-Gaulle airport.

➤ **Roissy-Charles-de-Gaulle** (CDG) is 27 km north-east of the city: flight times, ☎ 39 50 (from abroad, +33 1 70 36 39 50, premium rate; www.adp.fr); three main terminals, bureaux de change, cashpoints, tourist information and hotel booking desk. Links to the city: RER line B to Gare du Nord and on to Châtelet-Les Halles, 0456–2356, every 10 or 15 mins, taking about 35 mins to/from Châtelet-Les Halles; Roissybus to rue Scribe near L'Opéra 0600–2300 every 15–20 mins, taking 45 mins (15 mins more if the traffic is heavy). Noctilien night bus (same contact information for all public transport: ☎ 32 46, from abroad +33 8 92 69 32 46, premium rate; www.ratp.fr). Night buses 🚌 N140 and N143 to Gare du Nord and on to Gare de l'Est every hour or half-hour 2400–0430, between the last train in the evening and the first train in the morning. From either station you will find connections to other night buses. Fares vary. A taxi to the centre (40 mins to 2 hrs) should cost around €50.

➤ **Orly** is 14 km south; information service, ☎ 39 50 (from abroad, +33 1 70 36 39 50, premium rate, 24 hr; www.adp.fr); two terminals (Sud and Ouest), each with a tourist information booth and bureau de change. Orlyrail (shuttle bus then RER line C) to Gare d'Austerlitz, 0530–2330 every 20 mins, taking 50 mins; Orlyval (shuttle train); ☎ 32 46, premium rate (www.orlyval.com), connecting with RER B at Antony, 0600–2308, every 4–7 mins, taking 8 mins, then RER B, taking 25 mins, fare €10.75. Orlybus (☎ 08 92 68 77 14, premium rate; www.ratp.fr) to Denfert-Rochereau métro station, 0600–2320 (one hour later on Sat, Sun & holidays) every 15–20 mins, taking 30 mins, fare €6.60. If you arrive late, night buses 31/131 going to Gare de Lyon should help, leaving every hour from about 0100 to 0400.

You can see Paris on foot, but it's worth taking advantage of the efficient and well coordinated **public transport** system, made up of the métro and buses of RATP (Régie Autonome des Transport Parisiens) and RER (Réseau Express Régional) trains. Free maps of the networks are available from métro and bus stations (plus many hotels and big stores): the *Petit Plan de Paris* covers the centre; the *Grand Plan de Paris* is more extensive. The impressive **métro system** runs every few minutes 0530–0040 (0530–0140 Fri & Sat). Lines are coded by colour and number and named after their final destination.

RER trains run 0500–0030 (0500–0130 Fri & Sat), consisting of five rail lines (A, B, C, D and E), which are basically express services between the city and the suburbs. They form a cross through Paris and have a few central stops. The numbers following the letters (usually in the suburbs) indicate a branch from the main line. Not all trains stop at every station, so check the sign on the platform before boarding. There are computerised route-finders at the RER stations. These give you alternative ways to reach your destination — on foot, as well as by public transport.

Night buses (Noctilien) run 0030–0530 and have 35 routes throughout the Île-de-France. Good bus routes for seeing the city are 🚌 24/63/67/69. Flagging **taxis** down in the street is rarely successful. Licensed taxis have roof-lights; white indicates that the taxi is free, orange means it is occupied. Fares are determined by three time zones and a host of extras, but they are regulated. Rates increase 1900–0600.

INFORMATION

🛈 **Tourist information** can be found at the **Paris Convention and Visitors Bureau**, ☎ 08 92 68 30 00 (premium-rate number; 24 hr recorded information in English and French); www.parisinfo.com. This covers Paris and the surrounding Île-de-France and offers a booking service for excursions, a France-wide hotel reservation desk, desks for SNCF and Disneyland Paris. The main office is at 25 rue des Pyramides. You can find other offices at Gare de Lyon, Gare du Nord, Gare de l'Est, the Louvre Clemenceau (av. des Champs-Élysées/av. Marigny), Anvers (opposite 72 blvd. Rochechouart), Montmartre (21 pl. du Tertre) and Paris Expo (Porte de Versailles).

Paris Vision, 214 r. de Rivoli, ☎ 01 42 60 30 01, offer recorded commentary multilingual **bus tours** of all the main sights in about two hours. **The Batobus**, ☎ 08 25 05 01 01 (www.batobus.com), is a water-bus (without commentary) every 15–30 mins, 1000–2130 June & Aug, 1000-1900 Sept & Oct, 1030-1630 Nov & Dec. Check the website for other periods. The Batobus stops at the Eiffel Tower, Musée d'Orsay, St-Germain-des-Prés, Notre-Dame, Jardin des Plantes, Hôtel de Ville, the Louvre and Champs-Élysées. You can get a 1/2/5 day ticket, or even a 1 year pass (€14–€60).

ACCOMMODATION

Despite Paris's huge number of tourist beds, finding accommodation can be a problem at busy periods (usually May, June, Sept and Oct). Bureaux d'Accueil at the main tourist office and main-line stations offer a room-finding service for hostels or hotels and there are automated room-finding machines at airports.

🛏 **Hotels**: Cheaper accommodation is getting harder to find anywhere near the city centre, and if you're on a tight budget, you may have to stay a bit further afield, for instance in Bastille or République (11e), Montparnasse (14e) or Montmartre (9e and 18e). There's plenty of cheap accommodation around the Gare du Nord (10e), though it's a somewhat sleazy area. The Quartier Latin (5e) and St-Germain-des-Prés (6e), on the Left Bank, have some delightful medium-priced hotels. The fashionable Marais (3e and 4e) tends to be pricey now, but still has the odd gem here and there, like the **Hôtel du Septième Art**, 20 r. St-Paul, 4e, ☎ 01 44 54 85 00 (www.paris-hotel-7art.com), €€€, with a black-and-white movie theme and a lively bar (métro: Châtelet; Les Halles). Another very central budget option is **Hôtel Tiquetonne**, 6 r. Tiquetonne, 2e, ☎ 01 42 36 94 58, €, near Les Halles (métro: Étienne Marcel).

Out in Clichy, the **Hôtel Eldorado** is a trendy find at 18 r. Dames, 17e, ☎ 01 45 22 35 21 (www.eldoradohotel.fr), €€, métro: Place de Clichy. In Grands Boulevards, the **Hôtel Chopin**, 46 Passage Jouffroy, 9e (entrance 10 blvd. Montmartre), ☎ 01 47 70 58 10 (www.hotelbretonnerie.com), €€, is a friendly place in a glazed 19th-century shopping arcade (métro: (Richelieu Drouot). **Regyn's Montmartre**, 18 pl. Abbesses, 18e, ☎ 01 42 54 45 21 (www.regynsmontmartre.com), €€, is a Montmartre favourite (métro: Abbesses). **The Hôtel Langlois**, 63 r. St-Lazare, 9e, ☎ 01 48 74 78 24 (www.hotel-langlois.com), €€€, is a lovely place full of character and well worth the price-tag (métro: Trinité-d'Estienne d'Orves). The **Hôtel Garden Saint Martin**, 35 r. Yves Toudic, 10e, ☎ 01 42 40 17 72 (www.hotel-parisgardensaintmartin.com), €€, is a modest but charming find in an interesting area of cafés and shops (métro: République). On the Left Bank, the welcoming **Familia Hôtel**, 11 r. des Écoles, 5e ☎ 01 43 54 55 27 (www.hotel-paris-familia.com), €€€, has glimpses of Notre-Dame (métro: Cardinal Lemoine or Jussieu). The **Hôtel de Nesle**, in St-Germain, 7 r. de Nesle, 6e, ☎ 01 43 54 62 41 (www.hoteldenesleparis.com), €€, has a garden and loads of relaxing charm, every room with a different style and furniture (métro: Odéon).

There are lots of **hostels**, both official and independent, in Paris but sadly many have a deserved reputation for standards that do not compare favourably with hostels elsewhere in Europe. That said, there are a couple of good options, including the **St Christopher's Paris**, 68–72 quai de la Seine, ☎ 01 40 34 34 40 (www.stchristophers. co.uk), **Le Village Hostel**, 20 rue d'Orsel, ☎ 01 42 64 22 02 (www.villagehostel.fr), the amusingly-named **Oops Hostel**, 50 avenue des Gobelins, ☎ 01 47 07 47 00 (www. oops-paris.com) and the **Plug-Inn Hostel**, 7 rue Aristide Bruant, ☎ 01 42 58 42 58 (www.plug-inn.fr).

The official **HI youth hostels** are: **Le d'Artagnan**, 80 r. Vitruve, 20e, ☎ 01 40 32 34 56; **Cité des Sciences**, 24 r. des Sept Arpents, le Pré-St-Gervais, 19e, ☎ 01 48 43 24 11; **Jules Ferry**, 8 blvd. Jules Ferry, 11e, ☎ 01 43 57 55 60; **Léo Lagrange**, 107 r. Martre, 92110 Clichy, ☎ 01 41 27 26 90 and **Louvre**, 20 r. Jean-Jacques Rousseau, ☎ 01 53 00 90 90 (website for all official youth hostels is www.fuaj.org). Easily the most central **campsite** is **Camping du Bois de Boulogne**, 2, allée du Bord-de-l'Eau, 16e, ☎ 01 45 24 30 00 (www.campingparis.fr; métro: Porte Maillot). Next to the Seine and very popular, so book well in advance.

ITINERARIES

Half day

If you have only half a day in Paris, taking the Batobus the length of the Seine from the Notre-Dame to the Eiffel Tower or vice versa and visiting each monument at either end will give a compact, visually stunning introduction to Paris.

One day

As well as the Batobus or an hour-long tour on one of the many sightseeing boats, such as the **Bâteaux Parisiens**, you should fit in a half-day tour of either the **Musée du Louvre** or the **Musée d'Orsay**.

Two days

Adding to one of the above itineraries, climb to the top of the Arc de Triomphe for a real perspective of the grand design of Paris, especially the broad boulevards

THE BEST OF PARIS

Tour Eiffel (Eiffel Tower)
The graceful, filigreed metal tower, glowing burnished gold at night, is the symbol of France around the world. Climb the 1,665 steps for spectacular views across the city. (métro: Bir-Hakeim).

Arc de Triomphe
Built to honour Napoleon's victories, this grand, angular arch stands in the centre of 12 avenues, the most famous of which is the Champs-Élysées. Walk along the famous boulevard, or else take the métro to Charles de Gaulle-Étoile.

Notre-Dame
Like a silent sentinel, this magnificent Gothic cathedral on an island in the Seine has witnessed some of France's greatest events.

Montmartre
Many visitors may know Montmartre through the movies, since this, and the adjacent Pigalle, is the famed historic, artistic area of the Moulin Rouge and the picturesque, magical world of Amélie Poulain.

Musée du Louvre
Once home of the kings of France, the 800-year-old Louvre could be called the king of museums, renowned the world over and housing works from ancient civilisations to the mid-1900s. The Louvre is on the banks of the Seine (Right Bank) and has its own métro station. Closed Tue.

Cimetière du Père-Lachaise
Probably the world's most famous cemetery, Père-Lachaise is the final, beautiful resting place of some of France's most illustrious figures from Balzac to Piaf, as well as Oscar Wilde and Jim Morrison (métro: Père-Lachaise).

Quartier Latin (Latin Quarter)
This lively area is the heart of the Left Bank. Once famous for its students and literary legacy, it is now buzzing with cafés and bistros, nightclubs and chic boutiques.

Musée d'Orsay
The former 19th-century train station is now renowned for its collection of Western art from 1848 to 1914. The building is worth a visit in its own right (métro: Solférino); closed Mon.

stretching out like a star. A stroll down the **Champs-Élysées**, with its elegant shops and cafés, is a must. Over on the **Left Bank**, visit a gallery or museum, then have a coffee at one of the famous literary cafés, watching the *beau monde* go by and soaking up the ambience of the Latin Quarter.

More
Explore the *butte* (or hill) of Paris at Montmartre, where Place du Tertre behind the white-domed **Sacré-Cœur** is the quintessential Parisian painters' corner.

Licensed painters sell portraits or depictions of your favourite Parisian scene. From in front of the Sacré-Coeur, the rooftops of Paris stretch out below.

Montmartre, with its climbing cobbled streets, is a great area to have a coffee or a meal. If you have time to explore beyond Paris, you may wish to visit Versailles, the grand château and gardens built for Louis XIV, particularly if you can time your visit for the Grandes Eaux Musicales or the Nocturnes.

EXPLORING PARIS

One of the city's oldest areas, the **Marais** (a marsh drained to make aristocrats' mansions in the 16th century) is an intimate area of speciality boutiques, restaurants and museums.

The district is great for strolling, with its narrow streets, ancient timbered houses, cobbled cloisters, fountains, squares, surprising architectural details including a mosaic-covered building and houses so aged they lean into the street. Many Marais shops, particularly on rue des Francs-Bourgeois, are open on Sunday. To start exploring, take the métro to Saint-Paul.

Whatever you may think of the industrial-chic look, the **Centre Pompidou** (métro: Rambuteau) is France's most important modern art museum, showcasing the world's greatest 20th- and 21st-century artists. You can see great views from its top floor and the **Georges** restaurant. On the first Sunday of the month admission to the exhibitions is free.

Place Beaubourg in front of the Centre Pompidou is an animated gathering place, with musicians and other performers amusing the crowds, so you can enjoy this destination even if you don't wish to art-gaze. Not too far away, **La Cinémathèque Française** is a treasure trove of movie history and includes an exceptional collection of 40,000 films plus a movie-themed library, exhibition halls and four movie theatres showing classic films from all types of cinema year-round.

The **Left Bank** is the Paris of universities and bohemia, of literary cafés, student hang-outs and artists' *ateliers* and galleries. Such historically important buildings as the Sorbonne, the Panthéon, the Eiffel Tower and the Musée d'Orsay are all found here. While the Champs-Élysées is the grand thoroughfare of the Right Bank, **Boulevard Saint-Germain** is the main boulevard of the Left, where boutiques and bistros, cafés and cinemas, street entertainers and *flâneurs* (strollers) all converge. It is also known for its little jazz joints and art galleries on side streets such as rue de Seine, rue des Beaux-Arts and rue Bonaparte.

PARIS ON A BUDGET

In Paris many wonderful experiences are there for the taking. Thanks to a recent law, **national museums and monuments are now free** to residents of EU countries aged 18–25 inclusive. For everyone else, they are free on the first Sunday of every month. These include the Louvre, the Musée d'Orsay and the

MARKETS

Paris's markets are an attraction in themselves, reminiscent of the traditional form of country commerce, where vendors call out their wares to passers-by and goods range from fresh, tempting foodstuffs to books, birds and collectables. **Marché Bio Raspail** is an organic food market on blvd. Raspail between rue du Cherche-Midi and rue de Rennes, 6e (open 0900–1500 Sun, métro: Rennes). At **Marché Couvert Monge**, a covered food market in the Latin Quarter at pl. Monge, 5e, vocal vendors sell a wide range of produce, meat, cheese and delicacies (open 0700–1430 Wed & Fri, 0700–1500 Sun; métro: Place Monge). Past the polyester-clothing stalls and oddball junk, you can find some gems at the **Marché aux Puces de la Porte de Vanves** flea market, such as lace fabrics, antique tables and silverware. Located at av. Georges Lafenestre & av. Marc Sangnier, 14e (open: 0700–1500 or 17.00 Sat & Sun, métro: Porte de Vanves).

Panthéon among many others. Every Wednesday night the Maison Européenne de la Photographie has free entrance.

The permanent collections of all of Paris's municipal museums are also free. One of these, the **Musée Carnavalet** displays the history of Paris from the French Revolution to today. If you are interested in fashion, the **Palais Galliera** displays three centuries of history for free, but check before you go as the fragility of the costumes does not allow the museum to be opened to the public year-round.

Also in the Marais district is the 17th-century **Place des Vosges**. Ruddy-pink brick pavilions form a handsome square that is both a peaceful public space and a collection of art galleries. Nobility and literary figures, such as Victor Hugo, lived here and his house is now a museum. Nearby, the fence along the famous **Jardin du Luxembourg** has become an outdoor photo gallery. Huge photographs, many by news photographers and photojournalists, are exhibited. Each is lit at night, providing an enchanting nocturnal experience. During Paris's long, sultry summers, **free concerts** are held in some 20 parks and gardens and there is often a Latin or African drumbeat to be heard along the quays of central Paris.

The city itself is **a walkable feast**, and perhaps nowhere is this more true than strolling along the Seine.

FOOD

Paris is still a great place to eat, with many fabulous restaurants, both French and exotic, at relatively cheap prices. Cafés and bars are the cheapest, *brasseries* slightly more expensive. The closer to the bar you stand, the less you pay. Self-service restaurants are usually fine, if a little institutional, and a snack at a *crêperie* will keep hunger at bay.

Set lunches tend to be much better value than the evening equivalents. A trip to a *boulangerie* or market and an hour's picnic in the **Tuileries gardens** make a lovely way to lunch. Try the organic produce market, blvd. Raspail, on Sun morning (métro: Rennes). Alternatively, treat yourself to tea and a pâtisserie at one of the *salons de thé*.

For evening meals, study the set menus outside most restaurants; these often provide a reasonable choice at affordable prices. The **Bastille** area, the **Latin Quarter, Marais, Montmartre** and **Montparnasse** are good areas for cheap eating and multi-ethnic cuisine, especially Greek, North African, East European and Vietnamese. Vegetarian food is now much easier to find in Paris with bio (organic) cafés, soup shops and veggie restaurants springing up all over the city. The weekly listings magazine, *Pariscope*, provides a guide to Paris restaurants.

CULTURE AND NIGHTLIFE

From all-night discos to cosy wine bars and what some euphemistically call 'naughty Paris', the city truly has something for every nightlife temperament. To **find out what's on** during your stay, see the English-language www.parisnightlife.fr.

The long summer nights give Parisians several more hours of daylight after their work day, when they can dine or drink at outdoor restaurants and bars. **Free summer concerts** fill the parks and gardens from May to September, while festivals and music *fêtes* fill the streets and bars with a lively, late-night atmosphere during the warmer months.

Jazz lovers head for the numerous clubs on rue des Lombards near Les Halles and the famous Caveau de la Huchette on the street of the same name in the Saint-Michel district. Paris has some 100 **dance clubs**, so there's something for

MULTICULTURAL PARIS

In the last 50 years or so, immigrants from France's former colonies in Algeria, Morocco and West Africa, as well as those from China, the Caribbean and Eastern Europe, have made Paris their home. This infusion of cultures has brought with it a whole new selection of intriguing museums and galleries, shops selling goods from around the world, and a fine collection of restaurants serving foreign cuisine.

Some *quartiers* have a varied mix: in the culturally diverse **Belleville** area in the north, there are Thai and Vietnamese restaurants, Turkish cafés, Arab grocery stores and kosher butchers. **Ménilmontant**, east of République, is a neighbourhood of couscous and tagine restaurants competing with those serving Senegalese cuisine. Generally, though, individual ethnic groups have settled in well-defined areas such as the predominantly North African Goutte d'Or in the 18e *arrondissement* and the Cambodian, Vietnamese, Laotian and Chinese sections of the 13e. The main Jewish community is based around Rue des Rosiers in the Marais, with its delicatessens and restaurants. The area around the **Barbès-Rochechouart** métro station is a West African and West Indian neighbourhood, and a great place to buy dazzling dresses or browse in food markets selling tropical produce and exotic spices.

VERSAILLES

Versailles was the pride and joy of Louis XIV (RER line C5 to Versailles-Rive Gauche, then walk through the town), the long-reigning 'Sun King' who in 1668 transformed his father's hunting lodge in to this stupendous palace (www.chateauversailles.fr).

Most famous of all are the dazzling **Galerie des Glaces** (Hall of Mirrors) and the **Petit Trianon** and **Grand Trianon** — two elegant pavilions built for the king's mistresses — where the doomed Marie-Antoinette used to play at peasant life before the Revolution. Crowded at the height of summer, but the huge grounds, with their statuary, topiary and water parterres, are always rewarding. Gardens open daily, châteaux open daily except Mon, 0900–1830, Nov to Mar 0900–1730.

every music taste, from rock, hip-hop and techno to African rhythms, salsa and samba. Those who like to party all night long should ask bartenders or party-hearty Parisians where the 'after' bars, often unadvertised, are. Many are in the lively Pigalle area of Montmartre. In a country synonymous with fine wine, **wine bars** or quiet places to *boire un verre* (have a drink) are plentiful and varied.

The major museums have at least one late-night opening for culture vultures, while the **Opéra National de Paris** stages the best of opera and ballet performances at its sumptuous Palais Garnier and its modern **Opéra Bastille** is known for its daring productions.

Scantily-clad cancan girls in **cabaret-type performances** strut their stuff in le Lido, le Moulin Rouge and le Crazy Horse, among others.

EVENTS

There is always something going on in Paris, more than even a resident could ever hope to attend. For the latest information on events, see www.parisinfo.com.

From mid-June to mid-July a massive screen is set up in the Parc de la Villette for **Le Cinéma en Plein Air**, where you can settle in a deckchair and watch evening shows of classic films for free. The best jazz sounds are played from the end of July at the Paris Jazz Festival, whilst on 14 July the country comes to a standstill for **Bastille Day**, France's national holiday.

From mid-July to early August the **Quartier d'Été Festival** (Summer Festival) takes place, with music, movies and other happenings throughout the city. On Saturday evenings during the summer, sound-and-light shows fill the evening sky during **Nocturnes** in Versailles. Normally off-limits buildings such as the Palais de l'Élysée, the President's residence, are opened to the public for the third weekend in September for the annual **Journées du Patrimoine**. The **Festival d'Automne à Paris** (Paris Autumn Festival) celebrates autumnal events from mid-September to the end of December, whilst in October the **Nuit Blanche** gives you the chance to visit the normally hidden side of nocturnal Paris, revealed through performances, monument visits and installations.

Prague (Praha)

Even in the '70s and early '80s, a steady stream of travellers of all ages were making for Prague from the West. Before the **Iron Curtain** wavered in 1989, Prague was for many Westerners the only glimpse they'd had of life in 'the other Europe'. Two decades later and the stream of travellers has become a flood. During the spring and summer months, Prague is packed. Yet, for all the crowds, the Czech capital has a very special appeal.

You'll find architectural styles galore, everything from Gothic to cubist, on both sides of the **Vltava River**, which languidly loops through town. Plenty of parks, a pulsing nightlife and a galaxy of classical music offerings all add to Prague's heady mix. Prague locals have bittersweet feelings about the tourist crowds. Rowdy and inebriated Brits have done nothing to smooth ruffled feathers. And watch your pockets. Robbery in some parts of the city centre is all too common. That said, Prague, be it in spring sunshine or in the bitter cold of snowy winter, remains one of Europe's most engaging capital cities.

Prague has good connections to the neighbouring countries of the Czech Republic — Germany, Poland, Austria and Slovakia — as well as to countries and cities beyond. Bavaria-Prague-Kraków and Berlin-Prague-Budapest have long been extremely popular routes for the interrail/backpacking crowd, which can be found in this book on **Routes 47** (p385) and **48** (p394) respectively.

TRAVEL BASICS

🚃 **Praha Hlavní Nádraží** (Prague Main Station) is on Wilsonova, not far from the top end of Wenceslas Square. To reach the centre of town, either hop one stop (direction Háje) on the metro, which you will find clearly signed at basement level within the station concourse, to Muzeum or turn left out of the main station entrance, passing through the park. Both routes will take you to the top of Wenceslas Square in about five minutes although the park route is unsafe outside daylight hours.

Some long-distance and international services also use **Nádraží Praha-Holešovice**, Partyzanska, in Prague 7 (a little way out). From here take the metro, a few metres from the railway station, for four stops to Muzeum (direction Háje). Until 2010, some trains only served Holešovice, but this inconvenience is now a thing of the past. Both stations are on metro line C and have exchange bureaux, left luggage and accommodation services. Rail information service, ☎ 840 112 113 (24 hrs).

🚌 **Central Bus Station** (long-distance services) is at Křižíkova 6 at metro Florenc. Take metro line C two stops to Muzeum (direction Háje) or metro line B two stops to Můstek (direction Zličín) to reach the centre of town. ✈ **Ruzyně Airport** is 20 km north-west of the city centre (flight enquiries, ☎ 220 113 321; www.prg.aero). The Airport Express runs every 30 mins (0535–2205) to and from Praha Hlavní Nádraží railway station. Cedaz's excellent minibus service (☎ 221 111 111, www.cedaz.cz) runs every 30 mins (0730–1900) and to and from Náměstí Republiky, but costs more.

Prague's efficient, fast and clean public transport system is a good choice if you need to speed across town. With three metro lines, more than twenty tram routes and

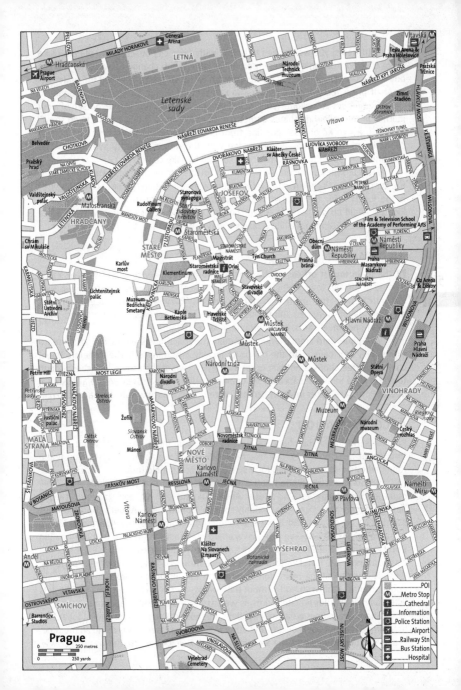

nine night trams, you won't need to bother with inner-city buses. If you plan to use a lot of transport or can't be bothered fiddling about with change and tickets, you can buy a 1/3-day pass for 110 Kč/310 Kč. Children under six travel free, and the under-15s pay half-price. You will need to buy a 16 Kč ticket for a large backpack or luggage.

Remember to validate your ticket by stamping it once at the outset of your journey in the yellow machines at metro entrances and on trams. Failure to do so will earn you a 950 Kč on-the-spot fine from one of the many transport controllers. A controller must show you a gold badge with the metro authority symbol on it as identification (some tourists have been conned by fake controllers).

Muzeum metro station is the junction for the green and red metro lines and is the centre of the Prague metro system. Florenc metro station (pronounced 'Florence') is the junction for the yellow and red lines, and is where the main bus station is located. Avoid taxis if possible – overcharging of foreigners is endemic. Always agree a fare before getting in. Calling a taxi is always cheaper than hailing on the street.

INFORMATION

🛈 The **main tourist offices** of the **Prague Information Service** (PIS) (www.pis.cz) is located in the Old Town Hall (Staroměstská radnice), Staroměstské náměstí 1 as well as branches at the main rail station and at Ruzyně Airport. Free brochures, accommodation services, information about cultural events, tickets, tours, trips, transport and travel cards. For information: ☎ 221 714 444.

A **Prague Card** from Prague Information Service gives admission to some 50 sights over four days, with the option to include city transport. The **Bohemia Bagel** chain of coffee shops is not just great for bagels. Two of their three branches around town (in Malá Strana at Lázeňská 19, open 0730–1900, and in Staré Město at Mazná 1, open 0800–2300) offer **internet access** (more details on www.bohemiabagel.cz).

ACCOMMODATION

Prague is no longer as cheap as it once was, but there are good-value options throughout the city. The Prague Information Service (see above) can help you find a room, whether you are looking for a swish hotel or a simple room in a *penzion*.

🛏 Some recommended hotels that might be worth trying include the small, quiet and perfectly located **Hotel Antik**, Dlouhá 22, ☎ 222 322 288 (www.hotelantik.cz), €€. Other reasonably priced options are **Anděl's Hotel**, Stroupežnického 21, ☎ 296 889 688 (www.andelshotel.com), €€, the **Aparthotel City 5**, Vltavská 667/11 ☎ 602 495 529 (www.aparthotelprague.com), €€, and the floating **Botel Admiral**, Hořejší nábř. 57, ☎ 257 321 302 (www.admiral-botel.cz), €€–€€€. The classic art nouveau **Hotel Paříž**, ul. Obecního domu 1, ☎ 195 195 (www.hotel-pariz.cz), €€€, is close to all the main sights and worth the financial splurge. For good-value double rooms, both with and without bathrooms, do not forget to check the hostels listed below: all offer private rooms as well as the more traditional dorms.

There are some great independent **hostels** in Prague, and the standard of accommodation for backpackers and other like-minded travellers is rising all the time. Especially recommended is the **Sir Toby's Hostel**, Delnicka 24, ☎ 246 032 610 (www.

THE BEST OF PRAGUE

Václavské náměstí (Wenceslas Square)
The Czech Champs-Élysées and the biggest and busiest shopping plaza in Prague, as well as being the focal point for political rallies, protests and parades, such as the unrest in 1968/1969 and the Velvet Revolution of 1989. Take the metro to Muzeum and then walk down the length of the square towards the Old Town.

Pražský hrad (Prague Castle)
Possibly the largest ancient castle complex in the world, boasting a magnificently elevated cliff-top position, and crammed with artistic and architectural treasures. Cross the Charles Bridge from the Old Town and walk up through the narrow, picturesque streets.

Karlův most (Charles Bridge)
A vibrant place day or night, bustling with vendors, entertainers, locals and tourists. Get up early if you want to take photographs that do not include hoards of tourists.

Petřín Hill and funicular
A 318 m hill covered in eight parks and topped with a 62 m copy of the Eiffel Tower. It offers fabulous views of Prague and the surrounding area. Trams 6/9/12/20/22 will get you to the start of the funicular at Újezd.

Josefov (Jewish Quarter)
A spot for quiet reflection among some beautiful historic buildings. From the Old Town square walk north to the winding side streets around Maiselova ul.

Staroměstské náměstí (Old Town Square)
Studded with cafés and inimitable baroque, Gothic and Romanesque architecture, including the Old Town Hall and its exquisite 14th-century Astronomical Clock, St Nicholas Church and the Jan Hus Monument.

Národní muzeum (National Museum)
A bastion of Czech history and prehistory at the south end of Wenceslas Square. Take the metro to Muzeum, or a short 5-min walk from the main train station.

sirtobys.com), a little out of the centre but a wonderfully cosy and friendly place. Other great hostels in Prague include **Miss Sophie's**, Melounova 3, ☎ 296 303 530 (www.miss-sophies.com) and the trendy and cutting-edge **Czech Inn**, Francouzská 76, ☎ 267 267 600 (www.czech-inn.com). Two further excellent choices are the **Mosaic House**, Odborů 278/4, ☎ 246 008 324 (www.mosiachouse.com), and the **Adam&Eva Hostel**, Zborovská 497/50, ☎ 732 666 423 (www.adamevahostel.com).

ITINERARIES
Half day
If you have only a few hours to spare, then concentrate on **Hradčany** (the Castle District) and **Malá Strana** (the Lesser Quarter). Visit the Gothic Chrám sv. Vita (St Vitus Cathedral) and Kostel sv. Jiří (St George's Basilica), and pass the

Lilliputian houses of Zlatá ulička (Golden Lane). Then descend into Malá Strana, where you'll find ancient burgher houses and the baroque, copper-domed Kostel sv. Mikuláše (St Nicholas Church).

Making your way across **Karlův most** (Charles Bridge) can take as little or as much time as you like; if you enjoy souvenir stands, performers, artists, musicians, or just beautiful city views, you may like to linger a while.

One day

After a morning in the Hradčany and Malá Strana areas, make your way from Karlův most (Charles Bridge) on the time- and tourist-worn cobblestones to the oldest part of Prague, the aptly named **Staré Město** (Old Town). At its centre is the fabulous Staroměstské náměstí (Old Town Square), home to some of Prague's most famous and beautiful monuments, such as the colourful **Orloj** (Astronomical Clock) and **Týn Church**.

From there, work your way up Celetná ulice towards the Prašná brána (Powder Tower) and the Obecní dům (Municipal House), and from there, walk southwest along Na příkopě to the tourist mecca that is **Václavské náměstí** (Wenceslas Square).

Two days

With a bit more time, you'll be able to do everything listed above in more depth, plus spend half a day in **Josefov** (Jewish Quarter), with its own pensive and reverent atmosphere.

Then visit a gallery or a museum, and maybe take in an evening concert. To keep your energy levels up, sample some wonderfully heavy **Czech cuisine** from one of the local restaurants.

More

Lucky you! Prague is more than just a sightseer's dream; it is a place to be savoured. With more than a few days here, you can get in all of the above sights at a leisurely pace, chill out at some funky cafés or clubs, and take a day trip to **Karlštejn** or **Terezín**.

PRAGUE ON A BUDGET

Prague is a great destination for budget travellers, as the whole city is an open-air museum, accessible 365 days a year, with free admission. If you enjoy **people-watching**, the Jan Hus Monument, in the middle of the Old Town Square, provides the perfect perch to watch the throngs of tourists. You may even catch some enlightening tour commentary in English from one of the passing groups.

An even livelier vantage point is **Karlův most** (Charles Bridge). Here you can hear amusing conversational snippets, cunning pick-up and convincing hard-sell lines, all set to the sound of street musicians and performers. For a bit of loose change, you can stay and watch for as long as you like. Some beautiful, central spots in Prague are made for rest and relaxation. The gardens leading up to **Petřín Hill**, the largest of Prague's parks, are magical on a hot summer's day and are frequented by frisbee throwers, lovers and only a smattering of tourists. The view from here is enchantingly spire-filled and the clamour of the city is far away.

Prague's **hidden churches and cloisters** are often used for musical concerts and, therefore, rehearsals. Slip in through the side door, pay your respects, and, if possible, stay for the angelic acoustics.

For museum goers, the **Národní muzeum** (National Museum) offers visitors free admission from 1400–1800 on the first Tuesday of the month. When you pick up the *The Prague Post*, check for any gallery exhibition openings.

There is free wi-fi access in many cafés and pubs in the centre of town, though owners do expect you to buy at least something small to eat or drink while surfing the internet.

Food

There are three main categories of eating house: *restaurace* (restaurant), *vinárna* (wine bar/restaurant) and *pivnice* (pub). The Old Town, Malá Strana and Castle District are all groaning with places to eat of all shapes and sizes, but bear in mind that, the nearer the major sights, the higher the price, but not necessarily the quality.

It is well worth wandering fractionally off the beaten track to find cheaper grub in more plentiful portions, washed down with a range of beers and spirits — restaurants with menus only in Czech are normally a safe bet, and it can make ordering great fun!

Prague 3 Žižkov district, for example, is blessed with the city's largest collection of authentic **pubs**. In addition to Czech and international dishes, Italian cuisine is becoming popular here and almost every street in the centre boasts its pizzeria. Wenceslas Square is the home of fast-food joints, both home-grown and household names, as well as booths offering grilled sausage, roast chicken and sandwiches.

Culture and nightlife

There are clubs all over Prague, but each area has its own distinctive style. For an upmarket tipple, try the **Malá Strana** area, where jazz and cocktails successfully mix with the lamplight and smoky alleyways. For a more eclectic mix of performance art while nuzzling your neighbour and guzzling beer, try **Josefov** and the **Old Town**.

The glittery club scene is most attractive in the New Town. For a night you won't remember, the **Žižkov** and **Vinohrady** areas have a great mix of places, ranging from grungy local hang-outs to sleekly designed gay and lesbian bars that

ŽIŽKOV TV TOWER

Rising like a futuristic spaceship above the working-class quarter of Žižkov, this is one of Prague's most interesting, if controversial, buildings. At 216 m, the TV tower is the tallest building in the city, and they say that on a clear day you can see it from a full 100 km away. Often regarded as a relic of the communist era, the tower was actually completed after the Velvet Revolution in 1992. The restaurant closed in 2010, but visitors can still take the lift up to the viewing tower. Artist David Černý's black, computer-inspired babies climbing up the side of the tower lend a bit of whimsy to the structure. On ground level, check out the beautifully haunting Jewish cemetery. Information: ☎ 420 242 418 784, www.tower.cz, Open: 1000–2330 (metro: Jiřího z Poděbrad). Admission charge.

stay open late and don't charge steep entry prices. Along with the dedicated concert halls, Prague's many churches and baroque palaces also serve as **performance venues**, staging choral performances, organ recitals, and concerts by string quartets, brass ensembles and, occasionally, full orchestras. You can get details of these concerts from PIS (Prague Information Service) offices. If you go to a concert in a church, remember to take an extra layer of clothing, even on a hot summer day.

As soon as you hit town, buy the English-language weekly, *The Prague Post*, at any newspaper stand, sit down at a café and make your plan of attack (www.praguepost.com). Its *Night & Day* section is thick with cultural offerings.

EVENTS

There are plenty of events taking place throughout the year in Prague, and what follows is just a selection. Check out www.prague.tv for gigs, festivals and other events.

In March, the **One World International Film Festival** showcases films from around the world and is one of Europe's leading human rights festivals. Later in the month, the **Febiofest** is an audiovisual showcase of over 600 movies by independent film-makers from around the world.

In May and June the **Prague Spring Music Festival** serves up music and dance performances at venues throughout the city, whilst the **Khamoro** (also in May) is a festival of gypsy culture, with performers from communities throughout central and eastern Europe taking part.

Prague is famous for its puppet shows, and the **World Festival of Puppet Art** in late May and early June has performances from marionettes and their masters that makes for one of Prague's most wonderfully creepy events. The **anniversary of the Velvet Revolution** is celebrated on 17 November each year, whilst later in the month the smooth sound of jazz can be heard in bars and venues across Prague, as the **International Jazz Festival** comes to town.

Rome (Roma)

The Romans have an inbuilt resistance to schedules and short lunch breaks. Life is too Latin for a Protestant work ethic. Indeed, they have no qualms about playing the tourist in their own city, from eating ice creams on **Piazza Navona** to tossing a coin in the **Trevi Fountain**, visiting the **Vatican museums** on a Vespa, lolling around the Villa Borghese Gardens, or peeking into the Pantheon while on a café crawl. In Italy's most bewildering but beguiling city, it has somehow never made more sense to 'do as the Romans do'.

The **Eternal City**, dominated by its seven hills (Aventine, Capitoline, Celian, Esquiline, Palatine, Quirinal and Viminal), is cut by the fast-flowing River Tiber. Don't expect Rome's legendary 'seven hills' to stand out as landmarks: they are too gentle, and merge into one another. Instead, treat the **Colosseum** and the **Forum** as the city centre, set on the east bank of the Tiber, with the Pantheon just north, and the chic **Spanish Steps** beyond. On the west bank of the Tiber lies bohemian **Trastevere**, a great restaurant and nightlife centre, with the mausoleum-fortress of **Castel Sant'Angelo** further north, and the **Vatican City** to the west. If this sounds exhausting (and it is), **Villa Borghese** is Rome's green heart, but with baroque fountains and galleries attached — you'll find there's no escape from several millennia of art and architecture in a city that spawned a civilisation. Rome is on **Routes 36** (p304) and **37** (p312) of this book.

TRAVEL BASICS

≥ There are four main railway stations. **Termini**, Pza dei Cinquecento, is Rome's largest, handling all the main national and international lines; bureaux de change, tourist and hotel information; well served by taxis, buses and night buses, and at the hub of the metro system. **Tiburtina**, Pza della Stazione Tiburtina, serves some long-distance north–south trains. Services to Bracciano (1 hr 9 mins) and Viterbo (1 hr 50 mins) depart from **Ostiense**. **Porta San Paolo** serves the seaside resort of Lido di Ostia (45 mins).

✈ **Leonardo da Vinci** (Fiumicino) is 36 km south-west of Rome, ☎ 06 65 951 (www.adr.it). Taxis into the centre are hassle-free, but expensive. Much cheaper (€8) is the 45-min train service, every 15 mins (every 30 mins late evenings, Sundays and holidays), to Tiburtina and Ostiense stations. Trenitalia runs an express rail link taking 30 mins to Termini (0636-2336), €14; **Aeroporto Ciampino** (same phone number and website as Fiumicino) is just 16 km south-east of Rome with frequent rail services to Termini station.

Luckily, the *centro storico* (historic centre) is fairly compact, traffic-free and easy to see on foot. However, many of the most important sights lie outside this area so you will need to use the **public transport system**. To save time and money, buy a 1 day pass, called a BIG ticket (€4), a 3 day BTI pass (€11) or a 1 week Carta Settimanale (€16). These are valid for all forms of transport (bus, metro and tram) in Rome. Individual combined bus/metro tickets, called BIT (*biglietto integrato a tempo*, €1), are valid for 75 mins. Tickets can be bought at newsstands and tobacconists or at railway

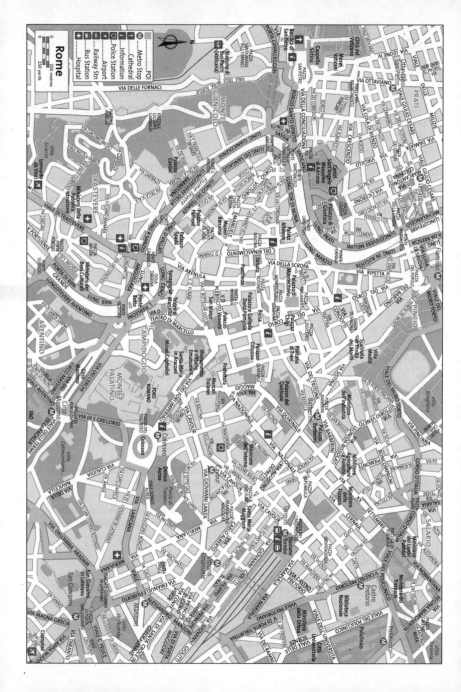

and underground stations and bus termini. Validate (time-stamp) the ticket in the machine as you enter the bus (or risk a fine). The BIG ticket needs to be validated once only.

INFORMATION

🄳 The **main tourist office** is run by the APT (Rome provincial Tourist Board) and can be found at Via XX Settembre 26, ☎ 06 421 381 (www.aptprovroma.it), metro: Repubblica. There are also a number of tourist information points throughout the city: at both airports, at Termini station and on Via Nazionale near Palazzo delle Esposizioni (see also http://en.turismoroma.it).

The **Roma Pass** (www.romapass.it) is valid for three days and includes free admission to two museums plus discounts on others, theatre events and exhibitions, and free transport on city buses, metro lines and some trains (€25).

ACCOMMODATION

Hotels range from the opulent — mainly located close to the Spanish Steps and the Via Veneto — to the basic, largely clustered around the Via Nazionale and Termini station. Central, reasonably-priced hotels get booked quickly so reserve ahead.

Hotels: Close to Termini Station, the **Aphrodite**, Via Marsala 90, ☎ 06 491 096 (www.aphroditehotelrome.com), €€, is not only comfortable, but boasts its own roof terrace. The **Arenula**, Via S Maris de'Calderari 47, ☎ 06 687 9454 (www.hotelarenula.com), €€, is set in a charming 19th-century building, whilst the **Cervia**, Via Palestro 55, ☎ 06 491 057 (www.hotelcerviaroma.com), €–€€, is a great-value pension in the heart of the city. Also conveniently situated is the **Gerber**, Via degli Scipioni 241, ☎ 06 321 6485 (www.hotelgerber.it), €€, or for those looking to splash out, the **Isa**, Via Cicerone 39, ☎ 06 321 2610 (www.hotelisa.net), €€€, is a boutique hotel close to the Spanish Steps.

Hostels: The two **Alessandro Hostels** are extremely well regarded. The Alessandro Palace Hostel is at Via Vicenza 42, ☎ 06 446 1958 (www.hostelalessandropalace.com), whilst the Alessandro Downtown Hostel can be found on Via C Cattaneo 23, ☎ 06 443 40147 (www.hostelsalessandro.com). Other hostel options include the **Funny Palace Hostel**, Via Varese 33, ☎ 06 447 03523 (www.funnyhostel.com), the **Mosaic Hostel**, Via Cernaia 39b, ☎ 06 9893 7179 (www.hostelmosaic.com) and the **Ciak Hostel**, Viale Manzoni 55, ☎ 06 7707 6703 (www.ciakhostel.com). The official youth hostel (HI) is the **Ostello Foro Italico AF Pessina**, Viale delle Olimpiadi 61, ☎ 06 323 6267 (www.ostellodiroma.it).

ITINERARIES

Half day

Head to the **Roman Forum** to get a sense of what life was like during the Roman Republic. This was home to political and religious institutions, shops and markets, and remained the most important area until the republic became an empire in 50 BC and Julius Caesar built the Imperial Fora nearby.

THE BEST OF ROME

Piazza Navona
Rome's most famous square is also its vibrantly beating heart in the middle of the *centro storico* (historic centre).

Roman Forum (Foro Romano)
The centre of Ancient Rome and thus the one-time centre of the world.

Capitoline Hill
The political hub of the Roman Empire.

Pantheon
A magnificent feat of architecture.

Vittorio Emanuele Monument
This awe-inspiring building gives panoramic views of the city from the Piazza Venezia.

The Colosseum (Colosseo)
The largest amphitheatre in the Roman Empire witnessed many a gladiatorial epic.

Trevi Fountain (Fontana di Trevi)
Magnificent baroque fountain of iconic significance. Located on Trevi Square, not far from the Spanish Steps, another city landmark with an intriguing history (see box p560).

Sistine Chapel (Cappella Sistina)
Priceless artwork made glorious by the genius of Michelangelo.

One day

Continue the ancient Rome itinerary with the **Palatine Hill** and the **Colosseum**. At the bottom of the hill, turn right at the Arch of Titus to get to the main entrance of the Colosseum. Clinging to the side of the hill are the ruins of the **Baths of Septimius Severus**. One of the crown jewels in Rome's ancient monuments is the Colosseum. Awe-inspiring, it needs little historical knowledge to explain its function. Imagine the clanging of the gladiators, cries of the Christians and the roar of the crowds. After each battle or sacrifice, sand was thrown on the arena floor to soak up the blood. To avoid the crowds visit in the early morning or late afternoon.

Two days

Walk behind the **Pantheon** to **Piazza della Minerva** and you will find Bernini's diminutive and whimsical *Elephant* statue. In front of you is the grand facade of **Santa Maria sopra Minerva**, the only Gothic church in Rome, built in the late 13th century over the ruins of a temple to Minerva. The **Fontana di Trevi** (Trevi Fountain) and the **Spanish Steps** have been drawing tourists since the 18th century when Rome was on the itinerary of the Grand Tour. A good place to find some shade on a sweltering summer day is the **Villa Borghese**, a series of parks to the north that form the core of Rome's largest central open space. Made up of the grounds of the 17th-century *palazzo* of Cardinal Scipione Borghese, it's a huge area, with a boating lake, a zoo and three of the city's finest museums. The **Piazza Navona** is crowded day and night with tourists, street musicians, buskers and artists. Hang out at the fountains or pricey cafés with those who want to see and be seen.

More

Allow several days to explore the **Vatican**; Castel Sant'Angelo, St Peter's Basilica, the gardens, galleries and museums all make up the richest but most exhausting museum complex in the world. The **Sistine Chapel**, a barn-like structure built between 1473 and 1481 for Pope Sixtus IV, is the Pope's private chapel. The ceiling and wall murals here are regarded by many as the greatest masterpieces in Western art executed by one man, Michelangelo.

ROME ON A BUDGET

Rome can be as expensive or inexpensive as you want it to be. In fact the cheapest and most enjoyable pastime in Rome is simply **walking** around the city's piazzas, parks, outdoor artwork, monuments, fountains, ancient architecture and colourful gardens. Many **churches**, particularly those located in out-of-the-way neighbourhoods, are free, offering a splendid chance to see beautiful interiors and liturgical artwork.

From June to September there are **free performances** of music, dance and opera at many of the city's open parks and squares. Something new that's catching on well at wine shops are *degustazioni* (wine tastings), which offer a chance to sample new, interesting vintages, often at no cost. At the cocktail hour, bistros and cafés put out tempting food samplings, so dust off your backpacks, change your clothes and join the foray — for the price of a drink you can dine well.

Festas (festivals) are a Roman way of life, bringing a huge number of free events to enjoy: music, parades, live theatre, fireworks and food. In **mid-August** everything shuts down for two weeks to celebrate *Ferragosto* (the Feast of the Assumption). The entire city is rife with celebrations, parades, hot-air balloon rides and music jam sessions, to name just a few events. Streets are clogged with food kiosks where you can eat free, or very inexpensively, on wonderful specialities such as *calamari* (squid), fresh pasta dishes, cheeses, *gelato* (ice cream) and pastries.

Or, when in Rome do as the Romans do and simply **people-watch** from an outdoor café or the steps of an ancient church.

FOOD

Italians as a whole are in love with food, so it comes as no surprise that the capital also places cuisine very high on its agenda. In even the most modest of establishments, your food is likely to be the **freshest** that is available that day — Italians hold little sway with frozen meat or vegetables. Their insistence on quality is also shown by the amount of time they like to spend savouring the produce — even busy Romans will take hours out of their day to spend them eating and socialising over lunch or dinner.

The typical **Italian meal** starts with *antipasti*, which are tapas-style bite-size variations of cold cuts, seafood and vegetables. Next, *Il Primo* (first course) is usually a soup or pasta dish, followed by *Il Secondo* (second course), consisting of meat or fish. Italians rarely eat pasta as a main course, so portions are smaller than you would find in Italian restaurants at home. Vegetables (*contorni*) are ordered separately, so don't assume your main course will come with an accompaniment unless you order them. The meal usually ends with *frutta* (fresh fruit) and a selection of *dolci* (sweet desserts), followed by coffee and a *digestivo*. Five courses may seem like a lot, but remember that portion sizes reflect this, and no one will frown on you if you order less, as many now do.

One **speciality** in Rome that may not appeal to all tastes is the use of animal offal — the *quinto quarto*, or 'fifth quarter' parts of a beast that are left over after the prime cuts of meat are sold off. That means *cervello* (brains), *nervetti* (beef tendons), *coda* (oxtail), *pajata* (baby veal intestines) and *animelle* (the thymus glands in an animal's throat) can often be seen on menus. *Trattorie* in the neighbourhoods of Testaccio and Trastevere are known for these delicacies.

CULTURE AND NIGHTLIFE

Everything you've ever thought about Italian style and posing becomes apparent when you walk through the door of Rome's more popular clubs. If you want cheaper prices and less fashion pressure, however, head for the smaller venues —

THE SPANISH STEPS

These beautiful broad, tiered steps and the adjoining Piazza di Spagna get their name from the Spanish Embassy that used to have its headquarters here. The steps were constructed in 1725 by Francesco de Sanctis as a means of reaching the Trinità dei Monti church at the top of the hill, and the three tiers were intended to reflect the three figures of the Holy Trinity.

Their popularity as a general meeting place and social spot began in the 18th century at the height of the **Grand Tour** period because this was the area where most of the hotels and boarding houses were located. Facing onto the **Piazza di Spagna** on the eastern side of the foot of the Spanish Steps is the **Keats-Shelley Memorial House**, set up as a library in honour of the poet John Keats, who died here at the age of 25 in 1821, and Percy Bysshe Shelley, poet and husband of *Frankenstein* author Mary Shelley. Manuscripts and mementos of these and other Romantic poets are on display within the elegant rooms (closed Sun). Closest metro: Spagna.

VATICAN CITY

On the west bank of the Tiber lies the Vatican City State, the smallest independent state in the world, covering just over 40 hectares. The state was established as an autonomous sovereignty in 1929 after an agreement between the King of Italy and the papacy acknowledged that the Church could not be ruled under political regimes but needed to establish its own rules according to the Roman Catholic faith.

Today, the Vatican is populated by fewer than 1,000 citizens and has its own militia, the **Swiss Guards**. The area might be small in terms of world geography, however, it can take visitors several days to explore the entire area and only the very dedicated will have the stamina to do so. The public entrance into Vatican City is through Bernini's glorious **Piazza San Pietro** (St Peter's Square), which offers a breathtaking introduction to the glories that are to come. Straight in front is the towering facade of **St Peter's Basilica** and the pillared colonnade decorated with statues of 140 saints. In front of this is an obelisk brought here from the ancient Egyptian city of Heliopolis and two fountains also placed here by Bernini.

Do note that proper dress is required for visiting the Vatican; this means long trousers for men, long trousers or knee-length skirts for women, covered shoulders (no sleeveless tops) and no bare feet. Unless you comply with these regulations you will not be allowed into the Vatican, St Peter's or any of the museums.

you'll find details in local listings magazines. To beat the licensing laws, many of Rome's clubs are listed as private, which means they charge a membership fee just to enter, although this usually includes the price of a drink.

The best areas for nightlife can be found in Trastevere, the *centro storico* (around Piazza Navona in particular), Testaccio and Ostiense (to the south-west of Trastevere). Pick up a copy of *Roma C'e* (www.romace.it), published every Wednesday and available from newsagents (€1) which has a section in English.

EVENTS

Tourists and pilgrims pour into Rome on the Saturday before Palm Sunday, filling St Peter's Square (Piazza San Pietro) for the open-air Mass. **Holy Week** brings numerous religious services, culminating with the Papal Address on Easter Sunday. On **Pasquetta** (Easter Monday), by tradition Romans head for the mountains and parks outside the city to relax and feast on picnics of *uove sode* (hard-boiled eggs) and *salumi* (cured meats).

In addition to the innumerable independently run arts festivals that cram the summer calendar, there are many city-run cultural events under the banner of **Estate Romana** (Roman Summer). For three months open-air concerts, plays and ballet performances are staged in venues dotted around the city. Many of the *Estate Romana* events are free: check newspapers, online and tourist boards for details (www.estateromana.comune.roma.it). Following on from Estate Romana, **Romaeuropa Festival** is an autumn arts festival of music, dance and theatre.

St Petersburg (Санкт-Петербург)

Russia's second-largest city is first in the hearts of its population due to its collection of showpiece museums, elegant pastel-hued palaces, tree-lined parks and boulevards, not to mention its proud history of decadence and defiance. Home to the Russian tsars for over three hundred years, St Petersburg has seen more than its share of political power struggles since it was founded on the banks of the Neva River by **Peter the Great** in 1703. Sheer determination built this city up to become the fourth largest in Europe within a century of its founding — and it's also what got its citizens through such moments as the storming of the **Winter Palace** by Communist revolutionaries and the two-and-a-half year blockade by the Nazis during World War II.

A visit to St Petersburg will intoxicate and captivate you. Whether it's a summer night flooded with late sunlight — the so-called **White Nights** — along the banks of the river, or a winter's evening sharing a bottle of Georgian wine in a basement bar next to a cosy fireplace, you're sure to find your perfect corner. So take a stroll down **Nevskiy Prospekt** and enjoy a caviar-covered *bliny*. The city is included in **Route 45** (p365) and has direct fast trains to Moscow (ERT 1900) and Helsinki (ERT 1910), plus a bus service to Tallinn (ERT 1870).

TRAVEL BASICS

≋ **Moscow Station** (Moskovskiy vokzal; metro: Mayakovskaya or Ploshchad Vosstaniya) for trains to Moscow and onwards to the south. **Vitebsk Station** (Vitebskiy vokzal; metro: Pushkinskaya) for trains to Belarus, Ukraine, Poland and the Baltic States. **Finland Station** (Finlyandskiy vokzal; metro: Ploshchad Lenina) for trains to Helsinki. Buy your ticket at the Central Railway Booking Office (Tsentralnye Zhelezno-dorozhnye Kassy), Naberezhnaya Kanala Griboedova 24, at windows 100–104, 2nd floor (metro: Nevskiy Prospekt). ⛴ **Sea Terminal**, Morskoy Vokzal, Morskoy Slavy Ploshchad 1, ☎ 812 322 6052 (numerous buses, trolleybuses and *marshrutkas*). Boats from Moscow arrive at the **River Passenger Terminal**, Obukhovskoy oborony 195 (metro: Proletarskaya), ☎ 812 262 0239. ✈ **Pulkovo**, ☎ 812 704 3444. St Petersburg's international airport is located 17 km south of the city centre. *Marshrutkas* (shared taxis on pre-defined routes) link both terminals (domestic: Pulkovo 1; international: Pulkovo 2) to Moskovskaya metro station 0700–2200, taking 10–15 mins. **Public**

RECOGNISE YOUR STATIONS

train station (вокзал): Moscow (Московский), Vitebsk (Витебский), Finland (Финляндский), Ladozhski (Ладожский); **metro:** Chernyshevskaya (Чернышевская), Elektrosila (Электросила), Gorkovskaya (Горковская), Gostinyy Dvor (Гостиный двор), Leninskiy Prospekt (Ленинский проспект), Mayakovskaya (Маяковская), Moskovskaya (Московская), Nevskiy Prospekt (Невский проспект), Park Pobedy (Парк Победы), Ploshchad Lenina (Площадъ Ленина), Ploshchad Vosstaniya (Площадъ Восстания), Proletarskaya (Пролетарская)

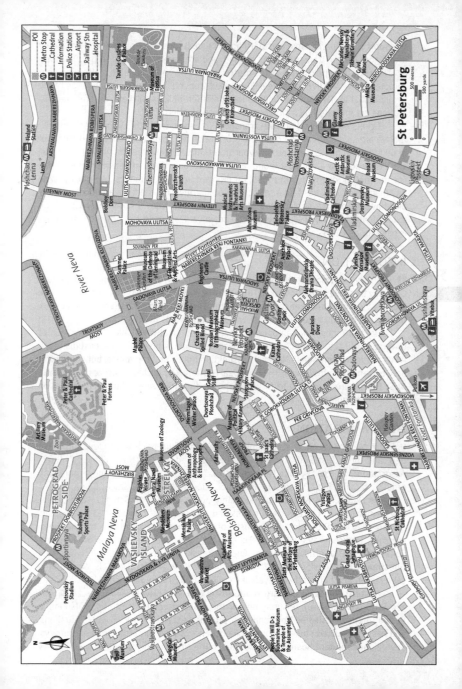

transport is comprehensive and startlingly cheap. It runs 0530–0100, but is infrequent after 2300. Official transport maps abound, and are available in English (try *Dom Knigi* at Nevskiy Prospekt 28). The **metro** is cheap and reliable, although not comprehensive. All five lines are colour coded, but you'll need basic knowledge of the Cyrillic alphabet. Two intersecting stations on different lines will have different names. Stations are indicated by a sign bearing a large blue letter 'M'.

Tickets for all **local surface transport** (buses, trams, trolleybuses and *marshrutkas*) are sold on board by conductors or the driver. There are ticket inspectors (not in uniform), so make sure you buy your ticket immediately. A *yedinyy bilet* covers all state transport for a calendar month and is good value if you are staying a long time. For the metro, tokens (*jetony*) must be dropped into the turnstiles, but most people buy magnetic cards, valid for a set number of journeys. Official **taxis** are mostly yellow and have an orange light on top. If you order a cab from a hotel the cost will be extortionate, but will at least be fixed in advance. Flagging a cab down on the street is risky for non-Russian speakers.

INFORMATION

🛈 The **City Information Office** is at 14/52 Sadovaya ul, ☎ 812 310 2231 (metro: Gostinyy Dvor, Nevskiy Prospekt). The useful *St Petersburg in your pocket* is available online (www.inyourpocket.com) or check the *St Petersburg Times* (www.sptimes.ru), the English weekly entertainment newspaper, for events listings.

Hard currency is not an option in many shops, so always have plenty of roubles for small services, although larger retailers and hotels now all accept credit cards. ATMs are fairly common in Nevskiy Prospekt, in hotels and the metro, but some offer only extremely limited sums. The best deal is offered by exchange offices. The centre of St Petersburg is quite safe to wander around in the evening but keep an eye on personal belongings.

ACCOMMODATION

Unlike in Moscow, there is a broadening range of medium-price and budget hotels. For bed and breakfast, go for the long-established HOFA (Host Families' Guest Association), ☎ 812 275 1992 (www.hofa.ru). They can do visas and find a room with ordinary families in St Petersburg and other cities of the former Soviet Union.

🛏 **Hotels**: The **Nevsky Inn**, Kirpichny per. 2, flat 19, ☎ 812 972 6873 (www.nevskyinn.com), €–€€, has clean rooms and a kitchen that can be used by residents (metro: Nevskiy Prospekt). For a taste of communist-era 'glamour', try the **Hotel Mercury**, Tavricheskaya ul. 39, ☎ 812 576 4555, €€, once the address of choice for Communist Party officials (metro: Chernyshevskaya). The simple, yet welcoming **Guesthouse**, Grechesky pr. 13, ☎ 812 271 3089 (www.ghspb.ru), €€, is located on a calm street, just behind the Oktyabrsky Concert Hall (metro: Ploshchad Vosstaniya).

Hostels: The **St Petersburg Youth Hostel** (HI), 3-ya Sovetskaya ulitsa 28, ☎ 812 329 8018 (www.ryh.ru), is surely one of the most successful ventures of its kind in Russia (metro: Ploshchad Vosstaniya). It provides excellent back up in all situations, and has an attached student/youth travel agency, which can book onward journeys. Several **independent hostels** have opened in the city, and the standards are high. Try

THE BEST OF ST PETERSBURG

The Hermitage
The royal family's Winter Palace was transformed into the world's largest art gallery (closed Mon). The Impressionist collection alone is worth the cost of admission. The closest metro station is Nevskiy Prospekt.

The Peter & Paul Fortress
The oldest large-scale building in St Petersburg was built to defend against the Swedes — yet never saw any action. The Fortress is on the opposite bank of the Neva from the Hermitage. Take the metro to Gorkovskaya.

Russian Museum
The finest Russian art available. A must-see for those wanting to expand their knowledge of Russian culture (metro: Gostinyy Dvor or Nevskiy Prospekt); closed Tue.

Peterhof
Peter the Great built this Russian palace to rival Versailles, and it certainly does. Peterhof is outside the city, and you can take a picturesque voyage by hydrofoil from the jetty at the Hermitage. Otherwise, catch the bus from Leninskiy Prospekt metro station (30 mins).

Sweating in a banya (steam bath)
Sit down, get hot, whip yourself with twigs — it's all in a day's relaxation.

Tsarskoe Selo
The favoured summer retreat of the royal family during the years of Catherine the Great — and it's easy to see why. Tsarskoe Selo is about 45 mins out of town, via the suburban train from Vitebsk station.

Nevskiy Prospekt
Shop for caviar, step into the Grand Hotel or just watch the hordes go by.

MIR Hostel, Nevskiy Prospekt 16, ☎ 962 680 9830 (www.mirhostel.com), the **Soul Kitchen**, 1-ya Sovietskaya 12, ☎ 911 237 7969 (www.soulkitchenhostel.com) or the **Marmalade Hostel**, Malaya Morskaja 8, ☎ 911 966 4455 (www.marmaladeru.com).

ITINERARIES

Half day

Head straight to the **Hermitage**. The Winter Palace is massive, so if you want to see the highlights, you'll have to do some planning.

One day

Start your day at the souvenir market near **St Isaac's Cathedral** before popping into the church itself. Cross the Admiralty gardens to spend a few hours in the Hermitage. Continue along until you reach Dvortsovaya Ploshchad. Once you hit the canal, follow it until you arrive at **Nevskiy Prospekt**. End your day with caviar at the Grand Hotel Europe.

Two days

Follow the plan suggested for a one-day trip and then get out of town to explore the wonders of **Peterhof**. There are plenty of tour operators who offer a full-day package. If you have extra time, either plan a full day in the Hermitage or head over to the **Russian Museum**.

More

Divide the city into equal sections, making sure to give the Hermitage a full day. Discover the **Peter & Paul Fortress** and the sights on Vasilevsky Island for a day. Budget two days for the sights within the area of the **Fontanka** River, and then venture beyond the canal, taking a look at sights outside the downtown core. Book a **cruise along the Neva** and then explore the **royal palaces** outside the city for a couple of days.

St Petersburg on a budget

Unfortunately, even the most minor of museums charges an admission fee. This is due to the fact that most artistic and cultural institutions receive absolutely no other financial assistance. Your best bet if you're on a budget is to admire the architecture and history of the city from the street. A stroll through the city's squares brings you into contact with some of the most important locations in St Petersburg, including **Dvortsovaya Ploshchad**, considered by most to be the square that launched the revolution of 1905, for it was here where tsarist troops fired on peaceful workers protesting the harsh regime.

Another favoured public area is the **Summer Garden**, once the private gardens of Peter the Great. This path-filled green space nestles on the banks of the Neva and boasts a number of lime trees that provide shade during the summer. A weekend walk along **Nevskiy Prospekt** has long been the height of fashion for locals, whether they are up for a shop or not. This elegant boulevard is 4.5 km long and measures up to 60 m across in some places. Street life is varied and can include encounters with beggars, babushkas and fur-clad members of the *nouveau riche*.

Food

St Petersburg is truly a hit-and-miss town when it comes to dining out. For every memorable meal there will be one you would prefer to forget. This is due to the fact that the transition from the years of communist frugality has been a slow-moving process, with quality control and organic produce low on the list of priorities. The old saying that breakfast is the most important meal of the day is heartily endorsed by Russians, with a typical morning meal packed with stodgy favourites such as curd cheese (*tvorog*), porridge (*kasha*) and pancakes (*bliny*). The main meal of the day is always lunch, usually eaten between 1300 and 1600. Typical dishes boast peasant origins and make free use of ingredients such as

THE WHITE NIGHTS

When summer arrives, locals truly know how to take advantage of the warmer and sunnier weather. The best (and wildest) time to experience this carefree period is during the White Nights Festival, which is held through the last two weeks of June and into early July. The term White Nights is due to the fact that the city is so far north, which ensures that the sun stays up for an extraordinary length of time in and around the summer solstice. Locals party all day and through the (short) night, flooding the streets that surround Nevskiy Prospekt and the Neva embankment.

cabbage, potatoes and dense, black bread. A typical lunch begins with soup, usually cabbage or beetroot (*borscht*). In summer, chilled soups are also popular. Following this will be a meat dish of either pork or beef in sauce (usually cream). Alternatively, the meat may be formed into a type of ravioli known as *pelmeni* that is served in a light broth. Ethnic influences drawn from across the Soviet world also crop up in the form of Georgian kebabs or lightly-spiced Uzbek meats complete with pilau rice.

CULTURE AND NIGHTLIFE

A night at the **theatre** or **ballet** is a major event for locals and they dress up for the occasion. Tuxedos and evening gowns are commonplace, even when it's not an opening night. Tickets often sell out well in advance, so if you are arriving at a peak time you will either have to buy them through your hotel concierge for a hefty fee or reserve them. The most in-demand seats are always for performances at the world-renowned **Mariinsky Theatre**, especially for the Kirov Ballet.

A little over a decade ago, **nightlife** in St Petersburg was fairly limited and centred around consuming incredible quantities of alcohol. Times have changed and the city has now become one of the most decadent on the planet. Anything goes in this town (if you have the money), with an evening out potentially costing a hefty sum, depending on what you're after. Trips to clubs and bars start late, with venues getting going not much before midnight. To find out what is going on take a look at the listings in the English-language *St Petersburg Times*.

EVENTS

Some events worth noting are **Orthodox Easter** (usually around April) when banners are hung from churches and midnight mass brings out the crowds. In June it is the **Beer Festival**, one of the most popular annual events in the city. In November the national holiday — the **Day of Reconciliation and Accord** — is held on the anniversary of the Revolution. Demonstrations and parades celebrating the 'good old days' are common. In December, the **Arts Square Winter Festival** brings the best of classical music and opera to the city, and is regarded by locals as the highlight of the musical calendar.

Stockholm

Spread over 14 islands with countless inlets, Stockholm has a stunning **waterfront** that rivals those of San Francisco and Sydney, and most visitors would probably rate it the most rewarding of the Scandinavian capitals. At its heart is the impressively intact original part of the city, **Gamla Stan**, with an enticing blend of dignified old buildings, cafés, and craft and designer shops; in contrast, the **Djurgården** is a huge natural park where the city comes to swim, canoe, fly kites, visit the zoo and the superb outdoor museum Skansen, or just admire the views.

Stockholm is airy and very much a **harbour capital**, a lovely place to be outdoors in summer (winter is perfectly romantic, if a bit austere), whether listening to an outdoor concert or taking a cruise, but there are plenty of superb indoor attractions, such as the **Nationalmuseum** and the historic *Vasa* **warship**. It's also a clean, safe and friendly place, and you get the sense that everything runs like clockwork. Stockholm is on **Routes 25** (p236) and **26** (p240) of this book.

TRAVEL BASICS

🚆 **Centralstationen** has a bus information/ticket office, currency exchange and good food stalls. For train information, ☎ 0771 75 75 75 (www.sj.se). 🚌 **Cityterminalen** (long-distance bus station) is between Klarabergsviadukten and Kungsbron, not far from both Centralstationen and the metro and linked to them by tunnels, ☎ 08 762 59 97 (www.cityterminalen.com). Swebus Express is the largest domestic company, ☎ 0771 21 82 18 (www.swebusexpress.se).

🚢 **Ferries to Helsinki**: the overnight ships to Finland are run by **Silja Line**, with offices at Sveavägen 14 and at Cityterminalen, ☎ 08 440 59 90 (www.tallinksilja.com), and **Viking Line**, office at Cityterminalen, ☎ 08 452 40 00 (www.vikingline.se).

✈ **Stockholm Arlanda**, ☎ 08 797 60 00, www.arlanda.se, is 45 km north of Stockholm. The Arlanda Express (airport rail link to Centralstationen), ☎ 0771 72 02 00 (www.arlandaexpress.com), takes 20 mins (every 15 mins, daily, 0505–2305, then every 30 mins until 0105).

🚌 Storstockholms Lokaltrafik (SL) runs the excellent **bus** and **metro** (T-bana) network. Main office: lower level of Sergels Torg; ☎ 08 600 10 00 (www.sl.se) and a branch in Centralstationen.

Buy tickets for buses and the T-bana at SL Centers or ticket agents located in most ticket halls and visibly displayed with the SL logo. The one-hour ticket allows unlimited travel during that time in one zone (SEK36), two zones (SEK54), or three zones (SEK72). Validate your ticket before you enter the T-bana or bus, or bypass the machines by buying a pass for free transit within 24 hours (SEK115), 72 hours (SEK230), or seven days (SEK300). The T-bana has three main lines (red, green and blue). Trains are fast and frequent, 0500–0100.

Metro stations display a blue 'T' on a white circle. The decor on some lines is among the most imaginative in Europe: walls are moulded to look like caves, are painted in strident colours and hold original murals.

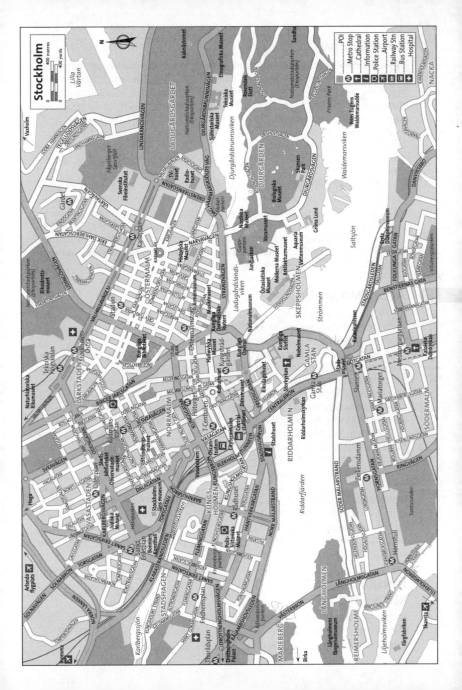

INFORMATION

ℹ Tourist office: Stockholm Tourist Centre, Sverigehuset (Sweden House), Hamngatan 27, Kungsträdgården, ☎ 08 50 82 85 08 (www.stockholmtown.com). From Central-stationen, walk up Klarabergsg. to Sergels Torg (marked by an oddly-shaped pillar), then right on Hamngatan for the tourist office. Also try the digital guide in the main hall of Centralstationen (tourist info and hotel bookings). Small city maps are freely available, but a larger-scale one might come in handy. A wealth of free English-language literature includes *What's On Stockholm* (free bi-monthly tourist and events guide), *Hotels and Hostels Stockholm* (free hotel and youth hostel guide) and the official guide to Stockholm.

The **Stockholm Card** (Stockholmskortet, SEK425 for 24 hrs, SEK550 for 48 hrs or SEK650 for 72 hrs; www.stockholmtown.com/stockholmcard) from tourist offices, stations, the Silja Line terminal and most hotels, youth hostels and campsites, provides free public transport, free boat tour, free bike tour (both May–Sept), free entrance to 80 museums and attractions as well as other discounts. Stockholm is fairly well wired when it comes to **internet cafés**. Try the **Sidewalk Express Internet Points** that can be found on levels 1 and 2 at Centralstationen or in 7-eleven stores.

ACCOMMODATION

If you are struggling to find a place to stay, the **Hotellcentralen** is the official accommodation booking service and can be found in the main hall of Centralstationen; ☎ 08 50 82 85 00 (www.stockholmtown.com/hotels).

⊨ Hotels: The **Story Hotel**, Riddargatan 6, ☎ 08 54 50 39 40 (www.storyhotels.com), €€, offers smart design and arty details — perfect for guests who like their hotel room to be modern and trendy. **Den Röda Båten**, Söder Mälarstrand 6, ☎ 08 644 43 85 (www.theredboat.com), €–€€, once sailed the Gota Canal and the Vättern. Nowadays it's one of two boats that form the hotel and hostel at the Lake Mälaren locks into the Baltic. Hotel cabins have private baths.

Hostels: The **Af Chapman** and **Skeppsholmen**, Flaggmansvägen 8, ☎ 08 463 22 66 (www.stfchapman.com) offer inexpensive sea and land hostel accommodation at two adjacent facilities. The sea rooms are aboard the striking white three-masted barque A*f Chapman* in the harbour across from the Royal Palace.

Otherwise try the **City Backpackers**, Upplandsgatan 2A, ☎ 08 20 69 20 (www.citybackpackers.org); and **Castanea Old Town Hostel**, Kindstugatan 1, ☎ 08 22 35 51 (www.castaneahostel.com). **Campsites**: The most central campsite is **Öster-malms Citycamping**, Fiskartorpsvägen 2, Östermalm, ☎ 08 10 29 03 (www.camping.se), 1.5 km from the city centre at Östermalm sports ground, 🚌 55 (late June–late August).

ITINERARIES
Half day

If the weather is nice, wander and treat your eyes to all the sights around the watery rim of downtown Stockholm. Begin at the **Royal Opera** in Kungsträdgården (pick up a map at Sweden House) and follow the water past the

THE BEST OF STOCKHOLM

Changing of the Guard at the Kungliga Slott
Christopher Robin would love it — all that pomp and marching to military band music. It takes place at the Royal Palace daily in summer, and three times a week in winter.

Gamla Stan
The beautiful remnants of Stockholm's medieval heritage — amid the brand new.

Vasa Ship
Dredged from the mud and restored to reveal its full 17th-century glory. The Vasa Museum that houses the ship is located on the island of Djurgården, which can be reached by boat from Nybroplan, Slussen or Steppsholmen or by tram no. 7 from Norrmalmstorg.

Skansen Park
Also on the island of Djurgården, Skansen Park is best described as Sweden in a day, revealed through buildings and living exhibits in a massive open-air museum.

Stadshuset
The City Hall, one of the city's landmarks and where modern architecture was born. All that, and a tower providing stunning views over Stockholm.

Nordiska Museet (Nordic Museum)
Cultural overdose, as a collection of over a million artefacts explains the country's traditions and way of life. You find the museum on the island of Djurgården.

Drottningholm Palace
How the other half regally lives, in a residence fit for a king and his family.

Grand Hôtel and the white ferries and around the corner by the **National Museum of Fine Arts**, following the line of boats along Nybrokajen to Berzelii Park and Nybroplan. Step inside the **Royal Dramatic Theatre** to see the lobby, if it's open, then hop on a ferry to **Djurgården** to see the *Vasa* ship. If you still have some time, take a ferry to **Slussen** and stroll through the narrow streets of Gamla Stan, browsing for a place to have lunch or dinner. Give in to the urge to stop for coffee in a cosy café or at a pavement table at any time.

One day

The half-day route above makes a good beginning for a full day, leaving time to spend the afternoon in **Skansen Park**. The highlights not to miss there are the historic buildings, which are set along walking routes. These are arranged chronologically, so you get a mini tour of the whole country in past centuries. The mid-19th-century village has working artisans, including a baker.

Two days

While you could spend a whole day at Skansen alone, there is a great deal more to see in the city. With an extra day you can either visit two or three of the many museums or begin the day in **Gamla Stan**, touring the Royal Palace. In that case, plan to remain for the midday Changing of the Guard.

If the weather is good, you might spend the day visiting either the Viking island town of **Birka**, **Drottningholm Palace** and its gardens, or one of the islands in the archipelago. The ride is as much the point as reaching an island. **Vaxholm** is the closest, but other islands are accessible for a day trip.

More

With more time, and a rented car, you could follow the route of the **Göta Canal** across the narrow country to Gothenburg, stopping off at Söderköping and later exploring the shores of the Vättern and Vänern lakes. Gothenburg highlights include the excellent art museum and the world's largest collection of floating museum ships, at the **Maritime Centre**. In the evening you might catch a show at Liseberg, or just enjoy the rides at Scandinavia's biggest amusement park.

STOCKHOLM ON A BUDGET

While many cities are decorated by monumental statues, few have such a continuing commitment to public art as Stockholm. And few make their most treasured museum collections of world-famous art available free to the public. This city is one big, free art gallery. Several works by **Carl Milles**, Sweden's premier sculptor, adorn the city, including his *Orpheus* in front of the Concert Hall on Hötorget. Contemporary sculptures pop up here and there, and in the newly regenerated western edge of **Södermalm**, a 183 m long wall of colourful mosaic dresses up the buildings facing the lakeside promenade. At **Kulturhuset**, you'll find free changing exhibits of art by both Swedish and international artists.

The **world's longest art exhibition** — more than 100 km of it — is claimed to be in the city's underground system, the T-bana. Trains pull into 100 stunning stations, each individually designed by different artists. In some, the lighting creates designs on the ceilings; others have massive, three-dimensional wall murals; others still are decorated with tiles or sculptures. Top Swedish artists began competing for these commissions as long ago as the 1950s, and the work still continues. *Art in the Stockholm Metro* is a free brochure that describes the various stations, with information on the artists. Ask at the tourist office about free guided tours of the stations. Those on the Blue Line are the most outstanding.

The **National Museum of Fine Arts** contains paintings by Rembrandt, Rubens, Degas and other well-known artists, as well as decorative arts from the Middle Ages to modern Swedish design treasures.

Across the bridge on the island of Skeppsholmen, **Moderna Museet** is considered to be one of Europe's top museums of modern art. Its collections include works by Picasso and Salvador Dalí, as well as leading contemporary names. Next door is the **Museum of Architecture**, whose exhibition hall is chock-full of fascinating exhibits on the country's architecture, including models of buildings from all periods of its history. Excellent interactive stations offer photographs and artistic information in English.

While you're on Skeppsholmen, follow the path around its perimeter to **Stockholmsbriggen**. Lining the quay are dozens of historic wooden ships, some of which you can visit.

FOOD

Swedish cooking is much more than meatballs and *gravad lax*. Hot young chefs have donned their toques, fusing highly flavourful local ingredients with cooking styles pulled from all over the world. The short growing season and long summer daylight hours intensify the flavours of berries and vegetables, elevating the humble potato to new heights and turning strawberries into juicy sweets. Swedish chefs shine brightest with garden-fresh vegetables and the readily available coldwater fish and shellfish from surrounding seas. Add autumn woodland mushrooms, wild lingonberries and cloudberries from the northern bogs, as well as venison — the red meat of choice — and you have the basics of Swedish cuisine.

Eating out in Stockholm can be expensive, and as in most cities, Stockholm's trendier eateries with designer decor and celebrity chefs are among the priciest, and the neighbourhood places and Asian or Middle Eastern restaurants are the cheapest. Cafés serve salads and sandwiches and some have all-you-can-eat buffets at lunch.

Traditional local dishes include several varieties of pickled herring, blackened herring (*strömming* or *sill*) with potatoes, salmon (*lax*), cured salmon (*gravad lax*), cod (*torsk*), meatballs (*köttbullar*), and roasted game meats. Occasionally found on menus, a popular homestyle dish known as Jansson's Temptation (*Janssons frestelse*) includes potatoes, onions, butter, anchovies and cream baked together.

CULTURE AND NIGHTLIFE

Stockholm has a thriving and diverse nightlife scene, and whatever your interest when it comes to evening entertainment you should be able to find it. **Stureplan** is the undisputable entertainment hub, its bars and clubs packed with young and glamorous party animals. **Södermalm** is hottest with bohemian and alternative sets, including much of the gay/lesbian scene, the rest of which is in **Gamla Stan**.

Although things don't begin to rock until after midnight (Thursday, Friday and Saturday are the nights to prowl), arrive well before 2300 to avoid the queues. It's not fashionably late, but you'll get in. Södermalm bars begin to close at about 0100, clubs at 0300, but the Stureplan scene continues as late as 0500.

THE ARCHIPELAGO

Less than half an hour from the heart of Stockholm is a watery wonderland of 24,000 islands, a scenic playground where city residents spend weekends and holidays. Some are little more than skerries; others lie in clusters that form mini-archipelagos within. A steady stream of ferries and historic boats connects these, making day trips or longer island-hopping adventures easy. Romantic lodging, camping, fine dining, local crafts, paddle sports, fishing, sailing, walking trails, historic sights, beaches and a variety of natural environments offer enough attractions to occupy several days. From June to mid-August, everything is open on the islands. In spring and autumn many places are still open, but only a few operate all winter, and the boat service is limited then.

The scenery and the laid-back atmosphere of the islands are the greatest attraction, each island with its own character. Some, such as **Gustavsberg** and **Vaxholm**, are connected to Stockholm by causeway or bridge. Boats to the others (and to Vaxholm) depart from Strömkajen and Strandvägen, in central Stockholm. At the tourist office in Sweden House you can book excursions that include boat trips and activities, such as sailing or cycling and even meals and lodging, or you can buy an Island Hopper card, good for five days of unlimited travel on Waxholmsbolaget and Cinderella boats throughout the archipelago.

Thankfully for those who like rather more gentle evening entertainment, it's not all nightclubs and noisy bars in Stockholm. **Classical music and opera** fans have a ball in this city, where heavily subsidised ticket prices are among the lowest in Europe and hundreds of concerts each year are free. The music season, for both the Royal Opera and the philharmonic and symphony orchestras, extends from September to May. In summer, seek outdoor venues for concerts and music festivals.

EVENTS

On 30 April bonfires and choral singing fill the night sky as Sweden celebrates **Walpurgis Night**, which is a national holiday. The major festivities in Stockholm can be found at the terrace of Riddarholmen or in Skansen Park. In June the city's top restaurants set up booths for an entire week as part of the **Taste of Stockholm** festival, and it is a great way to try the specialities of some of Sweden's culinary superstars without forking out for a whole meal. Even cheaper is the free **Parkteatren**, which runs from June to August and brings a range of dance and music performances to the city's public parks.

In early summer Stockholm gets into the swing of things with the annual **Jazz Festival**, whilst in August the **Cultural Festival of Stockholm** brings over 300 events and attractions to locations throughout the city. In December it is time for the **Christmas Markets**, the best of which can be found at Kungsträdgården, Skansen Park, Rosendal Palace and Stortorget.

Venice (Venezia)

Venice can play cultural one-upmanship better than most cities. Even the cafés of **St Mark's Square** (Piazza San Marco) are awash with famous ghosts, and tourism is almost as ancient as the city itself. Built on 118 tiny islands, this former maritime republic once held sway over an empire stretching from northern Italy to Cyprus. Around 1,000 residents leave each year, driven out by exorbitant rents. Ironically, for a city built on water, Venice numbers around 450 souvenir shops but fewer than ten plumbers. Most day trippers fail to stray far from Piazza San Marco, which is a huge mistake. Beyond the crowds at the major sights, especially around St Mark's and the **Rialto Bridge**, Venice exudes a village-like calm. Even 15 minutes walk from the main drag can deposit you alone in a Gothic square, with just pigeons for company.

Surprisingly for a city built on water, walking is the best way to explore. Prepare yourself for serious walking as there are 400 bridges and around 180 canals to discover. Expect to get lost, especially at night, which is part and parcel of the charm of this mysterious **lagoon** world. However, you're never far from the **Grand Canal**, which snakes through the centre, and Venice is perfectly safe. The best way to feel the spirit of the city is simply to wander its narrow streets (*calli*), popping into churches as you pass and pausing to sit at a waterside café whenever the whim takes you. Venice is included in the book on **Route 35** (p296), between Milan and Trieste. From these cities it is possible to connect with other routes to Switzerland (Milan) or to Slovenia, Croatia and the Balkans (Trieste), and of course to other destinations in Italy.

TRAVEL BASICS

≈ To get to Venice itself, take a train to **Santa Lucia station** (some terminate 10 mins earlier at **Mestre** on the mainland). A local service operates between Mestre and Santa Lucia, which has its own *vaporetto* (waterbus) stop, at the north-west end of the Grand Canal. A rapid-transit system opened in 2010, providing a fast link between Tronchetto and Piazzale Roma with an intermediate stop at Station Marittima.
➔ Marco Polo International Airport is 13 km north-east of Venice; flight information, ☎ 041 260 9260 (www.veniceairport.it). The regular motorboat service of Alilaguna operates from the airport (year-round, www.alilaguna.com) via the Lido to the Pza San Marco in the heart of Venice, and costs €13 for a one-way trip.

Venice's sturdy **waterbuses**, *vaporettos*, are operated by the ACTV transport authority (www.actv.it) and run at 10- to 20-min intervals in daytime and approximately hourly from midnight to 0600. Lines 1 (slow) and 82 (faster) run the length of the Grand Canal, connecting Santa Lucia station to Pza San Marco. Piers bear the line numbers — but make sure you go in the right direction. Lines 41 and 42 are round-the-islands services taking in Murano. Lines that run at night are identified with a moon symbol on local timetables and in publicity.

There are quite a few **travelcards** available for tourists including 12/36/48/72-hr, or 7-day options, and the popular 24-hr pass for €18. With these tourists can travel on

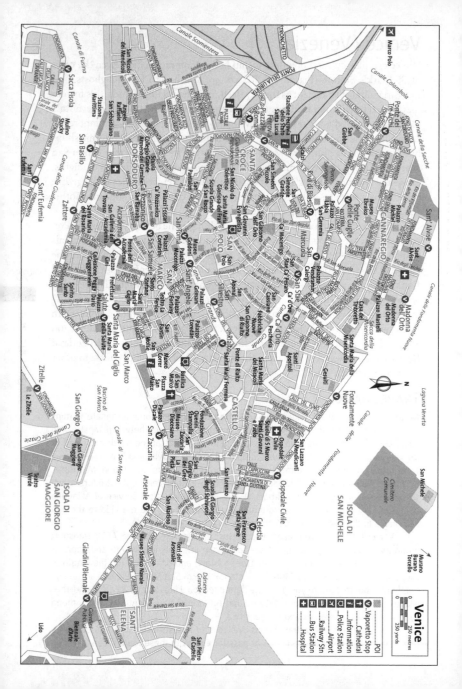

Venice

Marco Polo

ISOLA DI SAN GIORGIO MAGGIORE

ISOLA DI SAN MICHELE

SANT'ELENA

---

0   250 metres
0   250 yards

- Vaporetto Stop
- Cathedral
- Information
- Police Station
- Airport
- Railway Stn
- Bus Station
- Hospital

city buses and all *vaporetto* routes run by ACTV (including to outlying islands such as Torcello, Burano and Murano). They can be purchased at Hellovenezia offices (www.hellovenezia.com) or pre-booked online at www.veniceconnected.com, which offers discounted rates depending on the season (high, mid or low).

Water taxis are sleek but expensive. They can be found at major strategic positions such as outside the train station or the airport, Piazza San Marco and the Lido. The city's 400 gondolas, which can take up to six passengers each, provide a costly, conceivably romantic, means of getting around. Rates are fixed. You can also try the short gondola ride on the *traghetto* (gondola ferry), which crosses the Grand Canal at eight points (signposted *traghetto*) for only 50 cents.

INFORMATION

🅸 The **main tourist office** at Pza San Marco 71 is often overwhelmed — it can be better to try the one at Venice Pavilion, on the waterfront by the Giardini Ex Reali. There is also a branch at Santa Lucia station. Contact: ☎ 041 529 8711 (www.turismovenezia.it). A *mappa sconti* (discount map) is given together with the **Rolling Venice Card** for young people aged 14 to 29 (must present ID when purchasing the card). A three-day **transport pass** (city buses and vaporetti) can be bought with the Rolling Venice Card and costs €18. Buy the card at the tourist office or online (www.veniceconnected.com). The **Chorus Pass** is a combined ticket to some of the best churches (www.chorusvenezia.org).

For **internet access**, try **Venetian Navigator** (www.venetiannavigator.com) which has a convenient branch in Calle Stagneri, between the Rialto Bridge and Campo Fava and another in Calle Caselleria, not far from Pza San Marco.

ACCOMMODATION

Check the Venice Tourism website (www.turismovenezia.it) for booking accommodation (including B&Bs). ⊨ **Hotels**: The **Agli Alboretti,** Dorsoduro 882, Rio Terra Foscarini, ☎ 041 523 0058 (www.aglialboretti.com), €–€€, is a popular hotel near the Accademia with a good restaurant and pleasant rooms. **Da Zorzi**, Fondamenta San Giacomo, Giudecca 197, ☎ 041 528 6380, €€, has apartments and rooms in a family-run B&B with garden on un-touristy island of Giudecca.

A recommended B&B within walking distance of the station is **Campiello Zen**, Santa Croce, 1285 Rio Tera`, ☎ 041 710 365 (www.campiellozen.com), €€. Those on a budget can check out the **Collegio Armeno Moorat**, Raphael, Dorsoduro 2596, 041 522 8770 (www.collegioarmeno.com), €, a grand baroque palace with budget rooms in a quiet part of Venice. Splurgers should head for the **Locanda Leon Bianco**, Corte Leon Bianco, ☎ 041 523 3572 (www.leonbianco.it), €€€, a romantic hotel overlooking the Grand Canal. **Hostels**: The HI youth hostel is **Ostello Venezia**, Fondamenta Zitelle 86, Isola della Giudecca, ☎ 041 523 8211 (*vaporetto* line 82: Zitelle stop). One of the best-located hostels in Italy, set in an ancient granary on the lively (and 'real') island of Giudecca, a quick crossing to Pza San Marco. Ten mins from the railway station is **Santa Fosca Hostel** (non-HI), Cannaregio 2372, ☎ 041 715 775 (www.santafosca.com). If Venice is full, do not stay in grim Mestre; opt for Padua or Treviso, 30 mins by train.

ITINERARIES

Half day

Head to the heart of the city, **Piazza San Marco**, where you'll find most main sights, attractions and shops. Have a drink in the legendary Florian or Quadri cafés, take the lift to the top of the Campanile, and admire St Mark's Basilica. Then choose between shopping in the nearby arts and crafts shops, art in the **Correr Museum**, or history in the **Doge's Palace**. Take a water bus, water taxi or gondola down the **Grand Canal** to see Venice from another perspective.

One day

A full day in Venice means you can also visit the **Accademia Gallery** and see the glories of Venetian art. **Ca' Rezzonico** is nearby and will give you an idea of the lush interior design during Venice's heyday. Find time to walk across **Rialto Bridge** in the morning and soak up the atmosphere of its lively food market.

Two days

When you've discovered the city centre and want to escape the day-tourists, head for the **Dorsoduro, Santa Croce** and **San Polo** areas. In Dorsoduro, you will find the famous Peggy Guggenheim Collection and the nearby church of Santa Maria della Salute, one of the city's major landmarks. Santa Croce and San Polo contain the magnificent church of Santa Maria Gloriosa dei Frari and the Scuola Grande di San Rocco. Relax at a café or restaurant along **Zattere** with a view of the island of Giudecca.

More

To get away from the bustle, head to **Cannaregio** for the lovely church of Madonna dell'Orto. If you are interested in ships and naval history, don't miss the **Museo Storico Navale** in the Arsenale area.

You should also make time for a trip to the island of **Giudecca**, where you will have fine views of Venice. For a change in atmosphere and some time on the beach, go to the **Lido**. Alternatively, head out to the charming small islands of Torcello, Murano and Burano.

VENICE ON A BUDGET

Venice is not the place to come for a cheap holiday. On the other hand, some of the most enjoyable things about the city are absolutely free. **Strolling along the canals**, standing on the bridges, admiring the views, soaking up the atmosphere, chatting and pointing, are a real pleasure when there are no cars to distract you from the stunningly beautiful architecture.

Treat the streets as a museum and take closer looks at the impressive buildings and elaborate designs you will come across. For a lazy afternoon in a **free park**, try the gardens in the Castello district or the Giardini Pubblici. Churches

THE BEST OF VENICE

St Mark's Basilica (Basilica di San Marco)
The oldest and most famous building in Venice is part of the city's soul.

Boat trips on the canals
Take a water bus from the airport, Lido or islands. Alternatively splash out on a water taxi or gondola ride. One of the best ways to travel around Venice, see its impressive buildings and churches and re-live its history.

Piazza San Marco and the Campanile
The heart of the city, with museums and shopping all around. You can get great views of Venice from the top of the Campanile, or bell tower.

Accademia Gallery
The place to see the works of the city's greatest artists. Located on Campo della Carità, Dorsoduro no. 1050. Closed Mon afternoon.

Rialto Bridge
One of the focal points of the city with a buzzing market.

Murano and Burano
Tiny islands where the traditional skills of glass- and lace-making still thrive today.

Peggy Guggenheim Collection
Venice's finest collection of modern art in a popular but peaceful museum on the Grand Canal at Dorsoduro no. 704. Closed Tues.

charge lower admission fees than museums but often contain artworks that are just as impressive. Look out for posters advertising free concerts in churches.

FOOD

There is a huge choice of places to eat and drink in Venice, ranging from ordinary bars and cafés to *bacari* (casual wine bars which serve tapas-style snacks called *cichetti*), more sophisticated *enoteche* (wine bars with more elaborate food), simple *trattorias* and *osterias*, plus the more formal *ristorante*. You will also find *pizzerias*, *gelaterie* (ice cream parlours), tea shops, bakeries, and some excellent cake and pastry shops. Most restaurants near **Pza San Marco** cater solely for the tourist industry and as a general rule, the closer you are to this area the pricier a meal or a drink will be. Cheaper and better-quality food and wine can often be found in the outlying areas such as **Cannaregio, Castello, San Polo** and **Santa Croce**.

There are many tasty local specialities in Venice, particularly **fish and seafood**. Try *anguilla* (eel), *baccalà* (a salt-cod dip), *folpi* (baby octopus), *granchio* (crab), *sarde in soar* (sardines marinated with onions, pine nuts, raisins and vinegar) or, for a more filling meal, *risotto di mare* or *in nero* (seafood risotto or risotto with squid ink). If you prefer meat, there is some excellent *carpaccio* (raw, lean, thinly sliced fillet of beef), *prosciutto San Daniele* (local ham) and *fegato alla veneziana* (calves' liver and onions).

WHERE THE 'REAL' PEOPLE LIVE

The district of Cannaregio, once Venice's main manufacturing area, is spacious and pleasant with broad canal sides and a fairly simple layout. Shops, bars and hotels tend to be cheaper and the area is more popular with locals than the city centre. The backstreets here in Cannaregio, where over a third of the city's population live, are where you will find the 'real' people in Venice. The Strada Nova is a broad, hectic street running along the **Grand Canal**, leading from the Rialto Bridge to the Ca' d'Oro museum and packed with shops and cafés as well as tourists. Equally bustling is the Lista di Spagna near the railway station, full of touristy cafés and shops. To see a bit more of the 'real' Venice you have to venture away from these streets.

The Fondamenta della Sensa and the parallel Fondamenta della Misericordia both offer peaceful walks. From the quayside of Fondamente Nuove you can get fine views of the lagoon, the cemetery island of **San Michele** and, beyond it, **Murano**.

CULTURE AND NIGHTLIFE

Carnival excepted, Venice's **nightlife** tends to be relaxed and quiet. Lazy dinners and evening strolls are more popular than loud music and wild dancing, and many bars and cafés close by 2200 or earlier. Restaurants tend to stop serving at 2230 or 2300. For **late-night activity**, head for Campo Santa Margherita, Campo Santo Stefano, Campo San Polo, Fondamenta della Misericordia and Campo San Barnaba.

If you enjoy the **performing arts** and you speak Italian it is worth seeing a play at the beautiful Teatro Carlo Goldoni (www.teatrostabileveneto.it). There are also performances of **opera, dance and ballet** at the La Fenice opera house and the Teatro Malibran. Contemporary dance events are usually held at the Teatro Fondamente Nuove. Concerts of classical music and opera are held around the city and are particularly pleasant when held in a church. There is the occasional live jazz session but strict noise-reduction laws mean concerts of rock and other contemporary music are rare.

EVENTS

The most important cultural events in Venice, apart from **carnival**, are the **Biennale festivals**. The Art and Architecture festivals are held in alternate years, with 2012 being Architecture's turn. Every September Venice welcomes the **International Film Festival**. Some of the most attractive celebrations to attend, however, are the smaller, more traditional events such as the **gondola race** on the feast day of St Mark or the 1,000-year-old ceremony of La Sensa.

Also worth checking out is the **Venezia Suona**, a one-day rock, folk and jazz festival, usually held on a Sunday in late June, and the **Festa della Salute**, celebrating the end of the plague of 1630. A bridge of boats is laid across the Grand Canal to the church of Santa Maria della Salute on 21 November.

Vienna (Wien)

Not for nothing does Austria's capital regularly top surveys to find Europe's most liveable city, for Vienna is an enviably civilised place, safe and manageable yet rarely dull. The **Altstadt**, or historic core, is traffic-calmed if not entirely pedestrianised, with cobbled streets, old merchants' houses, spacious gardens and hundreds of atmospheric places to eat and drink, though some of the most charming — and least touristy — lie in the districts just beyond the ring.

A visit to one of the classic coffee houses for coffee and home-made cake is de rigueur. Most sights are on or inside the famous **Ringstrasse**, which encircles the city centre. For architectural splendours of the late 19th century, take trams 1 or 2, passing the neo-Gothic **Rathaus** (City Hall), Burgtheater, Parliament and **Staatsoper**. Vienna is extremely well placed to be part of a rail tour of Europe, with extremely good connections to Germany, the Czech Republic, Slovakia, Hungary, Slovenia, Switzerland, Italy and beyond. Vienna is included on **Route 32** (p279).

TRAVEL BASICS

⇌ A new main station is under construction on the site of the current **Südbahnhof**. To be called Hauptbahnhof, it is due to open in 2013. In the meantime, trains to and from the south and east serve Wien **Meidling**, linked to the centre by frequent S-Bahn trains, whilst trains to Bratislava leave from temporary platforms called **Südbahnhof (Ostbahn)**. The west, also Germany, Switzerland and Hungary, is served by the **Westbahnhof**, Europapl., whilst the area north-west of Vienna is served by **Franz-Josefs-Bahnhof**, Julius-Tandler-Pl. All stations are linked by tram or underground services and have good facilities. ✈ **Vienna International Airport** (www.viennaairport.com) is 19 km south-east of the city at Schwechat. Flight information, ☎ 01 700 722 233 (24 hrs). Express bus transfers (Vienna Airport Lines) run from the airport to City Air Terminal (U-Bahn and S-Bahn station: Landstrasse/Wien Mitte) and back and to Westbahnhof and Südbahnhof every 30 mins 0500–2400 (journey time 20 mins). There are also S-Bahn trains to Wien Mitte.

The U-Bahn (underground trains), S-Bahn (suburban trains) inside city limits, trams and buses all use the same tickets, with transfers allowed. Single tickets €2.20 if bought on board. Also sold in blocks of four. Under-6s travel free, under-15s travel free on Sundays, public holidays and school holidays; photo ID required. You can get a 24 hour (€5.70) or 72 hour (€13.60) rover ticket; there are also 8-day network tickets for €28.80, which can be used by several people travelling together. Just before travelling, validate (time-stamp) the ticket. Another option is the **Wien-Karte** (Vienna Card €18.50, from hotels, Vienna Transport ticket offices and tourist offices), valid for 72 hrs transport, plus four days discounts on museums, sights, shops, restaurants, concert, theatre tickets and more.

INFORMATION

Pick up the free city map from the **Vienna Tourist Board**, Albertinapl. (corner of Maysedergasse), ☎ 01 245 55 (www.info.wien.at), the *Vienna Scene* for an overview

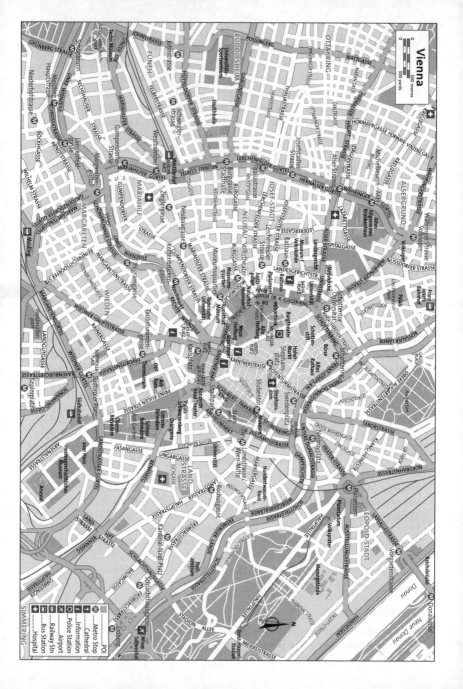

of the city and the monthly *Programm*, which lists events. Information and accommodation bureaux are also at Westbahnhof, Südbahnhof and Schwechat Airport. Finding **internet access** in Vienna poses no problem at all — over 120 free wi-fi hot spots across the city should do the trick.

Accommodation

📧 Moderately priced **hotels** and guesthouses include **Pension Dr Geissler**, Postgasse 14, ☎ 01 533 2803 (www.hotelpension.at), €€; some cheaper rooms with shared facilities are available at the very central **Hotel Austria**, Fleischmarkt 20, ☎ 01 515 23 (www.hotelaustria-wien.at), €€. South-west of the cathedral is **Pension Quisisana**, Windmühlgasse 6, ☎ 01 587 3341, (www.quisisana.at), €€. Close to the new Museumsquartier, **Pension Wild**, Lange Gasse 10, ☎ 01 406 5174 (www.pension-wild.com), €€, has great rooms and is both backpacker- and gay-friendly.

Hostels: The two stand-out hostels in Vienna are both close to the Westbahnhof; the **Hostel Ruthensteiner**, Robert-Hamerlinggasse 24, ☎ 01 893 4202 (www.hostelruthensteiner.com) is very friendly and has a wonderfully peaceful courtyard, whilst the **Wombat's City Hostel**, Grangasse 6, ☎ 01 897 2336 (www.wombats-hostels.com) is known for its lively atmosphere. Another well-regarded independent hostel is the relaxed **Believe It Or Not Hostel**, Myrthengasse 10, ☎ 01 526 4658 (www.believe-it-or-not-vienna.at). **My MOjO vie Home** (www.mymojovie.at) is a network of private accommodation providers, who offer everything from dorms to private rooms.

Itineraries
Half day
Whizz around **the Ring** on a tram to spot highlights including the Rathaus and Staatsoper (State Opera). Pause at the **Hofburg** palace to take a peek at the sumptuous state apartments, then scale the tower of **Stephansdom** (St Stephen's Cathedral) for sweeping views over Vienna's rooftops.

One day
Make a beeline for the **MuseumsQuartier** to seek out Klimt masterpieces in the **Leopold Museum** and quirky gifts in **quartier21**. Nip over to Spittelberg for an alfresco lunch on the cobblestones. Get your cultural fix with Rembrandt and Warhol originals in the splendid **Albertina**.

Two days
See Lipizzaner stallions perform at the **Spanische Hofreitschule** (Spanish Riding School) and head to **Leopoldstadt** to stand in awe of Hundert-wasserhaus's crazed colours.

By night enjoy theatrical highs at the illuminated **Burgtheater** (National Theatre). Rent a bike to cycle trails weaving through the **Prater** (stopping for a ride on the iconic Ferris wheel). Before you return, pick up gifts from the high-street stores lining Mariahilfer Strasse.

More

If time isn't a problem, stay longer to discover the region's rich pickings. Go west to the **Wienerwald** to see the Seegrotte Hinterbrühl (Europe's largest subterranean lake), glimpse precipitous gorges and hill walk in tranquil nature reserves. Climb **Leopold-Figl-Warte** for some spectacular alpine views. An hour's drive from Vienna, the River Danube snakes through the **Wachau Valley**. This UNESCO World Heritage Site has a clutch of Benedictine abbeys, cliff-top castles and gently sloping vineyards (see box p586).

VIENNA ON A BUDGET

For the cost of a tram ticket, you can arrange your **personalised tour** of the sights on the Ring — take tram lines 1 or 2 for fleeting glimpses of the immense Hofburg and Rathaus. Pause to admire the Volksgarten's attractive fountains, flowers and sculptures. Stepping over to Landstrasse, you don't have to be a dedicated art lover to be enthralled by the **Hundertwasserhaus**, an amazingly vibrant explosion of colour and mosaics that doesn't cost a penny to admire.

You can easily spend an afternoon combing the hip **Spittelberg** district's warren of cobbled streets, punctuated with beautiful Biedermeier town houses, art studios and pavement cafés.

Nature costs nothing in the **University of Vienna Botanic Gardens**, where you can spot alpine species, tropical ferns and Antarctic beech trees. Join the locals to stroll through the shady **Prater** on a Sunday morning and pop into **MUK** (the Museum for the Art of Entertainment) for a free taste of circus life. On the city's fringes, visit the **Lainzer Tiergarten** with its peaceful oak woods, where you can spy red deer, wild boar and woodpeckers.

ART IN VIENNA

Unrivalled in the art department, Vienna offers a kaleidoscopic palette of Old Masters and new talent. Start off at the Hofburg, which showcases glittering jewels and Biedermeier portraits, then head over to the Albertina, with its riot of Rembrandts, Picassos and Warhols, or gaze on the **Kunsthistorisches Museum's riches**, which include works by Velázquez and Caravaggio. Design reaches a peak at the **MAK** (Museum of Applied Arts), which houses precious *Wiener Werkstätte* pieces. Visit the Upper Belvedere for great Impressionist works and a fine Klimt collection; or see Hundertwasser's colours make a secessionist splash at KunstHaus Wien. For a modern twist to the city's art offerings visit the **MuseumsQuartier**. Take a trip to the cube-shaped Leopold Museum, which houses an impressive collection of Egon Schiele paintings, or the **Kunsthalle Wien** where contemporary art comes boldly to the fore. The monolithic **MUMOK** (Museum of Modern Art Ludwig Foundation) gives you a shove into the 20th century with works by Warhol, Magritte and Kandinsky.

THE BEST OF VIENNA

Hofburg (Imperial Palace)
Admire the lavish state apartments and some seriously glittering crown jewels at this vast palace complex, which was once home to the Austrian Habsburgs.

MuseumsQuartier
Explore one of the ten biggest cultural districts in the world, full of avant-garde architecture, modern art and funky boutiques. Located at Museumsplatz 1/5 (www.mqw.at); U-Bahn: Museumsquartier/Volkstheater.

Prater
The big wheel turns, carousels tinkle and roller coasters offer eye-popping thrills at this massive funfair set in acres of parkland. U-Bahn: Praterstern.

Stephansdom (St Stephen's Cathedral)
Gaze up at the filigree spires and mosaic roof of Vienna's Gothic cathedral and climb to the top for giddy views.

Staatsoper (Vienna State Opera)
See world-class opera and ballet at the 19th-century Opera House.

Österreichische Galerie Belvedere (Belvedere Gallery)
Roam manicured gardens and see works by Monet at Prince Eugene of Savoy's rococo summer palace. One end, the Upper Belvedere, is close to Südbahnhof.

Hundertwasserhaus
Curvy walls, twisting trees and shimmering mosaics characterise Friedensreich Hundertwasser's house. The Hundertwasserhaus is to the east of the centre at Kegelgasse 34–38, close to the Danube canal. U-Bahn: Landstrasse/Wien Mitte.

FOOD

Vienna serves fine food at far more affordable prices than many other European capitals. There are thousands of places to eat, including sleek tapas bars, elegant Michelin-starred restaurants and the ubiquitous *Würstelstände* (sausage stands). Whether it's a cavernous pub with homebrews and tasty snacks or a wood-panelled wine tavern, this city defies anyone to go hungry.

When it comes to dining districts, the centre's eateries are a mouth-watering fusion of Viennese classics and world flavours. Tucked down the streets fanning out from Stephansplatz are relaxed *trattorias* and gourmet haunts, sleek, ultra-modern sushi bars and snug cafés serving cheap and seriously tasty fare. These are fantastic places for striking up a conversation with the locals.

In the Wieden district, Vienna's vibrant **Naschmarkt** is an attraction in its own right. Alongside the mounds of fresh fruit are huge cheeses, seafood, olives and racks of colourful spices. You can spend hours wandering from stall to stall, popping into cafés for an espresso and eating your way around the world at hole-in-the-wall restaurants dishing up everything from falafel and curries to sushi and sizzling stir-fries fresh from the wok.

THE WACHAU VALLEY

A heady mix of world-class culture and natural highs, this UNESCO World Heritage Site beckons — explore it on foot, by bike, or accompanied by a llama. While many people flit past en route to Vienna, it's worth lingering to explore the hidden nooks of this **Eden-like valley** that wears every season well. In summer, boats chugging along the river reveal snapshot views of **gravity-defying castles**, in autumn, vines kindle into colour and apple orchards hang heavy, while winter is time to retreat to a cosy *Heurige* (wine cellar) to relax with a glass of Grüner Veltliner by an open fire. Sounds tempting? It is.

There are frequent train connections between the Westbahnhof and towns like Krems (1 hr 10 mins), Melk (1 hr 20 mins) and Ybbs (1 hr 30 mins — see ERT 950 or 990). There are also buses from Vienna.

CULTURE AND NIGHTLIFE

Vienna positively twinkles by night, as the Hofburg shines and the capital's bars and restaurants glow. Whether you're looking for a relaxed pub in which to chill out, a sleek lounge bar to sip on a cocktail, or you just want to let loose on a crowded dance floor, this 24-hour city always comes up with the goods.

No staid old maid of a town, Vienna has a vibrant **alternative pulse** that throbs around the desperately hip **Gürtel** area, where you can party to urban and electro beats in bars with an industrial edge beneath the railway arches. When you tire of the pulsating bass, make for nearby **Spittelberg**, where creaking pubs, delectable cocktail lounges and vibrant bars huddle in a web of narrow streets waiting to be explored.

As night falls, Vienna's stages light up with stars. Culture vultures should take a perch and catch contemporary and classic performances at the sumptuous **Burgtheater** (National Theatre), and opera, ballet and classical music at the grand 19th-century **Staatsoper** (Vienna State Opera). If you want something a bit less mainstream, the MuseumsQuartier's **Halle E & G** and **Tanzquartier Wien** are at the crest of cutting-edge performing arts.

EVENTS

If you are into 'high' culture with a side order of kitsch, the **Vienna Ball Season** in January and February is the time to pull out your tux or your gown. Later in the year, the **Vienna Festival** (May-June) brings some of the world's greatest performers of classical arts to stages across the city.

In June, the **Danube Island Festival** is a three-day, open-air event with acts from Austria and around the world, whilst in July the cool cats hit town for the annual **Jazz Fest Wien**. In October, the **Viennale** is Austria's biggest film festival, showcasing the best of local and international cinematic talent on screens around the city.

Warsaw (Warszawa)

Warsaw, a city of some one-and-three-quarter million and capital of a resurgent Polish nation, is once again punching its weight as a major European city. Straddling the **River Wisła** (Vistula), its location between the old powers of Germany and Russia has ensured that it has been a victim of history on more than one occasion. After the horrors of World War II, the communist period saw the meticulous reconstruction of the city's historic buildings and a rash of **Socialist Realist building**. During the same time, cultural activity was suppressed and the spirit of the city forced underground.

Warsaw emerged from the communist era determined to rejoin the European mainstream and shed its Eastern Bloc image. The transition to capitalism was painful at first, but Warsaw residents took to market economics with typical gusto. Poland joined the EU in 2004 allowing Warsaw to enjoy the economic benefits of Union membership. One consequence of these benefits was a renewed vigour in the city's **cultural life**. While it may not be able to rival Kraków's museums, galleries and historic legacy, Warsaw is the hub of modern Polish culture and it's where the trends and fashions are set. It is also Poland's **centre of academia** and the large student and young professional contingent has ensured one of Europe's most happening nightlife scenes. Warsaw is on **Routes 45** (p365) and **46** (p374).

TRAVEL BASICS

⇌ **Warszawa Centralna** is the principal rail station at Al. Jerozolimskie 54, ☎ 22 194 36 (www.intercity.pl). Other large stations in the city are: **Warszawa Wschodnia** on the east bank of the Wisła River, and the western suburban station, **Warszawa Zachodnia**, 3 km west of Centralna, opposite the PKS bus station.

✈ **Warsaw Frédéric Chopin Airport**, ul. Żwirki i Wigury 1, ☎ 22 650 42 20, lies 10 km south of the city, with two terminals (arrivals and departures). Airport City Bus 175 (N32 at night) every 20 mins (30 mins weekends and holidays), stopping at major hotels and Warszawa Centralna rail station.

Trams and 🚌 **buses** operate on a frequent network, ☎ 22 194 84 (www.ztm. waw.pl). Buses run from 0500–2300 on weekdays. Prepaid tickets (from kiosks etc.) are cheaper than paying on the bus. Night buses operate every 30 mins and cost three times the normal fare. The useful PPWK-published Warsaw map shows bus routes. The single underground (metro) line runs north to south through the centre of the city (red 'M' on yellow background denotes a metro station); trains run every six minutes, 0430–2330. Covering all public transport, 24 hr tickets are excellent value.

INFORMATION

ℹ There are **tourist offices**, ☎ 22 194 31, with English-speaking staff who will also help with accommodation at Warsaw Frédéric Chopin Airport (open until 2000), at Warszawa Centralna (central railway station), main hall upstairs; and also at ul. Krakowskie Przedmieście 39.

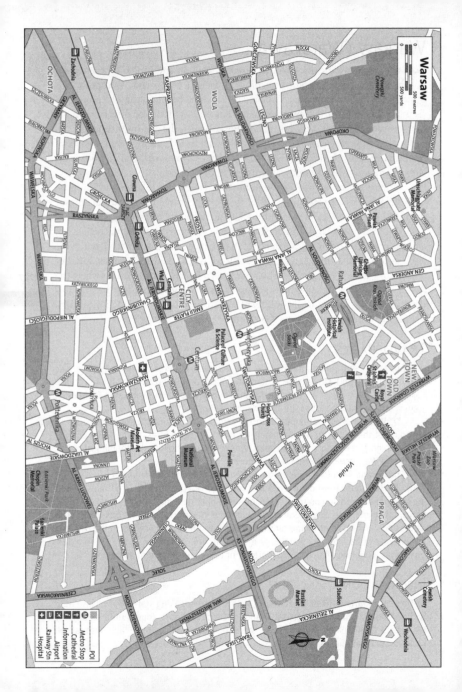

The monthly *Warsaw Insider* magazine, is an expat publication full of useful tips. The English-language *Warsaw Voice* has good features and local news items.

ACCOMMODATION

Hotels: The **Campanile**, ul. Towarowa 2, ☎ 22 582 72 00 (www.campanile.com), €€, remains one of the best value options in town. The rooms are bright and modern and the bathrooms are shiny. Other budget options include the **Harenda**, ul. Krakowskie Przedmieście 4/6, ☎ 22 826 00 71 (www.harenda.pl), €–€€, good central location with a 'ranch' underneath that's a favourite with drinkers, and **Hetman**, ul. Kłpotowskiego 36, ☎ 22 511 98 00 (www.hotelhetman.pl), €, which is clean, cheap and friendly.

Hostels: Extremely popular are **Nathan's Villa**, ul. Piekna 24/26, ☎ 22 622 29 46 (www.nathansvilla.com) and **Oki Doki**, Plac Dąbrowskiego 3, ☎ 22 826 51 12 (www.okidoki.pl), so in the summer it is recommended to call ahead to book a bed. Other hostels include the **Moon Hostel**, Foksal 16, ☎ 50 620 31 22 (www.moonhostel.pl), and the **Hostel Helvetia**, Sewerynów 7, ☎ 22 826 71 08 (www.hostel-helvetia.pl).

ITINERARIES

Half day
Pushed for time? An afternoon is just about enough time to glimpse Warsaw's Jekyll and Hyde nature. Start off by visiting the communist monstrosity otherwise known as the **Palace of Culture and Science**, and don't forgo a visit to the panoramic viewing platform at the top. Follow this by getting a cab up to the **Old Town** for a quick walk around its atmospheric streets, making enough time for a gut-busting traditional meal.

One day
As above, though more time on your hands means a proper opportunity to nose around the Old Town, with a visit to the **Museum of Modern Art** or the **Pawiak Prison**. Don't forget to stray north of the **Barbakan** to have a look around the New Town area.

Finish off with a visit to the **Warsaw Uprising Museum**, a powerful tribute to the heroism of those who died fighting for liberty. A visit here is not just for war buffs, but vital in understanding modern Warsaw.

Two days
Set aside a day to visit **Wilanów**, a supreme throwback to the days of Imperial Poland and packed with interesting exhibitions and collections. Do dress up and enjoy **the clubs and bars** of Warsaw, but try to limit the hangover so you can make an early-morning visit to the **Russian Market** before it's gone forever. Escape from the chaos and babble of a thousand tongues by walking through Warsaw's largest and most beautiful cemetery, **Powązki**, and don't miss the neighbouring **Jewish Cemetery**, a forlorn and thoughtful walk.

More

When you've done the above, make time to potter around Warsaw's series of churches and cathedrals, many of which come dripping with stories and sacral art. Make the foray into the **Praga district** to see a side of Warsaw left off most itineraries, and while you're there, temper your sightseeing with a drawn-out coffee in one of the many artsy cafés that have sprung up this part of the city.

WARSAW ON A BUDGET

Warsaw can be a financially draining city and you may leave feeling rather empty in the pocket. But that's not to say it's impossible to enjoy Warsaw if you find yourself skint. First off, remember that most **Polish museums** are in the habit of waiving admission charges once a week (usually Sun). Even better, many **museums of martyrdom and national suffering** are free all week. To leave on good terms just drop a few coins into the donations tin at the end.

Take some time to explore the **churches and cathedrals**, of which Poland has no shortage, making sure not to miss St John's Cathedral. Save on time and money with the **Warsaw Tourist Card**, which provides reduced or free entry to museums, galleries and other institutions, as well as discounts in hotels, clubs, theatres and restaurants, tour companies and bike rental amongst others. It also includes a public transport ticket, and prices start from 20 PLN for 24 hours.

FOOD

Polish food is a simple, filling affair. Starters include a range of tasty soups such as *żurek* (a sour rye soup) and *barszcz* (beetroot) and more traditional restaurants will serve up a plate of bread and *smalec* (lard) as a complimentary prelude to your meal. One particular **Polish speciality** to look for is *pierogi*, a ravioli-style offering filled with either meat or cabbage and sometimes even with seasonal fruit. Polish sausages, otherwise known as *kiełbasa*, are famous the world over, and for good reason, while the local game dishes also impress.

To enjoy Polish food the real way then visit one of the **milk bars** (*bar mleczny*) that stubbornly refuse to die. You'll need to place an order with the monolingual lady before claiming your winnings through a hatchway. Quite often what you'll

A FOOTBALL SUMMER

In June 2012, the elite footballing nations of Europe will be coming to Poland and their co-hosts Ukraine for the Euro 2012 tournament. Warsaw will be hosting five games during the tournament, including one of the semi-finals. Although it will be nearly impossible to get a ticket unless you do so well in advance, one of the great things about tournaments such as these are the 'fan zones' in host cities such as Warsaw, where you can join fellow fans to **watch games** on the big screen. For more information on what is going on in Warsaw, visit www.warsaw2012.eu.

THE BEST OF WARSAW

Muzeum Sztuki Nowoczesnej (Museum of Modern Art)
Cutting-edge contemporary Polish art inside a delightful 18th-century castle. Not far from the Palace of Culture and Science on ul. Pańska 3, the closest metro station is Centrum. Open Tues–Sun 1200–2000. Free entry.

The Old Town
A bewitching network of cobbled streets, church spires and hidden courtyards.

Palace of Culture and Science
Stalin's gift to Poland, and one of the most notorious existing examples of Socialist Realist architecture.

Muzeum Więzienia Pawiak (Pawiak Prison Museum)
A grim reminder of Nazi terror, the museum is located on ul. Dzielna 24/26 (metro: Ratusz). Closed Mon & Tues.

Royal Castle
A symbol of Warsaw rebuilt, as with much of the surrounding Old Town.

Warsaw's Jewish past
Learn more about Warsaw's fascinating, and ultimately tragic, history.

Muzeum Powstania Warszawskiego (Warsaw Uprising Museum)
Warsaw's most heroic moment relived inside one of Poland's finest museums. Located on ul. Grzybowska 79. Closed Tues. Tram 22/24 from Centrum.

Wilanów
A majestic palace likened to Versailles. Wilanów is to the south of the city centre, and can be reached using bus 116.

receive will resemble little more than a steaming plate of mashed objects, though you'll pay next to nothing for the honour.

However, Warsaw's international popularity has led to an explosion of new cuisines arriving in the capital, with sushi and fusion food being the most popular. Practically every venue will have an English menu, and English-speaking service is guaranteed in all but the old-school restaurants.

CULTURE AND NIGHTLIFE

As befits a capital city, Warsaw offers a **rich and varied social life** with something to please every taste. There is no particular centre for nightlife, rather numerous areas with clusters of nightspots. On the whole, most clubbers find themselves in the area between **pl. Trzech Krzyży** and **pl. Teatralny**. In particular, ul. Foksal and ul. Nowy Świat have heaps of bars and clubs, and you'll find the garden furniture coming out at the first hint of summer.

Although Warsaw is not really a 24-hour city, venues do tend to stay open late with bar staff rarely calling last orders. **Friday is the biggest night out**, so

Warsaw Jazz

Although it comes as a surprise to most Western Europeans, jazz has a long tradition in Poland. Pre-war dance club bands in Warsaw and other cities got Poles moving to swing-based jazz in the 1930s. After World War II the communist government suppressed the music and it was forced underground. During this so-called 'Catacomb Period', performances were confined to private homes and musicians risked arrest. The death of Stalin in 1953 and the subsequent political thaw afforded jazz musicians a new-found freedom to perform in public.

In the early 1960s the first Warsaw Jazz Jamboree Festival was staged. Now called the **JVC Jazz Festival Warsaw**, it is one of the longest-running jazz festivals in Europe and has hosted many of the great names in jazz including Miles Davis, Thelonious Monk, Dizzy Gillespie and Ray Charles. It takes place every October in the awe-inspiring Palace of Culture and Science. Not content with just one jazz festival, Warsaw also plays host to the **Warsaw Summer Days Jazz** and the **Jazz in the Old Town** festivals. The latter is a series of free open-air performances in the Rynek (Main Square) of the Old Town and is held every Saturday evening in July and August. These concerts often attract large crowds and they are a great way to spend a balmy summer's evening in historic surroundings. Even outside the festival season, Warsaw has a vibrant year-round jazz scene.

don't be surprised to find Saturday nights quiet in comparison; this is when many locals choose to get out of the city for the weekend, especially in summer.

Foreigners will not be able to grasp much of the Polish language theatre productions in town, but there is ample opportunity to enjoy **opera and classical music**. Before its destruction in World War II, Warsaw was a royal, baroque city and it has seen many composers and performers come and go. **Chopin** is Poland's most famous composer, and his music can be heard at the festival and the famous piano competition dedicated to him and at concerts held throughout the year.

Events

Warsaw may not have a packed calendar of festivals like its rival Kraków, but nevertheless has a number of interesting annual events, with most of them taking place in the summer months. Local and international musicians gather each Easter for the **Ludwig van Beethoven Easter Festival** to honour the master in a series of concerts and related events. The **Anniversary of the Warsaw Ghetto Uprising** is 19 April, when flowers are laid at the Monument to the Ghetto Heroes to remember those who died in the 1943 uprising.

In June and August it is time for the **Warsaw Summer Jazz Days** when free contemporary jazz concerts are held all around the city, whilst in July streets, squares and parks become the stage for theatrical performances as part of the **International Street Art Festival**. In early October over 100 films are presented on the big screen during the annual **Warsaw International Film Festival**.

Zurich (Zürich)

There's more to Switzerland's largest city than gold bars and chocolate bars. It's a classical city with a contemporary edge, preserving its architectural and cultural heritage, yet surprising the world with the latest innovations in art and architecture, fashion, shopping and design. Most of Zurich's sights fall within a compact, walkable area either side of the **Limmat River**, which bisects the city centre. The ancient hilly **Niederdorf** district to the east is a veritable labyrinth of ancient, cobbled lanes brimming with trendy bars, cafés and quirky shops. To the west, the **Altstadt** (Old Town) contains many of the city's finest historic buildings, and broad, leafy **Bahnhofstrasse** counts among the world's most sophisticated shopping boulevards. The newly trendy former industrial quarter of **Zurich West** reflects the city's radical change in recent years, while the lake, with its beautiful grassy parks and lakeside promenades, is framed by majestic, snow-capped mountains. Zurich is on **Routes 29** (p257), **30** (p265) and **32** (p279).

TRAVEL BASICS

⇌ **Zurich Hauptbahnhof** (HB) is on the west side of the River Limmat, leading out onto Bahnhofstr., the main shopping street. ✈ **Zurich Airport** is 10 km north-east of the city centre; flight information, ☎ 0900 300 313 (premium rate); general enquiries ☎ 043 816 22 11 (www.zurich-airport.com). There are 6 to 8 trains an hour from the rail station, taking approx. 10 mins (ERT 529). The centre of Zurich is small enough to explore on foot. All **buses and trams**, run by VBZ Züri-Linie (www.vbz.ch), leave the terminal outside the HB every 6–12 mins 0530–2400. Buy your ticket from machines at stops before boarding. An all-zones day ticket valid after 0900 is available for CHF24. The **Zurich Card** covers public transport and visitor attractions (24 hrs CHF20, 72 hrs CHF40). **Bikes** can be borrowed (free with a refundable CHF20 deposit) at the rail station and, from May–Oct, at several other central locations including Enge, Oerlikon Swissôtel, the Opera House and the Globus City department store (www.zuerirollt.ch).

INFORMATION

🛈 **Tourist office**: on the station concourse at the Hauptbahnhof, ☎ 044 215 40 00 (www.zuerich.com). This efficient, well-stocked office sells a street map, provides a free accommodation service and the monthly *Zurich City Guide*. **Internet access** in Switzerland is exemplary and almost ubiquitous. A variety of companies provide a vast number of free access points throughout the city.

ACCOMMODATION

⛨ **Hotels**: The **Dakini's Bed & Breakfast**, Brauerstr. 87, ☎ 044 291 42 20 (www.dakini.ch), €–€€, is two apartment houses, including colour-coded rooms, while **ZicZac Rock-Hotel**, Marktgasse 17, ☎ 044 261 21 81 (www.ziczac.ch), €–€€, has a great atmosphere and is good value for money. The **St Josef**, Hirschengraben 64–68, ☎ 044 250 57 57 (www.st-josef.ch), €€, is between the rail station and university. For

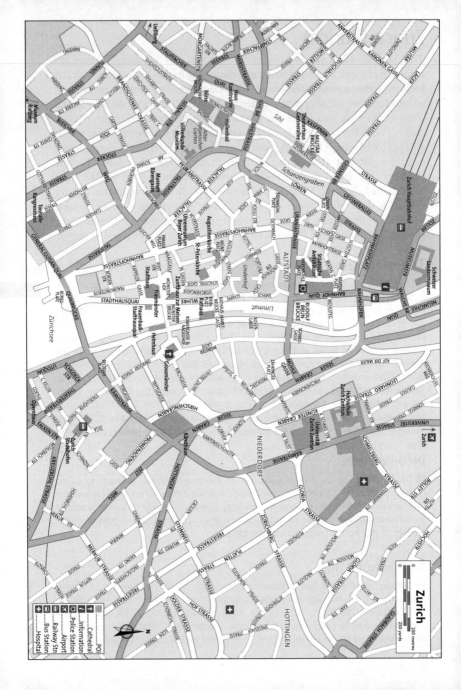

something a little different, try the **Rigihof**, Universitätsstr. 101, ☎ 044 360 12 00 (www.leonardo-hotels.com), €€€, which is a Bauhaus-style hotel with rooms dedicated to people who once lived or worked in the city, including Max Bill, Carl Jung, and many more. **Hostels**: **Hotel Biber/City Backpacker**, Niederdorfstr. 5, ☎ 044 251 90 15 (www.city-backpacker.ch), is in the lively Niederdorfer area and has dorms and private rooms. A brand new hostel, small, cosy and right in the heart of the city, is the **Langstars Hostel**, Langstrasse 120, ☎ 043 317 96 55 (www.langstars.ch). The (HI) **youth hostel** is in Mutschellenstr. 114, ☎ 043 399 78 00 (www.youthhostel.ch/zuerich), south of the city in Wollishofen (tram 7 to Morgental, then a 5 min-walk).

ITINERARIES

Half day

If you only have a few hours, start at the Hauptbahnhof and stroll along the celebrated **Bahnhofstrasse**, admiring the glittering window displays. Stop for coffee before heading down to the **lake** to glimpse the city's impressive mountainous backdrop. Head back along the river to visit **Fraumünster** with its dazzling stained-glass windows by Chagall, or the **Grossmünster** on the east bank of the Limmat, before enjoying a snack in a typical Zurich café.

One day

After you have completed the recommended half-day sightseeing, add a museum visit to your itinerary. The **Schweizerisches Landesmuseum** provides a fascinating historical background to the city, while the **Kunsthaus** is the city's finest gallery. Spend the rest of the day exploring **Niederdorf**, dipping into its delightful quirky boutiques, and its trendy cafés and bars.

Two days

The extra day provides plenty of time to **explore the lake** (see box p596). Stroll along the east bank and take time out to watch the world go by. Then take a boat trip for a new perspective of the city. Alternatively, take in another museum — modern art lovers in particular will enjoy the **Migros Museum** — or climb to the summit of **Uetliberg**, Zurich's very own mountain. You'll also have time to eat some chocolate, buy some souvenirs, and check out the city's nightlife.

More

A longer stay enables you to soak up the **café culture** of Niederdorf, appreciate the relaxed lifestyle of the Zürchers, and top up your tan at one of the city's legendary lidos. Take a trip **out of town** to explore the beautiful surroundings.

ZURICH ON A BUDGET

Strapped for cash in one of the world's most expensive cities? Don't worry! There are plenty of sights and attractions to amuse you, without placing demands on your wallet. Art aficionados on a budget need not be disappointed in Zurich, as many of the **museums and galleries** are free, including the Helmhaus and the Spielzeugmuseum (Toy Museum). Even the beautiful **Botanischer Garten**, the pièce de résistance of all the city parks and gardens, is free.

For a taste of historic Zurich, explore the **Altstadt**, where the hilly, cobbled streets are lined with romantic, shuttered houses, many painted in pastel shades and adorned with cascading geraniums. Then soak up the atmosphere and people-watch in the sociable **Niederdorf** quarter. Better still, why not explore the city on one of the free-to-hire bikes?

On a fine day, there is nothing more enjoyable than walking along the quaysides of the **Limmat and the lake**. The lake draws visitors and locals alike to its shores to relax, snooze, sunbathe or simply watch the world go by. If you're feeling really energetic, climb to the top of **Uetliberg** for stunning views of the city and the Alps and a picnic spot to take your breath away.

Food

Zurich has a large selection of restaurants of most nationalities, as well as its own local cuisine. Local specialities include *Kalbgeschnetzeltes* (veal in cream sauce) and the less expensive pork version, *Schweingeschnetzeltes*.

There are numerous fast-food and conventional restaurants around the huge station complex. The largest selection of eating places is on or just off Niederdorfstr., the main nightlife area, which stretches for about 1 km on the east side of the river, a block back from it. Fierce competition keeps prices at a relatively reasonable level.

Culture and nightlife

Zurich has plenty going on. In summer there are a number of **outside bars**, particularly by the lake. Around 500 venues stay open into the small hours at weekends, and cater for most tastes.

Exploring Lake Zurich

Lake Zurich offers an enormous choice of short excursions. Near the city, its shores are dominated by grassy parks, lakeside promenades and early 20th-century mansions. Further afield, picturesque villages such as Rapperswil and Küsnacht punctuate the shoreline, flanked by lush, green countryside and gentle hills. Even the lake itself offers a wide variety of activities, including sailing, pleasure-boat cruising and swimming. The *Zürichsee Schifffahrtsgesellschaft*, ☎ 044 487 13 33 (www.zsg.ch) offers a variety of excursions from two-hour mini-cruises to full-day outings. During summer months ZSG ferries stop at every lakeside town. The S-Bahn lines run the length of both shores, offering an easy, scenic journey to such destinations as Rapperswil and Küsnacht.

THE BEST OF ZURICH

Schweizerisches Landesmuseum (Swiss National Museum)
Once you have a grasp of the nation's colourful history, walks around town are all the more rewarding. Located next to the Hauptbahnhof on Museumstrasse. Closed Mon.

Kunsthaus
Switzerland's top art gallery spans the centuries from the Middle Ages to the present, but specialises in 19th- and 20th-century Swiss art. The Kunsthaus is in Niederdorf, on Heimplatz. Closed Mon.

Fraumünster
Renowned for its five world-famous stained-glass windows by Chagall, which together represent a lavish fusion of colour and ethereality, the church is one of the highlights of the Zurich Altstadt.

Niederdorf
This ancient quarter, distinguished by its picturesque cobbled streets, tiny specialist shops, bars and restaurants, is especially atmospheric by night.

Altstadt (Old Town)
The city's most charming quarter, south of the Hauptbahnhof, with its steep, cobbled lanes, beautiful mansions and tranquil, shady squares.

Grossmünster
The city's cathedral and the birthplace of the Swiss Reformation. Climb the tower for the best views over the city. The Grossmünster is in Niederdorf, on the opposite side of the Limmat from the Altstadt.

There's no shortage of bars, clubs and street performers around **Niederdorfstrasse**, a lively, safe area, despite its reputation as the red-light district. Fans of the classical arts should definitely check out Zurich's acclaimed **opera company**, which performs at the Opernhaus Zürich, Falkenstr. 1, ☎ 044 268 64 00 (www.opernhaus.ch).

EVENTS

There are a number of top-quality events taking place throughout the year. In February/March it is time for the first major festival of the year, the **ZüriCarneval**, as the Niederdorf comes alive with parades, fancy-dress, street entertainment and fireworks. More sedate is the **Zurich Festival**, which takes place in June and July and is one of Europe's top cultural events, with an extensive programme of opera, music, theatre and cultural exhibitions throughout the city. In August nearly a million party-goers take to the streets as part of the **Street Parade**, a colourful techno event that is Europe's largest street party. In September and October it is time for the **Zurich Film Festival**. Although it has only been going since 2006, it has already become established as one of the most important on the circuit.

Gazetteer

Countries from A to Z

AlbaniaAndorraAustriaBelarusBelgium
Bosnia and HerzegovinaBulgariaCroatia
Czech RepublicDenmarkEstonia
Faroe IslandsFinlandFranceGermany
GreeceHungaryIcelandIrelandItaly
KosovoLatviaLiechtensteinLithuania
LuxembourgMacedoniaMaltaMoldova
MonacoMontenegroNetherlandsNorway
PolandPortugalRomaniaRussia
San MarinoSerbiaSlovakiaSloveniaSpain
SwedenSwitzerlandTurkeyUkraine
United KingdomVatican City

There is some information that is best presented on a **country-by-country** basis. In our gazetteer we give key data such as language, time zone and currency. For countries that feature in our 50 rail routes, we give additional travel information.

In the gazetteer, you will find 14 maps of varying scales which together cover the entire area described in our 50 routes. Beside the respective country headings in the gazetteer, we give the page where you can locate that country on a map. The maps show **main rail routes**, and on the larger scale maps some lesser rail routes are included too. The red lines indicate **international boundaries** and red is also used to show country names in capitals. You can use the maps in conjunction with the *Thomas Cook European Rail Timetable* to plot your own itineraries across Europe by rail. For more comprehensive mapping, refer to the *Thomas Cook Rail Map of Europe*.

Within the gazetteer, you'll find photos that capture the flavour of a country or region. A photo credit to 'hidden europe' shows that the image comes from the editors' collection. All other images, in each case duly credited to the original photographer, were sourced through dreamstime.com.

ALBANIA — SEE MAP P608

The small republic in the eastern Adriatic features on few tourist itineraries, but there is no reason why it should not, for Albania offers remarkable old Ottoman towns, stunning beaches and some of Europe's finest mountain scenery. And it boasts some deliciously antiquated trains (see ERT 1390). No passenger trains cross the country's borders, so the Albanian rail network is effectively isolated from the rest of Europe. Read more in our **Sidetracks** on p329.

ESSENTIALS: Local name: Shqipëria — Population: 3.6m — Capital: Tirana — Currency: Lek — Language: Albanian (Italian and English often understood in main towns) Accommodation costs: low — Time zone: winter GMT+1, summer GMT+2 — International dialling code: +355

ANDORRA — SEE MAPS P621 AND P665

The mountain principality in the **Pyrenees** is one of just a handful of rail-free countries in mainland Europe. Tacky shops and concrete aplenty in the capital but fine hiking and skiing in the hills around. The nearest you'll get to Andorra by train is **L'Hospitalet** (on **Route 8**). The canny French have recently renamed this station Andorre-L'Hospitalet, and a limited bus service (ERT 313) connects the station with the principality. There are also direct buses to Andorra from Barcelona (ERT 664).

ESSENTIALS: Local name: Andorra — Population: 84k — Capital: Andorra la Vella — Currency: Euro — Language: Catalan (Spanish and French also widely spoken) Accommodation costs: high — Time zone: winter GMT+1, summer GMT+2 — International dialling code: +376

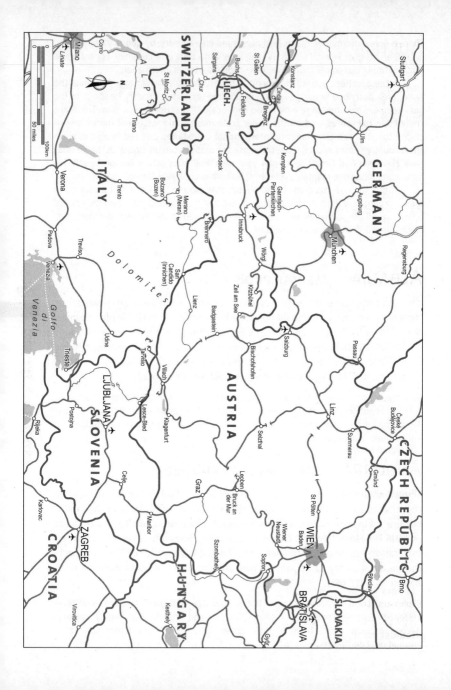

AUSTRIA – SEE MAP P600

Austria feels very much **at the centre** of Europe. Staples in the promotional literature designed to woo visitors are lush green Alpine meadows, steep-roofed chalets with heavy wooden balconies full of geraniums, and onion-domed churches. But Austria has much more, with extremely beautiful lake regions and fine historic cities such as Salzburg and Vienna.

TRAIN TRAVEL IN AUSTRIA

Austria is most conspicuously included in this book in **Route 32**. In addition, **Route 28** crosses the country from north to south, and **Route 39** starts in Austria. Rail travel in Austria is very efficient. Trains are generally clean and modern, and the great majority of internal services run precisely to time. A big plus point for touring Austria by rail is that there are no compulsory reservations or supplements on day trains, including the latest **Railjet high-speed trains**. International services (particularly night trains) arriving in Austria from the Czech Republic, Slovenia and Hungary are prone to delays, and you should be cautious about relying on too tight connecting times when arriving on these trains.

There is an impressive programme of **infrastructure renewal**. For example, throughout 2012 Salzburg Hauptbahnhof is being rebuilt. In Vienna, the entire rail network is being remodelled in anticipation of a new central station which is

ESSENTIALS (AUSTRIA)

Local name: Österreich – Population 8.2m – Capital: Vienna/Wien (p581) – Currency: Euro – Language: German (English is widely spoken in tourist areas) – Accommodation costs: high (see p16) – Time zone: winter GMT+1, summer GMT+2 – International dialling code: +43

OPENING HOURS
Shops: Mon–Fri 0900–1900 (some closing for a 1- or 2-hr lunch break), Sat 0800–1800. Museums: check locally.

PUBLIC HOLIDAYS
1, 6 Jan; Easter Mon; 1 May; Ascension Day; Whit Mon; Corpus Christi; 15 Aug; 26 Oct; 1 Nov; 8, 25, 26 Dec.

PUBLIC TRANSPORT
Long-distance: bus system run by Österreichische Bundesbahnen (ÖBB); usually based by rail stations/post offices. City transport: tickets cheaper from Tabak/Trafik booths; taxis: metered; extra charges for luggage (fixed charges in smaller towns).

TIPPING
Hotels, restaurants, cafés and bars: service charge of 10–15%, but tip of around 10% still expected. Taxis 10%.

TOURIST INFORMATION
Website: www.austria-tourism.at. Look for green 'i' sign; usually called a *Fremdenverkehrsbüro*.

expected to open in 2013 (see p581). Until the new Hauptbahnhof becomes available some trains to, from or through Vienna are calling at stations that are less than perfectly convenient for the city centre. The principal operator is Österreichische Bundesbahnen (ÖBB). The national rail website at www.oebb.at has a good journey planner and downloadable timetables.

RAIL PASSES

Both Eurail and InterRail passes are valid. Many areas within Austria have regional passes, some of which include private railways and local buses. For travel throughout the whole country, the **Einfach-Raus-Ticket** gives a day's second-class travel on regional trains for groups of 2–5 people for €28 (not before 0900 Mon–Fri).

ACCOMMODATION

Hotels are pricey. Standards of cleanliness and comfort are usually high even in simpler places. *Gasthaus/Gasthof* indicates a guesthouse or inn and *Frühstückspension* a bed and breakfast place. **Independent hostels** are a good bet for both private rooms and beds in dorms, although they are mainly limited to the major cities and principal tourist destinations. More widespread, but more institutional, are the *Jugendherbergen* (youth hostels), of which there are more than 100 around the country (www.oejhv.or.at). **Camping** is popular and there are lots of sites, mostly very clean and well run, but pricey. Many sites are open summer only.

FOOD AND DRINK

Food tends towards the **hearty**, with wholesome soups and **meat-dominated** main courses (famously *Wiener Schnitzel* — a thin slice of fried veal or pork), while *Goulasch* (of Hungarian origin) and dumplings are also prevalent. Cakes may be sinfully cream-laden, high in calories, but are rarely sickly; *Apfelstrudel* is the best option for those watching their waistlines. A filling snack, sold by most butchers, is *Wurstsemmel* — slices of sausage with a bread roll. Beer and wine are equally popular. The Austrians also take their coffee seriously.

BELARUS — SEE MAP P636

Rivalling Moldova for the prize of Europe's least known country, the Republic of Belarus is almost certainly Europe's most misunderstood country. For some the country is a reminder of what the Soviet Union was like in its heyday, but more realistically modern Belarus treads a **delicate path** between **Russia** (on its eastern border) and the **European Union** (to the west). For those who take the trouble to visit, a tantalising landscape of beautiful forests and wetlands awaits — all nicely offset by a huge dose of history, not all of it easy to get to grips with.

ESSENTIALS (BELARUS)

Local name: Belarus/Беларусь— Population: 9.5m — Capital: Minsk/Мінск (p371) — Currency: Belarusian rouble (BYR) — Language: Russian and Belarusian (young people in urban areas might speak some English) — Accommodation costs: medium (see p16) — Time zone: GMT+3 (summer and winter) — International dialling code: +375

OPENING HOURS
Food shops: Mon—Sat 0900–2000, else 1100–1900. Opening times of museums vary.

PUBLIC HOLIDAYS
1, 7 Jan; 8 Mar; Easter Mon; 1, 9 May; 3 July; 7 Nov; 25 Dec.

PUBLIC TRANSPORT
Buses and minibuses (*marshrutkas*) are a cheap means of travelling within Belarus. *Marshrutkas* can be very crowded. City transport: trolleybuses, *marshruktas* and buses.

TIPPING
No tipping expected, but in restaurants and cafés a tip of 5% for good service is appreciated.

TOURIST INFORMATION
The Republic of Belarus has a useful and informative government website at www.belarus.by/en. If you want to travel more extensively within Belarus, it is good to bring a map of the country (city maps are however easily available). Tourist offices are still rare and you might only encounter them in larger places.

TRAIN TRAVEL IN BELARUS

You will find Belarus on **Route 45** in this book. Many long-distance trains are international services to neighbouring Russia, Ukraine, Poland and Lithuania with the capital Minsk lying on the busy Warsaw to Moscow corridor. There are high-quality daytime services on principal axes, and slow **overnight trains** linking provincial centres at opposing corners of the country.

Reservation is compulsory on almost all long-distance trains. The Belarusian Railways' website (www.rw.by) is mainly in Russian, but you can check long-distance services, even trains wholly within Belarus, on the CIS rail website www.poezda.net.

RAIL PASSES
Neither Eurail nor InterRail are valid. There are no local rail passes for Belarus, but fares are cheap.

ACCOMMODATION

Forget the normal distinction you might make, perfectly correctly in western Europe, between cheap **hotels** and posher top-end places to rest your head. In the bigger Belarusian cities, many hotels offer several grades of accommodation from simple singles with shared bathroom to luxury suites. Note that foreign visitors usually pay more than locals for the same class of accommodation. There is a buoyant market for **private apartments**, which can be let for just a night or two, and the real growth area is staying out-of-town as Belarus develops its own take on **agritourism**. Find out more at www.ruralbelarus.by. There is no established hostel network.

FOOD AND DRINK

Few options for fine dining. Smart restaurants are few and far between in Belarus, and many Belarusians never eat out. But there is no shortage of good value places where you can linger over a beer and pizza. Standard Belarusian fare mainstreams on potatoes and root vegetables, and you can savour a hundred varieties of *pierogi*.

When it comes to meat dishes, pork reigns supreme, often served in hearty stews. High-quality coffee, beer and vodka are ubiquitous. Although there is no real wine culture in Belarus, you will find in supermarkets, and sometime also in restaurants, wonderful Georgian wines that never seem to make it onto the west European market.

BELGIUM — SEE MAP P645

If folk have told you Belgium is dull, ignore them! Belgium is homely, intimate and immensely interesting. It is a place to really explore, from the surreal urban landscapes of the coast, through historic cities like Bruges and Brussels, to the hill country of the Ardennes in the east and south-east of the country. You will find edgy modern culture cheek by jowl with magnificent medieval squares. Throw in some of Europe's finest art nouveau, a population that is enviably multilingual, and you have a beguiling mix.

TRAIN TRAVEL IN BELGIUM

Route 14 in this book features Belgium. The country has a busy and efficient rail network, reaching most parts of the country with frequent trains. In Brussels the

main hub is the Midi/Zuid station. No reservations are required for domestic services. The national rail operator is SNCB (in French) or NMBS (in Dutch), website www.b-rail.be.

There are two sets of time-tables, one for Mondays to Fridays

De Haan station on the coastal tram route in Belgium, which at 68 km is the longest in the world (photo © hidden europe).

Essentials (Belgium)

Local name: Belgique/België – Population: 10.8m – Capital: Brussels/Bruxelles/Brussel (p459) – Currency: Euro – Language: Dutch (north), French (south), German (east); many speak both French and Dutch plus often English and/or German – Accommodation costs: high (see p16) – Time zone: winter GMT+1, summer GMT+2 – International dialling code: +32

Opening Hours
Some establishments close 1200–1400. Shops: Mon–Sat 0900–1700/1800 (often later Fri). Museums: vary, but most open six days a week: 1000–1700 (usually Tues–Sun, Wed–Mon or Thur–Tues).

Public Holidays
1 Jan; Easter Mon; 1 May; Ascension Day; Whit Mon; 21 July; 15 Aug; 1, 11 Nov; 25 Dec. Transport and places that open usually keep Sun times.

Public Transport
National bus companies: De Lijn (Flanders), TEC (Wallonia, i.e. the French-speaking area), and STIB (Brussels); few long-distance buses. Buses, trams and metros: board at any door with ticket or buy ticket from driver. Fares depend on length of journey, but are cheaper if bought before boarding. Tram and bus stops: red and white signs (all stops are request only – raise your hand).

Tipping
Tipping in cafés, bars, restaurants and taxis not generally the norm, as service is supposed to be included in the price. About 10-15% in more touristy areas for good service.

Tourist information
Websites: www.belgium-tourism.net (Wallonia and Brussels), www.visitflanders.com (Flanders). *Office du Tourisme* in French, *Toerisme* in Dutch and *Verkehrsamt* in German.

and one for weekends, when even the route network can vary. Beware that only Dutch or French spellings may be shown on departure boards; for example Lille in France may be rendered at Dutch-speaking stations as Rijsel.

Rail passes
Both InterRail and Eurail are valid. The **Nettreinkaart/Carte Train Réseau** gives unlimited travel within Belgium for one week from €82 (photocard required, longer periods available). Weekend tickets give 50% discount, and there is an off-peak flat fare for senior citizens.

Accommodation

Hotels tend to be pricey, and during the summer months it is advisable to book ahead when visiting the main cities and tourist destinations. If you arrive without a reservation, the tourist office can help find a bed. As with many things in Belgium there are two official **youth hostel** organisations, the *Vlaamse Jeugdherbergen* (www.vjh.be), and the *Les Auberges de Jeunesse* (www.laj.be). **Independent hostels** are often more relaxed and friendly. A useful resource that covers all types of budget accommodation is www.use-it.be, which provides

tourist information 'for young people', but there is no age limit on making use of
their website!

FOOD AND DRINK

Most restaurants have good value fixed-price menus (*plat du jour, tourist menu,
dagschotel*). There's a wide variation in prices; establishments in the main squares
can charge two or three times as much as similar places in nearby streets. Try
waffles (*wafels/gaufres*) and sweet or savoury **pancakes** (*crêpes*), **mussels** (*moules*)
and freshly baked pastries. The most common snacks are *frieten/frites* (French
fries with mayonnaise or other sauce). You'll be tempted by the deservedly
famous **chocolates**, but be warned: the ones containing cream have a very short
shelf life. Belgium produces literally hundreds of types of **beer** (both dark and
light); **wheat beer** (*blanche*) comes with a slice of lemon in it in the summer.

BOSNIA AND HERZEGOVINA — SEE MAP P611

'The heart-shaped land' claim the tourist brochures produced by the Sarajevo
government, trying to give a suitably warm and cuddly feel to a country that has
had a very difficult time since the demise of socialist Yugoslavia. The country has
two 'entities' which operate in many respects as independent states. One is
referred to as the **Federation** and the other as **Republika Srpska**. The tiny **Brčko**
district remains apart from either entity. But cut through the troubled politics
and you'll discover a country with a rich Ottoman history, superb landscape and,
in Sarajevo, one of Europe's most interesting capital cities.

TRAIN TRAVEL IN BOSNIA AND HERZEGOVINA

Route 44 in this book is a wonderful journey through Bosnia and Herzegovina.
It relies on one of a number of new rail services linking Bosnia with its
neighbours. New trains are due for introduction in 2012 which will dramatically
improve the rolling stock on principal lines. In the entity known as the Federation
the railways are run by ZFBiH (www.zfbh.ba), whilst in the Republika Srpska the
operator is ZRS (www.zrs-rs.com).

RAIL PASSES

The Eurail pass is not valid. The InterRail global pass is valid, but there is no InterRail
one-country pass for Bosnia and Herzegovina. Domestic rail fares are very cheap.

ACCOMMODATION

Great value **hotels** that compensate for the sparse hostel network (though the
first hostels are now appearing in Sarajevo). Our experience is that there is
something of a gap between scruffy one-star hotels and modern posh hotels

ESSENTIALS (BOSNIA AND HERZEGOVINA)

Local name: Bosna i Hercegovina/Босна и Херцеговина — Population: 4.6m — Capital: Sarajevo (p362) — Currency: Convertible mark (KM) — Language: Bosnian, Croatian, Serbian (young people will speak some English; try German in northern Bosnia & western Herzegovina) — Accommodation costs: low (see p16) — Time zone: winter GMT+1, summer GMT+2 — International dialling code: +387

OPENING HOURS
Shops: in cities Mon–Sat 0900–2000, sometimes longer. Museum opening times vary.

PUBLIC HOLIDAYS
There is not (yet) a unified system so holidays are regional. 1, 2, 7, 14 Jan, 1 Mar, Easter Mon, 1 May, 25 Nov, 25 Dec plus entity-specific holidays such as Eid ul-Fitr and Eid ul-Adha (called Bajram) or Orthodox and Catholic feast and Saint's days. Victory Day (9 May) is celebrated only in the Republika Srpska.

PUBLIC TRANSPORT
Both public and private bus companies (and *marshrutkas*) connect every city and most villages within the country. Travel is cheap but standards may vary. One long-standing company with a good bus network hubbed on Sarajevo is Centrolines (www.centrolines.ba). Bus links between the entities may be sparse.

TIPPING
No tipping expected.

TOURIST INFORMATION
Website: www.bhtourism.ba/eng.

aimed at the business market. There is a growing **B&B market**, often aimed at budget German travellers.

FOOD AND DRINK

Even the most budget-conscious traveller can eat extremely well in Bosnia and Herzegovina. Good **fresh food** costs next to nothing in local markets, and restaurant fare is very reasonably priced. Look for superb grilled lamb and other meats, good salads and the inevitable *burek* — always tasty with a variety of fillings. Good local beer, decent **local wines** (that deserve to be much better known outside the country), and wonderful Turkish coffee all add to the mix and help make Bosnia and Herzegovina a really great destination for food lovers.

BULGARIA — SEE MAP P608

Bulgaria joined the EU in 2007, and is now being considered for full membership of the Schengen area for late 2012. These are two more milestones in the destiny of the Black Sea nation which has come a long way since political plurality was introduced in November 1989. The Bulgarian coast has long been popular with summer visitors, but now travellers are discovering the beauty of the Bulgarian

Memorial celebrating the First Bulgarian Empire (in the 8th century) (photo ©Corepics Vof).

Essentials (Bulgaria)

Local name: Balgarija/България — Population: 7.6m — Capital: Sofia/София (p347) — Currency: Lev (Lv); credit cards increasingly accepted — Language: Bulgarian (English, German, Russian and French in tourist areas); nodding the head indicates 'no' (ne), shaking it means 'yes' (da) — Accommodation costs: low (see p16) — Time zone: winter GMT+2, summer GMT+3 — International dialling code: +359

Opening hours
Banks: Mon–Fri 0900–1700. Some exchange offices open longer hours and weekends. Shops: Mon–Fri 0800–2000, closed 1200–1400 outside major towns, Sat open 1000–1800. Museums: vary widely, but often 0800–1200, 1400–1830. Many close Mon or Tues.

Public holidays
1 Jan; 3 Mar; Orthodox Easter Sunday and Monday, 1, 6, 24 May; 6, 22 Sept; 1 Nov; 25, 26 Dec.

Public transport
Buses (good network) slightly more expensive than trains; both very cheap compared with western Europe. Sofia: buses and trams use same ticket but different tickets for the subway; punch it at machines inside, get new ticket if you change. Daily/weekly cards available.

Tipping
Waiters and taxi drivers expect a tip of about 10%.

Tourist information
Website: www.bulgariatravel.org. Main tourist office: 1 Sveta Nedelya Sq., Sofia 1000, ☎ 02 987 9778 (closed Sat&Sun).

mountains. There are remarkable monasteries and old cities, the latter often revealing a rich vein of Ottoman influence.

Train travel in Bulgaria

Bulgaria might not have the fastest or most frequent services in Europe, but the network covers the major cities and there are good services linking Sofia with the Black Sea resorts. A handful of the fastest trains (category Exp) have compulsory reservation and higher fares, but you may also want to reserve on other express trains as they can be busy. On-board catering is not commonplace but is improving. Bulgaria is on **Routes 40** and **41** of this book. The Bulgarian State Railways (BDŽ) website includes an English version (www.bdz.bg). Signs at stations, however, are mostly in Cyrillic. Reservations can be made at Rila travel agencies as well as at stations.

Rail passes
InterRail is valid, as is Eurail. Domestic rail fares are cheap.

Accommodation

Beyond the main hotels, smaller private hotels and B&B-type accommodation are increasingly becoming available. As for hostels, Bulgaria is really only just getting started, although things are changing, especially in Sofia, Varna and Veliko Târnovo. Outside these cities, and particularly in rural areas, private rooms might be the best bet for the budget traveller.

FOOD AND DRINK

Bulgaria produces a wide variety of excellent fruits and vegetables. Soups are popular all year round, with yoghurt-based cold ones on offer in summer. Meat is generally pork or lamb, either cooked slowly with vegetables or grilled. Desserts include seasonal fruit, ice cream, gateaux and sweet pastries. Vegetarians can go for the varied and generally excellent salads, and dishes such as stuffed peppers or aubergine dishes like *kyopolou*.

Local beers are lager-style and good value. **Grozdova**, **slivova** and **mastika** are strong, served in large measures, traditionally with cold starters. Bulgarian wine is often of high quality, and very good value.

CROATIA — SEE MAP OPPOSITE

First of the countries to break from the Yugoslav fold by controversially declaring independence in 1991, Croatia is now gearing up to join the EU in late 2013. This deeply Catholic country is blessed with a vast stretch of Adriatic coast. Over a thousand islands are dotted along Croatia's sinewy littoral. The area north and west of the capital, Zagreb, is mountainous, while to the east are the vast Slavonian plains, the area worst hit by the 1990s war.

TRAIN TRAVEL IN CROATIA

Routes 38 and **39** feature Croatia. Additionally **Route 44**, which focuses more on Bosnia, includes a final leg in Croatia. Hubbed on Zagreb, the Croatian rail

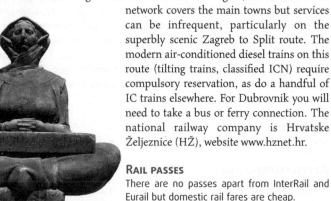

network covers the main towns but services can be infrequent, particularly on the superbly scenic Zagreb to Split route. The modern air-conditioned diesel trains on this route (tilting trains, classified ICN) require compulsory reservation, as do a handful of IC trains elsewhere. For Dubrovnik you will need to take a bus or ferry connection. The national railway company is Hrvatske Željeznice (HŽ), website www.hznet.hr.

RAIL PASSES

There are no passes apart from InterRail and Eurail but domestic rail fares are cheap.

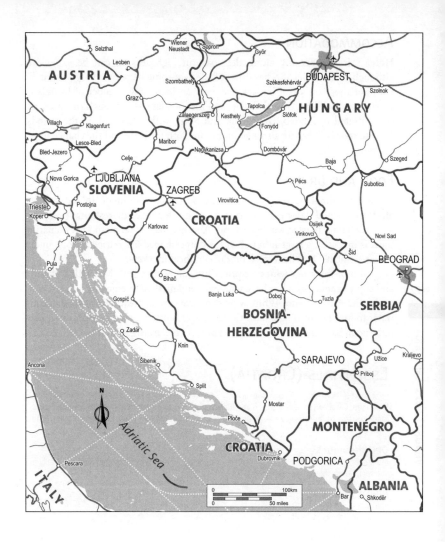

LEFT: The 'History of the Croats' sculpture is more than merely a work of art. Crafted by Croatian sculptor Ivan Meštrović, the piece has come to symbolise the Croatian spirit. The sculpture is outside the Law Faculty of the University of Zagreb. The tablet that rests on the knees of the seated figure is inscribed in the ancient Glagolitic script that was used in Croatia until the late eighteenth century (photo © Gordana Sermek).

Accommodation

Hotel prices, especially along the coast in high season, can be expensive, although if you travel at other times of the year some incredible bargains can be had. For those on a real budget, there are an increasing number of **hostels** in Croatia, both official (www.hfhs.hr) and independent — although the latter are concentrated in Zagreb, Dubrovnik and Split, with a handful on the islands. **Private rooms** (*sobe*) are also a good option, both for price and the chance to get to know your hosts.

Food and drink

Along the Dalmatian coast, fish and other seafood predominate. Inland, meat in all its guises and dairy produce rule. Look out for roadside restaurants serving *janjetina* (lamb) roasted whole on a spit. Another traditional method of preparing meat is in a *peka*, a large iron pot with a dome-shaped lid, buried to cook under glowing embers. Excellent fresh produce in **local markets**.

Top-of-the-range **wines** are pricey but can be excellent. Mix with still water and enjoy *bevanda* — a less headache-inducing method of enjoying rich red wine under the Adriatic sun. White wine can have similar treatment with sparkling water to make refreshing *gemišt*. Coffee (*kava*) is often served as espresso or cappuccino in bars, though some families prepare it Turkish-style at home.

Essentials (Croatia)

Local name: Hrvatska — Population: 4.5m — Capital: Zagreb (p325) — Currency: Kuna (Kn) — Language: Croatian (English, German and Italian spoken in tourist areas) — Accommodation costs: medium (see p16) — Time zone: winter GMT+1, summer GMT+2 — International dialling code: +385

Opening hours
Most shops: Mon–Fri 0800–2000, Sat 0800–1400/1500; many shops also open Sun, especially in summer. Some shops close 1200–1600.

Public holidays
1, 6 Jan; Good Friday; Easter Mon; 1 May; Corpus Christi; 22, 25 June; 5, 15 Aug; 8 Oct; 1 Nov; 25–26 Dec. Many local saints' holidays.

Public transport
Jadrolinija maintains most domestic ferry lines; main office in Rijeka, ☎ 051 666 111 (www.jadrolinija.hr). Buses and trams are cheap, regular and efficient. Avoid overpriced taxis.

Tipping
Leave 10% for good service in a restaurant. It's not necessary to tip in bars.

Tourist information
Website: www.croatia.hr. Croatian National Tourist Board, Iblerov trg 10/4, 10000 Zagreb, ☎ 01 469 9300.

ESSENTIALS (CZECH REPUBLIC)

Local name: Česka republika — Population: 10.5m — Capital: Prague/Praha (p548) — Currency: Czech koruna (Kč) — Language: Czech (English is widely spoken among young people, especially in the cities. German and Russian are also encountered, particularly among older folk) — Accommodation costs: medium (see p16) — Time zone: winter GMT+1, summer GMT+2 — International dialling code: +420

OPENING HOURS
Shops: Mon–Fri 0900–1700, Sat 0900–1200 (often longer in Prague on Sat and also open Sun; smaller shops might be closed 1200–1300). Museums: (usually) Tues–Sun 1000–1800. Most castles close Nov–Mar.

PUBLIC HOLIDAYS
1 Jan; Easter Mon; 1, 8 May; 5, 6 July; 28 Sept; 28 Oct; 17 Nov; 24–26 Dec.

PUBLIC TRANSPORT
Good long-distance bus network, run by Student Agency (http://jizdenky.studentagency.cz/) or private companies. You can buy tickets from the driver; priority to those with reservations.

TIPPING
You should tip at pubs and restaurants, in hotels and taxis. In general, round up the nearest 10Kč unless you are somewhere upmarket, when you should tip 10%.

TOURIST INFORMATION
Website: www.czechtourism.com, www.czech.cz/en/tourism. Information: Vinohradská 46, 120 41 Praha 2, ☎ 221 580 610.

CZECH REPUBLIC — SEE MAP P670

One half of former Czechoslovakia which, having defiantly despatched a lacklustre communist government with the Velvet Revolution in autumn 1989, then proceeded to a Velvet Divorce less than four years later. Thus was the Czech Republic born. The move to a market economy hasn't always been easy. An urban elite in Prague has undoubtedly made good, but in more rural areas the supposed benefits of capitalism are not so evident. You'll run across stunning areas of mountains and forests, towns with delightful squares, sleepy villages and imposing castles.

TRAIN TRAVEL IN THE CZECH REPUBLIC

Routes 47 and **48** both traverse the Czech Republic, connecting with each other in Prague. The well-run and generally punctual rail network covers every corner of the country, with express trains hourly or every two hours on most routes. The latest tilting **high-speed trains** are classified SuperCity (SC) on the Prague to Ostrava and Bratislava routes; these are the only trains to require compulsory reservation. If you have time on your hands, however, there is no better way to explore than on the many slow and **windy rural routes**, many operated by vintage railcars, which criss-cross the countryside.

The national rail company is České Dráhy (ČD), www.cd.cz. The winds of competition are bringing change. In late 2011, for example, private operator Student Agency launched a new thrice-daily service from Prague to Ostrava. Following a major revamp of the tracks around Prague, all principal routes now serve the main station, Praha hlavní, which has also been thoroughly modernised.

RAIL PASSES

InterRail and Eurail passes are both valid. The **ČD Net** ticket gives one day's unlimited second-class travel for 550 Kč; the 7-day version is particularly good value at 1,250 Kč (SC trains are extra). A wide range of regional day passes is also available, including several which include border areas of Germany or Poland. At weekends, the **SONE+ day pass** is valid for up to five people (max. two adults) and also has cross-border variants.

ACCOMMODATION

There is a wide choice of accommodation types in the Czech Republic, from the standard **hotels** to **private rooms** and **pensions**, and an ever-increasing number of hostels. Quality in the more budget hotels can often leave a lot to be desired, so for the cost-conscious a private room might be a better choice.

You can find a well-developed network of **independent hostels**, concentrating on favourite backpacker destinations such as Prague, Olomouc, Brno and Český Krumlov, whilst you can find more about the **youth hostel** organisation at www.czechhostels.com.

FOOD AND DRINK

Czech cuisine is hearty, and features lashings of meat with cream-based sauces, but vegetarian options include fried cheese (*smažený sýr*), risotto and salads. Pork with cabbage and dumplings (*vepřové–zelí–knedlíky*) is on virtually every menu, as is *guláš*, a bland beef stew. The cost of eating and drinking is reasonable. *Kavárny* and *cukrány* serve coffee and very sweet pastries. Pubs (*pivnice*) and wine bars (*vinárny*) are good places to eat. Czech beers are excellent, as is Moravian wine.

DENMARK — SEE MAP P668

Situated between the Baltic and the North Sea, watery Denmark incorporates some 400 islands, 78 of which are inhabited, as well as the peninsula of **Jutland**. It is low-lying and undramatic terrain, where you sense you're never far from the sea. The long maritime tradition inflects the townscapes too, a reminder that even towns that now seem well inland (like Roskilde) once lived from the sea.

While an impressive programme of bridge building has linked many of Denmark's islands, you will still need to take to ferries to reach remote islands. Ferries remain a credible choice for some other journeys (eg. Århus to Kalundborg).

ESSENTIALS (DENMARK)

Local name: Danmark — Population: 5.5m — Capital: Copenhagen/København (p472) — Currency: Danish kroner (DKr.) — Language: Danish (English is almost universally spoken) — Accommodation costs: high (see p16) — Time zone: winter GMT+1, summer GMT+2 — International dialling code: +45

OPENING HOURS
Shops: (mostly) Mon–Thur 1000–1730, Fri 1000–1900/2000, Sat 1000–1200/1300. Museums: (mostly) daily 1000/1100–1600/1700. In winter, hours are shorter and museums usually close Mon.

PUBLIC HOLIDAYS
1 Jan; Maundy Thursday–Easter Monday; Common Prayer Day (4th Fri after Easter); Ascension Day; Whit Mon; 5 June; 24–26, 31 Dec.

PUBLIC TRANSPORT
Long-distance travel is easiest by train. Excellent regional and city bus services, many dovetailing with trains; modern metro in Copenhagen. Ferries or bridges link all the big islands.

TIPPING
Usually not expected, and often included in the bill in restaurants, but appreciated.

TOURIST INFORMATION
Website: www.visitdenmark.com. Nearly every decent-sized town in Denmark has a tourist office (*turistbureau*), normally found in the town hall or central square; they distribute maps, information and advice. Some also book accommodation for a small fee.

TRAIN TRAVEL IN DENMARK

Denmark features in **Route 22** in this book. **Route 17** starts in Germany but then crosses the Baltic to end in Denmark, while **Routes 21** and **25** set off in Copenhagen, but both immediately track east into Sweden.

Denmark's efficient rail network relies on modern and frequent InterCity (IC) services that fan out from Copenhagen's main station, usually abbreviated to København H, which also has frequent trains across the Øresund to Malmö in Sweden, serving Copenhagen Airport (Kastrup) on the way. There is also an efficient rail-sea link to the Danish island of Bornholm (ERT 727). You don't need to reserve on InterCity trains but it is recommended at busy times. Most IC trains have refreshment trolleys.

Danske Statsbaner (DSB), www.dsb.dk, is the principal operator, although some regional services are run by private operators such as Arriva. There is a national multi-modal journey planner at www.rejseplanen.dk which includes an English and a German version.

RAIL PASSES
InterRail and Eurail are valid. Fares are based on a national zonal system. Tickets in the Greater Copenhagen area include local transport as well as trains and are available for various zones for 24 hours or, in the case of the **FlexCard**, 7 days.

ACCOMMODATION

Hotels in Denmark are of a high standard, and can be expensive. In rural areas the **old inns**, known as *kros*, are charming places to stay and often have good restaurants serving traditional food. To find these and other quirky places to stay, visit www.tourist-in-denmark.dk. **Dansk Bed & Breakfast** publish a brochure of around 300 bed & breakfast establishments throughout Denmark; it can also make bookings (www.bbdk.dk).

There are around 100 official (HI) **hostels** (*vandrerhjem*), and the general standard is excellent, which might explain why the growth of independent hostels in the country has not been as dramatic as elsewhere. Check out www.danhostel.dk for more details.

If you enjoy camping, you will find a wide choice of **campsites**, many of which also offer self-catering cabins which can work out great value for those travelling in a small group.

FOOD AND DRINK

Danish cuisine is simple, based on excellent local produce; standards are uniformly high, but with prices to match. Look for *dagens ret* (today's special), which is noticeably cheaper than eating à la carte.

Fish features a lot — most commonly herring served in a sauce. *Smørrebrød* are elaborately topped open sandwiches of meat, fish or cheese with accompaniments, served on *rugbrød* (rye bread) or *franskbrød* (wheat bread). You can also try

filling up on the ubiquitous *frikadeller* (pork meatballs). There are many local **lagers** in addition to the internationally known Carlsberg and Tuborg. The local firewater is *akvavit*. All alcohol is expensive.

ESTONIA — SEE MAP P636

Smallest of the three Baltic States, Estonia joined the EU in 2004. The country looks more to Finland than its Baltic neighbours to the south. Estonia offers a fetching mixture of forests with old manorial estates. You will also find some strikingly beautiful coast, desolate islands and appealing lake country. Relations with

Alexander Nevsky cathedral in Tallinn is a wonderful fragment of Orthodox life in the heart of the Estonian capital (photo © Arsty).

ESSENTIALS (ESTONIA)

Local name: Eesti — Population: 1.3m — Capital: Tallinn (p382) — Currency: Euro — Language: Estonian, Russian (English is widely spoken, though less so in rural areas) — Accommodation costs: medium (see p16) — Time zone: winter GMT+2, summer GMT+3 — International dialling code: +372

OPENING HOURS

Shops: Mon–Fri 0900/1000–1800/1900, Sat 0900/1000–1500/1700; many also open Sun. Museums: days vary (usually closed Mon and/or Tues); hours commonly 1100–1700.

PUBLIC HOLIDAYS

1 Jan; 24 Feb; Good Fri; 1 May; 23 June (Victory Day), 24 June; 20 Aug; 25, 26 Dec.

PUBLIC TRANSPORT

Bus services often quicker, cleaner and more efficient than rail but getting pricier (see www.peatus.ee for routes and timetables). Book international services in advance from bus stations or online at www.luxexpress.eu. Pay the driver at rural stops or small towns.

TIPPING

Not necessary to tip service at the bar or counter, but tip 10% if served at your table. Round up taxi fares to a maximum of 10%.

TOURIST INFORMATION

Website: www.visitestonia.com (with links to other useful Baltic websites). Turismiamet (Estonian Tourist Board), Lasnamäe 2, 11412 Tallinn, ☎ 627 9770. Ekspress Hotline, ☎ 1182, is an English-speaking information service covering all Estonian towns.

adjacent Russia are not always easy, but that should not deter you from combining the two countries in a single visit (provided you have a Russian visa of course).

TRAIN TRAVEL IN ESTONIA

Estonia is included in **Route 46** in this book. Whilst Tallinn has its electrified suburban trains (operated by Elektriraudtee, www.elektriraudtee.ee), regional train services, operated by Edelaraudtee (www.edel.ee), are somewhat thin on the ground, though it is possible to travel to Pärnu, Narva and Tartu by train, albeit infrequently. There are no trains from Tallinn to St Petersburg, this being the preserve of bus operator Eurolines (see ERT 1870). There is, however, a nightly sleeper train to Moscow with yet another operator, GoRail (www.gorail.ee). One train a day from Tallinn to Valga connects with an onward service into Latvia.

RAIL PASSES

Eurail and InterRail are not valid and there are no local rail passes, but fares are cheap.

ACCOMMODATION

There should be no problem with accommodation in Estonia, which has a variety of hostels and inexpensive hotels. Though prices in Tallinn are often twice as high as elsewhere. **Home stays** offer accommodation in farmhouses, summer cottages, homes and small boarding houses.

For **hostels**, the Estonian Youth Hostel Association can make reservations at 40 hostels throughout the country (www.balticbookings.com/eyha), whilst Tallinn in particular has seen a massive growth in independent, backpacker-orientated establishments.

FOOD AND DRINK

Particularly outside Tallinn, many restaurants close early in the evenings, so you may think of lunch as a main meal opportunity. For value, look to the dish of the day (*päevapraad*). Cheap cuts of meat, particularly pork, with potatoes and bread are staples. Not a place for the sweet-toothed or for vegetarians. Estonian beers (both dark and light) have a growing reputation. In winter, try mulled wine or the excellent Estonian liqueur, **Vana Tallinn** (great in tea or in cocktails).

FAROE ISLANDS

This curious little island polity in the North Atlantic has loose links to Denmark, but enjoys a high measure of independence with its own parliament. Stunning wild mountain and coastal landscapes across 17 inhabited islands which are linked by efficient ferries, bridges and undersea road tunnels. There are no railways at all in the entire archipelago. The Faroes are easily reached by ship from Hirtshals in Denmark (see **Route 22**).

ESSENTIALS: Local name: Føroyar — Population: 49k — Capital: Tórshavn — Currency: Faroese króna — Language: Faroese, Danish (English widely understood) — Accommodation costs: high — Time zone: winter GMT, summer GMT+1 — International dialling code: +298

FINLAND — SEE MAP P668

Often classified as part of Scandinavia, Finland is a world apart from the two Scandinavian neighbours with which it shares common borders, Norway and Sweden. The cultural landscape reflects Finland's historic links with Russia, even to the extent that the Orthodox Church is an official state church. The Grand Duchy of Finland was part of the Russian Empire until 1917. And the west has a good dose of Swedish influence. Pure air, glistening lakes, an abundance of wildlife and deep winter snow all help sustain Finland's appeal to travellers.

TRAIN TRAVEL IN FINLAND

Finland features on **Routes 26** and **27** in this book. Additionally, **Route 46** from Warsaw through the Baltic States concludes with a journey by sea across the Gulf

Essentials (Finland)

Local name: Suomi — Population: 5.3m — Capital: Helsinki (p491) — Currency: Euro — Language: Finnish (Sámi in the north); Swedish, the second language, often appears on signs after the Finnish (English widely spoken, esp. in Helsinki; German reasonably widespread) — Accommodation costs: high (see p16) — Time zone: winter GMT+2, summer GMT+3 — International dialling code: +358

Opening hours
Shops: Mon–Fri 0900–2000, Sat 0900–1500. Museums: usually close Mon, hours vary. Many close in winter.

Public holidays
1, 6 Jan; Good Fri; Easter Sun–Mon; 1 May; Ascension Day; Whit Sun; Midsummer's Day (Sat falling 20–26 June); All Saints Day (Sat falling 31 Oct–6 Nov); 6 Dec; 25–26 Dec.

Public transport
Timetables for trains, buses and boats dovetail conveniently. Matkahuolto covers timetables online (www.matkahuolto.info). Buses: stops are usually a black bus on a yellow background for local services; white bus on a blue background for longer distances. Cheaper to buy tickets from stations or agents than on board. Bus stations usually have good facilities. Taxis: for hire when the yellow taksi sign is lit; hailing them in the street is acceptable; metered.

Tipping
Service charge included in hotel and restaurant bills, but leave coins for good service. Hotel and restaurant porters and sauna attendants expect a euro or two.

Tourist information
Website: www.visitfinland.com. Every Finnish town has a Tourist Office (Matkailutoimisto) where staff speak English.

of Finland from Tallinn to Helsinki. The modern and efficient Finnish rail system now includes the brand-new Allegro high-speed trains that have served the **Helsinki to St Petersburg** route since December 2010 (making it very easy now to reach Helsinki after following **Route 45** from Berlin to St Petersburg).

The premium daytime services from Helsinki to Turku, Tampere and the north use high-speed tilting Pendolino trains, dubbed S220 thanks to their top speed of 220 km/h (reservation is compulsory). Other than for purely local journeys, tickets are sold for specific trains, the fare level varying according to the train type: Pendolino, InterCity, Express, or Regional (seat reservations are included except for Regional trains).

Most long-distance trains have a restaurant car, buffet car or trolley service, whilst overnight trains to the north have sleepers, seats and a restaurant car. The national rail company is VR (www.vr.fi).

Rail passes
Both InterRail and Eurail are valid. The **Finnrailpass** gives unlimited rail travel for 3, 5 or 10 days within one month. Available to non-Finnish residents, it can be purchased at main stations in Finland; seat reservation fees are required for Pendolino trains.

Accommodation

Hotels tend to be stylish, immaculate and pricey. Budget travellers might want to check out **matkustajakoti** (the relatively cheap tourist hotels) or the 80 **hostels** (*retkeilymajat*) that are well spread across the country (www.hostellit.fi). Note that just over half are open year-round. Many hostels have activity programmes, plus canoes, skis, boats and cycles. **Campsites** are widespread too (about 350; around 200 belong to the Finnish Campingsite Association www.camping.fi). Rough camping is generally allowed providing you keep 150 m from residents and remove any trace of your stay.

Food and drink

Fixed-price menus in a *ravintola* (upmarket restaurant) are the best value, or you may want to try a *grilli* (fast-food stand), *kahvila* (self-service cafeteria) or a *baari* (snack bar). For self-caterers, try Alepa, Siwa, K-market or Valintatalo supermarkets. Some specials are *muikunmäti* (a freshwater fish roe served with onions and cream and accompanied by toast or pancakes) and for dessert *kiisseli* (berry fool). Finns are very dedicated coffee drinkers. Lower-alcohol beers are sold in supermarkets, but for stronger beers and all wines and spirits, turn to **Alko**, the aptly named state-owned distributor of stronger drinks.

France – see map opposite

France boasts such varied culture and heritage, so rich a mix of scenery and architecture, that you could comfortably return every year of a long life and still discover something new. Impressive medieval cities in the north, although humdrum landscapes. Move to the centre for wilderness, east for the Alps, and south for sun, sea and sand. Throw in fine food and wine to create the perfect ensemble.

But be warned! Try it once and you may become an addict who can never be weaned off the country that is by far the most popular destination for tourists on the planet.

Train travel in France

France is on **Routes 1 to 7** in this book. In addition **Routes 8** and **12** start in south-west France and then cross the border into Spain. France's well-developed high-speed network means we now take for granted journeys such as Paris to Marseille (750 km) taking a mere three hours or so. Many parts of France have similarly impressive journey times from Paris by high-speed TGV, although in contrast cross-country routes can often be slow and infrequent.

France is not a country for hopping on and off trains at will, since reservation is compulsory on all TGV, Téoz, and night-train services, and some trains have

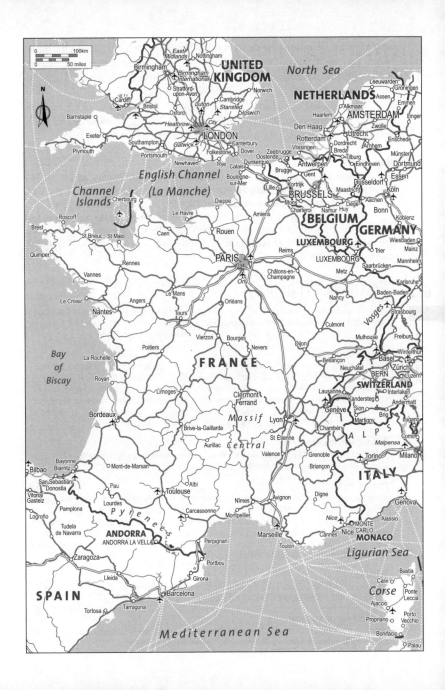

only a limited allocation of seats for pass holders. Fares are higher during the busier 'white' periods. Tickets (not passes) must be validated in the orange 'composteurs' at the entrance to platforms. Domestic night trains have couchettes (and often reclining seats), sleeping cars being confined to international services.

The national operator is Société Nationale des Chemins de fer Français (SNCF), www.sncf.com. ☎ 3635 (premium rate, in French), followed by 1 for traffic status, 2 for timetables, 3 for reservations and tickets, 4 for other services.

RAIL PASSES
InterRail and Eurail passes are valid, but beware the supplements on French TGV services. There is a **France Railpass** for non-European residents, valid for 3–9 days within one month. European residents should use the InterRail one-country pass.

Some of the regions offer day tickets, for example the **Alsa+ 24h-ticket** that allows travel throughout Alsace on local (TER) trains for €33. Elsewhere, such passes are generally only valid at weekends, and some are summer only; see www.ter-sncf.com for further details.

ESSENTIALS (FRANCE)

Local name: France — Population: 65.5m — Capital: Paris (p538) — Currency: Euro — Language: French (many people speak some English, particularly in Paris) — Accommodation costs: high (see p16) — Time zone: winter GMT+1, summer GMT+2 — International dialling code: +33

OPENING HOURS
Paris and major towns: shops, banks and post offices generally open 0900/1000–1900/2000 Mon–Fri, plus often Sat am/all day. Small shops can be open Sun am but closed Mon. Provinces: weekly closing is mostly Sun pm/all day and Mon; both shops and services generally close 1200–1430; services may have restricted opening times. Most super-/hypermarkets open to 2100/2200. Museums: (mostly) 0900–1700, closing Mon and/or Tues; longer hours in summer; often free or discount rate on Sun. Restaurants serve 1200–1400 and 1900–2100 at least.

PUBLIC HOLIDAYS
1 Jan; Easter Mon; 1, 8 May; Ascension Day; Whit Sun–Mon; 14 July; 15 Aug; 1, 11 Nov; 25 Dec. If on Tues or Thur, many places also close Mon or Fri.

PUBLIC TRANSPORT
The metro systems in Paris and several other major cities are clean, efficient and relatively cheap. For urban and peri-urban transport, carnets (multiple-ticket packs) are cheaper than individual tickets. Some city transport passes combine discount entries to certain tourist attractions. Bus and train timetables are available from bus and train stations and tourist offices; usually free. Always ask if your rail pass is valid on local transport. Bus services may be infrequent after 2030 and on Sun. Rural areas are often poorly served.

TIPPING
Not necessary to tip in bars or cafés although it is common practice to round up the price. In restaurants there is no obligation to tip, but if you wish to do so leave €1–2.

TOURIST INFORMATION
Website: www.franceguide.com. At a new destination, call at the local tourist office: look for *Syndicat d'Initiative* or *Office de Tourisme*; staff generally speak English.

Paris looks wonderful from all angles, but never more so than from some of the city's rooftops. Gargoyles often get the very finest views of many European capital cities (photo © Mrusty).

ACCOMMODATION

For **hotels**, half-board (i.e. breakfast and evening meal included) can be excellent value in smaller towns and villages, often having only a modest supplement over the regular room rate. As so often elsewhere in Europe, budget hotels are often clustered near stations. In summer, it is advisable to book ahead in larger towns and resort areas. **Gîtes de France** produces directories of B&Bs, *gîtes d'étape*, farm accommodation and holiday-house rentals for each *département* (www.gites-de-france.com). There are hundreds of **hostels** in France, including those which are members of Hostelling International (HI — www.fuaj.org) and those more independently minded. The useful website www.hostelz.com offers listings of both types. **Camping** is a national obsession, and there are hundreds of campsites all across France. *Camping Municipal* is usually basic but cheap. High-grade sites provide entertainment and facilities such as watersports. In mountain areas, a chain of **refuge huts** is run by *Club Alpin Français d'Île-de-France* (www.clubalpin-idf.com).

FOOD AND DRINK

France's gastronomic reputation often lives up to its promise, providing you're prepared to look beyond mere tourist fodder such as *steak frites* (steak and fries). In restaurants, eating à la carte can be expensive, but the *menu* (set menu, of which there may be several) or the *plat du jour* (dish of the day) is often **superb value**, especially at lunchtime. Strictly vegetarian restaurants are rare, but just about anywhere can rustle up a salad or an omelette and many offer far more imaginative fare. **Coffees and beers** can be surprisingly expensive: wine is generally cheaper — order a *pichet* of house red (*rouge*), white (*blanc*) or rosé. If you ask for *café*, you'll get a small black coffee; coffee with milk is *café crème*. Tea is usually served black. Beer is mostly yellow, cold, French and fizzy, though gourmet and foreign beers are popular. *Une pression* or *un demi* is draught beer, better value than bottled. *Baguettes* (French bread sticks) with a variety of fillings from cafés and stalls are cheap — as are *crêpes* and *galettes* (sweet and savoury

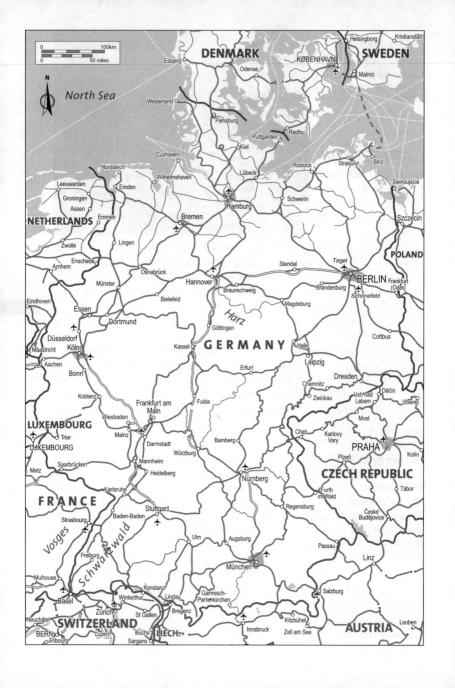

pancakes). **Morning markets** are excellent for stocking up on picnic items. Buy provisions before noon as shops can be closed for hours at lunchtime.

GERMANY — SEE MAP OPPOSITE

Germany, bang in the middle of Europe, is hard to miss. Nor should anyone wish to: from the heathlands of the north to the Alpine peaks of the south there is scenery galore. There are idyllic offshore islands and sandy beaches on both the North Sea and the Baltic coasts, great tracts of lakes and forests, especially in the north-east, and three of Europe's great rivers: the Rhine, the Danube and the Elbe. Plus a galaxy of historic cities that includes Cologne, Munich and Berlin.

TRAIN TRAVEL IN GERMANY

Germany features on **Routes 16 to 20** in this volume. In addition, **Routes 28, 45, 47, 48** and **49** start in Germany before crossing the country's southern or eastern borders. Germany's **comprehensive** and generally efficient **rail network** is served by many different types of train, from sleek high-speed ICE trains and the only slightly less modern IC and EC services to sleepy rural branch lines winding along picturesque river valleys. Apart from a handful of peak-hour ICE Sprinter trains, there is no compulsory reservation on daytime trains and no supplements for pass holders. Most long-distance trains have refreshments. Good facilities at main-line stations, such as showers and even (at Cologne) an automated left-luggage system which whisks away your bags into the subterranean depths of the station for storage.

Principal operator is Deutsche Bahn (DB), www.bahn.de, ☎ 0180 5 99 66 33 (premium rate) for timetable or fares information, also to purchase tickets and reservations. ☎ 0800 1 50 70 90 is a free automated service for timetables. For longer journeys, prices tumble if you can purchase tickets well in advance. Some local services are privately operated.

RAIL PASSES
The full range of InterRail and Eurail passes are valid. A **German Rail Pass** is available for those living outside Europe; residents

Assertively modern architecture at Potsdamer Platz bridges the former border between East Berlin and West Berlin (photo © Christian Draghici).

of Europe can buy the InterRail one-country pass. The **Schönes-Wochenende** ticket gives one day's travel at weekends on local trains for 1–5 people (buy on the day, cheapest from machines), whilst a range of regional **Ländertickets** is available (from €20 for one person, from €28 for groups of up to 5 people), giving the freedom to roam any day of the week on all but the fastest trains through one or more of the federal states of Germany or often even over Germany's borders. For example, the area in which the **Schleswig-Holstein ticket** is valid extends from Tønder and Padborg in Denmark to Świnoujście in Poland.

ACCOMMODATION

You'll find a range of accommodation options at all price levels in Germany, but prices for rooms of comparable standards vary enormously across the country. Areas that were, until 1990, part of the GDR still offer the best value, and Berlin is noticeably cheaper than, say, Munich. Expect to pay peak prices if you coincide with major festivals (eg. **Karneval** in the Rhineland or the **Oktoberfest** in Munich) or trade fairs.

Pensionen (**pensions**) and *Privatzimmer* (**private rooms**) represent particularly good value. They're usually meticulously kept, and many rural and small town family-run establishments are very welcoming and comfortable. In many cities, a

ESSENTIALS (GERMANY)

Local name: Deutschland — Population: 82m — Capital: Berlin (p450) — Currency: Euro — Language: German (English and French widely spoken in the west, less so in the east) — Accommodation costs: high (see p16) — Time zone: winter GMT+1, summer GMT+2 — International dialling code: +49

OPENING HOURS
Shops: Mon–Fri 0900–1830 (large department stores may open 0830/0900–2000) and Sat 0900–1600. Museums: Tue–Sun 0900–1700 (until 2100 Thur).

PUBLIC HOLIDAYS
1, 6* Jan; Good Fri; Easter Mon; 1 May, Ascension Day; Whit Mon; Corpus Christi*, 15 Aug*; 3 Oct; 1 Nov*; 24 Dec (afternoon); 25, 26 Dec;
(*Religious feasts celebrated as public holiday only in Catholic areas.)

PUBLIC TRANSPORT
Most large cities have U-Bahn (U) underground railway and S-Bahn (S) urban rail service. City travel passes cover both and other public transport, including ferries in some cities. International passes usually cover S-Bahn. Single fares are expensive; day card (*Tagesnetzkarte*) or multi-ride ticket (*Mehrfahrtenkarte*) pays its way if you take more than three rides.

TIPPING
10% is usual, but for small items, just round up to the nearest 50 cents or whole euro.

TOURIST INFORMATION
Website: www.germany-tourism.de. Tourist offices are usually near stations, with English-speaking staff. Most offer room-finding service.

new generation of design-orientated **budget hotels** are providing rooms of high quality at reasonable prices. Hostel accommodation is widely available in Germany, and it has a network of **independent hostels** — most of which are members of the German Backpacker Network (www.backpacker-network.de) — that can rival any country in Europe. There are also around 600 official (HI) *Jugendherbergen* (youth hostels) which often cater to school groups and can have an institutional feel. The *Deutscher Camping-Club (DCC)* (www.camping-club.de), compiles an annual list of 1,600 **camping** sites. The standard of German campsites is very high.

FOOD AND DRINK

Germans tend to have biological clocks that run in advance of the rest of Europe. Families at home eat early, with supper often done and dusted by soon after six. In restaurants, hotels and hostels expect breakfast from 0630 to 1000. Lunch is around 1200–1400 (from 1130 in rural areas) and dinner 1800–2030 (but much later in cities). Breakfast is often substantial (and usually included in the price of a room), consisting of a variety of bread, cheese and cold meats and possibly boiled eggs. Germans eat their **main meal at midday**, with a light supper (*Abendbrot*) in the early evening, but restaurants and pubs also offer light lunches and cooked evening meals. For lunch, the best value is the daily menu (*Tageskarte*); in rural parts of southern Germany, there's often a snack menu (*Vesperkarte*) from mid-afternoon onwards.

Traditional German cuisine is widespread, both in towns and rural areas, and traditional recipes, which vary greatly by region, are produced with pride. Expect **hearty fare**, with large portions, and often good value. Look for home-made soups, high-quality meat, piquant marinated pot roasts (known as *Sauerbraten*) and creamy sauces. For really cheap but generally appetising eats, there are *Imbisse* (stalls) serving *Kartoffelsalat* (potato salad) and *Wurst* (sausage) in its numerous variations, plus fish in the north.

GREECE — SEE MAP P608

Beset by financial woes, but still inexpensive, friendly and beautiful, and with a wonderful array of archaeological sites, Greece offers a seductive mix of culture and relaxation, with plenty of opportunity to linger in tavernas or laze on a beach as well as visiting ancient ruins. There is an edgy buzz about the capital, but it is easy to escape to the islands, some of which are full of cosmopolitan glitz, while others are refreshingly unspoilt and provincial.

TRAIN TRAVEL IN GREECE

Greece is on **Route 41** in this book. In addition **Route 43** south through the Balkans crosses the border from Macedonia and ends at Thessaloniki in northern

Greece. Both these routes presently involve crossing the Greek border by bus, the country having suspended all international rail services in 2011. The situation for 2012 remains uncertain. The **domestic rail network** is limited, but many routes around Athens and the main line to Thessaloniki have been much improved. Modernisation of the narrow-gauge lines on the Peloponnese came to an abrupt halt in 2011 due to the financial crisis. Fast trains run on main routes, but rail pass supplements are amongst the highest in Europe and reservation is essential. Trains are run by TrainOSE, www.trainose.com; ☎ 1110 (within Greece).

RAIL PASSES

InterRail, Eurail and the Balkan Flexipass are the main passes, but a multiple-journey card for 10, 20 or 30 days in second class is available from main stations.

ACCOMMODATION

Greece is over-supplied with accommodation. You should have no problem finding a bed in **Athens, Pátra** or **Thessaloniki** even in high summer (though the very cheapest Athens dorms and pensions are often very crowded in July and Aug). Rooms are hardest to find over the Greek Easter period (note this date is different from Easter elsewhere, as it's based on the Orthodox calendar), so try to

ESSENTIALS (GREECE)

Local name: Elláda/Ελλάδα — Population: 11.3m — Capital: Athens/Αθήνα (p430) — Currency: Euro — Language: Greek (English widely spoken in Athens and tourist areas; some German, French or Italian too, but less so in remote mainland areas) — Accommodation costs: medium (see p16) — Time zone: winter GMT+2, summer GMT+3 — International dialling code: +30

OPENING HOURS

Shops: vary; in summer most close midday and reopen in the evening (Tue, Thur, Fri) 1730–2030. Sites and museums: mostly 0830–1500; Athens sites and other major archaeological sites open until 1900 or open until sunset in summer.

PUBLIC HOLIDAYS

1, 6 Jan; Shrove Mon; 25 Mar; Easter; 1 May; Whit Mon; 15 Aug; 28 Oct; 25, 26 Dec. Everything closes for Easter; Greeks use the Orthodox calendar and dates may differ from western Easter.

PUBLIC TRANSPORT

KTEL buses (www.ktel.org): fast, punctual, fairly comfortable long-distance services; well-organised stations in most towns (tickets available from bus terminals). Islands connected by ferries and hydrofoils; see the Thomas Cook Publishing guide *Greek Island Hopping*. City transport: bus or (in Athens) trolleybus, metro and electric rail; services are crowded. Outside Athens, taxis are plentiful and good value.

TIPPING

Not necessary for restaurants or taxis.

TOURIST INFORMATION

Website of the Greek National Tourism Organisation: www.gnto.gr.

book ahead. Outside the Easter and July–Sept peaks, accommodation costs up to 30% less. The **youth hostel** network is sparse, but you will find hostels in Athens, Corfu and some of the more popular islands. **Campsites** at major sights (including Delphi, Mistra and Olympia) can be good value with excellent facilities.

FOOD AND DRINK

Greeks rarely eat breakfast. Traditional Greek meals are unstructured, with lots of dishes brought at once or in no particular order. Lunch is any time between 1200 and 1500, after which most restaurants close until around 1930. Greeks dine late, and you will find plenty of restaurants open until well after midnight.

The best Greek food is fresh, seasonal and simply prepared. Seafood dishes are usually the most expensive. Pork, chicken and squid are relatively cheap, and traditional salad — olives, tomatoes, cucumber, onions, peppers and feta cheese drowned in oil, served with bread — is a meal in itself (though Greeks eat it as a side dish). Coffee is easier to find than tea. Aniseed-flavoured **ouzo** is a favourite aperitif. **Retsina** (resinated wine) is an acquired taste. Greek brandy, **Metaxa**, is on the sweet side. Draught lager is not widely available and is neither as good nor as cheap as bottled beer: Amstel, Heineken and Mythos, brewed in Greece and sold in half-litre bottles.

HUNGARY —SEE MAP P649

Melding central European panache with a dash of Balkan style, Hungary is assertively different from any of its neighbouring countries. The **Great Plain**, Alföld, extends across more than half this landlocked country, with the most appreciable hills rising in the far north. Hungary's most scenic moments occur along **Lake Balaton** and the **Danube Bend** just north of Budapest, with a trio of fine towns — **Szentendre**, **Visegrád** and **Esztergom** (dominated by a huge basilica).

TRAIN TRAVEL IN HUNGARY

Hungary is on **Routes 40, 42** and **48** is this book. In recent years the country has developed its InterCity network to link all the main towns and cities, but there are plenty of slower trains from which to savour Hungary's largely rural nature, in particular along the north and south shores of Lake Balaton. IC trains require reservation and a supplement, whilst most of the international EC trains have a supplement but no compulsory reservation. International sleepers should be booked well in advance, particularly in summer. Free second-class travel for EU pensioners on most trains (yet not on cross-border services).

Hungarian State Railways (MÁV) owns the network, with MÁV-Start running the trains (www.mav-start.hu). Cross-border services between Sopron and Austria are run by GySEV.

Rail passes

InterRail and Eurail passes are valid. The **Turista Bérlet** is a 7- or 10-day network ticket available in first or second class; a separate version is available for GySEV services. **Balaton Mix** gives rail and shipping services around Lake Balaton, available May to Sept, allowing either 1 or 2 days travel, plus discounted travel to and from the area within 3 or 7 days respectively (family version also available).

ACCOMMODATION

There is a wide range of accommodation. For the medium to lower price bracket, **private rooms** are very good value, as is the **small pension**. Steer clear of the old Soviet-style tourist hotels and youth hostels as they are very basic with limited facilities. However, in Budapest especially, a new generation of **independent hostels** are offering dorm rooms at a much higher standard. **Campsites** are, on the whole, very good and can be found near the main resorts. Many have cabins to rent.

FOOD AND DRINK

Cuisine has been much influenced by Austria, Germany and Turkey. Portions are generous and most restaurants offer a cheap fixed-price menu. Lunch is the main meal of the day, and a bowl of *gulyás* (goulash) laced with potatoes and spiced with paprika is a 'must'.

Try smoked sausages, soups (sour cherry soup is superb) and paprika noodles or pike-perch. Dinner is early and you should aim to begin eating well before 2100. Hungary has some very decent wines, such as Tokaji and Egri Bikavér (Bull's Blood), while pálinka is a fiery schnapps.

Széchenyi Chain Bridge, the first permanent bridge over the Danube in Budapest, still links the two halves of the Hungarian capital, Buda and Pest (photo © Andre Gnat).

Essentials (Hungary)

Local name: Magyarország — Population: 10m — Capital: Budapest (p465) — Currency: Forint (Ft) — Language: Hungarian (English and German widely understood) — Accommodation costs: medium (see p16) — Time zone: winter GMT+1, summer GMT+2 — International dialling code: +36

Opening hours
Food shops: Mon–Fri 0700–1900, others: 1000–1800 (Thur until 1900); shops close for lunch and half-day on Sat (1400). Food/tourist shops, markets, malls open Sun. Museums: usually Tues–Sun 1000–1800, free one day a week, closed public holidays.

Public holidays
1 Jan; 15 Mar; Easter Mon; 1 May; Whit Mon; 20 Aug; 23 Oct; 25, 26 Dec.

Public transport
Long-distance buses operated by Volánbusz (www.volanbusz.hu). Boat services along the Danube. A hydrofoil service connects Budapest, Bratislava and Vienna (ERT 959, summer only).

Tipping
Round up by 10–15% for restaurants and taxis. People do not generally leave coins on the table; instead the usual practice is to make it clear that you are rounding up the sum when paying the bill.

Tourist information
Websites: www.hungary.com. Tourinform branches exist throughout Hungary.

Iceland

This remote North Atlantic island did a great favour to railway operators over much of Europe in spring 2010 by exporting so much volcanic ash that flights across Europe were paralysed. Of course, you'll not get to Iceland by train but there is an excellent ferry link from Hirtshals in Denmark (see **Route 22**). A land of wild fjords and volcanoes awaits. And it is not quite devoid of trains. On the dockside in Reykjavík you'll see a preserved steam locomotive that once ran on the local harbour railway. Read more in **Sidetracks** on p221.

Essentials: Local name: Ísland — Population: 32k — Capital: Reykjavík — Currency: Icelandic króna (kr) — Language: Icelandic (Danish and English are widely spread) — Accommodation costs: high — Time zone: winter and summer GMT — International dialling code: +354

Ireland

Much more than merely Britain's sidekick, the Republic of Ireland is assertively independent and punches far above its weight on the European stage. Eurail and InterRail are both valid (not just throughout the Republic but in neighbouring Northern Ireland too). Good ferry links with Cherbourg and Roscoff (see **Routes 3** and **4** respectively) allow Ireland conveniently to be combined with French rail

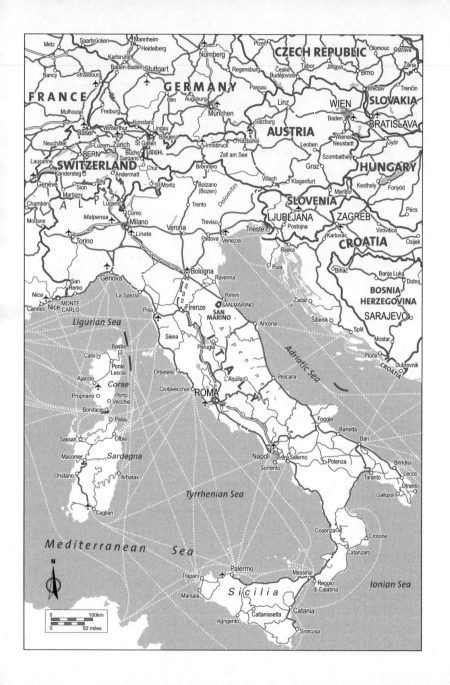

routes. Ireland has a modern rail network hubbed on Dublin with one route extending across the border to Belfast (for an onward connection by rail to Derry).

ESSENTIALS: Local name: Poblacht na hÉireann (or Éire for short) — Population: 4.3m — Capital: Dublin — Currency: Euro — Language: Gaeilge (Irish), English — Accommodation costs: high — Time zone: winter GMT, summer GMT+1 — International dialling code: +353

ITALY — SEE MAP OPPOSITE

Italy has been on the tourist trail since the days of the 18th-century 'Grand Tour', offering a mix of art, history and landscape arguably unrivalled in any other European country. It is not for nothing that the pundits say 'see Rome and die'. But Italian passion and flair comes with a nice dose of chaos too, and for unhurried travellers prepared to slip gently into the Italian way of life, the country is deeply seductive.

TRAIN TRAVEL IN ITALY

Italy features on **Routes 33 to 37** in this book. In addition, **Routes 6, 28, 29, 31** and **38**, while more focused on territory beyond Italy's borders, start or end in Italy. Although headlined by its showpiece 1,000-km-long Torino to Salerno **high-speed line**, with sleek Frecciarossa and Frecciargento trains linking the principal cities in double-quick time, there is also no shortage of railways of the slow and scenic variety in Italy. The fastest trains (at premium fares) are classified Alta Velocità (AV), Eurostar Italia (ES) or Eurostar City (ESc), and all apart from regional and local trains require advance reservation, with the exception of EC trains to Austria via Bolzano and the Brenner Pass. There are **refreshments** on most long-distance trains.

The national rail company is Trenitalia, www.trenitalia.com, a division of Ferrovie dello Stato (FS). National rail information ☎ 89 20 21 (+39 06 68 47 54 75 from outside Italy). Queues at stations are often long but you can buy tickets and make reservations online or at travel agencies (look for FS symbol).

RAIL PASSES
InterRail and Eurail are both valid. There are no locally sold national passes in Italy, but some city passes include trains and cover a wide area. There are 3- and 7-day passes for public transport in the Südtirol region around Bolzano.

ACCOMMODATION

Hotel prices are often per room rather than per person, with Venice and Capri particularly pricey. Most establishments style themselves *hotel* or *albergo*, but some more basic hotels are still called *locande*. **B&Bs** are booming, with lists available from tourist offices.

HI **youth hostels** are plentiful, with around 90 members; prices include sheets and breakfast (www.ostellionline.org). **Independent hostels**, of varying standards, can be found in all the main tourist destinations. Some 'hostels' are glorified guesthouses, and are small, family-run affairs often with restricted check-in times and lacking in common rooms or other social areas. In short, hostelling in Italy can be un-standardised and informal, much like the Italians themselves.

Camping is popular, but sites are often tricky to reach without a car. Most tend to be upmarket camping villages with bars, restaurants and pools, often also with accommodation in cabins. **Farm stays** and **B&B** in cottages and estates is well-established. *Agriturismo* (www.agriturismo.it) is a good first port of call.

FOOD AND DRINK

In Italy, meals are an important social occasion, but food is far more varied than the pasta and pizza stereotypes. A full meal may consist of *antipasti* (cold cuts, grilled vegetables, bruschetta), followed by pasta, a main course, then fruit, cheese or a *semi-freddo* (cold desserts, like tiramisu) or superb ice cream (*gelato*). Much of the pleasure of eating in Italy is derived from the sheer freshness and

ESSENTIALS (ITALY)

Local name: Italia — Population: 60m — Capital: Rome/Roma (p555) — Currency: Euro — Language: Italian (many speak English in cities and tourist areas) — Accommodation costs: medium (see p16) — Time zone: winter GMT+1, summer GMT+2 — International dialling code: +39

OPENING HOURS
Shops: (usually) Mon–Sat 0830/0900–1230, 1530/1600–1900/1930; closed Mon am/Sat pm July/Aug. Museums/sites: usually Tues–Sun 0930–1900; last Sun of month free.

PUBLIC HOLIDAYS
All over the country: 1, 6 Jan; Easter Sun and Mon; 25 Apr; 1 May; 2 June; 15 Aug (virtually nothing opens); 1 Nov; 8, 25, 26 Dec. Regional saints' days: 25 Apr in Venice; 24 June in Florence, Genoa and Turin; 29 June in Rome; 11 July in Palermo; 19 Sept in Naples; 4 Oct in Bologna; 6 Dec in Bari; 7 Dec in Milan.

PUBLIC TRANSPORT
Various regional bus companies operate. Buses often crowded, but regular; serve many areas inaccessible by rail. Services drastically reduced at weekends; not always shown on timetables.

TIPPING
In restaurants you need to look at the menu to see if service charge is included. If not, a tip of 10% is fine depending on how generous you feel like being (same for taxis).

TOURIST INFORMATION
Website: www.enit.it. All regions and most towns have Tourist Boards and tourist offices, usually now called APT or IAT but, confusingly, the name depends on the area.

quality of the ingredients. *Trattorie* are simple establishments and are cheaper than *ristoranti* while *osterie* vary from simple and unpretentious to pricey gentrified-rustic restaurants. For drinking, try an *enoteca*, a wine bar, which may do light meals. *Alimentari* stores often prepare good picnic rolls while *rosticcerie* sell meaty takeaways, and *tavole calde* have cheap self-service.

Coffee (*caffè*) comes in tiny shots of **espresso**. There are many fine Italian **wines**, though Italian beer tends to be bottled. Bars are good places to get a snack, such as a roll or toasted sandwich. If you're gathering picnic items, be aware that food shops close for a lengthy lunch break.

In restaurants, be aware of cover charges (*coperto*) and service (*servizio*), both of which will be added to your bill. Places serving a *menu turistico* include taxes and service charges but are best avoided — a sign the place caters to tourists and is of a lower standard, and not necessarily cheaper. You would be better off in a pizzeria or tiny trattoria.

KOSOVO — SEE MAP P608

Europe's newest nation state, Kosovo controversially seceded from Serbia in 2008, leaving the international community divided on whether the upstart country deserved recognition.

As of late 2011, less than half of UN members recognise Kosovo. Kosovo is best visited as a detour from **Route 43** in this book, entering from Macedonia and leaving again the same way. Limited train services within Kosovo are operated by Hekurudhat e Kosovës (HK). Read more in **Sidetracks** on p359.

ESSENTIALS: Local name: Kosovë / Kosova — Population: 1.8m — Capital: Priština — Currency: Euro — Language: Albanian, Serbian — Accommodation costs: low — Time zone: winter GMT+1, summer GMT+2 — International dialling code: +381

LATVIA — SEE MAP P636

Baltic State that secured independence from the Soviet Union in 1991 and joined the EU in 2004. Silvery beaches, the finest forests you've ever seen and some showpiece cities combine to make affordable Latvia one of Europe's most promising destinations. You'll find an interesting ethnic mix, with about one third of the population speaking Russian and preserving many aspects of Russian culture and customs.

TRAIN TRAVEL IN LATVIA

Latvian is on **Route 46** in this book. Domestic train services are sparse and international services even more so. To reach Vilnius from Riga you will almost certainly have resort to a bus. However, comfortable overnight trains operate

from Riga to St Petersburg and Moscow. The Latvian Railways website www.ldz.lv has an English-language version.

RAIL PASSES
Neither InterRail nor Eurail are valid. There are no local passes, but rail fares are unbelievably cheap.

ACCOMMODATION

The best selection of **hotels** in Latvia is available in Riga, the nearby seaside resort of Jūrmala and the bohemian city of Liepāja on the west coast of Latvia. Most camping facilities are located near the nation's 495 km of coastline, but cheap **country lodging** and **homestays** can be arranged online via Lauku ceļotājs (www.celotajs.lv). The Latvian capital offers dozens of good **hostels**.

FOOD AND DRINK

Many Latvian dishes are accompanied by a richly seasoned gravy, and are usually eaten with superb rye bread. Pork and peas are staples. Latvian **beer** (*alus*) is good and strong — try Bauskas, Tērvetes or Užavas. The bitter Riga **balsam** is famous throughout the former Soviet Union and is considered very good for health. Add it to coffee, cheap sparkling wine and cocktails, or just drink it on its own, whether you're ailing or not.

COUNTRIES A TO Z | LATVIA

ESSENTIALS (LATVIA)

Local name: Latvija — Population: 2.2m — Capital: Riga/Rīga (p379) — Currency: Lat (Ls) — Language: Latvian (spoken by two thirds of the population), Russian (English spoken by younger people) — Accommodation costs: medium (see p16) — Time zone: winter GMT+2, summer GMT+3 — International dialling code: +371

OPENING HOURS
Shops: Mon–Fri 0900/1000–1800/1900 and Sat–Sun 0900/1000–1700. Museums: days vary, but usually open Tues/Wed–Sun 1100–1700. Often closed on national holidays.

PUBLIC HOLIDAYS
1 Jan; Good Fri; Easter Sun/Mon; 1 May; 4 May (Independence Day); 23-24 June (Midsummer celebrations); 18 Nov; 25, 26, 31 Dec.

PUBLIC TRANSPORT
Cheap for Westerners. The long-distance train network has improved, but buses provide a more extensive service. Bus tickets can be purchased at bus stations or directly from the driver.

TIPPING
Not necessary to tip service at the bar or counter, but tip 10% if served at your table. Round up taxi fares to a maximum of 10%.

TOURIST INFORMATION
Website: www.latvia.travel.

LIECHTENSTEIN — SEE MAPS P600 AND P670

Bite-sized Alpine principality that nestles between the River Rhine and the mountains to the east. Enigmatic Liechtenstein shares borders with Austria and Switzerland and is traversed by **Route 32** which takes in the only railway line to cross Liechtenstein territory. All rail passes valid in Austria are deemed to also include Liechtenstein. Read more in **Sidetracks** on p285.

ESSENTIALS: Local name: Fürstentum Liechtenstein — Population: 36k — Capital: Vaduz — Currency: Swiss franc (CHF) — Language: German (English is widely spoken) — Accommodation costs: high — Time zone: winter GMT+1, summer GMT+2 — International dialling code: +423

LITHUANIA — SEE MAP P636

Largest of the three Baltic States (though only fractionally larger than Latvia), Lithuania is able to refer back to a more glorious history than its Baltic neighbours, having been part of the influential Polish-Lithuanian Commonwealth from 1569 to 1795. Nowadays a place for sculptural stork nests, Europe's finest sand spit and a glorious capital city in Vilnius, Lithuania is cheap, friendly and desperate to welcome visitors.

ESSENTIALS (LITHUANIA)

Local name: Lietuva — Population: 3.3m — Capital: Vilnius (p378) — Currency: Litas (Lt) — Language: Lithuanian, Russian (English is widely spoken, as is German on the coast) — Accommodation costs: medium (see p16) — Time zone: winter GMT+2, summer GMT+3 — International dialling code: +370

OPENING HOURS
Shops: department stores and smaller shops of interest to tourists in Vilnius and Kaunas usually open every day from 1000–1900. Supermarkets stay open until 2200. Specialist shops all close Sun and around 1700 on Sat. Museums: vary; see www.lnm.lt.

PUBLIC HOLIDAYS
1 Jan; 16 Feb; 11 Mar; Easter Sun and Mon; 1 May; the first Sun in May (Mothers' Day); 6 July; 15 Aug; 1 Nov; 25, 26 Dec.

PUBLIC TRANSPORT
Cheap for Westerners. The long-distance train network has improved, but buses provide a more comprehensive network and are the only way to Riga in Latvia.

TIPPING
Not necessary to tip service at the bar or counter, but tip 10% if served at your table. Round up taxi fares to a maximum of 10%.

TOURIST INFORMATION
Website: www.tourism.lt; www.lithuaniatourism.co.uk. Lithuanian State Department of Tourism, Švitrigailos g. 11M, LT-03228 Vilnius, ☎ 52 10 87 96.

TRAIN TRAVEL IN LITHUANIA

Vilnius features on **Route 46** in this volume. Lithuania has a thin domestic network with services from Vilnius to Kaunas and Klaipėda and a new link to Vilnius airport. There is a through train to St Petersburg, as well as good services to Minsk, Moscow and Russia's Baltic exclave at Kaliningrad. The once-daily train connection to Warsaw requires a change en route. The Lithuanian Railways website, www.litrail.lt, has an English version.

RAIL PASSES
Neither Eurail nor InterRail are valid. There are no local passes, but rail fares are very cheap.

ACCOMMODATION

Useful agencies to book accommodation are **Lithuanian Hotels Reservation Centre Service** (www.lithuanianhotels.com), Litinterp (www.litinterp.lt), who can arrange accommodation with local families (B&B) and the **Lithuanian Youth Hostels Association**, Filaretai Youth Hostel (www.lithuanianhostels.org). If you have no luck with these agencies, Lithuania has an extensive system of tourist information offices that cover all the main towns (for Vilnius see p378) and can help you find accommodation.

FOOD AND DRINK

Local specialities include: *cepelinai* (the national dish — dumplings stuffed with meat), *blynai* (mini pancakes) and *kotletas* (not the cutlets you might expect, but minced meat balls).

Fish and dairy products are common in all dishes. Lithuanians eat their **evening meal** early and in smaller restaurants you should aim to order by 2000. Vodka (the best is Kvietine) is the main spirit. Lithuanian **beer** (Utenos, Svyturys and other brands) is easily available.

The Hill of Crosses near Šiauliai is an outstanding piece of Lithuanian folk art that reflects the country's enduring Catholicism (photo © Andrey Butenk).

LUXEMBOURG – SEE MAP P645

The Grand Duchy of Luxembourg covers some pretty terrain for hiking, with river valleys, forests and hills, that give way to a more industrial landscape along the southern border (with neighbouring France). The forested sandstone hills of the north-east, abutting onto Germany, are an oasis of calm rurality in an otherwise rather crowded part of Europe. The country's eponymous capital has a dramatic and picturesque setting, straddling two gorges.

TRAIN TRAVEL IN LUXEMBOURG

This small, modern and efficient network links Luxembourg city with most areas, the longest line being the picturesque route northwards to the Belgian border at Gouvy and on to Liège (part of **Route 14** in this book). Most stations are small with few facilities. The national rail company is CFL, www.cfl.lu.

RAIL PASSES

Both Eurail and InterRail are valid. The **Dagesbilljee/Billet longue durée** gives a day's unlimited second-class travel on all public transport throughout the country for just €4 (not valid to border points); a carnet of 5 day tickets is also available. At weekends there is also a day ticket for up to 5 people costing just €6.

ESSENTIALS (LUXEMBOURG)

Local name: Luxembourg/Lëtzebuerg – Population: 0.5m – Capital: Luxembourg (p160) – Currency: Euro – Language: Lëtzebuergesch, French and German (most people speak some English) – Accommodation costs: high (see p16) – Time zone: winter GMT+1, summer GMT+2 – International dialling code: +352

OPENING HOURS
Many establishments take long lunch breaks. Shops: Mon 1300/1400–1800; Tues–Sat 0800/0900–1800; closed Sun. Museums: most open six days a week (usually Tues–Sun).

PUBLIC HOLIDAYS
1 Jan; Feb (Carnival); Easter Mon; 1 May; Ascension; Whit Mon; 23 June; 15 Aug; early Sept (Luxembourg City Fête); 1 Nov; 25, 26 Dec. When holidays fall on Sun, the Mon usually becomes a holiday, but only twice in one year.

PUBLIC TRANSPORT
Good bus network linking Luxembourg city with towns and villages across the Grand Duchy (operated by RGTR). Timetables are online at www.horaires.lu.

TIPPING
Essential in staffed public toilets and always welcome in restaurants, cafés and bars.

TOURIST INFORMATION
Luxembourg City Tourist Office, 30 place Guillaume II, PO Box 181, L-2011 Luxembourg, ☎ 22 28 09 (www.lcto.lu). The National Tourist Office has a branch located in the main hall of Luxembourg City railway station, ☎ 42 82 82 20 (www.ont.lu).

Accommodation

The national tourist office has free brochures featuring **hotels** (of all grades, plus restaurants), **holiday apartments, farm holidays** and **camping** in the Grand Duchy, plus a bed and breakfast booklet that covers all three Benelux countries.

There are 11 **youth hostels**. The price of bed and breakfast includes linen and varies from 'standard' category to the slightly pricier 'comfort' category. Non-members pay a supplement. See *Centrale des Auberges de Jeunesse Luxembourgeoises* (www.youthhostels.lu) for details.

Food and drink

Cuisine has been pithily described as 'French quality, German quantity', but eating out is pricey. Keep costs down by making lunch your main meal and looking out for special deals: *plat du jour* (single course) or *menu* (two–three courses). Local specialities include: Ardennes ham, *treipen* (black pudding), *gromperekichelcher* (fried potato patties) and (in Sept) *quetschentaart* (a flan featuring dark, violet plums).

Macedonia — see map p608

One of several countries that appeared on the political map of Europe 20 years ago following the break-up of Yugoslavia. Since then the country has had an ongoing spat with neighbouring Greece over the use of the name Macedonia (hence the common rendering FYRO Macedonia). Too often overlooked by travellers, Macedonia is a wonderful kaleidoscope of Balkan life and culture, and we hope that its inclusion in *Europe by Rail* helps it become better known.

ESSENTIALS: Local name: Republika Makedonija/Република Македонија — Population: 2.2m — Capital: Skopje/Скопје (p358) — Currency: Macedonian denar (MKD) — Language: Macedonian, Albanian — Accommodation costs: low (see p16) — Time zone: winter GMT+1, summer GMT+2 — International dialling code: +389

Rail travel in Macedonia

The small rail network of this former Yugoslav Republic centres on Skopje, on the international corridor linking Belgrade in Serbia with Thessaloniki in Greece — although services across the Greek border were suspended in 2011. This main north-south axis is described in some detail in **Route 43** in this book. Delightfully antiquated but slow and infrequent domestic services link Skopje with Bitola (Битола), Kočani (Кочани) and Kičevo (Кичево). The Macedonian Railways website, www.mz.com.mk, has no English version.

Rail passes

The only passes that are valid here are InterRail (not Eurail).

MALTA

Island archipelago (with three inhabited islands) in the Mediterranean. Explore the densely populated main island (Malta itself) and you'll find old railway stations in Mdina and Birkirkara.

But the railway line that linked them was closed in 1931 and Malta is now a country without trains. The islands are superbly well served by international ferries, with good links from Sicily, so you can conclude **Route 37** in this book with a sea voyage to Malta.

There are also ferries from Livorno, useful if you wish to combine **Routes 33** or **34** with a visit to Malta.

ESSENTIALS: Local name: Repubblika ta' Malta — Population: 0.4m — Capital: Valletta — Currency: Euro — Language: Maltese, English (Italian widely understood) — Accommodation costs: medium — Time zone: winter GMT+1, summer GMT+2 — International dialling code: +356

MOLDOVA — SEE MAP P654

Landlocked country that just touches the Danube and shares common borders with Ukraine and Romania. Moldova slipped quietly to independence as the Soviet Union was preoccupied with the August 1991 coup attempt in Moscow, and has been riven by strife ever since with the easternmost part of the country, called Transnistria, insisting that it is a separate state.

Despite those difficulties, Moldova is an engagingly different place to visit with some beautiful wetlands, amazing old monasteries and charmingly antiquated railways. A paradise for those who appreciate slow travel! Easily visited as an offshot of **Route 50** (see the **Sidetracks** on p419).

ESSENTIALS: Local name: Republica Moldova — Population: 3.5m — Capital: Chișinău — Currency: Moldovan leu (MDL) — Language: Moldovan (very similar to Romanian), Russian also widely used — Accommodation costs: low — Time zone: winter GMT+2, summer GMT+3 — International dialling code: +373

MONACO — SEE MAP P621

This tiny sovereign city state, a constitutional monarchy presided over by the Grimaldi family, is tucked away on a prime bit of real estate in the middle of the French Riviera. The main railway line from Nice to the Italian border at Ventimiglia (part of **Route 6** in this book) cuts through Monaco or, more properly, *under* Monaco for most of this stretch is buried away in a tunnel. So not a lot of potential for sightseeing by train, but you can stop off at the sole station, called Monaco-Monte Carlo (in ERT 360 and ERT 361). All rail passes valid for France are deemed to include Monaco.

ESSENTIALS: Local name: Principauté de Monaco — Population: 32k — Capital: Monaco Ville (p97) — Currency: Euro — Language: French, Monégasque (Italian and English commonly understood) — Accommodation costs: high — Time zone: winter GMT+1, summer GMT+2 — International dialling code: +377

MONTENEGRO — SEE MAPS P608 AND P611

Small Adriatic republic that was part of socialist Yugoslavia. Upon demise of the latter, it remained in a loose union with Serbia. Montenegro eventually split from Serbia in 2006 (without any of the problems associated with the later secession of Kosovo, for Montenegro was never politically integrated into Serbia). Fabulous coastal scenery, backed with wild mountain landscapes. One of Europe's last frontiers that cries out for inclusion in a future edition of *Europe by Rail*.

The country is served by direct train from Belgrade (ERT 1370), so a visit to Montenegro can easily be combined with **Routes 42, 43, 44** or **50**. There are direct buses from Bar and Kotor in Montenegro to Dubrovnik to join **Routes 38** and **44**. The InterRail global pass is valid, but there is no InterRail one-country pass for Montenegro. The Eurail global pass is not valid, but Eurail do have a select pass covering Montenegro, Serbia and Bulgaria.

ESSENTIALS: Local name: Crna Gora — Population: 0.6m — Capital: Podgorica — Currency: Euro — Language: Montenegrin (English and Italian widely understood in coastal resorts) — Accommodation costs: low — Time zone: winter GMT+1, summer GMT+2 — International dialling code: +382

NETHERLANDS — SEE MAP P645

Canals and 17th- and 18th-century gabled buildings are abiding memories of a visit to the Netherlands, whose numerous historic towns and cities have a strikingly uniform appearance. In between, the bulb fields and windmills lend the Dutch farmland a distinctive character. **Amsterdam**, laid-back and bustling at the same time, justifiably draws most visitors.

TRAIN TRAVEL IN THE NETHERLANDS

Route 15 in this book, one of only two circular routes in this entire volume, focuses on the Netherlands. Frequent and modern electric trains, many of which are double-deckers, whizz around the country's dense rail network, linking well-kept stations, some completely modernised, others retaining traditional features such as Delft Blue tiles. There is no advance booking on domestic services, which fall into three categories: Intercity, Sneltrein, and Sprinter (also called Stoptrein). Domestic services on the **high-speed line** south towards Belgium are branded as Fyra and a supplement is payable.

ESSENTIALS (NETHERLANDS)

Local name: Nederland — Population: 16.6m — Administrative Capital: Amsterdam (p421), Legislative Capital: The Hague (Den Haag) — Currency: Euro — Language: Dutch (English and German widely spoken) — Accommodation costs: high (see p16) — Time zone: winter GMT+1, summer GMT+2 — International dialling code: +31

OPENING HOURS

Shops: Mon 1300–1800, Tues–Fri 0900–1800 (until 2100 Thur or Fri), Sat 0900–1700. Museums: vary, but usually 1000–1700 (some close Mon). Many attractions close Oct–Easter, Apr–May is tulip season, and the country gets very crowded.

PUBLIC HOLIDAYS

1 Jan; Good Fri; Easter Sun–Mon; 30 Apr; 5 May; Ascension Day; Whit Sun–Mon; 25, 26 Dec. Note that although Good Friday is a 'holiday' in The Netherlands, no one gets a day off and nothing closes (apart from some banks). The same is largely true of 5 May.

PUBLIC TRANSPORT

Centralised (premium rate) number for all rail and bus enquiries: national, ☎ 0900 9292 (www. 92920v.nl). In many cities (not Amsterdam), shared Treintaxis have ranks at stations and yellow roof signs. *Strippenkaarten* (from stations, city transport offices, post offices, supermarkets and VVVs) are strip tickets valid nationwide on metros, buses, trams and some trains (2nd class) within city limits; zones apply; validate on boarding; valid 1 hr; change of transport allowed. *Strippenkaarten* will eventually be replaced by a new electronic ticketing system, the *OV-Chipkaart* (similar to the Oyster Card used in London). This is currently being phased in across the country, and will become the norm during 2012 for all public transport, including trains. *Strippenkaarten* and normal NS railway tickets will cease to be issued. For more information, see www.ov-chipkaart.nl.

TIPPING

Service charges are included, but it is customary to round off the bill in restaurants to a convenient figure. If paying by credit card, pay the exact amount on the card and leave a few coins.

TOURIST INFORMATION

Website: www.holland.com. Tourist bureaux are VVV (Vereniging voor Vreemdelingenverkeer): signs show a triangle with three Vs.

Most services are run by the national rail company Nederlandse Spoorwegen (NS), www.ns.nl. Tickets are mostly sold from machines, or online with e-tickets being printed at home. Credit cards are not accepted over the counter except at Schiphol Airport. A contactless smartcard, OV-chipkaart, is being introduced for all public transport. More on this in the 'Essentials' box above.

RAIL PASSES

Both InterRail and Eurail are valid. The **NS Dagkaart** allows unlimited travel for one day, and for a little extra the **OV Dagkaart** adds buses, trams and metro throughout the country. Lentetoer and Zomertoer are seasonal day tickets for two people available in spring and summer (not before 0900 Mon-Fri).

ACCOMMODATION

Hotel standards are high and lower prices reflect limited facilities rather than poor quality. Booking is advisable. As a backpacker-magnet, Amsterdam has a

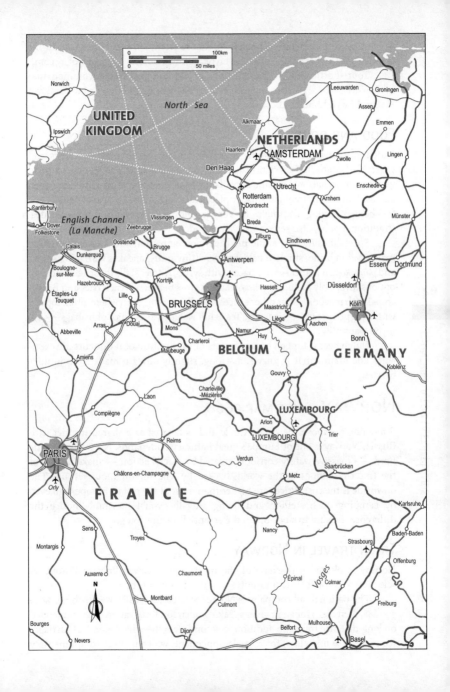

wide range of **independent hostels** to choose from, although elsewhere in the country a better bet are the official **Stayokay youth hostels** (www.stayokay.com).

Tourist offices (VVV) have listings of **bed and breakfast** accommodation in their area, where it exists, or you can book nationwide through Bed & Breakfast Holland (www.bbholland.com).

FOOD AND DRINK

Dutch cuisine is mainly simple and substantial: fish or meat, potatoes and vegetables. Many Indonesian restaurants offer spicy food and in cities a good variety of international cuisine is available. Most cheaper eating joints stay open all day. Some restaurants in smaller places take last orders by 2130 or 2200. Look for boards saying *dagschotel* (a very economical 'special'). 'Brown cafés' (traditional pubs) also serve good-value food.

Specialities include **apple pie** (heavy on cinnamon and sultanas), herring marinated in brine, **smoked eels**, *poffertjes* (tiny puff-pancakes with icing sugar) and *pannekoeken* (pancakes: try bacon with syrup). Street stalls for snacks abound, options invariably including *frites/patates* (a cross between French fries and British chips) with mayonnaise or other sauces. Excellent coffee everywhere, often topped with whipped cream — *slagroom*. Tea is hot water with a choice of teabags — ask if you want milk.

Dutch beer is topped by two fingers of froth. Most local **liqueurs** are excellent. The main **spirit** is *jenever*, a strong, slightly oily gin made from juniper berries.

NORWAY — SEE MAP P668

Stretching far above the Arctic Circle and as far east as a shared frontier with Russia, Norway is one of Europe's great natural wonderlands. Norway's majestic fjords — massive watery corridors created by glacial action — make up one of the finest coastlines in the world, backed by wild mountainous terrain. The downside is the cost. Prices are higher than most of the rest of Europe, and even by camping or hostelling and living frugally, you'll inevitably notice the difference. Be sure to stock up on the essentials before you go.

TRAIN TRAVEL IN NORWAY

Norway is blessed with some of the most scenic railway lines in Europe. A selection of those feature on **Routes 21, 23** and **24** in this book.

The national rail company is Norges Statsbaner (NSB), www.nsb.no, ☎ 81 500 888, then dial 9 for an English-speaking operator. Reservation is recommended on long-distance trains. In addition to second class these have Komfort carriages (equivalent to first class) for a fixed supplement, which include complimentary

ESSENTIALS (NORWAY)

Local name: Norge — Population: 4.9m — Capital: Oslo (p532) — Currency: Norwegian krone (NKr./NOK) — Language: Norwegian, i.e. Bokmål and Nynorsk (English widely spoken) — Accommodation costs: high (see p16) — Time zone: winter GMT+1, summer GMT+2 — International dialling code: +47

OPENING HOURS

Shops: Mon–Wed and Fri 0900–1700/2000 (supermarkets), Thur 0900–1900, Sat 0900–1500/1800 (supermarkets). Museums: usually Tues–Sun 1000–1700/1800. Some open Mon, longer in summer and close or have shorter opening hours in winter.

PUBLIC HOLIDAYS

1 Jan; Maundy Thur–Good Fri; Easter Sun–Mon; 1 May; Ascension Day; Pentecost; 17 May (National Day); Whitsun; 25–26 Dec.

PUBLIC TRANSPORT

Train, boat and bus schedules are interlinked to provide good connections. Often worth using buses or boats to connect two dead-end lines (e.g. Bergen and Stavanger), rather than retracing your route. Rail passes sometimes offer good discounts, even free travel, on linking services. NorWay Bussekspress, Oslo bussterminalen, avgangshallen, Schweigaards gt 8–10, 0185 Oslo, ☎ 81 54 44 44 (premium rate), (www.nor-way.no), has the largest bus network, routes going as far north as Alta. Long-distance buses: comfortable, with reclining seats, ample leg room. Tickets: buy on board or reserve, ☎ 81 54 44 44 (premium rate). Another long-distance bus company is Lavprisekspressen, which has routes between the largest cities, and also to Copenhagen through Sweden, ☎ 67 98 04 80 (www.lavprisekspressen.no).

TIPPING

Tip 10% in restaurants (but not bars/cafés) if you are satisfied with the food, service etc. Not necessary for taxis.

TOURIST INFORMATION

Website: www.visitnorway.com. Tourist offices (*Turistinformasjon*) amd tourist boards (*Reise-livslag*) can be found in virtually all towns; free maps, brochures etc available.

tea and coffee. Reserved seats are not marked other than on your confirmation. Sleeping cars have one, two and three berth compartments, all available with a second-class ticket plus a fixed fee. Long-distance trains convey a bistro car serving hot and cold meals, drinks and snacks.

RAIL PASSES

Norway is covered by the InterRail and Eurail schemes, but the Flåm line is treated like a private line and gives 30% discount.

ACCOMMODATION

Because Norway is so expensive, the **youth hostel** network is indispensable if you don't want to break the bank. There are some 75 hostels (*vandrerhjem*), many of which unfortunately open only mid-June–mid-Aug. The standard of hostel accommodation is very high, with singles, doubles and dormitories, and there's a good geographical spread. Booking ahead is highly recommended, especially in summer (www.hihostels.no). **Private houses** can be quite good value, and in some cases almost the same price as hostels. More upscale are **guesthouses** and **pensions**.

Hotels are generally very pricey, but many cut rates at weekends and in summer. Advance booking is important, especially in Oslo, Bergen and Stavanger. Many of the more than 1,200 official **campsites** have cabins (*hytter*), sleeping two–four people and equipped with kitchen and maybe a bathroom. Rough camping is permitted as long as you don't intrude on residents (you must be 150 m from them) and leave no trace of your stay. Never light fires in summer.

Food and drink

Eating out is very pricey and you will save a lot by self-catering. Stock up at supermarkets and at *konditori* (bakeries), which often serve sandwiches and pastries cheaply. Restaurants sometimes have *dagens rett* (daily specials), relatively inexpensive full meals. Self-service cafeterias are also generally reasonable. Bigger towns have the usual array of fast food, plus hot dog and baked-potato stalls on the street; you may find *smørbrød*, the ubiquitous and diverse open sandwich, more appetising. Refill cups of coffee often come free or half price, while tea with lemon is the norm — ask specifically if you want it with milk (*te med melk*). The range of vegetarian food is generally pretty limited.

Breakfast served in hotels and hostels is buffet-style, with a wide choice: a good chance to fill up for free on the likes of porridge, herring, cheese, meats and bread and jam. Lunch is normally 1200–1500, and sometimes features all-you-can-eat *koldtbord* at fixed price, for a lot less than the equivalent evening meal. Dinner is 1800–2200 in towns, but may end earlier in rural areas.

Fresh **fish** is in abundant supply, with numerous dishes based on salmon and trout. Meat is generally costlier, and includes *elg* (elk) and *reinsdyr* (reindeer), as well as hearty stews, sausages and *kjøttkaker* (meatballs). **Alcohol** can raise the cost of living from expensive to exorbitant. Many bars, especially in the capital, are voluntarily restricting the drinking age to 21, and rigorously checking ID. Nevertheless in winter you might like to warm up on *gløgg* (mulled wine).

Poland — see map opposite

In the space of just a few years, Poland has established itself as one of Europe's prime travel destinations. Superb old city squares, many quite Italianate in character, and some dazzling Baltic beaches are just the start. There are stunning lake landscapes (especially in Mazuria), memorably beautiful mountains (in the south of the country), tremendous nightlife and enough shrines to keep a shine on your rosary.

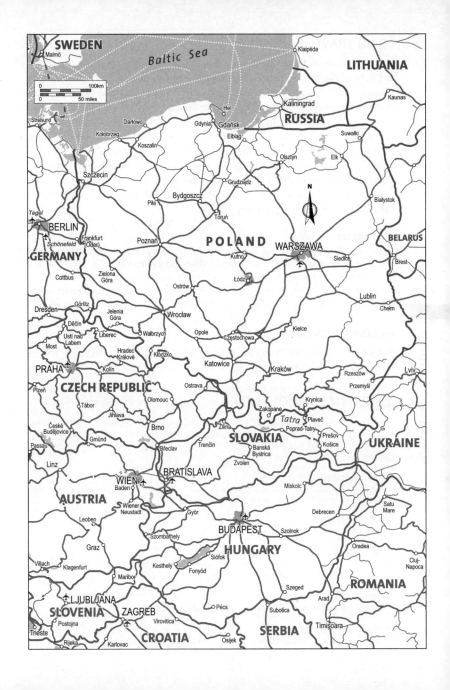

TRAIN TRAVEL IN POLAND

Poland features on **Route 45, 46, 47** and **49** in this book. The country has a decent rail network linking all major cities, though services in some rural areas can be infrequent. Timetables change with disconcerting frequency and the various rail operators lurch from one financial crisis to the next. Services are provided by two separate subsidiaries of the national railway: PKP Intercity (www.intercity.pl) operates EIC and TLK trains, in addition to international EC trains, whilst Przewozy Regionalne operates the more localised REGIO, InterREGIO (IR) and REGIO Ekspres trains, some of which nevertheless cover quite long distances. Reservation is compulsory on EIC, EC and some TLK trains. Not all long-distance trains have refreshments. Polish railway staff are famously mono-lingual. It helps to know some key phrases.

RAIL PASSES

InterRail is valid in Poland, but Eurail is not. PKP Intercity has a weekend ticket valid 1900 Friday to 0600 Monday, plus a similar **Bilet Podróznika** (Traveller ticket) for TLK trains only. Przewozy Regionalne has the REGIOkarnet valid for any 3 days out of 2 months, and **Bilet Turystyczny** valid 1800 Friday to 0600 Monday, both valid across the German border, e.g. to Görlitz or Frankfurt (Oder).

ACCOMMODATION

Expect huge variations in prices. A Kraków hotel in high season might charge several times more than a comparable place in a grim industrial city. Agencies

ESSENTIALS (POLAND)

Local name: Polska — Population: 38.2m — Capital: Warsaw/Warszawa (p587) — Currency: Złoty (Zł.) — Language: Polish (English spoken by younger Poles, German by older ones) — Accommodation costs: medium (see p16) — Time zone: winter GMT+1, summer GMT+2 — International dialling code: +48

OPENING HOURS

Shops: Mon–Fri 1000–1900, Sat 0900–1300. Many supermarkets are now open daily or round the clock in major cities. Museums: usually Tues–Sun 1000–1600.

PUBLIC HOLIDAYS

1 Jan; Easter Sun–Mon; 1, 3 May; Corpus Christi; 15 Aug; 1, 11 Nov; 25–26 Dec.

PUBLIC TRANSPORT

PKS buses are cheap and practical. Tickets normally include seat reservations (book at bus station). In rural areas, bus drivers often halt between official stops if you wave them down.

TIPPING

Tipping is normal and expected: 10% (bars, cafés and restaurants).

TOURIST INFORMATION

Website: www.poland.travel. Tourist offices can usually help with accommodation.

like www.polhotels.com offer online booking options, often with a small discount on rack rates. There is a growing range of **pensions** (*pensjonaty*), which can be great value, but note that breakfast is often charged as an extra. Rooms in **private houses** (*kwatera prywatna*), often touted to young travellers at main railway stations, are a bit hit and miss. Check you won't be staying out in some distant estate before committing.

Youth hostels are often lacklustre and spartan, but there are a growing number of **independent hostels**, especially in Kraków, Wrocław, Warsaw and Zakopane.

FOOD AND DRINK

Kiosks and cafés serve the ubiquitous pizzas, chips and unappealing burgers. A common Polish fast food is *zapiekanka* (cheese and mushrooms on toast). The wholesome local food is often excellent value. Look particularly for *pierogi* (tiny dumplings often filled with vegetables or meat), fried or grilled pork, and a great range of soups. *Barszcz* is one of the classics. Beer and vodka are very cheap, the latter coming in a thousand varieties. Try **vodka** flavoured with honey, juniper or lemon.

PORTUGAL – SEE MAP P665

Portugal once prospered as a great maritime power and ruled a far-flung empire across Africa, the Far East and South America. Much of northern Portugal looks positively lush, with landscapes of rolling hills dotted with orange, lemon and olive groves. Head inland to explore hill country, dotted with ancient fortified towns, and south to the Algarve for sun, sea and sand.

TRAIN TRAVEL IN PORTUGAL

Travel to Portugal by train, following **Route 9** in this book, and then use **Route 11** to explore Portugal a little more. Extensive modernisation in recent years has given Portugal a first-rate rail network, at least on the main lines, with tilting AP (Alfa Pendular) trains providing the fastest services on the core Porto — Lisbon — Faro route, alongside InterCity trains. AP and IC trains all require compulsory reservation. Semi-fast IR trains also run on many routes, including the picturesque Douro Valley line to Régua and Pocinho. National operator is Comboios de Portugal (CP), www.cp.pt, ☎ 808 208 208.

RAIL PASSES

Apart from InterRail and Eurail, CP has its own **Intra-Rail**, a zonal pass for ages 12-30 with free nights at youth hostels, valid either Friday to Sunday in one zone, or 10 days in two adjacent zones (not valid on AP trains).

Accommodation

A good bet in most places is to find rooms (*quartos* or *dormidas*) in a **private house**, or in a **pension** (*pensão* — more of a business than a house, and graded from 1 to 3 stars). Other inexpensive places are **boarding houses** (*hospedarias/casas de hóspedes*) and 1 star hotels.

Pousadas are state-run establishments in four categories. Some are converted national historic monuments (*Pousadas Históricas, Historic Pousadas*); those in historic buildings but which incorporate stylish new renovations are the Pousadas Históricas Design. The *Pousadas Charme* (Charm Pousadas) are unusual and romantic, while the *Pousadas Natureza* (Nature Pousadas) are in remote locations. More information from www.pousadas.pt. For details on **youth hostels** contact *Movijovem* (www.pousadasjuventude.pt). For **campsites**, contact the *Federação de Campismo e Montanhismo de Portugal* (www.fcmportugal.com).

Food and drink

The Portuguese pattern of eating is to have a fairly frugal breakfast and two big main meals: **lunch** (1200–1500) and **dinner** (1930–2230). Places that have evening entertainment may stay open until around midnight and, if so, tend to offer a late supper. The **cafés** and **pastry shops** usually stay open all day.

Eating is not expensive but, if your budget is strained, go for the meal of the day, *prato do día* or *menú*. Eating is taken seriously, the cuisine flavoured with herbs rather than spices and rather heavy on olive oil. There is lots of delicious seafood, such as grilled sardines and several varieties of *caldeirada* (fish stew). Other local dishes are *bacalhau* (dried salted cod in various guises) and *leitão* (roasted suckling pig). The most popular pudding is a sweet egg custard.

Portugal is, of course, the home of **port**, but there are also several excellent (and often inexpensive) **wines**, such as the *vinho verde* 'green' wines and the rich reds

Lisbon's distinctive yellow *elevadores* (funiculars) tackle steep gradients on their routes across the Portuguese capital. Here the Elevador da Bica (photo © Edyta Pawlowska).

ESSENTIALS (PORTUGAL)

Local name: Ripública Portuguesa — Population: 11.3m — Capital: Lisbon/Lisboa (p502) — Currency: Euro — Language: Portuguese (English is a good bet, French or Spanish may be understood) — Accommodation costs: medium (see p16) — Time zone: winter GMT, summer GMT+1 — International dialling code: +351

OPENING HOURS

Shops: Mon–Fri 0900/1000–1300 and 1500–1900, Sat 0900–1300. City shopping centres often daily 1000–2300 or later. Museums: Tues–Sun 1000–1700/1800; some close for lunch.

PUBLIC HOLIDAYS

1 Jan; National Carnival – end Feb/beginning March; Shrove Tues; Good Fri; 25 Apr; 1 May; 10 June; Corpus Christi; 15 Aug; 5 Oct; 1 Nov; 1, 8, 25 Dec. Many local saints' holidays.

PUBLIC TRANSPORT

Usually buy long-distance bus tickets before boarding. Bus stops: paragem; extend your arm to stop a bus. City transport: can buy single tickets as you board, but books of tickets or passes are cheaper; on boarding, insert 1–3 tickets (according to length of journey) in the machine behind the driver.

TIPPING

Not necessary in hotels. Tip 5–10% in restaurants and taxis.

TOURIST INFORMATION

Websites: www.visitportugal.com. Multilingual telephone information service for tourists, ☎ 808 781 212 (within Portugal). The police (dark blue uniforms in towns, brown in rural areas) wear red arm bands if they are bilingual.

of the **Dão** and **Bairrada** regions. Do not be surprised if you are charged for pre-dinner bread, olives or other nibbles that are brought to your table unordered. If you don't want them, say so.

ROMANIA — SEE MAP P654

A member of the EU since 2007, and still hoping to admitted to the Schengen area in late 2012, Romania is a world apart from its neighbours. Its linguistic and cultural heritage is more Romance than Slavic, and many rural areas of the country are caught in a time warp. This is Europe as it used to be. Travel comes with a few inevitable frustrations, but stay cool and take time to interact with the warmly hospitable locals. The country covers a remarkable range of landscapes from the rugged Carpathians to the wetlands of the Danube delta.

TRAIN TRAVEL IN ROMANIA

The natural landscapes and historic cities of Romania are easily explored by rail, with 11,000 km of track to chose from. In this book we feature Romania in **Routes 40** and **50**. With only a small number of InterCity trains, services can be quite slow, particularly on branch lines. Reservations are required for long-distance trains, either at the station or CFR agents. Fares for locally-purchased

Essentials (Romania)

Local name: România — Population: 22.2m — Capital: Bucharest/Bucureşti (p338) — Currency: Romanian Leu (RON) — Language: Romanian (English understood by younger people, plus some German, and Hungarian throughout Transylvania) — Accommodation costs: low (see p16) — Time zone: winter GMT+2, summer GMT+3 — International dialling code: +40

Opening hours

Shops: usually 0900–1800, closed Sun; shopping malls open until 2200, including Sun. Local food shops and kiosks often 0600–late. Museums: usually 0900/1000–1700/1800; open weekends, almost all closed Mon.

Public holidays

1–2 Jan; Easter Mon (Romanian Orthodox); Pentecost (50 days after Easter Sunday); 1 May; 1 Dec (National Unity Day); 25–26 Dec.

Public transport

Buy bus/tram/metro (*metrou*) tickets in advance from kiosks (as a rule) and cancel on entry. Trains are best for long-distance travel, although bus routes are expanding and connect important towns and cities.

Tipping

A tip of 5–10% will be appreciated for good service at restaurants and by taxis.

Tourist information

Website: www.romaniatourism.com. Romanian National Tourism Authority, Dinicu Golescu Blvd, 010873, Bucharest 1, ☎ 021 314 9957.

tickets depend on the type of train. Food is only available on a handful of the best trains, but drinks are occasionally available.

The national railway is CFR (www.cfr.ro), but some services are run by private operators, including some longer distance trains; tickets are not interchangeable.

Rail passes

InterRail and Eurail are valid, but beware the large supplements demanded of pass holders reserving seats on the fastest trains. The Balkan Flexipass is also valid.

Accommodation

At the bottom end, **hotels** can be basic and inexpensive, while some match the highest international standards and prices. **Private rooms** may be booked at tourist offices in some towns, and in a few tourist areas touts will meet trains at the station to offer their rooms — which may be centrally located in attractive old houses, or far out in grim suburban tower blocks, so make sure you know what you're agreeing to.

Book in advance for hotels on the **Black Sea coast** in summer and in **mountain ski** resorts at winter weekends. There are a few decent **hostels**: see www.hostelz.com for an overview.

FOOD AND DRINK

A small piece of meat (*cotlet*) and chips is staple fare in many restaurants. You could do a lot better by samping *sarmale* which are tasty stuffed cabbage leaves, often without meat. Try the local soup (*ciorbă*), stews and rissoles. And if all else fails, there are plenty of takeaway stalls and pizzerias.

Cafés serve excellent cakes (*prăjitură*), soft drinks, beer and coffee; *turceasca* is Turkish-style ground coffee, while *ness* is instant coffee. **Wines** are superb and very cheap. Try the plum brandy known as *ţuică* (pronounced 'tswica'), or its double-distilled version *palinca*.

RUSSIA — SEE PART OF RUSSIA ON MAP P636

That part of Russia that lies within Europe (viz. west of the Ural Mountains) is very much larger than the entire European Union. Russia is Europe's *terra incognita*, and deserves to be explored much more. But a strict visa regime deters many visitors.

The Russian Federation borders eight other countries featured in this book, and even the European part of the country includes constituent republics that hardly figure in Europe's collective consciousness. When did you last hear of Komi, Mordovia or Chuvashia? We dip a toe in the Russian pond with a route from Berlin to St Petersburg (see **Route 45**).

ESSENTIALS (RUSSIA)

Local name: Rossiya/Россия — Population: 142m — Capital: Moscow/Москва — Currency: Russian rouble (Rbl) — Language: Russian. Several other languages are co-official in various regions (English or German spoken by young people in larger cities) — Accommodation costs: medium (see p16) — Time zone (for the area covered in this book): GMT+4 (summer and winter) — International dialling code: +7

OPENING HOURS
Shops: Mon–Sat 1000–2000, food shops open earlier. Opening times of museums vary.

PUBLIC HOLIDAYS
1, 5, 7 Jan; 23 Feb; 8 Mar; Easter Mon; 1, 9 May; 12 June; 4 Nov. If a public holiday falls on a Sun, then the next working day becomes a holiday.

PUBLIC TRANSPORT
St Petersburg and Moscow both have the full range of public transport options: metro, trams, buses, trolleybuses and *marshrutkas*.

TIPPING
Tipping is increasingly expected in restaurants in major cities. Leave a tip between 10 and 15%.

TOURIST INFORMATION
Website: www.visitrussia.org.uk. Tourist offices exist in major cities.

Train travel in Russia

The train was the making of the Russian Empire in tsarist times, and trains were a mainstay of Soviet life — hardly surprising given the essential roadlessness of much of the country in the first decades after the revolution. The vast distances covered have dictated that the traditional Russian train is one of **sleeping cars** of various grades (even including dormitory-style bunks in many cases), designed for daytime use as well as overnight.

A revolution has taken place, however, on the 650 km Moscow to St Petersburg line with the introduction of **Sapsan high-speed trains** on daytime services, the fastest taking just four hours. A further Sapsan train was introduced in 2010 between St Petersburg and Nizhni Novgorod (Нижний Новгород), and a new fast link from St Petersburg to Helsinki opened in late 2010.

Trains in Russia are operated by RZD, www.rzd.ru. All except suburban trains require advance reservation. Some long-distance services run on alternate days. Sleeping cars to western European countries are of the standard European type with single and double compartments in first class, 3- or 4-berth compartments in second class.

Rail passes
Eurail and InterRail are not valid, and there are no other rail passes available for Russia.

Accommodation

There is a great advantage to staying in proper **hotels**, as they will handle the essential business of local registration for you. Your visa must be registered with the authorities in every city you stay. But in the main cities, the smarter hotels geared to western visitors are formidably expensive. There is a new breed of **Mini hotels**, some **independent hostels** and a lot of **apartment rentals** — the latter often very good value compared with hotels, but you will need then to handle your own visa registration.

Food and drink

If you have travelled east to Russia across the vast North European Plain, enjoying along the way the local diet of meat and potatoes, then Russia comes as a pleasant surprise.

The great Soviet experiment of the 20th century brought a wave of new culinary influences and you might run across an Azeri or Armenian restaurant in even a smallish Russian city. These exotic influences have tempered traditional Russian cooking too. Look for a wonderful range of **soups**, served both hot and cold, stuffed **pelmeni** or **pirozhki**, good grilled meat (especially *shashlik*) and all manner of spicy stews.

The Russian drinks list is as engaging as the food menu. According to season, try *kvass* or *sbiten*, the first a refreshing yeasty concoction sold ubiquitously from yellow barrels in summer, and the latter a mead-like hot winter drink. First class beer and a flood of vodka compete with tea. The Russians are the most dedicated tea drinkers on the planet.

SAN MARINO — SEE MAP P632

Serenissima Repubblica di San Marino. What a gracious name for a country! The Most Serene Republic of San Marino. Serene is not quite the word that springs to mind on a hot summer day when this little microstate is packed with tourists. This affluent territory, enclaved within eastern Italy, is not a member of the EU. Stunning scenery and its quirky political status pull the crowds, and it is well worth a visit.

The railway from the Italian city of Rimini to San Marino has long gone, so you'll have to take a bus nowadays. Although the territory is now train-less, you see relics of the old railway at several places in San Marino and some former railway tunnels have now been converted for pedestrian use.

ESSENTIALS: Local name: San Marino — Population: 31k — Capital: City of San Marino — Currency: Euro — Language: Italian — Accommodation costs: medium — Time zone: winter GMT+1, summer GMT+2 — International dialling code: +378

SERBIA — SEE MAP P608

Landlocked Serbia is a country that has reinvented itself. A dozen years ago, NATO was pounding Serbia with aerial bombardment, and the Belgrade government was widely denigrated, at least in the West, for its renegade ways. How times change! Now Serbia is hip, and angling to become a member of the EU. Serbia may be short on beaches, but it offers other ingredients that make for great travel. The country has good affordable food, a famously vibrant nightlife, mountain scenery aplenty (with some decent skiing), some remarkable Orthodox churches and monasteries and bags of cultural history.

TRAIN TRAVEL IN SERBIA

The Balkan nation is on **Routes 42, 43, 44** and **50** of *Europe by Rail*. No one travels by train in Serbia if they are in a rush. The country's rail network is engagingly antiquated. New Russian rolling stock, introduced in late 2011 as part of a broader investment package, is bringing improvements to some regional services across the country, but for now most Serbian trains are slow but fun. The national rail operator is Železnice Srbije (ZS) which has a good English-language website at www.serbianrailways.com.

Essentials (Serbia)

Local name: Republika Srbija/Република Србија — Population: 7.3m — Capital: Belgrade/Београд (p444) — Currency: Serbian dinar (RSD) — Language: Serbian (in the Vojvodina region also Hungarian, Slovak, Croatian, Rusyn and Romanian); note that many signs in Serbia are written in the Cyrillic alphabet (many younger Serbs know at least some English) — Accommodation costs: low (see p16) — Time zone: winter GMT+1, summer GMT+2 — International dialling code: +381

OPENING HOURS
Shops: Mon–Fri 0800-2000, Sat 0800-1500, many shops close 1200-1500 and most are closed Sun, although food shops may open 0700-1100. Museums: Most closed Mon.

PUBLIC HOLIDAYS
1, 7 Jan; 15 Feb; 1, 2 May; Orthodox Good Friday and Easter Monday.

PUBLIC TRANSPORT
Good network of buses connecting towns throughout the country. Buy tickets in advance at the bus station. Buses are usually comfortable though they might get very crowded on popular routes.

TIPPING
No tipping expected, but a tip of 10% for good service is appreciated.

TOURIST INFORMATION
Website: www.serbia-tourism.org, run by National Tourism Organisation of Serbia (NTOS).

RAIL PASSES
InterRail and the Balkan Flexipass are valid, but the Eurail global pass is not. Eurail do market a select pass that bundles in Serbia with Montenegro and Bulgaria. There are no locally available rail passes sold within Serbia.

ACCOMMODATION
If you don't mind staying in a charmless concrete block, you'll find cheap rooms aplenty in legacy state-run **hotels** constructed in the Yugoslav period. A growing private sector is bringing new standards with prices to match. There are **hostels** in Belgrade and Novi Sad, but elsewhere they are few and far between.

FOOD AND DRINK
Serbia is a carnivore's dream and you'll find excellent grilled-meat dishes at rock-bottom prices. Expect kebabs and *ćevapčići* aplenty, along with tasty tomatoes and peppers. A good range of snack food includes *burek* and *gibanica*. Serbs are notably restrained in their use of herbs and spices. Try the decent local wines, Serbian beer and the fiery plum brandy.

SLOVAKIA — SEE MAP P649
Slovakia has progressed enormously since joining the EU in 2004, adopting the euro in advance of any of its neighbours. Easy to get around, tourist-friendly and

still good value, Slovakia is beginning to cut a dash on the central European travel circuit. For real highlights, look to the High Tatras for fabulous mountain scenery and Carpatho-Ruthenia for picture-perfect wooden churches and the remarkable Rusyn culture.

TRAIN TRAVEL IN SLOVAKIA

The country is included in **Routes 47** and **48** in this book. Additionally, **Route 32** through Austria crosses the Slovakian border and ends in Bratislava. The country's main trunk route from Bratislava to Košice through Žilina and the foothills of the impressive Tatra Mountains at Poprad-Tatry is well provided for, with fast trains every two hours supplemented by a smattering of InterCity trains making fewer stops. A good network covers the rest of the country, although some minor branch lines were closed in 2011. An excellent **narrow-gauge network** covers the resorts of the Tatry area.

The national rail company is ŽSSK (www.slovakrail.sk), running on the network of ŽSR. Trains can be crowded, so reservation is recommended on express and night trains (at station counters marked R).

RAIL PASSES
Eurail and InterRail passes are both valid, plus the European East pass for non-European residents. 2012 is the first year in which the Eurail scheme covers Slovakia.

ACCOMMODATION

There is a wide choice of **hotels, private rooms** and **pensions**, and, at a much more basic level, **hostels** and **inns** with a few spartan rooms, plus *chaty* (simple chalets) and *chalupy* (traditional cottages) in the country-side. **Private rooms** are often much better than similarly priced cheap hotels. Note that **youth hostels** are not very common in Slovakia, only in bigger towns (official HI youth hostels association is at www.ckm.sk). Bratislava has an increasing number of stylish **independent hostels**.

Slovenes may be the gentlest folk on earth, but this assertive dragon on a Ljubljana bridge reveals another side of Slovenia (photo © Pablo Debat).

Essentials (Slovakia)

Local name: Slovensko — Population: 5.4m — Capital: Bratislava (p398) — Currency: Euro — Language: Slovak (German, Hungarian in the south, some English and French) — Accommodation costs: medium (see p16) — Time zone: winter GMT+1, summer GMT+2 — International dialling code: +421

Opening hours

Shops: Mon–Fri 0900–1800, Sat 0800–1200. Food shops usually open 0800 and Sun. Museums: (usually) Tues–Sun 1000–1700.

Public holidays

1, 6 Jan; Good Fri; Easter Mon; 1, 8 May; 5 July; 29 Aug; 1, 15 Sept; 1, 17 Nov; 24–26 Dec.

Public transport

Comprehensive long-distance bus network, often more direct than rail in upland areas. You can buy tickets from driver, though priority might be given to those with bookings.

Tipping

Tipping is expected at hotels, eateries and taxis. In general, round up a little, unless you are somewhere very upmarket, where you should tip 10%.

Tourist information

Website: www.slovakia.travel. Slovak Tourist Board (SACR), Námastie Ľ. Štura 1, PO Box 35, 974 05 Banská Bystrica, ☎ 048 413 61 46. SACR in Bratislava: Dr. V. Clementisa 10, 821 01 Bratislava, ☎ 02 507 00 801.

Food and drink

Slovak food has a lot in common with Hungarian; a typical dish is *bryndzové halušky*, gnocchi with grated **bryndza**, a ewes' milk cheese that's only produced in Slovakia and Romania.

You'll find *schnitzel* (usually pork), fried chicken and goulash-style stews everywhere, the latter often accompanied by steamed dumplings (tasty, even though the habit of serving them in slices looks distinctly unappetising). Good local beers, and decent local wines, many of which are rarely seen outside Slovakia.

Slovenia — see maps p600 and p611

Slovenia, a pocket-sized land of beautiful Alpine mountains and lakes, undulating farmland and vineyards, blends Mediterranean style with central European efficiency.

Not quite the first breakaway from the Yugoslav fold, for Croatia declared independence one day earlier, Slovenia was the first part of former Yugoslavia to join the EU. That was in 2004, and in the eight years since, the country has made fast progress. No other European country is quite so consummately dedicated to the outdoors and adventure.

Train travel in Slovenia

Slovenia features in **Routes 35, 38** and **39** in this book. The country's small and efficient rail network hubbed on Ljubljana mixes the traditional and charming aspects of this mountainous country with more modern features, such as the tilting ICS trains on the Maribor route.

The national operator is Slovenske Železnice (SŽ), www.slo-zeleznice.si, ☎ 01 29 13 332. ICS trains have compulsory reservation. Tickets are available from stations or travel agents.

Rail passes

InterRail and Eurail passes are valid.

Accommodation

Refurbished **hotels** and high standards make for prices comparable to those of other EU countries. **Private rooms** are an option for the budget conscious, as are hostels. The official youth organisation can be found at www.youth-hostel.si, although the **hostel** network is concentrated on the alpine north, plus a few options — including independent hostels — in Ljubljana. There are numerous small but well-equipped **campsites**.

Essentials (Slovenia)

Local name: Republika Slovenija — Population: 2m — Capital: Ljubljana (p323) — Currency: Euro — Language: Slovene (English, German and Italian often spoken in tourist areas) — Accommodation costs: medium (see p16) — Time zone: winter GMT+1, summer GMT+2 — International dialling code: +386

Opening hours

Shops: mostly Mon–Fri 0700/0900–1900/2100, Sat 0700/0900–1300/1500. Museums: 0900–1700/1800; closed Mon.

Public holidays

1–2 Jan; 8 Feb; Easter Mon; 27 Apr; 1–2 May; 25 June; 15 Aug; 31 Oct; 1 Nov; 25–26 Dec.

Public transport

Long-distance bus services frequent and inexpensive; usually buy ticket on boarding. Information: Trg Osvobodilne Fronte 5, next to Ljubljana station, ☎ 01 234 4606. City buses have standard fare, paid with correct change into box by driver; cheaper to buy tokens from newsstands/post offices. Daily or weekly bus passes in main cities.

Tipping

No need to tip bar staff or taxi drivers, although you can round sums up as you wish. In restaurants add 10%.

Tourist information

Website: www.slovenia.info. Slovenian Tourist Board, Dunajska 156, SI-1000 Ljubljana, ☎ 01 589 1858.

FOOD AND DRINK

Places to eat go by many different names in Slovenia. A restaurant where you are served by a waitress is a *restauracija*, while a *gostilna* is an inn, which typically serves national dishes in a rustic setting. Both sometimes have a set menu (*dnevna kosila*) at lunch, which is usually the least expensive option. There are also a variety of self-service places (*samopostrežna restauracija*) where you can often eat standing. Slovenian cuisine reflects historic ties with Vienna. Meat and dairy products predominate: *Wiener schnitzel* (veal in breadcrumbs) is a speciality, as is *pohana piska* (breaded fried chicken), and French fries are served with almost everything. Coffee shops offer a wide range of pastries, cakes and ice creams. A *zavitek* is a light pastry filled with cream cheese, either sweet or savoury.

SPAIN — SEE MAP P665

Inexpensive to travel in and blessed with a warm climate, Spain is astonishingly varied, ranging from the fashion-conscious sophistication and pulsing atmospheres of Madrid and Barcelona to rural scenes that look as if they might belong to another continent, or even another century.

It's not consistently beautiful — views from the train might take in ugly high-rise developments or monotonous cereal plains, while on much of the coast there are concrete resorts that sprang up in the 1950s and 1960s to provide cheap holidays. But the classic Spanish elements are there too: parched landscapes dotted with cypresses and cacti, backed by rugged sierras; lines of poplars receding to hazy horizons, and red-roofed fortified towns clustered around castles. Some scenes are peculiarly regional: the luxuriant greenness of Galicia; the snowy pinnacles of the Picos de Europa; the canyon-like badlands of **Aragon** on the southern fringes of the **Pyrenees**.

TRAIN TRAVEL IN SPAIN

Spain has long had a prominent place in successive editions of *Europe by Rail*. In this edition, you'll find Spain well covered by **Routes 9, 10, 12** and **13**. In addition, **Routes 8** and **11**, which commence in France and Portugal respectively, both end in Spain. Massive investment in **high-speed rail** has put Spain in the major league of European high-speed players, most notably with the Madrid to Barcelona line and the more established line to Seville, 20 years old in 2012, with its newer branch to Málaga. Madrid to Valencia is the latest scheme to come to fruition (in December 2010). An extension of the Albacete branch to Alicante will follow soon. All cities have good links to Madrid and there are many useful cross-country and regional links. There are different train categories, AVE being the principal high-speed trains, along with Alvia, Altaria and Avant.

The highest-quality night trains are known as **Trenhotel**, which include compartments with en suite facilities. Reservation is essential on the majority of trains, including some regional services, whilst supplements are payable on all high-speed and certain other long-distance trains.

The national railway company is RENFE, www.renfe.es, ☎ 902 320 320. Of several **narrow-gauge railways** the largest is FEVE (www.feve.es), which operates an extensive network, chiefly in the northern coastal provinces.

RAIL PASSES

InterRail and Eurail passes are all valid. EuskoTren has a seasonal day ticket valid from San Sebastián across the French border, including SNCF trains to Bayonne.

ACCOMMODATION

There's generally no problem finding somewhere to stay, outside major festivals and other peak periods; however, some large cities (notably Madrid and Barcelona) can be problematic. By strolling around, you'll often find **budget places** congregated near the station and around the main square.

Thanks to a useful hierarchy imposed by regional tourist authorities, accommodation is graded according to facilities, from *albergues juveniles* (youth hostels) via basic boarding houses, known variously as *Fondas* (look for plaques marked F), *Pensiones* (P), *Posadas*, *Ventas* and *Casas de Huéspedes*; then come *Hostales* (HS) and *Hostales Residencias* (HR) up to *hoteles* (H), ranging from 1 to 5 stars.

Private homes that offer rooms are known as *Casas Particulares*. They seldom have much in the way of facilities, but are usually centrally located and almost invariably very cheap. *Casas rurales* are **farmhouses** and *Refugios* are **mountain huts**. The hostel scene in Spain is developing fast. There are dozens of HI **youth hostels** around the country (www.reaj.com), as well as an increasing number of **independent hostels**. Barcelona, Madrid, Sevilla, San Sebastián and Granada all have a particularly good choice of hostel options. There are over 500 **campsites** (some

open all year, others just in summer); the Spanish Tourist Office issues a list of the approved ones (*Guía de Campings*), which are classified as luxury, first, second and third class.

The Plaza de España in Seville, built for the 1929 World Fair, is a superb example of Moorish Revival architecture (photo © Nick Stubbs).

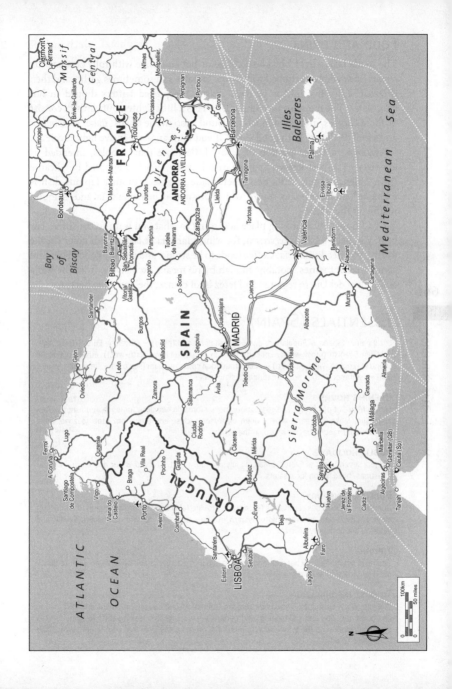

FOOD AND DRINK

The locals take a light breakfast: coffee or hot chocolate with rolls or a *pan con tomate* (toasted bread rubbed with a ripe tomato, and sometimes garlic, and then drizzled with olive oil) or perhaps *churros* (deep-fried fritters dipped in hot chocolate). The main meal is lunch. Dinner is a little lighter, but can still consist of three courses, and is eaten later, around 2200 in the towns. *Platos combinados* and *menú del día* are both good value. If you want an inexpensive light meal, ask for *raciones*, a larger portion of *tapas* (little more than nibbles, intended as aperitifs). The best-known Spanish dish is *paella*, which originated in Alicante (near Valencia); it is at its best when made to order. Another famous dish is *gazpacho* (chilled tomato soup), which originated in Andalucía and is found mainly in the south.

Choose your drinking place according to what you want to consume. For beer, you need a bar or *cervecería*, for wine a *taberna* or *bodega*. For cider (in the north), you need a *sidrería*. Coffee tends to be strong, and usually good. There are some excellent **wines** (notably, though by no means exclusively, from the Rioja and Ribera del Duero regions) and Jerez is, of course, the home of **sherry**.

ESSENTIALS (SPAIN)

Local name: España — Population: 46m — Capital: Madrid (p519) — Currency: Euro — Language: Castilian Spanish (most widely spoken), Catalan (east), Galego (north-west), Euskera (Basque country) (English widely spoken) — Accommodation costs: medium (see p16) — Time zone: winter GMT+1, summer GMT+2 — International dialling code: +34

OPENING HOURS
Shops: Mon–Sat 0930–1330 and 1630–2000; major stores do not close for lunch, food shops often open Sun. Museums: vary; mostly open 0900/1000, close any time from 1400 to 2030. Most places closed 1300–1500/1600, esp. in the south.

PUBLIC HOLIDAYS
1, 6 Jan; several days at Easter; 1 May; 25 July; 15 Aug; 12 Oct; 1 Nov; 6, 8 Dec and several days at Christmas; holidays on local saints' days.

PUBLIC TRANSPORT
Numerous regional bus companies (*empresas*) provide fairly comprehensive, cheap (if confusing) service. City buses and the metro system in large cities like Madrid, Barcelona, Seville and Valencia are both very efficient.

TIPPING
Tipping is not mandatory but common practice in bars, restaurants and taxis. If you want to tip for good service, add around 5–10%.

TOURIST INFORMATION
Website: www.spain.info. *Oficinas de Turismo* (tourist offices) can provide maps and information on accommodation and sightseeing, and generally have English-speaking staff. Regional offices stock information on the whole region, municipal offices cover only that city; larger towns have both types of office.

SWEDEN — SEE MAP P668

Scandinavia's largest country includes huge tracts of forest and thousands of lakes, with mildly rolling, fertile terrain to the south, and excitingly rugged uplands spilling over the Norwegian border and beyond the Arctic Circle into Lapland. The sheer amount of space is positively exhilarating, and it's the northern stretches that are easily the least populated.

TRAIN TRAVEL IN SWEDEN

You will find Sweden included in **Routes 21, 25** and **26** in this book. In addition, **Routes 22** and **24**, which start respectively in Denmark and Norway, end in Sweden. Since 1990 the prestigious X2000 tilting train has allowed the progressive development of faster services on Sweden's main routes, whilst the new **Botniabanan** has begun to revolutionise services from Stockholm to the north.

Services are efficient and frequent, though understandably sparse in the far north. Seat reservations are compulsory on night trains and X2000, the latter also requiring a supplement. Most long-distance trains have refreshments, some also have play areas for children. First-class sleeping cars have en suite facilities.

ESSENTIALS (SWEDEN)

Local name: Sverige — Population: 9.3m — Capital: Stockholm (p568) — Currency: Krona (SEK) — Language: Swedish (English widely spoken) — Accommodation costs: high (see p16) — Time zone: winter GMT+1, summer GMT+2 — International dialling code: +46

OPENING HOURS
Shops: mostly Mon–Fri 0930–1800, Sat 0930–1400. In larger towns department stores open until 1900; also some on Sun 1200–1600. Museums: vary widely; some closed Mon. In winter, many outdoor attractions close altogether.

PUBLIC HOLIDAYS
1, 6 Jan; Good Friday; Easter Sun–Mon; Labour Day (1 May); Ascension Day; Whit Sun–Mon; 6 June; Midsummer's Eve–Day; All Saints Day; 24–26 Dec. Many places close early the previous day, or Fri if it's a long weekend.

PUBLIC TRANSPORT
Transport system is highly efficient; ferries covered (in whole or part) by rail passes and city transport cards. Biggest operator of long-distance buses is Swebus Express ☎ 0771 21 82 18 (www.swebus.se). Advance booking is required on some routes and always advisable in summer; bus terminals usually adjoin train stations.

TIPPING
Restaurants include a service charge but a tip of 10–15% is appreciated. Taxis 10%.

TOURIST INFORMATION
Website: www.visit-sweden.com. Tourist offices are called *Turistbyrå*. Often a numerical waiting system in public places.

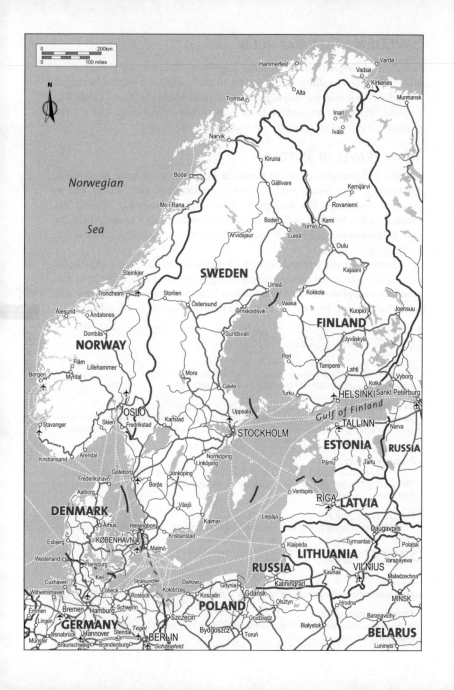

The national rail company is Statens Järnvägar (SJ), www.sj.se. Information line ☎ 0771 75 75 75. Several other operators are involved on certain routes, but InterRail and Eurail passes are generally valid whatever the operator. SJ fares are dictated by demand, with best-value fares available to early bookers.

RAIL PASSES
InterRail and Eurail passes are valid. **Öresund Rundt** gives two days of travel on trains and buses in the Malmö and Copenhagen area.

ACCOMMODATION

You can sleep in fair comfort at a reasonable price in Sweden. Tourist offices have listings of most places to stay and charge a small booking fee (www.visitsweden.com). Bed and Breakfast Service Stockholm (www.bedbreakfast.se) can provide rooms and flats in the capital.

Hotel standards are high and the cost usually includes breakfast. There are more than 300 HI **hostels** (*vandrarhem*), about half of which open only in summer; some are extremely characterful places and include castles and boats. Family rooms are available (www.stfturist.se). There are also more than 190 **independent hostels** operated by *Sveriges Vandrarhem i Förening (SVIF)* (www.svif.se). Room-only accommodation in **private houses** is a good budget alternative (contact local tourist offices).

Sveriges Campingvärdars Riksförbund (SCR), Swedish Camping Site Owners' Association, ☎ 031 355 60 00 (www.camping.se) lists more than 600 **campsites**. You can camp rough for one night if you keep more than 150 m from the nearest house and leave no litter.

FOOD AND DRINK

Hearty buffet breakfasts are a good start to the day. Cafés and fast-food outlets are budget options for later on. *Pytt i panna* is a hefty fry-up; other traditional dishes are pea soup served with pancakes, and Jansson's temptation (potatoes, onions and anchovies). **Systembolaget** is the state-owned outlet for alcohol — shoppers must be over 20, but you can buy alcoholic beverages in some restaurants, pubs and bars at 18.

SWITZERLAND — SEE MAP P670

Even by European standards, Switzerland packs a lot into a small space, and, despite its admirable transport system, it can take a surprisingly long time to explore the country thoroughly, though it's predominantly scenery rather than sights that attracts the appreciable crowds. There are marked regional differences, and four separate languages.

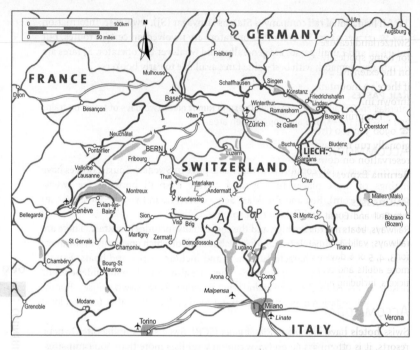

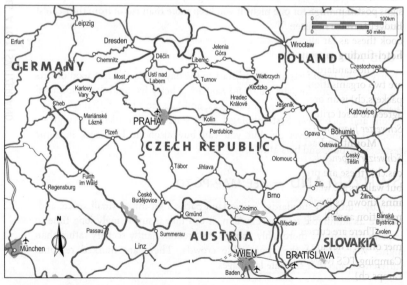

Train travel in Switzerland

Switzerland features on **Routes 29 to 32** in this volume. The country's reputation for being spotlessly clean, efficient, and above all punctual, certainly holds true on the extensive Swiss rail system, which covers every town and valley. Of course, if there's a mountain, there will often be a railway involved, with incredible views thrown in.

The principal carrier is Swiss Federal Railways (SBB/CFF/FFS), www.sbb.ch, ☎ 0900 300 300 (from within Switzerland). There are many small private or regionally run railways, particularly in mountainous areas. There is no compulsory reservation on domestic services, apart from the popular **Glacier Express** and **Bernina Express** narrow-gauge tourist trains.

Rail passes

InterRail and Eurail passes are valid. **Swiss Pass** gives consecutive days on Swiss Railways, boats and most Alpine postbuses and city buses, plus discounts on mountain railways; valid 4, 8, 15, 22 days or one month. The **Swiss Flexi Pass** is similar but valid for 3, 4, 5 or 6 days within one month. Both offer a discount when booking for two or more adults and provide free entrance to 400 museums. There are several regional tickets, including a summer-only 7-day pass for the Bernese Oberland.

Accommodation

Swiss **hotels** have high standards but are expensive. In rural areas and Alpine resorts, it is often possible to get rooms in **private houses** (look for *Zimmer frei* signs posted in windows and gardens), but these are few and far between in cities. Budget travellers (unless they are camping) rely heavily on youth hostels — so book these as far ahead as possible. Every major town and major station has a **hotel-finding service**, sometimes free and seldom expensive.

The standard of hostel accommodation in Switzerland is excellent, and there are two organisations worth checking out. **Swiss Backpackers** (www.swissbackpackers.ch) is an organisation of 34 privately-run independent hostels, that have agreed to a set criteria of standards, whilst the official **youth hostel** organisation *Schweizer Jugendherbergen* has locations across the country (www.youthhostel.ch).

Mountain backpackers can stay at huts of the *Swiss Alpine Club (SAC)/ Schweizer Alpenclub*, Monbijoustr. 61, CH-3000 Berne 23, ☎ 31 370 18 (www.saccas.ch); these are primarily climbing huts based at the start of climbing routes, but walkers are welcome. There are also (in more accessible locations) **mountain inns** known as *Berghotels* or *Auberges de Montagne*, with simple dormitory accommodation as well as private rooms ranging from basic to relatively luxurious.

There are currently around 450 **campsites** in Switzerland (most open summer only). They are graded on a one- to five-star system. Useful websites include Camping TCS (www.tcs.ch) and the *Verband Schweizerischer Campings* (www.swisscamps.ch).

Essentials (Switzerland)

Local name: Schweiz/Suisse/Svizzera — Population: 7.7m — Capital: Berne/Bern (p273) — Currency: Swiss Francs (CHF) — Language: German, French, Italian, Romansch (English is widespread) — Accommodation costs: high (see p16) — Time zone: winter GMT+1, summer GMT+2 — International dialling code: +41

Opening hours
Shops: Mon–Fri 0800–1200 and 1400–1900, Sat 0900–1200 and 1330–1600. Many close Mon morning. Museums: usually close Mon. Hours vary.

Public holidays
1–2 Jan; Good Fri; Easter Mon; Ascension Day; Whit Mon; 1 Aug; 25, 26 Dec. Also 1 May and Corpus Christi in some areas.

Public transport
Swiss buses are famously punctual. Yellow postbuses stop at rail stations; free timetables from post offices.

Tipping
Not necessary or expected in restaurants or taxis.

Tourist information
Website: www.myswitzerland.com. Tourist offices in almost every town or village. The standard of information is excellent.

Food and drink

Pork and veal are common menu items, but in the lake areas you'll also find fresh fish. Portions tend to be ample. Swiss cheese is often an ingredient in local dishes; the classic Swiss fondue, for instance, is bread dipped into a pot containing melted cheese, garlic, wine and *kirsch*. *Raclette*, a speciality of the canton of Valais, is simply melted cheese, served with boiled potatoes, gherkins and silverskin onions.

The ubiquitous meal accompaniment in German-speaking areas is *Rösti*, fried potatoes and onions, while French Switzerland goes in for stronger tastes, such as smoked sausages. In the Grisons, *Bündnerfleisch* is a tasty raw smoked beef, sliced very thin. Swiss wines are also excellent and very difficult to get in other countries.

Turkey — see part of Turkey on map p608

Europe meets Asia in Turkey. But before you write off Turkey as not being really European at all, bear it mind that it has in Istanbul the largest city anywhere in Europe. Even on the west side of the Bosphorus, you will find mosques, Islamic monuments and oriental-style bazaars and it is important to remember that Islam has been an important aspect of the cultural fabric of Europe for many centuries. Turkey has outstanding relics of Greek and Roman settlement, superb

The railway station at Haydar-paşa, on the east of the Bosphorus, is the grand point of departure for journeys from Istanbul to Anatolia and beyond. Read more in Sidetracks L on p342 (photo © Ahmet Ihsan Ariturk).

mountain and coastal scenery and a population that is ever welcoming to visitors.

TRAIN TRAVEL IN TURKEY

Turkey plays a bit-part role in this book, featuring only in **Route 40**. Many journeys by train are still tortuously slow, but high-speed lines are transforming Turkish rail travel. When the new Ankara to Konya route opened in August 2011, it slashed the journey time from over ten hours to less than two. Services are operated by Turkish State Railways (TCDD). The website at www.tcdd.gov.tr has an excellent English-language section with fares and timetables.

RAIL PASSES

In addition to InterRail and the Balkan Flexipass, Turkey has its own 30-day network pass called **Tren Tur Kartı**, in various versions. Eurail passes are not valid.

ACCOMMODATION

Turkey's accommodation spectrum is as varied and colourful as the country itself. You can hang your hat in converted **Ottoman palaces** (known as 'Special Licence Hotels') that aren't as expensive as you might think and almost define the word 'atmospheric'. Or choose a usual-suspect, international hotel that will deliver neither nice surprises nor hideous shocks, or go for a hostel. The Turkish **hostel scene** is particularly well developed and organised, and two great sites to check out are www.youthhostelturkey.com and www.eurohostels.co.uk.

Perhaps surprisingly, the *Turkish Touring and Automobile Association (TTAA)* is the best organisation to consult for all-round accommodation options, and the 'Touristic Facilities' page on their website (www.turing.org.tr/eng) changes daily, to show the TTAA's current best-hotel selections.

FOOD AND DRINK

Turkish cuisine has many fans, and generally the fare is more varied than in Greece. Try vegetable stews, *shish* (lamb) kebabs, pizza and spicy meat dishes, or

Essentials (Turkey)

Local name: Türkiye — Population: 73m — Capital: Ankara — Currency: Turkish Lira (TL); credit cards widely accepted — Language: Turkish (English and German often understood) — Accommodation costs: low (see p16) — Time zone: winter GMT+2, summer GMT+3 — International dialling code: +90

Opening hours
Shops: 0930–1900; until around 2400 in tourist areas. In Aegean and Mediterranean regions, many establishments stay open very late in summer. Museums: many close on Mon.

Public holidays
1 Jan; 23 Apr; 19 May; 30 Aug; 29 Oct.

Public transport
Excellent long-distance bus system (generally quicker than rail), run by competing companies (the best are Varan and Ulusoy). Shorter rides via *dolmuş* (shared taxis) that pick up passengers like a taxi, but only along a route and much cheaper. IDO runs the ferries (www.ido.com.tr). Ankara and Istanbul have a modern metro line, Istanbul also has a light-rail and tram route (see p496).

Tipping
A 10% tip is usual in restaurants, unless service is included.

Tourist information
Website: www.tourismturkey.org.

for a real blowout the all-encompassing *meze*, with a bit of everything. Tea is the national drink, but there are good-value wines and beers, and *raki* is the highly distinctive aniseed-flavoured brandy.

Ukraine — see part of Ukraine on map p654

The former Soviet republic, now assertively independent for over 20 years, is the largest country entirely within Europe. Russia and Turkey, though both larger, each extend over the European-Asian border. The rich, fertile steppes so often associated with Ukraine give way to the Carpathian hills in the west and memorable coastal landscapes in the Crimea.

Although sometimes hard work for travellers, Ukraine has a lot to offer and is remarkably good value. The country is oddly split, very oriented to the EU in the west, but as you move east more aligned to Russia. Read more in our **Side-tracks** feature on p411.

Train travel in Ukraine

Routes 49 and **50** both end in Ukraine. There are good overnight services from Lviv and Kiev to Moscow. International links include services to Germany, Poland, the Czech Republic and Hungary. Long-distance trains in Ukraine are similar to Russian types with sleeping accommodation in various configurations designed for both night and daytime use. Advance reservation is essential. The operator is Ukrainian Railways (UZ), www.uz.gov.ua.

RAIL PASSES
There are no rail passes available. InterRail and Eurail are not valid.

ACCOMMODATION
Inexpensive, but frankly uninspiring, **hotels** aplenty in the main cities, many of them concrete blocks that have had little maintenance since the day, long ago, when they first opened their doors to the public. Hot water may be a rarity in these old Soviet piles. The short-lived spate of new entrepreneurialism that followed the Orange Revolution of 2004/5 led to a rash of new small **privately owned hotels**, particularly in Kiev and western Ukraine, many of which are half empty and offer good value for money (with hot water too). There is a nascent **independent hostel movement**, most conspicuously in Kiev, Lviv and the Ukrainian Carpathian region. Since 2008, **farm-stay** opportunities have blossomed in the Carpathians.

FOOD AND DRINK
This is a country where even urbanites profess an intimate relationship with the land, and the food reflects that. Fertile Ukraine produces a wealth of vegetables that find their way into soups and stews — of which the most celebrated is *borscht*

ESSENTIALS (UKRAINE)

Local name: Ukrayina/Україна — Population: 45.8m — Capital: Kiev/Київ — Currency: Hryvnia (UAH) — Language: Ukrainian, Russian (English spoken esp. by younger people in major cities) — Accommodation costs: low (see p16) — Time zone: winter GMT+2, summer GMT+3 (but check for possible changes from late October 2012) — International dialling code: +380

OPENING HOURS
Shops: 0900/1000–1900/2100. Supermarkets in larger cities might be open round the clock. Opening times of museums vary.

PUBLIC HOLIDAYS
1, 7 Jan; 8 Mar; Easter Mon; 1, 2, 9 May; 28 June; 24 Aug; 25 Dec.

PUBLIC TRANSPORT
Extensive and cheap bus network with buses of varying comfort level. *Marshrutkas* (minibuses) are also used. Buy tickets at bus stations in advance or directly from the driver.

TIPPING
In larger cities a tip of 10% is appreciated.

TOURIST INFORMATION
Website: www.ukrtourism.com.uk.

(beetroot soup). Crescent-shaped dumplings called **vareniki** are a Ukrainian staple, usually served stuffed with cabbage, potato or cheese. Pork and chicken dishes aplenty, though many Ukrainians may eat meat only rarely. Drinkwise, vodka rules. But there are good local beers and some splendid red wines from the Crimea. Try the sweet **kagor**, produced in southern Ukraine or imported from neighbouring Moldova.

UNITED KINGDOM — SEE PART OF UK ON MAP P621

The UK does not properly feature in this volume, which has as its focus the exploration of continental Europe by rail. However, many readers will begin their journey in Britain, so three routes in this book now start in London — each offering a different itinerary to reach the continent. They are **Routes 1, 2** and **3**. Although a member of the EU, the UK stands curiously apart from the mainstream of European life and the lively cultural agenda of the continent. It does not use the euro and is not a member of Schengen. The preoccupation with security means strict border controls that deter many would-be visitors.

Yet continental Europeans who venture across the Channel will find an **extensive rail network** that is by no means as bad as most UK residents assert. A dense network extends even to the distant extremities of the British mainland, and those willing to book far in advance can secure some of the cheapest tickets in Europe for long-distance journeys. The downside is crowded trains. Great Britain is not part of the Eurail scheme, so passes are not valid. But note that Northern Ireland is part of Eurail. InterRail is valid in the entire UK, but note that UK residents may not use an InterRail pass within their home country.

ESSENTIALS: Local name: United Kingdom — Population: 62m — Capital: London (p509) — Currency: Pound sterling (£) — Language: English, Welsh, Scottish Gaelic — Accommodation costs: high (see p16) — Time zone: winter GMT, summer GMT+1 — International dialling code: +44

VATICAN CITY

Tiny theocratic state that survives as a political island within the Italian capital, and the sole remaining territory of the once much more extensive *Stato Pontificio* or Papal States. Churches, fabulous art collections and remarkable gardens characterise the planet's smallest country. And there is something for rail travellers too. The Vatican has a few hundred metres of railway line and its own **train station**. Sadly, there are no regular passenger services.

ESSENTIALS: Local name: Stato della Città del Vaticano — Population: 820 — Capital: Vatican City — Currency: Euro — Language: Latin, Italian (English and French spoken) — Time zone: winter GMT+1, summer GMT+2 — International dialling code: +3906

Reference Section

The reference section that follows is packed with factual detail that will help you both as you **plan your journey** and while you are on the road (or, more precisely, on the rails). Top of the list are our **city links tables**, which start overleaf. Use them to check how long it will take to travel by train between key cities across Europe.

A WORD ON PLACE NAMES

To kick off this final section of the book, we just want to throw in a thought on a topic that confounds many novice travellers. Place-names are infinitely mutable. Even within a country you will find multiple renderings of the same place name. Luik, Lüttich and Liège are all the same place — the town in eastern Belgium that English speakers most commonly refer to as Liège.

The city you knew as Cologne when you were planning your journey turns out to be Köln when you reach it. The Viennese, it transpires, don't call their city Vienna, but favour Wien. And the Danish capital is København. Before you throw up your hands in despair, rest assured that you'll quickly get used to these various renderings. The maps at the start of each of our fifty routes show local renderings of place names (or an accurate transliteration of the Cyrillic), while the route details superimposed on those same maps use the English version where there is one. With just a little practice, you'll master the knack of mapping one version onto the other, and by the time you get back home you'll be referring to Venezia and Firenze rather than Venice and Florence. In areas which use the Cyrillic alphabet, you'll pick up some interesting variations. Russia's second city (Санкт-Петербург to the locals) is commonly called St Petersburg by English speakers. A more accurate transliteration of the Cyrillic would be Sankt Peterburg.

CITY LINKS

The following list shows, for all 26 hub cities in this book and for 13 other cities on Europe's rail network, the availability of trains between principal cities. The **numbers in brackets** after the emboldened name of each departure city indicates on which **routes** in this book the city features. Cities may be linked by a **direct overnight train service (N)** and/or by a **daytime service (D)**. These letters follow the destination name. Some night trains may run seasonally or only on certain days of the week. Overnight services that operate less than thrice weekly are generally not included (eg. the weekly Russian Railways' Moscow to Nice train which provides a useful, and rather exotic, way of travelling overnight in comfort between Warsaw and Milan or from Vienna to Nice). Many night trains carry hefty supplements over and above the regular fares. Pass holders will be liable for supplements on most night trains. For daytime services we give a **typical travel time** (in hours and minutes). Night trains are generally slower than daytime trains — a device which usually nicely allows you to sleep longer.

Where the **destination city is in black**, it shows that the two cities are connected by a direct train (whether by day or night). **Listings in red indicate an easy daytime journey with just one change of train**. The letter after the travel time indicates where that change of train would often take place (see box opposite).

Of course, many other daytime connections across Europe are easily accomplished, but these require two or more changes of train, so are not shown in the list. Please note that the list is based on the pattern of train services in late 2011. Schedules for summer 2012 may vary slightly. The latest edition of the *Thomas Cook European Rail Timetable* will always have the up-to-date schedules.

Amsterdam (15)
Berlin N D (6h20)
Brussels D (1h55)
Cologne D (2h40)
Copenhagen N
Frankfurt D (4h00)
Hamburg N D (5h10Y)
London D (4h50X)
Milan D (11h30P)
Munich N D (7h30F)
Nice D (10h10P)
Paris D (3h20)
Prague N D (12h30B)
Vienna D (11h50F)
Warsaw N D (13h10B)
Zurich N D (8h00C)

Athens (41)
Thessaloniki N D (5h20)

Barcelona (8, 9)
Madrid N D (2h50)
Milan N
Paris N D (7h50f)
Zurich N

Belgrade (42, 43, 44, 50)
Bratislava D (10h50)
Bucharest N
Budapest N D (8h00)
Istanbul N
Ljubljana N D (10h20)
Munich D (16h20T)
Prague D (15h30)
Sarajevo D (9h20)
Sofia N D (8h40)
Venice N
Vienna D (11h15E)
Zagreb N D (7h30)

Zurich N

Berlin (16, 20, 45, 48, 49)
Amsterdam N D (6h30)
Bratislava N D (9h05)
Brussels D (6h50K)
Budapest N D (12h00)
Cologne N D (4h20)
Copenhagen N D (6h50)
Frankfurt D (4h10)
Hamburg D (1h40)
Milan D (13h00C)
Munich N D (5h50)
Paris N D (8h20K)
Prague D (5h25)
St Petersburg N
Vienna N D (9h30)
Warsaw D (5h40)
Zurich N D (8h30C)

WHERE TO CHANGE TRAINS

On those daytime journeys marked in red, one en route train change is required. The letter codes below show where to change. A change of train in Budapest, Paris or Vienna may require a change of station. The code F refers to a change of train at *either* Frankfurt Flughafen *or* at Frankfurt Hauptbahnhof (no change of station required). Refer to the *Thomas Cook European Rail Timetable* or to http://bahn.hafas.de to check the best change point(s) for your specific itinerary.

Codes: A: Irún; **a:** Hendaye; **B:** Berlin; **C:** Basel; **E:** Budapest; **e:** Gothenburg; **F:** Frankfurt; **f:** Figueres; **G:** Ventimiglia; **H:** Hamburg; **J:** Břeclav; **K:** Cologne; **L:** Linz; **M:** Munich; **P:** Paris; **Q:** Milan; **r:** Šeštokai; **R:** Nuremberg; **S:** Salzburg; **T:** Villach; **U:** Innsbruck; **V:** Bologna; **W:** Vienna; **X:** Brussels; **Y:** Osnabrück; **Z:** Zurich

§: Journey requires use of an express bus service run by a rail operator. Regular rail tickets and passes are accepted. **N***: Overnight service by ship. Rail tickets not accepted. Discounts for rail pass holders on some sailings.

Bratislava (32, 48)
Belgrade D (10h40)
Berlin N D (9h10)
Budapest D (2h40)
Hamburg D (11h20)
Prague N D (4h10)
Sarajevo D (16h20E)
Vienna D (1h10)
Warsaw N D (7h20J)
Zagreb D (8h40W)
Zurich D (9h50W)

Brussels (14)
Amsterdam D (2h00)
Berlin D (6h50K)
Cologne D (1h50)
Frankfurt D (3h10)
Hamburg D (6h50K)
London D (2h00)
. Munich D (6h40F)
Nice D (7h50)
Paris D (1h20)
Vienna D (12h00K)
Zurich D (8h20)

Bucharest (40, 41)
Belgrade N
Budapest N
Istanbul N
Sofia N D (9h20)
St Petersburg N

Vienna N

Budapest (40, 42, 48)
Belgrade N D (7h50)
Berlin N D (11h50)
Bratislava D (2h40)
Bucharest N
Cologne D (13h00W)
Frankfurt D (10h30W)
Hamburg D (14h00)
Ljubljana D (9h15)
Munich N D (7h20)
Prague N D (6h50)
Sarajevo D (11h20)
Sofia N
Venice N
Vienna D (3h00)
Warsaw N D (10h00J)
Zagreb D (6h50)
Zurich N D (11h20)

Cologne (16, 18)
Amsterdam D (2h40)
Berlin N D (4h20)
Brussels D (1h50)
Budapest D (13h00W)
Copenhagen N D (9h00H)
Frankfurt D (1h10)
Hamburg D (4h00)
Ljubljana D (10h50M)
London D (4h30X)

Munich N D (4h40)
Paris D (3h20)
Prague N D (8h00R§)
Vienna N D (9h30)
Warsaw N D (10h40B)
Zurich N D (6h00)

Copenhagen (17, 21, 22, 25)
Amsterdam N
Berlin N D (6h40)
Cologne N D (9h50H)
Frankfurt N D (9h20H)
Hamburg D (4h30)
Munich D (11h20H)
Oslo N* D (7h50e)
Prague N D (11h40B)
Stockholm D (5h10)
Zurich D (14h20H)

Florence (34, 36)
Milan D (1h50)
Munich N D (8h00V)
Paris N D (9h20Q)
Rome D (1h40)
Venice D (2h10)
Vienna N
Zurich D (5h50Q)

Frankfurt (18)
Amsterdam D (4h00)
Berlin D (4h10)

Brussels D (3h10)
Budapest D (10h30W)
Cologne D (1h10)
Copenhagen N D (9h00H)
Hamburg D (3h50)
Ljubljana D (10h20)
London D (6h50X)
Milan D (8h00C)
Munich D (3h10)
Nice D (10h30P)
Paris D (3h50)
Prague N D (6h00R§)
Vienna N D (7h10)
Warsaw N D (10h00B)
Zagreb D (12h40)
Zurich D (4h00)

Hamburg (17)
Amsterdam N D (5h20Y)
Berlin D (1h40)
Bratislava D (11h20)
Brussels D (6h50K)
Budapest D (14h00)
Cologne N D (4h00)
Copenhagen D (4h40)
Frankfurt N D (4h00)
Ljubljana D (12h40M)
Milan D (11h40C)
Munich N D (5h50)
Paris N D (8h10K)
Prague D (7h00)
Vienna N D (9h20)
Warsaw D (8h10B)
Zagreb D (15h00M)
Zurich N D (7h40)

Helsinki (26, 27, 46)
St Petersburg N* D (3h40)
Stockholm N*

Istanbul (40)
Belgrade N
Bucharest N
Sofia N

Lisbon (9, 11)
Madrid N

Ljubljana (38, 39)
Belgrade N D (9h00)

Budapest D (9h00)
Cologne D (11h00M)
Frankfurt D (10h30)
Hamburg D (12h40M)
Munich N D (6h20)
Venice D (7h00T§)
Vienna D (6h00)
Warsaw D (14h10T)
Zagreb D (2h20)
Zurich N D (11h20M)

London (1, 2, 3)
Amsterdam D (4h50X)
Brussels D (2h00)
Cologne D (4h20X)
Frankfurt D (6h10X)
Milan D (11h30P)
Munich D (10h20P)
Nice D (9h30P)
Paris D (2h20)
Zurich D (8h20P)

Madrid (9, 10)
Barcelona N D (2h50)
Lisbon N
Paris N D (13h30a)

Milan (29, 31, 35)
Amsterdam D (11h30P)
Barcelona N
Berlin D (12h00C)
Florence D (1h50)
Frankfurt D (7h50C)
Hamburg D (14h10Z)
London D (11h30P)
Munich D (7h40)
Nice D (5h30G)
Paris N D (7h10)
Rome N D (3h00)
Venice D (2h40)
Vienna N D (11h30U)
Zurich D (3h40)

Munich (19, 20, 28)
Amsterdam N D (7h30F)
Belgrade D (15h10T)
Berlin N D (5h50)
Brussels D (6h40F)
Budapest N D (7h20)
Cologne N D (4h40)

Copenhagen D (11h00H)
Florence N D (8h00V)
Frankfurt D (3h10)
Hamburg N D (5h50)
Ljubljana N D (6h10)
London D (9h20P)
Milan D (8h00)
Paris N D (6h20)
Prague D (4h50§)
Rome N D (9h20V)
Venice N D (6h40)
Vienna N D (4h20)
Warsaw D (12h30B)
Zagreb N D (8h50)
Zurich D (4h10)

Narvik (24)
Stockholm N

Nice (6)
Amsterdam D (10h10P)
Brussels D (8h15)
Frankfurt D (11h30P)
London D (9h00P)
Milan D (5h00G)
Paris N D (5h40)

Oslo (21, 23, 24)
Copenhagen N* D (8h00e)
Stockholm D (6h10)

Paris (1, 2, 3, 4)
Amsterdam D (3h20)
Barcelona N D (7h50f)
Berlin N D (8h20K)
Brussels D (1h20)
Cologne D (3h20)
Florence N D (9h10Q)
Frankfurt D (3h50)
Hamburg N D (8h10K)
London D (2h20)
Madrid N D (13h30A)
Milan N D (7h10)
Munich N D (6h20)
Nice N D (5h40)
Rome N D (11h00Q)
Venice N D (10h00Q)
Vienna D (12h20F)
Zurich D (4h10)

Prague (47, 48)
Amsterdam N D (12h30B)
Belgrade D (15h00)
Berlin D (5h15)
Bratislava N D (4h10)
Budapest N D (6h50)
Cologne N D (9h30R§)
Copenhagen N D (11h40B)
Frankfurt D (6h00R§)
Hamburg D (7h00)
Munich D (4h45§)
St Petersburg N
Vienna N D (4h40)
Warsaw N D (8h20)
Zagreb D (12h00W)
Zurich N D (11h40M)

Rome (36, 37)
Florence D (1h40)
Milan N D (3h00)
Munich N D (9h40V)
Paris N D (11h10Q)
Venice D (3h50)
Vienna N
Zurich D (7h40Q)

St Petersburg (45)
Berlin N
Bucharest N
Helsinki N* D (3h40)
Prague N
Vilnius N
Warsaw N

Sarajevo (44)
Belgrade D (8h40)
Bratislava D (16h00E)
Budapest D (11h10)
Vienna D (15h10E)
Zagreb N D (9h30)

Sofia (41)
Belgrade N D (8h40)
Bucharest N D (9h30)
Budapest N
Istanbul N

Stockholm (25, 26)
Copenhagen D (5h20)
Helsinki N*

Narvik N
Oslo D (6h10)

Thessaloniki (41, 43)
Athens N D (5h20)

Venice (35)
Belgrade N
Budapest N
Florence D (2h10)
Ljubljana D (7h10T§)
Milan D (2h40)
Munich N D (7h00)
Paris N D (10h30Q)
Rome D (3h50)
Vienna N D (8h10T§)
Zagreb N D (9h40T§)
Zurich D (7h00Q)

Vienna (32)
Amsterdam D (11h50F)
Belgrade D (10h50E)
Berlin N D (9h50)
Bratislava D (1h10)
Brussels D (11h00F)
Bucharest N
Budapest D (3h00)
Cologne N D (9h40)
Florence N
Frankfurt N D (7h00)
Hamburg N D (9h20)
Ljubljana D (6h00)
Milan N D (11h50U)
Munich N D (4h20)
Paris D (12h20F)
Prague N D (4h50)
Rome N
Sarajevo D (15h20E)
Venice N D (8h00T§)
Warsaw N D (8h00)
Zagreb D (6h20)
Zurich N D (8h10)

Vilnius (46)
St Petersburg N
Warsaw D (9h30r)

Warsaw (45, 46)
Amsterdam N D (12h30B)
Berlin D (5h40)

Bratislava N D (7h20J)
Budapest N D (10h00J)
Cologne N D (10h40B)
Frankfurt N D (10h10B)
Hamburg D (8h30B)
Ljubljana D (14h40T)
Munich D (12h00B)
Prague N D (8h20)
St Petersburg N
Vienna N D (8h00)
Vilnius D (9h2or)

Zagreb (38, 39)
Belgrade N D (6h20)
Bratislava D (8h40W)
Budapest D (6h50)
Frankfurt D (13h00)
Hamburg D (16h10M)
Ljubljana D (2h20)
Munich N D (8h40)
Prague D (12h00W)
Sarajevo N D (9h10)
Venice N D (9h30T§)
Vienna D (6h00)
Zurich N D (14h00M)

Zurich (29, 30, 32)
Amsterdam N D (8h20F)
Barcelona N
Belgrade N
Berlin N D (8h30C)
Bratislava D (9h30W)
Brussels D (8h20)
Budapest N D (11h20)
Cologne N D (6h00)
Copenhagen D (14h10H)
Florence D (5h50Q)
Frankfurt D (4h00)
Hamburg N D (7h30)
Ljubljana N D (9h50S)
London D (8h10P)
Milan D (3h40)
Munich D (4h10)
Paris D (4h10)
Prague N D (12h00L)
Rome D (7h40Q)
Venice D (7h00Q)
Vienna N D (8h10)
Zagreb N D (12h20S)

NIGHT TRAINS

It is very likely that, sooner or later on your explorations of Europe by rail, you will end up taking an overnight train. Here we offer a few thoughts on what to expect. The first important distinction to make is between a **regular train** that just happens to run through the night and a properly designed **night train**. The first kind of train is, we feel, generally to be avoided. Yes, we have done it, but just take our word that the overnighter from Timișoara to Sighetu Marmației is not a lot of fun. Following part of **Route 50** through northern Romania, this train has few creature comforts and even our considerable enthusiasm for slow trains waned after a dozen hours aboard. If you must travel by night, then make sure that the train you choose is equipped for overnight travel. Many Romanian overnight trains are. We just opted for the wrong one.

At their best, Europe's night trains are superb. They offer various **grades of sleeping accommodation**. Top of the range are luxury sleepers with en suite facilities. You'll only find these on a small number of trains, and they are not cheap. You will need a first-class ticket (or first-class rail pass) and in addition you'll have to pay a supplement. Second-class (or standard-class) ticket holders can opt for regular sleeping compartments designed for one or more passengers (but usually bookable as a single for an extra charge) or couchettes. The latter are a down-market version of a sleeper. A normal compartment by day converts to simple bunk beds by night. Some night trains also convey carriages with seats. These are often designed to recline, thus affording a little more comfort.

Our advice is that, while only the most demanding travellers really need the luxury of the very poshest **sleeping compartments** (some of which may include minibars and flat screen TVs), it is worth trading up to a regular sleeper if you can possibly afford it. They are *much* more comfortable than couchettes. Remember you are saving a night's hotel or hostel accommodation and your appreciation of your destination in the morning will be vastly more positive if you have enjoyed a good night's sleep in crisp linen sheets.

Couchettes usually have four to six places per compartment. They are basic, but adequate. Bear in mind that a full six-berth couchette may be no fun in midsummer heat. **Sleepers** are usually air-conditioned and typically have one to four berths per compartment. Sheets and towels are all provided, and generally beds are made up for you. Russia, Belarus and Ukraine are rare exceptions. In those countries, the carriage attendant (called a *provodnik*) gives you the sheets, and you make your own bed. Help is always available for the elderly or less agile.

A shared **two-berth** sleeper compartment usually provides a reasonable measure of comfort. Single travellers booking a berth in a multiple-berth compartment must expect to share with strangers (usually segregated by gender). This is a travel experience that, as you move east across the continent, becomes ever more convivial. In Russia, it often involves sharing salami, hard-boiled eggs and life

NIGHT TRAIN OPERATORS

Germany, so strategically positioned at the heart of Europe, offers a fine network of night train services, and you can research details of Deutsche Bahn's **City Night Line** trains by going to www.bahn.co.uk (click on 'trains' and then select 'City Night Line'). Note that some of these services, such as Prague or Amsterdam to Copenhagen, do not start or end in Germany but merely traverse Germany by night.

There are particularly **high-quality hotel trains** from Spain to Paris, Milan and Zurich (details at www.elipsos.com) and a new operator will have replaced unlamented Artesia on Paris to Italy routes by the time this book is published. Austrian Railways (ÖBB) have good night trains to Italy and Germany (www.oebb.at). You will find useful domestic night train links within most larger European countries. It is always worth checking as a night train can usefully complement daytime travel on some of the journeys described in this book. For example, there is a daily Croatian night train linking Zagreb with the Adriatic coastal town of Split (**Route 38**). There are night trains across Austria, from Helsinki to the north of Finland, from northern Italy to Sicily, from one corner of Poland to the other and so on.

France is a little unusual in that overnight trains entirely within France have no sleeping cars, so a couchette is your best option. Conversely, some night trains within Spain have no couchette option, and offer only sleeping cars. Where Spanish night trains also have reclining seats, such carriages are reserved for first-class ticket holders (and on most of these trains there is no second-class seating).

Europe's most distinctive night trains run from Russia to central and western Europe and the Balkans. **Russian Railways** (RZD) offer through carriages from Moscow to far-flung destinations in Switzerland and the Netherlands. They operate several Balkan services. In late 2010 RZD inaugurated a direct train from Moscow to Nice, and in December 2011 upgraded their long-standing Moscow – Berlin – Paris service. Night trains are included in the *Thomas Cook European Rail Timetable*. And check our **city links table** (on pp678–81) where the letter 'N' behind the destination in a city pair indicates that those two cities are linked by a direct night train.

stories with complete strangers. There is no requirement that the stories you tell be true. Some sleeper trains are ideal for **families**. Many Finnish overnight services, the Caledonian Sleeper from London to Scotland and Elipsos trains from Spain to France, Switzerland and Italy have interconnecting doors between compartments that can be opened to create a larger space for a family.

Especially in central and eastern Europe, a train may include sleeping cars from several different countries. For many night trains, you can check the provenance of sleeping cars and what facilities they have (eg. air conditioning, electric sockets, etc) on *vagonWEB* (www.vagonweb.cz). Choose the English-language version, then select 'composition' and find your service through its train number. **Standards may vary** widely between the carriages of the various railway administrations. Don't assume that 'east' is bad and 'west' is good. Some of the most comfortable night trains we have used are Russian ones.

It also pays to know in advance if there will be a **restaurant car** on your train. Many menus on night trains nicely anticipate the destination. Thus on the journey from London to the Scottish Highlands you can enjoy haggis and neeps for supper and round off the evening with a good malt whisky in the lounge car. And on the train from Stockholm to Narvik in northern Norway, a magnificent overnight journey that takes you beyond the Arctic Circle, reindeer stew is standard fare on the dinner menu. You may have mixed feelings about this next morning when you awake and gaze out of the window to see rather forlorn looking reindeer standing beside the railway lines. On a limited number of trains, such as Elipsos services, the cost of an excellent dinner with wine is included in the highest-fare class (called *gran classe* on those Elipsos trains).

Some overnight trains may have no restaurant car. Go prepared! On most Russian trains, tea, coffee and a small selection of drinks and light snacks are available from the carriage attendant. In Germany and Austria, the train staff can usually provide drinks, soup and sandwiches on night trains with no restaurant car.

Night trains are of course the stuff of romance. They are a scriptwriter's delight — and a cameraman's nightmare, for the sleeping compartment offers few great panoramas when fixed on **celluloid**. That didn't stop Carol Reed in *Night Train to Munich* (1940) and Alfred Hitchcock in *North by Northwest* (1959) from both having a very good try. The mystery of the night train was forever sealed by *Murder on the Orient Express* (1974), where the accomplished music and superb cinematography that attend the train's departure from Istanbul's Sirkeci station more than compensate for the impish Belgian detective's subsequent difficulty in solving the murder that takes place at some unspecified but decidedly Balkan point along the route. Hercule Poirot will not be on your night train, so the chances are that you'll get a good night's sleep. Try it once, and you'll surely be hooked.

LONDON CONNECTIONS

Britain lost its last night train to the continent more than 30 years ago with the demise of *The Night Ferry*, a train with comfortable Wagons-Lits sleeping cars that provided a direct overnight service from London to Paris and Brussels. But travellers from Britain bound for many parts of the continent can conveniently use the excellent range of **night trains from Paris**. An afternoon journey from London to Paris with Eurostar and pre-dinner drinks in the French capital are the natural prelude to an overnight train journey. Climb aboard and leave your luggage in your sleeping compartment. Then enjoy dinner on board and a good night's sleep. International night trains from Paris serve many cities including Barcelona and Madrid (both with Elipsos); Munich, Berlin and Hamburg (City Night Line). There is also a thrice-weekly direct train from Paris to Minsk and Moscow (which will increase in frequency to five times weekly in summer 2012; ERT 24). In addition French trains, all sadly without restaurant cars, leave Paris every night for over 30 destinations in southern France.

When a train is not a train

There may be times when your train turns out not to be a train at all. Sometimes this might be because of a festival of track maintenance, meaning that for a day or two buses replace trains on a particular stretch of line. At other times buses **permanently replace trains** on a 'rail' journey. For example, the daytime services operated by Austrian Railways (ÖBB) from Venice via Udine to Austria are not trains at all, but comfortable double-decker coaches.

Similarly, the 'trains' between **Munich** or **Nuremberg** and **Prague** (both operated by Deutsche Bahn) are in fact buses. Here at least there is a choice, and devotees of rail travel will much prefer the slow trains from Nuremberg to the Czech capital (**Route 47**). The train follows deep wooded valleys and climbs over the hills that separate Bavaria from Bohemia. As so often in Europe, the rail route reveals a perspective on the landscape that is just not visible from the motorway.

Rail ferries

On a few routes in Europe, rail travellers may be surprised to find themselves afloat on a ship. The night train from Malmö to Berlin is a fine example (ERT 50). Scarcely an hour into its journey, the train shudders to a halt on the quayside at Trelleborg. The entire train is then shunted onto a ship for a nocturnal voyage **across the Baltic** to Sassnitz in Germany. We have met sound sleepers who, when alighting from the train on arrival in Berlin, had no idea that they had spent four hours afloat during the night. At the time of going to press in late 2011, it was not yet confirmed if this service would run in 2012.

There are routes where a daytime journey by train includes a stretch by ship. One is the Hamburg to Copenhagen part of **Route 17**, where the entire train is shipped on a ferry from Puttgarden to Rødby (ERT 720). Passengers can leave the train, stroll the decks of the ship, and enjoy the Baltic breeze on the 45-minute crossing. On **Route 37** trains are regularly loaded onto ships between the Italian mainland and Sicily.

The famous five gaps

On some of our 50 routes, you will find that we recommend a bus link to bridge a gap in Europe's rail network. The five key gaps in the continent's rail infrastructure include the journey across the Tatra Mountains between Slovakia and Poland (**Route 47**), heading south from Ploče to Dubrovnik (**Route 44**), the stretch along the Norwegian coast linking the railheads at Bodø and Narvik (**Route 24**), crossing the border from Sweden into Finland (**Route 26**) and travelling between Vilnius and Riga (**Route 46**). There are other areas where train connections exist but are very poor. Moving east from Trieste into Slovenia (**Routes 35** and **38**) is an example, and there we suggest taking a bus.

CRUISE TRAINS

The emphasis in this book is on independent travel. The rail journeys we recommend rely on regular scheduled train services. We think that's the best way to explore Europe by rail, but we understand that it is not for everyone. Some travellers prefer the more cosseted feel of a specialist cruise train that caters only to the tourist market.

The most celebrated of Europe's cruise trains is the **Venice Simplon-Orient-Express** (VSOE). The company styles London to Venice as its signature route. In 2012 VSOE will run once or twice weekly to Venice from late March to early November. The 30-hour journey includes a night aboard an **elegant heritage train** with beautiful Lalique glass panels and art deco marquetry. Such style does not come cheap. One-way from London to Venice for a couple sharing a double compartment costs €4,740 (including meals). The fare per couple in a larger cabin is €7,500. You can check schedules and fares on www.vsoe.com.

VSOE marks its 30th birthday in 2012 and boasts an enviable record of fine service and reliability. So no surprise that many entrepreneurs have tried to emulate the VSOE model. Their track record is very mixed.

The much vaunted **TransBaltZug** looked set to link Berlin and St Petersburg, with an imaginative route that nicely combined elements of Routes 45 and 46 in this book and also included Russia's Baltic exclave at Kaliningrad. Great idea, but no train ever ran.

A British-Hungarian venture called **Danube Express** was launched in 2008, but then cancelled its entire 2009 programme. Full programmes in 2010 and 2011 revived the fledgling company's reputation and you can see their 2012 programme on www.danube-express.com. Journeys start in Budapest, Istanbul and Warsaw. A one-way journey from Budapest to Istanbul (or vice versa), including three nights accommodation on the train and all meals costs over €3,000 per person.

El Transcantábrico has run since 1983 and is ultra-reliable. The company's cruise trains explore minor rail routes in **northern Spain**. The eight-day journey from San Sebastián to Santiago de Compostela includes on-board accommodation (seven nights), all meals, excursions and admission charges. For a couple sharing, the list price for 2011 was €7,500. No discount is available for single travellers.

A proposed new venture, already very much delayed, but now looking to launch in April 2012 is the **European Hotel Train** (EuHoTra) which promises a weekly cruise train making a circuit through Germany. The brochure price for a six-night tour for a couple is €4,980, which includes on-board accommodation on a refurbished Talgo train that until late 2009 was used on regular night train services within Germany. The fare covers breakfast each day and just one dinner (served on a boat on the eve of departure). Given that all other meals, and all excursions and sightseeing tours, are extras, this is certainly not a cheap holiday. Details about the European Hotel Train are available at www.hoteltrain.eu.

Rail pass directory

If you have just stumbled on this section of the book by chance, we strongly suggest you first read our **feature on tickets** and rail passes at the start of this book (see pp21–27). There we discuss whether or not a rail pass is even worth considering at all. You may find that individual tickets for the specific journeys you wish to make would together amount to less than the cost of a rail pass. But if you have considered those arguments and still judge that a pass is a plausible option, here are a few key facts. Beyond the various passes mentioned below, there are many other passes, often valid only in a particular country or just part of a country, which are not marketed under the Eurail or InterRail banner. You will find many of these mentioned in the **gazetteer section** of this book (see pp598–676) under the appropriate country entry.

And remember that the *Thomas Cook European Rail Timetable (ERT)* has detailed listings of rail passes in its regular rail pass feature which appears in the summer and winter seasonal editions, as well as in the May edition of the regular monthly timetable.

InterRail passes

Available only to residents of Europe (in this case defined as including everywhere you might expect plus all of Russia and Turkey as well as Cyprus), the InterRail pass comes in **two main varieties**. Firstly, there is a global pass, which covers most of Europe west of the borders of the former Soviet Union. Secondly, InterRail offer a range of one-country passes for individual countries. In either case you need to be a national of a European country, or have lived in Europe for at least six months to be eligible for an InterRail pass.

Passes are **not valid** in the passholder's country of residence, although discounts may be available on rail journeys to and from the border or an airport (though not in Britain). The prices quoted below are the provisional rates for 2012.

InterRail global pass

The global pass is **valid in 30 European countries**, namely Austria, Belgium, Bosnia-Herzegovina, Bulgaria, Croatia, the Czech Republic, Denmark, Finland, France, Germany, Great Britain, Greece, Hungary, Ireland (including Northern Ireland), Italy, Luxembourg, Macedonia, Montenegro, the Netherlands, Norway, Poland, Portugal, Romania, Serbia, Slovakia, Slovenia, Spain, Sweden, Switzerland and Turkey. The InterRail global pass is also valid on the railway lines that traverse Monaco and Liechtenstein. The area of validity of the global pass is highlighted on the **Europe map** on pp10–11 of this book.

For the global pass there are five different options on the period of validity. Two are flexi passes valid either for 5 days within 10, or 10 days within 22. You are free to choose which days you use your flexi pass, writing the date on the pass before the first journey of the day. The other options are for a set number of consecutive days, either 15, 22 or one month. Most are available in either first or second class (but the youth pass for those under 26 is valid only for second-class travel).

Youth prices start at €175 for the 5-day flexi pass, ranging to €422 for one month (the 15-day pass is €298). **Adult prices** for those 26 and over range from €267 to €638, with the 15-day pass costing €422. First-class passes range from €409 to €977. Children aged four to 11 pay 50% of the adult price, and there is a 10% discount for seniors (60+) which applies only to the global pass.

Full details of latest prices are available from the official **InterRail website** at www.interrailnet.com. Passes can be purchased online in advance directly from InterRail or from its agents, and are also available from principal stations in Europe. You will find a list of reliable agents on p22 of this book.

Supplements are payable on many high-speed and premium-priced trains: for further information see the panel on page p27. As well as the principal railway companies, passes are often valid on private or locally-run railways, or in some cases the latter may offer a discount to pass holders. Occasionally there is no discount at all, for example on the narrow-gauge railways in the Jungfrau area of Switzerland. Many ferry companies also give **discounts**, and in fact the pass gives free deck passage on the popular sailings between Italy and Greece operated by SuperFast Ferries, Blue Star Ferries and Minoan Lines (you will, however, pay port taxes and there are high-season surcharges of €10–€20 in summer). The pass may also give you discounts on a limited number of tourist attractions, hostels and even bike hire, so it's worth asking around.

InterRail one-country passes

These are flexi passes, valid for either 3, 4, 6 or 8 days within one month, and can be bought for most of the participating countries mentioned above. They do not exist for Bosnia-Herzegovina and Montenegro (in each case train fares are so cheap that a pass would make no sense anyway). As with the InterRail global pass, you cannot purchase the one-country pass for use in your country of residence. The **Benelux countries** of Belgium, Luxembourg and the Netherlands are grouped together and count as one. Monaco and Liechtenstein are so small that they have no one-country pass, but passes valid in France and Austria are deemed to be valid in Monaco and Liechtenstein respectively.

Once again there are youth and adult versions in second class, as well as a first-class adult variant. **Prices** fall into **five bands** according to the size of the country. The top-priced band covers France, Germany or Great Britain with youth prices ranging from €139 for 3 days to €211 for 8 days (adult second class €205–€319, first class €314–€489). The cheapest band covers Bulgaria, Macedonia, Serbia or Turkey, with prices €36–€82 for youth, €56–€128 for adult

SEDUCED BY FREEDOM

The seductive appeal of a global Eurail or InterRail pass lies in the chance to roam freely across Europe. Of course, as we have seen in our section on tickets at the front of this book (p21), this freedom is rather illusory as too many railway operators nowadays demand hefty supplements of pass holders. But the very idea of being able to speed from Hamburg to Budapest on a mere whim is quite tantalising. We know of one young Irish traveller who had never once set foot outside his home country until he purchased a global InterRail pass. He set off from Cork by ferry for France and a month later was back, having visited 31 countries in 31 days. It was, he said, the worst month of his entire life. He has not once set foot on a train since.

second class, and €86–€196 for first class. Supplements are the same as for the global pass. In some cases there are locally available passes which may offer better value (see the country listings in the gazetteer starting on p598), but buying an InterRail one-country pass in advance allows you to start travelling on arrival without queueing to buy tickets in local currency.

EURAIL PASSES

Eurail passes are for **non-European residents**. As with InterRail there is a global pass covering most of Europe, although there are a few countries in eastern Europe which, although participating in InterRail, are not part of the Eurail scheme. As well as a global pass there are select passes covering a group of adjacent countries, regional passes — which usually cover just two countries — and one-country passes. Note that Great Britain is not part of the Eurail scheme, as it is covered by the separate Britrail pass, itself with several options.

As the biggest market for Eurail passes is in the United States of America, we quote in the notes below the 2011 prices in US dollars. Non-residents of Europe can of course purchase Eurail passes from agents in their home countries with the prices denominated in local currency.

EURAIL GLOBAL PASS

The Eurail global pass is valid for **unlimited travel** on the national railways of 23 European countries, namely Austria, Belgium, Bulgaria, Croatia, the Czech Republic, Denmark, Finland, France, Germany, Greece, Hungary, Ireland (including Northern Ireland), Italy, Luxembourg, the Netherlands, Norway, Portugal, Romania, Slovakia (newly added for 2012), Slovenia, Spain, Sweden and Switzerland. The Eurail global pass is also valid on the railway lines that traverse Monaco and Liechtenstein. The area of validity of the global pass is highlighted on the **Europe map** on pp10–11 of this book. Note that additional countries, beyond those mentioned above and shaded on the map, participate in the select pass, regional pass and one-country pass schemes described below.

As with InterRail there are both **flexi passes** and **continuous passes**. The flexi pass gives you either 10 days or 15 days within a period of two months, allowing you to decide on a day by day basis exactly when you want to use the pass.

The continuous passes are for 15 days, 21 days or one month, and there are even two- and three-month versions for those planning a longer stay in Europe. The adult pass is for first-class travel (but is obviously also valid in second class), with only the youth pass (under 26) being restricted to second class.

Prices in US dollars for the 10- and 15-day flexi passes are $519/679 youth and $799/1,049 adult. The passes for 15, 21 days or 1 month are $439/569/709 youth or $679/879/1,089 adult. The 2- and 3-month passes come in at $999/1,239 youth and $1,539/1,899 adult. When two or more adults are travelling together there is a 15% discount for each person, known as the saver pass, but this is not available for the youth version. Children aged four to 11 pay half fare, and children under four travel free (except if a reservation for a separate seat or bed is required).

For the latest prices and **precise details** of supplements (which are sometimes different to those which apply to InterRail) see the Eurail website www.eurailgroup.org, or for additional information and details of Eurail's main agents worldwide see www.eurailtravel.com.

EURAIL SELECT PASSES

For those visiting a smaller area of Europe, the Eurail select pass allows unlimited travel in 3, 4 or 5 adjoining countries selected from the following: Austria, Denmark, Finland, France, Germany, Greece, Hungary, Ireland, Italy, Norway, Portugal, Romania, Spain, Sweden, or Switzerland. And in addition there are three country groupings which each count as one country: Belgium/Netherlands/Luxembourg, Croatia/Slovenia and Montenegro/Serbia.

Adjoining means linked by a direct train (not through another country) or shipping line included in the Eurail scheme; for example Italy's links include Spain and Greece, and France can be linked with Ireland.

The select pass is available for 5, 6, 8 or 10 travel days within a two-month period (the 5-country pass is also available for 15 days). **Prices** start at $346 for the 5-day 3-country youth version (or $531 for adult first class). Saver (for two or more adults travelling together) and child discounts are available.

EURAIL REGIONAL PASSES

Eurail regional passes allow unlimited travel in two European countries — or defined country combinations such as Scandinavia. There is a wide range of options available. Popular choices include Austria and Hungary, France and Germany, Portugal and Spain, and the Scandinavia pass mentioned above which covers Denmark, Norway, Sweden and Finland. Conditions vary but regional-pass options generally include 5, 6, 8 or 10 days within two months, and some are also available for 4, 7 or 9 days. Many have first- and second-class versions.

Sample second-class adult prices are France and Spain or France and Italy (4–10 days) $299–$509, Hungary and Romania first class (5–10 days) $249–$375. The youth versions give around 30% discount.

EURAIL ONE COUNTRY PASSES

These allow unlimited travel in a single European country selected from the following: Austria, Bulgaria, Croatia, the Czech Republic, Denmark, Finland, Greece, Hungary, Ireland, Italy, Norway, Poland, Portugal, Romania, Slovenia, Spain or Sweden. Each pass has its own characteristics regarding class of travel, number of travel days, and availability of saver, youth and child versions. A few also have discounts for seniors. For prices see www.eurailgroup.org.

OTHER PASSES

There are a handful of other passes covering more than one country. They are available to people who are resident outside the countries covered. These include the **Balkan Flexipass**, which gives unlimited first-class travel in Bulgaria, Greece, Macedonia, Montenegro, Romania, Serbia and Turkey for any 5, 10 or 15 days in one month. A second-class version is also available if actually purchased in one of the countries where it is valid.

The **Benelux Tourrail** gives unlimited rail travel throughout Belgium, Luxembourg and the Netherlands for any five days in a month and can be purchased from stations in Belgium and Luxembourg, but not in the Netherlands.

The **European East Pass** is available to non-European residents and offers unlimited rail travel throughout Austria, the Czech Republic, Hungary, Poland and Slovakia for any five days within a month.

There are several day or two-day passes which cover the border regions of two or more countries. These can be purchased by anyone, regardless of where they live. Examples include the **Öresund Rundt, Pass Alsace – Rhein-Neckar, Passbask, Saar-Lor-Lux Ticket**, the **Euro-Neisse Ticket** and a range of passes covering border areas of the Czech Republic and adjoining countries.

A–Z of travel in Europe

Bicycles

Before you start planning a comprehensive tour of Europe by train and bike, just be aware that many railway operators do not take an especially benign view of bicycles. Across much of Europe you can, usually for a small fee, take a bike on many local and regional trains, although restrictions may apply in many urban areas during peak travel times. Move to long-distance trains and the situation becomes much more varied.

For example, German ICE trains simply have no allocated bike space, so the only way you can transport your bicycle on those trains is if it is folded and carried in a proper **bike bag**. There is **limited space** for pre-booked bicycles on many German IC trains. Spain is a problem area with bikes barred from all daytime long-distance services, even if they are folded and packed in a bike bag. In Finland and the Czech Republic, bicycles can be transported on Pendolino services, but only if pre-booked.

There is a limited amount of space for **pre-booked** bicycles on Eurostar. Some TGVs have bike space, others do not. On Thalys, a bicycle must be folded and packed. Okay, so you get the idea. This is a formidably complicated subject. In summary, many local trains are bike-friendly, but if you are planning stretches on fast trains, you will need to research carefully what trains are able to take your bike and at what price. You can see why many travellers decide to **rent a bike** at their destination.

Borders

Most travellers will need a **valid passport** to travel through Europe. A dispensation allows citizens of any of the 30 members of the **European Economic Area** (EEA), plus Switzerland too, to travel throughout the participating countries with just a National Identity Card. In practice, passport checks are very low-key in much of Europe nowadays and the only occasions your documents are likely to be seriously checked is if you venture outside the **Schengen area**. The latter consists of more than two dozen countries which are either formally or de facto party to the Schengen Agreement, allowing freedom of movement across their mutual borders. Romania and Bulgaria may join the Schengen region in late 2012. The UK and Ireland are conspicuously not members of Schengen and the UK in particular maintains strict border controls, even to the extent that you must pass through UK immigration in Brussels or Paris before joining Eurostar trains bound for London.

So it is really only as you enter the UK, Russia, Belarus, Ukraine, Turkey and certain Balkan countries that you will encounter any significant **border bureaucracy**. See also **Visas** and **Customs checks** in this section.

Cellphones – see Telephones

Children

Kids and trains just go together. Many children will tolerate a much longer journey on a train than in a car. But don't test their patience too much. Too packed an itinerary just won't wash with most youngsters. On some trains, such as Thalys and selected German ICE services, you'll even find dedicated family space. Some trains in Scandinavia and Switzerland have a children's play area. Almost without exception, European rail operators offer **discounted fares** for children.

Climate – see Seasons

Credit cards

If you come from a country with a strong credit card culture (such as the UK or USA), you may be surprised how little you can use your credit cards in some parts of Europe. Train ticket machines in many countries will not accept credit card payment and you may find that, especially once you get off the main tourist trails, hotels and restaurants will want payment in cash. Of course in **major cities** payment with plastic is absolutely accepted, but just be aware that this may not apply to more **rural areas**. Where cards are accepted, VISA and MasterCard are your best bets. Some cards, such as AmEx and Diners Club, are quite unknown in many rural regions of Europe.

Cycles – see Bicycles

Currency

With the uncertainties affecting some of the peripheral countries in the **eurozone**, most notably Greece, currency looks set to be a hot topic throughout 2012 and beyond. At least for now, the euro remains by far the most useful currency for travellers exploring Europe by train, but do bear in mind that national currencies are still cherished in the UK, Denmark, Norway, Sweden and Switzerland. In central and eastern Europe, as also in the Balkan region, you will find many more countries that use currencies other than the euro. Our country gazetteer (pp598–676) gives currency details for every territory in Europe.

Customs checks

With the development of the single European market, customs checks are becoming a thing of the past. Just be aware that there are still strict limits on importing cigarettes and alcohol from non-EU areas into the European Union. No-one will quibble over 200 cigarettes and a bottle of spirits, but that's about the limit. It goes without saying that narcotics, weapons and pornographic publications can all get you into serious trouble. See also **Borders** in this section.

DISABILITIES

Travellers with disabilities need to take special care in planning their journeys. The exemplary service provided by **Eurostar** (even with concessionary fares) is not emulated across the continent. On premium long-distance services (TGV, AVE, ICE, etc) there is designated space for wheelchairs and boarding assistance is available if pre-booked. Move to regional and local trains and accessibility is much more patchy. It pays to check carefully before booking.

ELECTRICITY

The invisible stuff that comes out of plugs isn't quite the same the world over. Most of the planet, including Europe, uses a 220 to 240 volt system (230 volts is standard across the EU). A small number of countries (including Japan, Taiwan, Mexico, Canada, USA and a handful of Caribbean and central American states) use 110 volts. If you are travelling with dual voltage appliances such as a hair dryer, check that they are correctly set.

Much more troublesome are **plugs** which vary enormously. A universal plug adaptor is a wise investment. And ponder on a continent that devotes enormous effort to standardising the size of strawberries but still has a bewildering variety of electrical sockets. See www.kropla.com for details.

INSURANCE

If you live in one of the 31 countries that are party to the **EHIC scheme**, make sure you get a European Health Insurance Card before leaving home. That will cover some (but by no means all) emergency medical expenses within the EHIC area. So best to take out **travel insurance** that covers additional medical expenses (including repatriation if necessary) as well as theft or loss of your belongings. Remember to take out insurance at an early stage, as most policies only provide cancellation cover for transport bookings and hotel reservations made *after* you have taken out the insurance.

LANGUAGE

Use our gazetteer (pp598–676) to check which languages are spoken in each country. English will get you a long way across most of Europe, but it is presumptuous to assume that everyone you meet speaks English. Make sure you master at least a few words of the local lingo. And as you head east, it is important you are able to decipher the **Cyrillic alphabet**, if only to be able to transliterate place names.

Mobile phones – see Telephones

Passports – see Borders

Plugs – see Electricity

Rail passes – see pp21–27 and pp687–691

See the validity of the global **Eurail** and **InterRail** mapped on pp10–11.

Seasons

As an area significantly larger than the continental United States, it'll be no surprise that Europe encompasses a great range of **climate zones**. Mainland Europe alone takes in 65° of longitude and 35° of latitude. Of course you really can follow the routes in this book at *any* time of year, but there can be a special pleasure in travelling to places at times when there are fewer folk on the move. Trains in many parts of Europe are significantly quieter in winter than in summer (provided of course you can avoid the Christmas and New Year rush and you are not bound for the main skiing areas). Our view is that **spring and autumn** are the best seasons for exploring Europe by rail. So April, May, September and October. But bear in mind that the timing of seasons varies greatly across the continent. The southern areas of Spain and Italy may have idyllic spring weather in late March, while at the same time northern Scandinavia and the Alps may still have deep snow.

Smoking bans

A smoking ban on all **public transport** and in some **public places** has prevailed in some European countries for over 20 years, augmented since 2004 with more bans extended to cover cafés, bars and restaurants. Most of Europe now has such bans, with smoking rarely allowed on trains. Finland is an oddball exception, with some long-distance trains having a designated smoking cell equipped with special exhaust ventilation.

Telephones

If your mobile phone (**cellphone**) is enabled for roaming (ask your provider before leaving home if you're unsure), you'll be able to use it anywhere in Europe where your phone picks up an adequate signal and can log onto a network.

Remember you'll generally incur a charge to receive a call when abroad. Thanks to an EU initiative, the costs of receiving and making calls and sending texts has plummeted in recent years. This benefits only those with EU SIM cards and applies only to communications within the EU.

If you plan on making a lot of calls from one country, you might consider the merits of buying a local SIM card. **Payphones** are available in cities and at major rail stations. Increasingly they rely on **prepaid cards** (commonly available from newsstands and in some countries from post offices) rather than cash. Avoid making long calls from phones in hotel rooms. They are invariably expensive.

Time zones

Europe's great longitudinal spread from west to east means that it extends over **several time zones**. When it is noon in the easternmost parts of European Russia, it is only 0500 (in winter) or 0600 (in summer) in Europe's westernmost island communities (in the Azores). You can check the time zone for each country in the gazetteer section of this book (see pp598–676). All but three countries mentioned in this book seasonally **adjust their clocks**, moving them forward an hour on the last Sunday in March and putting them back on the last Sunday in October. The three exceptions are Iceland, Belarus and the Russian Federation. You will find some dramatic leaps in time on some European borders. Kirkenes in Norway and Boris Gleb in Russia (both mentioned on p235) are just 10 km apart, but their clocks are two hours adrift in summer and three hours adrift in winter.

Train tickets – SEE PP21–27

Visas

EU passport holders can follow all but one of the routes in this book without having to worry about visas. The exception is **Route 45**, and you can read more about what's needed there by way of visas on p366. Much the same applies to citizens of EEA member states outside the EU, and passport holders from Switzerland, Japan, Australia, Canada and the United States. Yet even within these general precepts there are some intriguing exceptions. Australians need a visa to enter Ukraine (which features in **Routes 49** and **50** in this book).

We live in a divided world and citizens of most African countries, as well as those from Asia (except for Japan and one or two others), will need to secure one or more visas for almost every route described in this book. The same applies to holders of passports from the Commonwealth of Independent States (including the Russian Federation) and some Latin American countries. If in doubt, check out what visas might be necessary before purchasing tickets. The consular departments of the embassies of countries you propose to visit will always advise.

MEET THE TEAM BEHIND THE BOOK

The 2011 edition of *Europe by Rail* was given a totally new look. It was completely revised with many new routes added and every existing route thoroughly reworked. For this 2012 edition, we have further improved coverage of the Alps, added a host of new accommodation options and taken into account many new rail services that debut in 2012. The successive annual editions of Europe by Rail are produced by **Susanne Kries** and **Nicky Gardner,** who together run a Berlin-based editorial bureau called hidden europe. Together they also edit *hidden europe* magazine, which showcases good travel writing with a focus on Europe's unsung corners. Susanne and Nicky were together responsible for the overall look and feel of this 2012 edition of *Europe by Rail*. Nicky penned most of the new prose that features in this volume, and Susanne handled the design and layout of the book. Words and images by Nicky and Susanne have featured regularly in many European media, often with a focus on rail travel to far-flung parts of the continent. You can find out more about their work on www.hiddeneurope.co.uk. The two women also maintain a website dedicated to supporting this book at www.europebyrail.eu.

Paul Scraton and **Greg Gardner** were editorial assistants for the duration of the project, each bringing a fine eye for detail to *Europe by Rail*. Paul is a Berlin-based travel writer and magazine editor, and has an appreciation of the European hotel and hostel scene that few can rival. Greg cut his journalistic teeth by writing regularly for the student newspaper at uni, worked for a spell in economic policy analysis and is now undertaking postgraduate studies in Oxford. The maps were commissioned by Thomas Cook Publishing and created by **Sally Cooney** of PCGraphics (UK) Ltd.

The editors were aided and abetted by the team who edit the *Thomas Cook European Rail Timetable*. Between them, that **timetable team** based in Peterborough (England) has nearly 100 years of experience of rail, bus and ferry timetables from throughout the world. Led by **Brendan Fox**, the others who worked hard to ensure that the rail information and many other details in this book are correct are Chris Woodcock, John Potter, Reuben Turner and David Turpie. Without the sustained commitment and interest of Brendan and his team, this book would be much the poorer.

Tim and Anne Locke served as consultants to the 2011 edition, bringing their experience as writers and editors of travel guidebooks to bear, as the structure and scope of the new *Europe by Rail* was developed and refined. As Tim had served for ten years as editor of earlier editions, he was keen to see that the book would be in safe hands as he handed editorial responsibility for the book over to Susanne and Nicky. That input by Tim and Anne feeds through very strongly into this 2012 edition.

The book still draws in some measure upon prose included in earlier editions of the book. Whether those legacy authors will find any vestiges of their fine efforts in this edition will vary by section, but the editors acknowledge their indebtedness to the writers who contributed various sections to the 2008 and 2010 editions of *Europe by Rail*: Lisa Gerard-Sharp, Roger Norum, Neil Taylor, Neville Walker, Paul Murphy, Lindsay Hunt, Jane Foster, Gorana Nad-Conlan and Robin McKelvie.

The texts of the 26 hub city descriptions that feature in this book draw to some extent on the **Thomas Cook Pocket Guides** for the respective cities. That series covers over 100 pocket-sized guides to many of the best destinations across Europe.

COUNTRY INDEX

Use this index only to identify which sections of *Europe by Rail* relate to specific countries. If you wish to search by place name (eg. Florence or Lisbon) or by topic (eg. visas), please use the general index that starts on the opposite page.

General index

Geographic names are in recto and the names of the 26 hub cities in this book are emboldened. Index entries which are not strictly place names are in italics.

REFERENCE | INDEX

Feedback request

We hope you've valued using this book as much as we've enjoyed creating this new edition for 2012. Now we would like to ask for your help. If you identify errors, or if you'd just like to give us a little feedback, we'd love to hear from you. Which routes did you follow? What did you find good about the book? And what worked less well? You can send your comments to editors@europebyrail.eu. We'll certainly acknowledge any thoughts you send, and take them into account as we prepare the next edition. Note that there is a website to support this book at **www.europebyrail.eu**.